Frommer's®
Mexico

My Mexico

by David Baird

THERE ARE MANY REASONS TO TRAVEL, BUT THE ONE THAT MOST often prompts me to leave home is a foreign culture's ability to jostle me from complacency. Mexico is good for this. It's vibrant and full of vivid sights and sensations. In the mountains, the contrast between strong sun and cool air makes me feel alive. There's a lifetime's worth of beaches to explore. But above all, I appreciate the Mexican people, who have a love of vigorous expression in just about every form of human endeavor. Witness the country's emphatically flavored food and drink, its over-the-top music and dance, its bold creations in art and architecture. After spending time in Mexico, I find other places to be dull and lackluster.

If this were all Mexico had to offer, it would be enough. But beneath the color lies a deep-seated complexity that makes the country fascinating. The national culture was born of two distinct civilizations: the Spanish and the Indian. The end result after centuries of synthesizing these contradictory forces is a rich symbolism that encapsulates multiple, often opposing, meanings. To get to know and understand Mexico in its entirety would be the work of several lifetimes. But to enjoy Mexico need take no more than an open mind and heart. These photos give you a taste of Mexico's complex allure.

Few experiences inspire as much awe as close contact with a whale in its natural habitat. Along Baja's Pacific coast, various protected bays and lagoons have become the preferred winter waters for migrating **GRAY WHALES (left)** as they journey south to mate and give birth to their calves. Naturally friendly and curious, these whales frequently come up to the sightseeing boats and stay close by. Baja's whale-watching season generally runs from January to March.

The megalithic **OLMEC HEADS (above)** are some of the most intriguing pre-Colombian artifacts. Seventeen have been discovered, and though they share a common style, the variations in their facial features suggest that they might depict something part human, part Jaguar god. Most of the heads are in out-of-the-way places such as Villahermosa and Xalapa. This modern reproduction can be found at the Chankanaab National Park, on the island of Cozumel.

The various regional cuisines of Mexico lend great variety to eating in Mexico, especially when you choose to eat in a local *FONDA* (above), or food stall, like this one at Libertad Market in Guadalajara. I love the guisados (stews), such as the ones this woman has prepared here.

I always enjoy visiting **MARKETS** (right) like this one, Oaxaca's Abastos Market. You see a variety of produce in most of them that would put a supermarket to shame. They also serve as a place for friends and neighbors to meet, eat, and chat about local events and the latest scandals.

Mexicans have a genius for working with their hands. When given the opportunity many artisans really shine, but more often they produce the everyday goods that demand dictates. I seek out the less commonplace work that is created from the need for personal expression. Even if I have no success, the effort often bears other fruit. This **MAYA VENDOR IN SAN CRISTOBAL DE LAS CASAS** is selling nontraditional garments to tourists. She may have other, more interesting pieces, but the highland Maya are often difficult to engage in conversation.

One of my favorite pastimes in Puerto Vallarta is strolling along its waterfront boardwalk, known as the malecón. Here, you'll find a collection of majestic monumental sculptures, including these, part of the *FANTASY OF THE SEA COLLECTION* (above) by noted Mexican artist Alejandro Colunga. Especially at sunset, or on Sunday evenings, the malecón buzzes with activity: vendors selling balloons, street musicians, and romantics of all ages holding hands.

No trip to Acapulco is complete without witnessing the dramatic performance of the **CLIFF-DIVERS** (right) at La Quebrada. For just a moment, when the diver springs from his perch, he seems suspended, weightless in the still air high above the roiling sea. It's almost impossible to tear your eyes away as he plummets more than 40m (130 ft.) toward the rocks and surf below.

I don't know of a place more emblematic of travel to Mexico than the **RUINS OF TULUM (right)**. Facing the blue Caribbean from a rocky promontory is the elegant form of a Maya temple platform. I like it best in the early morning when the sun glimmers off the water.

In the early '70s, the Mexican government ran a computer analysis to determine the best place to build the country's premier beach resort. But given **CANCUN'S (below)** gorgeous white-sand beaches, large sheltered lagoon, and proximity to America's eastern seaboard, could the decision have been that difficult?

The 17th and 18th centuries, when a European art form known as baroque arrived, was a time of great artistic achievement in Mexico, especially in architecture. This church in Oaxaca City, **SANTO DOMINGO (above)**, is one of my favorite examples. Think of it as an expression of ecstatic religious feeling that rejects limitations of structure, proportion, and balance.

Mexicans have a direct, almost personal, relationship with their Catholic saints. You need go no further than Mexico City to see this dynamic unfold. Stalls selling **RELIGIOUS ICONS (right)** line the way to the Basilica of Our Lady of Guadalupe.

The towers of this parochial church are all that can be seen of **THE BURIED TOWN OF PARANGARICUTIRO** in the southwestern state of Michoacán. In the 1940s, this area was an unremarkable little corner of Mexico—then steam began spewing up from a cornfield. Fissures appeared and from them lava and ash rose to the surface. Just like that the Paracutín volcano was born, expanded for a few years, and then, as promptly as it had begun, it stopped.

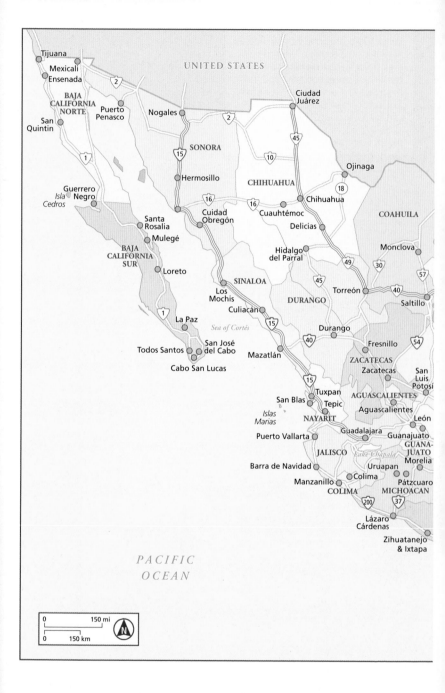

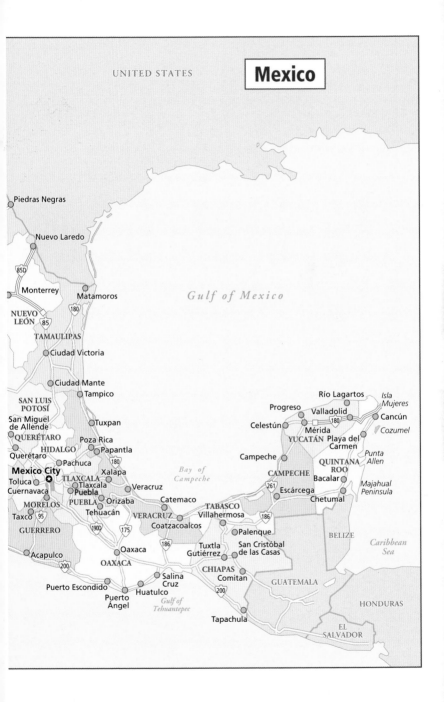

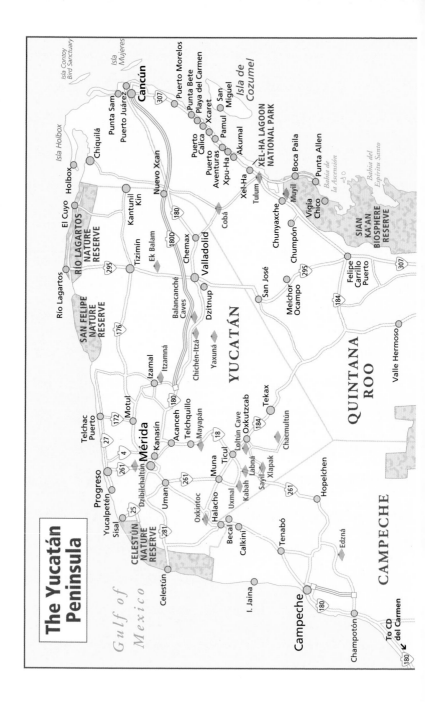

The Yucatán Peninsula

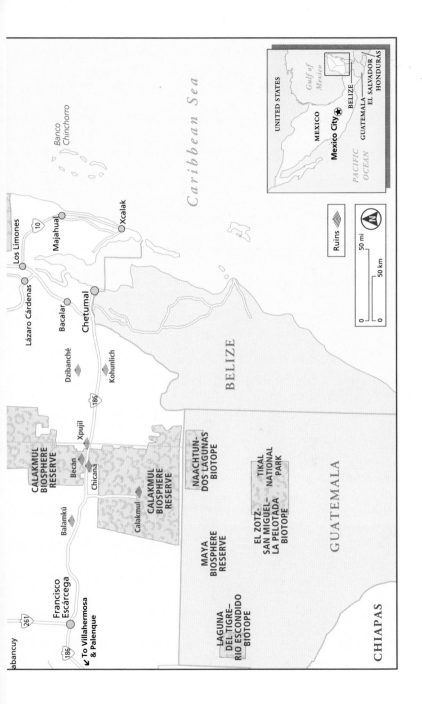

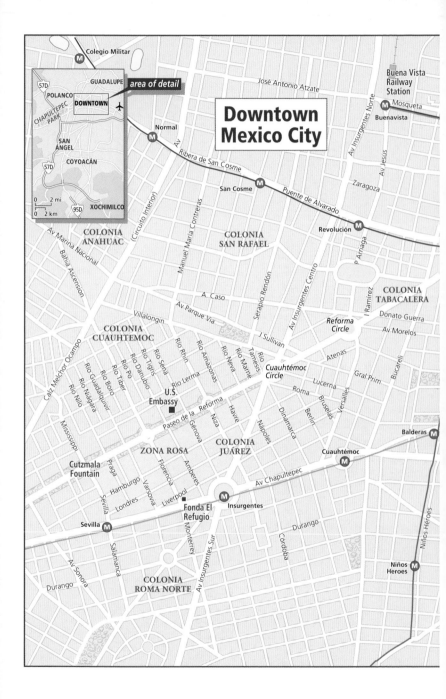

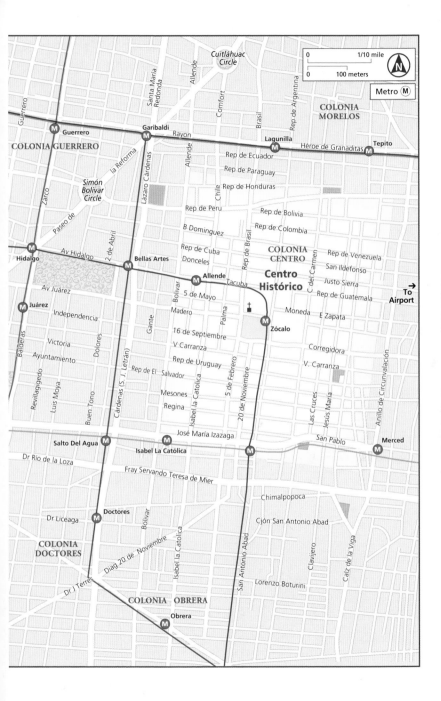

Cuitláhuac
Circle

0 | 1/10 mile
0 | 100 meters

N

Metro Ⓜ

Ⓜ Guerrero
COLONIA GUERRERO

Ⓜ Garibaldi
Rayon

Ⓜ Lagunilla
Héroe de Granaditas

Ⓜ Tepito

Santa María
Redonda

Allende

Comfort

Brasil

Rep de Argentina

**COLONIA
MORELOS**

Guerrero

la Reforma

Lázaro Cárdenas

Allende

Chile

Rep de Ecuador
Rep de Paraguay
Rep de Honduras

Rep de Peru

Rep de Bolivia
Rep de Colombia

Rep de Venezuela
San Ildefonso
Justo Sierra
Rep de Guatemala

C del Carmen

Simón
Bolívar
Circle

Zarco

Paseo de

2 de Abril

B Dominguez

Rep de Cuba

Rep de Brasil

**COLONIA
CENTRO**

Ⓜ Hidalgo
Av Hidalgo

Ⓜ Bellas Artes

Donceles

Ⓜ Allende
Tacuba

**Centro
Histórico**

→
**To
Airport**

Av Juárez

Bolívar

5 de Mayo

Palma

†

Moneda

E Zapata

Ⓜ Juárez
Independencia

Gante

Madero

16 de Septiembre

Ⓜ Zócalo

Av Juárez

Victoria

Dolores

V Carranza

Corregidora

Balderas

Ayuntamiento

Rep de El Salvador

Isabel la Católica

5 de Febrero

V. Carranza

Anillo de Circunvalación

Revillagigedo

Luis Moya

Buen Tono

Cárdenas (S. J. Letrán)

Rep de Uruguay

20 de Noviembre

Las Cruces

Jesús María

Mesones
Regina

José María Izazaga

San Pablo

Ⓜ Merced

Ⓜ Salto Del Agua
Dr Río de la Loza

Ⓜ Isabel La Católica

Ⓜ

Fray Servando Teresa de Mier

Chimalpopoca

Dr Liceaga

Ⓜ Doctores

Bolívar

Isabel la Católica

Cjón San Antonio Abad

Clavijero

Calz de la Viga

**COLONIA
DOCTORES**

Diag 20 de Noviembre

San Antonio Abad

Lorenzo Boturini

Dr J Terres

COLONIA OBRERA

Ⓜ Obrera

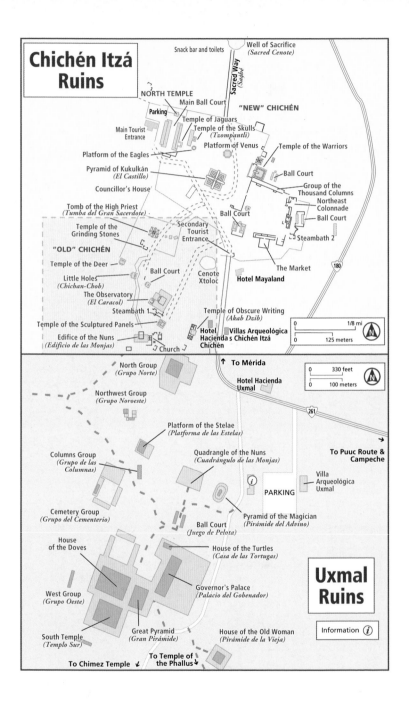

Chichén Itzá Ruins

Snack bar and toilets

Well of Sacrifice (Sacred Cenote)

Sacred Way (Sacbé)

NORTH TEMPLE

North Ball Court

Parking

Temple of Jaguars

Main Tourist Entrance

Temple of the Skulls (Tzompantli)

Platform of Venus

"NEW" CHICHÉN

Temple of the Warriors

Platform of the Eagles

Pyramid of Kukulkán (El Castillo)

Ball Court

Councillor's House

Group of the Thousand Columns

Northeast Colonnade

Tomb of the High Priest (Tumba del Gran Sacerdote)

Ball Court

Ball Court

Temple of the Grinding Stones

Secondary Tourist Entrance

Steambath 2

"OLD" CHICHÉN

Temple of the Deer

Ball Court

Cenote Xtoloc

The Market

Little Holes (Chichan-Chob)

Hotel Mayaland

The Observatory (El Caracol)

180

Steambath 1

Temple of the Sculptured Panels

Temple of Obscure Writing (Akab Dzib)

Edifice of the Nuns (Edificio de las Monjas)

Hotel Villas Arqueológica Haciendas Chichén Itzá Chichén

Church

0 ——— 1/8 mi
0 ——— 125 meters

N

North Group (Grupo Norte)

↑ To Mérida

0 ——— 330 feet
0 ——— 100 meters

N

Hotel Hacienda Uxmal

Northwest Group (Grupo Noroeste)

261

Platform of the Stelae (Platforma de las Estelas)

Columns Group (Grupo de las Columnas)

Quadrangle of the Nuns (Cuadrángulo de las Monjas)

To Puuc Route & Campeche →

i

Villa Arqueológica Uxmal

PARKING

Cemetery Group (Grupo del Cementerio)

Pyramid of the Magician (Pirámide del Advino)

Ball Court (Juego de Pelota)

House of the Doves

House of the Turtles (Casa de las Tortugas)

West Group (Grupo Oeste)

Governor's Palace (Palacio del Gobenador)

Uxmal Ruins

South Temple (Templo Sur)

Great Pyramid (Gran Pirámide)

House of the Old Woman (Pirámide de la Vieja)

Information i

To Chimez Temple ↓

To Temple of the Phallus ↓

Frommer's®

Mexico

2008

by David Baird, Juan Cristiano, Lynne Bairstow, & Emily Hughey Quinn

BICENTENNIAL
1807
WILEY
2007
BICENTENNIAL

Wiley Publishing, Inc.

Published by:

Wiley Publishing, Inc.
111 River St.
Hoboken, NJ 07030-5774

ISBN: 978-0-470-14574-6

Editor: Jennifer Moore
Production Editor: Jana M. Stefanciosa
Cartographer: Roberta Stockwell
Photo Editor: Richard Fox
Anniversary Logo Design: Richard Pacifico
Production by Wiley Indianapolis Composition Services

Front cover photo: Mexico City, National Palace: Fresco painted by Diego Rivera
Back cover photo: Cabo San Lucas: People walking under monumental natural stone arch.

For information on our other products and services or to obtain technical support, please contact our Customer Care Department within the U.S. at 800/762-2974, outside the U.S. at 317/572-3993 or fax 317/572-4002.

Wiley also publishes its books in a variety of electronic formats. Some content that appears in print may not be available in electronic formats.

Manufactured in the United States of America

5   4   3   2

Contents

List of Maps ix

What's New in Mexico 1

1 The Best of Mexico 7

by David Baird, Juan Cristiano & Emily Hughey Quinn

1 The Best Beach Vacations 7

2 The Best Cultural Experiences 10

3 The Best Archaeological Sites 11

4 The Best Active Vacations 12

5 The Best of Natural Mexico 13

6 The Best Places to Get Away from It All 14

7 The Best Art, Architecture & Museums .15

8 The Best Shopping 16

9 The Best Luxury Hotels 17

10 The Best Inexpensive Inns 18

11 The Best Spa Resorts 19

12 The Best Mexican Food & Drink 20

2 Planning Your Trip to Mexico 22

1 The Regions in Brief 22

2 Visitor Information & Maps 24

Destination Mexico: Red-Alert Checklist 24

3 Entry Requirements 25

4 When to Go 26

Calendar of Events 27

5 Getting There 33

Luxury Bus Service from the Mexico City Airport 34

Getting Through the Airport 35

6 Money & Costs 39

7 Travel Insurance 42

8 Health 43

9 Safety 46

10 Specialized Travel Resources 48

11 Sustainable Tourism/Ecotourism 52

Frommers.com: The Complete Travel Resource 52

12 Staying Connected 53

Online Traveler's Toolbox 55

13 Packages for the Independent Traveler 55

14 Special-Interest Trips 57

15 Getting Around Mexico 60

16 Tips on Accommodations 63

17 Tips on Dining 66

Fast Facts: Mexico 69

3 Suggested Mexico Itineraries   78

by David Baird

1 Central Mexico's Pre-Columbian
Treasures in a Week 78
2 The Best of Western Mexico
in a Week 80

3 Los Cabos to Copper Canyon 81
4 La Ruta Maya in 2 Weeks 82

4 Mexico City   85

by Juan Cristiano

1 Orientation 86
*Important Taxi Safety Precautions
in Mexico City* 89
The Neighborhoods in Brief 93
2 Getting Around 95
Fast Facts: Mexico City 100
3 Where to Stay 103
4 Where to Dine 111

¡Café, Por Favor! 116
5 Exploring Mexico City 117
6 Organized Tours 136
7 Shopping 137
8 Mexico City After Dark 140
9 A Side Trip to the Pyramids
of San Juan Teotihuacán 144

5 Silver, Spas & Spiritual Centers: From Taxco to Tepoztlán   149

by Juan Cristiano

1 Taxco: Cobblestones & Silver 149
Spanish & Art Classes in Taxco 154
2 Ixtapan de la Sal: A Thermal
Spa Town 160
3 Valle de Bravo & Avándaro:
Mexico's Switzerland 162

4 Cuernavaca: Land
of Eternal Spring 164
Fast Facts: Cuernavaca 167
5 Tepoztlán 174

6 San Miguel de Allende & the Colonial Silver Cities   179

by David Baird

1 San Miguel de Allende 180
*Fast Facts: San Miguel
de Allende* 184
*Learning at the Source: Going
to School in San Miguel* 186
2 Guanajuato 196
Fast Facts: Guanajuato 199
The Redolent Mexican Cantina 210

3 Santiago de Querétaro 211
Fast Facts: Querétaro 213
All Things Querétaro 215
Shopping for Opals 217
4 Zacatecas 221
Fast Facts: Zacatecas 222
5 San Luis Potosí 230
Fast Facts: San Luis Potosí 232

7 Michoacán   237

by David Baird

1 Morelia 238
   Fast Facts: Morelia 240
   Free-Market Forces 242
   A Brief Pause for
   the Food Cause 243
   Michoacán's Monarch Migration ...248

2 Pátzcuaro 249
   Fast Facts: Pátzcuaro 251
3 Uruapan: Handicrafts
   & Volcanoes 259

8 Guadalajara   262

by David Baird

1 Orientation 262
   The Neighborhoods in Brief 263
2 Getting Around 264
   Fast Facts: Guadalajara 265
3 Where to Stay 266
4 Where to Dine 270

5 Exploring Guadalajara 274
   Guadalajara Bus Tours 274
6 Shopping 279
   Tequila: The Name Says It All 280
7 Guadalajara After Dark 282

9 Puerto Vallarta & the Central Pacific Coast   283

by Lynne Bairstow

1 Puerto Vallarta 283
   Fast Facts: Puerto Vallarta 289
   A Huichol Art Primer:
   Shopping Tips 303
2 Mazatlán 332
   Fast Facts: Mazatlán 336

   Mazatlán's Carnaval:
   A Weeklong Party 340
3 Costa Alegre: Puerto Vallarta
   to Barra de Navidad 349
4 Manzanillo 359
   Fast Facts: Manzanillo 362

10 Acapulco & the Southern Pacific Coast   370

by Juan Cristiano

1 Acapulco 371
   Fast Facts: Acapulco 376
2 Northward to Zihuatanejo
   & Ixtapa 394
   Fast Facts: Zihuatanejo & Ixtapa ...397
3 Puerto Escondido 410

   Fast Facts: Puerto Escondido 414
   Ecotours & Other Adventurous
   Explorations 416
4 Bahías de Huatulco 425
   Fast Facts: Bahías de Huatulco 427

11 The Southernmost States: Oaxaca & Chiapas   433

by David Baird

1 Oaxaca City 434
  Social Unrest in Oaxaca 436
  Fast Facts: Oaxaca 440
  Oaxacan Street Food 450
2 Villahermosa 460
3 Palenque 463

4 San Cristóbal de las Casas 471
  The Zapatista Movement
  & Chiapas 472
  Fast Facts: San Cristóbal
  de las Casas 475

12 Veracruz & Puebla: On the Heels of Cortez   486

by David Baird

1 Veracruz City 486
  Fast Facts: Veracruz 488
2 Exploring North of Veracruz: Ruins,
  More Ruins & a Great Museum . . .495

3 Colonial Puebla 502
  Fast Facts: Puebla 504
  Cinco de Mayo & the Battle
  of Puebla 505

13 Cancún   516

by Juan Cristiano

1 Orientation 517
  The Best Websites for Cancún 518
  Fast Facts: Cancún 521
2 Where to Stay 523
3 Where to Dine 531

4 Beaches, Watersports
  & Boat Tours 536
5 Outdoor Activities & Attractions . . .540
6 Shopping 541
7 Cancún after Dark 542

14 Isla Mujeres & Cozumel   545

by Juan Cristiano & David Baird

1 Isla Mujeres 545
  The Best Websites for Isla
  Mujeres & Cozumel 546
  Fast Facts: Isla Mujeres 549

2 Cozumel 560
  An All-Inclusive Vacation
  in Cozumel 562
  Fast Facts: Cozumel 564

15 The Caribbean Coast: The Riviera Maya, Including
Playa del Carmen & the Costa Maya   578

by David Baird

1 Playa del Carmen 580
  Fast Facts: Playa del Carmen 582

Choosing an All-Inclusive
in the Riviera Maya 590

2 North of Playa del Carmen 592

3 South of Playa del Carmen 597

4 Tulum, Punta Allen
& Sian Ka'an 603

*The Sian Ka'an Biosphere
Reserve* .607

5 Cobá Ruins 608

6 Majahual, Xcalak & the
Chinchorro Reef 611

7 Lago Bacalar 613

8 Chetumal 615

9 Side Trips to Maya Ruins
from Chetumal 617

16   Mérida, Chichén Itzá & the Maya Interior   619

by David Baird

*The Best Websites for Mérida,
Chichén Itzá & the Maya Interior* . . .621

1 Mérida: Gateway to the
Maya Heartland 621

*Festivals & Special Events
in Mérida* 624

Fast Facts: Mérida 625

Of Haciendas & Hotels 636

2 The Ruins of Uxmal 647

3 Campeche 654

Fast Facts: Campeche 656

4 The Ruins of Chichén Itzá 660

5 Valladolid 666

17   The Copper Canyon   672

by David Baird

1 The Copper Canyon Train &
Stops along the Way 674

*Choosing a Package or
Tour Operator* 675

2 Los Mochis: The Western
Terminus 683

3 Chihuahua: The Eastern Terminus . . .686

Fast Facts: Chihuahua 688

18   Los Cabos & Baja California   692

by Lynne Bairstow & Emily Hughey Quinn

1 Los Cabos: Resorts, Watersports
& Golf 695

Fast Facts: San José del Cabo 698

Fast Facts: Cabo San Lucas 712

Surf & Sleep 718

2 Todos Santos: A Creative Oasis . . .724

3 La Paz: Peaceful Port Town 727

Fast Facts: La Paz 729

4 Mid Baja: Loreto, Mulegé
& Santa Rosalía 736

Whale-Watching in Baja 743

5 Tijuana & Rosarito Beach 744

*First Crush: The Annual
Harvest Festival* 747

A Northern Baja Spa Sanctuary 749

Surfing, Northern Baja Style 752

6 Ensenada: Port of Call 753

Appendix A: Mexico in Depth   756

by David Baird

1 The Land & Its People 756   3 Recommended Books 763
2 A Look at the Past 757

Appendix B: Useful Terms & Phrases   764

Index   767

List of Maps

Mexico 8

Central Mexico's Pre-Columbian
    Treasures 79

The Best of Western Mexico 81

Los Cabos to Copper Canyon 82

La Ruta Maya 83

Mexico City & Environs 87

Downtown Mexico City 96

Polanco/Chapultepec Area 105

Historic Downtown (Centro
    Histórico) 119

Chapultepec Park 121

Coyoacán 123

San Angel 125

Alameda Park Area 127

Teotihuacán 145

Side Trips from Mexico City 150

Taxco 153

Ixtapan de la Sal 161

Valle de Bravo & Avándaro 163

Cuernavaca 165

The Colonial Silver Cities 181

Where to Stay in San Miguel
    de Allende 183

Guanajuato 197

Santiago de Querétaro 212

Zacatecas 223

San Luis Potosí 231

Morelia 239

Pátzcuaro 251

Uruapan 261

Downtown Guadalajara 275

Puerto Vallarta: Hotel Zone
    & Beaches 285

Downtown Puerto Vallarta 301

Mazatlán Area 333

Costa Alegre & Central Pacific
    Coast 351

Barra de Navidad Bay Area 355

Manzanillo Area 361

Acapulco Bay Area 372

Zihuatanejo & Ixtapa Area 395

Downtown Zihuatanejo 403

Puerto Escondido 411

Oaxaca Area 435

Downtown Oaxaca 437

Monte Albán 455

Palenque Archaeological Site 465

Where to Stay & Dine
    in Palenque 467

San Cristóbal de las Casas 473

Downtown Veracruz 487

Xalapa Orientation 497

Puebla 503

Tlaxcala 513

Downtown Cancún 519

Isla Cancún (Zona Hotelera) 525

Isla Mujeres 547

Cozumel 561

San Miguel de Cozumel 567

Playa del Carmen   581

The Yucatán's Upper Caribbean
  Coast   593

The Yucatán's Lower Caribbean
  Coast   612

Where to Stay & Dine in Mérida   633

The Copper Canyon   673

Chihuahua   687

The Baja Peninsula   693

San José del Cabo   697

The Two Cabos & the Corridor   708

Cabo San Lucas   713

The Lower Baja Peninsula   737

Tijuana   745

The Upper Baja Peninsula   751

An Invitation to the Reader

In researching this book, we discovered many wonderful places—hotels, restaurants, shops, and more. We're sure you'll find others. Please tell us about them, so we can share the information with your fellow travelers in upcoming editions. If you were disappointed with a recommendation, we'd love to know that, too. Please write to:

Frommer's Mexico 2008
Wiley Publishing, Inc. • 111 River St. • Hoboken, NJ 07030-5774

An Additional Note

Please be advised that travel information is subject to change at any time—and this is especially true of prices. We therefore suggest that you write or call ahead for confirmation when making your travel plans. The authors, editors, and publisher cannot be held responsible for the experiences of readers while traveling. Your safety is important to us, however, so we encourage you to stay alert and be aware of your surroundings. Keep a close eye on cameras, purses, and wallets, all favorite targets of thieves and pickpockets.

About the Authors

A writer, editor, and translator, **David Baird** has lived several years in different parts of Mexico. Now based in Austin, Texas, he spends as much time in Mexico as possible.

A resident of Mexico City, **Juan Cristiano** is a native of Los Angeles who has written extensively about destinations in Mexico and Latin America, the United States, and Western Europe. **Lynne Bairstow** has lived in Puerto Vallarta for most of the past 16 years. Her travel articles on Mexico have appeared in numerous publications, including the *New York Times, Los Angeles Times, Private Air* magazine, and *Luxury Living* magazine.

Fresh out of Kansas, **Emily Hughey Quinn** moved to Los Cabos, Mexico, in 2003 after launching *Cabo Living* magazine. Enchanted by the desert landscape, the Sea of Cortez, the people, and the tacos al pastor, Quinn now considers Baja's brazen wilderness to be as much a part of her as the prairie.

Frommer's Star Ratings, Icons & Abbreviations

Every hotel, restaurant, and attraction listing in this guide has been ranked for quality, value, service, amenities, and special features using a **star-rating system.** In country, state, and regional guides, we also rate towns and regions to help you narrow down your choices and budget your time accordingly. Hotels and restaurants are rated on a scale of zero (recommended) to three stars (exceptional). Attractions, shopping, nightlife, towns, and regions are rated according to the following scale: zero stars (recommended), one star (highly recommended), two stars (very highly recommended), and three stars (must-see).

In addition to the star-rating system, we also use **eight feature icons** that point you to the great deals, in-the-know advice, and unique experiences that separate travelers from tourists. Throughout the book, look for:

Finds	Special finds—those places only insiders know about
Fun Fact	Fun facts—details that make travelers more informed and their trips more fun
Kids	Best bets for kids and advice for the whole family
Moments	Special moments—those experiences that memories are made of
Overrated	Places or experiences not worth your time or money
Tips	Insider tips—great ways to save time and money
Value	Great values—where to get the best deals
Warning	Warning—traveler's advisories are usually in effect

The following **abbreviations** are used for credit cards:

AE	American Express	DISC	Discover	V	Visa
DC	Diners Club	MC	MasterCard		

Frommers.com

Now that you have this guidebook to help you plan a great trip, visit our website at **www.frommers.com** for additional travel information on more than 3,600 destinations. We update features regularly to give you instant access to the most current trip-planning information available. At Frommers.com, you'll find scoops on the best airfares, lodging rates, and car rental bargains. You can even book your travel online through our reliable travel booking partners. Other popular features include:

- Online updates of our most popular guidebooks
- Vacation sweepstakes and contest giveaways
- Newsletters highlighting the hottest travel trends
- Online travel message boards with featured travel discussions

What's New in Mexico

The year 2007 brought new leadership to Mexico, with Felipe Calderon of the center-right National Action Party (PAN, the same political party that former President Fox belonged to) elected as the new president following a close and contested race. President Calderon promised to focus his government on tackling domestic insecurity, poverty, and joblessness. Throughout this transition, Mexico's economy remained stable and the government committed to attracting investment and tourism. Although drug-related violence and organized crime remained a concern in some areas of the country, this seldom affected Mexico's major tourist areas. Tensions in Oaxaca related to a protracted teachers strike in 2006 had mostly dissipated by 2007 and tourists were returning to that lovely state capital once again.

For visitors, this means that they can go ahead and plan their Mexican vacation in advance without having to worry about the unknown—except when it comes to the weather (Mexico has had particularly difficult hurricane seasons in recent years). Thankfully, the damage caused by Hurricane Wilma in 2005 has been overcome and the tourist infrastructure of Cancun—which was especially hard hit—has been rebuilt and the beaches replenished.

PLANNING YOUR TRIP TO MEXICO As of January 23, 2007, citizens of the United States, Canada, Mexico, and Bermuda are required to present a passport or other accepted document that establishes the bearer's identity and nationality to enter the United States when arriving by air from any part of the Western Hemisphere. This change in travel document requirements is the result of recommendations made by the 9/11 Commission, which the U.S. Congress subsequently passed into law in the Intelligence Reform and Terrorism Prevention Act of 2004. A separate proposed rule addressing land and sea travel will be published at a later date, proposing specific requirements for travelers entering the United States through land and sea border crossings. As early as January 1, 2008, U.S. citizens traveling between the United States and Canada, Mexico, Central and South America, the Caribbean, and Bermuda by land or sea could be required to present a valid U.S. passport or other documents as determined by the U.S. Department of Homeland Security.

Travelers to Mexico are now able to make tax-free purchases while vacationing, thanks to a law passed by Mexico's Congress. The law grants international visitors a full refund of the tax added to purchases if the buyer adheres to certain criteria. The merchandise must be purchased in Mexico and verified by airport or seaport Customs, and be verified with a receipt presented at time of departure to be worth at least 1,200 Mexican pesos (approximately US$110 at current exchange rates). Reimbursement to tourists is contingent upon any added costs a possible return may generate.

Here are highlights on new flight services to and within Mexico:

- **Alaska Airlines** (www.alaskaair.com) now serves Cancún, Los Cabos, and Puerto Vallarta from Seattle and Portland.
- **Aviacsa Airlines** (www.aviacsa.com) flies to destinations throughout Mexico from Los Angeles, Las Vegas, and Houston.
- **Click Mexicana** (www.clickmx.com), a low-cost subsidiary of Mexicana Airlines, has continued to expand its domestic routes, with connections to international destinations via Mexico City on Mexicana.
- **Delta Airlines** (www.delta.com) now offers nonstop flights from LAX to Mexico City.
- **Frontier Airlines** (www.frontier airlines.com) has expanded service to include Acapulco, Cabo San Lucas, Cancún, Cozumel, Ixtapa/ Zihuatanejo, Mazatlán, and Puerto Vallarta.
- **InterJet** (www.interjet.com.mx) offers low-cost flights connecting Toluca (near Mexico City) with most Mexican resort destinations.

MEXICO CITY For complete information, see chapter 4.

Starwood Hotels and Resorts plans to open the first **St. Regis Hotel** (www. starwoodhotels.com) in Latin America in 2007, on Paseo de la Reforma in Mexico City. Owned by Mexican real estate investors Grupo 1818 and developed by Ideurban Consultores, the St. Regis Hotel, Mexico City, will have 189 hotel rooms and suites, as well as 100 private residences.

The **Angel de la Independencia** (The Angel of Independence Monument, often referred to simply as the "Angel") completed an extensive renovation in 2006, as did the roundabout surrounding it on Paseo de la Reforma, the city's main thoroughfare.

SILVER CITIES For complete information, see chapter 6.

San Miguel de Allende The **Casa de Sierra Nevada** (© 800/701-1561; www. casadesierranevada.com), under the ownership of Orient Express, is step-by-step doing an extensive makeover of the guest rooms. For several months this year the section in Parque Juárez will be closed for remodeling.

Bill Levasseur, owner of the B&B **Casa de la Cuesta** (© 415/154-4324; www. casadelacuesta.com), and a long-time collector of masks, has opened a jewel of a museum featuring his treasures. It's located behind the B&B and called **La Otra Cara de México** (The Other Face of Mexico). It's open by appointment by calling the B&B.

Guanajuato This city's tourist information office has changed phone numbers, as it is apt to do every 3 years. The new number is © 473/732-1574, ext. 1437.

A small property called **Hotel Antiguo Vapor** (© 473/732-3211; www.hotel avapor.com) adds to the variety of lodging available downtown. It has some pretty rooms and will soon be opening a restaurant and a bar.

A new **Hotel Camino Real** (www. caminoreal.com) will open by the summer of 2007 on the site of the former Hacienda San Javier (where the old Parador San Javier was). It's downtown, above the Alhóndiga.

The new restaurants in town include the following: **El Abue** (© 473/732-6242), for Mexican with an Italian slant. **El Midi** (no phone) for fresh salads and light lunch fare, with a Mediterranean touch. **México Lindo y Sabroso** (© 473/731-0529) for good honest Mexican food. There was one notable loss—**Chez Nicole** has closed its doors.

Querétaro The tourism office has provisionally spun off its city bus tours to private concessionaires. These companies have set up tourist information kiosks in some of the downtown plazas, but up until now, they don't offer very good information. Their real function is to sell tickets for the tours. For visitor info, go to the regular office on Calle Pasteur just off the Plaza de Armas.

Gran Hotel (© 442/241-8050; www. granhoteldequeretaro.com.mx), which had stood vacant for years, has been reopened. It's the first 50-room hotel I've seen in provincial Mexico that is all non-smoking. The rooms are luxurious, the location stellar, and the character of the old place singular.

Another property that looks to be an attractive and well-priced hotel should open sometime in 2007. It's in the historic center and has a swimming pool. But it doesn't yet have a name, much less a website. Ask at the front desk of Hotel Posada Acueducto (© 442/224-1289).

San Luis Potosí The city is better looking than ever now that it has finished an extensive renovation of the historic center, which includes the illumination of several of its most remarkable buildings.

The tourism office has moved. It's now at Manuel José Othón 130, and faces the side of the cathedral.

The **National Mask Museum** remains closed until sometime in 2007.

MICHOACAN For complete information, see chapter 7.

With Continental offering **nonstop service** between Morelia and Los Angeles, AeroMéxico has decided to offer competing service from southern California's Ontario airport.

One of the first acts of the new president was to send 8,000 troops to Michoacán to root out the drug gangs, which are enmeshed in a brutal turf war that has killed over a hundred gang members and police officers. I was recently in the state, and everything appeared quite normal. There seems to be no disruption, and the army's campaign wasn't even the most common topic of conversation.

GUADALAJARA For complete information, see chapter 8.

There's another lodging option for downtown Guadalajara: **Hotel Morales** (© 33/3658-5232; www.hotelmorales. com.mx), was a landmark hotel in Guadalajara until it closed many years ago. It's now quite a comfortable, well-located place to stay.

PUERTO VALLARTA & THE CENTRAL PACIFIC COAST For complete information, see chapter 9.

Punta Mita will welcome the **St. Regis Resort** (www.starwoodhotels.com) in early 2008. The resort will include 100 guest rooms—each with private outdoor shower, as well as 65 luxury villas, a spa and fitness center, two restaurants, and the second Jack Nicklaus Signature Golf Course to be located in Punta Mita.

ACAPULCO & SOUTHERN PACIFIC COAST For complete information, see chapter 10.

By early 2006, over $5 billion was spent on improvements for Acapulco, with an additional $2.5 billion planned in the following 3 years. The city's newest hotels and investment projects are in Punta Diamante (the "Diamond Acapulco" section of town), between the airport and Las Brisas, heading toward Acapulco Bay.

OAXACA & CHIAPAS For complete information, see chapter 11.

Oaxaca After the civil unrest that practically closed down the city for half a year, things are returning to normal. Tourists are returning in growing numbers. Businesses have reopened, but a few have closed or changed owners. This was the case with **El Naranjo.** Chef Iliana de la Vega sold her restaurant and has left the city.

VERACRUZ & PUEBLA   For complete information, see chapter 12.

There are new hotel options in both cities. In Veracruz, the **Gran Hotel Diligencias** (© 229/923-0280; www.gran hoteldiligencias.com) has completely refurbished an old building on the Zócalo that had been abandoned for years. It's now the place to stay when visiting the downtown port area. In downtown colonial Puebla, an unrepentantly modern hotel, the **NH Puebla** (© 888/726-0528; www.nh-hotels.com), has created an attractive space where there was once only an old office building.

CANCUN   For complete information, see chapter 13.

On October 21, 2005, the Category 4 **Hurricane Wilma** came ashore Mexico's Yucatán peninsula with winds reaching 242kmph (150 mph). It toppled trees, washed away portions of Cancún's famed white beaches, and damaged the majority of the resort's hotels, restaurants, and attractions. However, relief came quickly, and by 2007 most of the city resort had been rebuilt to look even better than before.

Foremost among Cancún's renewal and restoration projects was the recovery of 14km (9 miles) of beaches. The $21-million **beach restoration project** used the same silky white sand that the area is known for, dredging it from the sea floor not far from Cancún's coastline to create miles of new beach along the hardest-hit areas. The project, centered primarily on the southernmost stretch of the city's famous hotel strip, is now complete.

The majority of damaged hotels took the opportunity to upgrade their facilities and redecorate their rooms, which has led to a new and improved Cancún. Other enhancements included the replanting of thousands of palm trees, as well as new gardens and sidewalks for the hotel strip's main thoroughfare, Bulevar Kukulcán.

Highway 307, which services the Riviera Maya, is being expanded. Currently the highway has two lanes south and two lanes north from downtown Cancún to just south of Playa del Carmen. The expansion project extends this configuration all the way to Tulum.

At **Cancún's International Airport,** construction on a second runway and third terminal will be completed by mid-2007. These steps should greatly improve logistics at the airport.

Accommodations ME (© 866/436-3542; www.mebymelia.com) brings to Cancún a new level of minimalist chic by the Spanish Meliá hotel group. This new hotel includes trendy bars, sensual artwork, and chill-out music in the public spaces; guest rooms have distinctive contemporary furnishings and modern amenities like plasma TVs. The stylish Yhi Spa overlooks the ocean and offers every type of facial and body treatment. If you're looking for a hotel to see-and-be-seen, ME is the place to go.

The **Ritz-Carlton Cancún** (© 800/241-3333; www.ritzcarlton.com), re-opened on December 15, 2006, after a multimillion-dollar repair and refurbishment project that generated new facilities and expanded services, including a culinary center. The resort also added a tennis program, operated by former pro and ESPN commentator Cliff Drysdale, and upgraded and expanded its fitness center.

Opened in early 2007, the **Royal** (© 800/760-0944; www.realresorts.com. mx) is an over-the-top, all-inclusive, adults-only resort. Luxury abounds, from the stunning infinity pools and gorgeous beach to the gourmet restaurants and sophisticated spa. The elegant marble lobby looks out one side to the Caribbean and the other to the lagoon, and the guest suites offer every conceivable amenity, including two-person Jacuzzis. Guests in the top-category suites have access to

BMW Mini Coopers. The all-inclusive package includes gourmet meals, premium drinks, and evening entertainment.

ISLA MUJERES & COZUMEL For complete information, see chapter 14.

Cozumel The **Presidente InterContinental Cozumel** (℡ 800/327-0200 in the U.S.; www.intercontinentalcozumel. com) reopened in November of 2006. It was the final hotel to reopen after the hurricane. The company decided not just to refurbish the hotel, but to also make some serious changes and upgrades. There's a new pool, just for adults. There are several new amenities, but the change is most noticeable in the guest rooms, which are far more comfortable and attractive than they used to be. The hotel is now a member of Leading Hotels of the World.

A new condo development on the south side of town, **El Cantil Condominiums** (℡ 954/323-8491 in the U.S.; www.elcantilcondos.com), offers handsome studio and multi-bedroom condos for lease by the night or the week. The developer is the owner of Prima Restaurant, a favorite restaurant on the island. He also has plans to open another restaurant on the top of one of the condo towers and has brought a chef from New York to run the show. It's called **The Wynston** (℡ 987/869-1517). It had not yet opened when I was last there.

There are a few other new eateries in the town. One that might be particularly convenient is **Le Chef** (℡ 987/876-3437) a gourmet grocery store and deli where you can get all the fixings for a picnic on the beach. Another is **Capicúa** (℡ 987/869-8265), a tapas bar with an ample menu of main courses.

THE RIVIERA MAYA For complete information, see chapter 15.

Playa del Carmen Playa is still growing fast. Most of the new growth is residential and condos. But the core part of Playa has remained largely the same.

Acanto Hotel and Suites (℡ 631/882-1986 in the U.S.; www.acantohotels. com) is a lovely little property in a great part of Playa, just off Avenida La Quinta. The property was originally small condos, but it makes a lot better sense as a hotel.

Puerto Morelos & Environs All the exclusive spa resorts have reopened after recovering from Hurricane Wilma and are more luxurious than ever. Ikal del Mar has changed hands and has a new name: **The Tides Riviera Maya** (℡ 800/578-0281 in the U.S. and Canada). **Maroma** (℡ 866/454-9351 in the U.S.) has added some new suites that are beyond any suites it had before. **Ceiba del Mar** (℡ 877/545-6221 in the U.S.) has invested a great deal in its suites and added penthouses to the top of each of the seven buildings. It has also added another restaurant.

Mayakoba (www.mayakoba.com) is a new golf course resort development between Playa and Puerto Morelos that has attracted a stellar lineup of resorts including The Fairmount, Rosewood, and Banyan Tree—all have spas and border a grand golf course designed by Greg Norman. At present only the Fairmount has been completed. The other resorts will be completed in 2008.

Tulum The highway to Tulum is under construction. It is being widened to four lanes. When I was last there, construction was completed as far as Paamul.

In the Tulum hotel zone, one of my favorite properties, Sueños Tulum, was closed because of a legal challenge to the property deed. Several properties along this coast have clouded titles, and I suspect a couple more may close.

MERIDA, CHICHEN ITZA & THE MAYA INTERIOR For complete information on this region, see chapter 16.

Mérida A new U.S. consulate was built at Calle 60 #338-K, just north of the Hyatt hotel. The new number is © **999/942-5700.**

Amate Books (www.amatebooks.com), the English-language bookstore in Oaxaca, has opened up a branch store in Mérida at the corner of Calle 60 and Calle 51.

Campeche My favorite restaurant in Campeche, **La Pigua** (© **981/811-3365**) now stays open until the evening to accommodate visitors (locals don't believe in eating seafood at night). It also enlarged the dining room to accommodate more guests, which will make it a lot easier to get a table now.

LOS CABOS & BAJA CALIFORNIA

For complete information on this region, see chapter 18.

SeaWatch, a La Paz-based organization dedicated to exposing and stopping destructive fishing practices in the Sea of Cortez for the past 15 years, is launching a public awareness campaign in Southern Baja to stop commercial fishermen from wiping out reefs and snaring hammerhead schools in nets. Despite promotional materials constantly quoting Jacques Cousteau's claim that the Sea of Cortez is the "world's aquarium," fisheries have declined between 70% and 90% since the 1960s, and nothing is being done to ensure future generations will have fish in the sea. The **Bay of La Paz Project,** under the auspices of SeaWatch, hopes to limit commercial fishing in various high-pressure areas, thereby allowing fish populations to reproduce. To find out more, visit **www.seawatch. org** or call © **503/616-4421.**

Accommodations Sol Meliá rolled out its new brand, ME by Meliá, this year, transforming The Meliá San Lucas into **ME Cabo** (© **624/145-7800;** www.mebymelia.com), a chic resort for young-at-heart travelers looking to party in an ultrafabulous setting. New rooms, new style, a new V.I.P. floor called "The Level," and the creation of Passion, already one of the most popular nightclubs in Cabo, all contribute to ME Cabo's new reign as the flagship of hip in Cabo San Lucas.

Desire Resorts opened Los Cabos' first couples-only, clothing-optional luxury resort in the hotel zone of San José del Cabo. Call it decadent, hedonistic, and even downright racy; there's a thriving market that's willing to pay top-dollar for exotic encounters at the all-inclusive **Desire Resort & Spa,** Los Cabos (© **888/201-7551** in the U.S.; 624/142-9300; www.desireloscabos.com)

Attractions A new, 18-hole Jack Nicklaus–designed championship golf course is open for play at **Club Campestre** (© **624/142-5327;** www.clubcampestre. com) in San José del Cabo. Grupo Questro, the masterminds behind Cabo Real and Puerto Los Cabos, are the developers of this new golf course and residential community.

Canopy Costa Azul Xtreme Tours (© **624/105-9311;** www.canopycosta azul.com) may not be your typical "canopy" tour—there's no canopy—but you will feel the thrill of sailing across the void of the Costa Azul Canyon. Nearly 5km (3 miles) of zip lines crisscross the canyon at varying lengths and heights, all of which elicit gleeful squeals from zip liners of all ages.

The Best of Mexico

by David Baird, Juan Cristiano & Emily Hughey Quinn

Across Mexico, in villages and cities, in mountains, tropical coasts, and ⸻tings, enchanting surprises await travelers. These might take the form of ⸻small-town festival, delightful dining in a memorable restaurant, or even ⸻road through heavenly countryside. Below is a starter list of our favorite ⸻you'll have the pleasure of adding your own discoveries.

1 The Best Beach Vacations

- **Puerto Vallarta:** Spectacularly wide Banderas Bay offers 42km (26 miles) of beaches. Some, like Playa Los Muertos—the popular public beach in town—abound with *palapa* restaurants, beach volleyball, and parasailing. The beaches of Punta Mita, the exclusive development north of Vallarta, are of the white-sand variety, with crystalline waters and coral reefs just offshore. Others around the bay nestle in coves, accessible only by boat. Puerto Vallarta is the only place where authentic colonial ambience mixes with true resort amenities. See "Puerto Vallarta" in chapter 9.

- **Puerto Escondido:** The best overall beach value in Mexico is principally known for its world-class surfing beach, Playa Zicatela. The surrounding beaches all have their own appeal; colorful fishing *pangas* dot the central town beach, parked under the shade of palms leaning so far over they almost touch the ground. Puerto Escondido offers unique accommodations at excellent prices, with exceptional budget dining and nightlife. See "Puerto Escondido" in chapter 10.

- **Ixtapa/Zihuatanejo:** These side-by-side resorts offer beach-goers the best of both worlds: serene simplicity and resort comforts. For those in search of a back-to-basics beach, the best and most beautiful is Playa La Ropa, close to Zihuatanejo. The wide beach at Playa Las Gatas, with its restaurants and snorkeling sites, is also a great place to play. The high-rise hotels in Ixtapa, on the next bay over from Zihuatanejo, front Playa Palmar, a fine, wide swath of beach. See "Northward to Zihuatanejo & Ixtapa" in chapter 10.

- **Cancún:** In terms of sheer beauty, Cancún and the coastline of the Yucatán state of Quintana Roo have always boasted Mexico's most enticing beaches. The powdery, white-sand beaches have water the color of a Technicolor dream. Cancún offers the widest assortment of luxury beachfront hotels, with more restaurants, nightlife, and activities than any other resort destination in Mexico. See chapter 13.

- **Tulum:** Fronting some of the best beaches on Mexico's Caribbean coast,

Mexico

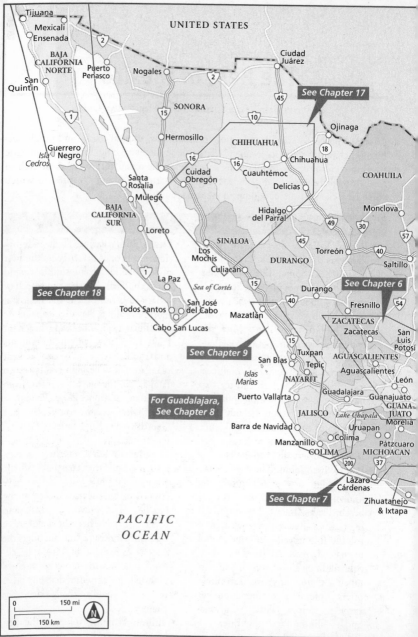

UNITED STATES

Tijuana
Mexicali
Ensenada
BAJA
CALIFORNIA
NORTE
Puerto
Peñasco
San
Quintin
Nogales
2
SONORA
15
Hermosillo
Isla
Cedros
Guerrero
Negro
Santa
Rosalia
Mulegé
BAJA
CALIFORNIA
SUR
Loreto
1
La Paz
1
Sea of Cortés
Todos Santos
San José
del Cabo
Cabo San Lucas

Ciudad
Juárez
45
Ojinaga
10
CHIHUAHUA
16
16
Chihuahua
18
Cuidad
Obregón
Cuauhtémoc
Delicias
COAHUILA
Hidalgo
del Parral
Monclova
49
30
57
SINALOA
Los
Mochis
Culiacán
45
Torreón
40
Saltillo
DURANGO
Durango
40
Fresnillo
54
Mazatlán
15
ZACATECAS
Zacatecas
San
Luis
Potosí
15
Tuxpan
San Blas
Tepic
AGUASCALIENTES
Aguascalientes
León
Islas
Marias
NAYARIT
Puerto Vallarta
Guadalajara
Guanajuato
GUANA-
JUATO
JALISCO
Lake Chapala
Morelia
Barra de Navidad
Uruapan
Pátzcuaro
Manzanillo
Colima
MICHOACAN
COLIMA
200
37
Lázaro
Cárdenas
Zihuatanejo
& Ixtapa

See Chapter 17

See Chapter 6

See Chapter 18

See Chapter 9

For Guadalajara,
See Chapter 8

See Chapter 7

PACIFIC
OCEAN

0   150 mi
0   150 km

N

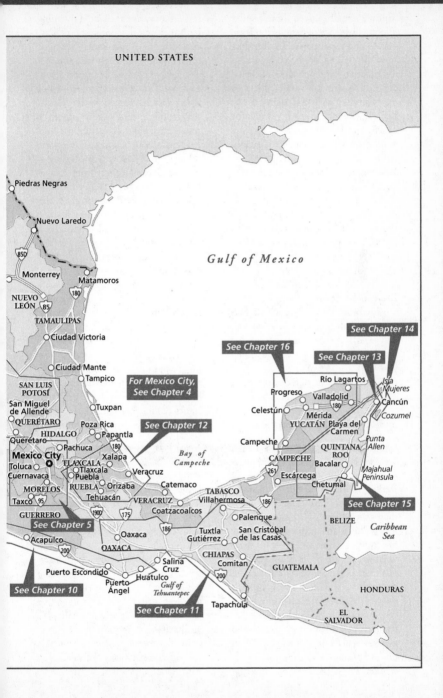

UNITED STATES

Gulf of Mexico

Piedras Negras

Nuevo Laredo

850

Monterrey
Matamoros
NUEVO
LEÓN   85
180
TAMAULIPAS

Ciudad Victoria

Ciudad Mante
Tampico
SAN LUIS
POTOSÍ
San Miguel
de Allende
QUERÉTARO
Tuxpan
HIDALGO
Poza Rica
Papantla
Querétaro
Pachuca
180
Mexico City
Toluca
Xalapa
TLAXCALA
Cuernavaca
Tlaxcala
Veracruz
MORELOS
PUEBLA
Puebla
Orizaba
Taxco   95
Tehuacán
GUERRERO
VERACRUZ
1900
175
Coatzacoalcos
See Chapter 5

Acapulco
200
Oaxaca
186
OAXACA

Puerto Escondido
Salina
Cruz
Puerto
Ángel
Huatulco
Gulf of
Tehuantepec
See Chapter 10

See Chapter 11

For Mexico City,
See Chapter 4

See Chapter 12

Bay of
Campeche

Catemaco
TABASCO
Villahermosa
Palenque
Tuxtla
Gutiérrez
San Cristóbal
de las Casas
CHIAPAS
Comitan
200
Tapachula

See Chapter 16

See Chapter 13

See Chapter 14

Río Lagartos
Progreso
Valladolid
Celestún
180
Mérida
YUCATÁN
Playa del
Carmen
Campeche
QUINTANA
ROO
CAMPECHE
261
Escárcega
Bacalar
Chetumal
186
Isla
Mujeres
Cancún
Cozumel
Punta
Allen
Majahual
Peninsula
See Chapter 15

BELIZE
Caribbean
Sea

GUATEMALA

HONDURAS

EL
SALVADOR

Tulum's small *palapa* hotels offer guests a little slice of paradise far from crowds and megaresorts. The bustling town lies inland; at the coast, things are quiet and will remain so because all these hotels are small and must generate their own electricity. If you can pull yourself away from the beach, nearby are ruins to explore and a vast nature preserve. See chapter 15.

- **Isla Mujeres:** There's only one main beach here—Playa Norte—but it's superb. From this island, you can dive El Garrafón reef, snorkel offshore, and take a boat excursion to the Isla Contoy national wildlife reserve, which features great birding and a fabulous, uninhabited beach. See "Isla Mujeres" in chapter 14.
- **Playa del Carmen:** "Playa" is Mexico's hip beach destination with a dash of third-world chic. Above all, it's easy and low key. You walk to the beach, you walk back to the hotel, you walk to one of the many good restaurants. Next day, you repeat. The beaches are white sand; the water is clear blue and perfect for swimming. If you feel the urge to be active,

not far away are ancient Maya ruins, Cozumel, and the megaresort of Cancún, offering all the variety that you might want in a beach vacation. See "Playa del Carmen" in chapter 15.

- **La Paz:** This state capital borders a lovely beach, dotted with colorful playgrounds and lively open-air restaurants. Take a cue from the local residents, though, and pass on swimming here in favor of the exquisite beaches just minutes from downtown. La Paz's beaches and the islets just offshore have transformed this tranquil town into a center for diving, sea kayaking, and other adventure pursuits. See "La Paz: Peaceful Port Town" in chapter 18.
- **Los Cabos:** Dramatic rock formations and crashing waves mix with wide stretches of soft sand and rolling surf breaks. Start at Playa Palmilla and work your way down the Tourist Corridor to the famed Lovers' Beach at Land's End. Some beaches are more appropriate for contemplation than for swimming, which isn't all bad. See "Los Cabos: Resorts, Watersports & Golf" in chapter 18.

2 The Best Cultural Experiences

- **Passing Time in the Plazas & Parks:** All the world may be a stage, but some parts have richer backdrops than others. Town plazas are the perfect settings for watching everyday life unfold. Alive with people, these open spaces are no modern product of urban planners, but are rooted in the traditional Mexican view of society. Several plazas are standouts: **Veracruz**'s famous *zócalo* (see chapter 12) features nearly nonstop music and tropical gaiety. One look tells you how important **Oaxaca**'s *zócalo* (see chapter 11) is to the local citizenry;

the plaza is remarkably beautiful, grand, and intimate all at once. **Mexico City**'s Alameda (see chapter 4) has a dark, dramatic history—heretics were burned at the stake here during the colonial period—but today it's a people's park where lovers sit, cotton-candy vendors spin their treats, and the sound of organ grinders drifts over the changing crowd. **San Miguel de Allende**'s Jardín (see chapter 6) is the focal point for meeting, sitting, painting, and sketching. During festivals, it fills with dancers, parades, and elaborate fireworks. **Guanajuato** and **Querétaro** (see chapter 6) have the coziest of plazas, while El Centro in **Mérida** (see chapter 16) on a Sunday can't be beat.

- *Música Popular:* Nothing reveals the soul of a people like music, and Mexico boasts many kinds in many different settings. You can find brassy, belt-it-out **mariachi** music in the famous Plaza de Garibaldi in Mexico City (see chapter 4), under the arches of El Parián in Tlaquepaque, and in other parts of Guadalajara (see chapter 8). Or perhaps you want to hear romantic **boleros** about love's betrayal sung to the strumming of a Spanish guitar, or what Mexicans call *música tropical* and related *cumbias,* mambos, and cha-cha-chas (see chapter 13).

- **Regional Folk Dancing:** Whether it's the Ballet Folklórico in Mexico City or the Ballet Folclórico in Guadalajara (see chapters 4 and 8), the almost-nightly park performances in Mérida (see chapter 16), or celebrations countrywide, these performances are diverse and colorful expressions of Mexican traditions.

- **Fireworks:** Mexicans share such a passion for fireworks and such a cavalier attitude toward them that it's a

good thing the buildings are stone and cement, or the whole country would have burned down long ago. Many local traditions surround fireworks, and every festival includes a display. The most lavish are the large constructions known as *castillos,* and the wildest are the *toros* that men carry over their shoulders while running through the streets, causing festival-goers to dive for cover.

- **Strolling** *El Malecón:* Wherever there's a seafront road, you'll find *el malecón* bordering it. This is generally a wide sidewalk for strolling, complete with vendors selling pinwheels and cotton candy. In some places, it has supplanted the plaza as a centerpiece of town life. The best examples are in **Puerto Vallarta, Mazatlán** (see chapter 9), **La Paz** (see chapter 18), **Cozumel** (see chapter 14), and **Veracruz** (see chapter 12).

- **Regional Fairs:** Almost every city and town has its regional fair *(feria regional).* They showcase the best products of the region—tequila or fruit liquors, livestock, carved silver, or clay handicrafts. One of the most notable regional fairs is La Feria del Caballo in Texcoco, which takes place in late March or early April.

3 The Best Archaeological Sites

- **Teotihuacán:** So close to Mexico City, yet centuries away. You can feel the majesty of the past in a stroll down the pyramid-lined Avenue of the Dead, from the Pyramid of the Sun to the Pyramid of the Moon. Imagine what a fabulous place this must have been when the walls were stuccoed and painted brilliant colors. See "A Side Trip to the Pyramids of San Juan Teotihuacán" in chapter 4.

- **Monte Albán:** A grand ceremonial city built on a mountaintop overlooking the valley of Oaxaca, Monte

Albán offers the visitor panoramic vistas; a fascinating view of a society in transition, reflected in the contrasting methods of pyramid construction; and intriguing details in ornamentation. See "Oaxaca City" in chapter 11.

- **Palenque:** Like the pharaohs of Egypt, the rulers of Palenque built tombs deep within their pyramids. Imagine the magnificent ceremony in A.D. 683 when King Pacal was entombed in his magnificent burial chamber, which lay unspoiled until its discovery in 1952. See "Palenque" in chapter 11.

- **Ek Balam:** Archaeologists at this site have made the most astonishing discoveries of the decade. Ek Balam's main pyramid is taller than Chichén Itzá's, and it holds a sacred doorway bordered with elaborate stucco figures of priests and kings and rich iconography. See "Ek Balam: Dark Jaguar" in chapter 16.

- **Uxmal:** No matter how many times you see Uxmal, the splendor of its stone carvings is awe-inspiring. A stone rattlesnake undulates across the facade of the Nunnery complex, and 103

masks of the rain god Chaac project out from the Governor's Palace. See "The Ruins of Uxmal" in chapter 16.

- **Chichén Itzá:** Stand beside the giant serpent head at the foot of El Castillo pyramid and marvel at the architects and astronomers who positioned the building so precisely that shadow and sunlight form a serpent's body slithering from the peak to the earth at each equinox (Mar 21 and Sept 21). See "The Ruins of Chichén Itzá" in chapter 16.

4 The Best Active Vacations

- **Scuba Diving in Cozumel & along the Yucatán's Caribbean Coast:** The coral reefs off the island, Mexico's premier diving destination, are among the top five dive spots in the world. See chapter 14. The Yucatán's coastal reef is part of the second-largest reef system in the world and affords excellent diving. Especially beautiful is the Chinchorro Reef, 32km (20 miles) offshore from Majahual or Xcalak. You can also dive in the clear, cool water of the many caverns and *cenotes* (sinkholes, or natural wells) that dot the interior. See chapter 15. Other excellent dive sites are in and around **Puerto Vallarta** and off **Los Cabos.** See chapters 9 and 18.

- **Fly-Fishing off the Punta Allen Peninsula:** Serious anglers will enjoy the challenge of fly-fishing the saltwater flats and lagoons of Ascension Bay, near Punta Allen. See "Tulum, Punta Allen & Sian Ka'an" in chapter 15.

- **Hiking & Horseback Riding in the Copper Canyon:** Miles and miles of beautiful, remote, challenging canyon lands are paradise for the serious hiker or rider. **Canyon Travel** (© 800/843-1060 in the U.S.; www.canyontravel.com) can set hikers up with a Tarahumara Indian guide, who can take you

deep into the canyons to places rarely viewed by tourists. Doug Rhodes of **Paraíso del Oso** (© 800/884-3107 in the U.S.) leads tours of experienced horseback riders on a 12-day ride that tests a rider's skill in mountainous terrain. It has to be the most challenging ride in North America. See "The Copper Canyon Train & Stops along the Way" in chapter 17.

- **Golf in Los Cabos & Puerto Vallarta:** Puerto Vallarta, with its seven championship courses, is *the* new destination for golfers to watch. Added to the appeal of golf here are courses within easy driving distance along the Pacific Coast at El Tamarindo, Isla Navidad, and Manzanillo. See chapter 9. The Corridor between San José del Cabo and Cabo San Lucas is one of the world's premier golf destinations, with seven championship courses open and a total of 207 holes slated for the area. See chapter 18.

- **Surfing Zicatela Beach in Puerto Escondido:** This world-class break is a lure for surfers from around the globe. It challenges the best in the sport each September and October, when the waves peak and the annual surf competitions take place. See chapter 10. Other noted surf breaks in Mexico include Sayulita, Punta Mita, and Las Islitas Beach near **San Blas** (all north of Puerto Vallarta); Playa Costa Azul, on the outskirts of **San José del Cabo;** and "Killers" at Todos Santos Island in northern Baja. See chapters 9 and 18.

- **Sportfishing in La Paz:** Billfishing for magnificent marlin and sailfish is a popular sport throughout southern Baja, and La Paz pulls in the most consistent share. See chapter 18. Fishing is also excellent in Los Cabos,

Mazatlán, Manzanillo, and Zihuatanejo. See chapters 9, 10, and 18.

- **Sea Kayaking in the Sea of Cortez:** From Cabo San Lucas to La Paz, and continuing north, the Sea of Cortez is a sea kayaker's dream. It has dozens of tiny coves and impressive inlets to pull into and explore, under the watchful gaze of sea lions and dolphins. Professional outfitters provide gear, guides, and instruction for novices. See chapter 18.

5 The Best of Natural Mexico

- **Michoacán's Million Monarch March:** Mexico is an exotic land, and no place drives this home more forcefully than a mountain forest where you stand surrounded by the fluttering wings of millions of monarch butterflies—it's like being in a fairy tale. The setting is the rugged highlands of Michoacán, from mid- to late November through March. See "Morelia" in chapter 7.

- **Whale-Watching:** Each winter, between December and April, magnificent humpback and gray whales return to breed and instruct their young in the waters of Banderas Bay, fronting **Puerto Vallarta,** and in **Los Cabos.** See "Puerto Vallarta" in chapter 9, and "Los Cabos: Resorts, Watersports & Golf" in chapter 18.

- **Sea Turtle Nesting Beaches:** Between June and November, sea turtles return to the beaches of their birth to lay their eggs in nests on the sand. With poaching and natural predators threatening these species, communities along Mexico's Pacific coast have established protected nesting areas. Many are open for public viewing and participation in the egg collection and baby-turtle release processes. Turtles

are found along the Yucatán coast, in Baja Sur, on the Oaxaca coast, in Puerto Vallarta, and on Costa Alegre. See chapters 9, 15, and 18.

- **Lago Bacalar** (Yucatán Peninsula): The waters of this crystal-clear, spring-fed lake—Mexico's second largest—are noted for their vibrant color variations, from pale blue to deep blue-green and turquoise. The area surrounding the lake is known for birding, with over 130 species identified. See "Lago Bacalar" in chapter 15.

- **The Rugged Copper Canyon:** The canyons, known collectively as the Copper Canyon, are beautiful, remote, and unspoiled. The entire network is larger than the Grand Canyon; it incorporates high waterfalls, vertical canyon walls, mountain forests in the canyon-rim country, and semiarid desert inside the canyons. This is the land of the Tarahumara Indians, who gained their legendary endurance from adapting to this wilderness. See chapter 17.

- **Desert Landscapes in Baja Sur:** The painted-desert colors and unique plant life are a natural curiosity in **Los Cabos,** where horseback, hiking, and ATV trips explore the area. The arid desert contrasts sharply with the intense blue of the strong sea surrounding the peninsula. See "Los Cabos: Resorts, Watersports & Golf" in chapter 18.

6 The Best Places to Get Away from It All

- **Costa Alegre:** Between Puerto Vallarta and Manzanillo, a number of superexclusive hotels cater to those with both time and money. These resorts—Hotelito Desconocido, Las Alamandas, Hotel Careyes, and El Tamarindo—are miles from civilization on private beaches. See "Costa Alegre: Puerto Vallarta to Barra de Navidad" in chapter 9.

- **San Sebastián:** A 15-minute flight from Puerto Vallarta takes you a century back in time. The colonial mountain town of San Sebastián used to be the center of Mexico's mining operations; today, it's simply a place of delicious seclusion in a magical mountain setting. See "Puerto Vallarta" in chapter 9.

- **Punta Mita:** Its ancient inhabitants considered the northern tip of the Bay of Banderas sacred ground. Today, the point where the Sea of Cortez, the Pacific Ocean, and Banderas Bay meet has evolved into Mexico's most exclusive residential resort development. The beaches are white and the waters crystalline. See "Puerto Vallarta" in chapter 9.

- **Riviera Maya & Punta Allen Peninsula:** Away from the popular resort of Cancún, the Riviera Maya's heavenly quiet getaways offer tranquillity at low prices on beautiful palm-lined beaches. South of the Tulum ruins, Punta Allen's beachside budget inns offer some of the most peaceful getaways in the country. See chapter 15.

- **Lago Bacalar:** The spring-fed waters of Lake Bacalar make an ideal place to unwind. South of Cancún, near Chetumal, there's nothing around for miles. If you want adventure, you can paddle a kayak on the lake, follow a birding trail, or venture to Belize or nearby Maya ruins. See "Lago Bacalar" in chapter 15.

- **Cerocahui:** Up in the high Sierra Tarahumara, far from where the large tours stop, you'll find a peaceful little town surrounding a former mission. Nearby are two small hotels that are even more peaceful—no phones, no crowds, no traffic, just beautiful mountains and canyons clothed in pine forest. See "The Copper Canyon Train & Stops along the Way" in chapter 17.

- **Cabo Pulmo:** It's only a 60-mile drive from the Los Cabos airport to Cabo Pulmo, yet if the mounded Sierra de La Laguna peaks weren't a dead giveaway for Baja, you could be in the South Pacific. Swaying in the shade of a palapa-roofed bungalow at Cabo Pulmo Beach Resort, you won't care where you are—you just won't want to leave. The Sea of Cortez breaks on a coral reef, allowing only the finest bits of sand and smooth pebbles to pad the coast. The coral itself is a sight to behold, but the real attraction is the sea life in this protected marine park. Extensive hiking/mountain biking trails loop through the mountains for those who prefer the peace of the desert. See chapter 18.

7 The Best Art, Architecture & Museums

- **Museo Nacional de Antropología:** Among the world's most outstanding museums, the Museum of Anthropology in Mexico City contains riches representing 3,000 years of the country's past. Also on view are fabulous artifacts of still-thriving indigenous cultures. The award-winning building, designed by architect Pedro Ramírez Vázquez, is stunning. See p. 120.

- **Palacio Nacional:** Mexico's national center of government overlooks one of the three biggest public squares in the world (the *zócalo*) and was originally built in 1692 on the site of Moctezuma's "new" palace, to be the home of Hernán Cortez. The top floor, added in the late 1920s, holds a series of stunning Diego Rivera murals depicting the history of Mexico. See p. 120.

- **Palacio de Bellas Artes in Mexico City:** The country's premier venue for the performing arts, this fabulous building is the combined work of several masters. The theater's exterior is early-20th-century Art Nouveau, covered in marble; the interior is 1930s Art Deco. See p. 124.

- **The Templo Mayor's Aztec Splendor:** The Templo Mayor and Museo del Templo Mayor constitute an archaeological excavation and museum with 6,000 objects on display. They showcase the variety and splendor of the Aztec Empire as it existed in the historic center of what is now Mexico City. See p. 122.

- **Catedral Metropolitana:** This towering cathedral, begun in 1567 and finished in 1788, blends baroque, neoclassical, and Mexican churrigueresque architecture, and was constructed primarily from the stones of destroyed Aztec temples. See p. 126.

- **Santa Prisca y San Sebastián Church:** One of Mexico's most impressive baroque churches, completed in 1758, this church in Taxco has an intricately carved facade, an interior decorated with gold-leafed saints and angels, and paintings by Miguel Cabrera, one of Mexico's most famous colonial-era artists. See p. 156.

- **Mexican Masks in Zacatecas:** Masks are a ubiquitous feature in Mexican festivals and folk art, and the Museo Rafael Coronel in Zacatecas has the greatest collection in the country. See p. 226.

- **Museo Virreinal de Guadalupe:** Six kilometers (4 miles) southeast of Zacatecas in the small town of Guadalupe, this Franciscan convent and art museum holds a striking collection of 17th- and 18th-century paintings by such masters as Miguel Cabrera and Cristóbal de Villalpando. The expressive, dramatic works will fascinate art lovers. See p. 227.

- **Morelia's Cathedral:** Sober lines, balanced proportions, a deft blending of architectural styles, and monumental height—Morelia's cathedral is the most beautiful in the country. It's built of brownish-pink stone that turns fiery rose in the late-afternoon sun. See p. 241.

- **Museo Antropología de Xalapa:** With the finest examples of Olmec and Totonac sculpture and ceramics, this museum includes the best collection of the Olmec megalithic heads. See p. 498.

- **Puebla's Capilla del Rosario:** Located in the church of Santo Domingo, this chapel is a tour de force of baroque expression, executed in molded plaster, carved wood, Talavera tile, and gold leaf. The overall effect is to overpower the senses. See p. 505.

- **Puebla's Museo Amparo:** This museum contains a magnificent collection of pre-Columbian and colonial art, which is beautifully displayed. See p. 506.

8 The Best Shopping

- **Bazar del Sábado in San Angel:** This festive Saturday market in colonial San Angel, one of Mexico City's more exclusive southern neighborhoods, offers exceptional crafts of a more sophisticated nature than you'll see in most *mercados.* Furnishings, antiques, and collectibles are also easy to find in surrounding shops and street plazas. See p. 138.
- **Polanco, Mexico City:** This fashionable neighborhood is noted for its designer boutiques, formal dress shops, fine jewelers, and leather-goods offerings. See "Shopping" in chapter 4.
- **Contemporary Art:** Latin American art is surging in popularity. Galleries in Mexico City feature Mexico's masters and emerging stars, with Oaxaca, Puerto Vallarta, and San Miguel de Allende galleries also offering excellent selections. See chapters 4, 6, 9, and 11.
- **Taxco Silver:** Mexico's silver capital, Taxco, has hundreds of stores featuring fine jewelry and decorative objects. See "Taxco: Cobblestones & Silver" in chapter 5.
- **Talavera Pottery in Puebla & Dolores Hidalgo:** An inheritor of the Moorish legacy of ceramics, Puebla produces some of the most sought-after dinnerware in the world. The tiles produced there adorn building facades and church domes throughout the area. See chapter 12. Dolores Hidalgo, 40km (25 miles) northwest of San Miguel de Allende, produces attractive, inexpensive Talavera of less traditional design. See "San Miguel de Allende" in chapter 6.
- **San Miguel de Allende's Diverse Crafts:** Perhaps it's the influence of the Instituto Allende art school, but something has given storekeepers here real savvy about choosing their merchandise. The stores have fewer typical articles of Mexican handicrafts and more interesting and eye-catching works than you'll find in other towns. See "San Miguel de Allende" in chapter 6.
- **Pátzcuaro's Fine Crafts:** Michoacán is known for its crafts, and Pátzcuaro is at the center of it all. You can find beautiful cotton textiles, woodcarvings, pottery, lacquerware, woven straw pieces, and copper items in the market, or you can track the object to its source in one of the nearby villages. See "Pátzcuaro" in chapter 7.
- **Decorative Arts in Tlaquepaque & Tonalá:** These two neighborhoods of Guadalajara offer perhaps the most enjoyable shopping in Mexico. Tlaquepaque has attracted sophisticated and wide-ranging shops selling a wide variety of decorative art. In Tonalá, more than 400 artisans have workshops, and you can visit many of them; on market days, wander through blocks and blocks of market stalls seeking that one perfect piece. See "Shopping" in chapter 8.
- **Huichol Art in Puerto Vallarta:** One of the last indigenous cultures to remain faithful to their customs, language, and traditions, the Huichol Indians come down from the Sierra Madre to sell their unusual art to Puerto Vallarta galleries. Inspired by visions received during spiritual ceremonies, the Huichol create their art

with colorful yarn or beads pressed into wax. See "Shopping" in chapter 9.

- **Oaxacan Textiles:** The valley of Oaxaca produces the best weavings and naturally dyed textiles in Mexico; it's also famous for its pottery, and colorful, imaginative woodcarvings. See "Oaxaca City" in chapter 11.

- **The Markets of San Cristóbal de las Casas:** This city, deep in the heart of the Maya highlands, has shops, open plazas, and markets featuring distinctive waist-loomed wool and cotton textiles, as well as leather shoes, handsome pottery, genre dolls, and Guatemalan textiles. See "San Cristóbal de las Casas" in chapter 11.

9 The Best Luxury Hotels

- **Hotel Four Seasons** (Mexico City; ℂ 800/332-3442 in the U.S.): The standard of excellence in Mexico, and the most stylish choice in Mexico City, this hotel captures both serenity and elegance in a palace-style building that surrounds a picturesque courtyard. The gracious staff and offerings of unique cultural tours are bonuses. See p. 107.

- **W Mexico City** (Mexico City; ℂ 888/625-5144 in the U.S.): Stylish and high-tech, this dramatic addition to Mexico City hotels has set the city abuzz. With its super-*caliente* red hues and lively bar scene, the W Mexico City has infused the country's capital with a dose of minimalist urban chic. Luxury extras include expansive bathrooms with circular tubs. See p. 104.

- **Hacienda Xcanatún** (outskirts of Mérida; ℂ 888/883-3633 in the U.S.): Large, boldly designed suites built with extravagance in mind, extensive grounds, private spa, excellent restaurant, and ample staff—this hotel does the difficult trick of being small in size but large in offerings. See "Of Haciendas & Hotels" on p. 636.

- **Maroma** (north of Playa del Carmen; ℂ 866/454-9351 in the U.S.): You can't ask for a better setting for a resort than this beautiful stretch of Caribbean coast with palm trees and manicured gardens. You'll start to relax before you even take the first sip of your welcome cocktail. Service is very attentive, and the rooms are luxurious. See p. 595.

- **Villa Montaña** (Morelia; ℂ 800/223-6510 in the U.S., or 800/448-8355 in Canada): The Villa Montaña defines perfection. From the layout of the grounds to the decoration of the rooms, every detail has been skillfully handled. The hotel perches on a ridge overlooking Morelia; from its terraces, guests can survey the city below. The restaurant is one of the city's best. See p. 245.

- **Four Seasons Resort Punta Mita** (north of Puerto Vallarta; ℂ 800/332-3442 in the U.S.): This luxury resort offers an unrivaled location (on a remote, pristine stretch of beach) and the stellar service characteristic of the Four Seasons chain. Also on-site are an expansive spa and a private Jack Nicklaus Signature golf course. See p. 329.

- **El Tamarindo** (between Manzanillo and Puerto Vallarta; ℂ 315/351-5032): The most exclusive remote resort in Mexico, this stylish place combines large private casitas facing the Pacific with a stunning private oceanfront golf course. Fellow guests are likely to be Hollywood celebrities and the well-to-do from around the world. It's about 1 hour north of Manzanillo along Costa Alegre. See p. 352.

- **Villa del Sol** (Zihuatanejo; ℂ **888/ 389-2645** in the U.S.): This stunning hotel sits on one of Mexico's calmest and most beautiful beaches. Modern rooms and suites overlook the bay or a man-made lagoon, and many have private plunge pools. This is a luxurious retreat you won't want to leave. See p. 405.
- **Hotel Camino Real** (Oaxaca; ℂ **800/ 722-6466** in the U.S.): No other hotel in Mexico captures the sense of antiquity as well as this one. It occupies a 16th-century convent in the middle of the best part of Oaxaca City and has several beautiful, tranquil courtyards where renovation efforts have carefully preserved the marks of time. See p. 447.
- **Ritz-Carlton Cancún** (Cancún; ℂ **800/241-3333** in the U.S.): Thick carpets, sparkling glass and brass, and rich mahogany surround guests at this hotel, for years the standard-bearer of luxury in Cancún. The service is impeccable, leaving guests with an overall sense of pampered relaxation. And, post–Hurricane Wilma, the Ritz received a significant makeover. See p. 526.
- **Le Méridien Cancún Resort & Spa** (Cancún; ℂ **800/543-4300** in the U.S.): This is the most intimate of the luxury hotels in Cancún, with an understated sense of highly personalized service. Most notable is its 4,570 sq. m (49,190-sq.-ft.) Spa del Mar. See p. 526.
- **Las Ventanas al Paraíso** (Los Cabos; ℂ **888/767-3966** in the U.S.): Stunning in its relaxed elegance, Las Ventanas boasts a deluxe European spa, excellent gourmet restaurant, and elegantly appointed rooms and suites. From fireplaces and telescopes to private pools and rooftop terraces, each suite offers a slice of heaven. See p. 708.
- **Esperanza** (Los Cabos; ℂ **866/311- 2226** in the U.S.): This Auberge resort pampers guests in a desert-chic setting, on a bluff overlooking twin coves below. Spacious, sumptuous rooms are enhanced by ample terraces, and the resort's spa and dining services make a stay here even more memorable. See p. 708.
- **One&Only Palmilla** (Los Cabos; ℂ **800/637-2226** in the U.S.): A popular Mexican resort with the Hollywood crowd, the completely renovated Palmilla has regained its spot as the most deluxe hotel in this seaside playground known for sumptuous accommodations and great golf. The exceptional spa, fitness center, and yoga garden, as well as a restaurant under the direction of renowned chef Charlie Trotter, are added bonuses. See p. 709.

10 The Best Inexpensive Inns

- **Best Western Hotel de Cortés** (Mexico City; ℂ **800/528-1234** in the U.S.): This historic building and former home of Augustinian friars offers exceptionally clean, comfortable, value-priced accommodations. It's on La Alameda park, near the Palace of Fine Arts and the Franz Mayer Museum. See p. 109.
- **Hotel Los Flamingos** (Acapulco; ℂ **744/482-0690**): Once a private club for Hollywood's elite during the heyday of Acapulco, this hotel will enchant you with its pervasive mid-century charm, the funky profusion of hot pink, and absolutely breathtaking cliff-top views. See p. 387.

- **Hotel San Francisco Plaza** (Guadalajara; © **33/3613-8954**): This two-story colonial-style hotel is a more agreeable place to stay than lodgings charging twice as much, and it's every bit as comfortable. It's in the downtown area, near the main plaza and several good restaurants and nightspots. See p. 269.
- **Paraíso Escondido** (Puerto Escondido; © **954/582-0444**): This eclectic inn is a great bargain, especially for the originality of the decor and the excellent service. It's a short walk to both the beach and the action along Puerto's main street. See p. 418.
- **Misión de los Arcos** (Huatulco; © **958/587-0165**): Just 1 block from the central plaza, this hotel has a similar style to the elegant Quinta Real, at a fraction of the cost. An all-white facade and intriguing decorative touches give it an inviting feel. There's shuttle service to the Huatulco beaches. See p. 431.
- **Las Golondrinas** (Oaxaca; © **951/514-3298**): We receive more favorable letters about this hotel than about any other in the country. It's small, simple, and colorful, with homey touches of folk art and pathways lined with abundant foliage. See p. 449.
- **Rey del Caribe Hotel** (Cancún; © **998/884-2028**): An ecological oasis in downtown Cancún, this hotel has considered every detail to achieve the goal creating in an organic and environmentally friendly setting. Set in a tropical garden, the combination of sunny rooms, warm service, yoga and meditation classes, and healthful dining is a welcome respite to party-hearty Cancún. See p. 530.
- **Cabo Inn** (Cabo San Lucas; © **624/143-3348**): This former bordello is the area's best budget inn. Rooms are small but extra clean and invitingly decorated, amenities are generous, and the owner-managers are friendly and helpful. Ideally located, close to town and near the marina, the inn caters to sportfishers. See p. 721.

11 The Best Spa Resorts

- **Hotel Ixtapan Spa and Golf Resort** (Ixtapan; © **800/638-7950** in the U.S.): In operation since 1939, this resort is a classic, traditional spa with consistently upgraded amenities and services. It's also close to the region's renowned thermal baths. See p. 161.
- **El Santuario Resort Spa** (Valle de Bravo; © **726/262-9104** in the U.S.): The suites at this newest offering in the region of spa resorts overlook a vast lake and are built into the foot of a quartz mountain. A 1,858 sq. m (20,000 sq.-ft.) spa offers a wealth of therapies, plus yoga, Pilates, Tai Chi, and meditation classes. See p. 164.
- **Misión Del Sol Resort & Spa** (Cuernavaca; © **777/321-0999** in the U.S.): Mexico's finest spa resort, with every architectural and functional detail designed to soothe body and soul—from meditation rooms to reflexology showers to magnets under your mattress. The sumptuous, full-service spa and fitness center and delicious vegetarian cuisine make this a heavenly base for personal renewal. See p. 172.
- **Paradise Village** (Nuevo Vallarta; © **800/995-5714**): Excellent fitness facilities combined with pampering yet affordable spa services make this one of the best all-around spas in

Mexico. It actively promotes the beneficial properties of indigenous Mexican spa therapies and natural treatments. See p. 326.

- **Le Méridien Cancún Resort & Spa** (Cancún; ℂ **800/543-4300** in the U.S.): The Spa del Mar is a state-of-the-art, 1,400 sq. m (15,069-sq.-ft.) facility bordering the brilliant Caribbean. It boasts the most complete spa in the area, with inhalation rooms, saunas, steam, Jacuzzis, cold plunges, Swiss showers, a cascading waterfall whirlpool, and 14 treatment rooms. See p. 526.
- **The Tides Riviera Maya** (ℂ **800/578-0281** in the U.S. and Canada); **Maroma** (ℂ **866/454-9351** in the U.S.); and **Paraíso de la Bonita** (ℂ **866/751-9175** in the U.S.): The area north of Playa del Carmen, around Puerto Morelos, is a hotbed of spa-resort luxury. These three establishments, in lovely settings, offer guests an impressive range of pampering treatments. See p. 595.
- **ME** (Cancún; ℂ **866/436-3542** in the U.S.): The ultrachic Yhi Spa of Cancún's new ME hotel overlooks the ocean and offers body glows and exfoliations, aromatherapy massages, body masks, and wraps—this is a place to indulge yourself until you're

convinced that you've landed in heaven. See p. 528.
- **Casa de los Sueños Resort & Spa Zenter** (Isla Mujeres; ℂ **998/877-0651**). This luxury B&B has a small but well-appointed spa and "Zenter," which is also accessible to nonguests. Highlights include yoga classes, massages, and holistic spa treatments, which take place either indoors or out, in one of the most tranquil places you'll find. See p. 554.
- **One&Only Palmilla** (Los Cabos; ℂ **800/637-2226** in the U.S.): Home to Mexico's most extravagant spa, 13 private treatment rooms set among gardens offer the most pampering array of services, complemented by a yoga garden, fitness center, and menu of classes for getting in touch with—or indulging—your inner self. See "The Best Luxury Hotels" above, and p. 709.
- **Rancho La Puerta** (Baja Norte; ℂ **800/443-7565** in the U.S.): One of Mexico's best-known spas, Rancho La Puerta is a spa-vacation pioneer, having opened its doors—at the time, tent flaps—in 1940. A steady stream of guests returns to this pristine countryside for the constantly expanding facilities, spa services, and outdoor opportunities. See p. 749.

12 The Best Mexican Food & Drink

- **Aguila y Sol** (Mexico City; ℂ **55/5281-8354**): One of the world's best Mexican restaurants, Aguila y Sol serves haute Mexican cuisine incorporating indigenous and pre-Hispanic ingredients. Acclaimed chef-owner Martha Ortiz has written numerous cookbooks, and her magical dishes overflow with imagination. See p. 111.
- **La Opera** (Mexico City; ℂ **55/5512-8959**): This legendary cantina, in the style of an opulent European

cafe, has attracted the capital's most illustrious personalities for decades—Pancho Villa once shot a still-visible hole through the roof. Located in the historic center, the cantina doubles as a restaurant but is best saved as a late afternoon watering stop. See p. 116.
- **Adobe Fonda** (Tlaquepaque; ℂ **33/3657-2792**): Delicious Mexican food is served inside one of those gorgeous decorative arts stores that line Tlaquepaque's Calle Independencia.

The point of departure for the food is some uncommon Mexican recipes, which are then given sparkling Italian and Argentine accents. See p. 270.

- **El Sacromonte** (Guadalajara; ☎ 33/3825-5447): Various dishes delight the senses with novel tastes and textures and skillful presentation. The menu describes each dish in Spanish couplets. See p. 271.

- **El Arrayán** (Puerto Vallarta; ☎ 322/222-7195): The colorful atmosphere may be casual, funky, and fun, but the food is seriously and authentically Mexican. The owner, Carmen, has taken her prime beef filet tacos off the menu—wanting guests to try more traditional Mexican fare—but you can still ask for them. Or, take her cue and order the duck confit, shrimp *pozole,* or homemade ice creams from indigenous fruits. Don't miss her martini made from *raicilla,* Mexico's version of moonshine. See p. 317.

- **El Mirador** (Acapulco, in the Hotel Plaza Las Glorias; ☎ 744/483-1221 in the U.S.): You can enjoy a great margarita at many places in Mexico, but this is the only one that serves them with a view of the spectacular La Quebrada cliff divers. See p. 387.

- **Los Flamingos** (Acapulco; ☎ 744/482-0690): If in Acapulco on a Thursday, you can enjoy a bowl of *pozole,* a traditional hominy and meat stew. Although you'll find it served at lunchtime throughout town, the best place to savor it is at the cliff-top restaurant at Los Flamingos. Order a Coco Loco to accompany it, and you're in for a real treat! See p. 387.

- **El Naranjo** (Oaxaca; ☎ 951/514-1878): Oaxaca has an elaborate regional cuisine, and we're delighted by what El Naranjo does with it. Each day offers a different *mole* in addition to several uncommon dishes. This is a wonderful place for throwing caution to the wind—the owner is meticulous about cleaning and sterilizing foods. See p. 451.

- **Mariscos Villa Rica Mocambo** (Veracruz; ☎ 229/922-2113): Nobody else does seafood the way Veracruz does seafood, and this restaurant is the showcase for the region's cuisine. See p. 494.

- **Don Emiliano** (downtown San José del Cabo; ☎ 624/142-0266): Don Emiliano wields farm-fresh ingredients laced with Mexican tradition and emerges from the kitchen with modern delights such as stepped-up *chile en nogada* for Día de Independencia and *lemon atole* with candied pumpkin for Day of the Dead. Apart from holiday menus, don't miss the regular menu, which combines the likes of locally made cheeses with roasted tomatillos and dried hibiscus flowers with beef tenderloin. See p. 704.

Planning Your Trip to Mexico

A little planning can make the difference between a good trip and a great trip. When should you go? What's the best way to get there? How much should you plan on spending? What festivals or special events will occur during your visit? What safety or health precautions should you take? We'll answer these and other questions in this chapter. In addition to these basics, I highly recommend taking a little time to learn about the culture and traditions of Mexico. It can make the difference between simply getting away for a few days and truly adding cultural understanding to your trip. See the appendix for more details.

1 The Regions in Brief

BAJA CALIFORNIA A peninsula longer than Italy, Baja stretches 1,402km (869 miles) from its border with California at Mexico's northernmost city of **Tijuana** to **Cabo San Lucas** at its southern tip. On one side is the Pacific Ocean; on the other, the **Sea of Cortez.** Volcanic uplifting created the craggy desertscape you see today. Culturally and geographically, Baja sits apart from mainland Mexico, and it remained isolated for centuries. The southern tip of Baja has evolved into a vacation haven, offering golf, fishing, diving, and whale-watching in beautiful settings and at posh resorts. Mid-Baja is known more for its ecological excursions.

THE COPPER CANYON The Copper Canyon is the common name for a region of roughly 16,800 sq. km (6,487 sq. miles) in the northern state of Chihuahua, midway between the state's capital city and the Pacific coast. Here you'll find a network of canyons deeply etched into the volcanic rock of the **Sierra Tarahumara.** The dramatic canyon area is one of those rare places where one can sense the earth's creation. To get there, you ride the famous Chihuahua al Pacífico railroad. It starts at the seaport of Topolobampo, outside **Los Mochis,** and runs 624km (387 miles) to **Chihuahua City,** climbing to 2,425m (7,954 ft.) above sea level in the process. The train skirts the edge of more than 20 canyons. Tours can accommodate any kind of traveler, from primitive camper to modern hotel patron.

THE PACIFIC COAST The Pacific coast has virtually every kind of beach and landscape imaginable. You can stay in modern resorts that offer inexhaustible arrays of amenities and activities, from sailing to scuba diving to golf, capped off by exuberant nightlife. Or you can stay in a sleepy coastal town where the scenery abounds with rustic charm, life is slower, and the beaches are quieter. By **Mazatlán,** the northern desert disappears, replaced by tropical vegetation and plantations of coconut and other fruit. At **Puerto Vallarta,** mountains covered in tropical forests meet the sea. For many, this is the most appealing place on the coast. From here, it's a 5-hour car ride inland to **Guadalajara,** the most Mexican of cities

Map Pointer

To locate these regions, please turn to the map of Mexico on p. 8.

and a superb place to shop. Tropical forests interspersed with banana, mango, and coconut palm plantations cover the coast from Puerto Vallarta to **Manzanillo.** Well south of Manzanillo, in the state of Guerrero, are the beach towns **Zihuatanejo** and **Ixtapa.** Tree-covered mountains remain around **Acapulco,** though hillside development has marred them. From Acapulco, a road leads inland to **Taxco,** a mountainside colonial city famed for its hundreds of silver shops. Farther south along the coast are the beach villages of **Puerto Escondido** and **Puerto Angel,** and beyond them, the nine gorgeous bays of **Huatulco.**

THE NORTH-CENTRAL REGION

This funnel-shaped region stretches from the northern border with Texas and New Mexico to **Mexico City** and includes the beautiful colonial **silver cities.** The majority of this territory lies in the vast Chihuahua/Coahuila desert of the north between the two great **Sierra Madre ranges,** which meet in the south to form the central valley of Mexico. The colonial cities nestle in the mountains not far north and west of Mexico City.

THE GULF COAST

Of all Mexico, this region is probably the least known, yet the whole coast, which includes the long, skinny state of Veracruz, holds marvelous pockets of scenery and culture. Highway 180 leads from **Matamoros** at the Texas border and offers a few glimpses of the Gulf of Mexico. Highlights of this region are the ruins of **El Tajín,** near the mountain village of Papantla; the mountain town of **Xalapa,** Veracruz's capital and home of the magnificent Museo de Antropología; and the lively, colorful port of **Veracruz.** This is a good region to visit if you're longing for the Mexico of yesteryear.

TARASCAN COUNTRY

This region, in the state of Michoacán, presents two distinct visions of colonial architecture: **Pátzcuaro,** a town of tile roofs and adobe walls painted traditional white with dark-red borders; and **Morelia,** a stately city of stone mansions, broad plazas, and a monumental cathedral. The eastern part of the state consists of high mountains with large tracts of pine and fir forests. Every year, millions of **monarch butterflies** make the long journey to congregate in a small part of the forest here. The central part of the state, a land of lakes, is the homeland of the Purépecha or Tarascan Indians. The villages throughout this area specialize in crafts for which the region is well known. Farther west lie the hot lands and the coast. Tourists largely neglect Michoacán, except during the Days of the Dead.

OAXACA & CHIAPAS

This is the southern land of the Zapotec, Mixtec, and Maya cultures. Most people fly around this region, but a toll highway from near Puebla to **Oaxaca City** makes the area more accessible by car. The valley of Oaxaca is one of the grandest places in Mexico: fascinating Indian villages, beautiful ruins, and a wonderful colonial city. **San Cristóbal de las Casas,** in Chiapas, is harder to get to, but definitely worth the effort. Approaching San Cristóbal from any direction, you see small plots of corn tended by colorfully clad Maya. Oaxaca and Chiapas are rich in craftspeople, from woodcarvers to potters to weavers.

THE YUCATAN PENINSULA

Travelers to the peninsula have an opportunity to see pre-Hispanic ruins—such as **Chichén Itzá, Uxmal,** and **Tulum**—and the living descendants of the cultures that built them, as well as the ultimate in resort Mexico: **Cancún.** The peninsula borders the dull aquamarine Gulf of Mexico on the west and north, and the clear blue Caribbean on the east. It covers almost 217,560 sq. km (84,000 sq. miles), with nearly 1,600km (1,000 miles) of shoreline.

Lovely rock-walled Maya villages and crumbling *henequén* haciendas dot the interior of the peninsula. The placid interior contrasts with the hubbub of the Caribbean coast. From Cancún south to **Chetumal,** the jungle coastline is spotted with all kinds of development, from posh to budget. It also boasts an enormous array of wildlife, including hundreds of species of birds. National parks near **Celestún** and **Río Lagartos** on the Gulf Coast are home to amazing flocks of flamingos.

2 Visitor Information & Maps

The **Mexico Tourism Board** (© 800/ 446-3942) is an excellent source for general information; you can request brochures on the country and get answers to the most common questions from the exceptionally well-trained, knowledgeable staff.

More information (15,000 pages' worth) about Mexico is available on the official site of Mexico's Tourism Board, **www.visitmexico.com.** The **U.S. Department of State** (© 888/407-4747) or 202/501-4444; fax 202/647-1488; www. travel.state.gov) offers a **Consular Information Sheet** on Mexico with safety, medical, driving, and general travel information gleaned from reports by its offices in Mexico, and consistently updated. The **Centers for Disease Control and Prevention Hot Line** (© 800/311-3435 or 404/639-3534; www.cdc.gov) is a source of medical information for travelers to Mexico and elsewhere. For travelers to Mexico and Central America, the number

Destination Mexico: Red-Alert Checklist

- Did you pack your passport or a current, government-issued ID, necessary to clear immigration both into Mexico and to return to your country of origin? If you are planning to be in the outdoors, did you pack bug repellent? Appropriate attire?
- Did you check to see if any travel advisories have been issued by the U.S. Department of State (www.travel.state.gov) regarding your destination?
- Do you have the address and phone number of your country's embassy or consulate with you?
- Do any excursion, restaurant, or travel reservations need to be booked in advance?
- Did you find out your daily ATM withdrawal limit?
- Do you have your credit card PINs?
- If you purchased traveler's checks, have you recorded the check numbers, and stored the documentation separately from the checks?
- Do you have a safe, accessible place to store money?
- Did you bring emergency drug prescriptions and extra glasses and/or contact lenses?
- Did you leave a copy of your itinerary with someone at home?

with recorded messages is © **877/394-8747.** Information is also available at **www.cdc.gov/travel**. The U.S. Department of State's website (see above) also offers medical information for Americans traveling abroad and a list of air ambulance services.

The **Mexican Government Tourist Board** has offices in major North American cities, in addition to the main office in Mexico City (© **55/5278-4200**). In the **United States:** Chicago (© **312/228-0517,** ext. 14), Houston (© **713/772-2581,** ext. 105, or 713/772-3819), Los Angeles (© **310/282-9112**), Miami (© **786/621-2909**), and New York (© **212/308-2110**).

The **Mexican Embassy** in the United States is at 1911 Pennsylvania Ave. NW, Washington, DC 20005 (© **202/728-1750** or -1600). In Canada: 2055 Rue Peel, Suite 1000, Montreal, QUE, H3A 1V4 (© **514/288-2502**); Commerce Court West, 199 Bay St., Suite 4440, Toronto, ON, M5L 1E9 (© **416/925-0704**); 710 West Hastings St., Suite 1177, Vancouver, BC V6E 2K3 (© **604/684-1859**); 1500-45 O'Connor St., Ottawa, ON, K1P 1A4 (© **613/233-8988;** fax 613/235-9123).

3 Entry Requirements

PASSPORTS

All travelers to Mexico are required to present **photo identification** and **proof of citizenship,** such as a valid passport, naturalization papers, or an original birth certificate with a raised seal, along with a driver's license or official ID, such as a state or military issued ID. Driver's licenses and permits, voter registration cards, affidavits and similar documents are not sufficient to prove citizenship for readmission into the United States. If the last name on the birth certificate is different from your current name, bring a photo identification card *and* legal proof of the name change, such as the original marriage license or certificate. *Note:* Photocopies are *not* acceptable.

Effective January 23, 2007, all U.S. citizens traveling by **air** to Mexico are required to have a valid passport to enter or reenter the United States. As early as January 1, 2008, U.S. citizens traveling between the United States and Mexico by **land** or **sea** may also be required to present a valid U.S. passport or other documents as determined by the Department of Homeland Security.

Safeguard your passport in an inconspicuous, inaccessible place like a money belt, and keep a copy of the critical pages with your passport number in a separate place. If you lose your passport, visit the nearest consulate of your native country as soon as possible for a replacement.

For information on how to get a passport, go to "Passports" in the "Fast Facts" section of this chapter—the websites listed provide downloadable passport applications as well as the current fees for processing passport applications. For an up-to-date, country-by-country listing of passport requirements around the world, go to the "Foreign Entry Requirement" Web page of the U.S. Department of State at **http://travel.state.gov**.

VISAS

You must carry a **Mexican Tourist Permit (FMT),** the equivalent of a tourist visa, which Mexican border officials issue, free of charge, after proof of citizenship is accepted. Airlines generally provide the necessary forms aboard your flight to Mexico. The FMT is more important than a passport, so guard it carefully. If you lose it, you may not be permitted to leave until you can replace it—a bureaucratic hassle that can take anywhere from a few hours to a week.

The FMT can be issued for up to 180 days. Sometimes officials don't ask but just stamp a time limit, so be sure to say "6 months," or at least twice as long as you intend to stay. If you decide to extend your stay, you may request that additional time be added to your FMT from an official immigration office in Mexico.

In **Baja California,** immigration laws have changed; they allow FMTs for a maximum of 180 days per year, with a maximum of 30 days per visit. This is to encourage regular visitors, or those who spend longer periods in Mexico, to obtain documents that denote partial residency.

For travelers entering Mexico by car at the border of Baja California, note that FMTs are issued only in Tijuana, Tecate, and Mexicali, as well as in Ensenada and Guerrero Negro. If you travel anywhere beyond the frontier zone without the FMT, you will be fined $40. Permits for driving a foreign-plated car in Mexico are available only in Tijuana, Ensenada, Tecate, Mexicali, and La Paz.

U.S. citizens do not require a visa or a tourist card for tourist stays of 72 hours or less within "the border zone," defined as an area from 20 to 30km (12–19 miles) of the border with the U.S., depending on the location.

Note: Children younger than age 18 that are traveling without parents or with only one parent must have a notarized letter from the absent parent(s) authorizing the travel. Mexican law requires that any non-Mexican younger than age 18 departing Mexico must carry notarized written permission from any parent or guardian not traveling with the child. This permission must include the name of the parent, the name of the child, the name of anyone traveling with the child, and the notarized signature(s) of the absent parent(s). The child must carry the original letter (not a copy) as well as proof of the parent/child relationship (usually a birth certificate or court document) and an original custody decree, if applicable.

MEDICAL REQUIREMENTS

For information on medical requirements and recommendations, see "Health," p. 43.

CUSTOMS

For information on what you can bring into and take out of Mexico, go to **"Customs"** in the **"Fast Facts"** section of this chapter.

4 When to Go

SEASONS

Mexico has two principal travel seasons. **High season** begins around December 20 and continues to Easter; in some places it begins as early as mid-November. **Low season** is from the day after Easter to mid-December; during low season, prices may drop 20% to 50%. In beach destinations popular with Mexican travelers, such as Veracruz and Acapulco, prices will revert to high season during July and August, the traditional national summer vacation period. Prices in inland cities seldom fluctuate from high to low season, but may rise dramatically during the weeks of **Easter** and **Christmas.** Taxco and Pátzcuaro raise prices during their

popular Easter-week celebrations. In Isla Mujeres and Playa del Carmen, on the Yucatán Peninsula, high season starts earlier than in the rest of the country and includes the month of August, when many European visitors and Mexican families arrive. The chapters that follow mention all of these exceptions and others.

Mexico has two main climate seasons: **rainy** (May to mid-Oct) and **dry** (mid-Oct to Apr). The rainy season can be of little consequence in the dry, northern regions of the country. Southern regions typically receive tropical showers, which begin around 4 or 5pm and last a few hours. Though these rains can come on suddenly and be quite strong, they usually

Moments Our Favorite Mexico Events

All of the activities mentioned in the "Calendar of Events," below, are worth checking out. But several unforgettable festivals and celebrations deserve special mention. They are: **Carnaval, Holy Week, Assumption of the Virgin Mary, Festival Cervantino,** and the **Feast of the Virgin of Guadalupe.** Consult the calendar for more information.

end just as quickly and cool off the air for the evening. **Hurricane season** particularly affects the Yucatán Peninsula and the southern Pacific coast, especially June through October. However, if no hurricanes strike, the light, cooling winds, especially September through November, can make it a perfect time to tackle the pre-Hispanic ruins that dot the interior of the peninsula.

Norte **(northern) season** runs from late November to mid-January, when the jet stream dips far south and creates northerly winds and showers in many resort areas. These showers usually only last for a couple of days.

June, July, and August are unrelentingly hot on the Yucatán Peninsula and in most coastal areas, though temperatures rise only into the mid-80s to 90°F (mid-20s to 32°C). Most of coastal Mexico experiences temperatures in the 80s°F (20s°C) in the hottest months. The northern states that border the United States experience very high summer temperatures.

Elevation is another important factor. High-elevation cities such as Mexico City and San Cristóbal de las Casas can be surprisingly cold. Temperatures can drop close to freezing at night in winter even in San Miguel de Allende and Guanajuato, which are at lower elevations.

CALENDAR OF EVENTS

Keep in mind that during national holidays, Mexican banks and governmental offices—including immigration—are closed. For an exhaustive list of events beyond those listed here, check http://events.frommers.com, where you'll find a searchable, up-to-the-minute roster of what's happening in cities all over the world.

January

Año Nuevo (New Year's Day), nationwide. This national holiday is perhaps the quietest day in all of Mexico. Most people stay home or attend church. All businesses are closed. In traditional indigenous communities, new tribal leaders are inaugurated with colorful ceremonies rooted in the pre-Hispanic past. January 1.

Día de los Reyes (Three Kings' Day), nationwide. This day commemorates the Three Kings' bringing of gifts to the Christ Child. On this day, children receive gifts, much like the traditional Christmas gift-giving in the United States. Friends and families gather to share the Rosca de Reyes, a special cake. Inside the cake is a small doll representing the Christ Child; whoever receives the doll must host a tamales-and-*atole* (a warm drink made of corn dough) party on February 2. January 6.

Regional Fair, León, Guanajuato. One of Mexico's largest fairs celebrates the founding of this shoemaking and leather-craft city. The fair features parades, theater, craft exhibits, music, and dance. Month of January.

Feast of San Antonio Abad, Mexico City. This feast is celebrated through the Blessing of the Animals at the Santiago Tlatelolco Church on the Plaza of Three Cultures, at San Juan Bautista Church in Coyoacán, and at the

Church of San Fernando, 2 blocks north of the Juárez-Reforma intersection. January 17.

February

Día de la Candelaria (Candlemas), nationwide. Music, dances, processions, food, and other festivities lead up to a blessing of seed and candles in a ceremony that mixes pre-Hispanic and European traditions marking the end of winter. Those who attended the Three Kings celebration reunite to share *atole* and tamales at a party hosted by the recipient of the doll found in the Rosca. Celebrations are especially festive in Tlacotalpan, Veracruz. February 2.

Día de la Constitución (Constitution Day), nationwide. This national holiday is in honor of the current Mexican constitution, signed in 1917 as a result of the revolutionary war of 1910. It's celebrated through small parades. February 5.

Carnaval, nationwide. Carnaval takes place the 3 days preceding Ash Wednesday and the beginning of Lent. The cities of Tepoztlán, Huejotzingo, Chamula, Veracruz, Cozumel, and Mazatlán celebrate with special gusto. In some places, such as Veracruz, Mazatlán, and Cozumel, the celebration resembles New Orleans's Mardi Gras, with a festive atmosphere and parades. In Chamula, the event harks back to pre-Hispanic times, with ritualistic running on flaming branches. On Shrove Tuesday in Tepoztlán and Huejotzingo, brilliantly clad *chinelos* (masked dancers) fill the streets. Transportation and hotels are packed, so it's best to make reservations 6 months in advance and arrive a couple of days ahead of the beginning of celebrations.

Ash Wednesday, nationwide. The start of Lent and time of abstinence, this is a day of reverence nationwide; some towns honor it with folk dancing and fairs.

March

Annual Witches Conference, Lake Catemaco, Veracruz. Shamans, white witches, black witches, and practitioners of Caribbean, Afro, and Antillean ritualistic practices gather on the shores of the lake. Taking place the first Friday night of March every year, the annual gathering is a spectacle of witches, healers, magicians, and wizards.

Benito Juárez's Birthday, nationwide. This national holiday celebrating one of Mexico's most beloved leaders is observed through small hometown celebrations, especially in Juárez's birthplace, Guelatao, Oaxaca. March 21.

Spring Equinox, Chichén Itzá. On the first day of spring, the Temple of Kukulkán—Chichén Itzá's main pyramid—aligns with the sun, and the shadow of the plumed serpent moves slowly from the top of the building down. When the shadow reaches the bottom, the body joins the carved stone snake's head at the base of the pyramid. According to ancient legend, at the moment that the serpent is whole, the earth is fertilized. Visitors come from around the world to marvel at this sight, so advance arrangements are advisable. Elsewhere, equinox festivals and celebrations welcome spring, in the custom of the ancient Mexicans, with dances and prayers to the elements and the four cardinal points. It's customary to wear white with a red ribbon. March 21 (the shadow appears Mar 19–23).

April

Semana Santa (Holy Week), nationwide. Mexico celebrates the last week in the life of Christ, from Palm Sunday to Easter Sunday, with somber religious processions, spoofing of Judas, and reenactments of biblical events, plus food and craft fairs. Among the Tarahumara Indians in the Copper Canyon, celebrations have pre-Hispanic overtones. Pátzcuaro, Taxco, and Malinalco hold special celebrations. Businesses close during this traditional week of Mexican national vacations.

If you plan on traveling to or around Mexico during Holy Week, make your reservations early. Seats on flights into and out of the country will be reserved months in advance. Buses to these towns and to almost anywhere else in Mexico will be full, so try arriving on the Wednesday or Thursday before Good Friday. Easter Sunday is quiet, and the week following is a traditional vacation period. Early April.

Festival de México en el Centro Histórico (Annual Mexico City Festival), Mexico City. Regarded as one of Latin America's most vibrant celebrations of art and culture, this 2-week festival features diverse events including opera, concerts, theater, art exhibits, dance productions, and gourmet fare. Proceeds go toward the rescue and restoration of the art and architecture of Mexico City's historic downtown area. For a detailed schedule and more information visit www.fchmexico.com. Mid-March to early April.

San Marcos National Fair, Aguascalientes. Mexico's largest fair, first held in 1604, lasts 22 days. About a million visitors come for bullfights and rodeos as well as *ranchera* music and mariachis. There are craft and industrial exhibits, markets, fireworks, and folk dancing. April 12 to May 4.

May

Labor Day, nationwide. Workers' parades countrywide; everything closes. May 1.

Cinco de Mayo, Puebla and nationwide. This national holiday celebrates the defeat of the French at the Battle of Puebla. May 5.

Feast of San Isidro, nationwide. A blessing of seeds and work animals honors the patron saint of farmers. May 15.

June

Día de la Marina (Navy Day), various towns. All coastal towns celebrate the holiday, with naval parades and fireworks. June 1.

Corpus Christi, nationwide. This day, celebrated nationwide, honors the Body of Christ (the Eucharist) with processions, Masses, and food. Festivities include performances of *voladores* (flying pole dancers) beside the church and at the ruins of El Tajín, Veracruz. In Mexico City, children dressed as Indians and carrying decorated baskets of fruit for the priest's blessing gather with their parents before the National Cathedral. *Mulitas* (mules), handmade from dried cornhusks and painted, are traditionally sold outside all churches on that day to represent a prayer for fertility. Dates vary, but celebrations take place on the Thursday following "Holy Trinity" Sunday.

National Ceramics Fair and Fiesta, Tlaquepaque, Jalisco. This pottery center on the outskirts of Guadalajara offers craft demonstrations and competitions as well as mariachis, dancers, and colorful parades. June 14 to July 14.

Día de San Pedro y San Pablo (St. Peter and St. Paul Day), nationwide. This feast day is celebrated wherever St. Peter is the patron saint; it also honors anyone named Pedro or Peter. It's especially festive at San Pedro Tlaquepaque, near Guadalajara, with numerous mariachi bands, folk dancers, and parades with floats. June 29.

July

Guelaguetza Dance Festival, Oaxaca. This is one of Mexico's most popular events. Villagers from the seven regions around Oaxaca gather in the city's amphitheater. They dress in traditional costumes, and many wear colorful "dancing" masks. The celebration dates from pre-Hispanic times. Make advance reservations—this festival attracts visitors from around the world. Call ℂ **800/446-3942** for details and schedule. Late July.

August

International Chamber Music Festival, San Miguel de Allende. Held since 1982 in this beautiful town, the festival features international award-winning classical music ensembles. August 1 to 15.

Fall of Tenochtitlán, Mexico City. The last battle of the Spanish Conquest took place at Tlatelolco, ruins that are now part of the Plaza of Three Cultures. Wreath-laying ceremonies there and at the Cuauhtémoc monument on Reforma commemorate the surrender of the last Aztec king, Cuauhtémoc, to Cortez, and the loss of thousands of lives. August 13.

Assumption of the Virgin Mary, nationwide. This day is celebrated throughout the country with special Masses, and in some places with processions. In Huamantla, flower petals and colored sawdust carpet the streets. At midnight on August 15, a statue of the Virgin is carried through the streets; on August 16 is the running of the bulls. On August 15 in Santa Clara del Cobre, near Pátzcuaro, Our Lady of Santa Clara de Asis and the Virgen de la Sagrado Patrona are honored with a parade of floats, dancers on the main square, and an exposition of regional crafts. Buses to Huamantla from Puebla and Mexico City will be full,

and there are few hotels in Huamantla. Plan to stay in Puebla and commute to the festivities. August 15 to 17.

Fiestas de la Vendimia (Wine Harvest Festival), Ensenada, Baja California. A food and wine festival celebrating the annual harvest, with blessings, seminars, parties, and wine tastings. Call ℂ **800/446-3942** for details and schedule. Mid- to late August.

September

Mariachi Festival, Guadalajara, Jalisco. These public concerts of mariachi music include visiting mariachi groups from around the world (even Japan!). Workshops and lectures focus on the history, culture, and music of the mariachi in Mexico. Call ℂ **800/446-3942** (www.mariachi-jalisco.com.mx) to confirm dates and the schedule of performances. September 2 to 16.

Reto al Tepozteco (Tepozteco Challenge), Tepoztlan, Morelos. A celebration of King Tepoztecatl's conversion to the Catholic religion, including a performance depicting the event. A procession leads toward the Tepozteco Pyramid, where people offer food and beverages. This event includes hypnotic *chinelo* dances, fireworks, and a food festival. September 7 to 8.

Independence Day, nationwide. Celebrates Mexico's independence from Spain with parades, picnics, and family reunions. At 11pm on September 15, the president gives the famous independence *grito* (shout) from the National Palace in Mexico City. At least half a million people crowd into the *zócalo* (main plaza), and the rest of the country watches on TV or participates in local celebrations. Tall buildings downtown are draped in the national colors (red, green, and white), and the *zócalo* is ablaze with lights. Many people drive downtown at night to see the lights. Querétaro and San Miguel de Allende, where Independence conspirators lived and met, also celebrate elaborately; the schedule of events is exactly the same in every village, town, and city across Mexico. September 15 and 16.

Fall Equinox, Chichén Itzá. The same shadow play that occurs during the spring equinox repeats. September 21 and 22.

Sanmiguelada (Running of the Bulls at San Miguel), San Miguel de Allende. Also known as the Pamplonada because it is Mexico's imitation of Spain's running of the bulls, the Sanmiguelada is an annual festival usually taking place the third Saturday of September in honor of Saint Michael the Archangel. The event involves dances, concerts, fireworks, and bulls running through town. Daring participants meet at high noon. For more information visit www.sanmiguelguide.com/tour-pamplonada.htm. Third Saturday of September.

October

Fiestas de Octubre (October Festivals), Guadalajara. This "most Mexican of cities" celebrates for a month with its trademark mariachi music. It's a bountiful display of popular culture and fine arts, and a spectacular spread of traditional food, Mexican beer, and wine. All month.

Festival Cervantino, Guanajuato. This festival began in the 1970s as a cultural event bringing performing artists from all over the world to this picturesque village northeast of Mexico City. Now the artists travel all over the republic after appearing in Guanajuato. Call © 800/446-3942 or visit www.festivalcervantino.gob.mx for details. Mid- to late October.

Taste of Oaxaca Festival, Oaxaca, Oaxaca. Formerly called the Food for the Gods Festival, this week-long event is a culinary exploration of the indigenous cultures of Oaxaca. Known globally for its culinary creativity, Oaxaca is the birthplace of chocolate. More information on this weeklong event is available at www.taste-of-oaxaca.com. October 2 to 9.

Día de la Raza ("Ethnicity Day," or Columbus Day), nationwide. This day commemorates the fusion of the Spanish and Mexican peoples. October 12.

Feria Nacional del Mole, Mexico City. Just south of Mexico City, thousands of varieties of *mole* will be prepared for sampling and competition. This spicy sauce is a Mexican staple and made of unsweetened chocolate, peppers, and spices, often served with meat or poultry. Between October 1 and 15.

November

Day of the Dead, nationwide. This holiday (Nov 1) actually lasts for 2 days: All Saints' Day—honoring saints and deceased children—and All Souls' Day, honoring deceased adults. Relatives gather at cemeteries countrywide, carrying candles and food, and often spend the night beside graves of loved ones. Weeks before, bakers begin producing bread in the shape of mummies or round loaves decorated with bread "bones." Sugar skulls emblazoned with glittery names are sold everywhere. Many days ahead, homes and churches erect altars laden with bread, fruit, flowers, candles, favorite foods, and photographs of saints and of the deceased. On both nights, costumed children walk through the streets, often carrying mock coffins and pumpkin lanterns, into which they expect money to be dropped.

The most famous celebration—which has become almost too well known—is on Janitzio, an island on

Lake Pátzcuaro, Michoacán, west of Mexico City. Mixquic, a mountain village south of Mexico City, hosts an elaborate street fair, and around 11pm on both nights solemn processions lead to the cemetery in the center of town. Cemeteries around Oaxaca are well known for their solemn vigils, and some for their Carnaval-like atmosphere. November 1 and 2.

Fiestas de Noviembre (November Festivals), Puerto Escondido, Oaxaca. The events during this month include the annual Pipeline of Mexico, Zicatela Beach's International Surfing Tournament, the International Sailfish Tournament, and the Coastal Dance Festival. Check local calendars or call © 800/446-3942 for details. All month.

Gourmet Festival, Puerto Vallarta, Jalisco. In this culinary capital of Mexico, chefs from around the world join with local restaurateurs to create special menus, as well as host wine and tequila tastings, cooking classes, a gourmet food expo, and other special events. For a detailed schedule and more information visit www.festival gourmet.com. Dates vary, but the festival generally takes place for 10 days in mid-November.

Revolution Day, nationwide. Commemorates the start of the Mexican Revolution in 1910 with parades, speeches, rodeos, and patriotic events. November 20.

Sixth Annual Yucatán Bird Festival, Mérida, Yucatán. Bird-watching sessions, workshops, and exhibits are the highlights of this festival designed to illustrate the special role birds play in our environment and in the Yucatán territory. Call © 800/446-3942 or visit www.yucatanbirds.org.mx for details. Mid-November.

National Silver Fair, Taxco. A competition of Mexico's best silversmiths and some of the world's finest artisans. There are exhibits, concerts, dances, and fireworks. Check local calendars or call © 800/446-3942 for details. Late November to early December.

December

Annual Hot Air Balloon Festival, León, Guanajuato. Largest festival in Latin America with more than 60 balloons and pilots from all over the globe participating. Call © 800/446-3942 or visit www.festivaldelglobo.com.mx for details. Early December.

Feast of the Virgin of Guadalupe, nationwide. Religious processions, street fairs, dancing, fireworks, and Masses honor the patroness of Mexico. It is one of the country's most moving and beautiful displays of traditional culture. The Virgin of Guadalupe appeared to a young man, Juan Diego, in December 1531 on a hill near Mexico City. It's customary for children to dress up as Juan Diego, wearing mustaches and red bandanas. One of the most famous and elaborate celebrations takes place at the Basílica of Guadalupe, north of Mexico City, where the Virgin appeared. But every village celebrates this day, often with processions of children carrying banners, and with *charreadas* (rodeos), bicycle races, dancing, and fireworks. In Puerto Vallarta, the celebration begins on December 1 and extends through December 12, with traditional processions to the church for a brief Mass and blessing. In the final days, the processions and festivities take place around the clock. There's a major fireworks exhibition on the feast day at 11pm. December 12.

Festival of San Cristóbal de las Casas, San Cristóbal de las Casas, Chiapas. This 10-day festival in Chiapas includes a procession by the Tzotzil and Tzetzal Indians, *marimba* music, and a parade of horses. December 12 to 21.

Christmas Posadas, nationwide. On each of the 9 nights before Christmas, it's customary to reenact the Holy Family's search for an inn. Door-to-door candlelit processions pass through cities and villages nationwide, especially Querétaro and Taxco. Hosted by businesses and community organizations, these take the place of the northern tradition of a Christmas party. December 15 to 24.

Fiesta de los Rábanos (Festival of the Radishes), Oaxaca, Oaxaca. Local artisans and sculptors set up stalls around the main square to display their elaborate pieces of art—made entirely from radishes! The local crop is used for creating nativity scenes and famous Mexican figures. Balloons and birds crafted from local flowers add even more color. December 23.

Christmas, nationwide. Mexicans often extend this national holiday and take vacations for up to 2 weeks before Christmas, returning after New Year's. Many businesses close, and resorts and hotels fill. Significant celebrations take place on December 23 (see above). Querétaro has a huge parade. On the evening of December 24 in Oaxaca, processions culminate on the central plaza. On the same night, Santiago Tuxtla in Veracruz celebrates by dancing the *huapango* and with *jarocho* bands in the beautiful town square. December 24 and 25.

New Year's Eve, nationwide. Like the rest of the world, Mexico celebrates New Year's Eve with parties, fireworks, and plenty of noise. Special festivities take place at Santa Clara del Cobre, near Pátzcuaro, with a candlelit procession of Christ, and at Tlacolula, near Oaxaca, with commemorative mock battles. December 31.

5 Getting There

BY PLANE

The airline situation in Mexico is rapidly improving, with many new regional carriers offering scheduled service to areas previously not served. In addition to regularly scheduled service, charter service direct from U.S. cities to resorts is making Mexico more accessible.

THE MAJOR INTERNATIONAL AIR-LINES The main airlines operating direct or nonstop flights from the United States to Mexico include **AeroMéxico** (© 800/237-6639; www.aeromexico. com), **Air France** (© 800/237-2747; www.airfrance.com), **Alaska Airlines** (© 800/252-7522; www.alaskaair.com), **American Airlines** (© 800/223-5436; www.aa.com), **Continental** (© 800/537-9222; www.continental.com), **Frontier**

Airlines (© 800/432-1359; www.frontier airlines.com), **Mexicana** (© 800/531-7921; www.mexicana.com), **Northwest/KLM** (© 800/225-2525; www.nwa.com), **Taca** (© 800/400-8222; www.taca.com), **United** (© 800/538-2929; www.united. com), and **US Airways** (© 800/428-4322; www.usairways.com). **Southwest Airlines** (© 800/435-9792; www.south west.com) serves the U.S. border.

The main departure points in North America for international airlines are Atlanta, Chicago, Dallas/Fort Worth, Denver, Houston, Las Vegas, Los Angeles, Miami, New York, Orlando, Philadelphia, Phoenix, Raleigh/Durham, San Antonio, San Francisco, Seattle, Toronto, and Washington, D.C.

Tips **Luxury Bus Service from the Mexico City Airport**

An airport-to-destination service to a number of cities in central Mexico takes the hassle out of travel. The deluxe buses serving these routes are air-conditioned and have video movies and a restroom. The price usually includes soft drinks (and passengers tend to stock up when they board).

If you're going to **Puebla** (see chapter 12), Estrella Roja buses ($18/£9.90) depart hourly beginning at 6 or 7:30am from in front of the airport's Sala D (Gate D) exit. The bus runs every hour until midnight. Buses for **Querétaro** ($24/£13), **Toluca** ($10/£5.50), **Pachuca** ($11/£6.05), and **Cuernavaca** ($14/£7.70) are in front of the covered concourse outside the terminal between exit doors for Gate D. If you have trouble locating them, ask for help at an information desk on the main concourse. If precise scheduling is essential, call the **Airport Information Office** (✆ 55/5786-9341, -9342, -9358, or 55/5571-3600) to verify names of buses, where to find them, and current schedules.

FLYING FOR LESS: TIPS FOR GETTING THE BEST AIRFARE

- Passengers who can book their ticket either **long in advance or at the last minute,** or who **fly midweek** or **at less-trafficked hours** may pay a fraction of the full fare. If your schedule is flexible, say so, and ask if you can secure a cheaper fare by changing your flight plans.
- Search **the Internet** for cheap fares. The most popular online travel agencies are **Travelocity.com** (www.travelocity.co.uk); **Expedia.com** (www.expedia.co.uk and www.expedia.ca); and **Orbitz.com**. In the U.K., go to **Travelsupermarket** (✆ 0845/345-5708; www.travelsupermarket.com), a flight search engine that offers flight comparisons for the budget airlines whose seats often end up in bucket-shop sales. Other websites for booking airline tickets online include **Cheapflights.com, SmarterTravel.com, Priceline.com,** and **Opodo** (www.opodo.co.uk). Meta search sites (which find and then direct you to airline and hotel websites for booking) include

  Sidestep.com and **Kayak.com**—the latter includes fares for budget carriers like Jet Blue and Spirit as well as the major airlines. **Site59.com** is a great source for last-minute flights and getaways. In addition, most **airlines** offer online-only fares that even their phone agents know nothing about. British travelers should check **Flights International** (✆ 0800/0187050; www.flights-international.com) for deals on flights all over the world.
- Keep an eye on local newspapers for **promotional specials** or **fare wars,** when airlines lower prices on their most popular routes.
- Try to book a ticket **in its country of origin.** If you're planning a one-way flight from Johannesburg to Bombay, a South Africa–based travel agent will probably have the lowest fares. For multileg trips, book in the country of the first leg; for example, book New York–London–Amsterdam–Rome–New York in the U.S.
- **Consolidators,** also known as bucket shops, are wholesale brokers in the airline-ticket game. Consolidators

buy deeply discounted tickets ("distressed" inventories of unsold seats) from airlines and sell them to online ticket agencies, travel agents, tour operators, corporations, and, to a lesser degree, the general public. Consolidators advertise in Sunday newspaper travel sections (often in small ads with tiny type), both in the U.S. and the U.K. They can be great sources for cheap international tickets. On the down side, bucket shop tickets are often rigged with restrictions, such as stiff cancellation penalties (as high as 50% to 75% of the ticket price). And keep in mind that most of what you see advertised is of limited availability. Several reliable consolidators are worldwide and available online. **STA Travel** (www.statravel.com) has been the world's leading consolidator for students since purchasing Council Travel, but their fares are competitive for travelers of all ages. **Flights.com** (℃ 800/TRAV-800; www.flights.com) has excellent fares worldwide, particularly to Europe. They also have "local" websites in 12 countries. **FlyCheap** (℃ 800/FLY-CHEAP; www.1800fly cheap.com) has especially good fares to sunny destinations. **Air Tickets Direct** (℃ 800/778-3447; www.air ticketsdirect.com) is based in Montréal and books trips to places that U.S. travel agents won't touch, such as Cuba.

- Join **frequent-flier clubs.** Frequent-flier membership doesn't cost a cent, but it does entitle you to free tickets or upgrades when you amass the airline's required number of frequent-flier points. You don't even have to fly to earn points; **frequent-flier credit cards** can earn you thousands of miles for doing your everyday shopping. But keep in mind that award seats are limited, seats on popular

---

⌐Tips **Getting Through the Airport**

- Arrive at the airport 1 hour before a domestic flight and 2 hours before an international flight. You can check the average wait times at your airport by going to the TSA **Security Checkpoint Wait Times** site (http://waittime/tsa.dhs.gov/index.html).
- Know what you can carry on and what you can't. For the latest updates on items you are prohibited to bring in carryon luggage, go to **www.tsa.gov/travelers/airtravel**.
- Beat the ticket-counter lines by using the self-service electronic ticket kiosks at the airport or even printing out your boarding pass at home from the airline website. Using curbside check-in is also a smart way to avoid lines.
- Help speed up security before you're screened. Remove jackets, shoes, belt buckles, heavy jewelry, and watches and place them either in your carryon luggage or the security bins provided. Place keys, coins, cellphones, and pagers in a security bin. If you have metallic body parts, carry a note from your doctor. When possible, pack liquids in checked baggage.
- Use a TSA-approved lock for your checked luggage. Look for Travel Sentry certified locks at luggage or travel shops and Brookstone stores (or online at www.brookstone.com).

routes are hard to snag, and more and more major airlines are cutting their expiration periods for mileage points—so check your airline's frequent-flier program so you don't lose your miles before you use them. *Inside tip:* Award seats are offered almost a year in advance, but seats also open up at the last minute, so if your travel plans are flexible, you may strike gold. To play the frequent-flier game to your best advantage, consult the community bulletin boards on **FlyerTalk** (www.flyertalk.com) or go to Randy Petersen's **Inside Flyer** (www.insideflyer.com). Petersen and friends review all the programs in detail and post regular updates on changes in policies and trends.

LONG-HAUL FLIGHTS: HOW TO STAY COMFORTABLE

- Your choice of airline and airplane will definitely affect your leg room. Find more details about U.S. airlines at **www.seatguru.com**. For international airlines, the research firm Skytrax has posted a list of average seat pitches at **www.airlinequality.com**.
- Emergency exit seats and bulkhead seats typically have the most legroom. Emergency exit seats are usually left unassigned until the day of a flight (to ensure that someone able-bodied fills the seats); it's worth getting to the ticket counter early to snag one of these spots for a long flight. Many passengers find that bulkhead seating (the row facing the wall at the front of the cabin) offers more legroom, but keep in mind that bulkhead seats have no storage space on the floor in front of you.
- To have two seats for yourself in a three-seat row, try for an aisle seat in a center section toward the back of coach. If you're traveling with a companion, book an aisle and a window seat. Middle seats are usually booked

last, so chances are good you'll end up with three seats to yourselves. And, in the event that a third passenger is assigned the middle seat, he or she will probably be more than happy to trade for a window or an aisle.

- Ask about entertainment options. Many airlines offer seatback video systems where you get to choose your movies or play video games—but only on some of their planes. (Boeing 777s are your best bet.)
- To sleep, avoid the last row of any section or the row in front of an emergency exit, as these seats are the least likely to recline. Avoid seats near highly trafficked toilet areas. Avoid seats in the back of many jets—these can be narrower than those in the rest of coach. Or reserve a window seat so you can rest your head and avoid being bumped in the aisle.
- Get up, walk around, and stretch every 60 to 90 minutes to keep your blood flowing. This helps avoid **deep vein thrombosis,** or "economy-class syndrome."
- Drink water before, during, and after your flight to combat the lack of humidity in airplane cabins. Avoid alcohol, which will dehydrate you.
- If you're flying with kids, don't forget to carry on toys, books, pacifiers, and snacks and chewing gum to help them relieve ear pressure buildup during ascent and descent.

BY CAR

Driving is not the cheapest way to get to Mexico, but it is the best way to see the country. Even so, you may think twice about taking your own car south of the border once you've pondered the bureaucracy involved. One option is to rent a car once you arrive and tour around a specific region. Rental cars in Mexico generally are new, clean, and well maintained. Although they're pricier than in the United States,

Tips Carrying Car Documents

You must carry your temporary car-importation permit, tourist permit (see "Entry Requirements," earlier in this chapter), and, if you purchased it, your proof of Mexican car insurance (see below) in the car at all times. The temporary car-importation permit papers are valid for 6 months to a year, while the tourist permit is usually issued for 30 days. It's a good idea to overestimate the time you'll spend in Mexico so if you have to (or want to) stay longer, you'll avoid the hassle of getting your papers extended. Whatever you do, don't overstay either permit. Doing so invites heavy fines, confiscation of your vehicle (which will not be returned), or both. Also remember that 6 months does not necessarily equal 180 days—be sure that you return before the earlier expiration date.

discounts are often available for rentals of a week or longer, especially when you make arrangements in advance from the United States. (See "Car Rentals," later in this chapter, for more details.)

If, after reading the section that follows, you have additional questions or you want to confirm the current rules, call your nearest Mexican consulate or the Mexican Government Tourist Office. Although travel insurance companies generally are helpful, they may not have the most accurate information. To check on road conditions or to get help with any travel emergency while in Mexico, call ℰ **01-800/482-9832,** or 55/5089-7500 in Mexico City. English-speaking operators staff both numbers.

In addition, check with the **U.S. Department of State** (see "Visitor Information," earlier in this chapter) for warnings about dangerous driving areas.

CAR DOCUMENTS

To drive your car into Mexico, you'll need a **temporary car-importation permit,** which is granted after you provide a required list of documents (see below). The permit can be obtained through Banco del Ejército (Banjercito) officials, who have a desk, booth, or office at the *aduana* (Mexican Customs) building after you cross the border into Mexico.

The following strict requirements for border crossing were accurate at press time:

- **A valid driver's license,** issued outside of Mexico.
- **Current, original car registration and a copy of the original car title.** If the registration or title is in more than one name and not all the named people are traveling with you, a notarized letter from the absent person(s) authorizing use of the vehicle for the trip is required; have it ready. The registration and your credit card (see below) must be in the same name.
- **A valid international major credit card.** With a credit card, you are required to pay a $29.70 car-importation fee. The credit card must be in the same name as the car registration. If you do not have a major credit card (American Express, Diners Club, MasterCard, or Visa), you must post a bond or make a deposit equal to the value of the vehicle. Check cards are not accepted.
- **Original immigration documentation.** This is either your tourist permit (FMT) or the original immigration booklet, FM2 or FM3, if you hold more permanent status.
- **A signed declaration promising to return to your country of origin**

with the vehicle. Obtain this form *(Carta Promesa de Retorno)* from AAA or Sanborn's (see below for contact information) before you go, or from Banjercito officials at the border. There's no charge. The form does not stipulate that you must return by the same border entry through which you entered.

- **Temporary Importation Application.** By signing this form, you state that you are only temporarily importing the car for your personal use and will not be selling it. This is to help regulate the entry and restrict the resale of unauthorized cars and trucks. Make sure the permit is canceled when you return to the U.S.

If you receive your documentation at the border, Mexican officials will make two copies of everything and charge you for the copies. For up-to-the-minute information, a great source is the Customs office in Nuevo Laredo, or *Módulo de Importación Temporal de Automóviles, Aduana Nuevo Laredo* (© **867/712-2071**).

Important reminder: Someone else may drive, but the person (or relative of the person) whose name appears on the car-importation permit must *always* be in the car. (If stopped by police, a nonregistered family member driving without the registered driver must be prepared to prove familial relationship to the registered driver—no joke.) Violation of this rule subjects the car to impoundment and the driver to imprisonment, a fine, or both. You can drive a car with foreign license plates only if you have a foreign (non-Mexican) driver's license.

MEXICAN AUTO INSURANCE

Liability auto insurance is legally required in Mexico. U.S. insurance is invalid; to be insured in Mexico, you must purchase Mexican insurance. Any party involved in an accident who has no insurance may be sent to jail and have his or her car impounded until all claims are settled. This is true even if you just drive across the border to spend the day. U.S. companies that broker Mexican insurance are commonly found at the border crossing, and several quote daily rates.

You can also buy car insurance through **Sanborn's Mexico Insurance,** P.O. Box 52840, 2009 S. 10th, McAllen, TX (© **800/222-0158;** fax 800/222-0158 or 956/686-0732; www.sanbornsinsurance. com). The company has offices at all U.S. border crossings. Its policies cost the same as the competition's do, but you get legal coverage (attorney and bail bonds if needed) and a detailed mile-by-mile guide for your proposed route. Most of the Sanborn's border offices are open Monday through Friday, and a few are staffed on Saturday and Sunday. **AAA** auto club (www.aaa.com) also sells insurance.

RETURNING TO THE UNITED STATES WITH YOUR CAR

You *must* return the car documents you obtained when you entered Mexico when you cross back with your car or at some point within 180 days. (You can cross as many times as you wish within the 180 days.) If the documents aren't returned, heavy fines are imposed ($250 for each 15 days late), your car may be impounded and confiscated, or you may be jailed if you return to Mexico. You can only return the car documents to a Banjercito official on duty at the Mexican *aduana* building *before* you cross back into the United States. Some border cities have Banjercito officials on duty 24 hours a day, but others do not; some do not have Sunday hours.

BY SHIP

Numerous cruise lines serve Mexico. Some cruise from California to the Baja Peninsula (such as Carnival and Royal

Caribbean) and ports of call on the Pacific coast, or from Houston or Miami to the Caribbean (which often includes stops in Cancún, Playa del Carmen, and Cozumel). Several cruise-tour specialists sometimes offer last-minute discounts on unsold cabins. One such company is **CruisesOnly** (© **800/278-4373;** www.cruisesonly.com).

BY BUS
Greyhound-Trailways (or its affiliates) offers service from around the United States to the Mexican border, where passengers disembark, cross the border, and buy a ticket for travel into Mexico. Many border crossings have scheduled buses from the U.S. bus station to the Mexican bus station.

6 Money & Costs

It's always advisable to bring money in a variety of forms on a vacation: a mix of cash, credit cards, and traveler's checks. You should also exchange enough petty cash to cover airport incidentals, tipping, and transportation to your hotel before you leave home, or withdraw money upon arrival at an airport ATM.

CURRENCY
The currency in Mexico is the **peso.** Paper currency comes in denominations of 20, 50, 100, 200, and 500 pesos. Coins come in denominations of 1, 2, 5, 10, and 20 pesos, and 20 and 50 **centavos** (100 centavos = 1 peso). The current exchange rate for the U.S. dollar, and the one used in this book, is around 11 pesos; at that rate, an item that costs 11 pesos would be equivalent to US$1.

Getting **change** is a problem. Small-denomination bills and coins are hard to come by, so start collecting them early in your trip. Shopkeepers and taxi drivers everywhere always seem to be out of change and small bills; that's doubly true in markets.

Many establishments that deal with tourists, especially in coastal resort areas, quote prices in dollars. To avoid confusion, they use the abbreviations "Dlls." for dollars and "M.N." (*moneda nacional,* or national currency) for pesos.

Don't forget to have enough pesos to carry you over a weekend or Mexican holiday, when banks are closed. In general, avoid carrying the U.S. $100 bill, the bill most commonly counterfeited in Mexico and therefore the most difficult to exchange, especially in smaller towns. Because small bills and coins in pesos are hard to come by in Mexico, the $1 bill is very useful for tipping. A tip of U.S. coins, which cannot be exchanged into Mexican currency, is of no value to the service provider.

The bottom line on exchanging money: Ask first, and shop around. Banks generally pay the top rates.

Casas de cambio (exchange houses) are generally more convenient than banks because they have more locations and longer hours; the rate of exchange may be the same as at a bank or slightly lower. Before leaving a bank or exchange-house window, count your change in front of the teller before the next client steps up.

Large airports have currency-exchange counters that often stay open whenever flights are operating. Though convenient, they generally do not offer the most favorable rates.

Money Matters
The **universal currency sign ($)** is used to indicate pesos in Mexico. The use of this symbol in this book, however, denotes U.S. currency.

> ### ⌒ *Tips* A Few Words about Prices
>
> The peso's value continues to fluctuate—at press time, it was roughly 11 pesos to the dollar. Prices in this book (which are always given in U.S. dollars) have been converted to U.S. dollars at 11 pesos to the dollar. Most hotels in Mexico—with the exception of places that receive little foreign tourism—quote prices in U.S. dollars. Thus, currency fluctuations are unlikely to affect the prices most hotels charge.
>
> Mexico has a **value-added tax** of 15% (*Impuesto de Valor Agregado,* or IVA; pronounced "ee-bah") on most everything, including restaurant meals, bus tickets, and souvenirs. (Exceptions are Cancún, Cozumel, and Los Cabos, where the IVA is 10%; as ports of entry, they receive a break on taxes.) Hotels charge the usual 15% IVA, plus a locally administered bed tax of 2% (in most areas), for a total of 17%. In Cancún, Los Cabos, and Cozumel, hotels charge the 10% IVA plus 2% room tax. The prices quoted by hotels and restaurants do not necessarily include IVA. You may find that upper-end properties (three or more stars) quote prices without IVA included, while lower-priced hotels include IVA. Always ask to see a printed price sheet and always ask if the tax is included.

A hotel's exchange desk commonly pays less favorable rates than banks; however, when the currency is in a state of flux, higher-priced hotels are known to pay higher rates than banks, in an effort to attract dollars. *Note:* In almost all cases, you receive a better rate by changing money first, then paying.

You'll avoid lines at airport ATMs (automated teller machines) by exchanging at least some money—just enough to cover airport incidentals and transportation to your hotel—before you leave home (though don't expect the exchange rate to be ideal). You can exchange money at your local American Express or Thomas Cook office or at your bank. American Express also dispenses traveler's checks and foreign currency via www. americanexpress.com or ⓒ **800/673-3782,** but they'll charge a $15 order fee and additional shipping and handling costs.

BANKS & ATMs

Banks in Mexico are rapidly expanding and improving services. They tend to be open weekdays from 9am until 5pm, and often for at least a half day on Saturday.

In larger resorts and cities, they can generally accommodate the exchange of dollars (which used to stop at noon) anytime during business hours. Some, but not all, banks charge a service fee of about 1% to exchange traveler's checks. However, you can pay for most purchases directly with traveler's checks at the establishment's stated exchange rate. Don't even bother with personal checks drawn on a U.S. bank—the bank will wait for your check to clear, which can take weeks, before giving you your money.

Travelers to Mexico can easily withdraw money from **ATMs** in most major cities and resort areas. The U.S. Department of State has an advisory against using ATMs in Mexico for safety reasons, stating that they should only be used during business hours, but this pertains primarily to Mexico City, where crime remains a significant problem. In most resorts in Mexico, the use of ATMs is perfectly safe—just use the same precautions you would at any ATM. Universal bank cards (such as the Cirrus and PLUS systems) can be used. This is a convenient way to withdraw money and avoid carrying too much with you at any time. The exchange rate is generally more favorable than that at *casas de cambio*. Most machines offer Spanish/English menus and dispense pesos, but some offer the option of withdrawing dollars.

The **Cirrus** (© 800/424-7787; www.mastercard.com) and **PLUS** (© 800/843-7587; www.visa.com) networks span the globe. Go to your bank card's website to find ATM locations at your destination. Be sure you know your daily withdrawal limit before you depart. *Note:* Many banks impose a fee every time you use a card at another bank's ATM, and that fee can be higher for international transactions (up to $5 or more) than for domestic ones (where they're rarely more than $2). In addition, the bank from which you withdraw cash may charge its own fee. For international withdrawal fees, ask your bank.

CREDIT CARDS

Credit cards are another safe way to carry money. They also provide a convenient record of all your expenses, and they generally offer relatively good exchange rates. You can withdraw cash advances from your credit cards at banks or ATMs, but high fees make credit-card cash advances a pricey way to get cash. Keep in mind that you'll pay interest from the moment of your withdrawal, even if you pay your monthly bills on time. Also, note that many banks now assess a 1% to 3% "transaction fee" on **all** charges you incur abroad (whether you're using the local currency or your native currency).

In Mexico, Visa, MasterCard, and American Express are the most accepted cards. You'll be able to charge most hotel, restaurant, and store purchases, as well as almost all airline tickets, on your credit card. Pemex gas stations have begun to accept credit card purchases for gasoline, though this option may not be available everywhere—check before you pump. You can get cash advances of several hundred dollars on your card, but there may

be a wait of 20 minutes to 2 hours. Charges will be made in pesos, then converted into dollars by the bank issuing the credit card. Generally you receive the favorable bank rate when paying by credit card. However, be aware that some establishments in Mexico add a 5% to 7% surcharge when you pay with a credit card. This is especially true when using American Express. Many times, advertised discounts will not apply if you pay with a credit card.

For tips and telephone numbers to call if your wallet is stolen or lost, go to "Lost & Found" in the "Fast Facts" section of this chapter.

TRAVELER'S CHECKS

You can buy traveler's checks at most banks. They are offered in denominations of $20, $50, $100, $500, and sometimes $1,000. Generally, you'll pay a service charge ranging from 1% to 4%.

The most popular traveler's checks are offered by **American Express** (© 800/807-6233 or © 800/221-7282 for card holders—this number accepts collect calls, offers service in several foreign languages, and exempts AmEx gold and platinum cardholders from the 1% fee) and **Visa** (© 800/732-1322)—AAA members can obtain Visa checks for a $9.95 fee (for checks up to $1,500) at most AAA offices or by calling © 866/339-3378. Call © 800/223-9920 for information on MasterCard traveler's checks.

Be sure to keep a record of the traveler's checks serial numbers separate from your checks in the event that they are stolen or lost. You'll get a refund faster if you know the numbers.

American Express, Thomas Cook, Visa, and **MasterCard** offer **foreign currency traveler's checks,** useful if you're traveling to one country or to the Euro zone; they're accepted at locations where dollar checks may not be.

Another option is the new prepaid traveler's check cards, reloadable cards that work much like debit cards but aren't linked to your checking account. The **American Express Travelers Cheque Card,** for example, requires a minimum deposit, sets a maximum balance, and has a one-time issuance fee of $14.95. You can withdraw money from an ATM (for a fee of $2.50 per transaction, not including bank fees), and the funds can be purchased in dollars, euros, or pounds. If you lose the card, your available funds will be refunded within 24 hours.

7 Travel Insurance

The cost of travel insurance varies widely, depending on the destination, the cost and length of your trip, your age and health, and the type of trip you're taking, but expect to pay between 5% and 8% of the vacation itself. You can get estimates from various providers through **Insure MyTrip.com**. Enter your trip cost and dates, your age, and other information for prices from more than a dozen companies.

U.K. citizens and their families who make more than one trip abroad per year may find an annual travel insurance policy works out cheaper. Check **www.money supermarket.com**, which compares prices across a wide range of providers for single- and multitrip policies.

Most big travel agents offer their own insurance and will probably try to sell you their package when you book a holiday. Think before you sign. **Britain's Consumers' Association** recommends that you insist on seeing the policy and reading the fine print before buying travel insurance. **The Association of British Insurers** (© 020/7600-3333; www.abi. org.uk) gives advice by phone and publishes *Holiday Insurance,* a free guide to policy provisions and prices. You might also shop around for better deals: Try **Columbus Direct** (© 0870/033- 9988; www.columbusdirect.net).

If you'll be driving in Mexico, see "Getting There" earlier in this chapter, and "Getting Around Mexico," later in this chapter, for information on **collision, damage** and **personal accident insurance.**

TRIP-CANCELLATION INSURANCE

Trip-cancellation insurance will help retrieve your money if you have to back out of a trip or depart early, or if your travel supplier goes bankrupt. Trip cancellation traditionally covers such events as sickness, natural disasters, and Department of State advisories. The latest news in trip-cancellation insurance is the availability of **expanded hurricane coverage** and the **"any-reason"** cancellation coverage—which costs more but covers cancellations made for any reason. You won't get back 100% of your prepaid trip cost, but you'll be refunded a substantial portion. **TravelSafe** (© **888/885-7233;** www.travelsafe.com) offers both types of coverage. Expedia also offers any-reason cancellation coverage for its air–hotel packages.

For details, contact one of the following recommended insurers: Access America (© 866/807-3982; www.access america.com); Travel Guard International (© 800/826-4919; www.travelguard. com); Travel Insured International (© 800/243-3174; www.travelinsured. com); and Travelex Insurance Services (© 888/457-4602; www.travelex-insurance.com).

MEDICAL INSURANCE

For travel overseas, most U.S. health plans (including Medicare and Medicaid) do not provide coverage, and the ones that do often require you to pay for services up front and reimburse you only after you return home.

Travel in the Age of Bankruptcy

Airlines go bankrupt, so protect yourself by **buying your tickets with a credit card.** The Fair Credit Billing Act guarantees that you can get your money back from the credit card company if a travel supplier goes under (and if you request the refund within 60 days of the bankruptcy). **Travel insurance** can also help, but make sure it covers against "carrier default" for your specific travel provider. And be aware that if a U.S. airline goes bust midtrip, a 2001 federal law requires other carriers to take you to your destination (albeit on a space-available basis) for a fee of no more than $25, provided you rebook within 60 days of the cancellation.

As a safety net, you may want to buy travel medical insurance, particularly if you're traveling to a remote or high-risk area where emergency evacuation might be necessary. If you require additional medical insurance, try **MEDEX Assistance** (✆ 410/453-6300; www.medexassist.com) or **Travel Assistance International** (✆ 800/821-2828; www.travelassistance.com; for general information on services, call the company's Worldwide Assistance Services, Inc., at ✆ 800/777-8710).

Canadians should check with their provincial health plan offices or call **Health Canada** (✆ 866/225-0709; www.hc-sc.gc.ca) to find out the extent of their coverage and what documentation and receipts they must take home in case they are treated overseas.

LOST-LUGGAGE INSURANCE

On international flights (including U.S. portions of international trips), baggage coverage is limited to approximately $9.07 per pound, up to approximately $635 per checked bag. If you plan to check items more valuable than what's covered by the standard liability, see if your homeowner's policy covers your valuables, get baggage insurance as part of your comprehensive travel-insurance package, or buy Travel Guard's "BagTrak" product.

If your luggage is lost, immediately file a lost-luggage claim at the airport, detailing the luggage contents. Most airlines require that you report delayed, damaged, or lost baggage within 4 hours of arrival. The airlines are required to deliver luggage, once found, directly to your house or destination free of charge.

---

8 Health

GENERAL AVAILABILITY OF HEALTH CARE

In most of Mexico's resort destinations, health care meeting U.S. standards is now available. Mexico's major cities are also known for their quality health care, although the facilities available may be fewer, and equipment older than what is available at home. Prescription medicine is broadly available at Mexico pharmacies; however, be aware that you may need a copy of your prescription or to obtain a prescription from a local doctor. This is especially true in the border towns, such as in Tijuana, where many Americans have been crossing into Mexico specifically for the purpose of purchasing lower-priced prescription medicines.

Contact the **International Association for Medical Assistance to Travellers (IAMAT;** ✆ 716/754-4883 or, in Canada, 416/652-0137; www.iamat.org) for tips on travel and health concerns in the countries you're visiting and for lists of local, English-speaking doctors. The United States **Centers for Disease Control and Prevention** (© **800/311-3435;** www.cdc.gov) provides up-to-date information on health hazards by region or country and offers tips on food safety. **Travel Health Online** (www.tripprep.com), sponsored by a consortium of travel medicine practitioners, may also offer helpful advice on traveling abroad. You can find listings of reliable medical clinics overseas at the **International Society of Travel Medicine** (www.istm.org).

COMMON AILMENTS

SUN EXPOSURE   Mexico is synonymous with sunshine, with most of the country blanketed in intense sunlight most of the year. Avoid excessive sun exposure, especially in the tropics where UV rays are more dangerous. The hottest months in Mexico are April and May in the south, and July through September along the Pacific Coast, including Baja California. The deserts of northern Mexico are extremely hot during summer months.

DIETARY RED FLAGS   Travelers' diarrhea or *turista,* the Spanish word for "tourist": persistent diarrhea, often accompanied by fever, nausea, and vomiting, used to attack many travelers to Mexico. (Some in the U.S. call this "Montezuma's revenge," but you won't hear it called that in Mexico.) Widespread improvements in infrastructure, sanitation, and education have greatly diminished this ailment, especially in well-developed resort areas. Most travelers make a habit of drinking only bottled water, which also helps to protect against unfamiliar bacteria. In resort areas, and generally throughout Mexico, only purified ice is used. If you do come down with this ailment, nothing beats Pepto Bismol, readily available in Mexico. Imodium is also available in Mexico and

is used by many travelers for a quick fix. A good high-potency (or "therapeutic") vitamin supplement and even extra vitamin C can help; yogurt is good for healthy digestion.

Since dehydration can quickly become life-threatening, the Public Health Service advises that you be careful to replace fluids and electrolytes (potassium, sodium, and the like) during a bout of diarrhea. Drink Pedialyte, a rehydration solution available at most Mexican pharmacies, or natural fruit juice, such as guava or apple (stay away from orange juice, which has laxative properties), with a pinch of salt added.

The U.S. Public Health Service recommends the following measures for preventing travelers' diarrhea: **Drink only purified water** (boiled water, canned or bottled beverages, beer, or wine). **Choose food carefully.** In general, avoid salads (except in first-class restaurants), uncooked vegetables, undercooked protein, and unpasteurized milk or milk products, including cheese. Choose food that is freshly cooked and still hot. Avoid eating food prepared by street vendors. In addition, something as simple as **clean hands** can go a long way toward preventing *turista.*

HIGH-ALTITUDE HAZARDS   Travelers to certain regions of Mexico occasionally experience **elevation sickness,** which results from the relative lack of oxygen and the decrease in barometric pressure that characterizes high elevations (more than 1,500m/5,000 ft.). Symptoms include shortness of breath, fatigue, headache, insomnia, and even nausea. Mexico City is at 2,100m (6,720 ft.) above sea level, as are a number of other central and southern cities, such as San Cristóbal de las Casas (even higher than Mexico City). At high elevations, it takes about 10 days to acquire the extra red blood corpuscles you need to adjust to the scarcity of oxygen. To help your body acclimate, drink plenty of

Tips Over-the-Counter Drugs in Mexico

Antibiotics and other drugs that you'd need a prescription to buy in the States are often available over the counter in Mexican pharmacies. Mexican pharmacies also carry a limited selection of common over-the-counter cold, sinus, and allergy remedies.

---

fluids, avoid alcoholic beverages, and don't overexert yourself during the first few days. If you have heart or lung problems, talk to your doctor before going above 2,400m (7,872 ft.).

BUGS, BITES & OTHER WILDLIFE CONCERNS Mosquitoes and **gnats** are prevalent along the coast and in the Yucatán lowlands. *Repelente contra insectos* (insect repellent) is a must, and it's not always available in Mexico. If you'll be in these areas and are prone to bites, bring along a repellent that contains the active ingredient DEET. Avon's Skin So Soft also works extremely well. Another good remedy to keep the mosquitoes away is to mix citronella essential oil with basil, clove, and lavender essential oils. If you're sensitive to bites, pick up some antihistamine cream from a drugstore at home.

Most readers won't ever see an *alacrán* (scorpion). But if one stings you, go immediately to a doctor. The one lethal scorpion found in some parts of Mexico is the *Centruroides,* part of the Buthidae family, characterized by a thin body, thick tail, and triangular-shaped sternum. Most deaths from these scorpions result within 24 hours of the sting as a result of respiratory or cardiovascular failure, with children and elderly people most at risk. Scorpions are not aggressive (they don't hunt for prey), but they may sting if touched, especially in their hiding places. In Mexico, you can buy scorpion toxin antidote at any drugstore. It is an injection, and it costs around $25. This is a good idea if you plan to camp in a remote area where medical assistance can be several hours away.

TROPICAL ILLNESSES You shouldn't be overly concerned about tropical diseases if you stay on the normal tourist routes and don't eat street food. However, both dengue fever and cholera have appeared in Mexico in recent years. Talk to your doctor or to a medical specialist in tropical diseases about precautions you should take. You can also get medical bulletins from the U.S. Department of State and the Centers for Disease Control and Prevention (see "Visitor Information," earlier in this chapter). You can protect yourself by taking some simple precautions: Watch what you eat and drink; don't swim in stagnant water (ponds, slow-moving rivers, or wells); and avoid mosquito bites by covering up, using repellent, and sleeping under netting. The most dangerous areas seem to be on Mexico's west coast, away from the big resorts.

WHAT TO DO IF YOU GET SICK AWAY FROM HOME
Any foreign consulate can provide a list of area doctors who speak English. If you get sick, consider asking your hotel concierge to recommend a local doctor—even his or her own. You can also try the emergency room at a local hospital. Many hospitals also have walk-in clinics for emergency cases that are not life-threatening; you may not get immediate attention, but you won't pay the high price of an emergency room visit. We list hospitals and emergency numbers under "Fast Facts," in each destination's chapter.

For travel abroad, you may have to pay all medical costs up front and be reimbursed later. Medicare and Medicaid do not provide coverage for medical costs outside the U.S. Before leaving home, find out what medical services your health insurance covers. To protect yourself, consider buying medical travel insurance (see "Medical Insurance," under "Travel Insurance," above).

Very few health insurance plans pay for medical evacuation back to the U.S. (which can cost $10,000 and more). A number of companies offer medical evacuation services anywhere in the world. If you're ever hospitalized more than 150 miles from home, **MedjetAssist** (© **800/ 527-7478**; www.medjetassistance.com) will pick you up and fly you to the hospital of your choice, virtually anywhere in the world, in a medically equipped and staffed aircraft—24 hours day, 7 days a week. Annual memberships are $225 individual, $350 family; you can also purchase short-term memberships.

We list **hospitals** and **emergency numbers** under "Fast Facts," p. 69.

If you suffer from a chronic illness, consult your doctor before your departure. Pack **prescription medications** in your carry-on luggage, and carry prescription medications in their original containers, with pharmacy labels—otherwise they won't make it through airport security. Also bring along copies of your prescriptions in case you lose your pills or run out. Carry the generic name of prescription medicines, in case a local pharmacist is unfamiliar with the brand name.

9 Safety

CRIME

Crime in Mexico, especially in Mexico City, in selected cities along the U.S. border, and in some states affected by drug violence, has received attention in the North American press over the past several years. Many feel this unfairly exaggerates the real dangers, but it should be noted that crime rates, including taxi robberies, kidnappings, and highway carjackings, have risen in recent years. The most severe problems have been concentrated in Mexico City, where even longtime foreign residents will attest to the overall lack of security. Violent crime has also continued at high levels in Tijuana, Ciudad Juarez, Nuevo Laredo, Acapulco, and the state of Sinaloa. The U.S. Department of State recommends caution in traveling to the southern states of Oaxaca, Chiapas, and Guerrero due to sporadic incidents of politically motivated violence there. Check the U.S. Department of State Consular Information Sheet (and any applicable travel advisories) for Mexico before you travel to any notable "hot spots." See "Visitor Information," earlier in this chapter, for information on the latest **U.S. Department of State Consular Information Sheet** for Mexico.

Precautions are necessary, but travelers should be realistic. Common sense is essential. You can generally trust a person whom you approach for help or directions, but be wary of anyone who approaches you offering the same. The more insistent the person is, the more cautious you should be. The crime rate is, on the whole, much lower in Mexico than in many parts of the United States, and the nature of crime, in general, is less violent.

Although these general comments on crime are basically true throughout Mexico, the one notable exception is in **Mexico City,** where violent crime is serious. Do not wear fine jewelry, expensive watches, or any other obvious displays of wealth. Muggings—day and night—are common. Theft is even common at the Benito Juárez International Airport, where items such as briefcases, cameras, or laptops are common targets. Arriving passengers wanting to obtain pesos should use the exchange counters or

ATMs in the arrival/departure gate area, where access is restricted, rather than changing money after passing through Customs, to avoid being targeted by criminals. Avoid the use of the **green Volkswagen** and **libre taxis** taken off the street, many of which have been involved in "pirate" robberies, muggings, and kidnappings. These taxis are also common in incidents where a passenger is "hijacked," and released only when the limit on their ATM bank cards have been withdrawn. Car theft and carjackings are also a common occurrence. More specific precautions appear in chapter 4. (See also "Emergencies" under "Fast Facts," later in this chapter.)

Travelers should also exercise caution in traveling Mexico's highways, avoiding travel at night, and using toll *(cuota)* roads rather than the less secure "free" *(libre)* roads whenever possible. It is also advised that you should not hike alone in backcountry areas nor walk alone on less-frequented beaches, ruins, or trails.

All bus travel should be during daylight hours and on first-class conveyances. Although there have been several reports of bus hijackings and robberies on toll roads, buses on toll roads have a markedly lower rate of incidents than buses (second and third class) that travel the less secure "free" highways. The Embassy advises caution when traveling by bus from Acapulco toward Ixtapa or Huatulco. Although the police have made some progress in bringing this problem under control, armed robberies of entire busloads of passengers still occur.

BRIBES & SCAMS

As is the case around the world, there are the occasional bribes and scams in Mexico, targeted at people believed to be naive—such as the telltale tourist. For years, Mexico was known as a place where bribes—called *mordidas* (bites)—were expected; however, the country is rapidly changing. Frequently, offering a bribe today, especially to a police officer, is considered an insult, and it can land you in deeper trouble.

If you believe a **bribe** is being requested, here are a few tips on dealing with the situation. Even if you speak Spanish, don't utter a word of it to Mexican officials. That way you'll appear innocent, all the while understanding every word.

When you are crossing the border, should the person who inspects your car ask for a tip, you can ignore this request—but understand that the official may suddenly decide that a complete search of your belongings is in order. If faced with a situation where you feel you're being asked for a *propina* (literally "tip"; colloquially, "bribe"), how much should you offer? Usually $3 to $5 or the equivalent in pesos will do the trick. Many tourists have the impression that everything works better in Mexico if you "tip"; however, in reality, this only perpetuates the *mordida* attitude. If you are pleased with a service, feel free to tip, but you shouldn't tip simply to attempt to get away with something illegal or inappropriate, whether it is crossing the border without having your car inspected or not getting a ticket that's deserved.

Whatever you do, **avoid impoliteness;** under no circumstances should you insult a Latin American official. Extreme politeness, even in the face of adversity, rules Mexico. In Mexico, *gringos* have a reputation for being loud and demanding. By adopting the local custom of excessive courtesy, you'll have greater success in negotiations of any kind. Stand your ground, but do it politely.

As you travel in Mexico, you may encounter several types of **scams,** which are typical throughout the world. One involves some kind of a **distraction** or feigned commotion. While your attention is diverted, a pickpocket makes a grab for your wallet. In another common scam, an **unaccompanied child** pretends to be lost and frightened and takes your hand for safety. Meanwhile the child or an accomplice plunders your pockets. A third involves **confusing currency.** A shoeshine boy, street musician, guide, or other individual might offer you a service for a price that seems reasonable—in pesos. When it comes time to pay, he or she tells you the price is in dollars, not pesos. Be very clear on the price and currency when services are involved.

10 Specialized Travel Resources

TRAVELERS WITH DISABILITIES

Mexico may seem like one giant obstacle course to travelers in wheelchairs or on crutches. At airports, you may encounter steep stairs before finding a well-hidden elevator or escalator—if one exists. Airlines will often arrange wheelchair assistance to the baggage area. Porters are generally available to help with luggage at airports and large bus stations, once you've cleared baggage claim.

Mexican airports are upgrading their services, but it is not uncommon to board from a remote position, meaning you either descend stairs to a bus that ferries you to the plane, which you board by climbing stairs, or you walk across the tarmac to your plane and ascend the stairs. Deplaning presents the same problem in reverse.

Escalators (and there aren't many in the country) are often out of order. Stairs without handrails abound. Few restrooms are equipped for travelers with disabilities; when one is available, access to it may be through a narrow passage that won't accommodate a wheelchair or a person on crutches. Many deluxe hotels (the most expensive) now have rooms with bathrooms designed for people with disabilities. Those traveling on a budget should stick with one-story hotels or hotels with elevators. Even so, there will probably still be obstacles somewhere. Generally speaking, no matter where you are, someone will lend a hand, although you may have to ask for it.

One exception is Puerto Vallarta, which has renovated the majority of its downtown sidewalks and plazas with ramps that accommodate wheelchairs (as well as baby strollers). Even the airport has ramps adjacent to all stairways, and special wheelchair lifts. A local disabled citizen deserves the credit for this impressive task—hopefully setting the stage for greater accessibility in other towns and resorts.

Most disabilities shouldn't stop anyone from traveling. There are more options and resources out there than ever before.

Organizations that offer a vast range of resources and assistance to disabled travelers include **MossRehab** (© 800/ CALL-MOSS; www.mossresourcenet. org); the **American Foundation for the Blind (AFB;** © 800/232-5463; www.afb. org); and **SATH (Society for Accessible Travel & Hospitality;** © 212/447-7284; www.sath.org). **AirAmbulance Card.com** is now partnered with SATH and allows you to preselect top-notch hospitals in case of an emergency.

Access-Able Travel Source (© 303/ 232-2979; www.access-able.com) offers a comprehensive database on travel agents from around the world with experience in accessible travel; destination-specific access information; and links to such resources as service animals, equipment rentals, and access guides.

Many travel agencies offer customized tours and itineraries for travelers with disabilities. Among them are **Flying Wheels Travel** (© 507/451-5005; www.flying wheelstravel.com); and **Accessible Journeys** (© 800/846-4537 or 610/521-0339; www.disabilitytravel.com).

Flying with Disability (www.flying-with-disability.org) is a comprehensive information source on airplane travel. **Avis Rent a Car** (℃ 888/879-4273) has an "Avis Access" program that offers services for customers with special travel needs. These include specially outfitted vehicles with swivel seats, spinner knobs, and hand controls; mobility scooter rentals; and accessible bus service. Be sure to reserve well in advance.

Also check out the quarterly magazine *Emerging Horizons* (www.emerging horizons.com), available by subscription ($16.95 year in the U.S.; $21.95 outside the U.S.).

The "Accessible Travel" link at **Mobility-Advisor.com** (www.mobility-advisor.com) offers a variety of travel resources to disabled persons.

British travelers should contact **Holiday Care** (℃ 0845-124-9971 in the U.K. only; www.holidaycare.org.uk) to access a wide range of travel information and resources for disabled and elderly people.

GAY & LESBIAN TRAVELERS

Mexico is a conservative country, with deeply rooted Catholic religious traditions. Public displays of same-sex affection are rare and still considered shocking for men, especially outside of urban or resort areas. Women in Mexico frequently walk hand in hand, but anything more would cross the boundary of acceptability. However, gay and lesbian travelers are generally treated with respect and should not experience any harassment, assuming they give the appropriate regard to local culture and customs.

In Mexico City, the **Zona Rosa** is a gay-friendly neighborhood with numerous bars and cafes dedicated to gay and lesbian patrons. Puerto Vallarta is perhaps the most welcoming and accepting destination in Mexico. Susan Weisman's travel service, **Bayside Properties** (℃ 322/223-4424; www.baysidepropertiespv.

com), rents gay-friendly condos, villas, and hotels for individuals and large groups. Her services are customized to individual needs, and she can offer airport pickups and in-villa cooks.

The International Gay and Lesbian Travel Association (IGLTA; ℃ 800/448-8550 or 954/776-2626; www.iglta.org) is the trade association for the gay and lesbian travel industry, and offers an online directory of gay- and lesbian-friendly travel businesses and tour operators.

Many agencies offer tours and travel itineraries specifically for gay and lesbian travelers. Among them are **Above and Beyond Tours** (℃ 800/397-2681; www.abovebeyondtours.com); **Now, Voyager** (℃ 800/255-6951; www.nowvoyager.com); and **Olivia Cruises & Resorts** (℃ 800/631-6277; www.olivia.com).

Gay.com Travel (℃ 800/929-2268 or 415/644-8044; www.gay.com/travel or www.outandabout.com) is an excellent online successor to the popular *Out & About* print magazine. It provides regularly updated information about gay-owned, gay-oriented, and gay-friendly lodging, dining, sightseeing, nightlife, and shopping establishments in every important destination worldwide. British travelers should click on the "Travel" link at **www.uk.gay.com** for advice and gay-friendly trip ideas.

The Canadian website **GayTraveler** (http://gaytraveler.ca) offers ideas and advice for gay travel all over the world.

The following travel guides are available at many bookstores, or you can order them from any online bookseller: *Spartacus International Gay Guide, 35th Edition* (Bruno Gmünder Verlag; www.spartacus world.com/gayguide) and *Odysseus: The International Gay Travel Planner, 17th Edition* (www.odyusa.com); and the *Damron* guides (www.damron.com), with separate, annual books for gay men and lesbians.

SENIOR TRAVEL

Mexico is a popular country for retirees. For decades, North Americans have been living indefinitely in Mexico by returning to the border and recrossing with a new tourist permit every 6 months. Mexican immigration officials have caught on, and now limit the maximum time in the country to 6 months within any year. This is to encourage even partial residents to acquire proper documentation.

Some of the most popular places for long-term stays are Guadalajara, Lake Chapala, Ajijic, and Puerto Vallarta, all in the state of Jalisco; San Miguel de Allende and Guanajuato in Guanajuato state; Cuernavaca in Morelos; Alamos in Sinaloa; and increasingly destinations in Baja California.

AIM, Apartado Postal 31–70, 45050 Guadalajara, Jal., is a well-written, informative newsletter for prospective retirees. Issues have evaluated retirement in Aguascalientes, Puebla, San Cristóbal de las Casas, Puerto Angel, Puerto Escondido and Huatulco, Oaxaca, Taxco, Tepic, Manzanillo, Melaque, and Barra de Navidad. Subscriptions are $18 to the United States and $25 to Canada. Back issues are three for $5.

Sanborn Tours, 2015 S. 10th St., P.O. Drawer 519, McAllen, TX 78505-0519 (© **800/395-8482;** www.sanborns.com), offers a "Retire in Mexico" orientation tour.

Mention the fact that you're a senior citizen when you make your travel reservations. Although all the major U.S. airlines have canceled their senior discount and coupon book programs, many hotels still offer lower rates for seniors. In most cities, people older than 60 qualify for reduced admission to theaters, museums, and other attractions, and discounted fares on public transportation.

Members of **AARP,** 601 E St. NW, Washington, DC 20049 (© **888/687-2277;** www.aarp.org), get discounts on hotels, airfares, and car rentals. AARP offers members a wide range of benefits, including *AARP: The Magazine* and a monthly newsletter. Anyone older than 50 can join.

Many reliable agencies and organizations target the 50-plus market. **Elderhostel** (© **800/454-5768;** www.elderhostel.org) arranges study programs for those ages 55 and older. **ElderTreks** (© **800/741-7956;** www.eldertreks.com) offers small-group tours to off-the-beaten-path or adventure-travel locations, restricted to travelers 50 and older.

Recommended publications offering travel resources and discounts for seniors include: the quarterly magazine *Travel 50 & Beyond* (www.travel50andbeyond.com) and the bestselling paperback *Unbelievably Good Deals and Great Adventures That You Absolutely Can't Get Unless You're Over 50 2005–2006, 16th Edition* (McGraw-Hill), by Joann Rattner Heilman.

FAMILY TRAVEL

If you have enough trouble getting your kids out of the house in the morning, dragging them thousands of miles away may seem like an insurmountable challenge. But family travel can be immensely rewarding, giving you new ways of seeing the world through the eyes of children.

Children are considered the national treasure of Mexico, and Mexicans will warmly welcome and cater to your children. Many parents were reluctant to bring young children into Mexico in the past, primarily due to health concerns, but I can't think of a better place to introduce children to the exciting adventure of exploring a different culture. Some of the best destinations include Puerto Vallarta, Cancún, and La Paz. Hotels can often arrange for a babysitter.

Before leaving, ask your doctor which medications to take along. Disposable diapers cost about the same in Mexico but are of poorer quality. You can get Huggies Supreme and Pampers identical

Tips Advice for Female Travelers

Mexicans in general, and men in particular, are nosy about single travelers, especially women. If a taxi driver or anyone else with whom you don't want to become friendly asks about your marital status, family, and so forth, my advice is to make up a set of answers (regardless of the truth): "I'm married, traveling with friends, and I have three children." Saying you are single and traveling alone may send the wrong message. U.S. television—widely viewed now in Mexico—has given many Mexican men the image of American single women as being sexually promiscuous. Check out the award-winning website **Journey-woman** (www.journeywoman.com), a "real-life" women's travel information network where you can sign up for a free e-mail newsletter and get advice on everything from etiquette and dress to safety; or the travel guide *Safety and Security for Women Who Travel* by Sheila Swan and Peter Laufer (Travelers' Tales, Inc.), offering common-sense tips on safe travel.

to the ones sold in the United States, but at a higher price. Many stores sell Gerber's baby foods. Dry cereals, powdered formulas, baby bottles, and purified water are easily available in midsize and large cities or resorts.

Cribs may present a problem; only the largest and most luxurious hotels provide them. However, rollaway beds are often available. Child seats or high chairs at restaurants are common.

Consider bringing your own car seat; they are not readily available for rent in Mexico.

Every country's regulations differ, but in general children traveling abroad should have plenty of documentation on hand, particularly if they're traveling with someone other than their own parents (in which case a notarized form letter from a parent is often required). For details on entry requirements for children traveling abroad, go to the U.S. Department of State website (www.travel.state.gov); click on "International Travel," "Travel Brochures," and "Foreign Entry Requirements."

To locate accommodations, restaurants, and attractions that are particularly kid-friendly, refer to the "Kids" icon throughout this guide.

Recommended family travel websites include **Family Travel Forum** (www.familytravelforum.com), a comprehensive site that offers customized trip planning; **Family Travel Network** (www.familytravelnetwork.com), an online magazine providing travel tips; and **Travel WithYourKids.com** (www.travelwithyourkids.com), a comprehensive site written by parents for parents offering sound advice for long-distance and international travel with children.

STUDENT TRAVEL

Because Mexicans consider higher education more a luxury than a birthright, there is no formal network of student discounts and programs. Most Mexican students travel with their families rather than with other students, so student discount cards are not commonly recognized.

However, more hostels have entered the student travel scene. **Hostelling International México** (© 55/5518-1726; www.hostellingmexico.com) offers a list of hostels that meet international standards in Mexico City, Cuernavaca and surrounding areas, Oaxaca, and Veracruz. Hostels.com offers a list of hostels in Mexico City, Zacatecas, Guanajuato, Puerto Escondido, Uxmal, Palenque, Tulum, Cancún, and Playa del Carmen.

11 Sustainable Tourism/Ecotourism

Each time you take a flight or drive a car CO_2 is released into the atmosphere. You can help neutralize this danger to our planet through "carbon offsetting"—paying someone to reduce your CO_2 emissions by the same amount you've added. Carbon offsets can be purchased in the U.S. from companies such as **Carbon fund.org** (www.carbonfund.org) and **TerraPass** (www.terrapass.org), and from **Climate Care** (www.climatecare.org) in the U.K.

Although one could argue that any vacation that includes an airplane flight can't be truly "green," you can go on holiday and still contribute positively to the environment. You can offset carbon emissions from your flight in other ways. Choose forward-looking companies that embrace responsible development practices, helping preserve destinations for the future by working alongside local people. An increasing number of sustainable tourism initiatives can help you plan a family trip and leave as small a "footprint" as possible on the places you visit.

Responsible Travel (www.responsible travel.com) contains a great source of sustainable travel ideas run by a spokesperson for responsible tourism in the travel industry. **Sustainable Travel International** (www.sustainabletravelinternational.org) promotes responsible tourism practices and issues an annual Green Gear & Gift Guide.

You can find eco-friendly travel tips, statistics, and touring companies and associations—listed by destination under "Travel Choice"—at **The International Ecotourism Society's (TIES)** website, www.ecotourism.org. Also check out **Ecotravel.com,** an online magazine and ecodirectory that lets you search for touring companies in several categories (water-based, land-based, spiritually oriented, and so on).

In the U.K., **Tourism Concern** (www. tourismconcern.org.uk) works to reduce

Frommers.com: The Complete Travel Resource

It should go without saying, but we highly recommend **Frommers.com,** voted Best Travel Site by *PC Magazine.* We think you'll find our expert advice and tips; independent reviews of hotels, restaurants, attractions, and preferred shopping and nightlife venues; vacation giveaways; and an online booking tool indispensable before, during, and after your travels. We publish the complete contents of over 128 travel guides in our **Destinations** section, covering nearly 3,600 places worldwide, to help you plan your trip. Each weekday, we publish original articles reporting on **Deals and News** via our free **Frommers.com Newsletter** to help you save time and money and travel smarter. We're betting you'll find our new **Events** listings (http:// events.frommers.com) an invaluable resource; it's an up-to-the-minute roster of what's happening in cities everywhere—including concerts, festivals, lectures and more. We've also added weekly **Podcasts, interactive maps,** and hundreds of new images across the site. Check out our **Travel Talk** area featuring **Message Boards** where you can join in conversations with thousands of fellow Frommer's travelers and post your trip report once you return.

social and environmental problems connected to tourism and find ways of improving tourism so that local benefits are increased.

The **Association of British Travel Agents (ABTA;** www.abta.com) acts as a focal point for the U.K. travel industry and is one of the leading groups spearheading responsible tourism.

The **Association of Independent Tour Operators (AITO;** www.aito.co.uk)

is a group of interesting specialist operators leading the field in making holidays sustainable.

For information about the ethics of swimming with dolphins and other outdoor activities, visit the **Whale and Dolphin Conservation Society (WDCS;** www.wdcs.org) and **Tread Lightly** (www.treadlightly.org).

12 Staying Connected

TELEPHONES

Mexico's telephone system is slowly but surely catching up with modern times. All telephone numbers have 10 digits. Every city and town that has telephone access has a two-digit (Mexico City, Monterrey, and Guadalajara) or three-digit (everywhere else) area code. In Mexico City, Monterrey, and Guadalajara, local numbers have eight digits; elsewhere, local numbers have seven digits. To place a local call, you do not need to dial the area code. Many fax numbers are also regular telephone numbers; ask whoever answers for the fax tone *("me da tono de fax, por favor")*. Cellular phones are very popular for small businesses in resort areas and smaller communities. To call a cellular number inside the same area code, dial 044 and then the number. To dial the cellular phone from anywhere else in Mexico, first dial 01, and then the three-digit area code and the seven-digit number. To dial it from the U.S., dial 011-52, plus the three-digit area code and the seven-digit number.

The **country code** for Mexico is **52.**

To call Mexico: If you're calling Mexico from the United States:

1. Dial the international access code: 011 from the U.S.; 00 from the U.K., Ireland, or New Zealand; or 0011 from Australia.

2. Dial the country code: 52.

3. Dial the two- or three-digit area code, then the eight- or seven-digit number. For example, if you wanted to call the U.S. consulate in Acapulco, the entire number would be 011-52-744-469-0556. If you wanted to dial the U.S. embassy in Mexico City, the entire number would be 011-52-55-5209-9100.

To make international calls: To make international calls from Mexico, first dial 00, then the country code (U.S. or Canada 1, U.K. 44, Ireland 353, Australia 61, New Zealand 64). Next, dial the area code and number. For example, to call the British Embassy in Washington, you would dial 00-1-202-588-7800.

For directory assistance: Dial ✆ **040** if you're looking for a number inside Mexico. *Note:* Listings usually appear under the owner's name, not the name of the business, and your chances to find an English-speaking operator are slim to none.

For operator assistance: If you need operator assistance in making a call, dial ✆ **090** to make an international call, and ✆ **020** to call a number in Mexico.

Toll-free numbers: Numbers beginning with 800 within Mexico are toll-free, but calling a U.S. toll-free number from Mexico costs the same as an overseas call. To call an 800 number in the U.S., dial 001-880 and the last seven digits of the toll-free number. To call an 888 number in the U.S., dial 001-881 and the last seven digits of the toll-free number. For a number with an 887 prefix, dial 882; for 866, dial 883.

CELLPHONES

The three letters that define much of the world's wireless capabilities are **GSM** (Global System for Mobile Communications), a big, seamless network that makes for easy cross-border cellphone use throughout Europe and dozens of other countries worldwide. In the U.S., T-Mobile, AT&T Wireless, and Cingular use this quasi-universal system; in Canada, Microcell and some Rogers customers are GSM, and all Europeans and most Australians use GSM. GSM phones function with a removable plastic SIM card, encoded with your phone number and account information. If your cellphone is on a GSM system, and you have a world-capable multiband phone, such as many Sony Ericsson, Motorola, or Samsung models, you can make and receive calls across civilized areas around much of the globe. Just call your wireless operator and ask for "international roaming" to be activated on your account. Unfortunately, per-minute charges can be high—usually $1 to $1.50 in Western Europe and up to $5 in places such as Russia and Indonesia.

For many, **renting** a phone is a good idea. While you can rent a phone from any number of overseas sites, including kiosks at airports and at car-rental agencies, we suggest renting the phone before you leave home. North Americans can rent one before leaving home from **InTouch USA** (© **800/872-7626;** www. intouchglobal.com) or **Roadpost** (© **888/ 290-1606** or **905/272-5665;** www.road post.com). InTouch will also, for free, advise you on whether your existing phone will work overseas; simply call © **703/222-7161** between 9am and 4pm EST, or go to **http://intouchglobal. com/travel.htm**.

Buying a phone can be economically attractive, as many nations have cheap prepaid phone systems. Once you arrive at your destination, stop by a local cellphone shop and get the cheapest package; you'll probably pay less than $100 for a phone and a starter calling card. Local calls may be as low as 10¢ per minute, and in many countries incoming calls are free.

VOICE-OVER INTERNET PROTOCOL (VOIP)

If you have Web access while traveling, you might consider a broadband-based telephone service (in technical terms, Voice over Internet protocol, or VoIP) such as Skype (www.skype.com) or Vonage (www.vonage.com), which allows you to make free international calls if you use their services from your laptop or in a cybercafe. Check the sites for details.

INTERNET/E-MAIL
WITHOUT YOUR OWN COMPUTER

To find cybercafes in your destination, you can check **www.cybercaptive.com** and **www.cybercafe.com**, but it's hard nowadays to find a city or town in Mexico that *doesn't* have a few cybercafes. The "Fast Facts" sections in this book list cybercafes in major destinations.

WITH YOUR OWN COMPUTER

More and more hotels, resorts, airports, cafes, and retailers are going **Wi-Fi** (wireless fidelity), becoming "hotspots" that offer high-speed Wi-Fi access free or for a small charge. Most laptops sold today have built-in wireless capability. To find public Wi-Fi hotspots at your destination, go to **www.jiwire.com**; its Hotspot Finder holds the world's largest directory of public wireless hotspots.

For dial-up access, most business-class hotels throughout the world offer dataports for laptop modems, and a few thousand hotels in Europe now offer free high-speed Internet access.

Online Traveler's Toolbox

Veteran travelers usually carry some essential items to make their trips easier. Following is a selection of handy online tools to bookmark and use.

- **Airplane Food** (www.airlinemeals.net)
- **Airplane Seating** (www.seatguru.com and www.airlinequality.com)
- **Foreign Languages for Travelers** (www.travlang.com)
- **Maps** (www.mapquest.com)
- **Subway Navigator** (www.subwaynavigator.com)
- **Time and Date** (www.timeanddate.com)
- **Travel Warnings** (http://travel.state.gov, www.fco.gov.uk/travel, www.voyage.gc.ca, or www.smartraveller.gov.au)
- **Universal Currency Converter** (www.xe.com/ucc)
- **Visa ATM Locator** (www.visa.com); **MasterCard ATM Locator** (www.mastercard.com)
- **Weather** (www.intellicast.com and www.weather.com)

Wherever you go, bring a **connection kit** of the right power and phone adapters, a spare phone cord, and a spare Ethernet network cable—or find out whether your hotel supplies them to guests. For information on the electric current in Mexico, see "Electricity" in the "Fast Facts" section later in this chapter.

13 Packages for the Independent Traveler

Package tours are simply a way to buy the airfare, accommodations, and other elements of your trip (such as car rentals, airport transfers, and sometimes even activities) at the same time and often at discounted prices.

One good source of package deals is the airlines themselves. Most major airlines offer air/land packages, including **American Airlines Vacations** (© 800/321-2121; www.aavacations.com), **Delta Vacations** (© 800/654-6559; www.deltavacations.com), **Continental Airlines Vacations** (© 800/301-3800; www.covacations.com), and **United Vacations** (© 888/854-3899; www.unitedvacations.com). Several big online travel agencies—**Expedia, Travelocity, Orbitz, Site59,** and **Lastminute.com**—also do a brisk business in packages.

Travel packages are also listed in the travel section of your local Sunday newspaper. Or check ads in the national travel magazines such as *Arthur Frommer's Budget Travel Magazine, Travel + Leisure, National Geographic Traveler,* and *Condé Nast Traveler.*

RECOMMENDED PACKAGERS

- **AeroMéxico Vacations** (© 800/245-8585; www.aeromexico.com) offers year-round packages to almost every destination it serves, including Acapulco, Cancún, Cozumel, Ixtapa/Zihuatanejo, Los Cabos, and Puerto Vallarta. AeroMéxico has a large selection (more than 100) of resorts in these destinations and more, in a variety of price ranges. The best deals are from Houston, Dallas, San Diego, Los Angeles, Miami, and New York, in that order.
- **Alaska Airlines Vacations** (© 800/468-2248; www.alaskaair.com) sells

packages to Ixtapa/Zihuatanejo, Loreto, Los Cabos, Manzanillo/Costa Alegre, Mazatlán, and Puerto Vallarta. Alaska flies direct from Los Angeles, San Diego, San Jose, San Francisco, Seattle, Vancouver, Anchorage, and Fairbanks. The website offers unpublished discounts that are not available through the phone operators.

- **American Airlines Vacations** (© 800/ 321-2121; www.aavacations.com) has year-round deals to Acapulco, Cancún, the Riviera Maya, Guadalajara, Los Cabos, Mexico City, and Puerto Vallarta. You don't have to fly with American if you can get a better deal on another airline; land-only packages include hotel, hotel tax, and airport transfers. American's hubs to Mexico are Dallas/Fort Worth, Chicago, and Miami. The website offers unpublished discounts that are not available through the operators.

- **US Airways Vacations** (© 800/235- 9298; www.usairwaysvacations.com) has deals to Acapulco, Cancun, Cozumel, Guadalajara, Ixtapa, Los Cabos, Manzanillo, Mexico City, and Puerto Vallarta. Many packages to Los Cabos include car rentals. The website offers discounted featured specials that are not available through the operators. You can also book hotels without air by calling the toll-free number.

- **Apple Vacations** (© 800/365-2775; www.applevacations.com) offers in-clusive packages to all the beach resorts, and has the largest choice of hotels in Acapulco, Cancún, Cozumel, Huatulco, Ixtapa, Loreto, Los Cabos, Manzanillo, Mazatlán, Puerto Vallarta, and the Riviera Maya. Scheduled carriers for the air portion include American, United, Mexicana, Delta, US Airways, Reno Air, Alaska Airlines, and AeroMéxico. Apple perks include baggage handling and the services of a company representative at major hotels.

- **Classic Vacations** (© 800/635-1333; www.classicvacations.com) specializes in package vacations to Mexico's finest luxury resorts. It combines discounted first-class and economy airfare on American, Continental, Mexicana, Alaska, America West, and Delta with stays at the most exclusive hotels in Cancún, the Riviera Maya, Mérida, Oaxaca, Guadalajara, Mexico City, Puerto Vallarta, Mazatlán, Costa Alegre, Manzanillo, Ixtapa/ Zihuatanejo, Acapulco, Huatulco, and Los Cabos. The prices are not for bargain hunters but for those who seek luxury, nicely packaged.

- **Continental Vacations** (© 800/ 301-3800; www.covacations.com) has year-round packages to Acapulco, Cancún, Cozumel, Guadalajara, Huatulco, Ixtapa, Los Cabos, Mazatlán, Mexico City, and Puerto Vallarta. The best deals are from Houston; Newark, N.J.; and Cleveland. You must fly Continental. The Internet deals offer savings not available elsewhere.

- **Delta Vacations** (© 800/654-6559; www.deltavacations.com) has year-round packages to Acapulco, Cancún, Cozumel, Guadalajara, Ixtapa/ Zihuatanejo, Los Cabos, Mazatlán, Mérida, and Puerto Vallarta. Atlanta is the hub, so expect the best prices from there.

- **Funjet Vacations** (© 800/888/558- 6654; www.funjet.com) is one of the largest vacation packagers in the United States. Funjet has packages to Acapulco, Cancún, Cozumel, the Riviera Maya, Los Cabos, Mazatlán, Ixtapa, and Puerto Vallarta. You can choose a charter or fly on American, Continental, Delta, AeroMéxico, US Airways, Alaska Air, or United.

(Finds Out-of-the-Ordinary Places to Stay

Mexico lends itself beautifully to the concept of small, private hotels in idyllic settings. They vary in style from grandiose estate to palm-thatched bungalow. **Mexico Boutique Hotels** (www.mexicoboutiquehotels.com) specializes in smaller places to stay with a high level of personal attention and service. Most options have less than 50 rooms, and the accommodations consist of entire villas, *casitas,* bungalows, or a combination. The Yucatán is especially noted for the luxury haciendas throughout the peninsula.

- **GOGO Worldwide Vacations** (© **888/636-3942;** www.gogowwv.com) has trips to all the major beach destinations, including Acapulco, Cancún, Mazatlán, Puerto Vallarta, and Los Cabos. It offers several exclusive deals from higher-end hotels. Book through any travel agent.
- **Mexicana Vacations,** or MexSeaSun Vacations (© **800/531-7921;** www.mexicana.com) offers getaways to all the resorts. Mexicana operates daily direct flights from Los Angeles to Los Cabos, Mazatlán, Cancún, Puerto Vallarta, Manzanillo, and Ixtapa/Zihuatanejo.
- **Mexico Travel Net** (© **800/511-4848** or 619/474-0100; www.mexicotravelnet.com) offers most of the well-known travel packages to Mexico beach resorts, plus offers last minute specials.
- **Pleasant Holidays** (© **800/742-9244;** www.pleasantholidays.com) is one of the largest vacation packagers in the United States, with hotels in Acapulco, Cancún, Cozumel, Huatulco, Ixtapa/Zihuatanejo, Los Cabos, Mazatlán, Mérida, Mexico City, Oaxaca, and Puerto Vallarta.

REGIONAL PACKAGERS

From the East Coast: Liberty Travel (© **888/271-1584;** www.libertytravel.com), one of the biggest packagers in the Northeast, often runs a full-page ad in the Sunday papers, with frequent Mexico specials. You won't get much in the way of service, but you will get a good deal.

From the West: SunTrips (© **800/248-7471** for departures within 14 days; www.suntrips.com) is one of the largest West Coast packagers for Mexico, with departures from San Francisco and Denver; regular charters to Cancún, Cozumel, Los Cabos, and Puerto Vallarta; and a large selection of hotels.

From the Southwest: Town and Country (book through travel agents) packages regular deals to Los Cabos, Mazatlán, Puerto Vallarta, Ixtapa, Manzanillo, Cancún, Cozumel, and Acapulco with America West from the airline's Phoenix and Las Vegas gateways.

14 Special-Interest Trips

ARCHAEOLOGICAL TOURS

The **Archaeological Conservancy,** 5301 Central Ave. NE, Suite 402, Albuquerque, NM 87108 (© **505/266-1540;** www.americanarchaeology.com), presents one trip per year led by an expert, usually an archaeologist. The trips change from year to year and space is limited; make reservations early.

ATC Tours and Travel, Av. 16 de Septiembre 16, 29200 San Cristóbal de las Casas, Chis. (© **967678-2550** or -2557; fax 967/678-3145; www.atctours.com), a Mexico-based tour operator with an excellent reputation, offers specialist-led

> ## *Tips* The Mexican Sports Scene
>
> Mexico has more than 120 **golf** courses, concentrated in the resort areas, with excellent options in Mexico City and Guadalajara. Los Cabos, in Baja Sur, has become the country's preeminent golf destination; the Puerto Vallarta area enjoys a growing reputation. For details on courses and events, see chapters 9 and 18. Visitors to Mexico can also enjoy **tennis, racquetball, squash, water-skiing, surfing, bicycling,** and **horseback riding.** **Scuba diving** is excellent, not only off the Yucatán's Caribbean coast (especially Cozumel), but also on the Pacific coast at Puerto Vallarta and Manzanillo, and off Baja in the Sea of Cortez. **Mountain and volcano climbing** is a rugged sport that allows you to meet like-minded folks from around the world. The top peaks are just 80km (50 miles) south of Mexico City—the snowcapped volcanoes Ixtaccihuatl (5,255m/17,236 ft.) and Popocatépetl (5,420m/17,778 ft.). Popocatépetl was not accepting visitors at press time, due to recent volcanic activity. For information on visiting and climbing the volcanoes, contact the **Club de Exploraciones de México A.C.** in Mexico City (© **55/5740-8032;** www.cemac.org.mx).

trips, primarily in southern Mexico. In addition to trips to the ruins of Palenque and Yaxchilán (extending into Belize and Guatemala by river, plane, and bus if desired), ATC offers horseback tours to Chamula or Zinacantán, and day trips to the ruins of Toniná around San Cristóbal de las Casas; birding in the rainforests of Chiapas and Guatemala (including in the El Triunfo Reserve of Chiapas); hikes to the shops and homes of native textile artists of the Chiapas highlands; and walks from the Lagos de Montebello in the Montes Azules Biosphere Reserve, with camping and canoeing. The company can also prepare custom itineraries.

ART & CULTURE TOURS

Mexican Art Tours, 1233 E. Baker Dr., Tempe, AZ 85282 (© **888/783-1331** or 480/730-1764; fax 480/730-1496; www.mexicanarttours.com) offers unique tours focusing on the authentic arts and cultures of Mexico. Groups are accompanied by compelling speakers who are themselves respected scholars and artists. Itineraries include visits to Oaxaca, Chiapas, Guadalajara, Puerto Vallarta, Mexico City, Veracruz, and other locales. Special tours include a Day of the Dead tour and architecture and interior-design tours.

Mexico Travel Link Ltd., 300-3665 Kingsway, Vancouver, BC V5R 5W2 Canada (© **604/454-9044;** fax 604/454-9088; www.mexicotravel.net), offers cultural, sports, and adventure tours to Mexico City and surrounding areas, Baja, Veracruz, the Copper Canyon, the Mayan Route, and other destinations.

Oaxaca Reservations/Zapotec Tours, 4955 N. Claremont Ave., Suite B, Chicago, IL 60625 (© **800/446-2922** outside Illinois, or 773/506-2444; fax 773/506-2445; www.oaxacainfo.com), offers a variety of tours to Oaxaca City and the Oaxaca coast (including Puerto Escondido and Huatulco). Its specialty trips include Day of the Dead and the Taste of Oaxaca Festival, both in Oaxaca. The coastal trips emphasize nature, while the Oaxaca City tours focus on the immediate area, with visits to weavers, potters, markets, and archaeological sites. This is also the U.S. contact for several hotels in Oaxaca City that offer a 10% discount for reserving online.

COOKING TOURS

Culinary Adventures, 6023 Reid Dr. NW, Gig Harbor, WA 98335 (© **253/ 851-7676;** fax 253/851-9532; www. marilyntausend.com), specializes in a short but select list of cooking tours in Mexico. They feature well-known cooks and travel to regions known for excellent cuisine. The owner, Marilyn Tausend, is the co-author of *Mexico the Beautiful Cookbook* and *Cocinas de la Familia* (Family Kitchens).

NATURAL HISTORY TOURS

Natural Habitat Adventures, 2945 Center Green Court, Suite H, Boulder, CO 80301 (© **800/543-8917** or 303/449-3711; www.nathab.com), offers naturalist-led natural history and adventure travel. Expeditions focus on monarch butterfly watching in Michoacán and gray whale–watching in Baja.

NatureQuest, 30872 South Coast Hwy., Suite PMB, Laguna Beach, CA 92651 (© **800/369-3033** or 949/499-9561; www.naturequesttours.com), specializes in the natural history, culture, and wildlife of the Copper Canyon and the remote lagoons and waterways off Baja California. A 10-day hiking trip ventures into rugged areas of the canyon; a less strenuous trip goes to Creel and Batopilas, in the same area. Baja trips get close to nature, with special permits for venturing by two-person kayak into sanctuaries for whales and birds.

OUTDOOR ADVENTURE TOURS

AMTAVE (Asociación Mexicana de Turismo de Aventura y Ecoturismo, A.C.) is an active association of ecotour and adventure tour operators. It publishes an annual catalog of participating firms and their offerings, all of which must meet certain criteria for security, quality, and training of the guides, as well as for sustainability of natural and cultural environments. For more information, contact AMTAVE (© **55/5688-3883;** www.amtave.org).

Far Flung Adventures, P.O. Box 377, Terlingua, TX 79852 (© **800/359-2627;** www.farflung.com), organizes specialist-led river trips to the Antigua, Actopan, and Filobobos rivers, in Veracruz.

Tour Baja, P.O. Box 827, Calistoga, CA 94515 (© **800/398-6200** or 707/942-4550; fax 707/942-8017; www.tourbaja.com), offers sea-kayaking tours in the Loreto area. Owner Trudi Angell has guided these trips for more than 20 years. She and her guides offer firsthand knowledge of the area. Kayaking, mountain biking, and pack trips as well as sailing charters combine these elements with outdoor adventures.

Sea Kayak Adventures, P.O. Box 3862, Coeur d'Alene, ID 83816 (© **800/616-1943** or 208/765-3116; fax 208/765-5254; www.seakayakadventures.com), features kayak trips in both the Sea of Cortez and Magdalena Bay, with a focus on whale-watching. This company has the exclusive permit to paddle Magdalena Bay's remote northern waters, and they guarantee gray whale sightings. Trips combine paddling of 4 to 5 hours per day, with hiking across dunes and beaches, while nights are spent camping.

Sea Trek Ocean Kayaking Center, P.O. Box 1987, Sausalito, CA 94966 (© **415/488-1000;** fax 415/332-8790; www.seatrekkayak.com), has been alternating sea-kayaking trips between Alaska and Baja for 20 years, which has provided them an intimate knowledge of the peninsula's coastline. Eight-day trips depart from and return to Loreto, and a 12-day expedition travels from Loreto to La Paz. An optional day excursion to Bahía Magdalena for gray whale–watching is available. Full boat support is provided, and no previous paddling experience is necessary.

Trek America, P.O. Box 189, Rockaway, NJ 07866 (© **800/221-0596** or

973/983-1144; fax 973/983-8551; www. trekamerica.com), organizes lengthy, active trips that combine trekking, hiking, van transportation, and camping in the Yucatán, Chiapas, Oaxaca, the Copper Canyon, and Mexico's Pacific coast, and a trip that covers Mexico City, Teotihuacán, Taxco, Guadalajara, Puerto Vallarta, and Acapulco.

Veraventuras, Santos Degollado 81-8, 91000 Xalapa, Ver. (© **228/818-9579,** or 01-800/712-6572 in Mexico; fax 228/ 818-9680; www.veraventuras.xalapa.net), uses specially trained leaders on well-organized and -outfitted adventures into the state of Veracruz, including hiking, mountain climbing, repelling, extreme sports, and rafting the rapids of the Antigua, Actopan, Barranca, and Filobobos rivers.

Baja Expeditions, 2625 Garnet Ave., San Diego, CA 92109 (© **800/843-6967** or 858/581-3311; fax 858/581-6542; www.bajaex.com), offers natural-history cruises, whale-watching, sea kayaking, camping, scuba diving, and resort and day trips out of Loreto or La Paz, Baja California, and San Diego, California. Small groups and special itineraries are Baja Expeditions' specialty.

The California Native, 6701 W. 87th Place, Los Angeles, CA 90045 (© **800/** 926-1140 or 310/642-1140; www.calnative.com), offers small-group deluxe 7-, 8-, 9-, and 11-day escorted tours through the Copper Canyon. Many trips visit the towns of Batopilas, Urique, and Tejeban as well as the customary destinations of Creel, El Fuerte, Divisadero, Chihuahua, and Cerocahui. The guides are known throughout the area for their work with the Tarahumara Indians. In addition to escorted trips, the company offers a full range of custom itineraries.

Canyon Travel, 900 Rich Creek Lane, Bulverde, TX 78163-2872 (© **800/843-1060** in the U.S. and Canada, or 830/ 885-2000; fax 830/885-2010; www. canyontravel.com), specializes in the Copper Canyon and has a variety of adventures, ranging from easy to challenging. It designs trips for special-interest groups of agriculturists, geologists, rock hounds, and birders, and custom trips to the Copper Canyon. The owner works with the Tarahumara Indians.

Mountain Travel Sobek, 6420 Fairmount Ave., El Cerrito, CA 94530 (© **888/687-6235** or 510/594-6000; www.mtsobek.com), takes groups kayaking in the Sea of Cortez, whale-watching in Baja, and river rafting, hiking, and camping in Veracruz. Sobek is one of the world's leading ecotour outfitters.

15 Getting Around Mexico

An important note: If your travel schedule depends on a vital connection—say, a plane trip or a ferry or bus connection—use the telephone numbers in this book or other resources to find out if the connection is still available.

BY PLANE

Mexico has two large private national carriers: **Mexicana** (© **800/531-7921;** www. mexicana.com) and **AeroMéxico** (© **800/ 237-6639;** www.aeromexico.com), in addition to several up-and-coming low-cost carriers. Mexicana and AeroMéxico offer extensive connections to the United States as well as within Mexico.

Up-and-coming low-cost carriers include **Aviacsa** (www.aviacsa.com), **Click Mexicana** (www.click.com.mx), and **InterJet** (www.interjet.com.mx). Regional carriers include **Aerovega** (www.oaxaca-mio.com/aerovega.htm), **Aero Tucán** (www.aero-tucan.com), and AeroMéxico's **Aerolitoral** (www.aerolitoral.com.mx). The regional carriers can be expensive, but they go to difficult-to-reach places. In each applicable section of this book, we've mentioned regional carriers with all pertinent telephone numbers.

Because major airlines can book some regional carriers, read your ticket carefully to see if your connecting flight is on one of these smaller carriers—they may use a different airport or a different counter.

AIRPORT TAXES Mexico charges an airport tax on all departures. Passengers leaving the country on international flights pay $24—in dollars or the peso equivalent. It has become a common practice to include this departure tax in your ticket price, but double-check to make sure so you're not caught by surprise at the airport. Taxes on each domestic departure within Mexico are around $17 (£9.35), unless you're on a connecting flight and have already paid at the start of the flight.

Mexico charges an $18 (£9.90) "tourism tax," the proceeds of which go into a tourism promotional fund. Your ticket price may not include it, so be sure to have enough money to pay it at the airport upon departure.

RECONFIRMING FLIGHTS Although Mexican airlines say it's not necessary to reconfirm a flight, it's still a good idea. To avoid getting bumped on popular, possibly overbooked flights, check in for an international flight 1½ hours in advance of travel.

BY CAR

Most Mexican roads are not up to U.S. standards of smoothness, hardness, width of curve, grade of hill, or safety markings. Driving at night is dangerous—the roads are rarely lit; trucks, carts, pedestrians, and bicycles usually have no lights; and you can hit potholes, animals, rocks, dead ends, or uncrossable bridges without warning.

The spirited style of Mexican driving sometimes requires super vision and reflexes. Be prepared for new customs, as when a truck driver flips on his left turn signal when there's not a crossroad for miles. He's probably telling you the road's clear ahead for you to pass. Another custom that's very important to respect is turning left. Never turn left by stopping in the middle of a highway with your left-turn signal on. Instead, pull onto the right shoulder, wait for traffic to clear, then proceed across the road.

GASOLINE There's one government-owned brand of gas and one gasoline station name throughout the country—**Pemex** (Petroleras Mexicanas). There are two types of gas in Mexico: *magna*, 87-octane unleaded gas, and *premio* 93 octane. In Mexico, fuel and oil are sold by the liter, which is slightly more than a quart (1 gallon equals about 3.8 liters). Many franchise Pemex stations have bathroom facilities and convenience stores—a great improvement over the old ones. Gas stations accept both credit and debit cards for gas purchases.

TOLL ROADS Mexico charges some of the highest tolls in the world for its network of new toll roads; as a result, they are rarely used. Generally speaking, though, using toll roads cuts travel time. Older toll-free roads are generally in good condition, but travel times tend to be longer.

BREAKDOWNS If your car breaks down on the road, help might already be on the way. Radio-equipped green repair trucks operated by uniformed English-speaking officers patrol major highways during daylight hours. These **"Green Angels"** perform minor repairs and adjustments free, but you pay for parts and materials.

Your best guide to repair shops is the Yellow Pages. For repairs, look under *Automóviles y Camiones: Talleres de Reparación y Servicio;* auto-parts stores are under *Refacciones y Accesorios para Automóviles.* To find a mechanic on the road, look for a sign that says TALLER MECÁNICO.

Places called *vulcanizadora* or *llantera* repair flat tires, and it is common to find them open 24 hours a day on the most traveled highways.

MINOR ACCIDENTS When possible, many Mexicans drive away from minor accidents, or try to make an immediate settlement, to avoid involving the police. If the police arrive while the involved persons are still at the scene, everyone may be locked in jail until blame is assessed. In any case, you have to settle up immediately, which may take days. Foreigners who don't speak fluent Spanish are at a distinct disadvantage when trying to explain their version of the event. Three steps may help the foreigner who doesn't wish to do as the Mexicans do: If you were in your own car, notify your Mexican insurance company, whose job it is to intervene on your behalf. If you were in a rental car, notify the rental company immediately and ask how to contact the nearest adjuster. (You did buy insurance with the rental, right?) Finally, if all else fails, ask to contact the nearest Green Angel, who may be able to explain to officials that you are covered by insurance. See also "Mexican Auto Insurance" in "Getting There," earlier in this chapter.

CAR RENTALS You'll get the best price if you reserve a car at least a week in advance in the United States. U.S. car-rental firms include **Advantage** (© 800/777-5500 in the U.S. and Canada; www.arac.com), **Avis** (© 800/331-1212 in the U.S., 800/879-2847 in Canada; www.avis.com), **Budget** (© 800/527-0700 in the U.S. and Canada; www.budget.com), **Hertz** (© 800/654-3131 in the U.S. and Canada; www.hertz.com), **National** (© 800/227-7368 in the U.S. and Canada; www.nationalcar.com), and **Thrifty** (© 800/847-4389 in the U.S. and Canada; www.thrifty.com), which often offers discounts for rentals in Mexico. For European travelers, **Kemwel**

Holiday Auto (© 800/678-0678; www.kemwel.com) and **Auto Europe** (© 800/223-5555; www.autoeurope.com) can arrange Mexican rentals, sometimes through other agencies. These and some local firms have offices in Mexico City and most other large Mexican cities. You'll find rental desks at airports, all major hotels, and many travel agencies.

Cars are easy to rent if you are 25 or older and have a major credit card, valid driver's license, and passport with you. Without a credit card, you must leave a cash deposit, usually a big one. One-way rentals are usually simple to arrange, but they are more costly.

Car-rental costs are high in Mexico because cars are more expensive. The condition of rental cars has improved greatly over the years, and clean new cars are the norm. You will pay the least for a manual car without air-conditioning. Prices may be considerably higher if you rent around a major holiday. Also double-check charges for insurance—some companies will increase the insurance rate after several days. Always ask for detailed information about all charges you will be responsible for.

Car-rental companies usually write credit card charges in U.S. dollars.

Deductibles Be careful—these vary greatly; some are as high as $2,500, which comes out of your pocket immediately in case of damage. On a VW Beetle, Hertz's deductible is $1,000 and Avis's is $500.

Insurance Insurance is offered in two parts: **Collision and damage** insurance covers your car and others if the accident is your fault, and **personal accident** insurance covers you and anyone in your car. Read the fine print on the back of your rental agreement and note that insurance may be invalid if you have an accident while driving on an unpaved road.

Damage Always inspect your car carefully and note every damaged or missing

> **⟨Warning⟩ Bus Hijackings**
>
> The U.S. Department of State notes that bandits target long-distance buses traveling at night, but there have been daylight robberies as well. Buses are more common targets than individual cars—they offer thieves more bucks for the bang.

item, no matter how minute, on your rental agreement, or you may be charged.

BY TAXI

Taxis are the preferred way to get around almost all of Mexico's resort areas, and around Mexico City. Fares for short trips within towns are generally preset by zone, and are quite reasonable compared with U.S. rates. (Los Cabos is one exception; another is taxi service to the north side of the bay from Puerto Vallarta. Travelers are better off renting a car than paying these exorbitant taxi fares—about $100/£55 for a one-way trip to Punta Mita.) For longer trips or excursions to nearby cities, taxis can generally be hired for around $10 to $15 (£5.50-£8.25) per hour, or for a negotiated daily rate. A negotiated one-way price is usually much less than the cost of a rental car for a day, and a taxi travels much faster than a bus. For anyone who is uncomfortable driving in Mexico, this is a convenient, comfortable alternative. A bonus is that you have a Spanish-speaking person with you in case you run into trouble. Many taxi drivers speak at least some English. Your hotel can assist you with the arrangements.

BY BUS

Except for the Baja peninsula, where bus service is not well developed, Mexican buses run frequently, are readily accessible, and can get you to almost anywhere you want to go. They're often the only way to get from large cities to other nearby cities and small villages. Don't hesitate to ask questions if you're confused about anything, but note that little English is spoken in bus stations.

Dozens of Mexican companies operate large, air-conditioned, Greyhound-type buses between most cities. Classes are *segunda* (second), *primera* (first), and *ejecutiva* (deluxe), which goes by a variety of names. Deluxe buses often have fewer seats than regular buses, show video movies, are air-conditioned, and make few stops. Many run express from point to point. They are well worth the few dollars more. In rural areas, buses are often of the school-bus variety, with lots of local color.

Whenever possible, it's best to buy your reserved-seat ticket, often using a computerized system, a day in advance on long-distance routes and especially before holidays.

16 Tips on Accommodations

MEXICO'S HOTEL RATING SYSTEM

The hotel rating system in Mexico is called "Stars and Diamonds." Hotels may qualify to earn one to five stars or diamonds. Many hotels that have excellent standards are not certified, but all rated hotels adhere to strict standards. The guidelines relate to service, facilities, and hygiene more than to prices.

Five-diamond hotels meet the highest requirements for rating: The beds are comfortable, bathrooms are in excellent working order, all facilities are renovated regularly, infrastructure is top-tier, and services and hygiene meet the highest international standards.

Five-star hotels usually offer similar quality, but with lower levels of service and detail in the rooms. For example, a five-star hotel may have less luxurious linens or, perhaps, room service during limited hours rather than 24 hours.

Four-star hotels are less expensive and more basic, but they still guarantee cleanliness and basic services such as hot water and purified drinking water. Three-, two, and one-star hotels are at least working to adhere to certain standards: Bathrooms are cleaned and linens are washed daily, and you can expect a minimum standard of service. Two- and one-star hotels generally provide bottled water rather than purified water.

The nonprofit organization Calidad Mexicana Certificada, A.C., known as **Calmecac** (www.calmecac.com.mx), is responsible for hotel ratings; visit their website for additional details about the rating system.

HOTEL CHAINS

In addition to the major international chains, you'll run across a number of less-familiar brands as you plan your trip to Mexico. They include:

- **Brisas Hotels & Resorts** (www.brisas.com.mx). These were the hotels that originally attracted jet-set travelers to Mexico. Spectacular in a retro way, these properties offer the laid-back luxury that makes a Mexican vacation so unique.
- **Fiesta Americana** and **Fiesta Inn** (www.posadas.com). Part of the Mexican-owned Grupo Posadas company, these hotels set the country's midrange standard for facilities and services. They generally offer comfortable, spacious rooms and traditional Mexican hospitality. Fiesta Americana hotels offer excellent beach-resort packages. Fiesta Inn hotels are usually more business oriented. Grupo Posadas also owns the more luxurious Caesar Park hotels and the eco-oriented Explorean hotels.
- **Hoteles Camino Real** (www.caminoreal.com). Once known as the premier Mexican hotel chain, Camino Real still maintains a high standard of service at its properties, although the company was sold in 2005, and many of the hotels that once formed a part of it have been sold off or have become independent. Its beach hotels are traditionally located on the best beaches in the area. This chain also focuses on the business market. The hotels are famous for their vivid and contrasting colors.
- **NH Hoteles** (www.nh-hoteles.com). The NH hotels are noted for their family-friendly facilities and quality standards. The beach properties' signature feature is a pool, framed by columns, overlooking the sea.
- **Quinta Real Grand Class Hotels and Resorts** (www.quintareal.com). These hotels, owned by Summit Hotels and Resorts, are noted for architectural and cultural details that reflect their individual regions. At these luxury properties, attention to detail and excellent service are the rule.

HOUSE RENTALS & SWAPS

House and villa rentals and swaps are becoming more common in Mexico, but no single recognized agency or business provides this service exclusively for Mexico. In the chapters that follow, we have provided information on independent services that we have found to be reputable.

With regard to general online services, the most extensive inventory of homes is found at **Vacation Rentals by Owner** (**VRBO;** www.vrbo.com). They have over 33,000 homes and condominiums worldwide, including a large selection in Mexico. Another good option is **VacationSpot** (© 888/903-7768; www.vacationspot.com), owned by Expedia and a part of its sister company Hotels.com. It has fewer choices, but the company's criteria for adding inventory is much more selective and often includes on-site inspections. They also offer toll-free phone support.

SURFING FOR HOTELS

In addition to the online travel booking sites **Travelocity, Expedia, Orbitz, Priceline,** and **Hotwire,** you can book hotels through **Hotels.com; Quikbook** (www.quikbook.com); and **Travelaxe** (www.travelaxe.net).

HotelChatter.com is a daily webzine offering smart coverage and critiques of hotels worldwide. Go to **TripAdvisor.com** or **HotelShark.com** for helpful independent consumer reviews of hotels and resort properties.

It's a good idea to **get a confirmation number** and **make a printout** of any online booking transaction.

SAVING ON YOUR HOTEL ROOM

The **rack rate** is the maximum rate that a hotel charges for a room. Hardly anybody pays this price, however, except in high season or on holidays. To lower the cost of your room:

- **Ask about special rates or other discounts.** You may qualify for corporate, student, military, senior, frequent flier, trade union, or other discounts.
- **Dial direct.** When booking a room in a chain hotel, you'll often get a better deal by calling the individual hotel's reservation desk rather than the chain's main number.
- **Book online.** Many hotels offer Internet-only discounts, or supply rooms to Priceline, Hotwire, or Expedia at rates much lower than the ones you can get through the hotel itself.
- **Remember the law of supply and demand.** You can save big on hotel rooms by traveling in a destination's off-season or shoulder seasons, when rates typically drop.
- **Look into group or long-stay discounts.** If you come as part of a large group, you should be able to negotiate a bargain rate. Likewise, if you're planning a long stay (at least 5 days), you might qualify for a discount. As a general rule, expect 1 night free after a 7-night stay.
- **Sidestep excess surcharges and hidden costs.** Many hotels have adopted the unpleasant practice of nickel-and-diming its guests with opaque surcharges. When you book a room, ask what is included in the room rate and what is extra. Avoid dialing direct from hotel phones, which can have exorbitant rates. And don't be tempted by the room's minibar offerings: Most hotels charge through the nose for water, soda, and snacks. Finally, ask about local taxes and service charges, which can increase the cost of a room by 15% or more.
- Consider the pros and cons of **all-inclusive** resorts and hotels. The term "all-inclusive" means different things at different hotels. Many all-inclusive hotels include three meals daily, sports equipment, spa entry, and other amenities; others may include most alcoholic drinks. In general, you'll save money going the "all-inclusive" way—as long as you use the facilities provided. The down side is that your choices are limited and you're stuck eating and playing in one place for the duration of your vacation.
- **Book an efficiency.** A room with a kitchenette allows you to shop for groceries and cook your own meals. This is a big money saver, especially for families on long stays.
- **Consider enrolling in hotel chains' "frequent-stay" programs,** which are upping the ante lately to win the

loyalty of repeat customers. Frequent guests can now accumulate points or credits to earn free hotel nights, airline miles, in-room amenities, merchandise, tickets to concerts and events, and discounts on sporting facilities. Perks are awarded not only by many chain hotels and motels, but individual inns and B&Bs. Many chain hotels partner with other hotel chains, car-rental firms, airlines, and credit-card companies to give consumers additional incentive to do repeat business.

LANDING THE BEST ROOM

Somebody has to get the best room in the house. It might as well be you. You can start by joining the hotel's frequent-guest program, which may make you eligible for upgrades. A hotel-branded credit card usually gives its owner "silver" or "gold" status in frequent-guest programs for free. Always ask about a corner room. They're often larger and quieter, with more windows and light, and they often cost the same as standard rooms. When you make your reservation, ask if the hotel is renovating; if it is, request a room away from the construction. Ask about nonsmoking rooms, rooms with views, rooms with twin, queen- or king-size beds. If you're a light sleeper, request a quiet room away

from vending machines, elevators, restaurants, bars, and dance clubs. Ask for a room that has been most recently renovated or redecorated.

If you aren't happy with your room when you arrive, ask for another one. Most lodgings will be willing to accommodate you, within reason.

In resort areas, particularly in warm climates, ask the following questions before you book a room:

- What's the view like? Cost-conscious travelers may be willing to pay less for a back room facing the parking lot, especially if they don't plan to spend much time in their room.
- Does the room have air-conditioning or ceiling fans? Do the windows open? If they do, and the nighttime entertainment takes place alfresco, you may want to find out when show time is over.
- What's included in the price? Your room may be moderately priced, but if you're charged for beach chairs, towels, sports equipment, and other amenities, you could end up spending more than you bargained for.
- How far is the room from the beach and other amenities? If it's far, is there transportation to and from the beach, and is it free?

17 Tips on Dining

Authentic Mexican food differs dramatically from what is frequently served in the United States under that name. For many travelers, Mexico will be new and exciting culinary territory. Even grizzled veterans will be pleasantly surprised by the wide variation in specialties and traditions offered from region to region.

Despite regional differences, some generalizations can be made. Mexican food usually isn't chile-hot when it arrives at the table (though many dishes must have a certain amount of piquancy, and some

home cooking can be very spicy, depending on a family's or chef's tastes). Chiles and sauces add piquant flavor after the food is served; you'll never see a table in Mexico without one or both of these condiments. Mexicans don't drown their cooking in cheese and sour cream, a la Tex-Mex, and they use a great variety of ingredients. But the basis of Mexican food is simple—tortillas, beans, chiles, squash, and tomatoes—the same as it was centuries ago, before the Europeans arrived.

THE BASICS

TORTILLAS Traditional tortillas are made from corn that's boiled in water and lime, and then ground into *masa* (a grainy dough), patted and pressed into thin cakes, and cooked on a hot griddle known as a *comal*. In many households, the tortilla takes the place of fork and spoon; Mexicans merely tear them into wedge-shaped pieces, which they use to scoop up their food. Restaurants often serve bread rather than tortillas because it's easier, but you can always ask for tortillas. A more recent invention from northern Mexico is the flour tortilla, which is seen less frequently in the rest of Mexico.

ENCHILADAS The tortilla is the basis of several Mexican dishes, but the most famous of these is the enchilada. The original name for this dish would have been *tortilla enchilada,* which simply means a tortilla dipped in a chile sauce. In like manner, there's the *entomatada* (tortilla dipped in a tomato sauce) and the *enfrijolada* (a bean sauce). The enchilada began as a very simple dish: A tortilla is dipped in chile sauce (usually with ancho chile) and then into very hot oil, and then is quickly folded or rolled on a plate and sprinkled with chopped onions and a little *queso cotija* (crumbly white cheese) and served with a few fried potatoes and carrots. You can get this basic enchilada in food stands across the country. I love them, and if you come across them in your travels, give them a try. In restaurants you get the more elaborate enchilada, with different fillings of cheese, chicken, pork, or even seafood, and sometimes in a casserole.

TACOS A taco is anything folded or rolled into a tortilla, and sometimes a double tortilla. The tortilla can be served either soft or fried. *Flautas* and quesadillas are species of tacos. For Mexicans, the taco is the quintessential fast food, and the *taquería* (taco stand)—a ubiquitous sight—is a great place to get a filling meal. See the section "Eating Out: Restaurants, *Taquerías* & Tipping," below, for information on taquerías.

FRIJOLES An invisible "bean line" divides Mexico: It starts at the Gulf Coast in the southern part of the state of Tamaulipas and moves inland through the eastern quarter of San Luis Potosí and most of the state of Hidalgo, then goes straight through Mexico City and Morelos and into Guerrero, where it curves slightly westward to the Pacific. To the north and west of this line, the pink bean known as the *flor de mayo* is the staple food; to the south and east, including all of the Yucatán, the standard is the black bean.

In private households, beans are served at least once a day and, among the working class and peasantry, with every meal, if the family can afford it. Mexicans almost always prepare beans with a minimum of condiments—usually just a little onion and garlic and perhaps a pinch of herbs. Beans are meant to be a contrast to the heavily spiced dishes. Sometimes they are served at the end of a meal with a little Mexican-style sour cream.

Mexicans often fry leftover beans and serve them on the side as *frijoles refritos.* "Refritos" is usually translated as refried, but this is a misnomer—the beans are fried only once. The prefix "re" actually means "well" (as in thoroughly).

TAMALES You make a tamal by mixing corn *masa* with a little lard, adding one of several fillings—meats flavored with chiles (or no filling at all)—then wrapping it in a corn husk or in the leaf of a banana or other plant, and finally steaming it. Every region in Mexico has its own traditional way of making tamales. In some places, a single tamal can be big enough to feed a family, while in others they are barely 3 inches long and an inch thick.

CHILES Many kinds of chile peppers exist, and Mexicans call each of them by one name when they're fresh and another when they're dried. Some are blazing hot with only a mild flavor; some are mild but have a rich, complex flavor. They can be pickled, smoked, stuffed, stewed, chopped, and used in an endless variety of dishes.

MEALTIME

MORNING The morning meal, known as *el desayuno*, can be something light, such as coffee and sweet bread, or something more substantial: eggs, beans, tortillas, bread, fruit, and juice. It can be eaten early or late and is always a sure bet in Mexico. The variety and sweetness of the fruits is remarkable, and you can't go wrong with Mexican egg dishes.

MIDAFTERNOON The main meal of the day, known as *la comida* (or *el almuerzo*), is eaten between 2 and 4pm. Stores and businesses often close, and many people go home to eat and perhaps take a short afternoon siesta before going about their business. The first course is the *sopa*, which can be either *caldo* (soup) or *sopa de arroz* (rice) or both; then comes the main course, which ideally is a meat or fish dish prepared in some kind of sauce and served with beans, followed by dessert.

EVENING Between 8 and 10pm, most Mexicans have a light meal called *la cena*. If eaten at home, it is something like a sandwich, bread and jam, or perhaps a couple of tacos made from some of the day's leftovers. At restaurants, the most common thing to eat is *antojitos* (literally, "little cravings"), a general label for light fare. Antojitos include tostadas, tamales, tacos, and simple enchiladas, and are big hits with travelers. Large restaurants offer complete meals as well.

EATING OUT: RESTAURANTS, TAQUERIAS & TIPPING

Avoid eating at those inviting sidewalk restaurants that you see beneath the stone archways that border the main plazas. These places usually cater to tourists and don't need to count on getting any return business. But they are great for getting a coffee or beer.

Most nonresort towns have one or two restaurants (sometimes one is a coffee shop) that are social centers for a large group of established patrons. These establishments over time become virtual institutions, and change comes very slowly. The food is usually good standard fare, cooked as it was 20 years ago; the decor is simple. The patrons have known each other and the staff for years, and the *charla* (banter), gestures, and greetings are friendly, open, and unaffected. If you're curious about Mexican culture, eating and observing the goings-on is fun.

During your trip, you're going to see many **taquerías** (taco joints). These are generally small places with a counter or a few tables set around the cooking area; you get to see exactly how the cooks make their tacos before deciding whether to order. Most tacos come with a little chopped onion and cilantro, but not tomato and lettuce. Find one that seems popular with the locals and where the cook performs with brio (a good sign of pride in the product). Sometimes there will be a woman making the tortillas right there (or working the *masa* into *gorditas, sopes,* or *panuchos* if these are also served). You will never see men doing this—this is perhaps the strictest gender division in Mexican society. Men may do all other cooking and kitchen tasks, and work with prepared tortillas, but they will never be found working *masa.*

For the main meal of the day many restaurants offer a multicourse blue-plate special called **comida corrida** or **menú del día.** This is the least expensive way to get a full dinner. In Mexico, you need to ask for your check; it is generally considered inhospitable to present a check to someone who hasn't requested it. If you're in a hurry to get somewhere, ask for the check when your food arrives.

Tips are about the same as in the United States. You'll sometimes find a 15% **value-added tax** on restaurant meals, which shows up on the bill as "IVA." This is a boon to arithmetically challenged tippers, saving them from undue exertion.

To summon the waiter, wave or raise your hand, but don't motion with your index finger, which is a demeaning gesture that may even cause the waiter to ignore you. Or if it's the check you want, you can motion to the waiter from across the room using the universal pretend-you're-writing gesture.

Most restaurants do not have **non-smoking sections;** when they do, we mention it in the reviews. But Mexico's wonderful climate allows for many open-air restaurants, usually set inside a courtyard of a colonial house, or in rooms with tall ceilings and plenty of open windows.

DRINKS

All over Mexico you'll find shops selling *jugos* (juices) and *licuados* (smoothies) made from several kinds of tropical fruit. They're excellent and refreshing; while traveling, I take full advantage of them. You'll also come across *aguas frescas*—water flavored with hibiscus, melon, tamarind, or lime. Soft drinks come in more flavors than in any other country I know. Pepsi and Coca-Cola taste the way they did in the United States years ago, before the makers started adding corn syrup. The coffee is generally good, and **hot chocolate** is a traditional drink, as is *atole*—a hot, corn-based beverage that can be sweet or bitter.

Of course, Mexico has a proud and lucrative **beer**-brewing tradition. A lesser-known brewed beverage is *pulque,* a pre-Hispanic drink: the fermented juice of a few species of maguey or agave. Mostly you find it for sale in *pulquerías* in central Mexico. It is an acquired taste, and not every gringo acquires it. **Mezcal** and **tequila** also come from the agave. Tequila is a variety of mezcal produced from the *A. tequilana* species of agave in and around the area of Tequila, in the state of Jalisco. Mezcal comes from various parts of Mexico and from different varieties of agave. The distilling process is usually much less sophisticated than that of tequila, and, with its stronger smell and taste, mezcal is much more easily detected on the drinker's breath. In some places such as Oaxaca, it comes with a worm in the bottle; you are supposed to eat the worm after polishing off the mezcal. But for those teetotalers out there who are interested in just the worm, I have good news—you can find these worms for sale in Mexican markets when in season. *¡Salud!*

FAST FACTS: Mexico

Abbreviations Dept. (apartments); Apdo. (post office box); Av. (*avenida;* avenue); c/ (*calle;* street); Calz. (*calzada;* boulevard). "C" on faucets stands for *caliente* (hot); "F" stands for *fría* (cold). "PB" (*planta baja*) means ground floor; in most buildings the next floor up is the first floor (1).

ATM Networks See "Money & Costs," p. 39.

Business Hours In general, businesses in larger cities are open between 9am and 7pm; in smaller towns many close between 2 and 4pm. Most close on Sunday. In resort areas it is common to find stores open at least in the mornings on Sunday, and for shops to stay open late, often until 8 or even 10pm. Bank hours are Monday through Friday from 9 or 9:30am to anywhere between 3 and 7pm. Increasingly, banks open on Saturday for at least a half-day.

Cameras & Film Film costs about the same as in the United States. Tourists wishing to use a video or still camera at any archaeological site in Mexico or at many museums operated by the Instituto de Antropología e Historia (INAH) must pay $4 per camera at each site visited. Also, use of a tripod at any archaeological site requires a permit from INAH. It's courteous to ask permission before photographing anyone. It is never considered polite to take photos inside a church in Mexico. In some areas, such as around San Cristóbal de las Casas (see chapter 11), there are other restrictions on photographing people and villages.

Car Rentals See "Getting Around Mexico," earlier in this chapter.

Climate See "When to Go," earlier in this chapter.

Currency See "Money & Costs," earlier in this chapter.

Customs Mexican Customs inspection has been streamlined. At most points of entry, tourists are requested to press a button in front of what looks like a traffic signal, which alternates on touch between red and green. Green light and you go through without inspection; red light and your luggage or car may be inspected. If you have an unusual amount of luggage or an oversized piece, you may be subject to inspection anyway.

What You Can Bring into Mexico When you enter Mexico, Customs officials will be tolerant as long as you have no illegal drugs or firearms. Tourists are allowed to bring in their personal effects duty-free. A laptop computer, camera equipment, and sports equipment that could feasibly be used during your stay are also allowed. The underlying guideline is: Don't bring anything that looks as if it's meant to be resold in Mexico. **U.S. citizens** entering Mexico by the land border can bring in gifts worth a value of up to $50 duty-free, except for alcohol and tobacco products. Those entering Mexico by air or sea can bring in gifts worth a value of up to $300 duty-free. The **website for Mexican Customs** ("Aduanas") is www.aduanas.sat.gob.mx/webadunet/body.htm.

What You Can Take Home from Mexico U.S. Citizens: Returning U.S. citizens who have been away for at least 48 hours are allowed to bring back, once every 30 days, $800 worth of merchandise duty-free. You'll pay a flat rate of duty on the next $1,000 worth of purchases. Any dollar amount beyond that is subject to duties at whatever rates apply. On mailed gifts, the duty-free limit is $200. Be sure to keep your receipts for purchases accessible to expedite the declaration process. *Note:* If you owe duty, you are required to pay on your arrival in the United States—either by cash, personal check, government or traveler's check, or money order (and, in some locations, a Visa or MasterCard).

To avoid paying duty on foreign-made personal items you owned before your trip, bring along a bill of sale, insurance policy, jeweler's appraisal, or receipts of purchase. Or you can register items that can be readily identified by a permanently affixed serial number or marking—think laptop computers, cameras, and CD players—with Customs before you leave. Take the items to the nearest Customs office or register them with Customs at the airport from which you're departing. You'll receive, at no cost, a Certificate of Registration, which allows duty-free entry for the life of the item.

For specifics on what you can bring back and the corresponding fees, download the invaluable free pamphlet *Know Before You Go* online at **www.cbp. gov** (click on "Travel," and then click on "Know Before You Go! Online Brochure"). Or contact the **U.S. Customs & Border Protection (CBP),** 1300 Pennsylvania Ave. NW, Washington, DC 20229 (© **877/287-8667**) and request the pamphlet.

Canadian Citizens: For a clear summary of Canadian rules, write for the booklet *I Declare,* issued by the **Canada Border Services Agency** (© **800/461-9999** in Canada, or 204/983-3500; www.cbsa-asfc.gc.ca).

U.K. Citizens: For information, contact **HM Revenue & Customs** at © **0845/010-9000** (from outside the U.K., 020/8929-0152), or consult their website at www.hmrc.gov.uk.

Australian Citizens: A helpful brochure available from Australian consulates or Customs offices is *Know Before You Go.* For more information, call the **Australian Customs Service** at © **1300/363-263,** or log on to www.customs.gov.au.

New Zealand Citizens: Most questions are answered in a free pamphlet available at New Zealand consulates and Customs offices: *New Zealand Customs Guide for Travellers, Notice no. 4.* For more information, contact **New Zealand Customs Service,** The Customhouse, 17–21 Whitmore St., Box 2218, Wellington (© **04/473-6099** or 0800/428-786; www.customs.govt.nz).

Doctors & Dentists Every embassy and consulate can recommend local doctors and dentists with good training and modern equipment; some of the doctors and dentists speak English. See the list of embassies and consulates under "Embassies & Consulates," below. Hotels with a large foreign clientele can often recommend English-speaking doctors.

Driving Rules See "Getting Around Mexico," earlier in this chapter.

Drug Laws It may sound obvious, but don't use or possess illegal drugs in Mexico. Mexican officials have no tolerance for drug users, and jail is their solution, with very little hope of getting out until the sentence (usually a long one) is completed or heavy fines or bribes are paid. Remember, in Mexico the legal system assumes you are guilty until proven innocent. *Note:* It isn't uncommon to be befriended by a fellow user, only to be turned in by that "friend," who collects a bounty. Bring prescription drugs in their original containers. If possible, pack a copy of the original prescription with the generic name of the drug.

U.S. Customs officials are on the lookout for diet drugs that are sold in Mexico but illegal in the U.S. Possession could land you in a U.S. jail. If you buy antibiotics over the counter (which you can do in Mexico) and still have some left, U.S. Customs probably won't hassle you.

Drugstores Farmacias (pharmacies) will sell you just about anything, with or without a prescription. Most pharmacies are open Monday through Saturday from 8am to 8pm. The major resort areas generally have one or two 24-hour pharmacies. Pharmacies take turns staying open during off hours; if you are in a smaller town and need to buy medicine during off hours, ask for the *farmacia de turno.*

Electricity The electrical system in Mexico is 110 volts AC (60 cycles), as in the United States and Canada. In reality, however, it may cycle more slowly and overheat your appliances. To compensate, select a medium or low speed on hair dryers. Many older hotels still have electrical outlets for flat two-prong plugs; you'll need an adapter for any plug with an enlarged end on one prong or with three prongs. Many better hotels have three-hole outlets (*trifásicos* in Spanish). Those that don't may have loan adapters, but to be sure, it's always better to carry your own.

Embassies & Consulates They provide valuable lists of doctors and lawyers, as well as regulations concerning marriages in Mexico. Contrary to popular belief, your embassy cannot get you out of jail, provide postal or banking services, or fly you home when you run out of money. Consular officers can provide advice on most matters and problems, however. Most countries have an embassy in Mexico City, and many have consular offices or representatives in the provinces.

The Embassy of the **United States** in Mexico City is at Paseo de la Reforma 305, next to the Hotel María Isabel Sheraton at the corner of Río Danubio (✆ 55/5080-2000 or 5511-9980); hours are Monday through Friday from 8:30am to 5:30pm. Visit http://mexico.usembassy.gov for addresses of the U.S. consulates inside Mexico. There are U.S. Consulates at López Mateos 924-N, Ciudad Juárez (✆ 656/611-3000); Progreso 175, Guadalajara (✆ 333/268-2100); Av. Constitución 411 Pte., Monterrey (✆ 818/345-2120); Tapachula 96, Tijuana (✆ 664/622-7400); Monterrey 141, Hermosillo (✆ 662/289-3500); Primera 2002, Matamoros (✆ 868/812-4402); Paseo Montejo 453, Mérida (✆ 999/942-5700); Calle San Jose, Nogales, Sonora (✆ 631/313-4820); and Allende 3330, Col. Jardin, Nuevo Laredo (✆ 867/714-0512). In addition, there are consular agencies in Acapulco (✆ 744/469-0556); Cabo San Lucas (✆ 624/143-3566); Cancún (✆ 998/883-0272); Cozumel (✆ 987/872-4574); Ixtapa/Zihuatanejo (✆ 755/553-2100); Mazatlán (✆ 669/916-5889); Oaxaca (✆ 951/516-2853); Puerto Vallarta (✆ 322/222-0069); San Luis Potosí (✆ 444/811-7802); and San Miguel de Allende (✆ 415/152-2357).

The Embassy of **Australia** in Mexico City is at Rubén Darío 55, Col. Polanco (✆ 55/51101-2200). It's open Monday through Friday from 9am to 1pm.

The Embassy of **Canada** in Mexico City is at Schiller 529, Col. Polanco (✆ 55/5724-7900); it's open Monday through Friday from 9am to 1pm. At other times, the name of a duty officer is posted on the door. Visit www.dfait-maeci.gc.ca for addresses of consular agencies in Mexico. There are Canadian consulates in Acapulco (✆ 744/484-1305); Cancún (✆ 998/883-3360); Guadalajara (✆ 333/615-6215); Mazatlán (✆ 669/913-7320); Monterrey (✆ 818/344-2753); Oaxaca (✆ 951/513-3777); Puerto Vallarta (✆ 322/293-0098); San José del Cabo (✆ 624/142-4333); and Tijuana (✆ 664/684-0461).

The Embassy of **New Zealand** in Mexico City is at Jaime Balmes 8, 4th floor, Col. Los Morales, Polanco (✆ 55/5283-9460; kiwimexico@compuserve.com.mx). It's open Monday through Thursday from 8:30am to 2pm and 3 to 5:30pm, and Friday from 8:30am to 2pm.

The Embassy of the **United Kingdom** in Mexico City is at Río Lerma 71, Col. Cuauhtémoc (✆ 55/5242-8500; www.embajadabritanica.com.mx). It's open Monday through Friday from 8:30am to 3:30pm.

The Embassy of **Ireland** in Mexico City is at Bulevar Cerrada, Avila Camacho 76, 3rd floor, Col. Lomas de Chapultepec (© **55/5520-5803**). It's open Monday through Friday from 9am to 5pm.

The **South African** Embassy in Mexico City is at Andrés Bello 10, 9th floor, Col. Polanco (© **55/5282-9260**). It's open Monday through Friday from 8am to 4pm.

Emergencies In case of emergency, dial © **065** from any phone within Mexico. For police emergency numbers, turn to "Fast Facts" in the chapters that follow. The 24-hour **Tourist Help Line** in Mexico City is © **01-800/987-8224** or 55/5089-7500, or you can now simply dial **078**. The operators don't always speak English, but they are always willing to help. The tourist legal assistance office (Procuraduría del Turista) in Mexico City (© **55/5625-8153** or -8154) always has an English speaker available. Though the phones are frequently busy, they operate 24 hours.

Etiquette & Customs **Appropriate attire:** Mexicans tend to dress more formally than in other North American countries. Cities are considerably more formal than rural areas. Except in beach resorts, shorts, short skirts, and sandals are uncommon and a sure sign you're not Mexican. During the workday, men are usually in business attire, while women dress in pants or long skirts. At night, fitted jeans are common.

Gestures: In Mexico, men and women may greet each other with a handshake or, more commonly, with one kiss on the right cheek, with the woman usually initiating. Between women, one kiss on the right cheek is exchanged. Men shake hands and, if friends, hug with two pats on the back (a hug is called an *abrazo*). Showing someone the back of your hand means, "thank you." Wiggling an index finger means, "yes, that's right."

Avoiding offense: Mexican culture tends to be indirect and polite, so that directness can sometimes be interpreted as aggressive. Mexicans value patience over punctuality. Avoid putting hands on your hips, which is an offense. Disrespectful comments about someone's family—particularly their mother—are considered the greatest offense.

Holidays See "Calendar of Events," earlier in this chapter.

Internet Access In large cities and resort areas, most hotels now offer business centers or some area with Internet access. You'll also find cybercafes in destinations that are popular with expats and business travelers. Even in remote spots, Internet access is common. For more information on Internet access, see "Staying Connected" earlier in this chapter.

Language Spanish is the official language in Mexico. English is spoken and understood to some degree in most tourist areas. Mexicans are very accommodating with foreigners who try to speak Spanish, even in broken sentences. See Appendix B for a glossary of simple phrases for expressing basic needs.

Legal Aid **International Legal Defense Counsel,** 111 S. 15th St., 24th floor, Packard Building, Philadelphia, PA 19102 (© **215/977-9982**), is a law firm specializing in legal difficulties of Americans abroad. See also "Embassies & Consulates" and "Emergencies," above.

Liquor Laws The legal drinking age in Mexico is 18; however, asking for ID or denying purchase is extremely rare. Grocery stores sell everything from beer and wine to national and imported liquors. You can buy liquor 24 hours a day, but during major elections, dry laws often are enacted for as much as 72 hours in advance of the election—and they apply to tourists as well as local residents. Mexico does not have laws that apply to transporting liquor in cars, but authorities are beginning to target drunk drivers more aggressively. It's a good idea to drive defensively.

It is not legal to drink in the street; however, many tourists do so. If you are getting drunk, you shouldn't drink in the street, because you are more likely to get stopped by the police.

Lost & Found To replace a **lost passport,** contact your embassy or nearest consular agent. You must establish a record of your citizenship and fill out a form requesting another FMT (tourist permit) if it, too, was lost. If your documents are stolen, get a police report from local authorities; having one *might* lessen the hassle of exiting the country without all your identification. Without the FMT, you can't leave the country, and without an affidavit affirming your passport request and citizenship, you may have problems at U.S. Customs when you get home. It's important to clear everything up *before* trying to leave. Mexican Customs may, however, accept the police report of the loss of the FMT and allow you to leave.

If you lose your **wallet** anywhere outside of Mexico City, before panicking, retrace your steps—you'll be surprised at how honest people are, and you'll likely find someone trying to find you to return your wallet.

If your wallet is stolen, the police probably won't be able to recover it. Be sure to notify all of your credit card companies right away, and file a report at the nearest police precinct. Your credit card company or insurer may require a police report number or record of the loss. Most credit card companies have an emergency toll-free number to call if your card is lost or stolen; these numbers are not toll-free within Mexico (see "Telephone & Fax," below, for instructions on calling U.S. toll-free numbers). The company may be able to wire you a cash advance off your credit card immediately, and, in many places, can deliver an emergency credit card in a day or two. **Visa's** U.S. emergency number is ① **800/847-2911** or 410/581-9994. American Express cardholders and traveler's check holders should call ① **800/221-7282.** MasterCard holders should call ① **800/307-7309** or 636/722-7111. For other credit cards, call the toll-free number directory at ① **800/555-1212.**

If you need emergency cash over the weekend when all banks and American Express offices are closed, you can have money wired to you via **Western Union** (① **800/325-6000;** www.westernunion.com).

Identity theft or fraud are potential complications of losing your wallet, especially if you've lost your driver's license along with your cash and credit cards. Notify the major credit-reporting bureaus immediately; placing a fraud alert on your records may protect you against liability for criminal activity. The three major U.S. credit-reporting agencies are **Equifax** (① **800/766-0008;** www.equifax.com), **Experian** (① **888/397-3742;** www.experian.com), and **TransUnion**

(✆ **800/680-7289;** www.transunion.com). Finally, if you've lost all forms of photo ID, call your airline and explain the situation; they might allow you to board the plane if you have a copy of your passport or birth certificate and a copy of the police report you've filed.

Mail Postage for a postcard or letter is 8 pesos; it may arrive anywhere from 1 to 6 weeks later. The price for registered letters and packages depends on the weight, and unreliable delivery time can take 2 to 6 weeks. The recommended way to send a package or important mail is through FedEx, DHL, UPS, or another reputable international mail service.

Newspapers & Magazines The English language newspaper is the *Miami Herald* published in conjunction with *El Universal.* You can find it at most newsstands. Newspaper kiosks in larger cities also carry a selection of English-language magazines.

Passports Allow plenty of time before your trip to apply for a passport; processing normally takes 3 weeks but can take longer during busy periods (especially spring). And keep in mind that if you need a passport in a hurry, you'll pay a higher processing fee.

For Residents of Australia: You can pick up an application from your local post office or any branch of Passports Australia, but you must schedule an interview at the passport office to present your application materials. Call the **Australian Passport Information Service** at ✆ **131-232,** or visit the government website at www.passports.gov.au.

For Residents of Canada: Passport applications are available at travel agencies throughout Canada or from the central **Passport Office,** Department of Foreign Affairs and International Trade, Ottawa, ON K1A 0G3 (✆ **800/567-6868;** www.ppt.gc.ca).

For Residents of Ireland: You can apply for a 10-year passport at the **Passport Office,** Setanta Centre, Molesworth Street, Dublin 2 (✆ **01/671-1633;** www.dfa.ie). Those younger than age 18 and older than 65 must apply for a 3-year passport. You can also apply at 1A South Mall, Cork (✆ **021/272-525**) or at most main post offices.

For Residents of New Zealand: You can pick up a passport application at any New Zealand Passports Office or download it from their website. Contact the **Passports Office** at ✆ **0800/225-050** in New Zealand or 04/474-8100, or log on to www.passports.govt.nz.

For Residents of the United Kingdom: To pick up an application for a standard 10-year passport (5-yr. passport for children younger than 16), visit your nearest passport office, major post office, or travel agency or contact the **United Kingdom Passport Service** at ✆ **0870/521-0410** or search its website at www.ukpa.gov.uk.

For Residents of the United States: Whether you're applying in person or by mail, you can download passport applications from the U.S. Department of State website at **http://travel.state.gov**. To find your regional passport office, either check the U.S. Department of State website or call the **National Passport Information Center** toll-free number (✆ **877/487-2778**) for automated information.

Pets Taking a pet into Mexico is easy but requires a little planning. Animals coming from the United States and Canada need to be checked for health within 30 days before arrival in Mexico. Most veterinarians in major cities have the appropriate paperwork—an official health certificate, to be presented to Mexican Customs officials, that ensures the pet's vaccinations are up-to-date. When you and your pet return from Mexico, U.S. Customs officials will require the same type of paperwork. If your stay extends beyond the 30-day time frame of your U.S.-issued certificate, you'll need an updated Certificate of Health issued by a veterinarian in Mexico. To check last-minute changes in requirements, consult the Mexican Government Tourist Office nearest you (see "Visitor Information," earlier in this chapter).

Police In Mexico City, police are to be suspected as frequently as they are to be trusted; however, you'll find many who are quite honest and helpful. In the rest of the country, especially in the tourist areas, most are very protective of international visitors. Several cities, including Puerto Vallarta, Mazatlán, Cancún, and Acapulco, have a special corps of English-speaking Tourist Police to assist with directions, guidance, and more.

Restrooms Public toilets are not common in Mexico, but an increasing number are available, especially at fast-food restaurants and Pemex gas stations. These facilities and restaurant and club restrooms commonly have attendants, who expect a small tip (about 50¢).

Safety See "Safety," earlier in this chapter.

Smoking Smoking is permitted and generally accepted in most public places, including restaurants, bars, and hotel lobbies. Nonsmoking areas and hotel rooms for nonsmokers are becoming more common in higher-end establishments, but they tend to be the exception rather than the rule.

Taxes The 15% IVA (value-added) tax applies on goods and services in most of Mexico, and it's supposed to be included in the posted price. This tax is 10% in Cancún, Cozumel, and Los Cabos. There is a 5% tax on food and drinks consumed in restaurants that sell alcoholic beverages with an alcohol content of more than 10%; this tax applies whether you drink alcohol or not. Tequila is subject to a 25% tax. Mexico imposes an exit tax of around $24 on every foreigner leaving the country by plane (see "Airport Taxes" under "Getting Around Mexico: By Plane," earlier in this chapter).

Telephone & Fax See "Staying Connected" earlier in this chapter.

Time Zone Central Time prevails throughout most of Mexico. The states of Sonora, Sinaloa, and parts of Nayarit are on Mountain Time. The state of Baja California Norte is on Pacific Time, but Baja California Sur is on Mountain Time. All of Mexico observes **daylight saving time.**

Tipping Most service employees in Mexico count on tips for the majority of their income, and this is especially true for bellboys and waiters. Bellboys should receive the equivalent of 50¢ to $1 per bag; waiters generally receive 10% to 15%, depending on the level of service. It is not customary to tip taxi drivers, unless they are hired by the hour or provide touring or other special services.

Useful Phone Numbers There are several helpful numbers to know: **Tourist Help Line,** available 24 hours (© 01-800/987-8224 toll-free inside Mexico; or dial 078); **Mexico Hot Line** (© 800/446-3942); **U.S. Department of State Travel Advisory,** staffed 24 hours (© 202/647-5225); **U.S. Passport Agency** (© 877/487-2777); and the **U.S. Centers for Disease Control and Prevention International Traveler's Hot Line** (© 877/394-8747).

Water Most hotels have decanters or bottles of purified water in the rooms, and the better hotels have either purified water from regular taps or special taps marked *agua purificada.* Some hotels charge for in-room bottled water. Virtually any hotel, restaurant, or bar will bring you purified water if you specifically request it but will usually charge you for it. Drugstores and grocery stores sell bottled purified water. Some popular brands are Santa María, Ciel, and Bonafont. Evian and other imported brands are also widely available.

3

Suggested Mexico Itineraries

by David Baird

Mexico is a land of contrasts, which makes it the perfect destination for those seeking a little variety in their travels. Several of the suggested itineraries described below will take you through changing landscapes and both big-city and small-town Mexico. A few itineraries conclude at a beach resort so that you can relax a little at the end of your trip. But there's another reason for this: I wanted to make use of Mexico's major points of entry—the big international airports—and many of these happen to serve resorts. When I visit Mexico, I seldom book a round-trip ticket, preferring to enter through one airport and leave through another; usually I don't have to pay any extra for doing this. Times have changed and round-trip fares aren't what they used to be.

Once inside Mexico, most travel is by bus, rental car, or a hired car and driver. Domestic flights are expensive, and there is only one true passenger train still operating. This train runs along the Copper

Canyon to Chihuahua City and works well for the surf-to-sierra approach that I like (see "Los Cabos to Copper Canyon," below). I've tried to keep travel time to a minimum for obvious reasons. None of these itineraries can be called exhaustive explorations of Mexico, but neither are they exhausting. If you want to put together a tour linking all of Mexico's most famous sites, you can connect the central archaeological tour with the Ruta Maya. This would take 3 weeks and cover most of what Mexico is famous for.

Renting a car works really well for the Yucatán and a few other parts of the country. In other areas, it can be confusing, as road signs are not always posted. Hiring a car and driver or taking the bus for certain legs of the trip are reasonable options. Mexico has good buses with an array of categories of service. Once you're inside a town or city, it's usually best to use taxis, which are for the most part cheap and plentiful.

1 Central Mexico's Pre-Columbian Treasures in a Week

Most of Mexico's great archaeological sites, aside from those left by the Maya, are located in the center of the country, from Mexico City to the east. This trip takes you to the best of these and to the three most impressive archaeological museums in Mexico. The area in which all of this is located is relatively compact. It doesn't require a lot of travel time to cover, unless you add on a side trip to Oaxaca for the ruins of Monte Albán and Mitla.

Days ❶, ❷ & ❸: Arrive in Mexico City

If you arrive at an early hour, go straight to the very heart of the nation: Mexico's **zócalo,** or main square (p. 135). There, poetically situated between the nation's preeminent cathedral and its National Palace, are the ruins of the Aztec's **Templo Mayor** (p. 122), left buried and forgotten until 1978. Explore the ruins and the museum. Dedicate your first full day of activity to the **Museo Nacional de Antropología** (p. 120). By the third day, you should have adapted to the altitude and will be ready for a day trip to **Teotihuacán** (p. 144), "City of the Gods," where you can explore palaces and pyramids and climb to the summit of the **Pyramid of the Sun** (p. 147).

Day ❹: Tlaxcala

Drive or take a bus to colonial Tlaxcala to view the vivid murals of **Cacaxtla** and the hilltop stronghold of **Xochitécatl** (p. 512). The murals are painted in an intriguing Maya style, with rich symbolism that invites speculation. Stay the night here and enjoy the slow rhythms and street life of the town. Though it is a state capital (in the smallest state in Mexico), Tlaxcala is small and off the beaten path. It still retains an unhurried, graceful air. Stroll over to the **Government Palace** (p. 512) to view the modern murals of

artist Desiderio Hernández Xochitiotzin, which chronicle the history of the Tlaxcaltecans, ancient rivals of the Aztecs. See p. 512.

Day ❺: Puebla ✦✦ & Cholula

From Tlaxcala, it's a quick car or bus ride to colonial **Puebla** (p. 502) and its satellite town, Cholula, which was the ancient religious center of central Mexico. In the afternoon, visit the **Museo Amparo** (p. 506) to see its stunning collection of pre-Hispanic art, then head over to **Cholula** (p. 511) the next day to view the ruins of Mexico's largest pyramid, with the beautiful volcano "El Popo" as a backdrop. If you have time, visit the local churches of **Tonantzintla** (p. 512) and **San Francisco Acatepec** (p. 512) for their beautiful Indian baroque design.

Day ❻: Xalapa

From Puebla, it's on to bustling **Xalapa** (p. 496), a 3-hour drive from the dry central plateau to the misty slopes of the Sierra Madre Oriental. Visit the city's wonderful **Museo de Antropología** (p. 498), with a collection of megalithic Olmec heads and expressive Totonac art.

Day ❼: Veracruz City ✦

Next travel down to the old port city of **Veracruz** (p. 486). Enjoy a relaxing day in this lively town, with its coffee shops, tropical music, and dance. From here, you can fly out directly or via Mexico City. To extend your trip, you can head north to see the ruins of **El Tajín** (p. 499) or south to **Oaxaca** (p. 434) to see Monte Albán and Mitla.

2 The Best of Western Mexico in a Week

On this route, you enter Mexico through the León/Guanajuato International airport and leave from Ixtapa/Zihuatanejo. In between, you're treated to a variety of places and scenes—from the maze of streets and alleyways of the old mining town of Guanajuato, to the stately colonial city of Morelia, to the Indian town of Pátzcuaro, to the modern resort hotels of Ixtapa and Zihuatanejo. From November to March you can add a day trip from Morelia to a magical place in the mountain forests east of the city where millions of monarch butterflies congregate in a yearly ritual that is one of the most intriguing of nature's mysteries.

Day ❶: Guanajuato ⟡⟡⟡

Take it easy until you get used to the altitude. Contract a taxi to give you a tour of the city by taking you along the panoramic highway that circles the narrow valley where the old city is nestled. Stop to take in the **view** from the statue of **El Pípila** (p. 200) before descending to the subterranean highway to see the houses cantilevered out over the road. Once you're ready for a stroll, try navigating through the jumble of streets surrounding the city's main plaza, taking time to visit a couple of the downtown **museums.** See p. 201.

Days ❷ & ❸: Morelia ⟡

Take a taxi or bus for the 2½-hour drive to **Morelia** (p. 238). Build in some time to enjoy the **cathedral** from one of the many vantage points offered by the cafes and restaurants that front Avenida Madero. This is best done in late afternoon/early evening, when it appears to the casual visitor that no one in Morelia is at the office. Take a tour of the city the next day and enjoy coffee, a drink, or dinner on the terrace of the **Villa Montaña Hotel** (p. 245). In winter you can take a day trip to see the **monarch** **butterflies** (p. 248). Another option is a day trip to the dormant volcano **El Paricutín** (p. 260).

Days ❹ & ❺: Pátzcuaro ⟡⟡⟡ & the Lakeside Villages of the Purépecha

From Morelia it's only an hour's drive to the picturesque town of **Pátzcuaro** (p. 249) and the heart of the Purépecha homeland. This is the Indian version of colonial Mexico. Enjoy a stroll around the two principal plazas of the town and pay a visit to the **House of Eleven Patios** (p. 253) and the **Museo de Artes e Industrias Populares** (p. 253) for a fascinating examination of all the different art forms practiced in the region. On your next day, hire a car or guide to take a tour of the lakeside villages and perhaps take a taxi to the town of **Santa Clara** (p. 258) to watch the coppersmiths at work.

Days ❻ & ❼: Ixtapa ⟡ & Zihuatanejo

The new toll highway connecting the central highlands to these resorts will get you there in 4 hours. Relax for a couple of days and then catch a flight back home. See p. 394.

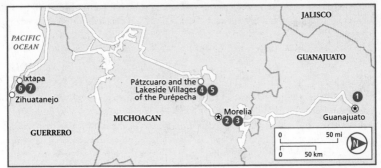

3 Los Cabos to Copper Canyon

This itinerary offers a great deal of contrast and starts in the resort area of Los Cabos. After enjoying any number of seaside activities, take a short tour of southern Baja that includes bohemian Todos Santos before crossing the Sea of Cortez and boarding a train that climbs up through rugged Sierra Tarahumara, hugging the sides of the Copper Canyon. Stop here to enjoy the peace and the beauty, and then reboard the train heading to the historical city of Chihuahua, which was home to Pancho Villa. This tour has been made easier by improvements to the ferry service between La Paz and Topolobampo.

Days ❶, ❷ & ❸: Cabo San Lucas, San José del Cabo & Todos Santos 🏛🏛

Spend your time enjoying the beauty of the area and the many activities offered in this large resort. Rent a car to drive along the coast and perhaps visit the town of **Todos Santos** (p. 724) to get a feel for the nonresort character of the region. See p. 692.

Day ❹: La Paz 🏛🏛 to Los Mochis

Take a bus or *colectivo* to **La Paz** and, from there, to the ferry dock. After a 5-hour voyage, you'll arrive at **Topolobampo** (p. 684), the port area of Los Mochis.

Days ❺ & ❻: Bahuichivo & Cerocahui 🏛🏛🏛

The train departs early in the morning and, by late morning, is snaking its way through some of the most beautiful canyon land on the trip. By midday, you

reach **Bahuichivo,** where you can get transportation to the town and mission of **Cerocahui.** This is a good place for hiking, horseback riding, and driving tours to the overlook of **Cerro Gallego.** See p. 678.

Days ❼ & ❽: Creel 🏛

Continue by train on to **Creel,** where you can get a car to take you to the nearby **Copper Canyon Sierra Lodge** (p. 681). Here you can enjoy the peace and quiet of the sierra, visit an old mission, hike to a nearby waterfall, and meet Tarahumara Indian women, who come to sell their pine-needle baskets and other handicrafts. See p. 680.

Days ❾ & ❿: Chihuahua 🏛

You'll arrive at night. Use part of the next day to enjoy the historic downtown area and visit **Pancho Villa's house** (p. 689) before flying back home. See p. 686.

Los Cabos to Copper Canyon

4 La Ruta Maya in 2 Weeks

This route, which connects all the major Maya sites in Mexico, could be done quickly in 2 weeks, or more slowly in a month, or perhaps broken up into two trips. There is a slight risk of overdosing on ruins by seeing too many in too short a time. I give you the fast-track approach, but that doesn't mean that I am encouraging you to move through this area that quickly. The best mode of travel would be a rental car: The highways are not terribly busy and are, for the most part, in good shape.

Day ❶: Arrive in Cancún

After you arrive, enjoy the remainder of the day with a swim in the Caribbean or a relaxing afternoon poolside. See p. 516.

Day ❷: Ek Balam 🐾🐾🐾 & Chichén Itzá 🐾🐾🐾

Get on the modern toll highway that heads toward Mérida and take the exit for Valladolid. Head north, away from the town, to visit the ruins of **Ek Balam** (p. 669). Highlights include a sacred doorway richly decorated with vivid figures of gods and men. Then it's back to the town of Valladolid for lunch before driving the short distance to **Chichén Itzá** (p. 660) on the old federal highway. Just outside of town, stop to see the *cenotes* of **Dzitnup** and **Sammulá** (p. 669). Farther on is the **cave of Balankanché** (p. 666). When you get to Chichén, check into your hotel, and then go to the **ruins** later in the evening for the **sound-and-light show.** See p. 661.

Day ❸: Continuing to Uxmal 🐾🐾🐾

Spend more time at the **ruins of Chichén Itzá** in the morning, then continue west on the toll highway toward Mérida, and turn off at Ticopó. Head south toward the town of **Acanceh** (p. 645) and Highway 18. Stop to see the small but interesting ruins in the middle of town, then proceed down Highway 18 to the ruins of **Mayapán** (p. 646). Afterward, continue through Ticul to Santa Elena and Uxmal. Experience the sound-and-light show. See p. 646.

Day ❹: Edzná

Visit **Uxmal** (p. 647) in the morning, then drive back toward Santa Elena and take Highway 261 south to Hopelchén and on to the impressive ruins of **Edzná** (p. 653). Nearby is a fancy hacienda turned hotel called **Uayamón** (p. 637) or drive into the town of Campeche and stay at more modest digs.

Days ⑤ & ⑥: Palenque 🐵🐵, Bonampak & Yaxchilán

Stay on Highway 261 to Escárcega, then head west on Highway 186 toward Villahermosa, then south on Highway 199 to the town of **Palenque** (p. 463) with its magnificent ruins. The next day, go to the **ruins of Bonampak and Yaxchilán** (p. 469) using one of the local tour operators.

Days ⑦ & ⑧: San Cristóbal de las Casas 🐵🐵

Keep south on Highway 199 toward **San Cristóbal** (p. 471). On the way, take a swimming break at **Misol Ha** (p. 470), and visit the ruins of **Toniná** outside of the town of Ocosingo. From San

Cristóbal, go with one of the local guides to see the present-day Maya communities of **Chamula** and **Zinacantan** (p. 478). Spend some time enjoying the town.

Day ⑨: En Route to Calakmul 🐵🐵🐵

Retrace your steps to Escárcega and continue east on Highway 186. If there's time, visit the fascinating sculptures of **Balamkú** (p. 618). Spend the night at one of the hotels in the vicinity of the turnoff for Calakmul, one of the prime city-states of the classic age of the Maya, and not often visited.

Day ⑩: Calakmul & Becán 🐵🐵🐵

Get to **Calakmul** (p. 618) early. Keep your eyes open for wildlife as you drive along a narrow jungle road. All the area surrounding the city is a **wildlife preserve.** For most of the city's history, Calakmul was the main rival to the city of Tikal, which is present day Guatemala. It eventually defeated Tikal and subjugated it for a hundred years. Calakmul's **Structure 2** is the highest Maya pyramid in Mexico. Afterward, continue east on Highway 186 to see the ruins of **Becán,** a large ceremonial center with tall temples. Also in the vicinity are **Xpujil** and **Chicanná.** Spend the night on the shores of **Lake Bacalar,** where you can cool off in its blue waters. See p. 613.

Days ⓫ & ⓬: Tulum

Drive north on Highway 307 to **Tulum** and settle into one of the small beach hotels there. In the morning, walk through the ruins and enjoy the lovely view of the coast. See p. 603.

Day ⓭: Back to Cancún

Drive back to Cancún. Depending on your schedule, you can enjoy some more beach time or simply head to the airport (25 min. south of Cancún) and depart. See p. 517.

4

Mexico City

by Juan Cristiano

Mexico City is experiencing a well-deserved renaissance in interest. In recent years, travelers dismissed Mexico's capital because of this grand city's problems with crime, pollution, and out-of-control growth. Now that these unsavory trends have begun to be reversed, the culturally curious are rediscovering what originally led so many to this magnificent place. I love Mexico City, with all of its urban energy and historic and cultural treasures. Although many compare it to the great cities of Europe, I find it a singular experience. Along with city sophistication, you also find riots of color, a constant background of music, and an endearing mix of the majestically ancient with the irresistibly new.

Standing 2,239m (7,347 ft.) high, on an enormous dry lakebed in a highland valley surrounded by mountains, this was the center of power of pre-Hispanic America, and it remains one of the most dynamic, fascinating, and charismatic cities in the world today.

For me, Mexico City is the only place you can find true insight into this captivating country—veiled in mysticism, infused with an appreciation of the moment, and proud of its heritage. Founded more than 675 years ago as the ancient city of Tenochtitlán and capital of the Aztec Empire, today it has some 22 million inhabitants—making it one of the most populated cities on the globe.

You only need to stand in the center of the *zócalo*—the central plaza—to visually comprehend the undisputed significance of this city. Here, the remains of an Aztec pyramid, a colonial church, and a towering modern office building face one another, a testament to the city's prominence in ancient and contemporary history. The Teotihuacán, Toltec, Aztec, and European conquistadors all contributed to the city's fascinating evolution, art, and heritage. Although residents refer to their city as simply México (*meh-hee-koh*), its multitude of ancient ruins, colonial masterpieces, and modern architecture has prompted others to call it "The City of Palaces."

The central downtown area resembles a European city, dominated by ornate buildings and broad boulevards, and interspersed with public art, parks, and gardens. This sprawling city is thoroughly modern and, in places, unsightly and chaotic, but it never strays far from its historical roots. In the center are the partially excavated ruins of the main Aztec temple; pyramids rise just beyond the city.

The sheer number of residents trying to exist here, combined with economic malaise, high unemployment, and government corruption, has created an environment where petty crime (principally robberies) is common. Several years ago, Mexico City's notoriety came from its rising crime rate, a trend that—thankfully—is in reverse. Over the past several years, the city has achieved admirable progress in making visitors feel more secure, with special safety programs, faster response to reports of crime, a vastly increased police presence, and programs that are effectively combating corruption—including hiring Rudy Giuliani as an anticorruption consultant. By 2006, Mexico City had reduced crime rates by almost 40% from 1994's historic highs, with only .02% related to visitors to the city.

Violent crime in Mexico is largely concentrated among drug traffickers and politicians, but kidnappings and murders of businesspeople, both Mexican and foreign, are numerous. Mexico City has many treasures to enjoy, but safety concerns demand that you dress and behave conservatively as you explore the city.

Technically, Mexico City is a federal district (similar to Washington, D.C.), called the Distrito Federal (D.F.). One finds here a microcosm of all that is happening in the rest of the country—it's not only the seat of government, but in every way the dominant center of Mexican life.

You've undoubtedly heard about Mexico City's pollution. Major steps to improve the air quality (restricted driving, factory closings, emission-controlled buses and taxis) have worked wonders, but the problem persists. On some days you won't notice it; on other days it will make your nose run, your eyes water, and your throat rasp. If you have respiratory problems, be very careful; the city's elevation makes matters even worse. Minimize your exposure to the fumes by refraining from walking busy streets during rush hour. Sunday, when many factories are closed and many cars escape the city, should be your prime outdoor day. One positive note: In the evenings, the air is usually deliciously cool and relatively clean. (See also "Pollution" under "Fast Facts," later in this chapter.)

Mexico City is a feast of urban energy, culture, dining, and shopping. The city has sidewalk cafes and cantinas; bazaars and boutiques; pyramids, monuments, and museums; and a multitude of entertainment options. And when you've had your fill of the city, memorable towns and historic national landmarks are only a couple of hours away in any direction.

1 Orientation

GETTING THERE & DEPARTING

BY PLANE   For information on carriers serving Mexico City from the United States, see chapter 2.

Mexico City's **Benito Juárez International Airport** is something of a small city, where you can grab a bite, have an espresso (including Starbucks!), or buy duty free goods, clothes, books, gifts, and insurance, as well as exchange money or stay in a hotel. It was recently expanded—filled with marble floors, upscale shops, and improved services—and has overall become a much more welcoming airport. International flights depart and arrive from gate F; domestic flights are accommodated by the other terminals.

Near Gate A is a guarded **baggage-storage area** (another is near Gate F). The key-operated metal lockers measure about .5×.5×.5m (2×2×1½ ft.) and cost $6 (£3.30) daily. Larger items are stored in a warehouse, which costs $6 to $9 (£3.30–£4.95) for each 24 hours, depending on the size. You may leave your items for up to a month.

The Mexico City Hotel and Motel Association offers a **hotel-reservation service** for its member hotels. Look for its booths before you leave the baggage-claim area, or near Gate A on the concourse. Representatives will make the call according to your specifications for location and price. If they book the hotel, they require 1 night's advance payment and will give you a voucher, which you must present at the hotel.

Mexico City & Environs

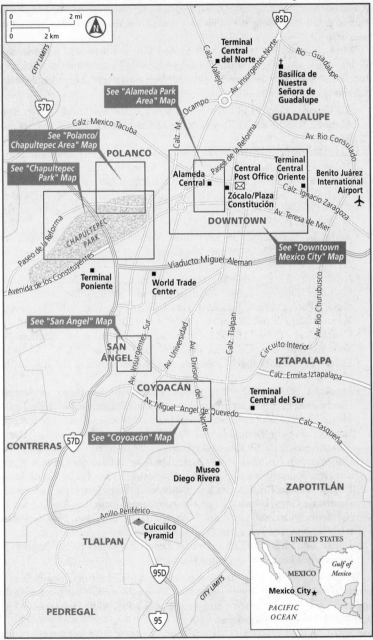

0   2 mi
0   2 km

CITY LIMITS

57D

Calz. Mexico Tacuba

See "Alameda Park Area" Map

See "Polanco/ Chapultepec Area" Map

POLANCO

See "Chapultepec Park" Map

CHAPULTEPEC PARK

Paseo de la Reforma

Avenida de los Constituyentes

Terminal Poniente

85D

Terminal Central del Norte

Calz. Vallejo

Av. Insurgentes Norte

Calz. M. Ocampo

Rio Guadalupe

† Basílica de Nuestra Señora de Guadalupe

GUADALUPE

Av. Rio Consulado

Paseo de la Reforma

Alameda Central

Central Post Office ⊠

Zócalo/Plaza Constitución

Terminal Central Oriente

Calz. Ignacio Zaragoza

Benito Juárez International Airport ✈

Av. Teresa de Mier

DOWNTOWN

See "Downtown Mexico City" Map

Viaducto Miguel Aleman

World Trade Center

See "San Ángel" Map

SAN ÁNGEL

Av. Insurgentes Sur

Av. Universidad

Av. División del Norte

Calz. Tlalpan

Av. Rio Churubusco

Circuito Interior

IZTAPALAPA

Calz. Ermita Iztapalapa

COYOACÁN

Av. Miguel Angel de Quevedo

Terminal Central del Sur

Calz. Tasqueña

CONTRERAS

57D

See "Coyoacán" Map

Museo Diego Rivera

ZAPOTITLÁN

Anillo Periférico

Cuicuilco Pyramid

TLALPAN

95D

CITY LIMITS

PEDREGAL

95

UNITED STATES

MEXICO

Gulf of Mexico

Mexico City ★

PACIFIC OCEAN

Ask about hotels with special deals. **Telephones** (operated by Telmex using prepaid Ladatel cards) are all along the public concourse; for instructions on how to use them, see chapter 2.

When you're getting ready to leave Mexico City and need local information on flights, times, and prices, contact the airlines directly (most airlines in Mexico City have English-speaking personnel). Although airline numbers change frequently, the following may be useful:

- **Air Canada** (© 55/9138-0280; www.aircanada.ca) serves Toronto (direct flight), Montreal, Vancouver, London, Paris, Hong Kong, Taipei, and Tokyo from inside Mexico.
- **AeroMéxico** (© 55/5133-4000; www.aeromexico.com.mx) serves Guadalajara, Monterrey, Tijuana, Chihuahua, Ciudad Juárez, La Paz, Los Cabos, Loreto, Mazatlán, Manzanillo, León, Aguascalientes, Ixtapa/Zihuatanejo, Puerto Vallarta, Veracruz, Acapulco, Huatulco, Oaxaca, Tapachula, Campeche, Mérida, Cancún, Tuxtla Gutiérrez, New York, Chicago, Houston, Los Angeles, San Diego, Paris, Madrid, São Paulo, Santiago de Chile, and Lima.
- **American Airlines** (© 55/5209-1400; www.aa.com) has direct flights from inside Mexico to Dallas, Miami, and Chicago, and connecting flights to all over the world.
- **Aviacsa** (© 55/5716-9005; www.aviacsa.com.mx) serves Acapulco, Cancún, Chetumal, Durango, León, Guadalajara, Mérida, Mexicali, Monterrey, Morelia, Oaxaca, Puerto Vallarta, Tapachula, Tijuana, Tuxtla Gutierrez, Villa Hermosa, and operates flights from Houston, Los Angeles, and Las Vegas.
- **Continental** (© 55/5283-5500; www.continental.com) serves Houston, New York, and other U.S., Canadian, and European destinations.
- **Delta** (© 55/5279-0909; www.delta.com) serves Atlanta, Los Angeles, and New York.
- **Mexicana** (© 55/5448-0990; www.mexicana.com) has flights to Acapulco; Guadalajara; Puerto Vallarta; Monterrey; Ixtapa/Zihuatanejo; Mexicali; Tijuana; Hermosillo; Loreto; Los Cabos; Nuevo Laredo; Monterrey; Mazatlán; Zacatecas; Saltillo; Tampico; León; Morelia; Poza Rica; Manzanillo; Colima; Veracruz; Xalapa; Oaxaca; Puerto Escondido; Huatulco; Minatitlán; Villa Hermosa; Tuxtla Gutiérrez; San Cristóbal de las Casas; Tapachula; Ciudad del Carmen; Mérida; Cancún; Cozumel; Santiago de Chile; Buenos Aires; São Paulo; Rio de Janeiro; Bogotá; Caracas; Panamá; San José (Costa Rica); Santo Domingo; San Salvador; Guatemala City; Havana; Miami; Orlando; San Antonio; Los Angeles; San Jose (California); Oakland; Las Vegas; Washington, D.C.; Chicago; New York; Montréal; Toronto; and Frankfurt.
- **United** (© 55/5627-0222; www.united.com) has flights to Los Angeles; San Francisco; Washington, D.C.; and Chicago.

Be sure to allow at least 45 to 60 minutes' travel time from the Zona Rosa or the *zócalo* (plaza) area to the airport—add about 30 minutes more if you're traveling during rush hour or bad weather. Check in at least 2 hours before international flights and 1 hour before domestic flights.

Getting to Town   Ignore those who approach you in the arrivals hall offering taxis; they are usually unlicensed and unauthorized. **Authorized airport taxis,** however, provide good, fast service. After exiting the baggage-claim area and before entering the public concourse (as well as near the far end of the terminal near Gate A), you'll see a

Tips Important Taxi Safety Precautions in Mexico City

There has been a marked increase in violent crime against both residents and tourists using taxis for transportation in Mexico City, concentrated among users of Volkswagen Beetle taxis. Robberies of taxi passengers have become increasingly violent, with beatings and even murders reported. Victims have included U.S. citizens. Many times the robberies involve taking passengers to an ATM, where they are forced to withdraw whatever limit their card or cards will allow.

If you plan to use a **taxi from the airport or bus stations,** use only an authorized airport cab with all the familiar markings: yellow car, white taxi light on the roof, and TRANSPORTACION TERRESTRE painted on the doors. Buy your ticket from the clearly marked taxi booth inside the terminal—nowhere else. After purchasing your ticket, go outside to the line of taxis, where an official taxi chief will direct you to the next taxi in line. Don't follow anyone else.

In Mexico City, *do not hail a passing taxi on the street.* Most hotels have official taxi drivers who are recognized and regulated by the terminal and city; they are considered safe taxis to use. These are known as **authorized** or *sitio* **taxis.** Hotels and restaurants can call the radio-dispatched taxis. **Official Radio Taxis** (© **55/5271-9146,** -9058, or 5273-6125) are also considered safe. You can hire one of these taxis from your hotel; the driver will frequently act as your personal driver and escort you through your travels in the city. This is a particularly advisable option at night.

All official taxis, except the expensive "turismo" cars, are painted predominantly yellow, orange, or green, have white plastic roof signs bearing the word TAXI, have TAXI or SITIO painted on the doors, and are equipped with meters. Look for all these indications, not just one or two of them. Even then, be cautious. The safest cars to use are sedan taxis (luxury cars without markings) dispatched from four- and five-star hotels. They are the most expensive, but worth it (taxi crime in Mexico City is very real).

Do not use VW Beetle taxis, which are frequently involved in robberies of tourists. Even though they are the least expensive taxis, you could be taking your life into your hands should you opt to use one. In any case, never get in a taxi that does not display a large 5×7-inch laminated **license card** with a picture of the driver on it; it's usually hanging from the door chain or glove box, or stuck behind the sun visor. *If there is no license, or if the photo doesn't match the driver, don't get in.* It's illegal for a taxi to operate without the license in view. No matter what vehicle you use for transportation, lock the doors as soon as you get in. Do not carry credit cards, your passport, or large sums of cash, or wear expensive jewelry when taking taxis.

booth marked TAXI. Staff members at these authorized taxi booths wear bright-yellow jackets or bibs emblazoned with TAXI AUTORIZADO (authorized taxi). Tell the ticket-seller your hotel or destination; the price is based on a zone system. Expect to pay around $17 (£9.35) for a *boleto* (ticket) to Polanco. Present your ticket outside to the driver. Taxi "assistants" who lift your luggage into the waiting taxi naturally expect a tip for their trouble. Putting your luggage in the taxi is the driver's job. (See also "Important Taxi Safety Precautions in Mexico City," below.)

The **Metro,** Mexico City's modern subway system, is cheap and faster than a taxi, but it seems to be gaining popularity among thieves who target tourists. If you try it, be forewarned: As a new arrival, you'll stand out. If you are carrying anything much larger than a briefcase, including a suitcase, don't even bother going to the station—they won't let you on with it. For Metro information, see "Getting Around," later in this chapter.

Here's how to find the Metro at the airport: As you come from your plane into the arrivals hall, turn left toward Gate A and walk all the way through the long terminal, out the doors, and along a covered sidewalk. Soon, you'll see the distinctive Metro logo that identifies the Terminal Aérea station, down a flight of stairs. The station is on Metro Line 5. Follow the signs for trains to Pantitlán. At Pantitlán, change for Line 1 ("Observatorio"), which takes you to stations that are just a few blocks south of the *zócalo* and La Alameda park: Pino Suárez, Isabel la Católica, Salto del Agua, and Balderas.

BY CAR Driving in Mexico City is as much a challenge and an adventure as driving in any major metropolis. Here are a few tips. First, ask the rental company whether your license-plate number permits you to drive in the city that day (break the rule and the fine can be as much as $1,600/£880). Traffic runs the course of the usual rush hours—to avoid getting tangled in traffic, plan to travel before dawn. Park the car in a guarded lot whenever possible.

Here are the chief thoroughfares for getting out of the city: Insurgentes Sur becomes Highway 95 to Taxco and Cuernavaca. Insurgentes Norte leads to Teotihuacán and Pachuca. Highway 57, the Periférico (loop around the city), is also known as Bulevar Manuel Avila Camacho, to denote street addresses; it goes north and leads out of the city to Tula and Querétaro. Constituyentes leads west out of the city past Chapultepec Park and connects with Highway 15 to Toluca, Morelia, and Pátzcuaro. (Reforma also connects with Hwy. 15.) Zaragoza leads east to Highway 150 to Puebla and Veracruz.

BY BUS Mexico City has a bus terminal for each of the four points of the compass: north, east, south, and west. You can't necessarily tell which terminal serves which area of the country by looking at a map, however.

Some buses leave directly from the **Mexico City airport.** Departures are from a booth located outside **Sala D (Gate D),** and buses also park there. Tickets to Cuernavaca and Puebla each run about $15 (£8.25), with departures every 45 minutes. Other destinations include Querétaro, Pátzcuaro, and Toluca.

If you're in doubt about which station serves your destination, ask any taxi driver—they know the stations and the routes they serve. All stations have restaurants, money-exchange booths or banks, post offices, luggage storage, and long-distance telephone booths where you can also send a fax.

Taxis from bus stations: Each station has a taxi system based on fixed-price tickets to various zones within the city, operated from a booth or kiosk in or near the entry foyer of the terminal. Locate your destination on a zone map or tell the seller where you want to go, and buy a *boleto.* See also the "Important Taxi Safety Precautions in Mexico City" box, above.

Terminal Central de Autobuses del Norte   Called "Terminal Norte," or "Central Norte" (© **55/5133-2444** or 5587-1552), Avenida de los Cien (100) Metros, is Mexico's largest bus station. It handles most buses coming from the U.S.–Mexico border. It also handles service to and from the Pacific Coast as far south as Puerto Vallarta and Manzanillo; the Gulf Coast as far south as Tampico and Veracruz; and such cities as Guadalajara, San Luis Potosí, Durango, Zacatecas, Morelia, and Colima. You can also get to the pyramids of San Juan Teotihuacán and Tula from here. By calling the above number, you can purchase tickets over the phone, charging them to a credit card. The operators can also provide exact information about prices and schedules, but few speak English.

To get downtown from the Terminal Norte, you have a choice: The **Metro** has a station (Terminal de Autobuses del Norte, or TAN) right here, so it's easy to hop a train and connect to all points. Walk to the center of the terminal, go out the front door and down the steps, and go to the Metro station. This is Línea 5. Follow the signs that say DIRECCION PANTITLÁN. For downtown, you can change trains at La Raza or Consulado (see the Mexico City Metro map on the inside back cover). Be aware that if you change at La Raza, you'll have to walk for 10 to 15 minutes and will encounter stairs. The walk is through a marble-lined underground corridor, but it's a long way with heavy luggage. If you have heavy luggage, you most likely won't be allowed into the Metro in the first place.

Another way to get downtown is by **trolleybus.** The stop is on Avenida de los Cien Metros, in front of the terminal. The trolleybus runs down Avenida Lázaro Cárdenas, the "Eje Central" (Central Artery). Or try the Central Camionera Del Norte–Villa Olimpica buses, which go down Avenida Insurgentes, past the university. Just like the Metro, the trolley will not let you board if you are carrying anything larger than a small carry-on suitcase. Backpacks seem to be an exception, but not large ones with frames.

Terminal de Autobuses de Pasajeros de Oriente (© **55/5542-0400,** 5133-2424)   The terminal is known as **TAPO.** Buses going east (Puebla, Amecameca, the Yucatán Peninsula, Veracruz, Xalapa, San Cristóbal de las Casas, and others) and Oaxaca buses, which pass through Puebla, arrive and depart from here.

To get to TAPO, take a Hipodromo–Pantitlán bus east along Alvarado, Hidalgo, or Donceles; if you take the Metro, go to the San Lázaro station on the eastern portion of Line 1 (DIRECCION PANTITLÁN).

Terminal Central de Autobuses del Sur (© **55/5689-9745**)   Mexico City's southern bus terminal is at Av. Taxqueña 1320, right next to the Taxqueña Metro stop, the last stop on Line 2. The Central del Sur handles buses to and from Cuernavaca, Taxco, Acapulco, Zihuatanejo, and intermediate points. The easiest way to get to or from the Central del Sur is on the Metro. To get downtown from the Taxqueña Metro station, look for signs that say DIRECCION CUATRO CAMINOS. Or take a trolleybus on Avenida Lázaro Cárdenas.

Terminal Poniente de Autobuses (© **55/5271-0038**)   The western bus terminal is conveniently located right next to the Observatorio Metro station, at Sur 122 and Tacubaya.

This is the smallest terminal; it mainly serves the route between Mexico City and Toluca. It also handles buses to and from Ixtapan de la Sal, Valle de Bravo, Morelia, Uruapan, Querétaro, Colima, Ixtapa/Zihuatanejo, Acapulco, and Guadalajara. In general, if the Terminal Norte also serves your destination, you'd be better off going there. It has more buses and better bus lines.

VISITOR INFORMATION

The Federal District Department provides several information services for visitors. **Infotur** (© **888/401-3880** from the U.S., or toll-free inside Mexico 01-800/987-8224) offices offer information in English and Spanish, including maps, a wide selection of brochures, and access to information from the Mexico Secretary of Tourism website. The most convenient office is in the Zona Rosa at Paseo de la Reforma and Florencia, across from the Angel de la Independencia (© **55/5208-1030**). Others are in Polanco at Av. President Masaryk 172 (© **55/3002-6300**), at the TAPO bus terminal (© **55/5784-3077**), and at the airport (© **55/5786-9002**). They're generally open daily from 9am to 6pm.

SECTUR, Mexico's Secretary of Tourism, developed a website to address safety concerns about travel to this city and other areas in Mexico. The website **www.sectur. gob.mx** offers perhaps not-so-objective assessments of destinations, as well as travel safety tips and help with lodging reservations throughout Mexico. **The Mexico City Secretary of Tourism** also has a website, **www.mexicocity.gob.mx**, which includes details on things to do, special events, safety precautions, and tourist services.

The **Mexico City Chamber of Commerce** (© **55/5592-2665**) maintains an information office with a very friendly, helpful staff that can sell you detailed maps of the city or country and answer questions. It's conveniently located at Reforma 42—look for the Cámara Nacional de Comercio de la Ciudad de México. It's open Monday through Thursday from 9am to 2pm and 3 to 6pm; Friday from 9am to 2pm and 3 to 5:30pm.

Day and night diversions are listed in the Spanish-language magazine *Tiempo Libre,* which is published each Thursday, and is available at hotels and newsstands. It also has a website, **www.tiempolibre.com.mx**. A good English-language source of visitor information is the Mexico File (**www.mexicofile.com**), and current event information and visitor tips are offered on the excellent site **www.mexicocity.gob.mx**.

CITY LAYOUT

FINDING AN ADDRESS   Despite its size, Mexico City is not hard to get a feel for. The city is divided into 350 *colonias,* or neighborhoods. Taxi drivers are notoriously ignorant of the city, including the major tourist sights and popular restaurants. Before getting into a taxi, always give a street address, *colonia,* and cross streets as a reference, and show the driver your destination on a map that you carry with you. Some of the most important *colonias* are Colonia Centro (historic city center); Zona Rosa (Colonia Juárez); Polanco (Colonia Polanco), a fashionable neighborhood immediately north of Chapultepec Park; colonias Condesa and Roma, south of the Zona Rosa, where there are many restaurants in quiet neighborhoods; all the Lomas—including Lomas de Chapultepec and Lomas Tecamachalco—which are exclusive neighborhoods west of Chapultepec Park; and San Angel and Coyoacán, the artsy neighborhoods toward the south of Mexico City. In addresses, the word is abbreviated *Col.,* and the full *colonia* name is vital in addressing correspondence.

STREET MAPS   Should you want more detailed maps of Mexico City than the ones included in this guide, you can get them easily. The **Infotur** office (see "Visitor Information," above) generally has several free maps available. Bookstores carry several local map/guides, with greater detail. The best detailed map is the ***Guía Roji***

(www.guiaroji.com.mx), available at bookstores in Mexico City. It features all the streets in Mexico City and is updated annually.

THE NEIGHBORHOODS IN BRIEF

Colonia Centro The heart of Mexico City, this business, banking, and historic center includes the areas in and around La Alameda and the *zócalo*, the capital's historic central square. The Spaniards built their new capital city on top of the destroyed capital of the conquered Aztec, and today, it is home to over 1,500 buildings. In the Centro Histórico—the concentrated historical center within Colonia Centro—you'll find the most historic landmarks, the most important public buildings, the partially unearthed Aztec ruins of the Great Temple, and numerous museums. There are restaurants, shops, and hotels in this area as well. In the past few years, public improvements have spurred the development of a few new hotels here, as well as a surge in nightlife and dining options, with some exquisite bars and clubs located in historic buildings.

A $300-million (£165-million) facelift was completed in 2003 in honor of the city's 675th anniversary. In addition to a beautification program for the *zócalo*—including the addition of a grassy knoll—other elements of the program included the restoration and conversion of more than 80 18th- and 19th-century buildings.

This neighborhood is also undergoing a residential renaissance. Investors are subsidizing rents in rehabbed loft buildings for students—especially artists, Web designers, and other creative types, hoping to turn it into a Latin version of New York City's Meatpacking District—and betting on a future escalation in real estate values. Accordingly, look for the hottest and hippest in nightlife catering to the 20-something crowd here.

A special corps of police on horseback outfitted in traditional *charro* attire (along with many female police on foot) now patrols the Centro Histórico and Alameda Park. Many speak English, and they have been specially trained in the history and culture of the area they patrol.

Chapultepec Park & Polanco A large residential area west of the city center and Zona Rosa, it centers on Chapultepec Park. The largest green area in Mexico City, it was dedicated as a park in the 15th century by the Aztec ruler Netzahualcóyotl. Together with the neighboring *colonia* of Polanco (north of the park), this is Mexico City's most exclusive address. With its zoo, many notable museums, antiques shops, stylish shopping, fine dining, and upscale hotels, it's an ideal place for discovering contemporary Mexican culture. **Avenida Presidente Masaryk** is the main artery—think of it as the Rodeo Drive or Madison Avenue of Mexico City. Some of the city's best high-rise hotels are located along **Campos Eliseos,** Polanco's version of the Champs Elysees.

Condesa & Roma With their new moniker "the SoHo of Mexico City," these side-by-side bohemian neighborhoods, located just south of the Zona Rosa, are home to the current hip clubs and hot spots, from cutting-edge restaurants to offbeat shops, art galleries, and cafes. The neighborhoods are also known for their parks and restored Art Deco buildings.

Coyoacán Eight kilometers (5 miles) from the city center, east of San Angel and north of the Ciudad Universitaria, Coyoacán (koh-yoh-ah-*kahn*) is an attractive, colonial-era suburb noted for its beautiful town square, cobblestone streets, fine old mansions, and several of the city's most interesting museums. This was the home of Frida Kahlo and Diego Rivera, and of Leon Trotsky after his exile from Stalin's USSR. With something of a hippy feel, it's a wonderful place to spend the day, but overnight accommodations are almost nonexistent. Attractions in Coyoacán are listed in the section "Southern Neighborhoods," later in this chapter.

From downtown, Metro Line 3 can take you to the Coyoacán or Viveros station, within walking distance of Coyoacán's museums. Iztacala–Coyoacán buses run from the center to this suburb. If you're coming from San Angel, the quickest and easiest way is to take a cab for the 15-minute ride to the Plaza Hidalgo. Francisco Sosa, a pretty street, is the main artery into Coyoacán from San Angel, which you can also walk. Or you can catch the Alcantarilla–Col. Agrarista bus heading east along the Camino al Desierto de los Leónes or Avenida Altavista, near the San Angel Inn. Get off when the bus reaches the corner of Avenida México and Xicoténcatl in Coyoacán.

San Angel   Eight kilometers (5 miles) south of the city center, San Angel (sahn *ahn*-hehl) was once a weekend retreat for Spanish nobles but has long since been absorbed by the city. It's a stunningly beautiful neighborhood of cobblestone streets and colonial-era homes, with several worthwhile museums. This is where the renowned Bazar del Sábado (Saturday Bazaar) is held. It's full of artistic and antique treasures and surrounded by excellent restaurants and cantinas—a wonderful place to spend a day. Other attractions in San Angel include a magnificent baroque fountain made of broken pieces of porcelain at the Centro Cultural Isidro Fabela, better known as the Casa del Risco (Plaza San Jacinto 15), and the ethereal Iglesia San Jacinto, a 16th-century church with an exquisite baroque altar, bordering the Plaza San Jacinto.

The nearest Metro station is M.A. de Quevedo (Line 3). From downtown, take a *colectivo* (minibus) marked SAN ANGEL, or bus marked INDIOS VERDES–TLALPAN or CENTRAL NORTE–VILLA OLIMPICA, south along Insurgentes near the Zona Rosa. Ask to get off at La Paz. To the east is a pretty park, the Plaza del Carmen, and to the west is a Sanborn's (a well-known department store chain in Mexico), on the eastern side of Insurgentes.

Xochimilco   Twenty-four kilometers (15 miles) south of the town center, Xochimilco (soh-chee-*meel*-coh) is noted for its famed canals and Floating Gardens, which have existed here since the time of the Aztec. Although the best-known attractions are the more than 80km (50 miles) of canals (see "Parks & Gardens," later in this chapter, for details), Xochimilco itself is a colonial-era gem: It seems small, with its brick streets, but they can become heavy with traffic—it has a population of 300,000. Restaurants are at the edge of the canal and shopping area, and historically significant churches are within easy walking distance of the main square. In the town of Xochimilco, you'll find a busy market, specializing in rugs, ethnic clothing, and brightly decorated pottery.

Xochimilco hosts an amazing 422 festivals annually, the most famous of which celebrate the **Niñopan,** a figure of the Christ Child that is believed to possess miraculous powers. The figure is venerated on January 6 (Three Kings' Day), February 2 (annual changing of the Niñopan's custodian),

April 30 (Day of the Child), and from December 16 to December 24 (*posadas* for the Niñopan). Caring for the Niñopan is a coveted privilege, and the schedule of approved caretakers is filled through 2031. From March 28 to April 4 (dates vary slightly) is the Feria de la Flor Más Bella del Ejido, a flower fair when the most beautiful girl with Indian features and costume is selected. For more information and exact dates, contact the **Xochimilco Tourist Office (Subdirección de Turismo),** Pino 36, Barrio San Juan (© **55/ 5676-8879;** fax 55/5676-0810), next to VIPS, 2 blocks from the main square. It's open daily from 9am to 7pm. Attractions in Xochimilco are listed in the section "Southern Neighborhoods," later in this chapter.

To reach Xochimilco, take the Metro to Taxqueña, then the *tren ligero* (light train), which stops at the main plaza of Xochimilco. From there, take a taxi to the main plaza of the town of Xochimilco. Buses run all the way across the city from north to south to end up at Xochimilco, but they take

longer than the Metro. Of the buses coming from the center, the most convenient is La Villa–Xochimilco, which you catch going south on Correo Mayor and Pino Suárez near the *zócalo,* or near Chapultepec on Avenida Vasconcelos, Avenida Nuevo León, and Avenida Division del Norte. Since Xochimilco is located in the far south of the city, it can take a long time to reach in traffic during the workweek. Consider visiting it on the weekend.

Zona Rosa West of the Centro, the "Pink Zone" was once the city's most exclusive residential neighborhood. It has given way to just about every segment of society, and offers an array of moderate hotels, antique and silver shops, casual restaurants, gay bars, and kitsch nightlife venues. Although the Zona Rosa has become increasingly tacky with time, many of the streets here are pedestrian-only, and you will find inviting cafes, ice cream shops, and shopping plazas along the way. It's a good place to shop or grab a bite, but there are few real historic or cultural attractions within the area.

2 Getting Around

Mexico City has a highly developed and remarkably cheap public transportation system. It is a shame that the sharp increase in crime and resulting safety concerns have made these less comfortable options for travelers. The Metro, first- and second-class buses, *colectivos,* and yellow or green VW Beetle taxis will take you anywhere you want to go for very little money—but the recent visitor warnings about the use of public transportation should be respected. Because *sitio* taxis (official taxis registered to a specific locale or hotel) are relatively inexpensive and the safest way to travel within the city, you are best off using them.

BY TAXI Taxis operate under several distinct sets of rules. *Warning:* Read the cautionary box "Important Taxi Safety Precautions in Mexico City," earlier in this chapter, before using any taxi.

"Turismo" Taxis These are by far the safest way to travel within Mexico City. The unmarked cabs, usually well-kept luxury cars assigned to specific hotels, have special license plates, and bags covering their meters. Although more expensive than the VW and *libre* taxis (usually Nissan Tsurus), "turismo" taxis, along with radio-dispatched *sitio* taxis, are the safest ones to use. The drivers negotiate rates with individual passengers for

Downtown Mexico City

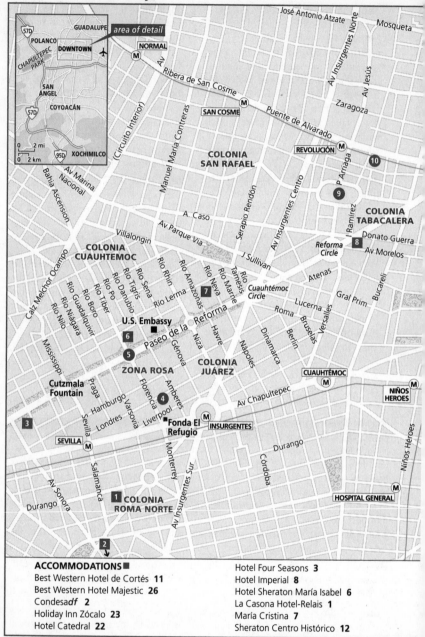

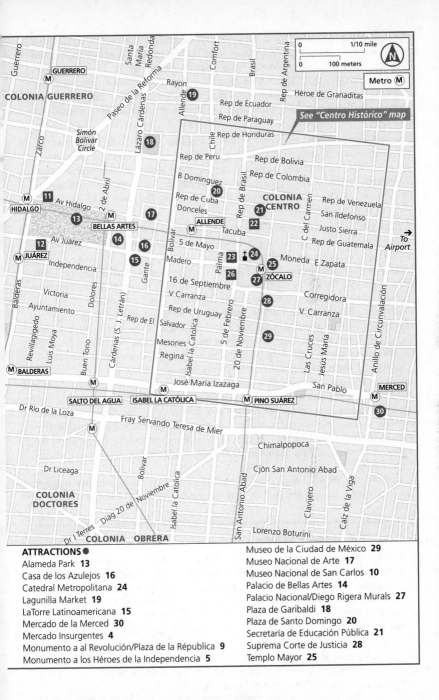

ATTRACTIONS ●

Alameda Park **13**
Casa de los Azulejos **16**
Catedral Metropolitana **24**
Lagunilla Market **19**
LaTorre Latinoamericana **15**
Mercado de la Merced **30**
Mercado Insurgentes **4**
Monumento a al Revolución/Plaza de la République **9**
Monumento a los Héroes de la Independencia **5**

Museo de la Ciudad de México **29**
Museo Nacional de Arte **17**
Museo Nacional de San Carlos **10**
Palacio de Bellas Artes **14**
Palacio Nacional/Diego Rigera Murals **27**
Plaza de Garibaldi **18**
Plaza de Santo Domingo **20**
Secretaría de Educación Pública **21**
Suprema Corte de Justicia **28**
Templo Mayor **25**

sightseeing, but rates to and from the airport are established. Ask the bell captain what the airport fare should be, and establish it before taking off. These drivers are often licensed English-speaking guides and can provide exceptional service. In general, expect to pay around $15 (£8.25) per hour for guided service, and about 15% more than metered rates for normal transportation. Often, these drivers will wait for you while you shop or dine to take you back to the hotel, or they can be called to come back and pick you up.

Metered Taxis Yellow or green VW Beetle and *libre* cabs provide low-cost service. Although you may encounter a gouging driver or one who advances the meter or drives farther than necessary to run up the tab, most service is quick and adequate. These taxis operate strictly by the meter: If the driver says his meter isn't working, find another taxi. But then, you will be heeding the warnings, and won't be using one anyway . . . now, will you?

BY METRO The subway system in Mexico City offers a smooth ride for one of the lowest fares anywhere in the world (20¢/10p per ride). Twelve lines crisscross the sprawling city. Each train usually has nine cars.

As you enter the station, buy a *boleto* at the glass *taquilla* (ticket booth). Insert your ticket into the slot at the turnstile and pass through; inside, you'll see two large signs showing the line's destination (for example, for Line 1, it's OBSERVATORIO and PANTITLÁN). Follow the signs in the direction you want and *know where you're going;* there is usually only one map of the routes, at the entrance to the station. You'll see two signs everywhere: **SALIDA** (exit) and **ANDENES** (platforms). Once inside the train, you'll see above each door a map of the station stops for that line with symbols and names.

CORRESPONDENCIAS indicates transfer points. The ride is smooth, fast, and efficient (although hot and crowded during rush hours). The beautifully designed stations are clean and have the added attraction of displaying archaeological ruins unearthed during construction. A subterranean passage goes between the Pino Suárez and Zócalo stations, so you can avoid the crowds and rain along Pino Suárez. The Zócalo station features dioramas and large photographs of the different periods in the history of the Valley of Mexico. At Pino Suárez you'll find the foundation of a pyramid from the Aztec Empire.

The Metro is crowded during daylight hours on weekdays and consequently pretty hot and muggy in summer. In fact, you may find it virtually unusable downtown

---

Tips **The Subway Skinny**

The Metro system runs workdays from 5am to 12:30am, Saturday from 6am to 1:30am, and Sunday and holidays from 7am to 12:30am. Baggage larger than a small carry-on is not allowed on the trains. In practice, this means that bulky suitcases or backpacks will make you persona non grata. On an average day, Mexico City's Metro handles more than five million riders—leaving little room for bags! But in effect, if no one stops you as you enter, you're in.

Watch your bags and your pockets. Metro pickpockets prey on the unwary (especially foreigners) and are very crafty—on a crowded train, they've been known to empty a fanny pack from the front. Be careful, and carry valuables inside your clothing. Women should avoid traveling alone.

between 4 and 7pm on weekdays, because of sardine-can conditions. At some stations, there are even separate lanes roped off for women and children; the press of the crowd is so great that someone might get molested. Buses, *colectivos*, and taxis are all heavily used during these hours, less so during off hours (such as 10:30am–noon). Avoid the crowds by traveling during off-peak hours, or simply wait a few minutes for the next train.

BY BUS Moving millions of people through this sprawling urban mass is a gargantuan task, but the city officials do a pretty good job of it. Bus stops on the major tourist streets usually have a map posted with the full route description.

The large buses that used to run on the major tourist routes (**Reforma** and **Insurgentes**) tended to become overpacked and have been phased out in favor of smaller, more frequent buses. Crowding is now uncommon except perhaps during peak hours. The cost in pesos is the U.S. equivalent of 25¢ to 50¢ (15p–30p). Although the driver usually has change, try to have exact fare or at least a few coins when you board.

One of the most important bus routes runs between the *zócalo* and the Auditorio (National Auditorium in Chapultepec Park) or the Observatorio Metro station. The route is Avenida Madero or Cinco de Mayo, Avenida Juárez, and Paseo de la Reforma. Buses marked ZÓCALO run this route.

Another important route is **Indios Verdes–Tlalpan**, which runs along Avenida Insurgentes, connecting the northern bus terminal (Terminal Norte), Buenavista railroad station, Reforma, the Zona Rosa, and, far to the south, San Angel and University City.

BY COLECTIVO Also called *peseros* or *combis*, these are sedans or minibuses, usually green and gray, that run along major arteries. They pick up and discharge passengers along the route, charge established fares, and provide slightly more comfort and speed than the bus. Cards in the windshield display routes; often a Metro station is the destination. One of the most useful routes for tourists runs from the *zócalo* along **Avenida Juárez**, along **Reforma** to **Chapultepec**, and back again. Board a *colectivo* with a sign saying ZOCALO, not VILLA. (The Villa route goes to the Basílica de Guadalupe.) Some of the minibuses on this route have automatic sliding doors—you don't have to shut them.

As the driver approaches a stop, he may put his hand out the window and hold up one or more fingers. This is the number of passengers he's willing to take on (vacant seats are difficult to see if you're outside the car).

BY TOURIST BUS An increasingly popular way to see the city is on one of the red double-decker **Turibuses** (© **55/5133-2488;** www.turibus.com.mx), put into service in 2002 to see sights around the capital. Each of the double-decker buses seats 75 and offers audio information in five languages, plus street maps. The buses operate from 9am to 9pm, with unlimited hop-on, hop-off privileges after paying $10 (£5.50) for a day pass ($11/£6.05 weekends). There are 25 stops at major monuments, museums, neighborhoods, and landmarks along the 35km (22-mile) route, which runs from the National Auditorium to the city center (including the *zócalo*) and from there to La Plaza de las Tres Culturas (Square of the Three Cultures), returning via Reforma Avenue towards the posh neighborhood of Polanco and finally to Museo del Niño (Children's Museum). The full circuit takes a little under 3 hours.

BY RENTAL CAR   If you plan to travel to Puebla (see chapter 12) or a surrounding area, a rental car might come in handy. But using taxis and the Metro eliminates the risk of getting lost in an unsavory area. And due to high rates of auto theft, I don't recommend renting a car. But if you do, the least-expensive rental car is the (old-style) manual-shift Volkswagen Beetle, manufactured in Mexico. The price jump is considerable beyond the VW Beetle, and you pay more for automatic transmission and air-conditioning in any car. (See also "Getting around Mexico," in chapter 2.)

If you still feel the need to rent a car in Mexico City, you can leave the driving to someone else—**Avis** offers chauffeur-driven rental cars at its nine locations in the Mexican capital. Prices begin at around $100 (£55) per day, which includes taxes, insurance, and unlimited mileage, with fuel extra. The chauffeur is on an 8-hour shift, but the car is available to the customer for 24 hours. For information and reservations, call Avis (© **800/331-1212** in the U.S.).

FAST FACTS: Mexico City

American Express   The Mexico City office is at Reforma 234 (© **55/5207-7282**), in the Zona Rosa. It's open for banking, the pickup of American Express clients' mail, and travel advice Monday through Friday from 9am to 6pm and Saturday from 9am to 1pm.

Banks   Banks are usually open Monday through Friday from 9am to 4pm; many now offer Saturday business hours. Bank branches at the airport are open whenever the airport is busy, including weekends. They usually offer ATMs and decent rates of exchange. Banks and money-exchange offices line Avenida Reforma. The Centro Histórico downtown also has banks and money-exchange booths on almost every block, as does the Zona Rosa.

Bookstores   In Mexico City, **Sanborn's** always has a great selection of books in English, as well as magazines and newspapers.

About the most convenient foreign- and Spanish-language bookstore in Mexico City, with a good selection of guidebooks and texts on Mexico, is

Librería Gandhi, Av. Juárez 4, near Avenida Lázaro Cárdenas (© **55/2625-0606;** www.gandhi.com.mx), right across from the Bellas Artes. It's open daily from 9am to 7pm and weekends from 10am to 4pm. The **New Option,** Rosas Moreno 152 (© **55/5705-3332** or -0585), is open Monday through Friday from 9am to 6pm and weekends from 10am to 4pm. The **Museo Nacional de Antropología,** in Chapultepec Park (© **55/5553-1902** or 5211-0754; www.mna.inah.gob.mx), also has a fair selection of books on Mexico, particularly special-interest guides. It's open Tuesday through Sunday from 9am to 7pm. Also in Chapultepec, the bookstore **Otro Lugar de la Mancha,** Esopo 11 Chapultepec (© **55/5280-4826),** offers a small but outstanding collection of books, music, and art, plus an upstairs cafe in a historic home. It's open Monday through Friday from 8am to 10pm, Saturday and Sunday from 9am to 10pm.

Currency Exchange The alternative to a bank is a currency-exchange booth, or *casa de cambio.* These often offer extended hours, with greater convenience to hotels and shopping areas, and rates similar to bank exchange rates. Usually, their rates are much better than those offered by most hotels. Use caution when exiting both banks and currency exchanges, which are popular targets for muggings.

Drugstores The drug departments at Sanborn's stay open late. Check the phone directory for the location nearest you. After hours, check with your hotel staff, which can usually contact a 24-hour drugstore.

Elevation Remember, you are now at an elevation of 2,239m (7,344 ft.)—over a mile in the sky. There's a lot less oxygen in the air than you're used to. If you run for a bus and feel dizzy when you sit down, it's the elevation. If you think you're in shape but huff and puff getting up Chapultepec Hill, it's the elevation. If you have trouble sleeping, it may be the elevation. If your food isn't digesting, again, it's the elevation. It takes about 3 days or so to adjust to the scarcity of oxygen. Go easy on food and alcohol the first few days in the city.

Emergencies The Mexico City government has an emergency number for visitors—dial © **060** for assistance 24 hours a day. The number is hard to reach, so have a local or Spanish speaker help you. In case of a crime or accident, contact the **Procuraduría del Turista** (© **55/5625-8153**). A government-operated service, **Locatel** (© **55/5658-1111**), is most often associated with finding missing persons anywhere in the country. With a good description of a car and its occupants, they'll search for motorists who have an emergency back home. **SECTUR** (Secretaría de Turismo; © **55/5250-0123,** -0493, -0027, -0151, -0292, or -0589; www.mexicocity.gob.mx), staffs telephones 24 hours daily to help tourists in difficulty.

Hospitals The **American–British Cowdray (ABC) Hospital** is at Calle Sur 136, at the corner of Avenida Observatorio, Col. las Américas (© **55/5230-8000;** www.abchospital.com).

Hot Lines If you think you've been ripped off on a purchase, call the **consumer protection office,** the Procuraduría Nacional del Consumidor (© **55/5625-6700** or 01-800/468-8722; www.profeco.gob.mx). SECTUR also sponsors **Infotur,** a 24-hour tourist-assistance line (© **55/5250-0123**).

Internet Access Surprisingly enough, it is easier to find cybercafes in some resort areas than in Mexico City. However, most hotels that cater to business travelers offer Internet connections in their business centers. The **Java Chat Café Internet,** Genova 44, in the Zona Rosa (© 55/5525-6853), is open daily from 7:30am to 11pm. The price per hour of access is around $2.50 (£1.40).

Pollution The rainy season, usually lasting from May to October, has less pollution than the dry season. Mid- to late November, December, and January are noted for heavy pollution. During January, schools may even close because of it, and restrictions on driving that are usually imposed only on weekdays may apply on weekends; be sure to check before driving into or around the city. (See "Rental Cars" under "Getting Around," above.) Be careful if you have respiratory problems. Just before your visit, call the Mexican Government Tourist Board office nearest you (see "Visitor Information" in chapter 2 for the address) and ask for the latest information on pollution in the capital. Minimize your exposure to fumes by refraining from walking busy streets during rush hour. Make Sunday, when many factories are closed and many cars escape the city, your prime outdoor sightseeing day.

Post Office The city's main post office, the **Correo Mayor,** is a block north of the Palacio de Bellas Artes on Avenida Lázaro Cárdenas, at the corner of Tacuba. For general postal information, call **FonoPost** (© 55/5385-0960); the staff is very helpful, and a few operators speak English.

If you need to mail a package in Mexico City, take it to the post office called Correos Internacional 2, Calle Dr. Andrade and Río de la Loza (Metro: Balderas or Salto del Agua). It's open Monday through Friday from 8am to noon. Don't wrap your package securely until an inspector examines it. Although postal service is improving, your package may take weeks, or even months, to arrive at its destination.

Restrooms There are few public restrooms. Use those in the larger hotels and in cafes, restaurants, and museums. Seasoned travelers frequently carry their own toilet paper and hand soap. Many public restrooms at museums and parks have an attendant who dispenses toilet paper for a "tip" of 5 pesos, in lieu of a usage charge.

Safety Read the "Safety" section in chapter 2 and the "Important Taxi Safety Precautions in Mexico City" box earlier in this chapter. In response to rising crime, Mexico City has added hundreds of new foot and mounted police officers, and there's a strong military presence. But they can't be everywhere. Watch out for pickpockets. Crowded subway cars and buses provide the perfect workplace for petty thieves, as do major museums (inside and out), crowded outdoor markets and bullfights, and indoor theaters. The "touch" can range from light-fingered wallet lifting or purse opening to a fairly rough shove by two or three petty thieves. Be extra careful anywhere that attracts a lot of tourists: on the Metro, in Reforma buses, in crowded hotel elevators and lobbies, at the Ballet Folklórico, and at the Museo de Antropología.

Robberies may occur in broad daylight on crowded streets in "good" parts of town, outside major tourist sights, and in front of posh hotels. The best way to avoid being mugged is to not wear any jewelry of value, especially expensive watches. If you find yourself up against a handful of these guys, the best thing to do is relinquish the demanded possession, flee, and then notify the police. (You'll need the police report to file an insurance claim.) If you're in a crowded place, you could try raising a fuss—whether you do it in Spanish or English doesn't matter. A few shouts of *"¡Ladrón!"* ("Thief!") might put them off, but that could also be risky. Overall, it's wise to leave valuables in the hotel safe and to take only the cash you'll need for the day, and no credit cards. Conceal a camera in a shoulder bag draped across your body and hanging in front of you, not on the side.

Taxes Posted prices generally include Mexico's 15% sales tax; however, it may be added. If in doubt, ask *"¿Mas IVA?"* ("Plus tax?") or *"¿Con IVA?"* ("With tax?"). There are also airport taxes for domestic and international flights, but the price of your ticket usually includes them. (See "Getting around Mexico" in chapter 2.)

Telephones Telephone numbers within Mexico City are eight digits; the first digit of the local phone number is always 5. Generally speaking, Mexico City's telephone system is rapidly improving (with new digital lines replacing old ones), offering clear, efficient service. Some of this improvement is resulting in numbers changing. As elsewhere in the country, the telephone company changes numbers without informing the telephone owners or the information operators. Business telephone numbers may be registered in the name of the corporation, which may be different than the name of a hotel or restaurant owned by the corporation. Unless the corporation pays for a separate listing, the operator uses the corporate name to find the number. The local number for **information** is © **040,** and you are allowed to request three numbers with each information call.

Coin-operated phones are prone to vandalism; **prepaid Ladatel card-only Telmex phones** have replaced most of them. Ladatel cards are usually available at pharmacies and newsstands near public phones. They come in denominations of 30, 50, and 100 pesos. **Long-distance calls** within Mexico and to foreign points can be surprisingly expensive. Consult "Fast Facts: Mexico" in chapter 2 for information on using phones.

Weather & Clothing Mexico City's high altitude means you'll need a warm jacket and sweater in winter. The southern parts of the city, such as the university area and Xochimilco, are much colder than the central part. In summer, it gets warm during the day and cool, but not cold, at night. From May to October is the rainy season (this is common all over Mexico)—take a raincoat or rain poncho.

3 Where to Stay

Not only is Mexico City one of the most exciting cities in the world, it can also be one of the most affordable when it comes to accommodations. For around $50 (£28), you can find a double room in a fairly central hotel, including a bathroom and often air-conditioning and TV. Many hotels have their own garages where guests can park free.

The best hotel values concentrate in the downtown **Centro Histórico (historic district),** which has recently undergone a dining and nightlife renaissance. Luxury hotels are mostly in the two most popular areas for mainstream tourism: The Financial District surrounding the **Zona Rosa** seems to attract predominantly those in the city for business or shopping, whereas the **Chapultepec Park** and **Polanco** neighborhood is ideally located near museums and other cultural attractions. This area is where you'll find trendy places to sleep, including the **W Mexico City** and the acclaimed **Hotel Habita** (see below).

Hotels in these zones not only offer more deluxe accommodations and amenities, but also generally have their own fleets of taxis (see "By Taxi" under "Getting Around," earlier in this chapter) and secured entrances for guests. The crime rate, though on the decline, is still quite high; given this unfortunate reality, visitors should consider staying in the most secure accommodations they can afford.

The ultrahip and happening **Condesa** neighborhood boasts the 40-room **Condesadf** (p. 110), which opened in 2005 to rave reviews.

CHAPULTEPEC PARK & POLANCO
VERY EXPENSIVE

Casa Vieja ⟨⟨ *(Finds)*   Pure Mexican style and service are the hallmarks of this luxury boutique hotel, a true gem known more to locals than tourists. Once a private residence, Casa Vieja is decorated with bold colors, unique handicrafts, exquisite antiques, and original furnishings. Each individually decorated suite includes a living and kitchen area, 36-inch TV, ample bedroom, and sizable bathroom with Jacuzzi tub. Notwithstanding the lovely decor, the real attraction is the highly personalized, gracious service. A rooftop bar and terrace serves made-to-order breakfasts (not included in the room rate). The only drawback is that in some rooms, you may overhear conversations in the halls and common areas.

Eugenio Sue 45 (a half block from Av. Presidente Masaryk), Col. Polanco, 11560 Mexico D.F. ✆ 55/5282-0067 or 5281-4468. Fax 55/5281-3780. www.casavieja.com. 10 suites. $300 (£165) junior suite; $430 (£237) master suite; $950 (£523) presidential suite. Rates include continental breakfast. AE, MC, V. Limited parking. Metro: Polanco. **Amenities:** Bar and cafe w/light meal service; concierge; room service; laundry service; dry cleaning. *In room:* A/C, TV/VCR, Wi-Fi, kitchenette, minibar, hair dryer, safe.

JW Marriott ⟨⟨   The JW Marriott is one of the city's most luxurious and expensive hotels, and a number of the city's most important visitors stay here. The refined marble lobby leads past world-class artwork and gorgeous flower displays to a dark wood library and a piano lounge. Spacious, state-of-the-art guest rooms have panoramic city and park views, plush furnishings, and separate showers and tubs with spray jets. The full-service spa includes body and facial treatments, massages, a well-equipped fitness center, and a lovely outdoor pool and Jacuzzi. Impeccable service complements the elegant surroundings. The JW Marriott lies within easy walking distance of Chapultepec Park and the fashionable shopping street, Avenida Presidente Masaryk, and is a short drive to the financial center.

Andrés Bello 29 (at Campos Eliseos), Col. Polanco, 11560 Mexico, D.F. ✆ 800/228-9290 in the U.S., or 55/5999-0000. Fax 55/5999-0001. www.marriott.com. 312 units. $239–$299 (£131–£164) double; $450 (£248) junior suite. AE, DC, MC, V. Parking $10 (£5.50) per day. Metro: Polanco. **Amenities:** Restaurant; piano lounge; outdoor pool; health club with spa services and fitness center; Jacuzzi; concierge; full-service business center; 24-hr. room service; laundry service; dry cleaning. *In room:* A/C, TV, Wi-Fi, minibar, hair dryer, safe.

W Mexico City ⟨⟨⟨   In late 2003, the W Mexico City opened to overwhelmingly rave reviews, living up to its billing as the choicest spot to stay in Mexico. This dramatic 26-story business hotel—with an all-glass entrance—is a sophisticated mixture

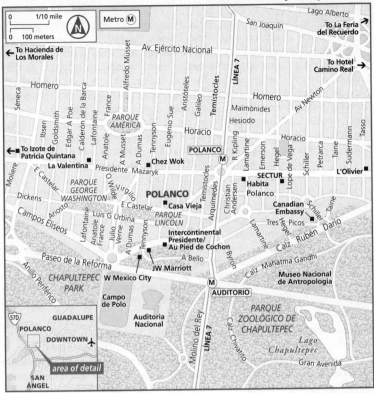

of style, comfort, and technology. The entry encompasses a series of stepped lounge areas with koi ponds, and the trendy lobby-level Red Lounge leads to a VIP bar and an outdoor terrace bar. The rooms are striking, decorated with brilliant cherry-red walls, white featherbeds, terrazzo floors, and a spacious and comfortable work area. Bathrooms break with tradition by being located on the far end of the room and feature windows, walk-in showers, and a hanging hammock. Some rooms have a large circular tub with massage jets. There are also nine high-ceiling "loft" suites, with views of Chapultepec Park, green-glass showers, and plasma TVs mounted on the ceiling above the beds. Targeting business travelers, the W Mexico City also has nine high-tech conference rooms that seat up to 400, a complete business center, and specially equipped "cyber rooms" with printers, scanners, and fax. The hotel features its own excellent full-service spa plus a glass-enclosed health club. Dining is available at Solea, a chic seafood restaurant with a Mexican and Asian flare, with alfresco terrace dining available for breakfast or lunch.

Campos Eliseos 252 (corner of Andrés Bello), Col. Polanco, 11560 Mexico, D.F. ⓒ 888/625-5144 in the U.S., or 55/9138-1800. Fax 55/9138-1899. www.starwood.com/whotels. 237 units. $339 (£186) double; $439 (£241) and up suite. AE, MC, V. Valet parking $5. Metro: Polanco. **Amenities:** Restaurant; 4 bars; full-service spa; concierge; tour services; business center; room service; laundry service; dry cleaning; CD and DVD library. *In room:* A/C, 27-in. TV, Wi-Fi, minibar, coffeemaker, hair dryer, safe.

EXPENSIVE

Hotel Camino Real ★★   Long one of the capital's leading hotels, the Camino Real is itself a work of art, set amid Mexico's finest museums. A perennial favorite, it remains one of the capital's top spots for business and social entertaining, and frequently sells out. Designed by renowned architect Ricardo Legorreta, the building is a classic example of contemporary Mexican architecture; over 400 works of art by Mexican masters and other celebrated contemporary artists complement the design. A stunning Rufino Tamayo mural, *Man Facing Eternity,* greets visitors as they enter, a mural by José Luis Covarrubias graces the La Huerta restaurant, and an impressive sculpture by Alexander Calder dominates the foyer. The spacious rooms, all with brightly colored decor and a sitting and desk area, contain armoires that conceal the TV and minibar. Executive Club rooms come with bathrobes; rates here include continental breakfast, evening cocktail hour, and daily newspaper. The hotel is also home to a branch of the trendy **China Grill** restaurant, the 24-hour **Bice Bistro,** and the first **Le Cirque** restaurant outside of the U.S. The lobby's "Blue Lounge"—a water-themed space with cascading waterfall and chairs set on an acrylic floor over a pool—occasionally features live music.

Mariano Escobedo 700, Col. Anzúrez, 11590 Mexico, D.F. ✆ **800/722-2646** in the U.S. and Canada, or 55/5263-8888. Fax 55/5263-8889. www.caminoreal.com/mexico. 712 units. $190–$250 (£105–£138) double; $250–$300 (£138–£165) executive club; $375 (£206) junior suite. AE, DC, MC, V. Parking $8 (£4). Metro: Chapultepec. **Amenities:** 5 restaurants; popular bar w/live entertainment; outdoor pool; gym; sauna; steam room; concierge; travel agency; car rental; full-service business center; salon; 24-hr. room service; massage; laundry service; dry cleaning. *In room:* A/C, TV, Wi-Fi, minibar, hair dryer, safe.

Hotel Habita ★★   If you're into the hot and the hip, and don't mind attitude with your stay, this is your place in Mexico City. I give Habita high points for changing the Mexico City hotel scene. A boutique hotel of modernist design and minimalist interiors, Habita quickly became a preferred hotel in the city's most stylish neighborhood. The white-and-steel room decor is understated, with striking extras like flat-panel TV displays and elegant gray Mexican marble lining the bathrooms from floor to ceiling. Beds are super-comfortable, with down comforters and pillows. Located on the rooftop terrace, the hotel's AREA bar remains among the city's most popular nightspots, despite newer arrivals. The lower level of the terrace features AREA's VIP section, along with a lap pool and small fitness center for guests. Adjacent to the lobby is an appropriately chic restaurant and lounge, AURA, serving fusion cuisine and exotic martinis. Habita belongs to Small Luxury Hotels and Design Hotels.

Av. Presidente Masaryk 201, Col. Polanco, 11560 Mexico, D.F. ✆ **800/337-4685** in the U.S., or 55/5282-3100. Fax 55/5282-3101. www.hotelhabita.com. 36 units. $195–$265 (£107–£146) double; $315 (£173) junior suite. AE, MC, V. Valet parking $3.50 (£1.90). Metro: Polanco. **Amenities:** Restaurant; 2 bars; rooftop heated pool and solarium; small gym; Jacuzzi; sauna; steam room; concierge; tour services; business center; room service; massage; laundry service; dry cleaning. *In room:* A/C, TV, Wi-Fi, minibar, hair dryer, safe.

Presidente InterContinental ★★   The popular Presidente is a leading destination for business executives and international visitors, a self-contained hotel city in a sleek 42-story building. Situated in the fashionable Polanco neighborhood, the Presidente is a short walk to some of the city's trendiest restaurants and nightlife and to Mexico City's world-class museums housed in Chapultepec Park. Among the hotel's excellent restaurants, **The Palm, Au Pied de Cochon,** and **Zen** are fed by the Presidente's wine cellar, the largest in Latin America. Contemporary Mexican designs decorate public areas and guest rooms, which are spacious, modern, and well-appointed.

Executive club rooms include private check-in service, breakfast, and evening hors d'oeuvres and cocktails; there is a floor dedicated to rooms with special amenities just for women. The hotel's numerous event salons make this as much of a business as a social center, and the large staff is known for its friendly, professional service. The knowledgeable concierges will help familiarize you with the area and point you in the direction you wish to travel.

Campos Eliseos 218, Col. Polanco, 11560 Mexico, D.F. © **800/424-6835** in the U.S., or 55/5327-7700. Fax 55/5327-7730. www.ichotelsgroup.com. 691 units. $239–$299 (£131–£164) double; $450 (£248) junior suite. AE, DC, MC, V. Parking $10 (£5.50) per day. Metro: Polanco. **Amenities:** 5 restaurants; lobby bar w/live entertainment; fitness center; concierge; travel agency; car rental; full-service business center; 24-hr room service; babysitting; laundry service; dry cleaning. *In room:* A/C, TV, Wi-Fi, minibar, hair dryer, safe.

ZONA ROSA & SURROUNDING AREAS

VERY EXPENSIVE

Hotel Four Seasons 𝄐𝄐𝄐 One of the finest hotels in all of Mexico, and a personal favorite, the Four Seasons sets the standard for service with a staff noted for gracious manners. In the style of an elegant Mexican hacienda, the hotel's rooms surround a beautiful interior courtyard—a veritable sanctuary in this busy city. Although you're only steps from the busy Paseo de la Reforma, the grounds of the eight-story hotel seem more like the quiet countryside surrounding a gracious manor house. Umbrella-covered alfresco dining with colonnaded walkways is found on the far side of the inviting outdoor courtyard, and the traditional English bar also offers courtyard tables.

The huge, airy rooms have high ceilings and are resolutely sumptuous. Each features plush bedspreads, beautiful Talavera lamps and bathroom accessories, Indonesian tapestries, and rich dark-wood furnishings, including a working desk. All rooms have bathrooms with separate shower and tub, dual sinks, and illuminated makeup mirrors. Most rooms face the interior courtyard, two deluxe suites have patios facing the courtyard, and most executive suites (with one to two separate bedrooms) overlook Reforma. About 100 rooms are reserved for nonsmokers. Expert-led private tours to many of the city's historic sites and museums are a unique offering; weekend guests have the option of joining a cultural tour. The Four Seasons lies at the western end of the Zona Rosa, near Chapultepec Park and Polanco and opposite the Hotel Marquís Reforma.

Paseo de la Reforma 500, Col. Juárez, 06600 Mexico, D.F. © **800/332-3442** in the U.S., 800/268-6282 in Canada, or 55/5230-1818. Fax 55/5230-1808. www.fourseasons.com. 240 units. $325 (£179) and up. Special weekend packages generally available. AE, DC, MC, V. Free valet parking. Metro: Sevilla. **Amenities:** Restaurant; bar; heated rooftop swimming pool; gym; spa; whirlpool; sauna; business center; salon; room service; massage; laundry service; dry cleaning; 1-hr. pressing service; 2 rooms for travelers w/disabilities. *In room:* A/C, TV, minibar, hair dryer, iron, safe.

EXPENSIVE

Hotel Sheraton María Isabel 𝄐 The Sheraton María Isabel's location in front of the Monumento de la Independencia is ideal: It's next to the U.S. Embassy and across Reforma from the heart of the Zona Rosa. A favorite for business travelers, the

---

ⓘ Tips **Weekend Deals**

Traveling business professionals make up most of the clientele of the top hotels, which often offer substantially lower rates Friday through Sunday.

updated 1950s-era hotel offers premium amenities in all its rooms. Tower suites, the most deluxe, occupy the 14th through 17th floors and have private check-in, butler service, and continental breakfast and evening canapés. Some have views of the beautiful Angel of Independence monument in front, and rooms on the 15th floor are specially designed for women travelers. The excellent health club includes two tennis courts, massage services, a fitness center, and small rooftop pool. The **Jorongo Bar,** a Mexico City institution, offers some of the best live Mexican music nightly from 7pm to 1am. (See "Mexico City After Dark," later in this chapter.)

Paseo de la Reforma 325 (at Río Tiber), 06500 Mexico, D.F. ✆ **800/325-3535** in the U.S., or 55/5242-5555. Fax 55/5207-0684. www.sheraton.com. 755 units. $179–$245 (£98–£135) double; $235–$355 (£129–£195) tower. AE, MC, V. Covered parking $12 (£6.60). Metro: Insurgentes (6 blocks away). **Amenities:** 3 restaurants; 2 bars; outdoor pool; privileges at nearby golf course; 2 tennis courts; full-service fitness center; travel agency; business center; salon; room service; laundry service; dry cleaning. *In room:* A/C, TV, Wi-Fi, minibar, hair dryer, safe.

MODERATE

Hotel Imperial *Value*   This classic hotel, which dates from 1904 and has been designated a historic monument, is one of the most memorable buildings along the Avenida Reforma. It has been the home of one Mexican president, the site of the assassination of another, and, for years, the U.S. Embassy. The Imperial changed hands several times before returning to its original name and status as a premier hotel in 1989. Popular with foreign—especially European—guests, it's one of the best values in the area. Rooms are extra large, with high ceilings and carpeting, although the traditional-style furnishings are dated. All have either a king or two double beds, plus desks and sitting areas. Bathrooms are large, with tubs and separate vanities. Each master suite, at the tip of one of the five floors of the building, has a unique triangular bedroom overlooking Reforma Avenue, living/dining room, bar, and whirlpool in the bathroom. All rooms are accessed from a central atrium with staircase (there's also an elevator).

Paseo de la Reforma 64 (at Morelos), Col. Juárez, 06600 Mexico, D.F. ✆ **55/5705-4911.** Fax 55/5703-3122. www.hotelimperial.com.mx. 65 units. $100–$130 (£55–£72) double; $150–$250 (£83–£138) suite. AE, DC, MC, V. Free parking. Metro: Revolución or Juárez. **Amenities:** Noted Spanish restaurant and bar Gaudi, w/live piano music nightly; concierge; business center; room service; laundry service; dry cleaning. *In room:* A/C, TV, minibar, hair dryer, safe.

INEXPENSIVE

Hotel María Cristina ✦   This classic choice for budget travelers is conveniently located just a 10-minute walk from the Zona Rosa. Resembling an aged Andalusian palace, the hotel is decorated with wrought-iron chandeliers, mahogany furnishings, and colonial patios and corridors. Standard rooms have one king or two double beds, ample closets, and modern bathrooms; the larger deluxe rooms include minibars and air-conditioning. The large lobby with overstuffed couches and a fireplace makes for a comfortable meeting place. A grassy courtyard offers lounge chairs for reading or relaxing. The hotel lies at Río Neva, on the north side of Reforma.

Río Lerma 31, Col. Cuauhtémoc, 06500 Mexico, D.F. ✆ **55/5703-1212** or 5566-9688. Fax 55/5566-9194. www.hotelmariacristina.com.mx. 150 units. $80 (£44) standard double; $100 (£55) deluxe double. AE, MC, V. Free guarded parking. **Amenities:** Restaurant; bar; travel agency; salon; private garden. *In room:* TV, Wi-Fi in most rooms, safe.

CENTRO HISTORICO & SURROUNDING AREAS
EXPENSIVE

Sheraton Centro Histórico Hotel & Convention Center ✦✦✦   Across from the Alameda Central park, this is the most luxurious option in the Historic Center. The striking marble-filled lobby leads to three outstanding restaurants, including the power lunch spot **El Cardenal,** and there's also an enticing wine bar. Spacious, modern guest rooms have separate marble showers and tubs, flat-screen TVs, and ample working spaces; corner rooms are even larger and suites include kitchenettes and Jacuzzi baths. Rooms on the east side boast views of the Alameda and adjacent Palace of Fine Arts; those looking west have city views. The Sports City gym features one of the best fitness centers of any hotel in the city, as well as an indoor pool, sun deck, and limited spa services. Despite the hotel's role as a convention center, the five-star service remains attentive and personalized. You can easily walk from here to the Palace of Fine Arts, and the major destinations in the Historic Center are a short walk or, at night, drive away.

Av. Juárez 70 (at Balderas), 06010 Mexico, D.F. ℂ 800/325-3535 in the U.S. and Canada, or 55/5130-5300. Fax 55/5130-5255. www.sheraton.com/centrohistorico. 457 units. $178–$425 (£98–£234) double; $620 (£341) suite. AE, DC, MC, V. Free covered guarded parking. Metro: Hidalgo. **Amenities:** 3 restaurants; wine bar; heated indoor swimming pool; fully equipped fitness center; limited spa services; steam room; Jacuzzi; concierge; full-service business center; room service; laundry service; dry cleaning. *In room:* A/C, TV, Wi-Fi, minibar, coffeemaker, hair dryer, iron, safe.

MODERATE

Best Western Hotel Majestic ✿   This classic hotel's prime location, facing the *zócalo*, is reason enough to stay here. The Majestic is somewhat of a Mexico City institution that visitors should experience at least once. The comfortable lobby has a glass ceiling that is also the floor of a sitting area surrounded by rooms. Rooms that don't look onto the *zócalo* overlook Avenida Madero or the hotel's inner court. The lobby and courtyard are decorated with stone arches, beautiful tiles, and stone fountains. Furnishings in the rooms are rather dated, and plans to upgrade them seem to continually stall. Tile bathrooms have tub/shower combos. In lower-floor rooms facing Avenida Madero, noise from the street may be a problem—quieter rooms look out onto the interior courtyard, which has its own aviary. Occupants of rooms facing the *zócalo* will get an unexpected jolt from the periodic early-morning flag-raising ceremony, complete with marching feet, drums, and bugle. The popular Terraza rooftop cafe/restaurant overlooking the *zócalo* serves all three meals. You can save quite a few dollars by booking directly with the hotel and by asking for promotional rates or discounts.

Av. Madero 73, Col. Centro, 06000 Mexico, D.F. ℂ 55/5521-8600. Fax 55/5512-6262. www.majestic.com.mx. 85 units. $134 (£74) double; $172 (£95) suite. AE, MC, V. Nearby parking $8. Metro: Zócalo. **Amenities:** Restaurant/bar; travel agency; room service; business services; babysitting; laundry services. *In room:* TV, coffeemaker.

INEXPENSIVE

Best Western Hotel de Cortés ✿ *Value*   This baroque-style hotel offers comfortable, modern accommodations in a fascinating historic building—a former home for Augustinian friars. The 18th-century stone structure features rooms on two floors surrounding a central colonial courtyard with a graceful fountain and Mexican restaurant. It's on La Alameda park, a short distance from the Palace of Fine Arts and the Franz Mayer Museum. Rooms, which were remodeled in 2005, vary in size and features, but all contain hand-woven bedspreads, carpeting, and a desk. The modern bathrooms have three-prong plugs and tile accents. Security boxes are available in the reception area.

Av. Hidalgo 85, 06300 Mexico, D.F. ℂ 800/528-1234 in the U.S., or 55/5518-2182. Fax 55/5512-1863. www.hotel decortes.com.mx. 28 units. $50 (£28) double; $80 (£44) suite. AE, DC, MC, V. Valet parking $10 (£5.50) per day. Metro: Hidalgo. **Amenities:** Courtyard restaurant/bar; gym; high-speed Internet; concierge; room service. *In room:* TV.

Holiday Inn Zócalo ✿✿ *Finds*   Located next to the city's historic central square, this unique Holiday Inn is decorated in colonial Mexican style with colorful art, antiques, handicrafts, and other charming touches. Photos of old Mexico City hang in the guest rooms, which have high ceilings, hardwood floors, marble bathrooms, robes, and modern conveniences such as wireless Internet access. Nonsmoking rooms are available. The rooftop terrace overlooks the *zócalo,* and the hotel also features a small restaurant, gym, concierge, and travel services. The multilingual staff caters to an international clientele that includes mostly Europeans and Americans.

Av. Cinco de Mayo 61, 06000 Mexico, D.F. © 55/5130-5130. Fax 55/5521-2122. www.hotelescortes.com. 105 units. $100 (£55) double; $150 (£83) suite. AE, MC, V. Free parking. Metro: Zócalo. **Amenities:** Restaurant; bar; gym; concierge; travel desk; room service; laundry service. *In room:* A/C, TV, Wi-Fi.

Hotel Catedral *(Value)*   This bargain hotel enjoys a stellar location 1 block north of Calle Tacuba on tree-shaded Calle Donceles, half a block from the Templo Mayor and a block from the Museo San Ildefonso. Guest rooms have purified drinking water from a special tap, over-bed reading lights, and TVs with U.S. cable channels. Some have tub/shower combinations, and others have whirlpool tubs. Rooms on the upper floors afford views of Mexico City's mammoth cathedral. On the seventh floor, a terrace with small tables and chairs offers great views. The Catedral's location is ideal for sightseeing in the Historic Center. Because heavily trafficked streets surround the hotel, add 45 minutes to your departure time if you go to the airport from here. In front of the big, marble-embellished lobby lies the bustling restaurant. The cozy bar beyond the reception desk also serves food. Ask for a top-floor room with a view.

Calle Donceles 95 (between Brasil and Argentina), 06020 Mexico, D.F. © 55/5518-5232. Fax 55/5512-4344. www. hotelcatedral.com. 116 units. $62 (£34) double; $70 (£39) junior suite. AE, MC, V. Free parking. Metro: Zócalo. **Amenities:** Restaurant; bar; travel agency; room service; laundry service. *In room:* TV, hair dryer, safe.

CONDESA/ROMA

Condesa*df* *(★★★)*   Developed by the same group that brought Hotel Habita to Polanco, Condesa*df* became the city's hottest place to stay after opening in 2005. Housed in a 1928 triangular Beaux Arts building, it features several rooms and bars that open onto a plant-filled interior courtyard. These spaces tend to be popular for small VIP parties and special events, which makes it a perfect place to check in on the local who's who. Interiors were fashioned by the French designer India Mahdavi, described as "Mexican with a twist"—stone floors, alpaca carpets, and a heavy dose of turquoise accents offset by cream leather sofas. Guest rooms feature high ceilings, balconies or terraces overlooking Parque España, hand-woven rugs, rocking chairs, flat-screen TVs, DVD players, and iPods. The rooftop sushi lounge is generally packed with the city's beautiful people, and a basement "cinema" screening room transforms into a sizzling nightclub Thursday through Saturday nights. You'll know the Condesa*df* when you see the life-sized car installation parked in front of the hotel.

Av. Veracruz 102, Col. Condesa, 06700 Mexico, D.F. © 800/337-4685 in the U.S., or 55/5241-2600. www.condesadf. com. 40 units. $175–$205 (£96–£113) double; $265–$395 (£146–£217) suites. AE, MC, V. Valet parking $4.50 (£2.50). Metro: Insurgentes. **Amenities:** 2 restaurants; bar; club; Jacuzzi; concierge; tour services; room service; massage; laundry service; dry cleaning. *In room:* A/C, plasma TV, Wi-Fi, minibar, hair dryer, safe.

La Casona Hotel-Relais *(★★)* *(Finds)*   Reminiscent of a small European luxury hotel, this exquisite establishment opened in 1996 after restoration of a dilapidated 1923 building. It has since been designated an artistic monument by Mexico's National Institute of Fine Arts. Each uniquely decorated room includes antique furniture. Tall interior shutter doors on guest-room windows keep out sound and light at night, and thick glass mutes street noise by day. Oriental-style rugs warm the hardwood floors throughout. A small wine cellar and bar below the lobby is a popular gathering place for drinks and conversation. The hotel lies 3 blocks south of the Diana Circle on Reforma, and 4 longish blocks west of the western edge of the Zona Rosa. Chapultepec Park is about a 20-minute walk to the northwest. More important than decor or location is the excellent service here—truly capable of pampering you.

Durango 280 (corner of Cozumel), Col. Roma, 06700 Mexico, D.F. © **800/223-5652** in the U.S., or 55/5286-3001. Fax 55/5211-0871. www.hotellacasona.com.mx. 29 units. $180 (£99) double. Rates include American breakfast. AE, MC, V. Gated parking $5. Metro: Sevilla (4 blocks away). **Amenities:** Restaurant; bar; small gym w/steam room; concierge; business center; room service; laundry service; safe; currency exchange. *In room:* A/C, TV, Wi-Fi.

NEAR THE AIRPORT
Hilton Airport Hotel ✦   This is the newest of the on-site airport hotels in terms of service and facilities. The lobby bar is a popular gathering place, and if the restaurant happens to be closed, there's 24-hour room service. The staff is attentive and the rooms nicely furnished, though small. Each has a color TV with U.S. channels, a nice-size work desk, and an ergonomic executive chair. It can't be beat for convenience and a guarantee of making an early morning plane. To get there, exit the terminal near Gate A and walk right, down the corridor to Sala F and the international departure gates.

International Mexico City Airport (Sala F1, 3rd floor), 15620 Mexico, D.F. © **800/228-9290** in the U.S., or 55/5133-0505. Fax 55/5133-0500. www.hilton.com. 129 units. $190 (£105) double; $300 (£165) junior suite. AE, DC, MC, V. Covered and uncovered parking $1 (55p) per hr. **Amenities:** Restaurant; lobby bar; small health club; concierge; business center; room service; laundry and pressing service. *In room:* A/C, TV w/pay movies, Wi-Fi, minibar, coffeemaker, hair dryer, iron, safe.

4 Where to Dine

As in most of the world's major cities, dining in Mexico City is sophisticated, with cuisine that spans the globe. From high chic to the Mexican standard of *comida corrida* (food on the go), the capital offers something for every taste and budget. The **Polanco** area in particular has become a place of exquisite dining options, with new restaurants rediscovering and modernizing classic Mexican dishes. The **Centro Histórico** led a resurgence of ultrahip restaurants and clubs open for late-night dining and nightlife, which has spread to the **Condesa** and **Roma** neighborhoods—now known as the SoHo of Mexico City. Cantinas, until not so very long ago the privilege of men only, offer some of the best food and colorful local atmosphere. **San Angel** houses some of Mexico City's finest traditional restaurants.

Everybody eats out in Mexico City, regardless of social class. Consequently, you can find restaurants of every type, size, and price range scattered across the city. Mexicans take their food and dining seriously, so if you see a full house, that's generally recommendation enough. But those same places may be entirely empty if you arrive early—remember, here, lunch is generally eaten at 3pm, with dinner not seriously considered before 9pm.

CHAPULTEPEC PARK & POLANCO
VERY EXPENSIVE
Aguila y Sol ✦✦✦ MEXICAN HAUTE CUISINE   One of Mexico City's most sophisticated and acclaimed restaurants is also one of the best Mexican restaurants you will find in the world. Chef-owner Martha Ortiz's enchanted cuisine matches indigenous and pre-Hispanic ingredients to contemporary creations, leaving you the sense that an outing to Aguila y Sol is as much an artistic as a dining experience (Ortiz has designed a number of excellent cookbooks on sale at the restaurant).

Among the delectable selections are duck mole, salmon in a maize crust, pork loin with gingered mango, and seared tuna with smoked chile. An outstanding wine list accompanies the exotic menu. Dishes are carefully presented but not overly big. The beautiful space reflects soft Mexican colors and is casually elegant, and the clientele includes some of the city's best-known personalities.

Moliere 42 (at Av. Presidente Masaryk), Col. Polanco. ℂ 55/5281-8354. Reservations recommended. Main courses $20–$35 (£11–£19). AE, MC, V. Mon–Sat 1:30–11:30pm; Sun 1:30–5:30pm. Metro: Polanco.

Chez Wok ⭐ HAUTE CHINESE   Opened in the fashionable Polanco area in 1992 with five chefs from Hong Kong and their incredible recipes, Chez Wok immediately became *the* place to feast on Chinese food. Years later, it hasn't lost its popularity, especially for power lunches. It's generally packed at lunch, although often quieter at night. The dining area, with large and small sections, has a combination of booths and tables with an elegant but simple yellow, black, and beige decor. Main courses include Cantonese, Peking, Szechuan, and Mandarin selections, such as steamed red snapper with white-wine sauce, chicken in shrimp paste with sesame and crab sauce, and the house specialty, Peking duck.

Tennyson 117, 2nd floor (at Av. Presidente Masaryk), Col. Polanco. ℂ 55/5281-3410 or -2921. www.chezwok.com. Reservations recommended. Main courses $18–$55 (£9.90–£30). AE, MC, V. Daily Mon–Sat 1:30–11pm; Sun 1:30–5pm. Metro: Polanco.

Hacienda de los Morales ⭐⭐ *Moments* MEXICAN HAUTE CUISINE   A 16th century oasis in the midst of the world's most populous city, the Hacienda de los Morales is an enchanted place for special occasions. The Spanish colonial decor includes dark wood furnishings, stone columns, and domed brick ceilings, with some tables looking out to garden fountains. The entrance patio doubles as an elegant bar, where you will find precious artwork and the original chapel where Spanish aristocrats once prayed. While the Hacienda is a bustling power lunch spot by day, it transforms into a romantic retreat at night. Expertly prepared food includes the best of Mexican dishes, with an excellent selection of meat, fish, and seafood, as well as pastas, crepes, and other selections. A constant stream of weddings and special events takes place in private salons surrounding the gardens. Jacket and tie are suggested.

Vázquez de Mella 525 (at Av. Horacio), Col. Polanco. ℂ 55/5096-3054. Reservations recommended. Main courses $20–$40 (£11–£22). AE, MC, V. Daily 1pm–1am. Metro: Polanco.

Izote ⭐⭐⭐ MEXICAN HAUTE CUISINE   A star of the city's superb dining scene, this signature venue of celebrated chef Patricia Quintana pays homage to the best of classic Mexican cooking. While there are only 19 tables in the simple atmosphere, what's on your plate will more than make up for it. Located on Mexico's version of Rodeo Drive, it remains one of the "must-dine" restaurants, so reservations are essential, even at lunch. The menu is a compilation of modern versions of pre-Hispanic dishes, and draws heavily on indigenous ingredients such as yucca flower, cactus, and *masa* (corn flour). Each dish is a delight. Try traditional Oaxacan *mole,* or lamb barbecued in a banana leaf. Endings are especially sweet here—save room for Tarta Zaachila, a chocolate pastry filled with nuts, accompanied by the traditional café de olla, coffee flavored with cinnamon and brown sugar. If you're curious, *izote* is the beautiful white flower that adorns the yucca plant.

Av. Presidente Masaryk 513 (between calles Sócrates and Platón), Col. Polanco. ℂ 55/5280-1671 or -1265. Reservations essential. Main courses $21–$55 (£12–£30). AE, MC, V. Mon–Sat 1pm–midnight; Sun 1–6pm. Metro: Polanco.

EXPENSIVE

Au Pied de Cochon ✹ FRENCH/BISTRO   The *capitalaños* seem to be having a love affair with French bistros these days, and this is a perennial hotspot. A direct import from Paris, this always-busy bistro packs in the city's jet set and fashion forward for classic cafe fare. Open 24-hours, it's the best late-night dining option in the city. The main dining room is a spirited scene of activity and conversation, in multiple languages. Two service bars offer singles places to dine without feeling "solo," and other tables are packed in together. Pâtés, cheese plates, and exquisite salads are standard starters. Steak frites, steamed mussels, and the specialty of *pied de cochon* (pigs' feet) are menu favorites—meat dishes are especially popular. There's also a raw bar, an excellent selection of French wines, and an ample choice of tequilas. Desserts are classically French and rich.

Campos Eliseos 218, in the Presidente InterContinental, Col. Chapultepec. ℂ 55/5327-7756. Reservations recommended. Main courses $15–$30 (£8.25–£17). AE, MC, V. Daily 24 hrs. Metro: Auditorio.

La Fonda del Recuerdo ✹✹ MEXICAN/SEAFOOD/VERACRUZ   For an all-out good time, no other restaurant in the city compares to this one. Come here if you want to immerse yourself in Mexico and join people eating, drinking, singing, and having the time of their lives (live Mexican music plays Tues–Fri nights). Diners enjoy their platters of food amid a glorious din created by *jarocho* musicians from Veracruz (several groups rove around the restaurant at once). The menu is authentically Mexican, with an emphasis on seafood; specials match the culinary traditions of whichever Mexican holiday is closest. Arrive before 2:30pm for lunch or you'll have to wait in line, which nonetheless will be worth it if you have all afternoon. At night, it's just as festive, but try to make it before 9pm, if you care to avoid the crowd. It's near the corner of Bahía de Santa Bárbara—take a taxi.

Bahía de las Palmas 37, Col. Verónica Anzures. ℂ 55/5260-0545 or 9112-7476. www.fondadelrecuerdo.com. Reservations recommended. Main courses $10–$20 (£5.50–£11). AE, DC, MC, V. Daily 11am–11pm. Metro: Polanco.

MODERATE

La Valentina ✹ TRADITIONAL MEXICAN   In the midst of posh Polanco, on the second floor of a small boutique-filled shopping center, sits this traditional Mexican restaurant within a haciendalike atmosphere. Pale-apricot stucco walls, shiny wood floors, and wood-beamed ceilings set off the cozy nooks of immaculately set tables. The menu features specialties from some of the country's best Mexican cooks. For example, there's Marta Chapa's breaded shrimp with sesame, lettuce, herbs, and chiles; cilantro soup by Suzanna Palazuelos; and Patricia Quintana's filet in butter and salsa. The bar is worth a visit on its own, with an impressive selection of premium tequilas, a selection of fine art, live trio music, and a festive cantina atmosphere that's popular among 30- and 40-somethings.

Av. Presidente Masaryk 393 (near the corner of Lafontaine), Col. Polanco. ℂ 55/5282-2297. Reservations recommended. Main courses $15–$35 (£8.25–£19). AE, DC, MC, V. Mon–Sat 1:30pm–1am; Sun 1:30pm–midnight. Metro: Polanco.

L'Olivier ✹✹ *Finds* COUNTRY FRENCH/BISTRO   This bright, bustling bistro would be reminiscent of an authentic French cafe—were it not for the fact that its patrons tend to be business professionals and sophisticated socialites rather than bohemians. Opened in 2000, L'Olivier packs in a crowd, and with good reason—the food is superb. Choices range from pâtés to soufflés (definitely plan ahead and save room for a chocolate soufflé!). There's an excellent representation of country French fare, including steak frites, cassoulets, and fricassees. The restaurant lies 12 blocks from the Polanco Metro station. You could venture in without a reservation, but depending on the night, you might not get in without one. There is no bar to wait in.

Masaryk 49-C (at Torcuato Tasso), Col. Polanco. ℂ 55/5545-3133. Reservations recommended. Main courses $12–$25 (£6.60–£14). AE, MC, V. Mon–Sat 1:30–11pm; Sun 1:30–5pm. Metro: Polanco.

ZONA ROSA & SURROUNDING AREAS

If you're up for a culinary adventure, dine at the student-staffed **Cordon Bleu Casa de Francia,** Havre 15, Zona Rosa (ℂ 55/5208-0660; www.lcbmexico.com/restaurante. cfm), a training ground for Mexico's up-and-coming chefs. The restaurants lies in two lovely dining rooms inside the Casa de Francia, a French cultural center. The menu varies, and this is a great way to sample imaginative culinary dishes. Wines by the glass are available. It's open Monday to Wednesday from 8:30am to 6pm, Thursday to Friday from 8:30am to 10pm, and Saturday 8:30am to 6pm.

EXPENSIVE

Casa Bell ⊛ INTERNATIONAL MEXICAN   A longtime favorite of Mexico City's political and business elite, Casa Bell is probably the capital's key power-lunch venue. The lovely terrace begins to fill up around 2pm, as birds chirp from strategically placed cages around the patio. Exceptionally well-trained waiters move attentively around the tables as lunch unfolds and are likely to recommend dishes such as the duck tacos, *filete Chemite* (filet mignon), or *robolo* (sea bass) prepared any way you like. Diners typically come dressed in suits and tend to linger over their meals and perhaps a few margaritas. Finish off with a delectable pastry from the dessert cart.

Praga 14 (off Paseo de la Reforma), Zona Rosa. ℂ 55/5208-3967. Reservations recommended. Main courses $20–$30 (£11–£17). AE, MC, V. Daily 1–6pm. Metro: Insurgentes.

Tezka ⊛⊛ SPANISH/MEXICAN HAUTE CUISINE   The sister of the Michelin three-star restaurant Arzak in Spain's Basque country, Tezka earns rave reviews of its own with innovative contemporary Spanish cuisine with Mexican influences. The atmosphere is spacious and relaxing, with several dining rooms, including one table for four on its own level. Some tables sit next to French windows that open to the street, one level below. Starters include an amuse-bouche of ceviche—raw tuna slivers and strawberries on tiny tostadas—and a mousse of foie gras wrapped in sliced mango. Entrees include sea bass in a pistachio sauce and lamb with a peanut sauce, served with peanuts and leeks, in thin slices of melon. For dessert, try the sweet-and-spicy chocolate-chile ice cream, or for more traditional palates, coconut soup with lemon ice cream. The $50 (£28) tasting menu is a great bargain for epicures.

Amberes 78, in the Hotel Royal, Zona Rosa. ℂ 55/5228-9918. Reservations recommended. Main courses $15–$40 (£8.25–£22). AE, DC, MC, V. Mon–Fri 1–5pm and 8–11pm; Sat 1–5pm. Metro: Insurgentes.

MODERATE

Fonda El Refugio ⊛⊛ MEXICAN   More than 40 years of tradition have shaped the service, food, and atmosphere here, making it a special place for authentic Mexican dining. It's small and unusually congenial, with a large fireplace decorated with gleaming copper pots and pans. The restaurant manages the almost impossible task of being both refined and informal. The menu runs the gamut of Mexican cuisine, from *arroz con plátanos* (rice with fried bananas) to *enchiladas con mole poblano,* topped with the rich, thick, spicy chocolate sauce of Puebla. Try chiles stuffed with ground beef or cheese, and for dessert have some coconut candy or the mouth-watering flan. The tortillas are handmade, and the margaritas potently delicious. Fonda El Refugio is very popular, especially on Saturday night, so get here early.

Liverpool 166 (between calles Florencia and Amberes), Col. Juárez Zona Rosa. © **55/5207-2732** or 5525-8128. Main courses $7–$16 (£3.85–£8.80). AE, MC, V. Mon–Sun 1–11pm. Metro: Insurgentes.

CENTRO HISTORICO & SURROUNDING AREAS
MODERATE
Café Tacuba ✹✹ MEXICAN   One of the city's most famous restaurants, Café Tacuba dates from 1912 and boasts a handsome colonial-era atmosphere. Guests are welcomed into one of two long dining rooms, with brass lamps, dark oil paintings, and a large mural of nuns working in a kitchen. The menu is authentic Mexican with traditional dishes, including tamales, enchiladas, chiles rellenos, *mole,* and *pozole.* Wednesday through Sunday from 6pm until closing, a wonderful group of medieval-costumed singers entertain; their sound is like the melodious *estudiantina* groups of Guanajuato accompanied by mandolins and guitars. A trio plays romantic boleros on Mondays and Tuesdays from 8 to 10pm.

Tacuba 28 (between República de Chile and Bolívar), Col. Centro. © **55/5512-8482** or 5518-4950. Breakfast $4–$14 (£2.20–£7.70); main courses $9–$17 (£4.95–£9.35); *comida corrida* $17–$23 (£9.35–£13). AE, MC, V. Daily 8am–11:30pm. Metro: Allende.

Restaurant Danubio SPANISH   Danubio has been a Mexico City tradition since 1936, and it remains an excellent choice for dining in the Historic Center. Photos of celebrity diners line the walls of the classically European-style room. The Basque-inspired menu offers a range of selections emphasizing seafood, and the house specialty is *langostinos* (baby crayfish). A five-course tasting menu with matching wines is available. Many dishes are prepared on an old coal and firewood stove. Danubio, which lies south of La Alameda, is also noted for its excellent wine cellar.

República de Uruguay 3 (near Bolívar). Alameda. © **55/5521-0976.** www.danubio.com. Main courses $10–$30 (£5.50–£17). AE, DC, MC, V. Daily 1–10pm. Metro: Bellas Artes or Salto del Agua.

CANTINAS
Cantina La Guadalupana ✹✹ *(Finds* MEXICAN   Opened in 1928, this cantina lies in Coyoacán, the southern neighborhood that was once the home of artists Diego Rivera and Frida Kahlo and the revolutionary Leon Trotsky. From the entrance—off a narrow, cobblestone, colonial street—to the antiquated bar, a sense of nostalgia permeates the comfortable, jovial cantina. The operation is as traditional as the menu. For those who are only drinking, waiters bring the customary small plates of complimentary snacks that range from crisp jicama slices with lime and chile to pigs' feet in a red sauce. It's easy to imagine the communist conversations that must have bounced off the walls here in Frida and Diego's day.

Higuera 2 and Caballo Calco (1 block from the central plaza), Coyoacán. © **55/5554-6253.** Main courses $5–$8 (£2.75–£4.40); mixed drinks $2.50–$8 (£1.40–£4.40), more for premium tequilas. AE, MC, V. Mon–Sat 1:30pm–1am. Metro: Coyoacán.

La México ✹ *(Finds* MEXICAN   The "queen of cantinas" as it is known, La México boasts three floors of nonstop tequila drinking, beer guzzling, music playing fun. A favorite among locals from all social classes, this authentic cantina offers live music Wednesday through Saturday nights, including salsa and traditional Mexican. Following their meals, or perhaps in the midst of them, patrons often take to dancing

Moments ¡Café, Por Favor!

If you think espresso bars are a new phenomenon, or coffee drinks a development of recent years, you may be intrigued to learn that in Mexico, drinking good coffee has been considered an art form for generations. Some of the best coffee can be found in small cafes that have a crowd of regulars who congregate to catch up on the local *chisme* (gossip).

Café La Habana, downtown at Bucareli and Morelos, is one of the most famous, a longstanding cafe with a rich history—and a reputation for strong coffee, all roasted and ground in-house. Ask the waiter and he'll tell you how Fidel Castro and Ché Guevara planned the Cuban revolution while sipping an espresso *cortao*. It's open Monday through Saturday from 7:30am to 10pm.

More European-style coffeehouses are in the Zona Rosa, frequented by businesspeople and trendy urban residents. Some of the most popular are **Salón de Té Auseba** and **Duca d'Este,** both on Hamburgo near Florencia. They serve excellent coffee and scrumptious cakes, as well as a variety of herbal teas. The sidewalk cafe **Konditori,** Genova 61, is another good option, on a pedestrian-only street. It's open daily 7am to midnight.

The Condesa neighborhood, east of Chapultepec Park, is another top cafe zone. **El Péndulo,** Nuevo León 115, close to Insurgentes, is a favorite. It combines its cafe setting with a book and music store and tends to draw intellectuals, writers, and students. It frequently hosts live music and poetry readings. It's open Monday through Friday from 8am to 11pm and weekends from 10am to 11pm. There's another branch in the Zona Rosa at Hamburgo 126.

between tables. Simple Mexican fare is offered. La México is located in San Jerónimo, toward the south end of the city.

Eje 10 Sur 75 (near Revolución), San Jerónimo. © 55/5550-2072. Main courses $4–$10 (£2.20–£5.50); mixed drinks $2–$7 (£1.10–£3.85), more for premium tequilas. No credit cards. Mon–Tues 1pm–12:30am; Wed 1pm–2am; Thurs–Fri 1pm–3am; Sat noon–2am.

La Opera ★★ *Moments* INTERNATIONAL   La Opera Bar, 3 blocks east of La Alameda, is the most opulent of the city's cantinas. Slide into a dark wood booth below gilded baroque ceilings, patches of beveled mirror, and exquisite small oil paintings. Or opt for a linen-covered table with a basket of fresh bread. La Opera is the Mexican equivalent of a London gentlemen's club, although it has become so popular for dining that fewer and fewer men play dominoes. In fact, you see people enjoying romantic interludes in cavernous booths—but tables of any kind are hard to find. Service is best if you arrive for lunch when it opens or go after 5pm when the throngs have diminished; the jacketed waiters cater to regulars at the expense of unknown diners. The menu is unimpressive, but the atmosphere and drinks are excellent. Try the incredible Aperital Batido—the bartender's special aperitif—or a classic tequila. Specialties include Spanish tapas, Caesar salad, and Veracruz-style red snapper with olives and tomatoes. While you wait for your meal, look to the ceiling for the bullet hole

A hotel can close for all kinds of reasons.
Our Guarantee ensures that if your hotel's undergoing construction, we'll let you know in advance. In fact, we cover your entire travel experience. See www.travelocity.com/guarantee for details.

You'll never roam alone.

that legend says Pancho Villa left when he galloped in on a horse. It's half a block toward the *zócalo* from Sanborn's House of Tiles.

Cinco de Mayo 10, Col. Centro. ℂ **55/5512-8959.** Reservations recommended at lunch. Main courses $4–$20 (£2.20–£11); mixed drinks $3.50–$6 (£1.95–£3.30), more for premium tequilas. AE, MC, V. Mon–Sat 1pm–midnight; Sun 1–6pm. Metro: Bellas Artes.

5 Exploring Mexico City

The diverse attractions in Mexico City spring from its complex layers of history. From the simple pleasure of a stroll through a bustling *mercado* to museums filled with treasures of artistic and historic significance, Mexico City has much to explore.

Mexico City was built on the ruins of the ancient city of Tenochtitlán. A downtown portion of the city, comprising almost 700 blocks and 1,500 buildings, has been designated Centro Histórico (Historic Center). The area has surged in popularity, and once-neglected buildings are rapidly being converted into chic clubs and trendy restaurants, recalling its former colonial charm.

Remember that this is a city, and a major one at that; dress is more professional and formal here than in other parts of the country. The altitude makes temperatures rather cool, which is often a surprise for travelers with preconceptions of Mexico as perpetually hot. In summer, always be prepared for rain, which falls almost daily. In winter, carry a jacket or sweater—stone museums are chilly inside, and when the sun goes down, the outside air gets quite cold.

THE TOP ATTRACTIONS

Basílica de Santa María de Guadalupe ⊛⊛

Within the northern city limits is the famous Basílica of Guadalupe—not just another church, but the central place of worship for Mexico's patron saint and the home of the image responsible for uniting pre-Hispanic Indian mysticism with Catholic beliefs. It is virtually impossible to understand Mexico and its culture without appreciating the national devotion for Our Lady of Guadalupe. The blue-mantled Virgin of Guadalupe is the most revered image in the country, and you will see her countenance wherever you travel. This is also one of the most important religious sites for Catholics.

The Basílica occupies the site where, on December 9, 1531, a poor Indian named Juan Diego reputedly saw a vision of a beautiful lady in a blue mantle. The local bishop, Zumarraga, was reluctant to confirm that Juan Diego had indeed seen the Virgin Mary, so he asked the peasant for evidence. Juan Diego saw the vision a second time, on December 12, and when he asked the Virgin for proof, she instructed him to collect the roses that began blooming in the rocky soil at his feet. He gathered the flowers in his cloak and returned to the bishop. When he unfurled his cloak, the flowers dropped to the ground and the image of the Virgin was miraculously emblazoned on the rough-hewn cloth. The bishop immediately ordered the building of a church on the spot, and upon its completion, the cloth with the Virgin's image was hung in a place of honor, framed in gold. Since that time, millions of the devout and the curious have come to view the miraculous image that experts, it is said, are at a loss to explain. So heavy was the flow of visitors—many approached for hundreds of yards on their knees—that the old church, already fragile, was insufficient to handle them. An audacious new Basílica, designed by Pedro Ramírez Vazquez, the same architect who designed the breathtaking Museo Nacional de Antropología, opened in 1987.

The miracle cloak hangs behind bulletproof glass above the altar. Moving walkways going in two directions transport the crowds a distance below the cloak. If you want to see it again, take the people-mover going in the opposite direction; you can do it as many times as you want.

A plaza with a visitor information center, museum, and auditorium were part of a $50-million (£28-million) face-lift and opened a couple of years ago.

In 2002, the pope declared Juan Diego a saint, a very big deal in this predominantly Catholic country; he was the first Mexican to achieve sainthood. The achievement was not, however, without controversy—Juan Diego's images have increasingly taken on a "European" appearance, and native Mexicans insist that Juan Diego be portrayed as the dark-skinned indigenous peasant he was.

To the right of the modern basilica is the Old Basílica, actually the second one built to house the cloak—the first one is higher up on the hill. Restoration of the Old Basílica, which had been tilting precariously, has been ongoing for at least 10 years. Lately it has progressed more rapidly, and the building is now open to the public. To the back of it is the entrance to the Basílica Museum, with a very good display of religious art in restored rooms. One of the side chapels, with a silver altar, is adjacent to the museum.

Outside the museum is a garden commemorating the moment Juan Diego showed the cloak to the archbishop. Numerous photographers with colorful backdrops gather there to capture your visit on film. At the top of the hill, behind the basilica, is the **Panteón del Tepeyac,** a cemetery for Mexico's more infamous folk (Santa Anna among them), and several gift shops specializing in religious objects and other folk art. The steps up this hill are lined with flowers, shrubs, and waterfalls, and the climb, though potentially tiring, is worthwhile for the view from the top.

If you visit Mexico City on **December 12,** you can witness the grand festival in honor of the **Virgin of Guadalupe.** The square in front of the basilica fills with the pious and the party-minded as prayers, dances, and a carnival atmosphere attract thousands of the devout. Many visitors combine a trip to the basilica with one to the **ruins of Teotihuacán,** as both are out of the city center in the same direction.

Plaza de las Américas 1, Villa de Guadalupe. ✆ **55/5577-6022.** www.virgendeguadalupe.org.mx. Free admission; museum 55¢ (30p). Daily 6am–9pm. Free guided tours (in Spanish) Fri–Sat noon. Metro: Basílica or La Villa. From Basílica, take exit marked SALIDA AV. MONTIEL; walk a block or so north of the station to a major intersection (Montevideo); turn right onto Av. Montevideo and cross the overpass; after about a 15-min. walk, you'll see the church ahead. From La Villa, walk north on Calzada de Guadalupe.

Museo Frida Kahlo 🌟🌟🌟   Although, during her lifetime, Frida Kahlo was known principally as the wife of muralist Diego Rivera, today her art surpasses his in popularity. Certainly the 2002 Salma Hayek movie *Frida* did much to bring this Mexican icon to the attention and appreciation of millions more. Kahlo dedicated her life to both her painting and her passionate, tortured love for her husband. Her emotional and physical pain—her spine was pierced during a serious streetcar accident in her youth—were the primary subjects of her canvases, many of which are self-portraits. Her paintings are now acknowledged as not only exceptional works of Latin American art, but as some of the purest artistic representations of female strength and struggle ever created. As her paintings have surged in renown and price, so has interest in the life of this courageous, provocative, and revolutionary woman.

Kahlo was born in this house on July 7, 1910, and lived here with Rivera from 1929 to 1954. During the 1930s and 1940s it was a popular gathering place for intellectuals. As you wander through the rooms of the cornflower-blue house, you'll get a glimpse of the life they led. Most of the rooms remain in their original state, with

Historic Downtown (Centro Histórico)

ACCOMMODATIONS ■
Best Western Hotel Majestic **7**
Gran Hotel Ciudad de México **8**
Hotel Catedral **3**
Holiday Inn Zócalo **5**

Church ✝
Metro Ⓜ

ATTRACTIONS ●
Catedral Metropolitana **9**
Museo de la Ciudad de México **15**
Museo del Templo Mayor **10**
Museo José Luis Cuevas **13**
Nacional Monte de Piedad **4**
Palacio de Minería **6**
Palacio Nacional **12**
Plaza de Santo Domingo **1**
Secretaría de Educacíon Pública **2**
Suprema Corte de Justicia **14**
Zócalo **11**

mementos everywhere. Tiny clay pots hang about; the names Diego and Frida are painted on the walls of the kitchen. In the studio upstairs, a wheelchair sits next to the easel with a partially completed painting surrounded by brushes, palettes, books, photographs, and other intimate details of the couple's art-centered lives. Much of the movie *Frida* was filmed in this house.

Frida and Diego collected pre-Columbian art, and many of the rooms contain jewelry and terra cotta figurines from Teotihuacán and Tlatelolco. Kahlo even had a mock-up of a temple built in the garden to exhibit her numerous pots and statues. On the back side of the temple are several skulls from Chichén Itzá. A cafe on the first floor serves light snacks, and the adjacent bookstore offers a full range of Kahlo and Rivera books and other commercialized memorabilia.

Londres 247, Coyoacán. (🕿 **55/5554-5999**. Admission $4.50 (£2.50). No cameras allowed. Tues–Sun 10am–5:45pm. Metro: Coyoacán.

Museo Nacional de Antropología ✩✩✩   Occupying approximately 4,100 sq. m (44,132 sq. ft.), Mexico City's anthropology museum is regarded as one of the top museums in the world. It offers the single best introduction to the culture of Mexico.

Inside the museum is an open courtyard (containing the Chávez Morado fountain) with beautifully designed rooms running around three sides on two levels. The **ground-floor rooms** are devoted to history—from prehistoric days to the most recently explored archaeological sites—and are the most popular among studious visitors. These rooms include dioramas of Mexico City when the Spaniards arrived, and reproductions of part of a pyramid at Teotihuacán. The Aztec calendar stone "wheel" occupies a proud place.

Save some time and energy for the livelier and more readily comprehensible **ethnographic rooms** upstairs. This section is devoted to the way people throughout Mexico live today, complete with straw-covered huts, recordings of songs and dances, crafts, clothing, and lifelike models of village activities. This floor, a living museum, strikes me as vital to the understanding of contemporary Mexico because of the importance of pre-Hispanic customs in Mexican village life.

A sweeping restoration took place during 2000 and 2001. The $13-million (£7-million) refurbishment project was the first since the museum opened in 1964. Over 2,000 new artifacts and information garnered from some 200 recent digs have been incorporated throughout the 23 rooms. In addition, new computerized touch-screen technology with video images and sound depicting rituals and customs are on display, providing visitors with a richer, more interactive experience. Exhibit signs now display English as well as Spanish explanations.

The museum has a lovely, moderately priced restaurant with cheerful patio tables. *Note:* Most of the museum is wheelchair accessible; however, assistance will be needed in places.

Paseo de la Reforma y Calzada Gandhi s/n, Chapultepec Polanco. (🕿 **55/5553-6266**. www.mna.inah.gob.mx. Admission $4.50 (£2.50); free Sun for residents of Mexico. Still camera $3 (£1.65), amateur video camera $4.50 (£2.50); no tripods or flash permitted. Tues–Sun 9am–7pm. Metro: Auditorio.

Palacio Nacional and the Diego Rivera Murals ✩✩   This complex of countless rooms, wide stone stairways, and numerous courtyards adorned with carved brass balconies is where the president of Mexico works. Even so, it's better known for the fabulous second-floor Diego Rivera murals depicting the history of Mexico. Begun in 1692 on the site of Moctezuma II's "new" palace, this building became the site of

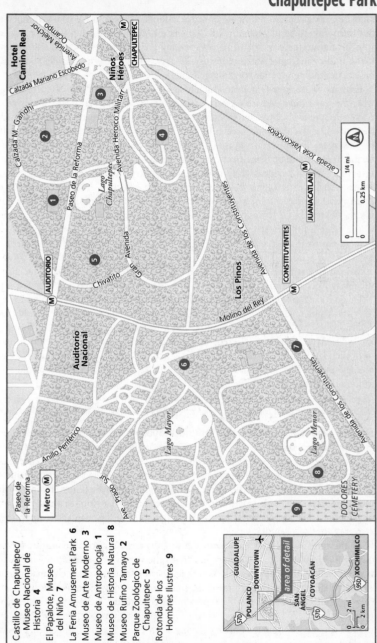

Castillo de Chapultepec/
Museo Nacional de
Historia **4**

El Papalote, Museo
del Niño **7**

La Feria Amusement Park **6**

Museo de Arte Moderno **3**

Museo de Antropología **1**

Museo de Historia Natural **8**

Museo Rufino Tamayo **2**

Parque Zoológico de
Chapultepec **5**

Rotonda de los
Hombres Ilustres **9**

Hernán Cortez's home and the residence of colonial viceroys. It has changed much in 300 years, taking on its present form in the late 1920s when the top floor was added. Just 30 minutes here with an English-speaking guide provides essential background for an understanding of Mexican history. The cost of a guide is negotiable: $8 (£4.40) or less, depending on your bargaining ability.

Enter by the central door, over which hangs the bell rung by Padre Miguel Hidalgo when he proclaimed Mexico's independence from Spain in 1810—the famous *grito.* Each September 15, Mexican Independence Day, the president of Mexico stands on the balcony above the door to echo Hidalgo's cry to the thousands of spectators who fill the *zócalo.* Take the stairs to the Rivera murals, which were painted over a 25-year period. The *Legend of Quetzalcoatl* depicts the famous tale of the feathered serpent bringing a blond-bearded white man to the country. When Cortez arrived, many Aztecs, recalling this legend, believed him to be Quetzalcoatl. Another mural tells of the American Intervention, when American invaders marched into Mexico City during the War of 1847. It was on this occasion that the military cadets of Chapultepec Castle (then a military school) fought bravely to the last man. The most notable of Rivera's murals is the *Great City of Tenochtitlán,* a study of the original settlement in the Valley of Mexico. The city is but a small part of the mural; the remainder is filled with what appear to be four million extras left over from a Hollywood epic, including the lovely Xochiquetzal, goddess of love, with her crown of flowers and tattooed legs.

Diego Rivera, one of Mexico's legendary muralists, left an indelible stamp on Mexico City, his painted political themes affecting the way millions view Mexican history. Additional examples of Rivera's stunning and provocative interpretations are found at the Bellas Artes, the National Preparatory School, the Department of Public Education, the National School of Agriculture at Chapingo, the National Institute of Cardiology, and the Museo Mural Diego Rivera (which houses the mural formerly located in the now-razed Hotel del Prado).

Palacio Nacional, Av. Pino Suárez, facing the *zócalo.* © 55/9158-1259. Free admission, but visitor tags required; be prepared to leave a form of photo identification in exchange. Mon–Fri 9am–4:45pm; Sat 10am–4:45pm. Metro: Zócalo.

Templo Mayor and Museo del Templo Mayor ★★★   In 1978, workmen digging on the east side of the Metropolitan Cathedral, next to the Palacio Nacional, unearthed an exquisite Aztec stone of the moon goddess Coyolxauhqui. Major excavations by Mexican archaeologists followed, and they uncovered interior remains of the Pyramid of Huitzilopochtli, also called the Templo Mayor (Great Temple)—the most important religious structure in the Aztec capital. What you see are the remains of pyramids that were covered by the great pyramid the Spaniards saw upon their arrival in the 16th century.

At the time of the 1521 Conquest, the site was the center of religious life for the city of 300,000. No other museum illustrates the variety and splendor of the Aztec Empire the way this one does. All 6,000 pieces came from the relatively small plot of excavated ruins just in front of the museum. Strolling along the walkways built over the site, visitors pass a water-collection conduit constructed during the presidency of Porfirio Díaz (1877–1911), as well as far earlier constructions. Shelters cover the ruins to protect traces of original paint and carving. Note especially the Tzompantli, or Altar of Skulls, a common Aztec and Maya design. Explanatory plaques with building dates are in Spanish.

The Museo del Templo Mayor (Museum of the Great Temple) opened in 1987. To enter it, take the walkway to the large building in the back portion of the site, which

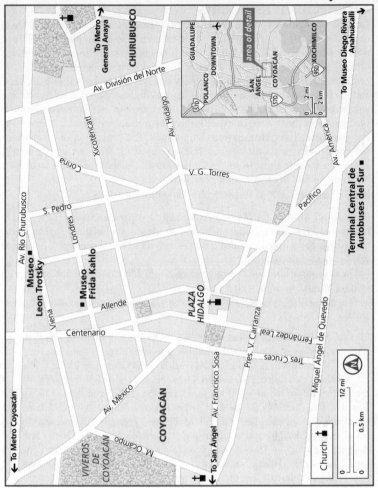

contains fabulous artifacts from on-site excavations. Inside the door, a model of
Tenochtitlán gives a good idea of the scale of the vast city of the Aztecs. The rooms
and exhibits, organized by subject, occupy many levels around a central open space.
You'll see some marvelous displays of masks, figurines, tools, jewelry, and other artifacts, including the huge stone wheel of the moon goddess Coyolxauhqui ("she with
bells painted upon her face") on the second floor. The goddess ruled the night, the
Aztec believed, but died at the dawning of every day, slain and dismembered by her
brother, Huitzilopochtli, the sun god.

Seminario 8, off the *zócalo*. © **55/5542-4943.** Fax 55/5542-1717. www.templomayor.inah.gob.mx. Admission to
museum and ruins $4.50 (£2.50); free Sun. Video camera permit $3.70 (£2.05); no flash photos. Tues–Sun 9am–5pm.
Metro: Zócalo.

ARCHITECTURAL HIGHLIGHTS

Casa de los Azulejos   This "House of Tiles" is one of Mexico City's most precious colonial gems and popular meeting places. Covered in gorgeous blue-and-white tiles, it dates from the end of the 1500s, when it was built for the count of the Valley of Orizaba. According to the oft-told story, during the count's defiant youth his father proclaimed: "You will never build a house of tiles." A tiled house was a sign of success, and the father was sure his son would amount to nothing. So when success came, the young count covered his house in tiles, a fine example of Puebla craftsmanship. The tiled murals in the covered courtyard, where the restaurant is located, were restored a few years back. Tile craftsmen from Saudi Arabia were brought in to ensure that the technique was true to the original 16th-century work. You can stroll through to admire the interior. Pause to see the Orozco mural, *Omniscience,* on the landing leading to the second floor (where the restrooms are).

Madero 4, Centro Histórico. ℭ 55/5512-9820. Daily 7am–1am. Metro: Bellas Artes.

Gran Hotel Ciudad de México   Originally a department store, the Gran Hotel boasts one of the most splendid interiors of any downtown building. Step inside to see the lavish lobby with gilded open elevators on both sides, topped with a breathtaking 1908 stained-glass canopy by Jacques Graber.

On the fourth floor, overlooking the *zócalo,* El Mirador restaurant makes a great stop for a coffee or drink with a view.

Av. 16 de Septiembre 82 at 5 de Febrero. ℭ 55/1083-7700. Free admission to view the lobby. Daily 24 hr. Metro: Zócalo.

Museo del Palacio de Bellas Artes ★★   Opulent and dramatic, the Bellas Artes is the masterpiece of theaters in this architecturally rich city. The exterior is early-20th-century Art Nouveau, built during the Porfiriato and covered in Italian Carrara marble. Inside, it's completely 1930s Art Deco. Since construction began in 1904, the theater (which opened in 1934) has sunk some 4m (13 ft.) into the soft belly of Lake Texcoco. The Palacio is the work of several masters: Italian architect Adamo Boari, who made the original plans; Antonio Muñoz and Federico Mariscal, who modified his plans considerably; and Mexican painter Gerardo Murillo ("Doctor Atl"), who designed the fabulous Art Nouveau glass curtain that was constructed by Louis Comfort Tiffany in the Tiffany Studios of New York. Made from nearly a million iridescent pieces of colored glass, the curtain portrays the Valley of Mexico with its two great volcanoes. You can see the curtain before important performances at the theater and on Sunday mornings.

In addition to being a concert hall, the theater houses permanent and traveling art shows. On the third level are famous murals by Rivera, Orozco, and Siqueiros. The controversial Rivera mural *Man in Control of His Universe* was commissioned in 1933 for Rockefeller Center in New York City. He completed the work there just as you see it: A giant vacuum sucks up the riches of the earth to feed the factories of callous, card-playing, hard-drinking white capitalist thugs—John D. Rockefeller himself among them—while all races of noble workers of the earth rally behind the red flag of socialism and its standard-bearer, Lenin. Needless to say, the Rockefellers weren't so keen on the new purchase. Much to their discredit, they had it painted over and destroyed. Rivera duplicated the mural here as *Man at the Crossing of the Ways* to preserve it. For information on tickets to performances of the **Ballet Folklórico,** see "Mexico City After Dark," later in this chapter.

San Angel

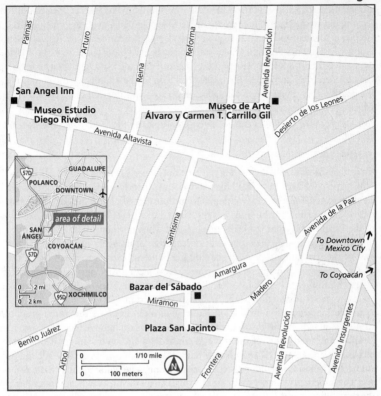

Warning: Avoid taxis parked in front of the Bellas Artes Theater and call for a radio taxi, instead.

Calle López Peralta, east end of La Alameda, Centro Histórico. ✆ 55/5512-2593, ext. 152. www.museobellasartes. artte.com. Free admission to view building when performances are not in progress; museum $3.50 (£1.95). Tues–Sun 10am–6pm. Metro: Bellas Artes.

Palacio de Minería Built in the 1800s, this "mining palace" is one of architect Manuel Tolsá's finest works—considered a masterpiece of Latin American neoclassicism—and one of the capital's handsomest buildings. Formerly the school of mining, it's occasionally used today for concerts and cultural events (and in those cases, the patio is often locked off). If it's open, step inside for a look at the patios and fabulous stonework. Guided tours are available.

Tacuba 5, Centro Histórico. ✆ 55/5623-2981. www.palaciomineria.unam.mx. Free admission. Wed–Sun 10am–6pm. Metro: Bellas Artes.

CEMETERIES
Rotonda de los Hombres Ilustres The din of traffic recedes in the serene resting place where Mexico's military, political, and artistic elite are buried. It's more like an outdoor monument museum than a cemetery; the stone markers stand in a double circle

around an eternal flame. A stroll here is a trip through who's who in Mexican history. Among the famous buried here are the artists Diego Rivera, David Alfaro Siqueiros, José Clemente Orozco, and Gerardo Murillo; presidents Sebastian Lerdo de Tejada, Valentín Gómez Farías, and Plutarco Calles; musicians Jaime Nunó (author of the Mexican national anthem), Juventino Rosas, and Agustín Lara; and outstanding citizens such as the philanthropist and writer Carlos Pellicer. Stop in the building at the entrance and the guard will give you a map with a list (in Spanish and English) of those buried here, which includes biographical information.

Constituyentes and Av. Civil Dolores, Dolores Cemetery, Chapultepec Park. Free admission. Daily 6am–6pm. Metro: Constituyentes.

CHURCHES

Catedral Metropolitana ★★★ The impressive, towering cathedral, begun in 1567 and finished in 1788, blends baroque, neoclassical, and Mexican churrigueresque architecture. As you look around the cathedral and the Sagrario (chapel) next to it, note how the building has sunk into the soft lake bottom beneath. The base of the facade is far from level and straight, and when one considers the weight of the immense towers—127,000 tons—it's no surprise. Scaffolding has become almost a part of the structure, in place to stabilize the building. However, much to the credit of Mexico City and its preservation efforts, the Catedral Metropolitana came off the World Monuments Fund's list of 100 Most Endangered Sites in 2000, as a result of an extensive reconstruction of the building's foundation.

In Mexico, the sacred ground of one religion often becomes the sacred ground of its successor. Cortez and his Spanish missionaries converted the Aztec, tore down their temples, and used much of the stone to construct a church on the spots of the temples that preceded it. The church they built was pulled down in 1628 while the present Metropolitan Cathedral was under construction. The building today has five naves and 14 chapels. As you wander past the small chapels, you may hear guides describing some of the cathedral's outstanding features: the tomb of Agustín Iturbide, placed here in 1838; a painting attributed to the Spanish artist Bartolomé Esteban Murillo; and the fact that the stone holy-water fonts ring like metal when tapped with a coin. Like many huge churches, it has catacombs underneath. The much older-looking church next to the cathedral is the chapel known as the Sagrario, another tour de force of Mexican baroque architecture built in the mid-1700s.

The Metropolitan Cathedral contains many prized works of art from the colonial era, in a variety of artistic styles. Jerónimo de Balbas built and carved the Altar de los Reyes (Altar of Kings) and the Altar del Perdón (Altar of Forgiveness) in 1737.

A sound-and-light show, "Voices of the Cathedral," takes visitors on a candlelit stroll through the cathedral, accompanied by period music. Tickets are $25 (£14), and are available through Ticketmaster (© **55/5325-9000**). The schedule of English-language performances changes periodically; call © **55/5521-7737** for details. Even if the presentation is in Spanish, it is mostly about choral music, so the language is not crucial for most visitors. Each Wednesday, the *Reforma* newspaper publishes the dates for the next 3 months of presentations.

As you walk around the outside of the cathedral, you will notice a reminder of medieval trade life. The west side is the gathering place of carpenters, plasterers, plumbers, painters, and electricians who have no shops. Craftspeople display the tools of their trades, sometimes along with pictures of their work. In front of the cathedral,

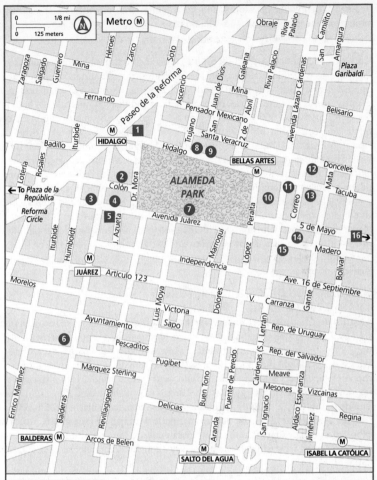

Metro Ⓜ

To Plaza de la República →

ALAMEDA PARK

GUADALUPE
POLANCO
DOWNTOWN
CHAPULTEPEC PARK
area of detail
SAN ÁNGEL
COYOACÁN
XOCHIMILCO

0   2 mi
0   2 km

ACCOMMODATIONS ■
Best Western Hotel de Cortés **1**
Holiday Inn Zócalo **16**
Sheraton Centro Histórico **5**

ATTRACTIONS ●
Casa de los Azulejos **14**
Correo (Post Office) **11**
FONART **3**
Juárez Monument **7**
La Torre Latinoamericana **15**

Mercado de la Ciudadela **6**
Museo Franz Mayer **8**
Museo Mural Diego Rivera **2**
Museo Nacional de Arte **12**
Museo Nacional de
la Estampa **9**
Palacio de Bellas Artes **10**
Palacio de Minería **13**
Plaza de la Solidaridad **4**

you can buy crystals, gemstones, and herbs, believed to provide special qualities of protection and cure from various afflictions.

The *zócalo*, on Cinco de Mayo, Centro Histórico. Free admission. Daily 7am–7pm. Metro: Zócalo.

Convent of San Bernardino de Siena   This 16th-century building is noted for its flower petals carved in stone—a signature of the Indians who did most of the work—on 16th-century *retablos* (painted boards) including one of three such altarpieces in the country that were created by pre-Hispanic Indians and that has miraculously been preserved for more than 400 years; most were destroyed by the Spaniards during the conquest and conversion to Christianity. The last Indian governor of Xochimilco, Apoxquiyohuatzin, is buried here. Inside and to the right, the skull over the font is from a pre-Hispanic skull rack signifying an Indian-Christian mixture of the concept of life and death. Eight lateral *retablos* date from the 16th to the 18th centuries. The fabulous gilt main altar, also from the 16th century, is like an open book with sculpture and religious paintings. A profusion of cherubic angels decorates columns and borders. Some of the altar paintings are attributed to Baltasar Echave Orio the Elder. Over the altar, above the figure of Christ, is San Bernardino with the *caciques* (local authorities) dressed in clothing with Indian elements, and without shoes.

Pino and Hidalgo (facing the main square), Xochimilco. Free admission. Daily 8am–8pm. *Tren ligero* (light train): Xochimilco.

HISTORIC BUILDINGS & MONUMENTS
CHAPULTEPEC PARK & POLANCO
Castillo de Chapultepec/Museo Nacional de Historia   This site had been occupied by a fortress since the days of the Aztec, although the present palace wasn't built until 1784. When open, the castle offered a beautiful view of Mexico City. During the French occupation of the 1860s, Empress Carlota (who designed the lovely garden surrounding the palace) could sit up in bed and watch her husband, Maximilian, proceeding down Reforma on his way to work. Later, this was the official home of Mexico's president until 1939. In 2004, archaeologists discovered an ancient Teotihuacán settlement behind the landmark, and are currently working on excavations, which are expected to demonstrate that the Teotihuacán culture spread and influenced the area around Mexico City earlier than previously thought, sometime between A.D. 300 and 600.

Chapultepec Park and Polanco. ✆ 55/5061-9211. www.castillodechapultepec.inah.gob.mx. Admission $4.50 (£2.50), free Sun. Tues–Sun 9am–5pm. Metro: Chapultepec.

ZONA ROSA & SURROUNDING AREAS
Monumento a los Héroes de la Independencia ✦   Without a doubt, the Monument to the Heroes of Independence is the most noted of Mexico City's exceptional public sculptures and monuments. The "Angel" is both a landmark and homage to those who lost their lives fighting for independence. It's also a central stage—along with the *zócalo*—for many of Mexico City's celebrations and mass demonstrations. Set upon a tall marble shaft, the golden angel is an important and easily discerned guidepost for travelers. A creation of Antonio Rivas Mercado, the 7m-high (23-ft.), gold-plated bronze angel, cast in Florence, Italy, was completed in 1906 at a cost of $2.5 (£1.5) million. With its base of marble and Italian granite, the monument's total height is 45m (148 ft.). It was renovated in 2006.

Intersection of Paseo de la Reforma, Florencia, and Río Tiber, Reforma/Zona Rosa. Metro: Sevilla.

CENTRO HISTORICO & SURROUNDING AREAS

Monumento a la Revolución and Museo Nacional de la Revolución The Art Deco Monument to the Revolution, in the large **Plaza de la República,** has a curious history. The government of Porfirio Díaz, who was perennially "reelected" president of Mexico, began construction of what was intended to be a new legislative chamber. However, only the dome was raised by the time the Mexican Revolution (1910) put an end to his plans, not to mention his dictatorship. In the 1930s, after the revolutionary turmoil had died down, the dome was finished as a monument. The remains of two revolutionary presidents, Francisco Madero and Venustiano Carranza, were entombed in two of its pillars, and it was dedicated to the Revolution. Later, presidents Plutarco Elías Calles and Lázaro Cárdenas were also buried there. (*Note:* At the time of his death, Calles was buried at La Rotonda de los Hombres Ilustres. His body was then moved to the Monumento a la Revolución by an order of President Díaz Ordaz in 1969. A plaque honoring him still remains at the Rotunda, but his actual body is at the Monumento.)

Beneath the Monument to the Revolution is the **Museo Nacional de la Revolución** (enter directly across from the Frontón). It chronicles the tumultuous years from 1867 to 1917—when the present constitution was signed—in excellent exhibits of documents, newspaper stories, photographs, drawings, clothing, costumes, uniforms, weapons, and furnishings.

Av. Juárez and La Fragua, Plaza de la República s/n, Col. Tabacalera beneath the Monumento a la Revolución. (C) 55/ 5536-2115 or 5566-1902. Admission $1.40 (80p); free Sun. Tues–Sun 9am–5pm. From the Colón Monument on Reforma, walk 2 blocks north on I. Ramírez; the monument looms ahead. Metro: Revolución.

Secretaría de Educación Pública Originally built in 1922 as a convent, it became the home of the Secretary of Public Education in 1922 and was decorated with a great series of more than 200 Diego Rivera murals, dating from 1923 and 1928, that cover over 1,500 sq. m (16,146 sq. ft.) of wall space. Other artists did a panel here and there, but the Rivera murals are the most outstanding.

República de Argentina 28, near República de Brasil. (C) 55/5328-1097. www.sep.gob.mx. Free admission. Mon–Fri 9am–5pm. Metro: Allende.

Suprema Corte de Justicia The Supreme Court of Justice, built between 1935 and 1941, is the highest court in the country. Inside, on the main staircase and its landings, are Orozco murals depicting a theme of justice.

Pino Suárez and Corregidora, Centro Histórico. No phone. Free admission. Mon–Fri 9am–5:30pm. Metro: Zócalo.

OTHER MUSEUMS & GALLERIES
CHAPULTEPEC PARK & POLANCO

Museo de Arte Moderno The Museum of Modern Art is known for having the best permanent exhibition of painters and sculptors from the modern Mexican art movement. It also features some of the most important temporary exhibitions of national and international modern art in the world. Representing the Mexican muralist movement are significant works by the three greats: Diego Rivera, José Clemente Orozco, and David Alfaro Siqueiros. The main building is a round, two-story structure with a central staircase. Two of the museum's four spaces showcase the permanent collection, which also contains works by Mexico's other modern masters—Tamayo, José Luis Cuevas, Alejandro Colunga, Francisco Toledo, and Vladamir Cora. The remaining two spaces house visiting exhibitions. The museum's surrounding gardens exhibit large-scale public sculptures.

Chapultepec Park. (✆ **55/5553-6233**. www.conaculta.gob.mx/mam. Admission $2 (£1.10); discounts for students and teachers w/ID; free Sun. Tues–Sun 10am–5:30pm. Metro: Chapultepec.

Museo de Historia Natural de la Ciudad de Mexico (*Kids*) The 10 interconnecting domes that form the Museum of Natural History contain stuffed and preserved animals and birds; tableaux of different natural environments with the appropriate wildlife; exhibits on geology, astronomy, biology, and the origin of life; and more. It's a fascinating place for anyone with the slightest curiosity about nature and is totally absorbing for youngsters.

Chapultepec Park, Section 2. (✆ **55/5516-2848**. Admission $2 (£1.10); free Tues. Tues–Sun 10am–5pm. Metro: Constituyentes.

Museo Rufino Tamayo (✦) Oaxaca-born painter Rufino Tamayo not only contributed a great deal to modern Mexican painting, but also collected pre-Hispanic, Mexican, and foreign works, including pieces by de Kooning, Warhol, Dalí, and Magritte. Tamayo's pre-Hispanic collection is in Oaxaca, but here you can see a number of his works and the remainder of his collection (unless a special exhibit has temporarily displaced them).

Chapultepec Park. (✆ **55/5286-6519**. www.museotamayo.org. Admission $1.50 (85p); free Sun. Tues–Sun 10am–6pm. Metro: Chapultepec.

Papalote, Museo del Niño (*Kids*) The Building of the Pyramids at this interactive children's museum holds most of the more than 350 exhibits, while two films alternate (10 shows daily) in the IMAX building. There's virtually nothing here that children can't touch; once they discover this, they'll want to stay a long time. As they say, adults must be accompanied by children, except on Thursday, when the museum is open until 11pm to give "big kids" a chance to enjoy it themselves.

Av. de los Constituyentes 268, Chapultepec Park, Section 2. (✆ **55/5237-1700** or 5237-1777. www.papalote.org. mx. Admission to museum $8.50 (£4.76) adults, $8 (£4.50) children; admission to museum and IMAX show $11 (£6.15) adults, $10 (£5.60) children. Mon–Fri 9am–6pm; Thurs 9am–11pm; Sat–Sun and holidays 10am–7pm. Metro: Constituyentes.

CENTRO HISTORICO & SURROUNDING AREAS

Museo de la Ciudad de México Before you enter the Museum of Mexico City, go to the corner of República del Salvador and look at the enormous stone serpent head, a corner support at the building's base. The stone was once part of an Aztec pyramid. At the entrance, a stone doorway opens to the courtyard of this mansion, built in 1778 as the House of the Counts of Santiago de Calimaya. This classic building became the Museum of the City of Mexico in 1964; it's a must for anyone interested in the country's past. Dealing solely with the Mexico Valley, where the first people arrived around 8000 B.C., the museum contains some fine maps, pictographic presentations of the initial settlements, and outlines of the social organization as it developed, as well as models of several famous buildings. Upstairs is the studio of Mexican Impressionist Joaquín Clausell (1866–1935). There's a good bookstore to the left after you enter.

Pino Suárez 30, Centro Histórico. (✆ **55/5542-0487**. www.cultura.df.gob.mx. Free admission. Tues–Sun 10am–6pm. Metro: Zócalo.

Museo Franz Mayer One of the capital's foremost museums, the Franz Mayer Museum opened in 1986 in a beautifully restored 16th-century building on Plaza de la Santa Veracruz on the north side of La Alameda. The extraordinary 10,000-piece collection of antiques, mostly Mexican objects from the 16th through 19th centuries, was amassed by one man: Franz Mayer. A German immigrant, he adopted Mexico as his home in 1905 and grew rich here. Before his death in 1975, Mayer bequeathed the collection to the country and arranged for its permanent display through a trust with the Banco Nacional. The pieces, mostly utilitarian objects (as opposed to pure art objects), include inlaid and richly carved furniture; an enormous collection of Talavera pottery; gold and silver religious pieces; sculptures; tapestries; rare watches and clocks (the oldest is a 1680 lantern clock); wrought iron; old-master paintings from Europe and Mexico; and 770 *Don Quixote* volumes, many of which are rare editions or typographically unique. There's so much here that it may take two visits to absorb it all. In the central courtyard, a pleasant cafe serves coffee and light snacks.

Av. Hidalgo 45, next to Plaza Santa Cruz, Col. Guerrero. ✆ 55/5518-2265. www.franzmayer.org.mx. Admission $3.40 (£1.90); free Tues. Tues–Sun 10am–5pm (Wed until 7pm). Guided tours by appointment Mon–Sat 10:30, 11:30am, and 12:30pm. Metro: Hidalgo or Bellas Artes.

Museo José Luis Cuevas　José Luis Cuevas is one of Mexico's leading contemporary artists, though early in his career, he was considered the "enfant terrible" of Mexican plastic arts. To this day, he can arouse controversy, and is known to draw throngs of women wherever he appears. The center that bears his name opened in 1992 and is filled with about 1,000 paintings, drawings, and sculptures donated by Cuevas, including many of his own. Don't miss the Erotic Room, a permanent exhibit of his erotic paintings, photographs, and erotic objects from the artist's personal collection. Housed in the 16th century Convento de Santa Inés, the museum includes many works by other contemporary Latin American artists, as well as a large collection of Picassos.

Calle Academia 13, 2 blocks northeast of the Palacio Nacional and across from the Academia de San Carlos, Centro Histórico. ✆ 55/5542-6198. www.museojoseluiscuevas.com.mx. Admission $1. Tues–Sun 10am–5:30pm. Metro: Zócalo.

Museo Mural Diego Rivera　This museum houses Diego Rivera's famous mural *Dream of a Sunday Afternoon in Alameda Park,* which was painted on a wall of the Hotel Prado in 1947. The hotel was demolished after the 1985 earthquake, but the precious mural, perhaps the best known of Rivera's works, was saved and transferred to its new location in 1986. The huge picture, 15m (49 ft.) long and 4m (13 ft.) high, chronicles the history of the park from the time of Cortez onward. Portrayed in the mural are numerous historical figures. More or less from left to right, but not in chronological order, they include: Cortez; a heretic suffering under the Spanish Inquisition; Sor Juana Inés de la Cruz, a brilliant, progressive woman who became a nun to continue her scholarly pursuits; Benito Juárez, seen putting forth the laws of Mexico's great Reforma; the conservative Gen. Antonio López de Santa Anna, handing the keys to Mexico to the invading American Gen. Winfield Scott; Emperor Maximilian and Empress Carlota; José Martí, the Cuban revolutionary; Death, with the plumed serpent (Quetzalcoatl) entwined about his neck; Gen. Porfirio Díaz, great with age and medals, asleep; a police officer keeping La Alameda free of "riffraff" by ordering a poor family out of the elitists' park; and Francisco Madero, the martyred democratic president who caused the downfall of Díaz, and whose betrayal and alleged murder by Gen. Victoriano Huerta (pictured on the right) resulted in years of civil turmoil.

Plaza de la Solidaridad (at Balderas and Colón), Centro Histórico–Alameda. ✆ 55/5512-0754. Admission $1.50 (85p); free Sun. Tues–Sun 10am–6pm. Metro: Hidalgo.

Museo Nacional de Arte (Munal)   The National Art Museum's palacelike building, designed by Italian architect Silvio Contri and completed in 1911—a legacy of Europe-loving Porfirio Díaz's era—was built to house the government's offices of Communications and Public Works. Díaz occupied the opulent second-floor salon, where he welcomed visiting dignitaries. The National Museum of Art took over the building in 1982. Wander through the immense rooms with polished wooden floors as you view the wealth of paintings showing Mexico's art development, primarily covering the period from 1810 to 1950. There's a nice cafe on the second floor.

Tacuba 8, Centro Histórico. ✆ **55/5130-3400** or -3410. Fax 55/5130-3401. www.munal.com.mx. Admission $3 (£1.65); free Sun. Tues–Sun 10:30am–5:30pm. Metro: Allende.

Museo Nacional de la Estampa   *Estampa* means "engraving" or "printing," and this museum is devoted to understanding and preserving the graphic arts. The beautifully restored 16th-century building holds both permanent and changing exhibits. Displays include those from pre-Hispanic times, when clay seals were used for designs on fabrics, ceramics, and other surfaces. But the most famous works here are probably those of José Guadalupe Posada, Mexico's famous printmaker, who poked fun at death and politicians through his skeleton figure drawings. If your interest in this subject is deep, ask to see the video programs on graphic techniques—woodcuts, lithography, etchings, and the like.

Av. Hidalgo 39 (next door to the Museo Franz Mayer), Centro Histórico–Alameda. ✆ **55/5521-2244**. Admission $1 (55p); free Sun. Tues–Sun 10am–5:30pm. Metro: Bellas Artes.

Museo Nacional de San Carlos   The San Carlos Museum exhibits 15th- to 19th-century European paintings. The museum was once the Academy of San Carlos, an art school that some of the country's great painters—Rivera and Orozco among them—attended. Architect Manuel Tolsá built the beautiful mansion in the early 1800s; it was later the home of the Marqués de Buenavista. The rooms on the first and second floors hold some of Mexico's best paintings, by both Mexican and European artists. Another gallery holds prints and engravings. In the mansion's elliptical court are displays of 19th-century Mexican statuary and busts by Manuel Vilar and his pupils, and off to one side is a pretty garden court shaded by rubber trees.

Puente de Alvarado 50 (at Arizpe). ✆ **55/5566-8085**. Fax 55/5535-1256. Admission $2.50 (£1.40); free Sun. Wed–Mon 10am–6pm. Walk 5½ blocks west of La Alameda (2½ blocks west of San Fernando Plaza). Metro: Revolución.

SOUTHERN NEIGHBORHOODS

Museo Arqueológico de Xochimilco   The building dates from 1904, when it was the pump house for the springs. It houses artifacts from the area, many of them found when residents built their homes. These include 10,000-year-old mammoth bones; figures dating from the Teotihuacán period, including representations of Tlaloc (god of water and life), Ehecatl (god of the wind), Xipe Totec (god of renewal and of plants), and Huehueteotl (god of fire); polychrome pottery; carved abalone; and tombs showing funerary practices. One unique piece is a clay figure of a child holding a bouquet of flowers.

Av. Tenochtitlán and Calle La Planta, Santa Cruz Acalpixcan. ✆/fax **55/2157-1757**. Free admission. Tues–Sun 10am–4:30pm. From Xochimilco (see "Mexico City Neighborhoods in Brief," earlier in this chapter), take a cab or microbus to Tulyehualco. The museum is at Tenochtitlán and La Planta, on the left.

Museo Diego Rivera Anahuacalli 🍀   Not to be confused with the Museo Estudio Diego Rivera near the San Angel Inn (see below), this is probably the most unusual museum in the city. Designed by Rivera before his death in 1957, it's devoted to his works as well as his extensive collection of pre-Columbian art. With over 52,000 pieces, it is the largest private collection displayed in Mexico. Constructed of pedregal (the lava rock in which the area abounds), it resembles Maya and Aztec architecture. Anahuacalli means "House of Mexico"; *Anahuac* was the old name for the ancient Valley of Mexico.

In front of the museum is a reproduction of a Toltec ball court, and the entrance to the museum is a coffin-shaped door. Twenty-three display rooms are arranged in chronological order, with thousands of pieces stashed on the shelves, tucked away in corners, and peeking out of glass cases.

Upstairs, in a replica of Rivera's studio, you'll find the original sketches for some of his murals and two in-progress canvases. There's a photo of his first sketch (of a train), done at the age of 3, plus a color photograph of him at work later in life. Rivera (1886–1957) studied in Europe for 15 years and spent much of his life as a devoted Marxist. Yet he came through political scrapes and personal tragedies with no apparent diminution of creative energy. A plaque in the museum proclaims him "a man of genius who is among the greatest painters of all time." This is one of the most popular places in Mexico to come for Day of the Dead on November 2.

Calle del Museo 150, Col. San Pablo Tepetlapa. (C) **55/5617-3797**. www.diegorivera.com. Admission $4.50 (£2.50). Tues–Sun 10am–5pm. Metro: Taxqueña; then *tren ligero* (light train) to Xotepingo; go west on Xotepingo (Museo) 3 short blocks; cross División del Norte and go another 6 blocks.

Museo de Arte Carrillo Gil (MACG)
Sometimes called the Museo de la Esquina (Corner Museum)—it's at a major intersection on Avenida de la Revolución—this modern gallery features a collection that includes rooms dedicated to the works of José Clemente Orozco (1883–1949), Diego Rivera (1886–1957), David Alfaro Siqueiros (1896–1974), and other Mexican painters. The museum is not accessible by Metro.

Revolución 1608 (at Desierto de los Leónes), Col. San Angel. (C) **55/5550-3983**. www.macg.inba.gob.mx. Admission $1.50 (85p); free Sun. Tues–Sun 10am–6pm.

Museo Dolores Olmedo Patiño 🔆
Art collector and philanthropist Olmedo left her former home, the grand Hacienda La Noria, as a museum featuring the works of her friend Diego Rivera. At least 137 of his works are displayed here, including his portrait of Olmedo, 25 paintings of Frida Kahlo, and 37 creations of Angelina Beloff (Rivera's first wife), many of them drawings and engravings. Among the notable Kahlo works here is her famed *The Broken Column*, which is considered the artistic embodiment of her physical suffering, the result of a trolley accident that pierced her spine when she was young. Besides the paintings, there are fine pre-Hispanic pieces on display, colonial furniture and other hacienda artifacts, and a collection of folk art. An excellent gift shop and a cafeteria are on the premises. Olmedo was the executor of both the Rivera and Kahlo estates, a close friend and former lover of Diego's, and a rival to Frida. Olmedo died in 2002, recognized as one of the most astute collectors of contemporary Mexican art.

Av. México 5843, Col. La Noria, Xochimilco. (C) **55/5555-1016** or -0891. Fax 55/5555-1642. Admission $3.50 (£1.95), free on Tues. Tues–Sun 10am–6pm. Metro: Taxqueña; then *tren ligero* (light train) to Xochimilco. Get off at the La Noria station.

Museo Estudio Diego Rivera
Here, in the studio designed and built by Juan O'Gorman in 1928, Rivera drew sketches for his wonderful murals and painted smaller works. He died here in 1957. Now a museum, the Rivera studio holds some

of the artist's personal effects and mementos, as well as changing exhibits relating to his life and work. (Don't confuse Rivera's studio with his museum, the Anahuacalli; see above.) The museum is not accessible by Metro.

Calle Diego Rivera and Av. Altavista (across from San Angel Inn), Col. San Angel. ✆ 55/5616-0996. Admission $1 (55p); free Sun. Tues–Sun 10am–6pm. By taxi, go up Insurgentes Sur to Altavista and make a left.

Museo León Trotsky   During Lenin's last days, Stalin and Trotsky fought a silent battle for leadership of the Communist Party in the Soviet Union. Trotsky stuck to ideology, while Stalin took control of the party mechanism. Stalin won, and Trotsky was exiled to continue his ideological struggle elsewhere. Invited by Diego Rivera, an ardent admirer of his work, he settled here on the outskirts of Mexico City to continue his writings on political topics and Communist ideology.

His ideas clashed with those of Stalin in many respects, and Stalin, wanting no opposition or dissension in the world Communist ranks, set out to have Trotsky assassinated. A first attempt failed, but it served as a warning to Trotsky, his wife, Natalia, and their household. The house became a veritable fortress, with watchtowers, thick steel doors, and round-the-clock guards, several of whom were Americans who sympathized with Trotsky's philosophies. Finally, a man thought to have been paid, cajoled, or blackmailed by Stalin, directly or indirectly, was able to gain admittance to the house by posing as a friend of Trotsky's and a believer of his political views. On August 20, 1940, he put an ice pick into the philosopher's head. The assailant was caught, and Trotsky died of his wounds shortly afterward. Because Trotsky and Rivera had previously had a falling out—Trotsky was having an affair with Rivera's wife, Frida Kahlo—Rivera was a suspect for a short time.

You can visit Natalia's study, the communal dining room, and Trotsky's study— with worksheets, newspaper clippings, books, and cylindrical wax dictating records still spread around—as well as the fortresslike bedroom. Some of the walls bear the bullet holes left from the first attempt on his life. Trotsky's tomb, designed by Juan O'Gorman, is in the garden. You can recognize this house by the brick riflemen's watchtowers on top of the high stone walls.

Av. Río Churubusco 410 (between Gómez Farías and Morelos), Col. Del Carmen Coyoacán. ✆ 55/5658-8732 or 5554-0687. Admission $3 (£1.65). Tues–Sun 10am–5pm. Metro: Coyoacán. From Plaza Hidalgo, go east on Hidalgo 3 blocks to Morelos, then north 8 blocks to Churubusco; house is on the left.

OUTDOOR ART/PLAZAS

Plaza de las Tres Culturas   Three cultures converge here: Aztec, Spanish, and contemporary Mexican. Surrounded by modern office and apartment buildings are large remains of the **Aztec city of Tlatelolco,** site of the last battle of the conquest of Mexico. Off to one side is the **Church of Santiago.** During the Aztec Empire, Tlatelolco was on the edge of Lake Texcoco, linked to the Aztec capital by a causeway. Bernal Díaz de Castillo, in his *True Story of the Conquest of New Spain,* described the roar from the dazzling market there, and the incredible scene after the last battle of the conquest in Tlatelolco on August 13, 1521—the dead bodies were piled so deep that walking there was impossible. That night determined the fate of the country and completed the Spanish takeover of Mexico. It was also here, in October 1968, that government troops fired on thousands of protesters who filled the square, killing hundreds.

View the pyramidal remains from raised walkways over the site. The church, off to one side, was built in the 16th century entirely of volcanic stone. The interior has been tastefully restored, preserving little patches of fresco in stark-white plaster walls, with a few deep-blue stained-glass windows and an unadorned stone altar. Sunday is a good day to combine a visit here with one to the Lagunilla street market (see "Shopping," below), which is within walking distance, south across Reforma.

Lázaro Cárdenas and Flores Magón, Centro Histórico. Metro: Tlatelolco.

Plaza de Santo Domingo   This fascinating plaza—a wonderful slice of Mexican life—has arcades on one side, a Dominican church on another. A statue of the Corregidora of Querétaro, Josefa Ortiz de Domínguez, dominates the plaza. The plaza is best known for the scribes who compose and type letters for clients unable to do so. Years ago, it was full of professional writers clacking away on typewriters, and a few still ply their trade on ancient electric typewriters among a proliferation of small print shops and presses. Emperor Cuauhtémoc's palace once occupied this land, before Dominicans built their monastery here.

Bordered by República de Venezuela, República de Brasil, República de Cuba, and Palma, Centro Histórico. Metro: Tacuba.

Zócalo ★★   Every Spanish colonial city in North America was laid out according to a textbook plan, with a plaza at the center surrounded by a church, government buildings, and military headquarters. Because Mexico City was the capital of New Spain, its *zócalo* is one of the grandest, graced on all sides by stately 17th-century buildings. The Plaza de la Constitución, as this square is officially called, is also one of the three biggest public squares in the world.

Zócalo actually means "pedestal" or "plinth." A grand monument to Mexico's independence was planned and the pedestal built, but the project was never completed. Nevertheless, the pedestal became a landmark for visitors, and soon everyone was calling the square the *zócalo,* even after the pedestal was removed. It covers almost 4 hectares (10 acres) and is bounded on the north by Cinco de Mayo, on the east by Pino Suárez, on the south by 16 de Septiembre, and on the west by Nacional Monte de Piedad. The downtown district—especially north of the Templo Mayor, one of the oldest archaeological sites in the city—is currently undergoing an important restoration project that is renewing much of its colonial charm. Occupying the entire east side of the *zócalo* is the majestic red tezontle-stone Palacio National, seat of the Mexican national government, and on the northern border is the Catedral Metropolitana.

Juárez and 20 de Noviembre, Centro Histórico. Metro: Zócalo.

PARKS & GARDENS
Alameda Park   Today the lovely tree-filled Alameda Park attracts pedestrians, cotton-candy vendors, strollers, lovers, and organ grinders. Long ago, the site was an Aztec marketplace. When the conquistadors took over in the mid-1500s, heretics were burned at the stake here under the Spanish Inquisition. In 1592, the governor of New Spain, Viceroy Luis de Velasco, converted it to a public park. Within the park, known as La Alameda, is the **Juárez Monument,** sometimes called the **Hemiciclo** (hemicycle, or half-circle), facing Avenida Juárez. Enthroned as the hero he was, Juárez assumes his proper place here in the pantheon of Mexican patriots. European (particularly French) sculptors created most of the other statuary in the park in the late 19th and early 20th centuries.

Av. Juárez and Lázaro Cárdenas. Free admission. Metro: Bellas Artes.

Chapultepec Park   One of the biggest city parks in the world, 220-hectare (543-acre) Chapultepec Park is more than a playground; it's virtually the centerpiece of the city. Besides accommodating picnickers on worn-away grass under centuries-old trees, it has canoes on the lake; jogging and bridle paths; vendors selling balloons, souvenirs, and food; a miniature train; and **Los Pinos,** home of Mexico's president. The park is also home to the **City Zoo** and **La Feria** amusement park. Most important for tourists, it contains a number of interesting museums, including the Museo Nacional de Antropología.

Between Paseo de la Reforma, Circuito Interior, and Av. Constituyentes. Free admission. Daily 5am–5pm. Metro: Chapultepec.

Floating Gardens of Xochimilco 🌟   In the southern neighborhood of Xochimilco are more than 80km (50 miles) of canals known as the Floating Gardens. They consist of two main parts. The first is the tourism-oriented area in the Historic Center of town, where colorful boats called *trajineras* take loads of tourists through a portion of the canals. Lively music, some of it provided by mariachi musicians for hire who board the gondolas, is a staple. Historic buildings, restaurants, souvenir stands, curio sellers, and boat vendors border this area. The other section, north of the center of town, is the ecology-oriented area, or Parque Natural Xochimilco. On Sunday, Xochimilco is jammed; on weekdays, it's nearly deserted. As you enter Xochimilco proper, you will see many places to board boats. Should you miss them, turn along Madero and follow signs that say LOS EMBARCADEROS (the piers).

Southern neighborhood of Xochimilco. ✆ 55/5673-7890. Admission to area $2 (£1.10); boat rides $14–$16 (£7.70–£8.80) per boat per hour, which up to 14–18 people may share. Daily 9am–6pm.

BEST VIEW

La Torre Latinoamericana   From the observation deck on the 44th floor of this soaring skyscraper, the Latin American Tower, you can take in fabulous views of the whole city. Buy a ticket for the deck at the booth as you approach the elevators. Tokens for the telescope are on sale here, too. You then take an elevator to the 42nd floor, cross the hall, and take another elevator to the 44th floor. An employee will ask for your ticket as you get off.

Madero and Lázaro Cárdenas, Centro Histórico. ✆ 55/5518-7423. www.ociopuro.org/torre. Admission $5 (£2.75) adults, $4 (£2.20) children. Daily 9am–10pm. Metro: Bellas Artes.

6 Organized Tours

Mexico City is a great place for looking around on your own, and in general this is the easiest and least expensive way to see what you like. But if your time is limited, you may want to acclimate yourself quickly by taking a tour or two.

Among the noncommercial offerings are **free guided tours** sponsored by the **Mexico City Historical Center** (✆ **55/5345-8000,** ext. 1499), in the 18th-century home of Don Manuel de Heras y Soto, at Donceles and República de Chile. Groups meet each Sunday at 10:45am at a central gathering place for that day's tour, which varies from week to week. These tours might explore a historic downtown street, cafes and theaters, cemeteries, or the colonial churches of Xochimilco. Most tours, which last about 2 hours, are in Spanish; as many as 300 people may be divided among 10 guides. Visitors can ask a day in advance for a guide who speaks their language. The center's phone is almost always busy, so you may opt to visit the office, in the far back

Tips **Tours: The Downside**

Many readers have written to say they were unhappy with the sightseeing tours of this or that company. The reasons are myriad: The tour was too rushed; the guide knew nothing and made up stories about the sights; the tour group spent most of its time in a handicrafts shop (chosen by the tour company) rather than seeing the sights. Do tour companies get a kickback from souvenir shops? Of course! If you meet someone who has recently taken a guided tour and liked it, go with the same company. Otherwise, you might do well to see the sights on your own, following the detailed information in this book. Your hotel can arrange a private car by the hour or day—generally with a driver who is also an English-speaking guide. This can cost less or only slightly more than an organized tour, with greater flexibility and personalized service.

of the building, on the right and up a spiral staircase, to get a list of upcoming tours and gathering locations. Office hours are Monday through Friday from 9am to 3pm and 6 to 9pm.

The many commercial tours include a 4-hour city tour of such sites as the **Metropolitan Cathedral,** the **National Palace,** and **Chapultepec Park and Castle;** a longer tour to the **Shrine of Guadalupe** and nearby pyramids at **Teotihuacán;** and the Sunday tour that begins with the **Ballet Folklórico,** moves on to the **Floating Gardens of Xochimilco,** and may or may not include lunch and the afternoon bullfights. Almost as popular are 1-day and overnight tours to Puebla, Cuernavaca, Taxco, and Acapulco. There are also several nightclub tours. Book through your hotel concierge or tour desk.

7 Shopping

From handicrafts to the finest in designer apparel, Mexico City, like any major metropolitan area, is a marvelous place for shopping. From malls to *mercados,* numerous places display fascinating native products and sophisticated goods.

The two best districts for browsing are on and off **Avenida Presidente Masaryk,** in Polanco, and the **Zona Rosa.** Polanco's shops include Burberrys of London, Christian Dior, Versace, Gucci, Hermès, Luis Vuitton, Giorgio Armani, Tiffany's, and Cartier. Think New York's Madison Avenue, Beverly Hills's Rodeo Drive, or Chicago's Magnificent Mile, and you'll get the picture. The 12 square blocks at the heart of the Zona Rosa are home to antiques shops, boutiques, art galleries, silver shops, and fine jewelers. A few unique shops deserve particular mention.

Several government-run shops and a few excellent private shops have exceptionally good collections of Mexico's arts and crafts. Here's the rundown on the best places to shop, from small crafts shops to vast general markets.

SHOPPING A TO Z
ART
Artesanos de México   This shop in the Zona Rosa sells crafts from all over Mexico. It isn't large, but it's a good place to see handsome displays of pottery, textiles, and original art. It's open Monday through Saturday from 10:30am to 7pm. Londres 117 Altos, Zona Rosa. ✆ 55/5514-7455. Metro: Insurgentes.

Arvil. Galería de Arte y Libros de Arte   Collectible works of art—auction-quality pieces—by Mexican masters. It's open by appointment only, Monday through Friday from 10am to 2:30pm and 4 to 7pm, and Saturday from 10am to 3pm. Cerrada de Hamburgo 7 and 9, Reforma/Zona Rosa. ℭ **55/5207-2647.** Fax 55/5207-3994. Metro: Insurgentes.

Exposición Nacional de Arte Popular (FONART)   This store is usually loaded with crafts: papier-mâché figurines, textiles, earthenware, colorful candelabras, hand-carved wooden masks, straw goods, beads, bangles, and glass. The Fonda Nacional para el Fomento de las Artes (FONART), a government organization that helps village craftspeople, operates the store. It's open daily from 9am to 8pm. Juárez 89, Centro Histórico. ℭ **55/5521-0171.** www.fonart.gob.mx. Metro: Hidalgo or Juárez.

López Quiroga Gallery   Auction-quality works of art by contemporary Latin American masters, including Toledo, Tamayo, and Siqueiros. The gallery is not accessible by Metro; take a cab. It's open Monday to Friday 10am to 7pm and Saturday from 10am to 2pm. Aristóteles 169, Polanco. ℭ **55/5280-1247.** Fax 55/5280-3960. www.arte-mexico.com.

O.M.R. Gallery   This gallery has earned a reputation for discovering and introducing emerging talents and new artists from Latin America. It's open Monday through Friday from 10am to 3pm and 4 to 7pm, Saturday from 10am to 2pm. Plaza Río de Janeiro 54, Col. Roma. ℭ **55/5511-1179,** 5525-3095, or 5207-1080. Fax: 55/5533-4244. Metro: Insurgentes.

Víctor Artes Populares Mexicanas   Owned by the Fosado family, which has been in the folk art business for more than 50 years, Víctor, near La Alameda, is a shop for serious buyers and collectors. The Fosados buy most of their crafts from Indian villages. It's open Monday through Friday from 12:30pm to 7pm, and Saturdays by appointment only. Fco. I. Madero 10 (3rd floor entrance, near the perfume store), room 305, Centro Histórico. ℭ **55/5512-1263.** Metro: Bellas Artes or Allende.

JEWELRY
Besides the shops mentioned below, dozens of jewelry stores and optical shops are on Madero from Motolinia to the *zócalo,* in the portals facing the National Palace. **Nacional Monte de Piedad (National Pawn Shop),** also opposite the National Palace, has an enormous jewelry selection. The first Latin American branch of **Tiffany's** is on Avenida Presidente Masaryk in Polanco.

Bazar del Centro   Located between La Alameda and the *zócalo,* this colonial-era building was the palace of the Counts of Miravale. Now it houses shops selling jewelry, precious stones, and silver. It's open Monday through Friday from 10am to 7pm and Saturday from 10am to 3pm. Isabel la Católica 30, Centro Histórico. No phone. Metro: Zócalo.

Tane   Tucked in the lobby of the hotel Presidente InterContinental, this is one of the branches of one of Mexico's top silver designers, with other locations found only in the best hotels and shopping centers. The quantity of good-quality silver work is enormous. You'll see jewelry, platters, pitchers, plates, cutlery, frames, candlesticks, and even the signature china, by Limoges. There are also branches in the Polanco and San Angel neighborhoods, and at the airport. It's open Monday through Friday from 10am to 7pm and Saturday from 11am to 3pm. Campos Eliseos 218 (at corner of Andrés Bello), Col. Polanco. ℭ **55/5281-0820.** www.tane.com.mx. Metro: Auditorio.

MARKETS
Bazar del Sábado *(Moments*   A festive and unique shopping experience, the Bazar del Sábado is held (as its name indicates) only on Saturday. Located in an expensive colonial-era suburb of cobblestone streets, mansions, and parks a few kilometers south of

the city, it's my top recommendation for passing a Saturday afternoon in Mexico City. The actual bazaar building is an elegant two-story mansion built around a courtyard.

The central area houses an excellent, authentic, hectic Mexican cafe where waiters hustle to serve tacos hot off the grill and frosty margaritas, plus *antojitos* (finger foods) and traditional main dishes such as enchiladas. Marimba music plays in the background. Dozens of small rooms surrounding the courtyard serve as permanent stalls featuring original works of high-quality decorative art. You'll find blown glass, original fine jewelry, papier-mâché figures, masks, and embroidered clothing. The prices are on the high side, but the quality is equally high, and the designs are sophisticated. On adjacent plazas, hundreds of easel artists display their paintings, and surrounding homes abound with antiques, fine rugs, and hand-carved furniture for sale. Members of indigenous groups from Puebla and elsewhere bring their folk art—baskets, masks, pottery, textiles, and so on—to display in the parks. Plan to spend Saturday touring the attractions on the southern outskirts of the city. (See also "San Angel" under "Mexico City Neighborhoods in Brief," earlier in this chapter.) It's open Saturday from 9am to 6pm. Plaza de San Jacinto, San Angel. Metro: Miguel Angel de Quevado.

Centro Artesanal (Mercado de Curiosidades)   This rather modern building set back off a plaza consists of a number of stalls on two levels, selling everything from leather to tiles. They have some lovely silver jewelry and, as in most non-fixed-price stores, the asking price is high but the bargained result is often very reasonable. It's open Monday through Saturday from 10am to 5:30pm. Corner of Ayuntamiento and Dolores, Reforma North. Metro: Guerrero.

Lagunilla Market   This is one of the most interesting and unusual markets in Mexico—but watch out for pickpockets. It's only open on Sundays, when the Lagunilla becomes a colorful outdoor market filling the streets for blocks. Arrive around 9am. Vendors sell everything from axes to antiques. The two enclosed sections, on either side of a short street, Calle Juan Salvages, are open all week. They have different specialties: The one to the north is noted for clothes, *rebozos* (shawls), and blankets; the one to the south for tools, pottery, and household goods, such as attractive hanging copper lamps. This is also the area to find old and rare books, many at a ridiculously low cost, if you're willing to hunt and bargain. It's open daily from 10am to 7pm. 3 blocks east of Plaza de Garibaldi, at the corner of Francisco Bocanegra. Metro: Allende.

Mercado de la Ciudadela   An excellent place to get authentic arts and crafts, this market has hundreds of stalls with arts and crafts from all over Mexico. It's across from the Escuela Nacional de Artes. A few places take credit cards. It's open daily from 9am to 8pm. Balderas, between Reforma and Chapultepec. Metro: Balderas.

Mercado de la Merced   This is the city's biggest market and among the most fascinating in the country; the intense activity and energy level are akin to those at Oaxaca's Abastos Market (see chapter 11). Officially it's housed in several modern buildings, but shops line the tidy, crowded streets all the way to the *zócalo*.

The first building is mainly for fruits and vegetables; the others contain about what you'd find if a department store joined forces with a discount warehouse—especially housewares, such as hand-held citrus juicers of all sizes, tinware, colorful spoons, and decorative oilcloth. The main market, east of the *zócalo* on Circunvalación between General Anaya and Adolfo Gurrión, is the place to stock up on Mexican spices. The easy 13-block walk from the *zócalo* zigzags past many shops. Or take the Metro; the stop is right outside the market. It's open daily from 7am to 6pm. Circunvalación between General Anaya and Adolfo Gurrión. Metro: Merced.

Mercado Insurgentes   Mercado Insurgentes is a full-fledged crafts market tucked into the Zona Rosa. Because of its address, you might expect exorbitant prices, but vendors in the maze of stalls are eager to bargain, and good buys aren't hard to come by. It's open Monday through Saturday from 9am to 5:30pm. Londres between Florencia and Amberes, Zona Rosa. Metro: Insurgentes.

Nacional Monte de Piedad (National Pawn Shop)   This building used to be a pawn shop for all sorts of items, but now is reserved for the more profitable and saleable jewelry, with a couple of small rooms set aside for art and antiques. Pedro Romero de Terreros, the Count of Regla, an 18th-century silver magnate from Pachuca, donated the present building so that Mexican people could get low-interest loans. It's open Monday through Friday from 8:30am to 6pm, Saturday from 8:30am to 3pm. Corner of Monte de Piedad and Cinco de Mayo, Centro Histórico. http://dns.montepiedad.com. mx. Metro: Zócalo.

8 Mexico City After Dark

From mariachi, reggae, and opera to folkloric dance, classical ballet, and dinner shows, the choice of nighttime entertainment in Mexico City is enormous and sophisticated. Prices are much lower than those for comparable entertainment in most of the world's major cities. If you're willing to let *la vida mexicana* put on its own fascinating show for you, the bill will be even less. People-watching, cafe-sitting, music, and even a dozen mariachi bands all playing at once can be yours for next to nothing. For those looking for the hottest spots in dance clubs, head straight for the **Condesa** and **Roma** neighborhoods.

THE ENTERTAINMENT SCENE

Mexico City boasts a world-class nightlife scene, with hot venues for downing tequila and dancing to music ranging from salsa to house. In recent years, the **Centro Histórico** downtown has earned a reputation for having a number of hip and edgy bars and clubs concentrated within walking distance. The posh **Polanco** neighborhood is known for its perennially hot nightclub scene, and in recent years many of the trendiest nightspots have opened in the **Condesa** and **Roma** neighborhoods (reputedly the SoHo of Mexico City, though the nightlife scene is more akin to New York's East Village). Some of the city's most exclusive nightclubs lie in the **Lomas** area. In the south of the city, **San Angel** remains highly popular, although it's a bit of a drive if you're not already staying in that area. Most bars don't even begin to get going until around 10 or 11pm and usually stay open until at least 3am; nightclubs get started

---

Tips Crime at Night

Make sure to leave valuables—especially watches and jewelry—at your hotel, and bring only the cash you will need. While I list Metro stops, these should probably be used only for orientation; take only authorized *sitio* taxis (see the advisory "Important Taxi Safety Precautions in Mexico City," at the beginning of this chapter) or hire a private taxi by the hour and have an escort wait for you as you sample the festivities of the city. Your hotel can help with these arrangements.

after midnight and continue into the wee hours. Many clubs operate only Thursday through Saturday.

Fiesta nights give visitors a chance to dine on typical Mexican food and see wonderful regional dancing, which seems always to be a treat no matter how many times you've seen it.

For lower-key nightlife and people-watching, outdoor cafes remain a popular option. Those on **Calle Copenhague,** in the thick of the Zona Rosa scene, are among the liveliest, but with one or two exceptions, they have become more expensive than they are good. Another tradition is **Garibaldi Square,** where mariachis tune up and wait to be hired, but *be especially careful*—it's now known as much for chronic street crime as for music.

Hotel lobby bars tend to have live entertainment of the low-key type in the late afternoon and into the evening. The exception is the Blue Lounge at the Camino Real, which occasionally books top-name Latin-American talent.

THE PERFORMING ARTS

Mexico City's performing arts scene is among the finest and most comprehensive in the world. It includes opera, theater, ballet, and dance, along with concerts of symphonic, rock, and popular music.

For current information on cultural offerings, *Donde Ir, Tiempo Libre,* and *Concierge,* free magazines found in hotels, are good sources for locating the newest places, though they don't have complete listings of changing entertainment or current exhibits. **Ticketmaster** (© 55/5325-9000) usually handles ticket sales for major performances.

The **Ballet Folklórico de México (Folkloric Ballet of Mexico),** with its stunning presentation of regional dance, is perhaps the city's most renowned entertainment for visitors.

Note: The majority of the theatrical performances at the Palacio de Bellas Artes and in other theaters around the city are presented in Spanish.

FOLKLORIC BALLET

Palacio de Bellas Artes   Although various groups perform around the city, the finest offering is at the Palacio de Bellas Artes, where the famed **Ballet Folklórico de México** performs twice a week. The Ballet Folklórico is a celebration of pre- and post-Hispanic dancing. A typical program includes Aztec ritual dances, agricultural dances from Jalisco, a fiesta in Veracruz, a wedding celebration—all linked with mariachis, marimba players, singers, and dancers.

Because the Bellas Artes books many other events—visits by foreign opera companies, for instance—the Ballet Folklórico occasionally moves. In that case, it usually appears in the **National Auditorium** in Chapultepec Park. Check at the Bellas Artes box office. The show is popular and tickets sell rapidly (especially to tour agencies at twice the cost). The box office is on the ground floor of the Bellas Artes, main entrance. Ballet Folklórico performances are on Sunday at 9:30am and 8:30pm and Wednesday at 8:30pm.

The Fine Arts theater not only offers the finest in performing arts, but is also architecturally worth a visit (see "Exploring Mexico City," earlier in this chapter). It's open Monday through Saturday 11am to 7pm, and Sunday 8:30am to 7pm. Eje Central and Av. Juárez, Centro Histórico–Alameda. © 55/5512-2593. www.cnca.gob.mx/palacio/ni.htm. Tickets $36–$60 (£20–£33). Metro: Bellas Artes.

THE CLUB & MUSIC SCENE

This warning can't be reiterated enough: **Take an authorized *sitio* taxi or hire a car for transportation to all nightspots.** Metro stops are given merely as a point of reference.

MARIACHIS

Mariachis play the music of Mexico. Although the songs they play may be familiar—ranging from traditional boleros to Mozart to the Beatles—their style and presentation are unique to Mexico. Known for their distinctive dress, strolling presentation, and mix of brass and guitars, they epitomize the romance and tradition of the country. They look a little like Mexican cowboys dressed up for a special occasion—tight trousers studded with silver buttons down the outside of the legs, elaborate cropped jackets, embroidered shirts with big bow ties, and grandiose sombrero hats. The dress dates to the French occupation of Mexico in the mid–19th century, as does the name. *Mariachi* is believed to be an adaptation of the French word for marriage; this was the type of music commonly played at weddings in the 15th and 16th centuries. The music is a derivative of *fandango,* which was the most popular dance music of the elite classes in 16th-century Spain. In Mexico, fandango became the peasant's song and dance.

In Mexico City, the mariachis make their headquarters around the **Plaza de Garibaldi,** 5 blocks north of the Palacio de Bellas Artes—up Avenida Lázaro Cárdenas, at Avenida República de Honduras. Mariachi players are everywhere in the plaza. At every corner, guitars are stacked together like rifles in an army camp. Young musicians strut proudly in their outfits, on the lookout for *señoritas* to impress. They play when they feel like it, when there's a good chance to gather some tips, or when someone orders a song—the going rate is $2.50 to $5 (£1.40–£2.75) per song.

Should you want to enjoy mariachi music in a more tourist-friendly venue, I can recommend:

Jorongo Bar   For wonderful mariachi and trio music of romantic boleros in plush surroundings, make your way to the Hotel María Isabel Sheraton, facing the Angel Monument. This bar has enjoyed a reputation for outstanding traditional music for decades—it's an institution, including among locals. Nightly from 7:30pm to 2am, you can enjoy the smooth and joyous sounds for the price of a drink ($5–$9/£2.75–£4.95) plus cover. Hotel María Isabel Sheraton, Reforma 325, Zona Rosa. (*C*) **55/5242-5555.** Cover $7 (£3.85). Metro: Insurgentes.

CLUBS & MUSIC BARS

AREA Bar and Terrace at Hotel Habita *(Finds)*   The rooftop bar of this boutique Polanco hotel is among Mexico City's enduring hotspots. Umbrellas top tables, but otherwise, you're under the stars—and, likely, surrounded by a few—among a trendy crowd sipping tequila cocktails and Cosmopolitans. Decor is minimalist, of course, with a few white couches. Barstools set along the railing look out over the city. If you can make it past the bouncer and down the circular stairway to the lower terrace and pool area, you've really arrived—that's the glitzy VIP section, not unlike what you'd find in a rooftop L.A. bar. Music is mainly Euro, chill, and house. It's open Monday to Wednesday from 7pm to midnight, and Thursday to Saturday until 2am. Hotel Habita, Av. Presidente Masaryk 201, Polanco. (*C*) **55/5282-3100.** Metro: Polanco.

Bar Fly *(Finds)*   The talented house band—direct from Cuba—makes this small but stylish bar sizzle. By midnight the tiny dance floor is shaking with hot salsa moves. It's

---

Tips **A Note of Caution in Garibaldi Square**

Plaza de Garibaldi, *both day and night,* is increasingly populated by thieves looking to separate tourists from their valuables. Although the police presence has increased, it's still best to visit by private taxi. If you go, don't take credit cards or excess money with you. Go with a crowd of friends rather than alone, or take a tour that includes Garibaldi.

---

on the first floor of an upscale shopping center, and open Wednesday through Saturday from 9pm to 3am. Live music starts around 11pm. Av. Presidente Masaryk 393, Polanco. (?) 55/5282-2906. 2-drink minimum. Metro: Polanco.

Bengala   Expats, world travelers, and internationally minded Mexicans have made Bengala one of the city's hottest bars, which features a diverse selection of music and dancing between tables. The 30-somethings crowd comes for live jazz on Tuesday and Thursday nights and a rocking DJ the rest of the week. Open Tuesday to Saturday from 8pm to 3am. Sonora 34 (at corner of Puebla), Col. Roma. (?) 55/5553-9219. Metro: Insurgentes.

Cafeina   The ultrastylish Cafeina attracts a beautiful crowd of models and young socialites, featuring a celeb-DJ serving up house, jazz, bossa nova, reggaeton, and—on Monday nights—the best Brazilian party in town with live music and samba dancers. First-rate Mediterranean cuisine and potent *caipirinhas* (the traditional Brazilian cocktail made with *cachaça,* lime, and sugar) are also on offer. It's open Monday to Saturday from 7pm to 4am and Sunday from 6 to 10pm. Nuevo León 73 (at corner of Juan Escutia), Col. Condesa. (?) 55/5212-0090. Metro: Insurgentes.

Living   Mexico City's most glamorous gay club is also a hotspot for open-minded heterosexuals, and its huge dance floor kicks off each weekend night with an exotic theme show. There's a special section for lesbians only, and music includes electronic, house, and trance. Open weekends from 10pm until 4am. Paseo de la Reforma 483, Col Cuauhtémoc. (?) 55/5286-0066. www.living.com.mx. During special shows or events, cover charge of up to $20 (£11) may apply. Metro: Insurgentes.

Rexo   Credited with changing Mexico City's nightlife scene by leading people to Condesa, this Mediterranean bar and restaurant still rules as one of the city's sexiest spots. A cube walled in by glass, Rexo consists of three contemporary floors which integrate the restaurant and bar crowds. The patrons are largely 30-somethings, mostly single, and very stylish. The club is not easily accessible by Metro. It's open daily from 1pm to 2am. Saltillo 1 (corner of Nuevo León), Col. Condesa. (?) 55/5553-5337.

Rioma   Hard to get into, this after-hours club commands a top spot for the ultrachic. A set of stairs leads down to the high-tech dance floor, with tables, lit from the inside, surrounding it. There's a long bar along one wall. Music is Euro, house, and techno. The crowd is among the most fashionable in the city—models, young socialites, celebrities, and hard-core clubbers. On weekends there's often a line out the door and down the street. Plan to arrive late (not before 1am unless you want to sit alone) and stay into the early morning. It's open Wednesday through Saturday from 10pm to 4am. Insurgentes Sur 377 (near the corner of Michoacán), Col. Condesa. (?) 55/5584-0613. Cover $10 (£5.50) and up. Metro: Insurgentes.

Zinco   Possibly the coolest jazz club south of the U.S. border, Zinco sits in an old basement vault in the Historic Center. Top performers play in the center of the intimate club, which attracts a crowd that's both cutting edge and unaffected. A full menu is available for those who wish to dine. It's open Wednesday to Saturday from 9pm to 3am. Motolinía 20 (corner of 5 de mayo), Centro Histórico. 🅒 55/5512-3369. $20 (£11) cover. Metro: Zócalo.

BARS

La Casa de las Sirenas   This old-school bar serves over 200 types of tequila—one of the widest selections available anywhere—in a stylish atmosphere. Although it also serves food, it's best known for its friendly bar crowd and ambience. Housed in a 17th-century colonial building, the "House of Mermaids" features a courtyard filled with flowering plants and trees, and lies almost in front of the Templo Mayor in the Centro Histórico. It's open Monday through Saturday from 1 to 11pm, Sunday from 1pm to 6pm. República de Guatemala 32, Centro Histórico, behind the cathedral. 🅒 55/5704-3345 or -3273. Metro: Zócalo.

Tierra de Vinos   Only drinks made with grapes are served in this lively wine bar and restaurant, which offers delicious tapas and other Spanish delights to accompany your wine tasting. The stylish bar boasts a terrific vibe and one of the city's most impressive wine cellars, with selections from all over the world. It's open Sunday to Tuesday from 1 to 6pm and Wednesday to Saturday from 1pm to 1am. Durango 197 (at corner of Oaxaca), Col. Roma. 🅒 55/5208-5133. Metro: Insurgentes.

Whiskey Bar/The Terrace 🅐🅐   If this bar is too crowded to get in—which it often is—you can at least view the action you're missing through the floor-to-ceiling glass windows, visible from the street. This first international location of Rande Gerber's hot chain of bars has created a sensation and is one of the hottest clubs in the city. Stunning design and the group's signature cool music are the features, but it's the buzz and the crowd that's the real attraction. The Whiskey is actually four bars in one, and includes an outdoor terrace lounge. Open until 2am Sunday through Wednesday, until 3am Thursday through Saturday. At the W Mexico City hotel, Campos Eliseos 252, at Andrés Bello. 🅒 55/9138-1800. Metro: Polanco.

9 A Side Trip to the Pyramids of San Juan Teotihuacán 🅐🅐🅐

50km (31 miles) NE of Mexico City

The ruins of Teotihuacán are among the most remarkable in Mexico—indeed, they are among the most important ruins in the world. Mystery envelops this former city of 200,000; although it was the epicenter of culture and commerce for ancient Mesoamerica, its inhabitants vanished without a trace. *Teotihuacán* (pronounced "teh-oh-tee-wa-*khan*") means "place where gods were born," reflecting the Aztec belief that the gods created the universe here.

Occupation of the area began around 500 B.C., but it wasn't until after 100 B.C. that construction of the enormous Pyramid of the Sun commenced. Teotihuacán's rise coincided with the classical Romans' building of their great monuments, and with the beginning of cultures in Mexico's Yucatán Peninsula, Oaxaca, and Puebla.

Teotihuacán's magnificent pyramids and palaces covered about 30 sq. km (12 sq. miles). At its zenith, around A.D. 500, the city counted more inhabitants than in contemporary Rome. Through trade and other contact, Teotihuacán's influence was known

Teotihuacán

SAN MARTÍN

Entrance
Peripheral Highway

Parking

Avenue of the Dead

Parking

To San Juan
Teotihuacán

Parking

Terraced Road

Parking

Río San Juan

Avenue of the Dead

Parking

To Mexico City

Entrance

Parking

Peripheral Highway

Roadside
Food Stands

La Cueva
Entrance

Villas
Arqueológicas

0   1/4 mi
0   0.25 km

HIDALGO
area of detail   SAN MARTÍN
MÉXICO
ECATEPEC DE MORELOS
MEXICO CITY

1 Tepantitla
2 Pyramid of the Moon
3 Palace of Quetzalpapálotl
4 Palace of the Jaguars
5 El Corso
6 Pyramid of the Sun
7 The High Priest's Home
8 New Museum Location
9 The Viking Group
10 The Temple of
   Quetzalcoatl
11 La Ciudadela
12 Old Museum Building
13 La Ventilla
14 Atetelco
15 Tetitla
16 Zacuala
17 Yayahuala

in other parts of Mexico and as far south as the Yucatán and Guatemala. Still, little information about the city's inhabitants survives: what language they spoke, where they came from, why they abandoned the place around A.D. 700. It is known, however, that at the beginning of the 1st century A.D., the Xitle volcano erupted near Cuicuilco (south of Mexico City) and decimated that city, which was the most prominent of the time. Those inhabitants migrated to Teotihuacán. Scholars believe that Teotihuacán's decline, probably caused by overpopulation and depletion of natural resources, was gradual, perhaps occurring over a 250-year period. In the last years, it appears that the people were poorly nourished and that the city was deliberately burned.

Ongoing excavations have revealed something of the culture. According to archaeoastronomer John B. Carlson, the cult of the planet Venus that determined wars and human sacrifices elsewhere in Mesoamerica was prominent at Teotihuacán as well. (Archaeoastronomy is the study of the position of stars and planets in relation to archaeology.) Ceremonial rituals were timed with the appearance of Venus as the morning and evening star. The symbol of Venus at Teotihuacán (as at Cacaxtla, 80km/50 miles away, near Tlaxcala) appears as a star or half-star with a full or half-circle. Carlson also suggests the possibility that people from Cacaxtla conquered Teotihuacán, as name glyphs of conquered peoples at Cacaxtla show Teotihuacán-like pyramids. Numerous tombs with human remains (many of them either sacrificial inhabitants of the city or perhaps war captives) and objects of jewelry, pottery, and daily life have been uncovered along the foundations of buildings. It appears that the primary deity at Teotihuacán was a female, called "Great Goddess" for lack of any known name.

Today, what remains are the rough stone structures of the three pyramids and sacrificial altars, and some of the grand houses, all of which were once covered in stucco and painted with brilliant frescoes (mainly in red). The Toltec, who rose in power after the city's decline, were fascinated with Teotihuacán and incorporated its symbols into their own cultural motifs. The Aztec, who followed the Toltec, were fascinated with the Toltec and with the ruins of Teotihuacán; they likewise adopted many of their symbols and motifs. For more information on Teotihuacán and its influence in Mesoamerica, see Appendix A.

ESSENTIALS

GETTING THERE & DEPARTING **By Car** Driving to San Juan Teotihuacán on the toll Highway 85D or the free Highway 132D takes about an hour. Head north on Insurgentes to leave the city. Highway 132D passes through picturesque villages but can be slow due to the surfeit of trucks and buses. Highway 85D, the toll road, is less attractive but faster.

By Private Sedan or Taxi If you prefer to explore solo or want more or less time than an organized tour allows, consider hiring a private car and driver for the trip. They can easily be arranged through your hotel or at the Secretary of Tourism (SECTUR) information module in the Zona Rosa; they cost about $15 to $20 (£8.25–£11) an hour. The higher price is generally for a sedan with an English-speaking driver who doubles as a tour guide. Rates can also be negotiated for the entire day.

By Bus Buses leave daily every half hour (5am–10pm) from the Terminal Central de Autobuses del Norte; the trip takes 1 hour. When you reach the Terminal Norte, look for the AUTOBUSES SAHAGUN sign at the far northwest end, all the way down to the sign 8 ESPERA. Be sure to ask the driver where you should wait for returning buses, how frequently buses run, and especially the time of the last bus back.

ORIENTATION The ruins of Teotihuacán (© 59/4956-0276 or 59/4956-0052) are open daily from 7am to 5pm. Admission is $4.50 (£2.50). Using a video camera costs $3 (£1.65).

A small trolley-train that takes visitors from the entry booths to various stops within the site, including the Teotihuacán museum and cultural center, runs only on weekends and costs $1 (55p) per person.

Keep in mind that you're likely to be doing a great deal of walking, and perhaps some climbing, at an altitude of more than 2,120m (7,000 ft.). Take it slow, bring sun block and drinking water, and during the summer be prepared for almost daily afternoon showers.

A good place to start is at the **Museo Teotihuacán** ☭. This excellent state-of-the-art museum holds interactive exhibits and, in one part, a glass floor on which visitors walk above mock-ups of the pyramids. On display are findings of recent digs, including several tombs, with skeletons wearing necklaces of human and simulated jawbones, and newly discovered sculptures.

The Layout The grand buildings of Teotihuacán were laid out in accordance with celestial movements. The front wall of the **Pyramid of the Sun** is exactly perpendicular to the point on the horizon where the sun sets at the equinoxes (twice annually). The rest of the ceremonial buildings were laid out at right angles to the Pyramid of the Sun.

The main thoroughfare, which archaeologists call the **Calzada de los Muertos (Avenue of the Dead),** runs roughly north to south. The **Pyramid of the Moon** is at the northern end, and the **Ciudadela (Citadel)** is on the southern part. The great street was several kilometers long in its prime, but only a kilometer or two has been uncovered and restored.

EXPLORING THE TEOTIHUACAN ARCHAEOLOGICAL SITE

LA CIUDADELA   The Spaniards named the Ciudadela. This immense sunken square was not a fortress at all, although the impressive walls make it look like one. It was the grand setting for the Feathered Serpent Pyramid and the Temple of Quetzalcoatl. Scholars aren't certain that the Teotihuacán culture embraced the Quetzalcoatl deity so well known in the Toltec, Aztec, and Maya cultures. The feathered serpent is featured in the Ciudadela, but whether it was worshipped as Quetzalcoatl or a similar god isn't known. Proceed down the steps into the massive court and head for the ruined temple in the middle.

The Temple of Quetzalcoatl was covered over by an even larger structure, a pyramid. As you walk toward the center of the Ciudadela's court, you'll approach the Feathered Serpent Pyramid. To the right, you'll see the reconstructed temple close behind the pyramid, with a narrow passage between the two structures.

Early temples in Mexico and Central America were often covered by later ones. The Pyramid of the Sun may have been built up in this way. Archaeologists have tunneled deep inside the Feathered Serpent Pyramid and found several ceremonially buried human remains, interred with precise detail and position, but as yet no royal personages. Drawings of how the building once looked show that every level was covered with faces of a feathered serpent. At the Temple of Quetzalcoatl, you'll notice at once the fine, large carved serpents' heads jutting out from collars of feathers carved in the stone walls. Other feathered serpents are carved in relief low on the walls.

AVENUE OF THE DEAD   The Avenue of the Dead got its strange and forbidding name from the Aztec, who mistook the little temples that line both sides of the avenue for tombs of kings or priests.

As you stroll north along the Avenue of the Dead toward the Pyramid of the Moon, look on the right for a bit of wall sheltered by a modern corrugated roof. Beneath the shelter, the wall still bears a painting of a jaguar. From this fragment, you might be able to reconstruct the breathtaking spectacle that must have been visible when all the paintings along the avenue were intact.

PYRAMID OF THE SUN   The Pyramid of the Sun, on the east side of the Avenue of the Dead, is the third-largest pyramid in the world. The first and second are the Great Pyramid of Cholula, near Puebla, and the Pyramid of Cheops on the outskirts of Cairo, Egypt. Teotihuacán's Pyramid of the Sun is 220m (722 ft.) per side at its base—almost as large as Cheops. But at 65m (213 ft.) high, the Sun pyramid is only about half as high as its Egyptian rival. No matter—it's still the biggest restored pyramid in the Western Hemisphere, and an awesome sight. Although the Pyramid of the Sun was not built as a great king's tomb, it is built on top of a series of sacred caves, which aren't open to the public.

The first structure of the pyramid was probably built a century before Christ, and the temple that used to crown the pyramid was completed about 400 years later (A.D. 300).

By the time the pyramid was discovered and restoration was begun (early in the 20th c.), the temple had disappeared, and the pyramid was just a mass of rubble covered with bushes and trees.

It's a worthwhile 248-step climb to the top. The view is extraordinary and the sensation exhilarating.

PYRAMID OF THE MOON   The Pyramid of the Moon faces a plaza at the northern end of the avenue. The plaza is surrounded by little temples and by the Palace of Quetzalpapalotl or Quetzal-Mariposa (Quetzal-Butterfly) on the left (west) side. You have about the same range of view from the top of the Pyramid of the Moon as you do from its larger neighbor, because the moon pyramid is built on higher ground. The perspective straight down the Avenue of the Dead is magnificent.

PALACE OF QUETZALPAPALOTL   The Palace of Quetzalpapalotl lay in ruins until the 1960s, when restoration work began. Today, it reverberates with its former glory, as figures of Quetzal-Mariposa (a mythical, exotic bird-butterfly) appear painted on walls or carved in the pillars of the inner court. Behind the Palace of Quetzalpapalotl is the Palace of the Jaguars, complete with murals showing jaguars.

WHERE TO DINE

Vendors at the ruins sell drinks and snacks, but many visitors choose to carry a box lunch—almost any hotel or restaurant in the city can prepare one for you. A picnic in the shadow of this impressive ancient city allows extended time and perspective to take it all in. There is a **restaurant** in the new Museo Teotihuacán, which is the most convenient place for a snack or a meal.

Silver, Spas & Spiritual Centers: From Taxco to Tepoztlán

by Juan Cristiano

It may seem as if the small towns in this region of Mexico are trying to capitalize on recent trends in travel toward spas and self-exploration, but in reality, they've helped define them. From the restorative properties of thermal waters and earth-based spa treatments to the mystical and spiritual properties of gemstones and herbs, the treasures and knowledge in these towns have existed for years—and, in some cases, for centuries.

This is only a sampling of towns south and west of Mexico City. They are fascinating in their diversity, history, and mystery, and make for a unique travel experience, either on their own or combined. They vary in character from mystical villages to sophisticated spa towns, with archaeological and colonial-era attractions in the mix. And with their proximity to Mexico City, all are within easy reach by private car or taxi—or by inexpensive bus—in under a few hours.

The legendary silver city of **Taxco,** on the road between Acapulco and Mexico City, is renowned for its museums, picturesque hillside colonial-era charm, and, of course, its silver shops. North of Taxco and southwest of Mexico City, over the mountains, are the venerable thermal spas at **Ixtapan de la Sal,** as well as their more modern counterparts in **Valle de Bravo.** Verdant **Cuernavaca,** known as the land of eternal spring, has gained a reputation for its exceptional spa facilities and its wealth of cultural and historic attractions. Finally, **Tepoztlán,** with its enigmatic charms and legendary pyramid, captivates the few travelers who find their way there.

1 Taxco: Cobblestones & Silver ★★

178km (110 miles) SW of Mexico City; 80km (50 miles) SW of Cuernavaca; 296km (184 miles) NE of Acapulco

In Mexico and around the world, the town of Taxco de Alarcón—most commonly known simply as Taxco (*tahs*-koh)—is synonymous with silver. The town's geography and architecture are equally precious: Taxco sits at nearly 1,515m (4,969 ft.) on a hill among hills, and almost any point in the city offers fantastic views.

Hernán Cortez discovered Taxco as he combed the area for treasure, but its rich caches of silver weren't fully exploited for another 2 centuries. In 1751, the French prospector Joseph de la Borda—who came to be known locally as José—commissioned the baroque Santa Prisca Church that dominates Taxco's *zócalo* (Plaza Borda) as a way of giving something back to the town. In the mid-1700s, Borda was considered the richest man in New Spain.

Side Trips from Mexico City

To Querétaro
Ruinas Tula
57D
126
55

0 25 mi
0 25 km
N

Presa Huapango

55D

MICHOACÁN

Atlacomulco

Villa del Carbon

Río Pearl

146

55D

← To Guadalajara

MEXICO

55

Río Lerma

134

15

15

Zitacuaro

Ruinas Calixtlahuaca

Toluca

15

1

Valle de Bravo

Metepec

PARQUE NACIONAL DESIERTO DE LOS LEONES

PARQUE NACIONAL NEVADO DE TOLUCA

Avándaro

PARQUE NACIONAL LAGUNAS DE ZEMPOALA

▲ *Nevado de Toluca (15,026')*

Temascaltepec

550

Ruinas Malinalco

134

Tenancingo

Ixtapan de la Sal

Tonatico

95

UNITED STATES

Gulf of Mexico

MEXICO

Mexico City ★

PACIFIC OCEAN

GUERRERO

Taxco

95

95D

95

95D

To Chilpancingo & Acapulco ↓

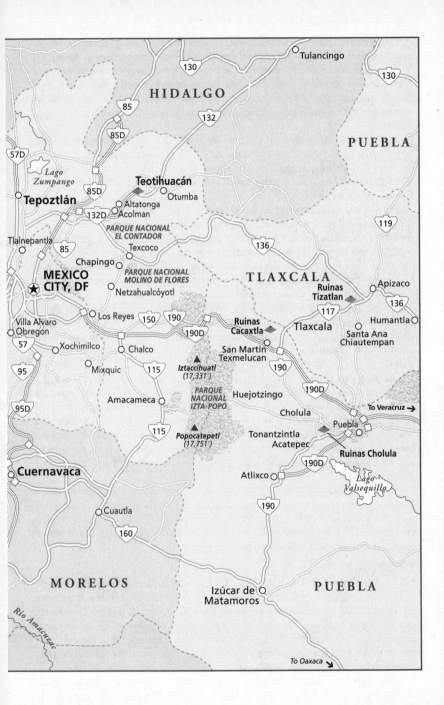

The fact that Taxco has become Mexico's most renowned center for silver design, even though it now mines only a small amount of silver, is the work of an American, William Spratling. Spratling arrived in the late 1920s with the intention of writing a book. He soon noticed the skill of the local craftsmen and opened a workshop to produce handmade silver jewelry and tableware based on pre-Hispanic art, which he exported to the United States in bulk. The workshops flourished, and Taxco's reputation grew.

Today, most of the residents of this town are involved in the silver industry in some way. Taxco is home to hundreds (some say up to 900) of silver shops and outlets, ranging from sleek galleries to small stands in front of stucco homes. You'll find silver in all of its forms here—the jewelry basics, tea sets, silverware, candelabras, picture frames, and napkin holders.

The tiny one-man factories that line the cobbled streets all the way up into the hills supply most of Taxco's silverwork. "Bargains" are relative, but nowhere else will you find this combination of diversity, quality, and rock-bottom prices. Generally speaking, the larger shops that most obviously cater to the tourist trade will have the highest prices—but they may be the only ones to offer "that special something" you're looking for. For classic designs in jewelry or other silver items, shop around, and wander the back streets and smaller venues.

You can get an idea of what Taxco is like by spending an afternoon, but there's much more to this picturesque town of 120,000 than just the Plaza Borda and the shops surrounding it. Stay overnight, wander its steep cobblestone streets, and you'll discover little plazas, fine churches, and, of course, an abundance of silversmiths' shops.

The main part of town is relatively flat. It stretches up the hillside from the highway, and it's a steep but brief walk up. White VW minibuses, called *combis*, make the circuit through and around town, picking up and dropping off passengers along the route, from about 7am until 9pm. These taxis are inexpensive (about 50¢/30p), and you should use them even if you arrive by car, because parking is practically impossible. Also, the streets are so narrow and steep that most visitors find them nerve-racking. Find a secured parking lot for your car, or leave it at your hotel and forget about it until you leave.

Warning: Self-appointed guides will undoubtedly approach you in the *zócalo* (Plaza Borda) and offer their services—they get a cut (up to 25%) of all you buy in the shops they take you to. Before hiring a guide, ask to see his SECTUR (Tourism Secretary) credentials. The Department of Tourism office on the highway at the north end of town can recommend a licensed guide.

ESSENTIALS

GETTING THERE & DEPARTING   By Car   From Mexico City, take Paseo de la Reforma to Chapultepec Park and merge with the Periférico, which will take you to Highway 95D on the south end of town. From the Periférico, take the Insurgentes exit and merge until you come to the sign for CUERNAVACA/TLALPAN. Choose either CUERNAVACA CUOTA (toll) or CUERNAVACA LIBRE (free). Continue south around Cuernavaca to the Amacuzac interchange, and proceed straight ahead for Taxco. The drive from Mexico City takes about 3½ hours.

From Acapulco you have two options: Highway 95D is the toll road through Iguala to Taxco, or you can take the old two-lane road (Hwy. 95) that winds more slowly through villages; it's in good condition.

Taxco

Church †

Tourism Office

Aqueduct

To Mexico City, Cuernavaca,
Ixtapan de la Sal & Toluca

12

HIDALGO

MICHOACÁN

MEXICO

Mexico City ★

MORELOS

PUEBLA

Taxco ●

GUERRERO

0   50 mi
0   50 km

0   330 feet
0   100 meters

Avenida J.F. Kennedy

Calle la Garita

Punte Ramonet

Chavarrieta †

Calle Reforma

Avenida J.F. Kennedy

† **Ex Convento**

† **Guadalupe**

Plazuela de Bernal

Calle Juan Ruiz de Alarcón

3

2

4

1 ■ **City Hall**

■ **Silver Museum**

5

Plaza Borda

Veracruz

Flecha Roja Bus Station ■

7 † **6**

Calle de la Veracruz & San Sebastián

Santa Prisca

8

Mercado de Artesanías

Calle San Agustín

■ **Bank**

Calle Santa Ana

■ **Bank**

Calle San Nicolás

La Santisima †

† ■ **San Nicolás**

Calle San Miguel

Plazuela San Juan

9

10

Calle Cena Obscuras

Calle San Nicolás

San Miguel †

To Panoramic Road ←

Calle Luis Montes de Oca

Estrella de Oro Bus Station ■

11 →

To Iguala & Acapulco →

↓ To Ixateopan

ATTRACTIONS ●

Casa de la Cultura de Taxco (Casa Borda) **1**
Humboldt House/Musseo Virreinal de Taxco **4**
Mercado Central **6**
Museo Arqueológical Guillermo Spratling **5**
Santa Prisca y San Sebastián Church **7**
Wholesale Silver Market **8**
Workshops: Los Castillo & Spratling **11**

ACCOMMODATIONS ■

Hotel Best Western Taxco **10**
Hotel Los Arcos **3**
Hotel Posada Emilia Castillo **2**
Hotel Santa Prisco **9**
Monte Taxco **12**

Spanish & Art Classes in Taxco

The Taxco campus of the **Universidad Nacional Autónoma de México (UNAM;** © **762/622-0124** for the Spanish school, or 622-3690 for the art school) sits on the grounds of the Hacienda del Chorrillo, formerly part of the Cortez land grant. Here, students learn silversmithing, Spanish, drawing, composition, and history under the supervision of UNAM instructors. Classes are small, and courses generally last 3 months. The school provides a list of prospective town accommodations that consist primarily of hotels. More reasonable accommodations for a lengthy stay are available, but best arranged once you're there. At many locations all over town, you'll find notices of furnished apartments or rooms for rent. For information about the school, contact either the Dirección de Turismo (tourist office) in Taxco (see "Visitor Information," above), or write the school directly at Hacienda del Chorrillo, 40200 Taxco, Gro.

By Bus   From Mexico City, buses depart from the Central de Autobuses del Sur station (Metro: Taxqueña) and take 2 to 3 hours, with frequent departures.

Taxco has two bus stations. Estrella de Oro buses arrive at their own station on the southern edge of town. Estrella Blanca service, including Futura executive-class buses, and Flecha Roja buses arrive at the station on the northeastern edge of town on Avenida Los Plateros ("Avenue of the Silversmiths," formerly Av. Kennedy). Taxis to the *zócalo* cost around $2 (£1.10).

VISITOR INFORMATION   The **State of Guerrero Dirección de Turismo** (©/fax **762/622-2274**) has offices at the arches on the main highway at the north end of town (Av. de los Plateros 1), which is useful if you're driving into town. The office is open Monday through Friday from 8am to 3:30pm. To get there from the Plaza Borda, take a ZOCALO-ARCOS *combi* and get off at the arch over the highway. As you face the arches, the tourism office is on your right.

CITY LAYOUT   The center of town is the tiny **Plaza Borda,** shaded by perfectly manicured Indian laurel trees. On one side is the imposing twin-towered, pink-stone **Santa Prisca Church;** whitewashed, red-tile buildings housing the famous silver shops and a restaurant or two line the other sides. Beside the church, deep in a crevice of the mountain, is the **wholesale silver market**—absolutely the best place to begin your silver shopping, to get an idea of prices for more standard designs. You'll be amazed at the low prices. Buying just one piece is perfectly acceptable, and buying in bulk can lower the per-piece price. One of the beauties of Taxco is that its brick and cobblestone streets are completely asymmetrical, zigzagging up and down the hillsides. The plaza buzzes with vendors of everything from hammocks and cotton candy to bark paintings and balloons.

FAST FACTS   The telephone area code is **762.** The main post office, Benito Juárez 6, at the City Hall building (© **762/622-8596**), is open Monday through Saturday from 9am to 2:30pm. The older branch of the post office (© **762/622-0501**), open Monday through Friday from 8am to 2:30pm, is on the outskirts, on the highway to Acapulco. It's in a row of shops with a black-and-white CORREO sign.

EXPLORING TAXCO

Shopping for jewelry and other items is the major pastime for tourists. Prices for silver jewelry at Taxco's shops are about the best in the world, and everything is available, from $1 (55p) trinkets to artistic pieces costing hundreds of dollars.

In addition, Taxco is the home of some of Mexico's finest stone sculptors and is a good place to buy masks. However, beware of so-called "antiques"—there are virtually no real ones for sale.

SPECIAL EVENTS & FESTIVALS   January 18 marks the annual celebration in honor of Santa Prisca, with public festivities and fireworks displays. **Holy Week** 𝕮𝕮 in Taxco is one of the most poignant in the country, beginning the Friday a week before Easter with processions daily and nightly. The most riveting, on Thursday evening, lasts almost 4 hours and includes villagers from the surrounding area carrying statues of saints, followed by hooded members of a society of self-flagellating penitents, chained at the ankles and carrying huge wooden crosses and bundles of thorny branches. On Saturday morning, the Plaza Borda fills for the **Procession of Three Falls,** reenacting the three times Christ stumbled and fell while carrying the cross.

Taxco's **Silver Fair** starts the last week in November and continues through the first week in December. It includes a competition for silver works and sculptures among the top silversmiths. In late April to early May, **Jornadas Alarconianas** features plays and literary events in honor of Juan Ruiz de Alarcón (1572–1639), a world-famous dramatist who was born in Taxco—and for whom Taxco de Alarcón is named. Art exhibits, street fairs, and other festivities are part of the dual celebration.

SIGHTS IN TOWN

Casa de la Cultura de Taxco (Casa Borda)   Diagonally across from the Santa Prisca Church and facing Plaza Borda is the home José de la Borda built for his son around 1759. Now the Guerrero State Cultural Center, it houses a bookstore, classrooms, and exhibit halls where period clothing, engravings, paintings, and crafts are on display. The center also books traveling art exhibits, theatrical performances, music concerts, and dance events.

Plaza Borda 1. ℂ 762/622-6617. Fax 762/662-6634. Free admission. Tues–Sun 10am–5pm.

Humboldt House/Museo Virreinal de Taxco   Stroll along Ruiz de Alarcón (the street behind the Casa Borda) and look for the richly decorated facade of the Humboldt House, where the renowned German scientist and explorer Baron Alexander von Humboldt (1769–1859) spent a night in 1803. The museum houses 18th-century memorabilia pertinent to Taxco, most of which came from a secret room discovered during a recent restoration of the Santa Prisca Church. Signs with detailed information are in Spanish and English. As you enter, to the right are very rare *túmulos funerios* (painted funerary altars). The bottom two were painted in honor of Charles III of Spain; the top one, with a carved phoenix on top, was supposedly painted for the funeral of José de la Borda.

Another section presents historical information about Don Miguel Cabrera, Mexico's foremost 18th-century artist. Fine examples of clerical garments decorated with gold and silver thread hang in glass cases, and on the bottom level there's an impressive 17th-century carved wood altar of Dolores. Next to it, a small room is devoted to Humboldt and his sojourns through South America and Mexico.

Calle Juan Ruiz de Alarcón 12. ℂ 762/622-5501. Admission $2 (£1.10) adults, $1.50 (85p) students and teachers w/ID. Tues–Sat 10am–6pm; Sun 10am–4pm.

Mercado Central   Located to the right of the Santa Prisca Church, behind and below Berta's, Taxco's central market meanders deep inside the mountain. Take the stairs off the street. In addition to a collection of wholesale silver shops, you'll find numerous food stands, always the best place for a cheap meal.

Plaza Borda. Shops daily 10am–8pm; food stands daily 7am–6pm.

Museo Arqueológico Guillermo Spratling   A plaque in Spanish explains that most of the collection of pre-Columbian art displayed here, as well as the funds for the museum, came from William Spratling (1900–1967). You'd expect this to be a silver museum, but it's not—for Spratling silver, go to the Spratling Ranch Workshop (see "Nearby Attractions," below). The entrance floor and the one above display a good collection of pre-Columbian statues and implements in clay, stone, and jade. The upper floor holds changing exhibits.

Calle Porfirio A. Delgado 1. ℂ 762/622-1660. Admission $2.50 (£1.40) adults, free for children younger than 13; free to all Sun. Tues–Sat 9am–5pm; Sun 9am–3pm. Leaving Santa Prisca Church, turn right and right again at the corner; continue down the street, veer right, then immediately left. The museum will be facing you.

Santa Prisca y San Sebastián Church 𝔾𝔾   This is Taxco's centerpiece parish church; it faces the pleasant Plaza Borda. José de la Borda, a French miner who struck it rich in Taxco's silver mines, funded the construction. Completed in 1758, it's one of Mexico's most impressive baroque churches. The ultracarved facade is eclipsed by the interior, where the intricacy of the gold-leafed saints and cherubic angels is positively breathtaking. The paintings by Miguel Cabrera, one of Mexico's most famous colonial-era artists, are the pride of Taxco. The sacristy (behind the high altar) contains more Cabrera paintings.

Guides, both children and adults, will approach you outside the church offering to give a tour. Make sure the guide's English is passable, and establish whether the price is per person or per tour.

Plaza Borda. ℂ 762/622-0184. Free admission. Daily 10am–8pm.

NEARBY ATTRACTIONS

The impressive **Grutas de Cacahuamilpa** 𝔾, known as the Cacahuamilpa Caves or Grottoes, are less than a half hour north of Taxco. Hourly guided tours run daily at the caverns, which are truly sensational and well worth the visit. To see them, you can join a tour from Taxco (see "Exploring Taxco," above) or take a *combi* from the Flecha Roja terminal in Taxco; the one-way fare is $3 (£1.65), and admission to the caves is $3 (£1.65). For more information, see "Sights near Tepoztlán," later in this chapter.

Los Castillo   Don Antonio Castillo was one of hundreds of young men to whom William Spratling taught silversmithing in the 1930s. He was also one of the first to branch out with his own shops and line of designs, which over the years have earned him a fine reputation. Castillo has shops in several Mexican cities. Now, his daughter Emilia creates her own noteworthy designs, including decorative pieces with silver fused onto porcelain. Emilia's work is for sale on the ground floor of the Posada de los Castillo, just below the Plazuela Bernal.

8km (5 miles) south of town on the Acapulco Hwy. Also at Plazuela Bernal, Taxco. ℂ 762/622-1016 or -1988 (workshop). Free admission. Workshop Mon–Fri 8am–2pm and 3–6pm; open to groups at other hours by appointment only.

Spratling Ranch Workshop   William Spratling's hacienda-style home and workshop on the outskirts of Taxco still bustles with busy hands reproducing unique designs. A trip here will show you what distinctive Spratling work was all about, for the designs crafted today show the same fine work. Although the prices are higher than at other outlets, the designs are unusual and considered collectible. There's no store in Taxco, and unfortunately, most of the display cases hold only samples. With the exception of a few jewelry pieces, most items are by order only. Ask about U.S. outlets.

10km (6¼ miles) south of town on the Acapulco Hwy. **762/622-0026.** Free admission. Mon–Sat 9am–5pm. The *combi* to Iguala stops at the ranch; fare is 70¢ (40p).

WHERE TO STAY
MODERATE
Best Western Taxco ★★ This is the newest and most modern hotel in the town center, with professional service and an international clientele. Rooms are smallish but very comfortable, with white tiles and bedspreads and Mexican architectural touches; some have windows (interior rooms do not) and the junior suite has a terrace with views of the surrounding hills. Near the Santa Prisca church, this hotel offers a quality Mexican restaurant and access to a nearby pool. The friendly staff will arrange in-room massages upon request.

Carlos J. Nibbi 2, Plazuela de San Juan, 40200 Taxco, Gro. © **762/627-6194.** Fax 762/622-3416. www.bestwestern taxco.com. 23 units. $110 (£61) double weekdays; $120 (£66) double weekends; $160 (£88) junior suite weekdays; $190 (£105) junior suite weekends. AE, MC, V. Free parking. **Amenities:** Restaurant; access to outdoor pool and massage services; business center; laundry service. *In room:* AC, TV, Wi-Fi.

Monte Taxco *Overrated* This resort and country club sits atop a hill near the entrance to Taxco coming from Mexico City. A longtime landmark of the city, it offers golf and tennis, spa services, and access to the mountain's cable car. Colonial-style rooms are a bit dated but comfortable. Open weekends for dinner only, Toni's boasts the best city views of any restaurant in Taxco, and you can finish the night at the flashy dance club next door. You'll need to drive or take a taxi to reach the city center.

Fracc. Lomas de Taxco s/n, 40210 Taxco, Gro. © **762/622-1300.** Fax 762/622-1428. www.montetaxco.com.mx. 156 units. $170 (£94) double. AE, MC, V. Free parking. **Amenities:** Restaurant (w/spectacular city view; see "Where to Dine," below); bar; dance club; heated outdoor pool; 9-hole golf course; 3 tennis courts; gym; spa services; travel desk; room service; laundry service. *In room:* A/C, TV.

INEXPENSIVE
Hotel los Arcos ★ Los Arcos occupies a converted 1620 monastery. The handsome inner patio is bedecked with Puebla pottery and rustic furnishings surrounding a central fountain. Guest rooms are nicely but sparsely appointed, with natural tile floors and colonial-style furniture; the spacious junior suite has two levels. You'll feel immersed in colonial charm and blissful quiet. To find the hotel from the Plaza Borda, follow the hill down (with Hotel Agua Escondida on your left) and make an immediate right at the Plazuela Bernal; the hotel is a block down on the left, opposite the Hotel Posada (see below).

Juan Ruiz de Alarcón 4, 40200 Taxco, Gro. © **762/622-1836.** Fax 762/622-7982. 21 units. $43 (£24) double; $50 (£28) triple; $56 (£31) quad; $62 (£34) junior suite. No credit cards. **Amenities:** Internet. *In room:* TV.

Hotel Emilia Castillo *Value* Each room in this delightful small hotel is simply but handsomely appointed with carved doors and furniture; the small tile bathrooms have showers only. Ask for an interior room, which are much quieter than those facing the street. A high-quality silver shop lies next to the colorful lobby. The hotel does not have parking but contracts with a local parking garage.

Juan Ruiz de Alarcón 7, 40200 Taxco, Gro. ℂ/fax **762/622-1396**. www.hotelemiliacastillo.com. 14 units. $45 (£25) double; $50 (£28) triple with TV. MC, V. From the Plaza Borda, go downhill a short block to the Plazuela Bernal and make an immediate right; the hotel is a block farther on the right, opposite the Hotel los Arcos (see above). **Amenities:** Internet. *In room:* TV.

Hotel Santa Prisca *Value*   The Santa Prisca, 1 block from the Plaza Borda on the Plazuela San Juan, is one of the older and best located hotels in town. Rooms are small but comfortable, with standard bathrooms (showers only), tile floors, wood beams, and a colonial atmosphere. For longer stays, ask for a room in the adjacent new addition, where the rooms are sunnier, quieter, and more spacious. There is a reading area in an upstairs salon overlooking Taxco, as well as a garden patio with fountains.

Cenaobscuras 1, 40200 Taxco, Gro. ℂ **762/622-0080** or -0980. Fax 762/622-2938. 34 units. $50 (£28) double; $65 (£36) superior double; $74 (£41) junior suite. AE, MC, V. Limited free parking. **Amenities:** Dining-room-style restaurant and bar; room service; laundry service; safe.

WHERE TO DINE

Taxco gets a lot of day-trippers, most of whom choose to dine close to the Plaza Borda. Prices in this area are high for what you get. Just a few streets back, you'll find some excellent, simple *fondas* (taverns) or restaurants.

VERY EXPENSIVE

Toni's 🏵 STEAKS/SEAFOOD   High on a mountaintop, Toni's is an intimate, classic restaurant enclosed in a huge, cone-shaped *palapa* with a panoramic view of the city. Eleven candlelit tables sparkle with crystal and crisp linen, and piano music accompanies dinner. The menu, mainly shrimp or beef, is limited, but the food is quite good. Try tender, juicy prime roast beef, which comes with creamed spinach and baked potato. To reach Toni's, it's best to take a taxi. Note that it's open for dinner on weekends only.

In the Hotel Monte Taxco. ℂ **762/622-1300**. Reservations recommended. Main courses $15–$26 (£8.25–£14). AE, MC, V. Fri–Sat 7pm–1am.

MODERATE

Cafe Sasha 🏵🏵 INTERNATIONAL/VEGETARIAN   One of the cutest places to dine in town, Cafe Sasha is very popular with locals, and offers a great array of vegetarian options—such as falafel and vegetarian crepes, as well as Mexican and international classics. Try their Thai chicken curry or a hearty burrito. Open for breakfast, lunch, and dinner, it's also a great place for a cappuccino and pastry, or an evening cocktail. The music is hip, and the atmosphere is inviting and chic. Local artists often exhibit here, and there's live music on Sundays.

Calle Juan Ruiz de Alarcón 1, just down from Plazuela de Berna. No phone. www.cafesasha.com. Breakfast $2–$7 (£1.10–£3.85); main courses $5–$15 (£2.75–£8.25). No credit cards. Daily 8am–11:30pm.

El Adobe 🏵 MEXICAN   This charming restaurant is an eclectic Mexican mix of adobe, brick, and wood with decor that includes regional art, old black and white photos of Mexican and American entertainers, and some kitsch memorabilia. There are a number of romantic balcony tables lit with candles and lamps after dark. The hearty fare includes *cecina taxqueña* (thin strip steak served with guacamole), *pollo al adobe* (chicken with onions, green chili, and ham diced with grated cheese and cooked in aluminum foil), and enchiladas prepared anyway you want. A guitar player/singer performs weekend nights, and brunch is offered on Sundays.

Plazuela de San Juan 13. ℂ **762/622-1416**. Breakfast $3–$5 (£1.65–£2.75); main courses $5.50–$14 (£3–£7.70). MC, V. Daily 7:30am–11pm.

La Terraza Café-Bar INTERNATIONAL   One of two restaurants at the Hotel Agua Escondida (on the *zócalo*), the rooftop La Terraza is a scenic spot for a meal or a drink, with a great view of the church and tasty food. The menu is ample—you can get anything from breaded veal to grilled pork chops or chicken fajitas, and desserts include crepes, chocolate cake, and flan. Frosty margaritas and rich cappuccinos are also on order. During the day, cafe umbrellas shade the sun, but you can stargaze here at night.

Plaza Borda 4. ℂ 762/622-1166. Main courses $4–$10 (£2.20–£5.50). MC, V. Daily noon–10pm.

Sotavento Restaurant Bar Galería ✿✿ ITALIAN/INTERNATIONAL   Paintings decorate the walls of this stylish restaurant, which offers tables inside, on the balcony, or in the garden patio. The extensive menu features Italian and Mexican dishes—try deliciously fresh spinach salad and large pepper steak for a hearty meal, or Spaghetti Barbara, with poblano peppers, onions, avocado, and crema for a vegetarian option. Savory crepes are also available.

Benito Juárez 12, next to City Hall. ℂ 762/627-1217. Main courses $4.50–$15 (£2.50–£8.25). MC, V. Tues–Sun 1pm–midnight. From the Plaza Borda, walk downhill beside the Hotel Agua Escondida, then follow the street as it bears left (don't go right on Juan Ruiz de Alarcón) about 1 block; the restaurant is on the left just after the street bends left.

Sr. Costilla's MEXICAN/INTERNATIONAL   The offbeat decor at "Mr. Ribs" includes old photos of Mexican and international performers and a ceiling decked out with an assortment of cultural curios (note the festive dangling skeletons). Several tiny balconies hold minuscule tables that afford a view of the plaza and church, and they fill up long before the large dining room does. The broad menu features steaks, sandwiches, barbecue chicken, shrimp, and spareribs, as well as desserts and an extensive selection of drinks.

Plaza Borda 1 (next to Santa Prisca, above Patio de las Artesanías). ℂ/fax 762/622-3215. Main courses $8–$22 (£4.40–£12). MC, V. Mon–Fri noon–midnight; Sat 9am–midnight; Sun 8am–8pm.

INEXPENSIVE

Restaurante Ethel MEXICAN   This family-run eatery opposite the Hotel Santa Prisca, 1 block from the Plaza Borda, is simple and cheap. It has colorful cloths on the tables and a tidy, homey atmosphere. The hearty *comida corrida* (food on the go) consists of soup or pasta, meat (perhaps a small steak), dessert, and good coffee. Full breakfasts, typical Mexican dishes, and rich *pozole* (a thick Mexican soup) are offered, too.

Plazuela San Juan 14. ℂ 762/622-0788. Breakfast $5.50–$6 (£3–3.30); main courses $5.50–$7 (£3–£3.85); *comida corrida* (served 1–5pm) $5.80 (£3.20). No credit cards. Daily 9am–9pm.

TAXCO AFTER DARK

Bar Acerto (ℂ 762/622-0064) is the most enticing place overlooking the square for cocktails, conversation, and people-watching, all of which continue until 11pm daily. Taxco's popular, modern dance club, **Windows,** sits high up the mountain in the **Hotel Monte Taxco** (ℂ 762/622-1300). The whole city is on view, and music runs the gamut from Latin pop to '80s hits. For a $5 (£2.75) cover, you can dance away Friday or Saturday night from 10pm to 3am.

Completely different in tone is **Berta's** (ℂ 762/622-0172), next to the Santa Prisca Church. Opened in 1930 by a lady named Berta, who made her fame on a drink of the same name (tequila, soda, lime, and honey), it's the traditional gathering place of the local gentry and more than a few tourists. Spurs and old swords decorate the walls.

Grab a seat on the balcony overlooking the plaza and church. A Berta (the drink, of course) costs about $5 (£2.75); rum, the same. It's open daily from 11am to 8pm.

La Concha Nostra (© **762/622-7944**), has a local, edgy feel and features live rock music Saturday nights for a $3 (£1.65) cover. It's located upstairs inside the Hotel Casa Grande at Plazuela de San Juan 7, and is open nightly until 1am. The gay-friendly **Aztec Disco** (© **762/627-3833**) features drag shows and dancing. It's located on Av. de los Plateros 184, and is open from 10pm until late.

2 Ixtapan de la Sal: A Thermal Spa Town

120km (74 miles) SW of Mexico City

The whitewashed town of Ixtapan de la Sal (not to be confused with Ixtapa, on the Pacific coast) is known for its thermal mud baths—this is an original spa town, with generations of healing traditions.

Hotels in Ixtapan (pronounced "*eeks*-tah-pahn") de la Sal tend to be full on weekends and Mexican holidays, as the town is a popular retreat from Mexico City. Cuernavaca, Taxco, and Toluca are all easy side trips.

ESSENTIALS

GETTING THERE & DEPARTING   By Car   From Mexico City, take Highway 15 to Toluca. In Toluca, Highway 15 becomes Paseo Tollocan. Follow Tollocan south until you see signs pointing left to Ixtapan de la Sal. After the turn, continue straight for around 15km (9⅓ miles). Just before the town of Tenango del Valle, you have a choice of the free road to Ixtapan de la Sal or the toll road. The free road winds through the mountains and takes 1½ hours. The inexpensive two-lane toll road has fewer mountain curves and takes around an hour—it's worth taking. The toll road stops about 15km (9⅓ miles) before Ixtapan; the rest of the trip is on a curvy mountainous drive.

By Bus   From Mexico City's Terminal Poniente, buses leave for Ixtapan de la Sal every few minutes. Request a bus that's taking the toll road, which cuts the travel time by 30 to 60 minutes, to about 2½ hours. To return, take a bus marked MEXICO DIRECTO, which leaves every 10 minutes and usually stops in Toluca. Buses from here also go to Cuernavaca and Taxco every 40 minutes.

A PUBLIC SPA

The **Balneario Ixtapan** (© **721/143-0331**), next to the Hotel Spa Ixtapan, is the town's original public spa and bathhouse. It's not a modern, pampering spa, but a spa in the traditional manner—think Turkish baths. Over the years, the *balneario* has melded its traditional thermal waters with some features that make it more of an aquatic park. In addition to the large pools of varying temperatures, it offers modern features such as water slides, a slow-moving river, and other attractions. Entrance is $15 (£8.25) for adults, $7 (£3.85) for children between .9 and 1.2m (3–4 ft.) tall; children under .9m (3 ft.) tall enter free. The *balneario* has restaurants, so you can spend the day. The entrance fee gives you access to all of the pools and rides. Lockers are 50¢ (30p) and dressers are $1 (55p). It's open Tuesday through Sunday from 8am to 7pm. The traditional spa amenities and services are next door, where you can take private thermal water baths or choose among massages, facials, hair treatments, paraffin wraps, pedicures, and manicures. Prices range from $15 to $50 (£8.25–£28). When you purchase a spa treatment you can include access to the *balneario* for $7

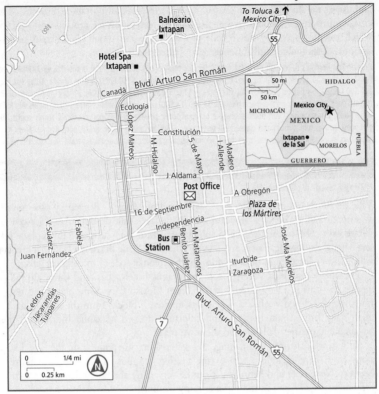

(£3.85). The spa is open daily from 8am to 8pm during holiday periods; at other times, Monday through Friday from 8am to 8pm, Saturday and Sunday from 7am to 8pm. For a spa menu, call Señora Silvia Rivas at ☎ **55/5254-0500**.

WHERE TO STAY & DINE

Hotel Spa Ixtapan 🌟🌟 *Value*   The town's only first-class hotel sits on 14 manicured and flower-filled hectares (35 acres). It's been in operation since 1939, and though it's continually upgraded, some areas that have been left untouched provide guests with the nostalgic feel of the original resort. When you compare this spa's comfort, weight-loss programs, good food, and relaxing pace to the offerings at other spas, you'll understand its continued popularity. It's one of the best spa values in Mexico, although very expensive for Ixtapan. The resort offers golf, tennis, riding, swimming, and miles of trails for walking, jogging, or biking. It also has freshwater and thermal mineral swimming pools, an outdoor whirlpool, and a host of spa facilities for body treatments. The guest rooms are large, comfortable, and stylishly furnished. You have your choice of two restaurants: One serves a menu focused on smart nutrition, with vegetarian options; the other offers a more traditional international menu. The hotel shows classic movies each night in its own private theater. The spa week goes from Monday to Friday, with Sunday arrival preferred. Spa facilities are closed on Sunday. Hotel guests not on the spa program can use the facilities on a per-treatment basis, and there's no daily admission charge. Round-trip taxi transportation from the Mexico City airport can be arranged at the time of reservation for around $300 (£165), which can be shared by up to four people. There are about 10 different package options. Rates include full American plan (three meals daily).

Bulevar San Román s/n, Ixtapan de la Sal, 51900 Edo. de México. © 800/638-7950 in the U.S., or 721/143-2440. Fax 721/143-0856. www.spamexico.com. 220 units, including 45 villas. $150 (£83) double or villa. 4-day spa package $604 (£332) per person double; 7-day spa package $1,075 (£591) per person double; 21-day spa package $2,700 (£1,485) per person double; 28-day spa package $3,600 (£1,980) per person double. Rates include meals. AE, MC, V. **Amenities:** 2 restaurants; bar; piano lounge; 2 outdoor pools; private 18-hole golf course; 2 tennis courts; fully equipped gym; aerobics room and classes; full-service spa; 2 indoor and 1 outdoor whirlpool; sauna; steam room; mountain bikes; tour desk; Internet room; room service; laundry service; solarium; hiking trails. *In room:* TV, minibar.

3 Valle de Bravo & Avándaro: Mexico's Switzerland

152km (94 miles) SW of Mexico City

Valle de Bravo has been called the "Switzerland of Mexico." Ringed by pine-forested mountains and set beside a beautiful man-made lake, Valle de Bravo is a 16th-century village with cobblestone streets and colonial structures built around a town plaza. Like San Miguel de Allende, Taxco, and Puerto Vallarta, Valle de Bravo is a National Heritage village; new construction must conform to the colonial style of the original village.

The village's cobbled streets, small restaurants, hotels, spas, and shops are full on weekends—this is a very popular retreat from Mexico City. Some shops and restaurants may be closed weekdays. The crafts market, 3 blocks from the main square, is open daily from 10am to 5pm, and colorfully dressed Mazahua Indians sell their handmade tapestries daily around the town plaza.

Sailing, windsurfing, bass fishing, and water-skiing are popular on the lake. Excursions from here include a trip to the nesting grounds of the monarch butterfly between November and February. It can be very rainy and chilly September through December, in addition to the summer rainy season.

The neighboring town of Avándaro, 6km (3¾ miles) away, is a popular place for weekend homes for well-to-do residents of Mexico City.

ESSENTIALS

GETTING THERE & DEPARTING   By Car   From Mexico City, the quickest and most direct route is Highway 15 to Toluca. In Toluca, Highway 15 becomes Paseo Tollocan. Follow Tollocan south until you see signs pointing left to Highway 134 and Valle de Bravo, Francisco de los Ranchos, and Temascaltepec. After the turn, continue on Highway 142 until Francisco de los Ranchos, where you bear right, following signs to Valle de Bravo. The drive from this point takes about 1½ to 2 hours.

By Bus   From Mexico City's Terminal Poniente, buses leave every 20 minutes for the 3-hour journey. First-class buses depart hourly.

WHERE TO STAY & DINE

Avándaro Golf and Spa Resort ★★   Nestled on 118 hectares (291 acres) amid large estates, lushly forested mountains, and a gorgeous, rolling 18-hole golf course, this resort occupies one of the loveliest settings in Mexico. Rooms come in two categories: large, beautifully furnished deluxe suites, and small, less luxurious cabañas. All have fireplaces and terraces or balconies overlooking the grounds. The extensive spa includes hot and cold whirlpools, sauna and steam rooms, and a full range of body and facial treatments. Transportation from Mexico City can be arranged.

Valle de Bravo & Avándaro

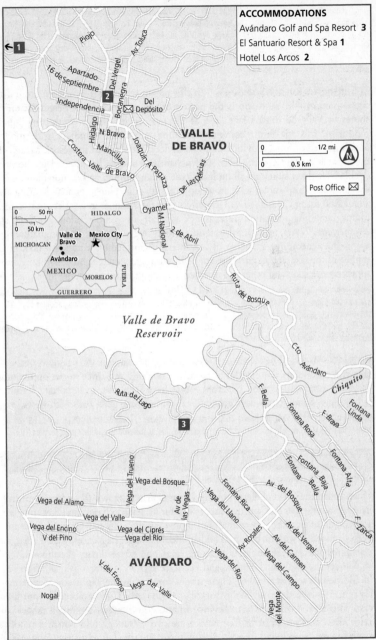

ACCOMMODATIONS

Avándaro Golf and Spa Resort **3**

El Santuario Resort & Spa **1**

Hotel Los Arcos **2**

Piojo

Av Toluca

Apartado

16 de Septiembre

Del Vergel

Bocanegra

Independencia

Del Depósito

2

Hidalgo

N Bravo

Mancillas

Joaquín A Pagaza

**VALLE
DE BRAVO**

Costera Valle de Bravo

De las Delicias

0   1/2 mi

0   0.5 km

Post Office ✉

Oyamel

M. Nacional

2 de Abril

0   50 mi

0   50 km

HIDALGO

MICHOACAN

Valle de
Bravo

Mexico City ★

Avándaro

MEXICO

MORELOS

PUEBLA

GUERRERO

Ruta del Bosque

Cto. Avándaro

*Valle de Bravo
Reservoir*

Chiquito

Fontana
Linda

Ruta del Lago

F. Bella

Fontana Rosa

F. Brava

Fontana Alta

3

Fontana Baja

Fontana
Bella

Vega del Trueno

Vega del Bosque

Av de las Vegas

Vega del Llano

Fontana Rica

Av. del Bosque

Vega del Alamo

Av del Vergel

Vega del Valle

Vega del Cíprés

Vega del Río

Av Rosales

Av del Carmen

Vega del Campo

F. Zarca

Vega del Encino

V del Pino

Vega del Río

AVÁNDARO

V del Fresno

Vega del Valle

Vega del Río

Vega
del Monte

Nogal

Fracc. Vega del Río s/n. Avándaro, 51200 Valle de Bravo. © **726/266-1651;** reservations 55/5280-1532, 5282-0954, 5280-5532, or 5282-0578 in Mexico City. www.grupoavandaro.com.mx. 82 units. $190 (£105) double cabaña; $250 (£138) deluxe suite. 7-day spa or golf package available. AE, MC, V. **Amenities:** 2 restaurants; 25m (82-ft.) junior Olympic-size pool; 18-hole golf course; 7 tennis courts; weight-training equipment; ultramodern spa w/well-trained staff and full range of services; hot and cold whirlpools; sauna; steam rooms; room service. *In room:* TV, hair dryer, safe.

El Santuario Resort Spa ★★★ In this region where spas have been around for ages—literally—El Santuario is the newest of the spa resorts to emerge. Set on the shores of Valle de Bravo's lake, and at the foot of an "energy-conducting" quartz mountain, this spa resort combines soothing natural surroundings with modern amenities, recreational activities, and spa services. Throughout the resort, natural elements such as slate, quartz, river stones, bamboo, and shells are used in the decor details. The guest suites are all built into the mountainside, with panoramic views of the lake. Each also comes with an indoor, infinity-edge plunge pool and sitting area. The 1,860 sq. m (20,020-sq.-ft.) spa offers over 60 therapies in a variety of treatment rooms, including a flotation suite, as well as a cafe, oxygen bar, salon, gym, and studio for yoga, Pilates, meditation, and other mind-body activities. Their signature therapy is the Yenecamú—2½ hours of treatments performed on a pontoon boat in the middle of the lake. If you grow tired of being pampered, there's also golf, hiking, water sports on the lake, and other eco-oriented activities to while away the time.

ExHacienda San Gaspar Carretera a Colorines, Km 4.5, 51200 Valle de Bravo. © **726/262-9104.** www.elsantuario spa.com. 64 suites. $270 (£149) double on weekdays; $400 (£220) double on weekends. Spa packages start at $200 (£110) extra per person, double occupancy for 2 nights, including all meals and selected spa services. Other packages are also available. MC, V. **Amenities:** Restaurant/bar; outdoor pool with whirlpools; 9-hole golf course; spa; tour desk; boutique; salon; laundry service; marina. *In room:* TV, minibar, hair dryer, safe.

Hotel los Arcos The Hotel los Arcos, close to the main square, has views of the village and mountains. Two stories of rooms on one side and three stories on the other surround a swimming pool. Nineteen rooms have fireplaces, an important feature in winter here. Some rooms have balconies, and most have glass walls with views.

Bocanegra 310, 51200 Valle de Bravo, Edificio de México. ©/fax **726/262-0042,** -0531, or -0168. 24 units. Mon–Thurs $85 (£47) double; Fri–Sun $110 (£61) double. AE, MC, V. **Amenities:** Outdoor pool. *In room:* TV.

4 Cuernavaca: Land of Eternal Spring ★★★

102km (63 miles) S of Mexico City; 80km (50 miles) N of Taxco

Often called the "land of eternal spring," Cuernavaca is known these days as much for its rejuvenating spas and spiritual sites as it is for its perfect climate and flowering landscapes. Spa services are easy to find, but more than that, Cuernavaca exudes a sense of deep connection with its historical and spiritual heritage. Its palaces, walled villas, and elaborate haciendas are home to museums, spas, and extraordinary guesthouses.

Wander the traditional markets and you'll see crystals, quartz, onyx, and tiger's eye, in addition to tourist trinkets. These stones come from the Tepozteco Mountains— for centuries considered an energy source—which cradle Cuernavaca to the north and east. This area is where Mexico begins to narrow, and several mountain ranges converge. East and southeast of Cuernavaca are two volcanoes, also potent symbols of earth energy: Ixtaccihuatl (the Sleeping Woman) and the recently active Popocatépetl (the Smoking Mountain).

Cuernavaca

0 1/8 mi
0 125 meters

V. Fábregas

Alvaro Obregón
Ricardo Linares
Ixtapa

Las Mañanitas ■

Chamilpa

Aldama

F. Madero

Calle del Arco

Calle de Cuoglia

M. Ocampo

PARQUE

Priv. Ocampo

Priv. M. León Díaz

Calle de la Selva

Calle Carlos Fuera

Pr. del Arco

Gómes Farias

Mariano

Guadalupe Victoria

Matamoros

Av. Gral. José María Morelos

Arista

Pirámide de
Teopanzolco

Degollado

No Reelección

Guerrero

Market ■

Obregón

Calle de Aragón y León

Pr. M. Salinas

Morrow

Calle de Arteaga

(ravine)

Hosteria
Las Quintas

Pr. de Rayón

Lerdo de Tejada

JARDÍN
JUÁREZ

Calle Central

Calle de Gutenberg

JARDÍN
BORDA

López Rayón

Governor's
Palace

Zócalo

Calle de

Salazar

Entrance ■

Alarcón

Comonfort

ALAMEDA

Catedral de
Cuernavaca ■ †

Hidalgo

Plaza de
Armas

Cortéz Palace
& Museo de
Cuauhnahuac

Callejón Borda

Museo Casa
Robert Brady ■

Netzahualcoyti

Galeana

Mercado ■

Jardín →
de los
Héroes

Palacio
Municipal

Bartolomé de las Casas

0 50 mi
0 50 km

HIDALGO

MICHOACÁN

Mexico City ★

MEXICO

Cuernavaca ●

MORELOS
GUERRERO

PUEBLA

Avenida Morelos

20 de
Noviembre

Hotel
Juárez

Hotel Posada
María Cristina

Juárez

Francisco Leyva

Jardín
Etnobotánico →

Abasolo

■ Bus Terminal
Pullman de Morelos

Information ⓘ
Post Office ✉

165

Cuernavaca, capital of the state of Morelos, is also a cultural treasure, with a past that closely follows the history of Mexico. So divine are the landscape and climate that both the Aztec ruler Moctezuma II and French Emperor Maximilian built private retreats here. Today, the roads between Mexico City and Cuernavaca are jammed almost every weekend, when city residents seek the same respite. Cuernavaca even has a large American colony, plus many students attending the numerous language and cultural institutes.

Emperor Charles V gave Cuernavaca to Hernán Cortez as a fief, and in 1532 the conquistador built a palace (now the Museo de Cuauhnáhuac), where he lived on and off for half a dozen years before returning to Spain. Cortez introduced sugar cane cultivation to the area, and African slaves were brought in to work in the cane fields, by way of Spain's Caribbean colonies. His sugar hacienda at the edge of town is now the impressive Hotel de Cortez.

After Mexico gained independence from Spain, powerful landowners from Mexico City gradually dispossessed the remaining small landholders, imposing virtual serfdom on them. This condition led to the rise of Emiliano Zapata, the great champion of agrarian reform, who battled the forces of wealth and power, defending the small farmer with the cry of *"¡Tierra y Libertad!"* (Land and Liberty!) during the Mexican Revolution of 1910.

Today, Cuernavaca's popularity has brought an influx of wealthy foreigners and industrial capital. With this commercial growth, the city has also acquired the less desirable by-products of increased traffic, noise, and air pollution—although still far, far less than nearby Mexico City, which you may be escaping.

ESSENTIALS

GETTING THERE & DEPARTING   By Car   From Mexico City, take Paseo de la Reforma to Chapultepec Park and merge with the Periférico, which will take you to Highway 95D, the toll road on the far south of town that goes to Cuernavaca. From the Periférico, take the Insurgentes exit and continue until you come to signs for Cuernavaca/Tlalpan. Choose either the CUERNAVACA CUOTA (toll) or CUERNAVACA LIBRE (free) road on the right. The free road is slower and very windy, but is more scenic.

By Bus   *Important note:* Buses to Cuernavaca depart directly from the Mexico City airport. (See "Getting There," in chapter 2, for details.) The trip takes an hour. The Mexico City Central de Autobuses del Sur exists primarily to serve the Mexico City–Cuernavaca–Taxco–Acapulco–Zihuatanejo route. Pullman de Morelos has two stations in Cuernavaca: downtown, at the corner of Abasolo and Netzahualcóyotl (© **777/318-0907** or 312-6063), 4 blocks south of the center of town; and Casino de la Selva (© **777/312-9473**), less conveniently located at Plan de Ayala 14, near the railroad station.

Autobuses Estrella Blanca (© **777/312-2626;** www.estrellablanca.com.mx), depart from the Central del Sur with 4 buses daily from Mexico City. They arrive in Cuernavaca at Av. Morelos Sur 329, between Arista and Victoria, 6 blocks north of the town center. Here, you'll find frequent buses to Toluca, Chalma, Ixtapan de la Sal, Taxco, Acapulco, the Cacahuamilpa Caves, Querétaro, and Nuevo Laredo.

Estrella de Oro (© **777/312-3055;** www.estrelladeoro.com.mx), Morelos 900, serves Iguala, Chilpancingo, Acapulco, and Taxco.

Estrella Roja (© **777/318-5934;** www.estrellaroja.com.mx), a second-class station at Galeana and Cuauhtemotzin in Cuernavaca, about 8 blocks south of the town center, serves Cuautla, Yautepec, Oaxtepec, and Izúcar de Matamoros.

VISITOR INFORMATION   Cuernavaca's **Municipal Tourist Office** is at Av. Morelos Sur 278, between Jalisco and Tabasco (© **777/314-3920;** www.cuernavaca. gob.mx), half a block north of the Estrella de Oro bus station and about a 15- to 20-minute walk south of the cathedral. The **Morelos State Tourism Office** is located on Av. Morelos Sur 187 (© **777/314-1880;** www.morelostravel.com). Both are open Monday through Friday from 9am to 5pm. There's also a **City Tourism kiosk** (© **777/329-4404**), on Morelos beside the El Calvario Church. It's open daily from 9am to 5pm.

CITY LAYOUT   In the center of the city are two contiguous plazas. The smaller and more formal, across from the post office, has a Victorian gazebo (designed by Gustave Eiffel, of Eiffel Tower fame) at its center. This is the **Alameda.** The larger, rectangular plaza with trees, shrubs, and benches is the **Plaza de Armas.** These two plazas are known collectively as the *zócalo* and form the hub for strolling vendors selling balloons, baskets, bracelets, and other crafts from surrounding villages. It's all easy-going, and one of the great pleasures of the town is hanging out at a park bench or table in a nearby restaurant. On Sunday afternoons, orchestras play in the gazebo. At the eastern end of the Alameda is the **Cortez Palace,** the conquistador's residence, now the Museo de Cuauhnáhuac.

Note: The city's street-numbering system is extremely confusing. It appears that the city fathers, during the past century or so, imposed a new numbering system every 10 or 20 years. An address given as "no. 5" may be in a building that bears the number "506," or perhaps "Antes no. 5" (former no. 5).

FAST FACTS: Cuernavaca

American Express The local representative is **Viajes Marín,** Edificio las Plazas, Loc. 13 (© **777/314-2266** or 318-9901; fax 777/312-9297). It's open daily from 9am to 7pm.

Area Code The telephone area code is **777.**

Banks Bank tellers (9am–3 or 5pm, depending on the bank), ATMs, and *casas de cambio* change money. The closest bank to the *zócalo* is **Bancomer,** Matamoros and Lerdo de Tejada, cater-cornered to Jardín Juárez (across López Rayón from the Alameda). ATMs at banks generally remain open until 6pm Monday through Friday and a half-day on Saturday.

Drugstore **Farmacias del Ahorro** (© **777/322-2277**) offers hotel delivery service, but you must ask the front desk of your hotel to place the order, because the pharmacy requires the name of a hotel employee. It has 12 locations around the city, but the individual pharmacies have no phone. They are open daily from 7am to 10pm.

Elevation Cuernavaca sits at 1,533m (5,028 ft.).

Hospital **Hospital Inovamed,** Calle Cuauhtémoc 305, Col. Lomas de la Selva (© **777/311-2482,** -2483, or -2484).

Internet Access **MarkSoft** Internet, Otilio Montano, Col. Altavista (www.marksoft solutions.com), serves coffee and Internet access for $3 (£1.65) per 15 minutes. You can also try **Café Internet Net-Conn,** Morelos Norte 360-A, Col. Carolina

(℃ **777/317-9496**), which offers high-speed access for $2.50 (£1.40) per hour, as well as color laser printers, Web cams, scanners, and other equipment. It's open Monday through Saturday from 8am to 11pm, closed Sunday.

Population Cuernavaca has 400,000 residents.

Post Office The *correo* (℃ **777/312-4379**) is on the Plaza de Armas, next door to Café los Arcos. It's open Monday through Friday from 8am to 6pm, Saturday from 10am to 2pm.

Spanish Lessons Cuernavaca is known for its Spanish-language schools. Generally, the schools will help students find lodging with a family or provide a list of places to stay. Rather than make a long-term commitment in a family living situation, try it for a week, then decide. Contact the **Universidad Internacional,** San Jerónimo 304 (Apdo. Postal 1520), 62000 Cuernavaca, Morelos (℃ **800/574-1583** in the U.S. or 777/317-1087; www.spanish.com.mx); **Instituto de Idioma y Cultura en Cuernavaca** (℃ **777/317-8947;** fax 777/317-0455); or **Universal Centro de Lengua y Comunicación Social A.C. (Universal Language School),** J. H. Preciado 171 (Apdo. Postal 1-1826, 62000 Cuernavaca, Morelos; ℃ **777/318-2904** or 312-4902; www.universal-spanish.com). Note that the whole experience, from classes to lodging, can be quite expensive; the school may accept credit cards for the class portion.

EXPLORING CUERNAVACA

On weekends, the whole city (including the roads, hotels, and restaurants) fills with people from Mexico City. This makes weekends more hectic, but also more fun. You can spend 1 or 2 days sightseeing pleasantly enough. If you've come on a day trip, you may not have time to make all the excursions listed below, but you'll have enough time to see the sights in town. Also notable is the traditional *mercado* **(public market)** adjacent to the Cortez Palace. It's open daily from 10am to 10pm, and the colorful rows of stands are a lively place for testing your bargaining skills as you purchase pottery, silver jewelry, crystals, and other trinkets. Note that the Cuauhnáhuac museum is closed on Monday.

Catedral de Cuernavaca 🌟 *Moments*   As you enter the church precincts and pass down the walk, try to imagine what life in Mexico was like in the old days. Construction on the church, also known as the *Catedral de Asunción de María,* began in 1529, a mere 8 years after Cortez conquered Tenochtitlán (Mexico City) from the Aztec, and was completed in 1552. The churchmen could hardly trust their safety to the tenuous allegiance of their new converts, so they built a fortress as a church. The skull and crossbones above the main door are a symbol of the Franciscan order, which had its monastery here. The monastery is still here, in fact, and open to the public; it's on the northwest corner of the church property. Also visible on the exterior walls of the main church are inlaid rocks, placed there in memory of the men who lost their lives during its construction.

Once inside, wander through the sanctuaries and the courtyard, and pay special attention to the impressive frescoes painted on the walls, in various states of restoration. The frescoes date from the 1500s and have a distinct Asian style.

The main church sanctuary is stark, even severe, with an incongruous modern feeling (it was refurbished in the 1960s). Frescoes on these walls, discovered during the refurbishing, depict the persecution and martyrdom of St. Felipe de Jesús and his companions in Japan. No one is certain who painted them. In the churchyard, you'll see gravestones marking the tombs of the most devout—or wealthiest—of the parishioners. Being buried on the church grounds was believed to be the most direct route to heaven.

At the corner of Hidalgo and Morelos (3 blocks southwest of the Plaza de Armas). ℭ 777/318-4590. Free admission. Daily 8am–2pm and 4–7pm.

Jardín Borda   Across Morelos Street from the cathedral lies the Jardín Borda (Borda Gardens). José de la Borda, the Taxco silver magnate, ordered a sumptuous vacation house built here in the late 1700s. When he died in 1778, his son Manuel inherited the land and transformed it into a botanical garden. The large enclosed garden next to the house was a huge private park, laid out in Andalusian style, with kiosks and an artificial pond. Maximilian took it over as his private summer house in 1865. He and Empress Carlota entertained lavishly in the gardens and held frequent concerts by the lake.

The gardens were completely restored and reopened in 1987 as the Jardín Borda Centro de Artes. In the gateway buildings, several galleries hold changing exhibits and large paintings showing scenes from the life of Maximilian and from the history of the Borda Gardens. One portrays the initial meeting between Maximilian and La India Bonita, a local maiden who became his lover.

On your stroll through the gardens, you'll see the little man-made lake on which Austrian, French, and Mexican nobility rowed small boats in the moonlight. Ducks have taken the place of dukes, however. There are rowboats for rent. The lake is now artfully adapted as an outdoor theater (see website for performance information), with seats for the audience on one side and the stage on the other. A cafe serves refreshments and light meals, and a weekend market inside the *jardín* sells arts and crafts.

Av. Morelos Sur 271, at Hidalgo. ℭ 777/318-1044. Fax 777/318-3706. www.arte-cultura-morelos.gob.mx. Admission $3 (£1.65) adult, $1.50 (85p) children; free Sun. Tues–Sun 10am–5:30pm.

Jardín Etnobotánico y Museo de Medicina Tradicional y Herbolaria ✸✸
This museum of traditional herbal medicine, in the south Cuernavaca suburb of Acapantzingo, occupies a former resort residence built by Maximilian, the Casa del Olvido. During his brief reign, the Austrian-born emperor came here for trysts with La India Bonita, his Cuernavacan lover. The building was restored in 1960, and the house and gardens now preserve the local wisdom of folk medicine. The shady gardens are lovely to wander through, and you shouldn't miss the 200 orchids growing near the rear of the property.

Matamoros 14, Acapantzingo. ℭ 777/312-5955, 312-3108, or 314-4046. www.inah.gob.mx. Free admission. Daily 9am–5pm. Take a taxi, or catch *combi* no. 6 at the mercado on Degollado. Ask to be dropped off at Matamoros near the museum; turn right on Matamoros and walk 1½ blocks; the museum will be on your right.

Museo Casa Robert Brady ✸✸   This private home and garden turned museum contains more than 1,300 works of exceptional art. Among them are pre-Hispanic and colonial pieces; oil paintings by Frida Kahlo and Rufino Tamayo; popular Mexican art; and handicrafts from America, Africa, Asia, and India. Robert Brady, an Iowa native with a degree in fine arts from the Art Institute of Chicago, assembled the collections.

He lived in Venice for 5 years before settling in Cuernavaca in 1960. The wildly colorful rooms remain exactly as Brady left them when he died here in 1986. Admission includes a guide in Spanish; English and French guides are available if requested in advance.

Calle Netzahualcóyotl 4 (between Hidalgo and Abasolo). (©) **777/318-8554.** Fax 777/314-3529. www.bradymuseum. org. Admission $3 (£1.65). Tues–Sun 10am–6pm.

Museo de Cuauhnáhuac   The museum is in the Cortez Palace, the former home of the greatest of the conquistadors, Hernán Cortez. Construction started in 1530 on the site of a Tlahuica Indian ceremonial center and was finished by the conquistador's son Martín. The palace later served as the legislative headquarters for the state of Morelos.

In the east portico on the upper floor is a large Diego Rivera mural commissioned by Dwight Morrow, U.S. ambassador to Mexico in the 1920s. It depicts the history of Cuernavaca from the coming of the Spaniards to the rise of Zapata (1910). On the lower level, the excellent bookstore is open daily from 11am to 8pm. Tour guides in front of the palace offer their services in the museum, and for other sights in Cuernavaca, for about $10 (£5.50) per hour. Make sure you see official SECTUR (Tourism Secretary) credentials before hiring one of these guides. This is also a central point for taxis in the downtown area.

In the Cortez Palace, Leyva 100. (©) **777/312-8171.** www.morelostravel.com/cultura/museo7.html. Admission $3.70 (£2.05); free Sun. Tues–Sun 9am–6pm.

ACTIVITIES & EXCURSIONS

GOLF   With its perpetually springlike climate, Cuernavaca is an ideal place for golf. The **Tabachines Golf Club and Restaurant,** Km 93.5 Carr. Mexico-Acapulco (© **777/314-3999**), the city's most popular course, is open for public play. Percy Clifford designed this 18-hole course, surrounded by beautifully manicured gardens blooming with bougainvillea, gardenias, and other flowers. The elegant restaurant is a popular place for breakfast, lunch, and especially Sunday brunch. Greens fees are $75 (£41) during the week and $190 (£105) on weekends. American Express, Visa, and MasterCard are accepted. It's open Tuesday through Sunday from 7am to 6pm; tee times are available from 7am to 2pm.

Also in Cuernavaca is the **Club de Golf Hacienda San Gaspar,** Avenida Emiliano Zapata, Col. Cliserio Alanis (© **777/319-4424;** www.sangaspar.com), an 18-hole golf course designed by Joe Finger. It's surrounded by more than 3,000 trees and has two artificial lagoons, plus beautiful panoramic views of Cuernavaca, the Popocatépetl and Ixtaccihuatl volcanoes, and the Tepozteco Mountains. Greens fees are $75 (£41) on weekdays, $130 (£72) on weekends (discounted after 2pm); carts cost an additional $28 (£15) for 18 holes, and a caddy is $17 (£9.35) plus tip. American Express, Visa, and MasterCard are accepted. Additional facilities include a gym with whirlpool and sauna, pool, four tennis courts, and a restaurant and snack bar. It's open Wednesday through Monday from 7am to 7pm.

LAS ESTACAS   Either a side trip from Cuernavaca or a destination on its own, Las Estacas, Km 6.5 Carretera Tlaltizapán–Cuautla, Morelos (© **777/312-4412** or -7610 in Cuernavaca, or 734/345-0350; www.lasestacas.com) is a natural water park. Its clear spring waters reputedly have healing properties. In addition to the crystal-clear rivers, Las Estacas has two pools, wading pools for children, horseback riding, and a *balneario* (traditional-style spa), open daily from 8am to 6pm. Several restaurants serve such simple food as quesadillas, fruit with yogurt, sandwiches, and *tortas*. Admission is $20 (£11) for adults, $12 (£6.60) for children under 1.2m (4 ft.) tall. A small, basic hotel charges $120 to $150 (£66–£83) for a double room; rates include the entrance fee to the *balneario* and breakfast. Cheaper lodging options are available, including a trailer and camping park; you can rent an adobe or straw hut with two bunk beds for $30 (£17). Visit the website for more information. MasterCard and Visa are accepted. On weekends, the place fills with families. Las Estacas is 36km (22 miles) east of Cuernavaca. To get there, take Highway 138 to Yautepec, then turn right at the first exit past Yautepec.

PYRAMIDS OF XOCHICALCO ✵   This beautiful ceremonial center provides clues to the history of the whole region. Artifacts and inscriptions link the site to the mysterious cultures that built Teotihuacán and Tula, and some of the objects found here would indicate that residents were also in contact with the Mixtec, Aztec, Maya, and Zapotec. The most impressive building in Xochicalco is the Pirámide de la Serpiente Emplumada (Pyramid of the Plumed Serpent), with its magnificent reliefs of plumed serpents twisting around seated priests. Underneath the pyramid is a series of tunnels and chambers with murals on the walls. There is also an observatory, where from April 30 to August 15 you can follow the trajectory of the sun as it shines through a hexagonal opening. The pyramids (𝒞 777/314-3920 for information) are 36km (22 miles) southwest of Cuernavaca. They're open daily from 9am to 5pm. Admission is $3 (£1.65).

WHERE TO STAY
EXPENSIVE
Camino Real Sumiya ✵✵   About 11km (7 miles) south of Cuernavaca, this unusual resort, whose name means "the place of peace, tranquillity, and longevity," was once the home of Woolworth heiress Barbara Hutton. Using materials and craftsmen from Japan, she constructed the estate in 1959 for $3.2 (£1.8) million on 12 wooded hectares (30 acres). The main house, a series of large connected rooms and decks, overlooks the grounds and contains restaurants and the lobby. Sumiya's charm rests in its relaxing atmosphere, which is best midweek (escapees from Mexico City tend to fill it on weekends). The guest rooms, which cluster in three-story buildings bordering manicured lawns, are simple in comparison to the striking Japanese architecture of the main house. Rooms have subtle Japanese accents, with austere but comfortable furnishings and scrolled wood doors. Hutton built a Kabuki-style theater and exquisite Zen meditation garden, which are now used only for special events. The theater contains vividly colored silk curtains and gold-plated temple paintings protected by folding cedar and mahogany screens. Strategically placed rocks in the garden represent the chakras, or energy points of the human body.

Interior Fracc. Sumiya s/n, Col. José Parres, 62550 Jiutepec, Mor. 𝒞 **01-800/901-2300** in Mexico, or 777/329-9888. Fax 777/329-9889. www.caminoreal.com/sumiya. 163 units. $180 (£99) double; $385 (£212) suite. Low-season packages and discounts available. AE, DC, MC, V. Free parking. From the freeway, take the Atlacomulco exit and follow signs to Sumiya. Ask directions in Cuernavaca if you're coming from there, as the route is complicated. **Amenities:** 2 restaurants; poolside snack bar; outdoor pool; golf privileges nearby; 10 tennis courts; business center; concierge; room service; convention facilities w/simultaneous translation capabilities. *In room:* A/C, TV, Wi-Fi, minibar, hair dryer, iron, safe, ceiling fan.

Las Mañanitas   This has been Cuernavaca's most renowned luxury lodging for years and is also a popular weekend dining spot for affluent visitors from Mexico City. Guest rooms are formal in style, with gleaming polished molding and brass accents, large bathrooms, and rich fabrics. Rooms in the original mansion, called terrace suites, overlook the restaurant and inner lawn; the large rooms in the patio section each have a secluded patio; and those in the luxurious, expensive garden section each have a patio overlooking the pool and emerald lawns. Sixteen rooms have fireplaces, and the hotel also has a heated pool in the private garden. The hotel is one of only two in Mexico associated with the prestigious Relais & Châteaux chain. Transportation to and from the Mexico City airport can be arranged through the hotel for $140 (£77) each way. The restaurant overlooking the peacock-filled gardens is one of the country's premier dining places (see "Where to Dine," below). It's open to nonguests for all meals.

Ricardo Linares 107 (5½ long blocks north of the Jardín Borda), 62000 Cuernavaca, Mor. ✆ 777/362-0000. Fax 777/318-3672. www.lasmananitas.com.mx. 32 units. Weekday $215–$325 (£118–£179) double; weekend $250–$350 (£138–£193) double. Rates include breakfast. AE, MC, V. Free valet parking. **Amenities:** Restaurant; outdoor pool; concierge; room service; laundry service. In room: TV, hair dryer.

Misión Del Sol Resort & Spa ★★★ (Finds) This adults-only hotel and spa offers an experience that rivals any in North America or Europe—and is an exceptional value. You feel a sense of peace from the moment you enter the resort, which draws on the mystical wisdom of the ancient cultures of Mexico, Tibet, Egypt, and Asia. Guests and visitors are encouraged to wear light-hued clothes to contribute to the harmonious flow of energy.

Architecturally stunning adobe buildings that meld with the natural environment house the guest rooms, villas, and common areas. Streams border the extensive gardens. Such group activities as reading discussions, a chess club, and painting workshops take place in the salon, where films are shown on weekend evenings. Spacious rooms are designed according to Feng-Shui principles; each looks onto its own garden or stream and has three channels of ambient music. Some have air-conditioning. Bathrooms are large, with sunken tubs, and the dual-headed showers have river rocks set into the floor, as a type of reflexology treatment. Beds contain magnets for restoring proper energy flow. Villas feature two separate bedrooms, plus a living/dining area and a meditation room. The spa has a menu of 32 services, with an emphasis on water-based treatments. Elegant relaxation areas are interspersed among the treatment rooms and whirlpool.

Av. General Diego Díaz González 31, Col. Parres, 62550 Cuernavaca, Mor. ✆ 01-800/999-9100 toll-free inside Mexico, or 777/321-0999. Fax 777/320-7981. www.misiondelsol.com.mx. 42 units, plus 12 villas. $243 (£134) deluxe double; $502 (£276) 2-bedroom villa (up to 4 persons); $595 (£327) 3-bedroom villa (up to 6 persons). Special spa and meal packages available. AE, MC, V. Free parking. Children younger than 13 not accepted. **Amenities:** Restaurant; 2 tennis courts; well-equipped gym; extensive spa services; basketball; volleyball; daily meditation, yoga, and Tai Chi classes. In room: Safe.

MODERATE
Hotel Posada María Cristina ★★ The María Cristina's high walls conceal many delights: a small swimming pool, lush gardens with fountains, a good restaurant, and patios. Guest rooms vary in size; all are exceptionally clean and comfortable, with firm beds and colonial-style furnishings. Bathrooms have inlaid Talavera tiles and skylights. Suites are only slightly larger than normal rooms; junior suites have Jacuzzis. La Calandria, the handsome little restaurant on the first floor, overlooks the gardens and serves excellent meals based on Mexican and international recipes. Even if you don't stay here, consider having a meal. The popular Sunday brunch ($16/£8.80 per person) features live classical music. The hotel lies half a block from the Palacio de Cortez.

Bulevar Juárez 300, Col. Centro (Apdo. Postal 203), 62000 Cuernavaca, Mor. © **777/318-2981.** Fax 777/312-9126 or 777/318-2981. www.maria-cristina.com. 20 units. $130 (£72) double; $135–$220 (£74–£121) suite or cabaña. AE, MC, V. Free parking. **Amenities:** Restaurant; bar; outdoor pool; concierge; tour desk. *In room:* A/C, TV, hair dryer, ceiling fan.

INEXPENSIVE

Hotel Juárez   Low rates and a prime location (downtown, 1 block from the Casa Borda) make the Juárez a good choice for those intent on exploring the town's cultural charms. Each of the simple rooms is old-fashioned but well kept.

Netzahualcóyotl 19, 62000 Cuernavaca, Mor. © **777/314-0219.** 12 units. $35 (£19) double. No credit cards. Limited street parking. From the Cathedral, go east on Hidalgo, then turn right on Netzahualcóyotl. The hotel is 1 block down on the left. **Amenities:** Outdoor pool; tour desk. *In room:* TV.

WHERE TO DINE
VERY EXPENSIVE

Restaurant Las Mañanitas MEXICAN/INTERNATIONAL   Las Mañanitas has set the standard for sumptuous, leisurely dining in Cuernavaca, filling with wealthy families from Mexico City on weekends and holidays. The setting is exquisite and the service superb, although the food is more standard than special. Tables stand on a shaded terrace with a view of gardens, strolling peacocks, and softly playing violinists or a trio playing romantic boleros. Diners have the option of ordering drinks and making their menu selections from chairs in the garden, waiting to take their seats at their tables when their meals are served. The cuisine is Mexican with an international flair, drawing on seasonal fruits and vegetables and offering a full selection of fresh seafood, certified Angus beef, lamb chops, baby back ribs, and free range chicken, but in standard preparations. Try the zucchini flower soup, filet of red snapper in curry sauce, and black-bottom pie, the house specialty.

In Las Mañanitas hotel, Ricardo Linares 107 (5½ long blocks north of the Jardín Borda). © **777/362-0019.** Fax: 777/318-3672. www.lasmananitas.com.mx. Reservations recommended. Main courses $19–$39 (£10–£21). AE, MC, V. Daily 8–11am, 1–5pm, and 7–11pm.

MODERATE

Casa Hidalgo ★★★ GOURMET MEXICAN/INTERNATIONAL   In a beautifully restored colonial building across from the Palacio de Cortez, this is a relatively recent addition to Cuernavaca dining. The food is more sophisticated and innovative than that at most places in town. Specialties include chilled mango and tequila soup, smoked rainbow trout, and the exquisite Spanish-inspired filet Hidalgo—breaded and stuffed with serrano ham and *manchego* cheese. There are always daily specials, and bread is baked on the premises. Tables on the balcony afford a view of the action in the plaza below. The restaurant is accessible by wheelchair.

Calle Hidalgo 6. © **777/312-2749.** www.casahidalgo.com. Reservations recommended on weekends. Main courses $14–$20 (£7.70–£11). AE, MC, V. Mon–Thurs 1:30–11pm; Fri–Sat 1:30pm–midnight; Sun 1:30–10pm.

Restaurant La India Bonita ★★ MEXICAN   Cuernavaca's oldest restaurant is housed among the interior patios and portals of the restored home—known as Casa Mañana—of former U.S. Ambassador Dwight Morrow. The beautiful setting features patio tables amidst trickling fountains, palms, and flowers. Specialties include *mole poblano* (chicken with a sauce of bitter chocolate and fiery chiles) and the signature *La India Bonita* plate with steak, enchiladas, rice, and beans. There are also several daily specials. A breakfast mainstay is *desayuno Maximiliano*, a gigantic platter of chicken enchiladas with an assortment of sauces.

Morrow 15 (between Morelos and Matamoros), Col. Centro, 2 blocks north of the Jardín Juárez. ☎ 777/318-6967 or 312-5021. Breakfast $4–$7 (£2.20–£3.85); main courses $7–$16 (£3.85–£8.80). AE, MC, V. Tues–Thurs 8am–10pm; Fri 8am–11pm; Sat 9am–11pm; Sun–Mon 9am–5pm.

INEXPENSIVE

La Universal 🌟🌟 *Value* MEXICAN/PASTRIES   This is a busy place, partly because of its great location (overlooking both the Alameda and Plaza de Armas), partly because of its traditional Mexican specialties, and partly because of its reasonable prices. It's open to the street and has many outdoor tables, usually filled with older men discussing the day's events or playing chess. These tables are perfect for watching the parade of street vendors and park life. The specialty is a Mexican grilled sampler plate, including *carne asada,* enchilada, pork cutlet, green onions, beans, and tortillas, for $12 (£6.60). A full breakfast special ($5/£2.75) is served Monday through Friday from 9:30am to noon. Live music is played weekdays from 3 to 5pm and again from 8 to 10pm.

Guerrero 2. ☎ 777/318-6732 or -5970. Breakfast $5–$8 (£2.75–£4.40); main courses $9–$14 (£4.95–£7.70); *comida corrida* $8.90 (£4.90). AE, MC, V. Daily 9:30am–1am.

CUERNAVACA AFTER DARK

Cuernavaca has a number of cafes right off the Jardín Juárez where people gather to sip coffee or drinks till the wee hours—check out La Universal (see "Where to Dine," above). Band concerts are held in the Jardín Juárez on Thursday and Sunday evenings. **La Plazuela,** a short, pedestrian-only stretch across from the Cortez Palace, features cafes, kitsch stores, and live-music bars. It's geared toward a 20-something, university crowd.

5 Tepoztlán 🌟🌟

72km (45 miles) S of Mexico City; 45km (28 miles) NE of Cuernavaca

Tepoztlán is one of the strangest and most beautiful towns in Mexico. Largely undiscovered by foreign tourists, it occupies the floor of a broad, lush valley whose walls were formed by bizarrely shaped mountains that look like the work of some abstract expressionist giant. The mountains are visible from almost everywhere in town; even the municipal parking lot boasts a spectacular view.

Tepoztlán remains small and steeped in legend and mystery—it lies adjacent to the alleged birthplace of Quetzalcoatl, the Aztec serpent god—and comes about as close as you're going to get to an unspoiled, magical mountain hideaway. Eight chapels, each with its own cultural festival, dot this traditional Mexican village. Though the town stays tranquil during the week, escapees from Mexico City descend in droves on the weekends, especially Sunday. Most Tepoztlán residents, whether foreigners or Mexicans, tend to be mystically or artistically oriented—although some also appear to be just plain disoriented.

Aside from soaking up the ambience, two things you must do are climb up to the Tepozteco pyramid and hit the weekend folkloric market. In addition, Tepoztlán offers a variety of treatments, cures, diets, massages, and sweat lodges. Some of these are available at hotels; for some, you have to ask around. Many locals swear that the valley possesses mystical curative powers.

If you have a car, Tepoztlán provides a great starting point for traveling this region of Mexico. Within 90 minutes are Las Estacas, Taxco, las Grutas de Cacahuamilpa, and Xochicalco (some of the prettiest ruins in Mexico). Tepoztlán lies 20 minutes

Cooking Classes in Tepoztlán

An engaging cooking school called **Cocinar Mexicano** offers weeklong programs in Mexican cuisine. The founder, Magda Bogin, conducts class from her large, sunny outdoor kitchen, tiled in blue-and-white Talavera. Participants study recipes typical of the festival that coincides with their visit. During the Day of the Dead workshop, for example, students learn to make tamales, the traditional dish that families bring to the gravesites of deceased love ones. For other festivals, the focus is *mole,* a typical fiesta food often made with chocolate and chiles that's arguably the most complex dish in Mexican cuisine. Cost for the class is $1,895 (£1,042), which includes round-trip transportation from Mexico City and most meals but not airfare or accommodations. Frommer's readers receive a $100 (£55) discount. For more information, visit www.cocinar mexicano.com.

from Cuernavaca and only an hour south of Mexico City (that is, an hour once you're able to get out of Mexico City), which—given its lost-in-time feel—seems hard to believe.

ESSENTIALS

GETTING THERE & DEPARTING   By Car   From Mexico City, the quickest route is Highway 95 (the toll road) to Cuernavaca; just before the Cuernavaca city limits, you'll see the clearly marked turnoff to Tepoztlán on 95D and Highway 115. The slower, free federal Highway 95D, direct from Mexico City, is also an option, and may be preferable if you're departing from the western part of the city. Take 95D south to Km 71, where the exit to Tepoztlán on Highway 115 is clearly indicated.

By Bus   From Mexico City, buses to Tepoztlán run regularly from the Terminal de Sur and the Terminal Poniente. The trip takes an hour.

In addition, you can book round-trip transportation to the Mexico City airport through **Marquez Sightseeing Tours** (© 777/315-5875; www.tourbymexico.com/ marqueztours) and some hotels. The round-trip cost is about $200 (£110).

EXPLORING TEPOZTLAN

Tepoztlán's **weekend folkloric market** is one of the best in central Mexico. More crafts are available on Saturdays and Sundays, but the market also opens on Wednesdays. Vendors sell all kinds of ceramics, from simple fired-clay works resembling those made with pre-Hispanic techniques, to the more commercial versions of majolica and pseudo-Talavera. There are also puppets, carved wood figures, and some textiles, especially thick wool Mexican sweaters and jackets made out of *jerga* (a coarse cloth). Very popular currently is the "hippie"-style jewelry that earned Tepoztlán its fame in the '60s and '70s. The market is also remarkable for its variety of food stands selling fruits and vegetables, spices, fresh tortillas, and indigenous Mexican delicacies.

The other primary activity is hiking up to **Tepozteco pyramid.** The climb is steep and fairly strenuous, although perfectly doable in a few hours and not dangerous. In fact, you'll see folks across three generations doing the hike. Dense vegetation shades the trail (actually a long natural staircase), which is beautiful from bottom to top. Once you arrive at the pyramid you are treated to remarkable views and, if you are lucky, a great show by a family of *coatis* (tropical raccoons), who visit the pyramid most mornings to beg for food; they especially love bananas. The pyramid is a Tlahuica construction that predates the Náhuatl (Aztec) domination of the area. It was the site of important celebrations in the 12th and 13th centuries. The main street in Tepoztlán, Avenida 5 de Mayo, takes you to the path that leads you to the top of the Tepozteco. The 2km winding rock trail begins where the name of Avenida 5 de Mayo changes to Camino del Tepozteco. The hike takes about an hour each way, but if you stop and take in the scenery and really enjoy the trail, it can take up to 2 hours each way. Water and drinks are available at the top. The trail is open daily from 9am to 5:30pm and, while the hike is free, the pyramid costs $3 (£1.65) to enter.

Also worth visiting is the **former convent Dominico de la Navidad.** The entrance to the Dominican convent lies through the religious-themed "Gate of Tepoztlán," constructed with beads and seeds, just east of the main plaza. Built between 1560 and 1588, the convent is now a museum open Tuesday through Sunday from 10am to 5pm.

SIGHTS NEAR TEPOZTLAN

Many nearby places are easily accessible by car. One good tour service is **Marquez Sightseeing Tours,** located in Cuernavaca (© 777/315-5875; www.tourbymexico. com/marqueztours). Marquez has four- and seven-passenger vehicles, very reasonable prices, and a large variety of set tours. The dependable owner, Arturo Marquez Diaz, speaks better-than-passable English and will allow you to design your own tour, including to archeological sites and museums. He also offers transportation to and from Mexico City airport for approximately $200 (£110).

Two tiny, charming villages, **Santo Domingo Xocotitlán** and **Amatlán,** are only a 20-minute drive from Tepoztlán and can be reached by minibuses, which depart regularly from the center of town. There is nothing much to do in these places except wander around absorbing the marvelous views of the Tepozteco Mountains and drinking in the magical ambience.

Las Grutas de Cacahuamilpa ⚘, the Cacahuamilpa Caves or Grottoes, are an unforgettable system of caverns with a wooden illuminated walkway for easy access. As you pass from chamber to chamber you'll see spectacular illuminated rock formations, including stalactites, stalagmites, and twisted rock formations with names like Dante's head, the champagne bottle, the tortillas, and Madonna with child. Admission for 2 hours is $3 (£1.65); a guide for groups, which can be assembled on the hour, costs an additional $8 (£4.40). The caverns are open daily from 10am to 7pm (last tickets sold at 5pm), and lie 90 minutes from Tepoztlán and 30 minutes from Taxco.

About 40 minutes southeast of Tepoztlán is **Las Estacas,** an ecological resort with a cold-water spring that is said to have curative powers (p. 170). The ruins of **Xochicalco** (see "Cuernavaca," earlier in this chapter) and the colonial town of **Taxco** (earlier in this chapter) are easily accessible from Tepoztlán.

WHERE TO STAY

The town gets very busy on the weekends, so if your stay will include Friday or Saturday night, make reservations well in advance. In addition to the choices noted below, consider two other excellent options just outside of town. **Casa Bugambilia** ⚘⚘⚘, Callejón de Tepopula 007, Valle de Atongo (© 739/395-0158; www. casabugambilia.com), is an 11-room hotel property 3km outside Tepoztlán. Don't confuse this hotel with Posada Bugambilia, a modest hotel in town. The spacious rooms are elegantly furnished with high-end, carved Mexican furniture, and every room has a

> ### ⟨Moments⟩ Tepoznieves: A Taste of Heaven
>
> Don't leave town without a stop at **Tepoznieves**, Av. 5 de Mayo 21
> (ⓒ **739/395-3813**), the sublime local ice-cream shop. The store's slogan, "nieve
> de dioses" (ice cream of the gods), doesn't exaggerate. Almost 200 types of ice
> cream and sorbet, made only with natural ingredients, come in flavors familiar
> (vanilla, bubble gum), exotic (tamarind, rose petal, mango studded with chile
> piquin), and off-the-wall (beet, lettuce, corn). It's open daily 8am to 9pm.

fireplace. Doubles average $180 to $250 (£99–£138). **Las Golondrinas** ✦✦✦, Callejón de Términas 4 (ⓒ **739/395-0649**; http://homepage.mac.com/marisolfernandez/LasGolondrinas), is a three bedroom B&B in the area behind Ixcatepec church; it's so off the beaten track that even cab drivers have trouble finding the place. But owner Marisol Fernández has imbued the house with her tranquil, down-to-earth charm; the guest rooms open onto a wraparound terrace that overlooks the garden, a small pool, and the Tepozteco Mountains beyond. Doubles cost $120 (£66), including breakfast.

Hotel Nilayam ✦   Formerly Hotel Tepoztlán, this holistic-oriented retreat lies in a colonial building, but the decor has been brightened up considerably. Stays here encourage self-exploration: The gracious, helpful staff offers complete detox programs and a full array of services, including body and facial treatments, reflexology, hot stone and shiatsu massages, and yoga, Tai Chi, and meditation. The hotel has a great view of the mountain, and the restaurant features a creative menu of vegetarian cuisine. Spa packages are available.

Industrias 6, 62520 Tepoztlán, Mor. ⓒ 739/395-0503. Fax 739/395-0522. www.nilayam.net. 35 units. $120 (£66) double. AE, MC, V. Free parking. **Amenities:** Restaurant; outdoor pool; spa services; private *temazcal* (pre-Hispanic sweat lodge). *In room:* TV.

Posada del Tepozteco ✦✦   This property looks out over the town and down the length of the spectacular valley; the views from just about anywhere are superb. Rooms are tastefully furnished in colonial style. All but the least expensive have terraces and views. All suites have small whirlpool tubs. The grounds are exquisitely landscaped, and the atmosphere is intimate and romantic.

Paraíso 3 (2 blocks from the town center), 62520 Tepoztlán, Mor. ⓒ 739/395-0010. Fax 739/395-0323. www.posadadeltepozteco.com. 21 units. $120–$175 (£66–£96) double; $200–$366 (£110–£201) suite. MC, V. Free parking. **Amenities:** Restaurant w/stunning view; small outdoor pool.

WHERE TO DINE

In addition to the two choices listed below, El Chalchi restaurant at the **Hotel Nilayam** (see above) offers some of the best vegetarian fare in the area. It's 3 blocks from the main square, with main courses priced around $6 (£3.30).

El Ciruelo Restaurant Bar ✦ GOURMET MEXICAN   This upscale restaurant surrounded by beautiful flowering gardens and adobe walls offers a sampling of Tepoztlán's essence. The service is positively charming, and the food divine. House specialties include chalupas of goat cheese, chicken with *huitlacoche*, and a regional treat: milk-based gelatin with brown sugar.

Zaragoza 17, Barrio de la Santísima, in front of the church. ⓒ 739/395-1203. Dinner $6–$20 (£3.30–£11). AE. Sun 1–7pm, Mon–Thurs 1–6pm; Fri–Sat 1–11pm.

Restaurant Axitla ★★★ *(Finds)* GOURMET MEXICAN/INTERNATIONAL Axitla is not only the best restaurant in Tepoztlán, but also one of the finest in Mexico for showcasing the country's cuisine. Gourmet Mexican delicacies are made from scratch using the freshest local ingredients. Specialties include chicken breast stuffed with wild mushrooms in a *chipotle chile* sauce, *chiles en nogada,* pepper steak, grilled octopus, and exceptional *mole.* There are also excellent steaks and fresh seafood. And, if the food isn't enough—and believe me, it is—the enchanted setting will make your meal even more memorable. The restaurant lies at the base of the Tepozteco Pyramid (about a 10-minute walk from the town center), surrounded by 1.2 hectares (about 3 acres) of junglelike gardens that encompass a creek and lily ponds. The views of the Tepozteco Mountains are magnificent. Memo and Laura, the gracious owners, speak excellent English and are marvelous sources of information about the area.

Av. del Tepozteco, at the foot of the trail to the pyramid. © **739/395-0519.** Lunch and dinner $8–$15 (£4.40–£8.25). MC, V. Wed–Sun 10am–7pm.

San Miguel de Allende & the Colonial Silver Cities

by David Baird

Mexico's colonial silver mining cities—San Miguel, Querétaro, San Luis Potosí, Guanajuato, and Zacatecas—lie northwest of Mexico City in the rugged mountains of the Sierra Madre Occidental. The towns, in colonial settings with backdrops of high mountains, feature an ideal climate, local handicrafts, good food, and many memorable vistas.

San Miguel de Allende is the smallest of the cities. Its cobblestone streets and fanciful church set it apart from the rest, as do its numerous restaurants and interesting shops. For many years it has supported a resident population of artists, writers, and expatriates. **Guanajuato** and **Zacatecas,** with their winding streets and alleys and their small, oddly shaped plazas, seem more like medieval towns than products of the Renaissance. In contrast, **Querétaro** and **San Luis Potosí** have stately colonial centers of broad plazas and monumental civil and religious architecture.

Travel through these parts is easy and relaxing; there is little crime, and the inhabitants are gracious. The region is a good introduction to Mexico's interior and is well suited for a family vacation. All Mexicans, but especially those in this region, are family-oriented and warm up quickly when they see a family traveling together.

The colonial silver cities are close to the Mexican capital by modern standards, but at the time of their founding, this land was the frontier. In pre-Columbian times, the great civilizations of central Mexico never established more than a tenuous sway here. Mountainous and arid, this was the land of the Chichimeca, a large nation of nomadic tribes that occasionally banded together for raids upon their civilized neighbors to the south. After the Spanish conquest of the Aztec empire in 1521, the conquistadors turned their attention to this region in search of precious metals. The Chichimecans resisted the encroachers, but epidemic diseases brought from Europe soon decimated the native population. The Spanish established mining cities in quick succession, stretching from Querétaro (established in 1531) north all the way to Zacatecas (1548) and beyond. They found quantities of gold, but silver proved so plentiful that it made Mexico world famous as a land of riches.

For 3 centuries of colonial rule, much of the mines' great wealth went to build urban centers of impressive and lasting architecture. It's wonderful to walk leisurely through these cities and view them, not one building at a time, but in broad views of colonial cityscapes. Of the five cities, three (Guanajuato, Querétaro, and Zacatecas) have been designated World Heritage Sites by UNESCO.

Life remains civilized here; it is savored and enjoyed at a relaxed pace. Many people have ancestors who lived here at least a century ago. They maintain a broad network of kinfolk, friends, and acquaintances. I've walked down streets with locals who would greet every third or fourth person we passed. Often, I've had conversations in which I mention someone from a completely different context, only to hear something like, "Oh, he's married to my cousin." This is the kind of intimate and close-knit world you enter when visiting these cities.

EXPLORING THE SILVER CITIES

The most common ways of getting here are flying into Mexico City and taking the bus that goes directly from the airport to Querétaro, or flying into the León/Guanajuato airport. Zacatecas, San Luis Potosí, and Querétaro also have international airports that receive a few flights from the U.S. Or you can get to this region by car or bus on one of the superhighways that run from the U.S. border. From Texas, the first of the silver cities you reach will be San Luis Potosí (which, by the way, bills itself to the rest of Mexico as the "Gateway to the United States").

Once in the region, you'll find the roads are good, but not great, and the smaller ones are poorly marked. Driving within these towns can be maddening due to convoluted, narrow streets and bizarre traffic routing (especially in Guanajuato and Zacatecas). If you ever have difficulty navigating into the center of town, simply hail a cab to lead the way. Parking can also be a problem; we have included, when possible, good motels where you can park and leave your car for the length of your visit. If you prefer to travel by bus, you'll find frequent, inexpensive first-class buses connecting all these cities, which are only a few hours apart from each other.

The region has a short rainy season from June through September, which is a good time to come. I also like late fall, winter, and early spring. The hottest month is May (and sometimes early June before the rains arrive). May can also be smoky because it's when many farmers burn the stubble in their corn fields before the next planting. As to how and where to spend your time, much depends on your interests. If your chief goal is to relax and enjoy the good life, spend more time in San Miguel. If it is to be active and do some exploring, spend more time in Guanajuato and Zacatecas. If you're already comfortable running around Mexico and are looking for cultural immersion, I would point you to Querétaro and San Luis Potosí. But whichever cities you elect to visit, I recommend a stay of at least 3 days per destination—a good part of their charm will go unappreciated if you're pressing too much to see everything.

1 San Miguel de Allende 🖈🖈🖈

288km (179 miles) NW of Mexico City; 120km (74 miles) E of Guanajuato; 64km (40 miles) NW of Querétaro

San Miguel de Allende mixes the best aspects of small-town life with the cosmopolitan pleasures of a big city. It is the smallest of the cities covered here and perhaps the most relaxed, but it offers such a variety of restaurants, shops, and galleries that urbanites find themselves quite at home. Most of the buildings in the central part of the town date from the colonial era or the 19th century; the law requires newer buildings to conform to existing architecture, and the town has gone to some lengths to retain its cobblestone streets.

Living in San Miguel is a large community of Americans: some retired, some attending art or language school, and some who have come here to live simply and follow their creative muses—painting, writing, and sculpting. The center of this community is the public library in the former convent of Santa Ana. It is a good place to find information on San Miguel or just to sit in the patio and read.

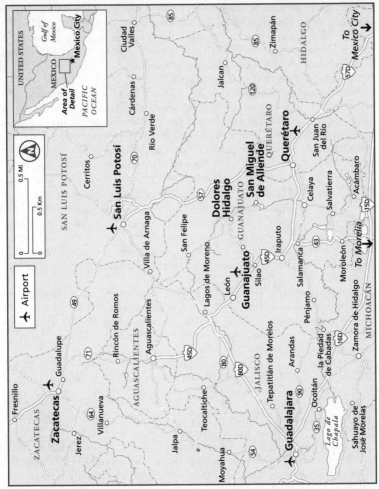

A notable aspect of San Migueleña society is the number of festivals it celebrates. In a country that needs only the barest of excuses to hold a fiesta, it is known far and wide for them. Most of these celebrations are of a religious character and are meant to combine social activity with religious expression. People practice Catholicism with great fervor—going on religious pilgrimages, attending all-night vigils, ringing church bells at the oddest times throughout the night (something that some visitors admittedly might not find so amusing). See "Special Events & Festivals," below.

ESSENTIALS

GETTING THERE & DEPARTING   By Plane   The two major airports are the Mexico City airport, which is 3½ hours away (and has direct bus transportation to nearby Querétaro) and the León/Guanajuato airport, 1½ hours away.

By Car   You have a choice of two routes for the 3½-hour trip from Mexico City—a Querétaro bypass or via Celaya. The former is shorter—take Highway 57, a four-lane freeway, north toward Querétaro. Past the Tequisquiapan turnoff is an exit on the right marked A SAN MIGUEL. This toll road bypasses Querétaro and crosses Highway 57 again north of town. Here it narrows to two lanes and becomes Highway 111. Some 30km (20 miles) farther is San Miguel.

From Guanajuato, the quick route is to go south from the city a short distance on Highway 110, then east on a secondary, paved road passing near the village of Joconoxtle. For the long but scenic route, which passes through Dolores Hidalgo, go northeast on Highway 110 through Dolores, then south on Highway 51. If you drive this route, take a break and experience a slice of rural Mexican life near the small community of Santa Rosa, where a few restaurants serve the local *mezcal de la sierra,* a locally distilled firewater that makes tequila taste positively smooth.

By Bus   From Mexico City airport: AeroPlus buses (© **55/5786-9357**) leave directly from the airport for Querétaro about every half-hour and cost $22 (£12). They leave from outside Gate E-2. Getting there is a little confusing, and the signs don't help much. When you get to the E-2 area take the ramp or elevator up one floor and walk down a concourse that crosses over the passenger pickup area. At the end of the concourse are the ticketing booths for the different buses. Buy your ticket there, then take the elevator down to the ground floor.

From Mexico City's Terminal Norte: First-class buses take 4 hours (with one stop in Querétaro). The company ETN has the best service, with wide seats that recline far back (four buses per day). Primera Plus has two buses per day. Regular service is handled by Flecha Amarilla with buses leaving every 40 minutes. Another option is to take a bus to Querétaro and change buses.

From Querétaro: Local buses run to San Miguel every 20 minutes (Flecha Amarilla and Herradura de Plata have alternating departures). If you arrive in Querétaro by first-class bus, you'll be in Terminal A. Go out the door, turn right, and walk to Terminal B.

From Guanajuato: ETN has three nonstop superdeluxe buses per day. Primera Plus/Servicios Coordinados has four nonstop buses per day.

To/from Laredo and Nuevo Laredo: Four companies offer an overnight first-class bus to/from Laredo or Nuevo Laredo: **Autobuses Americanos** (© **415/154-8233** or www.autobusesamericanos.com.mx) crosses the border to Laredo; **Futura** (© **415/152-2237**), **Primera Plus** (© **01-800/375-7587** in Mexico) and **Omnibus de México** (© **01-800/765-6636** in Mexico or www.odm.com.mx) go to Nuevo Laredo. The trip takes 12 hours and costs around $60. From San Miguel there is one departure per day per company. The four buses leave San Miguel between 6 and 7pm. Departure times from Laredo and Nuevo Laredo are also around 6 or 7pm.

The **bus station** in San Miguel is 2km (1½ miles) west of town on the westward extension of Calle Canal. Taxis to town are cheap ($3/£1.65) and available at all hours. An office in the center of San Miguel sells tickets for AeroPlus buses from Querétaro to the Mexico City airport, as well as for all other buses operated by Primera Plus or Servicios Coordinados. Its new location is at Calle Sollano 23 (© **415/152-5043**). Office hours are from 9am to 5pm Monday through Saturday.

VISITOR INFORMATION   The city's **tourist information office** is in the *ayuntamiento* (city hall) facing El Jardín. The address is Plaza Principal 8, and the

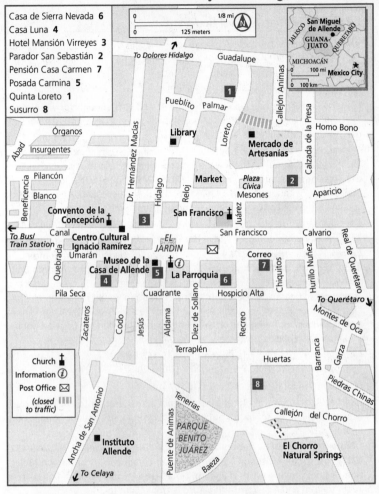

Where to Stay in San Miguel de Allende

Casa de Sierra Nevada **6**
Casa Luna **4**
Hotel Mansión Virreyes **3**
Parador San Sebastián **2**
Pensión Casa Carmen **7**
Posada Carmina **5**
Quinta Loreto **1**
Susurro **8**

San Miguel de Allende
JALISCO GUANA-JUATO QUERÉTARO
MICHOACÁN
Mexico City

0   1/8 mi
0   125 meters

0   100 mi
0   100 km

To Dolores Hidalgo
Guadalupe
Callejón Ánimas
Calzada de la Presa

1
Pueblito Palmar
Órganos
Insurgentes
Pilancón
Blanco
Beneficencia
Abad
Dr. Hernández Macías
Library
Loreto
Homo Bono
Mercado de Artesanías
Hidalgo
Reloj
Market
Plaza Cívica
Mesones
2
Aparicio
Convento de la Concepción ✝
3
San Francisco ✝
Juárez
Calvario
To Bus/ Train Station
Canal
Centro Cultural Ignacio Ramírez
Quebrada
Umarán
EL JARDÍN
San Francisco
Real de Querétaro
Correo
7
Chiquitos
Hurillo Núñez
Museo de la Casa de Allende
4   **5**
✝ ⓘ ✉
La Parroquia
6
Pila Seca
Cuadrante
Hospicio Alta
To Querétaro
Montes de Oca
Zacateros
Codo
Jesús
Aldama
Diez de Sollano
Recreo
Barranca
Garza
Terraplén
Huertas
Piedras Chinas
8
Church ✝
Information ⓘ
Post Office ✉
(closed to traffic)
Ancha de San Antonio
Tenerias
Puente de Ánimas
Callejón del Chorro
Instituto Allende
PARQUE BENITO JUÁREZ
Baeza
El Chorro Natural Springs
To Celaya

phone is ✆ **415/152-0900.** Office hours are Monday through Friday from 8:30am to 8pm, Saturday from 10am to 8pm, and Sunday from 10am to 5:30pm.

CITY LAYOUT   Groomed Indian laurel trees shade San Miguel's central square, **El Jardín.** The center of city life, El Jardín is the point of reference for all places in the middle of town and is bounded by Correo (Post Office St.), San Francisco, Hidalgo, and Reloj.

GETTING AROUND   Most places in San Miguel are within walking distance, so a car isn't necessary. Buses to outlying villages (La Taboada thermal pool, for example) leave from the little plaza by the *mercado.* Taxis to places inside town should not cost more than $3 (£1.65), unless ordered from a hotel.

FAST FACTS: San Miguel de Allende

American Express The local representative is **Viajes Vértiz,** Hidalgo 1 (© **415/ 152-1856;** fax 415/152-0499), open Monday through Friday from 9am to 2pm and 5pm, Saturday from 10am to 2pm.

Area Code The telephone area code is **415.**

Climate San Miguel can be warm in summer and cold enough for wool clothing in winter, especially at night or occasionally when a norther (a strong, sudden north wind) makes its way this far south.

Communication & Shipping Services Several services offer packing and shipping, mail boxes, telephone messages, long distance, and the like. One is **Border Crossings,** Mesones 57, Loc. 6 (© **415/152-2497;** fax 415/152-3672). **Pack 'n' Mail** is at Calle Canal 42 (©/fax **415/152-3191**). Both keep standard office hours: weekdays from 9 or 10am to 6pm, Saturday from 10am to 2pm.

Consular Office It's located at Hernández Macías 72, Int. 111. (© **415/152-2357**). Hours are Monday to Friday from 9am to 1pm.

Currency Exchange **Intercam** has three locations: Juárez 27, San Francisco 4, and Correo 15. Business hours are Monday through Friday from 9am to 6pm, Saturday from 9am to 2pm. **Dicambio** has three locations: Correo 3, Juárez 1, and Puente Umarán 16. Hours are Monday through Friday from 9am to 4pm, Saturday from 9am to 2pm, and Sunday from 10am to 2pm. Several banks have cash machines, including one on the corner of the Jardín in the Casa del Conde, and a few on Calle San Francisco.

Drugstore Try the **Farmacia Agundis** (© **415/152-1198**), Canal 26 at Macías. It's open daily from 10am to midnight.

Elevation San Miguel sits at 1,862m (6,107 ft.).

Internet Access Several places offer Internet access around town. These businesses come and go so fast it's not worth listing them. Ask at your hotel for the nearest cybercafe.

Library The **Biblioteca Pública (Public Library),** Insurgentes 25 (© **415/152-0293**), is a social institution for the American community. It has a good selection of books in Spanish and English. Hours are Monday through Friday from 10am to 2pm and 4 to 7pm, and Saturday from 10am to 2pm.

Newspaper An English-language paper, *Atención,* carries local news as well as full listings of what to see and do.

Parking San Miguel is congested, and street parking is scarce. White poles, signs, or both at the ends of streets mark the stopping point for parking (so that other cars can make a turn). Police are vigilant about parking and ticket with glee.

Population San Miguel has 130,000 residents.

Post Office The *correo,* Calle Correo 16, is open Monday through Friday from 9am to 2pm for all services (and sells stamps until 5pm), Saturday from 9am to 1pm.

Seasons Because of the fast freeway access from Mexico City, San Miguel is popular with weekenders from the capital. Arrive early on Friday or make a reservation ahead of time for weekends, especially long weekends. There's also a squeeze on rooms around the Christmas and Easter holidays and around the feast of San Miguel's patron saint, on September 29.

SPECIAL EVENTS & FESTIVALS

San Miguel celebrates 30 to 40 festivals a year. These are just the standouts: January 17 is the **Blessing of the Animals.** In the morning, locals bring their decorated pets and farm animals to the town's churches to be doused with holy water. The first Friday in March celebrates **Our Lord of the Conquest,** and the day before is filled with music, fireworks, and decorated teams of oxen. After a celebratory Mass, there is dancing by the *concheros* (traditional Aztec dancers). Two weeks before Holy Week is the procession of **Our Lord of the Col+umn.** Between then and Easter Sunday there are more processions, and altars are set up in honor of **La Virgen Dolorosa.** In May is the **Festival of the Holy Cross.** In June around Saint Anthony's Day is the **Fiesta de los Locos (Festival of the Madmen)** ☆☆, when many dress up in carnavalesque costumes and go cavorting about the center of town. August begins the preparatory festivals for September 29, the festival of San Miguel's **patron saint.** Parades, fireworks, and band concerts continue throughout September. On one weekend in September, the town holds a *pamplonada* (running of the bulls)—it produces a lot of public drunkenness and carousing in the central part of town. I would avoid it. At the beginning of November is the **Day of the Dead,** followed by the **Christmas fiestas.** In addition to all of this, you have the **Chamber Music Festival** in summer, **Jazz Music Festival** in the fall, and a couple of arts fairs that occur on varying dates.

EXPLORING SAN MIGUEL

It's difficult to be bored in San Miguel. The shopping is excellent, and you'll run out of time before you can try all the restaurants. The town is well situated for side trips to Dolores Hidalgo, Querétaro, and Guanajuato. It's also popular for Spanish and art classes.

The colonial architecture tends more toward domestic than monumental and offers much to see—fine courtyards, beautiful interiors, and rich architectural details. Of particular note are the town's lovely streetscapes with narrow cobblestone lanes that invite aimless strolling and make it advisable to wear walking shoes with thick soles.

THE TOP ATTRACTIONS

Centro Cultural Ignacio Ramírez (Bellas Artes/El Nigromante)   Housed in the former Convento de la Concepción (1755), 2 blocks west of El Jardín, the Centro is a branch of the Palacio de Bellas Artes of Mexico City. The two-story cloister, surrounding an enormous courtyard with large trees and a gurgling fountain, houses art exhibits and classrooms for drawing, painting, sculpture, lithography, textiles, ceramics, dramatic arts, ballet, regional dance, piano, and guitar. A mural by David Alfaro Siqueiros and some of his memorabilia are worth seeing. A bulletin board lists concerts and lectures at this institute and elsewhere in the city. You can also dine in

Learning at the Source: Going to School in San Miguel

San Miguel has several schools for learning Spanish. If you're wishing to take classes, shop around before you travel to San Miguel to find one that's a good fit for you. These schools cater to travelers and often can provide a list of apartments for long-term stays.

Instituto Allende, Calle Ancha de San Antonio 20, 37700 San Miguel de Allende, Gto. (© 415/152-0190; www.instituto-allende.edu.mx), began in 1950 as a fine arts school and later added Spanish courses. The main focus is still on the arts, with different classes and workshops offered throughout the year. Spanish students have the option of group and individual classes, short- and long-term. The school's credits are transferable to many colleges and universities in the United States and Canada; noncredit students are also welcome.

LanguagePoint, 20 de Enero Sur 42, 37750 San Miguel de Allende, Gto. (© 415/152-4115; www.languagepoint.org), offers instruction and immersion at all levels of competency. With a maximum of three students per instructor, students get a lot of individual attention, and the teaching method leans heavily toward conversation. Emphasis at the basic level is on gaining a working knowledge of everyday Spanish as a basis for further development of language skills.

these pleasant surroundings at the restaurant **Las Musas,** which serves pasta dishes, salads, sandwiches, and desserts. Before you leave, take a look at the magnificent dome behind the convent. It belongs to the Iglesia de la Concepción and was designed by the same unschooled architect who designed the Parroquia (see below).

Hernández Macías 75 (between Canal and Insurgentes). © 415/152-0289. Free admission. Mon–Fri 10am–5:30pm; Sat 10am–2pm.

La Parroquia ✦✦✦   Looking nothing like any other church in Mexico, La Parroquia has become the emblem of San Miguel. It is an object of great pride for the citizenry and a source of discomfort for architectural purists. Originally built in the colonial style, the church was remade in the late 19th century by a local builder named Zeferino Gutiér-rez, who reconstructed the towers and facade. Gutiérrez was supposedly unlettered but had seen picture postcards of European Gothic churches and worked from these alone, drawing his designs in the sand. I find the finished product fascinating—a very personal vision of the Gothic style that owes more to the builder's imagination and fancy than to the European churches that were its inspiration. The inside is not nearly so much fun as the outside; the church was looted on several occasions during times of social upheaval, and this kind of art criticism puts a damper on commissioning more paintings and deco-ration. Still, there are things to see. My favorite, and one often missed, is the crypt beneath the altar. You get to it through a door on the right side. You'll have to seek out the caretaker, who can unlock the door (for a small tip).

South side of El Jardín. No phone. Free admission. Daily 8am–2pm and 5–9pm.

Warren Hardy Spanish, San Rafael 6, 37700 San Miguel de Allende, Gto. (© 415/154-4017; www.warrenhardy.com), is a popular school for those who know little Spanish. Emphasis is on the spoken language, with special focus on the use of verbs. Mr. Hardy has taught Spanish for many years and has designed his own methodology for teaching it, which involves partnering students and using a lot of flash cards. It's best to contact the school through its website. Mr. Hardy's wife, Tuli, answers questions and handles registration.

Academia Hispano Americana, Mesones 4 (Apdo. Postal 150), 37700 San Miguel de Allende, Gto. (© 415/152-0349; www.ahaspeakspanish.com), has a reputation for offering an intensive language course with an emphasis on grammar as well as conversation. Classes are limited to 12 people and are much smaller than that on average. The school has a continuous program of study of 12 4-week sessions for 35 hours a week. Less intensive courses and private lessons are also available. It's a member of the International Association of Language Centers.

Habla Hispana, Calzada de la Luz 25, 37700 San Miguel de Allende, Gto. (© 451/152-1535; www.mexicospanish.com), is a small school with four experienced and dedicated instructors, all locals. Classes are arranged in four-week courses. Class size is limited to 10 students. The school likes to combine a personal touch with a clearly structured teaching program.

Museo Casa de Allende   The house of San Miguel's most famous son and namesake, the independence leader Ignacio Allende, is now a museum. It is of the genre known as *museos regionales* that you will find across Mexico. The objective of these museums is to present a view of the local area from prehistoric times to recent history; to explain what roles the region played in the context of national development; and to give some idea of how the great historical movements that swept across Mexico ran their courses at the local level. Featured is a small biographical exhibit on Allende as one of the initiators of the independence movement, which began in nearby Dolores Hidalgo, and on what national independence meant for San Miguel and the local area. Explanations are in Spanish only, but the artifacts—including fossils, pre-Hispanic pottery, colonial-era furnishings, and articles of daily life—and the beauty of the house are worth the price.

Southwest corner of El Jardín. No phone. Admission $3.50. Tues–Sun 9am–5pm.

MORE ATTRACTIONS

The **House and Garden Tour** ⭐, sponsored by the Biblioteca Pública, is universally enjoyed. The tour opens the doors of some of the city's most interesting colonial and contemporary houses. Tours leave Sunday at 11:30am from the library, Insurgentes 25 (© 415/152-0293), and last about 2 hours. A $15 (£8.25) donation goes to support various library projects benefiting the youth of San Miguel.

Bill Levasseur of Casa de la Cuesta Bed and Breakfast has recently opened a mask museum called **La Otra Cara de México (The Other Face of Mexico)** ⭐. It's a thoughtfully arranged exhibition of masks that provides a lot of cultural context. Masks have played an important role in many of the native cultures of Mexico, usually as part of a dance or ritual. Over the years Bill has collected some great pieces and has filmed dances and performances in which the masks were used. This museum is a treat for both the serious collector and the casual traveler. Visits are by appointment only (© **415/154-4324**).

A couple of the most enjoyable walks in town are to the lookout point **El Mirador,** especially at sunset, which colors the whole town and the lake beyond, and to **Parque Juárez,** a large and shady park.

NEARBY ATTRACTIONS

Just outside of San Miguel are several hot mineral springs that have been made into bathing spots. They're all just off the road leading to Dolores Hidalgo. **La Taboada, La Gruta,** and **Escondido** lie close to one another, just 8 to 10km (5–6 miles) outside San Miguel. La Gruta is perhaps the nicest, but La Taboada has a quiet, old hotel reminiscent of an earlier Mexico and makes for a relaxing stay.

Near these hot springs is the sanctuary of **Atotonilco el Grande,** a complex of chapels, dormitories, dining rooms, and a church. World Monuments Watch ranks the church among the most important buildings meriting preservation. Father Luis Felipe Neri Alfaro, an austere mystic, founded the church in 1740. He thought the area in dire need of a religious presence, as many people would gather at the thermal springs to bathe publicly and, in his eyes, licentiously. He commissioned a local artist, Martínez Pocasangre, to paint murals illustrating the instructive verses that Alfaro wrote with much emphasis on the dangers lying in wait for the human soul. The murals and verses cover the church's ceiling and walls. They add brightness and color to an otherwise dark and severe structure.

Father Alfaro built his sanctuary on the spot where he was granted an ecstatic vision of Christ. The location proved providential: 70 years later, when the Spanish authorities uncovered a plot to liberate Mexico that implicated Father Miguel Hidalgo, he was in the town of Dolores. Warned of the danger, he hastily declared independence and marched his impromptu army toward San Miguel. En route, he stopped at Atotonilco where he took the church's image of the Virgin of Guadalupe as his banner, declaring her the protector of the new nation—the first time that she was officially recognized as such.

The church and adjoining buildings still function throughout the year as a religious retreat for people who come from all over the country for a week of prayer, penance, and mortification. These spiritual exercises are conducted quietly, in private, with no public display. You can get to Atotonilco by cab or by taking the EL SANTUARIO bus at the market. It passes every hour on the hour, and goes through Taboada on its way to Atotonilco.

SHOPPING

San Miguel is a town of artists; you'll find art for sale not only in galleries but also in restaurants, offices, and just about anywhere there's space in a public area. San Miguel is also a town of artisans working mainly with clay, iron, brass, tin, blown glass, and papier-mâché. And San Miguel is a town of shopkeepers who sell locally produced items as well as folk art and decorative objects from across Mexico. There are so many stores, and they are so different from each other, that a list would not be helpful. The best advice I can give is to explore the streets around the main square. If you're looking for something in particular, ask around. One place that's easily walkable but a bit out-side the downtown area is **Fábrica La Aurora,** an old textile mill that's been converted into galleries and shops selling art, furnishings, and antiques. The old factory is an attractive space, with lots of open floor space and includes a restaurant and a cafe. It's a bit north of downtown on Calzada de La Aurora, just past the bridge.

Stores are usually open Monday through Saturday from 9am to 2pm and 4 to 7 or 8pm. Most stores close on Sunday. If you're interested in Talavera pottery, consider going to nearby Dolores Hidalgo (see "A Side Trip to Dolores Hidalgo: Fine Pottery & Shrimp Ice Cream," later in this chapter). Also, you can find some fun knickknacks at the **Mercado de Artesanías (handicrafts market),** but it will require hunting through lots of goods that are either too tacky or not tacky enough. The *mercado* occu-pies a walkway 3 blocks long that descends from the municipal market past the Hotel Quinta Loreto.

WHERE TO STAY

For longer stays, you might check with the language schools (see "Learning at the Source: Going to School in San Miguel," above) and other bulletin boards around town for lists of apartments or rooms to rent, or check websites such as www.internet sanmiguel.com or www.infosma.com. Most apartments have kitchens and bedding; some come with maid service. San Miguel is a popular weekend getaway for residents of the capital, and several hotels raise rates on weekends. Secured parking is at a pre-mium; if your hotel doesn't provide it, you'll pay around $12 to $15 (£6.60–£8.25) daily in a guarded lot. Most places can arrange airport transportation. The rates listed below already include taxes, which are 17%.

VERY EXPENSIVE

Casa de Sierra Nevada ★★   The hotel consists of several 16th-century town houses on a couple of streets just above El Jardín and a second grouping bordering Par-que Juárez. With picturesque terraces and courtyards bedecked in flowers and plants, some affording charming views and considerable privacy, this place feels like a true getaway from the modern world. When I was last in San Miguel, the new owner, Ori-ent Express, was doing major remodeling to some of the townhouses in the main part of the hotel. I'm told that these improvements will include climate control. This year the hotel will close the rooms and restaurant at Parque Juárez for remodeling. Rooms and suites vary in shape and design; most are very large and have private patios or secluded entrances and working fireplaces. The hotel is 2 blocks southeast of El Jardín. Transportation from either airport is available.

Hospicio 35 (between Diez de Sollano and Recreo), 37700 San Miguel de Allende, Gto. ⓒ **800/701-1561** in the U.S. and Canada, or 415/152-7040. Fax 415/154-9703. www.casadesierranevada.com. 33 units. $354 (£195) deluxe; $429–$522 (£236–£287) suite. AE, MC, V. Free valet parking. Children younger than 16 not accepted. **Amenities:** 2 restaurants; 2 bars; large outdoor heated pool; spa; concierge; tour and activities desk; room service; laundry service; dry cleaning. *In room:* TV, hair dryer, safe.

La Puertecita Boutique Hotel ★★ *Kids*   Those who can't find the charm in church bells and firecrackers going off at all hours of the night will appreciate this hotel, as will those who are traveling with children. Set on the side of a narrow canyon, the hotel is above and a little removed from the central part of town. A fence sur-rounds the grounds, with terraced gardens and the ruined remains of an aqueduct for a touch of local character. Rooms, especially deluxe units and suites, are large; many have vaulted brick ceilings, small terraces, and beautifully tiled large bathrooms. They are furnished and decorated in modern Mexican style. The junior and one-bedroom suites have living areas and, in some cases, a dining area for four. Six suites have kitchenettes. Superior rooms and villas come with a king or a queen bed; the deluxe rooms and suites have a king or two queen beds. There are also two-bedroom suites, which are the equivalent of a one-bedroom suite with a deluxe room attached.

Santo Domingo 75, 37740 San Miguel de Allende, Gto. ℂ 415/152-5011. Fax 415/152-5505. www.lapuerte cita.com. 32 units. $215–$270 (£118–£149) double; $295–$324 (£162–£178) suite. AE, MC, V. Free guarded parking. **Amenities:** Restaurant; bar; 2 small outdoor pools (1 heated); golf and tennis at local club; exercise equipment; outdoor whirlpool; game room; concierge; tour desk; courtesy car; room service; in-room massage; babysitting; laundry service; dry cleaning; nonsmoking rooms. *In room:* TV, hair dryer, safe.

EXPENSIVE

Casa de la Cuesta ★★★ In an upper *barrio* (neighborhood) stands this magnificent house, an example of how colonial architecture can be rethought in modern terms. The combined effect of architecture and location is dramatic. The entrance to the house is through a passage that opens up to the first of two courtyards. On three sides are structures of different heights, which make use wherever possible of rooftop terraces. In one of these structures is a studio and gallery, which the owners (who are art dealers) use for shows or workspace. Guest rooms encircle the arcaded rear courtyard, with a lot of terraces and common space, much of which has a fine view of the central part of town. Rooms are large and comfortable, with king-size beds, lots of color and detail, and a mix of modern and colonial furnishings. The house is about a 10-minute walk to the center of town, and the return is uphill. Breakfasts are great, and the hosts, Heidi and Bill Levasseur, are helpful and entertaining.

Cuesta de San José 32, 37700 San Miguel de Allende, Gto. ℂ/fax 415/154-4324. www.casadelacuesta.com. 6 units. $140–$160 (£77–£88) double. Rates include full breakfast. MC, V (for deposits). Limited street parking. **Amenities:** In-room massage; laundry service; nonsmoking rooms. *In room:* No phone.

Casa Luna Pila Seca/Casa Luna Quebrada ★★★ Casa Luna Pila Seca and the new Casa Luna Quebrada are both striking to look at and fun to stay in. Both are just a few blocks below the main square. The new house on Calle Quebrada is a large property, enjoys lots of open space, and is designed in the hacienda style. The original house on Pila Seca is more playful and has lovely nooks and crannies and riotous vegetation. Guest rooms in both houses are roughly the same in size and amenities. They are great fun—lots of color, lots of detail. Most have some Mexican theme but not exclusively. The owner, Dianne Kushner, has a real talent for bringing together disparate design elements and making them look like they naturally belong together. Most rooms are large and come with a king bed or two twins, down comforters, gas fireplaces, and large bathrooms with shower/tub combinations. Most have private patios. The common areas are lovely and relaxing (and now offer Wi-Fi connectivity) and get you right into that *mañana* attitude. Breakfasts are delicious, and cooking classes are sometimes offered.

Pila Seca 11, 37700 San Miguel de Allende, Gto. ℂ 210/200-8758 or 415/152-1117. www.casaluna.com. 25 units. $135–$165 (£74–£91) double. Rates include full breakfast. MC, V (for deposits). Children younger than 16 not accepted. Limited street parking. **Amenities:** Bar; outdoor pool at Quebrada house; Jacuzzi; tour information; massage; nonsmoking rooms; Wi-Fi. *In room:* Hair dryer, safe, no phone.

Susurro ★★★ *(Finds)* Spend any amount of time in places like San Miguel or Cuernavaca, and you realize that the domestic architecture is all about the creation of serene, private spaces. Susurro (which in Spanish describes the sound made by whispering wind and trickling water) has elegant interior spaces, and with only four guest rooms, you'll find plenty of time to enjoy these all to yourself. The soft sounds of flowing water can be heard all around the house. Three of the rooms are large and come with separate terraces. The fourth, the garden room, has now been enlarged and has a lovely patio area in the rear garden. All rooms have either a queen or a king bed and come beautifully decorated. The house is just a few blocks from the main square. Robert Waters, the owner, is an easy-going, agreeable man who makes an excellent host.

Recreo 78, 37700 San Miguel de Allende, Gto. ℭ **310/943-7163** or 415/152-1065. www.susurro.com.mx. 4 units. $155–$190 (£85–£105) double. Rates include full breakfast. AE, MC, V for deposits only. Children younger than 13 not accepted. Limited street parking. **Amenities:** Plunge pool; in-room massage; laundry service; nonsmoking rooms; computer access; Wi-Fi in half the property. *In room:* TV, hair dryer, no phone.

MODERATE

Hotel Mansión Virreyes   Soon after the Mexican Revolution ended, this became the first hotel in San Miguel. The rooms are simply furnished, but comfortable. Almost all face the interior courtyard. Half are carpeted, half are tiled. Bathrooms are small to medium. On the top floor are three suites, which are quite large and come with kitchenettes. These are usually rented out from January to March.

Canal 19, 37700 San Miguel de Allende, Gto. ℭ **415/152-3355,** -0851. Fax 415/152-3865. mansionvirreyes@ prodigy.net.mx. 23 units. Fri–Sun $100 (£55) double, $150 (£83]) suite; Mon–Thurs $90 (£50) double; $165 (£91) suite. Rates include full breakfast. AE, MC, V. Limited street parking. **Amenities:** Restaurant; room service. *In room:* TV.

Hotel Posada Carmina ★   This centrally located hotel is comfortable, beautiful, and well managed. It's a half-block south of the plaza, next to the Parroquia, in a large colonial mansion made from the same stone as the church. The two floors of rooms surround a stately courtyard with orange trees growing around a stone fountain, and bougainvillea and *llamarada* creeping up the walls. Rooms are ample and well furnished. Most of the bathrooms are comfortably sized but simple, with small mirrors (and, in some, little counter space) and plenty of hot water. Light sleepers will find that the bells of the Parroquia prove a nuisance in the front rooms. The new section in back is quieter. Rooms there are midsize with well-lit bathrooms and firm mattresses.

Cuna de Allende 7, 37700 San Miguel de Allende, Gto. ℭ **415/152-0458.** Fax 415/152-1036. www.posada carmina.com. 24 units. $120–$130 (£66–£72) double. Rates include full breakfast. MC, V. Limited street parking. **Amenities:** Restaurant; room service. *In room:* TV.

Pensión Casa Carmen ★   Every B&B has its own feel, and this one feels like a friendly Mexican household. A pretty little Mexican patio with orange trees and a fountain; large rooms that are comfortably but simply furnished; and a gracious, helpful landlady who speaks English—all help set you at ease. All rooms have gas heaters and come with either two twins or one queen-size bed. Of these, the penthouse is perhaps the most comfortable, but the ones in the first courtyard have the most character. Bathrooms vary in size. Breakfast (daily) and the afternoon meal (Mon–Sat) are served in a pleasant dining room; the cooking is good. You can reserve rooms by the day, week, or month, with discounts for extended stays. The location is very central, just 2 blocks east of the Jardín.

Correo 31, near Recreo (Apdo. Postal 152), 37700 San Miguel de Allende, Gto. ℭ/fax **415/152-0844.** www. infosma.com/casacarmen. 11 units. $85 (£47) double. Rates include breakfast and lunch (breakfast only Sun). No credit cards. Children younger than 14 not accepted. Limited street parking. *In room:* No phone.

INEXPENSIVE

Parador San Sebastián _Value_   The San Sebastián is another colonial house turned hotel with a central location and comfortable rooms for the price. Standard rooms are simple and quiet. They vary in size and choice of beds. Pricing is based on bed choices. The lower price is for a double bed or two twins; the higher price is for two doubles. Bathrooms are mostly medium size. Apartments come with a double or two twin beds, a kitchen, and a living/dining area. Guests can lounge in the chairs located in the courtyard and on the rooftop terrace. This hotel takes only walk-ins and won't accept reservations.

Mesones 7 (between Colegio and Núñez), 37700 San Miguel de Allende, Gto. ℂ **415/152-7084.** 30 units. $30–$52 (£17–£29) double; $50 (£28) apt. No credit cards. Free parking. _In room:_ No phone.

Quinta Loreto _Value_   This motel is a good place to stay whether traveling by car or not. It has good rooms for the price, a lovely garden, and a friendly atmosphere. Rooms come with ceiling fans and heaters. The cheaper rooms, without phones or televisions, are smaller than the others. Most rooms contain one double and one twin bed. The food is good and the laundry service a bargain. Make reservations—the Loreto is very popular and often books up weeks in advance. Nonguests can come for breakfast ($3–$5/£1.65–£2.75) and for lunch ($8/£4.40). The _quinta_ (country house) is on a small street below the crafts market off Calle Loreto, about 7 blocks from the main square.

Calle Loreto 15, 37700 San Miguel de Allende, Gto. ℂ **415/152-0042.** Fax 415/152-3616. hqloreto@cybermatsa. com.mx. 40 units. $45–$55 (£25–£30) double. Weekly and monthly discounts available. AE, MC, V. Free parking. **Amenities:** Restaurant; small outdoor pool; tour desk; laundry service. _In room:_ Some w/TV and phone; some w/neither.

WHERE TO DINE

In San Miguel vegetarians will have no problem—most restaurants have legitimate meat-free main courses. Reservations generally aren't necessary except during festival times. For the best baked goods (pastries, French bread, croissants, and cakes), try **El Petit Four,** Calle Mesones 99-1, down the street from the Angela Peralta Theater. It's open Tuesday through Saturday from 10am to 9pm, Sunday from 10am to 6pm. There's a small seating area, or you can take your baked goods with you. The shop also sells coffee.

To sample some of the people's food, you might try **Cenaduría La Alborada** at Sollano 11 (ℂ **415/513-0577**) by the main square. It's a traditional sort of supper place where you can get a nourishing bowl of _pozole_ or a plate of enchiladas. It's open Monday to Saturday from 2pm to 1am. For tacos, try **Los Faroles** at Ancha de San Antonio 28-C (ℂ **451/152-1849**). The owners sell a variety of _tacos de parrilla_ (tacos with grilled meats) and _volcanes_ (a toasted tortilla topped with meat and cheese).

Finally, there's another dining option that's a 10-minute ride east of town. An Italian chef has taken over a small part of the former **Hacienda de Landeta** and has a "country-kitchen" thing going on there—outdoor dining, chalkboard menu, unhurried personal service. Local residents love it. Amidst crumbling walls and ancient trees, the setting has a gracious Old World feel to it. The menu always includes fresh pasta dishes, usually a fish dish and three or four Italian specialties. Chef Andreas personally attends his customers from Thursday to Sunday starting around 2pm. He has only a few tables, so make reservations (ℂ **415/120-3481**).

EXPENSIVE

Bella Italia ★ ITALIAN   The chef, Anselmo, does wonders with just about anything. If you have time, order the risotto, which takes a little while but is worth it; it comes with asparagus, boletus mushrooms, or shrimp, depending on what's available. The chef's specials are good bets—duck breast with blueberry sauce or crabmeat pasta are both excellent choices. Pastas include fresh spinach ravioli.

Canal 21 (at Hernández Macías). ✆ 415/152-4989. Reservations recommended on weekends and during festivals. Main courses $15–$21 (£8.25–£12). AE, MC, V. Daily 1–10:30pm.

MODERATE

Azafrán ★★ NUEVA COCINA   Modern cooking, modern dining area, wide-ranging menu—such a combination is uncommon in San Miguel. The food might best be described as Mexico meets the Mediterranean, with dishes such as terrines, pastas, stuffed chiles, and *nopal* (cactus) soup. On my last visit, I tried a curried pumpkin and pear soup with a stuffed chile swimming in the middle, which, though not on the menu, was a frequent daily special. It was delicious. The jicama-crab salad was quite good, as was a spinach salad with mango, avocado, and bits of blue cheese. There's a back patio and a nonsmoking area. The main dining room is comfortable and decorated in a modern style that works well with the colonial house.

Hernández Macías 97. ✆ 415/152-7482. Reservations recommended during high season. Main courses $10–$18 (£5.50–£9.90). AE, MC, V. Thurs–Tues 1–11pm.

Chamonix ECLECTIC   A rustic little patio holds just a handful of tables. Review the chalkboard to see what the day's offerings are. You'll always find a few dishes from southern Europe and one or two things from south and southeast Asia. Sometimes these will have a little Mexican twist. The pastas and the salads are popular. The last time I was there, I had a very simple fish dish cooked perfectly with an attractive and well matched side dish. Service can be slow.

Sollano 12-A. ✆ 415/154-8363. Reservations recommended on weekends and during festivals. Main courses $7–$15 (£3.85–£8.25). MC, V. Tues–Sat 1:30–10pm.

Restaurant/Bar Bugambilia ★★★ MEXICAN   One can ask little more of a restaurant—delicious and attractive dishes, a large menu, good service, well-spaced tables, and a choice between dining in an elegant plant-filled courtyard and a large dining room, which in cool weather holds a roaring fire. Señora Arteaga offers a delicious variation on *chiles en nogada* (stuffed poblano chile with walnut cream sauce)—she marinates the pepper and serves it cold, not fried in batter. The *chiles en nogada* have been the object of many innovations, but most fail because they don't preserve the essence of this baroque dish, which balances opposites like the point and counterpoint of a fugue. Too spicy or too sweet, too strong a taste of meat or onions, and the magic is lost. Something simpler, perhaps? Start with the *caldo Xochitl* (the perfect soup for an irritable stomach), followed by traditional *enchiladas del portal* cooked in *chile ancho* sauce.

Hidalgo 42 (between Insurgentes and Calzada de la Luz). ✆ 415/152-0127. Reservations recommended on weekends. Main courses $10–$17 (£5.50–£9.35). MC, V. Daily noon–11pm.

Romano's *Value* ITALIAN   A beautiful location that offers indoor and outdoor dining has turned into a popular spot serving great food in generous portions. The ingredients are fresh (organic when possible), and most of the pastas are made on the premises. Pizzas and fresh bread are baked in a wood-burning brick oven. Among the locals, the extra-thick grilled pork chops earn lots of remarks, as do the pasta dishes or the pizzas.

Hernández Macías 93. ℂ **415/152-7454.** Reservations recommended. Main courses $8–$16 (£4.40–£8.80). No credit cards. Tues–Sat 5–11pm.

INEXPENSIVE

Cha-Cha-Cha *Finds* MEXICAN   An apt name for a fun place to eat home-style Mexican cooking. The house and dining area are informal and relaxing (made more so by being a bit distant from the hustle and bustle of downtown), and the friendly service makes you want to linger here well after the meal is over, perhaps to sample the excellent margaritas. Menu items include *albóndigas* (Mexican meat balls flavored with chipotle), chicken in a *huazontle* sauce (a vegetable vaguely similar to broccoli, but much milder), and quesadillas with a variety of fillings including beef in a chile pasilla sauce. Leave room for the coffee-flavored flan.

28 de Abril Norte 37. ℂ **415/152-6586.** Main courses $4–$6 (£2.20–£3.30). No credit cards. Tues–Sun 1–7pm.

El Correo ★ MEXICAN   This is a small place right across from the post office. I really like the owner's selection of menu items, offering in a small package quite a varied sampling of Mexican standards: *sopes* (little fried masa cakes topped with savory meats and veggies); *caldo tlalpeño* (chicken, rice, and vegetable soup; my preference over the tortilla soup, which is what most people come for); and *enchiladas del portal* (enchiladas with chile sauce), which are made in the classic western Mexican style. Other offerings include *mole* and *arrachera a la tampiqueña* (steak with an array of side dishes).

Correo 23. ℂ **415/152-4951.** Reservations accepted. Breakfast $4–$5 (£2.20–£2.75); main courses $7–$12 (£3.85–£6.60). MC, V. Wed–Mon 8am–11pm.

El Pegaso Restaurant & Bar INTERNATIONAL   Decorated in a cheerful, colorful style, and with a friendly, helpful staff, this restaurant is popular with expatriates and visitors. It's good for breakfast and light meals of sandwiches, soups, or salads. The restaurant is 1 block east of the Jardín.

Corregidora 6 (at Correo). ℂ **415/152-1351.** Breakfast $4–$8 (£2.20–£4.40); soups, salads, sandwiches $5–$7 (£2.75–£3.85); main courses $5–$15 (£2.75–£8.25). MC, V. Mon–Sat 8:30am–10pm.

Olé Olé MEXICAN   Festive and friendly, this small restaurant is a riot of red and yellow streamers and bullfight memorabilia. The small menu specializes in grilled main courses—beef or chicken fajitas, shrimp brochettes, and *arrachera* (skirt steak). It also includes dishes such as *champiñones al ajillo* (mushrooms in garlic and *guajillo* chile) and *chistorra* (Spanish-style sausage).

Loreto 66 (between Insurgentes and Calzada de la Luz). ℂ **415/152-0896.** Main courses $7–$12 (£3.85–£6.60). No credit cards. Daily 1–9pm.

SAN MIGUEL AFTER DARK

To see a calendar of events, find a copy of the local paper, *Atención,* or one of the free monthly periodicals for visitors. Bellas Artes and the Angela Peralta Theater also post announcements of performances around town. Local regulations favor restaurant-bars over simple bars, so live-music acts often perform in restaurants. Clubs and dance clubs tend to spring up and then die off quickly. One club that has persisted is **La Cava de la Princesa,** Recreo 3 (ℂ **415/152-1403**). It books a lot of live acts playing

Tips **Recommended Day-Trip Tours**

Dolores Hidalgo is the most popular destination for day-trippers from San Miguel (see "A Side Trip to Dolores Hidalgo: Fine Pottery & Shrimp Ice Cream," below). Some people make a day trip of Guanajuato or Querétaro (see "Guanajuato," and "Santiago de Querétaro," both later in this chapter). It's a hurried way of seeing them, but it can be done. Several tour guides and companies in San Miguel make trips to all of these places. **Leandro Delgado** (✆ 415/152-0155; leandrotours@hotmail.com) is an independent tour guide who is well informed and conscientious. He speaks English, is a good driver, and is familiar with the artisans of Dolores Hidalgo and Guanajuato. Another tour agency is **PMC,** Hidalgo 18 (✆ 415/152-0121). It offers several options for day trips and walking tours of San Miguel, too. Both of these businesses offer trips to see the **monarch butterflies,** 5 hours away in the state of Michoacán (see chapter 7). This is an exhausting trip; do it in 2 days, overnighting in the town of Angangueo, if you can. The season runs from mid- to late November to March.

different kinds of music, as well as impersonators of Mexican pop stars. The cover charge is $3 to $8 (£1.65–£4.40). A couple of restaurants are popular nightspots: **Tío Lucas** (✆ 415/512-4996) is a fun place to hear jazz, have a few drinks and perhaps a bite of dinner. It's located at Mesones 105 across from the Teatro Peralta. **Mama Mía,** Umarán 8, between Jesús and Hernández Macías (✆ 415/152-2063), has a bar area where salsa and jazz bands play on the weekends. There is a $4 (£2.20) cover. In the summer you can enjoy the late afternoon and early evening from its rooftop terrace. If you don't feel like hearing music, how about a drink and a movie? The **Cine Bar** at the Hotel Jacaranda (✆ 415/152-1015), Calle Aldama 53, shows recently released American movies on a large screen and includes popcorn and a drink with the $6 (£3.30) price of admission. Waiters come to your table with drinks and will bring the dinner menu as well. The film starts rolling at 7:30pm. A couple of bars near El Jardín are good places if you just want to enjoy a drink with friends. One is **La Fragua,** next to Allende's house.

A SIDE TRIP TO DOLORES HIDALGO: FINE POTTERY & SHRIMP ICE CREAM

Dolores Hidalgo lies 40km (25 miles) northwest of San Miguel on Highway 35. Most people go there to shop at the Talavera pottery companies, but the town itself merits a visit. It remains a quiet, provincial place with a lovely main square and parish church; on the church steps, Father Hidalgo proclaimed the independence of Mexico. The church has a charming facade that, if pressed, I would label late Mexican baroque, but that doesn't do it justice. The interior of the church was plundered at various times but retains a couple of altarpieces that are worth a peek.

The main square has a quaint, small-town feel to it. Vendors sell ice cream in exotic flavors—tequila, shrimp, and pulque (a fermented beverage made from agave) are just a few enticing examples—as well as mango, *guanábana,* and other more familiar standbys. It all started 30 years ago on a dare, and then caught on for the notoriety it gave the vendors. Ask for some impossibly bad flavor like cilantro–*mezcal*–chocolate chip or chicken *mole* swirl, and, without batting an eye, they'll tell you they're fresh out and to come back tomorrow. Most of these ice creams are known as *nieves* and are low in fat; for a richer ice cream ask for a *mantecado*. If you're hungry, there is a restaurant, El Patio, on the east side of the square.

Dolores has two small museums. The **Casa de Hidalgo** (admission $2/£1.10) is filled with letters and historical artifacts having to do with Father Hidalgo, and will be of most interest to history buffs. The **Museo de la Independencia** (admission 50¢/30p), a more dramatic approach to the theme of independence, also has a small collection of memorabilia of José Alfredo Jiménez, the king of *ranchera* music.

SHOPPING FOR TALAVERA

The **Talavera** pottery produced in Dolores is quite handsome and colorful, if less traditional than Talavera produced in Puebla. It's also inexpensive and plentiful. You can find all kinds of objects, from sink basins to napkin rings to hand-painted tiles. The pieces are formed with molds and then painted freehand. Prices here are considerably lower than those in San Miguel. Workshops are usually open from 10am to 6pm, but may or may not close for the afternoon meal. Almost all are closed on Sunday.

The first couple of Talavera workshops you'll encounter aren't even in town, but are on the highway just before you get there. **Talavera San Gabriel** (© 418/185-5037) has a warehouse full of large and small decorative objects, including picture frames, candlesticks, and ginger jars. And **Talavera Mora** (© 418/185-9002) has more dinnerware, including the popular blue-and-yellow fish pattern.

Once you get into town, you're best off just asking directions for different stores and factories. There are a lot of shops and each seems to have a different specialty. At the entrance to the town, on the left side of the first roundabout is **Hacienda Style** (© 418/182-2064 or 602/288-9122 in the U.S.). It is the outlet for two factories that produce tiles and sink basins and decorative objects in traditional and contemporary patterns. Another that specializes in decorative objects is **Talavera Cortés** (© 418/182-0900), at the corner of Distrito Federal and Tabasco streets. **Azulejos Talavera Vázquez** (© 418/182-0630) has a large store at the corner of Puebla and Tamaulipas streets. It has a bit of everything, and at that same intersection are a couple of other stores with lots of dinnerware.

1 APR 2009

2 Guanajuato ★★★

354km (219 miles) NW of Mexico City; 56km (35 miles) SE of León; 93km (58 miles) W of San Miguel de Allende; 208km (129 miles) SW of San Luis Potosí; 163km (101 miles) N of Morelia; 280km (174 miles) SE of Zacatecas

If you're going to Mexico to lose yourself, you'll have no problem doing so on the streets of Guanajuato (gwah-nah-*whah*-toh). They seem designed for just that purpose as they curl this way and that, becoming alleys or stairways, and intersecting each other at different angles. At times it can seem like the Twilight Zone; I've heard of people hurriedly passing by a curious-looking shop intending to return later, and then never being able to locate it again. To make matters worse, the streets are filled with things that can draw your attention away from the business of getting from one place to another. The town is so photogenic; everywhere you look is postcard material. Most buildings, like the streets, are irregular in shape, creating a jumble of walls, balconies, and rooftops meeting at anything but a right angle. The churches are the exception, having regular floor plans, but even they show asymmetry—despite the best efforts of their builders, none has two matching towers, which only adds to their charm.

Guanajuato

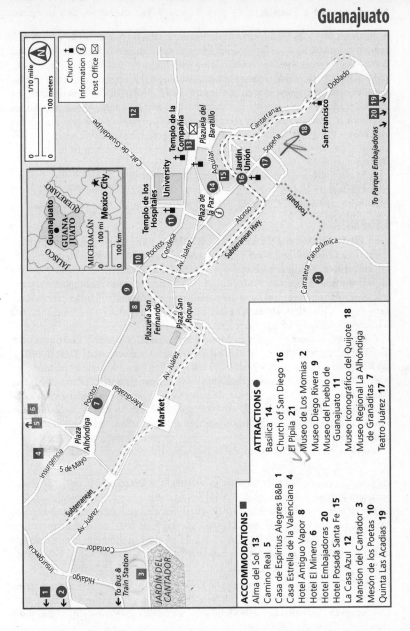

ATTRACTIONS ●

Basílica **14**
Church of San Diego **16**
El Pípila **21**
Museo de Los Momias **2**
Museo Diego Rivera **9**
Museo del Pueblo de
Guanajuato **11**
Museo Iconográfico del Quijote **18**
Museo Regional La Alhóndiga
de Granaditas **7**
Teatro Juárez **17**

ACCOMMODATIONS ■

Alma del Sol **13**
Camino Real **5**
Casa de Espíritus Alegres B&B **1**
Casa Estrella de la Valenciana **4**
Hotel Antiguo Vapor **8**
Hotel El Minero **6**
Hotel Embajadoras **20**
Hotel Posada Santa Fe **15**
La Casa Azul **12**
Mansion del Cantador **3**
Mesón de los Poetas **10**
Quinta Las Acadias **19**

Founded in 1559, Guanajuato soon became a fabulously rich town, with world-famous mines (such as La Valenciana, Mineral de Cata, and Mineral de Rayas) that earned their owners titles of nobility. Along with Zacatecas and San Luis Potosí, Guanajuato was one of Mexico's most important mining cities. From the 16th through the 18th centuries, the mines in these towns produced a third of all the silver in the world, and Guanajuato bloomed with elaborate churches and mansions. Floods plagued the city until it finally diverted the river and turned the old river bed into a road that winds into the old downtown area, with cantilevered houses jutting out high above the cars. The city has also opened an impressive network of tunnels (it is, after all, a mining town).

Still, on the surface, Guanajuato seems like an old Spanish city dumped into a Mexican highland valley. It's one of Mexico's great colonial cities. Picturesque and laden with atmosphere, Guanajuato should be high on your list of places to visit.

ESSENTIALS

GETTING THERE & DEPARTING   **By Plane**   Air access is good, with frequent flights in and out of the León/Guanajuato (also known as León/Bajío) airport, 27km (17 miles) from downtown Guanajuato. The taxi ride costs about $35 (£19) from the airport and $30 (£17) in the return direction. The airport has an ATM, pharmacy, and gift store. It also has the following car-rental counters: **Avis** (© 477/713-3003), **Budget** (© 477/713-1404), **Hertz** (© 477/771-5050), **National** (© 477/771-3371), and **Thrifty** (© 477/713-8522).

American Airlines's number in Mexico is © 01-800/904-6000; **Continental**'s is © 01-800/900-5000; **Delta**'s is © 01-800/902-2100. **AeroMéxico** (© 01-800/021-4000) and its affiliate, **Aerolitoral,** fly to and from Los Angeles, Tijuana, Mexico City, Puerto Vallarta, Monterrey, and Ciudad Juárez. **Mexicana** (© 01-800/502-2000) flies to and from Chicago, Oakland, Los Angeles, Denver, San Jose, Guadalajara, Mexico City, and Tijuana. **AeroMar** (© 01-800/704-2900) flies to and from Saltillo and Puebla. *Note:* For more information, including these airlines' toll-free phone numbers, please see chapter 2.

There are airline ticket offices in León and at the airport. In Guanajuato, travel agencies can arrange flights.

By Car   From Mexico City there are two routes. The faster one (4½ hr.), is Highway 57 north and northwest to Highway 45D at Querétaro, west through Salamanca to Irapuato, where you follow Highway 45 north to Silao and then take Highway 110 east. The route is a four-lane road almost all the way. The slower route continues north on Highway 57 past Querétaro, then west on Highway 110 through Dolores Hidalgo, and continues to Guanajuato. From San Luis Potosí, the quickest way to Guanajuato is through Dolores Hidalgo (3 hr.).

By Bus   The bus station in Guanajuato is 6km (3½ miles) southwest of town. From **Mexico City's Terminal Norte,** you'll have no trouble finding a *directo* (nonstop bus) to Guanajuato. **Servicios Coordinados/Primera Plus** (© 55/5567-4388) and **Estrella Blanca** (© 55/5729-4388) run express buses (5 hr.). You shouldn't have to wait more than a half-hour. Try to catch one of **ETN**'s (© 55/5785-1576) super-deluxe buses with extra-wide seats that recline far back (10 per day). They're worth the extra money.

From **San Miguel de Allende,** ETN has three nonstop buses, Primera Plus/Servicios Coordinados has nine. These go *vía la Presa* (the short route—1¼ hr.). Don't take buses that go via Dolores Hidalgo. There is also service to Guadalajara (4 hr.), Morelia (2½ hr.), and elsewhere.

ORIENTATION   Arriving by Plane   The only transportation from the León/Guanajuato airport, 27km (17 miles) from downtown, is a **private taxi.** You pay for the cab ($35) inside the airport. There is no shuttle service.

Arriving by Car   Try not to lose your sanity while finding a place to park. Such a winding, hilly town defies good verbal or written directions. Be alert for one-way streets. Consider parking your car until you leave town, because the frustration of driving in the city could spoil your visit.

Arriving by Bus   The bus station is about 6km (3¾ miles) southwest of town, on the road to Celaya. Cabs are easy to come by and should cost about $3 (£1.65).

VISITOR INFORMATION   The state **tourism information office** is at Plaza de la Paz 14, across from the basilica (© **473/732-1574,** ext. 1437). It's open Monday through Friday from 9am to 7pm.

CITY LAYOUT   Guanajuato is a town of narrow streets, alleys, and stairs, and small, picturesque plazas. The hilly terrain and tangle of streets are difficult to represent on a map. You'll soon learn that maps aren't drawn to scale, nor do they show every street and stairway. The best way to get oriented is to visit the overlook at El Pípila (see "The Top Attractions," below) and one by one make out the major landmarks.

The small plaza at the center of the city, **Jardín Unión** (known as the cheese wedge, for its shape)—is where students, locals, and visitors gather. Facing the Jardín from the direction of El Pípila are both the **Teatro Juárez** and **Templo de San Diego.** From this plaza, you are within walking distance of many of the major sights.

GETTING AROUND   Walking is the only way to get to know the historic district of this labyrinthine town. For longer stretches, taxis are reasonably priced and abundant, except between 2 and 4pm when office workers are trying to get home for the midafternoon meal. As usual, you should establish the price before setting out.

FAST FACTS: Guanajuato

Area Code   The telephone area code is **473.**

Climate   The city has temperatures that are mild in summer, cool in winter, with the occasional freeze at night.

Drugstores   **Farmacia Embajadoras,** Paseo Madero 10 (© **473/732-0996**), or **Farmacia La Perla,** Juárez 146 (© **473/732-1175**).

Elevation   Guanajuato sits at 2,008m (6,586 ft.).

Emergency & Police   Call © **473/732-0266** for the police.

Hospital   You have two reasonable choices: **Centro Médico La Presa,** Paseo de la Presa 85 (© **473/731-1074**), and **Clínica Plaza Mayor,** in the western part of the city (© **473/732-2305**).

Internet Access There are several Internet cafes in the downtown area, with a lot of turnover. Just keep your eyes peeled for any sign that says INTERNET or CYBERCAFE.

Language School There are five language schools in Guanajuato. The best known is **Academia Falcón,** Paseo de la Presa 80 (② 473/731-0745; www.academiafalcon.com; mailing address: Callejón de la Mora 158, 36000 Guanajuato, Gto.). The institute provides skilled and dedicated tutors for those at all levels, and gets high marks from students. It can also arrange boarding with local families.

Population Guanajuato has 145,000 residents.

Post Office The *correo*, on the corner of Ayuntamiento and Carcamanes, near the Templo de la Compañia, is open Monday through Friday from 9am to 6pm.

Seasons The rainy season is June through September. Occasionally the rain is hard, but mostly it's afternoon showers and presents no problems for travelers. The coldest part of the year is December and January; the hottest is April, May, and some of June, before the rains come.

SPECIAL EVENTS & FESTIVALS

Every year in October, the state of Guanajuato sponsors the **Festival** Internacional **Cervantino (International Cervantes Festival)** 🏵🏵, 2 weeks of performing arts from all over the world. In recent years, the festival has featured marionettes from the Czech Republic, the Eliot Feld Ballet from New York, the Kiev Ballet, and a host of Mexican artists. The shows are held in open plazas and theaters all over town. Book rooms well in advance during the festival; if Guanajuato is full, consider staying in San Miguel de Allende.

For ticket information and a schedule, contact Festival Cervantino, Plaza San Francisquito 1, 36000 Guanajuato, Gto. (② **473/731-1221;** www.festivalcervantino.gob.mx). Once you know the schedule, you can order tickets through **Ticketmaster** in Mexico City (② **55/5325-9000**). Keep your confirmation number; you'll need it to pick up your tickets in Guanajuato. The best time to be at the festival is during the week; on weekends it's absolute madness.

EXPLORING GUANAJUATO

THE TOP ATTRACTIONS

El Pípila   This is the best vantage point in Guanajuato for photographs—the whole city unfolds below you, with great views in every direction. A funicular railway runs up the hill from behind the church of San Diego. You can also climb the hill on foot up a rugged winding pathway. Just look for signs that read AL PÍPILA (to El Pípila).

The statue is the city's monument to José de los Reyes Martínez, better known as El Pípila. According to the story, El Pípila (if he really existed) was a brave young miner in Father Hidalgo's ragtag army of peasants and workers fighting for Mexican independence. Guanajuato was the first real battle of the war. The royalist forces took up their position inside the Alhóndiga de Granaditas. It seemed impregnable to Hidalgo's army, which lacked artillery. But El Pípila managed to breach the Spanish defenses by tying a flagstone to his back as protection, crawling to the fortress doors, and setting them ablaze. Today, El Pípila's statue raises a torch high over the city in everlasting vigilance; the inscription at his feet proclaims AUN HAY OTRAS ALHÓNDIGAS POR INCENDIAR (There still remain other *alhóndigas* to burn).

Free admission. Daily 24 hr.

Museo del Pueblo de Guanajuato ★★   Just north of the Plaza de la Paz is this 17th-century mansion that once belonged to the Marqués San Juan de Rayas. The first and third floors display traveling exhibits; the second holds a fascinating collection of colonial-era civil and religious pieces gathered by distinguished local muralist José Chávez Morado. As a collector, Chávez Morado had an eye for the macabre, acquiring death portraits, some even eerier portraits of the living, and religious paintings on the subject of mortality. Also in the collection are some paintings by the gifted Hermenegildo Bustos, a portrait artist of the 19th century. There is a small collection of pre-Hispanic artifacts and several folk-art testimonials dedicated to the miraculous powers of various saints. The museum contains a couple of Chávez's murals; other works by Bustos and Chávez can be found at La Alhóndiga, down the street.

Calle Positos 7. ⓒ 473/732-2990. Admission $2 (£1.10). Tues–Sat 10am–6:30pm; Sun 10am–2:30pm.

Museo Diego Rivera ★★   From the Museo del Pueblo, walk 1½ blocks farther down the street, and you'll find the house where the artist Diego Rivera was born on December 8, 1886. It has been restored and converted into a museum. The first floor is furnished as it might have been in the era of Rivera's birth. Upstairs there's a pretty good collection of his early works. He began painting when he was 10 years old and eventually moved to Paris, where he became a Marxist during World War I. The house contains a few sketches of some of the earlier murals that made his reputation, and paintings from 1902 to 1956. The fourth floor holds a small auditorium for lectures and conferences, and there you'll find a large representation of one of Rivera's most famous murals, *Un Sueño Dominical en la Alameda*.

Calle Positos 47. ⓒ 473/732-1197. Admission $2 (£1.10). Tues–Sat 10am–6:30pm; Sun 10am–2:30pm.

Museo Iconográfico del Quijote ★ *Finds*   There are only a few truly universal characters in the world of literature: Hamlet, Faust, Don Juan, and Don Quixote come to mind. Writers far and wide have taken up these characters and reworked their stories, but Don Quixote much more than the others has become a favorite subject of artists. The list includes Dalí, Picasso, Miró, Raul Angiano, José Guadalupe Posada, Daumier, José Moreno Carbonero, and Pedro Coronel. This museum, a long block southeast of the Jardín Unión, holds a fascinating collection of art based upon Don Quixote—all Quixote, all the time! Particularly forceful are the sculptures and murals, but the sheer variety of forms and thematic treatment is what makes a stroll through this museum so entertaining.

Manuel Doblado 1. ⓒ 473/732-6721. Free admission. Tues–Sat 10am–6:30pm; Sun 10am–2:30pm.

Museo Regional La Alhóndiga de Granaditas ★★   On the same street as the Rivera Museum, 2 blocks farther down, is La Alhóndiga de Granaditas, which was built between 1798 and 1809 as the town granary—hard to believe, because it is such a beautiful building. The Spanish took refuge here in 1810 when El Pípila (see above) and company captured Guanajuato. A slaughter ensued that Father Hidalgo was unable to stop. This convinced many people who had been leaning toward independence to remain loyal to Spain, although when the Spanish forces under Félix Calleja retook Guanajuato, they exacted an equally horrible revenge on the locals suspected of collusion. (The exhibits tell the story.) By the next year, the royalist forces triumphed, and the heads of the insurrectionists Hidalgo, Allende, Aldama, and Jiménez adorned the four corners of the building, where they remained until 1821 as a dissuasive reminder.

The old granary now houses a *museo regional* (regional museum). The interior courtyard is large and beautiful and shouldn't be missed. Two floors of rooms hold exhibits of pre-Columbian artifacts, displays on colonial history, and regional crafts. Adorning the two stairways to the second floor are the vivid murals of José Chávez Morado, who donated his pre-Hispanic art collection to the museum (and whose colonial-era collection is in the Museo del Pueblo de Guanajuato). The exhibits take you through the region's colonial era and its role in the struggle for independence, all the way up to the Mexican Revolution. Explanatory text is in Spanish only, but the artifacts are interesting and well displayed. Down the hill from the Alhóndiga is the Mercado Hidalgo (see "Shopping," below).

Mendizábal 6. ⓒ 473/732-1112. Admission $3.25 (£1.80), free for students w/ID. Video camera $3 (£1.65). Tues–Sat 10am–2pm and 4–6pm; Sun 10am–3pm.

Teatro Juárez   Built in 1903 during the opulent era of the Porfiriato, this theater is now the venue for many productions, especially during the Festival Cervantino. The exterior is starkly at odds with its surroundings—Greco-Roman portico adorned with *fin-de-siècle* bronze lions and lanterns. The interior is especially eye-catching. Box seats rise up four stories along the walls of the theater, and there's not a bad seat in the house.

Jardín de la Unión. ⓒ 473/732-0183. Admission $1 (55p). Still camera $1 (55p), video camera $2 (£1.10). Tues–Sun 9am–1:45pm and 5–7:45pm.

MORE ATTRACTIONS

The **Church of San Diego,** on the Jardín Unión, stands almost as it did in 1633, when it was built under the direction of Franciscan missionaries. A flood in 1760 nearly destroyed it. The reconstruction was completed in 1786, largely at the expense of the Count of La Valenciana. The pink cantera-stone facade is a fine example of the Mexican baroque.

The **Plazuela del Baratillo,** just behind the Jardín Unión, has a beautiful fountain (a gift from Emperor Maximilian) at its center. You'll always find people sitting around it peacefully, some in the shade and others in the sun. Its name derives from its former role as a weekly *tianguis* (market); vendors would yell *"¡Barato!"* ("Cheap!").

Just west of Baratillo is the **Church of the Compañía.** Built in 1747 by the Jesuit order, it was the biggest of their churches. The churrigueresque decoration lightens it somewhat, but the interior, which was restored in the 19th century, is neoclassical. This church was built as part of a Jesuit university, which was founded in 1732 on orders of Philip V. It's the last of 23 universities the Jesuit order built in Mexico. The main building of the **university** is on the same block as the church. Its entrance was rebuilt in 1945 in imposing neoclassical style.

Farther west, between the main street, Juárez, and Calle Positos are three plazas almost connected to each other and worth seeing: **Plaza San Roque, Jardín de la Reforma,** and **Plaza San Fernando,** where you can sit at one of the outdoor tables and enjoy coffee in a perfectly charming setting. This plaza is an increasingly popular hangout, and it's a good area to find an Internet cafe.

NEARBY ATTRACTIONS

The following attractions are all a short distance above the city, and the best way to get to them is by taxi. You can hire one for $10 (£5.50) per hour. I would recommend taking the panoramic highway around the city, which allows you to pass by La Valenciana, La Cata, and La Raya; each has a mine and a church. The highway circles around to El Pípila. The drive is enjoyable and lasts about an hour, with a couple of stops and a quick drive along the submerged highway to view the houses that are perched precariously above the road.

La Valenciana ★★★ The area around La Valenciana mine holds several attractions, shopping destinations, and a good restaurant. You might want to allot several hours for a visit, but keep in mind that everything closes by 6pm. The star attraction is the magnificent **church of San Cayetano,** built toward the end of the colonial period in the opulent style of Mexican baroque. The interior is a dazzling affair, with gilded carvings and *retablos* (altarpieces). The best time to see it is midafternoon, when sunlight pours through the windows, illuminating the golden carvings.

In the church plaza is an outstanding folk-art store called **Ojo de Venado** (see "Shopping," below) and a rock-and-mineral shop. Guides offer (in Spanish only) a short, so-so **tour of the mine** ($1/55p) and explain something of its operation. (Zacatecas has a more interesting mine tour.) Look for a sign that says BOCAMINA–LA VALENCIANA. Across the road from the church is the house of the Count of La Valenciana, which now holds a restaurant, **La Casa del Conde de la Valenciana** (see "Where to Dine," later in this chapter).

La Valenciana silver mine is still in operation. The mining operations are a couple of hundred yards west of the house. It's an eight-sided vertical shaft (500m/1,640 ft. deep) surrounded by a tall stone wall in the shape of a crown with large wooden doors and a miner's chapel at the entrance. The miners extract silver and about 50 other minerals and metals.

If you keep climbing on the road that runs alongside La Valenciana, you will shortly see the driveway up to Casa de Capelo (see "Shopping," below) and to Cerámica La Cruz. Continue for a few miles farther and you come to the small town of Santa Rosa, where you can see yet more beautiful ceramics at Mayólica Santa Rosa (see "Shopping," below).

Templo de la Valenciana, Valenciana. Free admission. Daily 9am–6pm.

Museo de Los Momias (Mummy Museum)   First-time visitors find this museum grotesque or fascinating, or both: Mummified remains of the dead, some of whom wear tattered clothing from centuries past, are on display. Dryness and the earth's gases and minerals in this particular *panteón* (cemetery) have halted decomposition. Because graveyards have limited space, bodies are eventually exhumed in Mexico to make room for newcomers. Those on display were exhumed between 1865 and 1985. The mummies stand or recline in glass cases, grinning, choking, or staring, while tour guides tell crowds of visitors macabre stories in Spanish of the fates of some of the deceased. Are they true? *¿Quién sabe?* But it's impossible to resist the temptation to go up and look at them, and this is the only graveyard I've seen with souvenir stands. They mostly sell sugar skulls and effigies of the mummies. Next to the mummy museum is a small exhibit called "El Culto a la Muerte" (Worship of the Dead) which is a bad mix of morbid and hokey.

Esplanada del Panteón. ✆ 473/732-0639. Admission $2 (£1.10). Still camera $1 (55p), video camera $2 (£1.10). Daily 9am–6pm. At the northwest end of town, the steep Esplanada del Panteón leads up to the municipal cemetery.

Templo de Cata   Up above the city, perched on the mountain to the north, is this small, elaborate "miners' church." Cata is also the name of the mine nearby and the *barrio* (neighborhood) that surrounds the church. A lovely baroque facade, with just one tower standing, decorates the outside. Until a few of years ago, this church held an enormous number of personal testimonials that covered the walls from floor to ceiling. Most of these took the traditional form of small square sheets of metal with painted scenes (in a primitive folk style) and explanatory text describing the miracles performed by the church's Señor de Villaseca. "El Trigueñito" (roughly translated as "the olive-skinned one"), as he is affectionately called, is a popular figure in Guanajuato, especially with miners and truck and taxi drivers. The testimonials were a touching display of the highly personal relationship these people have with El Trigueñito. What has become of all these testimonials is now the question. At first, the removal of the testimonials was supposed to be temporary, but I suspect they might not be coming back.

Carretera Panorámica. Free admission. Daily 9am–5pm.

A NEARBY MUSEUM   Surrounding Guanajuato were more than 150 haciendas of wealthy colonial mine owners. Most are now either in ruins or restored and privately owned, but one has been made into the **Museo Exhacienda San Gabriel de Barrera**. About 3km (2 miles) from town on the road to Marfil, it's a lovely place noted for its elaborate gardens in different styles (Moorish, English, and Spanish, for example). The hacienda house presents a good picture of 18th-century life in the grand style. As is often the case, the hacienda has its own chapel (baroque, of course), with a key identifying the various figures depicted in the *retablo*. There is also a state-run shop displaying all the handicrafts produced in the state. The grounds are open daily from 9am to 6pm; admission is $3 (£1.65), plus $1 (55p) for a still camera or $1.50 (85p) for a video camera. The store's hours are Wednesday through Sunday from 10am to 5pm.

SHOPPING

Stores in Guanajuato keep the usual hours—Monday through Saturday from 10am to 2pm and 4 to 8pm. The **Mercado Hidalgo,** or municipal market, is one of the most orderly in Mexico. You can browse on the main floor or watch the action from the raised walkway that encircles it. Aside from food and vegetable stalls, there's lots of pottery and ceramic ware.

Artesanías Vázquez   Outlet for a factory in Dolores Hidalgo, this place is small but loaded with the colorful Talavera-style pottery for which Dolores is famous. You'll see plates, ginger jars, frames, cups and saucers, serving bowls, and the like. Open Monday to Saturday from 9am to 9pm. Cantarranas 8. ✆ **473/732-5231.**

Casa de Capelo   Famous ceramist Javier de Jesús Hernández, known simply as Capelo, has his workshop and showroom high above Guanajuato, past La Valenciana church. You'll see signs for the store, which point to a dirt road that climbs steeply to the left of the highway. It's open Monday through Friday from 10am to 6pm. Carretera a Dolores Hidalgo s/n. ✆ **473/732-8964.**

Cerámica La Cruz   If you're on your way up to see Capelo's store, stop here, just below Capelo's, to view another style of ceramic ware that plays a lot with glazes producing crackleware, among other things. Its hours are Monday through Friday from 10am to 6pm. Carretera a Dolores Hidalgo s/n. ✆ **473/732-9037.**

The Gorky González Workshop   This prize-winning ceramist has dedicated himself to bringing back the traditional Talavera of Guanajuato. The workshop is a short cab ride from the historic center. The showroom is open Monday through Friday from

10am to 2pm and 4 to 6pm, Saturday from 10am to 1pm. Call first. Calle Pastita (by the baseball field). ℰ **473/731-0389.**

Mayólica Santa Rosa   This factory store is in the small town of Santa Rosa, on the way to Dolores Hidalgo. It carries high-quality *mayólica* for less money than in Guanajuato. It's open Monday through Friday from 8am to 5pm. On the highway. ℰ **473/739-0572.**

Ojo de Venado   A knowledgeable dealer of folk art, Randy Walz, sells a variety of pieces from Michoacán and other areas near Guanajuato. He's good at finding unique, highly expressive works. The store is open daily from 10am to 6pm. Below the church of San Cayetano. ℰ **473/734-1435.**

Rincón Artesanal   Objects in carved wood, wax, papier-mâché, pewter, and ceramic, produced in different workshops throughout the state of Guanajuato, stock this store. It also carries items from farther afield, including beautiful *catrina calaveras* (skeleton statues in fancy dress) from the state of Michoacán. The mother and daughter who own and run the place are very helpful. It's open daily from 10am to 9pm. Sopeña 5 (1 block east of Jardín Unión). ℰ **473/732-8632.**

WHERE TO STAY

Hotels have high-season rates for Christmas, Easter, and the Festival Cervantino. High season at moderate and inexpensive hotels also includes July and August, when schools are out and families vacation and any long weekend. During the Festival Cervantino, in October, rooms are virtually impossible to find without a reservation, and even then it's good to claim your room early in the day. Some visitors have to stay as far away as León or San Miguel de Allende. Rates quoted here include the 17% tax.

The old Parador San Javier is closed while being completely made over. It will reopen sometime in April or May of 2007 as a Camino Real (www.caminoreal.com), at rates considerably higher than the old ones.

VERY EXPENSIVE

Casa Estrella de la Valenciana ✦✦✦   This is a beautiful modern house perched on the mountainside above La Valenciana church. It's constructed in contemporary Mexican style in such a way as to take full advantage of the panoramic view of the city and surrounding valley. The owners—two American women, one of whom lives on the premises—have taken pains to create comfortable, spacious interiors decorated with the tiles, pottery, and arts of the area. The bathrooms, the fixtures, the linens—everything has been handled with meticulous attention. Guest rooms are named after local mines. All have their own balcony or terrace; two are handicap accessible. The two most expensive are quite large and have special amenities such as a private Jacuzzi (La Valenciana) or a steam locker (La Sirena). Each comes with a king bed. Another oversize room, the San Bernabé, comes with two queens and has both a tub and a shower. The others have either a queen or a king bed. La Cata and Guadalupe are the smallest and most economical, but are still of a good size. La Cata has a lovely bóveda ceiling. Common areas include a living room, an upstairs terrace, and a poolside patio. These are attractive and inviting, and there's a library and an honor bar. The hotel is nonsmoking.

Callejón Jalisco 10, Col. La Valenciana 36240 Guanajuato, Gto. ℰ **866/983-8844** in the U.S., or 473/732-1784. Fax 562/430-0648 in the U.S. www.mexicaninns.com. 8 units. $170–$190 (£94–£105) standard; $190–$210 (£105–£116) deluxe; $220–$250 (£121–£138) superior; $350 (£193) 2-bedroom casita. Rates include full breakfast and beverages. AE. Free parking. In the *colonia* above La Valenciana church. **Amenities:** Heated outdoor pool; Jacuzzi; in-room massage; babysitting; overnight laundry; nonsmoking rooms. *In room:* TV, DVD/VCR, hair dryer, iron, safe, no phone.

Quinta Las Acacias ✪✪ To stay here is to go back in time, not to the colonial period as with so many hotels, but to the late 19th century, when architecture and design in Mexico were borrowing heavily from French (called *afrancesado*) and Victorian styles. This elegant house, like so many on the Paseo de la Presa, was built then and has been painstakingly remodeled. The rooms are decorated and furnished with period furniture, wallpaper, and wainscoting. I prefer the three suites on the second floor (in Mexico, this is considered the first floor) to the three on the third floor. Behind the house are three larger, modern suites that have Jacuzzis. Rooms contain one king or two queen beds and have spacious, well-equipped bathrooms. Breakfast can be served in the dining room, on the terrace, or in the guest's room. The cocktail area serves drinks until 10pm.

Paseo de la Presa 168, 36000 Guanajuato, Gto. ⓒ 888/497-4129 in the U.S., or 473/731-1517. Fax 473/731-1862. www.quintalasacacias.com.mx. 10 units. $270 (£149) suite; $325 (£179) suite with Jacuzzi; $335 (£184) master suite. Rates include breakfast. AE, MC, V. Free limited parking. Children younger than 14 not accepted. **Amenities:** Restaurant; bar; large outdoor Jacuzzi; tour desk; laundry service; dry cleaning. *In room:* A/C, TV, hair dryer, safe.

EXPENSIVE

Hotel Antiguo Vapor ✪✪ Rooms at this small hotel have all the Mexican character you could wish for, from clay tile floors to beamed ceilings to Talavera tile bathrooms. They range in size from medium to large. All are colorful, and most have windows or balconies looking out over the city. For being downtown, the rooms are fairly quiet; there are some interior rooms that would be quite the thing for light sleepers. Room rates vary according to the choice of beds—the most economical have one queen, the most expensive have two doubles, rooms with king beds are in between. Bathrooms are very nicely finished and some are quite large. The location is good, close by the Diego Rivera Museum. Sometime in late 2007 the hotel hopes to open a restaurant and bar. Construction was in progress when I visited the hotel.

Galarza 5, 36000 Guanajuato, Gto. ⓒ 473/732-3211. www.hotelavapor.com. 10 units. $135–$175 (£74–£96) double. Rates are higher for Cervantino and holidays. MC, V. Free guarded parking. **Amenities:** Restaurant; bar; tour info; nonsmoking rooms. *In room:* TV, hairdryer.

La Casa de Espíritus Alegres B&B ✪✪✪ *Moments* Folk art and atmosphere abound in this idiosyncratic "house of happy spirits," a 16th-century colonial hacienda. The rooms are decorated and furnished in a vivacious and attractive style. Each fulfills the promise of "a skeleton in every closet," and each has its own fireplace. The grounds are so lovely you don't want to leave.

Breakfast, served overlooking the garden, features Californian and Mexican food, with generous helpings of fresh fruit. Check out the hand-painted chairs (decorated by artist friends of the owners). Guests have use of the folk art–decorated living room, and may borrow history, travel, and art books as well as paperback novels. The B&B is 3km (2 miles) from downtown (10 min. by taxi). The owner has opened a new B&B downtown (rates are $160–$180/£88–£99). It's partly a museum/gallery of folk textiles and has only four units (two of which are two-bedroom suites) and a lovely rooftop terrace. It's called **Alma del Sol** for being located on Sol street across from the grand church of La Compañía.

La Exhacienda la Trinidad 1, 36250 Marfil, Gto. ⓒ/fax 473/733-1013. www.casaspirit.com. 8 units. $145–$165 (£80–£91) double. Rates include breakfast. MC, V. Free guarded parking. **Amenities:** Tour info; massage; laundry service; nonsmoking rooms. *In room:* Hair dryer, no phone.

MODERATE

El Mesón de los Poetas

I love hotels that are unselfconscious expressions of their city, and this is just such a place. Set against a hillside, it makes the most of its space by clever positioning of rooms in an irregular jumble. Following the stairs and walkways that led to my room, I thought for a moment I was trapped in an M. C. Escher drawing.

Standard rooms are decorated in the attractive modern Mexican style. They vary in size, and a few come with kitchenettes. The largest hold two double beds. Others come with only one double or a double and a twin. The lighting in all the rooms is good. The bathrooms are adequate. Suites have king-size beds, but I prefer the two-bedroom suites, which have a spacious, attractive living room with dining table and chairs, a sitting area, and a nice kitchenette. (Kitchenettes come with little in the way of cooking implements, but ask for some and you may get them.) The hotel is right downtown by the Diego Rivera museum.

Positos 35, 36000 Guanajuato, Gto. ℂ/fax **473/732-6657**, -0705. www.mexonline.com/poetas.htm. 31 units. $100–$115 (£55–£63) double; $160 (£88) 2-bedroom suite; $150–$170 (£83–£94) suite. Extra person $9 (£4.95). MC, V. Limited off-site parking. **Amenities:** Tour info; laundry service; nonsmoking rooms. *In room:* TV, coffeemaker (on request).

Hotel Embajadoras

This is a quiet motel-like place in the historic center, on Parque Embajadoras, a tree-lined square that's a 10-minute walk east of the main square (not much climbing). The rooms are plain. They come with carpeted floors and midsize bathrooms. A reasonably priced restaurant with a pleasant outdoor dining area takes care of meals.

Parque Embajadoras, 36000 Guanajuato, Gto. ℂ **473/731-0105.** Fax 473/731-0063. hotelembajadoras@ hotmail.com. 27 units. $70–$85 (£39–£47) double. MC, V. Free parking. **Amenities:** Restaurant; travel agency; room service. *In room:* TV.

Hotel Posada Santa Fé ★

Right on the Jardín Unión, this hotel is for those who want to be in the thick of things from the moment they step out the door. It dates from the 1860s, having survived both the reform wars and the revolution, and the old lobby is a great place to have a drink. The hotel underwent extensive remodeling, and the wiring and plumbing in most of the building was replaced, which was money well spent. But the size of the rooms was one thing that couldn't be changed. They're small, except for the suites and some of the rooms with exterior views. They are, however, attractive, well kept, and comfortable. Standard rooms hold either one double or two twin beds. Exterior-view rooms and suites have larger bathrooms and fancier furniture; most have king-size beds.

Jardín Unión, 36000 Guanajuato, Gto. ℂ **473/732-0084.** Fax 473/732-4653. www.posadasantafe.com. 47 units. $95–$135 (£52–£74) double; $150–$170 (£83–£94) suite and exterior views. Rates include full breakfast during low-season. AE, MC, V. Free limited valet parking. **Amenities:** Restaurant; 2 bars; whirlpool; room service; laundry service. *In room:* TV.

INEXPENSIVE

Hotel El Minero (Value)

Only 3 blocks above the Museo Alhóndiga, this four-story (no elevator) hotel has a rare commodity: cheap rooms that aren't ugly or small. New tile floors, attractive paint jobs, ceiling fans, and cleanliness are the high points. The location is good, and the back rooms are quiet, but the lighting is just okay, the bathrooms are small, and the TVs don't add much to the experience of staying here. Most rooms have a double and a single bed.

Alhóndiga 12-A, 36000 Guanajuato, Gto. (©) **473/732-5251.** Fax 473/732-4739. 20 units. $40 (£22) double. MC, V. Limited street parking. **Amenities:** Restaurant. *In room:* TV.

La Casa Azul   This house is in an upper barrio above the Plazuela del Baratillo, which could be good or bad, depending on how you look at it. Staying here would give you an idea how the locals live, always going up or down through a network of alleys (good?). But, staying here means you, too, will be always going up and down (bad?). You decide. It's a good steep climb from the plaza to the hotel, but you get to stay in an interesting part of town for not a lot of money. The rooms have lots of character and are well maintained. They are small to medium in size and come with either a double or a king bed. One room is larger and has two doubles and a twin. There's a nice rooftop terrace, too. *Note:* Don't stay here if you have a car. This hotel is on a narrow, steep street far from any garage.

Carcamanes 57, 36000 Guanajuato, Gto. (©) **473/731-2288.** www.lacasaazul.com.mx. 5 units. $50–$70 (£28–£39) double. No credit cards. No parking. **Amenities:** Bar. *In room:* TV, no phone.

Mansión del Cantador   For a no-frills hotel, this isn't too bad. It offers large, cheerful rooms on the Jardín del Cantador for a good price. Being on this square cuts down on noise, and yet it's still close to the market and the Alhóndiga. Most rooms come with two double beds. In cold weather ask at the desk for extra blankets. The bathrooms are small but in good repair.

Cantador 19, 36000 Guanajuato, Gto. (©) **473/732-6888.** hmcr84@hotmail.com. 42 units. $50–$60 (£28–£33) double. Rates include full breakfast. MC, V. Limited street parking. **Amenities:** Restaurant; bar. *In room:* no phone.

WHERE TO DINE

Restaurants in the downtown area are improving. In addition to the ones I list below, try an outdoor table at the restaurant of the **Hotel Posada Santa Fé** (see above), which is a wonderful way of enjoying the Jardín de la Unión. The Jardín has a closed, intimate feel; if you want something more open with longer vistas, try the **Plaza de la Paz,** a block away. Here you can sit, have a drink, and perhaps nibble on an appetizer at one of the outdoor cafes in front of Guanajuato's cathedral. If you're in search of coffee, the best in town is at **Café Tal** (© 473/732-6212). It's just off the main street that runs between Jardín Unión and Plaza Embajadoras, on Calle Temezcuitate.

EXPENSIVE

La Casa del Conde de la Valenciana ★★ MEXICAN/INTERNATIONAL Dine in the former home of the count of La Valenciana, across the street from his other creation, La Valenciana church. You can eat on the patio or in one of the dining rooms. The menu is a combination of old standards and original recipes. For an appetizer, try a fresh salad or refreshing gazpacho served in a vessel encased in ice. For a main course, you can choose one of Mexico's traditional dishes, such as chicken *mole* or *enmoladas* (chicken-filled tortillas rolled in *mole*), or perhaps chicken breast *a la flor de calabaza* (in a mild, satisfying cream sauce of blended squash flowers and poblano chile). The shady patio is so relaxing and the chairs so comfortable that many linger here over coffee and dessert.

Carretera Guanajuato-Dolores Km 5, opposite La Valenciana church. (©)/fax 473/732-2550. Reservations accepted. Main courses $10–$18 (£5.50–£9.90). MC, V. Mon–Wed noon–6pm; Thurs–Sat noon–10pm.

MODERATE

El Abue ★★ MEXICAN/ITALIAN   A comfortable little downtown restaurant where you can enjoy some good cooking in a simple, understated dining room. The *sopa azteca* (tortilla soup) was well made and had a nice bite to it, the *tostadas yucate-cas* with *cochinita pibil* (braised pork marinated in sour orange and annatto) were good and tangy. The kitchen also produces *chiles en nogada* (if you're wanting something rich and elaborate) and fettuccine in a poblano cream sauce. There are a few standard Italian dishes, too.

San José 14 (at the top of the Plazuela del Baratillo). ℭ 473/732-6242. Reservations recommended on weekends. Main courses $7–$13 (£3.85–£7.15). MC, V. Daily 12:30pm–10:30pm.

El Claustro MEXICAN   A lot of locals really like this downtown hole-in-the-wall. Tables are outside on the square or inside in what was once the bodega of the build-ing now occupied by the restaurant. My favorite things to eat here are the enchiladas, especially the *rojas* ("red" enchiladas, because they are in a chile ancho sauce) and the *enmoladas* (enchiladas in a mole sauce). The *pollo con mole* (chicken with *mole* sauce) is good, too. Other dishes include various *antojitos* (small plates) and main dishes. The restaurant is within 50 paces of Avenida Juárez, almost across from the market.

Jardín de la Reforma 13-B. No phone. Main courses $5–$11 (£2.75–£6.05). No credit cards. Daily 8am–10pm.

México Lindo y Sabroso ☆☆ MEXICAN   This is a fun place to go for a quiet meal in the Colonia Paseo de la Presa, not far from downtown. The menu has lots of the dishes that Mexico is known for. These are cooked with care. The surroundings are attractive, and the service is great. For all these reasons, this restaurant is popular with the locals. The best time to avoid crowds is after 5pm. You can dine outside on the front veranda, in an attractive interior patio, or inside in one of the dining rooms. I tried several things and liked them all. The tostadas de *tinga* (meat stewed in chipo-tle sauce), the green pozole, and the flautas were all great. On the menu are some Yucatecan specialties, such as *cochinita pibil* and *panuchos* (masa cakes stuffed with refried black beans and topped with shredded turkey or chicken, lettuce, onion, and chile sauce)—these were delicious, too. You can take a cab there and then grab any bus to take you back to downtown.

Paseo de la Presa 154. ℭ 473/731-0529. Reservations accepted. Main courses $4–$11 (£2.20–£6.05). MC, V. Daily 9am–10:30pm.

INEXPENSIVE

El Midi ☆ SALADS/MEDITERRANEAN   The things I like best about eating at this small place are that you can serve yourself only as much food as you want; you can dine outside at a table in a corner of the Plazuela San Fernando, which is an oasis of tranquillity for the downtown area; and of course the food is good and healthful. The offerings change daily—different salad fixings, different quiches, different vegeta-bles, different desserts. And on Thursday and Friday evenings you can get a cheese and cold cuts plate, which goes well with the house bread and table wine. The owner is an open and personable woman from southern France who has been living in Guanaju-ato for a couple of years. She bakes a lot, including many cakes and pies. The food is always fresh, and it tends to run out late in the day, so don't show up too late.

Plazuela San Fernando 41. No phone. Salad, quiche, desserts sold by weight. No credit cards. Sun–Wed 1–6pm; Thurs–Fri 1–11pm.

Truco 7 ☆ MEXICAN   With its economical prices and warm atmosphere, this place is a solid choice for any meal. The three dining rooms are small and a bit crowded, yet nicely decorated with leather *equipal* (a rustic Mexican style) tables and chairs and paintings by local artists. The restaurant occupies an 18th-century structure originally

Moments **The Redolent Mexican Cantina**

If you're curious about Mexican cantinas, swinging saloon doors and all, Guanajuato is a good place to do your fieldwork. You should know, however, that most of these are *men-only* drinking dives.

The town's favorite son is José Alfredo Jiménez, the undisputed master of *ranchera* music. This is the quintessential drinking music (long laments punctuated by classic Mexican yelps) that drives most non-Mexicans screaming from the building. But after downing a few *copitas,* you may warm up to it, and after asking about Jiménez, you'll probably get a few more drinks on the house. Around the Jardín Unión are a couple of cantinas that aren't bad; I enjoyed a few shots at one called **El Incendio (The Fire),** Cantarranas 15. Unlike most cantinas, this place welcomes women. El Incendio opens at 10am and closes at 4am.

You may be surprised to see an open urinal at the end of the bar. While this is a standard feature in cantinas and part of the, er, authentic flavor, you still may wish to opt for a seat at the opposite end.

built for members of the Valenciana silver family. Calle Truco, a short street south of the basilica, runs between the Jardín Unión and the Plaza de la Paz.

Truco 7. ℭ **473/732-8374.** Reservations not accepted. Breakfast $2–$4 (£1.10–£2.20); *comida corrida* (served 2–4pm) $3 (£1.65); main courses $5–$8 (£2.75–£4.40). No credit cards. Daily 8:30am–11:30pm.

GUANAJUATO AFTER DARK

If city planners had known the **Jardín Unión** would be so popular, they might have made it larger. This tiny plaza, shaded by Indian laurel trees, is the heart of the city and the best hangout. No other spot in town rivals its benches and sidewalk restaurants.

You can catch some worthwhile free **theater** in Plazuela de San Roque at 8pm on Sunday when the university is in session. Students perform short theatrical pieces known as *entremeses* (literally, "intermissions"). These are usually costumed period pieces that rely more on action than dialogue, so you don't need to understand too much Spanish to get the point. The costumes are great and look curiously appropriate in this *plazuela.*

More conventional nightspots—such as dance clubs—aren't difficult to find; ask at your hotel. A different kind of place is **La Dama de las Camelias,** Sopeña 32 (no phone), an unpretentious second-floor bar that doesn't get going until late in the evening. The music is all classic recordings of *danzón,* mambo, *son cubano,* and salsa. It opens at 8pm, starts getting busy around midnight, and closes at 4am. **Bar Ocho** (no phone), another salsa bar, is behind the San Diego church at the foot of the hill where El Pípila stands.

3 Santiago de Querétaro ★★★

213km (132 miles) NW of Mexico City; 96km (60 miles) SE of San Miguel Allende; 200km (124 miles) S of San Luis Potosí

Querétaro is the most historic city in the region. During the colonial era, it played a central role in all the expeditions headed north. Later, it was at the center of events in the three wars that forged the Mexican nation: La Independencia, La Reforma, and La Revolución. Downtown Querétaro is lively, pedestrian-friendly, and filled with eye-opening colonial splendor. The local government has spruced up the city, keeps it neat with round-the-clock cleaning crews, and provides street vendors with attractive stands, regulating them so that they don't obstruct public streets and walkways. In the evenings, the downtown area fills with people who stroll about the plazas and *andadores* (pedestrian walkways), eat at one of the restaurants, outdoor cafes, or food stands. Since the city is only an hour by bus from San Miguel, it makes an easy day trip. But once you come, you'll be tempted to stay longer and get better acquainted with this lovely city.

The Spanish founded Querétaro in 1531 during their first large-scale expedition into the vast northern stretches of their new territory. There was a skirmish with the Chichimeca in which Santiago (St. James) appeared in the clouds. Santiago is the patron saint of Spain and of La Reconquista, the seven-century struggle to recapture all of Spain from the Moors, which had ended barely 40 years earlier. It is no wonder that the Spanish hoped he would again lend a hand in this new struggle for territory. For his appearance, Santiago also became the patron saint of Querétaro. (When you visit the Jardín Zenea at the center of town, look up at the facade of the church of San Francisco, and you will see a depiction of Santiago in battle, lopping off the turbaned head of a Moor.) In time, the city became the base of operations for all expeditions headed north.

While the conquistadors were setting out to conquer lands for the crown, the religious orders were setting out to convert souls for Christ. The Franciscans established a large community in Querétaro and eventually a college for the propagation of the faith, the first such institution in the New World. From here, the missionaries set out (always on foot, as the Franciscan Rule forbade riding on horseback or in carriages) to evangelize and establish missions as far away as Texas and California. Some of their histories are nothing short of astounding. Among them was Junípero Sierra, who went all the way to California establishing missions there.

Centuries later, Mexican independence began in Querétaro with the conspiracy of 1810 (of which Father Hidalgo was a member). A little more than 50 years after that, Querétaro was again in the thick of things when Emperor Maximilian made his last stand here, and was captured and executed. Another 50 years passed, and the city became the site of the laborious constitutional convention during the Mexican Revolution. The document that it produced, the Constitution of 1917, remains the law of the land.

ESSENTIALS

GETTING THERE & DEPARTING By Plane Querétaro's new airport is a good 25 minutes from downtown. At present, the only international service is to

Santiago de Querétaro

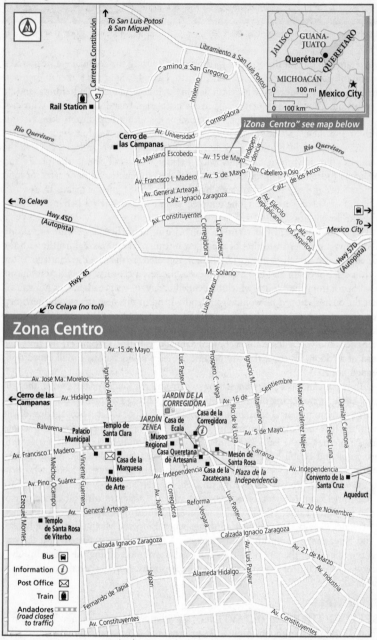

Zona Centro

Houston via **Continental ExpressJet** (℃ **800/231-0856** in the U.S., or 01-800/ 900-5000 in Mexico), but there is talk of adding other international flights. There are also connecting flights to nearby Mexico City, or you can take the bus that leaves directly for Querétaro from the Mexico City airport. Look for the elevated concourse in E-2 area of the terminal. A one-way ticket is $22 (£12). Departures are about every half hour.

By Car   From Mexico City, take the super toll road 57D (2½ hr.). From San Miguel, take Highway 111 to 57D, then turn right (1 hr.). From San Luis Potosí, take 57D south (2½ hr.).

By Bus   For directions from the Mexico City airport, see "By Plane," above. From Mexico City's northern bus terminal (Central del Norte), buses leave every 15 minutes. Make sure you get a *directo* (nonstop). From San Miguel, second-class buses leave every 20 minutes. The bus station is south of town. Look for a booth in the terminal that sells cab tickets. A cab ride downtown costs $3 (£1.65).

VISITOR INFORMATION   There is a good **tourism information office** at Pasteur Norte 4, just off the Plaza de la Independencia on the north side. It's open daily from 9am to 8pm. The phone numbers are ℃ **888/811-6130** in the U.S., or **442/238-5067;** or visit www.venaqueretaro.com. The office was operating 1-hour tours of the city by trolley-style bus. These tours are now operated by private companies who have a concession from tourism and also staff the information kiosks that you'll see in some of the plazas. You can get info from the staff at these kiosks, but you'll also get a pitch to take a bus tour. These concessions are, thus far, on a trial basis. Tourism still offers a self-guided audio walking tour of the *centro histórico*. At the information office, you can rent a digital player for $5 (£2.75) per day, using a credit card voucher for a deposit.

CITY LAYOUT   The heart of downtown is the Jardín Zenea, at the intersection of the main north-south and east-west streets, Corregidora and Madero. Just east is the Plaza de Armas, and farther east are the Convento de la Cruz and the famous aqueduct. West of Jardín Zenea are several plazas, churches, convents, and museums.

FAST FACTS: Querétaro

American Express The local representative is **Agencia Turismo Beverly,** Av. Tecnológico 118, Col. San Angel (℃ **442/216-1500**). Office hours are Monday through Friday from 9am to 2pm and 4 to 6pm, Saturday from 9am to noon.

Area Code The telephone area code is **442.**

Climate The average temperature in summer is 75°F (24°C), in winter 56°F (13°C).

Elevation Querétaro sits at 1,818m (5,963 ft.).

Emergency The central emergency number (similar to 911) is ℃ **066.**

Hospital The local hospital is the **Hospital Angeles** (℃ **442/215-5901** or 442/ 216-2751) at Bernardo del Razo 21, Colonia Ensueño.

Internet Access Cybercafes and Internet access providers are everywhere in the central historic district.

Parking To find parking in the downtown area, look for white square signs with the capital letter E in light blue. There are a couple of places at Pino Suárez 45 and 17. Rates run about $1 (55p) for the first hour, 25¢ (15p) for every hour after that.

Population Querétaro has 750,000 residents.

Post Office The *correo,* Arteaga 5, is open Monday through Saturday from 9am to 2:30pm.

A STROLL AROUND THE HISTORIC CENTER

In the center of Querétaro, you'll notice right away how many lovely plazas, churches, and convents there are. If you're really observant, you'll notice that the plazas are frequently next to the churches. In fact, most of these plazas were formed at the cost of the convents, which lost much of their real estate to the government during la Reforma. This is true of the town's most important plaza, **Jardín Zenea,** where we will begin. This plaza used to be part of the atrium of San Francisco Church and Convent, which you see facing the park across Corregidora Street. This park is popular every night, but especially on Sunday, when the municipal band plays dance music of the '40s, '50s, and '60s. Great fun! The old bandstand dates from 1900.

Turn toward **San Francisco Church** and you will see on the facade the depiction of St. James, mentioned earlier. From the beginning, this church was the most important in town; it remains so today, the more recent cathedral notwithstanding. It and the attached cloister are all that remain of a large complex that included several chapels and an orchard that extended a few blocks east and south. Inside the church, you will see a few interesting remains of baroque decoration. The main altar is a rather uninteresting piece of neoclassicism that replaced what reputedly was a masterpiece of baroque design. This is a common story with churches in Querétaro. Many of the baroque *retablos* escaped the plunderers, only to fall prey to the "improvers," as was the case here.

Next door to the church is the cloister, which is now the **Museo Regional** ✷. It's open Tuesday through Sunday from 10am to 7pm. Admission is $3.50 (£1.95). Exhibits include artifacts from pre-Hispanic, colonial, and republican times. The architecture shows common traits of Franciscan design in the simplicity of its lines and decoration, which you can contrast with the rich decoration (caryatids and all) of the former Augustinian convent, now a museum of colonial art (see below). Leaving the museum, turn left and then left again and you'll be on the pedestrians-only Andador Libertad. This leads to the small Plaza de Independencia or Plaza de Armas, with its carefully hedged Indian laurel trees, outdoor restaurants, and colonial mansions.

At the Plaza de Independencia are a few things to take note of. First is **Galería Libertad,** on your right just as you get to the Plaza. It's free, and, in past visits, I've come upon some entertaining exhibits. At the far end of the plaza is the **Casa de la Corregidora.** As you walk toward it, you will pass the **Casa de Ecala** on your left. A mansion built in magisterial baroque style with beautiful balconies and wrought iron, it dates from the 18th century.

La Corregidora was the wife of the mayor *(corregidor)* at the beginning of the struggle for independence. Her full name was Doña Josefa Ortiz de Domínguez, and she

All Things Querétaro

Walking up Andador Libertad, you will see a pergola of bougainvillea. Just past it, on the right hand side is the state-run store for arts and crafts, **Casa Queretana de Artesanía,** Andador Libertad 52 (📞 **442/224-3456**). Even though Querétaro is a small state, it has a wide variety of craft traditions. You can see a sampling of these in the three rooms in this part of the store, and in another three rooms that are further up the walkway. Everything in this store was made in the state. Hours are Tuesday and Wednesday 11am to 2pm and 4 to 7pm; Thursday and Friday 11am to 2pm and 4 to 8pm; Saturday 11am to 8pm; and Sunday 11am to 4pm.

was a member of the conspiracy to liberate Mexico from Spain. As the wife of Querétaro's mayor, she was in a useful position for gathering information. When the conspiracy was discovered, she was put under house arrest but still managed to warn Father Hidalgo. He eluded capture and rushed to Dolores, where he gave his famous *grito* (the cry for independence). For her actions, La Corregidora was imprisoned several times between 1810 and 1817. She died impoverished and forgotten, but was later remembered when she became the first woman to appear on a Mexican coin.

The fountain in the middle of the plaza honors Querétaro's greatest benefactor, a Spanish grandee named Don Juan Antonio de Urrutia y Arana, who built a large aqueduct to bring water to the city. This colonial aqueduct is the most famous landmark in the city. To view it, continue east on Andador Libertad. It ends in 1 block, so you must dogleg to the next eastbound street, either Independencia or Carranza. The street gradually climbs towards the church and convent of **La Santa Cruz** ⭐⭐, where missionaries were trained to evangelize the heathens as far away as California and Nicaragua. The church has one bell tower with an attractive tile dome. It and the convent are Franciscan. The convent continues in operation. You can take a short tour, usually led by an elderly monk, Fray Jesús Guzmán de León, who speaks English. He will show you how the water from the aqueduct arrived here and how it fed a system of fountains known as *cajas de agua* that provided water throughout the old city. From these, the citizens of Querétaro would fill their buckets. He will also show you a thorn tree said to have grown from the walking stick of Friar Antonio Margil de Jesús, a famous missionary who covered vast territories on foot. This thorn tree is considered miraculous because its thorns grow in the shape of the cross. The tour is free, but you will be given an opportunity to make a contribution to the preservation of the convent and church.

Behind the church is a small plaza from which you can view the aqueduct. Follow the rough stone wall partially covered by the branches of mesquite trees, and you can't miss it. The aqueduct extends across an expanse of bottomland from the hill in front. This feat of engineering required the construction of 74 arches. Work began in 1726 and finished in 1738.

From here, work your way back to the Jardín Zenea. If you go by way of Calle Independencia, you can pop into **La Casa de la Zacatecana** (look for a banner), Independencia 59 (📞 **442/224-0758**). It presents a vision of what many colonial mansions were like in Querétaro, with period furnishings and decor. Hours are from Tuesday to Sunday 10am to 6pm in winter (11am-7pm in summer). Entrance is $2 (£1.10). Associated with this house (as with a couple of others in town) is a tale of illicit love, murder, and retribution. Colonial Mexico is a fertile land for gothic tales.

Back at Jardín Zenea, head west on Calle Madero. At the first corner, just before the street becomes an *andador*, is **La Casa de la Marquesa** ★★★, an opulent colonial residence–turned–hotel. Walk in and check out the courtyard lobby, which has elaborate *mudéjar*-style (a Spanish architectural style with Moorish influences) arches and patterned walls.

Cater-corner from this hotel is the **church and former Convent of Santa Clara** ★★★. The church is a must-see; inside are six astonishing baroque *retablos* and a choir loft, all gilded and each a self-contained composition. In prominent positions are sculptures and paintings of saints; here and there, the faces of angels appear out of the enveloping, thickly textured ornament. Gazing upon these is like gazing upon a mandala. The juxtaposition of straight lines and multiple facets with overflowing curves that move inward and outward make the *retablos* appear fluid and rigid at the same time. The key to enjoying these *retablos* is not to look for proportion, balance, or an underlying structure, but to look at them as the expression of an ecstatic religious sentiment that rejects these very notions.

For a greater acquaintance with the colonial religious mind, walk south 1 block on Allende. On your right will be the **Museo de Arte** ★★★ (© **442/212-3523**), in the former **convent of San Agustín.** Admission is $2 (£1.10); it's free on Tuesday. The museum is open Tuesday through Sunday from 10am to 6pm. It contains one of the great collections of Mexican colonial art, but the architecture of the former convent alone is worth the price of admission. Highly stylized human forms, complex geometric lines, and vegetal motifs are everywhere. The art is organized by style of painting. The collection has works by Europeans, but its focus is on painters in New Spain, including the most famous of the land.

If you're still in the mood for colonial splendor, walk west 2 blocks on Pino Suárez. After you cross Melchor Ocampo, turn left down a narrow street graced with bougainvillea and you'll come to the **church and former convent of Santa Rosa de Viterbo** ★★★. Like Santa Clara, it is a masterpiece of baroque architecture. On the outside, notice the scroll-shaped flying buttresses (a style that as far as I know is unique to Querétaro) and the imaginative tower. Inside, the church is much like Santa Clara, with magnificent gilt *retablos* occupying all available wall space. Also like Santa Clara, the main altar failed to escape the "improvers."

Farther west (a bit too far to walk) is the **Cerro de las Campanas (Hill of Bells),** where Maximilian was executed. You'll find a large, ugly statue of Juárez installed there by the Mexican government to counter a small and sad memorial chapel for Maximilian erected by his brother, Emperor Franz Josef of Austria. Immediately south of downtown is a park called Alameda Hidalgo, which offers a lovely setting for a walk.

WHERE TO STAY

Rates below include the 17% tax. Most of the downtown hotels have high and low season. High season is Easter, July, August, December, and any long weekend. The city is a favorite weekend getaway from Mexico City; it's much easier to find a room during the week.

> ## Tips   Shopping for Opals
>
> The small state of Querétaro is one of the two principal places in the world that mine opals commercially (the other is southern Australia). The opal is a soft stone noted for its iridescent play of color. Prices vary depending on size, color, shape, and transparency. A few stores in Querétaro, usually called *lapidarias*, sell locally mined opals and other semiprecious stones. One is the **Lapidaria de Querétaro,** Corregidora Norte 149-A, a few blocks north of Jardín Zenea (℗ **442/212-0030**). It's open Monday through Friday from 10am to 2pm and 5 to 8pm and Saturday 10am to 3pm. Or stop by **El Artesano,** a little shop at Corregidora Norte 42, near the Jardín Zenea. Owner Alfredo Vázquez, who carves miniatures out of opals and other semiprecious stones, speaks mostly Spanish, and is a fountain of information on opals and the trade. He keeps interesting store hours: 12:30 to 5pm and 6 to 10pm Monday through Saturday. Another source is **Lapidaria Ramírez,** Pino Suárez 98.

VERY EXPENSIVE

La Casa de la Marquesa 𝄢𝄢𝄢   Few hotels in Mexico can match this one for sheer colonial opulence. Even if you don't stay here, make a point of walking into the courtyard lobby. Built for the wife of the Marqués de Urrutia, the house, with Moorish-inspired arches, tiles, and painted walls, has an Andalusian feel. Rooms are large, have all the amenities, and are furnished with period pieces and Persian rugs. Bed choices include one queen-size, two queen-size, or one king-size. The least expensive rooms (deluxe) are across the street in another colonial house, La Casa Azul. The hotel, a member of the Small Luxury Hotels of the World, prides itself on the attention it gives its guests. The location is excellent.

Madero 41, 76000 Querétaro, Qro. ℗ **442/212-0092.** Fax 442/212-0098. www.lacasadelamarquesa.com. 25 units. $212 (£117) deluxe; $248 (£136) royal suite; $412 (£227) imperial suite. AE, MC, V. Valet parking $5 (£2.75). **Amenities:** Restaurant; bar; concierge; tour desk; room service; in-room massage; laundry service; dry cleaning. *In room:* A/C, TV (with DVD in most rooms), coffeemaker, hair dryer.

EXPENSIVE

Gran Hotel 𝄢𝄢   After being boarded up for many years, the old Gran Hotel finally reopened in mid 2006 and looks grand, indeed. As is often the case with old hotels, there is a lavish use of space that is decidedly uneconomical (and attention-grabbing for precisely that reason). A grand stairway and cavernous galleries with vaulted ceilings lead the way to your room. The rooms have high ceilings and carpeted floors and are large and comfortable with independently controlled air conditioning and beautifully finished bathrooms. The hotel is set between two plazas, and most rooms have a view of one plaza or the other (with double-glazed windows and French doors). Unless you're a very light sleeper, noise is not a problem, but for the light sleeper the hotel has a few interior rooms *(ejecutivos),* which are oversize and come with a few extra amenities, while costing virtually the same. The entire property is nonsmoking. It lacks a restaurant, but given its location, this is hardly a drawback.

Juárez Sur 5 (between Jardín Zenea and Plaza Constitución), 76000 Querétaro, Qro. ⓒ 442/241-8050. www.
granhoteldequeretaro.com.mx. 50 units. $183 (£101) executive; $185 (£102) superior; $250 (£138) corner suite.
AE, MC, V. Valet parking $5 (£2.75). **Amenities:** Bar; fitness center; tour desk; car rental; membership in local spa;
laundry service; dry cleaning, nonsmoking rooms. *In room:* A/C, TV, high-speed Internet, hair dryer, safe.

Hotel Mesón del Alfarero ⭐⭐
This place will please those who like their hotels
small and with a modern aesthetic. Modern, yes, but definitely Mexican, in that it has
that distinctive look that contemporary architects in Mexico have developed and made
their own. Rooms are large and uncluttered. There's a lot of white and cream-colored
stucco with sharp accents. The mattresses are comfortable, and the furniture has character. Bathrooms are medium to large and attractive, with Talavera tiles, and two-person tubs in the master suites. The outdoor spaces are serene. An open-air restaurant
occupies a small area by the entrance.

Hidalgo 71 (between Ezequiel Montes and Melchor Ocampo), 76000 Querétaro, Qro. ⓒ 442/212-7053. Fax 442/
214-0552. www.mesondelalfarero.com.mx. 12 units. $153 (£84) standard; $160 (£88) junior suite; $178–$205
(£98–£113) master suite. Rates include continental breakfast. AE, MC, V. Limited street parking. **Amenities:** Restaurant; bar; concierge; tour info; airport transportation; car rental; room service; laundry service; dry cleaning. *In room:*
A/C, TV, Wi-Fi, minibar, hair dryer, safe.

Hotel Mesón de Santa Rosa ⭐⭐
With its large open courtyards, clean lines, and
simple stone and iron work, this hotel presents a colonial architecture that contrasts
sharply with La Casa de la Marquesa (see above). There are three elegant courtyards
variously holding a pool, a fountain, and a stone trough for watering your horses
(a vestige of the original tavern, which served wagon and mule drivers). Rooms are
quiet, large, and comfortable, with high ceilings, carpeted floors, and plain furniture
and decoration. Standard rooms come with either two doubles or a king-size bed;
superior rooms are much larger. Higher rates are for remodeled rooms with air-conditioning. The location, at the southwest corner of the Plaza de Armas, is ideal.

Pasteur 17 Sur (on Plaza de Armas, access from 5 de Mayo), 76000 Querétaro, Qro. ⓒ 442/441-5000. Fax 442/
212-5522. www.mesonsantarosa.com. 21 units. $139–$144 (£76–£79) standard double; $193–$210 (£106–£116)
superior double. AE, DC, MC, V. Valet parking $5 (£2.75). **Amenities:** Restaurant; bar; midsize heated outdoor pool;
tour desk; car rental; room service; babysitting; laundry service; dry cleaning. *In room:* A/C (in 7 rooms), TV, Wi-Fi,
minibar, coffeemaker, hair dryer, safe.

INEXPENSIVE
Hotel Posada Acueducto (*Value*)
You get a good room for the money at this hotel.
The rooms are on two floors running along one side of the narrow property. Almost
all face a thin strip of patio. Most are in back, in the new section (slightly preferable).
They are mostly medium size with ample bathrooms. The one upstairs in the very
back (Rm. 111) has a king-size bed and a little porch. The lower price listed is for a
room with one double bed; the higher price is for a room with two double beds; somewhere in between is the price for a room with a king bed.

Tip: Ask the staff about their new hotel. I recently saw this downtown property
while it was under construction. At that time, it didn't even have a name, but from
what I could see, the location and the layout were excellent, most of the rooms were
very large, and there was a pool and a fitness room. The rates the owners were considering seemed bargain rate—in the $60 to $80 (£33–£44) range.

Juárez 64 Sur (between Arteaga and Zaragoza), 76000 Querétaro, Qro. ⓒ 442/224-1289. 15 units. $28–$45
(£15–£25) double. No credit cards. Limited street parking. **Amenities:** *In room:* A/C, TV.

Hotel Señorial   This is a simple hotel with plainly furnished, medium size rooms. By and large they are a little more attractive than the rooms at Posada Acueducto (see above). The carpeting has been replaced with Pergo flooring (bathrooms still have tile.) The beds (usually two twins or two doubles) are comfortable. The important thing is to reserve an even-numbered room. Odd-numbered rooms are in the south wing, which has plumbing so noisy you think it will bring down the building.

Guerrero Norte 10-A (corner of Hidalgo), 76000 Querétaro, Qro. ℰ/fax 442/214-3700. www.senorial-hotel.com. 54 units. $45–$62 (£25–£34) double. MC, V. Free secure parking. **Amenities:** Restaurant; room service. *In room:* A/C (in 13 rooms), TV, Wi-Fi.

Mesón del Obispado   For better or worse, this colonial hotel is in the middle of the most popular part of downtown. For better, it's on a pedestrian *andador* and is close to everything. For worse, it's by the Plaza de la Corregidora, which doesn't settle down on weekends until well after midnight. The rooms in front have balconies overlooking the *andador* and are popular with the vacationing crowd that isn't going to bed early anyway. I had a room in back that looked out toward the courtyard of the hotel, and it was perfectly quiet. The rooms are medium to large in size, usually with two double beds or a king. The furniture is plain. The best thing about the bathrooms is that there's plenty of hot water and good water pressure.

Andador 16 de Septiembre 13, 76000 Querétaro, Qro. ℰ 442/224-2464. mesondelobispado@hotmail.com.mx. 16 units. $67 (£37) double. AE, DC, MC V. Limited street parking. **Amenities:** Restaurant; room service. *In room:* TV.

WHERE TO DINE

In addition to the restaurants listed below, you might want to try the restaurant at the Mesón de Santa Rosa on the Plaza de Armas. One local dish I can't recommend is the *enchiladas queretanas.* The problem is that the enchiladas typically come buried in a mountain of salty fresh cheese that completely overpowers the bland sauce. For fancy baked goods try **Panadería El Globo** (ℰ 442/212-8883) at Corregidora Sur 41. For tamales, go to one of the three vendors that are on the same block of Arteaga street between Allende and Guerrero. They serve tamales and the corn-based beverage, *atole,* all day long and well into the night. Open only at night is a pretty good taco place called **Tacos del 57** (ℰ 442/224-2211) at Calle del 57 #21. It's 1 block west of Ezequiel Montes, right before you get to the first traffic light (there's no sign). It sells great *tacos al pastor* (tacos made with thinly sliced pork and served with pineapple, onion, and cilantro), but for the most part sells *tacos de guisos* (called *tacos de cazuela* in other parts of Mexico, meaning any taco made with something cooked in a sauce, such as eggs cooked in a chile pasilla sauce or pork rinds cooked in a red sauce). It also offers delicious and safe fresh-fruit drinks. ***Tip:*** It's popular to go out for a late breakfast on weekends. If you're not having breakfast at your hotel, you can beat the crowds by showing up at a restaurant by 9am.

EXPENSIVE

El Caserío ★★ SPANISH   The favorite dining spot for Querétaro's well-heeled denizens, El Caserío owes its popularity in part to the stylish, comfortable, no-nonsense dining areas, in part to the cooking and the service, which are both good, and, I suspect, in part to its ample off-street parking (not that common in this city). The menu is broad enough to please a variety of tastes. I had the *crema de tres quesos* (three-cheese soup) and the *pescado en salsa verde a la vasca* (fish in a Basque-style herb sauce). Both were exquisite. It's a long walk from the Jardín Zenea; take a cab.

Constituyentes 101 Poniente (near intersection with Ezequiel Montes). ℂ 442/217-1777. Reservations recommended. Main courses $10–$20 (£5.50–£11). AE, MC, V. Mon–Sat 2pm–midnight; Sun 2–6pm.

San Miguelito ✪✪ MEXICAN   The least you should do is go for a drink and a view of the surroundings. The restaurant occupies the restored Casa de los Cinco Patios, a landmark colonial house that had been closed to the public for years. The first patio (which is the main dining area) impresses with the height of its arches and the fine wrought-iron work. It's beautifully lit at night, too. For appetizers, try the *infladitas* (small puffy tostadas topped with Yucatecan-style pork). Most of the main courses are steaks prepared with a variety of sauces (keep in mind that *medio* doesn't mean medium but medium rare; for medium, say *"tres cuartos"*). On one side of the main entrance is the bar **La Viejoteca,** with live music on the weekends. On the other side is **La Antojería,** which serves traditional supper foods—tacos, and such The decor is folksy and nostalgic for Mexicans. It's a fun place to have a bite.

Andador 5 de Mayo 39 (between Corregidora and Vergara). ℂ 442/224-2760. Reservations recommended on weekends. Main courses $10–$16 (£5.50–£8.80). AE, MC, V. Tues–Sat 1–11pm; Sun 1–5pm.

MODERATE

Apolonia ✪✪ CONTEMPORARY MEXICAN   At this restaurant not far from the Plaza de Armas you can dine on some inventive dishes that are well prepared, and enjoy them in attractive surroundings. There's a good selection of soups and salads, including a savory strawberry soup served hot, and a green salad with mango and cashews. The main courses include a chicken breast in a pool of apple/corn/poblano sauce or shrimp with tequila and roasted cactus leaves. Servings aren't overly large, and the desserts are mostly light dishes.

Andador Libertad 46. ℂ 442/212-0389. Reservations recommended. Main courses $8–$15 (£4.40–£8.25). MC, V. Wed–Mon 1:30pm–midnight.

Restaurante Bar 1810 ✪ MEXICAN/INTERNATIONAL   This is one of the restaurants on the Plaza de Armas across from the house of La Corregidora. It has a large and varied menu and is the perfect place to enjoy an afternoon or evening meal. Your best bet is to stick with traditional Mexican specialties, which are well prepared; the soups are wonderful. Sunday brunch is especially popular.

Andador Libertad 62 (on the Plaza de Armas). ℂ 442/214-3324. Reservations recommended on weekends and holidays. Main courses $7–$17 (£3.85–£9.35). AE, MC, V. Mon–Sat 8am–midnight; Sun 8am–10pm.

INEXPENSIVE

Cafetería Bisquets *(Value)* MEXICAN   This modest restaurant serves inexpensive *comida casera* (home cooking) on a little patio and in adjoining dining rooms. One of the specialties is paper-thin *milanesa* (lightly breaded round steak) served with green enchiladas on the side. Breakfasts are popular. Avoid the *bisquet*—something like an American biscuit, but larger and heavier—and try the *chilaquiles con pollo y crema* (fried tortilla strips cooked with chicken in a either a red or green sauce and served with Mexican sour cream) or any of the egg dishes and the *café con leche* (coffee with milk). The *menú del día* (daily menu) is a bargain.

Pino Suárez 7 (between Juárez and Allende). ℂ 442/214-1481. Main courses $4.50–$7 (£2.50–£3.85); *menú del día* $4–$6 (£2.20–£3.30). No credit cards. Daily 7:30am–11pm.

Cafetería La Mariposa MEXICAN   This coffee shop, sweet shop, and restaurant is a popular hangout with locals. The full breakfasts are probably better at Bisquets, but this place makes its own breads and yogurt and is a nice spot for a light breakfast.

The old-time dining room is comfortable (less cramped than at Bisquets). For lunch or dinner you can count on most of the Mexican standards on the menu.

Angela Peralta 7 (between Corregidora and Juárez). (✆ 442/212-1166. Main courses $3–$5 (£1.65–£2.75). No credit cards. Daily 8am–9:30pm. From the Jardín Zenea, walk north 2 blocks along Corregidora and turn left.

4 Zacatecas ⭑⭑⭑

627km (389 miles) NW of Mexico City; 198km (123 miles) NW of San Luis Potosí; 322km (200 miles) NE of Guadalajara; 298km (185 miles) SE of Durango

Zacatecas, like Guanajuato, owes its beauty to the wealth of silver extracted from its mines. The farthest flung of the silver cities, it still feels like an outpost of civilization. High above the center of town looms a rocky hill with a distinctive crest, which is accessible by cable car. From the summit you have a panoramic view of the wild and desolate terrain that surrounds the city. The scene makes you realize what a frontier town Zacatecas must have been, and after you have been in town for a few days, you appreciate its present sophistication all the more. You will find startlingly good museums, beautiful architecture, and good restaurants. The city has gone to the enormous trouble of burying all of its power and telephone cables, which adds greatly to the beauty of the town and makes strolling along the streets a pleasure.

ESSENTIALS

GETTING THERE & DEPARTING   By Plane   Mexicana (✆ **800/531-7921** in the U.S., 01-800/502-2000 in Mexico, or 492/922-7429; www.mexicana.com) flies nonstop to and from Chicago, Denver, and Los Angeles. Seats are hard to come by around Christmas, when native Zacatecans fly home in large numbers. Within Mexico, Mexicana flies nonstop to and from León/Guanajuato, Mexico City, and Tijuana.

Transportation from the airport, 29km (18 miles) north of Zacatecas, is about $15 by taxi.

By Car   From the south, you can take Highway 45D, a toll road, from Querétaro through Irapuato, León, and Aguascalientes (a 6-hr. drive). It's expensive (about $30/£17) but fast. Highway 54 heads northeast to Saltillo and Monterrey (a 5- to 6-hr. drive) and southeast to Guadalajara (a 41/2-hr. drive). Highway 49 leads north to Torreón (4 hr.) and southeast to San Luis Potosí (3 hr.). Highway 45 heads to Durango (4 hr.).

By Bus   Omnibus de México, Estrella Blanca, and their many affiliates handle first-class bus travel to and from Zacatecas. Together, they operate 30 buses a day to Guadalajara and to San Luis Potosí, more than that to Mexico City (via Querétaro), and 10 per day to Guanajuato. I usually don't buy a ticket ahead of time unless I'm traveling during a national holiday or during December and August (vacation months), or when I'm going all the way to the border. The **Central Camionera** (bus station) is on a hilltop a bit out of town. The taxi ride costs about $3 (£1.65).

VISITOR INFORMATION   The downtown office is at Hidalgo 401 at Callejón de la Caja (✆ **492/924-4047**); it's open daily from 9am to 9pm. Sometimes there's an information desk out on Hidalgo.

CITY LAYOUT   Understanding traffic circulation in the middle of town requires an advanced degree in chaos theory. I either walk or let the cab driver handle it. The city's main axis is Hidalgo. From the **Plaza de Armas (main square),** it goes 8 blocks southwest to the Enrique Estrada Park and Hotel Quinta Real (changing names as it goes);

in the opposite direction it reaches another 8 blocks to the Rafael Coronel Museum (again making a name change). The historical center of town extends several blocks on either side of this 1.5km (1-mile) stretch of Hidalgo.

GETTING AROUND I enjoy walking around Zacatecas, but the terrain is hilly and the air is thin. Cabs are inexpensive and readily available. Their availability declines somewhat between 2 and 4pm, when office workers snag them to get home for the midafternoon meal.

FAST FACTS: Zacatecas

American Express Visit travel agent **Viajes Mazzocco**, Enlace 115 (© **492/922-0859, -5159**; fax 492/924-0277). Hours are Monday through Friday from 9am to 6pm, Saturday from 9am to 2pm.

Area Code The telephone area code is **492**.

Climate It can get very cold in winter here. At other times it can be chilly in the evenings.

Elevation The city is at a lofty 2,485m (8,151 ft.). The air is always crisp and cool, but a tad thin for some people.

Emergency & Police The emergency number is © **066**.

Hospital The two hospitals in town are **Clínica Santa Elena**, Av. Guerrero 143 (© **492/922-6861**), and **Hospital San José**, Cuevas Cancino 208, near the clinic (© **492/922-3892**).

Internet Access Internet cafes are cheap and very popular with the young crowd. To find one all you have to do is ask at your hotel or get directions from any young person you meet on the street.

Population Zacatecas has 250,000 residents.

Post Office The *correo*, at Allende 111, a half-block from Avenida Hidalgo, is open Monday through Friday from 9am to 3pm, Saturday from 10am to 2pm.

SPECIAL EVENTS & FESTIVALS

During Semana Santa (Holy Week), Zacatecas hosts an **international cultural festival** that the town hopes will eventually rival the Festival Cervantino in Guanajuato. Painters, poets, dancers, musicians, actors, and other artists converge on the town.

The annual **Feria de Zacatecas,** which celebrates the founding of the city, begins the Friday before September 8 and lasts for 3 weeks, incorporating the national Fiestas Patrias (independence celebration). Cockfights, bullfights, sporting events, band concerts, and general hoopla prevail. Famous bullfighters appear, and the cheap bullfight tickets go for around $8 (£4.40).

EXPLORING ZACATECAS

SIGHTS In town you can visit museums and churches, tour an **abandoned silver mine,** ride a cable car up to the **Cerro de la Bufa,** perhaps take in a concert, and partake of an old tradition called *callejoneadas.* On Saturday nights, people go strolling and singing with tambourines, drums, and a burro laden with mezcal through the

Zacatecas

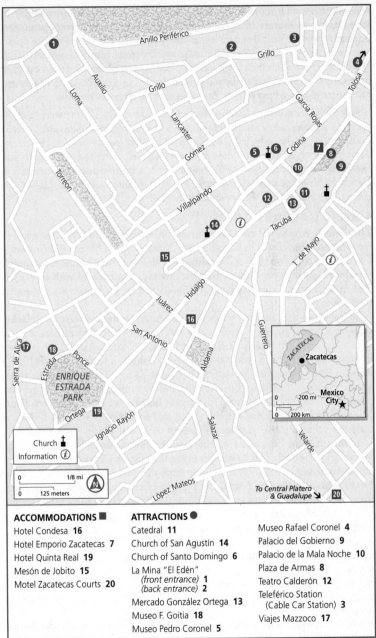

ACCOMMODATIONS ■

Hotel Condesa **16**
Hotel Emporio Zacatecas **7**
Hotel Quinta Real **19**
Mesón de Jobito **15**
Motel Zacatecas Courts **20**

ATTRACTIONS ●

Catedral **11**
Church of San Agustín **14**
Church of Santo Domingo **6**
La Mina "El Edén"
  (front entrance) **1**
  (back entrance) **2**
Mercado González Ortega **13**
Museo F. Goitia **18**
Museo Pedro Coronel **5**

Museo Rafael Coronel **4**
Palacio del Gobierno **9**
Palacio de la Mala Noche **10**
Plaza de Armas **8**
Teatro Calderón **12**
Teleférico Station
  (Cable Car Station) **3**
Viajes Mazzoco **17**

winding streets and *callejones* (alleyways) of the city. Zacatecas remains largely neglected by foreign tourists, though it is popular with Mexicans. Consequently, the various sights provide little descriptive material in English. If you don't speak Spanish, you might want to hire a bilingual tour guide. Try contacting **Viajes Mazzocco** (see "American Express" in "Fast Facts," above). It offers several tours that you can choose from for a fixed price. Some take you around the city; others take you to **nearby ruins** or to some of the old towns near Zacatecas, such as **Jerez** or **Fresnillo.**

SHOPPING **Zacatecan handicrafts** include stone-carving, leatherwork, and silver jewelry. Examples can be found in shops inside the old **Mercado González Ortega** on Hidalgo, next to the cathedral. There are a lot of silver jewelry shops in the center of town. A few other stores on Hidalgo and Tacuba sell crafts and antiques. Huichol Indians occasionally sell their crafts around the Plaza Independencia. Zacatecas is well known for its stone carvings. Many architects and builders from the United States come to Zacatecas when they need fancy stonework.

A STROLL AROUND TOWN

The **Plaza de Armas,** the town's main square on Avenida Hidalgo, is where you'll find the **cathedral** ★★★, with its famous facade. Nowhere else in Mexico is there anything like this; the depth of relief in the carving and wealth of detail create the impression that the images are formed not in stone but in some softer material, such as cake icing. The cathedral took 23 years to build (1729–52), and the final tower wasn't completed until 1904.

To the left of the cathedral, on the Plaza de Armas, is the 18th-century **Palacio de Gobierno,** where governors lived in colonial times. By the time of Mexico's revolt against Spain in 1810, Don Miguel de Rivera (Count of Santiago de la Laguna), owned it. Since 1834, it's been a government building. Inside is a modern **mural** (1970) by Antonio Pintor Rodríguez showing the history of Zacatecas. It is a fairly straightforward chronological presentation of history from left to right, except for the center panel, which represents prominent Zacatecans. Below it is a stone frieze depicting the economic underpinning that supports society and drives historical events. It flows into the mural's central panel, tying society's leaders to the soil of their motherland.

To the left of the Palacio de Gobierno is the **Residencia de Gobernadores,** with its multicolor stonework. This building is newer than the Palacio and served as the governor's house until 1950. Across the street from the plaza are the **Palacio de la Mala Noche (Palace of the Bad Night)** and the Hotel Emporio. The palace's name comes from the mine that brought great wealth to its original owner, Manuel de Rétegui, a philanthropic Spaniard. In case you're thinking that such fine stonework is becoming a lost art, look at the hotel's facade, which was done within the last 40 years.

Climb the small street next to the Palacio de la Mala Noche, and you'll face the massive walls of the **church of Santo Domingo,** which fronts an open space that it shares with the Museo Pedro Coronel (see "Museums," below). This church and the building that houses the museum belonged to the Jesuits until their expulsion in 1767. Afterward, the Dominicans occupied the church and convent. Inside are some lovely baroque gilt *retablos.*

Two blocks south of Santo Domingo, on Calle Dr. Hierro (the mostly level street that parallels Hidalgo), is another grand church, **San Agustín.** This one is in partial ruins. During the Reform Wars, Zacatecas's liberal leaders kicked out the Augustinian friars, converted the church and convent into a brothel and casino, and destroyed the reportedly beautiful gilt altarpieces. The bishop of Zacatecas promptly excommunicated these

Philistines. Twenty years later, a Presbyterian missionary society bought the property and dismantled the ultrabaroque facade that decorated the east door. Again, excommunication for all who aided the missionaries. Now the government has begun restoration of the church and has converted the inside into exhibition space.

Turn and go downhill, and you'll be back on Avenida Hidalgo. Walk back toward the cathedral (left), and you'll pass on your left the **Teatro Calderón** (inaugurated first in 1836 and again in 1891 after a fire). A stately building with lovely stained-glass windows, it is also a favorite spot for people to sit and watch passersby. The opera star Angela Peralta sang here several times in the 1800s. Zacatecas has a flourishing music school, and occasionally it offers performances here. A little farther down Hidalgo, a block before the cathedral on the same side of the street, is the 19th-century **Mercado Jesús González Ortega,** which used to be the town's main market. A pleasant, old-fashioned market, it now holds small stores selling handicrafts and some of the region's wines.

Backtrack along Hidalgo, and over the next few blocks you will pass by some lovely buildings and climb up to **Enrique Estrada Park** (the street changes names and becomes Av. General Jesús González Ortega). The **equestrian statue** (1898) portrays none other than the general himself, hero of the Battle of Calpulalpan. Behind it are a gazebo with marvelous acoustics and a pleasant, shady park that is a romantic spot for young couples at night. Beginning at Estrada Park and extending southward are the lovely arches of the **Aqueduct of Zacatecas.** Two of these arches frame the doorway to the Quinta Real Hotel, which you can enter to see the town's old bullring, a lovely sight. Go to the hotel bar and order a margarita—another lovely sight.

A RIDE UP CERRO DE LA BUFA ★★★

To get to the cable car station from the Plaza de Armas, you must climb one of the streets or alleys that lead up the hill that faces the cathedral. But first, glance up to see if the cars are running; if it's windy, they won't be. The first cross street will be Villalpando or Hierro; go right, and make a left when you get to the Callejón (alley) de García Roja. If you're unaccustomed to the thin air, this is quite a climb. An easier way to get there is to catch bus no. 7, which you can pick up along Juárez, or take a cab. The cable car (𝄢 **492/922-5694**) is a great ride up to the Cerro de la Bufa. The view from the top is best in the late afternoon and early evening, when the sun is low in the sky; if you intend to ride the cable car down, you can't stay too late. It operates only from 10am to 6pm, but the walk down isn't too bad should you want to stay later. A one-way ticket is $2.50 (£1.40).

On Cerro de la Bufa is the **Museo de la Toma de Zacatecas,** which will be of most interest to Spanish-speaking history buffs. It displays artifacts and enlarged newspaper articles about the capture of Zacatecas by Pancho Villa. This was a decisive battle of La Revolución, and one of Villa's greatest victories. The museum is in need of investment; admission is $2 (£1.10). Beside the museum is the beautiful church **La Capilla de la Virgen del Patrocinio,** patroness of Zacatecas. Around the far side of the *cerro* (hill) is the **Mausoleo de los Hombres Ilustres de Zacatecas,** where many of the city's heroes are entombed.

MUSEUMS

La Mina "El Edén" ★   This mine is a giant gash carved diagonally through the core of a mountain following the trail of a silver vein deeper and deeper underground. To see this gash and think that all the stone and ore that once occupied this space was mined and extracted by hand provokes a sense of wonder. The mine opened in 1586, using forced Indian labor. Accidents, tuberculosis, and silicosis caused the workers' early deaths. The mine was extremely rich, yielding gold, copper, zinc, iron, and lead in addition to silver, but it eventually closed when an attempt to use explosives resulted in an inundation of water in the lower levels. Unfortunately, there are no English-speaking guides here, although the tour is eye-opening even for those who don't speak Spanish. Mannequins illustrate some of the mining process. A visit also includes a short, unremarkable train ride.

The mine's back entrance is only a block from the cable-car terminal. I prefer this entrance because most people start at the main entrance, so you can avoid the crowds. When you get to the ticket office, buy your ticket right then. According to the rules, a tour must begin within 15 minutes after the first ticket is purchased. On my last two visits, I've had the guide all to myself (a tip is appreciated). After the tour is over, you can exit by the front entrance, which puts you on Juárez, just a few blocks above Hidalgo.

For directions on getting to the front entrance, see "La Mina Club" below, under "Zacatecas After Dark."

Cerro Grillo. ℂ 492/922-3002. Admission $6 (£ 3.30; includes train and tour). Daily 10am–6pm.

Museo F. Goitia 🟡🟡 I don't expect anybody to believe what they read about modern art, and because my credentials as a critic are nil, I'll be brief. I was surprised by this small museum and the work of Goitia and his Zacatecan comrades, Julio Relas and José Kuri Brença. I walked in expecting it to be a display of regional chauvinism, but I found the works moving, serious, and meaningful. Francisco Goitia (1882–1960) is famous in Mexico, and brothers Rafael and Pedro Coronel amassed great collections that became the basis for two highly touted museums.

Enrique Estrada 102, Col. Sierra de Alica. ℂ 492/922-0211. Admission $2 (£1.10). Tues–Sun 10am–5pm.

Museo Pedro Coronel 🟡🟡 Pedro Coronel, in addition to being an artist, was a collector of inspired tastes. He acquired works from all over the world, but the strongest parts of the collection are the works of European modern masters (Dalí, Picasso, Miró, Kandinsky, Braque, Rouault), pre-Columbian Mesoamerica, and West Africa. All but a few of the pieces of modern art are illuminating. Many date from early in the artist's career, and some display a seminal character that points in the direction of later works. This collection is not large; after a while you drift into the Mesoamerican room—beautiful stuff, and seeing it so quickly after the modern art gets your mind working out strange and improbable connections. There is no filler here; all of the pieces are outstanding. The same can be said of the African material, but in this case the connections with modern art are tangible.

Plaza de Santo Domingo. ℂ 492/922-8021. Admission $2 (£1.10). Fri–Wed 10am–5pm.

Museo Rafael Coronel 🟡🟡🟡 First stroll through the tranquil gardens and ruins of the former Franciscan convent, filled with trailing blossoms and framed by crumbling arches and the open sky. A small wing contains Coronel's drawings on paper. Once you step inside the mask museum, you'll be dazzled by the sheer number of fantastic masks. There are 4,500 of them from all over Mexico, and they're so exotic and dissimilar that you would think that they came from all over the world. One wing of the museum is dedicated to puppets. There are dioramas showing a bullfight, battling armies, and even a vision of hell. The puppets are some of the hundreds created during the last century by the famous Rosete-Aranda family of Huamantla, Tlaxcala, where there is also a puppet museum. Also in the museum, to the left after you enter, is the Ruth Rivera room, where some of Diego Rivera's drawings are on display. Ruth Rivera is the daughter of Diego Rivera and the wife of Rafael Coronel.

Calle Chevano (between Abasolo and Matamoros). ✆ 492/922-8116. Admission $2 (£1.10). Thurs–Tues 10am–5pm.

A SIDE TRIP TO NEARBY GUADALUPE

In the nearby town of Guadalupe, now almost a suburb of Zacatecas, is a large Franciscan convent and evangelical college founded by a famous member of the evangelical college of Querétaro, Fray Antonio Margil de Jesús. It remains an active monastery, but a large part of the convent houses a wonderful museum of colonial art, which will impress anyone interested in art and painting of any kind. Some people might skip this one because they suppose colonial art to be staid, scholastic, and full of arcane symbolism. Not true. The paintings, mostly from the 1700s, are by some of the greatest painters of New Spain—Cabrera, Villalpando, Correa, and others. They are detailed, expressive, dramatic, and eye-catching for their use of anachronisms and fantastical themes. There is also a smaller museum displaying antique carriages from colonial times and classic cars. Zacatecas had a lively carriage-building industry in the colonial era.

A taxi to Guadalupe runs about $12 (£6.60). Transportes de Guadalupe buses go to Guadalupe from the Central Camionera in Zacatecas. If you're driving, take López Mateos east, and follow the signs. When you enter the town, ask anyone for directions to the convent. The convent's church has a lovely facade and holds the famous 19th-century Capilla de Nápoles, a chapel in the shape of a cross with lots of gilding and beautiful designs. You cannot enter the chapel, but you can see it from the ground floor of the church or from the organ loft, which is accessible from the museum.

Convento de Guadalupe/Museo Virreinal de Guadalupe ✯✯✯   To a dedicated museumgoer, seeing these paintings exhibited in galleries with open-air circulation and no climate control is a little unsettling. But with Zacatecas's climate, there may not be much cause for concern. The museum has about 350 works. On the first floor are over 20 portraits depicting scenes of St. Francis's life. The stairway to the second floor has some large, striking paintings, including Cabrera's *Virgin of the Apocalypse* and Arnáez's *The Triumph of the Sweet Light of Jesus,* which is an amusing propagandistic work showing the victory of Rome over the pagans and the Reformation. Highlights on the second floor include the organ loft, 14 oval paintings by Cabrera, four by Villalpando, and the surprising work of a local artist named Gabriel José de Ovalle, who distorts space and deforms human features in a style that seems much more modern than the 1700s. Guides are available for a tour of the museum and to view the Capilla de Nápoles (if the resident monks aren't celebrating Mass).

Jardín Juárez, Oriente, Guadalupe. ✆ 492/923-2089 or -2386. Admission $4 (£2.20). Daily 9am–6pm.

Museo Regional de la Historia   This museum, to the right of the convent, contains examples of carriages and antique cars. Collected from all over Mexico, they formerly belonged to ex-presidents and famous historical figures.

Jardín Juárez, Guadalupe. ✆ 492/923-2386 or -2089. Free admission. Tues–Sun 9am–6pm.

WHERE TO STAY

Zacatecas has a great selection of hotels. In the fall and winter, heat can come in handy. Of the hotels listed here, all but the Condesa have heaters in the rooms, but many hotels in Zacatecas do not. Prices quoted here include the 17% tax. Rates go up for festivals and high season—Easter and August to September.

VERY EXPENSIVE

Hotel Quinta Real ★★★   Mexico is littered with hotels made from former colonial mansions, convents, and haciendas, but how many have risen from bullrings? And yet, it's the beauty, not the novelty, that makes this hotel so great. It has won several design awards, undoubtedly because the architects knew enough to leave the beautiful old bullring intact and keep the hotel small enough to be unobtrusive. A few of the graceful arches that remain from the town's colonial aqueduct frame the entrance. Inside the lobby, you can survey the whole arena, with its arches and stepped levels. The rooms were built along the outside of the bullring, and their windows open onto a small courtyard. Rooms are large, with spacious, well-equipped bathrooms, a writing desk, and a couch. Master suites are one room with a king or two double beds; *gran clase* suites are a good bit larger and have a sitting area and a whirlpool tub.

Av. Rayón 434, 98000 Zacatecas, Zac. © 800/445-4565 in the U.S. and Canada, or 492/922-9105. Fax 492/922-8440. www.quintareal.com. 49 suites. $309 (£170) master suite; $333 (£183) *gran clase* suite. AE, DC, MC, V. Free secure parking. **Amenities:** Restaurant; bar; golf and health club privileges at local club; fitness center, concierge; tour desk; business center; room service; in-room massage; babysitting; laundry service; dry cleaning; nonsmoking rooms. *In room:* A/C, TV, high-speed Internet, minibar, hair dryer, iron.

EXPENSIVE

Hotel Emporio Zacatecas ★★   A comfortable hotel across from the Plaza de Armas, it is a popular choice with Mexican tourists and businesspeople. The spacious rooms on its six floors are carpeted and well furnished. Rooms in the back are quiet. The rooms in front, mostly junior suites, are sunny and have balconies with good views of the cathedral and Cerro de la Bufa. The ones I like most are those on the fourth floor, which have terraces. These are set back a little and offer more shielding from street noise. The rooms in back face a small interior patio, complete with gurgling fountain. They contain one king or two double beds. Bathrooms are midsize, with a decent amount of counter space.

Av. Hidalgo 703, Col. Centro, 98000 Zacatecas, Zac. © 492/925-6500. Fax 492/922-6245. www.hotelesemporio.com. 113 units. $180 (£99) double; $193 (£106) junior suite. AE, MC, V. Free secure parking. **Amenities:** Restaurant; bar; golf and tennis at local club; fitness center; tour desk; car rental; business center; room service; babysitting; laundry service; dry cleaning; nonsmoking rooms. *In room:* TV, hair dryer, iron.

Mesón de Jobito ★★   This two-story hotel occupies a traditional *vecindad,* which was a common form of housing for the lower classes in olden days. The buildings ramble back from the entrance, forming private alleys decorated with ornamental plants and flowers and painted in traditional Mexican colors. The hotel has an intimate feel. The rooms are large, carpeted, and nicely furnished, with queen- or king-size beds and large bathrooms. A couple of the junior suites are large and stylishly decorated. Rates vary seasonally and are highest from September to December and during festival times. The hotel is 5 blocks from the cathedral and a block above Hidalgo.

Jardín Juárez 143, 98000 Zacatecas, Zac. ©/fax 492/924-1722, or 01-800/021-0040 in Mexico. www.mesondejobito.com. 53 units. $167 (£92) double; $175–$190 (£96–£105) suite. AE, MC, V. Free valet parking. **Amenities:** 2 restaurants; bar; tour desk; room service; babysitting; laundry service; dry cleaning. *In room:* A/C, TV, coffeemaker, hair dryer, iron.

INEXPENSIVE

Hotel Condesa *Value*   The good location, well-kept rooms, and economical price are the main attractions here. Many rooms, especially on the lower floors, have been remodeled and have modern furniture, cheerful paint, and new bathroom tile. These rooms have interior views. Rooms on the third floor have new bathrooms. Those facing east overlook Cerro de la Bufa and the market below the hotel. Some remodeled rooms contain king-size beds; other units have a double or two twins.

Av. Juárez 102, 98000 Zacatecas, Zac. ℭ/fax **492/922-1160.** www.hotelcondesa.com.mx. 60 units. $40–$50 (£22–£28) double. AE, MC, V. No parking. **Amenities:** Restaurant; cafe/bar; tour desk; room service; laundry service. *In room:* TV.

Motel Zacatecas Courts   Rooms have carpeting and comfortable beds. It is a 10-minute walk from the main square. Be sure to get a room in the back, away from the street. Also, you must ask to have the heat turned on in the room and for extra blankets in winter.

López Velarde 602, 98000 Zacatecas, Zac. ℭ **492/922-0328.** Fax 492/922-1225. 92 units. $45 (£25) double. MC, V. Free secure parking. **Amenities:** Restaurant; tour info; room service. *In room:* TV.

WHERE TO DINE

The dining in Zacatecas is good. Besides the establishments listed below, I've eaten well at the Quinta Real and Mesón del Jobito. The *gordita,* a thick tortilla that is split open and stuffed with any of several cooked fillings, might be considered the state food of Zacatecas, and the most popular *gordita* place is **Gorditas Doña Julia,** which operates three or four locations. The best coffee in town is at **Café San Patrizio** in the courtyard at 301 Hidalgo. It doesn't open until 9am.

Café Nevería Acrópolis MEXICAN   This restaurant and coffee shop with a soda fountain is a popular meeting spot for breakfast, afternoon coffee, or dessert. Behind the cash register are photos and signatures of famous patrons, including Gregory Peck and Jane Fonda.

Av. Hidalgo and Rinconada de Catedral. ℭ **492/922-1284.** Breakfast $4–$6 (£2.20–£3.30); main courses $5–$9 (£2.75–£4.95). AE, MC, V. Daily 8am–10pm.

La Cantera Musical Restaurant Bar ✦ MEXICAN/REGIONAL   This restaurant is best known for its regional cooking, especially typical dishes such as *asado de bodas* (a pork dish made with cinnamon and ancho and *guajillo* chiles) and *mole zacatecano* (a sweet and spicy chicken dish). You can also get a number of Mexican standards. The dining room is attractive. The restaurant is below the Mercado González Ortega, by the cathedral.

Tacuba 2, Centro Comercial El Mercado. ℭ **492/922-8828.** Main courses $6–$11 (£3.30–£6.05). AE, MC, V. Mon–Sat 1–11pm; Sun 2–10pm.

La Cuija ✦✦ INTERNATIONAL/REGIONAL   Set beneath the Centro Comercial, La Cuija's dining room has tables spaced between thick stone columns supporting close arches. The room is attractive and the seating is comfortable and well separated. The restaurant has its own vineyards (though the wine I tried was not good). The menu offers a selection of mostly Mexican dishes, such as a good *sopa azteca* (tortilla soup) and an ancho chile stuffed with *huitlacoche* (salty and mild-tasting corn fungus that is considered a delicacy in Mexico) in a sauce of ground corn, cream, and a bit of *chile mestizo* (dried chile).

Tacuba T-5, Centro Comercial El Mercado. ℭ **492/922-8275.** Reservations not accepted during Semana Santa. Main courses $8–$15 (£4.40–£8.25). AE, MC, V. Daily 1:30pm–midnight.

Los Dorados de Villa ✦✦ MEXICAN   If your grandmother were Mexican, this is how you would want her to cook. The green *pozole* (soup with chicken, hominy, lettuce, and radishes) is excellent and safe to eat, as are the enchiladas, which come in many varieties (I prefer the *valentinas* and the *rojas*). Other menu items include tostadas, tacos, soups, and guacamole. The name of the place refers to "the golden ones"—Pancho Villa's honor guard of fearless soldiers. The owner is a collector of memorabilia. Artifacts and reproductions from La Revolución cover the walls of the small dining room. Decorative paper cutouts hang from the ceiling, making the room feel even smaller, but festive, too. Los Dorados is not far from the Rafael Coronel Museum; from the cathedral walk north several blocks on Hidalgo, keeping to the left each time the street forks. Or take a cab. What's for dessert? *Buñuelos* (a fried pastry), of course.

Plazuela de García 1314. (©) 492/922-5722. Reservations recommended on weekends. Main courses $4–$6 (£2.20–£3.30). No credit cards. Mon–Sat 3pm–1am; Sun 3–11pm.

ZACATECAS AFTER DARK

La Mina Club   Disco music in a mine deep inside the earth—does "Disco Inferno" ring a bell? Whose life could be considered complete without having made the scene here? The entrance is at the end of Calle Dovali. From Hidalgo, walk up Juárez, which turns into Torreón. Just past the Seguro Social building on Avenida Torreón, you'll find Dovali; turn right. Take a cab if you don't want to be so bushed that you can't boogie. The club is open Thursday through Sunday from 9:30pm to 2am. Mina El Edén, Calle Dovali. (©) 492/922-3727. Cover $15 (£8.25).

5 San Luis Potosí

418km (259 miles) N of Mexico City; 346km (215 miles) NE of Guadalajara; 202km (125 miles) N of Querétaro; 189km (117 miles) E of Zacatecas

San Luis Potosí, more than a mile high in central Mexico's high-plains region, was among the country's most picturesque and prosperous mining cities. It is now the largest and most industrial of the silver cities, with almost a million inhabitants, but you would never know it if you stayed in the historic central district. It has rich colonial architecture and is known for its great plazas. Capital of the state of the same name, San Luis Potosí was named for Louis IX, saintly king of France; *Potosí*, the Quechua word for richness, was borrowed from the incredibly rich Bolivian Potosí mines.

ESSENTIALS

GETTING THERE & DEPARTING   By Plane   Continental ExpressJet (© **800/ 231-0856** in the U.S., or 01-800/900-5000 in Mexico; www.continental.com) and **American Eagle** (© **800/433-7300** in the U.S., or 01-800/904-6000 in Mexico) fly to and from Houston and Dallas. Several domestic carriers have flights to Mexico City and other destinations within the country.

The **airport** is about 11km (7 miles) from downtown. A taxi to the city center is $20 (£11). A *colectivo* van is more economical, but don't tarry in the terminal, because they leave quickly.

By Car   From Mexico City, take Highway 57D; from Guadalajara, take Highway 80. If you're coming from the north, it takes 6 to 7 hours to drive the 536km (332 miles) from Monterrey.

By Bus   The large Central Camionera is 3km (2 miles) east of downtown on Guadalupe Torres at Diagonal Sur. Taxis cost about $5 (£2.75). Most of the bus travel is through Estrella Blanca and its many affiliates, which occupy the counters to the left as you enter. You can buy a ticket for any of the affiliates from any counter. To the right as you enter are three other first-class bus companies: ETN (mostly to Mexico

San Luis Potosí

To Monterrey and Saltillo

To Ciudad Valles and Tampico →

Plaza España

Azteca

Old Train Station

New Train Station

Av. 20 de Noviembre

ALAMEDA PARK

Universidad

Templo de San José

Negrete

Lanzagorta

Parrodi

Xochitl

Othón

Insurgentes

Constitución

Arriaga

Juan Sarabia

11

10

9

8

Villerias

Plaza San Juan de Dios

Plaza del Carmen

Moctezuma

Escobedo

Morelos

Mercado Hidalgo

Plaza Arriaga

Los Bravo

Zaragoza

Juárez

JARDÍN COLÓN

Reforma

Hidalgo

6

Allende

Calle Bocanegra

Plaza de Armas

5

Iturbide

Guerrero

Galeana

5 de Mayo

7

Mier y Terán

J. de Los Reyes

Plaza de los Fundadores

Aldama

Plaza de San Francisco

Vallejo

2

J. de León

4

Madero

Universidad

1

Calle Abasolo

Calle Comonfort

Carmona

Carranza

Arista

Obregón

Independencia

Zapata

Ocampo

Bolívar

Reforma

F. Nieto

1/4 mi

0.25 km

3

Church

Information

Post Office

Train

---

100 mi

100 km

Gulf of Mexico

VERACRUZ

HIDALGO

San Luis Potosí

Mexico City

TAMAULIPAS

ZACATECAS

SAN LUIS POTOSÍ

JALISCO

GUANAJUATO

MICHOACÁN

ATTRACTIONS ●

Cathedral **6**

FONART store **2**

Museo Nacional
de la Máscara **8**

Palacio de Gobierno **5**

Teatro de la Paz **9**

Templo de San Francisco **1**

Templo del Carmen **10**

ACCOMMODATIONS ■

Hotel Filher **7**

Hotel María Cristina **11**

Hotel Panorama **4**

Hotel Real Plaza **3**

City and Guadalajara), Primera Plus (to Mexico City and Querétaro), and Omnibus de Mexico (to Mexico City, Guadalajara, and Querétaro).

VISITOR INFORMATION   The **State Tourism Office** (© **444/812-9939,** -9943; fax 444/812-6769) is at Manuel Jose Othon 130, to one side of the cathedral. The information office has a helpful staff, a good map of the city and historic district, and, of course, lots of brochures. It's open Monday through Friday from 8am to 9pm, Saturday from 9am to 2pm.

CITY LAYOUT   The **Plaza de Armas** is the center of the historic district. All the streets bordering it are pedestrian only. The principal pedestrian street runs north-south in front of the plaza; the southern part (called **Zaragoza**) extends 8 blocks to the Jardín Colón, and the northern part (called **Hidalgo**) runs 5 blocks to the main market. The city also has many plazas and a large downtown park called the **Alameda. Avenida Carranza** heads east from the Plaza de Armas, passes by the Plaza de Fundadores, and extends to the prosperous residential section of the city. Fronting this street are many banks, clubs, and restaurants.

FAST FACTS: San Luis Potosí

American Express   The local representative is **Grandes Viajes,** Av. Carranza 1077 (© **444/817-6084;** fax 444/811-1166). Hours are Monday through Friday from 9am to 2pm and 4 to 7pm, Saturday from 10am to 1pm.

Area Code   The telephone area code is **444.**

Climate   San Luis is on the high plateau more than a mile above sea level, but the weather can get hot during May, June, and sometimes July. In winter it occasionally drops to freezing at night. Rain is rare, with an average total of 14 inches per year; it falls between May and November, mostly in August.

Currency Exchange   Four *casas de cambios* near the main post office offer better rates and better service than the banks. Two are in the arcade on Julián de los Reyes, and two are on Mariano Escobedo. This is just a few blocks northeast of the Plaza de Armas. All are open Saturday. The historic district has many ATMs.

Emergency   San Luis's central emergency number is © **060.**

Hospital   The **Hospital Centro Médico,** Antonio Aguilar 155 (© **444/813-3797),** is one of the best in the country.

Population   San Luis Potosí has 850,000 residents.

Post Office   The *correo,* Morelos 235, 4 blocks north-northeast of the Plaza de Armas, is open Monday through Friday from 8am to 3pm, Saturday 9am to 1pm. Look for a narrow one-story building made of gray stone.

EXPLORING SAN LUIS POTOSI
A STROLL AROUND THE HISTORIC CENTER

San Luis has more streets dedicated solely for the use of pedestrians than any of the other silver cities. The center of town is the **Plaza de Armas,** dating from the mid-1700s and shaded by magnolia and flamboyant trees. The **bandstand** in the center of the plaza was built in 1947 (in colonial style), using pink volcanic stone. Free band concerts usually begin on Thursday and Sunday at around 7:30 or 8pm. On the west side of the plaza is the **Palacio de Gobierno.** It has been much repaired, restored, and added to through the centuries—the back and the south facade were redone as recently as 1973. The front of the building retains much of the original 18th-century decoration, at least on the lower floors. On the second floor, you'll find the rooms that Juárez occupied when he established his temporary capital here. It's worth a peek.

Across the plaza from the Government Palace is the **cathedral.** The original building had only a single bell tower; the one on the left was built in 1910 to match, although today the newer tower looks older. The Count of Monterrey built the **Palacio Municipal,** on the north side of the cathedral, in 1850. He filled it with paintings and sculptures, few of which survived the city's stormy history. When the count died in 1890, the palace was taken over by the bishop and, in 1921, by the city government. Since then, it has been San Luis's city hall. On January 1, 1986, it was fire-bombed in a moment of social unrest. It was restored and functions again.

East of the plaza is one of the city's most famous squares, **Plazuela del Carmen,** named for the **Templo del Carmen** ✦ church. From the *jardín,* walk east along Madero-Othón to Escobedo and the *plazuela.* The entire area you see was once part of the extensive grounds of the 18th-century Carmelite monastery. The church has a beautiful and complex facade, in which appear Elijah and Elisha, two prophets in the Old Testament who lived on Mount Carmel and are considered by the Carmelite order as spiritual founders. The other two large figures are St. Theresa of Avila and St. John of the Cross, both mystics, who in the 16th century reformed the order in Spain and founded the congregation of the discalced Carmelites. Inside the church are some beautiful baroque altarpieces.

The **Teatro de la Paz** and the **Museo Nacional de la Máscara** also face the plaza. The museum is scheduled to reopen in late 2007 after a thorough remodeling. Attached to the Teatro de la Paz (enter to the right of the theater's main entrance) is the **Sala German Gedovius** (✆ **444/812-2698**), with four art galleries. It's open Tuesday through Sunday from 10am to 2pm and 4 to 6pm. Admission is free.

One block east of the Plaza del Carmen is a large urban green area known as **La Alameda.** Vendors sell handicrafts, fruits, and all manner of snacks. Facing the park on Negrete is the **Templo de San José,** with lots of ornate gold decorations, huge religious paintings, and *El Señor de los Trabajos,* a miracle-working statue with many *retablos* testifying to the wonders it has performed.

PLAZAS

San Luis Potosí has more plazas than any other colonial city in Mexico. In addition to those mentioned above, the **Plaza de San Francisco** is south of the Plaza de Armas along Aldama, between Guerrero and Galeana. This shady square takes its name from the Franciscan monastery on the south side of the plaza and the church on the west side. The church holds some beautiful stained glass, many colonial-era statues and paintings, and a crystal chandelier shaped like a sailing ship.

Another square is **Plaza de los Fundadores (Founders' Square),** at the intersection of Obregón and Aldama, northwest of the Plaza de Armas. Facing it is the **Loreto Chapel,** with its exquisite baroque facade. The neighboring church of **El Sagrario** belonged to the Jesuits before the order was expelled from Mexico.

SHOPPING

The best one-stop shopping in San Luis is at the government-operated **FONART** crafts store (✆ **444/814-3868**) on the Plaza de San Francisco. The building was originally part of the Convent of San Francisco, founded in 1590. Today it houses the offices of the Casa de la Cultura, and a branch of FONART on the ground floor. It's open Monday through Friday from 9am to 2pm and 4 to 7pm, Saturday 10am to 5pm. Another place to try is the state-run store **La Casa del Artesano,** Carranza 540 (© **444/814-8990**). The store carries examples of every kind of craft made in the state. It's open Monday through Friday from 10am to 2pm and 4:30 to 8pm. It closes at 7pm on Saturday.

Several blocks along the pedestrian Calle Hidalgo from the Jardín Hidalgo, you'll find the city's **Mercado Hidalgo,** a mammoth building devoted mostly to food, but also offering, among other things, baskets, *rebozos* (shawls), and straw furniture. The walk along Hidalgo is an introduction to the city's commercial life. Hardware stores, crafts shops, shoe stores, groceries, and taverns crowd the street. Past the Mercado Hidalgo is another big market, the Mercado República.

A well-loved local candy factory is **Constanzo,** which has several outlets throughout the city, including three on Carranza. Most outlets are open Monday through Saturday from 10am to 1:30pm and 4 to 8:30pm.

WHERE TO STAY

There are no luxury hotels in the historic center. Most of them (the María Dolores, Real de Minas, and Holiday Inn) are to the east, where the highway from Mexico City enters the town. The Westin and the Camino Real are to the west, along the highway to Guadalajara. All rates listed below include the 17% tax. Expect higher rates for Easter, Christmas, and, in some hotels, August.

VERY EXPENSIVE

Westin San Luis Potosí ✦✦   Perhaps the loveliest hotel in San Luis, the Westin offers comfort and service in surroundings that exemplify how contemporary Mexican architects have worked the elements of colonial architecture to achieve an aesthetic that is new without being divorced from its past. The rooms are along a three-story stone arcade that surrounds a broad courtyard. All are large, carpeted, and decorated with flair. They come with either two full- or one king-size bed, a writing table, and a small dining table. Bathrooms are very large, with marble tiles, countertops, and shower/tub combinations. Suites are even larger and offer a stereo with a CD player, a large whirlpool tub, a safe, and bathrobes. I prefer the rooms that have an interior view of the courtyard. The center of town is 15 to 20 minutes away by car.

Real de Lomas 1000, 78210 San Luis Potosí, S.L.P. © **800/228-3000** in the U.S., or 444/825-0125. Fax 444/825-0200. www.westin.com. 123 units. $220 (£121) double; $235 (£129) suite. Rates include airport transfers and breakfast buffet. Children younger than 12 stay free in parent's room. AE, MC, V. Free valet parking. **Amenities:** Restaurant; bar; small heated outdoor pool; access to nearby health club w/tennis and racquetball; fitness center; kids' club; concierge; tour desk; car rental; airport transportation; business center; executive business services; room service; babysitting; laundry service; dry cleaning; nonsmoking rooms. *In room:* A/C, TV, Wi-Fi, minibar, hair dryer, iron.

MODERATE

Hotel Panorama   Aptly named, this hotel is in a 10-story glass building near the Plaza Fundadores. Many years ago, it was *the* hotel in San Luis, but newer, fancier competitors and a certain amount of decay changed that. Rooms vary in size from medium to large; none feel cramped. Bathrooms are a little small. Most rooms come with two full-size beds. All have an exterior view. Five floors of guest rooms have been completely remodeled. The difference in the remodeled rooms is substantial; they have air-conditioning, high-speed Internet, hair dryers, marble bathrooms with plenty of counter space, modern mahogany-stained furniture, and much better lighting.

Av. Carranza 315, 78000 San Luis Potosí, S.L.P. © 444/812-1777. Fax 444/812-4591. www.hotelpanorama.com.mx. 126 units. $75 (£41) standard double; $85 (£46) *piso ejecutivo* (remodeled). AE, MC, V. Free secure parking. **Amenities:** Restaurant; cafe; bar; dance club; midsize heated outdoor pool; tour desk; car rental; room service; babysitting; laundry service; dry cleaning; executive-level rooms. *In room:* TV, A/C (in remodeled rooms), high-speed Internet (in remodeled rooms), hair dryer (in remodeled rooms).

Hotel Real Plaza *Value* A modern nine-story hotel 8 blocks from the Plaza de Armas, the Real Plaza offers comfort and quiet at a good price. The midsize rooms are carpeted and well lit. They are preferable to the unremodeled rooms at the Panorama (see above). Bathrooms are a little larger than at the Panorama, but some rooms have no view. Try to get a corner room.

Av. Carranza 890, 78250 San Luis Potosí, S.L.P. © 444/814-6969. Fax 444/814-6639. www.realplaza.com.mx. 268 units. $65 (£36) double. AE, MC, V. Free secure parking. **Amenities:** Restaurant; bar; outdoor pool; fitness center; tour desk; business center; room service; laundry service. *In room:* A/C, TV, high-speed Internet.

INEXPENSIVE

Hotel Filher *Value* Good location and medium to large rooms painted in cheerful colors are the high points of this economical three-story hotel. If you want quiet, request a room on the third floor; if you want a window and a firm mattress, book a room on the second. Rates are higher for second-floor rooms. Of these, I like the ones facing the pedestrian-only Zaragoza. They have balconies with a good view, and though there may be street noise, you don't get the noise that reverberates through the rather loud lobby. This hotel is a good choice in warm weather because the rooms are airy and have tile floors rather than carpeting. They also have ceiling fans. Hot water can take as long as 5 minutes to get to the rooms.

Av. Universidad 375 (at Zaragoza), 78000 San Luis Potosí, S.L.P. © 444/812-1562. Fax 444/812-1564. 50 units. $45 (£25) double. MC, V. Free parking 3 blocks away. **Amenities:** Restaurant; bar; room service. *In room:* TV.

Hotel María Cristina The María Cristina is in a narrow nine-story building around the corner from the Plaza del Carmen. It's next door to (and often confused with) the Hotel Nápoles. All rooms are small and have a ceiling fan, and most don't offer much of a view. The bathrooms are small, with little counter space. Rooms are quiet, carpeted, and warmer in the winter than the rooms at the Filher (see above). They come with either one full or two twin beds.

Juan Sarabia 110, 78000 San Luis Potosí, S.L.P. © 444/812-9408. www.mariacristina.com.mx. 74 units. $60 (£33) double. MC, V. Free guarded parking. **Amenities:** 2 restaurants; bar; tour info; room service. *In room:* TV.

WHERE TO DINE

Downtown San Luis has a number of restaurants offering standard local fare. Try the **Posada del Virrey** on the Plaza de Armas; the 24-hour **Café Pacífico** at Los Bravos and Constitución, off the Plaza del Carmen; or **La Parroquia** on the Plaza Fundadores. For something a little more special, try one of the following.

MODERATE

El Callejón de San Francisco ★ MEXICAN If the night air is comfortable, there's no lovelier place for dinner than this restaurant's rooftop terrace, with San Francisco's cupola and bell towers for a backdrop. Even if it's a tad too chilly, you can still enjoy yourself; just ask the waiter for a *jorongo* (hoh-*rohn*-goh), a traditional woolen wrap for the shoulders. There's also a dining room downstairs. The menu has a number of Mexican standards at reasonable prices. The restaurant is on a pedestrian street beside San Francisco church and behind FONART.

Callejón de Lozada 1. © 444/812-4508. Reservations recommended on weekends. Main courses $6–$12 (£3.30–£6.60). AE, MC, V. Mon–Sat 2pm–midnight.

La Corriente Restaurant Bar ⚑ MEXICAN   The menu has several Mexican dishes, using mostly beef. I liked the *chamorro pibil* (pork cooked in a Huastecan *mole*), the *puntas al chipotle* (beef in a spicy chipotle sauce), and the *costillitas en chile ancho* (pork ribs in chile ancho sauce). It also offers a large selection of blended fruit and vegetable drinks with surprising combinations. These are filling; don't make the mistake of ordering one and a main course or a full breakfast; instead, try an appetizer such as the *quesadillas de huitlacoche*. The restaurant is in a large old house. The main dining room is a roofed patio with hanging plants, lots of photos, and tile wainscoting. Off to the sides are other dining rooms.

Carranza 700. © 444/812-9304. Main courses $5–$10 (£2.75–£5.50); blended juices $3 (£1.65). MC, V. Mon–Sat 8am–midnight; Sun 8am–6pm.

La Virreina ⚑⚑ REGIONAL/MEXICAN   Opened in 1959, this restaurant has for years been one of the places Potosinos go to dine when there's something to celebrate. It has been under the same ownership all this time, and service and food preparation are given attention. Of all the places I've tried here, this one had the best *enchiladas potosinas* (ask for them with strips of chile poblano instead of just cheese). Or order the *carne asada a la virreina* and you'll get a couple on the side. This dish is a steak topped with a little cheese and a sauce flavored with Mexican sausage (it sounds excessive now, but it didn't at the time). A more moderate option is the pepper steak or the baked fish with bleu cheese and bread crumbs. The large dining room was once an open courtyard. It is comfortable and attractive, with plenty of space between tables.

Av. Carranza 830. © 444/812-3750. Reservations recommended. Main courses $8–$15 (£4.40–£8.25). AE, MC, V. Mon–Sat 1pm–midnight; Sun 1–7pm.

Restaurant Orizatlán ⚑⚑ HUASTECAN   This colorful restaurant specializes in the traditional Huastecan cooking of eastern San Luis Potosí. If you are hungry, try the *parrillada a la Huasteca* for two. A large sampling of typical dishes, it includes portions of the *zacahuil*, Mexico's largest tamal. The waiters will keep the Huastecan enchiladas coming until you beg them to stop. Less ambitious eaters can order a la carte. After dinner, the restaurant serves complimentary home-style cordials made from several fruits and puts on a mini Huastecan fandango, with music and dance.

Pascual M. Hernández 240. © 444/814-6786. Breakfast $4 (£2.20); main courses $5–$10 (£2.75–£5.50). AE, MC, V. Mon–Thurs 8am–10pm; Fri–Sat 8am–11pm; Sun 8am–7pm. 8 blocks south of Plaza de Armas on Zaragoza, turn left at Jardín Colón; restaurant is about 30m (98 ft.) down.

SAN LUIS AFTER DARK

The most popular clubs in town are those where you can sit down to a late supper or drinks and hear guitarists and vocalists. Most of the music is romantic—*trovas*, or ballads. In the downtown area, a number of bars offer this kind of entertainment, usually on Thursday, Friday, and Saturday nights. They include **La Compañía,** Mariano Arista 350 (© 444/812-9693); **Viejo San Luis,** Carranza 485-A (© 444/814-0801); and **Restaurant Bar 1913,** Galeana 205 (© 444/812-8352). **Play,** Carranza 423 (© 444/814-7034), is a popular dance club for 20-somethings.

Michoacán

by David Baird

West of Mexico City and southeast of Guadalajara lies the state of Michoacán (mee-choh-ah-*kahn*), the homeland of more than 200,000 Tarascan Indians, properly known as the Purépecha. The land is mountainous in the east, north, and center, but, in the south and west, it drops to a broad lowland plain that meets the Pacific Ocean. The state gets more rain and is consequently greener than its neighbors Jalisco and Guanajuato, and many Mexicans consider it the most beautiful state in their country. And yet, it remains relatively unvisited by foreign tourists.

High in the mountains, in the northeastern part of the state, a miraculous ritual occurs every year. Millions of monarch butterflies congregate in an isolated highland forest. They are the final link in a migratory chain stretching as far away as Canada. During peak season (Dec–Mar), the tree limbs bend under their cumulative weight, and the undulation of so many wings creates a dazzling spectacle. (See "Michoacán's Monarch Migration," later in this chapter.) In central Michoacán are highland lakes and colorful Indian towns that evoke the Mexico of old. These towns are known for their handicrafts and all-night celebrations on the Day of the Dead. Farther west and south is the famous volcano Paricutín, the only major volcano born in modern times (1943).

The two most important cities in Michoacán, **Morelia** and **Pátzcuaro**, offer the visitor contrasting visions of the colonial past. Morelia is a city built of chiseled stone, planned with architectural considerations and possessed of a clearcut geometry, while Pátzcuaro is all about undulating adobe walls, crooked red-tile roofs, and narrow meandering streets. The former is proud of its Spanish heritage; the latter remains rooted in its Indian origins.

The native Purépecha are an intriguing people. Where they came from and how they got here we don't know. Their language is unlike any other in Mexico, the closest linguistic connection being with native peoples in Ecuador. Their civilization developed contemporaneously with that of the Aztec, and they successfully defeated Aztec expansionism—the only highland civilization to do so.

Since they were not vassals of the Aztec, they didn't simply submit to Spanish rule after the collapse of the Aztec empire. In the history of the conquest and conversion of the Purépecha, two men represent the extremes of Spanish attitudes toward the Indians. One was the conquistador Nuño de Guzmán, a man whose rapaciousness and cruelty made him infamous even among fellow conquistadors, eventually earning him a prison cell in Spain. The other was Vasco de Quiroga, a humanist who believed in the ideas of Erasmus and Thomas More. He joined the church late in life and came to Michoacán as the first bishop of the Purépecha, establishing his see in Pátzcuaro. Here, he strove to build a utopian society of cooperative communities, organizing and instructing each village in the practice of a specific craft. To this day, his organization of crafts among the different villages is largely followed.

EXPLORING MICHOACAN

Travel between the major cities of Michoacán takes only an hour or two at most, and public transportation is frequent. You should plan 3 days in **Morelia** (more if you intend to see the butterflies) and a minimum of 3 days in **Pátzcuaro,** but more like a week if you're interested in taking day trips to the lakes and the villages in the region and want to look into the local handicrafts. **Uruapan,** another important town, is an easy day trip from either city, although you may want to stay longer to visit the **Paricutín volcano.** During Easter week or Day of the Dead observances (Nov 1–2), the Plazas Grandes in Pátzcuaro and Uruapan overflow with regional crafts. Reserve rooms well in advance for these holidays. With the new highway from Ixtapa, it's possible to plan a vacation that combines the lovely colonial cities of Michoacán with quality beach time.

1 Morelia ⟨⋆

312km (193 miles) NW of Mexico City; 365km (226 miles) SE of Guadalajara

The first viceroy of Mexico ordered the founding of the city in 1541 under the name Valladolid. The name was later changed to Morelia to honor the revolutionary hero José María Morelos, who was born here.

Morelia was intended as a bastion of Spanish culture for the region's large population of Indians. The adjective people most frequently use to describe Morelia is "aristocratic." And indeed, the city's greatest appeal lies in its grand colonial architecture.

ESSENTIALS

GETTING THERE & DEPARTING

BY PLANE   Continental (© **800/231-0856** in the U.S., or 01-800/900-5000 in Mexico; www.continental.com) has direct flights from Houston and Los Angeles. **Mexicana** (© **800/531-7921** in the U.S., or 443/324-3808; www.mexicana.com) has flights to and from the U.S.; flights from San Francisco, Oakland, San Jose, Los Angeles, and Chicago are either one-stop or nonstop, depending on the day of the flight. Mexicana also flies direct to several destinations within Mexico. **AeroMéxico/ Aerolitoral** (© **800/237-6639** in the U.S., or 443/324-2424, -3604; www.aeromexico. com.mx) flies to and from Mexico City, Guadalajara, Querétaro, Tepic, and Tijuana, with connections to U.S. destinations.

Morelia's airport is **Aeropuerto Francisco J. Mújica,** a 45-minute drive from the city center on Km 27 of the Carretera Morelia-Zinapécuaro. Taxis meet each flight. **Budget** has a car-rental office there (© **800/527-0700** in the U.S. and Canada, or 443/313-3399).

BY CAR   The slow route from either Mexico City or Guadalajara is Highway 15— a winding and narrow road with beautiful vistas, which can be appreciated at leisure because you inevitably get stuck behind an old truck that can barely climb the mountains as it makes its way through a series of blind curves. The fast way is the modern **toll highway** that connects Mexico City and Guadalajara. Exit when the road crosses **Highway 43.** It's clearly marked. To Morelia from either city is about 4 hours and $20 (£11). From Guanajuato (2½ hr.), take this same Highway 43. From Morelia to

Morelia

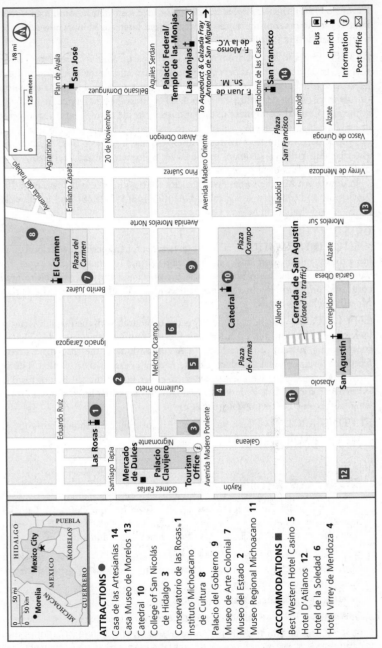

ATTRACTIONS ●

Casa de las Artesianías **14**
Casa Museo de Morelos **13**
Catedral **10**
College of San Nicolás
  de Hidalgo **3**
Conservatorio de las Rosas **1**
Instituto Michoacano
  de Cultura **8**
Palacio del Gobierno **9**
Museo de Arte Colonial **7**
Museo del Estado **2**
Museo Regional Michoacano **11**

ACCOMMODATIONS ■

Best Western Hotel Casino **5**
Hotel D'Atilanos **12**
Hotel de la Soledad **6**
Hotel Virrey de Mendoza **4**

Bus
Church
Information
Post Office

239

Pátzcuaro (1 hr.), there is **Highway 120,** a four-lane road. The new toll road from the Ixtapa beach resort connects to this highway. From Ixtapa to Morelia now takes about 4 hours and $15 (£8.25).

BY BUS   Buses to Morelia from Mexico City depart from the Observatorio station. ETN, Pegasso, Primera Plus/Servicios Coordinados, and Autovías all go to Morelia. Make sure to request a *directo* or *via autopista.* The trip takes 4 hours, and there are usually three or four departures every hour. ETN offers the best service. You will arrive at the new **Central Camionera** in the far northwest side of town, near the soccer stadium. First-class and deluxe bus service to and from Morelia uses terminal A, and regional service to and from Pátzcuaro uses terminal B. Service from Guadalajara is also frequent. From Guanajuato, your best bet is Primera Plus and Servicios Coordinados (a total of six departures per day).

In downtown Morelia some travel agencies sell bus tickets. At the corner of 20 de Noviembre and Obregón is one called **GAP** (✆ **443/317-2828**), and it sells tickets for ETN and Primera Plus.

ORIENTATION

VISITOR INFORMATION   The city government, in association with local guides, has a tourist information kiosk on the Plaza de Armas (main square). It's open from 9am until 8pm Monday to Saturday. The city operates a website (**www.visitmorelia. com**) and prints a free quarterly magazine with a calendar of events (**La Guía de Morelia),** which is handy.

CITY LAYOUT   The heart of the city is the **cathedral,** with the Plaza de Armas on its left (west side) and the Plaza Melchor Ocampo on its right (east side). The wide street passing in front of the cathedral is **Avenida Madero,** the city's main street. It meets the lovely colonial aqueduct .8km (a half mile) east of the cathedral. This segment of Madero, along with several blocks to either side, is the old part of town (see "Other Attractions," below.) From the fountain, the **aqueduct** heads southeast toward what has become the fashionable part of town.

GETTING AROUND   Taxis are a bargain here. Still, you should settle the fare before you enter the cab.

FAST FACTS: **Morelia**

American Express   The local representative is **Gran Turismo Viajes,** Av. Camelinas 3233, Int. 102–103, Fracc. Las Américas (✆ **443/324-0484**; fax 443/324-0495). Hours are Monday through Saturday from 9am to 2pm and 4 to 6pm.

Area Code   The telephone area code is **443.**

Climate   Morelia can be a bit chilly in the morning and evening, especially from November through February.

Elevation   Morelia sits at 1,950m (6,396 ft.).

Emergencies   The local number for emergencies is ✆ **066.**

Hospital   The best in town is the **Sanatorio de la Luz,** Calle Bravo 50, in the Chapultepec Norte neighborhood (✆ **443/314-4568** or -4464, or 315-2966).

Internet Access You can find Internet service without much effort in the Centro Histórico (historic district). The usual cost is about $2 (£1.10) per hour.

Population Morelia has 600,000 residents.

Post Office & Telegraph Office Both are in the Palacio Federal, on the corner of Madero and Serapio Rendón, 5 blocks east of the cathedral.

SPECIAL EVENTS & FESTIVALS

In April, the **International Guitar Festival** (www.figmorelia.com) attracts performers from Latin America and Europe. In May, the city holds the **International Organ Festival** (linked to the variable feast day of Corpus Christi). The cathedral has a very large pipe organ that sounds wonderful. Every year, four organists are invited to give concerts there. In October, the city holds its increasingly popular film festival, **Festival Internacional de Cine de Morelia** (www.moreliafilmfest.com). The **International Festival of Music** is held in November, with a series of concerts performed over 2 weeks. Performers come from all over.

The largest civic celebrations are in September, the month of the *fiestas patrias*. **Independence Day** is celebrated on September 15 and 16. Then, on September 29 and 30, Morelia celebrates the **birthday of its favorite son, José María Morelos,** a patriot and revolutionary hero. The second celebration is actually bigger than the first, but both include parades, a street party, and large fireworks displays.

EXPLORING MORELIA
A STROLL THROUGH THE COLONIAL CENTER

Downtown Morelia is a good town for walking. One comes across interesting details on just about any street, and crime poses little problem. The walk outlined below could take a whole day. The museums open at 9am; you'll find a lot of places closed on Mondays, holidays, and between 2 and 4pm. For a guided tour of the city, contact the guide mentioned in the section on the monarch butterfly migration ("Michoacán's Monarch Migration," p. 248). He can give a lot of local color and provide details about the city's history and architecture.

The **cathedral** ✸✸✸ is the place to begin. Built with the pink volcanic stone (*cantera* in Spanish) that Morelia is famous for, it's the most beautiful cathedral in Mexico. Notice how Avenida Madero widens as it passes in front of the cathedral, and how a cross street lines up with its facade. Morelia's planners sought to lend prominence to the city's churches by the placement of plazas and the alignment of streets to allow good views. This cathedral took the place of an earlier one; construction began in 1640 and ended in 1745. The new cathedral incorporated the styles of religious architecture already in the city, including plateresque, mannerist, and a reserved style of baroque. The cathedral's impressive size and monumental proportions were necessary to place it at the top of the hierarchy of the city's temples, and to make obvious Morelia's superiority to rival Pátzcuaro. The Italian architect who designed it worked closely with the authorities of Morelia's sizable religious community, and he did a masterful job balancing the architectural elements in the facade and shaping the proportions of the towers. The inside is stately, but much of the cathedral's most valuable possessions were plundered. Things to look for include the beautiful **organ** ✸ with 4,600 pipes

Free-Market Forces

Morelia's **city market** is 5 blocks south of San Francisco in a plain, ware-houselike structure. If you're a veteran marketgoer, you'll like this one. It's especially rich in regional manufactures, such as sombreros and huaraches, and has a good produce section where you can stock up on different kinds of dried chiles if you like cooking Mexican food.

To get to the market, continue downhill along Calle Vasco de Quiroga. Just before you get there you will see a little plaza and the **Templo de las Capuchinas.** It's a precious little baroque church with a gilt *retablo* (altarpiece) inside. Unfortunately, it is often closed; the best time to try is from 8 to 9am and from 5 to 6pm, when the priest opens the church for Mass. One block farther is the market.

(see "Special Events & Festivals," above); the silver baptismal font where Mexico's first emperor, Agustín de Iturbide, was baptized; and the elegant choir with carved wooden stalls. *Tip:* If you're in Morelia on a Saturday, make sure to be around the cathedral when the lights are turned on. This is accompanied by a fireworks display.

Across Avenida Madero from the cathedral is a two-story stone building crowned with finials and fanciful decorations on the corners. This is the **Palacio del Gobierno,** built in 1732 as a seminary. It now holds sweeping murals depicting the history of Michoacán and Mexico. Some are the work of a well-known local artist, Alfredo Zalce.

As you leave the *palacio,* turn left and walk down Madero for 2 blocks. Turn right at a small church on your right with a tall wrought-iron fence. The name of the street is Vasco de Quiroga. Walk 1 block, and to your left you'll see a broad plaza and the **church and convent of San Francisco** ✹✹. This is one of the two oldest religious buildings in Morelia. It draws on the Spanish Renaissance architectural style known as plateresque (already antiquated by the time of construction) because the builders wanted to accentuate their Spanish heritage. The convent is quite striking; it has elegant, Moorish windows on the second floor, borrowed from Spanish Mudéjar architecture. The interior courtyard, unlike any other in Morelia, has a medieval feel. Instead of being broad and open with light arches, it is closed and narrow, with heavy columns set closely together and thick buttressing. The former convent now houses a local **handicrafts museum** and the best shopping in Morelia (see "Shopping," below).

Back at San Francisco, take the street that lines up with the facade of the church and walk 2 blocks to Calle Morelos Sur (you'll see Plaza Melchor Ocampo). Turn left. One block down on the left-hand side is the **Casa Museo de Morelos,** Morelos Sur 323 (✆ **443/313-2651**). This is where José María Morelos lived as an adult (There's another Morelos museum, in the house where he was born, but it has little of interest). A grand house, with furniture and personal effects that belonged to the independence leader, as well as a period kitchen, this museum is worth a visit. For history buffs, there is an exhibition on his four campaigns against Spanish royalist forces. The museum is open daily from 9am to 7pm; admission is $3 (£1.65).

The next place to see is the **Museo Regional Michoacano** ✹, at the intersection of Allende and Abasolo (✆ **443/312-0407**). To get there, walk uphill the way you came and make a left when you get back to Plaza Melchor Ocampo. Walk through the stone arcades behind the cathedral.

At the end of the arcades and across the street, cater-corner to the Plaza de Armas, is the museum. It provides a colorful view of the state from prehistoric times to Mexico's Cardenist period of the 1930s. Isidor Huarte, father of Ana Huarte, Emperor Iturbide's wife, originally owned the building, which was finished in 1775. The museum is open Tuesday through Saturday from 9am to 7pm, Sunday from 9am to 4pm. Admission is $3 (£1.65).

To take a break, sit at one of the outdoor cafes under the stone arches along Avenida Madero. (No need really to over-exert one's self. Besides, sitting at a table having a little coffee or beer and watching the passersby is a favorite activity of the locals. In anthropology what you would be doing is called "participant observation.")

After having your fill of participant observation (or beer or coffee), head west on Madero for 1 block until you get to the corner of Nigromante. On the right corner, you'll see the **College of San Nicolás de Hidalgo,** a beautiful colonial building that claims to house the oldest university in the New World. Founded in Pátzcuaro in 1540 by Vasco de Quiroga, the university moved to Morelia in 1580 and became the University of Michoacán in 1917. On the other corner is another of Morelia's oldest church structures, the **Iglesia de la Compañía de Jesús,** built by the Jesuits. It is now a lovely library. Through a doorway to the right of the church is the state's **tourist information office.** Attached to the church is the former convent, now called the **Palacio Clavijero.** To see the graceful arches and rose-colored stone of its broad interior courtyard (the most photographed in Morelia), turn down Nigromante and follow it to the main entrance. The former convent now houses state government offices. Once you've seen the *palacio,* continue down the street to the little park. Facing the park is the **Conservatorio de las Rosas,** a former Dominican convent. It became a music school in 1785 and is now the home of the internationally acclaimed **Morelia Boys Choir.** The choir practices on weekday afternoons. If you would like to attend a concert, ask for information inside.

Cater-cornered from the conservatory, at the junction of Santiago Tapia and Guillermo Prieto, is the **Museo del Estado** (© **443/313-0629**). Exhibits include a display on the archaeology and history of the area and a 19th-century apothecary

A Brief Pause for the Food Cause

En route to the Museo Regional, you'll be walking by two local food vendors that are institutions in the city. One is an ice cream stand called **Nieves del Correo.** It's called that because for the first 30 years of its existence, it occupied a bit of sidewalk on Avenida Madero in front of the post office. Now it's in the last doorway under the arches before you cross the pedestrian-only Cerrada de San Agustín. You can't miss it. The specialty is fruit flavors such as mango and mammee. The other option is to enjoy a fruit cocktail known locally as a *gazpacho* (nothing like a gazpacho in Spain). Turn left on the Cerrada and you'll come to **Gazpachos La Cerrada.** Order one and you'll get chopped fruit (mango, pineapple, and jicama) swimming in orange and lime juice with a touch of powdered chile.

shop. The museum is open Monday through Friday from 9am to 2pm and 4 to 8pm, Saturday and Sunday from 9am to 2pm and 4 to 7pm. Admission is free. Look for or ask about concerts and other goings-on.

To visit another interesting museum, continue east on Santiago Tapia 2 blocks to Benito Juárez and turn north (left). The **Museo de Arte Colonial** ⊛, Av. Benito Juárez 240 (© **443/313-9260**), is a colonial mansion that houses a large collection of religious art from the 16th to the 18th centuries. One section displays Christ figures made from the paste of corn stalks. This was a pre-Columbian artistic technique among the Purépecha, and the missionaries soon had their Indian converts using it to create the Christ figures and saints that adorn many churches in Mexico. The museum is open Tuesday through Sunday from 10am to 2pm and 5 to 8pm. Admission is free.

Just around the corner from this museum (turn right as you exit) is the **Plaza del Carmen.** Across the plaza, behind a heavy wrought-iron fence, is the church and former convent of **El Carmen.** The entrance to the convent is on the opposite side of the block from the church, on Morelos Norte. The building is home to the state's **Instituto Michoacano de Cultura** (© **443/313-1320**), which has made this a comfortable and utilitarian destination; you can examine the calendars posted at the entrance to see whether a concert, film, or exhibition is happening during your stay. You can also view the large stone courtyard built in the style often used by the Carmelites. In and about the courtyard are a museum of native masks, a large bookstore, and a gallery. Entrance is free. The institute is open daily from 10am to 8pm.

OTHER ATTRACTIONS

On another day you might enjoy exploring Avenida Madero east from the cathedral. After a couple of blocks, you'll reach the **Templo de las Monjas (Nuns' Temple),** a lovely old church with a unique twin facade and B-shaped floor plan. Beside it is the massive **Palacio Federal,** which houses, among many other official bureaus, the post and telegraph offices. Continue on and you'll reach the colonial **aqueduct.** The graceful arches of the aqueduct stretch from here about a kilometer (less than a mile) eastward. A stone walkway, lined with trees and long stone benches, starts from one of the arches in front of the fountain. This is **La Calzada Fray Antonio de San Miguel** ⊛⊛. In the 1940's this walkway was used to shoot some scenes for a Hollywood movie with Tyrone Power called *Captains from Castile.* The Calzada leads to the **church of San Diego** ⊛⊛, the most ornate church in Morelia, San Diego is also known as **El Santuario de Guadalupe.** It has this wonderful interior done in neo-baroque, the product of a remodeling job done a century ago. In early December, food stands fill the entire plaza in front of the church, and a festival is held to celebrate the feast day of the Virgin of Guadalupe (Dec 12).

The distance from the cathedral to San Diego is about 1.6km (1 mile). You can take a taxi back or, if you still feel like walking, return by crossing the large plaza with the statue of Morelos on horseback. Go under the aqueduct, and enter Morelia's equivalent of Central Park, known as **El Bosque (The Woods).** Continue west and work your way back to the center of town. If you get turned around here, note that if you're walking on level ground, you're parallel to or heading toward Madero; if you're walking downhill, you're heading away from it.

SHOPPING

Casa de las Artesanías ⊛⊛   This place is both a museum and one of the best crafts shops in Mexico. In the showroom on the right, you'll find an array of objects produced in the Indian villages of Michoacán's central highlands, including carved-wood furniture from Cuanajo, pottery from Tzintzuntzan, wood masks from Tócuaro, lacquerware from Pátzcuaro and Uruapan, cross-stitch embroidery from Tarecuato, copperware from Santa Clara, guitars from Paracho, and close-woven hats from Jarácuaro. Straight ahead in the interior courtyard are showcases laden with the best regional crafts. Upstairs, individual villages have sales outlets. Sometimes you'll find artisans demonstrating their craft. The shop and museum are open daily from 9am to 2pm and 5 to 8pm. Exconvento de San Francisco, Plaza Valladolid. © 443/312-1248.

Mercado de Dulces   Along the back of the former Jesuit convent is the sweets market—a collection of stalls selling the typical sweets that Morelia is famous for, such as *ates* (a thick fruit paste), candied fruit wedges, pralines, toasted coconut, and milk candies. The *mercado* is open daily from 7am to 10pm. Behind the Palacio Clavijero, along Valentín Gómez Farías. No phone. From the cathedral, head west on Madero and turn right on Gómez Farías; entrance is a half block down on the right.

WHERE TO STAY

Rates listed here include the 17% tax. Rates at the inexpensive and moderately priced hotels can go up during holidays, long weekends (called *puentes* in Mexico), and the month of August.

VERY EXPENSIVE

Hotel Virrey de Mendoza 👰👰   This is one of the old-style grand hotels one occasionally finds in Mexico's colonial cities. Unlike others, this one was not allowed to decay; it's beautifully kept and most impressive. It's also right on the Plaza de Armas. Furnishings vary, but all rooms are comfortable. They have lots of character—wood floors with area rugs, period furniture, old-fashioned tile bathrooms with tub/shower combinations. Bed choices include two twins, one full, two queen-size, or one king-size. Standard rooms are midsize; of the eight exterior rooms, two have balconies. Suites are large, and master suites have separate sitting rooms. The *suite virreinal* (viceroy suite) is really grand, with a large third-floor terrace that looks out over the Plaza de Armas to the cathedral. Rooms have double-glazed windows, but traffic noises still leak in.

Av. Madero Poniente 310, 58000 Morelia, Mich. ©/fax **443/312-0633** or 443/312-0045. Fax 443/312-6719. www.hotelvirrey.com. 55 units. $190 (£105) double; $230–$390 (£127–£215) suite. Promotional rates sometimes available. AE, MC, V. Free valet parking. **Amenities:** Restaurant; lobby bar; tour desk; car rental; business center; room service; in-room massage; babysitting; laundry service; dry cleaning; nonsmoking rooms. *In room:* A/C (in 11 rooms), TV, hair dryer.

Villa Montaña Hotel and Spa 👰👰👰   High above the city on the Santa María Ridge, this hotel offers beauty and tranquillity. Rooms are in a small complex of buildings on a hillside, separated by gardens and connected by footpaths. The buildings are at different levels; this, as well as the placement of the entrances, allows for privacy. Villa Montaña, a member of the Small Luxury Hotels of the World, has no rough edges. Rooms are large, impressively furnished, and have working fireplaces. Most come with two doubles or a king-size bed. Bathrooms are large, with tub/shower combinations and lots of counter space. Most of the junior suites have a separate living area and a small terrace with table and chairs. Master suites have a lot of architectural details. The restaurant does a great job with local dishes, and having a drink on the terrace overlooking the city is one of the delights of staying here. Service is attentive.

Patzimba 201, Col. Vista Bella 58090 Morelia, Mich. ⓒ **443/314-0231** or -0179. Fax 443/315-1423. www.villa montana.com.mx. 36 units. $236 (£130) double; $325–$395 (£179–£217) suite; $510 (£281) 2-bedroom suite. Prices include service charge. Internet specials sometimes available. Weekday discounts available. AE, MC, V. Free secure parking. **Amenities:** Restaurant; terrace bar; heated outdoor pool; golf at local country club; lighted tennis court; fitness room; spa; concierge; tour desk; business center; executive business services; room service; in-room massage; babysitting; laundry service; dry cleaning. *In room:* TV, hair dryer, safe.

MODERATE

Best Western Hotel Casino *Value*   A colonial hotel that's not as striking as the Hotel de la Soledad, the Best Western should still be considered for its location—across the street from the cathedral—comfort, and price. The owners continue to invest money in improvements and upgrades. They've opened three new rooms on the top floor that are large, sunny, and quite comfortable. Most rooms are midsize and carpeted. They are, for the most part, more comfortable than the rooms at the Soledad. Some second-floor rooms in front have a balcony and view of the cathedral, but they can be noisy. Many rooms have two double beds or one double and one twin.

Portal Hidalgo 229, 58000 Morelia, Mich. ⓒ **800/528-1234** in the U.S., or 443/313-1328. Fax 443/312-1252. www.bestwestern.com. 43 units. $97–$110 (£53–£61) double. AE, MC, V. Free valet parking. **Amenities:** Restaurant; bar; tour desk; car rental; business center; room service; laundry service and courtesy washer and dryer; dry cleaning; nonsmoking rooms. *In room:* TV, Wi-Fi, coffeemaker, hair dryer, iron.

Hotel de la Soledad 𝒢   Past the massive wooden doors of this colonial hotel is a large, beautiful courtyard with antique carriages parked beneath stone arches. Some rooms have fireplaces and balconies. Standard rooms vary quite a bit and come with two twin beds, one double, or one king-size. The price depends on whether the room faces the more elegant front courtyard (these rooms are generally bigger) or the rear courtyard. Rooms have rugs or carpeting, Spanish-style furniture, and high ceilings. Bathrooms vary in size and quality; most are ample, and many contain tub/shower combinations. The location is great—1 block north of the cathedral.

Ignacio Zaragoza 90, 58000 Morelia, Mich. ⓒ **443/312-1888** or -1889. Fax 443/312-2111. www.hsoledad.com. 58 units. $100–$110 (£55–£61) double; $115–$130 (£63–£72) suite. AE, MC, V. Free valet parking. **Amenities:** Restaurant; bar; tour desk; car rental; room service; laundry service; dry cleaning. *In room:* TV, hair dryer (on request), safe.

INEXPENSIVE

Hotel D'Atilanos   This is the only decent inexpensive hotel in the downtown area. Two floors of rooms surround a simple patio. The rooms are simply furnished, with one or two double beds, two twins, or one king bed (king rooms are more expensive). Most rooms are midsize, but bathrooms are small. I prefer the downstairs rooms, which have high ceilings. Lighting is poor.

Corregidora 465, 58000 Morelia, Mich. ⓒ **443/313-3309** or 312-0121. 27 units. $40–$50 (£22–£28) double. No credit cards. Limited street parking. *In room:* TV.

WHERE TO DINE

Michoacán is known for a dish of slow-cooked pork called *carnitas*. To try it, you have to go to a *carnitas* establishment—restaurants don't offer it. Who serves the best *carnitas* is an never-ending discussion in Morelia. Many locals like **Los Tabachines,** in Colonia Ventura Puente. The address is Laguna de la Magdalena 430, but the taxi driver will know where it is. You can eat the *carnitas* there or buy it to go. In my opinion, nothing compares to the *carnitas* from the little town of Quiroga, near Pátzcuaro.

Cenaduría Lupita 𝒢 ANTOJITOS   Translated literally, *antojitos* means "little cravings." This is the traditional supper food of most Mexicans, but they usually eat it at home or in greasy-spoon joints whose cleanliness is doubtful. A good-looking, comfortable restaurant that specializes in *antojitos* is a rarity; rarer still is one that does such a good job. Take your pick of *tacos dorados,* tostadas, tamales, *huchepos* (like tamales, but made with fresh corn), and *pozole* prepared Michoacán style. The restaurant is a half-block off Avenida Lázaro Cárdenas; take a cab.

Sánchez de Tagle 1004. *(C)* **443/312-1340.** *Antojitos* $3–$6 (£1.65–£3.30). MC, V. Wed–Mon 7–11pm; Sun 7–10pm.

El Anzuelo &&& SEAFOOD/STEAKS   This simple outdoor restaurant in the modern part of town serves the best seafood in Morelia. It makes the perfect Mexican seafood cocktail and wonderful ceviche. After either of those, you might order *huachinango adobado* (red snapper in a chile-based marinade) or coconut shrimp. If you don't feel like fish, there's filet mignon. The owners are meticulous about food preparation. El Anzuelo is open only in the afternoon. On Sunday, it offers paella, and the restaurant gets very crowded. Take a taxi and keep the address handy.

Av. Camelinas 3180. *(C)* **443/314-8339** or 324-3237. Reservations recommended on weekends. Main courses $9–$17 (£4.95–£9.35). AE, MC, V. Daily noon–6pm.

La Casa del Portal REGIONAL/INTERNATIONAL   This upstairs restaurant is in a beautiful stone mansion facing the Plaza de Armas (entrance is on the side street). The floors, walls, and ceilings of the old house have remained virtually intact, including the antique wallpaper and other details. There are several dining rooms, and on occasion the rooftop terrace is open for dining. Most of the furniture comes from the owner's workshop—his colorful designs make use of many furniture-making traditions of the region. The restaurant doubles as a sort of factory outlet, and all the furniture is for sale. What's for dinner? The menu includes several regional standards, such as *enchiladas del portal* (Michoacán-style enchiladas) and *arrachera valladolid,* a skirt steak accompanied by a few Mexican sides.

Guillermo Prieto 30 (cater-cornered from Virrey de Mendoza; entrance is on the side street). *(C)* **443/313-4899.** Main courses $8–$17 (£4.40–£9.35). AE, MC, V. Daily 8:30am–10pm.

Las Trojes STEAKS/REGIONAL   A *troje* is the traditional dwelling of the highland Purépecha Indians, constructed of rough-cut wood planks. This restaurant is made of seven connected *trojes,* with windows added for light. For starters, try *sopa tarasca* (bean soup). Main courses include *cecina* (beef or pork sliced thin, spiced, and dried), a good steak *a la tampiqueña* (marinated and grilled), rib eye, *chistorra* (Spanish-style sausage), and chicken stuffed with cheese en brochette. Take a cab.

Juan Sebastián Bach 51, Col. La Loma. *(C)* **443/314-7344.** Main courses $9–$16 (£4.95–£8.80). AE, MC, V. Mon–Sat 1pm–midnight; Sun 1–6pm.

Los Mirasoles & REGIONAL   Los Mirasoles serves up good regional cooking including fish tacos, *corundas* (a kind of tamal in the form of a triangle without a filling and served in a chile sauce with Mexican cream), and *enchiladas placeras* (the traditional enchilada in Michoacán, cooked in a chile ancho sauce and topped with crumbled fresh cheese, with sautéed onions and potatoes on the side). A large selection of beer and wine is on offer to accompany your meal. The dining rooms are lovely, especially at night. Los Mirasoles is a few blocks west of the main square.

Av. Madero Poniente 549. *(C)* **443/317-5775.** Reservations recommended on weekends. Main courses $5–$10 (£2.65–£5.50); seafood/steaks $13–$18 (£7.15–£9.90). AE, MC, V. Daily 1–11pm. From cathedral, walk 4 blocks west on Madero.

Moments   Michoacán's Monarch Migration

A visit to the winter nesting grounds of the monarch butterfly, high in the mountains of northeast Michoacán, is a stirring experience. It might be the highlight of your trip. The season lasts from mid- to late November to March. Tour operators in Morelia offer a day trip to see the butterflies for $50 to $60 (£28–£33) per person. The tour takes 10 to 12 hours and involves hiking up a mountain at a high altitude. You shouldn't consider doing this if you're not in decent physical condition.

The best time to see the butterflies is on a sunny day, when they flutter through the air in a blizzard of orange and black. At the center of the group, the branches of the tall fir trees bow under their burden of butterflies, whose wings undulate softly as the wind blows through the forest; it's quite a spectacle.

From Morelia, you'll have no difficulty finding a tour; most hotels and all travel agencies can put you in contact with one. I particularly recommend **Luis Miguel López Alanís** (© **443/340-4632**). He speaks English, is federally licensed, and belongs to a small cooperative of guides called **Mex Mich Guías** (www.mmg.com.mx). The easiest way to contact him is through the website. Most tours provide transportation, guide, soft drinks, and usually lunch. A good guide is important, if only to answer all the questions that these butterflies and their strange migration provoke.

San Miguelito ★★ Finds MEXICAN   Perhaps the most popular restaurant in town, San Miguelito has a winning combination of an inventive menu, attentive service, and a setting loaded with icons of Mexican culture. One part of the main dining room is the Rincón de las Solteronas (the bachelorette corner), where many images of Saint Anthony hang upside down—the custom in Mexico when a girl is petitioning him for a boyfriend or husband. Guests are welcome to make a petition; the staff will be happy to show you how. I especially enjoy the appetizers here: tacos, *chicharrón de queso* (fried crispy cheese), and other finger foods. The sopa tarasca is among the best I've had in restaurants. There are several steak dishes, including one in tequila, *guajillo* chile, and orange sauce. For dessert there's a delicious version of cherries jubilee. Take a cab.

Av. Camelinas (at Ventura Puente). © 443/324-2300. Reservations recommended. Main courses $12–$19 (£6.60–£10). AE, MC, V. Mon–Wed 2–11pm; Thurs–Sat 2pm–midnight; Sun 2–5pm.

MORELIA AFTER DARK

For nighttime entertainment, be sure to check the calendar of events at the **Instituto Michoacano de Cultura** (see "A Stroll Through the Colonial Center," earlier in this chapter). In addition, you can sit at one of the cafes under the stone arches across from the Plaza de Armas to do some people-watching (a very Moreliano thing to do). Aside from the dance clubs that are mostly on the fashionable east side, there are few nightlife options. The following are my favorites. For dancing, go to **La Casa de la Salsa** (© **443/313-9362**), a large dance hall facing Plaza Morelos at the end of the

A few butterfly sanctuaries are open to the public. (The monarchs congregate at nine sites, but five are closed to visitors.) The sites with the best access are **El Rosario** (admission $4/£2.20; daily 10am–5 or 6pm) and the newer **Chincua** (same admission and hours as El Rosario). It is less of a drive, but usually more of a walk to the nucleus of the butterfly group—but not always. Throughout the season, the groups shift, moving up and down the mountains and making for a longer or shorter climb. A good guide will be aware of which is the shorter walk.

If you're driving, take the *autopista* to Mexico City, exit at Maravatío, and go right. Keep right after going through Maravatío and take the narrow two-lane road toward Angangueo. When you get to a T-junction, go right, toward San Felipe. Enter the town of Ocampo and look for a small sign pointing left to get to Rosario, where you will find a parking lot near the trail head. If you want to make this a leisurely trip, spend the night in the nearby town of Angangueo at **Hotel Don Bruno** (℗ **715/156-0026; $55/£30** double). It's a pretty hotel but a little overpriced, so you should ask to see the room before you accept it.

Travel agencies from **San Miguel de Allende** also book monarch tours, which take 1 or 2 days. See chapter 6 for details.

Calzada Fray Antonio de San Miguel. It's open Tuesday through Saturday from 9pm to 3am. It books live music on Friday and Saturday ($4/£2.20 cover). You can call ahead to reserve a table; the band plays a lot of salsa, merengue, and mambo.

If you want to hear live Latin American folk music, have a drink, and eat something, try **Peña Colibrí** (℗ **443/312-2261**), Galeana 36, behind the Virrey de Mendoza. It opens daily at 8pm and closes around midnight. There is another *peña* (bar where folk music is played) close by at Allende 3, **Bohemia V** (no phone). The food isn't good, but the music is great.

2 Pátzcuaro ⟨★⟨★⟨★

370km (229 miles) NW of Mexico City; 285km (177 miles) SE of Guadalajara; 69km (43 miles) SW of Morelia

Pátzcuaro is perhaps the loveliest town in Mexico. Crooked cobblestone streets, smooth stucco walls painted white with dark red borders, blackened tile roofs that join to form ramshackle rooflines—it is a town meant to be photographed and painted. During the rainy season, when low clouds roll in and curl through the tall trees, and water drips from the low-slung overhangs, a sweet melancholy descends upon the town.

Pátzcuaro is in the heart of the Purépecha homeland. Beside it is Lake Pátzcuaro (one of the world's highest at 2,200m/7,216 ft.), whose shores border dozens of Indian villages. In these villages and in town, visitors frequently hear the soft sounds of the Purépechan language in the background as they take in the sights. Although distinct

Pátzcuaro

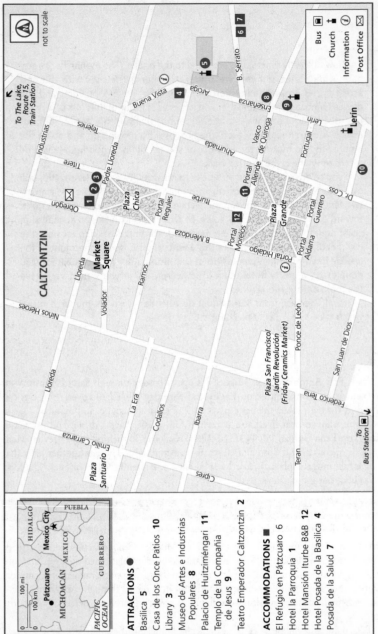

not to scale

To The Lake, Route 15, Train Station

Bus
Church
Information
Post Office

CALTZONTZIN

Market Square

Plaza Chica

Plaza Grande

Plaza San Francisco/ Jardín Revolución (Friday Ceramics Market)

To Bus Station

Industrias
Tejeres
Títere
Padre Lloreda
Obregón
Lloreda
Volador
Ramos
Niños Héroes
Lloreda
La Era
Codallos
Ibarra
Emilio Carranza
Cípres
Plaza Santuario
Buena Vista
Arciga
Enseñanza
B. Serrato
Ahumada
Vasco de Quiroga
Iturbe
Portal Regules
B. Mendoza
Portal Morelos
Portal Hidalgo
Portal Aldama
Portal Guerrero
Portal Allende
Lerín
Portugal
Dr. Coss
Ponce de León
San Juan de Dios
Federico Tena
Teran

PUEBLA
HIDALGO
Mexico City
MICHOACÁN
MEXICO
GUERRERO
PACIFIC OCEAN
Pátzcuaro
100 mi
100 km

ATTRACTIONS ●

Basílica **5**
Casa de los Once Patios **10**
Library **3**
Museo de Artes e Industrias Populares **8**
Palacio de Huitziméngari **11**
Templo de la Compañía de Jesús **9**
Teatro Emperador Caltzontzin **2**

ACCOMMODATIONS ■

El Refugio en Pátzcuaro **6**
Hotel la Parroquia **1**
Hotel Mansión Iturbe B&B **12**
Hotel Posada de la Basílica **4**
Posada de la Salud **7**

250

regional costumes are seldom seen today, Indian women still braid their hair with ribbons and wear the blue *rebozos* (long woolen wraps).

ESSENTIALS
GETTING THERE & DEPARTING

BY CAR   See "Getting There & Departing" under "Morelia," earlier in this chapter, for information from Mexico City, Guadalajara, and San Miguel de Allende. From Morelia there are two routes to Pátzcuaro; the faster is the new four-lane **Highway 120,** which passes near Tiripetío and Tupátaro/Cuanajo (see "Side Trips from Pátzcuaro," later in this chapter). The longer route, **Highway 15,** takes a little more than an hour and passes near the pottery-making village of Capula and then through Quiroga, where you follow signs to Pátzcuaro (see "Side Trips from Pátzcuaro," later in this chapter).

BY BUS   The bus station is on the outskirts of Pátzcuaro, 5 minutes away by taxi ($2/£1.10). If you're going anywhere outside of Michoacán, it's best to go to Morelia first. If you're going straight to Mexico City, the Pegaso bus company offers nonstop service. Buses between Morelia and Pátzcuaro run every 10 minutes. To visit any of the lakeside villages or nearby towns, public transportation is an option, but taxis are not that expensive. From the Pátzcuaro bus station, there are buses to Tócuaro and Erongarícuaro every 20 minutes; to Tupátaro and Cuanajo every hour; to Tzintzuntzan and Quiroga every 40 minutes; and to Santa Clara del Cobre every hour. For Ihuatzio, you can pick up a minivan or a bus from the Plaza Chica.

ORIENTATION

VISITOR INFORMATION   The **Tourism Office,** Cuesta Buenavista 7 (© **434/342-1214**), near the basilica, is open Monday through Saturday from 9am to 3pm and 4 to 7pm, and Sunday from 9am to 2pm. Although you might not find someone who speaks English, the staff can give you maps and point you in the right direction. There's also an office on the west side of the Plaza Grande (no phone). It keeps the same hours as the main office.

CITY LAYOUT   In a way, Pátzcuaro has two town centers, both plazas a block apart. **Plaza Grande,** also called Plaza Principal or Plaza Don Vasco de Quiroga, is picturesque and tranquil, with a fountain and a statue of Vasco de Quiroga. Hotels, shops, and restaurants in colonial-era buildings flank this plaza. **Plaza Chica,** also known as Plaza Gertrudis Bocanegra, flows into the market, and around it swirls the commercial life of Pátzcuaro. Plaza Chica is north of Plaza Grande.

GETTING AROUND   With the exception of Lake Pátzcuaro, the lookout, the bus station, and hotels on Lázaro Cárdenas, everything is within walking distance. Taxis are cheap. The lake is about a kilometer (less than a mile) from town; buses make the run every 15 minutes from both the Plaza Grande and the Plaza Chica, going all the way to the *embarcadero* or *muelle* (pier).

FAST FACTS: Pátzcuaro

Area Code   The telephone area code is **434.**

Climate   The climate is delightful most of the year, but occasional blustery days bring swirls of chilled air from across the lake, causing everyone to retreat indoors. October through April, it's cold enough for a heavy sweater, especially in the morning and evening. Few hotels have fireplaces or any source of heat in the rooms.

Elevation Pátzcuaro sits at an altitude of 2,200m (7,216 ft.).

Emergency Dial © **434/349-0209** for emergency assistance.

Hospital The **Hospital Civil Dr. Gabriel García** is at Calle Romero 18 (© **434/ 342-0285**).

Population Pátzcuaro has 70,000 residents.

Post Office The *correo,* located a half-block north of Plaza Chica, on the right side of the street, is open Monday through Friday from 10am to 2pm and 4 to 8pm.

SPECIAL EVENTS

The island of **Janitzio** has achieved international celebrity for the candlelight vigil that local residents hold at the cemetery during the nights of November 1 and 2, the Days of the Dead. **Tzintzuntzan,** a village about 15km (9⅓ miles) away, also hosts popular festivities, including folkloric dances in the main plaza and in the nearby *yácatas* (pre-Hispanic ruins), concerts in the church, and decorations in the cemetery. If you want to avoid the crowds, skip Janitzio and Tzintzuntzan and go to one of the smaller **lakeside villages or other islands** on the lake that also have extraordinary rituals. The tourism office (see "Visitor Information," above) has a schedule of events for the entire area and publishes an explanatory booklet, *Días de los Muertos.*

During the week surrounding **Days of the Dead,** artisans and vendors from all over Michoacán fill the Plaza Grande in Pátzcuaro with regional crafts. **Easter week,** beginning the Friday before Palm Sunday, is special, too. Most activity centers on the basilica. There are processions involving the surrounding villages almost nightly, and in Tzintzuntzan, there's a reenactment of the betrayal of Christ and a ceremonial washing of the feet.

EXPLORING PATZCUARO: A STROLL AROUND TOWN

The **Plaza Grande** is in the middle of town, surrounded by colonial buildings. A **stone fountain** in the center of the plaza holds a large figure of the beloved Vasco de Quiroga, "Tata Vasco," depicted in a benevolent posture. On the north side of the plaza is the **Palacio de Huitziméngari,** built by the Spaniards for the Tarascan emperor. Local Indian artisans now occupy the slowly deteriorating building.

One long block north is the **Plaza Chica,** crisscrossed by walkways and adorned with the statue of Gertrudis Bocanegra, a heroine of Mexican independence. This is the commercial center of town. On the west side of the plaza are **market** stalls selling pottery, copper, *rebozos, serapes* (a small woolen blanket that is sometimes carried over the shoulder), and food. On some days, the stalls extend a couple of blocks up the street. What was once San Agustín church is on the north side of the plaza. The cloister was remodeled in the 20th century and converted into the **Teatro Emperador Caltzontzin,** the municipal theater. The old church is now the public library; inside, all the way to the back, you'll find an early work of Juan O'Gorman—a large mural stretching the width and height of the nave.

Don Vasco built the **basilica,** on a hill just east of the Plaza Chica, although he died before it was inaugurated in 1554. It was designated a basilica by papal decree in 1907.

Tips **Festival Hotel Crunch**

Make hotel reservations months in advance for Holy Week or Days of the Dead. Most hotels require a 3-night minimum stay during these events. There are some other, less popular festivals in Pátzcuaro and surrounding towns; check with the tourist office to see if any will occur during your visit.

Now reconstructed, it has survived many catastrophes, human and natural—from earthquakes to the civil war of the mid-19th century. Be sure to visit the main altar to see the **Virgen de la Salud.** She is a sacred figure to the Indians of this region, who come from the villages to pay homage to her and petition her healing power on the eighth day of each month.

Two blocks south of the basilica is the **Museo de Artes Industrias Populares** ★★ (© 434/342-1029). It occupies yet another beautiful colonial building (1540), originally Don Vasco's College of San Nicolás. The rooms, filled with fine examples of regional popular art such as crafts and costumes, open to a central courtyard. The museum guides are well informed about the various crafts. The museum is open Tuesday through Saturday from 9am to 7pm, Sunday from 9am to 12:30pm. Admission is $3.50 (£1.95). Behind the museum are some recent excavations of Purépechan ruins.

Of the many old churches in Pátzcuaro, one of the most interesting is the **Templo de la Compañía de Jesús,** just south of the museum. This church was Don Vasco's cathedral before the basilica; afterward, it was given to the Jesuits. The buildings across the street from the church were once part of the complex, containing the hospital, soup kitchen, and living quarters for religious scholars.

The **Casa de los Once Patios (House of Eleven Patios)** ★, between José María Cos and Enseñanza, is another achievement of the colonial period. Formerly a convent belonging to the Catherine nuns, today it houses the **Casa de las Artesanías de Michoacán,** with every type of local artistry for sale (see "Shopping," below).

SHOPPING

Pátzcuaro is one of Mexico's best shopping towns: It has terrific textiles, copper, woodcarvings, lacquerwork, and straw weavings made in the region. Most shops are on the **Plaza Grande** and the streets leading from it to the **Plaza Chica,** the place of choice for copper vendors. There are also a couple of shops on the street facing the basilica. If you're interested in investigating a particular craft, you can find out which village or villages specialize in it, and if the villages have shops or a market. Tzintzuntzan, Ihuatzio, Cuanajo, Tupátaro, and Santa Clara del Cobre all have shops (see "Side Trips from Pátzcuaro," below).

Casa de las Artesanías de Michoacán/Casa de los Once Patios   This is the best one-stop shopping in the village. Small shops sell textile arts, pottery and ceramic dishes, lacquerwork, paintings, woodcarvings, jewelry, copper work, and musical instruments (including the famous Paracho guitars). Much of the merchandise was produced in the region. Most shops are open daily from 9am to 2pm and 4 to 6pm. Calle Madrigal de las Altas Torres, between Dr. Coss and Lerín. No phone.

Diseño Artesano   Owner Esperanza Sepúlveda designs one-of-a-kind clothing using locally made fabrics. Her shop, on the west side of the Plaza Grande, is open daily from 10am to 8pm. Dr. Coss 1. No phone.

Friday Pottery Market *Finds* Early each Friday morning this plaza, 1 block west of the Plaza Grande, fills with vendors of various styles of regionally made pottery, most of it not for sale in Pátzcuaro on other days. This is a market for locals that few tourists seem to hear about. Prices are *cheap.* Plaza San Francisco, Ponce de León at Federico Teña. No phone.

Galería del Arcángel Across from the Museo Regional, this store ("the Archangel's Gallery") offers a fine collection of quality regional pottery and hand-carved furniture, plus some of the best crafts from other parts of Mexico. It's open daily from 9am to 7pm. Arciga 30. ✆/fax **434/342-1774.**

Galería Iturbe Most of the artwork here is by local painters, mask makers, and other artists. You might also find a typical Day of the Dead altar. There's a small selection of books on Mexican art and culture. Enter through the Hotel Iturbe (go all the way to the back) or from Calle Iturbe, off the Plaza Grande. It's open daily from 10am to 8pm. Portal Morelos 59. ✆ **434/342-0368.**

Mantas Típicas *Value* A factory outlet for the company's textile mill, this is one of several textile outlets on the Plaza Grande. Colorful foot-loomed tablecloths, napkins, bedspreads, and bolts of fabric cover the shelves. It's open daily from 9am to 7pm. Dr. Coss 5. ✆ **434/342-1324.**

Market Plaza The House of Eleven Patios (see above) should be your first stop and this your second. The entire plaza fronting the food market holds covered stalls selling crafts, clothing, rugs, *rebozos,* and more. Locally knitted sweaters are a good buy. Streets surrounding the plaza churn with exuberant sellers of fresh vegetables and caged birds. West of Plaza Chica. No phone.

Palacio Huitziméngari On the north side of the Plaza Grande, in a colonial house, are a few shops run by folk from neighboring towns. Most of the merchandise is pottery and woodcarvings. Open daily from 8am to 10pm. Plaza Grande. No phone.

WHERE TO STAY

In addition to the hotels listed below, you can also contact **Casa Santiago** (✆ **434/ 344-0880;** tzipijo@ml.com.mx), which rents rooms in Ihuatzio, one of the lakeside villages in the area.

VERY EXPENSIVE

Hacienda Mariposas ✦✦✦ *Kids* This hotel is a retreat into the Mexican countryside. Most of the rooms are in separate bungalows. The rooms are big and the bathrooms are spacious and well equipped. Master suites come with Jacuzzi tubs. Emphasis is on personal attention and ecological practices. The hotel has plenty of educational activities for kids including collecting eggs and other farm activities, hiking, and pony riding. The entire hotel is nonsmoking. Breakfasts feature healthy versions of regional specialties, and there is a separate dining area with a low-fat menu. This is the first hotel in Mexico to be certified as ecological by the Mexican government.

Carretera Pátzcuaro–Santa Clara Km 3, 61600 Pátzcuaro, Mich. ✆ 434/342-4728. www.haciendamariposas.com. 17 units. $175 (£96) junior suite; $230 (£127) master suite; $290 (£160) 2-bedroom master suite. Rates include full breakfast, horseback rides, spa, and afternoon *antojitos.* AE, MC, V. Free secure parking. **Amenities:** Restaurant; bar; spa; Jacuzzi; steam room; children's activities; tours; business center; room service; in-room massage; babysitting; laundry service; nonsmoking rooms. *In room:* CD player and music library, minibar w/organic snacks, hair dryer, safe.

Tips **If Pátzcuaro's Packed Solid . . .**

During Easter week and Days of the Dead, Pátzcuaro's hotels fill up; visitors should be aware of three inexpensive hotels in the nearby town of Santa Clara. The **Hotel Oasis,** Portal Allende 144 ((C) **434/343-0040**), is the better of the two on the town's main plaza; **Hotel Real del Cobre,** Portal Hidalgo 19 ((C) **434/343-0205**), has a restaurant. The third hotel, **Camino Real** ((C) **434/343-0281**), is a few blocks away and is comparable to the Oasis.

EXPENSIVE

Hotel Mansión Iturbe Bed and Breakfast ☆☆   Located on the north side of the Plaza Grande, this 17th-century mansion has kept more of its original character than any of the other colonial buildings–turned–hotels. The owners have worked hard to keep the old local touches, such as raised thresholds. Rooms are on the second floor and have the original plank flooring, along with heavy, dark, Spanish-style wooden furniture and fresh-cut flowers. Exterior rooms have double-glazed windows to keep the noise down. Most bathrooms are large. All rooms are nonsmoking. Purified ice, instant coffee, and hot water are available. The free cocktail hour every night allows guests to make acquaintances and share experiences. Guests have the use of a solarium, a library, and a study.

Portal Morelos 59, 61600 Pátzcuaro, Mich. (C) **434/342-0368** or -3628. Fax (for reservations only) 443/313-4593. www.mexonline.com/iturbe.htm. 14 units. $90–$130 (£50–£72) double. Rates include full breakfast. Fourth night free (some restrictions apply). Ask about special promotions. AE, MC, V. Free secure parking. **Amenities:** 2 restaurants; 2 bars; complimentary bikes; tour desk; same-day laundry service. *In room:* TV, hair dryer (on request).

Hotel Posada la Basílica ☆   This colonial-style hotel in a great location across from the basilica has a lovely patio. The rooms, which border the patio on three sides, have tile floors and fireplaces. Seven have small balconies overlooking the street. The rooms were remodeled in the past year and new plumbing was installed. The restaurant has a fabulous view of the mountains, the tile rooftops, and the lake. Rooms come with one or two double beds.

Arciga 6 (at La Paz), 61600 Pátzcuaro, Mich. (C) **434/342-1108.** Fax 434/342-0659. www.posadalabasilica.com. 12 units. $135 (£74) double; $150–$180 (£83–£99) suites. AE, MC, V. Free secure parking. **Amenities:** Restaurant; bar; tour info; room service; babysitting; laundry service; dry cleaning. *In room:* TV, hair dryer.

MODERATE

El Refugio en Pátzcuaro ☆ *Value*   This house captures so well the feel of Pátzcuaro—its local flavor, its serenity. Qualities that the town is slowly losing, perhaps, but not here. The courtyard is perfectly what a courtyard of a provincial house should be. The rooms, with their clay tile floors and beamed ceilings, their artwork and their furniture, suggest the owner's affection for those days when life was simple and gracious. There is comfort, too. The rooms are spacious and well furnished. Each comes with a heater. The beds come with mattress heaters. The bathrooms are medium size and attractively finished in tile. Deborah, a young woman from Minnesota, manages the property.

Serrato 11, 61600 Pátzcuaro, Mich. (C)/fax **434/342-5237.** www.elrefugioenpatzcuaro.com.mx. 6 units. $65–$100 (£36–£55) double. 2-night minimum stay. No walk-ins. Rates include full breakfast. No credit cards. Free limited covered parking. **Amenities:** Tours, in-room massage, babysitting, laundry service, nonsmoking rooms. *In room:* TV, Wi-Fi in some rooms, hair dryer.

La Parroquia   This hotel has three stories of rooms (no elevator) around an open courtyard. In character with the region, it has dark-wood columns and beams and a tile roof, but it's not an old building. Wrought-iron banisters border wide arcades that hold attractive sitting areas. The comfortable rooms have pine furniture, carpets, and small, tiled bathrooms. All have windows that open onto the courtyard. The hotel faces the north side of the Plaza Chica.

Plaza Bocanegra 24, 61600 Pátzcuaro, Mich. ⓒ **434/342-2515** or ⓒ/fax 434/342-2516. 60 units. $90 (£50) double. MC, V. Free parking. **Amenities:** Restaurant; bar; room service; babysitting; laundry service. *In room:* TV.

INEXPENSIVE

Posada de la Salud *(value)*   This *posada* (inn) offers two floors of quiet, basic rooms built around an attractive courtyard. Rooms are clean and have simple wooden furniture. Two units have fireplaces. Rooms have one double bed, two double beds, two twins, or one twin and one double. The location is great—on the southeast side of the basilica, a long half-block up on the right.

Serrato 9, 61600 Pátzcuaro, Mich. ⓒ **434/342-0058.** www.posadadelasalud.com. 12 units. $30–$35 (£17–£19) double. No credit cards. Limited street parking. *In room:* No phone.

WHERE TO DINE

Restaurants open late and close early; don't plan on hot coffee if you're up early, but do plan ahead for late-evening hunger pangs. For inexpensive eats, try the **tamal and atole vendors** in front of the basilica and by the market. Housewives also sell steamy cups of *atole,* hot *corundas* (triangular tamales with no filling), and tamales.

In the evenings at the Plaza Chica, you can get a meal of chicken with simple enchiladas and heaps of fried potatoes and carrots. Look for a stand called **Don Emilio.** You can also get *buñuelos,* giant corn flakes that drip with cane syrup.

Cha Cha Cha ✦ MEXICAN/INTERNATIONAL   This is just the place to have a leisurely meal. You want to linger here in the relaxing and casual feel of the place. The service is friendly, and the food is good. The menu offers a variety of dishes, some traditional, some original. I tried the cream soup with chile poblano, the cabbage and sausage tostadas, and the pork loin with pecan stuffing in a pineapple and mango sauce. They were all worth recommending.

Buenavista 7. ⓒ **434/342-1627.** Reservations accepted. Main courses $8–$15 (£4.40–8.25). MC, V. Thurs–Tues 8:30am–9:30pm.

El Patio MEXICAN/REGIONAL   High ceilings, good lighting, and paintings of local scenes make this a pleasant place to dine. Specialties include *sopa tarasca* (bean soup to which you add cheese, fried tortilla strips, and toasted chiles), *trucha salmonada al vino blanco* (farm-raised trout—fed on special foods that turn the flesh salmon-colored—cooked in white-wine sauce). Standard Mexican dishes include enchiladas and more. El Patio is on the south side of Plaza Grande.

Plaza Grande 19. ⓒ **434/342-0484.** Breakfast $4–$6 (£2.20–£3.30); main courses $7–$12 (£3.85–£6.60). MC, V. Daily 8am–10pm.

El Primer Piso MEXICAN/INTERNATIONAL   El Primer Piso, which means "the first floor" (second floor in American usage), offers a bit of everything but focuses mostly on dishes of its own creation: *pechuga enogada* (chicken breast in walnut cream sauce) with cashews, for instance, and *pescado en salsa negra* (fish in a three-chile vinaigrette). These are good, as are the appetizers. The soups are more conventional—Tarascan, French onion, and Provençal. The restaurant is on the same block as El Patio.

Vasco de Quiroga 29. © **434/342-0122**. Main courses $8–$13 (£4.40–£7.15). AE, MC, V. Mon and Wed–Sat 1–10pm; Sun 1–8pm.

Restaurant Doña Paca ℛ MICHOACAN   This is one of the best places to try regional Michoacán cuisine. It serves fish in several ways, including in a cilantro sauce, *al mojo de ajo* (this is the most popular way of eating fish in Mexico—it's griddled with tiny toasted bits of garlic), or cooked in herbs. The restaurant also serves a fixed-price menu, which includes a glass of wine. For dessert, try a *buñuelo* topped with ice cream. The dining room is in the colonial Hotel Mansión Iturbe and is comfortable and welcoming. In the afternoon you can order at the tables outside under the archway.

Hotel Mansión Iturbe, Portal Morelos 59. © **434/342-3628**. Breakfast $6–$10 (£3.30–£5.50); main courses $9–$14 (£4.95–£7.70). AE, MC, V. Daily 8:30–11:30am, 2–5pm, and 6–9pm. Closed Sun night during low season.

PATZCUARO AFTER DARK

Generally speaking, Pátzcuaro closes down before 10pm, so bring a good book or plan to rest up. Late-night music lovers can go to **Viejo Gaucho** to hear Latin American folk music. The small restaurant serves salads and hamburgers. It's in the Hotel Mansión Iturbe (© **434/342-3627**; p. 255); enter from Calle Iturbe. It's open Wednesday through Saturday from 6pm to midnight. Music starts between 8:30 and 9pm. After the music starts, there's a $2.50 (£1.40) cover charge.

SIDE TRIPS FROM PATZCUARO

EL ESTRIBO: A SCENIC OVERLOOK   For a good view of the town and the lake, head for the lookout at El Estribo, on the hill 3km (2 miles) west of town. Driving from the main square on Calle Ponce de León and following the signs takes 10 to 15 minutes on an unpaved road. Walking up the steep hill will take about 45 minutes. Once you reach the gazebo, you can climb more than 400 steps to the summit of the hill. The gazebo area is great for a picnic; there are barbecue pits and sometimes a couple selling soft drinks and beer.

JANITZIO   No visit to Pátzcuaro would be complete without a trip on the lake to one or more of the islands. A hilltop statue of José María Morelos dominates the island of **Janitzio** ℛℛ. The village church is famous for the annual **Day of the Dead** ceremony, held at midnight on November 1. Villagers climb to the churchyard carrying lit candles in memory of their dead relatives, then spend the night in graveside vigil. The long day begins October 30 and lasts through November 2.

The cheapest way to get to Janitzio is by *colectivo* launch, which makes the trip when enough people have gathered to go, about every 20 to 30 minutes from about 7:30am to 6pm. It's best to go during the week when fewer travelers are around. Round-trip fare is $3.50 (£19); children younger than 5 ride free. A private boat costs around $55 (£30) for a trip to Janitzio for 1 hour and then a cruise by the other three islands. Sometimes the cooperative has launches available that are significantly cheaper. The **ticket office** on the pier, or *embarcadero* (© **434/342-0681**), is open daily from 8am to 6pm. The pier is less than a kilometer (about a half-mile) from the main square, and the 5-minute taxi ride costs $3 (£1.65).

At the ticket office, a map of the lake posted on the wall details boat trips to various islands and lakeshore towns. Launches will take you wherever you want to go. Up to 20 people can split the cost.

TZINTZUNTZAN: RUINS & HANDICRAFTS   Tzintzuntzan (tzeen-*tzoon*-tzahn) is an ancient village 15km (9⅓ miles) from Pátzcuaro on the road to Quiroga (see "By

Bus" under "Getting There & Departing," earlier in this chapter). In earlier centuries, Tzintzuntzan was the capital of the Purépechan kingdom (a confederation of more than 100 towns and villages). On a hill on the right before you enter town, pyramids, called *yácatas,* remind visitors of the town's past. There is also an interesting church and monastery dating from the time of Don Vasco. Today, the village is known for its straw handicrafts—mobiles, baskets, and figures (skeletons, airplanes, reindeer, turkeys, and the like)—as well as pottery and woven goods. Several open-air **wood-carving workshops,** full of life-size wooden saints and other figures, are across from the basket market.

LAKESIDE VILLAGES: A PORTRAIT OF INDIAN LIFE   For a close-up view of the Purépecha, contact Kevin Quigley or Arminda Flores, who live in Ihuatzio (see below), or **Francisco Castilleja** (© **434/344-0167**), an English-speaking Mexican who lives in Erongarícuaro. Mr. Castilleja conducts tours of the villages that explain their daily life, customs, and beliefs. He passes through the Restaurant Doña Paca in the Hotel Iturbe at 10am every day except Sunday and takes people to the villages of **Erongarícuaro, Uricho,** and **Tócuaro** to visit households, small workshops, and a well-known mask maker. The cost depends on the size of the group; tours usually run around $30 to $40 (£17–£22) per person.

SANTA CLARA DEL COBRE: COPPER SMITHERY   About 30 minutes away by car (a $10/£5.50 taxi ride), **Santa Clara del Cobre** 𝔊 is a good side trip if you want to purchase copper items or see how copper is worked. Although the copper mines of pre-Conquest times have disappeared, local artisans still make copper vessels using the age-old method of hammering pieces out by hand. They don't work on Sunday and are strict observers of "San Lunes"—taking Monday off to recover from the weekend. On other days, the sound of hammering fills the air. If you want to see someone practicing the craft, go to one of the larger stores and ask if you can visit the *taller* (studio). You can also visit the **Museo del Cobre (Copper Museum),** a half-block from the main plaza at Morelos and Pino Suárez. The museum section of the building displays copper pieces that date to pre-Columbian times. A sales showroom to the left of the entrance features the work of local craftsmen. Admission is 50¢ (30p); the museum is open Tuesday through Sunday from 10:30am to 3pm and 5 to 7pm.

The **National Copper Fair** is held here each August. It coincides with the **Festival de Nuestra Señora de Santa Clara de Asis** (second week in Aug), with folk dancing and parades. For information, call the tourism office in Morelia.

Buses for Santa Clara leave every few minutes from the Pátzcuaro bus station. If you want to spend the night in town, see "If Pátzcuaro's Packed Solid . . ." on p. 255.

TUPATARO & CUANAJO: A HISTORIC CHURCH & HAND-CARVED FUR-NITURE   Just off Highway 120 between Morelia and Pátzcuaro is the village of **Tupátaro** (pop. 600), which in Tarascan means "place of reeds."

The village church is the **Templo del Señor Santiago Tupátaro.** It was built in 1775. Indian artists painted the entire wood-plank ceiling with scenes of the life and death of Christ and the Virgin Mary. The gilt *retablo* (altarpiece) is adorned with Solomonic columns and paintings. Santiago (St. James) is in the center of the *retablo,* and the face of the Eternal Father is above him. The symbol of the dove crowns the *retablo.* The church and its ceiling were restored in 1994 by the National Institute of Anthropology and History, which oversees its maintenance. There's no admission charge, and photography is not permitted. The church is open daily from 8am to 5pm. Days of religious significance include the Tuesday of Carnaval week and July 25, which honors Santiago. From Tupátaro you can get back on Highway 120 or take a small road that leads to Cuanajo 8km (5 miles) away. From Cuanajo a small road leads directly to Pátzcuaro. It's not designated yet by any number.

Cuanajo (pop. 8,000) is a village of wood carvers who make brightly painted pine furniture. On the road as you enter, and around the pleasant, tree-shaded main plaza, you'll see storefronts with **colorful furniture** inside and on the street. Parrots, plants, the sun, the moon, and faces are carved on the furniture. Furniture is also sold at a **cooperative** on the main plaza. Here you'll also find soft-spoken women who weave tapestries and thin belts on waist looms. Everything is for sale. It's open daily from 9am to 6pm. Festival days in Cuanajo include March 8 and September 8, both of which honor the patron saint Virgen María de la Natividad.

IHUATZIO: TULE FIGURES & PRE-HISPANIC ARCHITECTURE   This little lakeside village is renowned for its **weavers of tule figures**—fanciful animals such as elephants, pigs, and bulls, made from a reed that grows on the edge of the lake—and for some ruins widespread through the area. Kevin Quigley, an American from San Francisco, and Arminda Flores, a Purépechan, live just outside the village (Casa Santiago; (C) **434/344-0880;** tzipijo@ml.com.mx). They rent comfortable rooms to guests at economical rates. Both Kevin and Arminda take people around the area, explaining the local culture, the society, and the local crafts. The turnoff to Ihuatzio is a paved road a short distance from the outskirts of Pátzcuaro on the road to Tzintzuntzan.

3 Uruapan: Handicrafts & Volcanoes

61km (38 miles) W of Pátzcuaro

Uruapan has long been a commercial center for western Michoacán. It's a larger, busier town than Pátzcuaro. For tourists, the best feature is the **Parque Nacional Eduardo Ruiz,** a lovely botanical garden with flowing water everywhere you look. Uruapan is also useful as a base for several interesting side trips, the most famous of which is to the **Paricutín volcano** and the lava-covered church and village near **Angahuan.** See "Angahuan, Paricutín Volcano," below.

ESSENTIALS

The **tourist office** ((C) 452/524-7199) is at Juan Ayala 16. It's open Monday through Saturday from 9am to 2pm and 4 to 7pm.

The main plaza, **Jardín Morelos/Plaza de los Mártires,** is actually a long, narrow rectangle running east to west, with the churches and La Huatápera Museum on the north side and a few hotels on the south. Everything you need is within 1 or 2 blocks of the square, including the market, which is behind the churches.

WHERE TO STAY & DINE

The best hotel in town is the **Hotel Cupatitzio** ((C) 452/523-2022), next to the national park. It has plenty of amenities, including a good restaurant, a large pool, and a lovely garden. A room for two people costs $97 (£53; American Express, Master-Card, and Visa are accepted). Also consider two inexpensive hotels by the main plaza: The comfortable **Hotel Villa de Flores,** Emiliano Carranza 15 ((C) **452/524-2800;** MasterCard and Visa are accepted), and the slightly less desirable, slightly cheaper **Hotel Nuevo Alameda,** Av. 5 de Febrero 11 ((C) **452/523-3635;** MasterCard and Visa are accepted). Rooms go for $30 to $40 (£17–£22). Both have restaurants, and there are restaurants on and near the plaza.

EXPLORING URUAPAN & BEYOND

Uruapan's main plaza fills with artisans and craft sellers from around the state before and during **Easter week.** Vendors sell an unbelievable array of wares.

La Huatápera ⚘, attached to the church on the main square, is a good museum of regional crafts. It occupies a former hospital built in 1533 by Fray Juan de San Miguel, a Franciscan. It's open daily from 9:30am to 1:30pm and 3:30 to 6pm. Admission is free.

For the finest in foot-loomed, brilliantly colored tablecloths, napkins, and other **textiles,** take a taxi to **Telares Uruapan** ⚘⚘ (✆ **452/524-0677** or -6135), in the **Antigua Fábrica de San Pedro,** Calle Miguel Treviño s/n. Call ahead, and the English-speaking owners may be able to give you a tour of the factory.

When you enter the **Parque Nacional Eduardo Ruiz,** a botanical garden 8 blocks west of the main plaza, you'll feel as if you're deep in the Tropics. This semitropical paradise contains jungle paths, deep ravines, rushing water, and clear waterfalls. The garden is open daily from 8am to 6pm, and there is a small admission fee.

A WATERFALL OUTSIDE OF URUAPAN

Eight kilometers (5 miles) outside of town is the **Tzaráracua** waterfall. The falls are pretty but not spectacular, and sometimes they smell bad. The real reason to come here is for the walk—a descent that takes you from cool pine forest to warm subtropical vegetation in no time. The return ascent takes 40 minutes, and the trail is good, with handrails in the steeper areas. You can catch a bus from Uruapan's bus station or take a cab, which costs only $5 (£2.75). Either one will drop you off at the trail head.

ANGAHUAN, PARICUTIN VOLCANO ⚘⚘

About 34km (21 miles) from Uruapan is **Angahuan,** a village serving as the point of departure for trips to **Paricutín volcano.** The volcano was born in 1943 and grew quickly, eventually enveloping portions of a village in lava. Autotransportes Galeana buses leave every 30 minutes from Uruapan's Central Camionera for the hour-long trip. To return, pick up the bus where it dropped you off. A taxi costs $15 (£8.25).

THE ERUPTION STORY   If you don't know the tale of Paricutín's volcanic blast, stop by the plaza in Angahuan. In the afternoon of February 20, 1943, a local man was plowing his cornfield in the valley when the ground began to boil and fissures opened up emitting steam. At first he tried to plug it up; when that proved impossible, he fled. By that evening, the earth was spitting fire and smoke. Some villagers fled that night; others, days later. The volcano remained active, continually spewing, until March 6, 1952, when it ceased as suddenly as it had begun.

USING A GUIDE   Angahuan has a little tourist center that rents cabins and runs a small cafeteria (✆ **452/520-8786**). It allows a good view of the volcano and the tower of the **Church of San Juan Parangaricutiro** (try saying that quickly five times), which is half-buried in lava. You will undoubtedly be offered a guide and horses for a trip to either or both places. Although a horse is not necessary, a guide is advisable.

CLIMBING THE VOLCANO   Allow at least 8 hours from Angahuan. The round-trip is about 22km (14 miles). *Take food and water—they are not available along the way.* The hike is mostly flat, with some steeper rises toward the end. Climbing the steep crater takes about 40 minutes for those who exercise regularly. Count on more time to walk around the crater's rim on top (1.5–3km/1–2 miles) and enjoy the view.

The trip to the volcano takes 6 to 7 hours on **horseback,** including the time spent climbing the crater, which you must do on foot. On the way, you can pass by the old church tower of Parangaricutiro. The asking price for a horse is around $20 (£11), and you'll need to pay for one for a guide. A good guide will climb to the top of the crater with you and point out various interesting features, including steaming fumaroles. Acting as a volcano guide is one of the conspicuously poor Angahuan villagers' few opportunities to earn money. Just withhold payment until the ride is over, and services are delivered as promised. Plan to spend an entire day for this outing.

8

Guadalajara

by David Baird

Guadalajara is the second-largest city in Mexico (with 3.5 million inhabitants, it's a very distant second to Mexico City), but because it's the homeland of mariachi music, the *jarabe tapatío* (the Mexican hat dance), and tequila, many consider it the most Mexican of cities. Despite its size, Guadalajara isn't hard to navigate, and the people are friendly and helpful. And unlike in Mexico City, visitors can enjoy big-city pleasures without big-city hassles.

While in Guadalajara, you will undoubtedly come across the word *tapatío* (or *tapatía*). In the early days, people from the area were known to trade in threes, called *tapatíos*. Gradually, the locals came to be called Tapatíos, too, and the word now signifies Guadalajaran when referring to a thing, a person, or a manner of doing something.

1 Orientation

GETTING THERE & DEPARTING

BY PLANE   Guadalajara's international airport is a 25- to 45-minute ride from the city. Taxi tickets to Guadalajara, priced by zone, are for sale in front of the airport ($15/£8.25 to downtown area). Taxis are the only transport.

Major Airlines   See chapter 2 for a list of toll-free numbers for international airlines serving Mexico. Numbers in Guadalajara are: **AeroMar** (© 33/3615-8509), **AeroMéxico** (© 01-800/021-4010), **American** (© 01-800/904-6000), **Click** (© 01-800/1225425), **Continental** (© 01-800/900-5000), **Delta** (© 33/3630-3530), **Mexicana** (© 01-800/502-2000), and **United** (© 33/3616-9489).

Of the smaller airlines, **Aviacsa** (© 33/3123-1751) connects to Los Angeles, Las Vegas, Houston, and Chicago. **Azteca** (© 33/3630-4615) offers service to and from Mexico City, and from there to several cities in Mexico. **Allegro** (© 33/3647-7799) operates flights to and from Oakland and Las Vegas via Tijuana. **Alaska Airlines** (© 01-800/426-0333) flies to Los Angeles and Reno.

BY CAR   Guadalajara is at the hub of several four-lane toll roads (called *cuotas* or *autopistas*), which cut travel time considerably but are expensive. From Nogales on the **U.S. border,** follow Highway 15 south (21 hr.). From **Tepic,** a quicker route is toll road 15D (5 hr.; $31/£17). From **Puerto Vallarta,** go north on Highway 200 to Compostela; toll road 68D heads east to join the Tepic toll road. Total time is 5½ hours, and the tolls add up to $29 (£16). From **Barra de Navidad,** on the coast southeast of Puerto Vallarta, take Highway 80 northeast (4½ hr.). From **Manzanillo,** you might also take this road, but toll road 54D through Colima to Guadalajara (3½ hr.; $26/£14) is faster. From **Mexico City,** take toll road 15D (7 hr.; $55/£30).

BY BUS   Two bus stations serve Guadalajara. The old one, south of downtown, is for buses to Lake Chapala and other nearby areas; the new one, 10km (6¼ miles) southeast of downtown, is for longer trips.

The Old Bus Station   For destinations within 100km (62 miles) of town, including the Lake Chapala area, go to the old bus terminal, on Niños Héroes off Calzada Independencia Sur. For Lake Chapala, take **Transportes Guadalajara-Chapala,** which runs frequent buses and *combis* (minivans).

The New Bus Station   The **Central Camionera** is 15 to 30 minutes from downtown. The station has seven terminals connected by a covered walkway. Each terminal houses different bus lines, offering first- and second-class service for different destinations. You can buy bus tickets from several travel agents in Guadalajara. Ask at your hotel for the closest to you. There are several major bus lines. The best service (big seats and lots of room) is provided by **ETN.**

VISITOR INFORMATION

The **State of Jalisco Tourist Information Office** is at Calle Morelos 102 (© **33/ 3668-1600** or -1601; http://visita.jalisco.gob.mx) in the Plaza Tapatía, at Paseo Degollado and Paraje del Rincón del Diablo. It's open Monday through Friday from 9am to 8pm, and Saturday, Sunday, and festival days 10am to 2pm. You can get maps, a monthly calendar of cultural events, and good information. The city operates several tourist information booths—one in Plaza Liberación (directly behind the cathedral), another in Plaza Guadalajara (directly in front of the cathedral). These are open daily from 9am to 1pm and 3 to 7pm.

CITY LAYOUT

The **Centro Histórico (city center),** with all its plazas, churches, and museums, will obviously be of interest to the visitor. The **west side** is Guadalajara's modern, cosmopolitan district. In the northwest corner is **Zapopan,** home of Guadalajara's patron saint. On the opposite side of the city from Zapopan, in the southeast corner, are the craft centers of **Tlaquepaque** and **Tonalá.**

The main artery for traffic from downtown to the west side is **Avenida Vallarta.** It starts downtown as **Juárez.** The main arteries for returning to downtown are **México** and **Hidalgo,** both north of Vallarta. Vallarta heads due west, where it intersects another major artery, **Avenida Adolfo López Mateos,** at **Fuente Minerva** (or simply La Minerva, or Minerva Circle). Minerva Circle, a 15-minute drive from downtown, is the central point of reference for the west side. To go to Zapopan from downtown, take **Avenida Avila Camacho,** which you can pick up on Alcalde; it takes 20 minutes by car. To Tlaquepaque and Tonalá, take **Calzada Revolución.** Tlaquepaque is 8km (5 miles) from downtown and takes 15 to 20 minutes by car; Tonalá is 5 minutes farther. Another major viaduct, **Calzada Lázaro Cárdenas,** connects the west side to Tlaquepaque and Tonalá, bypassing downtown.

THE NEIGHBORHOODS IN BRIEF

Centro Histórico The heart of the city contains many plazas, the cathedral, and several historic buildings and museums. Here, too, are the striking murals of José Clemente Orozco, one of the great Mexican muralists. Theaters, restaurants, shops, and clubs dot the area, and an enormous market rounds out the attractions. All of this is in a space roughly 12 blocks by 12 blocks, an easy area for a good walker to explore and enjoy the several plazas and pedestrian-only areas. To the south is a large green space called Parque Agua Azul.

West Side This is the swanky part of town, with the fine restaurants, luxury hotels, boutiques, and galleries, as well as the American, British, and Canadian consulates. It's a large area best navigated by taxi.

Zapopan Founded in 1542, Zapopan is a suburb of Guadalajara. In its center is the 18th-century basilica, the home of Guadalajara's patron saint, the Virgin of Zapopan. The most interesting part of Zapopan is clustered around the temple and can be explored by foot. It has a growing arts and nightlife scene.

Tlaquepaque This was a village of artisans (especially potters) that grew into a market center. In the last 30 years, it has attracted designers from all over Mexico. Every major form of art and craft is for sale here: furniture, pottery, glass, jewelry, woodcarvings, leather goods, sculptures, and paintings. The shops are sophisticated, yet Tlaquepaque's center retains a small-town feel that makes door-to-door browsing enjoyable and relaxing.

Tonalá This has remained a town of artisans. Plenty of stores sell mostly local products from the town's more than 400 workshops. You'll see wrought iron, ceramics, blown glass, and papier-mâché. A busy street market operates each Thursday and Sunday.

2 Getting Around

BY TAXI Taxis are the easiest way to get around town. Most have meters, and, though some drivers are reluctant to use them, you can insist that they do. There are three rates: for day, night, and suburbia. On my last visit, typical fares were: downtown to the west side, $6 to $8 (£3.30–£4.40); downtown or west side to Tlaquepaque, $7 to $9 (£3.85–£4.95); to the new bus station, $7 (£3.85); to the airport, $15 to $20 (£8.25–£11).

BY CAR Keep in mind the several main arteries (see "City Layout," above). Several important freeway-style thoroughfares crisscross the city. **González Gallo** leads south from the town center and connects with the road to Lake Chapala. **Avenida Vallarta** continues past La Minerva and eventually feeds onto **Highway 15,** bound for Tequila and Puerto Vallarta.

BY BUS For the visitor, the handiest route is the TUR **706,** which runs from the Centro Histórico southeast to Tlaquepaque, the Central Camionera (the new bus station), and Tonalá. You can catch this bus on Avenida 16 de Septiembre. The same bus runs in the reverse direction back to the downtown area.

The **electric bus** is handy for travel between downtown and the Minerva area. It bears the sign PAR VIAL and runs east along Hidalgo and west along the next street to the north, Calle Independencia (not Calzada Independencia). Hidalgo passes along the north side of the cathedral. The Par Vial goes as far east as Mercado Libertad and as far west as Minerva Circle. The city also has a light rail system, **Tren Ligero,** but it doesn't serve areas that are of interest to visitors.

FAST FACTS: Guadalajara

American Express The local office is at Av. Vallarta 2440, Plaza los Arcos, Local A-1 (© **33/3818-2323**); it's open Monday through Friday from 9am to 6pm, Saturday from 9am to noon.

Area Code The telephone area code is **33**.

Books, Newspapers & Magazines **Gonvil,** a popular bookstore chain, has a branch across from Plaza de los Hombres Ilustres on Avenida Hidalgo, and another a few blocks south at Av. 16 de Septiembre 118 (Alcalde becomes 16 de Septiembre south of the cathedral). It carries few English selections. **Sanborn's,** at the corner of Juárez and 16 de Septiembre, does a good job of keeping English-language periodicals in stock, but most are specialty magazines. Many newsstands sell the two English local papers, the *Guadalajara Reporter* and the *Guadalajara Weekly.* For the widest selection of English-language books, try **Sandi Bookstore,** Av. Tepeyac 718 (© **33/3121-0863**), in the Chapalita neighborhood on the west side.

Business Hours Store hours are Monday through Saturday from 10am to 2pm and 4 to 8pm.

Climate & Dress Guadalajara's weather is mostly mild. From November through March, you'll need a sweater in the evening. The warmest months, April and May, are hot and dry. From June through September, the city gets afternoon and evening showers that keep the temperature a bit cooler, but it seems to me that the local climate is getting warmer. Dress in Guadalajara is conservative; attention-getting sportswear (short shorts, halters, and the like) is out of place.

Consulates The **American consular offices** are at Progreso 175 (© **33/3268-2200** or -2100). Other consulates include the **Canadian consulate,** Hotel Fiesta Americana, Local 31 (© **33/3615-6215**); the **British consulate,** Calle Jesús Rojas 20, Col. Los Pinos (© **33/3343-2296**); and the **Australian consulate,** López Cotilla 2018, Col. Arcos Vallarta (© **33/3615-7418**). These offices all keep roughly the same hours: Monday through Friday from 8am to 1pm.

Currency Exchange Three blocks south of the cathedral, on López Cotilla, between Corona and Degollado, are more than 20 *casas de cambio.* Almost all post their rates, which are usually better than bank rates and without the long lines.

Elevation Guadalajara sits at 1,700m (5,576 ft.).

Emergencies The emergency phone number is © **060.**

Hospitals For medical emergencies, visit the **Hospital México-Americano,** Cólomos 2110 (© **33/3642-7152** or 33/3641-3141).

Internet Access Most of the big hotels have business centers that you can use. There are many Internet cafes in the Centro Histórico; the easiest way to find one is to ask a young person.

Language Classes Foreigners can study Spanish at the **Foreign Student Study Center,** University of Guadalajara, Calle Tomás V. Gómez 125, 44100 Guadalajara,

Jal. (📞 **33/3616-4399**). **IMAC** is a private Spanish school at Donato Guerra 180 in the Centro Histórico (📞 **33/3613-1080**).

Police Tourists should first try to contact the Jalisco tourist information office in Plaza Tapatía (📞 **33/3668-1600**). If you can't reach the office, call the municipal police at 📞 **33/3668-7983**.

Post Office The *correo* is at the corner of Carranza and Calle Independencia, about 4 blocks northeast of the cathedral. Standing in the plaza behind the cathedral, facing the Degollado Theater, walk to the left and turn left on Carranza; walk past the Hotel Mendoza, cross Calle Independencia, and look for the post office on the left. It's open Monday through Thursday from 9am to 5pm, Saturday from 10am to 2pm.

Safety Guadalajara doesn't have as much crime as Mexico City. Rarely do you hear of muggings. Crimes against tourists and foreign students are infrequent and most often take the form of purse snatching. Criminals usually work in teams and target travelers in busy places, such as outdoor restaurants. Keep jewelry out of sight. Should anyone spill something on you, be alert to your surroundings and step away from them—this is a common method for distracting the victim.

3 Where to Stay

Rates shown are the standard rack rates and include the 17% tax. In slow periods, look for discounts; the big hotels often give business discounts. I've noticed that in some of the cheaper hotels, air-conditioning is a relative concept.

Almost all of the luxury hotels in Guadalajara are on the west side, which has the majority of the shopping malls, boutiques, fashionable restaurants, and clubs. There is also a lot to do in the Centro Histórico, making it a good place to stay. Finally, Tlaquepaque is a comfortable suburb and is perfect for shoppers; the only drawback is that almost everything shuts down by 7 or 8pm. Chain hotels not included below are Hilton, Marriott, Camino Real, Howard Johnson, Crowne Plaza, and Best Western.

VERY EXPENSIVE

Hotel Presidente InterContinental ★★★ Housed in a 14-story glass building with an atrium lobby, this hotel offers the most comprehensive list of services and amenities in Guadalajara. There is little turnover in staff, and the concierge has proven more capable and knowledgeable than any other in the city. The health club here is a standout among other hotels. The rooms are comfortable and quiet, with modern furnishings that include a desk and a small table with two chairs. Club rooms have discreet check-in and are on limited-access hallways; rates include continental breakfast, newspaper, and evening cocktails. The extra privacy and services are good for Mexican soap opera stars or repeat guests who like having their preferences known in advance. If you're neither of these, opt for one of the other rooms. The lobby bar is popular; during the season, bullfighters relax here after *la corrida.* Standard rooms come as "superior" or "deluxe." Differences and price aren't that pronounced. The rooms are about the same size and come with attractive midsize bathrooms. Deluxe rooms have a few more amenities. The suites are very large and come with large, very attractive bathrooms.

Av. López Mateos Sur and Moctezuma (west side), 45050 Guadalajara, Jal. © **800/327-0200** in the U.S. and Canada, or 33/3678-1234. Fax 33/3678-1222. www.interconti.com. 409 units. $276–$290 (£152–£160) double; $317 (£174) club; $414 (£228) and up for suite. Internet promotional rates available. AE, DC, MC, V. Valet parking $5 (£2.75). **Amenities:** 2 restaurants; bar; outdoor heated pool; golf at nearby clubs; health club w/saunas, steam rooms, and whirlpools; concierge; tour desk; car rental; large business center; executive business services; salon; room service; in-room massage; babysitting; laundry service; dry cleaning; nonsmoking rooms; executive-level rooms. *In room:* A/C, TV w/pay movies, Wi-Fi, minibar, coffeemaker, hair dryer, iron, safe.

Quinta Real ⭐⭐⭐   This chain specializes in building properties that are suggestive of Mexico's heritage, in contrast to the comfortable but generic luxury hotels. No glass skyscraper here—two five-story buildings made of stone, wood, plaster, and tile occupy lush grounds. Suites vary quite a bit: Eight have brick cupolas, and some have balconies. All are large, with a split-level layout and antique decorative touches. And all come with large, great bathrooms with tub/shower combinations. The "grand-class" suites have even bigger bathrooms with Jacuzzi tubs. They are also a bit larger and come with a few extras, such as a stereo. You can choose between two doubles or one king-size bed. The hotel is 2 blocks from Minerva Circle in western Guadalajara. Ask for a room that doesn't face López Mateos.

Av. México 2727 (at López Mateos, west side), 44690 Guadalajara, Jal. © **866/621-9288** in the U.S. and Canada, or 33/3669-0600. Fax 33/3669-0601. www.quintareal.com. 76 suites. $418 (£230) master suite; $439 (£241) grand-class suite. AE, DC, MC, V. Free secure parking. **Amenities:** Restaurant; bar; small outdoor heated pool; golf at local club; fitness room; discounts at local day spa; concierge; tour desk; car rental; business center; executive business services; room service; in-room massage; babysitting; laundry service; dry cleaning; nonsmoking rooms. *In room:* A/C, TV, high-speed Internet, minibar, hair dryer, iron, safe.

Villa Ganz ⭐⭐⭐   This small, all-suite hotel is on the near west side of the city, near Avenida Chapultepec. It is one of the most comfortable places to stay in Guadalajara. Rooms are big, well furnished, and decorated with flair. Each holds a basket of fruit and a small bottle of wine on check-in. Bathrooms are large and well lit—some have tubs, others just showers. Bed choices include a king, a queen, or two twins. Beds come with down comforters (hypoallergenic option available). Rooms facing the garden are the quietest, but those facing the street are set back from the traffic and have double-glazed windows. The common rooms and rear garden are agreeable places to relax. Service is personal and helpful. Guests can contract with a guide or driver at the hotel. In-room dining can be arranged with one of three nearby restaurants or arrangements can be made to bring in a chef. Villa Ganz is a member of the Boutique Hotels of Mexico.

López Cotilla 1739 (between Bolivar and San Martín, west side), 44140 Guadalajara, Jal. © **800/728-9098** in the U.S. and Canada, 866/818-8342 in Canada, or 33/3120-1416. www.villaganz.com. 10 suites. $234 (£129) junior suite; $269 (£148) master suite; $304 (£167) grand master suite. Rates include continental breakfast. Internet specials often available. AE, MC, V. Free secure parking. Children younger than 12 not accepted. **Amenities:** Golf and tennis at local club; concierge; tour desk; room service; in-room massage; laundry service; dry cleaning. *In room:* A/C, TV, Wi-Fi, hair dryer, safe.

EXPENSIVE

Holiday Inn Hotel and Suites Centro Histórico ⭐⭐   This six-story downtown property has comfortable guest rooms and a good location—just a few blocks from the main square. Standard rooms are carpeted and decorated in Mexican architectural colors. The furniture is modern Mexican with a few wrought-iron pieces—the overall effect is cheerful. The size and lighting are good; bathrooms are midsize, recently upgraded, and well equipped, with ample counter space. For quiet, ask for a room off the street. The suites are larger, but otherwise not much different. Room rates include transportation to (but not from) the airport.

Av. Juárez 211, Centro Histórico, 44100 Guadalajara. Jal. ℂ 800/465-4329 in the U.S. and Canada, 01-800/009-9900 in Mexico, or 33/3560-1200. www.holiday-inn.com. 90 units. $140–$150 (£77–£83) double; $175 (£96) suite. Ask about promotional rates. AE, MC, V. Free secure parking. **Amenities:** Restaurant; bar; fitness room; business center; room service; laundry service; dry cleaning; nonsmoking rooms. *In room:* A/C, TV, Wi-Fi, minibar, |coffeemaker, hair dryer, iron, safe.

Hotel de Mendoza ⭐   On a quiet street next to the Degollado Theater and Plaza Tapatía, 2 blocks from the cathedral, the Mendoza has the best location of any downtown hotel. The decor would best be described as a stab at old Spanish, with wood paneling and old-world accents. Standard rooms are midsize. Bed choices are one queen, two full, or two queens. Bathrooms are midsize, with better than average lighting. Suites have an additional sitting area and larger bathrooms with the recent addition of Jacuzzi tubs. Rooms face the street, an interior courtyard, or the pool. *Note:* The bath towels are the narrowest I've ever seen—obviously the brainchild of a demented cost-cutting expert. If the hotel hasn't changed these, ask for a couple extra after you check in.

Carranza 16, Centro Histórico, 44100 Guadalajara, Jal. ℂ 33/3492-5151. Fax 33/3613-7310. www.demendoza. com.mx. 104 units. $125 (£69) double; $145 (£80) suite. Discounts sometimes available. AE, MC, V. Secure parking $4 (£2.20). **Amenities:** Restaurant; bar; small outdoor pool; fitness room; Jacuzzi; tour desk; business center; room service; laundry service; dry cleaning; nonsmoking rooms. *In room:* A/C, TV, Wi-Fi, hair dryer, safe.

MODERATE

Hotel Cervantes ⭐ *(Value*   This six-story downtown hotel offers modern amenities at a great price. The rooms are attractive and midsize. They have wall-to-wall carpeting and tile bathrooms with ample sink areas and shower/tub combinations. The air-conditioning is more in theory than in practice. The lower price is for one double bed; the higher price, for a king or two doubles. This is not a noisy hotel, but if you require absolute quiet, request an interior room. The Cervantes is 6 blocks south and 3 blocks west of the cathedral.

Prisciliano Sánchez 442, Centro Histórico, 44100 Guadalajara, Jal. ℂ/fax 33/3613-6686. www.hotelcervantes.com .mx. 100 units. $72–$80 (£40–£44) double; $105 (£58) suite. AE, MC, V. Free secure parking. **Amenities:** Restaurant; lobby bar; small outdoor heated pool; tour desk; room service; babysitting; laundry service; dry cleaning. *In room:* A/C, TV.

Hotel Morales ⭐⭐ *(Value*   A historical hotel that's attractive and comfortable, the Morales is a good choice for anyone wishing to stay downtown. Guest rooms are comparable to the Holiday Inn Hotel & Suites but a good bit cheaper. The standard rooms are called either "suite sencilla" (one queen bed) or "suite doble" (2 double beds). The beds are firm. The rooms are medium or large and come with Pergo floors. The bathrooms are quite attractive, with ceramic tile floors and good looking countertops. The showers are strong. The rooms that face the street have balconies with really good double-glazed windows that do a marvelous job at screening the noise. The imperial suites offer a lot for the money, with super large bathrooms equipped with a two-person Jacuzzi tub and a separate shower. All rooms are set around an arcaded lobby holding an attractive bar area. There's live music on Thursday and Friday evenings.

Av. Corona 243 (corner with Prisciliano Sánchez) Centro Histórico, 44100 Guadalajara, Jal. ℂ 33/3658-5232. Fax 33/3658-5239. www.hotelmorales.com.mx. 64 units. $105 (£58) suite double; $135 (£74) junior suite; $165 (£91) imperial suite. AE, MC, V. Free sheltered parking. **Amenities:** Restaurant; bar; fitness room; tour info; business center; room service; babysitting; laundry service; dry cleaning; nonsmoking rooms. *In room:* A/C, TV, high-speed Internet, coffeemaker, hair dryer, iron, safe.

La Villa del Ensueño ✦✦   This B&B in central Tlaquepaque is a lovely alternative to big-city hotels. A modern interpretation of traditional Mexican architecture, it is a delight to the eye—small courtyards and beautiful gardens bordered by old stucco walls, which have been painted in muted shades of orange oxide or covered in carefully trimmed ivy, with an occasional wrought-iron balcony or stone staircase. The rooms are individually decorated and have more character than most hotel lodgings. All contain ceiling fans and wireless Internet connections. Doubles have either two twin or two double beds. Guests receive a complimentary cocktail on arrival. The hotel is about 8 blocks from the main plaza.

Florida 305, 45500 Tlaquepaque, Jal. ✆ **800/220-8689** in the U.S., or 33/3635-8792. Fax 818/597-0637. www. villadelensueno.com. 18 units. $88 (£48) double; $100 (£55) deluxe double; $117 (£64) 2-bedroom unit; $140 (£77) suite. Rates include full breakfast and light laundry service. AE, MC, V. Free valet parking. **Amenities:** Bar; indoor and outdoor pool; laundry service. *In room:* A/C, TV, Wi-Fi, hair dryer.

Old Guadalajara ✦✦   This downtown bed and breakfast recommends itself in many ways. It's in a colonial house, and it's well located, quiet, and beautiful. The rooms reflect the local scene and speak of Mexico without shouting it. They are large and airy with high ceilings, tile floors, and comfortable bathrooms. The colonial architecture makes it possible to live without A/C in the warm months, and every room is equipped with a ceiling fan. The central courtyard is cool and shaded by tall bamboo. The common rooms are open to the courtyard and are stocked with material for readers curious about the city. Paul Callahan prepares filling breakfasts for his guests using only natural ingredients.

Belén 236, Centro Histórico, 44100 Guadalajara, Jal. ✆/fax **33/3613-9958**. www.oldguadalajara.com. 5 units. $125 double (£69). Rates include full breakfast. AE, MC, V for deposit; no credit cards at B&B. No children younger than 18. **Amenities:** Tour info; nonsmoking rooms. *In room:* Hair dryer, no phone.

Quinta Don José ✦✦ *Value*   Good value, great location, friendly English-speaking owners—there are a lot of reasons to like this small establishment just 2 blocks from Tlaquepaque's main square. Rooms run the gauntlet from midsize to extra large. They are comfortable, attractive, and quiet, with some nice local touches. Most of the standard and deluxe doubles have a king or two double beds and an attractive, midsize bathroom. A couple have small private outdoor spaces. Some of the suites in back come with a full kitchen and lots of space—more than twice the size of the usual suite, with one king and one double bed. The breakfasts are good, and plans are in the works to install a full restaurant. Some lodgings just have a good feel to them, and this is one.

Reforma 139, 45500 Tlaquepaque, Jal. ✆ **866/629-3753** in the U.S. and Canada, or 33/3635-7522. www.quintadon jose.com. 15 units. $93 (£51) standard; $105 (£58) deluxe; $128–$163 (£70–£90) suite. Rates include full breakfast. AE, MC, V. Free secure parking. **Amenities:** Restaurant; bar; heated outdoor pool; tour info; in-room massage; babysitting; laundry service; nonsmoking rooms. *In room:* A/C, TV, Wi-Fi, hair dryer, iron.

INEXPENSIVE

Hotel San Francisco Plaza *Value*   This colonial-style downtown hotel is both pleasant and a bargain. Its rooms are big and comfortable, with attractive furnishings. All have rugs or carpeting, and most have tall ceilings (except in the remodeled area behind the reception desk). The hotel is built in colonial style around four courtyards, which contain fountains and potted plants. Rooms along the Sánchez Street side are much quieter now that the management has installed double windows. Some units along the back wall of the rear patio have small bathrooms. The San Francisco Plaza is 6 blocks south and 2 blocks east of the cathedral. The air-conditioning is being upgraded.

Degollado 267, Centro Histórico, 44100 Guadalajara, Jal. ℂ **33/3613-8954** or -8971. Fax 33/3613-3257. www. sanfranciscohotel.com.mx. 76 units. $65 (£36) double. AE, MC, V. Free sheltered parking. **Amenities:** Restaurant; room service; laundry service; dry cleaning; ironing service. *In room:* A/C, TV.

Plaza Los Reyes *Value*   Okay, so the rooms in this 10-story downtown hotel aren't anything special to look at, but they do have good, individually controlled A/C and strong showers, all for not a lot of money. The location is downtown near the market. It's central, but it's not the prettiest part of town; it's not dangerous. For entertainment, there's a fancy new multiplex cinema across the street that shows first-run Hollywood movies. Guest rooms are midsize and come with either two doubles or a king-size bed. Those on the mezzanine level are larger and often cost the same. Ask for a room facing away from the busy Calzada Independencia. Midsize bathrooms are clean, with good water pressure and plenty of hot water.

Calzada Independencia Sur 168, 44100 Guadalajara, Jal. ℂ **33/3613-9770** or -9775. 189 units. $55 (£30) double. AE, MC, V. Free valet parking. **Amenities:** Restaurant; outdoor heated pool; tour info; room service; laundry service; nonsmoking rooms. *In room:* A/C, TV, Wi-Fi.

4 Where to Dine

Guadalajara has many excellent restaurants either for fine dining or for typical local fare. Most of the fine-dining spots are on the west side. Those in the Centro Histórico are uniformly bad, excepting **La Fonda de San Miguel.** Tlaquepaque has some good choices, but most close by 8pm. Popular eateries serving good local fare are abundant, especially in the Centro Histórico. For a quick bite, there are several **Sanborn's** in the city. This is a popular national chain of restaurants known for their *enchiladas suizas* (enchiladas in cream sauce). If you're downtown and looking for baked goods and coffee, go to **El Globo** (℃ **33/3613-9926**), an upscale bakery at the corner of Pedro Moreno and Degollado. This is also a chain with a couple more locations around Guadalajara. *Tip:* When taking a taxi, keep the address of the restaurant handy because taxi drivers cannot be relied upon to know where even the most popular restaurants are.

Local dishes include *birria* (goat or lamb covered in maguey leaves and roasted). It comes in a tomato broth or with the broth on the side. Another favorite is the *torta ahogada,* a sandwich with pork bathed in a tomato sauce. I'm not particularly fond of them. The most popular drink here is the *paloma,* which combines tequila, lots of lime juice, and grapefruit soda on ice. I am fond of these.

EXPENSIVE

Adobe Fonda 🎯🎯 NOUVELLE MEXICAN   This restaurant shares space with a large store on pedestrian-only Independencia. The dining area is open and airy. Homemade bread and tostadas come to the table with an olive oil-based chile sauce, pico de gallo, and *requezón de epazote* (ricotta-like cheese with a Mexican herb). Among the soups are *crema de cilantro* and an interesting mushroom soup with a dark-beer broth. The main courses present some difficult decisions, with intriguing combinations of Mexican, Italian, and Argentine ingredients. Shrimp quesadillas accompanied by *chimichurri* with *nopal* cactus, filet in creamy ancho sauce, and the crab salad tower were all excellent. Sample the margaritas, too.

Francisco de Miranda 27 (corner of Independencia, Tlaquepaque). ℂ **33/3657-2792.** Reservations recommended on weekends. Main courses $13–$19 (£7.15–£10). AE, MC, V. Daily 12:30–6:30pm.

Chez Nené ★★★ FRENCH   In a small and pleasant open-air dining room, you can enjoy a quiet and leisurely meal of delicious French food. After doing just this, I had to meet the owner to see who was behind such work. He turned out to be a French expatriate (whose Mexican wife, Nené, is the restaurant's namesake) with clear ideas about food and dining. Shorn of fads and pretense, his cooking aims at the essential in a dish. Freshness and quality of ingredients are what matter most, and everything (except stews and such) is cooked to order. The daily menu is on a chalkboard and depends on what the owner finds that morning at the market. There are always at least a dozen main courses. The waiter answered every question I put to him and gave excellent service.

Juan Palomar y Arias 426 (continuación Rafael Sanzio, west side). ℂ 33/3673-4564. Reservations recommended on weekends. Main courses $10–$20 (£5.50–£11). AE, MC, V. Tues 4–11pm; Wed–Sat 1–5:30pm and 7:30–11:30pm; Sun 1–6pm.

El Sacromonte ★★★ MEXICAN HAUTE CUISINE   The food here is so exquisite that I try to dine here every time I'm in Guadalajara. El Sacromonte emphasizes artful presentation and design: Order "Queen Isabel's crown," and you'll be served a dish of shrimp woven together in the shape of a crown and covered in divine lobster-and-orange sauce. Or try quesadillas with rose petals in a deep-colored strawberry sauce. For soup, consider *el viejo progreso* for its unlikely combination of flavors (blue cheese and chipotle chile). The menu features amusing descriptions in verse. The main dining area is a shaded, open-air patio. The restaurant isn't far from the downtown area, on the near west side.

In the building next door, the owners have opened an updated version of the classic Mexican bar where one drinks while snacking on complimentary *botanas* (the Mexican equivalent of tapas). There is also a menu, which is simpler than the restaurant's. The place is called **El Duende.**

Pedro Moreno 1398 (corner of Calle Colonias, west side). ℂ 33/3825-5447 or 3827-0663. Reservations recommended. Main courses $11–$18 (£6.05–£9.90). MC, V. Mon–Sat 1:30pm–midnight; Sun 1:30–6pm.

La Tequila ★★ MEXICAN   In its new location, about a block from where it used to be, this restaurant churns out Mexican standards such as *chalupas poblanas* (hand made tortillas lightly fried and topped with a chile sauce), as well as versions of the trendy contemporary Mexican cooking, including pasta stuffed with shrimp and *huitlacoche* (a salty and mild-tasting corn fungus), grilled-vegetable salad, and *molcajetes de arrachera* (fajitas with slices of chiles and onions that are cooked and served in a three-legged stone vessel). The cooking is great, the place is lively (the locals love it), and the decorative touches, such as trimmed agaves, give the dining areas a regional point of reference. Indoor/outdoor dining areas and a popular upstairs bar make up the majority of the restaurant. *Tip:* If this place is too crowded, or you're simply looking for quieter dining, go to the original site (Av. Mexico 2916) where you'll find a new restaurant called **La Divina Tentación** (ℂ 33/3642-7242). The menu is similar, and the cooking, from what I sampled, was even a little better, but I suspect it might not survive for long (though I hope I'm wrong). It's a little more sedate, but well run.

Av. México 2830 (at Napoleón, west side). ℂ 33/3640-3440 or 33/3640-3110. Reservations recommended. Main courses $10–$18 (£5.50–£9.90). AE, MC, V. Mon–Sat 1pm–midnight; Sun 1–6pm.

MODERATE

Hostería del Angel ★★ TAPAS/SPANISH DELI/WINE BAR   Sip wine and munch on a few tapas in this comfortable and casual restaurant and wine bar just a few blocks from the basilica in Zapopan. The chef-owner cooked for years in Spain and Italy, where he became fascinated with the making of cheeses and deli meats such as prosciutto and Spanish *jamón serrano*. He serves a variety of tapas, and his baguette sandwiches are very popular with the locals. The menu doesn't do a good job of explaining the dishes, so don't hesitate to ask the waitperson for explanations. The house specialty is the *rotolata*—vegetables and cold cuts surrounded by a thin layer of crispy cheese. Live music plays from 9 to 11pm Monday through Saturday. The restaurant is a half-block off the pedestrian-only *calzada*, which leads to the plaza in front of the basilica.

5 de Mayo 260, Zapopan (west side). ℂ/fax **33/3656-9516**. Reservations recommended. Menu items $5–$10 (£2.75–£5.50). MC, V. Mon–Sat 9am–midnight; Sun 9am–8pm.

I Latina FUSION   Warehouse chic with a porcine motif (the owner tells me that the pig is a symbol of abundance in Thailand) is the look here. The menu is absurdly small but is supplemented with lots of daily specials. On my last visit, I sampled a steak with a coffee crust sitting on a bed of mashed sweet potatoes with shoestring sweet potato fries and tossed greens scattered about the plate (quite good), a chicken in peanut sauce that was okay, and a stuffed filet of snapper that was quite tasty. This is a good place for people-watching—you get to see a portion of Guadalajara's hip, intellectual crowd, who enjoy the antiestablishment surroundings, including the metal and plastic tables and chairs. My main problem is the noise, which at times gets to be too much. If you're looking for quiet dining, go elsewhere. Cabs have a hard time finding this place despite being almost right off of Minerva Circle. It's not that difficult. Inglaterra faces the railroad tracks.

Av. Inglaterra (west side). ℂ **33/3647-7774**. Reservations recommended. Main courses $9–$15 (£4.95–£8.25). MC, V. Wed–Sat 7:30pm–1am; Sun 2–6pm.

La Fonda de San Miguel *Moments* MEXICAN   My favorite way to enjoy a good meal in Mexico is to have it in an elegant colonial courtyard. I love the contrast between the bright, noisy street and the cool, shaded patio. This restaurant is in the former convent of Santa Teresa de Jesús. While you enjoy the stone arches and gurgling fountain, little crisp tacos and homemade bread appear at the table. For main courses, try *chiles en nogada* (stuffed chile in a white walnut cream sauce) if it's in season, or perhaps a traditional *mole poblano*. The restaurant is 4 blocks west and 1 block south of the cathedral, between Pedro Moreno and Morelos. Thursday to Saturday musicians perform from 3 to 5 and 9 to 11pm.

Donato Guerra 25 (between Morelos and Pedro Moreno, downtown). ℂ **33/3613-0809**. Reservations recommended on weekends. Breakfast $4–$8 (£2.20–£4.40); main courses $9–$16 (£4.95–£8.80). AE, MC, V. Sun–Mon 8:30–11:30am, 1:30–6pm; Tues–Sat 8:30–11:30am, 1:30pm–midnight.

La Trattoria Pomodoro Ristorante *Finds* ITALIAN   Good food, good service, and moderate prices make this restaurant perennially popular. The price of pastas and main courses includes a visit to the well-stocked salad bar. Recommendable menu items include the combination pasta plate (lasagna, fettuccini Alfredo, and spaghetti), shrimp linguine, and chicken parmigiana. The Italian owner likes to stock lots of wines from the motherland. The dining room is attractive and casual, with comfortable furniture and separate seating for smokers and nonsmokers.

Niños Héroes 3051 (west side). ℂ **33/3122-1817**. Reservations recommended, but not accepted during holidays. Pasta $7–$9 (£3.85–£4.95); main courses $8–$10 (£4.40–£5.50). AE, MC, V. Daily 1pm–midnight.

Mariscos Progreso SEAFOOD   On a large, open patio shaded by trees and tile roofs, waiters navigate among the tables carrying large platters of delicious seafood. Mexicans do a wonderful job with seafood, and this popular restaurant does the tradition proud. Grilling over wood is the specialty here, but the kitchen's repertoire includes all the Mexican standards. For a sampling of grilled favorites, try the *parrillada* (a platter of grilled dishes) for two. Sometimes there's quite a bit of ambience, with mariachis adding to the commotion. At other times, the crowd thins and one can rest peacefully from the exertions of shopping with a cold drink. It's a half-block from the Parián.

Progreso 80, Tlaquepaque. © **33/3657-4995.** Reservations not accepted. Main courses $7–$15 (£3.85–£8.25). AE, MC, V. Daily 11am–7pm.

INEXPENSIVE

Café Madrid MEXICAN   This little coffee shop is like many coffee shops used to be—a social institution where people come in, greet each other and the staff by name, and chat over breakfast or coffee and cigarettes. Change comes slowly here. For example, despite the fact that it's an informal place, the waiters wear white jackets with black bow ties, as they did 20 years ago. The coffee and Mexican breakfasts are good, as is the standard Mexican fare served in the afternoon. The front room opens to the street, with a small lunch counter and another room in the back.

Juárez 264 (between Corona and 16 de Septiembre, downtown). © **33/3614-9504.** Breakfast $2–$4 (£1.10–£2.20); main courses $5–$7 (£2.75–£3.85). No credit cards. Daily 7:30am–10:30pm.

La Chata Restaurant REGIONAL/MEXICAN   If you're staying downtown, don't let this place slip off your radar. It does a good job with all the Mexican classics and some regional specialties as well. Unlike most restaurants, this one has the kitchen in front and the dining area in back. For a reasonable sum you can get a filling bowl of *pozole* (chicken, pork, and hominy in a broth to which you add onions, radishes, chile, and oregano). They also offer *flautas* (flour tortillas that are rolled up around a filling and deep fried), *sopes* (little fried masa cakes topped with savory meats and veggies), quesadillas, and guacamole. There's also traditional *mole* and a couple of combination plates. The chairs are comfortable, and you hang out with lots of locals.

Corona 126 (between Juárez and López Cotilla, downtown). © **33/3613-0588.** Reservations not accepted. Breakfast $4–$6 (£2.20–£3.30); main courses $6–$9 (£3.30–£4.95). AE, DC, MC, V. Daily 8am–midnight.

La Fonda de la Noche ★★ *Finds* MEXICAN   For a host of reasons this is my favorite place in the city for a simple supper. The limited menu is excellent, the surroundings are comfortable and inviting, the lighting is perfect, and there's a touch of nostalgia for the Mexico of the '40s, '50s, and '60s. It's not far from downtown or the west side; take a cab to the intersection of Jesús and Reforma and, when you get there, look for a door behind a small hedge. There's no sign. It's a house with five fun dining rooms. Only Spanish is spoken, but the menu is simple. To try a little of everything, order the *plato combinado,* a combination plate that comes with an *enchilada de "medio mole,"* an empanada called a *media luna,* a tostada, and a *sope.* The owner is Carlos Ibarra, an artist from the state of Durango. He has decorated the place with traditional Mexican pine furniture and cotton tablecloths and his personal collection of paintings, mostly the works of close friends. On weekends, La Fonda offers *chiles en nogada.*

Jesús 251 (corner with Reforma, Col. El Refugio). © **33/3827-0917.** Reservations not accepted. Main courses $6–$8 (£3.30–£4.40). MC, V. Tues–Sun 7:30pm–midnight.

Los Itacates Restaurant ✦ (Value) MEXICAN   The Mexican equivalent of down-home cooking at reasonable prices. Office workers pack the place between 2 and 4pm weekdays, and there's a good crowd weekend nights, but at other times there's no problem finding a table. You can dine outdoors in a shaded sidewalk area or in one of the three dining rooms. The atmosphere is bright and colorful. Specialties include *lomo adobado* (baked pork in dark chile sauce), and chiles rellenos. *Pollo Itacates* is a quarter of a chicken, two cheese enchiladas, potatoes, and rice. Los Itacates is 5 blocks north of Avenida Vallarta. In the evenings they serve tacos and other *antojitos.*

Chapultepec Norte 110 (west side). (𝄐) **33/3825-1106** or -9551. Reservations accepted on weekends and holidays. Breakfast buffet $6 (£3.30); tacos $1 (55p); main courses $5–$7 (£2.75–£3.85). MC, V. Mon–Sat 8am–11pm; Sun 8am–7pm.

5 Exploring Guadalajara

SPECIAL EVENTS

There's always something going on from September to December. In September, when Mexicans celebrate independence from Spain, Guadalajara goes all out, with a full month of festivities. The celebrations kick off with the **Encuentro Internacional del Mariachi** (www.mariachi-jalisco.com.mx), in which mariachi bands from around the world play before knowledgeable audiences and hold sessions with other mariachis. Bands come from as far as Japan and Russia, and the event takes on a curious postmodern hue. Concerts are held in several venues. In the Degollado Theater, you can hear orchestral arrangements of classic mariachi songs with solos by famous mariachis. You might be acquainted with many of the classics without even knowing it. The culmination is a parade of thousands of mariachis and *charros* (Mexican cowboys) through downtown. It starts the first week of September.

On **September 15,** a massive crowd assembles in front of the Governor's Palace to await the traditional *grito* (shout for independence) at 11pm. The *grito* commemorates Father Miguel Hidalgo de Costilla's cry for independence in 1810. The celebration features live music on a street stage, spontaneous dancing, fireworks,

---

Guadalajara Bus Tours

Two companies are now offering bus tours of the city. One is a local company, **Tranvías Turísticos** (no phone), which offers two tours on small buses that look like trolley cars. Get info and buy tickets from the kiosk in Plaza Guadalajara (in front of the cathedral) starting at 10am. There are two routes. One is a circuit through downtown and surrounding neighborhoods. It lasts 1 hour and 10 minutes. The second is a slightly longer tour, going to Tlaquepaque. It last 1½ hours. Both cost $9 (£4.95). The other company, **Tapatío Tours** ((𝄐) **33/3613-0887**), has modern, bright red double-decker buses. Its tour goes from downtown to western Guadalajara to Tlaquepaque. The tour costs $9 (£4.95) on weekdays, $11 (£6.05) on weekends. It goes further out, into western Guadalajara. There are 10 stops; you can get off at any and catch the next bus when it passes by, which is every 35 minutes. Catch the bus in the plaza on the north side of the cathedral. It also starts at 10 in the morning.

Downtown Guadalajara

Cathedral **3**
Instituto Cultural Cabañas **12**
Church of Santa María de Gracia **7**
Mercado Libertad **11**
Museo Regional de Guadalajara **5**
Palacio del Gobierno **2**
Plaza de Armas **1**

Plaza Guadalajara **4**
Quetzalcoatl Fountain **10**
Rotonda de los Hombres Ilustres **4**
Teatro Degollado **8**
Universidad de Guadalajara Facultad de Música
   & Iglesia de San Agustín **9**

and shouts of *"¡Viva México!"* and *"¡Viva Hidalgo!"* The next day is the official Independence Day, with a traditional parade; the plazas downtown resemble a country fair and market, with booths, games of chance, stuffed-animal prizes, cotton candy, and candied apples. Live entertainment stretches well into the night.

On **October 12,** a **procession** ★★ honoring Our Lady of Zapopan celebrates the feast day of the Virgin of Zapopan. Around dawn, her small, dark figure begins the 5-hour ride from the Cathedral of Guadalajara to the suburban Basilica of Zapopan (see "Other Attractions," below). The original icon dates from the mid-1500s; the procession began 200 years later. Today, crowds spend the night along the route and vie for position as the Virgin approaches. She travels in a gleaming new car (virginal in that it must never have had the ignition turned on), which her caretakers pull through the streets. During the months leading up to the feast day, the figure visits churches all over the city. You will likely see neighborhoods decorated with paper streamers and banners honoring the Virgin's visit to the local church.

The celebration has grown into a month-long event, **Fiestas de Octubre,** which kicks off with an enormous parade, usually on the first Sunday or Saturday of the month. Festivities include performing arts, *charreadas* (rodeos), bullfights, art exhibits, regional dancing, a food fair, and a Day of Nations incorporating all the consulates in Guadalajara. By the time this is over, you enter the **holiday season of November and**

December, with Revolution Day (Nov 20), the Virgin of Guadalupe's feast day (Dec 12), and several other celebrations.

DOWNTOWN GUADALAJARA

The most easily recognized building in the city is the **cathedral** ⚔, around which four open plazas make the shape of a Latin cross. Later, a long swath of land was cleared to extend the open area from Plaza Liberación east to the Instituto Cultural Cabañas, creating **Plaza Tapatía.**

Construction on the cathedral started in 1561 and continued into the 18th century. Over such a long time, it was inevitable that remodeling would take place before the building was ever completed. The result is an unusual facade that is an amalgam of several architectural styles, including baroque, neoclassical, and Gothic. An 1818 earthquake destroyed the original large towers; their replacements were built in the 1850s, inspired by designs on the bishop's dinner china. Blue and yellow are Guadalajara's colors. The nave is airy and majestic. Items of interest include a painting in the sacristy ascribed to the 17th-century Spanish artist Bartolomé Estaban Murillo (1617–82).

On the cathedral's south side is the **Plaza de Armas,** the oldest and loveliest of the plazas. A cast-iron Art Nouveau bandstand is its dominant feature. Made in France, it was a gift to the city from the dictator Porfirio Díaz in the 1890s. The female figures on the bandstand exhibited too little clothing for conservative Guadalajarans, who clothed them. The dictator, recognizing when it's best to let the people have their way, said nothing.

Facing the plaza is the **Palacio del Gobierno** ⚔⚔, a broad palace two stories high, built in 1774. The facade blends Spanish and Moorish elements and holds several eye-catching details. Inside the central courtyard, above the staircase to the right, is a spectacular mural of Hidalgo by the modern Mexican master José Clemente Orozco. The Father of Independence appears high overhead, bearing directly down on the viewer and looking as implacable as a force of nature. On one of the adjacent walls Orozco painted *The Carnival of Ideologies,* a dark satire on the prevailing fanaticisms of his day. Another of his murals is inside the second-floor chamber of representatives, depicting Hidalgo again, this time in a more conventional posture, writing the proclamation to end slavery in Mexico. The *palacio* is open daily from 10am to 8pm.

In the plaza on the opposite side of the cathedral from the Plaza de Armas is the **Rotonda de los Hombres Ilustres.** Sixteen white columns, each supporting a bronze statue, stand as monuments to Guadalajara's and Jalisco's distinguished sons. Across the street from the plaza, in front of the Museo Regional, you will see a line of horse-drawn buggies. A carriage ride around the Centro Histórico lasts about an hour and costs $20 (£11) for one to four people.

Facing the east side of the rotunda is the **Museo Regional de Guadalajara,** Liceo 60 (© **33/3613-2703**). Originally a convent, it was built in 1701 in the churrigueresque (Mexican baroque) style and contains some of the region's important archaeological finds, fossils, historic objects, and art. Among the highlights are a giant reconstructed mammoth's skeleton and a meteorite weighing 1,715 pounds, discovered in Zacatecas in 1792. On the first floor, there's a fascinating exhibit of pre-Hispanic pottery, and some exquisite pottery and clay figures recently unearthed near Tequila during the construction of the toll road. On the second floor is a small ethnography exhibit of the contemporary dress of the state's indigenous peoples, including the Coras, Huicholes, Mexicaneros, Nahuas, and Tepehuanes. It's open Tuesday through Saturday from 9am to 5:30pm and Sunday from 9am to 4:30pm. Admission is $4 (£2.20).

Behind the Cathedral is the Plaza Liberación, with the **Teatro Degollado** (deh-goh-*yah*-doh) on the opposite side. This neoclassical 19th-century opera house was named for Santos Degollado, a local patriot who fought with Juárez against Maximilian and the French. Apollo and the nine muses decorate the theater's pediment, and the interior is famous for both the acoustics and the rich decoration. It hosts a variety of performances during the year, including the Ballet Folclórico on Sunday at 10am. It's open Monday through Friday from 10am to 2pm and during performances.

To the right of the theater, across the street, is the sweet little **church of Santa María de Gracia,** built in 1573 as part of a convent for Dominican nuns. On the opposite side of the Teatro Degollado is the **church of San Agustín.** The former convent is now the **University of Guadalajara School of Music.**

Behind the Teatro Degollado begins the Plaza Tapatía, which leads to the Instituto Cabañas. It passes between a couple of low, modern office buildings. The **Tourism Information Office** is in a building on the right-hand side.

Beyond these office buildings, the plaza opens into a large expanse, now framed by department stores and offices and dominated by the abstract modern **Quetzalcoatl Fountain.** This fluid steel structure represents the mythical plumed serpent Quetzalcoatl, who figured so prominently in pre-Hispanic religion and culture, and exerts a presence even today.

At the far end of the plaza is the Hospicio Cabañas, formerly an orphanage and known today as the **Instituto Cultural Cabañas** ★★, Cabañas 8 (© **33/3617-4322**). This vast structure is impressive for both its size (more than 23 courtyards) and its grandiose architecture, especially the cupola. Created by the famous Mexican architect Manuel Tolsá, it housed homeless children from 1829 to 1980. Today, it's a thriving cultural center offering art shows and classes. The interior walls and ceiling of the main building display murals painted by Orozco in 1937. His *Man of Fire,* in the dome, is said to represent the spirit of humanity projecting itself toward the infinite. Other rooms hold additional Orozco works, as well as excellent contemporary art and temporary exhibits.

Just south of the Hospicio Cabañas (to the left as you exit) is the **Mercado Libertad** ★, Guadalajara's gigantic covered central market, the largest in Latin America. This site has been a market plaza since the 1500s; the present buildings date from the early 1950s (see "Shopping," below).

OTHER ATTRACTIONS

At **Parque Agua Azul (Blue Water Park),** plants, trees, shrubbery, statues, and fountains create a perfect refuge from the bustling city. Many people come here to exercise early in the morning. The park is open daily from 7am to 6pm. Admission is $1 (55p) for adults, 50¢ (30p) for children.

Across Independencia from the park, cater-cornered from a small flower market, is the **Museo de Arqueología del Occidente de México,** Calzada Independencia at Avenida del Campesino. It houses a fine collection of pre-Hispanic pottery from Jalisco, Nayarit, and Colima. The museum is open Tuesday through Sunday from 10am to 2pm and 4 to 7pm. There's a small admission charge.

The state-run **Casa de las Artesanías** (© **33/3619-4664**) is at the Instituto de la Artesanía Jalisciense, just past the park entrance at Calzada Independencia and González Gallo (for details, see "Shopping," below).

Also near the park is Guadalajara's rodeo arena, **Lienzo Charro de Jalisco** (© **33/ 3619-0315**). Mexican cowboys, known as *charros,* are famous for their riding and lasso work, and the arena in Guadalajara is considered the big time. There are shows and competitions every Sunday at noon. The arena is at Av. Dr. R. Michel 577, between González Gallo and Las Palomas.

Basílica de la Virgen de Zapopan 🎯   A wide promenade several blocks long leads to a large, open plaza and the basilica. This is the religious center of Guadalajara. On the Virgin's feast day (see "Special Events," above) the plaza fills with thousands of *tapatíos.* The 18th-century church is a lovely (and somewhat anachronistic) combination of baroque and plateresque styles. The cult of the Virgin of Zapopan practically began with the foundation of Guadalajara itself. She is much revered and the object of many pilgrimages. In front of the church are several stands selling religious figures and paraphernalia. On one side of the church is a lovely museum and store dedicated to the betterment of the Huichol Indians. It is well worth a visit.

Main Plaza, Zapopan (10km/6¼ miles northwest of downtown). No phone. Free admission. Daily 7am–7pm; museum daily 10am–7pm.

Museo de la Ciudad   This museum opened in 1992 in a former convent. It chronicles Guadalajara's past. The eight rooms, beginning on the right and proceeding in chronological order, cover the period from just before the city's founding to the present. Unusual artifacts, including rare Spanish armaments and equestrian paraphernalia, give a sense of what day-to-day life was like. Descriptive text is in Spanish only.

Independencia 684 (at M. Bárcenas). ☎ 33/3658-2531. 50¢ (30p). Tues–Sun 10am–5pm.

Museo de las Artes de la Universidad de Guadalajara   Inside the main lecture hall of this building are some more murals by Orozco. On the wall behind the stage is a bitter denunciation of corruption called *The People and Their False Leaders.* But in the cupola is a more optimistic work—*The Five-fold Man,* who works to create a better society and better self. There is also a small permanent collection of modern art, which will look all too familiar because the works seem so derivative of many of the modern masters.

Juárez 975 (enter on López Cotilla). ☎ 33/3134-2222. 50¢ (30p). Tues–Sun 10am–8pm.

Museo Pantaleón Panduro 🎯🎯🎯   This is the greatest collection of ceramic works I've ever seen. Collectors and connoisseurs of pottery will love it, but so will casual students of Mexican popular culture and the arts. This could be one of the great museums of Mexico, but someone in authority needs to come up with the money and the curators to exhibit the collection properly. Right now pieces are organized by state, which makes no sense because the collection is much more about individual artistic achievement than it is about tracing local and regional traditions in ceramics. Every year a prestigious competition is held in Tlaquepaque among ceramists from across the nation. Prizes are awarded in seven categories and a best of show among these. (*Tip:* The competition is held every June, which is a good time for visiting Tlaquepaque.) The president of Mexico even comes to town to give out the awards. After the competition, many of the winning pieces become part the museum's collection. The virtuosity manifested in some of them will take your breath away. It would be wonderful if they were organized by category, and exhibited with enough light and explanatory text to get a better appreciation and understanding of them. But for now, the best thing you can do is cajole someone into showing you around and explain something about the pieces that you're viewing. The staff is actually quite knowledgeable, and at least one speaks English. The museum occupies a third of a large complex that in colonial times was a large religious community. It's now called **Centro Cultural El Refugio,** and it's very much worth exploring after you've seen the museum's collection.

P. Sánchez 191 (at Calle Florida, Tlaquepaque). ☎ 33/3639-5656. Free admission. Tues–Sun 10am–6pm.

6 Shopping

Many visitors to Guadalajara come specifically for the shopping in Tlaquepaque and Tonalá (see below). If you have little free time, try the government-run **Instituto de la Artesanía Jalisciense** ⚔, González Gallo 20 at Calzada Independencia (✆ **33/3619-4664**), in Parque Agua Azul, just south of downtown. This place is perfect for one-stop shopping, with two floors of pottery, silver jewelry, dance masks, glassware, leather goods, and regional clothing from around the state and the country. As you enter, on the right are museum displays showing crafts and regional costumes from the state of Jalisco. The craft store is open Monday through Friday from 10am to 6pm, Saturday from 10am to 5pm, Sunday from 10am to 3pm.

Guadalajara is known for its shoe industry; if you're in the market for a pair, try the **Galería del Calzado,** a shopping center made up exclusively of shoe stores. It's on the west side, about 6 blocks from Minerva Circle, at avenidas México and Yaquis.

Mariachis and *charros* come to Guadalajara from all over Mexico to buy highly worked belts and boots, wide-brimmed sombreros, and embroidered shirts. Several tailor shops and stores specialize in these outfits. One is **El Charro,** which has a store in the Plaza del Sol shopping center, across the street from the Hotel Presidente Inter-Continental, and one downtown on Juárez.

To view a good slice of what constitutes the material world for most Mexicans, try the mammoth **Mercado Libertad** ⚔ downtown. Besides food and produce, you'll see crafts, household goods, clothing, magic potions, and more. Although it opens at 7am, the market isn't in full swing until around 10am. Come prepared to haggle.

SHOPPING IN TLAQUEPAQUE & TONALA

Almost everyone who comes to Guadalajara for the shopping has Tlaquepaque (tlah-keh-*pah*-keh) and Tonalá in mind. These two suburbs are traditional handicraft centers that produce and sell a wide variety of *artesanía* (crafts).

TLAQUEPAQUE

Located about 20 minutes from downtown, **Tlaquepaque** ⚔⚔⚔ has the best shopping for handicrafts and decorative arts in all of Mexico. Over the years, it has become a fashionable place, attracting talented designers in a variety of fields. Even though it's a suburb of a large city, it has a cozy, small-town feel; it's a pleasure simply to stroll through the central streets from shop to shop. No one hassles you; no one does the hard sell. There are some excellent places to eat (see "Where to Dine," earlier in this chapter), or you can grab some simple fare at **El Parián,** a building in the middle of town that houses a number of small eateries.

Tips **Packing It In**

If you need your purchases packed safely so that you can check them as extra baggage, or if you want them shipped, talk to **Margaret del Río.** She is an American who runs a large packing and shipping company at Juárez 347, Tlaquepaque (✆ **33/3657-5652**). Paying the excess baggage fee usually is cheaper than shipping, but less convenient.

Tequila: The Name Says It All

Tequila is an entertaining (and intoxicating) town, well worth a day trip from Guadalajara. Several taxi drivers charge about $55 (£30) to take you to the town, get you into a tour of a distillery, take you to a restaurant, and haul you back to Guadalajara. A few of them speak English. One recommended driver is José Gabriel Gómez (© 33/3649-0791; jgabriel-taxi@hotmail.com); he has a new car and drives carefully. Call him in the evening. Tour companies also arrange bus trips to Tequila; ask at the ticket kiosk of Tranvías Turísticos, mentioned above. That company has started a weekend tour to Tequila, taking people to the Cofradía distillery.

Tequila has many distilleries, including the famous brands **Sauza** and **José Cuervo.** All the distilleries—the big, modern ones and the small, more traditional ones—offer tours. If you're on your own, a good place to hook up with a tour is at the little booth outside the city hall on the main square; two young English-speaking women run tours to any of the local factories. Tours cost only $5 (£2.75) and last about 2 hours. All tours show how tequila is made, what traditions the process follows, and what differences exist between tequilas; they end, of course, with a tasting. Avenida Vallarta runs straight to the highway to Tequila, which is about an hour outside of Guadalajara.

A taxi from downtown Guadalajara costs $5 (£2.75), or you can take one of the TUR 706 buses that make a fairly quick run from downtown to Tlaquepaque and Tonalá (see "Getting Around," earlier in this chapter).

The **Tlaquepaque Tourism Office** (© 33/3562-7050, ext. 2320 or turismo tlaquepaque@yahoo.com.mx) has an information booth in the town's main square by El Parián. It's staffed from 9:30am to 8pm daily.

If you are interested in pottery and ceramics, make sure to see the Pantaleón Panduro Museum, listed above. Another is the **Regional Ceramics Museum,** Independencia 237 (© 33/3635-5404), which displays several aspects of traditional Jalisco pottery as produced in Tlaquepaque and Tonalá. The examples date back several generations and are grouped according to the technique used to produce them. Note the crosshatch design known as *petatillo* on some of the pieces; it's one of the region's oldest traditional motifs and is, like so many other motifs, a real pain to produce. Look for the wonderful old kitchen and dining room, complete with pots, utensils, and dishes. The museum is open Tuesday through Saturday from 10am to 6pm, Sunday from 10am to 3pm; admission is free.

The following list of Tlaquepaque shops will give you an idea of what to expect. This is just a small fraction of what you'll find; the best approach might be to just follow your nose. The main shopping is along **Independencia,** a pedestrian-only street that starts at El Parián. It was recently resurfaced in stone and looks pretty sharp. You can go door-to-door visiting the shops until the street ends, then work your way back on **Calle Juárez,** the next street over, south of Independencia.

Agustín Parra   So you bought an old hacienda and are trying to restore its chapel—where do you go to find traditional baroque sculpture, religious art, gold-leafed

Another approach is to take the **Tequila Express** to the town of Amatitán, home of the Herradura distillery. This excursion is more about having a good time and enjoying some of the things this area is known for than it is about sampling tequila. Serious tequila enthusiasts will be disappointed. There's a nice tour of the distillery, but most of the time is spent watching mariachis and Mexican cowboys perform. The tequila tastings are limited. Everyone has a good time and drinks a fair share, but a trip to the town proper is more informative and offers a greater opportunity for trying different tequilas.

The Tequila Express leaves from the train station on Friday and Saturday, and sometimes on Sunday during vacation and holiday season. It's well organized. You need to be there by 10am. The Guadalajara Chamber of Commerce (Cámara de Comercio), at Vallarta and Niño Obrero (© **33/3880-9099**), organizes this trip. Buy tickets ahead of time at the main office; at the small office in the Centro Histórico at Morelos 395, at Calle Colón (no phone); or through Ticketmaster (© **33/3818-3800**). Office hours are Monday through Friday from 9am to 2pm and 4 to 6pm. Tickets cost $65 (£36) for adults, $35 (£19) for children 6 to 12. The tour includes food and drink. It returns to Guadalajara at about 8pm. Travel time is 1¾ hours each way. For more information, see www.tequilaexpress.com.mx.

objects, and even entire *retablos* (altarpieces)? Parra is famous for exactly this kind of work, and the store is lovely. It's open Monday through Saturday from 10am to 7pm. Independencia 158. © **33/3657-8530**.

Bazar Hecht   One of the village's longtime favorites. Here you'll find wood objects, handmade furniture, and a few antiques. It's open Monday through Saturday from 10am to 2:30pm and 3:30 to 7pm. Juárez 162. © **33/3657-0316**.

Sergio Bustamante   Sergio Bustamante's imaginative, original bronze, ceramic, and papier-mâché sculptures are among the most sought-after in Mexico—as well as the most copied. He also designs silver jewelry. This exquisite gallery showcases his work. It's open Monday through Saturday from 10am to 7pm, Sunday from noon to 4pm. Independencia 238 at Cruz Verde. © **33/3639-5519**.

Teté Arte y Diseño   Architectural decorative objects, especially hand-wrought iron hardware for the "Old Mexico" look is what this store is mainly known for. It also has a large collection of wrought iron chandeliers. It's open Monday through Saturday from 10am to 7:30pm. Juárez 173. © **33/3635-7347**.

TONALA: A TRADITION OF POTTERY MAKING

Tonalá ★★ is a pleasant town 5 minutes from Tlaquepaque. The streets were paved only recently, and there aren't fancy shops here. The village has been a center of pottery making since pre-Hispanic times; half of the more than 400 workshops here produce a wide variety of high- and low-temperature pottery. Other local artists work with forged iron, cantera stone, brass and copper, marble, miniatures, papier-mâché, textiles, blown glass, and gesso. This is a good place to look for custom work in any of these materials; you can locate a large pool of craftspeople by asking around a little.

Market days are Thursday and Sunday. Expect large crowds, and blocks and blocks of stalls displaying locally made pottery and glassware, as well as cheap manufactured goods, food, and all kinds of bric-a-brac. "Herb men" sell a rainbow selection of dried medicinal herbs from wheelbarrows; magicians entertain crowds with sleight-of-hand; and craftspeople spread their colorful wares on the plaza's sidewalks. I prefer to visit Tonalá on non–market days, when it's much easier to get around and see the stores and workshops. This is the place for buying sets of margarita glasses, the widely seen blue-rimmed hand-blown glassware, as well as the pottery typically associated with Mexico and finely painted *petatillo* ware.

The **Tonalá Tourism Office** (© **33/3284-3092**) is in the Artesanos building, set back from the road at Atonaltecas 140 Sur (the main street leading into Tonalá) at Matamoros. There is an information booth in front. Hours are Monday through Friday from 9am to 3pm, Saturday from 9am to 1pm. The office offers **free walking tours** on Monday, Tuesday, Wednesday, and Friday at 9am and 2pm, Saturday at 9am and 1pm. They include visits to artisans' workshops (where you'll see ceramics, stoneware, blown glass, papier-mâché, and the like). Tours last 3 to 4 hours and require a minimum of five people. Visitors can request an English-speaking guide. Also in Tonalá, cater-cornered from the church, you'll see a small tourism information kiosk that's staffed on market days and provides maps and useful information.

Tonalá is also the home of the **Museo Nacional de Cerámica,** Constitución 104, between Hidalgo and Morelos (© **33/3284-3000,** ext. 1194). The museum occupies a two-story mansion and displays work from Jalisco and all over the country. There's a large shop in the front on the right as you enter. The museum is open Tuesday through Friday from 10am to 5pm, Saturday and Sunday from 10am to 2pm. Admission is free; the fee for using a video or still camera is $8.50 (£4.70) per camera.

7 Guadalajara After Dark
MARIACHIS
You can't go far in Guadalajara without coming across some mariachis, but seeing really talented performers takes some effort. Try **Casa Bariachi,** Av. Vallarta 2221 (© **33/3615-0029**). In Tlaquepaque, go to **El Parián,** the building on the town square where mariachis serenade diners under the archways.

THE CLUB & MUSIC SCENE
Guadalajara, as you might expect, has a lot of variety in entertainment. For the most extensive listing of clubs and performances, get your hands on a copy of *Ocio,* the weekly insert of *Público.* You'll find listings in the back, categorized by type of music. For good mariachis, you should go to Casa Bariachi, mentioned above. Across the street from that club is another called **La Bodeguita del Medio** (© **33/3630-1620**) at Av. Vallarta 2320. It offers live old-school Cuban son. The groups come from Cuba and rotate every few months. The last night I visited the place, a small combo was playing in a little corner partly mixing in with the crowd. The place is on the small side, but people were making room to dance. Another thing to do is track down a Cuban diva, named **Rosalia,** who lives in Guadalajara. She's a great talent and always has a tight band playing with her as she belts out salsa and merengue tunes. The last time I was in Guadalajara she was singing weekends at the bar at the Hotel Presidente InterContinental.

Puerto Vallarta & the Central Pacific Coast

by Lynne Bairstow

Known as the Mexican Riviera, Mexico's Pacific coastline—with its palm-studded jungles sweeping into the deep blue of the ocean—is a spectacular backdrop for some of the country's favored resort cities. From Mazatlán through Puerto Vallarta and curving down to Manzanillo, modern hotels, easy air access, and a growing array of activities and adventure tourism attractions have transformed this region into a premier resort area. And for those seeking an experience off the beaten track, the villages that border this stretch of coastline remain largely undiscovered.

Puerto Vallarta, with its traditional Mexican architecture and gold-sand beaches bordered by jungle-covered mountains, is the second-most-visited resort in Mexico (trailing only Cancún). The original town center of Vallarta maintains a small-town charm despite boasting sophisticated hotels, great restaurants, a thriving arts community, active nightlife, and a growing variety of ecotourism attractions. **Mazatlán** may be the greatest resort value in Mexico, luring visitors with exceptional fishing, a historic downtown, and the recent addition

of championship golf facilities. **Manzanillo** is surprisingly relaxed; even though it's one of Mexico's most active commercial ports, it also offers great fishing and golf. And along **Costa Alegre,** between Puerto Vallarta and Manzanillo, pristine coves are home to unique luxury and value-priced resorts that cater to travelers seeking seclusion and privacy. Just north of Puerto Vallarta, bordering Banderas Bay, are the increasingly popular coastal towns of **Nuevo Vallarta, Bucerías,** and, at the northern tip, **Punta Mita,** home of the first Four Seasons resort in Latin America and a Jack Nicklaus golf course. With more luxury resorts—including St. Regis—and a second Jack Nicklaus signature golf course opening in early 2008—it is emerging as Mexico's most exclusive luxury address.

Villages such as **Rincón de Guayabitos, Barra de Navidad,** and **Melaque** are laid-back and almost undiscovered. Starkly different from the spirited resort towns, they offer travelers a glimpse into local culture. Excursions to these smaller villages make easy day trips or extended stays.

1 Puerto Vallarta ★★★

885km (549 miles) NW of Mexico City; 339km (210 miles) W of Guadalajara; 285km (177 miles) NW of Manzanillo; 447km (277 miles) SE of Mazatlán; 239km (148 miles) SW of Tepic

No matter how extensively I travel in Mexico, Puerto Vallarta remains my favorite part of this colorful country, for its unrivaled combination of simple pleasures and sophisticated charms. No other place in Mexico offers both the best of the country's natural beauty and an authentic dose of its vibrant culture.

Puerto Vallarta's seductive innocence captivates visitors, beckoning them to return—and to bring friends. Beyond the cobblestone streets, graceful cathedral, and welcoming atmosphere, Puerto Vallarta offers a wealth of natural beauty and man-made pleasures. Hotels of all classes and prices, over 250 restaurants, a sizzling nightlife, and enough shops and galleries to tempt even jaded consumers make this town a perennial favorite.

Ecotourism activities flourish—from canopy tours to whale-watching, ocean kayak-ing, and diving with giant mantas in Banderas Bay. Forty-two kilometers (26 miles) of beaches, many in pristine coves accessible only by boat, extend around the bay. High in the Sierra Madre, the mystical Huichol Indians still live in relative isolation in an effort to protect their centuries-old culture from outside influences.

Vallarta (as locals refer to it) was never the "sleepy little fishing village" that many proclaim. It began life as a port for processing silver brought down from mines in the Sierra Madre—then was forever transformed by a movie director and two star-crossed lovers. In 1963, John Huston brought stars Ava Gardner and Richard Burton here to film the Tennessee Williams play *Night of the Iguana.* Burton's new love, Elizabeth Taylor, came along to ensure the romance remained in full bloom—even though both were married to others at the time. Titillated, the international paparazzi arrived, and when they weren't shooting photos of the famous couple—or of Gardner water-skiing back from the set, surrounded by a bevy of beach boys—they photographed the beauty of Puerto Vallarta.

Luxury hotels and shopping centers have sprung up north and south of the origi-nal town, allowing Vallarta to grow into a city of 350,000 without sacrificing its con-siderable charms. It boasts the services and infrastructure—and, unfortunately now the traffic—of a modern city, while still retaining the authenticity of a colonial Mexi-can village.

Cool breezes flow down from the mountains along the Río Cuale, which runs through the center of town. Fanciful public sculptures grace the *malecón* (boardwalk), which is bordered by lively restaurants, shops, and nightclubs. The *malecón* is a mag-net for both residents and visitors, who stroll the main walkway to take in an ocean breeze, a multihued sunset, or a moonlit, perfect wave.

If I sound partial, it's not just because Puerto Vallarta is my favorite of Mexico's sunny resorts; this has been my home for the past 16 years. I live here in good com-pany—there's a considerable colony of American, Canadian, and European residents. Perhaps they feel as I do: that the surrounding mountains offer the equivalent of a continual, comforting embrace, adding to that sense of welcome that so many visitors feel as well.

ESSENTIALS
GETTING THERE AND DEPARTING
BY PLANE   For a list of international carriers serving Mexico, see chapter 2. Local numbers of some international carriers serving Puerto Vallarta are **Alaska Airlines** (✆ **322/221-1350** or -1353), **American Airlines** (✆ **322/221-1799** or -1927), **Ameri-ca West** (✆ **322/221-1333,** or 001-880/235-9292 inside Mexico), **Continental** (✆ **322/221-1025** or -2212), **Frontier** (✆ **800/432-1359**), and **Ted** (United's lower-cost carrier offers direct service from San Francisco and Denver; ✆ **800/225-5833** in the U.S.).

Puerto Vallarta: Hotel Zone & Beaches

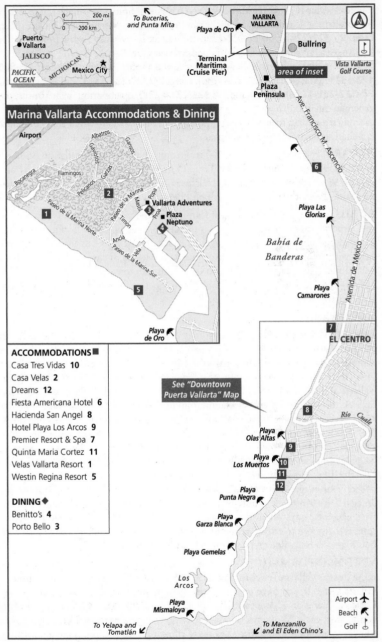

Marina Vallarta Accommodations & Dining

Airport

Albatros
Gaviotas
Bocanegra
Flamingos
Pelicanos
Garzas
Gansos
Paseo de la Marina Norte
Paseo de la Marina
Timon
Ancla
Paseo de la Marina Sur
Vela
Mastil
Proa
Popa

2

1

3 Vallarta Adventures
4 Plaza Neptuno

5

Playa de Oro

To Bucerias, and Punta Mita

Playa de Oro

MARINA VALLARTA

Bullring

Terminal Marítima (Cruise Pier)

area of inset

Vista Vallarta Golf Course

Plaza Peninsula

Ave. Francisco M. Ascencio

6

Playa Las Glorias

Bahía de Banderas

Avenida de México

Playa Camarones

7

EL CENTRO

See "Downtown Puerta Vallarta" Map

8

Río Cuale

Playa Olas Altas

9

Playa Los Muertos

10

11

12

Playa Punta Negra

Playa Garza Blanca

Playa Gemelas

Los Arcos

Playa Mismaloya

To Yelapa and Tomatlán

To Manzanillo and El Eden Chino's

Puerto Vallarta
JALISCO
PACIFIC OCEAN
MICHOACAN
Mexico City

0   200 mi
0   200 km

ACCOMMODATIONS ■
Casa Tres Vidas **10**
Casa Velas **2**
Dreams **12**
Fiesta Americana Hotel **6**
Hacienda San Angel **8**
Hotel Playa Los Arcos **9**
Premier Resort & Spa **7**
Quinta Maria Cortez **11**
Velas Vallarta Resort **1**
Westin Regina Resort **5**

DINING ◆
Benitto's **4**
Porto Bello **3**

Airport ✈
Beach 🏖
Golf ⛳

AeroMéxico (© **322/221-1204** or -1030) flies from Los Angeles, San Diego, Aguascalientes, Guadalajara, La Paz, León, Mexico City, Morelia, and Tijuana. **Mexicana** (© **322/224-8900** or 221-1266) has direct or nonstop flights from Chicago, Los Angeles, Guadalajara, Mazatlán, and Mexico City.

Major car rental agencies have counters at the airport, including **Budget** (© **800/472-3325** in the U.S., or 322/221-1730), **Hertz** (© **322/221-1473** or -1399), **National** (© **322/221-1226**), and **Alamo** (© **322/221-1228**), open during flight arrivals; they generally can also deliver a car to your hotel. Daily rates run $58 to $78. You need a car only if you plan to explore surrounding cities or are staying either along the southern coast, or north of Nuevo Vallarta.

BY CAR   The coastal Highway 200 is the only choice from Mazatlán (6 hr. north) or Manzanillo (3½–4 hr. south). Highway 15 from Guadalajara to Tepic takes 6 hours; to save as much as 2 hours, take Highway 15A from Chapalilla to Compostela, bypassing Tepic, then continue south on Highway 200 to Puerto Vallarta.

BY BUS   The bus station, **Central Camionera de Puerto Vallarta,** is just north of the airport, approximately 11km (7 miles) from downtown. It offers overnight guarded parking and baggage storage. Most major first-class bus lines operate from here, with transportation to points throughout Mexico, including Mazatlán, Tepic, Manzanillo, Guadalajara, and Mexico City. Taxis into town cost approximately $7.50 (£4.15) and are readily available; public buses operate from 7am to 11pm and regularly stop in front of the arrivals hall.

ORIENTATION

ARRIVING BY PLANE   The airport is close to the north end of town near the Marina Vallarta, about 10km (6¼ miles) from downtown. **Transportes Terrestres** minivans and **Aeromovil** taxis make the trip. They use a zone pricing system, with fares clearly posted at the ticket booths. Fares start at $10 (£5.50) for a ride to Marina Vallarta and go up to $35 (£19) for the south shore hotels. Federally licensed airport taxis exclusively provide transportation from the airport, and their fares are more than three times as high as city (yellow) taxi fares. A trip to downtown Puerto Vallarta costs $22 (£12), whereas a return trip using a city taxi costs only $8 (£4.40). Only airport cabs may pick up passengers leaving the airport. However, if you don't have too much baggage, you can cross the highway using the overpass, and there you'll find yellow cabs lined up. Note that when you arrive at the International Arrivals gate, after you collect your baggage, you enter into an enclosed area with colorful wall displays and an aggressive group of seemingly helpful greeters; beware—these are timeshare hustlers, and their goal, often in the guise of offering you free or discounted transportation, is to get you to attend a timeshare presentation. Keep walking—just outside this booth are the bona fide taxi and transportation alternatives.

VISITOR INFORMATION   Prior to arrival, a great source of general information is the **Puerto Vallarta Tourism Board** (© **888/384-6822** in the U.S.; www.visitpuerto vallarta.com). If you have questions after you arrive, visit the **Municipal Tourism Office** at Juárez and Independencia (© **322/223-2500,** ext. 230) in a corner of the white Presidencia Municipal building (city hall) on the northwest end of the main square. In addition to offering a listing of current events and promotional brochures for local activities and services, the employees can also assist with specific questions—there's usually an English speaker on staff. This is also the office of the tourist police.

It's open Monday through Friday from 8am to 9pm. During low season it may close for lunch between 2 and 4pm.

The **State Tourism Office,** Plaza Marina L 144, second floor (© **322/221-2676,** -2677, or -2678; fax 322/221-2680), also offers brochures and can assist with specific questions about Puerto Vallarta and other points in the state of Jalisco, including Guadalajara, Costa Alegre, the town of Tequila, and the program that promotes stays in authentic rural haciendas. It's open Monday through Friday from 9am to 5pm.

CITY LAYOUT   The seaside promenade, the *malecón,* is a common reference point for giving directions. It's next to **Paseo Díaz Ordaz** and runs north-south through the central downtown area. From the waterfront, the town stretches back into the hills a half-dozen blocks. The areas bordering the **Río Cuale** are the oldest parts of town— the original Puerto Vallarta. The area immediately south of the river, called **Olas Altas** after its main street (and sometimes Los Muertos after the beach of the same name), is home to a growing selection of sidewalk cafes, fine restaurants, espresso bars, and hip nightclubs. In the center of town, nearly everything is within walking distance both north and south of the river. **Bridges** on Insurgentes (northbound traffic) and Ignacio Vallarta (southbound traffic) link the two sections of downtown.

AREA LAYOUT   Beyond downtown, Puerto Vallarta has grown along the beach to the north and south. Linking downtown to the airport is **Avenida Francisco Medina Ascencio.** Along this main thoroughfare are many high-rise hotels (in an area called the **Zona Hotelera,** or Hotel Zone), plus several shopping centers with a variety of dining options.

Marina Vallarta, a resort city within a city, is at the northern edge of the Hotel Zone not far from the airport. It boasts modern luxury hotels, condominiums, and homes; a huge marina with 450 yacht slips; a golf course; restaurants and bars; and several shopping plazas. Because it was originally a swamp, the beaches are the least desirable in the area, with darker sand and seasonal inflows of cobblestones. The Marina Vallarta peninsula faces the bay and looks south to the town of Puerto Vallarta.

Nuevo Vallarta is a booming planned resort north of the airport, across the Ameca River in the state of Nayarit (about 13km/8 miles north of downtown). It also has hotels, condominiums, and a yacht marina, with a growing selection of restaurants and shopping, including the new Paradise Plaza mall. Most hotels there are all-inclusive, with some of the finest beaches in the bay, but guests usually travel into Puerto Vallarta (about $15/£8.25 a cab ride) for anything other than poolside or beach action. Regularly scheduled public bus service costs about $1.50 (85p) and runs until 10pm.

Bucerías, a small beachside village of cobblestone streets, villas, and small hotels, is farther north along Banderas Bay, 30km (19 miles) beyond the airport. Past Bucerías, following the curved coastline of Banderas Bay you'll find La Cruz de Huanaxcle, site of a new mega-marina project currently under construction, but still a charming seaside

---

⌜Tips⌝ Steer Clear of the Rambo Bus!

Buses in Vallarta tend to be rather aggressive, and some even sport names— including "Terminator," "Rambo," and "Tornado." Don't tempt fate by assuming these buses will stop for pedestrians. Although Vallarta has an extremely low crime rate, bus accidents are frequent—and frequently fatal.

(Tips **Don't Let Taxi Drivers Steer You Wrong**

Beware of restaurant recommendations offered by taxi drivers—many receive a commission from restaurants where they discharge passengers. Be especially wary if a driver tries to talk you out of a restaurant you've already selected.

---

town with *mucho* local color. Continue on to the end of the road and you'll reach **Punta Mita.** Once a rustic fishing village, it has been artfully developed as a luxury destination. In the works are a total of three exclusive luxury boutique resorts, private villas, and two golf courses. The site of an ancient celestial observatory, it is an exquisite setting, with white-sand beaches and clear waters. The northern shore of Banderas Bay is emerging as the area's most exclusive address for luxury villas and accommodations.

In the other direction from downtown is the southern coastal highway, home to more luxury hotels. Immediately south of town lies the exclusive residential and rental district of **Conchas Chinas.** Ten kilometers (6 miles) south, on **Playa Mismaloya** (where *Night of the Iguana* was filmed), lies the Barceló La Jolla de Mismaloya resort. There's no road on the southern shoreline of Banderas Bay, but three small coastal villages are popular attractions for visitors to Puerto Vallarta: **Las Animas, Quimixto,** and **Yelapa,** all accessible only by boat. The tiny, pristine cove of **Caletas,** site of John Huston's former home, is a popular day- or nighttime excursion (see "Boat Tours," later in this chapter).

GETTING AROUND By Taxi　Taxis are plentiful and relatively inexpensive. Most trips from downtown to the northern Hotel Zone and Marina Vallarta cost $4 to $9 (£4.40–£4.95); to or from Marina Vallarta to Mismaloya Beach (to the south) costs $12 to $15 (£6.60–£8.25). Rates are charged by zone and are generally posted in the lobbies of hotels. Taxis can also be hired by the hour or day for longer trips. Rates run $15 to $18 (£8.25–£9.90) per hour, with discounts available for full-day rates—consider this an alternative to renting a car.

By Car　Rental cars are readily available at the airport, through travel agencies, and through the most popular U.S. car rental services, but unless you're planning a distant side trip, don't bother. Car rentals are expensive, averaging $66 (£36) per day, and parking around town is very challenging, unless you opt for one of the two new parking garages constructed on either end of the *malecón* zone (at Park Hidalgo to the north, and adjacent to the northern border of the Cuale River to the south). If you see a sign for a $10 (£5.50) Jeep rental or $20 (£11) car rental, be aware that these are lures to get people to attend timeshare presentations. Unless you are interested in a timeshare, stopping to inquire will be a waste of your time.

By Bus　City buses, easy to navigate and inexpensive, will serve just about all your transportation needs. They run from the airport through the Hotel Zone along Morelos Street (1 block inland from the *malecón*), across the Río Cuale, and inland on Vallarta, looping back through the downtown hotel and restaurant districts on Insurgentes and several other downtown streets. To get to the northern hotel strip from old Puerto Vallarta, take the ZONA HOTELES, IXTAPA, or LAS JUNTAS bus. These buses may also post the names of hotels they pass, such as Krystal, Fiesta Americana, Sheraton, and others. Buses marked MARINA VALLARTA travel inside this area, stopping at the major hotels there.

Other buses operate every 10 to 15 minutes south to either Mismaloya Beach or Boca de Tomatlán (a sign in the front window indicates the destination) from Constitución and Basilio Badillo, a few blocks south of the river.

Buses run generally from 6am to 11pm, and it's rare to wait more than a few minutes for one. The fare is about 50¢ (30p). You do not have to have exact change; the driver will make change.

By Boat   The *muelle* (cruise-ship pier), also called Terminal Marítima, is where **excursion boats** to Yelapa, Las Animas, Quimixto, and the Marietas Islands depart. It's north of town near the airport, an inexpensive taxi or bus ride from town. Just take any bus marked IXTAPA, LAS JUNTAS, PITILLAL, or AURORA and tell the driver to let you off at the Terminal Marítima. *Note:* Odd though it may seem, you must pay a $1.50 (85p) fee (this is a federal tax) to gain access to the pier—and your departing excursion boat.

Water taxis to Yelapa, Las Animas, and Quimixto leave at 10:30 and 11am from the pier at Los Muertos Beach (south of downtown), on Rodolfo Rodríguez next to the Hotel Marsol. Another water taxi departs at 11am from the beachside pier at the northern edge of the *malecón*. A round-trip ticket to Yelapa (the farthest point) costs $25 (£14). Return trips usually depart between 3 and 4pm, but confirm the pickup time with your water taxi captain. Other water taxis depart from Boca de Tomatlán, about 30 minutes south of town by public bus. These water taxis are the better option if you want more flexible departure and return times from the southern beaches. Generally, they leave on the hour for the southern shore destinations, or more frequently if there is traffic. Prices run about $12 (£6.60) round-trip, with rates now clearly posted on a sign on the beach. A private water taxi costs $55 to $100 (£30–£55), depending on your destination, and allows you to choose your own return time. They'll take up to eight people for that price, so often people band together at the beach to hire one.

FAST FACTS: Puerto Vallarta

American Express   The local office is at Morelos 660, at the corner of Abasolo (© **01-800/504-0400** and 01-800/333-3211 in Mexico, or 322/223-2955). It's open Monday through Friday from 9am to 6pm, Saturday from 9am to 1pm. It offers excellent, efficient travel agency services in addition to money exchange and traveler's checks.

Area Code   The telephone area code is **322**.

Climate   It's warm all year, with tropical temperatures; however, evenings and early mornings in the winter can turn quite cool. Summers are sunny, with an increase in humidity during the rainy season, between May and October. Rains come almost every afternoon in June and July, and are usually brief but strong—just enough to cool off the air for evening activities. In September, heat and humidity are least comfortable and rains heaviest.

Consumer Assistance   Tourists with complaints about taxis, stores, abusive timeshare presentations, or other matters should contact **PROFECO**, the consumer protection office (© **322/225-0000**; fax 322/225-0018). The office is open

Monday through Friday from 8:30am to 3:30pm and may not have fluent English-speaking staff.

Currency Exchange Banks are found throughout downtown and in the other prime shopping areas. Most banks are open Monday through Friday from 9am to 5pm, with shorter hours on Saturday. ATMs are common throughout Vallarta, including the central plaza downtown. They are becoming the most favorable way to exchange currency, with bank rates plus 24-hour convenience. *Casas de cambio* (money exchange houses), located throughout town, offer longer hours than the banks with only slightly lower exchange rates.

Drugstores **CMQ Farmacia,** Basilio Badillo 365 (© **22/222-1330**), is open 24 hours and makes free deliveries to hotels between 11am and 10pm with a minimum purchase of $20 (£11). **Farmacias Guadalajara,** Emiliano Zapata 232 (© **322/224-1811**), is also open 24 hours.

Embassies & Consulates The **U.S. Consular Agency** office (© **322/222-0069**; fax 322/223-0074; 24 hr. a day for emergencies) is located in Nuevo Vallarta, in the Paradise Plaza, Local 1, on the street level between the plaza and the Paradise Village Yacht Club. It's open Monday through Friday from 10am to 2pm. The **Canadian Consulate** (© **322/293-0099** or -0098; 24-hr. emergency line 01-800/706-2900 in Mexico) is located in Plaza Las Glorias, 1951 Blvd. Francisco Medina Ascencio, Edificio Obelisco, Loc. 108 (you'll see the Canadian flag hanging from the balcony). It's open Monday through Friday from 9am to 3pm.

Emergencies **Police** emergency, © **060**; local police, © **322/290-0513** or -0512; intensive care **ambulance,** © **322/225-0386** (*Note:* English-speaking assistance is not always available at this number); **Cruz Roja (Red Cross),** © **322/222-1533**; **Global Life Ambulance Service** (provides both ground and air ambulance service), © **322/226-1010**, ext. 304.

Hospitals The following offer U.S.-standards service and are available 24 hours: **Ameri-Med Urgent Care,** Avenida Francisco Medina Ascencio at Plaza Neptuno, Loc. D-1, Marina Vallarta (© **322/221-0023**; fax 322/221-0026; www.amerimed-hospitals.com); **San Javier Marina Hospital,** Av. Francisco Medina Ascencio 2760, Zona Hotelera (© **322/226-1010**), and **Cornerstone Hospital,** Av. los Tules 136 (behind Plaza Caracol; © **322/224-9400**).

Internet Access Puerto Vallarta is probably the most wired destination in Mexico. Recommended is **Café.com** (© **322/222-0092**), Olas Altas 250, at the corner of Basilio Badillo, charges $2 (£1.10) for 30 minutes. It offers complete computer services, a full bar, and food service. It's open daily from 8am to 2am. Some hotels have lobby e-mail kiosks, but they're more expensive than the Net cafes.

Newspapers & Magazines ***Vallarta Today,*** a daily English-language newspaper (© **322/225-3323** or 224-2829), is a good source for local information and upcoming events. The bilingual quarterly city magazine ***Vallarta Lifestyles*** (© **322/221-0106**) is also very popular. Both are for sale at area newsstands and hotel gift shops. The weekly English-language *P.V. Tribune* (© **322/223-0585**) is distributed free throughout town and offers an objective local viewpoint.

Post Office The *correo* is at Colombia Street, behind Hidalgo park, and is open Monday through Friday from 9am to 6pm, Saturday from 9am to 1pm.

Safety Puerto Vallarta enjoys a very low crime rate. Public transportation is safe to use, and Tourist Police (dressed in white safari uniforms with white hats) are available to answer questions, give directions, and offer assistance. Most encounters with the police are linked to using or purchasing drugs—so don't (see chapter 2). *Note:* The tourist police conduct random personal searches for drugs. Although there is some question about their right to do this, the best course of action if they want to frisk you is to comply—objecting will likely result in a free tour of the local jail. However, you are within your rights to request the name of the officer. Report any unusual incidents to the local consular office.

BEACHES, ACTIVITIES & EXCURSIONS

Travel agencies can provide information on what to see and do in Puerto Vallarta and can arrange tours, fishing trips, and other activities. Most hotels have a tour desk on-site. Of the many travel agencies in town, I highly recommend **Tukari Servicios Turísticos,** Av. España 316 (© **322/224-7177;** fax 322/224-2350; www.tukari.com), which specializes in ecological and cultural tours. Another source is **Xplora Adventours** (© **322/223-0661**), in the Huichol Collection shop on the *malecón.* It has listings of all locally available tours, with photos, explanations, and costs; however, be aware that a timeshare resort owns the company, so part of the information you receive will be an invitation to a presentation, which you may decline. **American Express Travel Services,** Morelos 660 (© **322/223-2955**), also has a varied selection of high-quality, popular tours. One of the tour companies with the largest—and best quality—selection of boat cruises and land tours is **Vallarta Adventures** ★★★ (© **888/ 303-2653** in the U.S., or 322/297-1212, ext. 3; www.vallarta-adventures.com). I can highly recommend any of their offerings. Book with them directly and get a 10% discount when you mention Frommer's.

THE BEACHES

For years, beaches were Puerto Vallarta's main attraction. Although visitors today are exploring more of the surrounding geography, the sands are still a powerful draw. Over 42km (26 miles) of beaches extend around the broad Bay of Banderas, ranging from action-packed party spots to secluded coves accessible only by boat.

IN TOWN   The easiest to reach is **Playa Los Muertos** (also known as Playa Olas Altas or Playa del Sol), just off Calle Olas Altas, south of the Río Cuale. The water can be rough, but the wide beach is home to a diverse array of *palapa* restaurants that offer food, beverage, and beach-chair service. The most popular are the adjacent El Dorado and La Palapa, at the end of Pulpito Street. On the southern end of this beach is a section known as "Blue Chairs"—the most popular gay beach. Vendors stroll Los Muertos, and beach volleyball, parasailing, and jet-skiing are all popular pastimes. The **Hotel Zone** is also known for its broad, smooth beaches, accessible primarily through the hotel lobbies.

SOUTH OF TOWN   **Playa Mismaloya** is in a beautiful sheltered cove about 10km (6 miles) south of town along Highway 200. The water is clear and beautiful, ideal for snorkeling off the beach. Entrance to the public beach is just to the left of the **Barceló La Jolla de Mismaloya** (© **322/226-0600**). The movie *Night of the Iguana* was

Moments **Special Events in Puerto Vallarta**

Each November, the annual **Gourmet Festival** (www.festivalgourmet.com) is a standout reason to come here, with an agenda filled with culinary exhibitions, wine tastings, and guest chefs preparing special menus at area restaurants. Dates vary; call the Tourism Board (© **888/384-6822** in the U.S.) for a schedule, but the 2007 edition is slated for November 8 to 18. From December 1 to December 12, the **Festival of the Virgin of Guadalupe** ★—Mexico's patron saint—inspires one of the most authentic displays of culture and community in Mexico. Businesses, neighborhoods, associations, and groups make pilgrimages (called *peregrinaciones*) to the church, where they exchange offerings for a brief blessing by the priest. These processions, especially those created by hotels, often include floats, Aztec dancers, and mariachis, and are followed by fireworks. Hotels frequently invite guests to participate in the walk to the church. It's an event not to be missed.

---

filmed at Mismaloya, and the resort has a restaurant on the restored film set—**La Noche de la Iguana Set Restaurant,** open daily from noon to 11pm. The movie runs continuously in a room below the restaurant, and still photos from the filming hang in the restaurant. The restaurant is accessible by land on the point framing the south side of the cove. Just below the restaurant is **John Huston's Bar & Grill,** serving drinks and light snacks daily from 11am to 6pm.

The beach at **Boca de Tomatlán,** just down the road, has numerous *palapa* restaurants where you can relax for the day—you buy drinks, snacks, or lunch, and you can use their chairs and *palapa* shade.

The two beaches are accessible by public buses, which depart from the corner of Basilio Badillo and Insurgentes every 15 minutes from 5:30am to 10pm and cost just 50¢ (30p).

Las Animas, Quimixto, and **Yelapa** beaches offer a true sense of seclusion; they are accessible only by boat (see "Getting Around," above, for information about water-taxi service). They are larger than Mismaloya, offer intriguing hikes to jungle waterfalls, and are similarly set up, with restaurants fronting a wide beach. Overnight stays are available at Yelapa (see "Side Trips from Puerto Vallarta," later in this chapter).

NORTH OF TOWN   The beaches at **Marina Vallarta** are the least desirable in the area, with darker sand and seasonal inflows of stones.

The entire northern coastline from Bucerías to Punta Mita is a succession of sandy coves alternating with rocky inlets. For years the beaches to the north, with their long, clean breaks, have been the favored locale for surfers. The broad, sandy stretches at **Playa Anclote, Playa Piedras Blancas,** and **Playa Destiladeras,** which all have *palapa* restaurants, have made them favorites with local residents looking for a quick getaway—but come soon, because this area is slated for luxury development, easy access to these shores is likely to be limited in the coming years. At Playa Anclote you'll find a broad, sandy beach with protected swimming areas and a few great *palapa* restaurants. Of the restaurants, El Anclote and El Dorado have been the long-standing favorites, but **Mañana** (© **329/291-6374**), has raised the culinary bar of this casual dining area. It's open Tuesday through Sunday from 10am to 9pm, in summer 1 to 9pm. All have beach chairs available for your postmargarita nap in the sun. If you're seeking solace from the sun, head to the **Pink Bonsai** (📞 **329/291-6468**), which serves creative sushi, tempting tempuras, and the delectable changing specials of Chef/Owner Karl, who enjoys fusing Asian with Mexican flavors. It's located in the Plaza of Shops, second level, on the left-hand side of the short main road entering Playa Anclote (Av. de las Redes 75, Punta de Mita). It's open Monday through Saturday, 1pm to 6pm.

You can also hire a *panga* (small motorized boat) at Playa Anclote from the fisherman's cooperative on the beach and have the captain take you to the **Marietas Islands** ★★★ just offshore. These uninhabited islands are a great place for bird-watching, diving, snorkeling, or just exploring. Blue-footed booby birds (found only here, and in the Galapagos) can be spotted all along the islands' rocky coast, and giant mantas, sea turtles, and colorful tropical fish swim among the coral cliffs. The islands are honeycombed with caves and hidden beaches—including the stunning Playa de Amor (Beach of Love) that only appears at low tide. You enter a shallow passageway to access this semicircular stretch of sand. There's also a cave 12m (40 ft.) below the surface with an air pocket where divers can remove of their regulators and have an underwater conversation! Humpback whales congregate around these islands during the winter months, and *pangas* can be rented for a do-it-yourself whale-watching excursion. Trips cost about $30 (£17) per hour. You can also visit these islands aboard one of the numerous day cruises that depart from the cruise-ship terminal in Puerto Vallarta.

The stellar white-sand beach at **Punta Mita,** home of the Four Seasons, is closed to road access, except for owners in and guests of this residential resort development.

ORGANIZED TOURS

BOAT TOURS   Puerto Vallarta offers a number of boat trips, including sunset cruises and snorkeling, swimming, and diving excursions. They generally travel one of two routes: to the **Marietas Islands,** a 30- to 45-minute boat ride off the northern shore of Banderas Bay, or to **Yelapa, Las Animas,** or **Quimixto** along the southern shore. The trips to the southern beaches make a stop at **Los Arcos,** an island rock formation south of Puerto Vallarta, for snorkeling. Don't base your opinion of underwater Puerto Vallarta on this, though—dozens of tour boats dump quantities of snorkelers overboard at the same time each day, exactly when the fish know *not* to be there. It is, however, an excellent site for night diving. When comparing boat cruises, note that some include lunch, while most provide music and an open bar on board. Most leave around 9:30am, stop for 45 minutes of snorkeling, and arrive at the beach destination around noon for a 2½-hour stay before returning around 3pm. At Quimixto and Yelapa, visitors can take a half-hour hike to a jungle waterfall or rent a horse for the ride. Prices range from $45 (£25) for a sunset cruise or a trip to one of the beaches with open bar, to $85 (£47) for an all-day outing with open bar and meals.

One boat, the *Marigalante* (📞 **322/223-0309;** www.marigalante.com.mx), is an exact replica of Columbus's ship the *Santa María,* built in honor of the 500th anniversary of his voyage to the Americas. It features a daytime "Pirate Land" Morning Cruise daily from 8am until 3:30pm ($70/£39 per person), complete with breakfast, picnic barbecue and treasure hunt, as well as a sunset dinner (adult oriented) cruise from 6 to 10pm ($80/£44 per person) with fireworks and dance party. Children 3 to 11 are half price (children younger than 2 are free).

One of the best outings is a day trip to **Caletas** ★★, the cove where John Huston made his home for years. **Vallarta Adventures** (📞 **888/303-2653** in the U.S., or 322/297-1212, ext. 3; www.vallarta-adventures.com) holds the exclusive lease on the private cove and has done an excellent job of restoring Huston's former home, adding exceptional day-spa facilities, and landscaping the beach, which is wonderful for snorkeling. They also have a colony of sea lions that play with the visiting divers! You'll have a hard time deciding whether to kayak, take a yoga class, hike through surrounding trails, or simply relax in the hammocks strung between palms on the beach. The facilities and relative privacy have made this excursion $80 (£44) per person; $40 (£22) for children 4 to 11 one of the most popular. The evening cruise includes dinner and a spectacular contemporary dance show, "Rhythms of the Night" (see "Puerto Vallarta after Dark," later in this chapter).

Travel agencies sell tickets and distribute information on all cruises. If you prefer to spend more time at Yelapa or Las Animas without snorkeling and cruise entertainment, see the information about travel by water taxis, earlier in this chapter, under "Getting Around."

Whale-watching tours become more popular each year. Viewing humpback whales is almost a certainty from mid- to late November to March. The majestic whales have migrated to this bay for centuries (in the 17th c. it was called "Humpback Bay") to bear their calves. The noted local authority is **Open Air Expeditions,** Guerrero 339 (©/fax **322/222-3310;** www.vallartawhales.com). It offers ecologically oriented, oceanologist-guided 4-hour tours on the soft boat *Prince of Whales,* the only boat in Vallarta specifically designed for whale-watching. Cost is $83 (£46) for adults, $50 (£28) for children 5 to 10, and travel is in a group of up to 12. Twice-daily departures (8:30am and 1:30pm) include a healthful snack. **Vallarta Adventures** (see above) offers a variety of whale-watching excursions that may combine time for snorkeling, or simply focus on photographing these exquisite mammals. Prices range from $68 to $80 (£37–£44), and offer a choice of boat, ranging from small boats to bring you closest for photos, to graceful sailboats. All trips include a predeparture briefing on whale behavior.

LAND TOURS   **Tukari Servicios Turísticos** (see "Beaches, Activities & Excursions," above) can arrange trips to the fertile birding grounds near **San Blas,** 3 to 4 hours north of Puerto Vallarta in the state of Nayarit, and shopping trips to **Tlaquepaque** and **Tonalá** (6 hr. inland, near Guadalajara). A day trip to **Rancho Altamira,** a 20-hectare (50-acre) working ranch, includes a barbecue lunch and horseback riding, then a stroll through **El Tuito,** a small nearby colonial-era village. The company can also arrange an unforgettable morning at **Terra Noble Art & Healing Center** (©/fax (© **322/223-3530** or 222-5400; www.terranoble.com), a mountaintop day spa and center for the arts where participants can get a massage, *temazcal* (ancient, indigenous sweat lodge), or treatment; work in clay and paint; and have lunch in a heavenly setting overlooking the bay. Call ahead for reservations, and make sure to advise if you want to have lunch there.

Hotel travel desks and travel agencies, including Tukari and American Express, can also book the popular **Tropical Tour** or **Jungle Tour** ($30/£17), a basic orientation to the area. These excursions are expanded city tours that include a drive through the workers' village of Pitillal, the affluent neighborhood of Conchas Chinas, the cathedral, the market, the Taylor-Burton houses, and lunch at a jungle restaurant. Any stop for shopping usually means the driver picks up a commission for what you buy.

The **Sierra Madre Expedition** is another excellent tour offered by **Vallarta Adventures** (see "Boat Tours," above). The daily excursion travels in Mercedes all-terrain vehicles north of Puerto Vallarta through jungle trails, stops at a small town, ventures into a forest for a brief nature walk, and winds up on a pristine secluded beach for lunch and swimming. The $75 (£41) outing is worthwhile because it takes tourists on exclusive trails into scenery that would otherwise be off-limits.

AIR TOURS Speaking of off-limits, you can explore some of the most remote and undiscovered reaches of the Sierra Madre mountains in Vallarta Adventures' **San Sebastián Air Expedition** (© **888/303-2653** in the U.S., or 322/297-1212, ext. 3; www.vallarta-adventures.com). A 15-minute flight aboard a 14-seat turbo-prop Cessna Caravan takes you into the heart of the Sierra Madre. The plane is equipped with raised wings, which allow you to admire—and photograph—the mountain scenery. The plane arrives on a gravel landing strip in the old mining town of San Sebastián, a beautiful village that dates from 1603. One of the oldest mining towns in Mexico, it reached its prosperous peak in the 1800s, with over 30,000 inhabitants. Today, San Sebastián remains an outstanding example of how people lived and worked in a remote Mexican mountain town—it's a living museum. The half-day adventure costs $155 (£85), which covers the flight, a walking tour of the town (including a stop at the old Hacienda Jalisco, a favored getaway of John Huston, Liz and Dick, and their friends), and brunch in town. Other excursions include overnight stays and return trips by bike or horseback. If you prefer more leisurely travel, they offer a similar tour taking you by land in air-conditioned minivans for the 90-minute drive up the mountains, for $75 (£41) per person. Another **bus tour** to San Sebastián, which costs $75 (£41) per person, and includes a guide, departs at 9am and returns at 5pm. Call Pacific Travel (© **322/225-2270**) to make reservations.

Vallarta Adventures (see "Boat Tours," above) also offers a similar—yet different—air tour to the mountain villages of **Mascota** and **Talpa de Allende** ★★, where you'll learn about the religious significance of these traditional towns. In Mascota, stroll the cobblestone streets lined with adobe houses and colonial haciendas, stopping at the majestic town church, dedicated to the Virgen de los Dolores (Virgin of Sorrows), which was completed in 1880 and took more than 100 years to construct. You'll stop for lunch and tour a local *raicilla* distillery to sample this locally popular beverage before traveling on to Talpa. Talpa is known for being home to one of Mexico's most revered icons, the Virgen Rosario de Talpa, believed to grant miracles with her healing powers. Ask for one yourself, as you visit the Gothic church that bears her name, or simply wander around this pastoral village, set in a valley that is surrounded by pine-covered mountains. The 6-hour adventure includes airfare and lunch, for $175 (£96) per person. Departures are Mondays and Wednesdays at 10:30am, from the Aerotron private airport (adjacent to the Puerto Vallarta International Airport).

Vallarta Adventures also offers air tours to remote mountain villages where the **Huichol Indians** live (Fri departures, at a cost of $210/£116), as well as to the **Copper Canyon,** and the mystical village of **Mexcaltitan** (Mon departures, at a cost of $255/£140), all departing from Puerto Vallarta. Details and online booking options are available at www.vallarta-adventures.com.

TOURS IN TOWN Every Wednesday and Thursday in high season (late Nov–Easter), the **International Friendship Club** (© **322/222-5466**) offers a **private home tour** of four villas in town. It costs $35 (£19) per person, with proceeds donated to local charities. Arrive early, because this tour sells out quickly. It starts at the Hotel Posada Río Cuale, adjacent to the southbound bridge over the Río Cuale. Get there at 10am, and you can buy breakfast while you wait for the group to gather. The tour departs at 10:30am and lasts approximately 3½ hours. Also ask them about a new tour of the exquisite villas on the north shore planned to be inaugurated in late 2007.

A tour of the **Public Sculptures** of the *malecón* is hosted by Galería Pacífico owner Gary Thompson, each Tuesday at 9:30am, from December through April. Lasting a couple of hours, you'll stroll the *malecón* learning about the artists who created Vallarta's most visible art, and their inspirations. Frequently, Gary is joined by one or more of the artists on this tour. For more details, contact the gallery at © 322/221-1982.

STAYING ACTIVE

DIVING & SNORKELING   Underwater enthusiasts from beginner to expert can arrange scuba diving or snorkeling through **Vallarta Adventures** (© 888/303-2653 in the U.S., or 322/297-1212, ext. 3; www.vallarta-adventures.com), a five-star PADI dive center. You may snorkel or dive at Los Arcos, a company-owned site at Caletas Cove (where you'll dive in the company of sea lions!), Quimixto Coves, the Marietas Islands, or the offshore La Corbeteña, Morro, and Chimo reefs. The company also offers a full range of certification courses (up to Instructor). **Chico's Dive Shop,** Díaz Ordaz 772–5, near Carlos O'Brian's (© 322/222-1895; www.chicos-diveshop.com), offers similar diving and snorkeling trips and is also a PADI five-star dive center. Chico's is open daily from 8am to 10pm and has branches at the Marriott, Las Palmas, Holiday Inn, Fiesta Americana, Krystal, San Marino, Villa del Palmar, Paradise Village, and Playa Los Arcos hotels. You can also snorkel off the beaches at Mismaloya and Boca de Tomatlán; elsewhere, there's not much to see other than a sandy bottom.

ECOTOURS & ACTIVITIES   **Open Air Expeditions** (©/fax 322/222-3310; www. vallartawhales.com) offers nature-oriented trips, including birding and ocean kayaking in Punta Mita. **Ecotours de México,** Ignacio L. Vallarta 243 (©/fax 322/222-6606), has eco-oriented tours, including seasonal (Aug–Dec) trips to a turtle preservation camp where you can witness hatching baby Olive Ridley turtles.

A popular Vallarta adventure activity is **canopy tours.** You glide from treetop to treetop, getting an up-close-and-personal look at a tropical rainforest canopy and the trails far below. Expert guides assist you to the special platforms, and you move from one to another using pulleys on horizontal traverse cables, while the guides explain the tropical flora surrounding you. They also offer assistance—and moral support!—as you rappel back down to the forest floor. Tours depart from the **Vallarta Adventures** (see "Diving & Snorkeling," above) offices in both Marina Vallarta and Nuevo Vallarta at 8am, returning at 2pm. The price ($79/£43 for adults, $58/£32 for children 8–12) includes the tour, unlimited nonalcoholic beverages, and light snacks. Their newest offering is the **Outdoor Adventure,** which combines a ride on the canopy line with a day of adventure activities. You'll learn wilderness survival techniques while hiking through the Sierra Madre foothills, splashing through streams, rappelling down waterfalls, then taking a 300m (984-ft.) zip line over jungle landscape. The 6½ hour tour costs $110 (£61), for those who are physically fit, ages 12 and older.

A second option is available in the southern jungles of Vallarta, over the Orquidias River, through **Canopy Tours de Los Veranos** (© 322/223-6060; www.canopy tours-vallarta.com). This tour will pick you up at the Canopy office, near the south side Pemex station, to transport you to their facilities upriver from Mismaloya. Departures are on the hour, from 9am to 2pm. In addition to the 13 cables—the longest being a full 350m (1,148 ft.)—it also offers climbing walls, waterslides, and horseback riding. The guides here are noted for helping even the faintest of heart propel through the treetops. Price is $80 (£44) for adults, or $50 (£28) for children ages 6 and older. Use of the natural-granite climbing wall (helmets and climbing-shoe use included) is $18 (£9.90); the 1½-hour jungle horseback riding tour costs $35 (£19).

FISHING   Arrange fishing trips through travel agencies or through the **Cooperativa de Pescadores (Fishing Cooperative)**, on the *malecón* north of the Río Cuale, next door to the Rosita Hotel (© 322/222-1202). Fishing charters cost $100 (£55) per person, for one to eight people; or select from other options where the price varies with the size of the boat; a boat can be rented for 8 hours for $450 (£248). Although the posted price at the fishing cooperative is the same as you'll find through travel agencies, you may be able to negotiate a lower price at the cooperative, which does not accept credit cards. It's open Monday through Sunday from 7am to 10pm, but make arrangements a day ahead. You can also arrange fishing trips at the Marina Vallarta docks, or by calling **Fishing with Carolina** (© 322/224-7250; cell 044-322/292-2953; fishingwithcarolina@hotmail.com), which uses a 9m (30-ft.) Uniflite sports-fisher, fully equipped with an English-speaking crew. Fishing trips cost $350 (£193) for up to four people for 4 hours and include equipment and bait, but drinks, snacks, and lunch are optional, at $12 (£6.60) per person. If you mention Frommer's when you make your reservation, they'll offer a free lunch with your booking. All boats have brand new engines.

GOLF   Puerto Vallarta is an increasingly popular golf destination; five courses have opened in the past 6 years, bringing the total in the region to nine. The Joe Finger–designed private course at the **Marina Vallarta Golf Club** (© 322/221-0073) is an 18-hole, par-74 course that winds through the Marina Vallarta peninsula and affords ocean views. It's for members only, but most luxury hotels in Puerto Vallarta have memberships for their guests. Greens fees are $90 to $136 (£50–£75) in high season, $115 (£63) in low season. Fees include golf cart, range balls, and tax. Hiring a caddy costs $10 (£5.50). Club rentals, lessons, and special packages are available.

North of town in the state of Nayarit, about 15km (9⅓ miles) beyond Puerto Vallarta, is the 18-hole, par-72 **Los Flamingos Club de Golf** (© 329/296-5006; www.flamingosgolf.com.mx). It features beautiful jungle vegetation and underwent a renovation and upgrade of the course in 2005. It's open from 7am to 7pm daily, with a snack bar (but no restaurant) and full pro shop. The daylight greens fee is $140 (£77), which drops to $90 (£50) after 2:30pm. It includes the use of a golf cart; hiring a caddy costs $20 (£11) plus tip, and club rental is $30 to $40 (£17–£22). A free shuttle runs from downtown Puerto Vallarta; call for pickup times and locations.

The breathtaking Jack Nicklaus Signature course at the **Punta Mita Golf Club** 🏌🏌🏌 (© 329/291-6000; fax 329/291-6060) has 8 oceanfront holes and an ocean view from every hole. Its hallmark is the optional Hole 3B, the "Tail of the Whale," with a long drive to a green on a natural island—the only natural-island green in the Americas. It requires an amphibious cart to take you over when the tide is high, and there's an alternate hole for when the ocean or tides are not accommodating. The course is open only to guests staying in the Punta Mita resort or Four Seasons, or to members of other golf clubs with a letter of introduction from their pro. Other selected area hotels also have guest privileges—ask your concierge. Greens fees for hotel guests are $185 (£102) for 18 holes and $110 (£61) for 9 holes, and for nonguests are $230 (£127), including cart, with (Calloway) club rentals for $60 (£33). Lessons are also available. In early 2008, a second Jack Nicklaus Signature course will open in Punta Mita, adjacent to the new St. Regis Resort slated to open at the same time.

Another Jack Nicklaus course is located at the **Vista Vallarta Golf Club** (© 322/ **290-0030;** www.vistavallartagolf.com), along with one designed by Tom Weiskopf. These courses were the site of the 2002 PGA World Cup Golf Championships. The club is the foothills of the Sierra Madre, behind the bullring in Puerto Vallarta. A round costs $174 (£96) per person. Cart fee is an extra $46 (£25), with club rentals available for $49 (£27) per set/per round.

The Robert von Hagge–designed **El Tigre** course at Paradise Village (© **866/843- 5951** in the U.S., or **322/297-0773;** www.paradisevillage.com; www.eltigregolf.com), in Nuevo Vallarta, opened in March 2002. The 7,239-yard course is on a relatively flat piece of land, but the design incorporates challenging bunkers, undulating fairways, and water features on several holes. El Tigre also offers lessons and has an expansive clubhouse. This seems to be the favored course of local pros. Greens fees are $185 (£102) a round, or $85 (£47) if you play after 2pm. Club rentals are $45 (£25).

HORSEBACK-RIDING TOURS   Travel agents and local ranches can arrange guided horseback rides. **Rancho Palma Real,** Carretera Vallarta, Tepic 4766 (© 322/ **222-0501**), has an office 5 minutes north of the airport; the ranch is in Las Palmas, approximately 40 minutes northeast of Vallarta. It is by far the nicest horseback riding tour in the area. The horses are in excellent condition, and you enjoy a tour of local farms on your way to the ranch. The price ($62/£34; American Express or cash only) includes breakfast and lunch.

Another excellent option is **Rancho El Charro,** Av. Francisco Villa 895 (© **322/ 224-0114;** cell 044-322/294-1689; www.ranchoelcharro.com), which has beautiful, well-cared for horses, and a variety of rides for all levels, departing from their ranch at the base of the Sierra Madre Mountains. Rides range in length from 3 to 8 hours, and in price from $56 to $100 (£31–£55). There's even the $69 (£38) Wild Ride, where you gallop along a ridge to a jungle waterfall—too often, riders are disappointed with only trotting along well-marked trails on these excursions, and this ride allows experienced riders much more freedom. Rancho El Charro also has multiple-day rides— check their website for details. **Rancho Ojo de Agua,** Cerrada de Cardenal 227, Fracc. Las Aralias (©/fax **322/224-0607;** www.mexonline.com), also offers high-quality tours, from its ranch located 10 minutes by taxi north of downtown toward the Sierra Madre foothills. The rides last 3 hours (10am–1pm, 3–6pm, or 4–7pm) and take you up into the mountains overlooking the ocean and town. The cost is $59 (£32). Both of the ranches listed above have other tours available as well as their own comfortable base camp for serious riders who want to stay out overnight.

PARASAILING   Parasailing and other watersports are available at many beaches along the Bay of Banderas. The most popular spot is at Los Muertos Beach. WaveRunners, banana boats, and parasailing are available by the hour, half-day, or full day. Be forewarned, however, that the swiftly shifting winds in Banderas Bay can make this a dangerous proposition. Fly at your own risk!

SAILING   I personally believe that a trip to the Vallarta area is not complete without a journey out on the water—there's no better way to see the entirety of the area, the beauty of the surrounding mountains, and get a sense of the area than from the perspective of a sailboat. Banderas Bay is increasingly being used at the site of national and international regatta competitions.

A recent (2005) and welcome addition to Vallarta's sailing scene is most impressive— **Coming About** 🎖🎖 (© **322/222-4119;** www.coming-about.com) is a women-only

---

Tips **A Spectator Sport**

Bullfights are held December through April beginning at 5pm on Wednesday at the La Paloma bullring, across the highway from the town pier. Travel agencies can arrange tickets, which cost around $25 (£14).

---

sailing school that provides hands-on sailing instruction for day-sailing excursions, as well as week-long sailing classes at a variety of skill levels. Owned and operated by Pat Henry, who spent 8 years sailing around the globe, then wrote about it in her book *By the Grace of the Sea: A Woman's Solo Odyssey Around the World,* the classes are challenging, inspiring, and entertaining, as Pat shares her adventures with participants. Dubbed "any woman's sailing school," the goal is to take away the fear and the mystery, and make the skill of sailing accessible to everyone. Courses range from a 1-day introductory course to a 9-day bareboat charter captain course. Fees for the 1-day course are $475 (£261) for four people; $2,800 to $3,600 (£1,540–£1,980) per person, based on double occupancy, for the 9-day course, including hotel.

SWIMMING WITH DOLPHINS   Ever been kissed by a dolphin? Take advantage of a unique opportunity to swim with Pacific bottlenose dolphins in one of two facilities—a clear lagoon or a special swim facility that's part of the Vallarta Adventures offices. **Dolphin Adventure** ✦✦✦ (© **888/303-2653** in the U.S., or 322/297-1212, ext. 3; www.vallarta-adventures.com) operates an interactive dolphin-research facility—considered the finest in Latin America—that allows limited numbers of people to swim with dolphins Monday through Saturday at scheduled times. Cost for the swim is $135 (£74). Reservations are required, and they generally sell out at least a week in advance. You may prefer the **Dolphin Encounter** ($69/£38), which allows you to touch and learn about the dolphins in smaller pools, so you're ensured up-close-and-personal time with them. You can even be a **Trainer for a Day,** a special 7-hour program of working alongside the more experienced trainers and the dolphins, for a cost of $250 (£138). The **Dolphin Kids** program, for children ages 4 to 8, is a gentle introduction to dolphins, featuring the Dolphin Adventure baby dolphins and their mothers interacting with the children participants ($60/£33). I give this my highest recommendation. Not only does the experience leave you with an indescribable sensation, but it's also a joy to see these dolphins—they are well cared for, happy, and spirited. The program is about education and interaction, not entertainment or amusement, and is especially popular with children ages 10 and older.

TENNIS   Many hotels in Puerto Vallarta offer excellent tennis facilities; they often have clay courts. The full-service **Canto del Sol Tennis Club** (© **322/224-0123** and 322/226-0123; www.cantodelsol.com) is at the Canto del Sol hotel in the Hotel Zone. It offers indoor and outdoor courts (including a clay court), full pro shop, lessons, clinics, and partner matches.

A STROLL THROUGH TOWN

Puerto Vallarta's cobblestone streets are a pleasure to explore; they're full of tiny shops, rows of windows edged with curling wrought iron, and vistas of red-tile roofs and the sea. Start with a walk up and down the *malecón.*

Among the sights you shouldn't miss is the **municipal building** on the main square (next to the tourism office), which has a large Manuel Lepe mural inside in its stairwell.

Moments **A Spectacular Sight**

Performances of the **Voladores de Papantla (Papantla Flyers)** take place every day at 10 and 11am; and in the evenings, Friday to Wednesday at 7:30, 8:30, and 9:30pm on the *malecón,* adjacent to the "Boy on a Seahorse" statue. In this pre-Columbian religious ritual, four men are suspended from the top of a tall pole, circling around it (as if in flight), while another beats a drum and plays a flute while balancing himself at the top. It signifies the four cardinal points, and the mystic "center" of the self, a sacred direction for ancient Mexican cultures.

Nearby, right up Independencia, sits the picturesque **Parish of Nuestra Señora de Guadalupe church,** Hidalgo 370 (© **322/222-1326**), topped with a curious crown held in place by angels—a replica of the one worn by Empress Carlota during her brief time in Mexico as Emperor Maximilian's wife. On its steps, women sell religious mementos; across the narrow street, stalls sell native herbs for curing common ailments. Services in English are held each Saturday at 5pm, and Sunday at 10am. Regular hours are Monday through Saturday from 7:30am to 8:30pm, Sunday from 6:30am to 8:30pm. Note that entrance is restricted to those properly attired—no shorts or sleeveless shirts allowed. Three blocks south of the church, head east on Libertad, lined with small shops and pretty upper windows, to the **municipal market** by the river. (It's the Río Cuale Mercado, but I once overheard a tourist ask for the "real quality" market!) After exploring the market, cross the bridge to the island in the river; sometimes a painter is at work on its banks. Walk down the center of the island toward the sea, and you'll come to the tiny **Museo Río Cuale** (no phone; Mon–Sat 10am–5pm; free admission), which has a small but impressive permanent exhibit of pre-Columbian figurines.

Retrace your steps to the market and Libertad, and follow Calle Miramar to the brightly colored steps up to Zaragoza. Up Zaragoza to the right 1 block is the famous **pink arched bridge** that once connected Richard Burton's and Elizabeth Taylor's houses. In this area, known as **"Gringo Gulch,"** many Americans have houses.

SHOPPING

Shopping in Puerto Vallarta is generally concentrated in small, eclectic, independent shops rather than impersonal malls. You can find excellent **folk art,** original **clothing** designs, fine jewelry, and creative home accessories at great prices. Vallarta is known for having the most diverse and impressive selection of **contemporary Mexican fine art** outside Mexico City. It also has an abundance of tacky T-shirts and the ubiquitous **silver jewelry.**

THE SHOPPING SCENE

There are a few key shopping areas: central downtown, the Marina Vallarta *malecón,* the popular *mercados,* and on the beach—where the merchandise comes to you. Some of the more attractive shops are 1 to 2 blocks in **back of the *malecón.*** Start at the intersection of Corona and Morelos streets—interesting shops spread out in all directions from here. **Marina Vallarta** has two shopping plazas, Plaza Marina and Neptuno Plaza, on the main highway from the airport into town, which offer a limited selection of shops, with Plaza Neptuno primarily featuring home decor shops. Although still home to a few interesting shops, the *marina malecón* (marina boardwalk) is dominated by real estate companies, timeshare vendors, restaurants, and boating services.

Downtown Puerto Vallarta

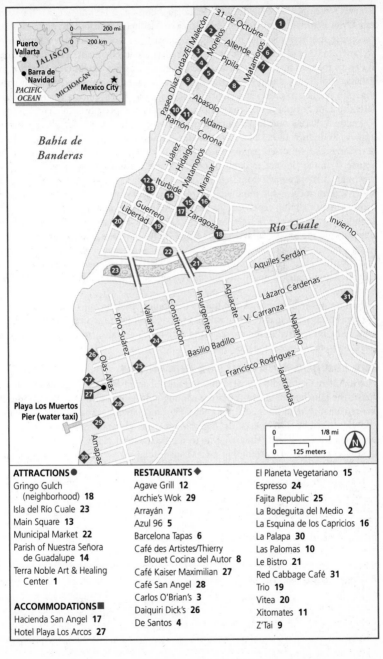

ATTRACTIONS ●

Gringo Gulch
(neighborhood) **18**
Isla del Río Cuale **23**
Main Square **13**
Municipal Market **22**
Parish of Nuestra Señora
de Guadalupe **14**
Terra Noble Art & Healing
Center **1**

ACCOMMODATIONS ■

Hacienda San Angel **17**
Hotel Playa Los Arcos **27**

RESTAURANTS ◆

Agave Grill **12**
Archie's Wok **29**
Arrayán **7**
Azul 96 **5**
Barcelona Tapas **6**
Café des Artistes/Thierry
Blouet Cocina del Autor **8**
Café Kaiser Maximilian **27**
Café San Angel **28**
Carlos O'Brian's **3**
Daiquiri Dick's **26**
De Santos **4**

El Planeta Vegetariano **15**
Espresso **24**
Fajita Republic **25**
La Bodeguita del Medio **2**
La Esquina de los Capricios **16**
La Palapa **30**
Las Palomas **10**
Le Bistro **21**
Red Cabbage Café **31**
Trio **19**
Vitea **20**
Xitomates **11**
Z'Tai **9**

A new (September 2006) addition to Vallarta's shopping and dining scene is the modern **Plaza Peninsula** (located on Av. Francisco Medina Ascencio 2485, just south of the cruise ship terminal and north of the Ameca River bridge; no phone number or website), in front of a large waterfront condominium development of the same name. It's home to more than 30 businesses including Vallarta's first **Starbuck's,** as well as art galleries, boutiques, and a varied selection of restaurants. There is underground parking, plus public sculptures and comfy outdoor seating. It has quickly emerged as Vallarta's current hotspot for hanging out in the evenings, especially with teens.

Puerto Vallarta's **municipal market** is just north of the Río Cuale, where Libertad and A. Rodríguez meet. The *mercado* sells clothes, jewelry, serapes, shawls, leather accessories and suitcases, papier-mâché parrots, stuffed frogs and armadillos, and, of course, T-shirts. Be sure to comparison-shop, and definitely bargain before buying. The market is open daily from 9am to 7pm. Upstairs, a **food market** serves inexpensive Mexican meals—for more adventurous diners, it's probably the best value and most authentic dining experience in Vallarta. An **outdoor market** is along Río Cuale Island, between the two bridges. Stalls sell crafts, gifts, folk art, and clothing. New to downtown is the **Small Vallarta** (© **322/222-7530**) on Paseo Díaz Ordaz 928, on the eastern side, just before the start of the *malecón*. It is a "small mall" featuring tourist-friendly shops and dining options, including Carl's Jr.'s burgers, Häagen-Dazs ice cream, Swatch watch shop, El Mundo de Tequila, and a Diamonds International jewelry store.

In most of the better shops and galleries, shipping, packing, and delivery to Puerto Vallarta hotels are available. Some will also ship to your home address. Note that while bargaining is expected in the *mercados* and with beach vendors, stores generally charge fixed—and fair—prices for their wares.

THE LOWDOWN ON HUICHOL INDIAN ART

Puerto Vallarta offers the best selection of Huichol art in Mexico. Descendants of the Aztec, the Huichol are one of the last remaining indigenous cultures in the world that has remained true to its ancient traditions, customs, language, and habitat. The Huichol live in adobe structures in the high Sierras (at an elevation of 1,400m/4,592 ft.) north and east of Puerto Vallarta. Due to the decreasing fertility (and therefore productivity) of the land surrounding their villages, they have come to depend more on the sale of their artwork for sustenance.

Huichol art has always been cloaked in a veil of mysticism—probably one of the reasons serious collectors seek out this form of *artesanía*. Colorful, symbolic yarn "paintings," inspired by visions experienced during spiritual ceremonies, characterize Huichol art. In the ceremonies, artists ingest peyote, a hallucinogenic cactus, which induces brightly colored visions; these are considered messages from their ancestors.

Tips Beware the Silver Scam

Much of the silver sold on the beach is actually alpaca, a lower-quality silver metal (even though many pieces are stamped with the designation ".925," supposedly indicating true silver). Prices for silver on the beach are much lower, as is the quality. If you're looking for a more lasting piece of jewelry, you're better off in a silver shop.

Fun Fact A Huichol Art Primer: Shopping Tips

Huichol art falls into two main categories: yarn paintings and beaded pieces. All other items you might find in Huichol art galleries are either ceremonial objects or items used in everyday life.

Yarn paintings are made on a wood base covered with wax and meticulously overlaid with colored yarn. Designs represent the magical vision of the underworld, and each symbol gives meaning to the piece. Paintings made with wool yarn are more authentic than those made with acrylic; however, acrylic yarn paintings are usually brighter and have more detail because the threads are thinner. It is normal to find empty spaces where the wax base shows. Usually the artist starts with a central motif and works around it, but it's common to have several independent motifs that, when combined, take on a different meaning. A painting with many small designs tells a more complicated story than one with only one design and fill-work on the background. Look for the story of the piece on the back of the painting. Most Huichol artists write in pencil in Huichol and Spanish.

Beaded pieces are made on carved wooden shapes depicting different animals, wooden eggs, or small bowls made from gourds. The pieces are covered with wax and tiny *chaquira* beads are applied one by one to form designs. Usually the beaded designs represent animals; plants; the elements of fire, water, or air; and certain symbols that give a special meaning to the whole. Deer, snakes, wolves, and scorpions are traditional elements; other figures, such as iguanas, frogs, and any animals not indigenous to Huichol territory, are incorporated by popular demand. Beadwork with many small designs that do not exactly fit into one another is more time-consuming and has a more complex symbolic meaning. This kind of work has empty spaces where the wax shows.

The visions' symbolic and mythological imagery influences the art, which encompasses not only yarn paintings but also fascinating masks and bowls decorated with tiny colored beads.

The Huichol might be geographically isolated, but they are learning the importance of good business and have adapted their art to meet consumer demand. Original Huichol art, therefore, is not necessarily traditional. Iguanas, jaguars, sea turtles, frogs, eclipses, and eggs appear in response to consumer demand. For more traditional works, look for pieces that depict deer, scorpions, wolves, or snakes.

The Huichol have also had to modify their techniques to create more pieces in less time and meet increased demand. Patterned fill-work, which is faster to produce, sometimes replaces the detailed designs that are used to fill the pieces. The same principle applies to yarn paintings. While some are beautiful depictions of landscapes and even abstract pieces, they are not traditional themes.

You may see Huichol Indians on the streets of Vallarta—they are easy to spot, dressed in white clothing embroidered with colorful designs. A number of fine Huichol galleries are in downtown Puerto Vallarta (see individual listings under "Crafts & Gifts" and "Decorative & Folk Art," below).

One place to learn more about the Huichol is **Huichol Collection,** Morelos 490, across from the sea-horse statue on the *malecón* (© **322/223-2141**). Not only does this shop offer an extensive selection of Huichol art in all price ranges, but it also has a replica of a Huichol adobe hut, informational displays explaining more about their fascinating way of life and beliefs, and usually a Huichol artist at work. However, note that this is a timeshare sales location, so don't be surprised if you're hit with a pitch for a "free" breakfast and property tour. **Peyote People,** Juarez 222 (© **322/222-2302,** and 222-6268; www.peyotepeople.com), is a more authentic shop specializing in Huichol yarn paintings and bead art from San Andres Cohamiata, one of the main villages of this indigenous group, up in the high Sierra. The shop is open Monday through Friday from 10am until 9pm and Saturday and Sunday 10am to 6pm.

CLOTHING

Vallarta's single true department store is **LANS,** with branches at Juárez 867 (© **322/ 226-9100;** www.lans.com.mx), and in Plaza Caracol, next door to the supermarket Gigante, in the Hotel Zone (© **322/226-0204**). Both offer a wide selection of name-brand clothing, accessories, footwear, cosmetics, and home furnishings. Along with the nationally popular **LOB, Carlos 'n' Charlie's,** and **Bye-Bye** brands, Vallarta offers a few distinctive shops.

Laura López Labra Designs The most comfortable clothing you'll ever enjoy. LLL is renowned for her trademark all-white (or natural) designs in 100% cotton or lace. Laura's fine gauze fabrics float in her designs of seductive skirts, romantic dresses, blouses, beachwear, and baby dolls. Men's offerings include cotton drawstring pants and lightweight shirts. Other designs include a line of precious children's clothing and some pieces with elaborate embroidery based on Huichol Indian designs. Personalized wedding dresses are also available. Open Monday through Saturday from 10am to 3:30pm and from 5 to 9pm. Basilio Badillo 329-A. © 322/113-0102.

Mar de Sueños ★★ This small shop carries stunning swimsuits and exquisite lingerie. Without a doubt, the finest women's beachwear, intimate apparel, and evening wear in Vallarta for those special occasions—or just to make you feel extra special. The shop also stocks a selection of fine linen clothing—and it's one of the few places in Mexico that carries the renowned Italian line La Perla. Other name brands include Gottex, D&G, and DKNY. Open daily from 10am to 9pm. Basilio Badillo 277-B. © 322/ 222-7362.

CONTEMPORARY ART

Known for sustaining one of the stronger art communities in Latin America, Puerto Vallarta has an impressive selection of fine galleries featuring quality original works. Several dozen galleries get together to offer art walks almost every week between November and April.

Corsica Among the newest and best of Vallarta's galleries, Corsica features an exquisite collection of sculptures, installations, and paintings, from world-renown contemporary artists from Mexico. They offer professional packing and worldwide shipping with purchases. There are three locations—at Guadalupe Sanchez 735, Leona Vicario 230, and Plaza Península. Open Monday through Saturday 11am to 2pm, and by appointment 5 to 11pm. © 322/223-1821. www.galeriacorsica.com.

Galería AL (Arte Latinoamericano) This gallery showcases contemporary works created by young, primarily Latin American artists, as well as Vallarta favorite Marta

Gilbert. Feature exhibitions take place every 2 weeks during high season. The historic building (one of Vallarta's original structures) has exposed brick walls; small rooms of exhibition spaces on the second and third floors surround an open courtyard. It's also rumored to have a friendly resident ghost, who partner Susan Burger says has been quite welcoming. Open Monday through Saturday from 10:30am to 9pm. Josefa Ortiz Domínguez 155. ℂ 322/222-4406. www.galeriaal.com.

Galería des Artistes This stunning gallery features contemporary painters and sculptors from throughout Mexico, including the renowned original "magiscopes" of Feliciano Bejar. Paintings by a Vallarta favorite Evelyn Boren, as well as a small selection of works by Mexican masters, including Orozco, can be found here, among the exposed brick walls and stylish interior spaces. It's open Monday to Saturday 11am to 10pm Just across the street, affiliate **Galería Omar Alonso** (ℂ 322/222-5587; www. galeriaomaralonso.com) exhibits photography by internationally renowned artists. Open Monday through Saturday 11am to 11pm. Leona Vicario 248. ℂ 322/223-0006.

Galería Pacífico Since opening in 1987, Galería Pacífico has been considered one of the finest in Mexico. On display is a wide selection of sculptures and paintings in various media by midrange masters and up-and-comers alike. The gallery is 1½ blocks inland from the fantasy sculptures on the *malecón*. Among the artists whose careers Galería Pacífico has influenced are rising talent Brewster Brockman, internationally renowned sculptor Ramiz Barquet, and Patrick Denoun. Open Monday through Saturday from 10am to 8pm; Sunday by appointment. Between May and October, check for reduced hours or vacation closings. Aldama 174, 2nd floor. ℂ 322/222-1982. galeriapacifico@prodigy.net.mx.

Galería Uno One of Vallarta's first galleries, the Galería Uno features an excellent selection of contemporary paintings by Latin American artists, plus a variety of posters and prints. During the high season, featured exhibitions change every 2 weeks. In a classic adobe building with open courtyard, it's also a casual, salon-style gathering place for friends of owner Jan Lavender. Open Monday through Saturday from 10am to 10pm. Morelos 561 (at Corona). ℂ 322/222-0908.

Galleria Dante This gallery-in-a-villa showcases contemporary art as well as sculptures and classical reproductions of Italian, Greek, and Art Deco bronzes—against a backdrop of gardens and fountains. Works by more than 50 Mexican and international artists are represented, including the acclaimed local talent Rogelio Diaz, as well as Alejandro Colunga and Tellosa. Located on the "Calle de los Cafés," the gallery is open during the winter Monday through Saturday from 10am to 5pm, and by appointment. Basilio Badillo 269. ℂ 322/222-2477. www.galleriadante.com.

Studio Cathy Von Rohr This lovely studio showcases the work of Cathy Von Rohr, one of the most respected artists in the area. For years, Cathy lived in the secluded cove of Majahuitas, on the bay's southern shore, and much of her work reflects the tranquillity and deep connection with the natural world that resulted. Paintings, prints, and sculptures are featured. It's open by appointment and does not accept credit cards. Manuel M. Diéguez 321. ℂ 866/256-2739 in the U.S., or 322/222-5875. www. cathyvonrohr.com.

CRAFTS & GIFTS

Alfarería Tlaquepaque Opened in 1953, this is Vallarta's original source for Mexican ceramics and decorative crafts, all at excellent prices. Talavera pottery and dishware, colored glassware, birdcages, baskets, and wood furniture are just a few of the many items in this warehouse-style store. Open Monday through Saturday, 9am to 9pm, and Sundays from 9am to 3pm. Av. México 1100. ℃ **322/223-2121.**

La Casa del Feng Shui   I am enchanted by this shop's selection of crystals, candles, talismans, fountains, and wind chimes—along with many more items designed to keep the good energy flowing in your home, office, or personal space. Why not take home something to add more harmony to your life? Open Monday through Saturday from 9am to 9pm. Corona 165, around the corner from Morelos. ℃ **322/222-3300.**

Safari Accents   Flickering candles glowing in colored-glass holders welcome you to this highly original shop overflowing with creative gifts, one-of-a-kind furnishings, and reproductions of paintings by Frida Kahlo and Botero. Open daily from 10am to 11pm. Olas Altas 224, Loc. 4. ℃ **322/223-2660.**

DECORATIVE & FOLK ART

Banderas Bay Trading Company ⭐   This shop features fine antiques and one-of-a-kind decorative objects for the home, including contemporary furniture, antique wooden doors, religious-themed items, original art, hand-loomed textiles, glassware, and pewter. This unique selection is handpicked by one of the area's most noteworthy interior designers, Peter Bowman. Open Monday to Saturday 9am to 9pm. Lázaro Cárdenas 263 (near Ignacio L. Vallarta). ℃ **322/223-4352** There's also a *bodega* (warehouse) annex of the shop located at Constitución 319 ℃ **322/223-9817.**

Lucy's CuCu Cabaña *(Finds*   Owners Lucy and Gil Givens have assembled an exceptionally entertaining and eclectic collection of Mexican folk art—about 70% of which is animal-themed. Each summer they travel Mexico and personally select the handmade works created by over 100 indigenous artists and artisans. Items include metal sculptures, Oaxacan wooden animals, *retablos* (altars), and fine Talavera ceramics. Open Monday through Saturday from 10am to 8pm. The store is closed from May 15 to October 15. Basilio Badillo 295. ℃ **322/222-4839.**

Olinala   This shop contains two floors of fine indigenous Mexican crafts and folk art, including an impressive collection of museum-quality masks and original contemporary art by gallery owner Brewster Brockman. Open Monday through Friday from 10am to 2pm and 5 to 8pm, Saturday from 10am to 2pm. Lázaro Cárdenas 274. ℃ **322/222-4995.**

Puerco Azul   Set in a space that actually has a former pig-roasting oven, Puerco Azul features a whimsical and eclectic selection of art and home accessories, much of it created by owner and artist Lee Chapman (aka Lencho). You'll find many animal-themed works in bright colors, including his signature *puercos azules* (blue pigs). Open Monday to Saturday from 10am to 8pm, closed on Sunday. Constitución 325, just off Basilio Badillo's "restaurant row." ℃ **322/222-8647.**

Tips Meet the Author

If you're shopping at Lucy's CuCu Cabaña, you may find yourself attended to by Lucy's husband, and Vallarta's favorite author, Gil Gevins. Gil's hilarious books include *Refried Brains, Puerto Vallarta on 49 Brain Cells a Day*, and the follow-up *Puerto Vallarta on a Donkey a Day*—laugh-out-loud tales of life in this town, perfect for beach reading. And, natch, they're available for sale at the shop. You couldn't buy a better souvenir.

Querubines *Finds* This is my personal favorite for the finest-quality artisanal works from throughout Mexico. Owner Marcella García travels across the country to select the items, which include exceptional artistic silver jewelry, embroidered and hand-woven clothing, bolts of loomed fabrics, tin mirrors and lamps, glassware, pewter frames and trays, high-quality wool rugs, straw bags, and Panama hats. Open Monday through Saturday from 9am to 9pm. Under the same ownership and open the same hours, **Serafina,** Basilio Badillo 260 (© **322/223-4594**), features a more extensive selection of cotton clothing and handmade jewelry. Juárez 501A (corner of Galeana). © **322/223-1727.**

JEWELRY & ACCESSORIES

Viva ★★★ *Finds* At Viva, both the shop and the jewelry are stunning. You enter through a long corridor lined with displays showcasing exquisite jewelry from over 450 international designers, including Mexico's finest silversmiths. Open daily from 10am to 11pm. Basilio Badillo 274. © **322/222-4078.** www.vivacollection.com.

TEQUILA & CIGARS

La Casa del Habano This fine tobacco shop has certified quality cigars from Cuba, along with humidors, cutters, elegant lighters, and other smoking accessories. It's also a local cigar club, with a walk-in humidor for regular clients. In the back, you'll find comfy leather couches, TV sports, and full bar service—in other words, a manly place to take a break from shopping. Open Monday through Saturday from noon to 9pm. Aldama 170. © **322/223-2758.**

La Casa del Tequila ★ Here you'll find an extensive selection of premium tequilas, plus information and tastings. Also available are books, tequila glassware, and other tequila-drinking accessories. The shop has recently (2005) been downsized to accommodate the **Agave Grill** (see "Where to Dine," later in this chapter) in the back, but now you can enjoy tasty Mexican fare and margaritas while you shop! Open Monday through Saturday from noon to 11pm. Morelos 589. © **322/222-2000.**

WHERE TO STAY

Beyond a varied selection of hotels and resorts, Puerto Vallarta offers many alternative accommodations. Oceanfront or marina-view condominiums and elegant private villas can offer families and small groups a better value and more ample space than a hotel. For more information on short-term rentals, check out **www.costavallartaboutique villas.com.** Prices start at $99 (£54) a night for nonbeachside condos and go to $3,000 (£1,650) for penthouse condos or private villas. Susan Weisman's **Bayside Properties,** Francisco Rodríguez 160, corner of Olas Altas (© **322/223-4424** and 222-8148; www.baysidepropertiespv.com), rents condos, villas, and hotels for individuals and large groups, including gay-friendly accommodations. She can arrange airport pickup and in-villa cooks. Another reputable option is the full-service travel agency, **Holland's** (© **415/841-1194** or 888/8672723; www.puertovallartavillas.com). For the ultimate, indulge in a Punta Mita Villa rental within this exclusive resort. Contact **Mita Residential** (© **877/561-2893** in the U.S., or 329/291-5300; www.mita residential.com).

This section lists hotels in directional order, moving south along Banderas Bay from the airport.

MARINA VALLARTA

Marina Vallarta is the most modern and deluxe area of hotel development in Puerto Vallarta. Located immediately south of the airport and just north of the cruise-ship terminal, it's a planned development whose centerpiece is a 450-slip modern marina.

The hotels reviewed below are on the beachfront of the peninsula. The beaches here are much less attractive than beaches in other parts of the bay; the sand is darker, firmly packed, and, during certain times of the year, quite rocky. These hotels compensate with oversize pool areas and exotic landscaping. This area suits families and those looking for lots of centralized activity. Marina Vallarta is also home to an 18-hole **golf course** designed by Joe Finger.

In addition to the hotels reviewed below, an excellent choice is **Casa Velas,** on the golf course at Pelícanos 311 (© **866/612-1097** in the U.S., or 322/226-6688; www. hotelcasavelas.com). The elegant, boutique-style hotel has extra large rooms, an on-site spa, and a lovely pool. Although it is not located on the beach, it has a stunning beach club with food and beverage service, a pool, and sun chairs, with shuttle service for guests. High-season rates average $650 (£358), all inclusive.

Due to traffic (rather than distance), a taxi from the Marina to downtown takes 20 to 30 minutes.

Velas Vallarta Grand Suite Resort ★★★ (Kids)

The beachside Velas Vallarta is an excellent choice for families. Each suite offers a full-size, fully equipped kitchen, ample living and dining areas, separate bedroom or bedrooms, and a large balcony with seating. Following a complete makeover in 2003, the suites are now decorated in a sophisticated, modern design featuring jewel-tone colors, Huichol art and Mexican textiles, feather beds with goose down comforters, 27-inch flatscreen TVs, modern kitchen appliances, and teak-wood furniture on balconies and terraces. Special extras include a pillow menu and luxury bathroom amenities. This property is part hotel, part full-ownership condominiums, which means each suite is the size of a residential unit. The suites all have partial ocean views; they face a central area where three freeform swimming pools, complete with bridges and waterfalls, meander through tropical gardens. A full range of services means you'd never need to leave the place if you don't want to. The Marina Vallarta Golf Club is across the street, and special packages are available for Velas guests. Guests may pay an extra fee for the Gold Crown All-Inclusive option, which is one of the most premium all-inclusive programs in Mexico.

Paseo de la Marina 485, Marina Vallarta, 48354 Puerto Vallarta, Jal. © **800/VELAS-PV (835-2778)** in the U.S. and Canada, or 322/221-0091. Fax 322/221-0755. www.velasvallarta.com. 361 units. $390 (£215) double; $740–$1,110 (£407–£611) suite. All inclusive prices. AE, DC, MC, V. Free indoor parking. **Amenities:** 2 restaurants; poolside snack bar; lobby bar; 3 outdoor pools; golf privileges at Marina Vallarta Golf Club; 3 lighted tennis courts; fitness center w/spa and massage; beach w/watersports equipment; complimentary bikes; activities program for children and adults; concierge; travel agency; car rental; minimarket; deli; salon; room service; laundry service. *In room:* A/C, TV, kitchen, coffeemaker, hair dryer, iron, safe.

Westin Resort & Spa Puerto Vallarta ★★

Stunning architecture and vibrant colors are the hallmark of this award-winning property, considered Puerto Vallarta's finest. Although the grounds are large—over 8 hectares (20 acres) with 260m (853 ft.) of beachfront—the warm service and gracious hospitality create the feeling of an intimate resort. Hundreds of tall palms surround the spectacular central freeform pool. You'll find hammocks strung between the palms closest to the beach, where there are also private beach cabañas. Rooms are contemporary in style, with oversize wood furnishings, tile floors, original art, and tub/shower combinations. Balconies have panoramic views. Eight junior suites and some double rooms have Jacuzzis, and the five grand suites and presidential suite are two-level, with ample living areas. Two floors of rooms make up the Royal Beach Club, with VIP services, including private concierge. The fitness center is one of the most modern, well-equipped facilities in Vallarta, with regularly scheduled spinning and yoga classes. **Nikki Beach** (www. nikkibeach.com), a renowned haven for the hip, opened an on-site, beachfront restaurant and club in 2004, complete with big, white bed-size lounges for taking in the sun, or enjoying libations anytime from noon until the early morning hours. Their Sunday champagne brunch is especially popular.

Paseo de la Marina Sur 205, Marina Vallarta, 48354 Puerto Vallarta, Jal. © 800/228-3000 in the U.S., or 322/226-1100. Fax 322/226-1144. www.starwoodhotels.com/westin. 280 units. High season $265–$529 (£146–£291) double, $559–$725 (£307–£399) suite; low season $119–$389 (£65–£214) double, $429–$659 (£236–£362) suite. AE, DC, MC, V. Free parking. **Amenities:** 2 restaurants; Nikki Beach Club; 2 poolside bars; lobby bar; oceanside pool; golf privileges at Marina Vallarta Golf Club; 3 lighted grass tennis courts; state-of-the-art health club w/treadmills, StairMasters, resistance equipment, sauna, steam room, solarium, whirlpool, massage, and salon; Kids' Club; travel agency; car rental; shopping arcade; room service; laundry service. *In room:* A/C, TV, minibar, coffeemaker, hair dryer, iron, safe.

THE HOTEL ZONE

The main street running between the airport and town is Avenida Francisco Medina Ascencio. The hotels here offer excellent, wide beachfronts with generally tranquil waters for swimming. From here it's a quick taxi or bus ride to downtown.

Fiesta Americana Puerto Vallarta ⊛

The Fiesta Americana's towering, three-story, thatched *palapa* lobby is a landmark in the Hotel Zone, and the hotel is known for its excellent beach and friendly service. An abundance of plants, splashing fountains, constant breezes, and comfortable seating areas in the lobby create a casual South Seas ambience. The nine-story terra-cotta building embraces a large plaza with a pool facing the beach. Marble-trimmed rooms in neutral tones with pastel accents contain carved headboards and comfortable rattan and wicker furniture. All have private balconies with ocean and pool views.

Av. Francisco Medina Ascencio Km 2.5, 48300 Puerto Vallarta, Jal. © 322/226-2100. Fax 322/224-2108. www.fiesta americana.com. 291 units. High season $209–$400 (£116–£222) double; low season $120–$196 (£66–£108) double; year-round $256–$819 (£141–£450) suite. AE, DC, MC, V. Limited free parking. **Amenities:** 3 restaurants; lobby bar w/live music nightly; large pool w/activities and children's activities in high season; travel agency; salon; room service; laundry service. *In room:* A/C, TV, minibar, hair dryer, safe.

Premier Hotel & Spa ⊛⊛

You couldn't ask for a better location to be close to all that Vallarta's vibrant *centro* has to offer. Located on a wide swathe of golden sand beach—and just a few blocks north of the start of the *malecón*—the Premier is easy walking distance or a quick taxi ride to the downtown restaurants, shops, galleries, and clubs. One of the newer hotels in Vallarta (opened 1999), the architecture is contemporary, but its size gives it an intimate feel. With a first-rate spa and a policy that restricts guests to ages 16 and older, it's a place that caters to relaxation. Four types of rooms are available, but all are decorated in warm colors with tile floors and light wood furnishings. Deluxe rooms have ocean views, a respectable seating area with comfortable chairs, plus a sizable private balcony—request one of several that has an outdoor whirlpool. There are also seven suites that have a separate living room plus a dining area with private bar, and a spacious terrace. These rooms also have a double whirlpool tub, and separate glass-enclosed shower. The top-of-the-line master suites have all that the above suites offer, plus an outdoor whirlpool on the spacious balcony.

The stunning bi-level spa is the real attraction of this hotel—scented with aromatherapy and glowing with candlelight, it uses top-notch, 100% natural products, most based on Mexico's natural treasures like coconut, aloe, and papaya. If you're not tempted by the nearby and accessible dining choices in downtown Vallarta, the Premier also offers an all-inclusive option, with all meals and drinks included.

San Salvador 117, behind the Buenaventura Hotel, Col. 5 de Diciembre, 48350 Puerto Vallarta, Jal. ℭ 877/886-9176 in the U.S., or 322/226-7001 and 322/226-7040. Fax 322/226-7043. www.premieronline.com.mx. 83 units. Room only: high season $135–$430 (£74–£237) double; low season $135–$370 (£74–£204) double. All-inclusive: high season $295–$545 (£162–£300) per person, based on double occupancy; low season $185–$360 (£102–£198) per person, double. AE, MC, V. Limited street parking. No children younger than 16 accepted. **Amenities:** 3 restaurants; 2 outdoor pools; fitness center; full spa; travel agency; salon; room service; laundry service. *In room:* A/C, TV, minibar, coffeemaker, hair dryer, safe.

DOWNTOWN TO LOS MUERTOS BEACH

This part of town has recently undergone a renaissance; economical hotels and good-value guesthouses dominate. Several blocks off the beach, you can find numerous budget inns offering clean, simply furnished rooms; most offer discounts for long-term stays. Much of Vallarta's nightlife activity now centers in the areas south of the Río Cuale and along Olas Altas.

Hacienda San Angel ⭐⭐⭐ *Finds*   This enchanting boutique hotel may not be on the beach, but you'll hardly miss it, you'll be so pampered in the stunning suites, or satisfied enjoying the view from the rooftop heated pool or Jacuzzi and sun deck. It's my top choice for a luxury stay in Puerto Vallarta. Once Richard Burton's home in Puerto Vallarta, it's located just behind Puerto Vallarta's famed church, making it easy walking distance to all of the restaurants, shopping, and galleries of downtown. The Hacienda consists of five villas; the first two are joined to the third villa by a path that winds through a lovely terraced garden filled with tropical plants, flowers, statuary, and a charming fountain, while the Las Campañas private one-bedroom villa is located on the northern border of the garden. The newest villa offers four suites, each with sweeping views. A large, heated pool and deck offer panoramic views of the city and Bay of Banderas, while a second sun deck with Jacuzzi literally overlooks the church's crown, across to the water beyond. Each of the Hacienda's 10 elegant suites is individually decorated, accented with exquisite antiques and original art. Bed linens and coverings are of the finest quality, with touches like Venetian lace and goose-down pillows. Each morning, you'll awake to continental breakfast served outside your suite at your requested hour. Sophisticated style, coupled with casual Vallarta charm, make Hacienda San Angel the top "find" in Mexico for the discriminating traveler. Hacienda is now open for dinner for nonguests to enjoy (see "Where to Dine," below).

Miramar 336, Col. Centro, 48300 Puerto Vallarta, Jal. ℭ 415/738-8220 or 322/222-2692. www.haciendasanangel. com. 10 units. High season $265-$565 (£146–£311) double; low season $235–$495 (£146–£272) double. All rates include daily continental breakfast. Rates for the entire Hacienda or separate villas consisting of 3 suites each are also available. MC, V. Very limited street parking available. **Amenities:** Menu of full breakfast, lunch, and dinner, or private chef available; 2 outdoor pools; rooftop sun deck w/Jacuzzi; concierge; tour services; complimentary Internet access. *In room:* A/C, TV/DVD, hair dryer, safe, CD player.

Hotel Playa Los Arcos ⭐⭐   This is one of Vallarta's perennially popular hotels and a favorite of mine, with a stellar location in the heart of Los Muertos Beach, central to the Olas Altas sidewalk-cafe action and close to downtown. The four-story structure is U-shaped, facing the ocean, with a small swimming pool in the courtyard. Rooms with private balconies overlook the pool. The 10 suites have ocean views; 5 of these have kitchenettes. The standard rooms are small but pleasantly decorated and immaculate, with carved wooden furniture painted pale pink. On the premises are a *palapa* beachside bar with occasional live entertainment, a gourmet coffee shop, and the popular Kaiser Maximilian's gourmet restaurant. It's 7 blocks south of the river.

Olas Altas 380, 48380 Puerto Vallarta, Jal. ⓒ **800/648-2403** in the U.S., or 322/222-1583 and 322/226-7100. Fax 322/226-7104. www.playalosarcos.com. 175 units. High season $105–$145 (£58–£80) double, $155–$175 (£85–£96) suite; low season $85–$120 (£47–£66) double, $118–$152 (£65–£84) suite. AE, MC, V. Limited street parking. **Amenities:** 2 restaurants; lobby bar; outdoor pool; tour desk; car-rental desk; babysitting; laundry; safe. *In room:* A/C, TV.

SOUTH TO MISMALOYA

Casa Tres Vidas 🌟🌟 *Value*   Terraced down a hillside to Conchas Chinas Beach, Casa Tres Vidas is three individual villas that make great, affordable lodgings for families or groups of friends. Set on a stunning private cove, Tres Vidas gives you the experience of your own private villa, complete with service staff. It offers outstanding value for the location—close to town, with panoramic views from every room—as well as for the excellent service. Each villa has at least two levels and over 460 sq. m (nearly 5,000 sq. ft.) of mostly open living areas, plus a private swimming pool, heated whirlpool, and air-conditioned bedrooms. The Vida Alta penthouse villa has three bedrooms, plus a rooftop deck with pool and bar. Vida Sol villa's three bedrooms sleep 10 (two rooms have two king-size beds each). Directly on the ocean, Vida Mar is a four-bedroom villa, accommodating eight. The staff prepares gourmet meals in your villa twice a day—you choose the menu and pay only for the food. If you're planning a wedding, Tres Vidas and its adjacent sister property, Quinta María Cortez, do a stunning job.

Sagitario 132, Playa Conchas Chinas, 48300 Puerto Vallarta, Jal. ⓒ **888/640-8100** or 801/531-8100 in the U.S., or 322/221-5317. Fax 322/221-53-27. www.casatresvidas.com. 3 villas. High season $700 (£385) villa; low season $500 (£275) villa. Rates include services such as housekeeping and meal preparation. Special summer 1- or 2-bedroom rates available; minimum 3 nights. AE, MC, V. Very limited street parking. **Amenities:** 2 prepared daily meals; private outdoor pool; concierge; tour desk; car rental. *In room:* A/C (in bedrooms), safe.

Dreams Puerto Vallarta Resort & Spa 🌟🌟   Formerly the Camino Real, this original luxury hotel in Puerto Vallarta was taken over by AMResorts in 2004 and turned into the premium all-inclusive Dreams Resort. It has the nicest beach of any Vallarta hotel, with soft white sand in a private cove. Set apart from other properties, with a lush mountain backdrop, it retains the exclusivity that made it popular from the beginning—yet it's only a 5- to 10-minute ride to town. The hotel consists of two buildings: the 250-room main hotel, which curves gently with the shape of the Playa Las Estacas, and the newer 11-story Club Tower, also facing the beach and ocean. An ample pool fronts the main building, facing the beach. Standard rooms in the main building are large; some have sliding doors opening onto the beach, and others have balconies. Club Tower rooms (from the sixth floor up) feature balconies with whirlpool tubs. The top floor consists of six two-bedroom suites, each with a private swimming pool, and with special concierge services. All rooms feature ocean views, and are decorated in vibrant colors, with marble floors and artwork by local renowned artist Manuel Lepe. In 2004, all rooms were completely renovated, with additions including two new swimming pools (including an adults-only tranquillity pool), a wedding gazebo, and upgraded health club and spa.

Carretera Barra de Navidad Km 3.5, Playa Las Estacas, 48300 Puerto Vallarta, Jal. ⓒ **866/237-3267** in the U.S. and Canada, or 322/226-5000. Fax 322/221-6000. www.dreamsresorts.com. 337 units. All-inclusive rates include all meals, premium drinks, activities, airport transfers, tips, and taxes. $360 (£198) double; $440 (£242) junior suite; $520

(£286) suite. AE, DC, MC, V. Free secured parking. **Amenities:** 5 restaurants; lobby bar; pool bar; 3 outdoor pools; 2 lighted grass tennis courts; fully equipped health club; spa; children's program (Easter and Christmas vacations only); travel agency; car rental; convenience store; room service; laundry service. *In room:* A/C, TV, minibar, hair dryer, iron, safe.

Quinta María Cortez *✦✦✦ Finds*   A sophisticated, imaginative B&B on the beach, this is Puerto Vallarta's most original place to stay—and one of Mexico's most memorable inns. Most of the seven large suites, uniquely decorated with antiques, whimsical curios, and original art, have a kitchenette and balcony. Sunny terraces, a small pool, and a central gathering area with fireplace and *palapa*-topped dining area (where an excellent full breakfast is served) occupy different levels of the seven-story house. A rooftop terrace offers another sunbathing alternative—and is among the best sunset-watching spots in town. The quinta is on a beautiful cove on Conchas Chinas beach. A terrace fronting the beach accommodates chairs for taking in the sunset.

The Quinta María wins my highest recommendation (in fact, I enjoyed living here for a few years when it still accepted long-term stays), but admittedly it's not for everyone. Air-conditioned areas are limited, due to the open nature of the suites and common areas. Those who love it return year after year, charmed by this remarkable place and by the consistently gracious service.

A new and very popular specialty of QMC and its adjacent sister property Casa Tres Vidas (see above) is planning and hosting weddings.

Sagitario 126, Playa Conchas Chinas, 48300 Puerto Vallarta, Jal. © **888/640-8100** or 801/536-5850 in the U.S., or 322/221-5317. Fax 322/221-53-27. www.quinta-maria.com. 7 units. High season $105–$235 (£58–£129) double; low season $95–$175 (£52–£96) double. Rates include breakfast. AE, MC, V. Very limited street parking. Children younger than 18 not accepted. **Amenities:** Small outdoor pool; concierge. *In room:* Fridge, coffeemaker, hair dryer, safe.

YELAPA

Verana *✦✦✦ Moments*   The magical Verana is my current favorite place to stay in Mexico. It has an unparalleled ability to inspire immediate relaxation and a deep connection with the natural beauty of the spectacular coast. Although Yelapa is 30 minutes by water taxi from town, even those unfamiliar with the village should consider it. Verana has eight rustic yet sophisticated suites located among seven bungalows, set into a hillside with sweeping views of the mountains and ocean. Each is a work of art, hand-crafted with care and creativity by owners Heinz Leger, a former film production designer, and prop stylist Veronique Lieve. Each has a private terrace and two beds—but you won't find TVs, telephones, or other distractions. My favorite suite is the Studio; it's the most contemporary, with a wall of floor-to-ceiling windows that perfectly frame the spectacular view. The European-trained chef prepares scrumptious creations—global cuisine with a touch of Mexico. Verana also has a magically crafted spa, and a yoga hut where daily classes take place. Compare this to the prices of the other rustic-chic resorts along Mexico's Pacific coast, and you'll find it's a true value. Adventurous travelers should not miss a stay at this unique place.

Domicilio Conocido, 48300 Yelapa, Jal. © **800/530-7176** or 310/360-0155 in the U.S., or 322/222-2360. www.verana. com. 7 villas. Winter/high season $280–$470 (£154–£259) villa per night with 5-night minimum; $700 (£385) 3-bedroom Casa Grande per night; extra person $60 (£33) per night. Mandatory daily breakfast and dinner charge $70 (£39) per person; lunch and beverages extra. Shorter stays based on availability. Closed during summer months. AE, MC, V. Management helps arrange transportation from Puerto Vallarta to Boca, where a private boat runs to Yelapa; from there, Verana is a gentle hike or mule ride. **Amenities:** Restaurant/bar; 2 prepared daily meals; outdoor pool; morning yoga classes; spa w/massage services; tours and excursions; library. *In room:* No phone.

WHERE TO DINE

Puerto Vallarta has the most exceptional dining scene of any resort town in Mexico. Over 250 restaurants serve cuisines from around the world, in addition to fresh seafood and regional dishes. Chefs from France, Switzerland, Germany, Italy, and Argentina have come for visits and stayed to open restaurants. In celebration of this diversity, Vallarta's culinary community hosts a 2-week-long gourmet dining festival each November (see box titled "Special Events in Puerto Vallarta" earlier in this chapter).

Dining is not limited to high-end options—there are plenty of small, family-owned restaurants, local Mexican kitchens, and vegetarian cafes. Vallarta also has branches of the world food-and-fun chains: Hard Rock Cafe, Outback Steakhouse, and even Hooters. I won't bother to review these restaurants, where the quality and decor are so familiar.

Of the inexpensive local spots, one favorite is **El Planeta Vegetariano,** Iturbide 270, just down from the main church (© **322/222-3073**), serving an inexpensive, bountiful, and delicious vegetarian buffet, which changes for breakfast and lunch/dinner. It's open daily. Breakfast ($4.50/£2.50) is served from 8am till noon; the lunch and dinner buffets ($6.50/£3.60) are served from noon to 10pm; no credit cards are accepted.

MARINA VALLARTA

Contrary to conventional travel wisdom, most of the best restaurants in the Marina are in hotels. Especially notable are **Andrea** (fine Italian cuisine), at Velas Vallarta, and **Nikki Beach** (fusion), on the beachfront of the Westin Resort & Spa. (See "Where to Stay," earlier in this chapter, for more information.) Other choices are along the boardwalk bordering the marina yacht harbor.

Benitto's CAFE   Wow! What a sandwich! Benitto's food would be reason enough to come to this tiny, terrific cafe inside the Plaza Neptuno—but added to that are the original array of sauces and the very personable service. This place is popular with locals for light breakfasts, filling lunches, and fondue and wine in the evenings. It's the best place in town to find pastrami, corned beef, or other traditional (gringo) sandwich fare, all served on your choice of gourmet bread. Draft beer and wine are available, as are the cafe's specialty infused waters.

Inside Plaza Neptuno. © **322/209-0287**. benittoscafe@prodigy.net.mx. Breakfast $3–$6 (£1.65–£3.30); main courses $5–$7 (£2.75–£3.85). No credit cards. Mon–Sat 8:30am–9:30pm.

Porto Bello ITALIAN   One of the first restaurants in the marina, Porto Bello remains a favorite for its authentically flavorful Italian dishes and exceptional service. For starters, fried calamari is delicately seasoned, and grilled vegetable antipasto could easily serve as a full meal. Signature dishes include fusilli prepared with artichokes, black olives, lemon juice, basil, olive oil, and Parmesan cheese, and sautéed fish filet with shrimp and clams in saffron tomato sauce. The elegant indoor dining room is air-conditioned, and there's also marina-front seating. The restaurant occasionally schedules live music in the evening.

Marina Sol, Loc. 7 (Marina Vallarta *malecón*). © **322/221-0003**. Reservations recommended for dinner. Main courses $8–$24 (£4.40–£13). AE, MC, V. Daily noon–11pm.

DOWNTOWN
Expensive
Café des Artistes/Thierry Blouet Cocina del Autor FRENCH/INTERNATIONAL   This sophisticated restaurant is known as the place in town for that very special evening. Creative in its menu and innovative in design, the dinner-only

restaurant rivals those in any major metropolitan city for its culinary sophistication. The award-winning chef and owner, Thierry Blouet, is both a member of the French Academie Culinaire and a Maitre Cuisinier de France. In late 2003, the singular dining experience of the Café evolved into a trio of special places, expanding to add the upscale Bar Constantini lounge, and separate, but connected Thierry Blouet Cocina del Autor dining area. All are located in a restored house that resembles a castle. The interior of the original Café des Artistes combines murals, lush fabrics, and an array of original works of art, with both an interior dining area as well as a lushly landscaped terraced garden area. The menu of this section is a changing delight of French gourmet bistro fare, which draws heavily on Chef Blouet's French training, yet uses regional specialty ingredients. Noteworthy entrees include sea bass filet served with a lentil, bacon, and coriander stew; and the renowned roasted duck glazed with honey, soy, ginger, and lime sauce, and served with a pumpkin risotto. At the Cocina de Autor, the atmosphere is sleek and stylish, and the fixed-priced tasting menu (prices depend on the number of plates you select, from three to six) offers you a choice of the chef's most creative and sumptuous creations, with each dish creatively combining ingredients to present one memorable "flavor"—choose any combination of starters, entrees, or desserts. After dining, you're invited to the cognac and cigar room, an exquisite blend of old adobe walls, flickering candles, and elegant leather chairs. Or, move on to the adjacent Bar Constantini, with its live jazz music and plush sofas, for a fitting close to a memorable meal. It's without a doubt worth the splurge.

Chef Thierry has also opened a new venue, **Thierry's Prime Steakhouse** in the Plaza Peninsula mall (Blvd. Francisco Medina Ascencio 2485, local Ancla Sub. A; © **322/ 331-1212;** www.thierrysprime.com). It features aged prime steaks, plus a limited selection of fish and chicken dishes. It's open for lunch and dinner daily.

Guadalupe Sánchez 740. © **322/222-3228,** -3229, or -3230. www.cafedesartistes.com. Reservations recommended. Main courses $9–$31 (£4.95–£17). Cocinade Autor tasting menu $25–$68 (£14–£37). AE, MC, V. Daily 6–11:30pm (lounge until 2am).

Moderate

Daiquiri Dick's 🦀🦀 MODERN AMERICAN   A Vallarta dining institution, Daiquiri Dick's has been around for over 22 years, evolving its winning combination of decor, service, and scrumptious cuisine. The menu is among Vallarta's most sophisticated, and the genuinely warm staff and open-air location fronting Los Muertos Beach add to the feeling of casual comfort. As lovely as the restaurant is, though, and as notorious as the fresh-fruit daiquiris are, the food is the main attraction. It incorporates touches of Tuscan, Thai, and Mexican. Start with grilled asparagus wrapped in prosciutto and topped with shaved Asiago cheese, then try an entree such as sesame-crusted tuna, grilled rare and served with wild greens; pistachio chicken served with polenta; or my favorite, simple yet indulgent lobster tacos. Chocolate banana bread pudding makes a perfect finish. Daiquiri Dick's is a great place for groups as well as for a romantic dinner. It's one of the few places that are equally enjoyable for breakfast, lunch, or dinner.

Olas Altas 314. © **322/222-0566.** www.ddpv.com. Main courses $6.50–$25 (£3.60–£14). AE, MC, V. Daily 9am– 10:30pm. Closed Sept.

de Santos 🦀 MEDITERRANEAN   After it opened a few years ago, de Santos quickly became the hot spot in town for late-night dining and bar action. Unfortunately, the food doesn't live up to the atmosphere and music, but it's still a worthwhile place to go, if the scene is as important in a dining experience as the substance. The menu is Mediterranean-inspired; best bets include lightly breaded calamari, paella Valenciana, and thin-crust pizza. The cool, refined interior feels more urban than resort, and it boasts the most sophisticated sound system in town—including a DJ who spins to match the mood of the crowd. It probably helps that one of the partners is also a member of the wildly popular Latin group Maná. There's an open-air terrace dining in the back. Prices are extremely reasonable for the quality and overall experience of an evening here. Be sure to stay and check out the adjacent club—still the hottest nightspot in town (see "Puerto Vallarta after Dark," later).

Morelos 771, Centro. (𝒞 322/223-3052. www.desantos.com.mx. Reservations recommended during high season. Main courses $5–$20 (£2.75–£5.50). AE, MC, V. Daily 5pm–1am; bar closes at 4am on weekends.

Hacienda San Angel 𝓕𝓕 MEXICAN   Meals at Hacienda San Angel were so popular with its guests, the owner decided to share the experience with other visitors to Puerto Vallarta as well. In addition to experiencing the exquisite beauty of the Hacienda itself, diners are treated to one of the most stunning views of town, overlooking the night lights of the city to the bay beyond. The very limited seating each night—by prior reservation only—is on the upper terrace of the Hacienda, near its main rooftop pool. Tables are elegantly set with linens and antique silverware. The menu changes periodically, but features classic Mexican fare, along with international favorites. Starters include crispy fried calamari with a selection of sauces, grilled seasonal vegetables in a tomato, olive oil, and basil balsamic vinaigrette, or a seafood soup flavored with mescal and thyme. The house specialty is the grilled *Cabreria,* a tender bone-in steak, served with black beans, garlic-stuffed portobello mushroom, and a three-chile sauce. Other standouts include their chicken *mole,* and the herb-encrusted rack of lamb in a green-pepper sauce. They offer full bar service, and an ample selection of wines to accompany your meal. Service is understated and attentive. Start the evening by arriving at 6pm for a cocktail hour with live music—you may also enjoy strolling the grounds of the Hacienda.

Miramar 336, Centro. (𝒞 322/222-2692. www.haciendasanangel.com. Reservations required. Main courses $17– $30 (£9.35–£17), with 20% gratuity added to all checks. MC, V. Mon–Sat 7pm–last guest (guests may arrive at 6pm for cocktail hour, but no later than 9pm to be served).

Las Palomas 𝓕 MEXICAN   One of Puerto Vallarta's first restaurants, this is the power-breakfast place of choice—and a popular hangout for everyone else throughout the day. Authentic in atmosphere and menu, it's one of Puerto Vallarta's few genuine Mexican restaurants. Breakfast is the best value. The staff pours mugs of steaming coffee spiced with cinnamon as soon as you're seated. Try classic *huevos rancheros* or *chilaquiles* (tortilla strips, fried and topped with red or green spicy sauce, cream, cheese, and fried eggs). Lunch and dinner offer traditional Mexican specialties, plus a selection of stuffed crepes. The best places for checking out the *malecón* and watching the sunset while sipping an icy margarita are the spacious bar and the upstairs terrace.

Paseo Díaz Ordaz 610. (𝒞 322/222-3675. www.laspalomaspvr.com. Breakfast $3.50–$10 (£1.95–£5.50); lunch $8.50–$20 (£4.70–£11); main courses $8.50–$22 (£4.70–£12). AE, MC, V. Daily 8am–11pm.

Trío 𝓕𝓕𝓕 *Finds* INTERNATIONAL   Trío is the darling of Vallarta restaurants, with local diners beating a path to the modest but stylish cafe where chef-owners Bernhard Güth and Ulf Henricksson's undeniable passion for food imbues each dish. Trío is noted for its perfected melding of Mexican and Mediterranean flavors; memorable entrees include San Blas shrimp in a fennel-tomato vinaigrette served over broiled

Tapas, Anyone?

Certainly, much of modern Mexico's culture draws on the important influence of Spain, so it only makes sense that Spanish culinary traditions would be evident as well. Within the last several years, dining on tapas has soared in popularity here. Of the many options, these are my favorites: the long-standing **Barcelona Tapas,** Matamoros and 31 de Octubre streets (© **322/222-0510**), a large and lovely restaurant on a terrace built high on a hillside, with sweeping views of the bay. They serve tapas and a selection of Spanish entrees, including paella, from 5pm to midnight. **La Esquina de los Caprichos,** Miramar 402, corner of Iturbide (© **322/222-0911**) is a tiny place, known as having the most reasonably priced ($2.50–$6/£1.40–£3.30) tapas in town, and perhaps the tastiest. Hours are Monday to Saturday from 1 to 10pm. It closes from mid-July to the end of August.

nopal cactus, herb risotto with toasted sunflower seeds and quail, and pan-roasted sea bass with glazed grapes, mashed potatoes, and sauerkraut in a white-pepper sauce. These dishes may not be on the menu when you arrive, though—it's a constantly changing work of art. The atmosphere is always comfortable and welcoming. The rooftop bar area allows for a more comfortable wait for a table or for after-dinner coffee. A real treat!

Guerrero 264. © 322/222-2196. www.triopv.com. Reservations recommended. Main courses $14–$26 (£7.70–£14). AE, MC, V. Year-round daily 6pm–midnight; high season Mon–Fri noon–3:30pm.

Xitomates ✪✪ MEXICAN Located in the heart of downtown, this creative Mexican restaurant has earned raves for its intimate atmosphere and chef/owner Luis Fitch's exceptionally creative versions of the country's culinary treasures. It's named for one of Mexico's contributions to gastronomy—the tomato (*xitomatl,* in the ancient Aztec language of Náhuatl). The menu mixes Mexican with Caribbean, Asian, and Mediterranean influences, and the presentation is as creative as the preparation. Starters include their signature coconut shrimp in a tangy tamarind sauce, thinly sliced scallops with cucumber and jicama julienne, or mushrooms stuffed with shrimp or *huitlacoche* (a mushroom that grows on corn stalks). Main courses range from grilled salmon filet in a poblano chile sauce, to a tender rib-eye steak with mushrooms, delicately flavored with the Mexican herb, epazote. The house specialty dessert is a Toluca ice-cream cake. The warmly decorated dining room is accented with tin star lamps and flickering candles. An excellent wine list and full bar complement the exquisite dining.

Morelos 570, across from Galería Uno. © 322/222-1695. www.losxitomates.com. Main courses $8–$22 (£4.40–£12). AE, MC, V. Daily 6pm–midnight.

Inexpensive

Agave Grill ✪ MEXICAN Opening its doors in late 2004, Agave Grill took over most of the space at the Casa de Tequila in central downtown. It's located in a beautiful garden setting in the back, within a classic hacienda-style building. The space has been put to excellent use: This cafe serves modern, casual Mexican cuisine and is an ideal spot to stop for a snack or a margarita while shopping. Start with an order of chiles anchos, stuffed with cream cheese and raisins, or the *antojitos mexicanos,* a sampler of Mexican snacks including sopes, quesadillas, a *tamal,* and guacamole. Favorite main courses include *chichilo negro,* a bone-in filet of beef with Oaxaca smoked mole, or the duck tacos in a *pipián* chile sauce. For a sweet finish, don't miss their tequila foam with chocolate sauce served with churros. All tortillas are handmade, as are the savory salsas. An elegant bar borders the room, serving undoubtedly Vallarta's most original selection of fine tequilas, many from small distilleries. In addition to the tequilas and fresh fruit margaritas, Agave Grill also serves a selection of fine Mexican wines.

Morelos 589. (*C*) **322/222-2000.** Main courses $6–$17 (£3.30–£9.35). MC, V. Mon–Sat noon–11pm.

El Arrayán ★★★ *(Finds)* MEXICAN   The traditional but original Arrayán is the pot of gold at the end of the rainbow for anyone in search of authentic Mexican cuisine. Owner Carmen Porras enlisted Mexico City chef Carmen Titita (praised by James Beard for her culinary work) to assist in the design of the kitchen and creation of the restaurant's concise menu, which features genuine regional dishes. The open-air dining area surrounds a cozy courtyard, while its exposed brick walls and funky-chic decor showcase a modern view of Mexican classics—tin tubs serve as sinks in the bathrooms, while colorful plastic tablecloths and primitive art enliven the dining room. Start with an order of sumptuous plantain fritters filled with black beans, or an unusual salad of diced *nopal* cactus paddles with fresh cheese. Favorite main courses include their tacos filled with prime beef filet, or Mexican duck *carnitas,* served in an *arrayán-*orange sauce. (*Arrayán,* the namesake of the place, is a small bittersweet fruit native to the region.) Homemade, fresh-fruit ice creams are an especially tasty finish to your meal. The full bar offers an extensive selection of tequilas and regional liquors, while nonalcoholic beverages center on *aguas frescas,* a blended drink of fresh fruit and water. Don't miss sampling their signature *raicilla* martini—made with the potent local spirit (raicilla) and infused with herbs for a unique flavor. The excellent service is a plus to this can't-miss dining experience—you can't miss the pink facade with the large bell at the entry.

Allende 344, just past Matamoros, on the corner with Miramar. (*C*) **322/222-7195.** www.elarrayan.com.mx. Main courses $11–$14 (£6.05–£7.70). AE, MC, V. Wed–Mon 6–11pm. Closed Aug.

Vitea ★★★ *(Finds)* INTERNATIONAL   This beachfront bistro was opened in late 2004 by the chef/owners of Trío, and their recipe for success took hold from day one—the place is bustling at any hour, and has become a favorite among locals. Due to strategically placed mirrors on the back wall, every seat has a view of the ocean, while the eclectic interior is cheerful and inviting. Seating is at small bistro-style tables, along a banquette that runs the length of the back wall, or at the small but beautiful bar. The long, narrow bistro faces the waterfront between the central plaza and river. But enough about looks—what counts here is the exceptional fare, which is both classic and original. Starters include a tomato and Roquefort salad with pecans, foie gras with Spanish plum sauce, and an exquisite bistro salad with bacon. Quiche is always on the menu, with changing selections, and main courses include chickpea ravioli with portobello mushrooms, Wiener schnitzel with salad, or a traditional steak frites. Lunch offers lighter fare, including heavenly deli sandwiches. You won't be disappointed here, no matter what you order! There's a full bar with an excellent selection of wines, and the service is exceptional.

Malecón no. 2, at Libertad. (*C*) **322/222-8703** or -8695. Reservations recommended during peak dining hours. Main courses $7–$19 (£3.85–£10). MC, V. Daily noon–midnight.

SOUTH OF THE RIO CUALE TO OLAS ALTAS

South of the river is the densest restaurant area, where you'll find Basilio Badillo, the street nicknamed "Restaurant Row." A second main dining drag has emerged along

Calle Olas Altas, with a variety of cuisines and price categories. Cafes and espresso bars, generally open from 7am to midnight, line its wide sidewalks.

Expensive

Café Kaiser Maximilian 𝕉𝕉 INTERNATIONAL   This bistro-style cafe has a casually elegant atmosphere with a genuine European feel. It's the prime place to go if you want to combine exceptional food with great people-watching. Austrian-born owner Andreas Rupprechter is always on hand to ensure that the service is as impeccable as the food is delicious. Indoor, air-conditioned dining is at cozy tables; sidewalk tables are larger and great for groups of friends. The cuisine merges old-world European preparations with regional fresh ingredients. My favorite is filet of trout with spinach, tomato, and almond ragout; but also notable is their mustard chicken with mashed potatoes; and the rack of lamb with polenta, endives, and lima beans is simply divine. Desserts are especially tempting, as are gourmet coffees—Maximilian has an Austrian cafe and pastry shop next door.

Olas Altas 380-B (at Basilio Badillo, in front of the Hotel Playa Los Arcos), Zona Romántica. 𝄍 322/223-0760. Reservations recommended in high season. Main courses $16–$26 (£8.80–£14). AE, MC, V. Mon–Sat 6–11pm.

Le Bistro MEXICAN/INTERNATIONAL   A long-standing favorite, Le Bistro is recommended here for their breakfast, though I would personally pass on it for dinner. I consider a morning meal here one of Vallarta's best values. Le Bistro is known for its elegant decor, great recorded jazz music, and open-air setting on the island in the midst of the Río Cuale—all creating a singular experience that blends sophistication with a typical Vallarta atmosphere. The specialty is crepes, which come in a variety of flavors for breakfast, lunch, or dinner. The lunch and dinner menu also features a selection of Mexican cuisine, including duck in Oaxacan black *mole,* and rock Cornish hen stuffed with herbed rice, dried tropical fruits, and nuts, finished in mango cilantro sauce. The vegetarian offerings are more creative than most. An extensive wine list and ample selection of specialty coffees complement the menu.

Isla Río Cuale 16-A (just east of northbound bridge). 𝄍 322/222-0283. www.lebistro.com.mx. Reservations recommended for dinner in high season. Breakfast $5–$8 (£2.75–£4.40); main courses $19–$25 (£10–£14). AE, MC, V. Mon–Sat 9am–midnight.

Moderate

Archie's Wok 𝕉𝕉𝕉 𝐹𝑖𝑛𝑑𝑠 ASIAN/SEAFOOD   Since 1986, Archie's has been legendary in Puerto Vallarta for serving original cuisine influenced by the intriguing flavors of Thailand, China, and the Philippines. Archie was Hollywood director John Huston's private chef during the years he spent in the area. Today his wife Cindy upholds his legacy at this tranquil retreat. The Thai mai tai and other tropical drinks, made from only fresh fruit and juices, are a good way to kick off a meal, as are the consistently crispy and delicious Filipino spring rolls. The popular Singapore fish filet features lightly battered filet strips in sweet-and-sour sauce; Thai garlic shrimp are prepared with fresh garlic, ginger, cilantro, and black pepper. Vegetarians have plenty of options, including broccoli, tofu, mushroom, and cashew stir-fry in black-bean-and-sherry sauce. Thursday through Saturday from 8 to 11pm, there's live classical harp and flute in Archie's Oriental garden.

Francisca Rodríguez 130 (a half block from the Los Muertos pier). 𝄍 322/222-0411. Main courses $6–$21 (£3.30–£12). MC, V. Mon–Sat 2–11pm. Closed Sept–Oct.

Espresso 𝕉𝕉 ITALIAN   This popular eatery is Vallarta's best late-night dining option. The two-level restaurant is on one of the town's busiest streets—across from

El Torito's sports bar, and cater-cornered from the lively Señor Frog's—meaning that traffic noise is a factor, though not a deterrent. The food is superb, the service attentive, and the prices more than reasonable. Owned by a partnership of lively Italians, it serves food that is authentic in preparation and flavor, from thin-crust, brick-oven pizzas to savory homemade pastas. My favorite pizza is the Quattro Stagioni, topped with artichokes, black olives, ham, and mushrooms. Excellent calzones and panini (sandwiches) are also options. I prefer the rooftop garden area for dining, but many patrons gravitate to the pool table in the air-conditioned downstairs, which features major sports and entertainment events on satellite TV. Espresso also has full bar service and draft beer. Espresso is especially popular with *vallartenses* (locals).

Ignacio L. Vallarta 279. 🕐 322/222-3272. Main courses $6.50–$18 (£3.60–£9.90). MC, V. Daily 9am–2am.

La Palapa 🏮🏮 SEAFOOD/MEXICAN   This colorful, open-air, *palapa*-roofed restaurant on the beach is a decades-old local favorite, and with each recent visit, I have found the quality of the food and the service keeps improving. It's an exceptional dining experience, day or night. Enjoy a tropical breakfast by the sea, lunch on the beach, cocktails at sunset, or a romantic dinner (on a cloth-covered table in the sand). For lunch and dinner, seafood is the specialty; featured dishes include macadamia-and-coconut-crusted prawns, and poached red snapper with fresh cilantro sauce. Its location in the heart of Los Muertos Beach makes it an excellent place to start or end the day; I favor it for breakfast or, even better, a late-night sweet temptation and specialty coffee, while watching the moon over the bay. A particular draw is the all-you-can-eat Sunday brunch, which entitles you to a spot on popular Los Muertos beach for the day. You can enjoy the extra-comfortable beach chairs for postbrunch sunbathing. A new classy bar area features acoustic guitars and vocals nightly from 8 to 11pm, generally performed by the owner, Alberto.

Pulpito 103. 🕐 322/222-5225. www.lapalapapv.com. Reservations recommended for dinner in high season. Breakfast $2.50–$12 (£1.40–£6.60); main courses $7–$28 (£3.85–£15); salad or sandwiches $5–$12 (£2.75–£6.60). AE, MC, V. Daily 9am–11pm.

Inexpensive

Café San Angel CAFE   This comfortable, classic sidewalk cafe is a local gathering place from sunrise to sunset. For breakfast, choose a burrito stuffed with eggs and chorizo sausage, a three-egg Western omelet, crepes filled with mushrooms, Mexican classics like *huevos rancheros* and *chilaquiles,* or a tropical fruit plate. Deli sandwiches, crepes, and pastries round out the small but ample menu. The cafe also serves exceptional fruit smoothies and perfectly made espresso drinks. Note that the service is reliably slow and frequently frustrating, so choose this place if you have time on your side—and keep in mind that it offers the best people-watching in the area. Bar service and Internet access are available.

Olas Altas 449 (at Francisco Rodríguez). 🕐 322/223-1273. Breakfast $3.50–$6 (£1.95–£3.30); main courses $3.50 (£1.95). No credit cards. Daily 8am–1am.

Fajita Republic 🏮 MEXICAN/SEAFOOD/STEAKS   Fajita Republic is consistently popular—and deservedly so. It has hit on a winning recipe: delicious food, ample portions, welcoming atmosphere, and low prices. The specialty is, of course, fajitas, grilled to perfection in every variety: steak, chicken, shrimp, combo, and vegetarian. All come with a generous tray of salsas and toppings. This "tropical grill" also serves sumptuous barbecued ribs, Mexican *molcajetes* with incredibly tender strips of marinated beef filet, and grilled shrimp. Starters include fresh guacamole served in a giant spoon and the ever-popular Mayan cheese sticks (breaded and deep-fried). Try an oversize mug or pitcher of Fajita Rita Mango Margaritas—or another spirited temptation. This is a casual, fun, festive place in a garden of mango and palm trees. A second location in Nuevo Vallarta, across from the Grand Velas Resort, is drawing equal raves with the same menu and prices.

Pino Suárez 321 (at Basilio Badillo), 1 block north of Olas Altas. ℂ **322/222-3131.** Main courses $9–$17 (£4.95–£9.35). MC, V. Daily 5pm–midnight.

Red Cabbage Café (El Repollo Rojo) ⭐⭐ *Finds* MEXICAN   The tiny, hard-to-find cafe is worth the effort—a visit here will reward you with exceptional traditional Mexican cuisine and a whimsical crash course in contemporary culture. The small room is covered wall-to-wall and table-to-table with photographs, paintings, movie posters, and news clippings about the cultural icons of Mexico. Frida Kahlo figures prominently in the decor, and a special menu duplicates dishes she and husband Diego Rivera prepared for guests.

Specialties from all over Mexico include divine *chiles en nogada* (poblanos stuffed with ground beef, pine nuts, and raisins, topped with sweet cream sauce and served cold), intricate chicken *mole* from Puebla, and hearty *carne en su jugo* (steak in its juice). In addition, the vegetarian menu is probably the most diverse and tasty in town. This is not the place for an intimate conversation, however—the poor acoustics cause everyone's conversations to blend together, although generally what you're hearing from adjacent tables are raves about the food. Also, this is a nonsmoking restaurant—the only one I'm aware of in town.

Calle Rivera del Río 204A (across from Río Cuale). ℂ **322/223-0411.** Main courses $9–$20 (£4.95–£11). No credit cards. Daily 5–10:30pm.

JUNGLE RESTAURANTS
One of the unique attractions of Puerto Vallarta is its "jungle restaurants," south of town toward Mismaloya. They offer open-air dining in a tropical setting by the sea or beside a mountain river. The many varieties of "jungle" and "tropical" tours (see "Organized Tours," earlier in this chapter) include a stop for swimming and lunch. If you travel on your own, a taxi is the best transportation—the restaurants are quite a distance from the main highway. Taxis are usually waiting for return patrons.

The most recommendable of the jungle restaurants is the ecologically sensitive **El Nogalito** ⭐ (ℂ/fax **322/221-5225**). Located beside a clear jungle stream, the exceptionally clean, beautifully landscaped ranch serves lunch, beverages, and snacks on a shady, relaxing terrace. Several hiking routes depart from the grounds, and the restaurant provides a guide (whom you tip) to point out the native plants, birds, and wildlife. It's much closer to town than the other jungle restaurants: To find it, travel to Punta Negra, about 8km (5 miles) south of downtown Puerto Vallarta. A well-marked sign points up Calzada del Cedro, a dirt road, to the ranch. It's open daily from noon to 5:30pm. No credit cards are accepted.

Just past Boca de Tomatlán, at Highway 200 Km 20, is **Chico's Paradise** (ℂ **322/223-6005**). It offers spectacular views of massive rocks—some marked with petroglyphs—and the surrounding jungle and mountains. There are natural pools and waterfalls for swimming, plus a small market selling pricey trinkets. The menu features excellent seafood as well as Mexican dishes. The quality is quite good, and the portions are generous, although prices are higher than in town—remember, you're paying for the setting. It's open daily from 10am to 6pm. No credit cards are accepted.

PUERTO VALLARTA AFTER DARK

Puerto Vallarta's spirited nightlife reflects the town's dual nature: part resort, part colonial town. In years past, Vallarta was known for its live music scene, but in recent years the nocturnal action has shifted to DJ clubs, spinning an array of eclectic, contemporary music. A concentration of nightspots lies along Calle Ignacio L. Vallarta (the extension of the main southbound road) after it crosses the Río Cuale. Along one 3-block stretch you'll find a live blues club, sports bar, live mariachi music, a gay dance club, a steamy live salsa dance club, and the obligatory **Señor Frog's.** Walk from place to place and take in a bit of it all!

The *malecón,* which used to be lined with restaurants, is now known more for hip dance clubs and a few more relaxed options, all of which look out over the ocean. You can first stroll the broad walkway by the water's edge and check out the action at the various clubs, which extend from **Bodeguita del Medio** on the north end to **Hooters** just off the central plaza.

Marina Vallarta's clubs offer a more upscale, indoor, air-conditioned atmosphere. South of the Río Cuale, the **Olas Altas** zone's small cafes and martini bars buzz with action. In this zone, there's also an active gay and lesbian club scene.

PERFORMING ARTS & CULTURAL EVENTS

Truth be told, cultural nightlife beyond the **Mexican Fiesta** is limited. Culture centers on the visual arts; the opening of an exhibition has great social and artistic significance. Puerto Vallarta's gallery community comes together in the central downtown area to present weekly **art walks,** where new exhibits are presented, featured artists attend, and complimentary cocktails are served. Check listings in the daily English-language newspaper, *Vallarta Today,* or the events section of www.virtualvallarta.com, to see what's on the schedule during your stay. Also of note are the free musical performances in the downtown plaza's gazebo—check with the municipal tourism office for the current schedule.

FIESTA NIGHTS

Major hotels in Puerto Vallarta feature frequent fiestas for tourists—extravaganzas with open bars, Mexican buffet dinners, and live entertainment. Some are fairly authentic and make a good introduction for first-time travelers to Mexico; others can be a bit cheesy. Shows are usually held outdoors but move indoors when necessary. Reservations are recommended.

Rhythms of the Night (Cruise to Caletas) ★★★ *Moments*   This is an unforgettable evening under the stars at John Huston's former home at the pristine cove called Las Caletas. The smooth, fast Vallarta Adventures catamaran travels here, entertaining guests along the way. Tiki torches and drummers dressed in native costumes greet you at the dock. There's no electricity—you dine by the light of candles, the stars, and the moon. The buffet dinner is delicious—steak, seafood, and generous vegetarian options. Everything is first class. The entertainment showcases indigenous dances in contemporary style. The cruise departs at 6pm and returns by 11pm. Departs from Terminal Marítima. ℂ 888/303-2653 in the U.S., or 322/297-1212, ext 3. www.vallarta-adventures.com. Cost $80 (£ 44; includes cruise, dinner, open bar, and entertainment).

THE CLUB & MUSIC SCENE
Restaurant & Bars

Azul 96   Among the newest clubs to open, Azul 96 is known more for its sand-floored, rooftop Sky Bar than its sleek ground-floor restaurant, which specializes in traditional gourmet fare. The architecture is stunning, but most people pass by as they climb the stairs—or take the elevator to the bar upstairs, with its panoramic views of the city. A long glass bar borders one side and serves sushi along with cocktails. In the "sandy beach" area, partiers settle into high tables or banquettes to enjoy the energizing dance music. The Sky Bar is open daily from 8pm to 4am. Morelos 696, Col. Centro. (ℭ 322/222-1022. www.azul96.com.

Bar Constantini ℛℛ   The most sophisticated lounge in Vallarta is set in the elegant eatery, Café des Artistes. It's become a popular option for those looking for a lively yet sophisticated setting for after-dinner drinks. The plush sofas are welcoming, and the list of champagnes by the glass, signature martinis, and specialty drinks is suitably tempting. Live jazz and blues in an intimate atmosphere are drawing crowds, as are weekly wine tastings, held each Thursday at 6pm. An ample appetizer and dessert menu make it appropriate for late-night dining and drinks. Open daily from 6pm to 2am. Guadalupe Sánchez 740. (ℭ 322/222-3229.

Carlos O'Brian's   Vallarta's original nightspot was once the only place for an evening of revelry. Although the competition is stiffer nowadays, COB's still packs them in—especially the 20-something set. The late-night scene resembles a college party. Open daily from noon to 2am; happy hour is from noon to 8pm. Paseo Díaz Ordaz (malecón) 786, at Pípila. (ℭ 322/222-1444 or -4065. Weekend cover $11 (£ 6.05; includes 2 drinks).

La Bodeguita del Medio   This authentic Cuban restaurant and bar is known for its casual energy, terrific live Cuban music, and mojitos. It is a branch of the original Bodeguita in Havana (reputedly Hemingway's favorite restaurant there), which opened in 1942. If you can't get to that one, the Vallarta version has successfully imported the essence—and has a small souvenir shop that sells Cuban cigars, rum, and other items. The downstairs has large wooden windows that open to the *malecón* street action, while the upstairs offers terrific views of the bay. Walls throughout are decorated with old photographs and patrons' signatures—if you can, find a spot and add yours! The food is less memorable here than the music and atmosphere, so I recommend drinks and dancing, nothing more. Open daily from 11:30am to 2am. Paseo Díaz Ordaz 858 (malecón); at Allende. (ℭ 322/223-1585.

Z'Tai ℛ   Opened in 2007, Z'Tai is a stunning array of spaces that span an entire city block. Enter from the *malecón,* and you'll discover ZBar, an upstairs lounge with chillout music, bay views, and comfy banquettes to relax on. Venture further into this club and you'll find an expansive open air garden area that serves cocktails as well as an array of Asian-inspired dining and snacking options, accompanied by electronic music at a level still appropriate for conversation. Seating is casual and spans several elevations, overlooking Zen gardens and flowing ponds. At the opposite end (Calle Morelos entrance), there's an air-conditioned dining area. They boast a 1,000-bottle wine menu, but the favorite drink here is their signature cucumber martini. Open daily for food service from 6pm to 2am, with bar service until 4am. They also offer valet service or shuttle service to wherever you parked your car. Morelos 737, Col. Centro. (ℭ 322/222-0306.

Rock, Jazz & Blues

El Faro Lighthouse Bar ℛ   A circular cocktail lounge at the top of the Marina lighthouse, El Faro is one of Vallarta's most romantic nightspots. Live or recorded jazz plays, and conversation is manageable. Drop by at twilight for the magnificent panoramic views, but don't expect anything other than a drink and, if you get lucky, some popcorn. Open daily from 5:30pm to 2am. Royal Pacific Yacht Club, Marina Vallarta. ℂ 322/221-0541 or -0542.

Mariachi Loco This lively mariachi club features singers belting out boleros and ranchero classics. The mariachi show begins at 9pm—the mariachis stroll and play as guests join in impromptu singing—and by 10pm it gets going. After midnight the mariachis play for pay, which is around $10 (£5.50) for each song played at your table. There's Mexican food from 8 to 10:30pm. Open daily from 8pm to 4am. Cárdenas 254 (at Ignacio Vallarta). ℂ 322/223-2205. Generally no cover, but varies depending on guest performances.

Route 66 A popular live-music club in Vallarta, Route 66 features a hot house band, playing a mix of reggae, blues, rock, and anything by Santana. Live music jams between 10pm and 2am Monday through Sunday nights. It's open daily from 6pm to 2am. Ignacio L. Vallarta 217 (between Madero and Cárdenas, south of the river). No phone.

Night Clubs & Dancing

A few of Vallarta's clubs charge admission, but generally you pay just for drinks: $5 (£2.75) for a margarita, $3 (£1.65) for a beer, more for whiskey and mixed drinks. Keep an eye out for discount passes frequently available in hotels, restaurants, and other tourist spots. Most clubs are open from 10pm to 4am.

Christine This dazzling club draws a crowd with an opening laser-light show, pumped-in dry ice, flashing lights, and a dozen large-screen video panels. Once a disco—in the true sense of the word—it received a needed face-lift in 2003, and is now a more modern dance club, with techno, house, and hip-hop the primary tunes played. The sound system is truly amazing, and the mix of music can get almost anyone dancing. Dress code: No tennis shoes or flip-flops, no shorts for men. Open daily from 10pm to 4am; the light show begins at 11pm. In the Krystal Vallarta hotel, north of downtown off Av. Francisco Medina Ascencio. ℂ 322/224-0202. Cover ladies $10 (£5.50), men $20 (£11).

Collage Club A multilevel monster of nighttime entertainment, Collage includes a pool salon, video arcade, bowling alley, and the always-packed Disco Bar, with frequent live entertainment. It's just past the entrance to Marina Vallarta, air-conditioned, and very popular with a young, mainly local crowd. Open daily from 10am to 6am. Calle Proa s/n, Marina Vallarta. ℂ 322/221-0505. Cover $5.50–$40 (£3.05–£22), which varies by theme party being offered that night.

de Santos 𝒶𝒶𝒶 Vallarta's chic dining spot is known more for the urban, hip crowd the bar draws—it is *the* hot spot for locals. The adjacent club has become known as the place for the superchic to party, although competition opened in late 2006 to lure some regulars away. The lower level holds an air-conditioned bar and dance floor (after midnight, when dining tables have been cleared away), where a DJ spins the hottest of house and techno. Upstairs, there's an open-air rooftop bar with chill-out music and acid jazz. Enjoy the tunes and the fresh air while lounging around on one of the several oversize beds. One partner, a member of the superhot Latin rock group Maná, uses Vallarta as a home base for writing songs. The crowd, which varies in age from 20s on up, shares a common denominator of cool style. The restaurant bar is open daily from 5pm to 1am; the club is open Wednesday through Saturday from 10pm to 6am. Morelos 771. ℂ 322/223-3052 or -3053.

Hilo You'll recognize Hilo by the giant sculptures that practically reach out the front entrance and pull you into this high-energy club, which has become a favorite with the 20-something set. Music ranges from house and electronic to rock. It seems the later the hour, the more crowded the place becomes. Open daily from 4pm to 6am. Malecón, between Aldama and Abasolo sts. ℭ 322/223-5361. Cover $7 (£3.85) weekends and holidays. No cover.

J & B Salsa Club This is the locally popular place to go for dancing to Latin music—from salsa to samba, the dancing is hot! On Fridays, Saturdays, and holidays the air-conditioned club features live bands. Open daily from 10pm to 6am. Av. Francisco Medina Ascencio Km 2.5 (Hotel Zone). ℭ 322/224-4616. Cover $10 (£5.50).

Nikki Beach This haven of the hip hails from South Beach, Miami, and St. Tropez, and has brought its ultracool vibe to Vallarta. White-draped bed-size lounges scatter the outdoor lounge area, under a canopy of tall palms and umbrellas. Indoor dining and lounge areas are also available. The music is the latest in electronic, house, and chill, with visiting DJs often playing on weekend nights. Sundays feature their signature beach brunch, and Thursday evenings feature "Beautiful People" night. It's a great choice for catching rays during the day, but its real appeal is the nocturnal action. Open Sunday to Wednesday from 11am to 1am (food service stops at 11pm); Thursday to Saturday from 11am to 3am (food service stops at 1am.). On the beach at the Westin Regina Resort, Marina Vallarta. ℭ 322/221-0252 or 226-1150. www.nikkibeach.com. No cover, unless for a special event, which will vary.

Señor Frog's The sheer size of this outpost of the famed Carlos 'n' Charlie's chain is daunting, but it fills up and rocks until the early morning hours. Cute waiters are a signature of the chain, and one never knows when they'll assemble on stage and call on a bevy of beauties to join them in a tequila-drinking contest. Occasionally live bands appear. Although mainly popular with the 20s set, all ages will find the air-conditioned club fun. There's food service, but it's better known for its dance-club atmosphere. Open daily from 11am to 4am. Ignacio L. Vallarta and Venustiano Carranza. ℭ 322/222-5171 or -5177. Cover–$11 (£6.05).

Zoo Your chance to be an animal and get wild in the night. The Zoo even has cages to dance in if you're feeling unleashed. This popular club has a terrific sound system and a great variety of dance music, including techno, reggae, and rap. Every hour's happy hour, with two-for-one drinks. It opens daily at noon and closes in the wee hours. Paseo Díaz Ordaz (malecón) 630. ℭ 322/222-4945. www.zoobardance.com. Cover $11 (£ 6.05; includes 2 drinks).

A SPORTS BAR

No Name Bar&Grill With a multitude of TVs and enough sports memorabilia to start a minimuseum, the No Name is a great venue for catching your favorite game. It shows all NBA, NHL, NFL, and MLB broadcast events, plus pay-per-view. No Name also serves great barbecued ribs and USDA imported steaks. It's open daily from 9am to midnight. Morelos 460 (malecón); at Mina. ℭ 322/223-2508.

GAY & LESBIAN CLUBS

Vallarta has a vibrant gay community with a wide variety of clubs and nightlife options, including special bay cruises and evening excursions to nearby ranches. The free *Gay Guide Vallarta* (www.gayguidevallarta.com) specializes in gay-friendly listings, including weekly specials and happy hours.

Disco Club Paco Paco This combination dance club, cantina, and rooftop bar stages a spectacular "Trasvesty" transvestite show every Thursday, Friday, Saturday, and

Sunday night at 1:30am. It's open daily from 1pm to 6am and is air-conditioned. Ignacio L. Vallarta 278. (©) 322/222-7667. www.club-pacopaco.com. Cover $6 (£3.30; includes 1 drink) 9pm to 6am.

Garbo   This small, cozy club is gay friendly, but not exclusively gay, and features great recorded music and occasional live music on weekends. It's open daily from 6pm to 2am and is air-conditioned. Pulpito 142. (©) 322/223-5753. www.bargarbo.com.

La Noche   A casual, intimate "neighborhood bar" catering to a gay clientele, with great prices on drinks, and a menu of tequila cocktails. Beers are always two-for-one. Open from 6pm to 2am, daily. Lazaro Cardenas 257 (2 doors from Ignacio Vallarta). (©) 322/222-3364.

Ranch Disco Bar   This place is known for the "Ranch Hand's Show," Wednesday through Sunday at 11:15pm and 1am. The club also has a dance floor. Open daily from 9pm to 6am. Venustiano Carranza 239 (around the corner from Paco Paco, and can also be accessed directly from Paco Paco). (©) 322/223-0537. Cover $6 (£3.30; includes 1 drink).

SIDE TRIPS FROM PUERTO VALLARTA

YELAPA: ROBINSON CRUSOE MEETS JACK KEROUAC ⊕   It's a cove straight out of a tropical fantasy, and only a 45-minute trip by boat from Puerto Vallarta. Yelapa has no cars, has one sole paved (pedestrian-only) road, and got electricity 5 years ago. It's accessible only by boat. Its tranquillity, natural beauty, and seclusion have made it a popular home for hippies, hipsters, artists, writers, and a few expats (looking to escape the stress of the world, or perhaps the law). A seemingly strange mix, but you're unlikely to ever meet a stranger—Yelapa remains casual and friendly.

To get there, travel by excursion boat or inexpensive water taxi (see "Getting Around," earlier in this chapter). You can spend an enjoyable day, but I recommend a longer stay—it provides a completely different perspective.

Once you're in Yelapa, you can lie in the sun, swim, snorkel, eat fresh grilled seafood at a beachside restaurant, or sample the local moonshine, *raicilla*. The local beach vendors specialize in the most amazing pies you've ever tasted (coconut, lemon, or chocolate). Equally amazing is how the pie ladies walk the beach while balancing the pie plates on their heads; they sell crocheted swimsuits, too. You can tour this tiny town or hike up a river to see one of two waterfalls; the closest to town is about a 30-minute walk from the beach. *Note:* If you use a local guide, agree on a price before you start out. Horseback riding, guided birding, fishing trips, and paragliding are also available.

For overnight accommodations, local residents frequently rent rooms, and there's also the rustic **Hotel Lagunita** ⊕ ((©) 322/209-5056 or -5055; www.hotel-lagunita. com). Its 32 cabañas have private bathrooms, and the hotel has electricity, a saltwater pool, primitive spa with massage, an amiable restaurant and bar, as well as the Barracuda Beach lounge and brick-oven pizza cafe, plus a gourmet coffee shop. Though the prices are high for what you get, it is the most accommodating place for most visitors. Double rates run $110 (£61) during the season and $75 (£41) in the off season (MasterCard and Visa are accepted). Lagunita has become a popular spot for yoga retreats, and regularly features yoga classes.

A stylish alternative is the fashionable **Verana** ⊕⊕⊕ ((©) **800/530-7176** or 322/ 222-2360; www.verana.com). See "Where to Stay," earlier, for details.

If you stay over on a Wednesday or Saturday during the winter, don't miss the regular dance at the **Yelapa Yacht Club** ⊕ (no phone). Typically tongue-in-cheek for Yelapa, the "yacht club" consists of a cement dance floor and a disco ball, but the DJ spins a great range of tunes, from Glenn Miller to 50 Cent, attracting all ages and types. Dinner ($5–$12/£2.75–£6.60) is a bonus—the food may be the best anywhere in the bay. The menu changes depending on what's fresh. Ask for directions; it's in the main village, on the beach.

NUEVO VALLARTA & NORTH OF VALLARTA: ALL-INCLUSIVES   Many people assume Nuevo Vallarta is a suburb of Puerto Vallarta, but it's a stand-alone destination over the state border in Nayarit. It was designed as a megaresort development, complete with marina, golf course, and luxury hotels. Although it got off to a slow start, it is finally coming together, with a collection of mostly all-inclusive hotels on one of the widest, most attractive beaches in the bay. The biggest resort, Paradise Village, has a growing marina and an 18-hole golf course inland from the beachside strip of hotels, plus a growing selection of condos and homes for sale. The Mayan Palace also recently opened an 18-hole course. The Paradise Plaza shopping center, next to Paradise Village, adds much to the area's shopping, dining, and services. It's open daily from 10am to 10pm. To get to the beach, you travel down a lengthy entrance road from the highway, passing by a few remaining fields (great for birding) but mostly real estate under construction.

Also worthwhile is a day spent at the **Etc. Beach Club,** Paseo de los Cocoteros 38, Nuevo Vallarta (© **322/297-0174**). This beach club has a volleyball net, showers, restroom facilities, and food and drink service on the beach, both day and night. To get there, take the second entrance to Nuevo Vallarta coming from Puerto Vallarta and turn right on Paseo de los Cocoteros; it is past the Vista Bahía hotel. It's open daily from 11am to 7pm. Drinks cost $2.50 to $7 (£1.40–£3.85), entrees $4.50 to $17 (£2.50–£9.35); cash only.

A trip into downtown Puerto Vallarta takes about 30 minutes by taxi, costs about $18 to $20 (£9.90–£11), and is available 24 hours a day. The ride is slightly longer by public bus, which costs $1.20 (65p) and operates from 7am to 11pm.

Marival Grand & Club Suites   This all-inclusive hotel sits almost by itself at the northernmost end of Nuevo Vallarta. Done in Mediterranean style, it offers a complete vacation experience, from its beautiful beach to the adjacent dance club. There are a large variety of room types, ranging from standard units with no balconies to large master suites with whirlpools. The master suites have minibars and hair dryers. The broad white-sand beach is one of the real assets here—it stretches over 450m (1,476 ft.). There is also an extensive activities program, including fun for children.

Paseo de los Cocoteros and Bulevar Nuevo Vallarta s/n, 63735 Nuevo Vallarta, Nay. © **450/686-0226** in Canada, and 322/297-0100 or 226-8200. Fax 322/297-0262. www.gomarival.com. 495 units. High season $409 (£225) double, low season $208 (£114) double; upgrade to junior suite $50 (£28) per day, to master suite with whirlpool $300 (£165) per day. Rates are all-inclusive. Ask for seasonal specials. AE, MC, V. From the Puerto Vallarta airport, enter Nuevo Vallarta from the 2nd entrance; Club Marival is the 1st resort to your right on Paseo de los Cocoteros. Free parking. **Amenities:** 6 restaurants; 8 bars; 3 outdoor pools and an adults-only whirlpool; 2 outdoor pools and a children's water park; 4 lighted tennis courts; spa; business center; salon. *In room:* A/C, TV, safe.

Paradise Village 🐾🐾   Truly a village, this self-contained resort on an exquisite stretch of beach offers a full array of services, from an on-site dance club to a full-service European spa and health club. The collection of pyramid-shaped buildings, designed in Maya-influenced style, houses well-designed all-suite accommodations in studio, one-, two-, and three-bedroom configurations. All have sitting areas and kitchenettes, making the resort ideal for families or groups of friends. The Maya theme extends to both oceanfront pools, with mythical creatures forming water slides and waterfalls. The exceptional spa is reason enough to book a vacation here, with treatments, hydrotherapy, massage (including massage on the beach), and fitness and yoga classes. Special spa packages are always available. A new and compelling attraction is their El Tigre golf course (details earlier in this chapter, under "Golf"), and their on-site marina continues to draw a growing number of boats and yachts.

Paseo de los Cocoteros 001, 63731 Nuevo Vallarta, Nay. © 800/995-5714 in the U.S., or 322/226-6770. Fax 322/226-6713. www.paradisevillage.com. 490 units. High season $185–$290 (£102–£160) junior or 1-bedroom suite, $390 (£215) 2-bedroom suite, $572 (£315) 3-bedroom suite; low season $159–$235 (£87–£129) junior or 1-bedroom suite, $290 (£160) 2-bedroom suite, $520 (£286) 3-bedroom suite. AE, DC, MC, V. Free covered parking. **Amenities:** 2 restaurants; 2 beachside snack bars; nightclub; 2 beachside swimming pools; lap pool; championship golf club w/18-hole course; 4 tennis courts; complete fitness center; European spa; watersports center; marina; kids' club; travel desk; guests-only rental-car fleet; basketball court; beach volleyball; petting zoo. *In room:* A/C, TV, minibar, coffeemaker, hair dryer, iron, safe.

BUCERÍAS: A COASTAL VILLAGE ✵
Only 18km (11 miles) north of the Puerto Vallarta airport, Bucerías ("boo-seh-*ree*-ahs," meaning "place of the divers") is a small coastal fishing village of 10,000 people in Nayarit state on Banderas Bay. It's caught on as an alternative to Puerto Vallarta for those who find the pace of life there too invasive. Bucerías offers a seemingly contradictory mix of accommodations—trailer-park spaces and exclusive villa rentals tend to dominate, although there's a small selection of hotels as well.

To reach the town center by car, take the exit road from the highway out of Vallarta and drive down the shaded, divided street that leads to the beach. Turn left when you see a line of minivans and taxis (which serve Bucerías and Vallarta). Go straight ahead 1 block to the main plaza. The beach, with a lineup of restaurants, is a half-block farther. You'll see cobblestone streets leading from the highway to the beach, and hints of villas and town homes behind high walls. Second-home owners and about 1,500 transplanted Americans have already sought out this peaceful getaway; tourists have discovered its relaxed pace as well.

If you take the bus to Bucerías, exit when you see the minivans and taxis to and from Bucerías lined up on the street that leads to the beach. To use public transportation from Puerto Vallarta, take a minivan or bus marked BUCERIAS (they run 6am–9pm). The last minivan stop is Bucerías's town square. There's also 24-hour taxi service.

Exploring Bucerías   Come here for a day trip from Puerto Vallarta just to enjoy the long, wide, uncrowded beach, along with the fresh seafood served at the beachside restaurants or at one of the cafes listed below. On Saturdays and Sundays, many of the streets surrounding the plaza are closed to traffic for a *mercado* (street market)—a shopping nirvana where you can buy anything from tortillas to neon-colored cowboy hats. If you are inclined to stay a few days, you can relax inexpensively and explore more of Bucerías.

The **Coral Reef Surf Shop,** Heroe de Nacozari 114-F (© 329/298-0261), sells a great selection of surfboards and gear, and offers surfboard and boogie board rentals, surf lessons, and ATV and other adventure tours to surrounding areas.

Where to Stay   Unfortunately, I cannot recommend any of the hotels in Bucerías; they're run-down, and most people who choose to stay here opt for a private home rental. Check out the villa rental bulletin board at **www.sunworx.com. Las Palmas** in Bucerías (© 329/298-0060; fax 329/298-0061) will book accommodations, including villas, houses, and condos. Call ahead, or ask for directions to the office when you get to Bucerías. It's open Monday through Friday from 9am to 2pm and 4 to 6pm, Saturday from 9am to 2pm.

Where to Dine   Besides those mentioned below, there are many seafood restaurants fronting the beach. The local specialty is *pescado zarandeado,* a whole fish smothered in tasty sauce and slow-grilled.

Karen's Place 𝕲 INTERNATIONAL/MEXICAN   This casual oceanside restaurant offers classic cuisine, plus Mexican favorites in a style that appeals to North American appetites. Known for Sunday champagne brunch (9am–3pm), it is a perfect place to enjoy a light beach lunch, or a romantic dinner. The best-selling entrees are barbeque ribs and coconut shrimp. The casual, comfortable restaurant features live music on Tuesday and Friday at 7pm. It also has a decked terrace dining area with spectacular views, as well as a sushi menu.

On the beach at the Costa Dorada, Calle Lázaro Cárdenas. ℭ **322/133-2186** or 329/298-0832. www.all.at/karens. Breakfast $4.50–$5.50 (£2.50–£3.05); Sun brunch (9am–3pm) $14 (£7.70); main courses $5.50–$13 (£3.05–£7.15). MC, V. Mon–Sat 9am–9pm, Sun 9am–3pm.

Le Fort 𝕲𝕲𝕲 FRENCH   What an unforgettable dining experience! It's more than dinner—the evening consists of watching as Chef Gilles Le Fort prepares your gourmet meal and teaches you how to re-create it. The U-shaped bar in the intimate kitchen accommodates diners, who sip fine wines and nibble on pâté while the master works. Chef Le Fort is the winner of numerous culinary awards, and his warm conviviality is the real secret ingredient of this unusual experience. Once dinner is served, the chef and his wife, Margarita, will join the table, entertaining with stories of their experiences in Mexico. The first group of six to book for the evening chooses the menu; the maximum class size is 16, so groups often blend together. Le Fort has probably the most extensive wine cellar in the bay—some 4,000 bottles. Hand-rolled Cuban cigars, homemade sausages, pâtés, and more delicacies are available in the adjoining shop.

Calle Lázaro Cárdenas 71, 1 block from the Hotel Royal Decameron. ℭ **329/298-1532**. www.lefort.com.mx. Reservations required. 3-course dinner, wines, and recipes $45 (£25) per person. No credit cards. Daily 8–10:30pm; cooking classes available 10am–1:30pm.

Mark's 𝕲𝕲 *Finds* ITALIAN/STEAK/SEAFOOD   It's worth a special trip to Bucerías just to eat at this covered-patio restaurant. The most popular American hangout in town, Mark's offers a great assortment of thin-crust pizzas and flatbread, baked in its brick oven and seasoned with fresh herbs grown in the garden. Everything has exquisite flavorings—some favorites include lobster-stuffed chile relleno, macadamia-crusted red snapper filet, ahi tuna served rare, and filet mignon with blue-cheese ravioli. Multitalented chef Jan Marie (Mark's charming wife and partner) runs an adjacent boutique, featuring elegant home accessories and unique gift items. The bar televises all major sporting events.

Calle Lázaro Cárdenas 56 (a half block from the beach). ℭ **329/298-0303**. Pasta $8.70–$19 (£4.80–£10); main courses $13–$22 (£7.15–£12). MC, V. High season daily lunch noon–4pm and dinner 5–11pm; low season daily 5–10pm. From the highway, turn left just after bridge, where there's a small sign for Mark's; double back left at next street (immediately after you turn left) and turn right at next corner; Mark's is on the right.

Mezzogiorno 𝕲𝕲 ITALIAN   The owners of this elegantly casual oceanfront *trattoria* built a reputation with their Mezzaluna restaurant in Vallarta, then moved the business to their former home in Bucerías when the traffic became too much to deal with a commute. And diners on the north shore are so very grateful! It's the most attractive dining option north of Vallarta, in a sleekly restored home overlooking the bay. Choose to dine indoors or under the stars, beneath a canopy of trees on a oceanview deck or on the sand itself. But as stunning as the minimalist decor of the restaurant is, it takes second place to the savory dishes served. Salads are ample in size, and varied in combination of ingredients. My favorite combines grilled chicken with mixed greens, sundried tomatoes, goat cheese, and a currant-balsamic vinaigrette. For main dishes, pastas are the specialty, with best-sellers that include their calamari and saffron ravioli in a creamy sauce. Also delightful are the shrimp, clams, and fish served over black fettuccine, with black olives, capers, and a spicy tomato sauce. There is an ample wine list, full bar service, and attentive service.

Av. del Pacífico 33. ⓒ 329/298-0350. www.mezzogiorno.com.mx. Main courses $7–$18 (£3.85–£9.90). MC, V. Daily 6–11pm.

PUNTA MITA: EXCLUSIVE SECLUSION ✸✸✸
At the northern tip of the bay is an arrowhead-shaped, 600-hectare (1,482-acre) peninsula bordered on three sides by the ocean, called Punta Mita. Considered a sacred place by the Indians, this is the point where Banderas Bay, the Pacific Ocean, and the Sea of Cortez come together. It's magnificent, with white-sand beaches and coral reefs just offshore. Stately rocks jut out along the shoreline, and the water is a dreamy translucent blue. Punta Mita is evolving into one of Mexico's most exclusive developments. The master plan calls for a total of four luxury hotels, several high-end residential communities, and up to three championship golf courses. It is the first luxury residential development in Mexico intended for the foreign market. Today, what you'll find is the elegant Four Seasons Resort, its Jack Nicklaus Signature golf course, and a selection of rental luxury villas and condos. But by early 2008, a new 100-room St. Regis Resort will open, along with Punta Mita's second Jack Nicklaus golf course.

Casa Las Brisas ✸✸ (Finds
Although not technically in Punta Mita, Casa Las Brisas is near enough to get the sense of relaxed seclusion of this area. It's located on the back road that runs from Punta Mita to Sayulita, on the small, pristine Careyeros Bay. The six rooms are set in a villa, overlooking the exquisite beach. The villa itself is a work of white stucco walls, tile floors and patios, thatch and tile roofs, and guayaba-wood balcony detailing. Patios and intimate indoor-outdoor seating areas on varying levels are ideal for an afternoon read or an evening cocktail. Interiors of the guest rooms are simple and elegant, with touches such as carved armoires, headboards, and doors from Michoacán. The colorful bathrooms feature large showers lined with hand-painted tiles. Private balconies with ocean views surround the pool, which features submerged sunning chairs and a small fountain. There are no TVs or telephones, but a cellphone in the lobby is available for guests. A big plus here is the delicious dining, included in the price of your stay.

Playa Careyeros, 63734 Punta de Mita, Nay. ⓒ 866/740-7999 in the U.S., 329/298-4114, or 322/225-4364. www.casalasbrisas.com. 7 suites. High season $445–$575 (£245–£316) suite; low season $385–$515 (£212–£283) suite. Rates include all meals and drinks. Minimum 3-night stay required. Credit cards for deposit only; cash payment upon booking. Limited street parking. **Amenities:** Restaurant; small outdoor pool; universal gym station; spa; tour services; entertainment room w/TV, DVD, and VCR. *In room:* A/C, minibar, safe, no phone.

Four Seasons Resort Punta Mita ✸✸✸
The Four Seasons Resort has brought a new standard of luxury to Mexico's Pacific Coast. The boutique hotel artfully combines seclusion and pampering service with a welcoming sense of comfort. Accommodations are in three-story *casitas* surrounding the main building, which holds the lobby, cultural center, restaurants, shopping arcade, and oceanfront pool. Every guest room offers breathtaking views of the ocean from a large terrace or balcony. Most

suites also offer a private plunge pool, a separate sitting room, a bar, and a powder room. Room interiors are typical Four Seasons—plush and spacious, with a king or two double beds, a seating area, and an oversize bathroom with a deep soaking tub, separate glass-enclosed shower, and dual vanity sink. More than the stylish luxury, this hotel boasts unerring service that is both warm and unobtrusive. At least 45 minutes from Puerto Vallarta's activities, it's the perfect get-away—but then, most guests feel so relaxed and at ease, it's hard to think of venturing beyond the resort at all. The full-service spa, tennis center, and private championship golf course seem to be options enough. In 2006, Four Seasons unveiled an adults-only tranquillity pool, complete with champagne and caviar bar, and surrounded by cabañas available for daily rent, that come equipped with wireless Internet, plasma TVs, and a comfy daybed. In 2007, they expanded their popular Kids for All Seasons club, plus added a building of rooms geared for family travelers, surrounded by a Lazy River, as well as yacht charters. In addition to the sumptuous rooms and suites, the resort now offers private 4- and 5-bedroom villas for guest stays, complete with private butler services.

63734 Bahía de Banderas, Nay. (C) **800/332-3442** in the U.S., or 329/291-6000. Fax 329/291-6060. www.fourseasons. com. 165 units. High season $545–$1,175 (£300–£646) double, $1,685–$4,485 (£927–£2,466) suite; low season $375–$925 (£206–£509) double, $1,025–$2,295 (£564–£1,262) suite. AE, DC, MC, V. Free valet parking. **Amenities:** 3 restaurants; lobby bar; beachfront bar, oceanfront pool; adults-only pool surrounded by private cabañas; tennis center w/4 courts of various surfaces; full-service fitness center; European-style spa; *temazcal* (pre-Hispanic sweat lodge); watersports equipment including sea kayaks, sailboards, surfboards, and sunfish sailboats; children's programs; game room, 24-hr. concierge; tour desk; room service; cultural center w/lectures and activities; complimentary video library. *In room:* A/C, TV/VCR, high-speed Internet, minibar, coffeemaker, hair dryer, iron, safe.

SAYULITA: MUCH MORE THAN A GREAT SURF SPOT   Sayulita is only 40km (25 miles) northwest of Puerto Vallarta, on Highway 200 to Tepic, yet it feels like worlds away. It captures the simplicity and tranquillity of beach life that has long since left Vallarta—but hurry, because it seems this place is on the verge of exploding in popularity. For years, Sayulita has been principally a surfers' destination—the main beach in town is known for its consistent break and long, rideable waves. Recently, visitors and locals who find Vallarta becoming too cosmopolitan have started to flock here.

An easygoing attitude seems to permeate the air in this beach town. Yet despite its simplicity, niceties are popping up all over among the basic accommodations, inexpensive Mexican food stands, and handmade, hippie-style-bauble vendors. It's quickly becoming gentrified with new restaurants, cafes, shops, and elegant villas for rent.

Sayulita is a popular stage for surfing tournaments; on any given weekend you might encounter perfect-swell-seeking surfers—or a Huichol Indian family that has come down to sell their wares. This eclectic mix of the cool, the unusual, and the authentic Mexican makes Sayulita a special place.

To get to Sayulita, you can rent a car, or take a taxi from the airport or downtown Vallarta. The rate is about $50 (£28) to get to the town plaza. You can also take a taxi back to Vallarta. The stand is on the main square, or you can call for pickup at your hotel. The trip from the airport to Sayulita costs $55 (£30). Guides also lead tours to Puerto Vallarta, Punta Mita, and other surrounding areas, including a Huichol Indian community.

Where to Stay   Sayulita offers several private homes for rent. One local expert on Sayulita rentals is **Upi Viteri** (upiviteri@prodigy.net.mx), who has access to some of the nicest rental properties.

Where to Dine   If you are in Sayulita, chances are you heard about it because of **Don Pedro's,** the most popular restaurant in town, in the heart of the main beach.

Don Pedro's INTERNATIONAL   Many say it's Don Pedro's that has brought so much attention to Sayulita in recent years—Vallarta area visitors came for the food, then booked their next vacation in this funky town. Choose between a two-level indoor dining area or shaded tables on the beach for breakfast, lunch, or dinner. Starters include crispy calamari, spring rolls, and fresh salads. Main courses include thin-crust pizzas, fresh fish artfully prepared, and a changing selection of savory pasta and chicken dishes, such as chicken Provençal, a whole chicken marinated in garlic and herbs, served with sautéed spinach, roasted tomatoes, and white beans. Grilled ahi tuna with mashed potatoes is also a favorite. In the bar area, TVs broadcast sporting events of any relevance, from the Super Bowl to Mexican soccer. I enjoy a relaxing lunch here, then stay for the beach action. Full bar service also available.

Marlin 2, on the beachfront. (© **329/291-3090.** Main courses $5–$25 (£2.75–£14). MC, V. Daily 8am–11pm.

Rollie's 𝄞𝄞 (Finds) BREAKFAST   Breakfast heaven! This family restaurant emanates a happy aura that puts its patrons in a good mood. The menu reflects the tone of the place, with options such as Rollie's Delight (blended fresh orange and banana), Adriana's Rainbow (an omelet with cheese, tomatoes, green peppers, and onions), and my personal favorite, Indian Pipe Pancakes. All dishes come with Rollie's famous lightly seasoned, pan-fried new potatoes. Rollie's recently expanded their offerings to dinner as well, served from 5:30 to 9pm. Specialties include paella. There's also an upstairs espresso bar.

Av. Revolución, 2 blocks west of the main square. (© **329/291-3567** or -3075. Breakfast $3–$8 (£1.65–£4.40); dinner $4–$15 (£2.20–£8.25). No credit cards. Daily Nov–Apr 8am–noon and 5:30–9pm. Closed May–Oct.

SAN SEBASTIAN: AN AUTHENTIC MOUNTAIN HIDEAWAY 𝄞𝄞𝄞   If you haven't heard about San Sebastián yet, it probably won't be long—its remote location and historic appeal have made it the Mexican media's new darling destination. Originally discovered in the late 1500s and settled in 1603, the town peaked as a center of mining operations, swelling to a population of over 30,000 by the mid-1800s. Today, with roughly 600 year-round residents, San Sebastián retains all the charm of a village locked in time, with an old church, a coffee plantation, an underground tunnel system—and wholly without a T-shirt shop.

Getting There   By car, it's a 2½-hour drive up the Sierra Madre from Puerto Vallarta on an improved road, but it can be difficult during the summer rainy season, when the road washes out frequently. **Vallarta Adventures** (© **888/303-2653** in the U.S., or 322/297-1212, ext. 3; www.vallarta-adventures.com) runs a daily plane service for half-day tours and can occasionally accommodate overnight visitors. The small private airport can arrange flights. **Aerotron** (© **322/221-1921;** www.aerotron.com.mx) charges about $130 (£72) round-trip, **Aéro Taxis de la Bahía** (© **322/221-1990** and 222-2049) about $92 (£51) round-trip, depending on the type of plane and number of passengers. For more information on air tours and horseback-riding excursions, see the "Organized Tours" section, earlier in this chapter.

Where to Stay   There are two places to stay in San Sebastián. The first is the very basic **El Pabellón de San Sebastián,** which faces the town square. Its nine simply furnished rooms surround a central patio. Don't expect extras here; rates run $50 (£28) per double. The town's central phone lines handle reservations—you call (© **322/297-0200)**

and leave a message or send a fax, and hopefully the hotel will receive it. Except on holidays, there is generally room at this inn. No credit cards.

A more enjoyable option is the stately **Hacienda Jalisco** ⟨★★⟩ (✆ **322/222-9638;** www.haciendajalisco.com), built in 1850 and once the center of mining operations in town. The beautifully landscaped, rambling old hacienda is near the airstrip, a 15-minute walk from town. Proprietor Bud Acord has welcomed John Huston, Liz Taylor, Richard Burton, Peter O'Toole, and a cast of local characters over the years.

The five extra-clean rooms have wood floors, rustic furnishings and antiques, and working fireplaces; some are decorated with pre-Columbian reproductions. The ample bathrooms are beautifully tiled and have skylights. Hammocks grace the upstairs terrace, while a sort-of museum on the lower level attests to the celebrity guests and importance the hacienda has enjoyed over the years. Because of its remote location, all meals are included. Rates are $80 (£44) per person per night, and includes full breakfast and dinner; alcoholic beverages are extra. Reserve through e-mail (pmt15@hotmail.com or info@haciendajalisco.com), through the town telephone (✆ **322/297-0200**), or on their website. Group rates and discounts for longer stays are available. No credit cards are accepted. Guided horseback, walking, or mine tours can be arranged through the Hacienda.

2 Mazatlán ⟨★⟩

1,078km (668 miles) NW of Mexico City; 502km (311 miles) NW of Guadalajara; 1,561km (968 miles) SE of Mexicali

Mazatlán is comfortable, casual, value-packed Mexico at its best. More than any other beach resort in the country, it probably best represents the golden beaches, fresh seafood, and inexpensive accommodations that typified Mexico's appeal to travelers in the first place. Although some developments are edging Mazatlán into the golf-playing, manicured resort that typifies most of Mexico today, it is going there grudgingly—most of Mazatlán remains refreshingly simple.

Mazatlán's lures continue to be its expansive beaches and renowned sportfishing. The evolving golf scene, luxury-yacht harbor, and growing selection of accommodations have yet to catch the attention of enough tourists to drive prices to the levels of other Mexican resorts, and that's good news for travelers looking for economy in a beach resort.

A city with a population of nearly 500,000, Mazatlán is the largest port between Los Angeles and the Panama Canal. Elegant reminders of its history, 27km (17 miles) of sandy beaches, and a geographically diverse environment are all added attractions in Mazatlán's efforts to become a premier beach resort.

Limited flight availability is the principal factor holding back Mazatlán's growth. Charter operators have picked up some of the slack and are the predominant means of arrival here.

Once known as a spring break haven and a place to party, Mazatlán is now attracting more families, mature travelers, and other tourists with an eye for value. It enjoys strong repeat business and positive word of mouth, as it continues to offer exceptional vacation values.

ESSENTIALS
GETTING THERE & DEPARTING
BY PLANE A number of airlines operate direct or nonstop flights to Mazatlán, though charters predominate. From the United States, **AeroMéxico** (✆ **800/237-6639**

Mazatlán Area

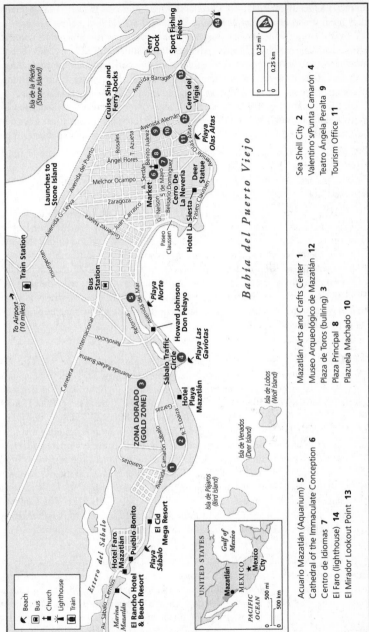

Isla de la Piedra (Stone Island)

Ferry Dock

Sport Fishing Fleets

Cruise Ship and Ferry Docks

Launches to Stone Island

Avenida Barragan

Cerro del Vigía

Playa Olas Altas

Rosales

Ángel Flores

Melchor Ocampo

Zaragoza

Avenida Alemán

Avenida Benito Juárez

Avenida del Puerto

Avenida G. Leyva

Avenida G. Nelson

5 de Mayo

A. Serdán

Belisario Domínguez

Gutiérrez Nájera

Juan Carrasco

Market

Deer Statue

Cerro La Nevería

Hotel La Siesta

Paseo Claussen

Train Station

Bus Station

Playa Norte

Howard Johnson Don Pelayo

Playa Las Gaviotas

Sábalo Traffic Circle

Hotel Playa Mazatlán

ZONA DORADO (GOLD ZONE)

To Airport (10 miles)

Avenida Rafael Buelna

Carretera Internacional

Revolución

Reforma

Avenida del Mar

Insurgentes

Garzas

Gaviotas

R.T. Loaiza

Avenida Camarón Sábalo

Av. Sábalo Cerritos

Marina Mazatlán

Estero del Sábalo

Hotel Faro Mazatlán

Pueblo Bonito

El Cid Mega Resort

Playa Sábalo

El Rancho Hotel & Beach Resort

Bahía del Puerto Viejo

Isla de Lobos (Wolf Island)

Isla de Venados (Deer Island)

Isla de Pájaros (Bird Island)

0   0.25 mi
0   0.25 km

Legend
- Beach
- Bus
- Church
- Lighthouse
- Train

UNITED STATES

PACIFIC OCEAN

Gulf of Mexico

Mazatlán

MEXICO

Mexico City

0   500 mi
0   500 km

Acuario Mazatlán (Aquarium) 5
Cathedral of the Immaculate Conception 6
Centro de Idiomas 7
El Faro (lighthouse) 14
El Mirador Lookout Point 13

Mazatlán Arts and Crafts Center 1
Museo Arqueológico de Mazatlán 12
Plaza de Toros (bullring) 3
Plaza Principal 8
Plazuela Machado 10

Sea Shell City 2
Valentino's/Punta Camarón 4
Teatro Ángela Peralta 9
Tourism Office 11

333

in the U.S., or 01-800/021-4000 in Mexico) flies from Los Angeles, Atlanta, Phoenix, and Tucson, via Mexico City. **Mexicana** (© **800/531-7921** in the U.S.) has direct service from Denver, Chicago, Los Angeles, Miami, and San Antonio, most connecting through Mexico City. **Alaska Airlines** (© **800/252-7522** in the U.S., or 669/985-2730) serves Vancouver, Seattle, Portland, San Francisco, and Los Angeles. Within Mexico, **AeroMéxico** (© **669/914-1111**) has flights from Hermosillo, Durango, Monterrey, Puerto Vallarta, Tijuana, and León, all via Guadalajara or Mexico City. **Mexicana** (© **669/982-5666**) offers service from Mexico City and Los Cabos. **Aero Calafia** (© **669/985-4300;** www.aereocalafia.com.mx) offers direct service from Puerto Vallarta and Los Cabos. Check with a travel agent for the latest **charter flights.**

BY BUS   First-class and deluxe buses connect Mazatlán to Guadalajara (7 hr.; $35 first class one-way) and Mexico City (16 hr.; $85/£47 first class one-way) almost hourly, and less often to other points within Mexico. The bus terminal is located on Highway 200 N. Km 1203; © **669/982-1949.**

BY CAR   To reach Mazatlán from the United States, take **International Highway 15** from Nogales, Arizona, to Culiacán. At Culiacán, change to the four-lane **tollway**—it costs about $40 but is the only road considered safe and in drivable condition. On the tollway, total trip time from the United States to Mazatlán is about 10 hours. Consider an overnight stop, because driving at night in Mexico can be dangerous. **From Puerto Vallarta,** the 560km (347-mile) drive is not easy—the road winds through the mountains, but is in generally good condition. Take **Highway 200** north to Las Varas. There it becomes four-lane **Highway 68;** follow that until you see a detour for **Highway 15.** Take 15 north to Mazatlán.

ORIENTATION

ARRIVING   The Rafael Buelna International Airport (airport code: MZT) is 27km (17 miles) southeast of the hotel-and-resort area of town. The following rental-car companies have counters in the airport, open during flight arrivals and departures: **Hertz** (© **800/654-3030** in the U.S., or 669/985-0845), **Budget** (© **800/472-3325** in the U.S., or 669/913-2000), and **National** (© **800/227-7368** in the U.S., or 669/982-4000). Daily rates run $65 to $145 (£36–£80). A car is desirable if you want to explore the surrounding coastline and villages, but it is not essential in Mazatlán.

Taxis and *colectivo* minivans run from the airport to hotels; the expensive airport-chartered taxis cost $40 to $50 (£22–£28), about twice as much as the *colectivo,* which runs $20 to $28 (£11–£15), depending on the location of your hotel. Only taxis make the return trip to the airport, which costs $20 to $30 (£11–£17). The **Central de Autobuses** (main bus terminal) is at Río Tamazula and Chachalacas. To get there from Avenida del Mar, walk 3 blocks inland on Río Tamazula; the station is on your right. Taxis line up in front of the bus station.

VISITOR INFORMATION   The extremely helpful and professional **City and State Tourism Office** is on Calle Carnaval 1317, corner of Mariano Escobedo, at the Plaza Machado (© **669/981-8886** or -8887; fax 669/981-8884; www.sinaloa-travel.com). The office is open Monday through Friday from 9am to 5pm; the staff speaks English. To preview what's going on in Mazatlán before you arrive, check the website of the local English-language newspaper (**www.pacificpearl.com**), or pick up a copy of their very helpful publication upon arrival for a complete schedule of current activities. Three other very helpful guides in English are the **Welcome Digest**

(© 669/913-3628), **Viejo Mazatlán** (© 669/985-3781; www.viejo-mazatlan.com), and **Mazatlán Interactivo** (© 669/981-8435; www.mazatlaninteractivo.com.mx).

CITY LAYOUT   Mazatlán extends north from the peninsula port area along Avenida Gabriel Leyva and Avenida Barragan, where the cruise ships, sportfishing boats, and ferries dock. Downtown begins with the historic area of **Viejo Mazatlán (Old Mazatlán)** and **Playa Olas Altas** to the south. A curving seaside boulevard, or *malecón,* runs 27km (17 miles) along the waterfront, all the way from Playa Olas Altas to **Playa Norte,** changing names often along the way. Traveling north, it begins as Paseo Olas Altas and becomes Paseo Claussen parallel to the commercial downtown area. The name changes to Avenida del Mar at the beginning of the Playa Norte area.

About 6km (4 miles) north of downtown lies the Sábalo traffic circle in the **Zona Dorada (Golden Zone)** near the **Punta Camarón,** a rocky outcropping over the water. The Zona Dorada begins where Avenida del Mar intersects Avenida Rafael Buelna and becomes **Avenida Camarón Sábalo,** which leads north through the abundant hotels and fast-food restaurants of the tourist zone. From here, the resort hotels, including the huge El Cid Resort complex, spread northward along and beyond **Playa Sábalo.** The **Marina Mazatlán** development has changed the landscape north of the Zona Dorada considerably; hotels, condo complexes, and private residences rise around the new marina. Although completion of the extensive project—to comprise the marina, condominiums, and commercial centers—is still years away, the new marina will be the largest on the western seaboard between Los Angeles and Panama, and one of the largest in all of Latin America. This area north of the Marina El Cid is increasingly known as Nuevo Mazatlán. North of here is **Los Cerritos (Little Hills),** the northern limit of Mazatlán.

GETTING AROUND

The downtown transportation center for buses, taxis, and *pulmonías* (see below) is on the central Plaza Principal, facing the cathedral.

BY TAXI   Eco Taxis are green-and-white cabs with posted set fares, but generally are about $3 or $5 (£1.65–£2.75) per trip. Taxis are easy to flag around town and can also be rented by the day or by the hour. Agree on a price in advance. Fares between the Zona Dorada and Old Mazatlán average $4.50 to $6.50 (£2.50–£3.60); within the Zona Dorada, you should pay about $3.50 to $5 (£1.95–£2.75). To request a taxi, call © **669/986-1111** or 985-2828.

BY *PULMONIA*   These open-air vehicles resembling overgrown golf carts carry up to three passengers. *Pulmonías* (literally "pneumonias") have surreylike tops and open sides. As a rule, they're slightly more expensive than taxis at about $5 (£2.75) per starting fare, but they're part of the Mazatlán experience.

BY BUS   Buses, some with air-conditioning, cover most of the city and are relatively easy to use, although knowing some Spanish is helpful. The fare is 80¢ (45p) for local routes. The SABALO CENTRO line runs from the Zona Dorada along the waterfront to downtown near the market and the central plaza; at Avenida Miguel Alemán, the buses turn and head south to Olas Altas. The CERRITOS-JUAREZ line starts near the train station, cuts across town to the *malecón* beside the Zona Dorada, and heads north to Los Cerritos and back. The SABALO COCOS line runs through the Zona Dorada, heads inland to the bus station, and goes on to downtown (also stopping at the market) by a back route. The PLAYA SUR line goes to the area where the sportfishing and tour boats depart. Buses run daily from 6am to 10:30pm. Fares are about 75¢ (40p) for air-conditioned green buses or 35¢ (20p) for the yellow buses.

FAST FACTS: Mazatlán

American Express The office is on Avenida Camarón Sábalo in the Centro Comercial Balboa shopping center, Loc. 15 and 16 (© **669/913-0600;** fax 669/916-5908), between the traffic circle and the El Cid Resort. It's open Monday through Friday from 9am to 6pm, Saturday from 9am to 1pm.

Area Code The telephone area code for Mazatlán is **669.**

Banks Most banks are generally open Monday through Friday from 9am to 6pm, and some have limited hours on Saturday.

Climate As the northernmost major beach resort on the mainland, Mazatlán can be cooler in summer than the resorts farther south. The wettest month is September.

Drugstore **Farmacias Hidalgo,** German Evers and Hidalgo s/n (© **669/985-4545** or -4646), is open 24 hours and delivers to hotels.

Emergencies Dial © **066.** For medical emergencies, contact the **Sharp Hospital,** Rafael Buelna and Las Cruces (© **669/986-5676** or -5678). The Traffic Police can be reached at © **669/983-2616.**

Internet Access Numerous places offer access, with one long-standing business being **Internet Café Netscape** (Av. Camarón Sábalo 222, between Farmacia Benavides and Taco Loco); it's open daily, including holidays, from 8am to 11pm. Access costs $3 (£1.65) per hour; $1.50 (85p) for 30 minutes (© **669/990-1289).**

Language Classes Spanish-language classes begin every Monday at the **Centro de Idiomas** (© **669/985-5606;** fax 669/982-2053; www.spanishlink.org), 3 blocks west of the cathedral near 21 de Marzo and Canizales. In addition to small-group (maximum 10 students) and individual instruction, the language center offers a home-stay program and a person-to-person program that matches students with local people. On Friday at 7pm, the center holds free Spanish and English conversation groups open to both visitors and locals. For more information, call or write Dixie Davis, Belisario Domínguez 1908, Mazatlán, Sin.

Post Office The *correo* is downtown on Benito Juárez just off Angel Flores, on the east side of the main plaza (© **669/981-2121).** Hours are Monday through Friday from 8am to 5pm, Saturday from 9am to noon.

ACTIVITIES ON & OFF THE BEACH

To orient yourself, walk up and enjoy the panoramic view from **El Faro,** the famous lighthouse on the point at the south end of town. It's the second-highest lighthouse in the world (only Gibraltar's is higher), towering 135m (443 ft.) over the harbor. Begin at the end of Paseo Centenario, near the sportfishing docks. There's a refreshment stand at the foot of the hill. Allow about 45 minutes for the climb. The view is nearly as spectacular from the top of **Cerro del Vigía (Lookout Hill),** which is accessible by car from Paseo Olas Altas.

BEACHES   At the western edge of downtown is rocky **Playa Olas Altas,** a lovely stretch of pounding surf not suitable for swimming. Around a rocky promontory north of Olas Altas is **Playa Norte,** which offers several kilometers of good sand beach.

At the Sábalo traffic circle, Punta Camarón juts into the water, and on either side of the point is **Playa Las Gaviotas.** Farther north, **Playa Sábalo** is perhaps the best beach in Mazatlán. The next point jutting into the water is Punta Sábalo, beyond which you'll find a bridge over a channel that flows in and out of a lagoon. Beyond the marina, more beaches stretch all the way to Los Cerritos. Remember that all beaches in Mexico are public property, so you have the right to enjoy the beach of your choice.

Mazatlán is one of only a few resorts in Mexico where surfing is common on central town beaches. The waves are best at **Los Pinos,** north of the fort—known in surfing circles as "the Cannon"—and at Playa Los Gaviotas and Playa Sábalo. Waves are most notable and consistent from May to September. Other notable surf breaks are found at Olas Altos, Cerritos, Isla de la Piedra, and El Camarón, at Playa Norte. For surf gear, board rentals, lessons, and surf reports, visit the **Mazatlán Surf Center** (© **669/913-1821;** www.mazatlansurfcenter.com) in the Zona Dorada, at Camarón Sábalo, 500-4, next to the Dairy Queen. Boogie boards are widely available for rent on the beaches in front of the Zona Dorada, for about $20 (£11) per day.

A good beach that makes a great day trip is on the ocean side of **Isla de la Piedra (Stone Island).** From the center of town, board a Circunvalación or Playa Sur bus from the north side of the Plaza Principal for the ride to the boat landing, Embarcadero–Isla de la Piedra. Small motorboats make the 5-minute trip to the island every 15 minutes or so from 7am to 6pm for a modest price. When you arrive on the island, walk through the rustic little village to the ocean side, where the pale-sand beaches, bordered by coconut groves, stretch for miles. On Sunday afternoons, the *palapa* restaurants on the shore have music and dancing, attracting mainly Mexican families; on other days the beach is almost empty. **Carmelita's** has delicious fish, called *lisamacho;* it's grilled over an open fire and served slightly blackened with fresh, hot corn tortillas and salsa. It's open daily from 10am to 6pm and doesn't accept credit cards.

The local gay beach is on **Isla de las Chivas.** Transportation to the island is by launches, which you can catch at the Muelle Puntilla, located next to the docks where the ferry to La Paz departs.

CRUISES & BOAT RENTALS   The **Kolonahe Sailing Adventure** departs for Isla de Venados (Deer Island) Tuesday through Sunday from Marina El Cid. Reserve through any travel agent or through El Cid directly (see below). This excursion sails aboard a 15m (50-ft.) trimaran to the island, where guests enjoy a picnic lunch and beverages, plus the use of snorkel equipment, boogie boards, kayaks, and canoes for a cost of $35 (£19) per person. Departure is at 9:15am, with the boat returning at 3:30pm.

Anfibios, amphibious vehicles that operate on land and in the water, head for Isla de Venados, one of three big islands off the coast. Trips last 2 to 2½ hours; they leave from the beaches of the **El Cid Resort** (© **669/913-3333,** ext. 3341; www.elcid.com) daily at 10am, noon, and 2pm. Round-trip tickets cost $10 (£11), plus $10 (£11) for snorkeling gear.

DEEP-SEA FISHING   Mazatlán claims to be the billfish and shrimp capital of the world, and whether or not it's a valid claim, deep-sea fishing in Mazatlán is generally less expensive than in other parts of Mexico. If you request it (please do!), your captain will practice "catch and release." Rates are around $250 (£138) per day for a 7m

(23-ft.) *lancha* for up to three persons and $430 (£237) per day for an 11m (36-ft.) cruiser for up to four passengers; rates do not include fishing licenses, drinks, or gratuities. Try the **Aries Fleet** located at the Marina El Cid harbormaster's office (© 669/916-3468). Locals suggest making fishing reservations for October through January at least a month in advance; at the very least, do it the minute you arrive in town. You may also choose to rent a *panga* (a small, uncovered, fiberglass boat with an outboard motor) at a rate of $50 (£28) per hour, with a minimum of 4 hours—it's the way the locals fish.

OTHER WATERSPORTS Among the best places to rent watersports equipment, from snorkeling gear to kayaks, are the Aqua Sport Center at the **El Cid Resort** (© 669/913-3333; www.mazatlan-aquasports.com) and the Ocean Sport Center at the **Hotel Faro Mazatlán** (© 669/913-1111; www.faromazatlan.com.mx).

SPECIAL EVENTS IN NEARBY VILLAGES On the weekend of the first Sunday in October, **Rosario,** a small town 45 minutes south on Highway 15, holds a **festival honoring Our Lady of the Rosary.** Games, music, dances, processions, and festive foods mark the event. From May 1 to May 10, Rosario holds its **Spring Festival.**

In mid-October, the village of **Escuinapa,** south of Rosario on Highway 15, holds a **Mango Festival.**

For more information, call the State Tourism Office at © 669/981-8886.

SPECTATOR SPORTS There's a bullring (Plaza de Toros) on Rafael Buelna about 1.5km (1 mile) from the Zona Dorada. From December to early April, **bullfights** take place every Sunday and on holidays at 4pm; locals recommend arriving by 2pm. Tickets range from $12 (£6.60) for general admission (ask for the shady side—*la sombra*) to $30 (£17) for the front of the shaded section; most travel agencies and tour desks sell advance tickets.

Rodeos, or *charreadas,* take place at the Lienzo Charro (bullring) of the Asociación de Charros de Mazatlán (© 669/986-3510) on Saturday or Sunday beginning at 4pm. Tickets (around $4.50/£2.50) are available through local travel agents and hotel concierge desks, which will have the current schedule.

At Playa Olas Altas, daring **cliff divers** take to the rock ledges of **El Mirador** and plunge into the shallow, pounding surf below, a la Acapulco. The divers perform sporadically during the day as tour buses arrive near their perch, sometimes diving with torches at 7pm. After the dive, they collect donations from spectators. Follow the *malecón* to the esplanade and look for the mermaid statue to find El Mirador.

TENNIS, GOLF & OTHER OUTDOOR SPORTS Mazatlán has more than 100 tennis courts. Try the **El Cid Resort,** on Camarón Sábalo (© 669/913-3333), although hotel guests have priority, or the **Racquet Club Gaviotas, Ibis,** and **Río Bravo** in the Zona Dorada (© 669/913-5939). Many larger hotels in Mazatlán also have courts.

Mazatlán is probably the best **golf** value in Mexico. Try the 27-hole course at the **El Cid Resort** (© 669/913-3333). Nine holes designed by Lee Trevino complement the 18 holes designed by Robert Trent Jones, Jr. It's open to the public, with preference given to hotel guests. Tee times book up quickly. Greens fees for nonguests are $60 (£33) for 18 holes, plus $17 (£9.35) for the caddy. El Cid guests pay $42 (£23), plus $17 (£9.35) for the caddy. El Cid's facilities include a John Jacobs golf school, the only one in Mexico. It's open daily, from 7am to 5:30pm.

Another option is the 9-hole course at the **Club Campestre Mazatlán** (© **669/ 980-1570**), which is open to the public. Greens fees are $22 (£12) for 9 holes, $33 (£18) for 18 holes; a caddy costs an extra $10 and $15 (£11 and 8.25), a cart $15 and $20 (£8.25 and £11), respectively. It's on Highway 15 on the outskirts of downtown.

Mazatlán's newest course is at the **Estrella del Mar Golf Club** (© **669/982-3300;** www.estrelladelmar.com). The 18-hole, 7,004-yard course, also designed by Robert Trent Jones, Jr., stretches along 3km (2 miles) of coastline on Isla de la Piedra, a penin- sula just south of downtown Mazatlán. There's a PGA pro on staff, and daily clinics. Greens fees run $110 (£60; $69/£38 after 1pm), including cart, but no caddies are available at present. It's open daily from 7:30am to sunset. Also on-site are a golf shop, restaurant, and bar. Clubs are available for rent for $30 (£17) plus tax.

You can go **horseback riding** on Isla de la Piedra for $6 (£3.30) per hour. Ask your hotel's travel agent to arrange a **kayaking excursion** on El Verde Camacho Ecological Lagoon, or take a trip to Teacapán for **birding** in one of Mexico's largest estuaries (see "Road Trips from Mazatlán," later in this chapter).

Bird-watching tours are also being offered by Sendero Mexico (www.senderomexico. com), an outfitter who has been offering a popular area kayaking tour. The birding tours can be arranged in conjunction with a kayak tour, or as a separate trip to either the foothills of the Sierra Madres or to the Palmito reserve (located just past Copala on the highway), home to the tufted-jay. The state of Sinaloa has 400 species of endemic birds—a bonanza for birders. The town of El Palmito, situated within 10,000 acres of wildlife preserve, is part of a government tourism program to promote sustainable and eco-friendly tourism to rural and isolated areas, which is supported in part by Cornell University. As a trip to El Palmito is a bit too far for a day trip, there are three small "safari tents," and two two-bedroom cabins available for overnight guests. Although the trip is possible to make on your own, it's best and highly recom- mend to notify Sendero Mexico of plans to visit, or simply set up a visit through them. Sendero Mexico has been approached by the national government to spearhead efforts to duplicate their success at El Palmito in other regions nationwide.

Kelly's Bicycle Shop, Av. Camarón Sábalo 204, Loc. 16 (© **669/914-1187;** www. kellys-bikes.com), in the Zona Dorada, arranges mountain-bike tours and rents alu- minum-frame bikes with full suspension. A half-day guided tour costs $28 (£15); rentals are $8 (£4.40) per half-day, $15 (£8.25) per full day. Bike rentals include water bottle, snack, map, and general route information.

EXPLORING MAZATLAN

Mazatlán may be best known for its wide, sandy beaches and sporting activities, but visitors who neglect to sample the city's cultural events and attractions are missing out on a multidimensional destination.

MUSEUMS

Acuario Mazatlán *Kids*   Children and adults interested in the sea will love the Mazatlán Aquarium. With over 200 species of fish, including sharks, eels, and sea horses, it is one of the largest and best in Mexico. Next to the aquarium are a play- ground and a botanical garden, with an aviary and a small crocodile exhibit. Staff feed the sea lions, birds, and fish at shows almost hourly.

Av. de los Deportes 111 (a half block off Av. del Mar). © **669/981-7815** or -7817. Admission $7 (£3.85) adults, $4.50 (£2.50) children 3–11. Daily 9:30am–5:30pm.

Moments   Mazatlán's Carnaval: A Weeklong Party

The week before Lent (usually in Feb) is Mazatlán's famous Carnaval, or Mardi Gras. People come from all over the country and abroad for this flamboyant celebration, topped in size and revelry only by those in Río de Janeiro and New Orleans. Highlights of the event include parades, special shows, the coronation of the Carnaval queen, outdoor concerts, more than 150 food and beverage vendors, all-night parties, and extravaganzas all over town. For event information, check with the major hotels or the tourism office, or look for posters around town. Every night during Carnaval week, all along the Olas Altas oceanfront drive in the southern part of town, the streets fill with music from roving mariachi groups, local traditional *bandas sinaloenses* (sporting lots of brass instruments), and electrified bands under tarpaulin shades. The crowd increases each day until the last night, Shrove Tuesday, when musicians, dancers, and people out for a good time pack the *malecón*. The following day, Ash Wednesday, the party is over. People receive crosses of ashes on their foreheads at church, and Lent begins.

Museo Arqueológico de Mazatlán   This small, attractive archaeological museum displays both pre-Hispanic artifacts and a permanent contemporary art exhibit. From Olas Altas, walk inland on Sixto Osuna 1½ blocks; the museum is on your right. Art exhibits sometimes take place in the Casa de la Cultura across the street from the museum.

Sixto Osuna 76 (1½ blocks from Paseo Olas Altas). (℗ 669/981-1455. Free admission. Tues–Sun 10am–7pm.

ARCHITECTURAL HIGHLIGHTS

Two blocks south of the central plaza stands the lovely **Teatro Angela Peralta,** Carnaval 1024, Centro (℗ 669/982-4444), a national historic monument. Built between 1869 and 1874, it most recently underwent renovation in 1998. The 841-seat Italian-style theater has three levels of balconies, two facades, and, in true tropical style, a lobby with no roof. The theater was named for one of the world's great divas, who, along with the director and 30 members of the opera, died in Mazatlán of cholera in an 1863 epidemic. Some city tours stop here; if you're visiting on your own, the theater is open daily from 9am to 6pm. The fee for touring the building is $1 (55p). It regularly schedules folkloric ballets, along with periodic performances of classical ballet, contemporary dance, symphony concerts, opera, and jazz. For information, call or check at the theater box office. This theater is the home of Delfos, one of the most important contemporary dance companies in Mexico.

The 20-block historic area near the theater, including the small square **Plazuela Machado** (bordered by Frías, Constitución, Carnaval, and Sixto Osuna), abounds with beautiful old buildings and colorful town houses trimmed with wrought iron and carved stone. The Plaza hosts local artists and vendors on Saturday afternoons, as well as offers arts and crafts activities and storytelling for children. Two new art galleries and art shops have opened near the plaza on Sixto Osuna: the Elena Chauvet Gallery and Casa Ethnica. Check out the **town houses** on Libertad between Domínguez and Carnaval and the two lavish **mansions** on Ocampo at Domínguez and at Carnaval.

For a rest stop, try the **Café Pacífico** (decorated with historic pictures of Mazatlán) on the Plazuela Machado.

The **Plaza Principal,** also called Plaza Revolución, is the heart of the city, filled with vendors, shoeshine stands, and people of all ages out for a stroll. At its center is a Victorian-style, wrought-iron bandstand with a diner-type restaurant underneath. Be sure to take in the **Cathedral of the Immaculate Conception,** built in the 1800s, with its unusual yellow-tiled twin steeples and partially tiled facade. It's on the corner of Calle 21 de Marzo and Nelson.

ORGANIZED TOURS

In addition to 3-hour **city tours** ($20/£11), tour operators offer excursions to many colorful and interesting villages nearby, such as Concordia and Copala (see below). Some towns date from the 16th-century Spanish Conquest; others are modest farming or fishing villages. Information and reservations are available at any travel agency or major hotel, and all accept American Express, MasterCard, and Visa. The premier provider of these and other tours is **Pronatours** (© 669/916-7720 or -3333, ext. 3490; www.elcid.com.mx), yet another part of the El Cid megacomplex of activities. In addition to the city tour, they offer a 5-hour Tequila Tour, visiting a distillery ($35/£19), a 5-hour sailing excursion to Isla de Venados ($42/£23), and a seasonal tour to visit protected turtle hatcheries ($42). Two other recommended tour agencies are the very helpful **Marlin Tours** (© 669/985-4875) and **Olé Tours** (© 669/916-6288;** fax 669/916-5134; www.ole-tours.com).

COPALA-CONCORDIA This popular countryside tour stops at several mountain villages where artisans craft furniture and other items. Copala is a historic mining village with a Spanish-colonial church. The tour ($45/£25), also known as the Mountain Tour or Country Tour, includes lunch and soft drinks. For more about Copala, see "Road Trips from Mazatlán," later.

MAZATLAN JUNGLE TOUR Some might say that David Pérez's (King David's) **Jungle Tour** (© 669/914-1444; fax 669/914-0451) is misnamed, but it's still worthwhile. It consists of a 1½-hour boat ride past a Mexican navy base, Mazatlán's shrimp fleet and packing plants, and into the mangrove swamps to Isla de la Piedra (Stone Island). There's a 3-hour stop at a pristine beach that has what could be the world's largest sand dollars (though fewer and fewer are left). Horseback rides on the beach are $6 (£3.30) for a half-hour. After the beach stop, feast on *pescado zarandeado* (fish cooked over coconut husks, green mangrove, and charcoal). Tours run from 9am to 3pm and cost $45 (£25) per person. Days vary, so call for dates and reservations. MasterCard and Visa are accepted.

WHERE TO STAY

The hotels in downtown Mazatlán are generally older and less expensive than those along the beachfront heading north. As a rule, room rates rise the farther north you go from downtown. The major areas to stay are the Zona Dorada, the Playa Norte (North Beach), and Olas Altas and downtown.

THE ZONA DORADA AND NORTH

The Zona Dorada is an elegant arc of gold sand linked by a palm-lined boulevard and bordered by the most deluxe hotels and a sprinkling of elaborate beach houses. A bonus here is the sunset view. Many hotels along this beach cut their prices from May through September.

El Cid Resort ✦✦✦   El Cid Resort is as much a destination as it is a hotel. Although it is large, bordering on imposing, El Cid offers every service and convenience you can think of, from deluxe rooms to ecotours. Both a hotel and a residential development, El Cid has three beachside buildings, private villas, and a 27-hole golf course on 360 hectares (889 acres). The main 17-story beachside tower, Castilla, was renovated in 1999; there's also the 28-story, all-suite El Moro Tower and the lower-rise, lower-priced Granada, near the golf course. Although room layouts vary, most are heavily detailed in marble and feature private balconies and contemporary, upscale furnishings. There are tons of extra services at El Cid as well, such as a program called Active Learning Vacations, encouraging more involved vacations and priced as special packages. There are opportunities to improve your golf, tennis, or sailing skills or indulge in a Fit for Life program through the on-site spa. Small boats are available, with departures every ten minutes, to take guests to nearby beaches. All-inclusive options are also available; ask for special deals. This resort has something for every type of traveler and is especially ideal when size matters.

Av. Camarón Sábalo s/n (between Av. Rodolfo T. Loaiza and Circuito Campeador), 82110 Mazatlán, Sin. ⓒ 800/525-1925 in the U.S., or 669/913-3333. Fax 669/914-131. www.elcid.com. 1,320 units. High season $126–$294 (£69–£162) double, $304 (£167) junior suite, $396–$536 (£218–£295) suite; low season $89–$244 (£49–£134) double, $244 (£134) junior suite, $343–$465 (£189–£256) suite. All-inclusive program $180 (£99) double occupancy, children 3–11 $30 (£17). AE, MC, V. Free guarded parking. **Amenities:** 11 restaurants; 8 bars; glitzy dance club; 8 outdoor swimming pools (including 1 saltwater pool); 9 tennis courts; tennis academy; fitness center; spa; watersports equipment; marina; sailing school; children's programs; concierge; tour desk; car-rental desk; business center; shopping arcade; salon; room service; babysitting; laundry service; dry cleaning. *In room:* A/C, TV, hair dryer, iron, safe.

El Rancho Hotel & Beach Resort ✦✦ *Kids*   Book a room at El Rancho, and you'll book yourself an apartment suite, complete with kitchen, making it a top choice for families. An intimate group of villas, the resort is located on a beautiful stretch of soft-sand beach, immediately to the north of the Zona Dorada. All units feature the same traditional Mexican-style decor, with colorful fabric accents, and are very well maintained. The difference in price depends on your view—garden, pool, or ocean. Each features two levels, with two spacious bedrooms (one with a king-size bed, the other with two queen-size beds) as well as two bathrooms, a fully equipped kitchen, and a living/dining area. The gardens are lovely, and the on-site restaurant is one level up, making it an ideal spot for watching sunsets. Note that this is also a timeshare resort, so be prepared for a sales pitch if you stay here.

Av. Sábalo-Cerritos 3000, 82110 Mazatlán, Sin. ⓒ 888/596-5760 in the U.S., or 01-800/717-1991 in Mexico. www.elrancho.com.mx. 28 units. High season $135–$200 (£74–£110) 2-bedroom suite (sleeps up to 6); low season $110–$170 (£61–£94) 2-bedroom suite (sleeps up to 6). Rates include free airport pickup and daily continental breakfast. AE, MC, V. Free parking. **Amenities:** 1 restaurant; outdoor pool; Jacuzzi; tour desk; laundry service. *In room:* A/C, TV.

Hotel Faro Mazatlán ✦✦   Formerly known as the Camino Real, this grande dame of Mazatlán hotels changed management in 2004, and underwent a much-needed renovation. Considered the most sophisticated place to stay in town, it's the best choice for those seeking seclusion. It has the best location in Mazatlán, on a rocky cliff overlooking the sea, and the beach edges a small cove that's perfect for swimming. Marble-floored hallways lead to rooms decorated in light, neutral colors, each with bathtubs and showers, large closets, and vanity tables. Junior suites have king-size beds and couches. The hotel is about a 10-minute drive from the heart of the Zona Dorada. Higher rates are for rooms with an ocean view; other rooms have a marina view.

Punta de Sábalo s/n, 82100 Mazatlán, Sin. © **800/716-9757** in the U.S., or 669/913-1111. Fax 669/916-5144 www.faromazatlan.com.mx. 165 units. High season $104–$195 (£57–£107) double, $220 (£121) junior suite; low-season discounts and special packages available. All-inclusive package $95 (£52) per person, with discounts available for families. AE, MC, V. Free guarded parking. **Amenities:** 2 restaurants; lobby bar; small heated outdoor pool; 2 tennis courts; gym; travel agency; business center; room service. *In room:* A/C, TV, minibar.

Pueblo Bonito ★★   The all-suite Pueblo Bonito continues to be a favored place to stay in Mazatlán. The kitchenettes and ample seating areas, along with architectural touches that include curved ceilings, arched windows, and tiled floors, make you feel more at home than traditional hotels do. The extra space means it's a good choice for families or friends traveling together. The grounds are gorgeous—peacocks and flamingos stroll lush lawns, a waterfall cascades into a large pool, and a row of *palapas* lines the beachfront.

Av. Camarón Sábalo 2121 (Apdo. Postal 6), 82110 Mazatlán, Sin. © **01-800/990-8250** in Mexico, or 669/989-8900. Fax 669/914-1723. www.pueblobonito.com. 250 units. $240 (£132) junior suite; $287 (£158) 2-bedroom suite (for up to 2 adults and 2 children). AE, MC, V. Free guarded parking; valet parking. **Amenities:** 3 restaurants; 2 large outdoor pools; gym; whirlpool; sauna; concierge; tour desk; car-rental desk; room service; massage; babysitting; laundry service. *In room:* A/C, TV.

PLAYA NORTE

The waterfront between downtown and the Zona Dorada is Mazatlán's original tourist hotel zone. Moderately priced hotels and motels line the street across from the beach. Señor Frog's, Mazatlán's most famous restaurant, is in this neighborhood, as is the bus station. From May to September, many hotels cut their prices.

Hotel Playa Mazatlán ★★ *Kids*   The most happening place on this stretch of the Zona Dorada, the Hotel Playa Mazatlán is enduringly popular with families, tour groups, and regulars who return annually for winter vacations or spring break. The quietest rooms are in the three-story section surrounding the well-tended interior gardens; those by the terrace restaurant and beach can be noisy. All rooms are decorated in bright colors, with dark-wood furnishings and colonial accents. The beach is one of the liveliest in town. The hotel hosts popular Mexican fiestas on Tuesday, Thursday, and Saturday, and a fireworks display on Sunday.

Av. Playa Gaviotas 202 Zona Dorada, 82110 Mazatlán, Sin. © **800/762-5816** in the U.S., or 669/989-0555. Fax 669/914-0366. www.playamazatlan.com.mx. 423 units. $135 (£74) gardenview double; $160 (£88) oceanview double. AE, MC, V. Free guarded parking. **Amenities:** 2 restaurants; bar; 3 outdoor pools; gym; 2 outdoor whirlpools; watersports rental equipment; tour desk; room service; laundry service. *In room:* A/C, TV, coffeemaker, hair dryer, iron.

Howard Johnson Don Pelayo   The Don Pelayo remains a top choice among budget inns. It's on the North Beach at the edge of the *malecón*. The very clean, regularly updated waterfront rooms have small balconies; all rooms have satellite TV, a king-size bed or two double beds, and central air-conditioning (without individual controls). Lighting and furnishings are gradually being improved. Suites have minibars. When you call to book, ask about seasonal specials; quite often you can get a junior suite for a substantial discount. The hotel is very popular with families and has ample RV parking.

Av. del Mar 1111 (Apdo. Postal 1088), 82000 Mazatlán, Sin. © **669/983-1866** or -1888. Fax 669/984-0799; www.hjdonpelayomazatlan.com.mx. 165 units. $140 (£77) double; $150 (£83) junior suite. AE, MC, V. Free enclosed parking. **Amenities:** Restaurant; bar; outdoor pool; wading pool w/slide; whirlpool. *In room:* A/C, TV.

DOWNTOWN SEAFRONT/PLAYA OLAS ALTAS

The old section of Mazatlán spreads around a picturesque beach a short walk from downtown. Movie stars of the 1950s and 1960s came here for sun and surf, and the hotels where they stayed are still here. There are a few seafront restaurants here, making it easy to dine near your hotel.

Hotel La Siesta The historic La Siesta occupies a well-maintained building surrounded by the old mansions of Mazatlán. Inside, three levels encircle a central courtyard; rooms facing the ocean have balconies opening to sea breezes and pounding waves. Guest rooms at the back of the hotel are quieter but less charming; all have two beds, a small table and chair, good lighting, and dependably hot water. For such functional accommodations, there's a surprising array of guest services. A bonus is the popular **El Shrimp Bucket** restaurant, in the courtyard, where live marimbas and recorded music play until 11pm. This is one of the most popular hotels in Old Mazatlán and fills up quickly. Reservations are strongly advised.

Av. Olas Altas 11 Sur, 82000 Mazatlán, Sin. © 669/981-2640 or -2334. Fax 669/982-2633. www.lasiesta.com.mx. 57 units. $85 (£47) interior double; $100 (£55) oceanview double. AE, MC, V. Street parking. From the deer statue on Olas Altas, go right 1 block. **Amenities:** Restaurant; bar; concierge; room service; in-room massage; laundry service; currency exchange; safe. *In room:* A/C, TV.

WHERE TO DINE

Mazatlán boasts one of the largest shrimp fleets in the world, so it's no surprise that shrimp and seafood are the specialties. Most restaurants are very casual and moderately priced, offering good value. A cheap-eats treat is to stop in one of the many *loncherías* (small establishments that are only for lunch, kind of like a home-cooking place, but not a counter) scattered throughout the downtown area. Here you can get a *torta* (a sandwich on a small French roll) stuffed with a variety of meats, cheeses, tomatoes, onions, and chiles for around $2 (£1.10). Also recommendable is the **Deli 28 Centro,** Belisario Domínguez 1503, Historic Downtown (© **669/981-1577**), serving gourmet baguettes, focaccia, brioche, quality deli meats and cheeses, as well as pizzas.

THE ZONA DORADA
Expensive

Angelo's ITALIAN/SEAFOOD   Even locals consider this hotel restaurant one of the best in town, as much for its ambience as for its food. Beveled glass doors reveal a dining room gleaming with brass, polished wood, and crystal chandeliers. A pianist plays in the background as formally dressed waiters present menus featuring homemade pastas; shrimp dishes, including superb scampi; and a large selection of imported wines. The dress code forbids beachwear, jeans, tennis shoes, and flip-flops.

In the Pueblo Bonito hotel, Av. Camarón Sábalo 2121. © 669/989-8900, ext. 8608. www.pueblobonito-mazatlan. com. Reservations required. Main courses $8–$24 (£4.40–£13). AE, MC, V. Daily 6–11:30pm.

Papagayo Restaurant INTERNATIONAL   Nestled on the beach, diners at Papagayo enjoy the natural beauty of the sea, with a choice of beach or open-air patio seating, and a view across the water to Las Tres Islas, the three imposing islands just offshore. The food is consistent and elegantly presented, with an extensive menu of international fare; favorites are shrimp CocoLoco, and tournedos Rossini in wild mushroom sauce.

The Inn at Mazatlán, Av. Camarón Sábalo 6291. © 669/913-4151. www.innatmazatlan.com.mx. Main courses $9.50–$28 (£5.25–£15). AE, MC, V. Daily 7am–11pm.

Señor Pepper's ✦✦ INTERNATIONAL   Managing to be both elegant and comfortable, this restaurant is known for serving the best steaks in Mazatlán. Potted plants, candlelight, and lots of polished crystal, silver, and brass give the dining room a romantic feeling, and some nights it seems as if all the diners are old friends. The enormous Sonoran beef steaks are grilled over mesquite; lobster and shrimp are also big hits. The nightly special includes appetizer, steak or seafood, vegetables, and soup or salad; those having only drinks at the bar receive a complimentary appetizer.

Av. Camarón Sábalo s/n, across from the Hotel Faro Mazatlán. ✆ 669/914-0101. Reservations recommended. Main courses $20–$39 (£11–£21). MC, V. Daily 5–11pm; bar daily 5pm–2am.

Moderate
Terraza Playa MEXICAN/INTERNATIONAL   During the day, diners enjoy the action on the beach plus a view across to Isla de Venados. After sundown, the stars overhead (in the open terrace) and the sound of the surging waves are a backdrop to live music and dancing from 7pm to midnight. The menu is standard international fare, well prepared, with excellent, friendly service. Especially popular is the breakfast buffet.

In the Hotel Playa Mazatlán, Av. Rodolfo T. Loaiza 202. ✆ 669/989-0555. Breakfast $3.50–$7 (£1.95–£3.85); Mexican plates $4.50–$9.50 (£2.50–£5.25); seafood and meat $7.50–$15 (£4.15–£8.25). AE, MC, V. Daily 6am–midnight.

Inexpensive
Jungle Juice ✦✦ 𝐹𝑖𝑛𝑑𝑠 MEXICAN/STEAKS/SEAFOOD   This comfortable patio and upstairs bar has a definite Mexican flair that gives the partially open-air restaurant a festive touch. Grilled meats and lobster are the specialties at this juice-and-smoothie joint, which has evolved into a full-fledged grill and bar. Smoothies and juices are still the specialties, as are vegetarian plates and meat dishes grilled over mesquite on the patio. This casual spot also serves good breakfasts and makes a nice stop after shopping in the Zona Dorada. Look for daily specials on the blackboard.

Las Garzas 101. ✆ 669/913-3315. Main courses $5–$20 (£2.75–£11). MC, V. Daily 8am–10pm; bar daily 6pm–2am. From Pastelería Panamá, take Sábalo and turn right on Las Garzas; it's 1 block down on your right. Heading north on Loaiza, Las Garzas and the Pastelería Panamá are on the right after the Sábalo traffic circle, before the Mazatlán Arts and Crafts Center.

Pura Vida I ✦ VEGETARIAN/HEALTH FOOD   Nearly hidden behind thick plants, Pura Vida has several small seating sections with wood picnic tables and white canvas umbrellas. A perfect morning spot, it specializes in juices and smoothies, from kelp to papaya. The energetic staff serves omelets and whole-wheat pancakes for breakfast, and burgers, purified salads, soups, and Mexican specialties for lunch. There are plenty of vegetarian dishes, like soy burgers. The veggie and white-chicken sandwiches served on whole-wheat rolls are fabulous.

Bugambilia 100. ✆ 669/916-5815. Main courses $2–$6 (£1.10–£3.30). No credit cards. Daily 8am–10pm. From Pastelería Panamá on Sábalo, turn right on Las Garzas, then left 1 block down onto Laguna; the cafe is on your right.

DOWNTOWN & PLAYA NORTE
Moderate
Copa de Leche ✦✦ 𝑀𝑜𝑚𝑒𝑛𝑡𝑠 MEXICAN   This shaded sidewalk cafe on the waterfront at Playa Olas Altas feels the way Mazatlán must have in the 1930s, and the food is consistently as good as the ocean view. The menu includes *pechugas en nogada* (chicken breast in pecan-and-pomegranate sauce); shrimp in tamarind sauce; traditional *alambre* barbecue (beef cooked with onion, peppers, mushrooms, ham, and

bacon); wonderful seafood soup loaded with squid, shrimp, and chunks of fish; and great shrimp with chipotle sauce. Inside, the decor is updated Mexican, the bar is an old wooden boat, and the dining tables are covered with linen cloths. They also have live music on Friday and Saturday nights.

Av. Olas Altas 1220 A Sur. ℂ 669/982-5753. Breakfast $4–$8 (£2.20–£4.40); main courses $5.50–$17 (£3.05–£9.35). MC, V. Daily 7am–11pm. From El Shrimp Bucket (at Mariano Escobedo and Olas Altas), turn south and walk half a block down Olas Altas; the cafe is on your left.

El Shrimp Bucket ⭐ MEXICAN/SEAFOOD   El Shrimp Bucket is among the most popular restaurants in town. The specialty is Mazatlán's famous shrimp, in the air-conditioned dining room or under umbrellas in the center courtyard. For wining, dining, and dancing, this is a great place for a rousing time.

In the Hotel La Siesta, Av. Olas Altas 111 (at Mariano Escobedo). ℂ 669/981-6350 or 982-8019. Mexican plates $4.50–$10 (£2.50–£5.50); seafood and steak $9–$22 (£4.95–£12). AE, MC, V. Daily 6:30am–11pm.

Señor Frog's INTERNATIONAL   A sign over the door says JUST ANOTHER BAR AND GRILL, but once inside you'll know that's just another of the Carlos Anderson chain's infamous understatements. The decor is delightfully wacky, the food consistently tasty, and the loud music extremely danceable. With an atmosphere this friendly and lively, revelers have been known to dance on the tables late into the night. Try the tasty ribs, Caesar salad, or caramel crepes. The restaurant is on the waterfront drive at Playa Norte.

North Beach *malecón,* Av. del Mar s/n. ℂ 669/985-1110 or 982-1925. Main courses $7–$22 (£3.85–£12). AE, MC, V. Daily 10am–1:30am.

SHOPPING

Mazatlán shopping runs the gamut from precious stones to seashells—with plenty of T-shirts in between. Most stores are open Monday through Saturday from 9 or 10am to 6 or 8pm. Very few close for lunch, and many stores are open on Sunday afternoon.

La Zona Dorada is the best area for shopping. For a huge selection of handicrafts from all over Mexico, visit the **Mazatlán Arts and Crafts Center,** Calle Gaviotas and Avenida Rodolfo T. Loaiza. It accepts cash only. Nearby **Sea Shell City,** Av. Playa Gaviotas 407 (ℂ 669/913-1301) is exactly what the name implies(more shell-covered decorative items than you ever dreamed could exist, from the tacky to the sublime. It's open daily 9am to 8pm. **Gallery Michael,** Av. Las Garzas 18, off Avenida Camarón Sábalo (ℂ 669/916-7816 or -5511; www.michaelgallerymexico.com), has an excellent selection of Tlaquepaque crafts and fine silver jewelry. It is near the Dairy Queen and does not accept credit cards.

For fine jewelry, seek out **Rubio Jewellers,** in the Costa de Oro Hotel, Av. Camarón Sábalo 710 (ℂ 669/914-3167; www.rubiojewellers.com). Shops throughout the Zona Dorada carry a good selection of clothing, fabrics, silver jewelry, leather, art, and crafts. They also carry Sergio Bustamante's jewelry and sculptures.

The **Centro Mercado** in Old Mazatlán is another kind of shopping experience. Here you'll find women selling fresh shrimp under colorful umbrellas; open-air food stalls; and indoor shops stacked with pottery, clothing, and crafts (mostly of lesser quality). Small galleries and shops are beginning to appear in Old Mazatlán; one of the nicest is **NidArt Galería,** Av. Libertad 45 and Carnaval (ℂ 669/981-0002, or 985-5991 for after-hours appointments; www.nidart.com), next to the Angela Peralta

Theater. It features changing exhibits of contemporary art. Open Monday through Saturday from 10am to 2pm or after hours by appointment.

La Gran Plaza is a large shopping mall 3 blocks from the waterfront on Avenida de los Deportes. The plaza has a large supermarket, department stores, and specialty shops. A good place for buying basic items, it's open daily from 10am to 9pm.

MAZATLAN AFTER DARK

Mazatlán is known for its vibrant Mexican fiestas and equally colorful local bar scene, where dancing on bars, atop tables, and inside cages can be a nightly event. Traditional mariachi groups, *tambora* bands, and live romantic music create a festive mood in many restaurants and hotel bars.

Happy hour specials abound in value-oriented Mazatlán. One particular favorite is **El Adobe,** in the Costa de Oro hotel (✆ **669/913-5344,** ext. 1166, or 913-5043). This three-level restaurant and bar has views to the Pacific, overlooking the cascading waterfalls and hotel gardens. From 7am to 10pm, El Adobe serves two-for-one tropical drinks in oversize brandy snifters.

A free **fireworks** show takes place every Sunday at 8pm on the beach fronting the Hotel Playa Mazatlán, Av. Rodolfo T. Loaiza 202, in the Zona Dorada (✆ **669/913-5320** or 989-0555). The display is visible from the beach and from the hotel's Terraza Playa restaurant (see "Where to Dine," above).

The same hotel presents Mazatlán's most popular **Fiesta Mexicana,** complete with buffet, open bar, folkloric dancing, and live music. Fiestas begin at 7pm Tuesday, Thursday, and Saturday year-round; try to arrive by 6pm to get a good table. Tickets are $32 (£18).

CLUBS & BARS

Joe's Oyster Bar Beer, burgers, fresh oysters, and high-volume dance music are the house specialties at this casual, *palapa*-topped, open-air club. It's open daily from 11am to 2am. On the beachfront at Los Sábalos Hotel, Av. Rodolfo T. Loaiza 100. ✆ **669/983-5333.**

Valentino's & the Fiestaland Complex If you're going out at night, chances are, you'll be headed here, because the popularity of the **Valentino's** club has resulted in its expansion to a whole array of nocturnal options. The centerpiece remains Valentino's, dramatically perched on a rocky outcropping overlooking the sea, in an all-white, Moorish-looking building, and featuring a good high-tech light show complete with green laser beams. For a break from the pulsating dance floor, there are pool tables in another room, and some (relatively) quiet areas for talking. Foam parties are the feature every Thursday night. Part of the complex is the **Bora Bora,** a pub-style bar complete with volleyball court and surfing simulator, the **Mikonos** piano bar, and **Canta Bar,** which features karaoke. Looking for televised sports? **Bali Hai** is your spot, while **Pepe's and Joe** offers a brew and pub ambience. Open daily from 9pm to 4am. Punta Camarón, near the Camarón Sábalo traffic circle. ✆ **669/989-1600.** Cover $5–$10 (£2.75–£5.50).

ROAD TRIPS FROM MAZATLAN

TEACAPAN: ABUNDANT WILDLIFE & A RUSTIC VILLAGE

Just 2 hours (131km/81 miles) south of Mazatlán is the fishing village of Teacapán, at the tip of an isolated peninsula that extends 29km (18 miles) down a coastline of pristine beaches. Mangrove lagoons and canals border its other side. Palm and mango groves, cattle ranches, and an occasional cluster of houses dot the peninsula, which ends at the Boca de Teacapán, a natural marina separating the states of Sinaloa and Nayarit. Shrimping boats line the beach at the edge of the marina, which backs up to the worn houses and dirt streets of town. A rugged place, it's recommended for those interested in birding.

Birders hire local fishermen to take them out around the lagoons, where they can see herons, flamingos, Canadian ducks, and countless other species. Inland, the sparsely populated land is a haven for deer, ocelot, and wild boars. There's talk of making the entire peninsula into an ecological preserve, and thus far, residents have resisted attempts by developers to turn the area into a large-scale resort. For now, visitors to Teacapán find the ultimate peaceful refuge.

GETTING THERE   By Car   Drive south from Mazatlán on the highway to Escuinapa. There are no signs marking the right turn for the road to Teacapán; ask for directions in Escuinapa. If you're arriving from the south, turn left at the Bancomer building.

By Bus   Autotransportes Escuinapa runs several second-class buses daily to Escuinapa; the fare is about $5. From there you can transfer to Teacapán (about $3/ £1.65). The second-class bus station is behind the first-class station, across the lot where the buses park.

Where to Stay

Villas Maria Fernanda   This small resort offers a selection of villas and one larger casa that sleeps up to 10 people. All are spacious, with simple, traditional furnishings in a colorful Mexican style, plus full kitchen facilities. Boat tours, bird-watching tours, and horseback riding are available. The hotel is adjacent to a small restaurant, which serves all meals. It's at the entrance to the estuary, making it ideal for bird-watchers who want to explore the area.

Domicilio Conocido, Teacapán, Sin. © **695/954-5393.** Fax 695/953-1343. www.villasmariafernanda.com. 6 units. Villas $65 (£36) double; houses $160 (£88). AE. Free parking. **Amenities:** Restaurant; outdoor pool; Jacuzzi; water slide; children's playground. *In room:* A/C, TV, kitchen.

COPALA: AN OLD SILVER TOWN

Popular tours from Mazatlán stop here for lunch only, but Copala is well worth an overnight stay. The town was founded in 1565, and from the late 1880s to the early 1900s it was the center of the region's silver-mining boom. When the mines closed, the town was nearly deserted. Today, it's a National Historic Landmark with 600 full-time residents and a part-time community of retired Canadian and U.S. citizens devoted to Copala's picturesque solitude.

Every building in town is painted white, and most have red-tile roofs splashed with bougainvillea. Cobblestone streets wind from the entrance to town up slight hills to the main plaza and the 1610 Cathedral of San José. The town kicks into high gear (relatively speaking) around noon, when tour buses arrive and visitors stroll the streets surrounded by small boys selling geodes extracted from the local hills. By 3pm, most of the outsiders have left. You can wander the streets in peace and visit the century-old cemetery, the ruins of haciendas, and the neighborhoods of white villas.

GETTING THERE   Tours go to Copala and Concordia (see "Organized Tours," earlier in this chapter). Copala is an easy 2-hour **drive** from Mazatlán; drive south for about 25 minutes until you get to the detour for Durango, then turn west and drive to Concordia. From there, follow the signs for Copala; it's about 22km (14 miles). The

Autotransportes Concordia **bus** service runs four buses daily from the second-class bus station, behind the first-class bus station. The fare is $4 (£2.20); check the schedule carefully before departing so you don't get stranded in Copala.

3 Costa Alegre: Puerto Vallarta to Barra de Navidad ⓡⓡⓡ

Costa Alegre is one of Mexico's most spectacular coastal areas, a 232km (144-mile) stretch that connects tropical forests with a series of dramatic cliff-lined coves. Tiny outpost towns line the coast, while dirt roads trail down to a succession of magical coves with pristine beaches, most of them steeped in privileged exclusivity. Considered one of Mexico's greatest undiscovered treasures, this area is becoming a favored hideaway for publicity-fatigued celebrities and those in search of natural seclusion.

The area is referred to as **Costa Alegre (Happy Coast)**—the marketer's term—and **Costa Careyes (Turtle Coast),** after the many sea turtles that nest here. It is home to an eclectic array of the most captivating and exclusive places to stay in Mexico, with a selective roster of activities that includes championship golf and polo. Along the line, however, you will encounter the funky beach towns that were the original lure for travelers who discovered the area.

Stops along Highway 200, as it meanders between Puerto Vallarta to the north and Manzanillo to the south, can be an enjoyable day trip, but travelers usually make the drive en route to a destination along the coast.

EXPLORING COSTA ALEGRE   Costa Alegre is more an ultimate destination than a place to rent a car and take a drive. Most of the beaches are tucked into coves accessible by dirt roads that can extend for kilometers inland. If you do drive along this coast, Highway 200 is safe, but it's not lit and it curves through the mountains, so travel only during the day. A few buses travel this route, but they stop only at the towns that line the highway; many of them are several kilometers inland from the resorts along the coast.

ALONG COSTA ALEGRE (NORTH TO SOUTH)
CRUZ DE LORETO'S LUXURY ECO-RETREAT

Hotelito Desconocido ⓡⓡⓡ *(Moments)*   The fact that the Hotelito Desconocido ("little unknown hotel") is ecologically minded is a bonus, but it's not the principal appeal. A cross between *Out of Africa* and *Blue Lagoon,* it is among my favorite places in Mexico. Think camping out with luxury linens, romantic candles everywhere, and a symphony performed by cicadas, birds, and frogs.

The rustic, open-air rooms, called *palafitos,* are in cottages perched on stilts over a lagoon. A grouping of suites is on the ample sand bar that separates the tranquil estuary from the Pacific Ocean. However, these are the least desirable units, and are often damp from the ocean air. Also here is a saltwater pool—the ocean is too aggressive for even seasoned swimmers.

Ceiling fans cool the air, and water is solar-heated. It's easy to disconnect here. In fact, it's mandatory: There's no electricity, no phones, no neighboring restaurants, nightclubs, or shopping—only delicious tranquillity. What the service lacks in polish it makes up for in enthusiasm. Rates do not include meals or drinks; a meal plan is mandatory, because there are no other options nearby (making the whole package somewhat pricey)—but it's a unique experience.

Playón de Mismaloya s/n, Cruz de Loreto, 48360 Tomatlán, Jal. ⓒ **800/851-1143** in the U.S. and Canada (reservations: ⓒ **01-800/013-1313** in Mexico, or 322/281-4010 or 222-2546). Fax 322/281-4130. www.hotelito.com. 24

units. High season $395–$478 (£217–£263) double, $520–$707 (£286–£389) suite; low season $312 (£172) double, $516–$561 (£284–£309) suite. Mandatory daily meal plan $90 (£50) per person. Children are discouraged. AE, MC, V. Take Hwy. 200 south for 1 hr., turn off at exit for Cruz de Loreto, and continue on clearly marked route on unpaved road for about 25 min. All activities are subject to an extra charge. Free parking. **Amenities:** 2 restaurant/bars; primitive-luxury spa; whirlpool; sauna; sailboards; kayaks; mountain bikes; massage; birding tours; hiking trails; horseback riding; billiards; beach volleyball. *In room:* No phone.

LAS ALAMANDAS: AN EXCLUSIVE LUXURY RESORT

Las Alamandas 🎦🎦🎦   Almost equidistant between Manzanillo (1½ hr.) and Puerto Vallarta (1¾ hr.) lies Mexico's original ultraexclusive resort. A dirt road winds for about a mile through a tiny village to the guardhouse of Las Alamandas, on 28 hectares (69 acres) set against low hills that are part of a 600-hectare (1,500-acre) estate. The resort consists of villas and *palapas* spread among four beaches, gardens, lakes, lagoons, and a bird sanctuary. It's designed for privacy—to the point that guests rarely catch a glimpse of one another. The resort has air-conditioning, telephones, and a new beachside massage *palapa*, yet manages to keep the experience as natural as possible. The resort accommodates only 22 guests.

The six spacious villas have brightly colored decor and tiled verandas with ocean views. They have several bedrooms (each with its own bathroom) and can be rented separately; guests who rent entire villas have preference for reservations. Some villas are on the beach, others across a cobblestone plaza. TVs with VCRs are available on request, but there's no outside reception. Van transportation to and from Manzanillo ($293/£161 one-way) and Puerto Vallarta ($289/£159 one-way) can be arranged when you reserve your room. Air transport from Puerto Vallarta is also available; call for details.

Hwy. 200, Km 83 48850 Manzanillo–Puerto Vallarta, Jal. Mailing address: Domicilio Conocido Costa Alegre QUEMARO Jalisco, Apdo. Postal 201, 48980 San Patricio Melaque, Jal. ⓒ **888/882-9616** in the U.S. and Canada, or 322/285-5500. Fax 322/285-5027. www.alamandas.com. 14 units. High season $460–$910 (£253–£501) double, $1,200–$1,990 (£660–£1,095) villa; low season $360–$680 (£198–£374) double, $960–$1,400 (£374–£528) villa. Meal plans available. AE, MC, V. Free parking. **Amenities:** Restaurant; 18m (59-ft.) outdoor pool; lighted tennis court; weight room; boogie boards; mountain bikes; concierge; tour desk; room service; birding boat tours; hiking trails; horseback riding; book and video library; landing strip (make advance arrangements). *In room:* A/C, minibar.

CAREYES

The Careyes Hotel 🎦🎦   The Careyes is a gem of a resort nestled on a small, pristine cove between dramatic cliffs that are home to the exclusive villas of Careyes. This area has practically defined the architectural style that defines Mexico beach chic— bold washes of vibrant colors, open spaces, and gardens that showcase the tropical flowers and palms indigenous to the area.

The pampering accommodations all face the ocean and have always been stylishly simple, however at press time, the resort was undergoing a major renovation (scheduled to reopen in June 2007); I'm not certain what the changes will entail, but they will provide a needed update. Although guests come here for isolation, you can enjoy many services, including a full European spa and polo. It's both rustic and sophisticated, with the room facades awash in scrubbed pastels forming a U around the center lawn and freeform pool. Some rooms have balconies; all have ocean views. Twenty rooms have private pools, and villas are available for rent.

The hotel offers a number of special-interest activities for guests. Named after the hawksbill turtle (*carey* in Spanish), the hotel sponsors a Save the Turtle program in which guests can participate between July and December.

Costa Alegre & Central Pacific Coast

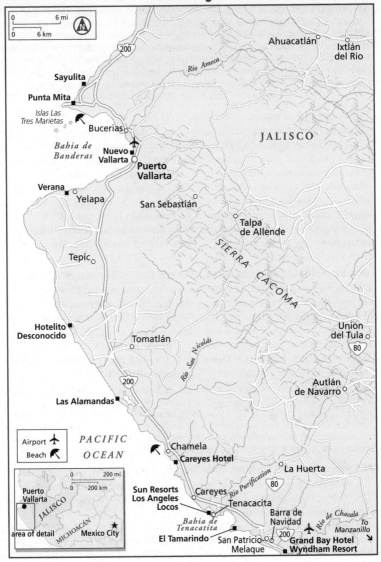

The Careyes is roughly 150km (93 miles) south of Puerto Vallarta. It's about a 2-hour drive north of Manzanillo on Highway 200, and about a 1-hour drive from the Manzanillo airport. Taxis from the Manzanillo airport charge around $100 (£55) one-way. There are car-rental counters at the Manzanillo and Puerto Vallarta airports. A car would be useful only for exploring the coast—Barra de Navidad and other resorts, for example—and the hotel can make touring arrangements.

Hwy. 200 Km 53.5, 48970 Careyes, Jal. CP. Mailing address: Apdo. Postal 24, 48970 Cihuatlán, Jal. © 800/525-4800 in the U.S. and Canada, 315/351-0000 or -0606. Fax 315/351-0100. www.elcareyesresort.com. 51 units. High season $345–$425 (£190–£234) double, $535–$625 (£294–£343) suite; low season $305–$379 (£168–£208) double, $479–$565 (£263–£311) suite. AE, MC, V. Free parking. **Amenities:** Restaurant; bar; deli; large beachside pool; privileges at exclusive El Tamarindo resort (40km/25 miles south), w/18-hole mountaintop golf course; 2 tennis courts; paddle court; weight equipment; state-of-the-art spa; steam room; hot and cold plunge pools; sauna; sailboards; kayaks; Aquafins; children's programs (during Christmas and Easter vacations only); Internet access; room service; massage; laundry service; book and video library. *In room:* A/C, TV/VCR, minibar, minifridge, hair dryer.

TENACATITA BAY

Located an hour (53km/33 miles) north of the Manzanillo airport, this jewel of a bay is accessible by an 8km (5-mile) dirt road that passes through a small village set among banana plants and coconut palms. Sandy, serene beaches dot coves around the bay (frolicking dolphins are a common sight), and exotic birds fill a coastal lagoon. Swimming and snorkeling are good, and the bay is a popular stop for luxury yachts. Just south of the entrance to Tenacatita is a sign for the all-inclusive **Sun Resorts Los Angeles Locos,** as well as the exclusive **El Tamarindo** resort and golf club. There is no commercial or shopping area, and dining options outside hotels are limited to a restaurant or two that may emerge during the winter months (high season). Relax— that's what you're here for.

Blue Bay Club Los Angeles Locos 🐠   On a 5km (3-mile) stretch of sandy beach, Los Angeles Locos offers an abundance of activities programs, entertainment, and dining options, which offer guests excellent value. It's a good choice for families and groups of friends. All rooms have ocean views, with either balconies or terraces. The three-story hotel is basic in decor and amenities, but comfortable. The attraction here is the wide array of on-site activities, plus a "Jungle River" cruise excursion (included in the room rate). **La Lagarta Disco** is a little on the dark and smoky side but can really rock, depending on the crowd—it's basically the only option on the bay.

Carretera Federal 200 Km 20, Tenacatita 48989, Municipio de la Huerta, Jal. © 800/483-7986 in the U.S., 315/351-5020 or -5100. Fax 315/351-5412. www.losangeleslocos.com. 204 units. High season $130 (£72) double; low season $110 (£61) double. Children 5–12 $35 (£19) year-round. Rates are all-inclusive. Ask about family specials. AE, MC, V. Free parking. **Amenities:** 2 restaurants and snack bar (w/buffets and a la carte dining); 3 bars; dance club; adult outdoor pool; kids' outdoor pool adjacent to the beach; 3 tennis courts; exercise room; sailboards; kayaks; Hobie cats; horseback riding; basketball court; pool tables; kids' club; massage; babysitting; laundry service. *In room:* A/C, TV.

El Tamarindo (Yellowstone Club World) 🐠🐠🐠 *Finds*   A personal favorite, El Tamarindo is a gem that combines stunning jungle surroundings with exquisite facilities, gracious service, and absolute tranquillity. In 2006, management of the resort was taken over by the prestigious Yellowstone Club World.

The bungalows exude an air of exclusivity—each thatched-roof villa has a splash pool and whirlpool, hammock, plus lounging and dining areas that overlook a private lawn and complement the stunning bedrooms. What they don't have are televisions. Service throughout the resort is exceptional. The bedrooms—with dark hardwood floors and furnishings—can be closed off for air-conditioned comfort, but the remaining areas are open to the sea breezes and heady tropical air.

The categories of bungalows denote their location—Beachfront (on a calm cove, but not as private as the others), Palm Tree, Garden, and Forest. The nonbeachside bungalows all have similar decor and amenities but feature more closed-in areas. Anyone squeamish about creepy-crawlies may be uncomfortable in the beginning, but listening to the life around you is a spectacular sensation. On 800 hectares (1,976 acres) of tropical rainforest bordering the Pacific Ocean, you'll feel as if you've found your own personal bit of heaven.

El Tamarindo has a championship 18-hole golf course designed by David Fleming; the approach to the first hole is through a forest of palms so tall they block the sun. The course has 7 oceanside holes and dramatic views. Equally exceptional are their spa services, with most massages and treatments provided in beachfront *cabañas,* or the resort's Spa Hut. The resort restaurant is the only dining option, but you won't be disappointed. The menu, which changes daily, has ample selections of fresh seafood selections, as well as pastas and beef, and all are artfully prepared. You can't leave without trying the resort's Tamarind Margarita.

Carretera Barra de Navidad–Puerto Vallarta Km 7.5, 48970 Cihuatlán, Jal. ℭ **315/351-5032.** Fax 315/351-5070. www.ycwtamarindo.com. 29 bungalows. High season $495–$975 (£272–£536) villas; low season $415–$839 (£228–£461) villas. AE, MC, V. From Puerto Vallarta (3 hr.) or the Manzanillo airport (40 min.), take Hwy. 200, then turn west at the clearly marked exit for El Tamarindo; follow signs for about 25 min. Free valet parking. **Amenities:** Restaurant; bar; large beachside pool w/whirlpool; 2 clay tennis courts; yoga classes; spa services; *temazcal* (pre-Hispanic sweat lodge); sailboards; kayaks; Aquafin sailboats; mountain bikes; estuary bird-watching tours; hiking trails; horseback riding; room service; TV and Internet-access room. *In room:* A/C, hair dryer, safe.

BARRA DE NAVIDAD & MELAQUE

This pair of rustic beach villages (only 5km/3 miles apart) has been attracting travelers for decades. Only 30 minutes north of Manzanillo's airport and about 100km (62 miles) north of downtown Manzanillo, Barra has a few brick or cobblestone streets, good budget hotels and restaurants, and funky beach charm. All of this lies incongruously next to the superluxurious Grand Bay Hotel, which sits on a bluff across the inlet from Barra.

In the 17th century, Barra de Navidad was a harbor for the Spanish fleet; from here, galleons first set off in 1564 to find China. Located on a crescent-shaped bay with curious rock outcroppings, Barra de Navidad and neighboring Melaque are connected by a continuous beach on the same wide bay. It's safe to say that the only time Barra and Melaque hotels are full is during Easter and Christmas weeks. **Barra de Navidad** has more charm, more tree-shaded streets, better restaurants, more stores, and more conviviality between locals and tourists. Barra is very laid-back; faithful returnees adore its lack of flash. Other than the Grand Bay Hotel, on the cliff across the waterway in what is called Isla Navidad (although it's not on an island), nothing is new or modern. But there's a bright edge to Barra, with more good restaurants and limited— but existent—nightlife.

Melaque, on the other hand, is larger, rather sun-baked, treeless, and lacking in attractions. It does, however, have plenty of cheap hotels available for longer stays, and a few restaurants. Although the beach between the two is continuous, Melaque's beach, with deep sand, is more beautiful than Barra's. Both villages appeal to those looking for a quaint, quiet, inexpensive retreat rather than a modern, sophisticated destination.

Isla Navidad Resort has a manicured 27-hole golf course and the superluxurious Grand Bay Hotel, but the area's pace hasn't quickened as fast as expected. The golf is challenging and delightfully uncrowded, with another exceptional course at nearby El Tamarindo. It's a serious golfer's dream.

ESSENTIALS

GETTING THERE & DEPARTING **Buses** from Manzanillo frequently run up the coast along Highway 200 on their way to Puerto Vallarta and Guadalajara. The fare is about $3.50 (£1.90). Most stop in the central villages of Barra de Navidad and Melaque. From the Manzanillo airport, it's only around 30 minutes to Barra, and **taxis** are available. The fare from Manzanillo to Barra is around $40 (£22); from Barra to Manzanillo, $30 (£17). From Manzanillo, the highway twists through some of the Pacific Coast's most beautiful mountains. Puerto Vallarta is 3 hours by **car** and 5 hours by bus, north on Highway 200 from Barra.

VISITOR INFORMATION The **tourism office** for both villages is at Jalisco 67 (between Veracruz and Mazatlán), Barra (©/fax **315/355-5100;** www.barradenavidad. com). The office is open daily Monday through Friday from 9am to 5pm.

ORIENTATION In Barra, hotels and restaurants line the main beachside street, **Legazpi.** From the bus station, beachside hotels are 2 blocks straight ahead, across the central plaza. Two blocks behind the bus station and to the right is the lagoon side. More hotels and restaurants are on its main street, **Morelos/Veracruz.** Few streets are marked, but 10 minutes of wandering will acquaint you with the village's entire layout. There's a taxi stand at the intersection of Legazpi and Sinaloa streets. Legazpi, Jalisco, Sinaloa, and Veracruz streets border Barra's **central plaza.**

ACTIVITIES ON & OFF THE BEACH

Swimming and enjoying the attractive beach and views of the bay take up most tourists' time. You can hire a small boat for a coastal ride or fishing in two ways. Go toward the *malecón* on Calle Veracruz until you reach the tiny boatmen's cooperative, with fixed prices posted on the wall, or walk two buildings farther to the water taxi ramp. The water taxi is the best option for going to Colimilla (5 min.; $2/£1.10) or across the inlet (3 min.; $1/55p) to the Grand Bay Hotel. Water taxis make the rounds regularly, so if you're at Colimilla, wait, and one will be along shortly. At the cooperative, a 30-minute **lagoon tour** costs $20 (£11), and a **sea tour** costs $25 (£14). **Sportfishing** is $80 (£44) for up to four people for a half-day in a small *panga* (open fiberglass boat, like the ones used for water taxis).

Surfing along Costa Alegre is gaining ground, thanks in large part to Germaine Badke, and the **South Swell Mex Surf Shop** (© 315/354-5497 or 100-4332; www. southswellmex.com), which he owns and operates. The shop offers boogie board and surfboard rentals, surfboard and surf supply sales, and will also create a custom-designed board. Surf lessons are also available. They're located in Suite 2 of the Hotel Alondra.

Isla Navidad Country Club (© 314/337-9024; http://navidad.wyndham-hotels. com) has a beautiful and challenging 27-hole, 7,053-yard, par-72 **golf course** that is open to the public. Grand Bay Hotel guests pay greens fees of $175 (£96) for 18 holes, $192 (£106) for 27 holes; nonguests pay $207 and $230 (£114 and £127), respectively. Prices include a motorized cart. Caddies are available, as are rental clubs.

Beer Bob's Books, Avenida Tampico, between Sinaloa and Guanajuato, is a booklover's institution in Barra and a sort of community service that the rather grouchy Bob does for fun. His policy of "leave a book if you take one" allows vacationers to select from hundreds of neatly shelved paperbacks, as long as they leave a book in exchange. It's open Monday through Friday from noon to 3pm and occasionally in the evenings. "Beer Bob" got his name because in earlier days, when beer was cheap, he kept a cooler stocked, and book browsers could sip and read. (When beer prices went up, Bob put the cooler away.)

Barra de Navidad Bay Area

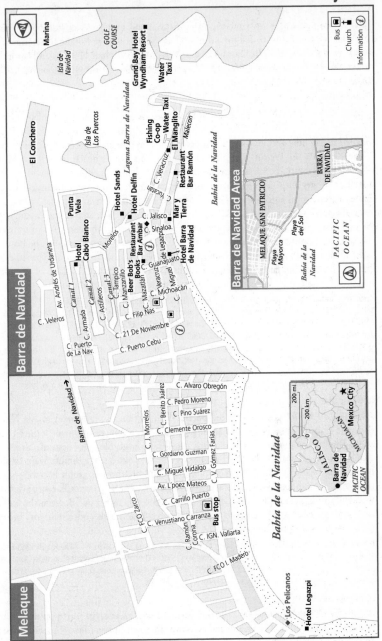

355

WHERE TO STAY

Low season in Barra is any time except Christmas and Easter weeks. Except for those 2 weeks, it doesn't hurt to ask for a discount at the inexpensive hotels. To arrange **real estate rentals,** contact **The Crazy Cactus,** Veracruz 165, a half-block inland from the town church on Legazpi (©/fax **315/355-6099;** crazycactusmx@yahoo.com). The store may be closed May through October.

Very Expensive

Grand Bay Hotel Isla Navidad Resort ☆ *(Overrated*   Across the yacht channel from Barra de Navidad, this luxurious hotel opened in 1997 on 480 hectares (1,186 acres) next to its 27-hole golf course. Now operated by Wyndham Resorts, it overlooks the village, bay, Pacific Ocean, and Navidad lagoon. The hotel's beach is narrow and on the lagoon. A better beach is opposite the hotel on the bay in Barra de Navidad. The spacious rooms are sumptuously outfitted with marble floors, large bathrooms, and hand-carved wood furnishings. Prices vary according to view and size of room, but even the modest rooms are large, and all have cable TV. Each comes with a king-size or two double beds, ceiling fans plus air-conditioning, and a balcony. All suites have a steam sauna and telephones in the bathroom as well as a sound system. The hotel is a short water-taxi ride across the inlet from Barra de Navidad; it is also on a paved road from Highway 200. Although the hotel bills itself as being on the Island of Navidad at Port Navidad, the port is the marina, and the hotel is on a peninsula.

Circuito de los Marinos s/n, 28830 Isla Navidad, Col. © **01-800/849-2373** in Mexico, or 310/937-5124 or 314/331-0500. Fax 314/331-0570. http://navidad.wyndham-hotels.com. 199 units. High season $499 (£274) double, $580–$892 (£319–£491) suite; low season $429 (£236) double, $507–$805 (£279–£443) suite. Rates include round-trip transportation to and from Manzanillo airport. AE, DC, DISC, MC, V. Free parking. **Amenities:** 2 restaurants; 2 bars; golf club w/food and bar service; outdoor swimming pool w/water slides and swim-up bar; 27-hole, par-72 golf course; golf club w/pro shop and driving range; 3 lighted grass tennis courts; small workout room; marina w/private yacht club; fishing, boat tours, and other excursions can be arranged; kids' club w/activity program; concierge; business center; salon; room service; babysitting; laundry service; dry cleaning. *In room:* A/C, TV, minibar, hair dryer, iron, safe.

Moderate

Hotel Cabo Blanco ☆☆   Located on the point where you cross over to Isla Navidad, the Cabo Blanco is an outstanding option for family vacations or longer-term stays. Rooms are pleasantly rustic, with tile floors, large tile tubs, separate dressing areas, and stucco walls. The hotel overlooks the bay, but it's a 5-minute walk to the beach. The beamed-ceiling lobby is in its own building; rooms are in hacienda-style buildings surrounded by gardens. The atmosphere is generally tranquil, except during weekends and Mexican holidays, when this hotel tends to fill up. Because the Cabo Blanco doesn't front the beach, it has an affiliated beach club and restaurant, Mar y Tierra (see "Where to Dine," below).

Armada y Bahía de la Navidad s/n, 48987 Barra de Navidad, Jal. © **315/355-6495** or -6496. Fax 315/355-6494. www.hotelcaboblanco.com. 101 units. $130 (£72) double; $256 (£141) suite with kitchenette. All-inclusive plans also available. AE, MC, V. Limited street parking. **Amenities:** 2 restaurants; 4 outdoor pools (2 adults only); 2 tennis courts; concierge; tour desk; car-rental desk; laundry service. *In room:* A/C, TV.

Inexpensive

Hotel Barra de Navidad ☆   At the northern end of Legazpi, this popular, comfortable beachside hotel is among the nicest in the town. It has friendly management, and some rooms with balconies overlooking the beach and bay. Other, less-expensive rooms afford only a street view. Only the oceanview rooms have air-conditioning. A nice swimming pool is on the street level to the right of the lobby.

Legazpi 250, 48987 Barra de Navidad, Jal. ⓒ 315/355-5122. Fax 315/355-5303. www.hotelbarradenavidad.com. 60 units. $72–$82 (£40–£45) double. MC, V. Free parking. **Amenities:** Outdoor pool. *In room:* A/C (in some rooms).

Hotel Delfín   One of Barra's better-maintained hotels, the four-story (no elevator) Delfín is on the landward side of the lagoon. It offers pleasant, basic, well-maintained, and well-lit rooms. Each has red-tile floors and a double, two double, or two single beds. The tiny courtyard, with a small pool and lounge chairs, sits in the shade of an enormous rubber tree. From the fourth floor, there's a view of the lagoon. A breakfast buffet is served from 8:30 to 10:30am (see "Where to Dine," below).

Morelos 23, 48987 Barra de Navidad, Jal. ⓒ 315/355-5068. Fax 315/355-6020. www.hoteldelfinmx.com. 24 units. $49 (£27) double; ask about low-season discounts. MC, V. Free parking. **Amenities:** Restaurant; heated outdoor pool, gym.

Hotel Sands   The colonial-style Sands, across from the Hotel Delfín (see above) on the lagoon side at Jalisco, offers small but homey rooms with red-tile floors and windows with both screens and glass. The remodeled bathrooms have new tiles and fixtures. Lower rooms look onto a public walkway and wide courtyard filled with greenery and singing birds; upstairs rooms are brighter. Twelve rooms (suites or bungalows) have air-conditioning and kitchenette facilities. The hotel is known for its warm hospitality and high-season happy hour (2–6pm) at the pool terrace bar beside the lagoon. On weekends from 9pm to 4am, an adjacent patio "disco" plays recorded music for dancing. Breakfast is served from 7:30am to noon. Fishing trips can be arranged, and tours to nearby beaches are available.

Morelos 24, 48987 Barra de Navidad, Jal. ⓒ/fax 315/355-5018. 42 units. High season $80 (£44) double; low season $54 (£30) double. Rates include breakfast. Room-only rates $10 (£5.50) less. Discounts for stays of 1 week or more. MC, V (6% surcharge). **Amenities:** Restaurant; bar; outdoor pool w/whirlpool overlooking lagoon beach; children's play area; tour desk. *In room:* A/C (in some rooms), kitchenette (in some rooms).

WHERE TO DINE

El Manglito 🦀 SEAFOOD/MEXICAN   On the placid lagoon, with a view of the palatial Grand Bay Hotel, El Manglito serves home-style Mexican food to a growing number of repeat diners. The whole fried fish accompanied by drawn garlic butter, boiled vegetables, rice, and french fries, is a crowd-pleaser. Other enticements include boiled shrimp, chicken in orange sauce, and shrimp salad.

Veracruz 17, near the boatmen's cooperative. No phone. Main courses $5–$10 (£2.75–£5.50). No credit cards. Daily 9am–11pm.

Hotel Delfín BREAKFAST   The second-story terrace of this small hotel is a pleasant place to begin the day. The self-serve buffet offers an assortment of fresh fruit, juice, granola, yogurt, milk, pastries, and unlimited coffee. The price includes made-to-order eggs and delicious banana pancakes—for which the restaurant is known.

Morelos 23. ⓒ 315/355-5068. www.hoteldelfinmx.com. Breakfast buffet $4 (£2.20). No credit cards. Daily 8:30am–noon.

Mar y Tierra INTERNATIONAL   Hotel Cabo Blanco's beach club is also a popular restaurant and bar and a great place to spend a day at the beach. On the beach, there are shade *palapas* and beach chairs, and a game of volleyball seems constantly in progress. The colorful restaurant is decorated with murals of mermaids. Perfectly seasoned shrimp fajitas come in plentiful portions.

Legazpi s/n (at Jalisco). ⓒ 315/355-5028. Main courses $10–$17 (£5.50–£9.35). MC, V. Wed–Mon 10am–6pm.

Restaurant Bar Ambar CREPES/ITALIAN/FRENCH   This cozy, thatched-roof, upstairs restaurant is open to the breezes. The crepes are named after towns in France;

the delicious *crêpe Paris,* for example, is filled with chicken, potatoes, spinach, and green sauce. International main dishes include imported (from the U.S.) rib-eye steak in Dijon mustard sauce, mixed brochettes, quiche, and Caesar salad. Ambar serves Spanish-style tapas from noon until 6pm, and adds French specialties during dinner. Pastas and pizzas are also served.

López de Legazpi 160, across from the church. (℃) **315/355-8169.** Crepes $9–$13 (£4.95–£7.15); main courses $15–$25 (£8.25–£14). No credit cards. Daily 5:30pm–midnight.

Restaurant Bar Ramón ✦ *Value* SEAFOOD/MEXICAN   It seems that everybody eats at Ramón's, where the chips and fresh salsa arrive unbidden, and service is prompt and friendly. The food is especially good—however, most options are fried. Try fresh fried shrimp with french fries or any daily special that features vegetable soup or chicken-fried steak. Great value!

Legazpi 260. (℃) **315/355-6435.** Main courses $6–$12 (£3.30–£6.60). No credit cards. Daily 7am–11pm.

BARRA DE NAVIDAD AFTER DARK

When dusk arrives, visitors and locals alike find a cool spot to sit outside, sip cocktails, and chat. Many outdoor restaurants and stores in Barra accommodate this relaxing way to end the day, adding extra tables and chairs for drop-ins.

During high season, the **Hotel Sands** poolside and lagoon-side bar has happy hour from 2 to 6pm. The colorful **Sunset Bar and Restaurant,** facing the bay at the corner of Legazpi and Jalisco, is a favorite for sunset watching and a game of oceanside pool or dancing to live or taped music. It's most popular with travelers ages 20 to 30. In the same vein, **Chips Restaurant,** on the second floor facing the ocean at the corner of Yucatán and Legazpi near the southern end of the *malecón,* has an excellent sunset vista. Live music follows the last rays of light, and patrons stay for hours. **Piper Lover Bar & Grill,** Legazpi 154 A ((℃) **315/355-6747;** www.piperlover.com) is done in the style of the Carlos Anderson's chain—but it's not one of them. Still, it is lively, with pool tables and occasional live music.

At the **Disco El Galeón,** in the Hotel Sands on Calle Morelos, cushioned benches and cement tables encircle the round dance floor. It's all open air, and about as stylish as you'll find in Barra. It serves drinks only. Admission is $6 (£3), and it's open Friday and Saturday from 9pm to 4am.

A VISIT TO MELAQUE (SAN PATRICIO)

For a change of scenery, you may want to wander over to Melaque (aka San Patricio), 5km (3 miles) from Barra on the same bay. You can walk on the beach from Barra or take one of the frequent local buses from the bus station near the main square in Barra. The bus is marked MELAQUE. To return to Barra, take the bus marked CIHUATLAN.

Melaque's pace is even more laid-back than Barra's, and though it's a larger village, it seems smaller. It has fewer restaurants and less to do. Although there are more hotels, or "bungalows," as they are usually called, few manage the charm of those in Barra; if Barra hotels are full on a holiday weekend, Melaque would be a second choice. The paved road ends where the town begins. A few yachts bob in the harbor, and the palm-lined beach is gorgeous.

If you come by bus from Barra, you can exit anywhere in town or stay on until the last stop, which is the bus station in the middle of town a block from the beach. Restaurants and hotels line the beach. Coming into town from the main road, you'll be on the town's main street, **Avenida López Matéos.** You'll pass the main square on the way to the waterfront, where there's a trailer park. The street going left (southeast) along the bay is **Avenida Gómez Farías;** the one going right (northwest) is **Avenida Miguel Ochoa López.**

WHERE TO DINE   At the north end of Melaque beach is **Los Pelícanos** (no phone). It serves the usual seafood specialties; the tender fried squid is delectable. In addition, you can find burritos, nachos, and hamburgers. Many Barra guests come here to stake a place on the beach and use the restaurant as headquarters for sipping and nipping. Open daily from 8am to 10pm, it's a peaceful place to watch the pelicans bobbing. The restaurant is at the far end of the bay before the **Hotel Legazpi** (© 315/355-5397), a pleasant place to stay. It has 20 rooms, charges $40 (£22) for a double, and doesn't accept credit cards.

In addition to the Los Pelícanos, there are many rustic *palapa* **restaurants** on the beach and farther along the bay at the end of the beach.

4 Manzanillo ⟨★⟩

256km (159 miles) SE of Puerto Vallarta; 267km (166 miles) SW of Guadalajara; 64km (40 miles) SE of Barra de Navidad

Manzanillo has long been known as a resort town with wide, curving beaches, legendary sportfishing, and a highly praised diversity of dive sites. Golf is also an attraction here, with two popular courses in the area.

One reason for its popularity could be Manzanillo's enticing tropical geography— vast groves of tall palms, abundant mango trees, and successive coves graced with smooth sand beaches. To the north, mountains blanketed with palms rise alongside the shoreline. And over it all lies the veneer of perfect weather, with balmy temperatures and year-round sea breezes. Even the approach by plane into Manzanillo showcases the promise—you fly in over the beach and golf course. Once on the ground, you exit the airport through a palm grove.

Manzanillo is a dichotomous place—it is both Mexico's busiest commercial seaport and a tranquil, traditional town of multicolor houses cascading down the hillsides to meet the central commercial area of simple seafood restaurants, shell shops, and a few salsa clubs. The activity in Manzanillo divides neatly into two zones: the downtown commercial port and the luxury Santiago Peninsula resort zone to the north. The busy harbor and rail connections to Mexico's interior dominate the downtown zone. A visit to the town's waterfront *zócalo* provides a glimpse into local life. The exclusive Santiago Peninsula, home to the resorts and golf course, separates Manzanillo's two golden sand bays.

ESSENTIALS

GETTING THERE & DEPARTING   By Plane   Alaska Airlines (© 800/252-7522 in the U.S., or 314/334-2211) offers service from Los Angeles; **US Airways (America West;** © 800/428-4322 in the U.S.) flies from Phoenix. Ask a travel agent about the numerous **charters** from the States in the winter.

The **Playa de Oro International Airport** is 40km (25 miles) northwest of town. *Colectivo* (minivan) airport service is available from the airport; hotels arrange returns. Make reservations for return trips 1 day in advance. The *colectivo* fare is based on zones and runs $8 to $10 (£4.40–£5.50) for most hotels. Private taxi service between the airport and downtown area is around $25 (£14). **Budget** (© 800/472-3325 in the U.S., or 314/333-1445), **Hertz** (© 314/333-3191), and **Alamo** (© 314/334-0124) have counters in the airport open during flight arrivals; they will also deliver a car to your hotel. Daily rates run $58 to $78 (£32–£43). You need a car only if you plan to explore surrounding cities and the Costa Alegre beaches.

By Car   **Coastal Highway 200** leads from Acapulco (south) and Puerto Vallarta (north). From Guadalajara, take **Highway 54** through Colima into Manzanillo. Outside Colima you can switch to a toll road, which is faster but less scenic.

By Bus   Buses run to Barra de Navidad (1½ hr. north), Puerto Vallarta (5 hr. north), Colima (1½ hr. east), and Guadalajara (4½ hr. north), with deluxe service and numerous daily departures. Manzanillo's **Central Camionera** (bus station) is about 12 long blocks east of town. If you follow Hidalgo east, the station will be on your right.

VISITOR INFORMATION   The **tourism office** (© 314/333-2277; fax 314/333-2264; www.manzanillo.com.mx) is on the Costera Miguel de la Madrid 875-A, Km 8.5. It's open Monday through Friday from 9am to 7pm, and Saturday from 9am to 2pm.

CITY LAYOUT   The town lies at one end of an 11km-long (7-mile) beach facing Manzanillo Bay and its commercial harbor. The beach has four sections—**Playa Las Brisas, Playa Azul, Playa Salahua,** and **Playa Las Hadas.** At the other end of the beaches is the high, rocky **Santiago Peninsula.** Santiago is 11km (7 miles) from downtown; it's the site of many beautiful homes and the best hotel in the area, Las Hadas, as well as the hotel's Mantarraya Golf Course. The peninsula juts out into the bay, separating Manzanillo Bay from Santiago Bay. Playa Las Hadas is on the south side of the peninsula, facing Manzanillo Bay, and **Playa Audiencia** is on the north side, facing Santiago Bay. The inland town of **Santiago** is opposite the turnoff to Las Hadas.

Activity in downtown Manzanillo centers on the *zócalo,* officially known as the Jardín Alvaro Obregón. A railroad, shipyards, and a basketball court with constant pickup games separate it from the waterfront. The plaza has flowering trees, a fountain, twin kiosks, and a view of the bay. It is a staple of local life, where people congregate on park benches to swap gossip and throw handfuls of rice to the ever-present *palomas* (doves—really just pigeons). Large ships dock at the pier nearby. **Avenida México,** the street leading out from the plaza's central gazebo, is the town's principal commercial thoroughfare. This area is currently undergoing a government-funded renaissance, so look for new improvements.

Once you leave downtown, the **Costera Miguel de la Madrid** highway (or just Costera Madrid) runs through the neighborhoods of Las Brisas, Salahua, and Santiago to the **hotel zones** on the Santiago Peninsula and at Miramar. Shell shops, minimalls, and several restaurants are along the way.

There are two main lagoons. **Laguna de Cuyutlán,** almost behind the city, stretches south for miles, paralleling the coast. **Laguna de San Pedrito,** north of the city, parallels the Costera Miguel de la Madrid; it's behind Playa Las Brisas beach. Both are good birding sites. There are also two bays. **Manzanillo Bay** encompasses the harbor, town, and beaches. The Santiago Peninsula separates it from the second bay, **Santiago.** Between downtown and the Santiago Peninsula is **Las Brisas,** a flat peninsula with a long stretch of sandy golden beach, a lineup of inexpensive but run-down hotels, and a few good restaurants.

GETTING AROUND   **By Taxi**   Taxis in Manzanillo are plentiful. Fares are fixed by zones; rates for trips within town and to more distant points should be posted at your hotel. Daily rates can be negotiated for longer drives outside the Manzanillo area.

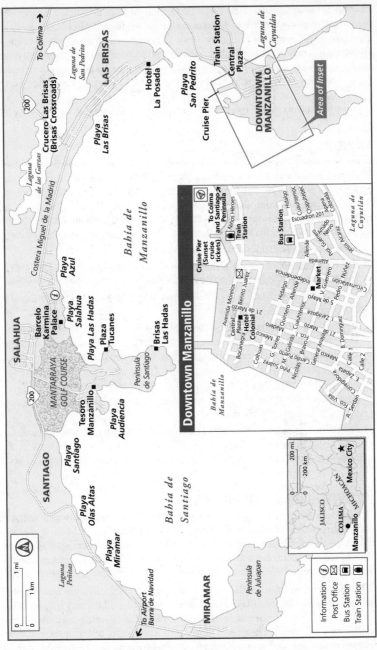

Downtown Manzanillo

By Bus   The *camionetas* (local buses) make a circuit from downtown in front of the train station, along the Bay of Manzanillo, to the Santiago Peninsula and the Bay of Santiago to the north; the fare is 10¢ (5p). The ones marked LAS BRISAS go to the Las Brisas crossroads, to the Las Brisas Peninsula, and back to town; MIRAMAR, SANTIAGO, and SALAHUA buses go to outlying settlements along the bays and to most restaurants mentioned below. Buses marked LAS HADAS go to the Santiago Peninsula and pass the Las Hadas resort and the Tesoro Manzanillo and Plaza Las Glorias hotels. This is an inexpensive way to see the coast as far as Santiago and to tour the Santiago Peninsula.

FAST FACTS: Manzanillo

American Express There is no local office for American Express in Manzanillo. However a highly recommendable agency (and American Express's former representative) is **Bahías Gemelas Travel Agency,** Blvd. Costero Miguel de la Madrid 1556, Las Gaviotas (© 314/333-1000; fax 314/333-0649). It's open Monday through Friday from 9am to 2pm and 4 to 7pm, Saturday from 9am to 2pm.

Area Code The telephone area code is **314.**

Bank **Banamex,** just off the plaza on Avenida Juárez, downtown (© **314/332-0115**), is open Monday through Friday from 9am to 4pm, Saturday 10am to 2pm.

Hospital Contact the **Cruz Roja (Red Cross)** at © **314/336-5770** or the **General Hospital** at © **314/332-1903.**

Internet Access **Digital Center,** Bulevar Miguel de la Madrid 96-B (© **314/333-9191**; www.digitalcenter.manzanillo.com), is located in the hotel zone, near the Hotel Marbella and Fiesta Americana hotels. It charges $2 (£1.10) per hour, and also has printers. It's open Monday through Friday from 9am to 8pm, Saturday from 9am to 2pm. They also have computer repair services available.

Police Both the general police and Tourism Police are available by calling © **314/332-1004** or -1002.

Post Office The *correo*, Dr. Miguel Galindo 30, opposite Farmacia de Guadalajara, downtown (© **314/332-0022**), is open Monday through Friday from 8:30am to 4pm, Saturday from 9am to 1pm.

ACTIVITIES ON & OFF THE BEACH

Activities in Manzanillo revolve around its golden sand beaches, which frequently accumulate a film of black mineral residue from nearby rivers. Most of the resort hotels are completely self-contained. Manzanillo's public beaches provide an opportunity to see more local color and scenery. They are the daytime playground for those staying at places off the beach or without pools.

BEACHES   **Playa Audiencia,** on the Santiago Peninsula, offers the best swimming as well as snorkeling, but **Playa San Pedrito,** shallow for a long way out, is the most popular beach for its proximity to downtown. **Playa Las Brisas,** located south of Santiago Peninsula as you're heading to downtown Manzanillo, offers an optimal combination of location and good swimming. **Playa Miramar,** on the Bahía de Santiago past the Santiago Peninsula, is popular with bodysurfers, windsurfers, and boogie boarders. It's accessible by local bus from town. The major part of **Playa Azul,** also south of the Santiago Peninsula, drops off sharply but is noted for its wide stretch of golden sand.

BIRDING   Several lagoons along the coast offer good birding. As you go from Manzanillo past Las Brisas to Santiago, you'll pass **Laguna de Las Garzas (Lagoon of the Herons),** also known as Laguna de San Pedrito, where you can see many white pelicans and huge herons fishing in the water. They nest here in December and January. Directly behind downtown is the **Laguna de Cuyutlán** (follow the signs to Cuyutlán), where you'll usually find birds in abundance; species vary between summer and winter.

DIVING   **Underworld Scuba** ☆☆ (©/fax **314/333-3678;** cell 314/358-0327; www.gomanzanillo.com), owned by longtime resident and local diving expert Susan Dearing, conducts highly professional diving expeditions and classes. Susan's warm enthusiasm and intimate knowledge of the area make this one of my top recommendations for dive outfitters in Mexico. Many locations are so close to shore that there's no need for a boat. Close-in dives include the jetty with coral growing on the rocks at 14m (46 ft.) and a nearby sunken frigate downed in 1959 at 8m (26 ft.). Divers can see abundant sea life, including coral reefs, seahorses, giant puffer fish, and moray eels. A dive requiring a boat costs $60 (£33) per person for one tank (with a three-person minimum) or $80 (£44) for two tanks ($10/£5.50 discount if you have your own equipment). You can also rent weights and a tank for beach dives for $10 (£5.50). A three-stop snorkel trip costs $45 (£25). All guides are certified divemasters, and the shop offers certification classes (PADI, YMCA, and CMAS) in very intensive courses of various durations. The owner offers a 10% discount on your certification when you mention Frommer's. MasterCard and Visa are accepted.

ESCORTED TOURS   Because Manzanillo is so spread out, you might consider a city tour. Reputable local tour companies include **HECtours** (© **314/333-1707;** www.hectours.com) and **Bahías Gemelas Travel Agency** (© **314/333-1000;** fax 314/333-0649). Schedules are flexible; a half-day city tour costs around $25 (£14). Other tours include the daylong Colima Colonial Tour ($67/£37), which stops at Colima's Archaeological Museum and principal colonial buildings, and passes the active volcano. Offerings change regularly, so ask about new tours.

FISHING   Manzanillo is famous for its fishing, particularly sailfish. Marlin and sailfish are abundant year-round. Winter is best for dolphin fish and dorado (mahimahi); in summer, wahoo and rooster fish are in greater supply. The international sailfish competition is held around the November 20 Revolution Day holiday, and the national sailfish competition is in February. You can arrange fishing through travel agencies or directly at the fishermen's cooperative (© **314/332-1031**), located downtown where the fishing boats moor. Call from 6am to 2pm or 5 to 8pm. A fishing boat is approximately $40 (£22) for 8 people to $50 (£28) for 12 people per hour, with most trips lasting about 5 hours.

GOLF   The 18-hole **La Mantarraya Golf Course** (© **314/331-0101**) is open to nonguests as well as guests of Las Hadas. At one time, La Mantarraya was among the top 100 courses in the world, but newer entries have passed it. Still, the compact, challenging 18-hole course designed by Roy and Pete Dye is a beauty, with banana trees, blooming bougainvillea, and coconut palms at every turn. A lush and verdant place (12 of the 18 holes are played over water), it remains a favorite.

When the course was under construction, workers dug up pre-Hispanic ceramic figurines, idols, and beads where the 14th hole now lies. It is believed to have been an important ancient burial site. The course culminates with its signature 18th hole, with a drive to the island green off El Tesoro (the treasure) beach, directly in front of the Karminda Palace Resort. Local lore says this beach still may hold buried treasure from Spanish galleons, whose crews were the first to recognize the perfection of this natural harbor, and who used it during the 16th century as their starting point for voyages to the Pacific Rim. Greens fees are $150 (£83) for 18 holes, $90 (£50) for 9 holes; cart rental costs $50 (£28) for 18 holes and $30 (£17) for 9 holes.

The fabulous Isla Navidad Country Club 27-hole golf course associated with the **Grand Bay Hotel** (© 314/337-9024) in Barra de Navidad, an easy distance from Manzanillo, is also open to the public. The Robert von Hagge design is long and lovely, with each hole amid rolling, tropical landscapes. It is wide open, with big fairways and big greens, and features plenty of water (2 lagoon holes, 13 lakeside holes, and 8 holes along the Pacific). The greens fees, including a motorized cart, are $166 (£91) for 18 holes, $192 (£106) for 27 holes for hotel guests; it's $207 and $230 (£114 and £127), respectively, for nonguests. Barra is about a 1- to 1½-hour drive north of Manzanillo on Highway 200.

A MUSEUM   The **Museum of Archaeology and History** (© 314/332-2256) is a small but impressive structure that houses exhibits depicting the region's history, plus rotating displays of contemporary Mexican art. It's on Avenida Niños Héroes at Avenida Teniente Azueta, on the road leading between the downtown and Las Brisas areas. Every Friday evening, the museum hosts free cultural events, which might be a trio playing romantic ballads or a chamber music ensemble. Performances begin at 8pm. Hours are Tuesday through Saturday from 10am to 2pm and 5 to 8pm, Sunday from 10am to 1pm. The museum completed an extensive renovation in November 2006.

SHOPPING   Manzanillo has a selection of shops carrying Mexican crafts and clothing, mainly from nearby Guadalajara. Almost all are downtown on the streets near the central plaza. Shopping downtown is an experience—for example, you won't want to miss the shop bordering the plaza that sells a combination of shells, religious items (including shell-framed Virgin of Guadalupe nightlights), and orthopedic supplies. The Plaza Manzanillo is an American-style mall on the road to Santiago, and there's a traditional *tianguis* (outdoor) market in front of the entrance to Club Maeva, with touristy items from around Mexico. Most resort hotels also have boutiques or shopping arcades.

SUNSET CRUISES   To participate in this popular activity, buy tickets from a travel agent or your hotel tour desk. Most cost around $25 (£14). The trips vary in their combinations of drinks, music, and entertainment and last 1½ to 2 hours. Departing from Las Hadas is the **El Explorer** and **Antares.**

WHERE TO STAY

Manzanillo's strip of coastline consists of three areas: **downtown,** with its shops, markets, and commercial activity; **Las Brisas,** the hotel-lined beach area immediately north of the city; and **Santiago,** the town and peninsula, now virtually a suburb, to the north at the end of Playa Azul. Transportation by bus or taxi makes all three areas fairly convenient to each other. Reservations are recommended during the Easter, Christmas, and New Year's holidays.

DOWNTOWN

Hotel Colonial ⚜   An old favorite, this three-story colonial-style hotel is in the central downtown district. Popular for its consistent quality, ambience, and service, it has beautiful blue-and-yellow tile and colonial-style carved doors and windows in the lobby and restaurant. Rooms are decorated with minimal furniture, red-tile floors, and basic comforts. The hotel is 1 block inland from the main plaza at the corner of Juárez and Galindo.

Av. México 100 and González Bocanegra, 28200 Manzanillo, Col. ℂ **314/332-1080**, -0668, or -1230. 42 units. $45 (£25) double. MC, V. Limited street parking. **Amenities:** Restaurant; bar. *In room:* A/C, cable TV.

LAS BRISAS

Some parts of the Las Brisas area look run-down; however, it still lays claim to one of the best beaches in the area and is known for its constant gentle sea breezes—a pleasure in the summer.

Hotel La Posada ⚜   This small inn has a bright-pink stucco facade with a large arch that leads to a broad tiled patio right on the beach. The rooms have exposed brick walls and simple furnishings with Mexican decorative accents. It remains popular with longtime travelers to Manzanillo. The atmosphere is casual and informal—help yourself to beer and soft drinks, and at the end of your stay, owners Juan and Lisa Martinez will count the bottle caps you deposited in a bowl labeled with your room number. The restaurant, which is open to nonguests, is open daily during high season from 8 to 11am and 1:30 to 8pm. A meal costs around $7 (£3.85). During low season, the restaurant is open from 8am to 3pm. Stop by for a drink at sunset; the bar's open until 9pm all year. The hotel is at the end of Las Brisas Peninsula, closest to downtown, and is on the local Las Brisas bus route.

Av. Lázaro Cárdenas 201, Las Brisas (Apdo. Postal 135), 28200 Manzanillo, Col. ℂ/fax **314/333-1899**. www.hotel-la-posada.info. 23 units. High season $78 (£43) double; low season $58 (£32) double. Rates include full breakfast. MC, V. Free parking. **Amenities:** Restaurant; bar; Internet cafe; laundry service; currency exchange; safe.

SANTIAGO

Five kilometers (3 miles) north of Las Brisas is the wide Santiago Peninsula. The settlement of Salahua is on the highway where you enter the peninsula to reach the hotels Las Hadas, Plaza Las Glorias, and Tesoro Manzanillo, as well as the Mantarraya Golf Course. Buses from town marked LAS HADAS pass by these hotels every 20 minutes. Past the Salahua turnoff, at the end of the settlement of Santiago, an obscure road on the left is marked ZONA DE PLAYAS and leads to the hotels on the other side of the peninsula and Playa de Santiago.

Barceló Karmina Palace ⚜⚜⚜ *Kids*   The quality of rooms and services at this all-inclusive resort makes the newest of Manzanillo's hotels one of the area's best values. It's the best choice for families visiting Manzanillo. The buildings resemble Maya pyramids, and even though the architecture at first might seem a little overdone, somehow it works. Rooms are all very large suites, with rich wood accents, comfortable recessed seating areas with pull-out couches, and two 27-inch TVs in each room. The extra-large bathrooms have marble floors, twin black marble sinks, separate tubs, and glassed-in showers. Most rooms have terraces or balconies with views of the ocean,

Film Fact

The movie *10* featured Manzanillo's signature property, Las Hadas—along with Bo Derek.

overlooking the tropical gardens and swimming pools. Master suites have spacious sun terraces with private splash pools, plus a full wet bar, full refrigerator, and a large living room area with 42-inch TV. Two full-size bedrooms close off from the living/dining area.

The kids' club offers a host of activities, while adults have numerous choices for fun—all included in the price. There's also an exceptionally well-equipped gym and European-style spa.

Av. Vista Hermosa 13, Fracc. Península de Santiago, 28200 Manzanillo, Col. **888/234-6222** in the U.S. and Canada, or 314/334-1300, 331-1313, or 01-800/507-4930 in Mexico. Fax 314/334-1108. www.barcelokarminapalace.com. 324 units. $278–$338 (£153–£186) double; $908 (£499) 2-bedroom suites for quad occupancy. Rates are all-inclusive. Special packages and Web specials available; ask about seasonal specials. 2 children younger than 8 stay free in parent's room. AE, MC, V. Free parking. **Amenities:** 2 restaurants; snack bar; 5 bars; 8 connected swimming pools; tennis courts; health club w/treadmills and Cybex equipment; full spa facilities; men's and women's sauna and steam rooms; sailboards; beach volleyball; kids' activity program; concierge; car rental; room service; currency exchange; safe. *In room:* A/C, TV, minibar, hair dryer, iron, safe ($2/£1.10).

Brisas Las Hadas Golf Resort & Marina 🌟🌟   For me, Las Hadas is synonymous with a visit to Manzanillo. This elegant beachside resort is built in Moorish style into the side of the rocky peninsula. The service is gracious, warm, and unobtrusive. Rooms were just updated in 2006, and are spread over landscaped grounds and overlook the bay; cobbled lanes lined with colorful flowers and palms connect them. The resort is large but maintains an air of seclusion. (Motorized carts are on call for transportation within the property.)

Views, room size, and amenities differentiate the six types of accommodations, which can vary greatly. If you're not satisfied with your room, ask to be moved—a few of the rooms are significantly less attractive than others. Understated and spacious, the better units have white-marble floors, sitting areas, and large, comfortably furnished balconies. Nine suites have private pools. The lobby is a popular place for curling up in one of the overstuffed seating areas or, at night, for enjoying a drink and live music. Pete and Roy Dye designed La Mantarraya, the hotel's 18-hole, par-71 golf course.

If you are visiting on a cruise ship or staying at another hotel, you can enjoy Las Hadas beach for a day by purchasing a day pass from the hotel's gate guard. In exchange, you'll receive coupons for beach chairs and towels.

Av. de los Riscos s/n, Santiago Peninsula, 28200 Manzanillo, Col. © **888/559-4329** in the U.S. and Canada, or 314/331-0101. www.brisas.com.mx. 234 units. High season $206–$327 (£113–£180) double, $386–$626 (£212–£344) Fantasy Suite; low season $175–$379 (£96–£208) double, $386–$626 (£212–£344) Fantasy Suite. AE, DC, MC, V. Free guarded parking. **Amenities:** 3 restaurants, including the elegant Legazpi (see "Where to Dine," below); 3 lounges and bars; 2 outdoor pools; small workout room; marina for 70 vessels; scuba diving; snorkeling; water-skiing; sailing and trimaran cruises; concierge; tour desk; travel agency; car rental; shopping arcade; room service; in-room massage; babysitting; laundry service; dry cleaning. *In room:* A/C, TV, minibar, hair dryer, safe.

Plaza Tucanes 🌟   The sunset-colored walls of this pueblolike hotel ramble over a hillside on the Santiago Peninsula. The restaurant on top and most rooms afford a broad vista of other red-tiled rooftops and either the palm-filled golf course or the bay. It's one of Manzanillo's undiscovered resorts, known more to wealthy Mexicans than to Americans. Originally conceived as private condominiums, the accommodations were designed for living; each spacious unit is stylishly furnished, and very comfortable. Each has a huge living room; a small kitchen/bar; one, two, or three large bedrooms with tile or brick floors; large bathrooms with Mexican tiles; huge closets; and large furnished private patios with views. Some units contain whirlpool tubs, and a few rooms can be partitioned off and rented by the bedroom only. Rooms can be a long walk from the main entrance, through a succession of stairways and paths. If stair climbing bothers you, try to get a room by the restaurant and pool—you'll have a great view, and a hillside rail elevator goes straight from top to bottom.

Av. de Tesoro s/n, Santiago Peninsula, 28200 Manzanillo, Col. (© 314/334-1098. Fax 314/334-0090. www.plaza tucanes.com.mx. 112 units. $146 (£80) double; $250 (£138) double all inclusive. Packages available. AE, MC, V. Free parking. **Amenities:** 2 restaurants, including Argentine steakhouse; outdoor pool; mini golf; recreational park; kids' club; game area; room service; babysitting (w/advance notice); beach club on Las Brisas beach, w/pool and small restaurant; transportation to and from beach club (once daily in each direction). In room: A/C, TV, safe.

Tesoro Manzanillo Resort 𝒦 (Kids)   This hotel (formerly the Gran Costa Real and Sierra) with all-inclusive package options, has 21 floors overlooking La Audiencia beach, and a full program of activities, dining, and entertainment. Its excellent kids' program makes it a top choice for families. Architecturally, it mimics the white Moorish style of Las Hadas that has become so popular in Manzanillo. Inside, it's palatial in scale and awash in pale-gray marble. Room decor picks up the pale-gray theme with armoires that conceal the TV and minibar. Most standard rooms have two double beds or a king-size bed, plus a small table, chairs, and desk. Several rooms at the end of most floors are small, with one double bed, small porthole-size windows, no balcony, and no view. Most rooms, however, have balconies and ocean or hillside views. The 10 honeymoon suites have king-size beds and chaises. Junior suites have sitting areas with couches and large bathrooms. Scuba-diving lessons take place in the pool, and excellent scuba-diving sites are within swimming distance of the shore.

Av. La Audiencia 1, Los Riscos, 28200 Manzanillo, Col. (© 800/543-7556 in the U.S., or 314/333-2000. Fax 314/333-2611 www.tesororesorts.com. 332 units. High season $230–$340 (£127–£187) double, $240–$370 (£132–£204) suite; low season $200 (£110) double, $220 (£121) suite. Rates are all-inclusive. AE, MC, V. Free parking. **Amenities:** 3 restaurants; 4 bars; grand pool on the beach; children's pool; 4 lighted tennis courts; health club w/exercise equipment, aerobics, and hot tub; men's and women's sauna and steam rooms; travel agency; salon w/massage; room service; laundry service; currency exchange. In room: A/C, TV, minibar, hair dryer.

WHERE TO DINE
DOWNTOWN
Roca del Mar MEXICAN/INTERNATIONAL   Join the locals at this informal cafe facing the plaza. The large menu includes club sandwiches, hamburgers, *carne asada a la tampiqueña* (thin grilled steak served with rice, poblano pepper, an enchilada, and refried beans), fajitas, fish, shrimp, and vegetable salads. A specialty is its paella (served on Sun and Tues), and the economical *pibil* tacos are outstanding. This cafe is very clean and offers sidewalk dining.

Blvd. Costero. (© 314/336-9097. Main courses $3–$12 (£1.65–£6.60). No credit cards. Daily 7:30am–11pm.

LAS BRISAS
The Hotel La Posada (see "Where to Stay," above) offers breakfast to nonguests at its beachside restaurant; it's also a great place to mingle with other tourists and enjoy the sunset and cocktails.

La Toscana 𝒦𝒦𝒦 (Finds) SEAFOOD/INTERNATIONAL   You're in for a treat at La Toscana (by the same owner of the now-closed Willy's), one of Manzanillo's most popular restaurants, located on the beach in Las Brisas. It's homey, casual, and small, so reservations are highly recommended. The exquisite cuisine belies the atmosphere, with starters that include escargot and salmon carpaccio. Among the grilled specialties are shrimp imperial wrapped in bacon, red snapper tarragon, dorado basil, sea bass with mango and ginger, and tender fresh lobsters (four to a serving). Live music frequently sets the scene.

Bulevar Miguel de la Madrid 3177. (℃) **314/333-2515.** Reservations highly recommended. Main courses $8–$20 (£4.40–£11). MC, V. Daily 6pm–2am. 100m (328 ft.) from Hotel Fiesta Mexicana.

SANTIAGO ROAD

The restaurants below are on the Costera Madrid between downtown and the Santiago Peninsula, including the Salahua area.

Benedetti's Pizza PIZZA   There are several branches in town, so you'll probably find a Benedetti's not far from where you are staying. The variety is extensive; add some *chimichurri* sauce to your sesame-crust pizza to enhance the flavor. Benedetti's specializes in seafood pizzas, such as smoked oyster and anchovy. You can also select from pastas, sandwiches, burgers, fajitas, salads, Mexican soups, cheesecake, and pie.

Bulevar Miguel de la Madrid, near the Las Brisas Glorietta on the ocean side (west). (℃) **314/333-1592** or 334-0141. Pizza $9–$12 (£4.95–£6.60); main courses $2–$5.55 (£1.10–£3.05). AE, MC, V. Daily 10am–11:30pm.

Bigotes II *(Finds* SEAFOOD   Locals flock to this large, breezy restaurant (the name translates as "Mustaches") by the water for the good food and festive atmosphere. Strolling singers serenade diners as they dig into large portions of grilled seafood.

Puesta del Sol 3. (℃) **314/333-1236.** Main courses $9.50–$23 (£5.25–£13). MC, V. Daily noon–10pm. From downtown, follow the Costera Madrid past the Las Brisas turnoff; the restaurant is behind the Penas Coloradas Social Club, across from the beach.

SANTIAGO PENINSULA

Legazpi ℱℱ INTERNATIONAL   This is a top choice in Manzanillo for sheer elegance, gracious service, and outstanding food. The candlelit tables are set with silver and flowers. Enormous bell-shaped windows on two sides show off the sparkling bay below. The sophisticated menu includes prosciutto with melon marinated in port wine, crayfish bisque, broiled salmon, roast duck, lobster, veal, and flaming desserts.

In the Brisas Las Hadas hotel, Santiago Peninsula. (℃) **314/331-0101.** Main courses $8.50–$16 (£4.70–£8.80). AE, MC, V. High season daily 7–11:30pm; closed low season.

MANZANILLO AFTER DARK

Nightlife in Manzanillo is much more exuberant than you might expect, but then Manzanillo is not only a resort town—it's a thriving commercial center. Clubs and bars tend to change from year to year, so check with your concierge for current hot spots. Some area clubs have a dress code prohibiting shorts or sandals, principally applying to men.

El Bar de Félix, between Salahua and Las Brisas by the Avis rental-car office (℃) **314/333-1875**), is open Tuesday through Sunday from 2pm to midnight, and has an $8 (£4.40) minimum consumption charge. Music ranges from salsa and ranchero to rock and house—it's the most consistently lively place in town, with pool tables. The adjacent (and related) **Vog Disco** (℃) **314/333-1875**), Bulevar Costera Miguel de la Madrid Km 9.2, features alternative music in a cavernous setting, with a midnight light show; it's Manzanillo's current late-night hot spot, open until 5am, but only on Friday and Saturday. The cover charge for women is $10 (£5.50), for men $15

(£8.25). Also very popular—with a built-in crowd—is the nightclub at the **Club Maeva Hotel & Resort** (☎ **01-800/849-1987** in Mexico), on the inland side of the main highway, north of the Santiago Peninsula. It's open Tuesday, Thursday, and Saturday from 11pm to 2am. Couples are given preferential entrance. Nonguests are welcome but must pay an entrance fee, typically $20 to $30 (£11–£17), after which all drinks are included. Note that when Club Maeva is fully booked, entrance to nonguests may be difficult to impossible—ask your hotel front desk if they can secure a pass for you. The fee varies depending on the night of the week and the time of year.

10

Acapulco & the Southern Pacific Coast

by Juan Cristiano

The exotic tropical beaches and rich jungle scenery of this part of Mexico first captured the imagination of travelers to this country. Although the geography of southern Pacific Mexico may be uniform, the resorts along this coast couldn't be more varied. They range from high-energy seaside cities to pristine, primitive coves.

Spanish conquistadors came to this coast for its numerous sheltered coves and protected bays, from which they set sail to the Far East. Centuries later, Mexico's first tourists found the same elements appealing, but for different reasons—they were seeking escape, and stretches of blue coves nicely complemented the tropical landscape of the adjacent mountains.

Over the years, the area developed a diverse selection of resorts. Each is distinct, and together they offer an ideal attraction for almost any type of traveler. The region encompasses the country's oldest resort, **Acapulco;** its newest, the **Bahías de Huatulco;** and a side-by-side pair of opposites, modern **Ixtapa** and the charming fishing village of **Zihuatanejo.** Between Acapulco and Huatulco lies **Puerto Escondido,** a laid-back beach town on a picturesque bay with world-class waves.

This chapter covers coastal towns in two Mexican states, Guerrero and Oaxaca. Stunning coastline and tropical mountains grace the whole region. Outside the urban centers, few roads are paved, and these two states remain among Mexico's poorest despite decades of incoming tourist dollars (and many other currencies).

EXPLORING THE SOUTHERN PACIFIC COAST

Time at the beach used to be the top priority for most travelers to this part of Mexico. Today, ecotourism, adventure tourism, and more culturally oriented travel are gaining ground. Each of the beach towns in this chapter is capable of satisfying your sand and surf needs. You could also combine several coastal resorts into a single trip or mix the coastal with the colonial—say, Puerto Escondido and Oaxaca (see chapter 11), or Acapulco and Taxco (see chapter 5).

The resorts have distinct personalities, but you get the beach wherever you go, whether you choose a city that offers virtually every luxury imaginable or a rustic town providing little more than seaside relaxation.

The largest and most decadent of Mexican resort destinations, **Acapulco** leapt into the international spotlight in the late 1930s when movie stars made it their playground. Today, though increasingly challenged by other seaside destinations, Acapulco still lures visitors with its glitzy nightlife and sultry beaches (even if the Hollywood celebrities who made it a household name have long since moved on). Of all the resorts in this chapter, Acapulco has the best airline connections, the broadest range of late-night entertainment, the most savory dining, and the widest range of accommodations. The beaches are generally wide and clean, and although the bay itself remains suspect, it's cleaner than in past years.

The resort of **Ixtapa** and its neighboring seaside village, **Zihuatanejo,** offer beach-bound tourist attractions on a smaller, less hectic scale than Acapulco. They attract travelers with their complementary contrasts—sophisticated high-rise hotels in one, local color and leisurely pace in the other. Their excellent beaches front clean ocean waters. To get there, many people fly into Acapulco, then make the 4- to 5-hour trip north by rental car or bus.

Puerto Escondido, noted for its celebrated surf break, laid-back village ambience, attractive and inexpensive inns, and nearby nature excursions, is a worthy destination and an exceptional value. It's 6 hours south of Acapulco on coastal Highway 200. Most people fly from Mexico City or drive up from Huatulco.

The **Bahías de Huatulco** encompass a total of nine bays—each lovelier than the last—on a pristine portion of Oaxaca's coast. Development of the area has been gradual and well planned, with great ecological sensitivity. The town of **Huatulco,** 130km (80 miles) south of Puerto Escondido, is emerging as Mexico's most authentic adventure tourism haven. In addition to an 18-hole golf course, cruise-ship pier, and a handful of resort hotels, it offers a growing array of soft adventures that range from bay tours to diving, river rafting, and rappelling. Dining and nightlife remain limited, but the setting is beautiful and relaxing.

1 Acapulco ★★

366km (227 miles) S of Mexico City; 272km (169 miles) SW of Taxco; 979km (607 miles) SE of Guadalajara; 253km (157 miles) SE of Ixtapa/Zihuatanejo; 752km (466 miles) NW of Huatulco

I like to think of Acapulco as a diva—maybe a little past her prime, perhaps overly made up, but still capable of captivating an audience. It's tempting to dismiss Acapulco as a passé resort, but the town's temptations are hard to resist. Where else do bronzed men dive from cliffs into the sea at sunset, and where else does the sun shine 360 days a year? Though most beach resorts are made for relaxing, Acapulco has non-stop, 24-hours-a-day energy. Its perfectly sculpted bay is an adult playground filled with water-skiers in *tanga* swimsuits and darkly tanned, mirror-shaded studs on jet skis. Visitors play golf and tennis with intensity, but the real sport is the nightlife, which has made this city famous for decades. Back in the days when there was a jet set, they came to Acapulco—filmed it, sang about it, wrote about it, and lived it.

It's not hard to understand why: The view of Acapulco Bay, framed by mountains and beaches, is breathtaking day or night. And I dare anyone to take in the lights of the city and not feel the pull to go out and get lively.

Though a few years ago, tourism to Acapulco was in a state of decline, it's now attempting a renaissance, in a style reminiscent of Miami's South Beach. Classic hotels are slowly being renovated and areas gentrified. Clean-up efforts have put an entirely new face on a place that was once aging less than gracefully.

International travelers began to reject Acapulco when it became clear that the cost of development was the pollution of the bay and surrounding areas. The city government responded, and invested over $1 billion in public and private infrastructure improvements. In addition, a program instituted in the early 1990s has cleaned up the water—whales have even been sighted offshore.

Acapulco Bay Area

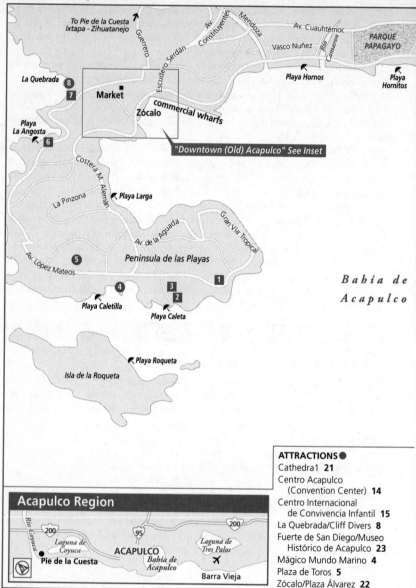

To Pie de la Cuesta
Ixtapa - Zihuatanejo

Av. Cuauhtémoc

PARQUE
PAPAGAYO

Guerrero

Escudero Serdán

Av. Constituyentes

Mendoza

Vasco Nuñez

Río Camaron

La Quebrada **8**
7

Market

Zócalo

commercial wharfs

Playa Hornos

Playa Hornitos

Playa
La Angosta
6

"Downtown (Old) Acapulco" See Inset

Costera M. Alemán

La Pinzona

Playa Larga

Av. de la Aguada

Gran Vía Tropical

Av. López Mateos

5

Peninsula de las Playas

*Bahía de
Acapulco*

4

3
2

1

Playa Caletilla

Playa Caleta

Playa Roqueta

Isla de la Roqueta

Acapulco Region

Río Coyuca

200

95

200

Laguna de
Coyuca

ACAPULCO

Laguna de
Tres Palos

Pie de la Cuesta

Bahía de
Acapulco

Barra Vieja

ATTRACTIONS ●
Cathedra1 **21**
Centro Acapulco
  (Convention Center) **14**
Centro Internacional
  de Convivencia Infantil **15**
La Quebrada/Cliff Divers **8**
Fuerte de San Diego/Museo
  Histórico de Acapulco **23**
Mágico Mundo Marino **4**
Plaza de Toros **5**
Zócalo/Plaza Álvarez **22**

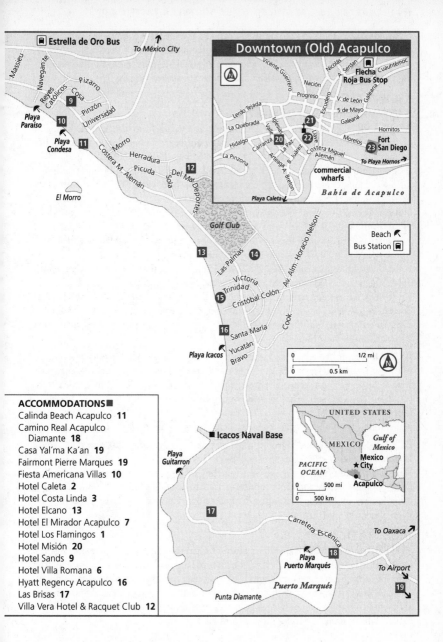

Estrella de Oro Bus

To México City

Navegante
Massieu
Reyes Católicos
Pizarro
Cosa
Pinzón
Universidad
Morro
Herradura
Picuda
Costera M. Alemán
Sola
Del Mar
Deportes

Playa Paraíso
Playa Condesa

9
10
11

El Morro

Golf Club

13
14

Las Palmas
Victoria
Trinidad
Cristóbal Colón
Av. Alm. Horacio Nelson
Cook

15

16

Santa María
Yucatán
Bravo

12

Playa Icacos

Beach
Bus Station

Downtown (Old) Acapulco

Vicente Guerrero
Nicolás
A. Serdán
Cuauhtémoc
Nación
V. de León
Galeana
Progreso
Escudero
5 de Mayo
Lerdo Tejada
La Quebrada
La Paz
Iglesias
Valle
Galeana
Hidalgo
Carranza
A. Bretón
La Paz
Hornitos
La Pinzona
Arteaga
A. Bretón
B. Juárez
Costera Miguel Alemán
Morelos

Flecha Roja Bus Stop

21
20
22
23

Fort San Diego

To Playa Hornos →

commercial wharfs

Bahía de Acapulco

Playa Caleta

0 ——— 1/2 mi
0 ——— 0.5 km

ACCOMMODATIONS

Calinda Beach Acapulco **11**
Camino Real Acapulco Diamante **18**
Casa Yal'ma Ka'an **19**
Fairmont Pierre Marques **19**
Fiesta Americana Villas **10**
Hotel Caleta **2**
Hotel Costa Linda **3**
Hotel Elcano **13**
Hotel El Mirador Acapulco **7**
Hotel Los Flamingos **1**
Hotel Misión **20**
Hotel Sands **9**
Hotel Villa Romana **6**
Hyatt Regency Acapulco **16**
Las Brisas **17**
Villa Vera Hotel & Racquet Club **12**

Icacos Naval Base

Playa Guitarron

17

UNITED STATES

MEXICO
Gulf of Mexico
PACIFIC OCEAN
★ Mexico City
Acapulco

0 ——— 500 mi
0 ——— 500 km

Carretera Escénica

To Oaxaca ↗

To Airport

18
19

Playa Puerto Marqués
Puerto Marqués
Punta Diamante

Acapulco tries hard to hold on to its image as the ultimate extravagant party town, and remains a top weekend and vacation destination for affluent residents of Mexico City, in particular. It's still the top choice for those who want to have dinner at midnight, dance until dawn, and sleep all day on a sun-soaked beach.

ESSENTIALS

GETTING THERE & DEPARTING

BY PLANE See chapter 2 for information on flying from the United States or Canada to Acapulco. Local numbers for major airlines with nonstop or direct service to Acapulco are **AeroMéxico** (© **744/485-1625** or 01-800/021-4010 and -4000 inside Mexico), **American** (© **744/466-9232,** or 01-800/904-6000 inside Mexico for reservations), **Continental** (© **744/466-9063**), **Mexicana** (© **744/466-9121** or 486-7586), and **US Airways** (© **744/466-9257**).

AeroMéxico flies from Guadalajara, Mexico City, Tijuana, and Monterrey; **Aviacsa** (© **01800/711-6733**) flies from Mexico City; **InterJet** (© **01800/01-12345**) is a new low-cost carrier that flies from Toluca, near Mexico City; **Mexicana** flies from Mexico City. Check with a travel agent about **charter** flights.

The airport (airport code: ACA) is 22km (14 miles) southeast of town, over the hills east of the bay. Private **taxis** are the fastest way to get downtown; they cost $30 to $50 (£17–£28). The major **rental-car** agencies all have booths at the airport. **Transportes Terrestres** has desks at the front of the airport where you can buy tickets for minivan *colectivo* transportation into town ($20/£11). You must reserve return service to the airport through your hotel.

BY CAR From Mexico City, take either the curvy toll-free **Highway 95D** south (6 hr.) or scenic **Highway 95,** the four- to six-lane toll highway (3½ hr.), which costs around $50 (£28) one-way. The free *"libre"* road from Taxco is in good condition; you'll save around $40 (£22) in tolls from there through Chilpancingo to Acapulco. From points north or south along the coast, the only choice is **Highway 200,** where you should (as on all Mexican highways) always try to travel by day.

BY BUS The **Estrella de Oro** terminal is at Av. Cuauhtémoc 1490, and the **Estrella Blanca** terminal is at Av. Cuauhtémoc 1605. **Turistar, Estrella de Oro,** and **Estrella Blanca** have almost hourly service for the 5- to 7-hour trip to Mexico City ($30–$50/£17–£28), and daily service to Zihuatanejo ($14/£7.70). Buses also serve other points in Mexico, including Chilpancingo, Cuernavaca, Iguala, Manzanillo, Puerto Vallarta, and Taxco.

ORIENTATION

VISITOR INFORMATION The **State of Guerrero Tourism Office** operates the **Procuraduría del Turista** (©/fax **744/484-4416**), on street level in front of the **International Center,** a convention center set back from the main Costera Alemán, down a lengthy walkway with fountains. The office offers maps and information about the city and state, as well as police assistance for tourists; it's open Monday to Saturday from 8am to 11pm, Sunday from 8am to 8pm.

CITY LAYOUT Acapulco stretches more than 6km (4 miles) around the huge bay, so trying to take it all in by foot is impractical. The tourist areas are roughly divided into three sections. On the western end of the bay is **Acapulco Viejo (Old Acapulco),** the original town that attracted the jet-setters of the 1950s and 1960s—and today it looks as if it's still locked in that era, though a renaissance is slowly getting under way.

> ## Tips Car & Bus Travel Warning Eases
>
> Car robberies and bus hijackings on Highway 200 south of Acapulco on the way
> to Puerto Escondido and Huatulco used to be common, and you may have
> heard warnings about the road. The trouble has all but disappeared, thanks to
> military patrols and greater police protection. However, as in most of Mexico,
> it's advisable to travel the highways during daylight hours only—not so much
> because of carjackings, but because highways are unlit, and animals can wan-
> der onto them.

The second section, in the center of the bay, is the **Zona Hotelera (Hotel Zone);** it
follows the main boulevard, **Costera Miguel Alemán** (or just "the Costera"), as it runs
east along the bay from downtown. Towering hotels, restaurants, shopping centers,
and strips of open-air beach bars line the street. At the far eastern end of the Costera
lie the golf course and the International Center (a convention center). **Avenida
Cuauhtémoc** is the major artery inland, running roughly parallel to the Costera.

The third major area begins just beyond the Hyatt Regency Hotel, where the name
of the Costera changes to **Carretera Escénica (Scenic Hwy.),** which continues all the
way to the airport. The hotels along this section of the road are lavish, and extravagant private villas, gourmet restaurants, and flashy nightclubs built into the hillside
offer dazzling views. The area fronting the beach here is **Acapulco Diamante,** Acapulco's most desirable address.

Street names and numbers in Acapulco can be confusing and hard to find—many
streets are not well marked or change names unexpectedly. Street numbers on the
Costera do not follow logic, so don't assume that similar numbers will be close
together.

GETTING AROUND   By Taxi   Taxis are more plentiful than tacos in Acapulco—
and practically as inexpensive, if you're traveling in the downtown area only. Just
remember that you should always establish the price with the driver before starting
out. Hotel taxis may charge three times the rate of a taxi hailed on the street, and
nighttime taxi rides cost extra, too. Taxis are also more expensive if you're staying in
the Diamante section or south. The minimum fare is $2 (£1.10) per ride for a roving
VW Bug-style taxi in town; the fare from Puerto Marqués to the hotel zone is $8
(£4.40), or $10 (£5.50) into downtown. *Sitio* taxis are nicer cars, but more expensive,
with a minimum fare of $4 (£2.20).

The fashion among Acapulco taxis is flashy, with Las Vegas–style lights—the more
colorful and pulsating, the better.

By Bus   Even though the city has a confusing street layout, using city buses is amazingly easy and inexpensive. Two kinds of buses run along the Costera: pastel color-
coded buses and regular "school buses." The difference is the price: New
air-conditioned tourist buses (Aca Tur Bus) are 50¢ (30p); old buses are 45¢ (25p).
Covered bus stops are all along the Costera, with handy maps on the walls showing
routes to major sights and hotels.

The best place near the *zócalo* to catch a bus is next to Sanborn's, 2 blocks east.
CALETA DIRECTO or BASE-CALETA buses will take you to the Hornos, Caleta, and
Caletilla beaches along the Costera. Some buses return along the same route; others
go around the peninsula and return to the Costera.

For expeditions to more distant destinations, there are buses to **Puerto Marqués** to the east (marked PUERTO MARQUES–BASE) and **Pie de la Cuesta** to the west (marked ZOCALO–PIE DE LA CUESTA). Be sure to verify the time and place of the last bus back if you hop on one of these.

By Car   Rental cars are available at the airport and at hotel desks along the Costera. Unless you plan on exploring outlying areas, trust me, you're better off taking taxis or using the easy and inexpensive public buses.

FAST FACTS: Acapulco

American Express The main office is in the Gran Plaza shopping center, Costera Alemán 1628 (© **744/435-2200**). It's open Monday through Friday from 9am to 6pm and Saturday 9am to 1pm.

Area Code The telephone area code is **744.**

Climate Acapulco boasts sunshine 360 days a year, with average daytime temperatures of 80°F (27°C). Humidity varies, with approximately 59 inches of rain per year. June through October is the rainy season, though July and August are relatively dry. Tropical showers are brief and usually occur at night.

Consular Agents The **United States** has an agent at the Hotel Acapulco Continental, Costera Alemán 121, Loc. 14 (© **744/469-0556**); the office is open Monday through Friday from 10am to 2pm. The **Canadian** office is at the Centro Comercial Marbella, Loc. 23 (© **744/484-1305**). The toll-free emergency number inside Mexico is © **01-800/706-2900.** The office is open Monday through Friday from 9am to 5pm. The **United Kingdom** office is at the Las Brisas Hotel on Carretera Escénica near the airport (© **744/481-2533**). Most other countries in the European Union also have consulate offices in Acapulco.

Currency Exchange Numerous banks along the Costera are open Monday through Friday from 9am to 6pm, Saturday from 10am to 2pm. Banks and their ATMs generally have the best rates. *Casas de cambio* (currency-exchange booths) along the street may have better rates than hotels.

Drugstores One of the largest drugstores in town is **Farmacía Daisy,** Francia 49, across the traffic circle from the convention center (© **744/48126350**). Sam's Club and Wal-Mart, both on the Costera, have pharmacy services and lower prices on medicine.

Hospital **Hospital Magallanes,** Av. Wilfrido Massieu 2, Fracc. Magallanes (© **744/485-6194** or -6197), has an English-speaking staff and doctors. For local emergencies, call the **Cruz Roja (Red Cross),** Av. Ruiz Cortines s/n (© **065** or 744/445-5912).

Internet Access **@canet,** Costera Alemán 1632 Int., La Gran Plaza, Loc. D-1, lower floor (©/fax **744/486-9186** or -8182), is open weekdays from 10am to 9pm and weekends from noon to 9pm. Internet access costs $2.50 (£1.40) per hour. This is a computer shop that also offers Internet access and has a very helpful staff. Also along the Costera strip is the **Santa Clara Cafe,** Costera Alemán 136, serving coffee, pastries, and ice cream, along with Internet service for $1 (55p) for 20 minutes. It's open 9am to 11pm. Internet access kiosks are also available inside **Wal-Mart,** Costera Miguel Alemán 500 (© **744-469-0203**), with varying rates depending on usage.

Parking It is illegal to park on the Costera at any time. Try parking along side streets or in one of the few covered parking lots, such as in Plaza Bahía and in Plaza Mirabella.

Post Office The *correo* is next door to Sears, close to the Fideicomiso office. It's open Monday through Friday from 9am to 5pm, Saturday from 9am to 2pm. Other branches are in the Estrella de Oro bus station on Cuauhtémoc, inland from the Acapulco Qualton Hotel, and on the Costera near Caleta Beach.

Safety Riptides claim a few lives every year, so pay close attention to warning flags posted on Acapulco beaches. Red or black flags mean stay out of the water, yellow flags signify caution, and white or green flags mean it's safe to swim.

As is the case anywhere, tourists are vulnerable to thieves. This is especially true when shopping in a market, lying on the beach, wearing jewelry, or visibly carrying a camera, purse, or bulging wallet.

Telephone Acapulco phone numbers seem to change frequently. The most reliable source for telephone numbers is the **Procuraduría del Turista,** on the Costera in front of the convention center (© **744/484-4416**), which has an exceptionally friendly staff.

Tourist Police Policemen in white and light-blue uniforms belong to the Tourist Police (© **065** for emergencies, or 744/485-0490), a special corps of English-speaking police established to assist tourists.

ACTIVITIES ON & OFF THE BEACH

Acapulco is known for its great beaches and watersports, and few visitors bother to explore its traditional downtown area. But the shaded *zócalo* (also called Plaza Alvarez) is worth a trip, to experience a glimpse of local life and color. Inexpensive cafes and shops border the plaza. At its far north end is the **cathedral Nuestra Señora de la Soledad,** with blue, onion-shaped domes and Byzantine towers. Though reminiscent of a Russian Orthodox church, it was originally (and perhaps appropriately) built as a movie set, then later adapted into a house of worship. From the church, turn east along the side street going off at a right angle (Calle Carranza, which doesn't have a marker) to find an arcade with newsstands and more shops. The hill behind the cathedral provides an unparalleled view of Acapulco. Take a taxi to the top of the hill from the main plaza, and follow signs to **El Mirador (lookout point).**

Local travel agencies book city tours, day trips to Taxco, cruises, and other excursions and activities. Taxco is about a 3-hour drive inland from Acapulco (see chapter 5 for more information).

THE BEACHES Here's a rundown on the beaches, going from west to east around the bay. **Playa la Angosta** is a small, sheltered, often-deserted cove just around the bend from **La Quebrada** (where the cliff divers perform).

South of downtown on the Peninsula de las Playas lie the beaches **Caleta** and **Caletilla.** Separating them is a small outcropping of land that contains the aquarium and water park **Mágico Mundo Marino,** which is open daily from 9am to 6pm

> ## *Tips* To Swim or Not to Swim in the Bay?
>
> In the past decade, the city has gone to great lengths (and great expense) to clean up the waters off Acapulco. Nevertheless, this is an industrial port that was once heavily polluted, so many choose to stick to the hotel pool. You may notice the fleet of power-sweeper boats that skim the top of the bay each morning to remove debris and oil.
>
> Among the bay beaches that remain popular with visitors and locals are **Caleta** and **Caletilla beaches**, as well as **Playa Puerto Marqués**.

(© **744/483-1215**) and costs $4 to enter. You'll find thatched-roofed restaurants, watersports equipment for rent, and brightly painted boats that ferry passengers to **Roqueta Island.** You can rent beach chairs and umbrellas for the day. Mexican families favor these beaches because they're close to several inexpensive hotels. In the late afternoon, fishermen pull their colorful boats up on the sand; you can buy the fresh catch of the day and, occasionally, oysters on the half shell.

Pleasure boats dock at **Playa Manzanillo,** south of the *zócalo.* Charter fishing trips sail from here. In the old days, the downtown beaches—Manzanillo, Honda, Caleta, and Caletilla—were the focal point of Acapulco. Today, beaches and resort developments stretch along the 6.5km (4-mile) length of the shore.

East of the *zócalo,* the major beaches are **Hornos** (near Papagayo Park), **Hornitos, Paraíso, Condesa,** and **Icacos,** followed by the naval base (La Base) and **Punta del Guitarrón.** After Punta del Guitarrón, the road climbs to the legendary Las Brisas hotel. Past Las Brisas, the road continues to the small, clean bay of **Puerto Marqués,** followed by **Punta Diamante,** about 20km (12 miles) from the *zócalo.* The fabulous Acapulco Princess, the Quinta Real, and the Pierre Marqués hotels dominate the landscape, which fronts the open Pacific.

Playa Puerto Marqués, in the bay of Puerto Marqués, is an attractive area for swimming. The water is calm and the bay sheltered. Water-skiing can also be arranged. Past the bay lies **Revolcadero Beach,** a magnificent wide stretch of beach on the open ocean, where many of Acapulco's grandest resorts are found.

Other beaches lie farther north and are best reached by car, though buses also make the trip. **Pie de la Cuesta** is 13km (8 miles) west of town. Buses along the Costera leave every 5 or 10 minutes; a taxi costs about $20 (£11). The water is too rough for swimming, but it's a great spot for checking out big waves and the spectacular sunset, especially over *coco locos* (drinks served in fresh coconuts with the tops whacked off) at a rustic beachside restaurant. The area is known for excellent birding and surrounding coconut plantations.

If you're driving, continue west along the peninsula, passing **Coyuca Lagoon** on your right, until almost to the small air base at the tip. Along the way, various private entrepreneurs, mostly young boys, will invite you to park near different sections of beach. You'll also find *colectivo* boat tours of the lagoon offered for about $10 (£5.50).

BAY CRUISES & ROQUETA ISLAND   Acapulco has virtually every kind of boat to choose from—yachts, catamarans, and trimarans (single- and double-deckers). Cruises run morning, afternoon, and evening. Some offer buffets, open bars, and live music; others just snacks, drinks, and taped music. Prices range from $24 to $40 (£13–£22). Cruise operators come and go, and their phone numbers change so frequently from year to year that it's pointless to list them here; to find out what cruises are currently operating, contact any Acapulco travel agency or your hotel's tour desk, and ask for brochures or recommendations.

Boats from Caletilla Beach to **Roqueta Island**—a good place to snorkel, sunbathe, hike to a lighthouse, visit a small zoo, or have lunch—leave every 15 minutes from 7am until the last one returns at 7pm. There are also primitive-style glass-bottom boats that circle the bay as you look down at a few fish and watch a diver swim down to the underwater sanctuary of the Virgin of Guadalupe, patron saint of Mexico. The statue of the Virgin—created by sculptor Armando Quesado—was placed there in 1958, in memory of a group of divers who lost their lives at the spot. You can purchase tickets ($5/£2.75) directly from any boat that's loading.

WATERSPORTS & BOAT RENTALS An hour of **water-skiing** at Coyuca Lagoon can cost as little as $35 (£19) or as much as $65 (£36).

Scuba diving costs $50 (£28) for 1½ hours of instruction if you book directly with the instructor on Caleta Beach. It costs about $70 (£39) if you book through a hotel or travel agency. Dive trips start at around $70 (£39) per person for one dive. One reputable shop, near Club de Esquís, is **Divers de México** (✆ 744/482-1398). Another recommended company, both PADI and NAUI certified, is the **Acapulco Scuba Center,** Paseo del Pescador 13–14, downtown Acapulco (✆ 744/482-9474; www.acapulcoscuba.com). They offer a variety of dives from half-day (9am–2pm) shallow dives for beginners to instructor training. Prices for two-tank dives are $90, and include transportation from your hotel, onboard lunch, boat, and gear. **Boat rentals** are cheapest on Caletilla Beach, where an information booth (✆ 744/482-2389) rents inner tubes, small boats, canoes, paddleboats, and chairs. It also arranges water-skiing and scuba diving.

For **deep-sea fishing** excursions, go to the boat cooperative's pink building opposite the *zócalo,* or book a day in advance (✆ 744/482-1099). Charter trips run $250 to $450 (£138–£248) for 6 hours, tackle and bait included, with an extra charge for ice, drinks, and lunch. Credit cards are accepted, but you're likely to get a better deal by paying cash. Boats leave at 7am and return at 2pm. If you book through a travel agent or hotel, prices start at around $250 (£138) for four people. Also recommendable is **Fish-R-Us,** Costera Alemán 100 (✆ 877/347-4787 in the U.S., or 744/482-8282). In addition to traditional fishing charters, they also offer private yacht charters, scuba diving, and a 3-hour Night of Delight cruise, complete with dinner served on board. Prices vary with the service requested and number of people, so call for details.

Parasailing, though not free from risk (the occasional thrill-seeker has collided with a palm tree or even a building), can be brilliant. Floating high over the bay hanging from a parachute towed by a motorboat costs about $25 (£14). Most of these rides

---

ⓘTips **Tide Warning**

Each year, at least one or two unwary swimmers drown in Acapulco because of deadly riptides and undertow (see "Safety" in "Fast Facts," above). Swim only in Acapulco Bay or Puerto Marqués Bay—and be careful of the undertow no matter where you go. If you find yourself caught in the undertow, head back to shore at an angle instead of trying to swim straight back.

Moments **Death-Defying Divers**

High divers perform at La Quebrada each day at 12:30, 7:15, 8:15, 9:15, and 10:30pm. Admission is $3.50 (£1.90). From a spotlit ledge on the cliffs, divers (holding torches for the final performance) plunge into the roaring surf of an inlet that's just 7m (23 ft.) wide, 4m (13 ft.) deep, and 40m (131 ft.) below—after wisely praying at a small shrine nearby. To the applause of the crowd, divers climb up the rocks and accept congratulations and gifts of money from onlookers. This is the quintessential Acapulco experience. No visit is complete without watching the cliff divers—and that goes for jaded travelers as well. To get there from downtown, take the street called La Quebrada from behind the cathedral for 4 blocks.

The public areas have great views, but arrive early, because performances quickly fill up. Another option is to watch from the lobby bar and restaurant terraces of the **Hotel Plaza Las Glorias/El Mirador**. The bar imposes a $19 (£10) cover charge, which includes two drinks. You can get around the cover by having dinner at the hotel's **La Perla restaurant**. Reservations (© **744/483-1155, ext. 802**) are recommended during high season.

---

operate on Condesa Beach, but they also can be found independently operating on the beach in front of most hotels along the Costera.

GOLF & TENNIS   Both the **Acapulco Princess** (© **744/469-1000**) and **Pierre Marqués** (© **744/466-1000**) hotels have top-notch courses. The Princess's course is a rather narrow, level, Ted Robinson design. The Marques course, redesigned by Robert Trent Jones, Sr., in 1972 for the World Cup Golf Tournament, is longer and more challenging. A morning round of 18 holes at either course costs $135 (£74) for guests and $150 (£83) for nonguests (discounted rates for afternoon rounds); American Express, Visa, and MasterCard are accepted, and the cart is included in the fee. Tee times begin at 7:30am, and reservations should be made a day in advance. Club rental is available for an extra $40 (£22). The **Mayan Palace Golf Club,** Geranios 22 (© **744/469-6043** or 466-2260), designed by Latin American golf great Pedro Guericia, lies farther east. Greens fees are $135 (£74) for visitors, and caddies are available for an additional $18 (£9.90). At the **Club de Golf Acapulco,** off the Costera next to the convention center (© **744/484-0781**), you can play 9 holes for $50 (£28) and 18 holes for $80(£44), with equipment renting for $16 (£8.80).

The newest addition to Acapulco's golf scene is the spectacular Robert von Hagge–designed course at the exclusive **Tres Vidas Golf Club,** Carretera a Barra Vieja Km 7 (© **744/444-5138** or -5126). The par-72, 18-hole course, right on the edge of the ocean, is landscaped with nine lakes, dotted with palms, and home to a flock of ducks and other birds. The club is open only to members, guests of members, and guests at Tres Vidas. Greens fees are $195 (£107), including cart; a caddy costs $15 (£8.25). Also here is a clubhouse with a restaurant (daily 7:30am–7:30pm), as well as a pool and beach club. American Express, Visa, and MasterCard are accepted.

The **Club de Tenis Hyatt,** Costera Alemán 1 (© **744/484-1225**), is open daily from 7am to 11pm. Outdoor and indoor courts cost $10 (£5.50) per hour during the day, $15 (£8.25) per hour at night; Rackets rent for $3 (£1.65) and a set of balls costs

$5.50 (£3). Many of the hotels along the Costera have tennis facilities for guests; the best are at the Acapulco Princess, Pierre Marqués, Mayan Palace, and Las Brisas hotels.

RIDING & BULLFIGHTS   You can go **horseback riding** along the beach. Independent operators stroll the Hotel Zone beachfront offering rides for about $25 to $45 (£25) for 1 to 2 hours. Horses are also commonly found on the beach in front of the Acapulco Princess Hotel. There is no phone; you go directly to the beach to make arrangements.

Traditionally called Fiesta Brava, **bullfights** are held during Acapulco's winter season at a ring up the hill from Caletilla Beach. Tickets purchased through travel agencies cost around $17 to $40 (£9.35–£22) and usually include transportation to and from your hotel. You can also buy a general admission ticket at the stadium for $4.50 (£2.50). Be forewarned that this is a true bullfight—meaning things generally do not fare well for the bull. The festivities begin at 5:30pm each Sunday from January to March.

A MUSEUM & A WATER PARK   The original **Fuerte de San Diego,** Costera Alemán, east of the *zócalo* (© **744/482-3828**), was built in 1616 to protect the town from pirate attacks. At that time, the port reaped considerable income from trade with the Philippine Islands (which, like Mexico, were part of the Spanish Empire). The fort you see today was rebuilt after considerable earthquake damage in 1776, and most recently underwent renovation in 2000. The structure houses the **Museo Histórico de Acapulco (Acapulco Historical Museum)** 🌟🌟, with exhibits that tell the story of Acapulco from its role as a port in the conquest of the Americas to a center for local Catholic conversion campaigns and for exotic trade with the Orient. Other exhibits chronicle Acapulco's pre-Hispanic past, the coming of the conquistadors (complete with Spanish armor), and Spanish imperial activity. Temporary exhibits are also on display. Admission to the museum is $3.50 (£1.90), free on Sunday. It's open Tuesday through Sunday from 9:30am to 6:30pm. To reach the fort, follow Costera Alemán past Old Acapulco and the *zócalo;* the fort is on a hill on the right.

A House of Art

Of all the exclusive villas and homes in Acapulco, one stands far apart from the others. Though not as elegantly impressive as the villas of Las Brisas, the **home of Dolores Olmedo** in Acapulco's traditional downtown area is a veritable work of art. In 1956, the renowned Mexican artist Diego Rivera covered its outside wall with a mural of colorful mosaic tiles, shells, and stones. The work is unique and one of the last he created. Rivera, considered one of Mexico's greatest artists, has been credited with being one of the founders of the 20th-century Mexican-muralist movement. The Olmedo mural, which took him 18 months to complete, features Aztec deities such as Quetzalcoatl and Tepezcuincle, the Aztec dog. Rivera and Olmedo were lifelong friends, and Rivera lived in this house for the last 2 years of his life, during which time he also covered the interior with murals. However, because this home isn't a museum, you have to settle for enjoying the exterior masterpiece. The house is a few blocks behind the Casablanca Hotel, a short cab ride from the central plaza, at Calle Cerro de la Pinzona 6. Have the driver wait while you look around.

The **Parque Acuático el CICI** ☆, Costera Alemán at Colón (© **744/484-8033**), is a sea-life and water park east of the convention center. It offers guests swimming pools with waves, water slides, and water toboggans, and has a cafeteria and restrooms. The park, which underwent a $3-million renovation, is open daily from 10am to 6pm. General admission is $10 (£5.50) and free for children younger than 2. There are **dolphin shows** (in Spanish) weekdays at 2pm and weekends at 2 and 4pm. There's also a dolphin swim program, which includes 30 minutes of introduction and 30 minutes to 1 hour of swim time. The cost for this option is $90 (£50) for a half-hour swim, $130 (£72) for an hour, and they are by prior reservation only. Shows are at 10am, 12:30, and 4pm. Reservations are required; there is a 10-person maximum per show for the dolphin swim option. The minimum age is 4 years.

SHOPPING

Acapulco is not among the best places to buy Mexican crafts, but it does have a few interesting shops, and the Costera is lined with places to buy tourist souvenirs, including silver jewelry, Mexico knickknacks, and the ubiquitous T-shirt.

The shopkeepers aren't pushy, but they'll test your bargaining mettle. The starting price will be steep, and dragging it down may take some time. Before buying silver, examine it carefully and look for ".925" stamped on the back. This supposedly signifies that the silver is 92.5% pure, but the less expensive silver metal called "alpaca" may also bear this stamp. (Alpaca is generally stamped MEXICO or MEX, often in letters so tiny that they are hard to read and look similar to the three-digit ".925"). The market is open daily from 9am to 6pm.

Sanborn's, a good department store and drugstore chain, offers an array of staples, including cosmetics, music, clothing, books, and magazines. It has a number of locations in Acapulco, including downtown at Costera Miguel Alemán 209, across from the boat docks (© **744/482-6167**); Costera Miguel Alemán 1226 at the Condo Estrella Tower, close to the convention center (© **744/484-2025**), and on Costera Miguel Alemán 163, at the Hotel Calinda (© **744/481-2426 or** 484-4465).

Acapulco also has a Sam's Club and a Wal-Mart on the inland side of the main highway just prior to its ascent to Las Brisas.

Boutiques selling resort wear crowd the Costera Alemán. These stores carry attractive summer clothing at prices lower than you generally pay in the United States. If there's a sale, you can find incredible bargains. One of the nicest air-conditioned shopping centers on the Costera is **Plaza Bahía,** Costera Alemán 125 (© **744/485-6939** or -6992), which has four stories of shops, movie theaters, a bowling alley, and small fast-food restaurants. The center is just west of the Costa Club Hotel. The bowling alley, **Aca Bol in Plaza Bahía** (© **744/485-0970** or -7464), is open daily from noon to 1am. Another popular shopping strip is the **Plaza Condesa,** adjacent to the Fiesta Americana Condesa, with shops that include Guess, Izod, and Bronce Swimwear. **Olvido Plaza,** near the restaurant of the same name, has Tommy Hilfiger and Aca Joe.

Acapulco has a few notable fine-art galleries. My favorite, **Galería Espacio Pal Kepenyes** ☆☆, Costera Guitarrón 140, on the road to the Radisson (© **744/484-3738**), carries the work of Pal Kepenyes, whose stunning bronzes are among Acapulco's most notable public sculptures. The gallery shows smaller versions, as well as signature pieces of jewelry in brass, copper, and silver, by appointment only.

Works by another notable Mexican artist, **Sergio Bustamante,** are available inside the gallery of the Hotel Mayan Palace, Costera de las Palmas (© **744/469-6003**). You can see his capricious suns, moons, and fantasy figures in a variety of materials.

WHERE TO STAY

The listings below begin with the very expensive resorts south of town (nearest the airport) and continue along Costera Alemán to the less expensive, more traditional hotels north of town, in the downtown or "Old Acapulco" part of the city. Especially in the Very Expensive and Expensive categories, inquire about promotional rates or check with the airlines for air-hotel packages. During Christmas and Easter weeks, some hotels double their normal rates. The rates below do not include the 17% tax.

Private **villas** are available for rent all over the hills south of town; staying in one of these palatial homes is an unforgettable experience. **Se Renta** (www.acapulcoluxury villas.com) handles some of the most exclusive villas.

SOUTH OF TOWN

Acapulco's most exclusive and renowned hotels, restaurants, and villas nestle in the steep forested hillsides here, between the naval base and Puerto Marqués. This area is several kilometers from the heart of Acapulco; you'll pay about $20 (£11) round-trip taxi fare every time you venture off the property into town.

Very Expensive

Camino Real Acapulco Diamante ★★ *(Kids)*   Tucked in a secluded location on 32 hectares (79 acres), this relaxing, self-contained resort is an ideal choice for families, or for those who already know Acapulco and don't care to explore much. I consider it one of Acapulco's finest places in terms of contemporary decor, services, and amenities. I like its location on the Playa Puerto Marqués, which is safe for swimming, but you do miss out on compelling views of Acapulco Bay. From Carretera Escénica, a handsome brick road winds down to the hotel, overlooking Puerto Marqués Bay. The lobby has an inviting terrace facing the water. The spacious rooms have balconies or terraces, small sitting areas, marble floors, ceiling fans (in addition to air-conditioning), and contemporary Mexican furnishings.

Carretera Escénica Km 14, Baja Catita s/n, Pichilingue, 39867 Acapulco, Gro. © **744/435-1010.** Fax 744/435-1020. www.caminoreal.com/acapulco. 157 units. High season $429 (£236) double; $611 (£336) master suite. Rates include buffet breakfast. Ask about low-season and midweek discounts. AE, MC, V. Parking $6. **Amenities:** 2 restaurants; lobby bar; 3 outdoor pools (1 for children); tennis court; health club w/aerobics, spa treatments, massage, and complete workout equipment (extra charge); watersports equipment rentals; children's activities; concierge; tour desk; car-rental desk; salon; room service; babysitting; laundry service. *In room:* A/C, TV, minibar, hair dryer, iron, safe.

Casa Yal'ma Ka'an ★★ *(Finds)*   A romantic hideaway 20 minutes south of Diamante, Casa Yal'ma Ka'an is a small ecological retreat with its own ocean beach. Stone paths with little bridges meander past several lookout towers and over lily ponds with palms and flowers, and the beautiful pool lies just steps from the Pacific. In addition to featuring its own beach club, Casa Yal'ma Ka'an offers a *temazcal*, a Mayan rustic steam bath that will be prepared for you with candles and aromatherapy amenities. Seven individual thatched-roof cottages have king beds, rustic wood furnishings, stone bathrooms, and private sitting decks. Gourmet breakfasts are served under a giant *palapa* overlooking the pool and beach. Service throughout this exclusive hotel is outstanding; children younger than 17 are not allowed.

Carretera hacia Barra Vieja Km 29 L189, 39867 Acapulco, Gro. © **744/444-6389** or -6390. www.casayalmakaan. com. 7 units. High season $280 (£154) double; low season $250 (£138) double. Rates include American breakfast. MC, V. Free parking. **Amenities:** Restaurant; pool bar; outdoor pool; beach club; spa treatments. *In room:* A/C, TV, safe.

Fairmont Pierre Marqués ★★★   The refined Fairmont Pierre Marqués is both more exclusive and relaxed than the famous Fairmont Princess next door, to which guests also have access. It once served as a private home for J. Paul Getty and is today one of Acapulco's most prestigious hotels. Together, the Pierre Marqués and the Princess offer more activities than you are likely to have time for, with three pools alone at the Pierre Marqués, a beautiful Pacific beach with watersports activities, championship golf, tennis, and a state-of-the-art fitness center. Luxurious guest rooms include villas, bungalows, and low-rise pavilions overlooking the pools, tropical gardens, or beach. Fine dining is available here or at the Princess, with a shuttle regularly connecting the two hotels. Service throughout the hotel is outstanding. The Fairmont is in Diamante, about a 20-minute drive from the center of Acapulco.

Playa Revolcadero s/n, Colonia Granjas del Marques, 39907 Acapulco, Gro. ℂ 800/441-1414 in the U.S. or 744/435-2600. Fax 744/466-1046. www.fairmont.com/pierremarques. 335 units. $259 (£142) and up double. AE, MC, V. Free parking. **Amenities:** Restaurant; cafe; 2 bars; 3 outdoor pools; health club and spa; championship golf course; 5 outdoor lighted tennis courts (10 additional courts at Fairmont Princess, including 2 indoor courts); concierge; room service; laundry service. *In room:* A/C, TV, safe.

Las Brisas ✦✦✦ (*Moments*)   This is a local landmark, often considered Acapulco's signature hotel, and my personal favorite. Perched on a hillside overlooking the bay, Las Brisas is known for its tiered pink stucco facade, private pools, and 50 pink Jeeps rented exclusively to guests. If you stay here, you ought to like pink, because the color scheme extends to practically everything. Las Brisas is also known for inspiring romance and is best enjoyed by couples indulging in time together—alone.

The hotel is a community unto itself: The simple, marble-floored rooms are like separate villas sculpted from a terraced hillside, with panoramic views of Acapulco Bay from a balcony or terrace. Each room has a private or semiprivate swimming pool. Las Brisas has a total of 150 pools. The spacious Regency Club rooms, at the apex of the property, offer the best views. You stay at Las Brisas more for the panache and setting than for luxury amenities, though rooms have been upgraded, with new bedding and a freshening up of the decor, although it still retains the beloved "Las Brisas" style. Early each morning, continental breakfast arrives in a cubbyhole. If you tire of your own pool, Las Brisas has a beach club less than a kilometer (a half-mile) away, on Acapulco Bay; continuous shuttle service departs from the lobby. The club offers casual dining, a large swimming pool, and a natural saltwater pool—actually a rocky inlet. Mandatory service charges cover shuttle service from the hillside rooms to the lobby and from the lobby to the beach club, plus tips. The hotel is on the southern edge of the bay, overlooking the road to the airport and close to the hottest area nightclubs.

Apdo. Carretera Escénica 5255, Las Brisas, 39868 Acapulco, Gro. ℂ 888/559-4329 in the U.S., or 744/469-6900. Fax 744/446-5332. www.brisas.com.mx. 263 units. High season $330 (£182) shared pool, $435 (£239) private pool, $540 (£297) Royal Beach Club; low season $230 (£127) shared pool, $345 (£190) private pool, $432 (£238) Royal Beach Club. $20 (£11) per day service charge plus 17% tax. Rates include continental breakfast. AE, MC, V. Free parking. **Amenities:** 2 restaurants; deli; private beach club w/fresh- and saltwater pools; 5 tennis courts; gym; concierge; guest-only tours and activity program; tour desk; Jeeps rental; shopping arcade; salon; room service; in-room massage; babysitting; laundry service; dry cleaning. *In room:* A/C, TV, minibar, hair dryer, safe.

Fun Fact **Acapulco, Queen of the Silver Screen**

Along with hosting some of the legendary stars of the silver screen, Acapulco has also played a few starring roles. Over 250 films have been shot here, including 1985's *Rambo II*, which used the Pie de la Cuesta lagoon as its backdrop.

COSTERA HOTEL ZONE
Expensive
Fiesta Americana Villas Acapulco • The Fiesta Americana is a long-standing favorite deluxe hotel in the heart of the beach-bar action. The 18-story structure towers above Condesa Beach, just east and up the hill from the Glorieta Diana traffic circle. The recently renovated studios, suites, and villas have marble floors, and can be loud if you're overlooking the pool area. Each has a private terrace or balcony with ocean view. The more expensive rooms have the best bay views, and all have purified tap water. The hilltop swimming pool affords one of the city's finest views. The location is great for enjoying the numerous beach activities, shopping, and more casual nightlife of Acapulco.

Costera Alemán 97, 39690 Acapulco, Gro. (C) **800/343-7821** in the U.S., or 744/484-2355. Fax 744/484-1828. www. fiestamericana.com. 324 units. High season $230 (£127) double, $290 (£160) suite; low season $100–$130 (£55–£72) double, $200 (£110) suite. AE, DC, MC, V. Free parking. **Amenities:** 3 restaurants; coffee shop; lobby bar; theme nights w/buffet dinner; 3 outdoor pools; travel agency; shopping arcade; salon; room service; laundry service. *In room:* A/C, TV, minibar, safe.

Hotel Elcano ••• *Finds*   An Acapulco classic, the Elcano is another personal favorite. It offers exceptional service and a prime location—on a broad stretch of beach in the heart of the hotel zone. The retro-style, turquoise-and-white lobby, and beachside pool area are the closest you can get to a South Beach, Miami, atmosphere in Acapulco, and its popular open-air restaurant adds to the lively waterfront scene. On the whole, the Elcano reminds me of a set from a classic Elvis-in-Acapulco movie. Rooms are continually upgraded, bright, and very comfortable. They feature classic navy-and-white tile accents, ample oceanfront balconies, and tub/shower combinations. The very large junior suites, all on corners, have two queen-size beds and huge closets. Studios are small but adequate, with king-size beds and small sinks outside the bathroom area. In the studios, a small portion of the TV armoire serves as a closet, and there are no balconies, only large sliding windows. All rooms have purified tap water. This is an ideal place if you're attending a convention or simply want the best of all possible locations, between hillside nightlife and the Costera beach zone. It's an excellent value.

Costera Alemán 75, 39690 Acapulco, Gro. (C) **744/435-1500**. Fax 744/484-2230. http://hotel-elcano.com. 180 units. High season $145 (£80) studio, $185 (£102) standard double, $195 (£107) junior suite, $250 (£138) master suite; low season about $50 (£28) less for each room type. Ask about promotional discounts. AE, MC, V. Free parking. **Amenities:** 2 restaurants; beachside pool; small workout room; video-game room; travel agency; shopping arcade; salon; room service; massage; babysitting; laundry service. *In room:* A/C, TV, minibar, hair dryer, safe.

Hyatt Regency Acapulco • A sprawling oasis, the Hyatt is one of the largest of Acapulco's hotels, although no longer as modern as many other resorts. The buzzing lobby encloses a sitting area and bar where there's live music every evening. A free-form pool fronts a broad stretch of beach with calm waters, one of the most inviting in Acapulco. The guest rooms are beginning to show their age, but they also have balconies with spectacular views of Acapulco Bay. Some contain kitchenettes. Regency Club guests receive continental breakfast, afternoon canapés, and other upgraded amenities. This hotel caters to a large Jewish clientele and has a full-service kosher restaurant, synagogue, and Sabbath elevator. Cruise passengers docking in Acapulco often stay here as well. The Alory Spa offers a broad menu of spa services and massage treatments.

Costera Alemán 1, 39869 Acapulco, Gro. © **800/233-1234** in the U.S. and Canada, 01-800/005-0000 in Mexico, or 744/469-1234. Fax 744/484-3087. www.acapulco.regency.hyatt.com. 640 units. High season $300–$360 (£165–£198) double, $390 (£215) Regency Club, $460 (£253) suite; low season $220 (£121) double, $290 (£160) Regency Club, $360 suite. AE, DC, MC, V. Valet parking $5. **Amenities:** 3 restaurants; cantina; lobby bar; 2 large, shaded free-form outdoor pools; small gym; spa; children's programs; concierge; tour desk; car-rental desk; business center; shopping arcade; salon; room service; in-room massage; babysitting; laundry service; dry cleaning; safe. *In room:* A/C, TV, minibar, hair dryer, iron, safe.

Moderate

Calinda Beach   You'll see this tall cylindrical tower rising at the eastern edge of Condesa Beach. Each room has a view, usually of the bay. Though not exceptionally well furnished, guest rooms are large and comfortable; most have two double beds. It's the most modern of the reasonably priced lodgings along the strip of hotels facing popular Condesa Beach. Package prices are available, and the hotel frequently offers promotions, such as rates that include breakfast.

Costera Alemán 1260, 39300 Acapulco, Gro. © **744/435-0600.** Fax 744/484-4676. www.hotelescalinda.com.mx. 357 units. High season $180 (£99) double; low season $140 (£77) double. Ask about promotional specials. AE, DC, MC, V. Limited free parking. **Amenities:** 2 restaurants; poolside snacks; lobby bar w/live music; 2 outdoor pools; small gym; travel agency; salon; room service; babysitting; laundry service; pharmacy. *In room:* A/C, TV, safe.

Sand's Acapulco *Kids* *Value*   A great option for budget-minded families, this unpretentious, comfortable hotel nestles on the inland side, opposite the giant resort hotels and away from the din of Costera traffic. A stand of umbrella palms and a pretty garden restaurant—with terrific, authentic Mexican food at reasonable prices—lead into the lobby. The rooms are light and airy, in the style of a good modern motel, with basic furnishings and wall-to-wall carpeting. Some units have kitchenettes, and all have a terrace or balcony. The family-friendly hotel includes a kids' pool and a special play area for youngsters. The rates are reasonable, the accommodations satisfactory, and the location excellent.

Costera Alemán 178, 39670 Acapulco, Gro. © **744/484-2260.** Fax 744/484-1053. www.sands.com.mx. 94 units. High season $150 (£83) standard double, $100 (£55) bungalow; low season $70 (£39) standard double, $50 (£28) bungalow. Rates include coffee in the lobby and are higher during Christmas, Easter, and other major holidays. AE, MC, V. Limited free parking. **Amenities:** Restaurant; 2 outdoor pools (1 for children); squash court; volleyball; Ping-Pong; children's playground; concierge; babysitting; laundry service; dry cleaning. *In room:* A/C, TV, minibar.

DOWNTOWN (ON LA QUEBRADA) & OLD ACAPULCO BEACHES

Numerous budget hotels dot the streets fanning out from the *zócalo.* They're among the best values in town, but be sure to check your room first to see that it meets your needs. Several hotels in this area are close to Caleta and Caletilla beaches, or on the back of the hilly peninsula, at Playa la Angosta.

Moderate

Hotel Caleta   The all-inclusive Hotel Caleta is more familiar to Mexican travelers than to their U.S. counterparts. This high-quality, nine-floor resort, adjacent to one of the liveliest beaches in Old Acapulco, offers excellent value. Stay here if you seek the authentic feel of a Mexican holiday, with all its boisterous, family-friendly charms. The hotel is built into a cliff on the Caleta peninsula, overlooking the beach. Rooms surround a plant-filled courtyard, topped by a glass ceiling. All have large terraces with ocean views, although some connect to the neighboring terrace. The simply decorated rooms are very clean and comfortable, with a large closet and desk. Each room has two queen beds with firm mattresses, and cable TV.

A succession of terraces holds tropical gardens, restaurants, and pools. A private beach and boat dock are down a brief flight of stairs. The resort has a changing agenda of theme nights and evening entertainment.

Cerro San Martín 325, Fracc. Las Playas, 39390 Acapulco, Gro. ℭ 744/483-9140. Fax 744/483-9125. meigaca@ prodigy.net.mx. 245 units. High season $140 (£77) double; low season $90 (£50) double. Rates are all-inclusive. Room-only prices sometimes available. AE, DC, MC, V. Free private parking. **Amenities:** Restaurant; snack bar; large fresh- and saltwater outdoor pools; tour desk; car-rental desk; shopping arcade. *In room:* A/C, TV, fan.

Hotel Mirador Acapulco ℭ

One of the landmarks of Old Acapulco, the El Mirador Hotel overlooks the famous cove where the cliff divers perform. Renovated with tropical landscaping and lots of Mexican tile, this hotel offers attractively furnished rooms. Each holds double or queen-size beds, a small kitchenette area with minifridge and coffeemaker, and a large bathroom with marble counters. Most have a separate living room, some have a whirlpool tub, and all are accented with colorful Saltillo tile and other Mexican decorative touches. Ask for a room with a balcony or ocean view.

A set-price dinner ($39/£21) offers great views of the cliff-diving show. The large, breezy lobby bar is a favorite spot to relax as day fades into night on the beautiful cove and bay. Nearby is a protected cove with good snorkeling.

Quebrada 74, 39300 Acapulco, Gro. ℭ **744/483-1221** for reservations. Fax 744/482-4564. www.hotelelmirador acapulco.com.mx. 132 units, including 9 junior suites with whirlpools. High season $185 (£102) double, $231 (£127) junior suite; low season $85 (£47) double, $110 (£61) junior suite. Add $13 (£7.15) for kitchenette. AE, MC, V. Street parking. **Amenities:** Restaurant; coffee shop; lobby bar; 3 outdoor pools, including 1 rather rundown saltwater pool; travel agency; room service; laundry service. *In room:* A/C, TV.

Inexpensive

Hotel Costa Linda *Value*

Budget-minded American and Mexican couples are drawn to the sunny, well-kept rooms of the Costa Linda, one of the best values in the area. All rooms have individually controlled air-conditioning and a minifridge, and some have a small kitchenette (during low season there is a $5/£2.75 charge for using the kitchenette). Closets and bathrooms are ample in size, and mattresses are firm. Cozy as the Costa Linda is, it is adjacent to one of the busier streets in Old Acapulco, so traffic noise can be bothersome. It's just a 1-block walk down to lively Caleta beach.

Costera Alemán 1008, 39390 Acapulco, Gro. ℭ **744/482-5277** or -2549. Fax 744/483-4017. 44 units. High season $100 (£55) double; low season $45 (£25) double. Children younger than 8 stay free in parent's room. MC, V. Free parking. **Amenities:** Restaurant; bar; small outdoor pool; tennis court; tour desk. *In room:* A/C, TV, minibar.

Hotel Los Flamingos ℭℭ *Finds*

An Acapulco landmark, Los Flamingos, perched on a cliff 150m (492 ft.) above Acapulco Bay, once entertained John Wayne, Cary Grant, Johnny Weissmuller, Fred McMurray, Errol Flynn, Red Skelton, Roy Rogers, and others. In fact, the stars liked it so much that at one point they bought it and converted it into a private club. The place is a real find in a kitschy campy sort of way—although the aged rooms are simple and lack modern luxuries, much of the hotel maintains the charm of a grand era. Photographs of the old movie stars line the hotel walls, and outdoor passages wind their way along the cliff overlooking the ocean. Most rooms have dramatic sea views and a large balcony or terrace, although few have air-conditioning and bathrooms are bare-bones. Thursdays at Los Flamingos are especially popular, with a *pozole* party and live music by a Mexican band that was probably around in the era of Wayne and Weissmuller—note the seashell-pink bass. Even if you don't stay here, plan to at least come for a margarita at sunset and a walk along the dramatic lookout point.

López Mateos s/n, Fracc. Las Playas, 39300 Acapulco, Gro. ℂ **744/482-0690.** Fax 744/483-9806. 40 units. High season $76 (£42) double, $95 (£52) superior double with A/C, $112 (£62) junior suite; low season $65 (£36) double, $78 (£43) superior double, $91 (£50) junior suite. AE, MC, V. **Amenities:** Restaurant; bar; outdoor pool; tour desk; car rental; room service; laundry service. *In room:* TV (in some), no phone.

Hotel Misión   Enter this hotel's plant-filled brick courtyard, shaded by two enormous mango trees, and you'll retreat into an earlier, more peaceful Acapulco. This tranquil 19th-century hotel lies 2 blocks inland from the Costera and the *zócalo.* The original L-shaped building is at least a century old. The rooms have colonial touches, such as colorful tile and wrought iron, and come simply furnished, with a fan and one or two beds with good mattresses. Breakfast is served on the patio.

Felipe Valle 12, 39300 Acapulco, Gro. ℂ **744/482-3643.** Fax 744/482-2076. 27 units. High season $50 (£28) double; low season $30 (£17) double. No credit cards. Limited free parking.

WHERE TO DINE

Diners in Acapulco enjoy stunning views and fresh seafood. The quintessential setting is a candlelit table with the glittering bay spread out before you. If you're looking for a romantic spot, Acapulco brims with such inviting places; most sit along the southern coast, with views of the bay. If you're looking for simple food or an authentic local dining experience, you're best off in Old Acapulco.

A deluxe establishment in Acapulco may not be much more expensive than a mass-market restaurant. The proliferation of U.S. franchise restaurants has increased competition, and even the more expensive places have reduced prices. Trust me—the locally owned restaurants offer the best food and the best value.

SOUTH OF TOWN: LAS BRISAS AREA
Very Expensive

Baikal ✹✹ FUSION/FRENCH/ASIAN   The exquisite and ultrahot Baikal is the best place in Acapulco for an over-the-top dining experience. You enter from the street, then descend a spiral staircase into the stunning bar and restaurant, awash in muted tan and cream colors of luxurious fabrics and natural accents of stone, wood, and water. The restaurant itself is constructed into the cliff, providing sweeping views of Acapulco Bay's glittering lights. The large dining room, with a two-story ceiling, has comfortable seating, including sofas that border the room. The creative menu combines fusion fare, and then adds a dash of Mexican flare. Start with the scallops in chipotle vinaigrette or the oriental-style salad. Notable entrees include steamed red snapper with lobster butter sauce, chicken breast rolled and stuffed with asparagus in a white-wine reduction, or medallions of New Zealand lamb in a sweet garlic sauce. The service is as impeccable as the presentation. There's also an extensive selection of wines, as well as live jazz and bossa nova music nightly. Periodically during the evening, large projector screens descend over the floor-to-ceiling glass windows and show short films of Old Acapulco or cavorting whales and dolphins, providing a brief reprise from conversation and dining. A fashionably late dining spot (expect a crowd at midnight), the attire is chic resort wear, as most patrons are headed to the clubs following dinner. Baikal also has wheelchair access, a private VIP dining room, a wine cellar, and an ample bar, ideal for enjoying a sunset cocktail or after-dinner drink. It's east of town on the scenic highway just before the entrance to the Las Brisas hotel.

Carretera Escénica 16 and 22. ℂ **744/446-6845** or -6867. www.baikal.com.mx. Reservations required (reservaciones@ baikal.com.mx). Main courses: $21–$74 (£12–£41). AE, MC, V. Sun–Thurs 7pm–1am, Fri–Sat 7pm–2am. Closed Mon during summer.

Moments **Dining with a View**

Restaurants with unparalleled views of Acapulco include **Baikal, Mezzanotte, Zibu,** and **Casa Nova** in the Las Brisas area, **El Olvido** along the Costera, **Su Casa** on a hill above the convention center, and the appropriately named **Bella Vista Restaurant** at the Las Brisas hotel.

Casa Nova ⟨R⟩ GOURMET ITALIAN   Enjoy an elegant though expensive meal and a fabulous view of glittering Acapulco Bay at this spot east of town. The cliffside restaurant offers several refined dining rooms, awash in marble and stone accents, and outdoor terrace dining with a stunning view. If you arrive before your table is ready, have a drink in the comfortable lounge. This is a long-standing favorite of Mexico City's elite; dress tends toward fashionable, tropical attire. The best dishes include veal scaloppine and homemade pastas, such as linguine with fresh clams. A changing tourist menu offers a sampling of the best selections for a fixed price. There's also an ample selection of reasonably priced national and imported wines. And there's live piano music nightly.

Carretera Escénica 5256. ⟨C⟩ **744/446-6237.** Reservations required. Main courses $28–$50 (£15–£28); fixed-price 4-course meal $39 (£21). AE, MC, V. Mon–Sat 7–11:30pm.

Mezzanotte Acapulco ⟨R⟩ ITALIAN   Mezzanotte offers a contemporary blending of classic Italian cuisines, but its strongest asset is the spectacular floor-to-ceiling view of the bay. This location has changed hands several times; it currently offers a mix of trendy international dishes served in an atmosphere that tries a bit too hard to be upscale and fashionable. Music is loud and hip, so if you're looking for a romantic evening, this is probably not the place. It's a better choice if you want a taste of Mexican urban chic. The view of the bay remains outstanding, though the food still strives for consistency. Dress up a bit for dining here. Mezzanotte is in the La Vista complex near the Las Brisas hotel.

Plaza La Vista, Carretera Escénica a Puerto Márquez 28-2. ⟨C⟩ **744/446-5727** or -5728. Reservations recommended. Main courses $20–$35 (£11–£19). AE, MC, V. Daily 6:30pm–midnight. Closed Mon during low season.

Zibu ⟨RRR⟩ SEAFOOD/THAI   With a gorgeous view over the sea, Zibu blends Mexican and Thai architectural and culinary styles to create a breathtaking dining experience. The open-air venue is furnished with rattan tables and chairs surrounded by warm lighting of candles, tiki torches, and lamps; a semi-circular pool serves as a moat between the ultrachic restaurant and *palapa*-topped lounge. Consider starting with the sea scallop carpaccio or sea bass tartare, and continue with the shrimp medallions with ginger and mango or grilled fish filet with almonds and soy (there are also meat dishes). The beautiful glass-enclosed wine cellar houses a well-balanced though expensive collection, including a thoughtful selection of French wines. Service is gracious and attentive, and Asian lounge and Thai music plays in the background.

Av. Escénica s/n, Fracc. Glomar. ⟨C⟩ **744/433-3058** or -3069. Reservations recommended. Main courses $14–$50 (£7.70–£28). AE, MC, V. Sun–Thurs 7pm–midnight; Fri–Sat 7pm–1am.

COSTERA HOTEL ZONE
Very Expensive
El Olvido ⟨RR⟩ FRENCH/MEXICAN   El Olvido gives you all the glittering bayview ambience of the posh Las Brisas restaurants, without the taxi ride. The menu is one of

the most sophisticated in the city. It's expensive, but each dish is delightful in presentation and taste. Start with 1 of the 12 house specialty drinks, such as Olvido, made with tequila, rum, Cointreau, tomato juice, and lime juice. Soups include delicious cold avocado, and thick black bean and chorizo. Among the innovative entrees are quail with honey and *pasilla* chiles, thick sea bass with a mild sauce of cilantro and avocado, and lamb chops with chipotle. For dessert, try chocolate fondue or *guanábana* (a tropical fruit) mousse in a rich *zapote negro* (black tropical fruit) sauce. El Olvido sits at the back of the Plaza Marbella shopping center fronting Diana Circle. Although the bay view is lovely, a drawback is that the dance clubs down the shoreline can often be heard after 10pm.

Glorieta Diana traffic circle, Plaza Marbella. © **744/481-0203**, -0256, or -0214. www.elolvido.com.mx. Reservations recommended. Main courses $15–$40 (£8.25–£22). AE, MC, V. Daily 6pm–midnight.

Su Casa/La Margarita 🍴🍴 INTERNATIONAL   Relaxed elegance and terrific food at reasonable prices are what you get at Su Casa. Owners Shelly and Angel Herrera created this pleasant, breezy, open-air restaurant on the patio of their hillside home overlooking the city (La Margarita is the indoor restaurant below Su Casa that's open during the rainy season). Both Shelly and Angel are experts in the kitchen and are on hand nightly to greet guests on the patio. The menu changes often. Some items are standard, such as shrimp *a la patrona* in garlic; grilled fish, steak, and chicken; and flaming *filet al Madrazo*, a delightful brochette marinated in tropical juices. Many entrees come with garnishes of cooked banana or pineapple. The margaritas are big and delicious. Su Casa is the hot-pink building on the hillside above the convention center.

V. Anahuac 110. © **744/484-4350** or -1261. Fax 744/484-0803. www.sucasa-acapulco.com. Reservations recommended. Main courses $17–$35 (£9.35–£19). MC, V. Daily 6pm–midnight.

Moderate
El Cabrito 🍴🍴 NORTHERN MEXICAN   With its hacienda-inspired entrance, waitresses in white dresses and *charro*-style neckties, and location in the heart of the Costera, this typical Mexican restaurant targets tourists. But its authentic and delicious food attracts Mexicans in the know—a comforting stamp of approval. Among its specialties are *cabrito al pastor* (roasted goat), *charro* beans, Oaxaca-style *mole,* and *burritos de machaca* (made with shredded beef). Bottles of beer are brought to your table in buckets of ice and then poured in frosty cold mugs. El Cabrito lies on the ocean side of the Costera, south of the convention center.

Costera Alemán 1480. © **744/484-7711**. Main courses $6.50–$18 (£3.60–£9.90). AE, MC, V. Daily 2pm–midnight.

Inexpensive
100% Natural 🍴 MEXICAN/HEALTH FOOD   Healthful versions of Mexican standards are the specialty at this clean, breezy, plant-filled restaurant, on the second level of the shopping center across from the Acapulco Plaza Hotel. (This chain has five other branches in Acapulco, including another one farther east on the Costera.) Especially notable are the fruit *licuados,* blended fresh fruit with your choice of yogurt or milk. Yogurt shakes, steamed vegetables, and cheese enchiladas are alternatives to their yummy sandwiches served on whole-grain breads. If you've over-indulged the night before, get yourself back on track here. It's wide selection of sandwiches and smoothies make this a great place for families.

Costera Miguel Alemán 200, across from the Costa Club Hotel. © **744/485-3982**. Sandwiches $5–$6; (£2.75–£3.30) other food items $5–$10. AE, MC, V. Daily 7am–11pm.

Ika Tako 🌟🌟 *Finds* SEAFOOD/TACOS These fresh fish, shrimp, and seafood tacos (served in combinations that include grilled pineapple, fresh spinach, grated cheese, garlic, and bacon) are so tasty that they're addicting. A spicy array of eight salsas accompanies them, and there are also excellent burritos, meat and chicken dishes, and vegetarian selections. Unlike most inexpensive places to eat, the setting is also lovely, with a handful of tables overlooking tropical trees and the bay below. The lighting may be bright, the atmosphere occasionally hectic, and the service dependably slow, but the tacos are delectable. You can also order beer, wine, soft drinks, and dessert. This restaurant is along the Costera, next to Beto's lobster restaurant. There's another branch across from the Hyatt Regency hotel that lacks the atmosphere of this one.

Costera Alemán 99. ✆ 744/484-9521. Main courses $5–$16 (£2.75–£8.80). AE, MC, V. Daily 5pm–3am.

DOWNTOWN: THE *ZOCALO* AREA

The old downtown area abounds with simple, inexpensive restaurants serving tasty eats. It's easy to pay more elsewhere and not get food as consistently good as you'll find in this part of town. To explore this area, start at the *zócalo* and stroll west along Juárez. After about 3 blocks, you'll come to Azueta, lined with small seafood cafes and street-side stands.

Moderate

El Amigo Miguel 🌟 *Finds* MEXICAN/SEAFOOD Locals know that El Amigo Miguel is a standout among downtown seafood restaurants—you can easily pay more elsewhere but not eat better. Impeccably fresh seafood reigns; the large, open-air dining room, 3 blocks west of the *zócalo,* is usually brimming with seafood lovers. When it overflows, head to a branch across the street, with the same menu. Try delicious *camarones borrachos* (drunken shrimp), in a sauce made with beer, ketchup, and bits of fresh bacon—it tastes nothing like the individual ingredients. *Filete Miguel* is a fresh fish filet (often red snapper or sea bass) stuffed with seafood and covered in a wonderful chipotle pepper sauce. Grilled shrimp with garlic and *mojo de ajo* (whole red snapper) are served at their classic best. Meat dishes are available, as well.

Juárez 31, at Azueta. ✆ 744/483-6981. Main courses $6.50–$15 (£3.60–£8.25). AE, MC, V. Daily 10am–9pm.

Mariscos Pipo 🌟 SEAFOOD Check out the photographs of Old Acapulco on the walls while relaxing in this airy dining room decorated with hanging nets, fish, glass buoys, and shell lanterns. The English-language menu lists a wide array of seafood,

---

Moments **If There's *Pozole*, It Must Be Thursday**

If you're visiting Acapulco on a Thursday, indulge in the local custom of eating *pozole*, a bowl of white hominy and meat in broth, garnished with sliced radishes, shredded lettuce, onions, oregano, and lime, served with crispy tostadas. The traditional version includes pork, but a newer chicken version has also become a standard. You can also find green *pozole*, which is made by adding a paste of roasted pumpkin seeds to the traditional *pozole* base. Green *pozole* is also traditionally served with a side of sardines. For a singular Acapulco experience, enjoy your Thursday *pozole* at the cliff-side restaurant of the Hotel Los Flamingos (see above).

including ceviche, lobster, octopus, crayfish, clams, baby-shark quesadillas, and fish prepared anyway you want. This local favorite is 2 blocks west of the *zócalo* on Breton, just off the Costera. Another bustling branch, open daily from 1 to 9:30pm, is at Costera Alemán and Canadá (© **744/484-0165**).

Almirante Breton 3. © **744/482-2237**. Main courses $8–$25 (£4.40–£14). AE, MC, V. Daily 11am–8pm.

ACAPULCO AFTER DARK

SPECIAL ATTRACTIONS   The **"Gran Noche Mexicana"** combines a performance by the Acapulco Ballet Folklórico with one by Los Voladores from Papantla (see chapter 12). It takes place in the plaza of the convention center Monday, Wednesday, and Friday at 7pm. With dinner and open bar, the show costs about $62 (£34); general admission (including three drinks) is $42 (£23). Call for reservations (© **744/435-0105**), or consult a local travel agency. Many major hotels also schedule Mexican fiestas and other theme nights that include dinner and entertainment. Local travel agencies will have information.

NIGHTCLUBS & DANCE CLUBS   Acapulco is even more famous for its nightclubs than for its beaches. Because clubs frequently change ownership—and often, names—it's difficult to give specific and accurate recommendations. But some general tips will help. Clubs have varying cover charges that are almost always higher for men. Drinks can cost anywhere from $5 to $15 (£2.75–£8.25). Don't even think about going out to one of the hillside dance clubs before 11pm, and don't expect much action until after midnight. But it will keep going until 4 or 5am, and possibly later.

Many dance clubs periodically waive their cover charge or offer some other promotion to attract customers. Look for promotional materials in hotel reception areas, at travel desks or concierge booths, in local publications, and on the beach.

The high-rise hotels have their own bars and sometimes dance clubs. Informal lobby or poolside cocktail bars often offer free live entertainment.

THE BEACH BAR ZONE   Prefer a little fresh air with your nightlife? The young, hip crowd favors the growing number of open-air oceanfront dance clubs along Costera Alemán, most of which feature techno or alternative rock. There's a concentration of them between the Fiesta Americana and Continental Plaza hotels. An earlier and more casual option to the glitzy dance clubs, these places include the jamming **Disco Beach** *** (© **744/484-8230**), **El Sombrero** (you'll know it when you see it), **Tabú,** and the pirate-themed **Barbaroja.** These mainly charge a cover (around $10/£5.50) and offer an open bar. Women frequently drink free or with a lesser charge (men may pay more, but then, this is where the beach babes are). Disco Beach is the most popular of the bunch and occasionally—such as during spring break—has live bands on the beachfront stage. Their Friday night foam parties are especially popular. Most of the smaller establishments do not accept credit cards; when they do, MasterCard and Visa are more widely accepted than American Express.

If you are brave enough—or inebriated enough—there's a **bungee jump** in the midst of the beach bar zone at Costera Alemán 101 (© **744/484-7529**). For $60 (£33) you get one jump, plus a T-shirt, diploma, and membership. Additional jumps are $20 (£11), and your fourth jump is free. For $90 (£50), you can jump as many times as you like from 4 to 11pm.

Alebrijes   Stadium seating, booths, and round tables surround the vast dance floor—the club (capacity 1,200) doubles as a venue for concerts and live performances by some of Mexico's most notable singers. Music includes pop, hip-hop, rock, and electronic music. The dress code forbids shorts, T-shirts, tennis shoes, flip-flops, and jeans. Average age here is late teens to early 20s. Open daily from 11pm to 5am. Costera Alemán 3308, across from the Hyatt Regency Acapulco. © 744/484-5902. Cover (including open bar with national drinks) $30 (£17) for women, $40 (£22) for men.

Baby-O ✰✰✰ This longtime Acapulco hot spot is a throwback to the town's heady disco days, although the music is exceptionally contemporary. The mid- to late-20s crowd dances to everything from house to hip-hop and techno to dance. Across from the Days Inn and Hooters, Baby-O has a dance floor surrounded by several tiers of tables and sculpted, cavelike walls, serviced by three bars. Drinks cost $5 to $7 (£2.75–£3.85). Three-dimensional laser shows and vapor effects keep the dancing going strong. Service is excellent. This is a high-class dance club attracting a beautiful clientele. It opens at 10:30pm, and you'd be wise to make a reservation. Costera Alemán 22. © 744/484-7474 or 481-1035. www.babyo.com.mx. Cover $20 (£11) for women, $60 (£33) for men.

Carlos 'n' Charlie's For fun, danceable music and good food, you can't go wrong with this branch of the Carlos Anderson chain. It's always packed. Come early and get a seat on the terrace overlooking the Costera. This is a great place to go for late dinner and a few drinks before moving on to a club. It's east of the Glorieta Diana traffic circle, across the street from the Fiesta Americana Condesa. It's open daily from 1pm to 1am. Costera Alemán 999. © 744/484-1285 or -0039. http://www.carlosandcharlies.com/acapulco/index.htm.

Mambo Café ✰✰ Part of a national chain, the vibrant Mambo Café hosts groups from the Dominican Republic, Cuba, Mexico, Venezuela, and Colombia. Sexy dancers swing their hips to salsa, merengue, cumbia, and pop. The tropical club attracts locals as well as tourists, and is considered the best Latin dance spot in town. Tables surround the dance floor, and patrons can order drinks by the glass or the bottle. Open Wednesday to Saturday from 10pm to 5am. Costera Alemán 1632. © 744/485-9688. www.gpofreedom.com.mx. Cover $8 (£4.40).

Mandara ✰✰ (Moments) Venture into this stylish chrome-and-neon extravaganza (formerly Enigma) perched on the side of the mountain for a true Acapulco nightlife experience. The plush, dim club has a sunken dance floor and panoramic view of the lights of Acapulco Bay. The club also has an intimate piano bar, Siboney, upstairs overlooking the dance floor; it has a special champagne menu and draws a more mature and moneyed crowd. The after-hours lounge Privado, also in the same building, opens its doors at 4:30am. Downstairs, there's pumped-in mood smoke, alternating with fresh oxygen to keep you dancing. Tight and slinky is the norm for women; no shorts for men. The club opens nightly at 10:30pm; fireworks rock the usually full house at 3am, which is when a stylized dance performance takes place on weekends, in the style of Euro clubs. Call to find out if you need reservations, this club tends to be busiest on Friday nights. Carretera Escénica, between Los Rancheros Restaurant and La Vista Shopping Center. © 744/446-5711 or -5712. www.acapulconightclubs.com (reservations: rsvpmandara@hotmail.com). Cover $30 (£17) for women, $40 (£22) for men, includes open bar; or pay $10 (£5.50) for entrance to Siboney, and purchase drinks separately.

Palladium ✰✰ This cliff-side club currently reigns as the top spot in town, and is found just down the road from Mandara. Generally, it welcomes a younger, rowdier crowd that enjoys the fabulous views and the dancing platforms set in the 50m-wide (164-ft.) glass windows overlooking the bay. Around 3:30am, Silver Man—complete with an Aztec headdress—performs, followed by a spray of fireworks outside the windows. Palladium has welcomed the world's finest DJs as special guests. The layout of the club is more open, which makes it easier than most places for meeting people. Carretera Escénica. ✆ **744/481-0330** or 446-5483. www.palladium.com.mx. Cover $30 (£17) for women, $40 (£22) for men, includes open bar.

Pepe's Piano Bar   Pepe's has surely been one of the most famous piano bars in the hemisphere, although it appears those days may be numbered. It has inspired patrons of all ages to sing their hearts out for decades, and it still draws a crowd, though it now caters to karaoke instead of piano—a big mistake, in my opinion. I keep hoping the owners will come to their senses and return to their roots. It's open Wednesday to Sunday from 10pm to 4am. Carretera Escénica, Comercial La Vista, Loc. 10. ✆ **744/446-5736.**

Salon Q   This place bills itself as "the cathedral of salsa," and it's a fairly accurate claim—Salon Q is *the* place to get down and enjoy the Latin rhythms. Frequently, management raises the cover and features impersonators of top Latin American musical acts. Open daily from 10pm to 4am. Costera Alemán 3117. ✆ **744/481-0114.** Cover $13–$25 (£7.15–£14).

2 Northward to Zihuatanejo & Ixtapa ✦

576km (357 miles) SW of Mexico City; 565km (350 miles) SE of Manzanillo; 253km (157 miles) NW of Acapulco

Side-by-side beach resorts, Ixtapa and Zihuatanejo share geography, but they couldn't be more different in character. Ixtapa is a model of modern infrastructure, services, and luxury hotels, while Zihuatanejo—"Zihua" to the locals—is the quintessential Mexican beach village. For travelers, this offers the intriguing possibility of visiting two distinct destinations in one vacation. Those looking for luxury should opt for Ixtapa (eex-*tah*-pah). You can easily and quickly make the 6.5km (4-mile) trip into Zihuatanejo for a sampling of the simple life in a *pueblo* by the sea. Those who prefer a more rustic retreat with real personality should settle in Zihuatanejo (see-wah-tah-*neh*-hoh). It's known for its long-standing community of Swiss and Italian immigrants, and its legendary beach playboys.

The area, with a backdrop of the Sierra Madre and a foreground of Pacific Ocean waters, provides a full range of activities and diversions. Scuba diving, deep-sea fishing, bay cruises to remote beaches, and golf are among the favorites. Nightlife in both towns borders on subdued; Ixtapa is the livelier.

This dual destination is the choice for the traveler looking for a little of everything, from resort-style indulgence to unpretentious simplicity. These two resorts are more welcoming to couples and adults than families, with a number of places that are off-limits to children younger than 16—something of a rarity in Mexico.

ESSENTIALS
GETTING THERE & DEPARTING
BY PLANE   These destinations tend to be even more seasonal than most resorts in Mexico. Flights are available year-round from U.S. gateways, but they operate less frequently in the summer. See chapter 2, "Planning Your Trip to Mexico," for information on flying to Ixtapa/Zihuatanejo from the United States and Canada. **AeroMéxico, Click Mexicana,** and **InterJet** fly daily from Mexico City. Here are the local numbers of some carriers: **AeroMéxico** (✆ 755/554-2018 or -2019), **Alaska Airlines** (✆ 755/554-8457), **Continental** (✆ 755/554-4219), **Click Mexicana** (✆ 01-800/112-5425 toll-free in Mexico), **InterJet** (✆ 01-800/011-2345 toll-free in

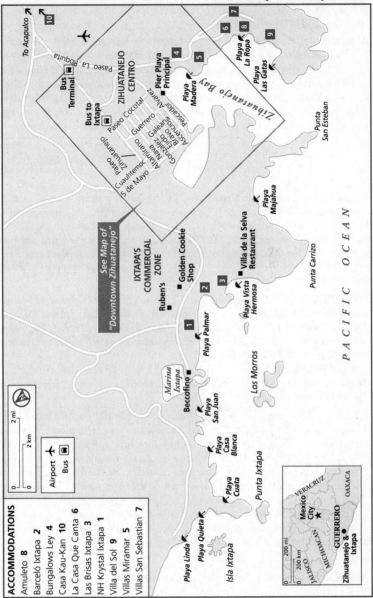

Zihuatanejo & Ixtapa Area

ACCOMMODATIONS

Amuleto **8**
Barceló Ixtapa **2**
Bungalows Ley **4**
Casa Kau-Kan **6**
La Casa Que Canta **6**
Las Brisas Ixtapa **3**
NH Krystal Ixtapa **1**
Villa del Sol **9**
Villas Miramar **5**
Villas San Sebastian **7**

Airport ✈
Bus ◼

To Acapulco

Paseo La Roquita

Bus Terminal
Bus to Ixtapa

ZIHUATANEJO CENTRO

Paseo Cocotal
Paseo Zihuatanejo

Álvarez
Ascencio
Bravo
Galeana
González
Guerrero
N. Bravo
Altamirano
Cuauhtémoc
15 de Mayo
pescador

Pier Playa Principal
Playa Madera

See Map of "Downtown Zihuatanejo"

Zihuatanejo Bay

Punta San Esteban

Playa La Ropa
Playa Las Gatas

Playa Majahua

4
5
6
7
8
9

IXTAPA'S COMMERCIAL ZONE

Ruben's ◼
Golden Cookie Shop ◼
Villa de la Selva Restaurant ◼

Playa Vista Hermosa

Punta Carrizo

2
3
1

Playa Palmar

Marina Ixtapa
Beccofino ◼

Playa San Juan

Los Morros

PACIFIC OCEAN

Playa Casa Blanca

Punta Ixtapa

Playa Cuata

Playa Quieta

Playa Linda

Isla Ixtapa

2 mi
2 km
0

200 mi
200 km
0

JALISCO
MICHOACÁN
GUERRERO
VERACRUZ
OAXACA
Mexico City ★
Zihuatanejo & Ixtapa ●

Tips Motorist Advisory

Motorists planning to follow Highway 200 northwest up the coast from Ixtapa or Zihuatanejo toward Lázaro Cárdenas and Manzanillo should be aware of reports of car and bus hijackings on that route, especially around Playa Azul, with bus holdups more common than car holdups. Before heading in that direction, ask locals and the tourism office about the status of the route. Don't drive at night. According to tourism officials, police and military patrols of the highway have increased, and the number of incidents has dropped dramatically.

Mexico), and **US Airways** (© 755/554-8634). Ask your travel agent about **charter flights** and packages.

The **Ixtapa/Zihuatanejo airport** (© **755/554-2070**) is about 11km (7 miles) and 15 minutes south of Zihuatanejo. Taxi fares are about $28 (£15). **Transportes Terrestres** *colectivos* (minivans) transport travelers to hotels in Zihuatanejo and Ixtapa and to Club Med; tickets cost $8 to $10 (£4.40–£5.50) and can be purchased just outside the baggage-claim area. Car-rental agencies with booths in the airport include **Hertz** (© **800/654-3131** in the U.S., or 755/554-2952), and **Budget** (© **800/527-0700** in the U.S., or 755/553-0397).

BY CAR   From Mexico City (about 8–9 hrs.), you can take **Highway 15** to Toluca, then **Highway 130/134** the rest of the way. On the latter road, highway gas stations are few. Another route is the four-lane **Highway 95D** to Iguala, then **Highway 51** west to **Highway 134.** A new toll road, **Highway 37** from Morelia to Ixtapa, cuts about an hour off the total trip time.

From Acapulco (2½–3 hr.) or Manzanillo (11 hr.), the only choice is the coastal **Highway 200.** The ocean views along the winding, mountain-edged drive from Manzanillo can be spectacular.

BY BUS   Zihuatanejo has two bus terminals: the **Central de Autobuses Estrella Blanca** (© 755/554-3477), Paseo Zihuatanejo at Paseo la Boquita, opposite the Pemex station and IMSS Hospital, from which most lines operate, and the **Estrella de Oro** station (© 755/554-2175), a block away. At the Central de Autobuses, several companies offer daily service to and from Acapulco, Puerto Escondido, Huatulco, Manzanillo, Puerto Vallarta, and other cities. At the other station, first-class Estrella de Oro buses run daily to Acapulco.

The trip from Mexico City to Zihuatanejo (bypassing Acapulco) takes 9 hours; from Acapulco, it's 4 to 5 hours. From Zihuatanejo, it's 6 or 7 hours to Manzanillo, and it's an additional 6 hours to Puerto Vallarta.

ORIENTATION

VISITOR INFORMATION   The **State Tourism Office** (©/fax **755/544-8361**) is in the center of Zihuatanejo on Galo 1, next to Plaza Kyoto; it's open Monday through Friday from 8am to 6pm and Saturday from 9am to 2pm. The **Zihuatanejo Tourism Office** (© **755/554-2001**; www.ixtapa-zihuatanejo.com) is on the main square by the basketball court at Alvarez; it's open Monday through Friday from 9am to 4pm and serves basic tourist-information purposes. The **Convention and Visitor's Bureau** is another source of information, it's in Ixtapa at Paseo de Las Gaviotas 12 (© **755/553-1270**; www.ixtapa-zihuatanejo.org).

CITY LAYOUT The fishing village and resort of **Zihuatanejo** spreads out around the beautiful Bay of Zihuatanejo, framed by downtown to the north and a beautiful long beach and the Sierra foothills to the east. The heart of Zihuatanejo is the waterfront walkway **Paseo del Pescador** (also called the *malecón*), bordering the Municipal Beach. Rather than a plaza, as in most Mexican villages, the town centerpiece is a **basketball court,** which fronts the beach. It's a point of reference for directions. The main thoroughfare for cars is **Juan Alvarez,** a block behind the *malecón.* Sections of several of the main streets are designated *zona peatonal* (pedestrian zone).

A cement-and-sand walkway runs from the *malecón* in downtown Zihuatanejo along the water to **Playa Madera.** The walkway is lit at night. Access to Playa La Ropa (Clothing Beach) is by the main road, **Camino a Playa La Ropa.** Playa La Ropa and Playa Las Gatas (Cats Beach) are connected only by boat.

A good highway connects Zihua to **Ixtapa,** 6km (4 miles) northwest. The 18-hole **Ixtapa Golf Club** marks the beginning of the inland side of Ixtapa. Tall hotels line Ixtapa's wide beach, **Playa Palmar,** against a backdrop of lush palm groves and mountains. Access is by the main street, **Bulevar Ixtapa.** On the opposite side of the main boulevard lies a large expanse of small shopping plazas (many with air-conditioned shops) and restaurants. At the far end of Bulevar Ixtapa, **Marina Ixtapa** has excellent restaurants, private yacht slips, and an 18-hole golf course. Condominiums and private homes surround the marina and golf course, and additional exclusive residential areas are rising in the hillsides past the marina on the road to Playa Quieta and Playa Linda. Ixtapa also has a paved bicycle track that begins at the marina and continues around the golf course and on toward Playa Linda.

GETTING AROUND Taxi fares are reasonable, but from midnight to 5am, rates increase by 50%. The average fare between Ixtapa and Zihuatanejo is $5.50 (£3). Within Zihua, the fare runs about $3 (£1.65); within Ixtapa it averages $3 to $5 (£1.65–£2.75). Radio cabs are available by calling © **755/554-3680** or -3311, however taxis are available from most hotels. A **shuttle bus** (35¢/20p) runs between Zihuatanejo and Ixtapa every 15 or 20 minutes from 5am to 11pm daily, but is almost always very crowded with commuting workers. In Zihuatanejo, it stops near the corner of Morelos/Paseo Zihuatanejo and Juárez, about 3 blocks north of the market. In Ixtapa, it makes numerous stops along Bulevar Ixtapa.

Note: The road from Zihuatanejo to Ixtapa is a broad, four-lane highway, which makes driving between the towns easier and faster than ever. Street signs are becoming more common in Zihuatanejo, and good signs lead in and out of both towns. However, both locations have an area called the Zona Hotelera (Hotel Zone), so if you're trying to reach Ixtapa's Hotel Zone, signs in Zihuatanejo pointing to that village's Hotel Zone may be confusing.

FAST FACTS: Zihuatanejo & Ixtapa

American Express The main office is in Av. Colegio Heróico Militar 38 in Plaza San Rafael, Loc. 7, Centro (© **755/544-6242;** fax 755/544-6242). It's open Monday through Friday from 9am to 6pm.

Area Code The telephone area code is **755.**

Banks Ixtapa's banks include **Bancomer,** in the La Puerta Centro shopping center. The most centrally located of Zihuatanejo's banks is **Banamex,** Cuauhtémoc 4. Banks change money during normal business hours, which are generally Monday through Friday from 9am to 3 or 5pm, Saturday from 10am to 1pm. ATMs and currency exchange are available during these and other hours.

Climate Summer is hot and humid, though tempered by sea breezes and brief showers; September is the peak of the tropical rainy season, with showers concentrated in the late afternoons.

Drugstore There's a branch of **Farmacías Coyuca** in Zihuatanejo, open from 8am to 11pm—hours that will also deliver; call ✆ **755/554-5390.**

Hospital **Hospital de la Marina Ixtapa** is at Bulevar Ixtapa s/n, in back of the artisans' market (✆ **755/553-0499**). In Zihuatanejo, there's the **Clinica Maciel** (✆ **755/554-2380;** La Palmas 12), or **Hospital Hernández Montejano,** Juan Alvarez s/n (✆ **755/554-5404**). Dial ✆ **065** from any phone for emergencies.

Internet Access Ixtapa has many Internet cafes. **Comunicación Mundial** is in Local 105 (✆ **755/553-1177**). Go to the back of the shopping center and take the stairs to the second level; Comunicación Mundial is to your right. The cost of Internet access is $3 (£1.65) per hour. Access is cheaper in Zihuatanejo; the most popular is **Zihuatanejo Bar Net,** Agustín Ramírez 9, on the ground floor of the Hotel Zihuatanejo Centro (✆ **755/554-3661**). Offering high-speed access for $2 (£1.10) per hour, it's open from 9am to 11pm daily.

Post Office The *correo* is in the SCT building, Edificio SCT, behind El Cacahuate in Zihuatanejo (✆ **755/554-2192**). It's open Monday through Friday from 8am to 6pm, Saturday from 9am to 1pm.

ACTIVITIES ON & OFF THE BEACH

The **Museo de Arqueología de la Costa Grande** (✆ 755/554-7552) traces the history of the area from Acapulco to Ixtapa/Zihuatanejo (the Costa Grande) from pre-Hispanic times, when it was known as Cihuatlán, through the colonial era. Most of the museum's pottery and stone artifacts give evidence of extensive trade with far-off cultures and regions, including the Toltec and Teotihuacán near Mexico City, the Olmec on the Pacific and Gulf coasts, and areas known today as the states of Nayarit, Michoacán, and San Luis Potosí. Local indigenous groups gave the Aztec tribute items, including cotton *tilmas* (capes) and *cacao* (chocolate), representations of which can be seen here. This museum, in Zihuatanejo near Guerrero at the east end of Paseo del Pescador, easily merits the half-hour or less it takes to stroll through; signs are in Spanish, but an accompanying brochure is available in English. Admission is $1, and it's open Tuesday through Sunday from 10am to 6pm.

THE BEACHES   In Zihuatanejo   At Zihuatanejo's town beach, **Playa Municipal,** the local fishermen pull their colorful boats up onto the sand, making for a fine photo op. The small shops and restaurants lining the waterfront are great for people-watching and absorbing the flavor of daily village life. **Playa Madera (Wood Beach),** just east of Playa Municipal, is open to the surf but generally peaceful. A number of attractive budget lodgings overlook this area.

All beaches in Zihuatanejo are safe for swimming. Undertow is rarely a problem, and the municipal beach is protected from the main surge of the Pacific. Beaches in Ixtapa are more dangerous for swimming, with frequent undertow problems.

South of Playa Madera is Zihuatanejo's largest and most beautiful beach, **Playa La Ropa** 🐱🐱, a long sweep of sand with a great view of the sunset. Some lovely small hotels and restaurants nestle in the hills; palm groves edge the shoreline. Although it's also open to the Pacific, waves are usually gentle. A taxi from town costs $3.50 (£1.90). The name Playa La Ropa (Clothing Beach) comes from an old tale of the sinking of a *galeón* during a storm. The silk clothing that it was carrying back from the Philippines washed ashore on this beach—hence the name.

The nicest beach for swimming, and the best for children, is the secluded **Playa Las Gatas (Cats Beach),** across the bay from Playa La Ropa and Zihuatanejo. The small coral reef just offshore is a nice spot for snorkeling and diving, and a little dive shop on the beach rents gear. Shop owner Jean Claude is a local institution—and the only full-time resident of Las Gatas. He claims to offer special rates for female divers and has a collection of bikini tops on display. The waters at Las Gatas are exceptionally clear, without undertow or big waves. Open-air seafood restaurants on the beach make it an appealing lunch spot. Small *pangas* (boats) with shade run to Las Gatas from the Zihuatanejo town pier, a 10-minute trip; the captains will take you across whenever you wish between 9am and 5pm for $3 (£1.65) round-trip. Usually the last boat back leaves Las Gatas at 6:30pm, but check to be sure.

Playa Larga is a beautiful, uncrowded beach between Zihuatanejo and the airport, with several small *palapa* restaurants, hammocks, and wading pools.

In Ixtapa Ixtapa's main beach, **Playa Palmar,** is a lovely white-sand arc on the edge of the Hotel Zone, with dramatic rock formations silhouetted in the sea. The surf can be rough; use caution, and don't swim when a red flag is posted. Several of the nicest beaches in the area are essentially closed to the public. Although by law all Mexican beaches are open to the public, it is common practice for hotels to create artificial barriers (such as rocks or dunes).

Club Med and Qualton Club have largely claimed **Playa Quieta,** on the mainland across from Isla Ixtapa. The remaining piece of beach was once the launching point for boats to Isla Ixtapa, but it is gradually being taken over by a private development. Isla Ixtapa–bound boats now leave from the jetty on **Playa Linda,** about 13km (8 miles) north of Ixtapa. Inexpensive water taxis ferry passengers to Isla Ixtapa. Playa Linda is the primary out-of-town beach, with watersports equipment and horse rentals available. **Playa las Cuatas,** a pretty beach and cove a few miles north of Ixtapa, and **Playa Majahua,** an isolated beach just west of Zihuatanejo, are both being transformed into resort complexes. Lovely **Playa Vista Hermosa** is framed by striking rock formations and bordered by the Las Brisas hotel high on the hill. All of these are very attractive beaches for sunbathing or a stroll but have heavy surf and strong undertow. Use caution if you swim here.

WATERSPORTS & BOAT TRIPS   Probably the most popular boat trip is to **Isla Ixtapa** for snorkeling and lunch at the El Marlin restaurant, one of several on the island. You can book this outing as a tour through local travel agencies, or go on your own from Zihuatanejo by following the directions to Playa Linda above and taking a boat from there. Boats leave for Isla Ixtapa every 10 minutes between 9am and 5pm, so you can depart and return as you like. The round-trip boat ride is $3 (£1.65). Along the way, you'll pass dramatic rock formations and see in the distance **Los Morros de**

Los Pericos islands, where a great variety of birds nest on the rocky points jutting out into the blue Pacific. On Isla Ixtapa, you'll find good snorkeling, diving, and other watersports. Gear is available for rent on the island. Be sure to catch the last water taxi back at 5pm, and double-check that time upon arrival on the island.

Local travel agencies can usually arrange day trips to Los Morros de Los Pericos islands for **birding,** though it's less expensive to rent a boat with a guide at Playa Linda. The islands are offshore from Ixtapa's main beach.

Sunset cruises on the sailboat *Picante,* arranged through **Yates del Sol** (© 755/554-2694 or -8270; www.picantecruises.com), depart from the Zihuatanejo town marina at Puerto Mío. The evening cruises cost $54 (£30) per person and include an open bar and hors d'oeuvres. There's also a "Sail and snorkel" day trip to **Playa Manzanillo** on the very comfortable, rarely crowded sailboat. It begins at 10am, costs $69 (£38) per person, and includes an open bar and lunch (snorkeling gear extra). Schedules and special trips vary, so call for current information.

You can arrange **fishing trips** with the **boat cooperative** (© 755/554-2056) at the Zihuatanejo town pier. They cost $150 to $450 (£83–£248), depending on boat size, trip length, and so on. Most trips last about 7 hours. The cooperative accepts Visa and MasterCard; paying cash saves you 20% tax, but don't expect a receipt. The price includes soft drinks, beer, bait, and fishing gear, but not lunch. You'll pay more for a trip arranged through a local travel agency. The least expensive trips are on small launches called *pangas;* most have shade. Both small-game and deep-sea fishing are offered. The fishing is adequate, though not on par with that of Mazatlán or Baja. Other trips combine fishing with a visit to the near-deserted ocean beaches that extend for miles along the coast. Sam Lushinsky at **Ixtapa Sport-fishing Charters,** 19 Depue Lane, Stroudsburg, PA 18360 (© 570/688-9466; fax 570/688-9554; www.ixtapasportfishing.com), is a noted outfitter. Prices range from $295 to $445 (£162–£245) per day, for 8 to 13m (26–42 ft.) custom cruisers, fully equipped. They accept MasterCard and Visa.

Boating and fishing expeditions from the new **Marina Ixtapa,** a bit north of the Ixtapa Hotel Zone, can also be arranged. As a rule, everything available in or through the marina is more expensive and more Americanized.

Sailboats, sailboards, and other **watersports equipment** rentals are usually available at stands on Playa La Ropa, Playa las Gatas, Isla Ixtapa, and at the main beach, Playa Palmar, in Ixtapa. There's **parasailing** at La Ropa and Palmar. **Kayaks** are available for rent at hotels in Ixtapa and some watersports operations on Playa La Ropa. **Villa del Sol** has a beach club in front of the hotel on La Ropa with sailboat, sailboard, and kayak rentals open to the public.

The PADI-certified **Carlo Scuba,** on Playa Las Gatas (© 755/554-6003; www.carloscuba.com), arranges **scuba-diving trips.** Fees start at $60 (£33) for a one-tank dive, or $80 (£44) for two dives, including all equipment and lunch. This shop has been around since 1962, and is very knowledgeable about the area, which has nearly 30 different dive sites, including walls and caves. Diving takes place year-round, though the water is clearest July to August and November to February, when visibility is 30m (100 ft.) or better. The nearest decompression chamber is in Acapulco. Advance reservations for dives are advised during Christmas and Easter.

Surfing is particularly good at **Petacalco Beach** north of Ixtapa.

GOLF, TENNIS & HORSEBACK RIDING In **Ixtapa,** the **Club de Golf Ixtapa Palma Real** (© 755/553-1062 or -1163), in front of the Barceló Hotel, has an 18-hole course designed by Robert Trent Jones, Jr. The greens fee is $80 (£44); caddies cost $20 (£11) for 18 holes, $15 (£8.25) for 9 holes; electric carts are $25 (£14); and clubs are $30 (£17). Tee times begin at 6:30am. The **Marina Ixtapa Golf Course** (© 755/ 553-1410; fax 755/553-0825), designed by Robert von Hagge, has 18 challenging holes. The greens fee is $80 (£44); carts cost $35 (£19); caddies cost $20 (£11), club rental is $35 (£19). The first tee time is 7am. Call for reservations 24 hours in advance. Both courses accept American Express, MasterCard, and Visa.

In Ixtapa, the **Club de Golf Ixtapa** (© 755/553-1062 or -1163) has lighted **public tennis courts**. Fees are $8 (£4.40) an hour during the day, $13 (£7.15) at night. Call for reservations. In Zihuatanejo, the hotel **Villa del Sol** (© 755/555-5500) has lit tennis courts open to the public for $20 (£11) an hour; private lessons cost $70 (£39) an hour.

For **horseback riding,** the largest local stable is on **Playa Linda** (no phone), offering guided trail rides from the Playa Linda beach (about 13km/8 miles north of Ixtapa). It's just next to the pier where the water taxis debark to Isla Ixtapa. Groups of three or more riders can arrange their own tour, which is especially nice around sunset (though you'll need mosquito repellent). Riders can choose to trace the beach to the mouth of the river and back through coconut plantations, or hug the beach for the entire ride (which usually lasts 1–1½ hr.). The fee is around $40 (£22), cash only. Travel agencies in either town can arrange your trip but will charge a bit more for transportation. Reservations are suggested in high season. Another good place to ride is in Playa Larga. There is a ranch on the first exit coming from Zihuatanejo (no phone, but you can't miss it—it is the first corral to the right as you drive toward the beach). The horses are in excellent shape. The fee is $40 (£22) for 1½ hours. To arrange riding in advance, call co-owner Ignacio Mendiola on his cellphone at © **755/559-8884.**

SHOPPING
ZIHUATANEJO

Zihuatanejo has its quota of T-shirt and souvenir shops, but it's becoming a better place to buy crafts, folk art, and jewelry. Shops are generally open Monday through Saturday from 10am to 2pm and 4 to 8pm. Many better shops close Sunday, but some smaller souvenir stands stay open, and hours vary.

The **artisans' market** on Calle Cinco de Mayo is a good place to start shopping before moving on to specialty shops. There's also a **municipal market** on Avenida Benito Juárez (about 5 blocks inland from the waterfront), but most vendors offer the same things—*huaraches,* hammocks, and baskets. The market sprawls over several blocks. Spreading inland from the waterfront some 3 or 4 blocks are numerous small shops well worth exploring.

Besides the places listed below, check out **Alberto's,** Cuauhtémoc 12 and 15 (no phone), for jewelry. Also on Cuauhtémoc, 2 blocks down from the Nueva Zelanda Coffee Shop, is a small shop that looks like a market stand and sells beautiful tablecloths, napkins, and other linens; all are handmade in Aguascalientes.

Casa Marina   This small complex extends from the waterfront to Alvarez near Cinco de Mayo and houses five shops, each specializing in handcrafted wares from all over Mexico. Items include handsome rugs, textiles, masks, colorful woodcarvings, and silver jewelry. Café Marina, the small coffee shop in the complex, sells shelves and shelves of used paperback books in several languages. Open daily from 9am to 9pm during the high season, 9am to 2pm and 5 to 9pm the rest of the year. Paseo del Pescador 9. © **755/554-2373.**

Coco Cabaña Collectibles   Next to Coconuts restaurant (p. 407), this impressive shop carries carefully selected crafts and folk art from across the country, including fine Oaxacan woodcarvings. Owner Pat Cummings once ran a gallery in New York, and the inventory reveals her discriminating eye. If you make a purchase, she'll cash your dollars at the going rate. Open Monday through Saturday from 10am to 2pm and 5 to 9pm; closed August and September. Guerrero 5 at Alvarez, opposite the Hotel Citali. © 755/554-2518.

Viva Zapatos   This shop carries bathing suits for every taste and shape, great casual and not-so-casual resort wear, sunglasses, and everything else for looking good in and out of the water. The store is 3 doors down from Apartamentos Amueblados Valle (see below). It's open Monday through Saturday from 10am to 2pm and 5 to 9pm. Vicente Guerrero 33. No phone.

IXTAPA

Shopping in Ixtapa is not especially memorable, with T-shirts and Mexican crafts the usual wares. **Ferrioni, Bye-Bye, Aca Joe,** and **Navale** sell brand-name sportswear. All of these shops are in the same area on Bulevar Ixtapa, across from the beachside hotels, and most are open daily from 9am to 2pm and 4 to 9pm.

La Fuente   This terrific shop carries gorgeous Talavera pottery, jaguar-shaped wicker tables, hand-blown glassware, masks, tin mirrors and frames, hand-embroidered clothing from Chiapas, and wood furniture. Open daily from 9am to 10pm during high season, daily from 10am to 9pm in low season. Los Patios Center, Bulevar Ixtapa. © 755/553-0812.

WHERE TO STAY

Larger high-rise hotels, including many all-inclusive resorts, dominate accommodations in Ixtapa and on Playa Madera. There are only a few choices in the budget range. If you're looking for lower-priced rooms, Zihuatanejo offers more selection and better values. Many long-term guests in Ixtapa and Zihuatanejo rent apartments and condos. **Lilia Valle** (© **755/554-2084** or 755/554-4649) is an excellent source for apartment and villa rentals. All lodgings in both towns offer free parking. The rates quoted below do not include the 17% tax.

ZIHUATANEJO

Some of the hotels in Zihuatanejo and its nearby beach communities are more economical than those in Ixtapa, while others are far more expensive and exclusive. The term "bungalow" is used loosely—it may mean an individual unit with a kitchen and bedroom, or just a bedroom. It may also be like a hotel, in a two-story building with multiple units, some of which have kitchens. It may be cozy or rustic, with or without a patio or balcony. Accommodations in town are generally very basic, though clean and comfortable.

Playa Madera and Playa La Ropa, separated by a craggy shoreline, are both accessible by road. Prices tend to be higher here than in town, but the value is much better, and people tend to find that the beautiful, tranquil setting is worth the extra cost. The town is 5 minutes away by taxi and 20 minutes by foot.

In Town
Apartamentos Amueblados Valle   These well-furnished apartments cost only as much as an inexpensive hotel room. Five one-bedroom units accommodate up to three people; the three two-bedroom apartments fit four comfortably. Units that do

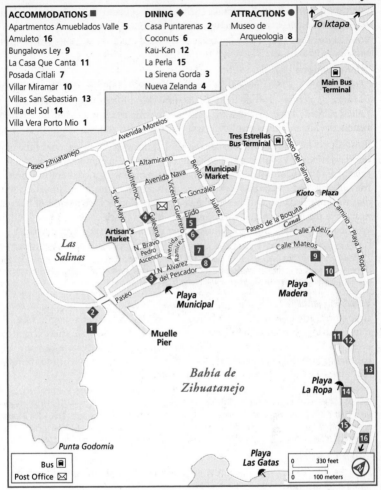

Downtown Zihuatanejo

ACCOMMODATIONS ■
Apartmentos Amueblados Valle **5**
Amuleto **16**
Bungalows Ley **9**
La Casa Que Canta **11**
Posada Citlali **7**
Villar Miramar **10**
Villas San Sebastián **13**
Villa del Sol **14**
Villa Vera Porto Mio **1**

DINING ◆
Casa Puntarenas **2**
Coconuts **6**
Kau-Kan **12**
La Perla **15**
La Sirena Gorda **3**
Nueva Zelanda **4**

ATTRACTIONS ●
Museo de
Arqueologia **8**

To Ixtapa

Main Bus Terminal

Avenida Morelos

Paseo Zihuatanejo

I. Altamirano

Cuauhtémoc

5 de Mayo

Galeana

Avenida Nava

Vicente Guerrero

Benito

C. González

Juárez

Tres Estrellas Bus Terminal

Paseo del Palmar

Municipal Market

Kioto   Plaza

Ejido

N. Bravo

Pedro Ascencio

Avenida Ramírez

J.N. Álvarez del Pescador

Artisan's Market

Las Salinas

Paseo de la Boquita

Canal

Calle Adelita

Calle Mateos

Camino a Playa la Ropa

Playa Municipal

Playa Madera

Paseo

Muelle Pier

Bahía de Zihuatanejo

Playa La Ropa

Punta Godomia

Playa Las Gatas

Bus ■
Post Office ✉

0   330 feet
0   100 meters

---

not face the street are less noisy than those that do. Each airy apartment is different; all have ceiling fans, private balconies, and kitchenettes. There's daily maid service, and a paperback-book exchange in the office. Owner Guadalupe Rodríguez and her son Luis Valle are good sources of information about cheaper apartments elsewhere, for long-term visitors. Reserve well in advance during high season. It's about 2 blocks from the waterfront.

Vicente Guerrero 33 (between Ejido and N. Bravo), 40880 Zihuatanejo, Gro. ② **755/554-2084.** Fax 755/554-3220. 8 units. High season $60 (£33) 1-bedroom apt, $90 (£50) 2-bedroom apt; low season $45 (£25) 1-bedroom apt, $80 (£44) 2-bedroom apt. Ask about low-season and long-term discounts. No credit cards. *In room:* Kitchenette, fan.

Posada Citlali   In this cheerful, three-story hotel, small rooms with fans surround a shaded, plant-filled courtyard that holds comfortable rockers and chairs. It's a good value for the price. Bottled water is in help-yourself containers on the patio. The stairway to the top two floors is narrow and steep.

Vicente Guerrero 3 (near Alvarez), 40880 Zihuatanejo, Gro. ℭ 755/554-2043. 19 units. $50 (£28) double. No credit cards. *In room:* No phone.

Playa Madera

Madera Beach is a 15-minute walk along the street, a 10-minute walk along the beach pathway, or a cheap taxi ride from Zihuatanejo. Most of the accommodations are on Calle Eva S. de López Mateos, the road overlooking the beach. Most hotels are set against the hill and have steep stairways.

Bungalows Ley   No two suites are the same at this small complex, one of the nicest on Playa Madera. If you're traveling with a group, you may want to book the most expensive suite (Club Madera); it has a rooftop terrace with a tiled hot tub, outdoor bar and grill, and spectacular view. All the units are immaculate; the simplest are studios with one bed and a kitchen in the same room. Rooms have terraces or balconies just above the beach, and all are decorated in Miami Beach colors. Bathrooms, however, tend to be small and dark. Guests praise the management and the service.

Calle Eva S. de López Mateos s/n, Playa Madera (Apdo. Postal 466), 40880 Zihuatanejo, Gro. ℭ 755/554-4087. Fax 755/554-1365. www.zihua.net/bungalosley. 8 units. $90 (£50) double with A/C; $170 (£94) 2-bedroom suite with kitchen (up to 4 persons). Low-season discounts available after 6 nights stay. No credit cards. Follow Mateos to the right up a slight hill; it's on your left. *In room:* A/C, TV.

Villas Miramar ⍟   This charming hotel with beautiful gardens offers a welcoming atmosphere, attention to detail, and superb cleanliness. Some of the elegant suites surround a shady patio that doubles as a restaurant. Those across the street center on a lovely pool and have private balconies and sea views. A terrace with a bay view has a bar that features a daily happy hour (5–7pm). TVs get cable channels, and the restaurant serves a basic menu for breakfast, lunch, and dinner.

Calle Adelita, Lote 78, Playa Madera (Apdo. Postal 211), 40880 Zihuatanejo, Gro. ℭ 755/554-2106 or -3350. Fax 755/554-2149. www.prodigyweb.net.mx/villasmiramar. 18 units. High season $95 (£52) suite, $100 (£55) oceanview suite, $190 (£105) 2-bedroom suite; low season $65 (£36) suite, $75 (£41) oceanview suite, $150 (£83) 2-bedroom suite. AE, MC, V. Free enclosed parking. Follow the road leading south out of town toward Playa La Ropa, take the 1st right after the traffic circle, and go left on Adelita. **Amenities:** Restaurant; bar; outdoor pool. *In room:* A/C, TV.

Playa La Ropa

Playa La Ropa is a 20- to 25-minute walk south of town on the east side of the bay, or it's a $3 taxi ride.

Amuleto ⍟⍟   Perched on a hill high above the beach, this intimate boutique hotel was designed for people who want to relax in luxury and exclusivity. Amuleto, which has only six units, boasts stunning panoramic views of Zihuatanejo Bay that make it seem like you're on top of the world. The *palapa*-covered restaurant serves innovative international food and overlooks a small infinity pool framed by the bay. Each of the bungalowlike units is individually decorated with Mexican and Asian designs using organic textures and earth colors. The *palapa* suite, for example, features meticulous stone, tile, and woodwork, a bed with 1,000-thread-count Egyptian cotton sheets, a separate sitting area with onyx lamps and bamboo chairs, a rooftop terrace with its own hammock surrounded by bougainvillea, and a private plunge pool. The eco-friendly hotel offers gourmet breakfasts and will customize dishes upon request.

Calle Escénica 9, Playa La Ropa, 40880 Zihuatanejo, Gro. ℭ 213/280-1037 in the U.S., or 755/544-6222. Fax 310/496-0286 in the U.S. www.amuleto.net. 6 units. High season $400–$700 (£220–£385) double; low season

$250–$550 (£138–£303) double. $100 (£55) extra person. AE, MC, V. **Amenities:** Restaurant; outdoor pool, gym, massage. *In room:* A/C, Wi-Fi, minibar.

La Casa Que Canta ✹✹✹   "The House that Sings" opened in 1992, an exclusive boutique hotel that sits on a mountainside overlooking Zihuatanejo Bay. Its striking molded-adobe architecture typifies the rustic-chic style known as Mexican Pacific, with gentle music that plays across the different walkways. Individually decorated rooms have handsome natural-tile floors, unusual painted Michoacán furniture, antiques, and stretched-leather *equipale*-style chairs and tables with hand-loomed fabrics throughout. All of the romantic accommodations offer large, beautifully furnished terraces with bay views. Hammocks hang under the thatched-roof terraces. Most of the spacious units are suites, and 10 of them have private pools. Rooms meander up and down the hillside, and while no staircase is terribly long, there are no elevators. An adjacent private villa, El Murmello, holds four suites, all with private plunge pools. A "well-being" center has been added, offering massage, spa services, and yoga. La Casa Que Canta sits off the road leading to Playa La Ropa, but not on any beach (Playa La Ropa is down a steep hill). The hotel's service is remarkably gracious, and you'll find La Casa Que Canta pretty close to heaven.

Camino Escénico a Playa La Ropa, 40880 Zihuatanejo, Gro. Ⓒ **888/523-5050** in the U.S., or 755/555-7000, -7030, or 554-6529. Fax 755/554-7900. www.lacasaquecanta.com. 21 units. $435–$785 (£239–£432) double; 5-night minimum stay required Jan–Apr. AE, MC, V. Children younger than 16 not accepted. **Amenities:** Small restaurant; bar; freshwater outdoor pool on main terrace; saltwater outdoor pool on bottom level; room service; laundry service. *In room:* A/C, minibar.

Villa del Sol ✹✹✹   A magnificent and timeless resort that caters to guests looking for exclusivity, Villa del Sol sits on one of Mexico's most beautiful beaches. Suites feature one or two bedrooms, living areas, large terraces, and private plunge pools. Rooms are decorated with modern Mexican touches and include comfy lounges, excellent reading lights, CD players, and hammocks that beckon at siesta time. There are 11 beachside suites and one presidential suite. Those units that don't overlook the beach surround a fountain-filled lagoon and tropical gardens with enchanted lighting at night. Service is refined and gracious; fresh flower petals are artistically arranged on guest beds in the evenings. A member of the Small Luxury Hotels of the World, Villa del Sol allows children only in two-bedroom suites and generally has a quiet feel. The meal plan (breakfast and dinner) is mandatory during the winter high season and includes an excellent variety of cuisine. In addition to the exquisite beach area, pools, restaurants, and bars, Villa del Sol offers a full-service spa, tennis courts, and beach club. You can even request a massage on the sand.

Playa la Ropa (Apdo. Postal 84), 40880 Zihuatanejo, Gro. Ⓒ **888/389-2645** in the U.S., or 755/555-5500. Fax 755/554-2758. www.hotelvilladelsol.com. 70 units. High season $365–$1,400 (£201–£770) double; low season $300–$1,100 (£165–£605) double. Meal plan $60 (£33) per person during high season (mandatory), or $45 (£25) during summer (optional). AE, MC, V. **Amenities:** 2 open-air beachside restaurants; 3 bars; 3 outdoor pools (including 18m/59-ft. lap pool); 2 tennis courts; full-service spa; tour desk; car rental; salon; room service. *In room:* A/C, TV, Wi-Fi, minibar, hair dryer, safe.

Villas San Sebastián   On the mountainside above Playa La Ropa, this nine-villa complex offers great views of Zihuatanejo's bay. The villas surround tropical vegetation and a central swimming pool. Each has a kitchenette and a spacious private terrace, and some have air-conditioning. The personalized service is one reason these villas come so highly recommended; owner Luis Valle, whose family has lived in this community for decades, is always available to help guests with any questions or needs.

Bulevar Escénico Playa La Ropa (across from the Dolphins Fountain). ✆ **755/554-4154**. Fax 755/554-3220. 11 units. High season $155 (£85) 1-bedroom villa, $275 (£151) 2-bedroom villa; low season $115 (£63) 1-bedroom villa, $165 (£91) 2-bedroom villa. No credit cards. **Amenities:** Outdoor pool. *In room:* A/C (some units); kitchenette.

Playa Zihuatanejo

Casa Kau-Kan 𝒦𝒦 Casa Kau-Kan is an upscale bohemian oasis on the long, secluded beach of Playa Larga. It's located about 20-minutes south of Zihuatanejo on the open Pacific Ocean. The spacious bungalowlike accommodations surrounded by palm trees feature private sitting areas, canopied beds, and bamboo furnishings; four have private terrace pools. Owned by Ricardo Rodriguez who also runs Kau-Kan restaurant (see review on p. 407), the hotel serves delicious fresh seafood. There's not much to do in the immediate surroundings except tan, swim, eat, read, and enjoy the quiet lazy days, although horseback riding is also offered on the beach immediately in front. You should be an experienced swimmer to go in the ocean here, which typically has waves perfect for body-surfing. Hotel service is friendly and extremely attentive (whether it's a coconut or a cocktail you desire, it'll be right up).

Playa Larga s/n, 40880 Zihuatanejo, Gro. ✆ **755/113-1379**. Fax 755/553-8168. www.casakaukan.com. 9 units. High season $120–$235 (£66–£129) double; low season $90–$200 (£50–£110) double. AE, MC, V. Children younger than 15 not accepted. **Amenities:** Restaurant; pool. *In room:* A/C.

IXTAPA
Expensive

Barceló Ixtapa 𝒦 *Kids* This grand 12-story all-inclusive resort hotel (formerly the Sheraton) has large, handsomely furnished public areas facing the beach; it's an inviting place to sip a drink and people-watch. Most rooms have balconies with views of the ocean or the mountains. Nonsmoking rooms are available. Gardens surround the large pool, which has a swim-up bar and a separate section for children. It's an excellent value and a great choice for families.

Bulevar Ixtapa, 40880 Ixtapa, Gro. ✆ **755/555-2000**. Fax 755/553-2438. www.barcelo.com. 341 units. High season $380 (£209) double all-inclusive; low season $275 (£151) double all-inclusive. AE, DC, MC, V. **Amenities:** 4 restaurants; lobby bar; nightclub; beachside pool; 3 tennis courts; fitness room; concierge; travel agency; car rental; salon; room service; laundry service; rooms for those w/limited mobility. *In room:* A/C, TV, minibar.

Las Brisas Ixtapa 𝒦𝒦 Set above the high-rise hotels of Ixtapa on a rocky promontory, Las Brisas is the best of Ixtapa's resorts. Notable for its striking stepped architecture, beautiful beach cove, and gracious service, Las Brisas features large stone and stucco public areas, minimalist guest rooms with Mexican-tile floors and plant-decked patios with hammocks, and multitier swimming pools with waterfalls. All rooms face the hotel's gorgeous private beach, which can be accessed by an elevator; although enticing, the water is often rough and can be dangerous for swimming. The six master suites come with private pools, and the 16th floor is reserved for nonsmokers. The hotel could use an upgrade but remains the best option in Ixtapa. Internet specials are usually available.

Bulevar Ixtapa s/n, 40880 Ixtapa, Gro. ✆ **888/559-4329** in the U.S., or 755/553-2121. Fax 755/553-1091. www. brisas.com.mx. 423 units. High season $285 (£157) deluxe double, $490 (£270) Royal Beach Club; low season $196 (£108) deluxe double, $230 (£127) Royal Beach Club. AE, MC, V. **Amenities:** 4 restaurants; 3 bars (including lobby bar w/live music at sunset); 4 outdoor pools (1 for children); 4 lighted tennis courts w/pro on request; fitness center; travel agency; car rental; shopping arcade; salon; room service; massage; babysitting; laundry service; rooms for those w/limited mobility; elevator to secluded beach. *In room:* A/C, TV, minibar, hair dryer, safe.

NH Krystal Ixtapa 𝒦 *Kids* Krystal hotels are known in Mexico for quality rooms and service, and this was the original hotel in the chain. It upholds its reputation for attentive service and is particularly welcoming toward families. Many staff members have been with the NH Krystal for its 20-some years of operation and are on hand to greet return guests. This large, V-shaped hotel has ample grounds and a terrific pool area. Most of the spacious guest rooms feature oceanview balconies and tile bathrooms, while master suites have larger balconies that double as living areas. Some rates include breakfast buffet. The center of Ixtapa nightlife is here, at Krystal's famed **Christine** dance club.

Bulevar Ixtapa s/n, 40880 Ixtapa, Gro. ℂ **888/726-0528** in the U.S., or 755/553-0333. Fax 755/553-0216. www.nh-hotels.com. 255 units. High season $224 (£123) double, $280 (£154) suite; low season $150 (£83) double, $230 (£127) suite. 2 children younger than 12 stay free in parent's room. Ask about special packages. AE, DC, MC, V. **Amenities:** 4 restaurants; lobby bar; nightclub; outdoor pool; gym; kids' club; travel agency; car rental; salon; room service; massage; laundry service. *In room:* A/C, TV, minibar.

WHERE TO DINE
ZIHUATANEJO

Zihuatanejo's **central market,** on Avenida Benito Juárez about 5 blocks inland from the waterfront, will whet your appetite for cheap and tasty food. It's best at breakfast and lunch, before the market activity winds down in the afternoon. Look for what's hot and fresh. The market area is one of the best on this coast for shopping and people-watching.

Expensive

Coconuts 🏵🏵 *Finds* INTERNATIONAL/SEAFOOD   What a find! Not only is the food innovative and delicious, but the restaurant is also in a historic building—the oldest in Zihuatanejo. This popular restaurant in a tropical garden was the weigh-in station for Zihua's coconut industry in the late 1800s. "Fresh" is the operative word on this creative, seafood-heavy menu. Chef David Dawson checks what's fresh at the market, then uses only top-quality ingredients in dishes like seafood pâté and grilled filet of snapper Coconuts. The bananas flambé (for two) has earned a loyal following, with good reason. Expect friendly, efficient service here.

Augustín Ramírez 1 (at Vicente Guerrero). ℂ 755/554-2518 or -7980. Reservations recommended. Main courses $12–$28 (£6.60–£15). AE, MC, V. High season daily 6–11pm. Closed July–Sept (rainy season).

Kau-Kan 🏵🏵🏵 NUEVA COCINA/SEAFOOD   A stunning view of the bay is one of the many attractions of this beautiful restaurant. Stucco and whitewashed walls frame the simple, understated furniture. Head chef Ricardo Rodriguez supervises every detail, from the ultrasmooth background music that invites after-dinner conversation to the spectacular presentation of all the dishes. Baked potato with baby lobster and mahimahi carpaccio are two of my favorites, but I recommend you consider the daily specials—Ricardo always uses the freshest seafood and prepares it with great care. For dessert, pecan and chocolate cake served with dark-chocolate sauce is simply delicious. If you're looking for a romantic dinner outside your hotel, reserve a candlelit table at Kau-Kan and try to arrive in time for the sunset.

Camino a Playa La Ropa. ℂ 755/554-8446. Reservations recommended. Main courses $10–$34 (£5.50–£19). AE, MC, V. Daily 5–10:30pm. From downtown on the road to La Ropa, Kau-Kan is on the right side of the road past the 1st curve.

Inexpensive

Casa Puntarenas MEXICAN/SEAFOOD   A modest spot with a tin roof and nine wooden tables, Puntarenas is one of the best places in town for fried whole fish served with toasted *bolillos* (crusty white-bread miniloaves), sliced tomatoes, onions, and avocado. The place is renowned for chiles rellenos, mild and stuffed with plenty of cheese; the meat dishes are less flavorful. Although it may appear a little too rustic for less experienced travelers, it is very clean, and the food is known for its freshness.

Calle Noria, Col. Lázaro Cárdenas. No phone. Main courses $5–$10 (£2.75–£5.50). No credit cards. Daily 6:30–9pm. From the pier, turn left on Alvarez and cross the footbridge on your left; turn right after you cross the bridge; the restaurant is on your left.

La Sirena Gorda MEXICAN   For one of the most popular breakfasts in town, head to La Sirena Gorda. "The Fat Mermaid," as it translates to in English, serves a variety of eggs and omelets, hotcakes with bacon, and fruit with granola and yogurt. The house specialty is seafood tacos—fish in a variety of sauces, plus lobster—but I consider them overpriced, at $6 and $23 (£3.30 and £13) respectively. A taco is a taco is a . . . you know. I'd recommend something from the short list of daily specials, such as blackened red snapper, steak, or fish kebabs. The food is excellent, and patrons enjoy the casual sidewalk-cafe atmosphere. Illustrations of colorful fat mermaids decorate the walls.

Paseo del Pescador. (℃ 755/554-2687. Breakfast $2–$5.50 (£1.10–£3); main courses $6–$15 (£3.30–£8.25). MC, V. Thurs–Tues 8am–10:30pm. From the basketball court, face the water and walk to the right; La Sirena Gorda is on your right just before the town pier.

Nueva Zelanda MEXICAN   This open-air snack shop serves rich cappuccino sprinkled with cinnamon, fresh-fruit *licuados* (milkshakes), and pancakes with real maple syrup. The mainstays of the menu are *tortas* and enchiladas, and service is friendly and efficient. There's a second location in Ixtapa, in the back section of the Los Patios shopping center (℃ 755/553-0838).

Cuauhtémoc 23 (at Ejido). (℃ 755/554-2340. *Tortas* $3.50 (£1.90); enchiladas $6 (£3.30); *licuados* $2.50 (£1.40); cappuccino $2.50 (£1.40). No credit cards. Daily 8am–10pm. From the waterfront, walk 3 blocks inland on Cuauhté-moc; the restaurant is on your right.

Playa Madera & Playa La Ropa

La Perla SEAFOOD   There are many *palapa*-style restaurants on Playa La Ropa, but La Perla, with tables under the trees and thatched roof, is the most popular. Somehow, the long stretch of pale sand and the group of wooden chairs under *palapas* combine with mediocre food and slow service to make La Perla a local tradition. Rumor has it that it is so hard to get the waiters' attention that you can get take-out food from a competitor and bring it here to eat, and they'll never notice. Still, it's considered the best spot for tanning and socializing.

Playa La Ropa. (℃ 755/554-2700. Breakfast $4–$6.50 (£2.20–£3.60); main courses $7.50–$24 (£4.15–£13). AE, MC, V. Daily 10am–10pm; breakfast served 10am–noon. Near the southern end of La Ropa Beach, take the right fork in the road; there's a sign in the parking lot.

IXTAPA
Very Expensive
Villa de la Selva ♔ MEXICAN/MEDITERRANEAN   Clinging to the edge of a cliff overlooking the sea, this elegant, romantic restaurant enjoys the most spectacular sea and sunset view in Ixtapa. The candlelit tables occupy three terraces; try to come early to get one of the best vistas, especially on the lower terrace. The cuisine is delicious, artfully presented, and classically rich. Filet Villa de la Selva is red snapper topped with shrimp and hollandaise sauce. Tortilla soup or hot lobster bisque makes a good beginning; finish with chocolate mousse or bananas Singapore.

Paseo de la Roca. © 755/553-0362. www.villadelaselva.com. Reservations recommended during high season. Main courses $19–$40 (£10–£22). AE, MC, V. Daily 6–11pm. Closed Sept.

Expensive

Beccofino ✿✿✿ NORTHERN ITALIAN   This restaurant is a standout in Mexico. Owner Angelo Rolly Pavia serves the flavorful northern Italian specialties he grew up knowing and loving. The menu is strong on pasta. Ravioli, a house specialty, comes stuffed with seafood (in season). The garlic bread is terrific, and there's an extensive wine list. A popular place in a breezy marina location, the restaurant tends to be loud when it's crowded, which is often. It's also an increasingly popular breakfast spot.

Marina Ixtapa. © 755/553-1770. Breakfast $4.50–$10 (£2.50–£5.50); main courses $16–$48 (£8.80–£26). AE, MC, V. Daily 9:30am–midnight.

Inexpensive

Golden Cookie Shop ✿ PASTRIES/INTERNATIONAL   Golden Cookie's freshly baked goods beg for a detour, and the coffee menu is the most extensive in town. Although prices are high for the area, the breakfasts are noteworthy, as are the deli sandwiches. Nutritional cookies, breads, pastries, and cakes are available, as well as vegetarian and low-carb selections. Large sandwiches on fresh soft bread come with a choice of sliced meats. An air-conditioned area is reserved for nonsmokers.

Los Patios Center. © 755/553-0310. www.goldencookieshop.com.mx. Breakfast $4–$6 (£2.20–£3.30); sandwiches $4–$6 (£2.20–£3.30); main courses $6–$8.50 (£3.30–£4.70). MC, V. Daily 8am–2:30pm. Go to the second floor of "Los Patios" commercial center, turn left, and you'll see the restaurant on your right.

Ruben's ✿✿ *Finds* BURGERS/VEGETABLES   The choices are easy here—you can order either a big, juicy burger made from top sirloin grilled over mesquite, or a foil-wrapped packet of baked potatoes, chayote, zucchini, or sweet corn. Ice cream, beer, and soda round out the menu, which is posted on the wall by the kitchen. It's kind of a do-it-yourself place: Patrons snare a waitress and order, grab their own drinks from the cooler, and tally their own tabs. Still, because of the ever-present crowds, it can be a slow process.

Centro Comercial Flamboyant. © 755/553-0027 or -0358. Burgers $4–$5 (£2.20–£2.75); vegetables $2 (£1.10); ice cream $1.50 (85p). No credit cards. Daily 11am–midnight.

ZIHUATANEJO & IXTAPA AFTER DARK

With an exception or two, Zihuatanejo nightlife dies down around 11pm or midnight. For a good selection of clubs, dance spots, hotel fiestas, special events, and fun watering holes with live music and dancing, head for Ixtapa. Just keep in mind that the shuttle bus stops at 11pm, and a taxi to Zihuatanejo after midnight costs 50% more than the regular price. During the off season (after Easter and before Christmas), hours vary: Some places open only on weekends, while others close completely. In Zihuatanejo, a lively bar showing satellite TV sports, is **Bandido's,** at the intersection of Cinco de Mayo and Pedro Ascencio in Zihuatanejo Centro, across from the Artisans' Market (© 755/553-8072). It features live music Wednesday through Saturday, and is open nightly until 2am, but is closed on Sunday from May to October. A popular hangout for local residents and expats is **Rick's Bar,** Av. Cuatemoc 5, in Zihuatanejo Centro (© 755/554-2535). On Friday's, it's known for its live music jam sessions, open to anyone wanting to share their unique talents. It's open Monday through Saturday from 7pm to midnight.

THE CLUB & MUSIC SCENE

Many dance clubs stay open until the last customers leave, so closing hours depend upon revelers. Most dance clubs have a ladies' night at least once a week—admission and drinks are free for women.

Carlos 'n' Charlie's   Knee-deep in nostalgia, bric-a-brac, silly sayings, and photos from the Mexican Revolution, this restaurant/nightclub offers party ambience and good food. The eclectic menu includes iguana in season (with Alka-Seltzer and aspirin on the house). Out back by the beach is a partly shaded open-air section with a raised wooden platform for "pier" dancing at night. The recorded rock 'n' roll mixes with sounds of the ocean surf. The restaurant is open daily from 10am to midnight; pier dancing is nightly from 9pm to 3am. Bulevar Ixtapa, just north of the Best Western Posada Real, Ixtapa. ✆ 755/553-0085. Cover (including drink tokens) after 9pm $10 (£5.50). No cover Sun–Fri during off season.

Christine   This glitzy streetside dance club is famous for its midnight light show, which features classical music played on a mega sound system. A semicircle of tables in tiers overlooks the dance floor. No sneakers, flip-flops, or shorts are allowed, and reservations are recommended during high season. Open Wednesday to Saturday at 10pm. Off-season hours vary. In the NH Krystal, Bulevar Ixtapa, Ixtapa. ✆ 755/553 0333. Cover free–$20 (£11).

Señor Frog's   A companion restaurant to Carlos 'n' Charlie's, Señor Frog's has several dining sections and a warehouselike bar with raised dance floors. Large speakers play electronic, rock, and Latin music, sometimes even prompting dinner patrons to shimmy by their tables between courses. The restaurant is open daily from 6 to 11:30pm; the bar stays open until 3am. In the La Puerta Center, Bulevar Ixtapa, Ixtapa. ✆ 755/553-2282. Friday cover $10 (£5.50).

Zen   This is Ixtapa's most progressive nocturnal option. Music includes acid jazz, drum and bass, and ambient, in a sleek setting. It draws a young, hip crowd. Bulevar Ixtapa, next to the Radisson Hotel. ✆ 755/553-0003 or -0293. Cover free–$10 (£5.50).

HOTEL FIESTAS & THEME NIGHTS

A number of hotels hold Mexican fiestas and other special events that include dinner, drinks, live music, and entertainment for a fixed price (generally $44/£24). The **Barceló Ixtapa** (✆ 755/555-2000) stages a popular Wednesday night fiesta; the **Dorado Pacífico** (✆ 755/553-2025) in Ixtapa hosts a Tuesday night fiesta. Only the Barceló Ixtapa offers them in the off season. Call for reservations or visit a travel agency for tickets, and be sure you understand what the price covers, as drinks, tax, and tip are not always included.

3 Puerto Escondido ★★★

368km (228 miles) SE of Acapulco; 240km (149 miles) NW of Salina Cruz; 80km (50 miles) NW of Puerto Angel

I consider Puerto Escondido (*pwer*-toh es-cohn-*dee*-doh) the best overall beach value in Mexico, and it retains the same casual beach feel that's drawn people here for decades. Although it has long been known as one of the world's top surf sites, today it's broadening its appeal. Think alternative therapies, great vegetarian restaurants, hip nightlife, awesome hotel and dining values, and some of the best coffee shops in Mexico. It's a place for those whose priorities include the dimensions of the surf break (big), the temperature of the beer (cold), the strength of the coffee (espresso), and the

Puerto Escondido

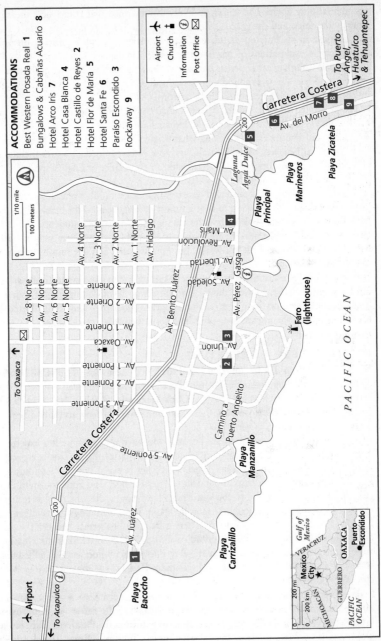

ACCOMMODATIONS

Best Western Posada Real **1**
Bungalows & Cabañas Acuario **8**
Hotel Arco Iris **7**
Hotel Casa Blanca **4**
Hotel Castillo de Reyes **2**
Hotel Flor de María **5**
Hotel Santa Fe **6**
Paraíso Escondido **3**
Rockaway **9**

Airport ✈
Church ✝■
Information ⓘ
Post Office ⊠

1/10 mile
100 meters

Av. 4 Norte
Av. 3 Norte
Av. 2 Norte
Av. 1 Norte
Av. Hidalgo

Av. 8 Norte
Av. 7 Norte
Av. 6 Norte
Av. 5 Norte

Av. 3 Oriente
Av. 2 Oriente
Av. 1 Oriente
Av. Oaxaca

Av. 1 Poniente
Av. 2 Poniente
Av. 3 Poniente
Av. 5 Poniente

Av. Benito Juárez

To Oaxaca →

Carretera Costera

To Acapulco ⓘ

Airport ✈

Av. Juárez

Playa Bacocho

Playa Carrizalillo

Playa Manzanillo

Camino a Puerto Angelito

Playa Principal

Av. Unión

Av. Soledad
Av. Libertad
Av. Revolución
Av. Maris
Av. Pérez Gasga

Faro (lighthouse)

Playa Marineros

Playa Zicatela

Carretera Costera

Av. del Morro

To Puerto Angel, Huatulco & Tehuantepec →

Laguna Agua Dulce

PACIFIC OCEAN

Gulf of Mexico
VERACRUZ
MICHOACÁN
OAXACA
GUERRERO
Mexico City ★
Puerto Escondido
PACIFIC OCEAN
200 mi
200 km

optimal tanning angle. The young and very aware crowd that comes here measures time by the tides, and the pace is relaxed.

The location of "Puerto," as the locals call it, makes it an ideal jumping-off point for ecological explorations of neighboring jungle and estuary sanctuaries, as well as indigenous mountain settlements. Increasingly, it attracts those seeking both spiritual and physical renewal, with abundant massage and bodywork services, yoga classes, and exceptional and varied healthful dining options.

People come from the United States, Canada, and Europe to stay for weeks and even months—easily and inexpensively. Expats have migrated here from Los Cabos, Acapulco, and Puerto Vallarta seeking what originally attracted them to their former homes—stellar beaches, friendly locals, and low prices. Added pleasures include an absence of beach vendors and time-share sales, an abundance of English speakers, and terrific, inexpensive dining and nightlife.

This is a real place, not a produced resort. A significant number of visitors are European travelers, and it's common to hear a variety of languages on the beach and in the bars. Puerto Escondido is also a favorite among Mexican college students. Solo travelers will probably make new friends within an hour of arriving. There are still surfers here, lured by the best break in Mexico, but espresso cafes and live music are becoming just as ubiquitous.

The city has been dismissed as a colony of former hippies and settled backpackers, but it's so much more. I have a theory that those who favor Puerto are just trying to keep the place true to its name (*escondido* means "hidden") and undiscovered by tourists. Don't let them trick you—visit, and soon, before it, too, changes.

ESSENTIALS
GETTING THERE & DEPARTING

BY PLANE **Aero Tucán** (© **954/582-3461**), and **Aerovega** (© **954/582-0151**) operate daily morning flights to and from Puerto Escondido on small planes; the fare is about $150 (£83) each way to Oaxaca. **Click Mexicana** (© **01-800/112-5425** toll-free in Mexico; www.click.com.mx) flies jets to and from Mexico City daily. The price is about $200 (£110) each way.

If flights to Puerto Escondido are booked, you have the (possibly less expensive) option of flying into **Huatulco** on a scheduled or charter flight. This is especially viable if your destination is Puerto Angel, which lies between Puerto Escondido and Huatulco. An airport taxi costs about $80 to Puerto Angel, and approximately $130 (£72) to Puerto Escondido. If you can find a local taxi, rather than a government-chartered cab, you can reduce these fares by about 50%, including the payment of a $5 (£2.75) mandatory airport exit tax. There is frequent bus service between the three destinations. **Budget** (© **958/581-9000** or 800/527-0700 in U.S) at the Huatulco airport, has cars available for one-way travel to Puerto Escondido, with an added drop charge of about $50 (£28). In Puerto Escondido, Budget is at the entrance to Bacocho (© **954/582-0312**).

Arriving: The Puerto Escondido **airport** (airport code: PXM) is about 4km (2½ miles) north of the center of town, near Playa Bacocho. The *colectivo* (**minibus**) to hotels costs $3.50 (£1.90) per person. **Aerotransportes de Pasajeros Turistas de Oaxaca** sells *colectivo* tickets to the airport through **Turismo Dimar Travel Agency** (©/fax **954/582-0737** or -2305) on Avenida Pérez Gasga (the pedestrian-only zone) next to Hotel Casa Blanca. The minibus will pick you up at your hotel.

BY CAR   From Oaxaca, **Highway 175** via Pochutla is the least bumpy road. The 240km (149-mile) trip takes 5 to 6 hours. **Highway 200** from Acapulco is also a good road and should take about 6 hours to travel. However, this stretch of road has been the site of numerous car and bus hijackings and robberies at night in recent years—travel only during the day.

From Salina Cruz to Puerto Escondido is a 5-hour drive, past the Bahías de Huatulco and the turnoff for Puerto Angel. The road is paved but can be rutty during the rainy season. The trip from Huatulco to Puerto Escondido takes just under 2 hours; you can easily hire a taxi for a fixed rate of about $50 (£28) an hour.

BY BUS   Buses run frequently to and from Acapulco and Oaxaca, and south along the coast to and from Huatulco and Pochutla, the transit hub for Puerto Angel. The main bus station for **Estrella Blanca, Oaxaca Pacífico,** and **Estrella del Valle** is the **Central Camionera,** just north of the city center. First-class buses go from here to Huatulco, Oaxaca, and Mexico City. Several buses also leave daily for Pochutla, Salina Cruz (5 hr.), and Oaxaca (7 hr. via second-class bus). **Cristóbal Colón** buses (© 954/ 582-1073) serve Salina Cruz, Tuxtla Gutiérrez, San Cristóbal de las Casas, and Oaxaca.

Arriving: Minibuses from Pochutla or Huatulco will let you off anywhere, including the spot where Pérez Gasga leads down to the pedestrians-only zone.

ORIENTATION
VISITOR INFORMATION   The **State Tourist Office, SEDETUR** (© 954/582-0175), which has a very helpful staff, is less than 1km (a half mile) from the airport at the corner of Carretera Costera and Bulevar Benito Juárez. It's open Monday through Friday from 9am to 7pm, Saturday from 10am to 2pm. A tourist kiosk at the west end of the Adoquín (in town center) is open Monday through Saturday from 9am to 1pm.

CITY LAYOUT   Looking out on the Bahía Principal and its beach, to your left you'll see the eastern end of the bay, consisting of a small beach, **Playa Marineros,** followed by rocks jutting into the sea. Beyond this is **Playa Zicatela,** unmistakably the main surfing beach. Zicatela Beach has come into its own as the most popular area for visitors, with restaurants, bungalows, surf shops, and hotels, well back from the shoreline. The west side of the bay, to your right, is about 1.5km long (1 mile), with a lighthouse and a long stretch of fine sand. Beaches on this end are not quite as accessible by land, but hotels are overcoming this difficulty by constructing beach clubs reached by steep private roads and jeep shuttles.

The town of Puerto Escondido has roughly an east-west orientation, with the long Zicatela Beach turning sharply southeast. Residential areas behind Zicatela Beach tend to have unpaved streets; the older town, with paved streets, is north of the Carretera Costera (Hwy. 200). The streets are numbered; Avenida Oaxaca divides east *(oriente)* from west *(poniente),* and Avenida Hidalgo divides north *(norte)* from south *(sur).*

South of this is the original **tourist zone,** through which Avenida Pérez Gasga makes a loop. Part of this loop is a paved pedestrians-only zone, known locally as the Adoquín, after the hexagonal bricks used in its paving. Hotels, shops, restaurants, bars, travel agencies, and other services are all here. In the morning, taxis, delivery trucks, and private vehicles may drive here, but at noon it closes to all but foot traffic.

Avenida Pérez Gasga angles down from the highway at the east end; on the west, where the Adoquín terminates, it climbs in a wide northward curve to cross the highway, after which it becomes Avenida Oaxaca.

The beaches—Playa Principal in the center of town and Marineros and Zicatela, southeast of the town center—are connected. It's easy to walk from one to the other, crossing behind the separating rocks. Puerto Angelito, Carrizalillo, and Bacocho beaches are west of town and accessible by road or water. Playa Bacocho is where you'll find the few more expensive hotels.

GETTING AROUND   Almost everything is within walking distance of the Adoquín. **Taxis** around town are inexpensive; call © **954/582-0990** or -0955 for service.

It's easy to hire a boat and possible to walk beside the sea from the Playa Principal to the tiny beach of Puerto Angelito, though it's a bit of a hike.

FAST FACTS: Puerto Escondido

Area Code The telephone area code is **954.**

Currency Exchange Banamex, Bancomer, Banorte, and HSBC all have branches in town, and all will change money during business hours; hours vary, but you can generally find one of the above open Monday through Saturday from 9am to 3pm. ATMs are also available, as are currency-exchange offices.

Drugstore **Farmacía de Más Ahorro,** Avenida 1 Norte at Avenida 2 Poniente (© **954/582-1911**), is open until 2am.

Hospital **Unidad Médico–Quirúrgica del Sur,** Av. Oaxaca 113 (© **954/582-1288**), offers 24-hour emergency services and has English-speaking staff and doctor. The number for the **Emergency Response Team** is (© **954/540-3816**).

Internet Access On Zicatela Beach, **Internet Acuario** is a small, extremely busy Internet service at the entrance to the Bungalows & Cabañas Acuario, Calle de Morro s/n (© **954/582-1026**). It's open daily from 8am to 10pm and charges just $1.50 per hour.

Post Office The *correo,* on Avenida Oaxaca at the corner of Avenida 7 Norte (© **954/582-0959**), is open Monday through Friday from 8am to 3pm.

Safety Depending on whom you talk to, you need to be wary of potential beach muggings, primarily at night. Lighting at Playa Principal and Playa Zicatela has caused the crime rate to drop considerably. Local residents say most incidents happen after tourists overindulge and then go for a midnight stroll along the beach. Puerto is so casual that it's an easy place to let your guard down. Don't carry valuables, and use common sense and normal precautions.

Also, respect the power of the magnificent waves here. Drownings occur all too frequently.

Seasons Season designations are somewhat arbitrary, but most consider high season to be from mid-December to January, around and during Easter week, July and August, and other school and business vacations.

Telephones Numerous businesses offer long-distance telephone service. Many are along the Adoquín; several accept credit cards. The best bet remains a prepaid Ladatel phone card.

WHAT TO SEE & DO IN PUERTO ESCONDIDO

BEACHES   **Playa Principal,** where small boats are available for fishing and tour services, and **Playa Marineros,** adjacent to the town center on a deep bay, are the best swimming beaches. Beach chairs and sun shades rent for about $5 (£2.75), which may be waived if you order food or drinks from the restaurants that offer them. **Playa Zicatela,** which has lifeguards and is known as the "Mexican Pipeline," adjoins Playa Marineros and extends southeast for several kilometers. The surfing part of Zicatela, with large curling waves, is about 4km (2½ miles) from the town center. Due to the size and strength of the waves, it's not a swimming beach, and only experienced surfers should attempt to ride Zicatela's powerful waves. Stadium-style lighting has been installed in both of these areas, in an attempt to crack down on nighttime beach muggings. It has diminished the appeal of the Playa Principal restaurants—patrons now look into the bright lights rather than at the sea. Lifeguard service has recently been added to Playa Zicatela, although the lifeguards are known to go on strike.

Barter with one of the fishermen on the main beach for a ride to **Playa Manzanillo** and **Puerto Angelito,** two beaches separated by a rocky outcropping. Here, and at other small coves just west of town, swimming is safe and the overall pace is calmer than in town. You'll also find *palapas,* hammock rentals, and snorkeling equipment. The clear blue water is perfect for snorkeling. Local entrepreneurs cook fresh fish, tamales, and other Mexican dishes right at the beach. Puerto Angelito is also accessible by a road that's a short distance from town, so it tends to be busier. You can also take a cab to the cliff above **Playa Carrizalillo,** and descend one hundred odd stone stairs to a calm and secluded swimming beach. **Playa Bacocho** is on a shallow cove (dangerous for swimming) farther northwest and is best reached by taxi or boat rather than on foot. It's also the location of the Villa Sol Beach Club. A charge of $10 (£5.50) gives you access to pools, food and beverage service, and facilities.

SURFING   **Zicatela Beach,** 2.5km (1½ miles) southeast of Puerto Escondido's town center, is a world-class surf spot. A surfing competition in August and Fiesta Puerto Escondido, held for at least 3 days each November, celebrate Puerto Escondido's renowned waves. There is also a surfing exhibition and competition in February, for Carnaval. The tourism office can supply dates and details. Beginning surfers often start out at Playa Marineros before graduating to Zicatela's awesome waves, although you will see intermediate surfers out at **La Punta,** at the southernmost end of Playa Zicatela. The waves and strong currents make Zicatela dangerous for swimming.

NESTING RIDLEY TURTLES   The beaches around Puerto Escondido and Puerto Angel are nesting grounds for the endangered Ridley turtle. During the summer, tourists, on lucky occasions, can see the turtles laying eggs or observe the hatchlings trekking to the sea.

Escobilla Beach near Puerto Escondido seems to be the favored nesting grounds of the Ridley turtle. In 1991, the Mexican government established the Centro Mexicano la Tortuga, known locally as the **Turtle Museum.** On view are examples of all species of marine turtles living in Mexico, plus six species of freshwater turtles and two species of land turtles. The center (© 958/584-3376) lies on **Mazunte Beach** ⸙, near the town of the same name. Hours are Wednesday through Saturday from 10am to 4:30pm, and Sunday from 10am to 2:30pm; suggested donation is $3 (£1.65). If you come between July and September, ask to join an overnight expedition to Escobilla Beach to see mother turtles scuttle to the beach to lay their eggs. The museum is near a unique shop that sells excellent naturally produced soaps, shampoos, bath oils, and

Ecotours & Other Adventurous Explorations

An excellent provider of ecologically oriented tour services is **Rutas de Aventura** ⟨ⅆ⟩, Hotel Santa Fe (ℂ **954/582-0170**; rutasdeaventura@gmail.com). Gustavo Boltjes speaks fluent English and offers kayak adventures, hiking excursions, and mountain-bike tours. He also leads waterfall hikes, camping trips, and agro-tourism adventures to learn about local farming and coffee production.

Turismo Dimar Travel Agency, on the landward side just inside the Adoquín (ℂ **954/582-0737** or -2305; fax 954/582-1551; www.viajesdimar.com; daily 8am–9pm), is another excellent source of information and can arrange all types of tours and travel. Manager Gaudencio Díaz Martinez speaks English and can arrange individualized tours or more organized ones, such as **Michael Malone's Hidden Voyages Ecotours.** Malone, a Canadian ornithologist, leads dawn and sunset trips in high season (winter) to **Manialtepec Lagoon,** a bird-filled mangrove lagoon about 20km (12 miles) northwest of Puerto Escondido. The tour ($40/£22) includes a stop on a secluded beach for a swim.

One of the most popular all-day tours offered by both companies is to **Chacahua Lagoon National Park,** about 65km (40 miles) west. It costs $45 (£25) with Dimar, $52 (£29) with Michael Malone. These are true ecotours—small groups treading lightly. You visit a beautiful sandy spit of beach and the lagoon, which has incredible bird life and flowers, including black orchids. Locals provide fresh barbecued fish on the beach. If you know Spanish and get information from the tourism office, it's possible to stay overnight under a small *palapa,* but bring plenty of insect repellent.

An interesting and slightly out-of-the-ordinary excursion is **Aventura Submarina,** Av. Pérez Gasga 601A, in front of the tourism office (ℂ **954/582-2353**). Jorge, who speaks fluent English and is a certified scuba instructor, guides individuals and small groups of qualified divers along the Coco trench just offshore. The price is $60 (£33) for a two-tank dive. This outfit offers a refresher scuba course at no extra charge. Jorge also arranges surface activities such as deep-sea fishing, surfing, and trips to lesser-known yet nearby swimming beaches. **Omar** (ℂ **954/559-4406**) offers dolphin watching tours in high season (winter).

Fishermen keep their colorful *pangas* (small boats) on the beach beside the Adoquín. A **fisherman's tour** around the coastline in a *panga* costs about $39 (£21), but a ride to Puerto Angelito beaches is only $5 (£2.75). Most hotels offer or will gladly arrange tours to meet your needs.

other personal-care products. All are made and packaged by the local community as part of a project to replace lost income from turtle poaching. Buses go to Mazunte from Puerto Angel about every half-hour, and a taxi ride is around $5.50 (£3). You can fit this in with a trip to Zipolite Beach (see "A Trip to Puerto Angel: Backpacking

Beach Haven," later in this chapter). Buses from Puerto Escondido don't stop in Mazunte; you can cover the 65km (40 miles) in a taxi or rental car.

The tourism cooperative at **Ventanilla** provides another chance to get up close to the turtles. The villagers here have created their own ecological reserve that encompasses a nearby lagoon, inhabited by crocodiles and dozens of species of birds, and a beach where sea turtles lay their eggs. A boat ride to see the crocs costs $4 and nothing on the menu at the restaurant is over $7. Turtles lay their eggs here year round, although summer is the prime season, so there's always a possibility that a nest is about to hatch. Helping the locals release the eggs is free. Ventanilla is a $2 taxi ride from Mazunte or the nearby beaches, but if you're planning on staying after sunset, ask your driver to wait, since it's a long walk in the dark back to the main highway.

GUIDED WALKING TOURS   For local information and guided walking tours, visit the **Oaxaca Tourist Bureau** booth (© 954/582-0276; ginainpuerto@yahoo.com). It's just west of the pedestrian street. Ask for Gina, who speaks excellent English and is incredibly helpful. She provides information with a smile, and many say she knows more about Puerto Escondido than any other person. On her days off, Gina offers walking tours to the market and to little-known nearby ruins. Filled with history and information on native vegetation, a day with Gina promises fun, adventure, and insight into local culture.

A Mixtec ceremonial center was discovered in early 2000 just east of Puerto Escondido and is considered a major discovery. The site covers many acres with about 10 pyramids and a ball court, with the pyramids appearing as hills covered in vegetation. A number of large carved stones have been found. Situated on a hilltop, it commands a spectacular view of Puerto Escondido and the Pacific coast. The large archaeological site spans several privately owned plots of land and is not open to the public, although Gina has been known to offer a guided walking tour to it.

SHOPPING

During high season, businesses and shops are generally open all day. During low season, many close between 2 and 4pm.

The Adoquín holds a row of tourist shops selling straw hats, postcards, and T-shirts, plus a few excellent shops featuring Guatemalan, Oaxacan, and Balinese clothing and art. You can also get a tattoo or rent surfboards and boogie boards. Interspersed among the shops, hotels, restaurants, and bars are pharmacies and minimarkets. The largest of these is **Oh! Mar,** Av. Pérez Gasga 502. It sells anything you'd need for a day at the beach, plus phone (Ladatel) cards and Cuban cigars.

Also of interest is **Bazar Santa Fe** 𝒦𝒦, Hotel Santa Fe lobby, Calle del Morro s/n, Zicatela Beach (© 954/582-0170), a small shop that sells antiques, vintage Oaxacan embroidered clothing, jewelry, religious artifacts, and gourmet local coffee. At either location of **Bikini Brazil,** Playa Zicatela, Calle del Morro s/n (© 954/582-2333), and on the Adoquín (© 954/582-0568), you'll find the hottest bikinis under the sun imported from Brazil, land of the *tanga* (string bikini). Another cool beach shop on Playa Zicatela, Calle del Moro s/n, is **Trapoy y Harapos** (© 954/582-0759), which sells bathing suits, sandals, and surfboards. The first surf shop in Puerto Escondido, **Central Surf** (© 954/582-2285; www.centralsurfshop.com), on Zicatela Beach, Calle del Morro s/n, rents and sells surfboards, offers surf lessons, and sells related gear, including custom-made surf trunks. Nearby, the **360 Surf Shop** sells everything for your out-of-town surf needs, and sells, trades, and rents boards. They don't have a phone number, but you can e-mail them at **360@puertoconnection.com**. Board rentals usually go for about $10 to $20 (£5.50–£11) per day, with lessons available for $60 (£33) for 2 hours. In front of the Rockaway Resort on Zicatela Beach, there's a 24-hour **minisuper** (no phone) that sells the necessities: beer, suntan lotion, and basic food.

WHERE TO STAY

The rates posted below do not include the 17% tax.

MODERATE

Best Western Posada Real *(Kids)*   On a cliff top overlooking the beach, the expanse of manicured lawn that backs this all-inclusive hotel is one of the most popular places in town for a sunset cocktail. The smallish standard rooms are less enticing than the hotel grounds. A big plus here is Coco's Beach Club, with a 1km (half-mile) stretch of soft-sand beach, large swimming pool, playground, and bar with occasional live music. A shuttle ride (or a lengthy walk down a set of stairs) will take you there. This is a great place for families, and it's open to the public (nonguests pay $2.50/£1.40 to enter). The hotel lies 5 minutes from the airport and about the same from Puerto Escondido's tourist zone, but you'll need a taxi to get to town. Rates include breakfast, lunch, dinner, and unlimited domestic drinks, tips, and taxes.

Av. Benito Juárez 1, Fracc. Bacocho, 71980 Puerto Escondido, Oax. ℭ **800/528-1234** in the U.S., or 954/582-0237. Fax 954/582-0192. www.posadareal.com.mx. 100 units. High season $130 (£72) double; low season $105 (£58) double. AE, MC, V. Free parking. **Amenities:** 2 restaurants; lobby bar; beach club w/food service; 2 outdoor pools; wading pool; putting green; tennis court; travel agency; car rental; laundry service. *In room:* A/C, TV, hair dryer, safe.

Hotel Santa Fe *★★★* *(Finds)*   If Puerto Escondido is the best beach value in Mexico, then the Santa Fe is without a doubt one of the best hotel values in Mexico. It boasts a winning combination of unique Spanish-colonial style, a welcoming staff, and comfortable if basic rooms. The hotel has grown up with the surfers who came to Puerto in the 1960s and 1970s and nostalgically return today. It's about 1km (a half mile) southeast of the town center, off Highway 200, at the curve in the road where Marineros and Zicatela beaches join—a prime sunset-watching spot. The three-story hacienda-style buildings have clay-tiled stairs, archways, and blooming bougainvillea. They surround two courtyard swimming pools. The ample but simply styled rooms feature large tile bathrooms, colonial furnishings, hand-woven fabrics, and both air-conditioning and ceiling fans. Most have a balcony or terrace, and the master and presidential suites enjoy ocean views. Bungalows are next to the hotel; each has a living room, kitchen, and bedroom with two double beds. The restaurant (see "Where to Dine," below) is one of the best on the southern Pacific coast.

Calle del Morro (Apdo. Postal 96), 71980 Puerto Escondido, Oax. ℭ **954/582-0170** or -0266. Fax 954/582-0260. www.hotelsantafe.com.mx. 61 units, 8 bungalows. High season $165 (£91) double, $180 (£99) junior suite, $260 (£143) suite, $175 (£96) bungalow; low season $120 (£66) double, $155 (£85) junior suite, $260 (£143) suite, $130 (£72) bungalow. AE, MC, V. Free parking. **Amenities:** Restaurant; bar; 3 outdoor pools; tour service; car rental; massage; babysitting; laundry. *In room:* A/C, TV, safe.

Paraíso Escondido *★★* *(Finds)*   This eclectic inn is hidden away on a shady street a couple of short blocks from the Adoquín and Playa Principal. A curious collection of Mexican folk art, masks, religious art, and paintings make this an exercise in Mexican magic realism, in addition to a tranquil place to stay. An inviting pool—surrounded by gardens, Adirondack chairs, and a fountain—affords a commanding view of the bay. The colonial-style rooms each have one double and one twin bed, a built-in desk, tile floors, a small bathroom, and a cozy balcony or terrace with French doors. The suites have much plusher decor than the rooms, with recessed lighting, desks set into bay windows, living areas, and large private balconies. The penthouse suite has a kitchenette, a tile chessboard inlaid in the floor, and murals adorning the walls—it is the owners' former apartment.

Calle Unión 10, 71980 Puerto Escondido, Oax. ℂ 954/582-0444. 25 units. $65 (£36) double; $120 (£66) suite; $150 (£83) penthouse suite. No credit cards. Free parking. **Amenities:** Restaurant; bar; outdoor pool. *In room:* A/C, TV.

INEXPENSIVE

Bungalows & Cabañas Acuario 🎯   Facing Zicatela Beach, this surfer's sanctuary offers cheap accommodations plus an on-site gym, surf shop, and Internet cafe. The two-story hotel and bungalows surround a pool shaded by great palms. Rooms are small and basic; bungalows offer basic kitchen facilities but don't have air-conditioning. The cabañas are more open and have hammocks. The adjoining retail area has public telephones, money exchange, a pharmacy, and a vegetarian restaurant. If you're traveling during low season, you can probably negotiate a better deal than the rates listed below once you're there.

Calle del Morro s/n, 71980 Puerto Escondido, Oax. ℂ 954/582-0357. Fax 954/582-1027. www.oaxaca-mio.com/bunacuario.htm. 40 units. High season $57 (£31) double, $69 (£38) double with A/C, $110 (£61) bungalow; 20% less in low season. No credit cards. Free parking. **Amenities:** Restaurant; Internet cafe; well-equipped gym; outdoor pool; Jacuzzi; tour desk. *In room:* No phone except in suite and 2 bungalows.

Hotel Arco Iris 🎯 *Value*   Rooms at the Arco Iris occupy a three-story colonial-style house that faces Zicatela Beach. Each is simple yet comfortable, with a spacious terrace or balcony with hangers for hammocks to rent—all have great views, but the upstairs ones are better (12 units include kitchenettes). Beds come draped with mosquito nets, with bedspreads made using beautifully worked Oaxacan textiles. The restaurant/bar features one of the most popular happy hours in town, daily from 5:30 to 7:30pm, with live music during high season. Hotel Arco Iris is often packed.

Calle del Morro s/n, Playa Zicatela, 71980 Puerto Escondido, Oax. ℂ 954/582-2344 and -1494 Fax 954/582-2963. www.puertoconnection.com/arco.html. 35 units. $55–$75 (£30–£41) double, $60–$80 (£33–£44) double with kitchen. Extra person $4 (£2.20). Rates 10%–20% higher at Easter and Christmas. MC, V. Ample free parking for cars and campers. **Amenities:** Restaurant; bar; outdoor pool; wading pool; TV/game room w/foreign channels; tour desk. *In room:* No phone.

Hotel Casa Blanca 🎯 *Value*   If you want to be in the heart of the Adoquín, this is your best bet for excellent value and ample accommodations. The courtyard pool and adjacent *palapa* make great places to hide away and enjoy a margarita or a book from the hotel's exchange rack. The bright, simply furnished rooms offer a choice of bed combinations, but all have at least two beds and a fan. Some rooms have both air-conditioning and a minifridge. The best rooms have a balcony overlooking the action in the street below, but light sleepers should consider a room in the back. Some rooms accommodate up to five ($68). This is an excellent and economical choice for families.

Av. Pérez Gasga 905, 71980 Puerto Escondido, Oax. ℂ 954/582-0168. 21 units. High season $52 (£29) double, $95 (£52) double with A/C; low season $38 (£21) double, $85 (£47) double with A/C. MC, V. Limited street parking. **Amenities:** Outdoor pool; safe; money exchange. *In room:* TV, A/C (in some rooms), minifridge (in some rooms), fan, no phone.

Hotel Castillo de Reyes   Proprietor Don Fernando has a knack for making his guests feel at home. Guests chat around tables on a shady patio near the office. Most of the bright, white-walled rooms have a special touch—perhaps a gourd mask or carved coconut hanging over the bed, plus over-the-bed reading lights. The rooms are shaded from the sun by palms and cooled by fans. The "castle" is on your left as you ascend the hill on Pérez Gasga, after leaving the Adoquín (you can also enter Pérez Gasga off Hwy. 200). This hotel is on one of Puerto's busiest streets, so traffic noise is a consideration.

Av. Pérez Gasga s/n, 71980 Puerto Escondido, Oax. © 954/582-0442. 18 units. High season $35 (£19) double; low season $25 (£14) double. No credit cards. Limited street parking. **Amenities:** Safe; money exchange. *In room:* Fans, no phone.

Hotel Flor de María   Though not right on the beach, the Flor de María offers a welcoming place to stay. This cheery, three-story hotel faces the ocean, which you can see from the rooftop. Built around a garden courtyard, each room is colorfully decorated with beautiful *trompe l'oeil* still lifes and landscapes. Rooms have double beds with orthopedic mattresses, and views that vary between the ocean, courtyard, and exterior. The roof holds a small pool, a shaded hammock terrace, and an open-air bar (noon–8pm during high season) with cable TV—all in all, a great sunset spot. The hotel lies about .5km (one-third mile) from the Adoquín, 60m (197 ft.) up a cobblestone road from Marineros Beach on Calle Marinero at the eastern end of the beach.

Playa Marineros, 71980 Puerto Escondido, Oax. © 954/582-0536. Fax 954/582-2617. 24 units. $45–$65 (£25–£36) double. Ask about off-season long-term discounts. MC, V. Limited parking. **Amenities:** Restaurant; bar; small outdoor pool; Internet kiosk; small gym.

Rockaway   Facing Playa Zicatela, this surfer's sanctuary offers very clean—and very cheap—accommodations geared for surfers. Every cabaña is equipped with a private bathroom, as well as ceiling fans and mosquito nets. The good-size swimming pool and *palapa* bar form a popular gathering spot. The cabañas in the older section do not have hot water; those in the newer section feature A/C, hot water, and cable TV.

Calle del Morro s/n, 71980 Puerto Escondido, Oax. © 954/582-0668. Fax: 954-582-2420. 14 units. High season $60 (£33) double, new rooms $80 (£44) double; low season $40 (£22) double, new rooms $60 (£33) double. No credit cards. Free parking. **Amenities:** Bar; outdoor pool. *In room:* A/C (in some), TV (in some), ceiling fans, mosquito nets, no phone.

WHERE TO DINE

In addition to the places listed below, a Puerto Escondido tradition is the *palapa* restaurants on Zicatela Beach, for early-morning surfer breakfasts or casual dining and drinking at night. One of the most popular is **Los Tíos,** offering very reasonable prices and surfer-sized portions. After dinner, enjoy homemade Italian ice cream from **Gelateria Giardino.** It has two locations, on Calle del Morro at Zicatela Beach, and Pérez Gasga 609, on the Adoquín (© **954/582-2243**).

EXPENSIVE

Pascal ★★★ *Finds* FRENCH   With an enchanted location on the edge of the bay, Pascal offers the only beachside terrace with views of the bobbing boats in front. Opened in 2006, it has quickly become one of the city's top restaurants. All of the French-inspired dishes are prepared by chef-owner Pascal on the outdoor grill using only fresh ingredients, and some of the specials include Chateaubriand, rack of lamb, fondue bourguignon, fish and seafood brochettes, and grilled lobster. The bouillabaisse tastes heavenly. Open only for dinner, Pascal offers candlelit tables amidst towering palm trees, a centerpiece fountain, and live music weekends. Service is refined, and the cuisine matches the quality you would expect from a fine French restaurant. There's an enticing selection of French and international wines, as well.

Playa Principal s/n (off the Adoquín). (✆ 954/103-0668. Reservations recommended. Main courses $6–$25 (£3.30–£14). No credit cards. Daily 6pm–midnight.

MODERATE
Cabo Blanco INTERNATIONAL   People come to this beachside bar and grill for a good time and simple beach food, which includes grilled fish, shrimp, steaks, and ribs topped with a variety of flavorful sauces. Favorites are dill-Dijon mustard, wine-fennel, and Thai curry. A bonus is that Cabo Blanco turns into a rowdy Zicatela Beach bar, with special Monday night parties featuring an all-you-can-eat buffet plus dancing, and a Friday night reggae dance. The top-notch team of bartenders keeps the crowd well-served, if not always well-behaved.

Calle del Morro s/n. (✆ 954/582-0337. www.geocities.com/oaxiki/cabo_blanco_pe.html. Main courses $7–$15 (£3.85–£8.25). V. Dec–Apr daily 6pm–2am.

Restaurant Santa Fe ★★ *Finds* INTERNATIONAL   The Hotel Santa Fe's beachside restaurant sits under a welcoming *palapa,* with the gentle waves crashing just in front. The excellent fish and seafood selections include crayfish, red snapper, tuna, octopus, and giant shrimp prepared any way you like. More traditional dishes, such as Oaxacan-style enchiladas with *mole,* are also available. The restaurant offers numerous vegetarian and vegan selections, including *chiles rellenos* and breaded tofu served with salad and rice. Even if you don't plan to dine, this is a beautiful spot to come for a sunset cocktail and perhaps an hors d'oeuvre.

In the Hotel Santa Fe, Calle del Morro s/n. (✆ 954/582-0170. Breakfast $4–$6; main courses $5.50–$25 (£3–£14). AE, MC, V. Daily 7am–10:30pm.

INEXPENSIVE
Arte la Galería ★ ITALIAN   At the east end of the Adoquín, La Galería offers a satisfying range of eats in a cool, creative setting. Dark-wood beams tower above, contemporary works by local artists grace the walls, and jazz music plays. Specialties include homemade pastas and brick-oven pizzas (the five cheese pizza is especially delicious), but burgers and steaks are also available. Cappuccino and espresso, plus desserts such as apple empanadas, finish the meal. Continental and American breakfasts are available in the morning.

Av. Pérez Gasga s/n. (✆ 954/582-2039. Breakfast $3–$5 (£1.65–£2.75); main courses $5–$18 (£2.75–£9.90). No credit cards. Daily 8am–11pm.

Cafecito ★ *Value* FRENCH PASTRY/MEXICAN   Carmen started with a small bakery in Puerto, and when she opened this cafe years ago on Zicatela Beach, with the motto "Big waves, strong coffee!," it quickly eclipsed the bake shop, and now is her main business. But not to worry—it still features all the attractions of her early *patisserie,* with the added attraction of serving full meals all day long. This café/restaurant sits under a big *palapa* facing the beach. Giant shrimp dinners cost less than $10 (£5.50), and creative daily specials are always a sure bet. An oversize mug of cappuccino is $2.20 (£1.21), and a mango éclair—worth any price—is a steal at $1.20 (£.66). Smoothies, natural juices, and a variety of coffee selections are available.

Calle del Morro s/n, Playa Zicatela. (✆ 954/582-0516. Pastries $1–$2 (55p–£1.10); breakfast $3–$4.50 (£1.65–£2.50); main courses $3–$9 (£1.65–£4.95). No credit cards. Daily 6am–10pm.

El Jardín ★★ *Value* ITALIAN   This wonderful restaurant facing Zicatela Beach is generally packed. It's known for its generous use of fresh, healthy ingredients, including lots of olive oil, tomatoes, and Italian vinaigrette. Among the choices are delicious

New York–style pizzas, vegetarian sandwiches, pastas, large salads, and crepes. There's also a wide selection of fresh fish and seafood. Under a *palapa* roof, El Jardín's extensive menu includes fruit smoothies, Italian and Mexican coffees, herbal teas, and a complete juice bar. The restaurant makes its own tempeh, tofu, pastas, and whole-grain breads. The rich tiramisu is to die for.

Calle del Morro s/n, Playa Zicatela. ℂ 954/582-2315. Main courses $3–$10 (£1.65–£5.50). No credit cards. Daily 8am–11pm.

Las Margaritas ☆ (Value) MEXICAN   One of the tastiest Mexican restaurants in town, Las Margaritas lies off a busy street that's a short drive from the Adoquín. The casual, open-air terrace offers wood tables and chairs as well as an open kitchen, bar, and tortilla stand where you can watch authentic dishes being made. This is Mexican food prepared as though you were in a family's home, featuring dishes like *empanadas*, quesadillas, fish and seafood brochettes, steaks, and *moles* that explode with flavor.

8 norte s/n (1 block from the market). ℂ 954/582-0212. Breakfasts $3–$4.50 (£1.65–£2.50); main courses $4–$12 (£2.20–£6.60). MC, V. Daily 8am–10pm.

Flor de María INTERNATIONAL   This first-floor, open-air hotel dining room near the beach is particularly popular with locals. The menu changes daily but always includes fresh fish, grilled meats, and pastas. The restaurant sits in the Hotel Flor de María, just steps from the center of town and up a cobblestone road from Playa Marinero at the eastern end of the beach.

In Hotel Flor de María, Playa Marinero. ℂ 954/582-0536. Breakfast $2–$3.50 (£1.10–£1.95); main courses $5–$14 (£2.75–£7.70). Daily 8–11am and 6–9pm. Closed May–June and Sept–Oct.

PUERTO ESCONDIDO AFTER DARK

Sunset watching is a ritual to plan your days around, and good lookout points abound. At Zicatela you can watch sun descend behind the surfers, and at **La Galería,** located on the third floor of the Arco Iris hotel, you can catch up on local gossip while enjoying a sundowner. It has a nightly happy hour (with live music during high season) from 5:30 to 7:30pm. Other great sunset spots are the **Hotel Santa Fe,** at the junction of Zicatela and Marineros beaches, and the rooftop bar of **Hotel Flor de María.** For a more tranquil, romantic setting, take a cab or walk a half-hour or so west to the cliff-top lawn of the **Hotel Posada Real.**

Puerto's nightlife will satisfy anyone dedicated to late nights and good music. Most nightspots are open until 3am or until customers leave; none of them have phones. The Adoquín offers an ample selection of clubs. Favorites include **Wipeout,** a multi-level club that packs in the crowds until 4am, and **El Tubo,** an open-air beachside dance club just west of Pascal on the Adoquín.

On Zicatela Beach, **El Son y la Rumba** features live Latino jazz, by its house band, each night from 8 to 11pm. It switches over to DJs playing house music Wednesday through Saturday, after 11pm. The cover is $5 (£2.75), and it's located at Calle de Moro 7. Within walking distance, **Bar Fly** sits upstairs overlooking the beach and features a DJ spinning Latin, retro, and electronic hits. It's open nightly from 9pm to 3am on Calle de Moro s/n. Don't miss **Cabo Blanco's** (see "Where to Dine," above) Monday night dine-and-dance party (all you can eat), or its Friday reggae night. An added draw is the complimentary snacks with drink purchase, in the style of Mexico's cantina tradition. **Casa Babylon,** a few doors down, is a bohemian beach bar with a book exchange and table games. It's open nightly from 7pm until late, and has a hip surfer vibe.

There's a movie theater on Playa Zicatela, **PJ's Book Bodega and Music Shop.** It's a pretty simple setup consisting of a large screen and some beach chairs, and it serves up popcorn and movies nightly.

A TRIP TO PUERTO ANGEL: BACKPACKING BEACH HAVEN

Seventy-four kilometers (46 miles) southeast of Puerto Escondido and 50km (30 miles) northwest of the Bays of Huatulco lies the tiny fishing port of **Puerto Angel** (*pwer*-toh *ahn*-hehl). With its beautiful beaches, unpaved streets, and budget hotels, Puerto Angel is popular with the international backpacking set and those seeking an inexpensive and restful vacation. Repeated hurricane damage and the 1999 earthquake took its toll on the village, driving the best accommodations out of business, but Puerto Angel continues to attract visitors. Its small bay and several inlets offer peaceful swimming and good snorkeling. The village's way of life is slow and simple: Fishermen leave very early in the morning and return with their catch before noon. Taxis make up most of the traffic, and the bus from Pochutla passes every half-hour or so.

ESSENTIALS

GETTING THERE & DEPARTING   By Car   North or south from **Highway 200,** take coastal **Highway 175** inland to Puerto Angel. The road is well marked with signs to Puerto Angel. From Huatulco or Puerto Escondido, the trip should take about an hour.

By Taxi   Taxis are readily available to take you to Puerto Angel or Zipolite Beach for a reasonable price (about $3/£1.65 to or from either destination), or to the Huatulco airport or Puerto Escondido (about $50/£28).

By Bus   There are no direct buses from Puerto Escondido or Huatulco to Puerto Angel; however, numerous buses leave Puerto Escondido and Huatulco for Pochutla, 11km (7 miles) north of Puerto Angel. Take the bus to Pochutla, and then switch to a bus going to Puerto Angel. If you arrive in Pochutla from Huatulco or Puerto Escondido, you may be dropped at one of several bus stations that line the main street; walk 1 or 2 blocks toward the large sign reading POSADA DON JOSE. The buses to Puerto Angel are in the lot just before the sign.

ORIENTATION   The town center is only about 4 blocks long, oriented more or less east-west. There are few signs in the village, and, off the main street, much of Puerto Angel is a narrow sand-and-dirt path. The navy base is toward the west end of town, just before the creek crossing toward Playa Panteón (Cemetery Beach).

Puerto Angel has several public (Ladatel) telephones that use widely available pre-paid phone cards. The closest bank is **Bancomer** in Pochutla, which changes money Monday through Friday from 9am to 6pm, Saturday from 9am to 1pm. The *correo*

(*Tips*   **Important Travel Note**

Although car and bus hijackings along Highway 200 north to Acapulco have greatly decreased (thanks to improved security measures and police patrols), you're still wise to travel this road only during the day.

(post office), open Monday through Friday from 9am to 3:30pm, is on the curve as you enter town.

BEACHES, WATERSPORTS & BOAT TRIPS

The golden sands and peaceful village life of Puerto Angel and the nearby towns are all the reasons you'll need to visit. Playa Principal, the main beach, lies between the Mexican navy base and the pier that's home to the local fishing fleet. Near the pier, fishermen pull their colorful boats onto the beach and unload their catch in the late morning while trucks wait to haul it off to processing plants in Veracruz. The rest of the beach seems light years from the world of work and commitments. Except on Mexican holidays, it's relatively deserted. It's important to note that Pacific coast currents deposit trash on Puerto Angel beaches. The locals do a fairly good job of keeping it picked up, but the currents are constant.

Playa Panteón is the main swimming and snorkeling beach. Cemetery Beach, ominous as that sounds, is about a 15-minute walk from the center, straight through town on the main street that skirts the beach. The *panteón* (cemetery), on the right, is worth a visit—it holds brightly colored tombstones and equally brilliant blooming bougainvillea.

In Playa Panteón, some of the *palapa* restaurants and a few of the hotels rent snorkeling and scuba gear and can arrange boat trips, but they tend to be expensive. Check the quality and condition of gear—particularly scuba gear—that you're renting.

Playa Zipolite (see-poh-*lee*-teh) and its village are 6km (4 miles) down a paved road from Puerto Angel. Taxis charge about $3 (£1.65). You can catch a *colectivo* on the main street in the town center and share the cost.

Zipolite is well known as a good surf break and as a nude beach. Although public nudity (including topless sunbathing) is technically illegal, it's allowed here—this is one of only a handful of beaches in Mexico that permits it. This sort of open-mindedness has attracted an increasing number of young European travelers. Most sunbathers concentrate beyond a large rock outcropping at the far end of the beach. Police will occasionally patrol the area, but they are much more intent on drug users than on sunbathers. The ocean and currents here are quite strong (that's why the surf is so good!), and a number of drownings have occurred over the years—know your limits. There are places to tie up a hammock and a few *palapa* restaurants for a light lunch and a cold beer.

Hotels in Playa Zipolite are basic and rustic; most have rugged walls and *palapa* roofs. Prices range from $10 to $50 (£5.50–£28) a night.

Traveling north on Highway 175, you'll come to another hot surf break and a beach of spectacular beauty: **Playa San Agustinillo.** If you want to stay in San Agustinillo, there are no formal accommodations, but you'll see numerous signs for local guesthouses, which rent rooms for an average of $10 to $20 (£5.50–£11) a night, often with a home-cooked meal included. One of the pleasures of a stay in Puerto Angel is discovering the many hidden beaches nearby and spending the day. Local boatmen and hotels can give details and quote rates for this service.

You can stay in Puerto Angel near Playa Principal in the tiny town, or at Playa Panteón. Most accommodations are basic, older, cement-block style hotels, not meriting a full-blown description. Between Playa Panteón and town are several bungalow and guesthouse setups with budget accommodations.

4 Bahías de Huatulco

64km (40 miles) SE of Puerto Angel; 680km (422 miles) SE of Acapulco

Huatulco has the same unspoiled nature and laid-back attitude as its neighbors to the north, Puerto Angel and Puerto Escondido, but with a difference. In the midst of natural splendor, you'll also encounter indulgent hotels and modern roads and facilities.

Pristine beaches and jungle landscapes can make for an idyllic retreat from the stress of daily life—and when viewed from a luxury hotel balcony, even better. Huatulco is for those who want to enjoy the beauty of nature during the day, and then retreat to well-appointed comfort by night.

Undeveloped stretches of pure white sand and isolated coves await the promised growth of Huatulco, but it's not catching on as rapidly as Cancún, the previous resort planned by FONATUR, Mexico's Tourism Development arm. FONATUR development of the Bahías de Huatulco is an ambitious project that aims to cover 21,000 hectares (51,870 acres) of land, with over 16,000 hectares (39,520 acres) to remain ecological preserves. The small local communities have been transplanted from the coast into Crucecita. The area consists of three sections: **Santa Cruz, Crucecita,** and **Tangolunda Bay** (see "City Layout," below).

Though Huatulco has increasingly become known for its ecotourism attractions—including river rafting, rappelling, and hiking jungle trails—it has yet to develop a true personality. There's little shopping, nightlife, or even dining outside of the hotels, and what is available is expensive for the quality. However, the service in the area shines.

The opening of a new cruise-ship dock in Santa Cruz Bay in 2005 is changing the level of activity in Huatulco, providing the sleepy resort with an important business boost. The new dock handles up to two 3,000-passenger cruise ships at a time (passengers are currently ferried to shore aboard tenders). Also recently opened, but still being refined, is the new 20,000-hectare (49,400-acre) "ecoarchaeological" park, **El Botazoo,** at Punta Celeste, where there is a recently discovered archeological site. Hiking, rappelling, and bird-watching are popular activities there. This new development is all being handled with ecological sensitivity in mind.

If you're drawn to snorkeling, diving, boat cruises, and simple relaxation, Huatulco nicely fits the bill. Nine bays encompass 36 beaches and countless inlets and coves. Huatulco's main problem has been securing enough incoming flights. It relies heavily on charter service from the United States and Canada.

ESSENTIALS
GETTING THERE & DEPARTING
BY PLANE **Click Mexicana** flights (© 01-800/112-5425 toll-free in Mexico; www.click.com.mx) connect Huatulco with Mexico City.

From Huatulco's international airport (airport code: HUX; © **958/581-9004** or -9005), about 20km (12 miles) northwest of the Bahías de Huatulco, private **taxis** charge $49 (£27) to Crucecita, $44 to Santa Cruz, and $49 (£27) to Tangolunda. **Transportes Terrestres** (© **958/581-9014**) *colectivos* fares are about $10 (£5.50) per person. When returning, make sure to ask for a taxi, unless you have a lot of luggage. Taxis to the airport run $42 (£23), but unless specifically requested, you'll get a Suburban, which costs $56 (£31).

Budget (© **800/527-0700** in the U.S., or 958/587-0010 or 958/581-9000) has an office at the airport that is open for flight arrivals. **Dollar** (© **958/587-1381**) also has rental offices downtown and offers one-way drop service for about $50 additional if you're traveling to Puerto Escondido. Because Huatulco is so spread out and has excellent roads, you may want to consider a rental car, at least for 1 or 2 days, to explore the area.

BY CAR   Coastal **Highway 200** leads to Huatulco (via Pochutla) from the north and is generally in good condition. The drive from Puerto Escondido takes just under 2 hours. The road is well maintained, but it's windy and doesn't have lights, so avoid travel after sunset. Allow at least 6 hours for the trip from Oaxaca City on mountainous **Highway 175.**

BY BUS   There are three bus stations in Crucecita, all within a few blocks, but none in Santa Cruz or Tangolunda. The **Gacela** and **Estrella Blanca** station, at the corner of Gardenia and Palma Real, handles service to Acapulco, Mexico City, Puerto Escondido, and Pochutla. The **Cristóbal Colón** station (© **958/587-0261**) is at the corner of Gardenia and Ocotillo, 4 blocks from the Plaza Principal. It serves destinations throughout Mexico, including Oaxaca, Puerto Escondido, and Pochutla. The **Estrella del Valle** station, on Jasmin between Sabali and Carrizal, serves Oaxaca.

ORIENTATION

VISITOR INFORMATION   The **State Tourism Office,** or Oficina del Turismo (© **958/581-0176;** fax 958/581-0177; www.baysofhuatulco.com.mx), has an information module in Tangolunda Bay, near the Grand Pacific hotel. It's open Monday to Friday from 8am to 5pm.

CITY LAYOUT   The overall resort area is called **Bahías de Huatulco** and includes nine bays. The town of Santa María de Huatulco, the original settlement in this area, is 27km (17 miles) inland. **Santa Cruz Huatulco,** usually called Santa Cruz, was the first developed area on the coast. It has a central plaza with a bandstand kiosk, which has been converted into a cafe that serves regionally grown coffee. It also has an artisans' market on the edge of the plaza that borders the main road, a few hotels and restaurants, and a marina where bay tours and fishing trips set sail. **Juárez** is Santa Cruz's 4-block-long main street, anchored at one end by the Hotel Castillo Huatulco and at the other by the Meigas Binniguenda hotel. Opposite the Hotel Castillo is the marina, and beyond it are restaurants in new colonial-style buildings facing the beach. The area's banks are on Juárez. It's impossible to get lost and you can take in almost everything at a glance. This bay is the site of Huatulco's cruise-ship dock.

About 3km (2 miles) inland from Santa Cruz is **Crucecita,** a planned city that sprang up in 1985. It centers on a lovely grassy plaza. This is the residential area for the resorts, with neighborhoods of new stucco homes mixed with small apartment complexes. Crucecita has evolved into a lovely, traditional town where you'll find the area's best, and most reasonably priced, restaurants, plus some shopping and several less-expensive hotels.

Until other bays are developed, **Tangolunda Bay,** 5km (3 miles) east, is the focal point of development. Over time, half the bays will have resorts. For now, Tangolunda has an 18-hole golf course, as well as the Las Brisas, Quinta Real, Barceló Huatulco, Royal, Casa del Mar, and Camino Real Zaashila hotels, among others. Small strip centers with a few restaurants occupy each end of Tangolunda Bay. **Chahué Bay,** between Tangolunda and Santa Cruz, is a small bay with a beach club and other facilities under construction along with houses and a few small hotels.

GETTING AROUND   Crucecita, Santa Cruz, and Tangolunda are too far apart to walk, but **taxis** are inexpensive and readily available. Crucecita has taxi stands opposite the Hotel Grifer and on the Plaza Principal. Taxis are readily available through hotels in Santa Cruz and Tangolunda. The fare between Santa Cruz and Tangolunda is roughly $2.50 (£1.40); between Santa Cruz and Crucecita, $2; between Crucecita and Tangolunda, $2.50(£1.40). To explore the area, you can hire a taxi by the hour (about $15/£8.25 per hr.) or for the day.

There is **minibus service** between towns; the fare is 50¢ (30p). In Santa Cruz, catch the bus across the street from Castillo Huatulco; in Tangolunda, in front of the Grand Pacific; and in Crucecita, cater-cornered from the Hotel Grifer.

FAST FACTS: Bahías de Huatulco

Area Code The area code is 958.

Banks All three areas have banks with ATMs, including the main Mexican banks, Banamex and Bancomer, and HSBC. They change money during business hours, Monday through Friday from 9am to 4pm. Banks line Calle Juárez in Santa Cruz, and surround the central plaza in Crucecita.

Drugstores **Farmacía del Carmen,** just off the central plaza in Crucecita (© 958/587-0878), is one of the largest drugstores in town. It's open Monday through Saturday from 8am to 10pm and Sunday from 8am to noon. **Farmacía La Clínica** (© 958/587-0591), Sabalí 1602, Crucecita, offers 24-hour service and delivery.

Emergencies **Police emergency** (© 060); **federal police** (© 958/587-0815); **transit police** (© 958/587-0186); and **Cruz Roja (Red Cross),** Bulevar Chahué 110 (© 958/587-1188).

Information **Oficina del Turismo,** the State Tourism Office (© 958/581-0176 or -0177; sedetur6@oaxaca.gob.mx) has an information module in Tangolunda Bay near the Campo de Golf. It's open weekdays, 8am to 5pm.

Internet Access Several Internet cafes are in Crucecita. One is at the cafe in the Misión de los Arcos, Av. Gardenia 902 (© 958/587-0165), which, in addition to paid service, is also a free wireless hot spot; another is on the ground-floor level of the **Hotel Plaza Conejo,** Av. Guamúchil 208, across from the main plaza (© 958/587-0054, -0009; conejo3@mexico.com). It's about $1 (55p) per hour.

Medical Care **Dr. Ricardo Carrillo** (© 958/587-0687 or -0600) speaks English.

Post Office The *correo,* at Bulevar Chahué 100, Sector R, Crucecita (© 958/587-0551), is open Monday through Friday from 8am to 3pm, Saturday from 9am to 1pm.

BEACHES, WATERSPORTS & OTHER THINGS TO DO

Attractions around Huatulco concentrate on the nine bays and their watersports. The number of ecotours and interesting side trips into the surrounding mountains is growing. Though it isn't a traditional Mexican town, the community of Crucecita is worth visiting. Just off the central plaza is the **Iglesia de Guadalupe,** with a large mural of Mexico's patron saint gracing the entire ceiling of the chapel. The image of the Virgin is set against a deep blue night sky, and includes 52 stars—a modern interpretation of Juan Diego's cloak.

You can dine in Crucecita for a fraction of the price in Tangolunda Bay, with the added benefit of some local color. Considering that shopping in Huatulco is generally poor, you'll find the best choices here, in the shops around the central plaza. They tend to stay open late, and offer a good selection of regional goods and typical tourist take-homes, including *artesanía*, silver jewelry, Cuban cigars, and tequila. A small, free trolley train takes visitors on a short tour of the town.

BEACHES   A section of the beach at Santa Cruz (away from the small boats) is an inviting sunning spot. Beach clubs for guests at nonoceanfront hotels are here. In addition, several restaurants are on the beach, and *palapa* umbrellas run down to the water's edge. For about $15 (£8.25) one-way, *pangas* from the marina in Santa Cruz will ferry you to **La Entrega Beach,** also in Santa Cruz Bay. There you'll find a row of *palapa* restaurants, all with beach chairs out front. Find an empty one, and use that restaurant for your refreshment needs. A snorkel equipment rental booth is about midway down the beach, and there's some fairly good snorkeling on the end away from where the boats arrive.

Between Santa Cruz and Tangolunda bays is **Chahué Bay.** The beach club has *palapas,* beach volleyball, and refreshments for an entrance fee of about $2.50 (£1.40). However, a strong undertow makes this a dangerous place for swimming.

Tangolunda Bay beach, fronting the best hotels, is wide and beautiful. Theoretically, all beaches in Mexico are public; however, nonguests at Tangolunda hotels may have difficulty entering the hotels to get to the beach.

BAY CRUISES & TOURS   Huatulco's major attraction is its coastline—a magnificent stretch of pristine bays bordered by an odd blend of cactus and jungle vegetation right at the water's edge. The only way to really grasp its beauty is to take a cruise of the bays, stopping at **Organo** or **Maguey Bay** for a dip in the crystal-clear water and a fish lunch at a *palapa* restaurant on the beach.

One way to arrange a bay tour is to go to the **boat-owners' cooperative** (© 958/ 587-0081) in the red-and-yellow tin shack at the entrance to the marina. Prices are posted, and you can buy tickets for sightseeing, snorkeling, or fishing. Beaches other than La Entrega, including Maguey and San Agustín, are noted for offshore snorkeling. They also have *palapa* restaurants and other facilities. Several of these beaches, however, are completely undeveloped, so you will need to bring your own provisions. Boatmen at the cooperative will arrange return pickup at an appointed time. Prices run about $25 (£14) for 1 to 10 persons to La Entrega, and $50 (£28) for a trip to Maguey and Organo bays. The farthest bay is San Agustín; that all-day trip will run $100 (£55) in a private *panga.*

Another option is to join an organized daylong bay cruise. Any travel agency can easily make arrangements. Cruises are about $30 (£17) per person, with an extra charge of $5 (£2.75) for snorkeling-equipment rental and lunch. One excursion is on the *Tequila,* complete with guide, drinks, and on-board entertainment. Another, more romantic option is the *Luna Azul,* a 13m (43-ft.) sailboat that also offers bay tours and sunset sails.

Ecotours are growing in both popularity and number throughout the Bays of Huatulco. The mountain areas surrounding the Copalita River are also home to other natural treasures worth exploring, including the **Copalitilla Cascades.** Thirty kilometers (19 miles) north of Tangolunda at 395m (1,296 ft.) above sea level, this group of waterfalls—averaging 20 to 25m (66–82 ft.) in height—form natural whirlpools and clear pools for swimming. The area is also popular for horseback riding and rappelling.

An all-day **Coffee Plantation Tour** takes you into the mountains east of Huatulco, touring various coffee plantations. You'll learn how Oaxacan coffee is cultivated and learn about life on the plantations. Lunch and refreshments are included. Cost for the day is $50 (£28); contact **Paraíso Tours** (www.paraisohuatulco.com) for reservations.

Guided **horseback riding** through the jungles and to Conejos and Magueyito beach makes for a wonderful way to see the natural beauty of the area. The ride lasts 3 hours, with departures at 9:45am and 1:45pm, and costs $35 to $45 (£19–£25). Contact **Caballo del Mar Ranch** (© 958/589-9387).

Another recommended guide for both **hiking** and **bird-watching** is Laura Gonzalez, of **Nature Tours Huatulco** (© 958/583-4047 or 589-0636; lauriycky@hotmail.com). Choices include a hike around Punta Celeste with views of the river, open sea, and forest, for sightings of terrestrial and aquatic birds. The 3½-hour tour can be made in the early morning or late afternoon, and costs $45 (£25). An 8-hour excursion to the Ventanilla Lagoons takes you by boat through a mangrove to view birds, iguanas, and crocodiles. The cost is $80 (£44), and lunch is included. Tours include transportation, binoculars, specialized bird guide, and beverages.

GOLF & TENNIS   The 18-hole, par-72 **Tangolunda Golf Course** (© 958/581-0037) is adjacent to Tangolunda Bay. It has tennis courts as well. The greens fee is $76, and carts cost $34. Tennis courts are also available at the **Barceló** hotel (© 958/581-0055).

SHOPPING   Shopping in the area is limited and unmemorable. It concentrates in the **Santa Cruz Market,** by the marina in Santa Cruz, and in the **Crucecita Market,** on Guamúchil, a half-block from the plaza. Both are open daily from 10am to 8pm (no phones). Among the prototypical souvenirs, you may want to search out regional specialties, which include Oaxacan embroidered blouses and dresses, and *barro negro,* pottery made from dark clay exclusively found in the Oaxaca region. Also in Crucecita is the Plaza Oaxaca, adjacent to the central plaza. Its clothing shops include **Poco Loco Club/Coconut's Boutique** (© 958/587-0279), for casual sportswear; and **Mic Mac** (© 958/587-0565), for beachwear and souvenirs. **Coconuts** (© 958/587-0057) has English-language magazines, books, and music.

WHERE TO STAY

Moderate- and budget-priced hotels in Santa Cruz and Crucecita are generally more expensive than similar hotels in other Mexican beach resorts. The luxury hotels have comparable rates, especially when they're part of a package that includes airfare. The trend here is toward all-inclusive resorts, which in Huatulco are an especially good option, given the lack of memorable dining and nightlife options. Hotels that are not oceanfront generally have an arrangement with a beach club at Santa Cruz or Chahué Bay, and offer shuttle service. Low-season rates apply August through November only. Parking is free at these hotels; the 17% tax is not included in the rack rates listed below.

EXPENSIVE

Camino Real Zaashila ★★ *Kids*   One of the original hotels in Tangolunda Bay, the Camino Real Zaashila sits on a wide stretch of sandy beach secluded from other beaches by small rock outcroppings. The calm water, perfect for swimming and snorkeling, makes it ideal for families. The white stucco building is Mediterranean in style and washed in colors on the ocean side. The boldly decorated rooms are large and have an oceanview balcony or terrace and a large bathroom with an Italian marble tub/shower combination. Each of the 41 club rooms on the lower levels has its own private plunge pool. The main pool is a free-form design that spans 500 feet of beach, with chaises built into the shallow edges. Well-manicured tropical gardens surround it and the guest rooms.

Bulevar Benito Juárez 5, Bahía de Tangolunda, 70989 Huatulco, Oax. ℂ 800/722-6466 in the U.S., or 958/581-0460. Fax 958/581-0468. www.camino-zaashila.com. 120 units. High season $345 (£190) double, $381 (£210) club room; low season $234 (£129) double, $284 (£156) club room. AE, DC, MC, V. **Amenities:** 3 restaurants (1 Oaxacan); lobby bar w/live music; 2 large outdoor pools; outdoor whirlpool; lighted tennis court; beachside watersports center; kids' club; concierge; tour and travel agency services; room service; laundry service. *In room:* A/C, TV, minibar, safe.

Quinta Real 🌟🌟🌟 Double Moorish domes mark this romantic, relaxed hotel, known for its richly appointed cream-and-white decor and complete attention to detail. From the welcoming reception area to the luxurious beach club below, the staff emphasizes excellence in service. The small groupings of suites are built into the sloping hill to Tangolunda Bay and offer spectacular views of the ocean and golf course. Suites on the eastern edge of the resort sit above the highway, which generates some traffic noise. Interiors are elegant and comfortable, with stylish Mexican furniture, original art, wood-beamed ceilings, and marble tub/shower combinations with whirlpool tubs. Balconies have overstuffed seating areas and stone-inlay floors. Eight Grand Class Suites and the Presidential Suite have private pools. The most luxurious hotel in Huatulco, the Quinta Real is perfect for weddings, honeymoons, or small corporate retreats.

Bulevar Benito Juárez Lt. 2, Bahía de Tangolunda, 70989 Huatulco, Oax. ℂ 888/561-2817 in the U.S, or 958/581-0428, -0430. Fax 958/581-0429. www.quintareal.com. 28 units. High season $390 (£215) Master Suite, $440 (£242) Grand Class Suite, $490 (£270) suite with private pool; low season $295 (£162) Master Suite, $345 (£190) Grand Class Suite, $395 (£217) suite with private pool. AE, MC, V. **Amenities:** Restaurant (breakfast, dinner); poolside restaurant (lunch); bar w/stunning view; beach club w/2 outdoor pools (1 for children); tennis court; concierge; tour desk; room service; in-room massage; laundry service; dry cleaning. *In room:* A/C, TV, minibar, hair dryer, safe.

MODERATE

Gala Resort 🌟 *Kids* With all meals, drinks, entertainment, tips, and a slew of activities included in the price, the all-inclusive Gala is a value-packed experience. It caters to adults of all ages (married and single) who enjoy both activity and relaxation. An excellent—but often overcrowded—kids' activity program makes it a great option for families. Rooms have tile floors and Oaxacan wood trim, large tub/shower combinations, and ample balconies, all with views of Tangolunda Bay.

Bulevar Benito Juárez s/n, Bahía de Tangolunda, 70989 Huatulco, Oax. ℂ 958/581-0000. Fax 958/581-0220. www. gala-resort-huatulco.com. 290 units. High season $258–$320 (£142–£176) double, $402 (£221) junior suite, for children 12–17 $78 (£43), children 8–11 $54 (£30); low season $198–$258 (£109–£142) double, $299 (£164) junior suite, children 12–17 $60 (£33), children 8–11 $40 (£22). Children younger than 8 stay free in parent's room. Ask about special promotions. AE, MC, V. **Amenities:** 4 restaurants (buffet, a la carte); 4 bars; 5 outdoor pools, including a large free-form pool; 3 lighted tennis courts; full gym; complete beachside watersports center. *In room:* A/C, TV, minibar, hair dryer, safe.

Hotel Meigas Binniguenda 🌟 Huatulco's first hotel retains the charm and comfort that originally made it memorable. Rooms have Mexican-tile floors, foot-loomed bedspreads, and colonial-style furniture; French doors open onto tiny wrought-iron balconies overlooking Juárez or the pool and gardens. There's a section with newer rooms that have modern teak furnishings. A nice shady area surrounds the small pool in back of the lobby. The hotel is away from the marina at the far end of Juárez, only a few blocks from the water. It offers free transportation every hour to the beach club at Santa Cruz Bay.

Bulevar Santa Cruz 201, 70989 Santa Cruz de Huatulco, Oax. © **958/587-0077** or -0078. Fax 958/587-0284. binniguenda@prodigy.net.mx. 165 units. Year-round $110 (£61) double. Children younger than 7 stay free in parent's room. AE, MC, V. **Amenities:** Large, *palapa*-topped restaurant and bar; small outdoor pool; shuttle to beach. *In room:* A/C, TV, safe.

INEXPENSIVE

Hotel Las Palmas The central location and accommodating staff add to the appeal of the bright, basic rooms at Las Palmas. Located a half-block from the main plaza, it's connected to the popular El Sabor de Oaxaca restaurant (see "Where to Dine," below), which offers room service to guests. Rooms have tile floors, cotton textured bedspreads, tile showers, and cable TV.

Av. Guamúchil 206, 70989 Bahías de Huatulco, Oax. © **958/587-0060.** Fax 958/587-0057. 25 units. High season $80 (£44) double; low season $45 (£25) double. AE, MC, V. **Amenities:** Currency exchange; safe. *In room:* A/C, TV.

Misión de los Arcos ★★ *Finds* This exceptional hotel, just a block from the central plaza, is similar in style to the elegant Quinta Real—but at a fraction of the cost. The hotel is mostly white, accented with abundant greenery, giving it a fresh, inviting feel. Simple rooms continue the theme, washed in white, with cream and beige bed coverings and upholstery. Built-in desks, French windows, and minimal but interesting decorative accents give this budget hotel a real sense of style. At the entrance level, an excellent cafe offers high-speed Internet access, Huatulco's regionally grown coffee, tea, pastries, and ice cream. It's open from 8am to midnight. The adjacent Terra-Cotta restaurant (see below) serves breakfast, lunch, and dinner, and is equally stylish and budget-friendly. Although there's no pool, for $2.50 (£1.40) guests can use the Castillo Beach Club, at Chahué bay, open daily from 9am to 7pm. The hotel lies next door to La Crucecita's central plaza, close to all the shops and restaurants.

Gardenia 902, La Crucecita, 70989 Huatulco, Oax. © **958/587-0165.** Fax 958/587-1904. www.misiondelosarcos.com. 13 units. High season $75 (£41) double, $80–$100 (£44–£55) suite; low season $50 (£28) double, $55–$75 (£30–£41) suite. Rates increase over Christmas and Easter holiday periods. AE, MC, V. Street parking. **Amenities:** Restaurant; nearby beach club; laundry service. *In room:* A/C, TV, Wi-Fi, safe.

WHERE TO DINE

El Sabor de Oaxaca ★★★ OAXACAN This is the best place in the area to enjoy authentic, richly flavorful Oaxacan food, among the best of traditional Mexican cuisine. This colorful restaurant is a local favorite that also meets the quality standards of tourists. Among the most popular items are mixed grill for two, with a Oaxacan beef filet, tender pork tenderloin, chorizo (zesty Mexican sausage), and pork ribs; and the Oaxacan special for two, a generous sampling of the best of the menu, with tamales, Oaxacan cheese, pork *mole,* and more. If you're feeling adventurous, try the salty grilled *chapulines* (grasshoppers, a Oaxacan specialty). Generous breakfasts include eggs, bacon, ham, beans, toast, and fresh orange juice.

Av. Guamúchil 206, Crucecita. © **958/587-0060.** Fax 958/587-0057. Breakfast $4; main courses $6–$20 (£3.30–£11). AE, MC, V. Daily 7am–11pm.

Noches Oaxaqueñas/Don Porfirio ★ SEAFOOD/OAXACAN This dinner show presents the colorful, traditional folkloric dances of Oaxaca in an open-air courtyard reminiscent of an old hacienda (but in a modern strip mall). The dancers clearly enjoy performing traditional ballet under the direction of owner Celicia Flores Ramírez, wife of Don Willo Porfirio. The menu includes the *plato oaxaqueño,* a generous, flavorful sampling of traditional Oaxacan fare, with a tamal, a *sope* (a thick tortilla), Oaxacan cheese, grilled filet, pork enchilada, and a chile relleno. Other house specialties include grilled lobster, shrimp with mezcal, and spaghetti marinara with seafood. Meat lovers can enjoy American-style cuts or a juicy *arrachera* (skirt steak).

Bulevar Benito Juárez s/n (across from Royal Maeva), Tangolunda Bay. © 958/581-0001. Main courses $10–$20 (£5.50–£11). AE, MC, V. Daily noon–11pm. Shows Tues, Thurs, and Sat from 8:30–10pm ($10/£5.50).

Restaurante Bar Doña Celia 🦀 SEAFOOD

Doña Celia, an original Huatulco resident, remains in business in the same area where she started her little thatch-roofed restaurant years ago. With outdoor tables fronting Santa Cruz, it offers fabulous seafood in picturesque surroundings. Among her specialties are *filete empapelado* (foil-wrapped fish baked with tomato, onion, and cilantro) and *filete almendrado* (fish filet covered with hotcake batter, beer, and almonds). The *ceviche* is terrific—one order is plenty for two—as is *platillo a la huatulqueño* (shrimp and young octopus fried in olive oil with chile and onion, served over white rice). There are also mouth-watering lobster selections, including lobster tacos. The restaurant is basic, but the food is the reason for its popularity.

Santa Cruz Bay. © 958/587-0128. Breakfast $3.50–$6 (£1.95–£3.30); seafood $8–$30 (£4.40–£17). MC, V. Daily 8:30am–11pm.

Terra-Cotta 🦀🦀 *(Finds)* INTERNATIONAL/MEXICAN

Located inside the Hotel Misión de los Arcos, this stylish yet casual restaurant is delicious for breakfast, lunch, or dinner. Start the day in this white-washed, Mediterranean setting with gourmet coffee, fruit salad, and an array of morning favorites, including specials such as French toast stuffed with cream cheese and orange marmalade. Lunch and dinner share the same menu, which offers standards such as fajitas, baby back ribs, and gourmet tacos. Scrumptious desserts such as caramelized pineapple with coconut ice cream offer a sweet finish.

Gardenia 902, at the Hotel Misión de los Arcos, in front of La Crucecita's central plaza. © 958/587-0165. Breakfast $1.50–$6 (85p–£3.30); lunch and dinner main courses $4–$14 (£2.20–£7.70). AE, MC, V. Daily 8am–10pm.

HUATULCO AFTER DARK

There's a very limited selection of dance clubs around Huatulco—meaning that's where everyone goes. Huatulco seems to have the least consistent nightlife of any resort in Mexico, and clubs seem to change ownership—and names—almost annually. Check with your hotel concierge to see if any new places have opened; none of the places listed below have phones. The current hot spot is **Bar La Crema,** in Crucecita (about 4 blocks south of the *zócalo,* at the corner of Bugambilia and La Ceiba), with a lounge atmosphere and a mix of tunes. Nearby is **Café Dublin,** Carrizal 504 (1 block east and a half-block south from the *zócalo*), an Irish pub with a book exchange. Both bars open in the evening during high season and stay open as long as the management sees fit; hours are sporadic in low season. On the east side of the *zócalo* lies **Bar La Iguana,** playing rock music and featuring televised sports. The bar is typically open daily from noon to 4am during high season, with limited hours in low season.

    La Papaya on Bulevar Chahué is a popular dance club open Thursday through Saturday into the wee hours. Each Wednesday, the Barceló Resort hosts its **Fiesta Mexicana** from 7 to 11pm, featuring folkloric dances, mariachi music, and a buffet of Mexican food and drinks.

The Southernmost States: Oaxaca & Chiapas

by David Baird

Oaxaca and Chiapas have larger Indian populations than the other states in Mexico. These Indians don't just keep to their own little villages; you see them everywhere. Over the centuries, their practices, beliefs, and customs have shaped the local culture, making these two states fascinating places to visit.

In **Oaxaca,** there is a large population of Zapotec and Mixtec Indians in the central highlands surrounding Oaxaca City. It's a land of mountains and valleys checkered with cornfields, at its prettiest during the rainy season (Jun–Oct), when the corn is green. The villages here are famous for their crafts and attract visitors from all over the world. For many families, selling handicrafts now contributes more to their livelihood than growing corn. But growing corn carries much more weight in their ordering of things— it's part of their identity, it's part of what makes them Indians.

Their ancestors established agriculture and civilization in these valleys centuries ago. They were the ones who built and rebuilt the magnificent ceremonial center of **Monte Albán** high upon a mountaintop above Oaxaca City. Up there you'll find an intriguing collection of buildings, ball courts, and plazas whose design is different from those of the Maya to the east and the many cultures of central Mexico to the northwest.

But, my favorite part of a trip here is visiting the **city of Oaxaca,** a colonial city of stone buildings, plazas, and courtyards. With the pleasures of elegant surroundings, good food, and warm, welcoming people, I find myself very much at home here.

Chiapas, too, has a central highland area that produces beautiful handicrafts. Its center is the town of **San Cristóbal de las Casas,** which is higher, cooler, and wetter than Oaxaca. It's best to come here during the relatively dry season (late Oct–May). San Cristóbal is much smaller and offers a provincial version of colonial architecture—narrow cobblestone streets, tile roofs, old adobe walls, and wooden balconies. It looks less monumental and more Indian.

Aside from the beauty of the mountains and the many handicrafts, what brings people here are the villages of the highland Maya, a people who cling so tenaciously to their beliefs and traditions that for a long time the area attracted more anthropologists than tourists. These communities have a high degree of autonomy in religious and social practices; a visit to the church in **San Juan Chamula** will bring this home in a way no description can.

North and east of San Cristóbal are the lowlands, where you can visit the famous ruins of **Palenque,** a Maya city of the

Classic age. Thanks to the deciphering work of epigraphers, we know much about the history of Palenque and its kings. One was King Pacal, who lay buried for centuries inside his pyramid until an archaeological team discovered him in the 1950s.

EXPLORING OAXACA & CHIAPAS

Airline service to Oaxaca has improved in the past few years. The same cannot be said of Chiapas, where the most common port of entry is still the airport at Villahermosa, Tabasco, for Palenque as well as the Chiapas highlands. There are fewer flights into Tuxtla Gutiérrez (near San Cristóbal), and the flight from Mexico City to San Cristóbal was canceled.

Most travelers should choose between visiting Oaxaca or Chiapas and not try to do both in the same trip unless they have a lot of time. First, the connections between these states are not good. So your choices will probably be to fly via Mexico City or take an overnight bus. Another thing to consider is that both Oaxaca and Chiapas offer so much to do that each place can easily absorb a week or 2-week vacation. And, if choosing Oaxaca, keep in mind that Oaxaca's coastal resorts—including Puerto Escondido and Puerto Angel—are not far away. See chapter 10 for more information.

1 Oaxaca City ★★★

520km (322 miles) SE of Mexico City; 230km (143 miles) SE of Tehuacán; 269km (167 miles) NE of Puerto Escondido

What you see today when you walk through the historic district of Oaxaca (wah-*hah*-kah) is largely the product of 3 centuries of colonial society. The city is famous for its green building stone and for its own particular style of colonial architecture—an adaptation to the frequent earthquakes that plagued the city in colonial times and still occasionally shake things up. Building walls and facades are thick and broad with heavy buttressing, colonnades are low and spaced closely, and bell towers are squat with wide bases. The impression is one of great mass and substantiality.

Before the arrival of the Spanish, the central valley of Oaxaca was an important and populous region. Olmec influence reached the area around 1200 B.C.; by 800 B.C. the Zapotec (the original builders of Monte Albán) occupied the valley. Their civilization flourished about the same time as Teotihuacán in central Mexico. Trade between the two areas intensified and remained important until the Conquest. There was also trade with the Maya to the east. In early post-Classic times, the Mixtec first appeared in the region and slowly, through war and conquest, gained ascendancy over much of the Zapotec homeland before both peoples were humbled by the Aztec and later the Spaniards. To this day, the two principal ethnic groups in Oaxaca remain the Zapotec and Mixtec, whose tonal languages are closely related to each other but far different from the Aztec language Náhuatl.

The city of Oaxaca, originally called Antequera, was founded just a few years after the Spanish vanquished the Aztec. Most of Oaxaca's central valley was granted to Hernán Cortez for his services to the crown. Three centuries of colonial rule followed, during which the region remained calm.

In the years following independence, there was more or less continuous upheaval. From the 1830s to the 1860s, the Liberals and Conservatives fought for control of Mexico's destiny, with the French eventually intervening on the side of the Conservatives. One man, a Zapotec Indian from Oaxaca, led the resistance against the French

Oaxaca Area

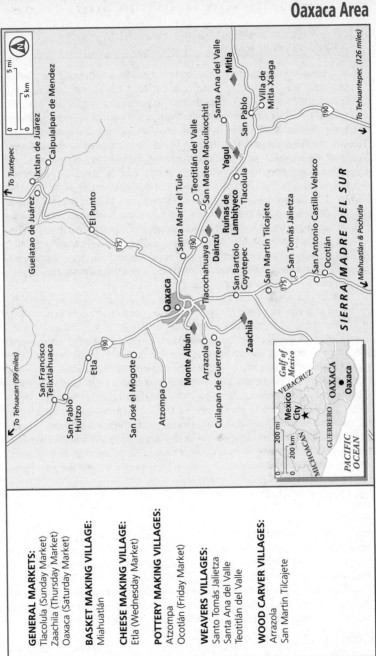

GENERAL MARKETS:
Tlacolula (Sunday Market)
Zaachila (Thursday Market)
Oaxaca (Saturday Market)

BASKET MAKING VILLAGE:
Miahuatlán

CHEESE MAKING VILLAGE:
Etla (Wednesday Market)

POTTERY MAKING VILLAGES:
Atzompa
Ocotlán (Friday Market)

WEAVERS VILLAGES:
Santo Tomás Jalietza
Santa Ana del Valle
Teotitlán del Valle

WOOD CARVER VILLAGES:
Arrazola
San Martín Tilcajete

Social Unrest in Oaxaca

What began in early June of 2006 as the annual teacher's strike for greater pay soon grew into a bitter struggle between Oaxaca's governor and a broad coalition of leftist groups protesting poverty, corruption in state government, and lack of fair elections. Matters turned bloody—some activists were shot by state police, and the protesters responded with marches, demonstrations, and the barricading of streets and highways, and, at times, even the airport. They demanded the resignation of the governor.

The city suffered greatly from the unrest, and the federal government did nothing to remedy the situation. The protests continued for months. The U.S. Department of State issued a travel advisory for Oaxaca. Tourism, the mainstay of the local economy, fell to a mere fraction of what it was. Hotels, restaurants, and stores closed across the city. Workers in the industry were left without jobs. Artisans were unable to sell their works. Finally, in October and November, the federal police entered the city and in violent confrontations retook possession of almost all of the public spaces, arresting many of the movement's leaders.

Now peace has returned to the city, and gradually things are returning to normal. Businesses have reopened—at least those that could survive. The Department of State repealed its travel advisory. Tourists are trickling in. Things may be okay now, but it bears mentioning that nothing has changed in the underlying conditions that brought on the protests, and, in fact, resentment of the government may be higher now than before. No one is sure what the teachers will do next time they want a raise. And the upcoming municipal elections, slated for 2007, could stir up bitter feelings.

So, if you want to plan a trip to Oaxaca, before you go, do a little research to make sure all is still peaceful there. Oaxaca is waiting for you. Just make sure that you see it in the best possible conditions. And exercise caution. In my travels through Latin America, I've found that when protest movements are suppressed, afterwards there's often a surge in petty crime. So keep your wits about you.

and played the key role in shaping Mexico's future. He was Benito Juárez, and his handiwork is known to history as *La Reforma*.

Born in the village of Guelatao, north of Oaxaca City, Juárez was adopted by a wealthy Oaxacan family who clothed and educated him in return for his services as a houseboy. He fell in love with the daughter of his benefactor and promised he would become rich and famous and return to marry her. He did all three and became president of the republic in 1861. Juárez is revered throughout Mexico.

ESSENTIALS
GETTING THERE & DEPARTING
BY PLANE **Continental ExpressJet** (© **800/231-0856** in the U.S., or 01-800/ 900-5000 in Mexico; www.continental.com) has nonstop service to/from Houston.

Downtown Oaxaca

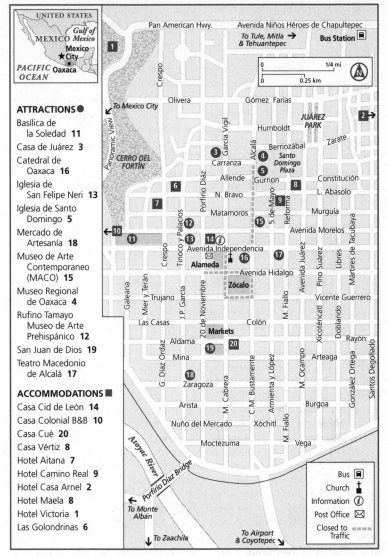

ATTRACTIONS ●

Basílica de
la Soledad **11**

Casa de Juárez **3**

Catedral de
Oaxaca **16**

Iglesia de
San Felipe Neri **13**

Iglesia de Santo
Domingo **5**

Mercado de
Artesanía **18**

Museo de Arte
Contemporaneo
(MACO) **15**

Museo Regional
de Oaxaca **4**

Rufino Tamayo
Museo de Arte
Prehispánico **12**

San Juan de Dios **19**

Teatro Macedonio
de Alcalá **17**

ACCOMMODATIONS ■

Casa Cid de León **14**

Casa Colonial B&B **10**

Casa Cué **20**

Casa Vértiz **8**

Hotel Aitana **7**

Hotel Camino Real **9**

Hotel Casa Arnel **2**

Hotel Maela **8**

Hotel Victoria **1**

Las Golondrinas **6**

Mexicana (☎ **800/531-7921** in the U.S., or 951/516-8414; www.mexicana.com) and **AeroMéxico** (☎ **800/237-6639** in the U.S., or 951/516-1066; www.aeromexico. com.mx) have several flights daily to and from Mexico City. **Click,** a Mexicana affiliate (☎ **01/800-122-5425** in Mexico; www.clickmx.com), has service to/from Mexico City. **Aviacsa** (☎ **01-800/006-2200** in Mexico, or 951/514-5187; www.aviacsa.com) connects Oaxaca to Mexico City and Acapulco. **Aerovega** (☎ **951/516-4982** or -2777) flies a six-passenger twin-engine Aero-Commander to and from Puerto Escondido and

Bahías de Huatulco once daily (twice if there are enough passengers). Make arrangements for Aerovega at the Monte Albán Hotel facing the Alameda (next to the *zócalo,* or town square).

BY CAR   It's a 5-hour drive from Mexico City on the toll road, **Highway 135D,** which begins at Cuacnoapalan, about 80km (50 miles) east-southeast of Puebla, and runs south, terminating in Oaxaca; the one-way toll is $30 (£17). For adventurous souls, the old federal **Highway 190** winds through the mountains and offers spectacular views; it takes 9 to 10 hours.

BY BUS   First-class and deluxe buses to and from Mexico City use the *autopista* (superhighway toll road) which takes 6 hours. A few make a short stop in Nochistlán, which isn't much of a delay. Almost all buses leave from Mexico City's **TAPO (east) bus station.** There is less frequent service to and from Mexico City's Central del Norte (north), and the Central del Sur (south, also called Taxqueña). There is no service from the Mexico City airport.

ADO (Autobuses del Oriente) and its affiliates handle most of the first-class and deluxe bus service. Your options are: *primera clase* (ADO), with almost hourly departures and a one-way fare of $35 (£19); *de lujo* (ADO GL) with seven or more departures per day for $43 (£24) one-way; and *servicio ejecutivo* (UNO), with five-plus departures per day for $60 (£33) one-way. *De lujo* has the same seats as first class, but more legroom, free soda and bottled water, and a better bathroom. *Servicio ejecutivo* has all this plus super-wide seats that recline far back. During holidays, you need to reserve a seat. Native Oaxaqueños living outside the state fill the buses for the Days of the Dead, Holy Week, and Christmas. It's possible to reserve seats over the Internet for the higher levels of service, and to check departure times and prices at **www.adogl. com.mx** and **www.uno.com.mx**.

In Oaxaca, the **ADO station** is on Calzada Niños Héroes. Buses serve Tuxtla Gutiérrez (five a day); San Cristóbal de las Casas (two overnight buses); Puebla (10 a day); Tehuacán (four a day); Tapachula (one a day); Veracruz (three a day); Villahermosa (two a day); and Huatulco, Pochutla, and Puerto Escondido on the coast (two a day, stopping at all three towns). These last buses take 9 hours to reach Puerto Escondido because they go by way of Huatulco; for a faster trip, see below.

Most of these buses are first-class; some are deluxe. When you walk through the station's main door, the passage to the buses is in front of you. The long counter to the right sells first-class tickets, and the shorter counter to the left sells deluxe. You can buy your tickets ahead of time at one of the offices of **Ticket Bus.** There's one on 20 de Noviembre 103-D, near the corner of Hidalgo, 1 block from the *zócalo* (© **951/ 514-6655**). Office hours are Monday through Saturday from 9am to 10pm, Sunday from 9am to 4pm.

The **Viajes Atlántida** agency, La Noria 101, near Armenta y López (© **951/514-7077**), offers daily service to Pochutla in Suburbans. It's much faster than the bus. There are nine runs daily (4 hr.; $12/£6.60). From Pochutla you can catch a *colectivo* (Volkswagen van) to **Puerto Escondido, Huatulco,** or **Puerto Angel** (which run 1–1½ hr.). You should buy your tickets in advance. The agency is open daily from 5:30am to 11:30pm.

The speediest buses to Puerto Escondido—6 hours away over a tortuous road— leave from the *terminal de segunda clase* (second-class terminal) Armenta y López 721, across from the Red Cross. Two lines serve the route. Pacífico Oaxaca buses leave daily at 8:30am and 10:30pm. One Estrella del Valle bus leaves at 11pm daily. Many people who go to Puerto Escondido on these buses say that if they had it to do over, they'd fly. Motion sickness is the main reason because of the hundreds of curves through the mountains.

ORIENTATION

ARRIVING BY PLANE   The airport is south of town; it's about a 20-minute cab ride. Buy a ticket at the window on your left as you exit the airport. A private cab is $11 (£6.05); a *colectivo* is $3 (£1.65) per person for downtown locations, more for outlying areas.

The same company provides service from the town to the airport. Go to **Transportes Aeropuerto Oaxaca** (© 951/514-4350), on the Alameda, in the building facing the cathedral. It doesn't accept phone reservations, so drop by Monday through Saturday from 9am to 2pm or 5 to 8pm to buy your ticket and arrange hotel pickup. The cost is $3.50 (£1.95) from downtown hotels, $7 (£3.85) and up from outlying hotels, and more if you have extra luggage.

ARRIVING BY BUS   The ADO first-class bus station is a short distance north of the center of town. A taxi ride to downtown is $3 (£1.65). If you're coming from the Pacific coast, you may arrive at the Central Camionera de Segunda Clase (second-class bus terminal) next to the Abastos Market. It's 10 long blocks southwest of the *zócalo*.

VISITOR INFORMATION   The **State Tourist Office** (©/fax **951/516-0123**) is at Murguía 206, between Reforma and 5 de Mayo. There you will find an information desk open every day from 8am to 8pm. Tourism also has an information office at Calle Independencia 607, corner of García Vigil, in front of the Alameda. It shares the building with a museum, Museo de los Pintores, and shares the same hours: Tuesday to Sunday from 10am to 8pm.

CITY LAYOUT   Oaxaca's east-west axis is **Independencia.** When streets cross Independencia and the north-south axis, **Alcalá/Bustamante,** their names change. The city's center is the *zócalo,* a large square surrounded by stone archways, and the **Alameda,** a smaller plaza attached to the northwest part of the *zócalo.* Oaxaca's cathedral faces the Alameda; its Palacio del Gobierno faces the *zócalo.* A few blocks to the north is the **Plaza de Santo Domingo.** The area between these two open spaces holds most of the historic district's shops, hotels, and restaurants. Two of the streets that run from Santo Domingo toward the *zócalo*—**Alcalá** and **Cinco de Mayo**—are partly closed to traffic.

GETTING AROUND   **By Car**   If you want to rent a car, try **Arrendadora Express,** 20 de Noviembre 103-B (© **951/516-6776**). Rental cars in Oaxaca are expensive, and the process is not exactly streamlined.

By Taxi   If you want to reach some of the outlying villages, I recommend hiring a taxi or signing up for a tour. Most taxi drivers have set hourly rates for touring the Oaxacan valleys. A trustworthy and careful taxi driver who speaks English is **Tomás Ramírez.** You can reach him at home (© **951/511-5061;** tomasramirez@prodigy. net.mx).

By Bus   Buses to the outlying villages of Guelatao, Teotitlán del Valle, Tlacolula, and Mitla leave from the second-class station just north of the Abastos Market. *Colectivos* leave for nearby villages from Calle Mercaderes, on the south side of the Abastos Market.

FAST FACTS: Oaxaca

American Express The office, in **Viajes Micsa,** is at Valdivieso and Hidalgo, at the northeast corner of the *zócalo* (✆ **951/516-2700;** fax 951/516-7475). American Express office hours are Monday through Friday from 9am to 2pm and 4 to 6pm, Saturday from 9am to 1pm. The travel agency stays open later and doesn't close for lunch.

Area Code The telephone area code is **951.**

Books, Newspapers & Magazines **Amate Books,** Alcalá 307-2, a few steps from Santo Domingo (✆ **951/516-6960),** has perhaps the best selection anywhere of books in English about Mexico. It stocks English-language magazines as well as a number of books about Oaxacan handicrafts. Hours are Monday through Saturday from 10:30am to 2:30pm and 3:30 to 7:30pm. A couple of monthly freebies, the English-language *Oaxaca Times* and the trilingual (English, Spanish, and French) *OAXACA,* circulate through the city and have information for tourists.

Consulates The **Canadian consulate,** Pino Suárez 700-11B (✆ **951/513-3777),** is open daily from 11am to 2pm. The **U.S. Consular Agency** is at Alcalá 407, Int. 20 (✆/fax **951/514-3054).** Hours are Monday through Friday from 10am to 3pm.

Currency Exchange *Casas de cambio* cluster on the streets at the northeast corner of the *zócalo,* at Alcalá and Valdivieso. These places post their rates, have short lines, and keep better hours than banks. Several exchange Canadian dollars.

Doctor Dr. Carlos Arnaud Carreño is a reputable internist at Calle Reforma 905 (✆ **951/515-4053).** Hours are Monday through Friday noon to 2pm and 4 to 8pm.

Emergencies The phone number for emergencies is ✆ **060.**

Internet Access In the downtown area, there are more than 20 Internet access services and cybercafes. Most are along Alcalá and around the *zócalo* and the Plaza Santo Domingo.

Population Oaxaca has 380,000 residents.

Post Office The *correo* is at the corner of Independencia and Alameda Park. It is open Monday through Friday from 8am to 5pm, Saturday from 9am to 1pm.

Seasons April and May are the hottest, driest months. (Also in May, rural teachers invade the *zócalo* and create havoc in the downtown area while they demonstrate for higher wages.) The rains come in June and improve things considerably. June through March, the city is most enjoyable. High seasons for tourists, when you can expect higher hotel rates, are late July and August (especially around the Guelaguetza), early November (around the Days of the Dead), the entire month of December, and during Easter.

Shipping The cheapest way to transport your goods is to have them packed securely so that you can check them as extra baggage on your flight home. Another way is to ship them. Many stores will pack and ship their own merchandise, but not other stores' goods. Recommended shippers are **Corazón del Pueblo** and **ARIPO** (see "Shopping," later in this chapter).

SPECIAL EVENTS & FESTIVALS

Oaxaca is famous for its exuberant traditional festivals. The most important ones are **Holy Week,** the **Guelaguetza** in July, **Días de los Muertos** in November, and the **Night of the Radishes** and **Christmas** in December. Make hotel reservations at least 2 months in advance if you plan to visit during these times.

At festival time in Oaxaca, sidewalk stands near the cathedral sell *buñuelos,* a thin, crisp, sweet snack food. It is the custom to serve *buñuelos* in cracked or otherwise flawed dishes; after you've finished eating, you smash the crockery on the sidewalk for good luck. Don't be timid! You can wash down the *buñuelos* with hot *ponche* (a steaming fruit punch) or *atole.*

HOLY WEEK   During Holy Week, figurines made of palm leaves are sold on the streets. On Palm Sunday, the Sunday before Easter, there are colorful parades. On the following Thursday, Oaxaca residents follow the Procession of the Seven Churches. Hundreds of the pious walk from church to church, praying at each one. The next day, Good Friday, many of the *barrios* (neighborhoods) have *encuentros:* Groups depart separately from the church, carrying religious figures through the neighborhoods, then "encounter" each other back at the church. Throughout the week, each church sponsors concerts, fireworks, fairs, and other entertainment.

FIESTA GUELAGUETZA   On the last two Mondays in July, Oaxaca holds the Fiesta Guelaguetza. In the villages of central Oaxaca, a *guelaguetza* (literally, a gift) is a celebration by a family in need of assistance to hold a wedding or some other community celebration. Guests bring gifts, which the family repays when they attend other *guelaguetzas.* The Fiesta Guelaguetza, begun in 1974, brings dancers from all the state's various ethnic groups to Oaxaca. For many communities, participation has become a matter of intense civic pride, and an opportunity to show people in the state capital and those from other ethnic groups the beauty of their traditional clothing and dance. Some 350 different *huipiles* (women's overblouses) and dresses can be seen during the performances. In the afternoon, there is an interpretive dance of the legend of Princess Donají.

The performances take place in the stadium that crowns the Cerro del Fortín each Monday from 10am to 1pm. Admission ranges from free (in Section C) to $50 to $75 (£28–£41; in Section A). Reserve tickets in advance—no later than May—through the State Tourism Office. A travel agency may be able to help you. I recommend Sections 5 and 6 in Palco (gallery) A for the best seating. The ticket color matches the color of your seat. You will be sitting in strong sunlight, so wear a hat and long sleeves.

Even if you don't attend the dances, you can enjoy the festival atmosphere that engulfs the city. There are fairs, exhibits, and a lot of gaiety. On the Sunday nights before the Guelaguetza, university students present an excellent program in the Plaza de la Danza at the Soledad church. The production, the *Bani Stui Gulal,* is an abbreviated history of the Oaxaca valley. The program begins at 9pm; arrive early, because the event is free and seating is limited.

DIAS DE LOS MUERTOS   The Mexican Days of the Dead festival (Nov 1–2) has garnered worldwide attention. It is celebrated across Oaxaca with more enthusiasm than in the rest of Mexico, which says quite a lot. Markets brim with marigolds—the flower of the underworld—and every household fills an altar with them and the favorite dishes, drinks, and cigarettes of the deceased. People visit relatives and friends, and anyone who visits is offered food. This is also the time to pay one's respects at the graveyard. Try to take one of the nocturnal cemetery tours offered around this time. **Hotel Casa Arnel** (© 951/515-2856) runs one. Another common form of celebrating is for young men to dress up in macabre outfits and frolic in the streets in Carnaval-like fashion.

DECEMBER FESTIVALS   The December Festivals begin on the 12th with the **Fiesta de la Virgen de Guadalupe (Festival of the Virgin of Guadalupe)** and continue on the 16th with a *calenda,* or procession, to many of the older churches in the *barrios,* all accompanied by dancing and costumes. Festivities continue on the 18th with the **Fiesta de la Soledad** in honor of the Virgen de la Soledad, patroness of Oaxaca State. A large fireworks construction known as a *castillo* is erected in Plaza de la Soledad. When it is ignited, look out. December 23 is **La Noche de Rábanos** (the Night of the Radishes), when Oaxaqueños build fantastic sculptures out of enormous radishes, flowers, and cornhusks. Displays on three sides of the *zócalo* are set up from 3pm on. By 6pm, when the show officially opens, lines to see the figures are 4 blocks long. It's well organized and overseen by a heavy police presence. On December 24, around 8:30pm, each Oaxacan church organizes a procession with music, floats, enormous papier-mâché dancing figures, and crowds bearing candles, all of which converge on the *zócalo.*

EXPLORING OAXACA

There is so much sightseeing to do inside and outside Oaxaca that you have to be sure to allow some idle time for enjoying the *zócalo.* In the traffic-free square, you can relax while getting a feel for the town and a good glimpse of Oaxacan society. I recommend going in the late afternoon and taking a seat at the outdoor cafe with the best view of the cathedral. You can get a beer or order a bowl of the traditional drink of Oaxaca: chocolate. The afternoon light filters through the shiny green leaves of the laurel trees, heightening the color of the cathedral's green stone. As dusk comes, a small drill corps enters stage left and performs a flag-lowering ceremony with much pomp and circumstance. Then the *marimba* or the municipal band usually strikes up in the central bandstand.

The city contains museums worth visiting, some interesting churches, and colorful markets. Outside town are the famous ruins of Monte Albán and Mitla and area villages known for their arts and crafts.

MUSEUMS

Museo de Arte Contemporáneo de Oaxaca   The MACO, 2½ blocks north of the *zócalo,* exhibits the work of contemporary artists, primarily from Oaxaca state (which has produced some of Mexico's most famous painters). It also books traveling exhibitions. A small bookstore is to your right as you enter. The 18th-century building housing the museum merits a visit for its own sake. It's called the Casa de Cortés, and some say that it was built by order of Hernán Cortez after he received the title of Marqués of the Valley of Oaxaca (in reality, it was built 2 centuries too late for that).

Alcalá 202, between Murguía and Morelos. © **951/514-2228.** Admission $2 (£1.10). Wed–Mon 10:30am–8pm.

Museo Regional de Oaxaca 👁👁👁   Next to the Santo Domingo Church (6 blocks north of the *zócalo*) is the most impressive museum in the city, housed in a former Dominican convent—one of the greatest of colonial Mexico. Construction was largely completed by the early 1600s. The government has spent millions to renovate the former convent, and it shows. The stairs, the arches, the cupolas—everywhere you look, there are lovely details in stone or in the remnants of colonial-era murals. The museum is an ambitious project that displays the course of human development in the Oaxaca valley from earliest times to the 20th century.

The most treasured possessions are the artifacts from Monte Albán's Tomb 7, which were discovered in 1932. The tomb contained 12 to 14 corpses and some 500 pieces of jewelry and art, making use of almost 8 pounds of gold and turquoise, conch shell, amber, and obsidian. This is part of a larger collection of artifacts from Monte Albán, which you would do well to see before going up to the ruins. In the many ceramics and carvings you can see definite Olmec and Teotihuacán influences, yet they display a style distinctly different from either culture. Other rooms are dedicated to the present-day ethnographic makeup of Oaxaca and a brief history of the efforts of the Dominican order in the region. Attached to the convent is the Santo Domingo Church (see "Churches," below). From some points on the north side of the convent you can look down over the recently opened botanical garden. Admission to the garden is free but by guided tour only (at 1 and 6pm). Sign up at the front desk of the museum the same day of the tour. There are two tours a week in English; ask for info at the front desk.

Gurrión at Alcalá. ✆ **951/516-2991.** Admission $4.25 (£2.35). Tues–Sun 10am–7:45pm.

Rufino Tamayo Museo de Arte Prehispánico de México ✶✶✶   The artifacts displayed in this museum were chosen "solely for the aesthetic rank of the works, their beauty, power, and originality." The result is a striking collection of pre-Hispanic art. The famed Oaxacan artist Rufino Tamayo amassed the collection over a 20-year period. The artifacts range from the pre-Classic period up to the Aztec, from far northwest Nayarit to southeastern Chiapas: terra-cotta figurines, scenes of daily life, lots of female fertility figures, Olmec and Totonac sculpture from the Gulf Coast, and Zapotec long-nosed figures. The well-displayed works reveal the great variety of styles of pre-Columbian art in Mexico.

Av. Morelos 503, north of the *zócalo* between Tinoco y Palacios and Porfirio Díaz. ✆ **951/516-4750.** Admission $3 (£1.65). Mon and Wed–Sat 10am–2pm and 4–7pm; Sun 10am–3pm. Closed holidays.

CHURCHES

Basílica de la Soledad ✶✶   The Basílica is the religious center of Oaxaca, and its Virgin is the patroness of the entire state. Adjoining the church is a former convent with a small but charming museum in back. A huge celebration on and around December 18 honors the Virgin, attracting penitents from all over Oaxaca. She is famous for her vestments, which are encrusted with pearls. (Until a few years ago, she had a crown of silver and jewels, which was stolen.) As with most Virgins, there is a story behind her. The short version is that her figure (actually just her hands and face) was found in a box on the back of a burro that didn't belong to anyone. The burro sat down on an outcropping of rock and refused to get up. This was the spot where the Virgin revealed herself and, consequently, where the basilica (completed in 1690) was constructed. You can still see the outcropping of rock, surrounded by a cage of iron bars, immediately to your right along the wall as you enter the church.

The concave facade of the church projecting forward from the building is unique in Mexico's religious architecture. The way the top is rounded and the tiers are divided suggests an imitation in stone of the baroque wooden *retablos* (altarpieces) common in Mexican churches. The interior is most impressive, too, but what I really like is the museum, which contains a curious blend of pieces—some museum quality, others mere trinkets that might as well have come from my grandmother's attic.

The Basílica's upper plaza is an outdoor patio and theater (Plaza de la Danza) with stone steps that serve as seats. Here, spectators view the famous Bani Stui Gulal (see "Fiesta Guelaguetza" under "Special Events & Festivals," above). When visiting the Basílica, it is traditional to eat ice cream; there are vendors in the lower plaza in front of the church.

Independencia at Galeana. No phone. Museum: Admission 50¢. Mon–Sat 10am–2pm and 4–6pm; Sun 11am–2pm. Basílica: Daily 7am–2pm and 4–9pm.

Catedral de Oaxaca 🎭🎭   The cathedral was built in 1553 and reconstructed in 1773. Its elaborate 18th-century baroque facade is an excellent example of the Oaxacan style. The central panel above the door depicts the assumption of the Virgin. Note the heavy, elaborate frame around the picture and the highly stylized wavelike clouds next to the cherubs—these elements, repeated in other churches in the region, are telltale signs of Oaxacan baroque. An uncommon and quite lovely detail is how the Virgin's cape and its folds are depicted in angular lines and facets. The cathedral's interior is not as interesting as its exterior because it was plundered during the Wars of Reform.

Fronting the Parque Alameda. No phone. Free admission. Daily 7am–9pm.

Iglesia de San Felipe Neri   This church, 2½ blocks northeast of the *zócalo*, was built in 1636 and displays all the architectural opulence of that period: The altar and nave are covered with ornately carved, gilded wood, and the walls are frescoed. In the west transept and chapel is a small figure of St. Martha and the dragon; the faithful have bedecked her with ribbons in hopes of obtaining her assistance.

Tinoco y Palacios at Independencia. No phone. Free admission. Daily 8am–11pm.

Iglesia de Santo Domingo 🎭🎭🎭 *(Moments*   There are 27 churches in Oaxaca, but none can equal the splendor of this one's interior. The church was started in the 1550s by Dominican friars and finished a century later; it contains the work of all the best artists of that period. Ornate plaster statues and flowers cover the extravagantly gilded walls and ceiling. When the sun shines through the yellow stained-glass window, it casts a golden glow over the whole interior and looks like a baroque vision of heaven. Just as you enter, look up at the ceiling formed by the choir loft to examine the elaborate genealogical tree of the Dominican order, which starts with don Domingo de Guzmán, Saint Dominic himself.

Corner of Gurrión and Alcalá. No phone. Free admission. Daily 7am–2pm and 4–11pm.

San Juan de Dios   This is the oldest church in Oaxaca, originally built in 1521 or 1522 of adobe and thatch. Construction of the present structure started during the mid-1600s and included a convent and hospital (where the 20 de Noviembre Market is now). The exterior is sweetly simple; the interior has an ornate altar and Urbano Olivera paintings on the ceiling. Oaxaqueños especially revere the glass shrine to the Virgin near the entrance, as well as one dedicated to Christ (off to the right). Because it's by the market, 1 block west and 2 blocks south of the *zócalo*, many of the people who visit the church are villagers who have come to Oaxaca to buy and sell.

20 de Noviembre s/n (corner of Aldama and Arteaga). No phone. Free admission. Daily 6am–11pm.

MORE ATTRACTIONS

Besides visiting the places mentioned below, try to get to the **Casa de Cortés,** which houses the Museo de Arte Contemporáneo (see above), and the former convent of **Santa Catalina,** home of the Hotel Camino Real (see below).

Casa de Juárez   This modest museum occupies the house where Benito Juárez first lived when he came to the city as a servant boy. It doesn't have any of his personal effects or any furniture belonging to the house, but it shows how a typical 19th-century household would have looked.

García Vigil 609. ⒸⓅ 951/516-1860. Admission $3 (£1.65). Tues–Sat 10am–7pm; Sun 10am–5pm.

Cerro del Fortín   To capture Oaxaca in a glance, take a cab to the top of this hill on the west side of town for a panoramic view. It's especially pretty just before sunset. Atop the hill are the statue of Benito Juárez and a stadium built to hold 15,000 spectators. The annual Fiesta Guelaguetza is held here. You can walk to the hill: Head up Díaz Ordaz/Crespo and look for the Escaleras del Fortín (Stairway to the Fortress) shortly after you cross Calle Delmonte; the 218 steps (interrupted by risers) are a challenge, but the view is worth it.

Díaz Ordaz at Calle Delmonte. No phone.

Teatro Macedonio de Alcalá   This beautiful 1903 Belle Epoque theater, 2 blocks east of the *zócalo*, holds 1,300 people and is still used for concerts and performances in the evening. Peek through the doors to see the marble stairway and Louis XV vestibule. Sometimes a list of events is posted on the doors.

Independencia at Armenta y López. No phone. Open only for events.

SHOPPING

Oaxaca and the surrounding villages are wonderful hunting grounds for handcrafted pottery, woodcarvings, and weavings. The hunt itself may be the best part. Specialties include the shiny **black pottery** for which Oaxaca is famous, **woolen textiles** with the deep reds and purples produced using the natural dye *cochineal*, and highly imaginative *alebrijes* **(wood carvings)**.

SHOPS & GALLERIES

Most of the shops, galleries, and boutiques are in the area between **Santo Domingo** and the *zócalo*, comprising the streets of **Alcalá, 5 de Mayo,** and **García Vigil** and the **cross streets.** Customary store hours are from 10am to 2pm and 4 to 7pm Monday through Saturday.

Artesanías e Industrias Populares del Estado de Oaxaca   ARIPO is a government store with a broader range of goods than most shops, including masks, baskets, clothing, furniture, and cutlery. The staff speaks English and will ship anywhere. Open Monday through Friday from 9am to 8pm, Saturday from 10am to 6pm, and Sunday from 11am to 4pm. It is 2 blocks above the Benito Juárez house. García Vigil 809 (at Cosijopi). ⒸⓅ 951/514-4030.

Galería Arte de Oaxaca   This gallery represents some of the state's leading contemporary artists. It's 2 blocks north and 1 block east of the *zócalo*. Murguía 105. ⒸⓅ 951/514-0910 or -1532.

Galería Quetzalli   A modest-looking art gallery behind the Church of Santo Domingo, Galería Quetzalli represents some of the big names in Mexican art—Francisco Toledo and José Villalobos—and some up-and-coming artists. Quetzalli also has a gallery at Murguía 400. Constitución 104. ⒸⓅ 951/514-0030.

Indigo   Beautiful and uncommon (and expensive) objects can be found here. The store can really test your resolution not to buy more artwork; go in and take a peek. Allende 104. ⒸⓅ 951/514-8338.

La Mano Mágica   Come here to see some of the best rug weaving in Oaxaca (by Arnulfo Mendoza) before you head to Teotitlán to see the work of other weavers. In the back rooms you can find well-chosen pieces of regional folk art. Shipping is available. The store is opposite the Museo de Arte Contemporáneo. Alcalá 203 (between Morelos and Matamoros). ⓒ 951/516-4275.

MARO   This is the store of Mujeres Artesanas de la Región de Oaxaca, a cooperative of women artisans. You'll find all the handicrafts of the state represented. Things are well priced and the quality of the goods is high. Open daily 9am to 8pm. 5 de Mayo 204 (between Murguía and Morelos). ⓒ 951/516-0670.

MARKETS

There are two market areas: one just south of the *zócalo,* and the newer Abastos Market, about 10 blocks west. Both areas bustle with people and are surrounded by small shops selling anything from hardware to leather goods to fabrics.

A few shops specialize in chocolate (not for eating, but for making hot chocolate) and *mole* paste. The neighboring state of Tabasco grows most of the cacao beans used for the chocolate. They are ground with almonds and cinnamon and pressed into bars or tablets. To prepare the drink, you dissolve the chocolate in hot milk or water (the more traditional drink) and beat until frothy. *Mole* paste, which contains chocolate, is used to make the classic Oaxacan dishes *mole negro* and *mole rojo.* A good place to hunt for chocolate and *mole* paste is along Mina street, on the south side of the 20 de Noviembre Market (see listing below). Here you'll find **Chocolate Mayordomo** and **Chocolate La Soledad.** Both offer a variety of preparations to fit American and European tastes, but I like the traditional Mexican best.

Note: Markets are generally open daily from 8am to 5pm.

Benito Juárez Market   One block south of the *zócalo,* this covered market is big and busy; stalls sell vegetables, flowers, medicinal preparation, meats, cheeses, and even clothing. Between calles Las Casas, Cabrera, Aldama, and 20 de Noviembre.

Mercado Abastos   The Abastos Market is open daily but is most active on Saturday, when Indians from the villages come to town to sell and shop. You'll see dried chiles, herbs, vegetables, crafts, bread, and even burros for sale at this bustling market. Ten blocks west of *zócalo,* between Calle Mercaderes and the *periférico.*

Mercado de Artesanía   Located 1 block south and 1 block west of the 20 de Noviembre Market, this market sells mostly textiles and articles of clothing at cheap prices. J. P. García and Zaragoza.

20 de Noviembre Market   This market is just south of the Benito Juárez Market, across Aldama. There are a lot of food stalls, but also some arts and crafts. On the south side, along Mina, are stores selling chocolate and *mole* paste. Between calles Aldama, Cabrera, Mina, and 20 de Noviembre.

OTHER THINGS TO DO

COOKING CLASSES   **Susana Trilling** (ⓒ 951/518-7726; www.seasonsofmyheart.com), author of the cookbook *Seasons of My Heart,* operates a cooking school of the same name just outside Oaxaca. In downtown Oaxaca, Señora Pilar Cabrera, owner of La Olla restaurant, gives cooking classes at Libres 205. She can be reached at ⓒ 951/516-5704 or at bugambilias2@yahoo.com.mx.

SPANISH CLASSES   Oaxaca has about a half-dozen language schools. With prior notice, most can arrange homestays with a Mexican family for students looking for total immersion. With little notice, most can arrange a week of classes for visitors to brush up their language skills. The **Instituto Cultural Oaxaca,** Av. Juárez 909 (Apdo. Postal 340, 68000 Oaxaca, Oax.; © **951/515-3404;** www.instculturaloax.com.mx), has the biggest name and perhaps the least flexibility. Besides language skill, classes focus on Oaxaca's history and archaeology. The **Instituto de Comunicación y Cultura,** Alcalá 307–312 (68000 Oaxaca, Oax.; ©/fax **951/516-3443;** www.iccoax.com), provides group and private instruction and uses music, art, and handicrafts to get students into the swing of things. Classes are small. **Becari Language School,** M. Bravo 210 (68000 Oaxaca, Oax.; © **951/514-6076;** www.becari.com.mx), was founded in 1994, and I'm hearing more and more good things from students—lots of flexibility and small classes.

HIKING & BIKING   Northwest of the city of Oaxaca is a mountain range known as the Sierra Norte that is cooler and wetter than the valley. The native communities offer guides and simple lodging for active sorts who are interested in seeing yet another side of Mexico. Several ecotourism outfits work with these communities. For information, ask at the State Tourism Office. **Zona Bici,** García Vigil 406 (© **951/516-0953;** boccaletti@prodigy.net.mx), does bike tours. This outfit also leads bike tours of the valley, which avoid car traffic and are less challenging than biking the mountains.

WHERE TO STAY

High season includes Easter, July, August, early November, and most of December. You should have no difficulty finding a room the rest of the time, and promotional rates are usually available. The prices listed below include the 18% tax. Most evenings are cool enough that you don't need air-conditioning, but for about 60 days a year, mostly from April to June, it comes in handy, and not every hotel has it.

VERY EXPENSIVE

Camino Real Oaxaca ✺✺✺   A magnificent hotel in a 16th-century landmark convent, this is the place to cloister yourself when in Oaxaca. Several beautiful courtyards with age-old walls bring to mind the original purpose of the building. The rooms, however, do not. All are comfortable and have the conveniences you would expect in a hotel of this caliber (no small feat given the constraints imposed by the infrastructure). Exterior rooms have triple-glazed windows to reduce noise. Higher prices are for interior rooms with views of the courtyards. The main difference between "deluxe" and "club" is the size of the room. Service is good. The location—between the *zócalo* and Santo Domingo on a pedestrian-only street—is ideal. All this said, I have to add that the prices keep going up and are getting harder and harder to justify. If you luck into a steep discount, then it might be worth it.

5 de Mayo 300, 68000 Oaxaca, Oax. © **800/722-6466** in the U.S. and Canada, or 951/501-6100. Fax 951/516-0732. www.caminoreal.com/oaxaca. 91 units. $350–$380 (£193–£21) deluxe; $425–$450 (£234–£248) club; $515 (£283) junior suite. Discounts and promotions available in low season. AE, MC, V. Valet parking $16 (£8.80). **Amenities:** Restaurant; 2 bars; large outdoor swimming pool; free membership for guests at local health club; children's activities in high season; tour desk; car-rental desk; room service; babysitting; laundry service; dry cleaning; nonsmoking rooms. *In room:* A/C, TV, minibar, hair dryer, safe.

Casa Cid de León ✺✺✺   Casa Cid de León has easily the largest suites in downtown Oaxaca. Each is extravagantly decorated in colonial style, with a few modern touches and fresh-cut flowers. The one that garners the most attention (La Bella Epoca) has three balconies facing the street and a large sitting room. The two-story, two-bathroom suite (El Mío Cid) would be perfect for a family. One of the downstairs suites, La Dominica, is my favorite for its space and comfort. Guests have access to a rooftop terrace. The location, 2 blocks north of the *zócalo,* is excellent, and Señora Cid de León is a most accommodating hotel owner. The hotel offers custom tours of the city and surrounding valley.

Av. Morelos 602, 68000 Oaxaca, Oax. © **951/514-1893**. Fax 951/514-7013. www.casaciddeleon.com. 4 units. $212–$260 (£117–£143) suite. Rates include juice, coffee, airport transfer, and tour of city. AE, MC, V. Valet parking $10 (£5.50). **Amenities:** Tour and limo service; business services; in-room salon services; room service; in-room massage; babysitting; laundry service. *In room:* A/C, TV, hair dryer.

EXPENSIVE

Hotel Victoria ✰✰ (Finds)   High above the downtown area, the Hotel Victoria offers that rare combination of proximity and the feeling of distance. It is ideal for those who want a little more peace than staying downtown can offer. And you're only a couple of minutes away on the hotel's shuttle bus. The Victoria also has a lovely view. You can enjoy it from a room or suite in one of the main buildings (three stories, no elevator), or you can stay in one of the villas distributed about the grounds, each with its own terrace. Rooms are large and carpeted and have modern furnishings.

Lomas del Fortín 1, 68070 Oaxaca, Oax. © **951/515-2633**. Fax 951/515-2411. www.hotelvictoriaoax.com.mx. 149 units. $166 (£91) standard double; $215 (£118) villa; $285 (£157) junior suite. AE, MC, V. Free parking. **Amenities:** Restaurant; bar; large outdoor swimming pool; tennis court; complimentary shuttle to downtown; babysitting; laundry service; dry cleaning; nonsmoking rooms. *In room:* A/C, TV, minibar, hair dryer, safe.

MODERATE

Casa Colonial Bed and Breakfast   The casual and comfortable setting created by attentive hosts Jane and Thornton Robison promptly sets guests at ease. This is an especially attractive place for first-timers to Oaxaca, who can tap into the owners' knowledge of the area and perhaps even tour some villages with them. The good-size rooms open to a large garden with tall jacaranda trees; they are simply but comfortably furnished. Breakfast is substantial: fresh fruit, yogurt, hot cereal, eggs, bacon, juice, and coffee. The hotel is farther from downtown than most of the others listed here. Rooms are not available for the Day of the Dead season or Christmas. Occasionally there is live music on Sunday afternoons. The place is closed in May.

Negrete 105 (Apdo. Postal 640), 68000 Oaxaca, Oax. © **800/758-1697** in the U.S., or ©/fax 951/516-5280. www.mexonline.com/colonial.htm. 15 units. $105 (£58) double. Rates include full breakfast. MC, V. Free parking. Pass La Soledad church on Av. Morelos, and angle right for a couple of blocks; the green house with purple trim (there's no sign) will be on your left. *In room:* No phone.

Casa Vértiz ✰ (Value)   Small courtyard hotel in good location. Rooms are medium size and come with either one or two queen-size beds. They are nicely done, with tile floor, beamed ceiling, stucco walls, and a few artsy decorations. There's good luggage space. Bathrooms are a little on the small side but attractive. A few come with tub/shower combinations.

Reforma 404, 68000 Oaxaca, Oax. © **951/516-1700**. www.hotelvertiz.com.mx. 14 units. $95–$105 (£52–£58) double. MC, V. No parking. **Amenities:** Restaurant; bar; room service; laundry service; dry cleaning. *In room:* A/C (in 12 units), TV, hair dryer, safe.

Hotel Aitana ✰ (Finds)   This stylish hotel is only 8 blocks from the *zócalo* and 6 blocks from Santo Domingo, but it's about 30m (98 ft.) uphill on a noisy street. All the rooms are away from the street, however, past a courtyard restaurant. They are well-lit and beautifully decorated. Most hold two twin beds; a few rooms have either two doubles or a king. Bathrooms are attractive and spacious, with shower/tub combinations.

Crespo 313, 68000 Oaxaca, Oax. (☏ 951/514-3788 or -3839. Fax 951/516-9856. www.hotelaitanaoaxaca.com. 23 units. High season $125 (£69) double; low season $65–$76 (£36–£42). Low-season rates include full breakfast, and often the 3rd night is free. MC, V. No parking. **Amenities:** Restaurant; bar; tour info; room service; laundry service; dry cleaning. *In room:* TV, coffeemaker, hair dryer.

Hotel Casa Cué (*Value*) A modern hotel 2 blocks from the *zócalo*, Casa Cué has good air-conditioning, good service, and bathrooms with instantly hot water. The lovely terrace on top of the three-story building (there's no elevator) has patio furniture and a fine view of the mountains. The midsize standard rooms are attractively furnished and well lit; most contain two twin beds. Junior suites are large and come with a sofa, coffee table, and writing table; most hold two double beds (some have one king and one double). The suites are still larger, and the second bedroom makes them perfect for a family. The hotel is well managed. It's across the street from the market, which can be a little noisy, but the double-glazed windows do a good job of blocking out the noise.

Aldama 103, 68000 Oaxaca, Oax. (☏/fax 951/516-1336. www.mexonline.com/casacue.htm. 23 units. $65–$72 (£36–£40) double; $79–$92 (£43–£51) junior suite; $96–$130 (£53–£72) suite. AE, MC, V. Free covered, secure parking. **Amenities:** Restaurant; bar; exercise equipment; tour info; car-rental desk; room service; laundry service; dry cleaning. *In room:* A/C, TV.

INEXPENSIVE

Hotel Casa Arnel (*Value*) (*Kids*) Not far from the bus station, this budget hotel is less than a kilometer (about a half-mile) from the *zócalo* but still within walking distance of most sights. It's a great choice for those traveling with kids: The Cruz family lives here with a couple of their children, and parrots hang out in the shady garden. From the rooftop terrace, you can admire the view and soak up some sun. Most rooms are plain but comfortable; some share bathrooms. Across the street in the new wing are three additional rooms with double beds and private bathrooms, plus four furnished, full-service apartments with fully equipped kitchens. Breakfast, at extra cost, is served on the patio. At Christmas, the family involves guests in the traditional Mexican celebrations, or *posadas*, which are held during the 12 nights before Christmas.

Aldama 404, Col. Jalatlaco, 68080 Oaxaca, Oax. (☏/fax 951/515-2856. www.casaarnel.com.mx. 40 units. $22–$25 (£12–£14) double w/shared bathroom, $40–$45 (£22–£25) with private bathroom; $70–$80 (£39–£44) suite; $450 (£248) apt monthly. Rates rise 30% for Easter, Guelaguetza, Día de los Muertos, and Christmas. No credit cards. Self-parking $3. **Amenities:** Tours; Internet access; laundry service. *In room:* No phone.

Hotel Maela This is a family hotel that the owners keep improving. The upkeep is good, the prices are good, and the location is excellent—a block behind Santo Domingo. Rooms are medium to small. Most have one double, two doubles, or one queen-size bed. The staff is very helpful.

Constitución 206, 68000 Oaxaca, Oax. (☏/fax 951/516-6022. www.mexonline.com/maela.htm. 26 units. High season $59 (£32) double; low season $51 (£28). No credit cards. Free guarded parking. *In room:* TV, safe.

Las Golondrinas (☆) This charming one-story hotel sits amid rambling patios with roses, Fuchsia, bougainvillea, and mature banana trees. Owned and managed by Guillermina and Jorge Velasco, Las Golondrinas (The Swallows) is very popular, so make reservations in advance. The simply furnished rooms, with windows and doors opening onto courtyards, all have tile floors and a small desk and chairs. Each holds either one full or two twin beds. A few rooms have a king-size bed and go for a higher

Finds Oaxacan Street Food

Unless it's during a festival, don't be surprised to find many restaurants empty. Oaxaqueños do not frequent restaurants but do like eating in market and street stalls. They favor foods such as tacos, tamales, *tlayudas* (12-in. tortillas, slightly dried, with a number of toppings), and quesadillas (in Oaxaca, large tortillas heated on the *comal*—a flat, earthenware pan—or among the coals, with several types of fillings). For adventurous diners, here are my picks for enjoying the people's food.

Quesadillas are a morning food, and the best place to eat them is in La Merced market (on Murguía, about 10 blocks east of Alcalá), where you'll find a number of food stalls. Everyone has a favorite; mine is La Florecita, and my favorite quesadilla comes with *huitlacoche*. The following places open only at night. For tacos, a little *taquería* (taco stand) called Tacos Sierra (on Morelos, a half-block west of Alcalá) is a Oaxacan institution. It makes simple tacos with pork filling and a spicy salsa, but I can never order enough. It closes when the pork runs out, usually by 10pm. Don't expect these tacos to come cheap. Another *taquería* is El Mesón, which is across from the northeast corner of the *zócalo* at Hidalgo 805. It offers *tacos de la parrilla* (grill) and *de olla* (clay pot). For *tlayudas,* seek out a hole-in-the-wall on Constitución around the corner from Libres, El Chepil. They come with a number of toppings, and with *tasajo* (dried beef) or *cecina* (pork rubbed with red chile) on the side. If you don't like lard, tell them that you want yours *sin asiento.* For tamales, find the woman who sets up her little stand on Avenida Hidalgo and 20 de Noviembre, in front of the pharmacy. She often doesn't get there until 7:30pm, but when she does, she quickly draws a crowd that buys tamales to go—six flavors, and my favorite is always the last one I've eaten. Since you're in Oaxaca, you might want to ask for a tamal made with *mole negro, mole amarillo,* or *chepil* (an herb).

---

price. Breakfast is served between 8 and 10am in a small tile-covered cafe in a garden setting ($3–$7/£1.65–£3.85); nonguests are welcome. The hotel is 6½ blocks north of the *zócalo*.

Tinoco y Palacios 411 (between Allende and Bravo), 68000 Oaxaca, Oax. ⓒ 951/514-3298 or ⓒ/fax 951/514-2126. lasgolon@prodigy.net.mx. 29 units. $48–$55 (£26–£30) double. No credit cards. Limited free parking. **Amenities:** Laundry service. *In room:* No phone.

WHERE TO DINE

Oaxacan cooking has a great reputation in Mexico. It makes use of more ingredients from the lowlands than central Mexican cooking. It's known for its *moles,* and for a wide variety of chiles, many of which you don't find in other parts of the country.

If you're curious to know more about Oaxacan cooking, **Zapotec Tours** (ⓒ 800/446-2922 in the U.S.) organizes a weeklong trip to the city in early October. The "Food of the Gods Festival" includes dining at different restaurants, cooking classes, a tour of the market, and field trips. For good coffee, espresso, or other, go to **Café Nuevo Mundo** (ⓒ 951/501-2122) at M. Bravo 206.

EXPENSIVE

El Ché 🍴 STEAKS   Need a break from spicy Mexican food? Have a steak and salad in attractive surroundings, and wash it down with a classic margarita. The restaurant offers both American and Argentine cuts of beef; the rib-eye and the *churrasco* are the most popular. Salads include Caesar and Roquefort prepared at the table.

5 de Mayo 413. 🕿 **951/514-2122.** Reservations recommended during special festivals. Steaks $13–$23 (£7.15–£13). MC, V. Daily 1–11pm.

MODERATE

El Asador Vasco INTERNATIONAL/MEXICAN   Of the restaurants circling the *zócalo,* this is the best bet. It certainly offers the most pleasant dining area: Tables overlook the *zócalo* from a second-floor stone archway. Take your pick of purely Mexican specialties (chiles rellenos, *moles, carne asada*) or dishes with a European twist (snapper filet cooked in olive oil and *guajillo* chile).

Portal de Flores 11. 🕿 951/514-4755. Main courses $8–$18 (£4.40–£9.90). MC, V. Daily 1–11:30pm.

El Naranjo OAXACAN/MEXICAN   This restaurant was closed for a long time and has now opened with a new owner. Chef Iliana de la Vega has left Oaxaca. I understand that the new owner has hired a chef to design a new menu that will focus on contemporary dishes. Call ahead for hours and other info.

Trujano 203. 🕿 **951/514-1878.** Reservations recommended. Main courses $8–$15 (£4.40–£8.25). AE, MC, V. Mon–Sat 1–10pm.

Marco Polo 🍴 SEAFOOD   If the weather's nice, you can enjoy dining outdoors in Marco Polo's shaded patio. The ceviche tostadas or the seafood cocktails are great starters (if you like your cocktail less tomato-y, tell the waiter you want it *a la marinera*). The specialty is the oven-baked fish (whole or filet), prepared several ways—I like their basic method, with just a *chile guajillo* marinade. For dessert, try the baked bananas. Marco Polo is just north of the central downtown area; it fronts the park known as Paseo Juárez.

Pino Suárez 806. 🕿 951/513-4308. Breakfast $3 (£1.65); main courses $9–$15 (£4.95–£8.25). AE, MC, V. Wed–Mon 8am–6pm.

María Bonita OAXACAN/MEXICAN   What I like best about this restaurant is that it offers some simple, classic Oaxacan dishes that are spurned by other restaurants in the city. The appetizer section, for example, has *tlayudas* and *memelitas* (the Oaxacan name for *sopes*), both rarely seen on restaurant menus. The soups are good as are the Oaxacan main courses. María Bonita occupies a house on Alcalá, 2 blocks north of the Santo Domingo. The three dining rooms are all simple, colorful, and attractive, with plain wooden chairs and tables.

Macedonio Alcalá 706-B. 🕿 951/516-7233. Main courses $6–$12 (£3.30–£6.60). AE, MC, V. Tues–Sat 8:30am–9pm; Sun 11am–6pm.

Yu Ne Nisa 🍴 OAXACAN ISTHMUS   In the hot lowlands of eastern Oaxaca, an area called the isthmus, a different kind of cooking is practiced, and you can sample some of the region's specialties at this restaurant located in a residential part of the Colonia Reforma, which is north of the Centro Histórico. Start off with some *garnachas* for appetizers—little corn patties covered in sauce—and then try one of the regional specialties like shrimp *mole* or another kind of *mole* called *gucheguiña.*

Seafood is a big part of isthmus cooking, and the menu offers seafood cocktails and soups.

Amapolas 1425, Col. Reforma. © 951/515-6982. Main courses $7–$14 (£3.85–£7.70). No credit cards. Daily 1–8pm.

INEXPENSIVE

Doña Elpidia *Finds* OAXACAN   The phrase "home-style cooking" is bandied about a lot, but in this case it really means something. For the traveler, it means a meal just like the main dinner in a well-run Mexican home. Finding this place is a bit of a trick; it's 5½ blocks south of the *zócalo*. Look for a small sign saying only RESTAURANT. When you enter, a chalkboard in front of you lists the day's meal. You will find some tables behind the overgrown garden. There is also indoor dining. The *comida corrida* includes a basket of bread, an appetizer, vegetable or pasta soup, rice, a meat or enchilada course, and dessert. Beer and other beverages are available.

Miguel Cabrera 413 (between Arista and Nuño del Mercado). © 951/516-4292. Fixed-price lunch $5 (£2.75). No credit cards. Daily 1–5pm.

Itanoni *Finds* MEXICAN/REGIONAL   This business began as a tortilla shop. The owner then decided to branch out into making other things besides tortillas. He is fascinated with the different forms of native corn and makes use of their varying characteristics in the cooking. The dishes are simple, traditional *antojitos* such as tacos, quesadillas, *memelitas,* and a couple I had never heard of: *tetelas,* and his own *"de ese."* I like these last two a lot. You can get them with a variety of fillings, including bean, cheese, mushrooms, *huitlacoche,* and others.

Belisario Domínguez 513, Col. Reforma. © 951/513-9223. Antojitos $1 (55p). No credit cards. Mon–Sat 8am–4pm; Sun 8am–2pm.

OAXACA AFTER DARK

If you are interested in seeing the region's traditional dances, you can check out the small-scale **Guelaguetza** performed by professional dancers at the Hotel Camino Real on Friday from 7 to 10pm. The cost ($30/£17) includes a buffet. **La Casa de Cantera,** Murguía 102 (© **951/514-7585**), offers something similar. The $11 (£6.05) cover is for the show only, which runs every night from 8:30 to 10:15pm. Drinks and supper cost extra. Call for reservations.

Concerts and dance programs take place all year at the **Teatro Macedonio de Alcalá,** Independencia and Armenta y López. Schedules are often posted by the front doors of the theater. In the early evening, the *zócalo* is a happening place, with all sorts of people out and about. The municipal brass band and marimba players perform free concerts on alternating nights. As the night wears on, you'll usually find some mariachis hanging about.

For salsa, go to **La Candela,** Murguía 413 (© **951/514-2010**), which offers live music Thursday through Saturday from 10:30pm to 2am. The cover is usually $3 (£1.65).

ROAD TRIPS FROM OAXACA

The countryside around Oaxaca is dotted with small archaeological sites and villages, and the most important are easy to reach. The landmark ruins in the region are **Monte Albán** (30 min.) and **Mitla** (1 hr.). If you're heading toward Mitla, you can make some interesting stops (see "The Road to Mitla: Ruins & Rug Weavers," below). A number of interesting villages in other directions make good day trips from Oaxaca. The State Tourism Office will give you a map that shows nearby villages where beautiful handicrafts are made. The visits are fun excursions by car or bus. If you would like a guided tour of archeological ruins or crafts villages, contact **Juan Montes Lara.** He is the thinking-person's guide to this area, as well as to most of southern Mexico. He speaks English and conducts tours for small groups throughout Oaxaca and Chiapas. He stays pretty busy, so contact him well in advance—the best way is by e-mail (ⓒ **951/515-7731;** jmonteslara@ yahoo.com).

Many villages have, in the past several years, developed fine small municipal museums. **San José El Mogote,** site of one of the earliest pre-Hispanic village-dweller groups, has a display of carvings and statues found in and around the town, and a display model of an old hacienda. **Teotitlán del Valle** also has a municipal museum; it features displays on the weaving process. Ask at the State Tourism Office for more information.

MONTE ALBAN: RUINS WITH A VIEW

Had I been the priest-king of a large Indian nation in search of the perfect site on which to build a ceremonial center, this would have been it. **Monte Albán** sits on a mountain that rises from the middle of the valley floor—or, rather, divides two valleys. From here you can see all that lies between you and the distant mountains.

Starting around 2000 B.C., village-dwelling peoples of unknown origin inhabited the Oaxaca valleys. Between 800 and 500 B.C., a new ceramic style appeared, indicating an influx of new peoples, now called Zapotec. Around 500 B.C., these peoples began the monumental exercise of leveling the top of a mountain, where they would build Monte Albán (*mohn*-teh ahl-*bahn*).

Very little of the original structures remain; they've either been obscured beneath newer construction or had their stones reused for other buildings. The **Danzantes friezes** (see below) date from this period.

A center of Zapotec culture, Monte Albán was also influenced by contemporary cultures outside the valley of Mexico. You can see Olmec influence in the early sculptures; more recent masks and sculptures reflect contact with the Maya. When Monte Albán was at its zenith in A.D. 300, it borrowed architectural ideas from Teotihuacán. By around A.D. 800, the significance of Monte Albán in Zapotec society began to wane. Although most likely never completely abandoned, it became a shadow of its former grandeur. At the beginning of the 13th century, the Mixtec appropriated Monte Albán. The Mixtec, who had long coexisted in the area with the Zapotec, began expanding their territory. At Monte Albán, they added little to the existing architecture; however, they seem to have considered it an appropriate burial ground for their royalty. They left many tombs, including **Tomb 7,** with its famous treasure.

Monte Albán centers on the **Great Plaza,** a man-made area created by flattening the mountaintop. From this plaza, aligned north to south, you can survey the Oaxacan valley. The excavations at Monte Albán have revealed more than 170 tombs, numerous ceremonial altars, stelae, pyramids, and palaces.

Begin your tour of the ruins on the eastern side of the Great Plaza at the I-shaped **ball court.** This ball court differs slightly from Maya and Toltec ball courts in that there are no goal rings, and the sides of the court slope. Also on the east side of the plaza are several **altars** and **pyramids** that were once covered with stucco. Note the sloping walls, wide stairs, and ramps; all are typical of Zapotec architecture and reminiscent of the architecture of Teotihuacán. The building, slightly out of line with the plaza (not on the north-south axis), is thought by some to have been an observatory;

it was probably aligned with the heavenly bodies rather than with the points of the compass.

The south side of the plaza has a large **platform** that bore several stelae, most of which are now in the National Museum of Anthropology in Mexico City. There's a good view of the surrounding area from the top of this platform.

The west side has more ceremonial platforms and pyramids. On top of the pyramid substructure are four columns that probably supported the roof of the temple at one time.

The famous building of **Los Danzantes (the dancers)** on the west side of the plaza, is the earliest known structure at Monte Albán. This building is covered with large stone slabs that have distorted naked figures carved into them (the ones you see are copies; the originals are protected in the site museum). There is speculation about who carved these figures and what they represent, although there is a distinct resemblance to the Olmec baby faces at La Venta, in Tabasco State. The distorted bodies and pained expressions might connote disease. Clear examples of figures representing childbirth, dwarfism, and infantilism are visible. Because of the fluid movement represented in the figures, they became known as Los Danzantes—merely a modern label for these ancient and mysterious carvings.

The **Northern Platform** is a maze of temples and palaces interwoven with subterranean tunnels and sanctuaries. Take time to wander here, for there are numerous reliefs, glyphs, paintings, and friezes along the lintels and jambs as well as the walls. In this section of the ruins, you are likely to see vendors discreetly selling "original" artifacts found at the site. These guys come from the nearby town of Arrazola, where the fabrication of "antiquities" is a long-standing cottage industry. I like to buy a piece from them occasionally and pretend I'm getting the real thing just to get an opportunity to talk with them.

Leaving the Great Plaza, head north to the **cemetery** and **tombs.** If you have a day to spend at Monte Albán, be sure to visit some of the tombs, which contain magnificent glyphs, paintings, and stone carvings of gods, goddesses, birds, and serpents. Lately, the tombs have been closed to the public, but check anyway. Of the tombs so far excavated, the most famous is **Tomb 7,** next to the parking lot. It yielded some 500 pieces of gold, amber, and turquoise jewelry, as well as silver, alabaster, and bone art objects. This amazing collection is on display at the Museo Regional de Oaxaca (p. 442).

As you enter the site, you'll see a museum, a shop with guidebooks to the ruins, a cafe, and a craft shop. I recommend purchasing a guidebook. Video camera permits cost $5 (£2.75). The site is open daily from 8am to 6pm. Admission to the ruins is $4 (£2.20). Licensed guides charge $15 (£8.25) per person for a walking tour.

To get to Monte Albán, take a bus from the Hotel Mesón del Angel, Mina 518, at Mier y Terán. **Autobuses Turísticos** makes seven runs daily, at 8:30, 9:30, 10:30, and 11:30am and 12:30, 1:30, and 3:30pm. Return service leaves the ruins at 11am, noon, 1, 2, 3, 4, and 5:30pm. The round-trip fare is $4 (£2.20). The ride takes a half-hour, and your scheduled return time is 2 hours after arrival. It's possible to take a later return for an additional $1 (55p), though you won't be guaranteed a seat; inform the driver of your intent. During high season there are usually additional buses. If you're driving from Oaxaca, take Calle Trujano out of town. It becomes the road to Monte Albán, about 10km (6¼ miles) away.

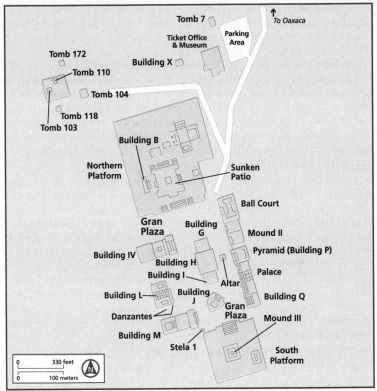

Tomb 7

Ticket Office & Museum

Parking Area

↑ To Oaxaca

Tomb 172

Tomb 110

Building X

Tomb 104

Tomb 118

Tomb 103

Building B

Northern Platform

Sunken Patio

Ball Court

Gran Plaza

Building G

Mound II

Building IV

Pyramid (Building P)

Building H

Building I

Palace

Altar

Building L

Building J

Building Q

Danzantes

Gran Plaza

Mound III

Building M

Stela 1

South Platform

0   330 feet
0   100 meters

THE ROAD TO MITLA: RUINS & RUG WEAVERS

East of Oaxaca, the Pan American Highway (Hwy. 190) leads to Mitla and passes several important archaeological sites, markets, and craft villages. You can visit the famous El Tule tree, an enormous, ancient cypress; the church at Tlacochahuaya, a lovely example of a 17th-century village church; the ruins at Dainzú, Lambityeco, and Yagul; the weaver's village of Teotitlán del Valle; and the village of Tlacolula, with its famous Dominican chapel.

There are a lot of little stops on this route, and some are a bit off the highway, so I recommend hiring a taxi, renting a car, or signing up with a small tour rather than using local bus transportation. If you take a tour, ask which sites it includes. To get to the highway, go north from downtown to Calzada Niños Héroes and turn right. This feeds directly on to the highway. All the sites are listed in order, from west (Oaxaca) to east (Mitla).

SANTA MARIA DEL TULE'S 2,000-YEAR-OLD TREE   Santa María del Tule is a small town 8km (5 miles) outside Oaxaca. It's famous for the immense **El Tule Tree,** an *ahuehuete* (Montezuma cypress, akin to the bald cypress) standing in a churchyard just off the main road. Now over 2,000 years old, it looks every bit its age, the way large cypresses do. However, this one is the most impressive tree I've ever seen for the sheer width of its trunk and canopy. It is said to have the broadest trunk of any tree in the world. When the tree was younger, the entire region around Santa María del Tule was marshland; in fact, the word *tule* means "reed." Now, the water table has dropped, so to protect the tree, a private foundation waters and takes care of it. The 25¢ admission fee goes toward these efforts.

The **Iglesia de San Jerónimo Tlacochahuaya,** 6km (4 miles) farther along, is the next stop. You'll see a sign pointing right; go less than another kilometer (about a half-mile) into town. Inside the church are an elaborately carved altar and a crucifix fashioned out of a ground paste made from the corn plant. The murals decorating the walls were the work of local artists of the 18th century and are a sweet mix of Spanish and Indian aesthetics. Make a point of seeing the beautifully painted baroque organ in the choir loft. The church is usually open daily from 10am to 2pm and 4 to 8pm.

DAINZU'S ZAPOTEC RUINS Three kilometers (2 miles) farther, visible from the highway (26km/16 miles from Oaxaca), you'll see a sign pointing to the right. It's less than a kilometer (under a mile) to the ruins, which were first excavated in the 1960s. Dainzú is a pre-Classic site that dates from between 700 and 600 B.C. Increasingly sophisticated building continued until about A.D. 300. The site occupies the western face of a hill, presumably for defense. The main building is a platform structure whose walls were decorated with carvings resembling Monte Albán's Danzantes. These carvings are now in a protective shed; a caretaker will unlock it for interested parties. These figures show Olmec influence but differ from the Danzantes because they wear the trappings of the "ball game," which make them, in all likelihood, the earliest representations of the ball game in Mexico. And, in fact, a partially reconstructed ball court sits below the main structure. The site provides an outstanding view of the valley. Admission is $3 (£1.65).

TEOTITLAN DEL VALLE'S BEAUTIFUL RUGS The next major turnoff you come to is 2km (1½ miles) farther along, 3km (2 miles) from the highway. This is Teotitlán, famous for weaving, and now an obviously prosperous town, to judge by all the current development. This is where you'll want to go for rugs, and you'll find no shortage of weavers and stores. Most weavers sell out of their homes and give demonstrations. The prices are considerably lower than in Oaxaca.

The church in town is well worth a visit. The early friars used pre-Hispanic construction stones to build the church and then covered them with adobe. When the townspeople renovated the church, they rediscovered these stones with carved figures, and now proudly display them. You'll see them in odd places in the walls of the church and sacristy. Teotitlán also has a small community museum, opposite the artisans' market and adjacent to the church. The museum has an interesting exhibit on natural dye-making, using herbs, plants, and cochineal (a red dye derived from insects).

For a bite to eat, consider the **Restaurant Tlamanalli,** Av. Juárez 39 (© **951/524-4006**), run by three Zapotec sisters who serve Oaxacan cuisine. Its reputation attracts lots of foreigners. It's on the right on the main street as you approach the main part of town, in a red brick building with black wrought-iron window covers. It's open Monday through Friday from 1 to 4pm. A bit farther on, there's another nice restaurant on the left where the main street intersects with the town center.

LAMBITYECO'S RAIN GOD Getting back to the highway and continuing eastward, in 3km (2 miles) you'll see a turnoff on the right for the small archaeological site of Lambityeco. Of particular interest are the two beautifully executed and preserved **stucco masks** of the rain god Cocijo. At Lambityeco, a major product was salt, distilled from saline groundwater nearby. Admission is $3 (£1.65).

TLACOLULA'S FINE MARKET & UNIQUE CHAPEL   Located about 30km (18 miles) from Oaxaca (1.5km/1 mile past Lambityeco), Tlacolula is in mezcal country, and along the road from here to Mitla, you'll see a couple of small distilleries and distillery outlets advertising their product. Feel free to stop by any one of them to taste their wares. Mezcal is distilled from a species of agave different from that of tequila. Most mezcal has a very strong smell and may or may not come with a worm in the bottle. Many of these small distilleries flavor their mezcal in much the same way that Russians flavor vodka.

Sunday is market day in Tlacolula, with rows of textiles fluttering in the breeze and aisle after aisle of pottery and baskets. If you don't go on market day, you have the advantage of not competing with crowds. The **Capilla del Mártir** of the parochial church is a stunning display of virtuosity in wrought iron. The doorway, choir screen, and pulpit, with their baroque convolutions, have no equals in Mexico's religious architecture. Also eye-catching are the realistic, almost life-size sculptures of the 12 apostles in their various manners of martyrdom. A few years ago, a secret passage was found in the church, leading to a room that contained valuable silver religious pieces. The silver was hidden during the Revolution of 1916, when there was a tide of anti-clerical sentiment; the articles are now back in the church.

YAGUL'S ZAPOTEC FORTRESS   Yagul, a fortress city on a hill overlooking the valley, is a couple of kilometers (about 1½ miles) farther on down the highway. You'll see the turnoff to the left; it's less than a kilometer (about a half mile) off the road. The setting is spectacular, and because the ruins are not as fully reconstructed as those at Monte Albán, you're likely to have the place to yourself. It's a good place for a picnic lunch.

The city was divided into two sections: the fortress at the top of the hill and the palaces lower down. The center of the palace complex is the plaza, surrounded by four temples. In the center is a ceremonial platform, under which is the **Triple Tomb.** The door of the tomb is a large stone slab decorated on both sides with beautiful hieroglyphs. The tomb may be open for viewing; if there are two guards, one can leave the entrance to escort visitors.

Look for the beautifully restored, typically Zapotec **ball court.** North of the plaza is the **palace** structure built for the chiefs of the city. It's a maze of rooms and patios decorated with painted stucco and stone mosaics. Visible here and there are ceremonial mounds and tombs decorated in the same geometric patterns found in Mitla. The panoramic view of the valley from the fortress is worth the rather exhausting climb.

Admission is $4 (£2.20). Still cameras are free, but use of a video camera costs $5 (£2.75). The site is open daily from 8am to 5:30pm.

It's just a few kilometers farther southeast to Mitla. The turnoff comes at a very obvious fork in the road.

MITLA'S LARGE ZAPOTEC & MIXTEC SITE   Mitla is 4km (2¾ miles) from the highway; the turnoff terminates at the **ruins** by the church. If you've come here by bus, it's less than a kilometer (about half a mile) up the road from the dusty town square to the ruins; if you want to hire a cab, there are some in the square.

The Zapotec settled Mitla around 600 B.C., and it became a Mixtec bastion in the late 10th century. This city was still flourishing at the time of the Spanish Conquest, and many of the buildings were used through the 16th century.

Tour groups often bypass the **town of Mitla** (pop. 7,000), but it is worth a visit. The University of the Americas maintains the **Museum of Zapotec Art** (previously known as the Frissell collection) in town. It contains some outstanding Zapotec and

Mixtec relics. Admission is $3 (£1.65). Be sure to look at the Leigh collection, which contains some real treasures. The museum is in a beautiful old hacienda.

You can easily see the most important buildings in an hour. Mixtec architecture is based on a quadrangle surrounded on three or four sides by patios and chambers, usually rectangular. The chambers are under a low roof, which is excellent for defense but makes the rooms dark and close. The stone buildings are inlaid with small cut stones to form geometric patterns.

There are five groups of buildings, divided by the Mitla River. The most important buildings are on the east side of the ravine. The **Group of the Columns** consists of two quadrangles, connected at the corners with palaces. The building to the north has a long chamber with six columns and many rooms decorated with geometric designs. The most common motif is the zigzag pattern, the same one seen repeatedly on Mitla blankets. Human and animal images are rare in Mixtec art. In fact, only one **frieze** has been found (in the Group of the Church, on the north patio). Here, you'll see a series of figures painted with their name glyphs.

Admission to the site is $4 (£2.20). Use of a video camera costs $5 (£2.75). Entrance to the museum is included in the price. It's open daily from 8am to 5pm.

Outside the ruins, vendors will hound you. The moment you step out of a car, every able-bodied woman and child for miles around will come charging over with shrill cries and a basket full of bargains—heavily embroidered belts, small pieces of pottery, fake archaeological relics, and cheap earrings. Offer to pay half the price the vendors ask. There's a modern handicrafts market near the ruins, but prices are lower in town.

SOUTH OF MONTE ALBAN: ARRAZOLA, CUILAPAN & ZAACHILA

ARRAZOLA: WOODCARVING CAPITAL   Arrazola lies in the foothills of Monte Albán, about 24km (15 miles) southwest of Oaxaca. The tiny town's most famous resident is **Manuel Jiménez,** the septuagenarian grandfather of the resurgence in woodcarving as folk art. Jiménez's polar bears, anteaters, and rabbits carved from copal wood are shown in galleries throughout the world; his home is a magnet for folk-art collectors. Now the town is full of other carvers, all making fanciful creatures painted in bright, festive colors. Little boys will greet you at the outskirts offering to guide you to individual homes for a small tip. Following them is a good way to get to know the town, and after a bit you can take your leave of them.

If you're driving to Arrazola, take the road out of Oaxaca City that goes to Monte Albán, then take the left fork after crossing the Atoyac River and follow the signs for Zaachila. Turn right after the town of Xoxo and you will soon reach Arrazola. You can also take a bus from the second-class station near the Abastos Market.

CUILAPAN'S DOMINICAN MONASTERY   Cuilapan (kwi-*lah*-pan) is about 15km (9⅓ miles) southwest of Oaxaca. The Dominican friars inaugurated their second **monastery** here in 1550. Parts of the convent and church were never completed due to political complications in the late 16th century. The roof of the monastery has fallen in, but the cloister and the church remain. The church, which is still in use, is being restored. There are three naves with lofty arches, large stone columns, and many frescoes. It is open daily from 10am to 6pm; entry is $5.50 (£3.05), plus $4 (£.20) for a video camera. The monastery is visible on the right a short distance from the main road to Zaachila, and there's a sign as well. The bus from the second-class station stops within a few hundred feet of the church.

ZAACHILA: MARKET TOWN WITH MIXTEC TOMBS   Farther on from Cuilapan, 24km (15 miles) southwest of Oaxaca, Zaachila (sah-*chee*-lah) has a **Thursday market;** baskets and pottery are sold for local household use, and the produce market is always full. Also take note of the interesting livestock section and a **mercado de madera (wood market)** just as you enter town.

Behind the church is the entrance to a small **archaeological site** containing several mounds and platforms and two interesting tombs. The artifacts found here now reside in the National Museum of Anthropology in Mexico City, but **Tomb 1** contains carvings that are worth checking out.

At the time of the Spanish Conquest, Zaachila was the last surviving city of the Zapotec rulers. When Cortez marched on the city, the Zapotec offered no resistance, and he formed an alliance with them. This outraged the Mixtec, who invaded Zaachila shortly afterward. The site and tombs are open daily from 9am till 4pm, and the entrance fee is $3 (£1.65).

To return to Oaxaca, your best option is to line up with locals to take one of the *colectivos* on the main street across from the market. If you're driving, see the directions for Arrazola, above.

SOUTH ALONG HIGHWAY 175

SAN BARTOLO COYOTEPEC'S POTTERY   San Bartolo is the home of the famous **black pottery** sold all over Oaxaca. It's also one of several little villages named Coyotepec in the area. Buses frequently operate between Oaxaca and this village, about 15km (10 miles) south on Highway 175. In 1953, a native woman named Doña Rosa invented the technique of smoking the pottery during firing to make it black and rubbing the fired pieces with a piece of quartz to produce a sheen. Doña Rosa died in 1979, and her son, **Valente Nieto Real,** carries on the tradition. Watching Valente change a lump of coarse clay into a work of art with only two crude plates (used as a potter's wheel) is an almost magical experience. The family's home and factory is a few blocks off the main road; you'll see the sign as you enter town. It's open daily from 9am to 5:30pm.

You can buy black pottery at many shops on the little plaza or in the artists' homes. Villagers who make pottery often place a piece of their work near their front door, by the gate, or on the street. It's their way of inviting prospective buyers to come in.

SAN MARTIN TILCAJETE: WOODCARVING VILLAGE   San Martín Tilcajete, about 15km (10 miles) past San Bartolo, is home to **woodcarvers** who produce *alebrijes*—fantastical, brightly painted animals and imaginary beasts—much like those produced in Arrazola. You can wander from house to house viewing the amazing collections of hot-pink rabbits; 1m (4-ft.), bright-blue twisting snakes; and two-headed Dalmatians.

SANTO TOMAS JALIETZA   About 2km (1½ mile) beyond San Martín, you'll see a sign on the left for this village of **weavers** who use backstrap looms. The village cooperative runs a market in the middle of town. Prices are fixed; you'll find the greatest variety of goods on Friday.

OCOTLAN   Twenty minutes farther on Highway 175 brings you to this fairly large market town. This city is notable for a few reasons: One is the **Aguilar sisters** (Josefina, Guillermina, Irene, and Concepción) and their families, who produce red clay pottery figures that are colorful, sometimes humorous, and prized by collectors. You'll see their row of home-workshops on the right as you enter. There are pottery figures on the fence and roof. (Don't go around town asking for the Aguilar family. Most of the town's inhabitants are named Aguilar.)

Ocotlán is also the home of **Rodolfo Morales,** a painter who, upon becoming wealthy and famous, took an active role in aiding his hometown with renovation projects. Two projects worth visiting are the parish church and former convent. Inside the convent, you can see some of the original decorations of the Dominicans. The noticeable sheen of the stucco walls is produced using the viscous innards of the nopal cactus. The convent is now a community museum.

Friday is market day in Ocotlán, and the town fills with people and goods. It's a very good market where you can find a variety of things at reasonable prices.

NORTH OF OAXACA
GUELATAO: BIRTHPLACE OF BENITO JUAREZ
High in the mountains north of Oaxaca, this lovely town has become a living monument to its favorite son, Benito Juárez. Although usually peaceful, the town comes to life on **Juárez's birthday** (Mar 21). The museum, statues, and plaza all attest to the town's obvious devotion to the patriot.

A second-class bus departs from Oaxaca's first-class station six times daily. There are also several departures from the second-class station. The trip takes at least 2 hours, through gorgeous mountain scenery. Buses return to Oaxaca every 2 hours until 8pm.

2 Villahermosa

142km (88 miles) NW of Palenque; 160km (100 miles) N of San Cristóbal de las Casas

Villahermosa (pop. 550,000) is the capital and the largest city of the state of Tabasco. It lies in a shallow depression about an hour's drive from the Gulf coast, at the confluence of two rivers: the Grijalva and the Carrizal. The land is marshy, with shallow lakes scattered here and there. For most of the year it's hot and humid. Why bother coming here? Because it has the giant Olmec heads set outside in something that's half museum and half park. Also, because it has the closest international airport to the ruins of Palenque and the highlands of Chiapas.

Oil has brought money to this town and raised prices. Villahermosa is one of the most expensive cities in the country and contrasts sharply with inexpensive Chiapas. The money is being sucked into the modern western sections surrounding a development called Tabasco 2000. This area, especially the neighborhoods around the **Parque–Museo La Venta,** is the most attractive part of town, surrounded, as it is, by small lakes. The historic center has been left to decay. It's gritty, crowded, and unpleasant. The main reason to be downtown is for the cheap hotels.

ESSENTIALS
GETTING THERE & DEPARTING
BY PLANE   **Continental ExpressJet** (© **800/525-0280** in the U.S., or 01-800/ 900-5000 in Mexico; www.continental.com) has direct service to/from Houston on a regional jet. **Mexicana** (© **800/531-7921** in the U.S., 01-800/502-2000; www. mexicana.com) and **AeroMéxico** (© **800/237-6639** in the U.S., or 01-800/021-4000; www.aeromexico.com) both have flights to and from Mexico City. **Aviación de Chiapas (Aviacsa;** © **993/316-5700** or 01-800/006-2200; www.aviacsa.com) flies to and from Mexico City and Mérida. The regional airline **Aerolitoral,** a subsidiary of AeroMéxico (© **800/237-6639** in the U.S., or 993/312-6991), goes through Mexico

City with a connection to Veracruz, Tampico, Monterrey, and Houston. **Click** (© **01-800/122-5425** in Mexico; www.clickmx.com), a Mexican budget airline, provides nonstop service to and from Mexico City.

BY CAR   Highway 180 connects Villahermosa to Campeche (6 hr.). **Highway 186,** which passes by the airport, joins **Highway 199** to Palenque and San Cristóbal de las Casas. The road to Palenque is a good one, and the drive takes 2 hours. Between Palenque and San Cristóbal the road enters the mountains and takes 4 to 5 hours. On any of the mountainous roads, road conditions are apt to get worse during the rainy season from May to October.

BY BUS   The **bus station** is at Mina and Merino (© **993/312-8900**), 3 blocks off Highway 180. There are eight nonstop buses per day to/from Palenque (2½ hr.). There are eight nonstop buses per day to Mexico City (10 hr.), six deluxe service on **ADO-GL,** and two super deluxe on **UNO.**

ORIENTATION

ARRIVING   Villahermosa's **airport** is 10km (6¼ miles) east of town. Driving in, you'll cross a bridge over the Río Grijalva, then turn left to reach downtown. Taxis to the downtown area cost $15 (£8.25).

Parking downtown can be difficult; it's best to find a parking lot. Use one that's guarded around the clock.

VISITOR INFORMATION   The **State Tourism Office** (© **993/316-5122,** ext. 229) has two information booths. The one at the **airport** is staffed daily from 10am to 5pm; the one at **Parque–Museo La Venta** (next to the ticket counter for the park) is staffed Tuesday to Sunday from 10am to 5pm.

CITY LAYOUT   The downtown area, including the pedestrian-only **Zona Luz,** is on the west bank of the Grijalva River. About 1.5km (1 mile) upstream (south) is **CICOM,** with the large archaeology museum named for the poet Carlos Pellicer Cámara. The **airport** is on the east side of the river. Highway 180 passes the airport and crosses the river just north of downtown, becoming **Bulevar Ruiz Cortines.** To get to the downtown area, turn left onto **Madero** or **Pino Suárez.** By staying on Ruiz Cortines you can reach the city's biggest attraction, the Parque–Museo la Venta. It's well marked. Just beyond that is the intersection with **Paseo Tabasco,** the heart of the modern hotel and shopping district.

GETTING AROUND   Taxis are your best way to get around town. Villahermosa is rare for being a Mexican city without meaningful public transportation.

FAST FACTS   American Express is represented by Turismo Creativo, Av. Paseo Tabasco 1404, Col. Tabasco 2000 (© **993/310-9900**). The telephone **area code** is **993.** There aren't a lot of *casas de cambio,* but you can exchange money at the airport, the hotels, and downtown banks on calles Juárez and Madero. ATMs are plentiful.

EXPLORING VILLAHERMOSA

Major sights include the **Parque–Museo La Venta** and the **Museo Regional de Antropología Carlos Pellicer Cámara.**

Museo Regional de Antropología Carlos Pellicer Cámara ✦✦   This museum on the west bank of the river about 1.5km (1 mile) south of the town center is well organized and has a great collection. The pre-Hispanic artifacts on display include not

only Tabascan finds (Totonac, Zapotec, and Olmec), but also those of other Mexican and Central American cultures.

The second floor is devoted to the Olmec. The third floor features artifacts from central Mexico, including the Tlatilco and Teotihuacán cultures; the Huasteca culture of Veracruz, San Luis Potosí, and Tampico states; and the cultures of Nayarit State, on the west coast. Photographs and diagrams provide vivid images, but the explanatory signs are mostly in Spanish. Look especially for the figurines that were found in this area and for the colorful Codex (an early book of pictographs).

CICOM Center, Av. Carlos Pellicer Cámara 511. (©) **993/312-6344**. Admission $3 (£1.65). Tues–Sun 9am–5pm.

Parque–Museo La Venta 🎏🎏 The Olmec created the first civilization in Mexico and developed several cultural traits that later spread to all subsequent civilizations throughout Mesoamerica. In addition to their monumental works, they carved small, exquisite figurines in jade and serpentine, which can be seen in the Museo Regional de Antropología (see above). Once inside the park and museum, a trail leads you from one sculpture to the next. Most of the pieces are massive heads or altars. These can be as tall as 2m (6 ft.) and weigh as much as 40 tons. The faces seem to be half adult, half infant. They have highly stylized mouths with thick fleshy lips that turn down. Known as the "jaguar mouth," this is a principal characteristic of Olmec art. At least 17 heads have been found: 4 at La Venta, 10 at San Lorenzo, and 3 at Tres Zapotes—all Olmec cities on Mexico's east coast. The pieces in this park were taken from La Venta, a major city during the pre-Classic period (2000 B.C.–A.D. 300). Most were sculpted around 1000 B.C. without the use of metal chisels. The basalt rock used for these heads and altars was transported to La Venta from more than 113km (70 miles) away. It is thought that the rock was brought most of the way by raft. Most of these pieces were first discovered in 1938. Now all that remains at La Venta are some grass-covered mounds that were once earthen pyramids. An exhibition area at the entrance to the park does a good job of illustrating how La Venta was laid out and what archaeologists think the Olmec were like.

As you stroll along, you will see labels identifying many species of local trees, including a grand ceiba tree of special significance to the Olmec and, later, the Maya. A few varieties of local critters scurry about, seemingly unconcerned with the presence of humans or with escaping from the park. Allow at least 2 hours for wandering through the junglelike sanctuary and examining the 3,000-year-old sculpture. *Note:* Don't forget the mosquito repellent.

Bulevar Ruiz Cortines s/n. (©) **993/314-1652**. Admission $4 (£2.20). Tues–Sun 8am–4pm.

WHERE TO STAY & DINE

You pay a little extra for rooms in Villahermosa, but you'll probably only spend 1 or 2 nights here. My favorites in descending order of price are the following: **Hyatt** Regency **Villahermosa** Hotel (© **800/233-1234** in the U.S., or 993/310-1234; www.villahermosa.regency.hyatt.com); **Best Western Hotel Maya Tabasco** (© **800/528-1234** in the U.S. and Canada, or 993/358-1111, ext. 822; www.hotelmaya.com.mx); **Hotel Plaza Independencia** (© **993/312-1299** or -7541; www.hotelesplaza.com.mx); and **Hotel Provincia Express** (© **993/314-5376**).

Like other Mexican cities, Villahermosa has seen the arrival of U.S. franchise restaurants, but as these things go, I prefer the Mexican variety: **Sanborn's,** Av. Ruiz Cortines 1310, near Parque–Museo La Venta (© **993/316-8722**), and **VIPS,** Av. Fco. I. Madero 402, downtown (© **993/312-3237**). Both usually do a good job with traditional dishes such as enchiladas or *antojitos* (supper dishes). But if you're looking for something beyond the standard fare, take a taxi to **Jangada** (© **993/317-6050**), an all-you-can-east seafood restaurant, with a wonderful variety of seafood cocktails, ceviches, grilled fish, and soups. It's on the west side of town in the La Choca neighborhood on Paseo de la Choca 126. The only problem is that it closes at 7pm. If you want to eat later, there's a sister restaurant next door that's a Brazilian-style steakhouse called Rodizio. It stays open until 9pm. It is quite good as well.

3 Palenque ⋆⋆

142km (88 miles) SE of Villahermosa; 229km (142 miles) NE of San Cristóbal de las Casas

The ruins of Palenque look out over the jungle from a tall ridge that juts out from the base of steep, thickly forested mountains. It is a dramatic sight colored by the mysterious feel of the ruins themselves. The temples here are in the Classic style, with high-pitched roofs crowned with elaborate combs. Inside many are representations in stone and plaster of the rulers and their gods, which give evidence of a cosmology that is—and perhaps will remain—impenetrable to our understanding. This is one of the grand archaeological sites of Mexico.

Eight kilometers (5 miles) from the ruins is the town of Palenque. There you can find lodging and food, as well as make travel arrangements. Transportation between the town and ruins is cheap and convenient.

ESSENTIALS
GETTING THERE & DEPARTING
BY PLANE   There is no regular commercial air service to Palenque.

BY CAR   The 230km (143-mile) trip from San Cristóbal to Palenque takes 5 hours and passes through lush jungle and mountain scenery. Take it easy, though, and watch out for potholes and other hindrances. **Highway 186** from Villahermosa should take about 2 hours. You may encounter military roadblocks that involve a cursory inspection of your travel credentials and perhaps your vehicle.

BY BUS   The two first-class bus stations are 2 blocks apart. Both are on Palenque's main street between the main square and the turnoff for the ruins. The smaller company, **Transportes Rodolfo Figueroa** (© **916/345-1322**), offers first-class service four times a day to and from San Cristóbal (5 hr.) and Tuxtla (6½ hr.). **ADO/ Cristóbal Colón** (© **916/345-1344**) offers service to those destinations and to Campeche (six per day, 5 hr.), Villahermosa (nine per day, 2 hr.), and Mérida (two per day, 9 hr.).

ORIENTATION
VISITOR INFORMATION   The downtown tourism office is a block from the main square at the corner of Avenida Juárez and Abasolo. It's open Monday to Saturday from 9am to 9pm, Sunday from 9am to 1pm. There's no phone at the downtown office. To get info over the phone, call the tourism office's business office (© **916/345-0356**).

CITY LAYOUT   **Avenida Juárez** is Palenque's main street. At one end is the **main plaza;** at the other is the oversized sculpture of the famous Maya head that was discovered here. To the right of the statue is the entrance to the Cañada; to the left is the road to the ruins, and straight ahead past the statue are the airport and the highway to Villahermosa. The distance between the town's main square and the monument is about 1.5km (1 mile).

La Cañada is a restaurant and hotel zone tucked away in the forest. Aside from the main plaza area, this is the best location for travelers without cars, because the town is within a few blocks, and the buses that run to the ruins pass right by.

GETTING AROUND   The cheapest way to get back and forth from the ruins is on the white **VW buses** (*colectivos*) that run down Juárez every 10 minutes from 6am to 6pm. The buses pass La Cañada and hotels along the road to the ruins and can be flagged down at any point, but they may not stop if they're full. The cost is $1 (55p) per person.

FAST FACTS   The telephone area code is **916.** As for the **climate,** Palenque's high humidity is downright oppressive in the summer, especially after rain showers. During the winter, the damp air can occasionally be chilly in the evening. Rain gear is handy at any time of year. **Internet service** and **ATMs** are easily available.

EXPLORING PALENQUE

The reason to come here is the ruins; although you can tour them in a morning, many people savor Palenque for days. There are no must-see sights in town.

PARQUE NACIONAL PALENQUE ★★★

A **museum and visitor center** sits not far from the entrance to the ruins. Though it's not large, the museum is worth the time it takes to see; it's open Tuesday to Sunday from 10am to 5pm and is included in the price of admission. It contains well-chosen and artistically displayed exhibits, including jade from recently excavated tombs. Explanatory text in Spanish and English explains the life and times of this magnificent city. New pieces are sometimes added as they are uncovered in ongoing excavations.

The **main entrance,** about 1km (½ mile) beyond the museum, is at the end of the paved highway. There you'll find a large parking lot, a refreshment stand, a ticket booth, and several shops. Among the vendors selling souvenirs are often some Lacandón Indians wearing white tunics and hawking bows and arrows.

Admission to the ruins is $5 (£2.75). The fee for using a video camera is $5 (£2.75). Parking at the main entrance and at the visitor center is free. The site and visitor center shops are open daily from 8am to 4:45pm.

TOURING THE RUINS   Pottery shards found during the excavations show that people lived in this area as early as 300 B.C. By the Classic period (A.D. 300–900), Palenque was an important ceremonial center. It peaked around A.D. 600 to 700.

When John Stephens visited the site in the 1840s, the ruins that you see today were buried under centuries of accumulated earth and a thick canopy of jungle. The dense jungle surrounding the cleared portion still covers unexcavated temples, which are easily discernible in the forest even to the untrained eye. But be careful not to drift too far from the main path—there have been a few incidents where tourists venturing alone into the rainforest were assaulted.

Of all Mexico's ruins, this is the most haunting, because of its majesty; its history, recovered by epigraphers; and its mysterious setting. Scholars have identified the rulers and constructed their family histories, putting visitors on a first-name basis with these ancient people etched in stone. You can read about it in *A Forest of Kings,* by Linda Schele and David Freidel.

As you enter the ruins, the building on your right is the **Temple of the Inscriptions,** named for the great stone hieroglyphic panels found inside. (Most of the panels, which portray the family tree of King Pacal, are in the National Anthropological

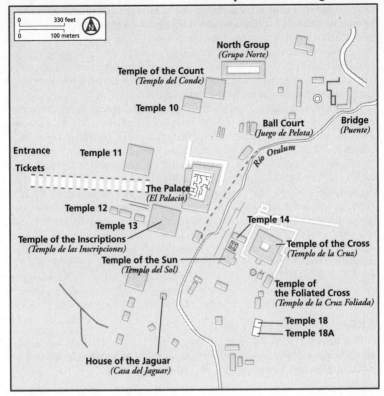

Museum in Mexico City.) This temple is famous for the crypt of King Pacal deep inside the pyramid, but the crypt is closed to the public. The archaeologist Alberto Ruz Lhuller discovered the tomb in the depths of the temple in 1952—an accomplishment many scholars consider one of the great discoveries of the Maya world. In exploratory excavations, Ruz Lhuller found a stairway leading from the temple floor deep into the base of the pyramid. The original builders had carefully concealed the entrance by filling the stairway with stone. After several months of excavation, Ruz Lhuller finally reached King Pacal's crypt, which contained several fascinating objects, including a magnificent carved stone sarcophagus. Ruz Lhuller's own gravesite is opposite the Temple of the Inscriptions, on the left as you enter the park.

Just to your right as you face the Temple of the Inscriptions is **Temple 13,** which is receiving considerable attention from archaeologists. They recently discovered the burial of another richly adorned personage, accompanied in death by an adult female and an adolescent. Some of the artifacts found there are on display in the museum.

Back on the main pathway, the building directly in front of you is the **Palace,** with its unique tower. The explorer John Stephens camped in the Palace when it was completely covered in vegetation, spending sleepless nights fighting off mosquitoes. A pathway between the Palace and the Temple of the Inscriptions leads to the **Temple of the Sun,** the **Temple of the Foliated Cross,** the **Temple of the Cross,** and **Temple**

14. This group of temples, now cleared and in various stages of reconstruction, was built by Pacal's son, Chan-Bahlum, who is usually shown on inscriptions with six toes. Chan-Bahlum's plaster mask was found in Temple 14 next to the Temple of the Sun. Archaeologists have begun probing the Temple of the Sun for Chan-Bahlum's tomb. Little remains of this temple's exterior carving. Inside, however, behind a fence, a carving of Chan-Bahlum shows him ascending the throne in A.D. 690. The panels depict Chan-Bahlum's version of his historic link to the throne.

To the left of the Palace is the North Group, also undergoing restoration. Included in this area are the **Ball Court** and the **Temple of the Count.** At least three tombs, complete with offerings for the underworld journey, have been found here, and the lineage of at least 12 kings has been deciphered from inscriptions left at this site.

Just past the North Group is a small building (once a museum) now used for storing the artifacts found during restorations. It is closed to the public. To the right of the building, a stone bridge crosses the river, leading to a pathway down the hillside to the new museum. The rock-lined path descends along a cascading stream on the banks of which grow giant ceiba trees. Benches are placed along the way as rest areas, and some small temples have been reconstructed near the base of the trail. In the early morning and evening, you may hear monkeys crashing through the thick foliage by the path; if you keep noise to a minimum, you may spot wild parrots as well. Walking downhill (by far the best way to go), it will take you about 20 minutes to reach the main highway. The path ends at the paved road across from the museum. The *colectivos* (minibuses) going back to the village will stop here if you wave them down.

WHERE TO STAY

English is spoken in all the more expensive hotels and about half of the inexpensive ones. The quoted rates include the 17% tax. High season in Palenque is Easter week, July to August, and December.

EXPENSIVE

Chan-Kah Resort Village ★   This hotel is a grouping of comfortable, roomy bungalows that offer privacy and quiet in the surroundings of a tropical forest. The hotel is on the road between the ruins and the town, but because the town of Palenque isn't particularly worth exploring, you won't miss much by staying here. The grounds are beautifully tended, and there is an inviting pool that resembles a lagoon. A broad stream runs through the property. Some of the bungalows can have a musty smell. Christmas prices will be higher than those quoted here, and you may be quoted a higher price if you reserve a room in advance from outside the country. The outdoor restaurant and bar serves only passable Mexican food. Room service is pricey.

Carretera Las Ruinas Km 3, 29960 Palenque, Chi. ℂ **916/345-1100.** Fax 916/345-0820. www.chan-kah.com.mx. 73 units. $140 (£77) double. MC, V. Free guarded parking. **Amenities:** Restaurant; bar; 3 outdoor pools (1 large w/natural spring); game room; room service; laundry service. *In room:* A/C, hair dryer.

Misión Palenque ★★   This hotel has returned to being the most comfortable in the city after a total remodeling of the rooms that includes new air-conditioning and other amenities. Rooms are medium-size and attractively furnished with light, modern furniture. Bathrooms are spacious with ample counters. The hotel has extensive grounds, and is very quiet. In one corner of the property, a natural spring flows through an attractive bit of jungle, where the hotel has installed the spa. Part of the

Where to Stay & Dine in Palenque

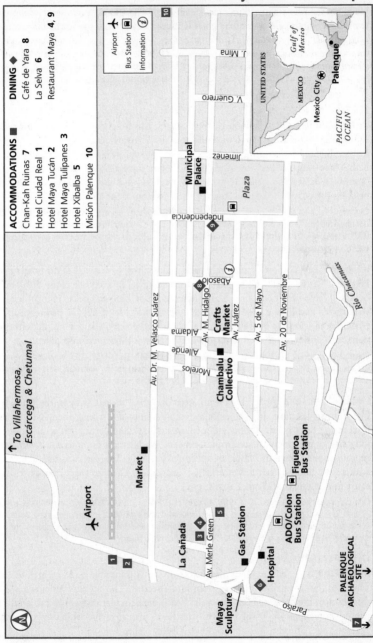

ACCOMMODATIONS ■

Chan-Kah Ruinas **7**
Hotel Ciudad Real **1**
Hotel Maya Tucán **2**
Hotel Maya Tulipanes **3**
Hotel Xibalba **5**
Misión Palenque **10**

DINING ◆

Café de Yara **8**
La Selva **6**
Restaurant Maya **4, 9**

Airport ✈
Bus Station ◼
Information ⓘ

↑ To *Villahermosa,
Escárcega & Chetumal*

Airport ✈

Market

La Cañada

Av. Merle Green

Gas Station

Maya
Sculpture

Hospital

Av. Dr. M. Velasco Suárez

Municipal
Palace

Jiménez

Plaza

Independencia

Abasolo

Av. M. Hidalgo
Aldama
Allende
Morelos

Crafts
Market

Chambalu
Collectivo

Av. Juárez

Av. 5 de Mayo

Av. 20 de Noviembre

Figueroa
Bus Station

ADO/Colon
Bus Station

Paraíso

PALENQUE
ARCHAEOLOGICAL
SITE →

J. Mina

V. Guerrero

Río Chacamax

UNITED STATES

Gulf of
Mexico

MEXICO

Mexico City ✳

Palenque

PACIFIC
OCEAN

spa is a *temazcal* or native American steam bath. There's also a mud bath along with the more common elements. The hotel is a few blocks east of the town's main square.

Periférico Oriente d/c, 29960 Palenque, Chi. ✆ **916/345-0241**, or 01/800-900-3800 in Mexico. Fax 916/345-0300. www.hotelesmision.com.mx. 156 units. $160 (£88) double. AE, MC, V. Free guarded parking that includes vehicle checkup. **Amenities:** Restaurant; bar; 2 outdoor pools; 2 tennis courts; fitness room; spa; Jacuzzi; tour service; car-rental desk; courtesy trips to ruins; room service; in-room massage; babysitting; laundry service. *In room:* A/C, TV, hair dryer (on request), safe.

MODERATE

Hotel Ciudad Real
Though not really fancy, this hotel does the important things right—the rooms are ample, quiet, and well lit. They are comfortably, if plainly, furnished. Suites have a sitting room with sleeping sofa. Most units hold two double beds; some king-size beds are available. All rooms have a small balcony, which in the best case overlooks an attractive garden. When making a reservation, specify the hotel in Palenque. It's at the edge of town in the direction of the airport.

Carretera a Pakal-Na Km 1.5, 29960 Palenque, Chi. ✆ **916/345-1343** (reservations: ✆ 967/678-4400). www. ciudadreal.com.mx. 72 units. High season $115 (£63) double, $135 (£74) suite; low season $100 (£55) double, $130 (£72) suite. AE, MC, V. Free secured parking. **Amenities:** Restaurant; bar; outdoor pool; baby pool; game room; travel agency; car-rental desk; room service; laundry service; nonsmoking rooms. *In room:* A/C, TV, hair dryer.

Hotel Maya Tucán
Get a room in back, and you will have a view of the hotel's natural pond. The cheerfully decorated rooms are adequate in size; they come with double beds and large bathrooms. Suites are larger and have king-size beds. The grounds are well tended and lush; scarlet macaws kept by the hotel fly about the parking lot. The Maya Tucán is on the highway to the airport. Bathrooms are larger and better lit but done with less polish than at Ciudad Real. Beds have rubber mattress covers.

Carretera-Palenque Km 0.5, 29960 Palenque, Chi. ✆ **916/345-0443**. Fax 916/345-0337. mayatucan@palenque. com.mx. 56 units. $110 (£61) double, $140 (£77) suit. MC, V. Free secured parking. **Amenities:** Restaurant; bar; outdoor pool; room service; laundry service. *In room:* A/C, TV, hair dryer, no phone.

Hotel Maya Tulipanes
This is an attractive hotel tucked away in the Cañada. I like it for its location, and the close attention paid by the management. Service and upkeep are both good. Rooms are medium to large and come with a queen-size, a king-size, or two double beds. Tropical vegetation adorns the grounds along with some reproductions of famous Mayan architecture. The Maya Tulipanes has an arrangement with a sister hotel at the ruins of Tikal, in Guatemala. The travel agency operates daily tours to Bonampak and other attractions.

Calle Cañada 6, 29960 Palenque, Chi. ✆ **916/345-0201** or -0258. Fax 916/345-1004. www.mayatulipanes.com.mx. 73 units. High season $110 (£61) standard. Internet packages available. AE, MC, V. Free secured parking. **Amenities:** Restaurant; bar; outdoor pool; travel agency; ground transportation to/from Villahermosa airport; room service; laundry service; nonsmoking rooms. *In room:* A/C, TV, Wi-Fi, hair dryer, no phone.

INEXPENSIVE

Hotel Xibalba
This modern small two-story hotel is inspired by Maya architecture. The medium-to-small rooms are clean and cheerful. The upstairs units are a little smaller than the downstairs. Most of the beds have firm mattresses. You can arrange a trip to Bonampak or Misol Ha with the hotel management, which owns a travel agency, Viajes Shivalva (pronounced like Xibalba: "shee-*bahl*-bah").

Calle Merle Green 9, Col. La Cañada, 29960 Palenque, Chi. ✆ **916/345-0392**. Fax 916/345-0411. www.palenquemx. com/shivalva. 15 units. $50–$60 (£28–£33) double. MC, V. No parking. **Amenities:** Restaurant; bar; laundry service; travel agency. *In room:* A/C, TV, no phone.

WHERE TO DINE

Palenque and, for that matter, the rest of backwater Chiapas, is not for gourmets. Who'd a thunk? I had an easy time eliminating a number of restaurants that didn't even seem to be keeping up the appearance of serving food. But the situation has been improving, and you can at least get some decent Mexican food.

MODERATE

La Selva ⭐ MEXICAN/INTERNATIONAL   At La Selva (the jungle), you dine under a large, attractive thatched roof beside well-tended gardens. The menu includes seafood, freshwater fish, steaks, and Mexican specialties. The most expensive thing on the menu is *pigua,* freshwater lobster caught in the large rivers of southeast Mexico. These can get quite large—the size of small saltwater lobsters. This and the finer cuts of meat have been frozen, but you wouldn't want otherwise in Palenque. I liked the fish stuffed with shrimp, and the *mole* enchiladas. La Selva is on the highway to the ruins, near the statue of the Maya head.

Carretera Palenque Ruinas Km 0.5. ℂ **916/345-0363.** Main courses $8–$17 (£1.65–£9.35). MC, V. Daily 11:30am–11:30pm.

INEXPENSIVE

Café de Yara MEXICAN   A small, modern cafe and restaurant with a comforting, not overly ambitious menu. The cafe's strong suit is healthy salads (with disinfected greens), and home-style Mexican entrees, such as the beef or chicken *milanesa* or chicken cooked in a *chile pasilla* sauce.

Av. Hidalgo 66 (at Abasolo). ℂ **916/345-0269.** Main courses $4–$7 (£2.20–£3.85). MC, V. Daily 7am–11pm.

Restaurant Maya and Maya Cañada ⭐ MEXICAN   These two are the most consistently good restaurants in Palenque. One faces the main plaza from the corner of Independencia and Hidalgo, the other is in the Cañada (ℂ **916/345-0216**). Menus are somewhat different, but much is the same. Both do a good job with the basics—good strong, locally grown coffee and soft, pliant tortillas. The menu offers a nice combination of Mexican standards and regional specialties. If you're in an exploratory mood, try one of the regional specialties such as the *mole chiapaneco* (dark red, like *mole poblano,* but less sweet) or any of the dishes based on *chaya* or *chipilin* (mild-flavored local greens), such as the soup with *chipilin* and *bolitas de masa* (corn dumplings). If you want something more comforting, go for the chicken and rice vegetable soup, or the *sopa azteca* (tortilla soup). The plantains stuffed with cheese and fried Mexican-style are wonderful. Waiters sometimes offer specials not on the menu, and these are often the thing to get. You can also try *tascalate,* a pre-Hispanic drink made of water, *masa,* chocolate, and *achiote,* and served room temperature or cold.

Av. Independencia s/n. ℂ **916/345-0042.** Breakfast $4–$5 (£2.20–£2.75); main courses $6–$12 (£3.30–£6.60). AE, MC, V. Daily 7am–11pm.

ROAD TRIPS FROM PALENQUE
BONAMPAK & YAXCHILAN: MURALS IN THE JUNGLE

Intrepid travelers may want to consider the day trip to the Maya ruins of Bonampak and Yaxchilán. The **ruins of Bonampak,** southeast of Palenque on the Guatemalan border, were discovered in 1946. The site is important for the vivid **murals** of the Maya on the interior walls of one temple. Particularly striking is an impressive battle scene, perhaps the most important painting of pre-Hispanic Mexico. Reproductions of these murals are on view in the Regional Archaeology Museum in Villahermosa.

Several tour companies offer a day trip. The drive to Bonampak is 3 hours. From there you continue by boat to the **ruins of Yaxchilán,** famous for its highly ornamented buildings. Bring rain gear, boots, a flashlight, and bug repellent. All tours include meals and cost about $50 (£28). No matter what agency you sign up with, the hours of departure and return are the same because the vans of the different agencies caravan down and back for safety. You leave at 6am and return at 7pm.

Try **Viajes Na Chan Kan** (© 916/345-2154), at the corner of avenidas Hidalgo and Jiménez, across from the main square, or **Viajes Shivalva,** Calle Merle Green 1 (© 916/345-0411;** fax 916/345-0392). A branch of Viajes Shivalva (© **916/345-0822**) is a block from the *zócalo* (main plaza) at the corner of Juárez and Abasolo, across the hall from the State Tourism Office. It's open Monday to Saturday from 9am to 9pm.

WATERFALLS AT MISOL HA & AGUA AZUL

A popular excursion from Palenque is a day trip to the Misol Ha waterfall and Agua Azul. **Misol Ha** is 20km (12 miles) from Palenque, in the direction of Ocosingo. It takes about 30 minutes to get there, depending on the traffic. The turn-off is clearly marked; you'll turn right and drive another 1½ km (1 mile). The place is absolutely beautiful. Water pours from a rocky cliff into a broad pool of green water bordered by thick tropical vegetation. There's a small restaurant and some rustic cabins for rent for $30 to $40 (£17–£22) per night, depending on the size of the cabin. The place is run by the *ejido* cooperative that owns the site, and it does a good job of maintaining the place. To inquire about the cabins, call © **916/345-1506.** Admission for the day is $1 (55p).

Approximately 44km (27 miles) beyond Misol Ha are the **Agua Azul waterfalls**— 270m (886 ft.) of tumbling falls with lots of water. There are cabins for rent here, too, but I would rather stay at Misol Ha. You can swim either above or below the falls, but make sure you don't get pulled by the current. You can see both places in the same day or stop to see them on your way to Ocosingo and San Cristóbal. Agua Azul is prettiest after 3 or 4 consecutive dry days; heavy rains can make the water murky. Check with guides or other travelers about the water quality before you decide to go. The cost to enter is around $2 (£1.10) per vehicle and $1 (55p) per person. Trips to both of these places can be arranged through just about any hotel.

OCOSINGO & THE RUINS OF TONINA

By the time you get to Agua Azul, you're half way to Ocosingo, which lies half way between Palenque and San Cristóbal. So, instead of returning for the night to Palenque, you can go on to Ocosingo. It's higher up and more comfortable than Palenque. It's a nice little town, not touristy, not a lot to do other than see the ruins of Toniná. But it is a nice place to spend the night so that you can see the ruins early before moving on to San Cristóbal. There are about a half dozen small hotels in town; the largest is not the most desirable. I would stay at the **Hospedaje Esmeralda** (© 919/673-0014) or the **Hotel Central** (© 919/673-0024) on the main square. Both of these are small and simple, but welcoming.

Ruins of Toniná ๑

The ruins of Toniná (the name translates as "house of rocks") are 14km (9 miles) east of Ocosingo. You can take a cab there and catch a *colectivo* to return. The city dates from the Classic period and covered a large area, but the excavated and restored part is all on one hillside that faces out towards a broad valley. This site is not really set up for lots of tourists. There's a lot of up and down, and some of it is a little precarious. It's not a good place to take kids. Admission is $3.50 (£1.95).

This complex of courtyards, rooms, and stairways is built on multiple levels that are irregular and asymmetrical. The overall effect is that of a ceremonial area with multiple foci instead of a clearly discernable center.

As early as A.D. 350, Toniná emerged as a dynastic center. In the 7th and 8th centuries it was locked in a struggle with rival Palenque and, to a lesser degree, with far-away Calakmul. This has led some scholars to see Toniná as more militaristic than its neighbors—a sort of Sparta of the classic Maya. Toniná's greatest victory came in 711, when, under the rule of Kan B'alam, it attacked Palenque and captured its king, K'an Joy Chitam, who is depicted on a stone frieze twisted and his arms bound with rope.

But the single most important artifact yet found at Toniná, is up around the fifth level of the acropolis—a large stucco frieze divided into panels by a feathered framework adorned with the heads of sacrificial victims (displayed upside down) and some rather horrid creatures. The largest figure is a skeletal image holding a decapitated head—very vivid and very puzzling. There is actually a stylistic parallel with some murals of the Teotihuacán culture of central Mexico. The other special thing about Toniná is that it holds the distinction of having the last ever date recorded in the long count (A.D. 909), which for all practical purposes marks the end of the Classic period.

4 San Cristóbal de las Casas ⭐⭐⭐

229km (142 miles) SW of Palenque; 80km (50 miles) E of Tuxtla Gutiérrez; 74km (46 miles) NW of Comitán; 166km (103 miles) NW of Cuauhtémoc; 451km (280 miles) E of Oaxaca

San Cristóbal is a colonial town of white stucco walls and red-tile roofs, of cobblestone streets and narrow sidewalks, of graceful arcades and open plazas. It lies in a green valley 2,120m (6,954 ft.) high. The city owes part of its name to the 16th-century cleric Fray Bartolomé de las Casas, who was the town's first bishop and spent the rest of his life waging a political campaign to protect the indigenous peoples of the Americas.

Surrounding the city are many villages of Mayan-speaking Indians who display great variety in their language, dress, and customs, making this area one of the most fascinating in Mexico. San Cristóbal is the principal market town for these Indians, and their point of contact with the outside world. Most of them trek down from the surrounding mountains to sell goods and run errands

Several Indian villages lie within reach of San Cristóbal by road: **Chamula,** with its weavers and unorthodox church; **Zinacantán,** whose residents practice their own syncretic religion; **Tenejapa, San Andrés,** and **Magdalena,** known for brocaded textiles; **Amatenango del Valle,** a town of potters; and **Aguacatenango,** known for embroidery. Most of these "villages" consist of little more than a church and the municipal government building, with homes scattered for miles around and a general gathering only for church and market days (usually Sun).

Many Indians now live on the outskirts of town because they've been expelled from their villages over religious differences. They are known as *los expulsados.* No longer involved in farming, they make their living in commerce and handicrafts. Most still wear traditional dress, but they've adopted Protestant religious beliefs that prevent them from partaking in many of the civic and religious celebrations of their communities.

The influx of outsiders hasn't created in most Indians a desire to adopt mainstream customs and dress. It's interesting to note that the communities closest to San Cristóbal are the most resistant to change. The greatest threat to the cultures in this area comes not from tourism but from the action of large market forces, population pressures, environmental damage, and poverty. The Indians aren't interested in acting or looking like the foreigners they see. They may steal glances or even stare at tourists, but mainly they pay little attention to outsiders, except as potential buyers for handicrafts.

You may see or hear the word *Jovel,* San Cristóbal's Indian name, incorporated often in the names of businesses. You'll hear the word *coleto,* used in reference to someone or something from San Cristóbal. You'll see signs for *tamales coletos, pan coleto* (Cristóbal bread), and *desayuno coleto* (Cristóbal breakfast).

ESSENTIALS
GETTING THERE & DEPARTING

BY PLANE   Flights from Mexico City have been canceled. The closest airport is in Tuxtla Gutiérrez.

BY CAR   From Tuxtla Gutiérrez, the 1½-hour trip winds through beautiful mountain country. From Palenque, the road is just as beautiful (if longer—5 hr.), and it provides jungle scenery, but portions of it may be heavily potholed or obstructed during rainy season. Check with the local state tourism office before driving.

BY TAXI   Taxis from Tuxtla Gutiérrez to San Cristóbal cost around $50 (£28). Another way to travel to and from Tuxtla is by *combi.* The Volkswagen vans, which can get extremely crowded, make the run every 15 to 30 minutes. They can be found just off the highway by the bus station. You'll have to ask someone to point them out to you because there isn't a sign.

BY BUS   The two bus stations in town are directly across the Pan American Highway from each other. The smaller one belongs to **Transportes Rodolfo Figueroa,** which provides first-class service to and from Tuxtla (every 40 min.) and Palenque (four buses per day, with a stop in Ocosingo—cheaper than the competition). For other destinations, go to the large station run by **ADO** and its affiliates, Altos, Cristóbal Colón, and Maya de Oro. This company offers service to and from Tuxtla (12 buses per day), Palenque (almost every hour), and several other destinations: Mérida (two buses per day), Villahermosa (two buses per day), Oaxaca (two buses per day), and Puerto Escondido (two buses per day). To buy a bus ticket without going down to the station, go to the **Ticket Bus** agency, Real de Guadalupe 5 (✆ **967/678-8503**). Hours are Monday to Saturday from 7am to 11pm, Sunday from 9am to 5pm.

The Zapatista Movement & Chiapas

In January 1994, Indians from this area rebelled against the Mexican government over health care, education, land distribution, and representative government. Their organization, the **Zapatista Liberation Army,** known as EZLN (Ejército Zapatista de Liberación Nacional), and its leader, Subcomandante Marcos, have become emblematic of the problems Mexico has with social justice. In the last couple of years, the rhetoric of armed revolt has ended, and the Zapatistas are talking about building a broad leftist coalition—but not a political party. What this means for Mexican politics is not clear, but for travelers it means not having to worry about violent political unrest. Yes, the underlying conditions for social unrest remain, as they do all over Mexico, but no one is talking about revolution.

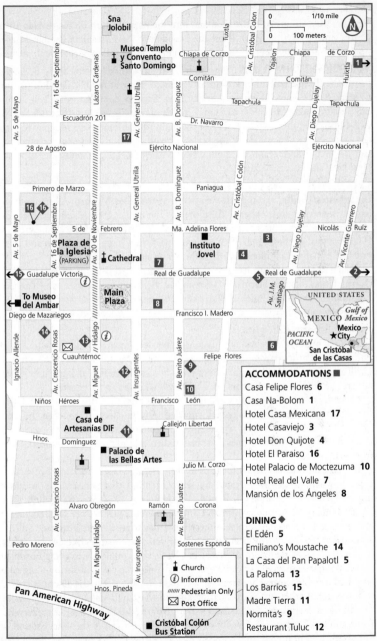

ACCOMMODATIONS ■
Casa Felipe Flores **6**
Casa Na-Bolom **1**
Hotel Casa Mexicana **17**
Hotel Casaviejo **3**
Hotel Don Quijote **4**
Hotel El Paraíso **16**
Hotel Palacio de Moctezuma **10**
Hotel Real del Valle **7**
Mansión de los Ángeles **8**

DINING ◆
El Edén **5**
Emiliano's Moustache **14**
La Casa del Pan Papalotl **5**
La Paloma **13**
Los Barrios **15**
Madre Tierra **11**
Normita's **9**
Restaurant Tuluc **12**

ORIENTATION

ARRIVING   To get to the main plaza from the highway turn on to **Avenida Insurgentes** (there's a traffic light). From the bus station, the main plaza is 9 blocks north up Avenida Insurgentes (a 10-min. walk, slightly uphill). Cabs are cheap and plentiful.

VISITOR INFORMATION   The **State Tourism Office** is better than the municipal office. It's just half a block south of the main plaza, at Av. Hidalgo 1-B (© **967/ 678-6570**); it's open Monday to Friday from 8am to 8pm, Saturday from 9am to 8pm, and Sunday from 9am to 2pm. The **Municipal Tourism Office** (©/fax **967/ 678-0665**) is in the town hall, west of the main square. Hours are Monday to Saturday from 9am to 8pm. Check the bulletin board here for apartments, shared rides, cultural events, and local tours. Both offices are helpful, but the state office is open an hour later and is better staffed.

CITY LAYOUT   San Cristóbal is laid out on a grid; the main north-south axis is **Insurgentes/Utrilla,** and the east-west axis is **Mazariegos/Madero.** All streets change names when they cross either of these streets. The *zócalo* (main plaza) lies where they intersect. An important street to know is **Real de Guadalupe,** which runs from the plaza eastward to the church of Guadalupe; located on it are many hotels and restaurants. The market is 7 blocks north of the *zócalo* along Utrilla.

Take note that this town has at least three streets named Domínguez and two streets named Flores. There's Hermanos Domínguez, Belisario Domínguez, and Pantaleón Domínguez, and María Adelina Flores and Dr. Felipe Flores.

GETTING AROUND   Most of the sights and shopping in San Cristóbal are within walking distance of the plaza.

Urbano **buses** (minibuses) take passengers between town and the residential neighborhoods. All buses pass by the market and central plaza on their way through town. Utrilla and Avenida 16 de Septiembre are the two main arteries; all buses use the market area as the last stop. Any bus on Utrilla will take you to the market.

Colectivos to outlying villages depart from the public market at Avenida Utrilla. Buses late in the day are usually very crowded. Always check to see when the last or next-to-last bus returns from wherever you're going, and then take the one before that—those last buses sometimes don't materialize, and you might be stranded. I speak from experience!

Rental cars come in handy for trips to the outlying villages and may be worth the expense when shared by a group, but keep in mind that insurance is invalid on unpaved roads. Try **Optima Car Rental,** Av. Mazariegos 39 (© **967/674-5409**). Office hours are daily from 9am to 1pm and 5 to 8pm. You'll save money by arranging the rental from your home country; otherwise, a day's rental with insurance will cost around $60 (£33) for a VW Beetle with manual transmission, the cheapest car available.

Scooters can be rented from Darren and Natasha, a couple of easygoing Australians who tell me that they've found the best way to enjoy the city and surrounding countryside. Look for **Croozy Scooters** (© **967/631-4329**) at Belisario Domínguez 7-A.

Bikes are another option for getting around the city; a day's rental is about $10 (£5.50). **Los Pingüinos,** Av. Ecuador 4-B (© **967/678-0202;** pinguinosmex@yahoo. com), offers bike tours to a few out-of-town locations. Tours in the valley around San Cristóbal last 4 to 6 hours and cost $25 to $30 (£14–£17). It's open daily from 10am to 2:30pm and 4 to 7pm.

FAST FACTS: San Cristóbal de las Casas

Area Code The telephone area code is **967**.

Books *The People of the Bat: Mayan Tales and Dreams from Zinacantán,* by Robert M. Laughlin, is a priceless collection of beliefs from that village near San Cristóbal. Another good book with a completely different view of today's Maya is *The Heart of the Sky,* by Peter Canby, who traveled among the Maya to chronicle their struggles (and wrote his book before the Zapatista uprising).

Bookstore For the best selection of new and used books and reading material in English, go to **La Pared,** Av. Hidalgo 2 (✆ **967/678-6367**). The owner, Dana Gay Burton, keeps a great collection of books on the Maya, and Mexico in general, both fiction and nonfiction.

Bulletin Boards San Cristóbal is a cultural crossroads for travelers, and several places maintain bulletin boards with information on Spanish classes, local specialty tours, rooms or houses to rent, rides needed, and so on. These include boards at the **Tourism Office, Café El Puente, Madre Tierra,** and **Casa Na-Bolom.**

Climate San Cristóbal can be chilly when the sun isn't out, especially during the winter. It's 2,120m (6,954 ft.) above sea level. Most hotels are not heated, although some have fireplaces. There is always a possibility of rain, but I would avoid going to San Cristóbal from late August to late October, during the height of the rainy season.

Currency Exchange There are at least five *casas de cambio* on Real de Guadalupe, near the main square, and a couple under the colonnade facing the square. Most are open until 8pm, and some are open Sunday. There are also a number of ATMs.

Doctor Try **Dr. Roberto Lobato,** Av. Belisario Domínguez 17, at Calle Flavio A. Paniagua (✆ **967/678-7777**). Don't be unsettled by the fact that his office is next door to Funerales Canober.

Internet Access There are Internet cafes everywhere.

Parking If your hotel does not have parking, use the *estacionamiento* (underground public lot) in front of the cathedral, just off the main square on 16 de Septiembre. Entry is from Calle 5 de Febrero.

Post Office The *correo* is at Crescencio Rosas and Cuauhtémoc, a block south and west of the main square. It's open Monday to Friday from 8am to 7pm, Saturday from 9am to 1pm.

Spanish Classes The **Instituto Jovel,** María Adelina Flores 21 (Apdo. Postal 62), 29250 San Cristóbal de las Casas, Chi. (✆/fax **967/678-4069**), gets higher marks for its Spanish courses than the competition. It also offers classes in weaving and cooking. The **Centro Bilingüe,** at the Centro Cultural El Puente, Real de Guadalupe 55, 29250 San Cristóbal de las Casas, Chi. (✆ **800/303-4983** in the U.S., or ✆/fax 967/678-3723), offers classes in Spanish. Both schools can arrange home stays for their students.

Telephone The best price for long-distance telephone calls and faxing is at **La Pared** bookstore (see "Bookstore," above) at Av. Hidalgo 2, across the street from the State Tourism Office.

EXPLORING SAN CRISTOBAL

San Cristóbal is a lovely town in a lovely region. A lot of people come for the beauty, but the main thing that draws most visitors here is the highland Maya. They can be seen anywhere in San Cristóbal, but most travelers take at least one trip to the outlying villages to get a close-up of Maya life.

ATTRACTIONS IN TOWN

Casa Na-Bolom 🌟🌟   If you're interested in the anthropology of the region, you'll want to visit this house museum. Stay here, if you can. The house, built as a seminary in 1891, became the headquarters of anthropologists Frans and Trudy Blom in 1951, and the gathering place of outsiders interested in studying the region. Frans Blom led many early archaeological studies in Mexico, and Trudy was noted for her photographs of the Lacandón Indians and her efforts to save them and their forest homeland. A room at Na-Bolom contains a selection of her Lacandón photographs, and postcards of the photographs are on sale in the gift shop (daily 9am–2pm and 4–7pm). A tour of the home covers the displays of pre-Hispanic artifacts collected by Frans Blom; the cozy library, with its numerous volumes about the region and the Maya (weekdays 10am–2pm); and the gardens Trudy Blom started for the ongoing reforestation of the Lacandón jungle. The tour ends with a showing of *La Reina de la Selva,* an excellent 50-minute film on the Bloms, the Lacandón, and Na-Bolom. Trudy Blom died in 1993, but Na-Bolom continues to operate as a nonprofit public trust.

The 12 guest rooms, named for surrounding villages, are decorated with local objects and textiles. All rooms have fireplaces and private bathrooms. Prices (including breakfast and admission to the museum) are $70 (£39) single, $90 (£50) double.

Even if you're not a guest here, you can come for a meal, usually an assortment of vegetarian and other dishes. Just be sure to make a reservation at least 2½ hours in advance, and be on time. The colorful dining room has one large table, and the eclectic mix of travelers sometimes makes for interesting conversation. Breakfast costs $5 to $7 (£2.75–£3.85); lunch and dinner cost $11 (£6.05) each. Dinner is served at 7pm. Following breakfast (8–10am), a guide not affiliated with the house offers tours to San Juan Chamula and Zinacantán (see "The Nearby Maya Villages & Countryside," below).

Av. Vicente Guerrero 3, 29200 San Cristóbal de las Casas, Chi. ☎ **967/678-1418.** Fax 967/678-5586. Group tour and film $5 (£2.75). Tours daily 11:30am (Spanish only) and 4:30pm. Leave the square on Real de Guadalupe, walk 4 blocks to Av. Vicente Guerrero, and turn left; Na-Bolom is 5½ blocks up Guerrero.

Catedral   San Cristóbal's main cathedral was built in the 1500s. It has little of interest inside besides a lovely, uncommon beam ceiling and a carved wooden pulpit.

Calle 20 de Noviembre at Guadalupe Victoria. No phone. Free admission. Daily 7am–6pm.

El Mercado   Once you've visited Santo Domingo (see listing below), meander through the San Cristóbal town market and the surrounding area. Every time I do, I see something different to elicit my curiosity.

By Santo Domingo church. No phone. Mon–Sat 8am–7pm.

Museo del Ambar 🌟   If you've been in this town any time at all, you know what a big deal amber is here. Chiapas is the third-largest producer of amber in the world, and many experts prefer its amber for its colors and clarity. A couple of stores tried calling themselves museums, but they didn't fool anybody. Now a real museum moves methodically through all the issues surrounding amber—mining, shaping, and identifying it, as well as the different varieties found in other parts of the world. It's interesting, it's cheap, and you get to see the restored area of the old convent it occupies. There are a couple of beautiful pieces of worked amber that are on permanent loan—make sure you see them. In mid-August, the museum holds a contest for local artisans who work amber. Check it out.

Exconvento de la Merced, Diego de Mazariegos s/n. (𝐶) **967/678-9716.** Admission $2 (£1.10). Tues–Sun 10am–2pm and 4–7pm.

Museo Templo y Convento Santo Domingo   Inside the front door of the carved-stone plateresque facade, there's a beautiful gilded wooden altarpiece built in 1560, walls with saints, and gilt-framed paintings. Attached to the church is the former Convent of Santo Domingo, which houses a small museum about San Cristóbal and Chiapas. The museum has changing exhibits and often shows cultural films. It's 5 blocks north of the *zócalo,* in the market area.

Av. 20 de Noviembre. (𝐶) **967/678-1609.** Free admission to church; museum $2 (£1.10). Museum Tues–Sun 10am–5pm; church daily 10am–2pm and 5–8pm.

Palacio de las Bellas Artes   Be sure to check out this building if you are interested in the arts. It periodically hosts dance events, art shows, and other performances. The schedule of events is usually posted on the door if the Bellas Artes is not open. There's a public library next door. Around the corner, the Centro Cultural holds a number of concerts and other performances; check the posters on the door to see what's scheduled.

Av. Hidalgo, 4 blocks south of the plaza. No phone.

Templo de San Cristóbal   For the best view of San Cristóbal, climb the seemingly endless steps to this church and *mirador* (lookout point). A visit here requires stamina. There are 22 more churches in town, some of which also demand strenuous climbs.

At the very end of Calle Hermanos Domínguez.

HORSEBACK RIDING

The **Casa de Huéspedes Margarita,** Real de Guadalupe 34, and **Hotel Real del Valle** (see "Where to Stay," below) can arrange horseback rides for around $15 (£8.25) for a day, including a guide. Reserve your steed at least a day in advance. A horseback-riding excursion might go to San Juan Chamula, to nearby caves, or up into the hills.

THE NEARBY MAYA VILLAGES & COUNTRYSIDE

The Indian communities around San Cristóbal are fascinating worlds unto themselves. If you are unfamiliar with these indigenous cultures, you will understand and appreciate more of what you see by visiting them with a guide, at least for your first foray out into the villages. Guides are acquainted with members of the communities and are viewed with less suspicion than newcomers. These communities have their own laws and customs—and visitors' ignorance is no excuse. Entering these communities is tantamount to leaving Mexico, and if something happens, the state and federal authorities will not intervene except in case of a serious crime.

The best guided trips are the locally grown ones. Three operators go to the neighboring villages in small groups. They all charge the same price ($10/£5.50 per person), use minivans for transportation, and speak English. They do, however, have their own interpretations and focus.

Pepe leaves from **Casa Na-Bolom** (see "Attractions in Town," above) for daily trips to San Juan Chamula and Zinacantán at 10am, returning to San Cristóbal between 2 and 3pm. Pepe looks at cultural continuities, community relationships, and, of course, religion.

Alex and Raúl can be found in front of the cathedral between 9:15 and 9:30am. They are quite personable and get along well with the Indians in the communities. They focus on cultural values and their expression in social behavior, which provides a glimpse of the details and the texture of life in these communities (and, of course, they talk about religion). Their tour is very good. They can be reached at © **967/678-3741** or chamul@hotmail.com.

For excursions farther afield, see "Road Trips from San Cristóbal," later in this chapter. Also, Alex and Raúl can be contracted for trips to other communities besides Chamula and Zinacantán; talk to them.

CHAMULA & ZINACANTAN A side trip to the village of San Juan Chamula will really get you into the spirit of life around San Cristóbal. Sunday, when the market is in full swing, is the best day to go for shopping; other days, when you'll be less impeded by eager children selling their crafts, are better for seeing the village and church.

The village, 8km (5 miles) northeast of San Cristóbal, has a large church, a plaza, and a municipal building. Each year, a new group of citizens is chosen to live in the municipal center as caretakers of the saints, settlers of disputes, and enforcers of village rules. As in other nearby villages, on Sunday local leaders wear their leadership costumes, including beautifully woven straw hats loaded with colorful ribbons befitting their high position. They solemnly sit together in a long line somewhere around the central square. Chamula is typical of other villages in that men are often away working in the "hot lands," harvesting coffee or cacao, while women stay home to tend the sheep, the children, the cornfields, and the fires.

Don't leave Chamula without seeing the **church interior.** As you step from bright sunlight into the candlelit interior, you feel as if you've been transported to another country. Pine needles scattered amid a sea of lighted candles cover the tile floor. Saints line the walls, and before them people are often kneeling and praying aloud while passing around bottles of Pepsi-Cola. Shamans are often on hand, passing eggs over sick people or using live or dead chickens in a curing ritual. The statues of saints are similar to those you might see in any Mexican Catholic church, but beyond sharing the same name, they mean something completely different to the Chamulas. Visitors can walk carefully through the church to see the saints or stand quietly in the background and observe.

In Zinacantán, a wealthier village than Chamula, you must sign a strict form promising *not to take any photographs* before you see the two side-by-side **sanctuaries.** Once permission is granted and you have paid a small fee, an escort will usually show you the church, or you may be allowed to see it on your own. Floors may be covered in pine needles here, too, and the rooms are brightly sunlit. The experience is an altogether different one from that of Chamula.

AMATENANGO DEL VALLE About an hour's ride south of San Cristóbal is Amatenango, a town known mostly for its **women potters.** You'll see their work in San Cristóbal—small animals, jars, and large water jugs—but in the village, you can visit the potters in their homes. Just walk down the dirt streets. Villagers will lean over the walls of family compounds and invite you in to select from their inventory. You may even see them firing the pieces under piles of wood in the open courtyard or painting them with color derived from rusty iron water. The women wear beautiful red-and-yellow *huipiles,* but if you want to take a photograph, you'll have to pay. To get here, take a *colectivo* from the market in San Cristóbal. Before it lets you off, be sure to ask about the return-trip schedule.

AGUACATENANGO   This village, 16km (10 miles) south of Amatenango is known for its **embroidery.** If you've visited San Cristóbal's shops, you'll recognize the white-on-white and black-on-black floral patterns on dresses and blouses for sale. The locals' own regional blouses, however, are quite different.

TENEJAPA   The **weavers** of Tenejapa, 28km (17 miles) from San Cristóbal, make some of the most beautiful and expensive work you'll see in the region. The best time to visit is on market day (Sun and Thurs, though Sun is better). The weavers of Tenejapa taught the weavers of San Andrés and Magdalena—which accounts for the similarity in their designs and colors. To get to Tenejapa, try to find a *colectivo* in the very last row by the market, or hire a taxi. On Tenejapa's main street, several stores sell locally woven regional clothing, and you can bargain for the price.

THE HUITEPEC CLOUD FOREST   **Pronatura,** Av. Benito Juárez 11-B (✆ **967/ 678-5000**), a private, nonprofit, ecological organization, offers environmentally sensitive tours of the cloud forest. The forest is a haven for **migratory birds,** and more than 100 bird species and 600 plant species have been discovered here. Guided tours run from 9am to noon Tuesday to Sunday. They cost $25 (£14) per group of up to eight people. Make reservations a day in advance. To reach the reserve on your own, drive on the road to Chamula; the turnoff is at Km 3.5. The reserve is open Tuesday to Sunday from 9am to 4pm.

SHOPPING

Many Indian villages near San Cristóbal are noted for **weaving, embroidery, brocade work, leather,** and **pottery,** making the area one of the best in the country for shopping. You'll see beautiful woolen shawls, indigo-dyed skirts, colorful native shirts, and magnificently woven *huipiles,* all of which often come in vivid geometric patterns. A good place to find textiles as well as other handicrafts, besides what's mentioned below, is in and around Santo Domingo and the market. There are a lot of stalls and small shops in that neighborhood that make for interesting shopping. Working in leather, the craftspeople are artisans of the highest caliber. Tie-dyed *jaspe* from Guatemala comes in bolts and is made into clothing. The town is also known for **amber,** sold in several shops, one of the best of which is mentioned below.

CRAFTS

Casa de Artesanías   The showroom has examples of every craft practiced in the state. It is run by the government in support of Indian crafts. You should take a look, if only to survey what crafts the region practices. It's open Monday to Friday from 9am to 9pm, Saturday 10am to 9pm, and Sunday 9am to 3pm. Niños Héroes at Hidalgo. ✆ **967/678-1180.**

El Encuentro   Noted for having reasonable prices, this shop carries many ritual items, such as new and used men's ceremonial hats, false saints, and iron rooftop adornments, plus many *huipiles* and other textiles. It's open Monday to Saturday from 9am to 8pm. Calle Real de Guadalupe 63-A (between Diego Dujelay and Vicente Guerrero). ✆ **967/ 678-3698.**

La Galería This art gallery beneath a cafe shows the work of well-known national and international painters. Also for sale are paintings and greeting cards by Kiki, the owner, a German artist who has found her niche in San Cristóbal. There are some Oaxacan rugs and pottery, plus unusual silver jewelry. It's open daily from 10am to 9pm. Hidalgo 3. © 967/678-1547.

Lágrimas de la Selva "Tears of the Jungle" deals in amber and jewelry, and no other amber shop in town that I know of has the variety, quality, or artistic flair of this one. It's not a bargain hunter's turf, but a great place for the curious to go. Often you can watch the jewelers in action. Open daily from 10am to 8pm. Hidalgo 1-C (half block south of the main square). © 967/674-6348.

TEXTILES

Plaza de Santo Domingo The plazas around this church and the nearby Templo de Caridad fill with women in native garb selling their wares. Here you'll find women from Chamula weaving belts or embroidering, surrounded by piles of loomed woolen textiles from their village. Their inventory includes Guatemalan shawls, belts, and bags. There are also some excellent buys on Chiapanecan-made wool vests, jackets, rugs, and shawls, similar to those at Sna Jolobil (described below), if you take the time to look and bargain. Vendors arrive between 9 and 10am and begin to leave around 3pm. Av. Utrilla. No phone.

Sna Jolobil Meaning "weaver's house" in Mayan, this place is in the former convent (monastery) of Santo Domingo, next to the Templo de Santo Domingo. Groups of Tzotzil and Tzeltal craftspeople operate the cooperative store, which has about 3,000 members who contribute products, help run the store, and share in the moderate profits. Their works are simply beautiful; prices are high, as is the quality. It's open Monday to Saturday from 9am to 2pm and 4 to 6pm; credit cards are accepted. Calzada Lázaro Cárdenas 42 (Plaza Santo Domingo, between Navarro and Nicaragua). © 967/678-2646.

Unión Regional de Artesanías de los Altos Also known as J'pas Joloviletic, this cooperative of weavers is smaller than Sna Jolobil (described above) and not as sophisticated in its approach to potential shoppers. It sells blouses, textiles, pillow covers, vests, sashes, napkins, baskets, and purses. It's near the market and worth looking around. Open Monday to Saturday from 9am to 2pm and 4 to 7pm, Sunday from 9am to 1pm. Av. Utrilla 43. © 967/678-2848.

WHERE TO STAY

Among the most interesting places to stay in San Cristóbal is the seminary-turned-hotel-museum **Casa Na-Bolom;** see "Attractions in Town," earlier in this chapter, for details.

Hotels in San Cristóbal are inexpensive. You can do pretty well for $30 to $50 (£17–£28) per night per double. Rates listed here include taxes. High season is Easter week, July, August, and December.

MODERATE

Casa Felipe Flores ★★ This beautifully restored colonial house is the perfect setting for getting a feel for San Cristóbal. The patios and common rooms are relaxing and comfortable, and their architectural details are so very *coleto*. The guest rooms are nicely furnished and full of character. And they are warm in winter. The owners, Nancy and David Orr, are gracious people who enjoy sharing their appreciation and knowledge of Chiapas and the Maya. Their cook serves up righteous breakfasts.

Calle Dr. Felipe Flores 36, 29230 San Cristóbal de las Casas, Chi. Ⓒ/fax **967/678-3996**. www.felipeflores.com. 5 units. $85–$105 (£47–£58) double. Rates include full breakfast. 10% service charge. No credit cards. Limited street parking. **Amenities:** Tour info; laundry service; library. *In room:* No phone.

Hotel Casa Mexicana ★★   Created from a large mansion, this beautiful hotel with a colonial-style courtyard offers comfortable lodging. Rooms, courtyards, the restaurant, and the lobby are decorated in modern-traditional Mexican style, with warm tones of yellow and red. The rooms are carpeted and come with two double beds or one king-size. They have good lighting, electric heaters, and spacious bathrooms. Guests are welcome to use the sauna, and inexpensive massages can be arranged. The hotel handles a lot of large tour groups; it can be quiet and peaceful one day, full and bustling the next. There is a new addition to the hotel across the street, but I like the doubles in the original section better. This hotel is 3 blocks north of the main plaza.

28 de Agosto 1 (at Utrilla), 29200 San Cristóbal de las Casas, Chi. Ⓒ **967/678-1348** or -0698. Fax 967/678-2627. www.hotelcasamexicana.com. 55 units. High season $95 (£52) double, $150 (£83) junior suite, $180 (£99) suite; low season $85 (£47) double, $140 (£77) junior suite, $170 (£94) suite. AE, MC, V. Free secure parking 1½ blocks away. **Amenities:** Restaurant; bar; sauna; tour info; room service; massage; babysitting; laundry service. *In room:* TV, hair dryer (on request).

Hotel Casavieja   The Casavieja is aptly named: It has a charming old feel that is San Cristóbal to a tee. Originally built in 1740, it has undergone restoration and new construction faithful to the original design in essentials such as wood-beam ceilings. One nod toward modernity is carpeted floors, a welcome feature on cold mornings. The rooms also come with electric heaters. Bathrooms vary, depending on what section of the hotel you're in, but all are adequate. The hotel's restaurant, Doña Rita, faces the interior courtyard, with tables on the patio and inside, and offers good food at reasonable prices. The hotel is 3½ blocks northeast of the plaza.

María Adelina Flores 27 (between Cristóbal Colón and Diego Dujelay), 29200 San Cristóbal de las Casas, Chi. Ⓒ/fax **967/678-6868** or -0385. www.casavieja.com.mx. 39 units. $60–$75 (£33–£41) double. AE, MC, V. Free parking. **Amenities:** Restaurant; bar; room service; laundry service. *In room:* TV.

Hotel El Paraíso   For the independent traveler, this is a safe haven from the busloads of tour groups that can disrupt the atmosphere and service at other hotels. Rooms are small but beautifully decorated. They have comfortable beds and good reading lights; some even have a ladder to a loft holding a second bed. Bathrooms are small, too, but the plumbing is good. The entire hotel is decorated in terra cotta and blue, with beautiful wooden columns and beams supporting the roof. The hotel's restaurant, El Edén (see "Where to Dine," below) may be the best in town.

Av. 5 de Febrero 19, 29200 San Cristóbal de las Casas, Chi. Ⓒ **967/678-0085** or -5382. Fax 967/678-5168. www.hotel posadaparaiso.com. 14 units. $55–$65 (£30–£36) double. AE, MC, V. No parking. **Amenities:** Restaurant; bar; tour info; room service; laundry service. *In room:* TV.

Mansión de los Angeles   This hotel with a good location offers good service and tidy rooms and public areas. Guest rooms are medium size and come with either a single and a double bed or two double beds. The rooms are warmer and better lit than at most hotels in this town. They are also quiet. Some of the bathrooms are a little small. Most rooms have windows that open onto a pretty courtyard with a fountain. The rooftop sun deck is a great siesta spot.

Calle Francisco Madero 17, 29200 San Cristóbal de las Casas, Chi. Ⓒ **967/678-1173** or -4371. hotelangeles@ prodigy.com.mx. 20 units. $55–$65 (£30–£36) double. MC, V. Limited street parking. *In room:* TV.

INEXPENSIVE

Hotel Don Quijote   Rooms in this three-story hotel (no elevator) are small but quiet, carpeted, and well lit, but a little worn. All have two double beds with reading lamps over them, tiled bathrooms, and plenty of hot water. There's complimentary coffee in the mornings. It's 2½ blocks east of the plaza.

Cristóbal Colón 7 (near Real de Guadalupe), 29200 San Cristóbal de las Casas, Chi. ℰ **967/678-0920.** Fax 967/678-0346. 24 units. $25–$40 (£14–£22) double. MC, V. Limited street parking. *In room:* TV.

Hotel Palacio de Moctezuma   This three-story hotel has open courtyards and more greenery than others in this price range. Fresh-cut flowers tucked around tile fountains are its hallmark. The rooms have carpeting and tiled bathrooms with showers; many are quite large but, alas, can be cold in winter. The restaurant looks out on the interior courtyard. On the third floor is a solarium with comfortable tables and chairs and great city views. The hotel is 3½ blocks southeast of the main plaza.

Juárez 16 (at León), 29200 San Cristóbal de las Casas, Chi. ℰ **967/678-0352** or -1142. Fax 967/678-1536. 42 units. $35–$40 (£19–£22) double. MC, V. Free limited parking. **Amenities:** Restaurant. *In room:* TV, no phone.

Hotel Real del Valle *(Value)*   This hotel has great location just off the main plaza. The rooms in the back three-story section have new bathrooms, big closets, and tile floors. The beds are comfortable, and the water is hot—all for a good price. In winter the rooms are a little cold. Amenities include a rooftop solarium.

Real de Guadalupe 14, 29200 San Cristóbal de las Casas, Chi. ℰ **967/678-0680.** Fax 967/678-3955. hrvalle@mundo maya.com.mx. 36 units. $25–$35 (£14–£19) double. No credit cards. Free parking. **Amenities:** Solarium; laundry service. *In room:* TV, no phone.

WHERE TO DINE

San Cristóbal is not known for its cuisine, but you can eat well at several restaurants. For baked goods, try the **Panadería La Hojaldra,** Mazariegos and 5 de Mayo (ℰ **967/678-4286**). It's open daily from 8am to 9:30pm. In addition to the restaurants listed below, consider making reservations for dinner at Casa Na-Bolom (see "Attractions in Town," earlier in this chapter).

MODERATE

El Edén *(★★)* INTERNATIONAL   This is a small, quiet restaurant where it is obvious that somebody who enjoys the taste of good food prepares the meals; just about anything except Swiss rarebit is good. The meats are especially tender, and the margaritas are especially dangerous (one is all it takes). Specialties include Swiss cheese fondue for two, Edén salad, and brochette. This is where locals go for a splurge. It's 2 blocks from the main plaza.

In the Hotel El Paraíso, Av. 5 de Febrero 19. ℰ **967/678-5382.** Breakfast $5 (£2.75); main courses $6–$10 (£3.30–£5.50). AE, MC, V. Daily 8am–9pm.

Los Barrios CONTEMPORARY MEXICAN   For Mexican food in San Cristóbal, I can't think of a better place than this. The tortilla soup was the best I've had here (called *sopa de la abuela*). For something different, there's a mushroom–and–cactus paddle soup. The main courses, while kept to a manageable number, offer enough variety to please several tastes. There are a couple of novel chile relleno combinations and a chicken breast *adobado* with plantain stuffing. The restaurant is in a patio with an interesting rough-wood enclosure. It's quiet and inviting.

Guadalupe Victoria 25 (between 3 de Mayo and Matamoros). ℰ **967/678-1910.** Main courses $6–$10 (£3.30–£5.50). MC, V. Mon–Sat 1–10pm; Sun buffet 1:30–6pm.

La Paloma INTERNATIONAL/MEXICAN   La Paloma I particularly like in the evening because the lighting is so well done. Both the Mexican and the other dishes are much more mainstream than what you get at Los Barrios—fewer surprises. For starters, I enjoyed the quesadillas cooked Mexico City style (small fried packets of *masa* stuffed with a variety of fillings). Don't make my mistake of trying to share them with your dinner companion; it will only lead to a quarrel over the last one. Mexican classics include *albóndigas en chipotle* (meatballs in a thick chipotle sauce, Oaxacan black *mole,* and a variety of chile rellenos). Avoid the *profiteroles.*

Hidalgo 3. (℃ **967/678-1547.** Main courses $6–$13 (£3.30–£7.15). MC, V. Daily 9am–midnight.

Pierre FRENCH   Who would have thought that you could get good French food in San Cristóbal? And yet, Frenchman Pierre Niviere offers an appealing selection of traditional French dishes, simplified and tweaked for the tropical surroundings. I showed up on a Sunday, enjoyed the fixed menu, and left well satisfied.

Real de Guadalupe 73. (℃ **967/678-7211.** Main courses $5–$16 (£2.75–£8.80); Sunday fixed menu $10 (£5.50). No credit cards. Daily 1:30–11pm.

INEXPENSIVE
Emiliano's Moustache *(finds)* MEXICAN/TACOS   Like any right-thinking traveler, I initially avoided this place on account of its unpromising name and some cartoonlike figures by the door. But a conversation with some local folk overcame my prejudice and tickled my sense of irony. Sure enough, the place was crowded with *coletos* enjoying the restaurant's highly popular *comida corrida* and delicious tacos, and there wasn't a foreigner in sight. The daily menu is posted by the door; if that doesn't appeal, you can choose from a menu of taco plates (a mixture of fillings cooked together and served with tortillas and a variety of hot sauces).

Crescencio Rosas 7. (℃ **967/678-7246.** Main courses $4–$8 (£2.20–£4.40); *comida corrida* $4 £2.20). No credit cards. Daily 8am–midnight.

La Casa del Pan Papalotl VEGETARIAN   This place is best known for its vegetarian lunch buffet with salad bar. The vegetables and most of the grains are organic. Kippy, the owner, has a home garden and a field near town where she grows vegetables. She buys high-altitude, locally grown, organic red wheat with which she bakes her breads. These are all sourdough breads, which she likes because she feels they are easily digested and have good texture and taste. The pizzas are a popular item. The restaurant shares space with other activities in the cultural center El Puente, which has gallery space, a language school, and cinema.

Real de Guadalupe 55 (between Diego Dujelay and Cristóbal Colón). (℃ **967/678-7215.** Main courses $5–$10 (£2.75–£5.50); lunch buffet $5–$6 (£2.75–£3.30). No credit cards. Mon–Sat 9am–10pm, lunch buffet 2–4pm.

Madre Tierra INTERNATIONAL/VEGETARIAN   A lot of vegetarians live in this town, and they have many options. This one is almost an institution in San Cristóbal. The restaurant is known for its baked goods, pastas, pizza, and quiche. They also offer fresh salads and international main courses that are safe and dependable. Good for breakfast, too. Madre Tierra is 3½ blocks south of the plaza.

Av. Insurgentes 19. (℃ **967/678-4297.** Main courses $4–$8; *comida corrida* (served after noon) $6 (£3.30). No credit cards. Restaurant daily 8am–9:45pm. Bakery Mon–Sat 9am–8pm; Sun 9am–2pm.

Normita's MEXICAN   Normita's is famous for its *pozole,* a hearty chicken and hominy soup to which you add a variety of things. It also offers cheap, dependable, short-order Mexican mainstays. Normita's is an informal "people's" restaurant; the open kitchen takes up one corner of the room, and tables sit in front of a large mural of a fall forest scene from some faraway place. It's 2 blocks southeast of the plaza.

Av. Juárez 6 (at Dr. José Flores). No phone. Breakfast $2–$2.50 (£1.10–£1.40); *pozole* $3 (£1.65); tacos $2.50 (£1.40). No credit cards. Daily 7am–11pm.

Restaurant Tuluc (Value) MEXICAN/INTERNATIONAL   A real bargain here is the popular *comida corrida*—it's delicious and filling. Other favorites are sandwiches and enchiladas. The house specialty is *filete Tuluc,* a beef filet wrapped around spinach and cheese served with fried potatoes and green beans; while not the best cut of meat, it's certainly priced right. The Chiapaneco breakfast is a filling quartet of juice, toast, two Chiapanecan tamales, and coffee. Tuluc also has that rarest of rarities in Mexico, a nonsmoking section. The restaurant is 1½ blocks south of the plaza.

Av. Insurgentes 5 (between Cuauhtémoc and Francisco León). (C) 967/678-2090. Breakfast $2–$3 (£1.10–£1.65); main courses $4–$5 (£2.20–£2.75); *comida corrida* (served 2–4pm) $3.75 (£2.05). No credit cards. Daily 7am–10pm.

COFFEEHOUSES

Because Chiapas-grown coffee is highly regarded, it's not surprising that coffeehouses proliferate here. Most are concealed in the nooks and crannies of San Cristóbal's side streets. Try **Café La Selva,** Crescencio Rosas 9 ((C) **967/678-7244**), for coffee served in all its varieties and brewed from organic beans; it is open daily from 9am to 11pm. A more traditional-style cafe, where locals meet to talk over the day's news, is **Café San Cristóbal,** Cuauhtémoc 1 ((C) **967/678-3861**). It's open Monday to Saturday from 9am to 10pm, Sunday from 9am to 9pm. There is also a coffee museum with a cafe inside with the confusing name **Café Museo Café.** It's at María Adelina Flores 10 ((C) **967/ 678-7876**)

SAN CRISTOBAL AFTER DARK

San Cristóbal is blessed with a variety of nightlife, both resident and migratory. There is a lot of live music, surprisingly good and varied. The bars and restaurants are cheap. And they are easy to get to: You can hit all the places mentioned here without setting foot in a cab. Weekends are best, but on any night you'll find something going on.

Almost of the clubs in San Cristóbal offer Latin music of one genre or another. **El Cocodrilo** ((C) **967/678-1140**), on the main plaza in the Hotel Santa Clara, has acoustic performers playing Latin folk music *(trova, andina).* Relax at a table in what usually is a not-too-crowded environment. After that your choices are varied. For Latin dance music there's a place just a block away on the corner of Madero and Juárez called **Latino's** ((C) **967/678-9972**)—good bands playing a mix of salsa, merengue, and cumbia. On weekends it gets crowded, but it has a good-size dance floor. Another club, **Blue** ((C) **967/678-2000**), is in the opposite direction on the other side of the main square. It has live music on weekends playing salsa, reggae, and some electronic music. The place is dark and has just a bit of the urban edge to it. From there you can walk down the pedestrian-only 20 de Noviembre to visit a couple of popular bars— **Revolución** and **El Circo.**

ROAD TRIPS FROM SAN CRISTOBAL

For excursions to nearby villages, see "The Nearby Maya Villages & Countryside," earlier in this chapter; for destinations farther away, there are several local travel agencies. But first you should try **Alex and Raúl** (p. 478). You can also try **ATC Travel**

and Tours, Calle 5 de Febrero 15, at the corner of 16 de Septiembre (© **967/678-2550;** fax 967/678-3145), across from El Fogón restaurant. The agency has bilingual guides and reliable vehicles. ATC regional tours focus on birds and orchids, textiles, hiking, and camping.

Strangely, the cost of the trips includes a driver but not necessarily a bilingual guide or guided information of any kind. You pay extra for those services, so when checking prices, be sure to flesh out the details.

PALENQUE, BONAMPAK & YAXCHILAN

For information on these destinations, see the section on Palenque, earlier in this chapter.

CHINCULTIC RUINS, COMITAN & MONTEBELLO NATIONAL PARK

Almost 160km (100 miles) southeast of San Cristóbal, near the border with Guatemala, is the **Chincultic** archaeological site and Montebello National Park, with **16 multicolored lakes** and exuberant pine-forest vegetation. Seventy-four kilometers (46 miles) from San Cristóbal is **Comitán,** a pretty hillside town of 40,000 inhabitants known for its flower cultivation and a sugar cane–based liquor called *comitecho.* It's also the last big town along the Pan-American Highway before the Guatemalan border.

The Chincultic ruins, a late Classic site, have barely been excavated, but the main **acropolis,** high up against a cliff, is magnificent to see from below and is worth the walk up for the view. After passing through the gate, you'll see the trail ahead; it passes ruins on both sides. More unexcavated tree-covered ruins flank steep stairs leading up the mountain to the acropolis. From there, you can gaze upon distant Montebello lakes and miles of cornfields and forest. The paved road to the lakes passes six lakes, all different colors and sizes, ringed by cool pine forests; most have parking lots and lookouts. The paved road ends at a small restaurant. The lakes are best seen on a sunny day, when their famous brilliant colors are optimal.

Most travel agencies in San Cristóbal offer a daylong trip that includes the lakes, the ruins, lunch in Comitán, and a stop in the pottery-making village of Amatenango del Valle. If you're driving, follow Highway 190 south from San Cristóbal through the pretty village of Teopisca and then through Comitán; turn left at La Trinitaria, where there's a sign to the lakes. After the Trinitaria turnoff and before you reach the lakes, there's a sign pointing left down a narrow dirt road to the Chincultic ruins.

12

Veracruz & Puebla: On the Heels of Cortez

by David Baird

The region of Veracruz and Puebla, in the east-central part of the country, was, for Hernán Cortez and his conquistadors, the door to Mexico. The region also played that role for most of the visitors who came to the area during colonial and early republic times. But today, only a small fraction of the multitudes that flock to Mexico each year passes through here.

This is a shame, for the area has much to recommend. For adventure travelers, it offers excellent white-water rafting, challenging climbs that include Mexico's highest mountain—a dormant volcano called the Pico de Orizaba—and scuba diving along Veracruz's coastal reefs. For the culture crowd, the region has three fascinating ruins, some excellent museums and historical sites, and great food.

Veracruz is a fun town for music and food, and for soaking up the easy-going rhythms of the Tropics. **Puebla** has the ideal highland climate, even better food, and a great historic district. The ruins in the area feature the startlingly vivid pre-Columbian murals of Cacaxtla, the great ceremonial center of El Tajín, and the New World's largest man-made structure, the great pyramid of Cholula.

1 Veracruz City ★

232km (144 miles) E of Mexico City; 109km (68 miles) SE of Xalapa

Veracruz has a reputation as a town with a rich history but little to show for it. True enough, because much of that rich history involved sackings by pirates; heavy bombardment by three different foreign powers (including during the wonderfully named French Pastry War); and epidemics of malaria, yellow fever, and cholera. One might not necessarily want to preserve such a history, even when those same events didn't destroy artifacts. For this reason, and for the character of the natives, Veracruz (unlike Puebla) is better suited to cafe-goers than museum-goers. With the exception of the old fort of San Juan de Ulúa and perhaps the aquarium, the museums can be missed. You come here for the feel of the tropics, the balmy air, and the carefree attitude of the locals.

Veracruz brings to mind other Gulf and Caribbean port cities—part New Orleans, part Maracaibo. Even more than in the rest of Mexico, things such as schedules are managed rather loosely. If you expect punctuality and order, you'll just be banging your head against a wall. Here, you relax: You get your coffee in the morning at the Café de la Parroquia, you stroll down the *malecón* (boardwalk) in the evening, you take in the party scene at the *zócalo* (town square) at night. The city attracts a lot of Mexicans, who come to take a break from the social constraints of their hometowns.

Downtown Veracruz

In many parts of Mexico, for instance, a woman walking into a bar by herself would be frowned upon; not here.

Music is important to Veracruz. Specific to the port city are *marimba, danzonera,* and *comparsa* (carnavalesque) music. Just south of the city begins the Jarocha region of the state, whose music is rhythmic, with sexually suggestive lyrics that depend on double meanings. This is the home of "La Bamba," popularized by Ritchie Valens. In the northern part of the state is the Huasteca region. Its music, the *huapango huasteco,* involves a violin, a couple of strumming guitars, and harmonized singing. Xalapa, the state's highland capital, is home to the largest and best music school in the country.

Cortez first landed a bit north of where the port is now, and his name for the place gives you an idea of what was on his mind: Villa Rica de la Vera Cruz ("Rich town of the true cross"). In colonial times, the Spanish galleons sailed for Spain from here, loaded with silver and gold. Pirates repeatedly attacked, and on occasion captured, the city. The citizens defended themselves, eventually constructing a high wall around the old town and a massive fort, San Juan de Ulúa. The walls surrounding the city are gone now, but the fort remains.

ESSENTIALS

GETTING THERE & DEPARTING   **By Plane**   **Continental** (✆ **800/231-0856** in the U.S., or 01-800/900-5000 in Mexico; www.continental.com) has nonstop service to and from Houston. **AeroMéxico** (© **800/237-6639** in the U.S., or 01-800/021-4000, or 229/935-0283 or 934-1534; www.aeromexico.com.mx) and **Mexicana** (© **800/531-7921** in the U.S., or 229/932-2242 or 938-0008; www.mexicana.com) and their affiliates offer service to and from Mexico City and other destinations within the country.

The **airport** is 11km (7 miles) from the town center. Getting there by **taxi** costs about $15 (£8.25). Major car-rental agencies with counters at the airport and locations in downtown hotels include **Avis** (© **800/331-1212** in the U.S., or 229/931-1580; www.avis.com), **Dollar** (© **800/800-4000** in the U.S., or 229/935-5231; www.dollar.com), and **National** (© **800/328-4567** in the U.S., or 229/931-7556; www.national.com).

By Car   From Mexico City (6 hr.) and Puebla (3½ hr.), take the *autopista* **(toll Hwy. 150D)** into Veracruz. From Xalapa (1½ hr.), take **Highway 140** to coastal toll **Highway 180** south.

By Bus   The **ADO** first-class bus station is 20 blocks south of the town center on Díaz Mirón between calles Orizaba and Molina. There is frequent service to Mexico City, Puebla, Xalapa, and other cities. Taxis wait in front of the terminal; the trip to the center costs around $3 (£1.65). You can buy a bus ticket downtown at the **Ticket Bus** agency (© **01-800/102-8000** in Mexico) at the corner of Allende and Zamora. It's open Monday through Saturday from 10am to 7pm.

VISITOR INFORMATION   The **tourism office** (©/fax 229/989-8817 or -8800, ext. 158), is downtown by the *zócalo,* on the ground floor of the Palacio Municipal (City Hall). It is open Monday through Friday from 8am to 8pm, Sunday from 10am to 6pm.

CITY LAYOUT   Downtown Veracruz is a jumble of streets. The social center of town is the *zócalo,* or town square (formally Plaza de Armas), where you'll find the tourism office. Two short blocks away is another landmark, *el malecón,* a long promenade fronting the harbor. Starting at the *malecón* and running south along the coast is **Bulevar Avila Camacho,** known as *el bulevar.* It connects downtown to Veracruz's hotel and restaurant zone, which stretches along the coast all the way to the onetime village of **Boca del Río.**

GETTING AROUND   Taxis are plentiful and inexpensive. Getting from the downtown area to the restaurant and hotel district to the south takes 5 to 10 minutes.

FAST FACTS: Veracruz

American Express **Viajes Reptur** represents American Express. The main office is at Serdán 690-B (© **229/931-0838**). Office hours for American Express–related business are Monday through Friday from 9am to 1:30pm and 4 to 6pm (but you can reach the staff during the lunch hour), and Saturday from 9am to 1pm.

Area Code The telephone area code is **229.**

Climate Veracruz is hot and humid most of the year, but the hottest months are May and June. In the winter, strong winds, known as *nortes,* occasionally bring cool, even chilly, weather.

Consulate The American consulate is closed, and there is no Canadian consulate. The **British Consulate** is at Independencia 1394 (©/fax **229/931-6694**). It's open Monday through Friday from 9am to 1pm.

Drugstore **Farmacía Las Torres,** Av. Díaz Mirón 295, between Abasolo and Paso y Toncoso (© **229/932-2885),** is open daily 24 hours.

Emergencies Dial © **060.**

High Season The peak tourist times are Carnaval, Easter, July and August, and December. Veracruz is more popular with Mexican nationals than with foreigners.

Hospital The **Hospital de María** is at Alacio Pérez 1004, between Carmen Serdán and 20 de Noviembre (© **229/931-3626** or **-3619).**

Police For nonemergencies, you can reach the police in Veracruz at © **229/ 938-0664;** in Boca del Río, © **229/986-1997.**

Post Office The *correo,* on Avenida de la República near the Maritime Customs House, is open Monday through Saturday from 8am to 4pm.

EXPLORING VERACRUZ

The *zócalo* ✹✹✹ is the social hub, where locals hang out in the cafes chatting with friends while the *marimbas, Jarocha* bands, and mariachis make a lively scene, playing well into the night. Bordering the *zócalo* are the **cathedral** and the **Palacio Municipal (City Hall).** There always seems to be some kind of performance on the square: exhibitions of *danzón* (see "Music, Dance & Carnaval," below), clown acts, band concerts, and comedy sketches.

One block east is the **Plaza de la República,** a long plaza where you'll find the **post office,** the old **Customs house,** and the civil registry, all built around the turn of the 19th century. On the north side is the old train station, **Estación de Ferrocarriles,** with its remarkable yellow-and-blue tile facade. From the east side of this plaza, you can board a bus to Veracruz's most famous tourist attraction, the fortress of **San Juan de Ulúa.** Around the corner from the south side of the plaza is the *malecón* (boardwalk), where you can take a boat ride or have coffee at the city's most popular gathering spot, **El Café de la Parroquia.**

A national company called **Turibus** (www.turibus.com.mx) has started to run sightseeing buses around the downtown area and then south along the shore past the hotel zone all the way to the township of Boca del Rio. Explanations are given in several languages including English. You buy a ticket on board the bus ($8/£4.40), which entitles you to get off at any of the 20 stops and catch any later bus that same day. Schedules and hours of operation vary depending on the season. You can get details from the tourism office (see above).

MUSIC, DANCE & CARNAVAL

Hang out in the *zócalo* and you'll be serenaded with *danzonera, marimba, Jarocha,* mariachi, and *norteño* music playing to a large crowd of Veracruzanos who've stopped to drink some coffee or beer and chat with friends. On Tuesday, Thursday, and Saturday a band plays in front of the Palacio Municipal for couples dancing the *danzón.* It's a stately affair: They alternate between dancing perfectly erect in a slow rumba-like fashion and promenading arm in arm while the women wave their fans. The *danzón* came to Veracruz from Cuba in the 1890s; today you won't often see it elsewhere. On Wednesday you can see more *danzón* at 8pm at the **Plaza de la Campaña** for free.

If you would like to see more styles of traditional dance, inquire at the tourist office in the *zócalo* (see above) about performances by the **Ballet Tradiciones de México.**

Several times throughout the year, the company appears at the **Teatro Clavijero** (⌖ **229/931-0574,** or 932-6693 for reservations). Tickets cost $5 to $7 (£2.75–£3.85). The shows are fun and colorful.

In the week before Ash Wednesday, Veracruz explodes with **Carnaval,** one of the best in Mexico. By local tradition, Carnaval begins with the ritual burning of "ill humor" and ends with the funeral of "Juan Carnaval." Visitors flood in from all over the country, packing the streets and hotels.

Carros alegóricos (floats) are made with true Mexican flair—bright colors, papier-mâché figures, flowers, and live entertainment. Groups from neighboring villages dance in peacock- and pheasant-feathered headdresses. Draculas, drag queens, and women in sparkling dresses fill the streets. The parades follow Bulevar Avila Camacho; most of the other activities center in the *zócalo* and begin around noon, lasting well into the night.

On the Sunday before Ash Wednesday, the longest and most lavish of the Carnaval parades takes place on the *malecón.* Parades on Monday and Tuesday are scaled-down versions of the Sunday parade (ask at the tourist office about these routes); by Wednesday, it's all over.

THE TOP ATTRACTIONS

El Acuario ⌖ *Kids*   For most Mexican visitors, the aquarium is one of the city's major attractions. The largest aquarium in Latin America, with 9 freshwater and 15 saltwater tanks, it's an impressive sight that can hold its own with American public aquariums. The doughnut-shaped tank gives the illusion of being surrounded by the ocean and its inhabitants. The large shark tank also impresses. To reach it, take a cab.

Plaza Acuario Veracruzano, Bulevar M. Avila Camacho. ⌖ **229/931-1020.** Admission $6 (£3.30) adults, $3 (£1.65) children 2–12. Daily 10am–7pm.

Fort of San Juan de Ulúa ⌖⌖⌖   Built to ward off pirates and foreign invasions, the fortress was enlarged throughout the colonial period until it became the massive work you see today. After independence, the fort served as a prison noted for its harsh conditions and for the famous people incarcerated there, among them Benito Juárez. It's a formidable example of colonial military architecture, with crenellated walls projecting straight up some 11m (36 ft.) from the water's edge, and bastions at each corner. Inside is a large courtyard, with wide ramps along the inside walls, storehouses, barracks, and old prison cells. English-speaking guides are available at the entrance. A narrow stretch of landfill connects the onetime island to the mainland.

⌖ **229/938-5151.** Admission $3.50 (£1.95). Tues–Sun 9am–4:30pm. Taxis charge $4 (£2.20). Cross the bridge that heads north between Av. de la República and Av. Morelos, then turn right past the container storage and piers.

MORE ATTRACTIONS

Baluarte Santiago   Built in 1635, this bastion is all that remains of the wall and fortifications that encircled the city. It was one of the nine original bastions protecting the wall. A small collection of pre-Hispanic gold jewelry, recovered several years ago by a fisherman along the coast some kilometers north of Veracruz, is on permanent display here.

Calle Canal, between Gómez Farías and 16 de Septiembre. ⌖ **229/931-1059.** Admission $3 (£1.65). Tues–Sun 10am–4:30pm.

Museo de la Ciudad   This small city museum is on the ground floor of a 19th-century building. The exhibits concern the history of the city and its social evolution from colonial times to the present. Text and audio are in Spanish; most of the exhibits are photos or dioramas.

Zaragoza 397. ② 229/989-8872. Admission $3 (£1.65). Tues–Sun 10am–6pm. From the Palacio Municipal, walk 5 blocks south on Zaragoza; it's on the right.

Museo Histórico Naval   This museum occupies the building that once housed Mexico's naval academy. Exhibits concern the history of navigation, including nautical paraphernalia, the history of the naval academy, and Mexico's struggles with other countries. In the courtyard, the foundations of the old wall that used to encircle the city are visible. As you enter, look for uniformed guides, who will show you around free.

Calle Arista between Landero y Coss and Gómez Farías. ② 229/931-4078. Free admission. Tues–Sun 10am–5pm.

OTHER THINGS TO SEE & DO

BEACHES   Veracruz has beaches, but they mostly have brown sand, and the Gulf water is a dull green. The nearest true beach is at the **Villa del Mar,** a little ways down *el bulevar,* followed by **Costa de Oro** and then **Mocambo** beach.

BOAT TRIPS   Boats tour the harbor (most narration is in Spanish only), around the tankers and ships docked in the port and San Juan de Ulúa fortress, and out to the Isle of Sacrifices. Departures are sporadic (depending on the weather and demand) from the *malecón* in front of the Hotel Emporio. The cost is $7 (£3.85) for adults and $4 (£2.20) for children ages 2 to 8.

EXCURSIONS   Popular day-trip destinations include **La Antigua;** the Totonac ruins at **Zempoala; Xalapa,** the state capital and home of an excellent anthropology museum; and the archaeological site at **El Tajín.** For prices and reservations, contact **VIP Tours** (② 229/922-3315 or -1918) or **Centro de Reservaciones de Veracruz** (② 229/935-6422).

For the actively inclined, **river rafting, mountain climbing,** and **diving** are all options. River rafting centers outside Xalapa (see "Xalapa: Museums & White Water," below). **Divers** can explore series of reefs and shipwrecks south of town toward Boca del Río. Contact **Dorado Divers** (② 229/931-4305) for details.

SHOPPING   Veracruz excels in one category of shopping and no other. It has sublimely **tacky souvenirs,** which make perfect payback for co-workers who have burdened you with white elephants. On the *malecón* across from Café de la Parroquia, you'll find a long row of small souvenir shops that constitute Veracruz's version of San Francisco's Fisherman's Wharf. Another place of interest (not so much for buying as for looking) is the **city market** at the corner of Madero and Cortez.

WHERE TO STAY

Most hotels have high- and low-season rates. High-season rates apply during Carnaval, Easter, July and August, December, and long weekends. Low season is the rest of the year. Prices quoted include the 17% tax.

VERY EXPENSIVE

Fiesta Americana Veracruz ★★ (Kids)   Veracruz's most resortlike hotel is six stories high and very long, stretching out across a wide beachfront. Spacious and decorated in muted colors, most rooms have either terraces or balconies, and all have ocean views. Each contains two full beds or one king. It's on the Playa Costa de Oro, one of Veracruz's nicest beaches, but there is also a large and inviting pool area, with an ample shaded section.

Bulevar Avila Camacho s/n, 94299 Boca del Río, Ver. © **800/343-7821** in the U.S. and Canada, or 229/989-8989. Fax 229/989-8909. www.fiestaamericana.com. 233 units. $215–$270 (£118–£149) double; $270–$310 (£149–£171) junior suite. AE, DC, MC, V. Free secure parking. **Amenities:** 3 restaurants; poolside snack bar; bar; 2 large pools (1 indoor); lighted tennis court; health club; spa; 2 whirlpools; watersports equipment rental; children's activities; concierge; tour desk; car rental; business center; salon; room service; babysitting; laundry service; dry cleaning; non-smoking rooms; executive-level rooms. *In room:* A/C, TV, minibar, coffeemaker, hair dryer, iron, safe.

EXPENSIVE

Gran Hotel Diligencias ★★★
This new hotel, in a completely refurbished building facing the *zócalo*, is now the place to stay downtown. The location is excellent and the rooms are better than anything else downtown. I had a large standard with a window looking out over the square, and yet the room was quiet. Bathrooms are large and attractive and the mattresses are comfortable. Plans are in the works to open a beach club so that guests can have a place to enjoy the water.

Independencia 1115, 91700 Veracruz, Ver. © **229/923-0280,** or 01-800/505-5595 in Mexico. www.granhotel diligencias.com. 120 units. High season $200 (£110) double; low season $110 (£61) double. AE, MC, V. Free valet parking. **Amenities:** Restaurant; bar; outdoor pool; fitness center; Jacuzzi; concierge; tour desk; car rental; business center; salon; room service; in-room massage; babysitting; laundry service; dry cleaning. *In room:* A/C, TV, high-speed Internet, coffeemaker, hair dryer, safe.

Hotel Emporio ★
Across from the *malecón* by the old lighthouse, the Emporio occupies an excellent location. Most of the rooms in the nine-story building have a view of the harbor. Some have balconies, others simply a large window. All are carpeted and have well-equipped bathrooms and double-glazed windows to keep out the noise. Rooms are furnished with rattan chairs and tables, with a choice of two double beds or one king. Sunday brunch on the top floor of the hotel is a popular event. In low season, a promotional rate is usually offered.

Paseo del Malecón s/n, 91700 Veracruz, Ver. © **229/932-0020,** or 01-/800-295-3000 in Mexico. Fax 229/931-2261. www.hotelesemporio.com. 203 units. High season $170–$190 (£94–£105) double; $210 (£116) junior suite; low season $120–$130 (£66–£72) double, $170 (£94) junior suite. AE, MC, V. Free guarded parking. **Amenities:** 2 restaurants; bar; 2 large outdoor pools, heated indoor pool; health club; game room; tour desk; car rental; business center; executive services; room service until midnight; babysitting; laundry service; nonsmoking rooms. *In room:* A/C, TV, high-speed Internet, coffeemaker, hair dryer, safe.

Hotel Lois ★
Good location, good service, and a wide variety of amenities for the price are the biggest reasons for staying here. The Lois is located on the coast between downtown and the hotel-and-restaurant zone. It's in a modern 10-story building. Newly remodeled rooms are competitively priced and comfortable. They are midsize, with two double beds or one king. Bathrooms are medium size. The lighting, though not great, is better than other hotels in this price range. The suites are larger, with larger bathrooms, and some contain Jacuzzi tubs. The large pool area on the third floor affords a good view of the coastline.

Calzada Ruiz Cortines 10, 94294 Boca del Río, Ver. © **229/937-8290,** or 01-800/712-9136 in Mexico. www.hotellois. com.mx. 116 units. High season $150 (£83) double; $170 (£94) suite; low season $88–$95 (£48–£52) double, $100–$120 (£55–£66) suite. AE, MC, V. Free secure parking. **Amenities:** Restaurant; 2 bars; large outdoor pool; squash courts; health club w/sauna, Jacuzzi; game rooms; tour desk; car rental; business center; salon; massage; babysitting; room service until 11:30pm; laundry service; dry cleaning. *In room:* A/C, TV, high-speed Internet, minibar, coffeemaker, hair dryer, safe.

Hotel Mocambo ★★ (Kids)
The Mocambo, built in 1932, was the city's first resort hotel, playing host to presidents and movie stars during the 1940s and 1950s. It overlooks some of Veracruz's finest beaches along the hotel zone south of downtown. In contrast to the bunched rooms and boxy corridors of the modern glass-enclosed

hotels, its low buildings make luxurious use of space, with wide, breezy open-air walkways and terraces that look out over the ocean, the gardens, and the coconut palms. The grounds and a small play area are fenced in so kids can't escape, and there's a water slide at the pool. The architecture and decor are simple and elegant. The hotel may show its age, but it echoes Mexico's Belle Epoque with stylish touches such as the Art Deco indoor pool. Most of the simply furnished rooms are large, with sea views and tile floors. My favorite rooms are those on the upper floors, which have balconies. The hotel serves good weekend brunches on the restaurant terrace.

Boca del Río (Apdo. Postal 263), 91700 Veracruz, Ver. *©* **229/922-0205.** Fax 229/922-0212. www.hotelmocambo. com.mx. 103 units. High season $170 (£94) junior suite; low season $105–$125 (£58–£69) junior suite. AE, MC, V. Free guarded parking. **Amenities:** 2 restaurants; 2 bars; 3 pools (1 indoor); lighted tennis court; gym w/sauna and steam room; spa; whirlpool; children's activities (high season only); tour desk; car rental; room service; babysitting; laundry service; dry cleaning; nonsmoking rooms. *In room:* A/C, TV.

MODERATE
Hotel Colonial   Two hotels sit next door to each other on the *zócalo:* the Hotel Colonial (which isn't so colonial), and the Hotel Imperial (which isn't so imperial). In terms of rooms, services, and price, they are much the same—comfortable, but not fancy. The location is great: you can enjoy the music and party atmosphere in the *zócalo* and then retire to your room (preferably an interior one). The Colonial has two sections. Rooms in the new section are larger, with better A/C and more light. Rooms in the old section are darker and more worn. Outside rooms, which are noisier and more expensive, have small balconies overlooking the plaza. The Imperial's lobby is more impressive, but the pool emits a smell of chlorine to parts of the hotel, and the Colonial seems to be better managed. Still, I think of these hotels for the most part as interchangeable. If you can't get a room at the Colonial, try the Imperial (*©* **229/932-1204**). Lower rates are for the old section.

Miguel Lerdo 117, 91700 Veracruz, Ver. *©*/fax **229/932-0193.** 174 units. High season $60–$78 (£33–£43) double, $90 (£50) balcony room; low season $45–$55 (£25–£30) double, $70 (£39) balcony room. AE, MC, V. Covered guarded parking $3 (£1.65). **Amenities:** Sidewalk cafe and bar; indoor pool. *In room:* A/C, TV.

WHERE TO DINE
The restaurants on the *zócalo* are the best spots for drinking a beverage and taking in the scene. While more expensive than places a few blocks away, their prices are still reasonable. If you want to have seafood with the locals, go to the city fish market on Landero y Coss around the corner from the *malecón.* Facing the street are several small restaurants. Find the one called **La Cría.**

Seafood and coffee are two readily available commodities. You will find *pescado a la veracruzana* (fish cooked in a sauce of tomatoes, onions, olives, garlic, and chiles) on menus across Mexico. And the mountains surrounding Xalapa, Orizaba, and Córdoba provide the ideal climate for growing coffee.

VERY EXPENSIVE
Restaurant El Cacharrito *★★* STEAKS   Midway between downtown and Mocambo beach is this family-run steakhouse. The steaks are expertly cooked and served Argentine style. They should be eaten Argentine style, too, meaning you should wash them down with ample amounts of wine. You'll find a large wine list for the purpose. The *bife de chorizo* (rib-eye) is the most popular cut. Also, you might want to try the Argentine *empanadas* or the *jugo de carne,* a rich and satisfying essence of beef. El Cacharrito is around the corner from the Hotel Lois.

Bulevar Ruiz Cortines 15. ℭ **229/937-7027.** Reservations recommended during Carnaval. Steaks $19–$40 (£10–£22). MC, V. Daily 2–11pm.

MODERATE

Gran Café del Portal *(Value)* MEXICAN   In the *portales* that face the front door of the cathedral is this dependable restaurant with good prices and local color. In the evenings a parade of strolling troubadours, harpists, marimba players, and shoeshine men passes by. For the midafternoon meal, the *comida del día* (blue-plate special) provides lots of food at a reasonable price. Avoid the overcooked pasta and most beef dishes, which are tough. The exception is the tenderized *milanesa* (breaded beef cutlet), done very well in the Mexican style. For seafood, ask the waiter what's freshest. The enchiladas and the soups are good, and the *flan napolitano* could feed a family of four.

Independencia at Zamora. ℭ **229/931-2759.** Main courses $6–$13 (£3.30–£7.15); *comida del día* Mon–Sat $6–$8 (£3.30–£4.40), Sun $8–$10 (£4.40–£5.50). No credit cards. Daily 7am–midnight.

Mariscos Villa Rica Mocambo ★★★ SEAFOOD   This establishment prides itself on cooking Veracruz style. The menu includes all the seafood standards, plus a few dishes that are harder to come by in Mexico, let alone north of the border. Everything I tried, I enjoyed enormously. For starters, try a classic seafood cocktail. Veracruzano specialties include *pampano al acuyo* (pompano cooked in a sauce of green herbs), conch filet *al ajillo* (with toasted strips of *guajillo* peppers), and *steak de camarón a la naranja* (shrimp pressed together and cooked in orange sauce). Service is excellent. Look for an open-air thatched structure below the Mocambo hotel.

Calzada Mocambo 527. ℭ **229/922-2113.** Main courses $8–$17 (£4.40–£9.35). AE, MC, V. Daily noon–10pm.

INEXPENSIVE

Gran Café de la Parroquia ★★ *(Moments)* MEXICAN/COFFEE   More than a coffeehouse, La Parroquia is an institution. Making the scene here for morning or afternoon coffee is mandatory on any trip to Veracruz. The action takes place in a large, bustling dining area facing the *malecón*. There's nothing fancy about it; the furniture is simple but comfortable and there's a minimum of decoration. The thing to order is *café lechero,* which is so good I would pit it against any other coffee-and-milk drink. You'll get two fingers of dark coffee in a glass. Add sugar, if desired, and stir, clinking your spoon against the glass. This will attract the attention of the waiter who circulates with the kettle of steaming milk. Don't be shy. The sound of clinking glass rings throughout the dining room. The cafe also offers pastries and decent breakfasts, but some of the main courses disappoint.

Av. Gómez Farías 34. ℭ **229/932-2584.** Breakfast $2–$5(£1.10–£2.75); coffee $1–$2 (55p–£1.10); main courses $4–$10 (£2.20–£5.50). No credit cards. Daily 6am–1am.

Samborcito ★ *(Finds)* REGIONAL   No need to say the name twice to any cab driver in town; everybody knows this place. Samborcito is simple eating at its best for either breakfast or lunch. The name pokes fun at Sanborn's, the oldest, best-known chain of restaurants in Mexico (never mind the difference in spelling). Classic dishes include *picadas* (thick *masa* pancake with cheese and sauce—a Veracruz tradition), and puffy *gordita negra* (*masa* cooked with black-bean paste and flavored with the toasted leaf of the aguacatillo—not spicy). Tamales are available on weekends. All the breakfasts are great. Samborcito is near downtown; a cab will run about $2 (£1.10).

16 de Septiembre 727. ℭ **229/931-4388.** Breakfast $3–$5 (£1.65–£2.75); *antojitos* $2–$5 (£1.10–£2.75); main courses $7–$12 (£3.85–£6.60). No credit cards. Daily 7am–6pm.

VERACRUZ AFTER DARK

The first thing that always comes to mind with Veracruz is the scene on the *zócalo,* which on a weekend can go on until the wee hours of the morning. The evening shows presented by the municipal government can be quite good. I've seen some great dance troupes perform *Jarocho.*

There's a small bar downtown with a real local feel, where on weekends you can hear live groups play *son montuno,* an old-style Latin tropical music. The bar's name is **Rincón de la Trova** (no phone) and it's at Plazuela de la Lagunilla 59. Live music is Thursday to Saturday. Friday and Saturday there's a $3 (£1.65) cover.

There are several dance clubs to choose from. Most play Latin music and are in or near the hotel zone. One that signs good acts is **La Casona de la Condesa** (© 229/933-5451) at Bulevar Avila Camacho 2014, Fracc. Costa de Oro. There are several clubs for dancing to salsa and such. Two are in the vicinity of the Hotel Lois. **Carioca** (© 229/937-8290) at Calz. A Ruiz Cortines 10, and **Kachimba** (© 229/927-1981) at Bulevar Avila Camacho s/n. Any taxi driver would know where these places are.

2 Exploring North of Veracruz: Ruins, More Ruins & a Great Museum

THE RUINS OF ZEMPOALA

On Highway 180, about 22km (14 miles) north of Veracruz, is the village of Antigua (on the river of the same name). It's not very well known today, but for 75 years beginning in 1525, it was a seat of Spanish power. The village is known locally for its seafood restaurants and is especially popular on weekends.

About 40km (25 miles) north of Veracruz, a little past Antigua, are the ruins of **Zempoala** (or Cempoala), surrounded by lush foliage and rich agricultural land. Though not as large as the site of El Tajín, they're still noteworthy. Zempoala was the principal city of the Totonac at the time of the Spanish Conquest. The name means "place of the 20 waters," for the several creeks that converge near the site. When the conquerors saw Zempoala, the whitewashed stucco walls glimmered like silver in the tropical sun, which of course brought the Spaniards running. Disappointed at seeing little in the way of precious metals, the Spaniards made allies of the Totonac Indians, who were resentful of Aztec domination.

Most buildings at Zempoala date from the 14th and 15th centuries. The area was populated at least 1,500 years earlier. The Great Temple is constructed in the Aztec style. The Temple of the Little Faces is decorated with stucco faces in the walls and hieroglyphs painted on the lower sections. The Temple of Quetzalcoatl, the feathered serpent god, is a square platform, and the Temple of Ehecatl, god of the wind, is (as usual) round. On weekends and during vacation months, you're likely to find a group of the famous *voladores* (flyers) from Papantla performing their acrobatic ritual (see the "The Ruins of El Tajín" on p. 500).

Admission to the archaeological site is $4 (£2.20); it's open daily from 9am to 6pm. A video camera permit costs $4 (£2.20). If you're going by car, driving time is 40 minutes north on Highway 180 through Cardel; the ruins of Zempoala are just north of Cardel. Transportes Regionales Veracruzanas (TRV) buses run hourly from Veracruz; the trip takes 1½ hours.

XALAPA: MUSEUMS & WHITE WATER

Xalapa (104km/65 miles northwest of Veracruz; pronounced "hah-*lah*-pa" and sometimes spelled "Jalapa") is a highland city in the middle of Mexico's prime coffee-growing area and the capital of the state of Veracruz. Less than 2 hours from the port of Veracruz, it offers an easy escape from the high temperatures there. It's a hilly city, crisscrossed by narrow, winding streets and alleys. A fine, misty rain known as *chipi chipi* often floats in the air, cloaking the views in a vaporous shroud. When the sky is clear, you can sometimes make out in the distance the snow-capped peak of Pico de Orizaba (also known as Citlaltépetl), an extinct volcano that is Mexico's tallest peak at 5,747m (18,850 ft.).

> **Tasty Fun Fact**
>
> Xalapa, or "Jalapa," lent its name to the famed jalapeño pepper.

Xalapa is a university town and has the best music school in the country, which is part of the University of Veracruz. Xalapa is also known for its symphony orchestra. If your interests are more archaeological, Xalapa's anthropology museum is second only to Mexico City's monster of a museum. For active sorts, there's excellent white-water rafting nearby.

ESSENTIALS

GETTING THERE   Veracruz, 1½ hours away, has the closest major airport, although some charter flights use the small Xalapa airport. If you're **driving** from Veracruz, take Highway 180 to Cardel, then west on Highway 140. From Papantla, you can avoid the mountains by taking Highway 180 south to Cardel. From Mexico City and Puebla, there's a turn-off for Highway 140 on the toll highway to Veracruz (150D). Fog is common and dangerous between Perote and Xalapa. The trip by bus to or from Papantla takes 4 hours.

The **bus station** (CAXA) is 2.5km (1½ miles) east of the town center just off Calle 20 de Noviembre. Taxis are downstairs, and prices are controlled. Tickets to downtown cost around $2.50 (£1.40). Buses run to Veracruz every 20 to 30 minutes and to Puebla 15 times a day. You can buy tickets downtown at the **Ticket Bus** agency, Av. Enríquez 13, a block east of the cathedral (© **228/841-1660**). The office is open Monday through Saturday from 10am to 8:30pm. Several travel agencies sell bus tickets as well.

VISITOR INFORMATION   Go to the **tourist information booth** at the Ayuntamiento (city hall), across from the Plaza Juárez. Hours are Monday through Friday from 9am to 3pm and 4 to 7pm.

CITY LAYOUT   Xalapa is a hilly town with streets that defy order. In the center of town is the large **Plaza Juárez,** where on a clear day the Pico de Orizaba is visible to the southwest. Across the street (north) from the plaza is the Ayuntamiento (city hall); just east is the Palacio del Gobierno (state capitol). The cathedral is across (north) from this.

GETTING AROUND   Most of the recommended hotels and restaurants (see "Where to Stay" and "Where to Dine," below) are within easy walking distance of the central Plaza Juárez. Taxis in Xalapa are inexpensive, as are city buses. Because streets in the center of town are busy and narrow, cabs aren't allowed to stop just anywhere. Sometimes you have to look for a TAXI sign.

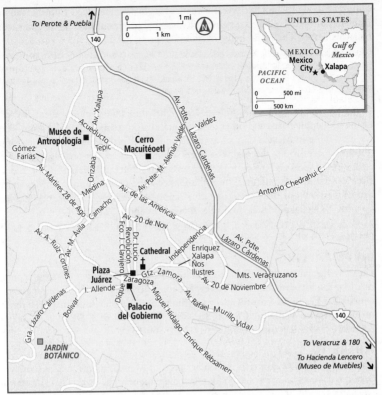

FAST FACTS   The telephone **area code** is ℂ **228.** The city is 1,430m (4,690 ft.) above sea level. The **climate** is humid and cool for the most part. It can be warm from March to early May. The light *chipi chipi* rain comes and goes at any time of year. The rainy season is May through July and can bring strong downpours. The **American Express** office is in Viajes Xalapa, Clavijero 311 (ℂ **228/817-4114**). Hours for traveler services are weekdays from 9am to 2pm and 4 to 7:30pm.

EXPLORING XALAPA

For information on cultural events, go to **El Agora,** a cultural center with a coffee shop beneath the Plaza Juárez (reached by steps on the south side of the plaza). Look for posters announcing upcoming concerts. There's usually something going on. Also, look in the local paper, *Diario de Xalapa* or in the "Cartelera," a monthly publication of the Instituto Veracruzano de Cultura.

Hacienda El Lencero   Occasionally called the Museo de Muebles (Furniture Museum), this country estate 14km (8⅔ miles) southeast of the town center was, for 14 years (1842–56), the home of Antonio López de Santa Anna, the 11-time president of Mexico. Here, he retreated from the world, though on occasion he opened his doors to receive notable visitors. Furniture from Mexico, Europe, and Asia fills the rooms, illustrating the cosmopolitan tastes of Mexico's upper classes during the 19th century. Among the notable pieces is the leader's bed, embellished with the national emblem (an eagle holding a serpent in its beak). The grounds are lovely and shaded by ancient trees. The grand house overlooks a spring-fed pond.

Carretera Xalapa-Veracruz Km 10. No phone. Admission $2.50 (£1.40); free guided tours (in Spanish only) on request. Tues–Sun 10am–5pm. Bus: Banderilla–P. Crystal–Lencero from Av. Lázaro Cárdenas to village of Lencero or nearby spot along the highway. Drive or take a taxi ($10/£5.50) about 10km (6 miles) south of town on Hwy. 140 toward Veracruz, past the country club; watch for the signs on the right.

Museo Antropología de Xalapa ★★★ This museum exhibits excellent examples of the megalithic heads and other monumental sculptures made by the Olmec—better than those in Mexico City or at the museum in Villahermosa. The collection of Totonac pieces, from the highly stylized smiling faces to the unadorned, realistic sculptures of faces and heads, is the best anywhere. The museum is laid out in order from earliest to latest cultures, from the Olmec—the mother culture of Mesoamerican civilization—to the post-Classic civilizations of Veracruz. Explanatory text is in Spanish. Bilingual guides are available. A taxi runs about $2 (£1.10).

Av. Xalapa s/n. ⓒ 228/815-0920 or -0708. Admission $4 (£2.20); free for children younger than 12. Tues–Sat 9am–5pm.

RIVER RAFTING

Close by Xalapa are three popular rivers for rafting and a number of rafting companies that can accommodate you. No experience is necessary. If you're planning ahead, contact **Far Flung Adventures** at www.farflung.com. Another outfit that I can recommend is **México Verde** (ⓒ 01-800/362-8800 in Mexico, or 228/812-0134). Either company can do day trips from Xalapa (about $60/£33).

WHERE TO STAY

Mesón del Alférez ★★ In most other parts of Mexico, rooms such as these, in a beautiful colonial house, would go for much more money. The owners have thoroughly renovated the old house and retained its residential feel. Rooms are spacious and beautifully decorated. Standard rooms and junior suites come with one double bed, suites with a choice of two doubles or one king. Rooms are colonial in style, accented by bright colors and stone. In some, a loft creates extra space. There are two smaller rooms in front that get noise from the street. Additional rooms are around the corner in a modern house, Balcones del Alférez. They are comfortable, modern, and a little quieter. The hotel faces the back of the Palacio del Gobierno. Suites have two double beds.

Sebastián Camacho 2, corner of Zaragoza, 91000 Xalapa, Ver. ⓒ/fax 228/818-0113. www.pradodelrio.com. 28 units. $59 (£32) standard; $68 (£37) junior suite; $82 (£45) suite. Rates include continental breakfast. AE, MC, V. Free secure parking 2 blocks away. **Amenities:** Restaurant; tour desk; car rental; room service; laundry service. *In room:* TV, coffeemaker, hair dryer.

Posada del Cafeto *(Value* This colorful, comfortable hotel has three stories of rooms surrounding a tidy garden. Furnishings and decor are simple and attractive, with handsome wood furniture and cheerful colors. Each room is slightly different. Some are small, but all have ample bathrooms. Bed choices include one double, two twins, a twin and a double, or two doubles for a higher rate.

Canovas 8 and 12, 91000 Xalapa, Ver. ⓒ 228/817-0023. www.pradodelrio.com. 32 units. $40 (£22) double; $78 (£43) suite. Rates include continental breakfast. AE, MC, V. No parking. From Plaza Juárez, walk 4 blocks east on Zaragoza, then 1 block south where it bends; Canovas is the first street on the right; the *posada* is farther down on the right. Limited street parking. **Amenities:** Cafe (breakfast and supper); tour info; room service; laundry service. *In room:* TV, coffeemaker, hair dryer.

WHERE TO DINE

Because Xalapa is a student town, you can eat well for little money. **Callejón del Diamante** is an alley near the cathedral, with a half-dozen inexpensive restaurants that cater to office workers and students. One, **La Sopa,** offers a daily blue-plate special for $3 (£1.65). Most of these restaurants are open Monday through Saturday from 8am to 10pm. To find them, turn your back to the cathedral and walk left on Enríquez across Lucio 1 block; the Callejón will be on the left.

Churrería del Recuerdo MEXICAN   This is a very popular place for supper, and I've eaten well here, but on my last visit I was a little disappointed—effort was lacking. Perhaps it will be fixed by the time you get there. The traditional supper fare is *antojitos*—enchiladas, *gorditas,* and tamales, which you can wash down with *tepache* (fermented pineapple drink). You might want to try the *churros,* best described as the Spanish equivalent of doughnuts, but crispy and usually eaten with hot chocolate. The restaurant is across from the Hotel Xalapa; take a cab ($3/£1.65 from downtown).

Victoria 158. ℂ 228/841-4961. *Antojitos* $3–$5 (£1.65–£2.75). No credit cards. Daily 6pm–midnight.

La Casona del Beaterio MEXICAN   This restaurant occupies a colonial house near the main square. You can dine in a small patio by a fountain or in one of the large dining rooms under high, beamed ceilings. The menu offers variety—in addition to Mexican standards, you'll find pastas, crepes, and burgers. The soups I tried, *sopa azteca* (tortilla soup) and *sopa de frijol* (bean soup), were good. Among the main courses is a platter of traditional dishes called *cazuelitas mexicanas,* which allows you to try a bit of several things. La Casona is 2 blocks east of Parque Juárez on the south side of the street. Live music begins at 9pm from Thursday to Sunday.

Zaragoza 20. ℂ 228/818-2119. Breakfast $4–$6 (£2.20–£3.30); *comida corrida* Mon–Sat $6 (£3.30); main courses $6–$12 (£3.30–£6.60). AE, MC, V. Tues–Sun 9am–midnight; Mon 9am–11pm.

EL TAJIN & THE CITY OF PAPANTLA

El Tajín (ehl tah-*heen*) is among the most important archaeological sites in Mexico. It has a large ceremonial center with several pyramids, platforms, and ball courts, some in the architectural styles of other cultures (Olmec, Teotihuacán, Maya) and some in the city's own unique style. It was probably built and inhabited (at least in its last stages) by the Totonac Indians who still live in this region. The Totonac culture is most famous for the "dance" of the *voladores,* a pre-Columbian religious ritual in which four men are suspended from the top of a tall pole while another beats a drum and plays a flute while balancing himself at the top.

The major stopover for seeing these ruins is **Papantla,** a hilly city of 165,000 in the coastal lowlands 225km (140 miles) north of Veracruz. In many respects, it's a typical Mexican town with lots of clay tile roofs, a jumble of small shops, and a lively street scene. One of the major products of Papantla, since the time of the Aztecs, is vanilla beans. Vanilla is native to Mexico and was used principally to flavor chocolate, also indigenous to Mexico.

ESSENTIALS

GETTING THERE   By Car   If you're driving from the south, follow the coastal road, **Highway 180,** from Veracruz. From Xalapa, it's best to do the same: drive down to the coast and then north.

By Bus   The quaint **ADO station** (ℂ 784/842-0218) is at the corner of Venustiano Carranza and Benito Juárez, 4 blocks below the main square. Almost all buses are *de* *paso* (originating elsewhere), so departure times can be a little earlier or later than the schedule says. Taxis pass in front of the station frequently.

CITY LAYOUT   Easily visible from many parts of town, the parish church and the Hotel El Tajín are at the top of a hill. This is where you'll find the *zócalo*.

GETTING AROUND   Taxis are available around the central plaza, and **city buses** go to the ruins of El Tajín (see below). Almost everything worth seeing is within easy walking distance of the central plaza.

FAST FACTS   The telephone **area code** is **784.** The **climate** is steamy for most of the year except for a few occasions in winter when a north wind blows.

SPECIAL EVENTS   The **Feast of Corpus Christi,** the ninth Sunday after Easter, is part of a very special week in Papantla. Well-known Mexican entertainers perform, and the native *voladores* (see "The Ruins of El Tajín," below) make special appearances. Lodging is scarce during this week, so be sure to book ahead.

EXPLORING PAPANTLA & EL TAJIN

In Papantla, the shady *zócalo* built of ceramic tile is where couples and families come in the evenings to sit or stroll. The large wall below the church facing the *zócalo* is covered with the image of El Tajín and a modern depiction of Totonac carved reliefs.

THE RUINS OF EL TAJIN   The ruined city sits among some low hills clothed in thick tropical forest. The views are lovely, but climbing on any of the pyramids is forbidden; your best view is from a high, man-made terrace that supports the Tajín Chico buildings towards the back. The city is divided into **Tajín Viejo** and **Tajín Chico**—the old and new sections. Of the 150 buildings identified at the site, 20 have been excavated and conserved, resurrecting their forms from what were grass-covered mounds. At least 12 ball courts have been found, of which 6 have been excavated. The most impressive structure, in the old section, is the **Pyramid of the Niches,** which is a unique stone-and-adobe pyramid with 365 recesses extending to all four sides of the building. The pyramid was formerly covered in red-painted stucco, and the niches were painted black. Try to imagine how that must have looked. Near the Pyramid of the Niches is a restored **ball court** with beautiful carved reliefs depicting gods and kings.

The most important building in the Tajín Chico section is the **Temple of the Columns.** A stairway divides the columns, three on either side, each decorated with reliefs of priests and warriors and hieroglyphic dates. Many mounds remain unexcavated, but with the reconstruction that has been done so far, it's increasingly easier to visualize the ruins as a city.

In a clearing near the museum, a group of local Totonac Indians called *voladores* **(flyers)** performs their acrobatic and symbolic ritual. This is a traditional, solemn ceremony that dates back centuries. The Totonac perform the unusual ritual in honor of the four directions of the earth. There's no set schedule for performances; the sound of a slow-beating drum and flute signals that the *voladores* are preparing to perform. Five flyers, dressed in brightly colored ceremonial garments and cone-shaped hats with ribbons and small round mirrors, climb to a square revolving platform at the top of a 25m (82-ft.) pole. While four flyers perch on the sides of the platform and attach themselves by the waist to a rope, the fifth stands and plays an instrument called a *chirimía,* used in rituals by the Toltec and Olmec. The instrument is a small bamboo flute with a deerskin drum attached. The performer plays the three-holed flute with his left hand and beats the drum with his right hand. When the time is right, the four fall backward, suspended by the rope, and descend as they revolve around the post.

The small but impressive **museum** is worth seeing as well. A small snack and gift shop and small restaurant are across from the museum. Admission to the site and museum is $5 (£2.75). The fee to use a personal video camera is $3.50 (£1.95). If you look like a professional photographer, the authorities will ask you to get a permit from the **Instituto Nacional de Antropología e Historia** in Mexico City. If you watch a performance of the *voladores,* one of them will collect an additional $2 (£1.10) from each spectator. The site is open daily from 9am to 5pm.

To El Tajín from Papantla, taxis charge about $20 (£11), but it's easy to take a local bus for 75¢. Look for buses marked CHOTE/TAJIN, which run beside the town church (on the uphill side) every 15 minutes beginning at 7am. Buses marked CHOTE pass more frequently and leave you at the Chote crossroads; from there, take a taxi for around $5 (£2.75). From Veracruz, take Highway 180 to Papantla, then Route 127, a back road to Poza Rica that runs through El Tajín.

SHOPPING   There are two markets in Papantla, both near the central plaza. **Mercado Juárez** is opposite the front door of the church. **Mercado Hidalgo** is 1 block downhill on the same street. The former has more food stalls, where you can order a bowl of *zacahuil,* a typical dish of the region. The latter has locally made baskets; vanilla extract; *Xanath,* a locally produced vanilla liqueur; and whole vanilla beans.

WHERE TO STAY

Hotel Provincia Express   Opened in 1990, this hotel is a good choice in a place with meager selections. Rooms are nicely furnished, with tile floors, and hold a king-size or two double beds. The medium-to-small bathrooms have showers. On occasion it takes a while for water to heat up, but it will. Nos. 1 to 6 have small balconies overlooking the *zócalo.* Others, toward the back, are windowless and quiet, and are reached through a tunnel-like hallway.

Enríquez 103, 93400 Papantla, Ver. (*C*) **784/842-1645.** Fax 784/842-4213. hotprovi@prodigy.net.mx. 20 units. $45–$60 (£25–£33) double. No credit cards. Free secure parking half a block away. **Amenities:** Cafe; room service; laundry service. *In room:* A/C, TV.

Hotel Tajín   At the top of the hill toward the back of the church sits this large, easily visible hotel. Rooms are small and tidy. Bed choices include one or two doubles or one king. Thirty-one rooms have air-conditioning, the rest have fans, and some have a view.

Núñez 104, 93400 Papantla, Ver. (*C*) **784/842-0121** or -1623. Fax 784/842-1062. hoteltajin@hotmail.com. 73 units. $32–$55 (£18–£30) double. MC, V. Free secure parking a half-block away. **Amenities:** Laundry service. *In room:* A/C or fan, TV.

WHERE TO DINE

In the morning, numerous stands at the Mercado Juárez offer the local specialty, *zacahuil* (a huge tamal cooked in a banana leaf). In Papantla, the *zacahuil* is cooked in enough liquid to be served in a bowl. Look around until you see a cook with a line of patrons—that's where you'll get the best *zacahuil.*

Plaza Pardo MEXICAN   This upstairs restaurant facing the main plaza serves plenty of Mexican standards and a couple of regional dishes. A few tables are on a balcony looking out over the *zócalo,* church, and giant statue of the *volador.* Specialties include *bocales* (small *gorditas* with different fillings), enchiladas, and *mole.*

Enríquez 105-altos. (*C*) **784/842-0059.** Breakfast $2–$4 (£1.10–£2.20); sandwiches $2–$3 (£1.10–£1.65); main courses $3–$7 (£1.65–£3.85). No credit cards. Daily 7:30am–11pm.

3 Colonial Puebla ★★

128km (79 miles) E of Mexico City; 285km (177 miles) W of Veracruz

The city of Puebla sits on a broad plane that lies between mountain ranges and snow-capped volcanoes. It's 2,155m (7,068 ft.) above sea level and has a mostly mild climate. It's considered the cradle of Mexican cuisine, having produced some of the country's classic dishes—the intricate *mole poblano* and *chiles en nogada,* as well as *tinga* (pork or chicken stewed in chiles) and *mixiotes* (spiced rabbit, lamb, or chicken wrapped and steamed in a sauce).

Puebla has a large colonial center, which has so many convents, churches, and public palaces that it has been named a UNESCO World Heritage Site. Its architecture differs from that of the rest of Mexico in the extensive use of painted tiles, gold leaf, and molded plaster. Facades and walls are commonly surfaced with clay and Talavera tiles to cover the unattractive gray-black color of the local building stone. Early in the city's history, artisans from the Spanish town of Talavera settled here and established their craft of making hand-painted tiles—a tradition the Moors originally brought to Spain in the 8th century. These tiles, along with dishes, pots, and other objects made in the same tradition, are referred to as Talavera.

Puebla is a very Catholic city, even for Mexico; there are so many churches and former convents that even most Poblanos can't keep them all straight. The **cathedral,** one of the largest in Mexico, and the **Capilla del Rosario,** with its overpowering baroque decoration, are perhaps the two most famous religious structures in the city. Modern Puebla surrounds the historic district. The principal industry of the city is a large Volkswagen plant on the outskirts. It produces most of the Volkswagens sold in the United States.

ESSENTIALS

GETTING THERE & DEPARTING   By Plane   Continental (© 800/231-0856 in the U.S., or 01-800/900-5000 in Mexico; www.continental.com) has a direct flight to/from Houston. Air travelers coming from other places fly into Mexico City and take the bus directly from the airport to Puebla. Look for area E-2 and find the upstairs concourse that spans the passenger pickup area. You'll find ticket counters at the end of the concourse. Buses for Puebla leave every half-hour and cost $15 (£8.25).

By Car   There are two roads to Puebla from the capital: **Highway 150,** an old, winding two-lane road with the likelihood of slow traffic; and **Highway 150D,** a four-lane modern toll road that's much faster. From Veracruz, take Highway 150D west. From Xalapa, take **Highway 140** west to the intersection with 150D. Tolls from Mexico City run $14 (£7.70); from Veracruz, $30 (£17).

By Bus   The ride from **Veracruz** to Puebla takes 3½ hours and costs $18 (£9.90). From **Mexico City,** it takes 2 hours and costs $12 (£6.60). Several bus lines have regular departures from Mexico City's **TAPO bus station,** as frequently as every 15 minutes. You can also catch a bus to Puebla directly from the **Mexico City airport** (see "By Plane," above).

You'll probably arrive at a large **bus station,** known by its acronym, CAPU. To get to downtown Puebla, look for one of several booths marked TAXI AUTORIZADO. Many buses to and from the Mexico City airport use the **Estrella Roja station** at 4 Poniente 2110, which is closer to downtown.

Puebla

ACCOMMODATIONS ■
Crowne Plaza Hotel **1**
Hotel Camino Real Puebla **20**
Hotel Colonial **14**
Hotel Posada San Pedro **8**
Hotel Puebla Plaza **19**
Hotel Royalty **9**
Mesón Sacristia de la Compañia **15**
Mesón Sacristia de las Capuchinas **21**
NH Puebla **11**

DINING ◆
Fonda de Santa Clara **13**
La Conjura **23**
La Guadalupana **25**

ATTRACTIONS ●
Biblioteca Palafoxiana **18**
Callejón de los Sapos **24**
Casa de la Cultura **17**
Casa de los Muñecos **10**
Casa del Alfeñique **6**
Cathedral **16**
Exconvento de Santa Mónica **4**
Exconvento de Santa Rosa **3**
Igleesia de Santo Domingo **5**
Mercado de Artesanías (El Parián) **7**
Museo Ampara **22**
Museo Bello y González **12**
Museo Nacional del Ferrocarril **2**

VISITOR INFORMATION The **State Tourism Office** (© 222/246-2044) is your best bet. It's at Calle 5 Oriente 3, across the street from the south side of the cathedral. The office is open Monday through Saturday from 8am to 8pm, Sunday from 9am to 2pm. The staff can answer questions, provide a map, and set you up with a guide if you want a private tour of the city. They can also help in case of emergencies, like losing your documents.

CITY LAYOUT Puebla's streets are laid out on a Cartesian quadrant, with the two main avenues as the *x* and *y* axes. Instead of positive and negative numbers, you have even and odd. Streets north of the **horizontal axis** (Reforma/Palafox y Mendoza) are numbered 2, 4, 6, and so on. Streets to the south are 3, 5, 7, and so on. The **north-south axis** (5 de Mayo/16 de Septiembre) does the same thing. East of it are even-numbered streets, and west are odd-numbered. Street names also include a direction—*norte, sur, oriente, poniente* (north, south, east, west). So if someone tells you that a church is on Calle 7 Oriente, then you know what part of town it's in: "Oriente" tells you that it's the eastern portion of an east-west street, and the odd number indicates that it's south of Palafox y Mendoza.

Don't count on taxi drivers to know where certain restaurants, hotels, or attractions are located; keep addresses handy.

FAST FACTS: Puebla

American Express The office is at Plaza Dorado 2, Loc. 21, Col. Ansures (© 222/229-1500). Hours are Monday through Friday from 9am to 6pm, Saturday 9am to 1pm.

Area Code The telephone area code is **222**.

Drugstores Pharmacies are almost as common as churches. They usually close around 9pm but take turns staying open late *(de turno)*. Should you need something overnight, **Farmatodo** (© 222/237-7133) delivers around the clock.

Emergency The emergency number is © **066**.

Hospital **Beneficiencia Española** is at 19 Norte 1001 (© 222/232-0500).

Internet Access There are several Internet access businesses downtown. Ask around; preferably ask young people.

Population Puebla has 1.8 million residents; the metro area has more than 2.5 million.

Post Office The *correo* is around the corner from the State Tourism office, on Av. 16 de Septiembre. Hours are Monday through Friday from 9am to 6pm, and Saturday mornings.

EXPLORING PUEBLA

Puebla is a city full of stories and anecdotes that color the colonial houses and convents of the historic district. For historical tours of the city or a tour of surrounding area, you might want a guide. One I can recommend is **Carlos Rivero Tours** (© 222/304-2855; www.riveros.com.mx). He speaks English, knows his city, and is very capable. For a quick sightseeing tour of the city, you can hop on one of the buses that park on the street between the *zócalo* and the cathedral (Calle 3 Oriente). Tours are in

Cinco de Mayo & the Battle of Puebla

In the United States, the Mexican holiday Cinco de Mayo is often compared to the Fourth of July, but it's not Mexican Independence Day. The date commemorates the Battle of Puebla, on May 5, 1862, which resulted in a memorable victory against foreign invaders.

At the time, Napoleon III of France was scheming to occupy Mexico. A well-trained and handsomely uniformed army of 6,000, under the command of General Laurencez, landed in Veracruz with the objective of occupying Mexico City. In its path were 4,000 ill-equipped Mexicans under General Ignacio Zaragoza. Despite the odds, the Mexicans won a resounding victory. The French were humiliated and suffered their first defeat in nearly a half-century at the hands of the penniless, war-torn republic of Mexico.

For Mexico, it marked the nation's first victory against foreign attack, and the battle remains a matter of national pride. Never mind that by the following year the French were in possession of both Puebla and Mexico City. Today, the Cinco de Mayo holiday is an enduring symbol of Mexico's sense of patriotism.

On a trip to Puebla, you can visit the forts of Guadalupe and Loreto, where the battle took place, just north of the old part of the city.

Spanish, depart every half-hour, and cost $4 (£2.20). Or you can climb on to one of the new **Turibus** (www.turibus.com.mx) open-air double-decker buses, with narrative in several languages. The circuit of both buses includes a quick view of the site where the Battle of Cinco de Mayo was fought. Your ticket is valid for the entire day and allows you to get off at any location and board the next bus that comes along.

CHURCHES

If you were to stop to examine every church you pass, you would be in for a long stay. Still, it is something I enjoy doing, even with the smaller churches. Many have simple, austere interiors that express a sweetness and humility that I like. Three churches in the historic district require special mention.

The **cathedral** ✦✦✦, completed in 1649, has the tallest bell towers in Mexico. Its dark-stone exterior and severe Herrerian design lend it a lugubrious appearance that perhaps befits a cathedral but takes a little while to warm up to. In the country, only Mexico City's cathedral has a more interesting interior. In front, you can usually find guides (or they'll find you) who offer a short tour.

The **Iglesia de Santo Domingo** ✦✦✦, on the corner of 5 de Mayo and 4 Poniente, was originally part of a Dominican monastery completed in 1611. Lining the walls of the nave are some exquisite baroque altars. In the left transept you'll find the **Capilla del Rosario,** built in 1690. It is a masterpiece of gold leaf and plaster convolutes dedicated to the Virgin of the Rosary. Some point to it as the epitome of Mexican baroque architecture. Note, too, the intricate Talavera wainscoting.

Last, there is the massive **church of the Compañía,** built by the Jesuits, where "La China Poblana" (a princess from India who converted to Catholicism) worshipped and was briefly entombed. Look to the right of the church doorway and you'll see a curious bit of text in Talavera. It marks the date of the execution of a con man who arrived in Mexico on a boat from Spain carrying papers identifying him as a *visitador* (papal emissary and inspector). He was wined and dined by the bishops in the capital and in Puebla and lived the good life for several weeks before being found out. As the text notes, he was executed and his head was hung above the doorway. The message, I guess, was that it's not nice to fool the mother church.

MUSEUMS

In addition to those listed below, there are a couple of smaller attractions worth visiting: The **Biblioteca Palafoxiana** ✦ is an impressive colonial library, the collection of the famous 17th-century bishop who went on to become viceroy, Juan Palafox y Mendoza. The library is on the second floor of the Casa de Cultura, next to the state tourism office. The **Casa de Alfeñique** is a colonial mansion and a landmark for its exterior plaster decoration, which reminds one of cake icing; the museum collection, a hodgepodge of things Poblano, is fun if you have time. It's at the intersection of calles 4 Oriente and 6 Norte. The **Casa de los Muñecos,** Calle 2 Norte 4, is more important for its exterior than for the museum collection inside. Large grotesques, said to be caricatures of the town council, adorn the late-18th-century facade, though this story is apocryphal.

Exconvento de Santa Mónica After independence, a long political struggle ensued between the national government and the Church. It climaxed in the Reform Wars of the 1850s, when the liberal government instituted several anticlerical measures, including appropriation of the convents. The nuns at Santa Mónica discreetly walled up their doors and kept functioning as a religious community with the aid of their neighbors and the blind eye of local officials. They survived with little assistance from the outside as, over the years, the convent slowly crumbled around them. Then, in 1934 (during another political feud between the government and the church), a local official "discovered" them. This history makes for an interesting visit: displays include the contents of this and two other clandestine convents confiscated at the same time. These nuns weren't sitting on great treasures—most of the paintings are poor examples of their era—but you will find a rare set of paintings on velvet that predate Elvis or the poker-playing dogs. Things not to miss are the crypt, the chapel, and the upper and lower *coros* (choirs).

Calle 18 Poniente 103. ✆ 222/232-0178. Admission $3 (£1.65). Tues–Sun 9am–6pm.

Exconvento de Santa Rosa ✦ Unlike its neighbor, this former convent was unable to postpone confiscation and served variously as barracks, hospital, and public housing. It is now the home of the **Museo de Arte Popular.** You can see the kitchen where *mole* was invented, and afterward the museum guide will take you upstairs to see displays of the crafts practiced in the state. If you enjoy handicrafts, don't miss this place; it has some rare and lovely examples of artisanship. The main door is usually closed; enter through the public parking lot at 14 Poniente 305.

Calle 3 Norte (at 14 Poniente). ✆ 222/232-9240. Admission $2 (£1.10). Tues–Sun 10am–4:30pm.

Museo Amparo ✦✦✦ The finest museum in the city, the Museo Amparo (named for the deceased wife of the founder) has a stunning collection of pre-Columbian pieces from across Mexico, beautifully displayed and intelligently organized. Its collections of colonial and modern art are quite good, and the museum frequently gets important traveling exhibitions, which usually don't require an additional admission charge. The collection of *arte virreinal* (colonial art) is on the second floor and includes decorative objects and furniture. It is exhibited in the restored living quarters of the original mansion. The interiors are all from the Porfiriato (1870s), with the elaborate decoration that the period is known for. Audio tours of the pre-Columbian collection are for rent ($1/55p, plus $1/55p deposit). You can hire an English-speaking guide for the entire museum ($20/£11). Signs are in Spanish and English; no cameras are permitted.

Calle 2 Sur 708. No phone. Admission $3 (£1.65) adults; $2 (£1.10) children 3–12 and students; free Mon. Wed–Mon 10am–6pm.

Museo Bello y González ⭐⭐   Located near the corner of Calle 3 Sur and Calle 3 Poniente, a block west of the *zócalo,* this museum houses a fine collection of 17th-, 18th-, and 19th-century art, furniture, and antiques from all over the world. Many of the Oriental objects in the museum were brought over in colonial times on the Philippine galleon. Viewing the house is another reason for seeing the place. At present, only the first floor is open to the public. My favorite room is almost completely covered in Talavera, and the display cabinets are filled with Talavera from several centuries. The museum is named for José Luis Bello y González, the father of Mariano Bello, the man who gathered this collection. A guided tour (in English or Spanish) is included in the price of admission.

Calle 3 Poniente 302. © 222/232-9475. Admission $1 (55p). Tues–Sun 10am–5pm.

Museo Nacional del Ferrocarril   This is a treat for railroad buffs. It consists of a large open area with several train engines (both steam and diesel), baggage cars, passenger cars, a presidential car, a dining car, Pullman coaches, and a caboose. You can board and inspect the cars. Even those not interested in railroads might enjoy seeing the design and details of some of these—they sketch a microcosm of a bygone era. A small gallery exhibits railway landscapes.

Calle 11 Norte and Calle 12 Poniente. © 222/232-4988. Free admission. Tues–Sun 10am–5pm.

SHOPPING

Puebla is the home of **Talavera** ⭐⭐⭐, a type of majolica earthenware. The Moors developed the technique for making it, and later started making it in Spain, in a town called Talavera. After the discovery of the New World, artisans brought the method to Puebla. And now, ironically, the making of Talavera has all but died out in Spain, but here it is practiced with great pride and fervor. There is even an association of Talavera factories that has established standards and certifies manufacturers. To be officially certified, a workshop must use only the traditional ingredients (no commercial ceramic mix or glazes) and methods; practically everything must be done by hand. There's no restriction on artistic taste, just the methods for making Talavera. So there's a good bit of variety from one workshop to another. Talavera pieces are not cheap, so you should look around in the showrooms until you find something you prefer over other styles. You should learn how to discern the cheap knock-offs from the real stuff.

And if you're interested in watching people make Talavera, several workshops offer tours. **Uriarte Talavera,** Calle 4 Poniente 911 (© 222/232-1598), charges $2 (£1.10) for its tour, but other places are free. The factory showroom has an impressive facade made completely of Talavera. And inside you'll see some great pieces displayed. There are nine or ten other certified manufacturers. Some use more modern patterns; some are more traditional. A couple of makers are in nearby Cholula. One workshop has a small restaurant in downtown Puebla that serves meals on its own Talavera. It's a pretty little place called **Talavera Celia** at Calle 5 Oriente 608 (© 222/242-3663). There's one workshop in the Parián area—**Talavera Armando,** at Calle 6 Norte 408 (© 222/232-6468). If enough people are around, they'll get a free tour. **Talavera de la Luz** specializes in making large maps and panoramic views in Talavera tiles. It has exhibited some of its largest pieces in museums in the United States.

The **Mercado de Artesanías (El Parián),** is a pedestrian-only, open-air shopping area just east of Calle 6 Norte between calles 2 and 6 Oriente. You'll see rows of neat brick shops selling inexpensive crafts and souvenirs. Don't judge all Talavera pottery by what you see here, though; the style in many cases is overblown. The shops are open daily from 10am to 8pm. Bargain to get a good price. While you're in this area, you can take a look at the **Teatro Principal.**

For antiques browsing, go to **Callejón de los Sapos (Alley of the Frogs),** about 3 blocks southeast of the *zócalo* near Calle 4 Sur and Calle 7 Oriente. Wander in and out; there's good stuff large and small. Shops are generally open daily from 10am to 2pm and 4 to 6pm. On Saturday mornings there's a flea market in the little square. If you're there between 12:30 and 5:30pm, stop by **La Pasita,** across Calle 5 from the Plaza de los Sapos, to taste homemade cordials and browse through the owner's humorous collection of Mexicana. Start with a *pasita,* then work your way up to a *China Poblana*—a layered cordial of red, white, and green liqueurs. The owner is an inveterate leg-puller.

WHERE TO STAY

Prices quoted include the 17% tax. All hotels listed here are in the historic district. Puebla's comfortable **Crowne Plaza Hotel** (© 800/465-4329 in the U.S. and Canada) is a short taxi ride from the center of town. Room rates are about $200 (£110) for a standard double. From late March to May, Puebla can experience heat waves. Consider getting a room with air-conditioning at this time of year.

VERY EXPENSIVE

Hotel Camino Real Puebla ★★★   This hotel, in the 16th-century former convent of the Immaculate Conception, is a nicely restored colonial gem. Courtyards spill into more courtyards, and remnants of poly-chromed colonial-era frescos are everywhere, even in the rooms. Rooms are decorated in handsome blue-and-yellow schemes inspired by Talavera colors. All have tile floors and original paintings, and some contain antiques. The hotel is 2½ blocks south of the *zócalo.*

Calle 7 Poniente 105 (between Calle 3 Sur and Av. 16 de Septiembre), Centro Histórico, 72000 Puebla, Pue. © 800/722-6466 in the U.S., or 222/229-0909 or -0910. Fax 222/232-9251. www.caminoreal.com/puebla. 84 units. $215 (£118) deluxe; $315 (£173) superior deluxe; $375 (£206) junior suite. AE, DC, MC, V. Valet parking $3.50. **Amenities:** 2 restaurants; bar; whirlpool; salon; tour desk; car rental; business center; room service; babysitting; laundry service; dry cleaning, nonsmoking rooms. *In room:* A/C, TV, minibar, coffeemaker, hair dryer, iron, safe.

Hotel La Quinta Luna ★★★   This small hotel in nearby Cholula is simple and elegant. The owners rescued this single-story colonial house from ruins and must have spent a fortune on it. The six rooms are all off a large courtyard. The rooms are spacious, comfortable, and simply perfect in some of the details. The windows are double glazed for quiet. The bathrooms are modern and are finished differently, but they are large and functional. Some come with tubs, others just showers. The service is personal, and the food at the little restaurant is quite good.

Calle 3 Sur 702, 72760 Cholula, Pue. © 800/728-9098 in the U.S. and Canada, or 222/247-8915. Fax 222/247-8916. www.laquintaluna.com. 7 units. $180 (£99) double; $220 (£121) junior suite; $260 (£14) master suite. AE, MC, V. Free valet parking. **Amenities:** Restaurant; bar; library; concierge; tour guide; complimentary airport pickup; room service; in-room massage; laundry service; dry cleaning, nonsmoking rooms. *In room:* TV w/DVD, Wi-Fi, minibar, coffeemaker, hair dryer, safe.

Mesones Sacristía ★★★   Two small hotels offer different ways to delve into Puebla's colonial past. If you're looking for modern convenience rather than atmosphere, stay at the Holiday Inn or the Crowne Plaza. If you want some colonial flavor mixed with sophistication or gaiety, try one of these unique hotels. Both are elegant adaptations of colonial houses, excellently located, but otherwise very different. The *Mesón Sacristía* **Capuchinas** offers quiet rooms, lots of privacy, and a smart blend of colonial and modern architecture. The small restaurant has won praise for its modern international cooking. The sister hotel, **Mesón Sacristía de la Compañía,** is less quiet and more fun. It offers an experience of the old city in all its antiquity and even quirkiness. For starters, you receive a massive colonial skeleton key to your room. And the rooms feel as colonial as the hotel could get away with. In the courtyard, a great restaurant and popular nightspot serves Poblano specialties. A guitarist performs romantic songs and ballads until about 11pm. Sometimes the entertainment is a guitar trio or some members of a *tuna* (traditional Spanish music sung to the accompaniment of string instruments)—not for those who like to retire early. The hotels offer packages for those interested in cooking lessons or Talavera.

Calle 6 Sur 304, Callejón de los Sapos, 72000 Puebla, Pue. ✆/fax **222/232-4513** or 242-3554. www.mesones-sacristia. com. 8 units at Mesón Sacristía Capuchinas; 7 units at Mesón de la Sacristía de la Compañía. $160 (£88) junior suite; $190 (£105) suite. Rates include full breakfast. AE, MC, V. Free secure parking. **Amenities:** Restaurant; bar; access to local health club; tour and activities desk; car rental; room service; in-room massage; laundry service; dry cleaning. *In room:* TV, coffeemaker, hair dryer.

NH Puebla ★★   This new property is unabashedly modern, spare, attractive, and calming. The common areas all have soft diffuse lighting, the surfaces and colors are muted, and the people seemed to respond by relaxing and talking in mellow tones. The rooms have lots of modern design elements. Good space, good lighting, comfortable furniture (as opposed to some other modern hotels) and nicely styled functional bathrooms. The location is right downtown.

Calle 5 Sur 105, 72000 Puebla, Pue. ✆ **888/726-0528** in the U.S., or 222/309-1919. www.nh-hotels.com. 128 units. $112–$178 (£62–£98) double; $144–$260 (£79–£143) junior suite. AE, MC, V. Valet parking $4 (£2.20). **Amenities:** Restaurant; bar; small heated outdoor pool; room service; babysitting; laundry service; dry cleaning; nonsmoking rooms. *In room:* A/C, TV, high-speed Internet, coffeemaker, hair dryer, iron.

EXPENSIVE
Hotel Posada San Pedro *(Kids)*   A better bargain than most downtown hotels offering the same level of amenities, especially for families, this place is convenient and comfortable. Spacious rooms come with plain wooden furniture, carpeting, and mid-size bathrooms. One section of the hotel has air-conditioning. There is a well-manicured courtyard with a small pool, surrounded by four stories of rooms. It's a family hotel, with afternoon videos for the kids and child care by prior arrangement.

Calle 2 Oriente 202, 72000 Puebla, Pue. ✆ **222/246-5077.** Fax 222/246-5376. www.hotelposadasanpedro.com.mx. 80 units. $110 (£61) double. Promotional rates available. AE, MC, V. Free covered parking. **Amenities:** Restaurant; 2 bars; outdoor heated pool; fitness room; tour info; car rental; business center; room service; babysitting; laundry service; dry cleaning, nonsmoking rooms. *In room:* AC, TV, Wi-Fi, minibar, coffeemaker, safe.

MODERATE
Hotel Colonial   This four-story hotel (with elevator) offers a great location. The rooms are ample and attractive, but avoid units along Calle 3. The furnishings are

simple; standard rooms usually contain twin beds with thin pillows. Bathrooms are basic but sufficient. The hotel's restaurant is good. The Colonial is 1 block east of the *zócalo,* on a pedestrian way.

Calle 4 Sur 105 (between Palafox y Mendoza and 3 Oriente), 72000 Puebla, Pue. © **222/246-4199.** Fax 222/246-0818. www.colonial.com.mx. 67 units. $62 (£34) double. AE, MC, V. No parking. **Amenities:** Restaurant; tour info; room service; laundry service; dry cleaning. *In room:* TV, safe.

Hotel Royalty   This hotel on Puebla's main square is a pretty good deal. You get the good location and the rooms are pretty quiet. They are small to medium (there's a good bit of variation) and have either two double or two twin beds. Most of the suites have balconies or at least windows that look out over the square. Some of these have larger size beds and go for not that much more.

Portal Hidalgo 8, 72000 Puebla, Pue. © **222/242-4740,** or 01-800/638-9999 in Mexico. www.hotelr.com. 45 units. $55–$75 (£30–£41) double. Rates include full breakfast. AE, MC, V. No parking. **Amenities:** Restaurant; tour info; room service; laundry service; dry cleaning. *In room:* TV, Wi-Fi, safe.

INEXPENSIVE

Hotel Puebla Plaza *Value*   The most attractive and comfortable of the budget hotels in the historic district, the Puebla Plaza is almost in the shadow of the cathedral. Rooms are small to midsize, with small bathrooms equipped with showers. Get a room in back to avoid the commotion in the front courtyard and at the restaurant next door. Lower prices are for rooms with one double bed.

Calle 5 Poniente 111, 72000 Puebla, Pue. © **222/246-3175.** Fax 222/242-5792. www.hotelpueblaplaza.com.mx. 48 units. $40–$50 (£22–£2.75) double. AE, MC, V. Secure parking $4 (£2.20). **Amenities:** Restaurant; tour info. *In room:* TV, Wi-Fi.

WHERE TO DINE

Puebla is known throughout Mexico for *mole poblano,* a spicy sauce with more than 20 ingredients (including chocolate), as well as *mixiotes* (mee-*shoh*-tehs), a dish of beef, pork, or lamb in a spicy red sauce baked in maguey paper. Another regional specialty, *pipián,* is somewhat like *mole* but based on ground toasted squash seeds. *Dulces* (sweets) shops are scattered about, with display windows brim-full of marzipan crafted into various shapes and designs, candied figs, and guava paste. If you're in the city during the season for *chiles en nogada* (July–Sept), make a point of trying one. It's a dish of elegant contrasts involving a poblano chile, a spicy-sweet filling made of pork, chicken, and sweetmeats, and a walnut cream sauce. The city goes crazy for this dish, and you'll see it everywhere. Besides the restaurants listed below, try those in the **Mesones Sacristía** (see above). I love the *mole* and traditional chalupas at the **Compañía** hotel restaurant.

VERY EXPENSIVE

La Conjura ★★★ SPANISH   It seems strange to eat Spanish food in this city known for its Mexican cuisine, but this restaurant is special. It plays with combinations of Old- and New-World ingredients, like tapas of *chistorra* (Spanish sausage) cooked with a small amount of *guajillo* peppers, or a shrimp dish with locally made goat cheese and passion fruit sauce. The ambitious menu changes daily, with offerings of seafood, lamb, and beef. On my last visit, I was especially impressed by the *arroz negro con calamares* (rice with squid cooked in the squid's ink), the *huachinango en alberino* (snapper in a scented wine sauce topped with mussels, clams, and shrimp), and a cream soup of sweet peppers and clams. The small, attractive dining room with its low, vaulted ceiling was formerly a bodega.

Calle 9 Oriente 201. ⓒ **222/232-9693**. Reservations recommended. Tapas $3–$10 (£1.65–£5.50); main courses $14–$36 (£7.70–£20). AE, DC, MC, V. Sun–Tues 2–6pm; Wed–Sat 2–11pm.

MODERATE

Fonda de Santa Clara *Overrated* REGIONAL   This is one of those restaurants invariably associated with a particular city. For many people, it is the automatic choice in Puebla, and unfortunately, this has caused a decline in quality. Still, many visitors love it. The *mole* is worth trying. It's 1½ blocks west of the *zócalo*.

Calle 3 Poniente 307. ⓒ **222/242-2659**. Main courses lunch $5–$10 (£2.75–£5.50), dinner $7–$14 (£3.85–£7.70). AE, DC, MC, V. Daily 9am–10pm.

La Guadalupana REGIONAL/MEXICAN   This restaurant off the Callejón de Los Sapos serves good regional specialties, including *mole, mole verde,* and *pipián.* The restaurant has two dining areas—the central front courtyard of a colonial house and the narrow patio of a former working-class *vecindad* (an enclosed grouping of simple apartments that share kitchen and bathroom areas).

Calle 5 Oriente 605. ⓒ **222/242-4886**. Main courses $6–$12 (£3.30–£6.60). AE, MC, V. Daily 8am–9pm.

Mi Ciudad ⭐⭐ MEXICAN   For an excellent *mole* or *pipián,* take a cab to this restaurant, in the middle of Puebla's restaurant and club district along Avenida Juárez. The dining room is large, with lots of references to Puebla in the decoration. The menu is large as well. The *chile atole* and *sopa poblana,* both cream soups, are excellent choices. Not on the menu, but you can ask for it anyway, is a half-and-half combination of either *mole* and *pipián* or *pipián rojo* and *pipián verde.* I like these dishes better here than at La Guadalupana. Also on the menu are several dishes from other parts of Mexico, including grilled meats, enchiladas, and so on.

Av. Juárez 2507. ⓒ **222/231-5326**. Reservations recommended. Main courses $7–$14 (£3.85–£7.70). AE, DC, MC, V. Tues–Sat 1:30pm–midnight; Sun 1:30–6:30pm.

PUEBLA AFTER DARK

Mariachis play daily, beginning at 6pm, on **Plaza de Santa Inés,** Calle 11 Poniente and Calle 3 Sur. They stroll through the crowds that gather at the sidewalk cafes. Another square where you can hear live music is **Plaza de los Sapos,** Calle 7 Oriente near Calle 6 Sur. To get there, walk 2 blocks south from the *zócalo* and take a left onto Calle 7 Oriente, toward the river. The plaza will be on your left, spreading out between Calle 7 and Calle 5 Oriente just past Calle 4 Sur. If you take Calle 5 Oriente from the cathedral to reach the Plaza de los Sapos, you'll pass several local hangouts where students, artists, and others gather for conversation, coffee, drinks, snacks, and live music.

Another place to hear live music is down the block from los Sapos at **Mesón Sacristía de la Compañía,** Calle 6 Sur 304. A singer-guitarist entertains with popular ballads from 9pm to midnight. The moderately priced restaurant serves a complete selection of Puebla specialties.

Teorema, Reforma 540 near Calle 7 Norte (ⓒ **222/242-1014**), is a good coffee shop and bookstore that features guitarists and folksingers every evening. It's open daily from 9:30am to 2:30pm and 4:30pm to midnight.

SIDE TRIPS FROM PUEBLA
CHOLULA, TONANTZINTLA & SAN FRANCISCO ACATEPEC

Ten minutes outside of Puebla on the old highway to Mexico City is the small town of **Cholula.** In pre-Columbian times, this was a large city—the religious capital of highland Mexico. The Spanish razed the hundreds of temples that stood here, and we know little about them. But the **Great Pyramid** still sits there, the largest pyramid in the New World. At first glimpse, it looks more like a hill crowned by a church (Nuestra Señora de los Remedios). But if you climb the unreconstructed pyramid beside it, you will see plainly the geometric outline of the original structure, which rises from the ground in four levels. From this viewpoint, you also get a good look at El Popocatépetl, the majestic snow-capped volcano that separates this valley from the valley of Mexico. The entrance fee for the Cholula pyramid is $3.50 (£1.95); the site is open Tuesday through Sunday from 9am to 5pm. Archaeologists have reconstructed one side of one of the lower segments of the pyramid and have dug tunnels into the pyramid, which visitors are free to explore.

A perfect complement to this trip is a visit to the church of **Tonantzintla** 🕮🕮🕮, just to the south. Leave the town on Bulevar Miguel Alemán, which becomes the road to Tonantzintla. Less than 1.5km (1 mile) ahead, the church is within plain sight of the road. It's justly famous for its jewel-box interior, executed in an endearing style that people have come to call Indian baroque. It has mesmerized many visitors, including R. Gordon Wasson, who saw in its manifold imagery allusions to a secret mushroom cult. If this visit hasn't quenched your appetite for visiting churches, proceed a bit farther down the road, and you will imperceptibly cross into the neighboring community of **San Francisco Acatepec** 🕮🕮. Its church is also along the road and cannot be missed; it has a stunning tile facade.

COLONIAL TLAXCALA & THE CACAXTLA & XOCHITECATL RUINS

Tlaxcala, 40km (25 miles) north of Puebla and 120km (75 miles) east of Mexico City, is the capital of Mexico's smallest state (also named Tlaxcala) and a colonial-era city with several claims to fame. Tlaxcalan warriors allied with Cortez against the Aztec played an essential role in the conquest. Tlaxcalan chiefs were the first to be baptized by the Spaniards; the baptismal font is in the **Templo de San Francisco** (2 blocks from the main plaza, just above the bullring). The church is noted for the elaborately inlaid Moorish ceiling below the choir loft. A painting inside the Chapel of the Third Order shows the baptism of the chiefs.

To the right of the Templo is the **Exconvento,** now a museum containing early paintings and artifacts from nearby archaeological sites. The **Government Palace** 🕮🕮, on the handsome, tree-shaped central *zócalo,* contains vivid murals by a local artist, Desiderio Hernández Xochitiotzin, that illustrate the city's history. The expanded **Museo de Artesanías,** on Sanchez Piedras between Lardizábal and Primera de Mayo, showcases the state's wide-ranging crafts and customs. Here, local artisans give visitors demonstrations in such crafts as embroidery, weaving, and *pulque*-making (juice of fermented *agaves*). Don't plan to breeze through; tours are mandatory and rather structured, and they take an hour or more—but are very interesting. The museum is open Tuesday through Sunday from 10am to 6pm; admission (including tour) is $1 (55p).

Tlaxcala's **tourist information office** is at the intersection of avenidas Juárez and Lardizábal (𝒞 **246/465-0961,** or 01-800/509-6557 in Mexico). Office hours are Monday through Friday from 9am to 7pm, Saturday and Sunday from 10am to 2pm.

Tlaxcala's main attractions are **Cacaxtla-Xochitécatl** 🕮🕮🕮 (pronounced "kah-*kahsh*-tlah soh-shee-*teh*-kahtl"), unique pre-Hispanic hilltop sites 19km (12 miles) southwest of the city. Tlaxcala attracts few tourists and retains its small-town atmosphere and overall low prices. If you are there on a weekend, the State Tourism Office sponsors a Saturday tour of the city and a Sunday tour of the Cacaxtla-Xochitécatl sites (both in Spanish). Tours leave from the front of the Museo de Arte at 10am. Board the

Tlaxcala

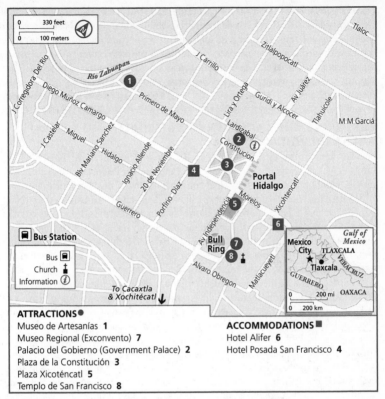

ATTRACTIONS●

Museo de Artesanías **1**
Museo Regional (Exconvento) **7**
Palacio del Gobierno (Government Palace) **2**
Plaza de la Constitución **3**
Plaza Xicoténcatl **5**
Templo de San Francisco **8**

ACCOMMODATIONS■

Hotel Alifer **6**
Hotel Posada San Francisco **4**

bus; the guide will collect the $2 (£1.10) fee. The city also offers a tour of the city in an old trolley bus Friday, Saturday, and Sunday. Ask at the information office.

Less than 1km (just over half a mile) from the town center is the famed **Ocotlán Sanctuary** ✛, constructed after Juan Diego Bernardino claimed to have seen an apparition of the Virgin Mary on that site in 1541. Baroque inside and out, it has elaborate interior decorations of carved figures and curling gilded wood that date from the 1700s. The carvings are attributed to Francisco Miguel Tlayotehuanitzin, an Indian sculptor who labored for more than 20 years to create them.

WHERE TO STAY & DINE IN TLAXCALA

Tlaxcala has several restaurants beneath the portal on the east side of the *zócalo*. One of them, Los Portales, has handmade corn tortillas all day and makes good breakfasts.

Hotel Alifer The Alifer's rooms are carpeted and have midsize tile bathrooms with showers. The rooms are a little worn (you can see it in the carpeting) but they aren't dirty or uncomfortable. The poor lighting is the only other thing that I can complain about, which is saying quiet a lot for a hotel in this price range with this kind of location. The price varies by number and size of beds.

Morelos 11, 90000 Tlaxcala, Tlax. ☎ **246/462-5678.** www.hotelalifer.com. 40 units. $35–$55 (£19–£30) double. MC, V. Free parking. **Amenities:** Restaurant. *In room:* TV.

Hotel Posada San Francisco   This occupies a 19th-century mansion on the town's main square known as the Casa de Piedra (House of Stone). Rooms are in the back of the property and most face the pool and patio. They're comfortable, simply furnished rooms with medium soft mattresses. Five rooms in the *zona rústica* have more character but are a little smaller. They are grouped around a small stone courtyard.

Plaza de la Constitución 17, 90000 Tlaxcala, Tlax. (✆ 246/462-6022. Fax 246/462-6818. www.posadasanfrancisco.com. 68 units. $105 (£58) double; $155 (£85) suite. AE, MC, V. Free sheltered parking. **Amenities:** Restaurant; bar; outdoor pool; tennis court; game room; room service; massage; laundry service; dry cleaning. *In room:* TV, Wi-Fi, hair dryer.

EXPLORING THE CACAXTLA-XOCHITECATL ARCHAEOLOGICAL SITE

Scholars were startled by the discovery in 1975 of vivid murals in red, blue, black, yellow, and white, showing Maya warriors (from the Yucatán Peninsula). Since then, more murals, more history, and at least eight construction phases have been uncovered.

Scholars attribute the influence of the site to a little-known tri-ethnic group (Náhuatl, Mixtec, and Chocho-popoloca) known as Olmec-Xicalanca, from Mexico's Gulf Coast. Among the translations of its name, "merchant's trade pack" seems most revealing. Like Casas Grandes north of Chihuahua City and Xochicalco between Cuernavaca and Taxco, Cacaxtla appears to have been an important crossroads for merchants, astronomers, and others in the Mesoamerican world. Its apogee, between A.D. 650 and 900, corresponds with the abandonment of Teotihuacán (near Mexico City), the decline of the Classic Maya civilization, and the emergence of the Toltec culture at Tula.

How—or even if—those events affected Cacaxtla isn't known. The principal **mural** apparently is a vividly detailed victory scene, with triumphant dark-skinned warriors wearing jaguar skins, and the vanquished dressed in feathers and having their intestines extracted. Numerous symbols of Venus (a half-star with five points) found painted at the site have led archaeoastronomy scholar John Carlson to link historical events such as wars, captive taking, and ritual sacrifice with the appearance of Venus; all of this was likely undertaken in hopes of assuring the continued fertility of crops.

The latest mural discoveries show a wall of corn plants from which human heads sprout, next to a merchant whose pack is laden with goods. The murals flank a grand **acropolis** with unusual architectural motifs. A giant steel roof protects the grand plaza and murals.

Xochitécatl is a small ceremonial center located on a hilltop overlooking Cacaxtla, about 1km (a half mile) to the east and in plain sight of Cacaxtla. It was probably inhabited, at least in the classical period, by the same people living in Cacaxtla. A curious **circular pyramid** stands atop this hill, 180km (590 ft.) above the surrounding countryside. Beside it are two other **pyramids** and three massive **boulders** (one about 3m/10 ft. in diameter), which were hollowed out for some reason. Hollowed boulders appear to have been restricted to the Puebla-Tlaxcala valley. Excavation of the Edificio de la Espiral (circular pyramid), dated between 1000 and 800 B.C. (middle formative period), encountered no stairways. Access is thought to have been by its spiral walkway. Rounded boulders from the nearby Zahuapan and Atoyac rivers were used in its construction. Rounded pyramids in this part of Mexico are thought to have been dedicated to Ehecatl, god of the wind. The base diameter exceeds 55m (180 ft.); it rises to a height of 15m (50 ft.).

The stepped and terraced **Pyramid of the Flowers,** made of rounded boulders, was started during the middle formative period. Modifications continued into colonial times, as exemplified by faced-stone and stucco-covered adobe. Of the 30 bodies found during excavations, all but one were children. Little is known about the people who built Xochitécatl. Evidence suggests that the area was dedicated to Xochitl, goddess of flowers and fertility. The small **museum** contains pottery and small sculpture, and a **garden** holds larger sculpture.

To get to Cacaxtla from Tlaxcala, take a *combi* (collective minivan) or city bus to Nativitas (also called San Miguel Milagro), the village nearest the Cacaxtla ruins. *Combis* depart from behind the Hotel Posada San Francisco. From there, walk the paved road less than 1km (about a half mile) or take a taxi to the entrance. From the parking lot, the archaeological site is a 90m (295-ft.) climb.

From Puebla, take Highway 119 north to the crossroads near Zacualpan and turn left, passing Tetlatlahuaca; turn right when you see signs to Nativitas and Cacaxtla. From Mexico City, take Highway 190 to San Martín Texmelucan, where you should ask directions for the road leading directly to the ruins, which are about 10km (6 miles) ahead. (This is the southern road you can use without going through Tlaxcala.) Admission is $4 (£2.20; a single ticket is good for both sites), plus $6 (£3.30) for a video or still camera. Both sites are open Tuesday through Sunday 10am to 5pm.

13

Cancún

by Juan Cristiano

Cancún turns 33 in 2008, and like many 30-somethings, the town is hitting its prime. In 1974, a group of Mexican government computer analysts picked Cancún for tourism development due to its ideal mix of elements: transparent blue oceans, powdery white beaches, and immense potential for growth. Since then, the city has faced considerable natural challenges, emerging stronger and more irresistible each time. The wreckage of Hurricane Wilma, which tore through the Yucatán peninsula in 2005, has been replaced by exacting renovations, luxurious upgrades, and brand new destinations throughout this slice of Caribbean paradise.

Cancún, or "golden snake" in Mayan, stretches from the old city to a 24km (15-mile) sliver of land connected to the mainland by two bridges. Between the old and the new rests the expansive Nichupté lagoon, a lush reminder of Cancún's jungle past.

Cancún remains Mexico's calling card to the world, perfectly showcasing both the country's breathtaking natural beauty and the depth of its 1,000-year history. One astonishing statistic suggests that more Americans travel to Cancún than to any other overseas destination in the world. Indeed, almost three million people visit this enticing beach resort annually—most of them on their first trip to Mexico.

The reasons for Cancún's allure have not changed since the government turned this once isolated beach into a five-star destination. In addition to its stunning coastline, Cancún also offers the highest quality accommodations, easy access by air, an unrivaled range of shopping, world-class dining and nightlife, and endless outdoor activities. Your day may begin with a jet-ski tour of the jungles near Cancún or a visit to one of several Mayan ruins, followed by an afternoon of water sports or lounging poolside. After soaking up the sun, browse through a Mexican *mercado* (market) searching for bargains or visit upscale stores for duty-free deals. Several five-diamond rated restaurants await the discriminating palate, and rocking bars and dance clubs summon those who cannot bear to go to bed until dawn.

Cancún embodies Caribbean splendor and the exotic joys of Mexico, but it is also a modern megaresort. Even a traveler feeling apprehensive about visiting foreign soil will feel completely at ease here. English is spoken and dollars accepted; roads are well-paved and lawns manicured. Most travelers feel comfortable in Cancún, while some also feel surprised to find that it almost resembles a U.S. beach resort more than authentic Mexico. Indeed, signs of Americanism are everywhere here.

In addition to attractions of its own, Cancún is a convenient distance from the more traditional resorts of Isla Mujeres and the coastal zone now known as the Riviera Maya—extending down from Cancún, through Playa del Carmen, to the Maya ruins at Tulum, Cozumel, Chichén Itzá, and Cobá. All lie within day-trip distance.

You will run out of vacation days before you run out of things to do in Cancún. Snorkeling, dolphin swims, jungle tours, and visits to ancient Mayan ruins and modern ecological theme parks are among the most popular diversions. There are a dozen malls with name-brand and duty-free shops (with European goods at prices better than in the U.S.), and more than 350 restaurants and nightclubs. The tens of thousands of hotel rooms in the area offer something for every taste and every budget.

Cancún's luxury hotels have pools so spectacular that you may find it tempting to remain poolside, but don't. Set aside some time to simply gaze into the ocean and wriggle your toes in the fine, brilliantly white sand. It is, after all, what put Cancún on the map—and not even a tempest of nature has been able to take that away.

1 Orientation

GETTING THERE

BY PLANE If this is not your first trip to Cancún, you'll notice that the airport's facilities and services continue to expand. **AeroMéxico** (℡ 800/237-6639 in the U.S., or 01/800-021-4000 in Mexico; www.aeromexico.com) offers connecting service to Cancún through Mexico City. **Mexicana** (℡ 800/531-7921 in the U.S., 01/800-502-2000 in Mexico, or 998/881-9090; www.mexicana.com.mx) offers connecting flights to Cancún through Miami or Mexico City. In addition to these carriers, many **charter** companies—such as Apple Vacations and Funjet—travel to Cancún; these package tours make up as much as 60% of arrivals by U.S. visitors (see "Packages for the Independent Traveler," in chapter 2).

Regional carrier **Click Mexicana,** a Mexicana affiliate (℡ 01-800/112-5425 toll-free in Mexico; www.click.com.mx) flies from Cozumel, Havana, Mexico City, Mérida, Chetumal, and other points within Mexico. You'll want to confirm departure times for flights to the U.S. **Aviacsa** (℡ 01-800/711-6733 toll-free in Mexico; www.aviacsa.com) and **InterJet** (℡ 01-800/01-12345 toll-free in Mexico; www.interjet.com.mx) are two other regional carriers that fly to Cancún from Mexico City.

Here are the U.S. numbers of major international carriers serving Cancún: **Alaska** (℡ 800/426-0333; www.alaskaair.com), **American** (℡ 800/433-7300; www.aa.com), **Continental** (℡ 800/231-0856; www.continental.com), **Delta** (℡ 800/221-1212; www.delta.com), **Northwest** (℡ 800/225-2525; www.nwa.com), and **US Airways** (℡ 800/428-4322; www.usairways.com).

Most major car-rental firms have outlets at the airport, so if you're renting a car, consider picking it up and dropping it off at the airport to save on airport-transportation costs. Another way to save money is to arrange for the rental before you leave home. If you wait until you arrive, the daily cost will be around $50 to $75 (£28–£41) for a Chevrolet Atos. Major agencies include **Avis** (℡ 800/331-1212 in the U.S., or 998/886-0221; www.avis.com); **Budget** (℡ 800/527-0700 in the U.S., or 998/886-0417; fax 998/884-4812; www.budget.com); **Dollar** (℡ 800/800-3665 in the U.S., or 998/886-2300; www.dollar.com); **National** (℡ 800/227-7368 in the U.S., or 998/886-0153; www.nationalcar.com); and **Hertz** (℡ 800/654-3131 in the U.S. and Canada, or 998/884-1326; www.hertz.com). If you're looking for an exotic car rental (such as a Porsche or Mercedes convertible) and don't mind paying a small fortune for it, try **Platinum** (℡ 998/883-5555; www.platinumcarrental.com), with an office inside the JW Marriott hotel. The Zona Hotelera (Hotel Zone) lies 10km (6¼ miles)—a 20-minute drive—from the airport along wide, well-paved roads.

Rates for a **private taxi** from the airport are around $25 (£14) to downtown Cancún, or $28 to $40 (£15–£22) to the Hotel Zone, depending on your destination.

Tips   **The Best Websites for Cancún**

- **All About Cancún: www.cancunmx.com**   This site is a good place to start planning. There's a database of answers to the most common questions, called "The Online Experts." It's slow, but it has input from lots of recent travelers to the region.
- **Cancún Convention & Visitors Bureau: www.cancun.info**   The official site of the Cancún Convention & Visitors Bureau lists excellent information on events and attractions. Its hotel guide is one of the most complete available, and it has an active message board of recent visitors to Cancún.
- **Cancún Online: www.cancun.com**   This comprehensive guide has lots of information about things to do and see in Cancún, with most details provided by paying advertisers. You can even reserve a tee time or conduct wedding planning online.
- **Cancún Travel Guide: www.go2cancun.com**   This group specializing in online information about Mexico has put together an excellent resource for Cancún rentals, hotels, and attractions. Note that it lists only paying advertisers, but you'll find most of the major players.
- **Mexico Web Cancún Chat: www.mexicoweb.com/chats/cancun**   This is one of the more active chats online specifically about Cancún. The users share inside information on everything from the cheapest beer to the quality of food at various all-inclusive resorts.

Colectivos (vans) run from the airport into town. Buy tickets, which cost about $10 (£5.50), from the booth to the far right as you exit the airport terminal. There's **minibus** transportation ($9.50/£5.25) from the airport to the Puerto Juárez passenger ferry to Isla Mujeres, or you can hire a private taxi for about $40 (£22). There is no *colectivo* service returning to the airport from Ciudad Cancún or the Hotel Zone, so you'll have to take a taxi, but the rate will be much less than for the trip from the airport. (Only federally chartered taxis may take fares *from* the airport, but any taxi may bring passengers *to* the airport.) Ask at your hotel what the fare should be, but expect to pay about half what you paid from the airport to your hotel.

BY CAR   From Mérida or Campeche, take **Highway 180** east to Cancún. This is mostly a winding, two-lane road that branches off into the express **toll road 180D** between Izamal and Nuevo Xcan. Nuevo Xcan is approximately 40km (25 miles) from Cancún. Mérida is about 80km (50 miles) away.

BY BUS   Cancún's **ADO bus terminal** (© 998/884-4352 or -4804) is in downtown Ciudad Cancún at the intersection of avenidas Tulum and Uxmal. All out-of-town buses arrive here. Buses run to Playa del Carmen, Tulum, Chichén Itzá, other nearby beach and archaeological zones, and other points within Mexico.

VISITOR INFORMATION

The **State Tourism Office,** Cancún Center, Bulevar Kukulkán Km 9, 1st floor, Zona Hotelera (© **998/881-9000;** www.qroo.gob.mx), is open Monday to Friday from 9am to 8pm. The **Cancún Municipal Tourism Office** is found downtown on

Downtown Cancún

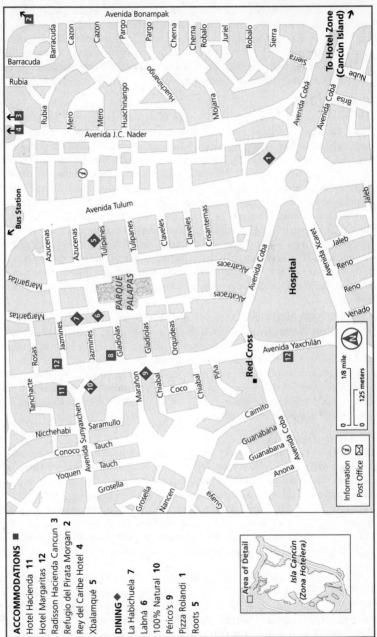

ACCOMMODATIONS ■
Hotel Hacienda 11
Hotel Margaritas 12
Radisson Hacienda Cancun 3
Refugio del Pirata Morgan 2
Rey del Caribe Hotel 4
Xbalamqué 5

DINING ◆
La Habichuela 7
Labná 6
100% Natural 10
Périco's 9
Pizza Rolandi 1
Roots 5

Avenida Cobá at Avenida Tulum (© **998/887-3379**). It's open Monday through Friday from 9am to 7pm. Each office lists hotels and their rates, and ferry schedules. For information prior to your arrival in Cancún, visit the Convention Bureau's website, **www.cancun.info**.

Pick up copies of the free monthly booklet, *Cancún Tips* (www.cancuntips.com.mx), and a seasonal tabloid of the same name.

CITY LAYOUT

There are really two Cancúns: **Isla Cancún (Cancún Island)** and **Ciudad Cancún (Cancún City).** The latter, on the mainland, has restaurants, shops, and less expensive hotels, as well as pharmacies, dentists, automotive shops, banks, travel and airline agencies, and car-rental firms—all within an area about 9 square blocks. The city's main thoroughfare is **Avenida Tulum.** Heading south, Avenida Tulum becomes the highway to the airport and to Tulum and Chetumal; heading north, it intersects the highway to Mérida and the road to Puerto Juárez and the Isla Mujeres ferries.

The famed **Zona Hotelera,** or Hotel Zone (also called the Zona Turística, or Tourist Zone), stretches out along Isla Cancún, which is a sandy strip 22km (14 miles) long, shaped like a "7." It connects to the mainland by the Playa Linda Bridge at the north end and the Punta Nizuc Bridge at the southern end. Between the two areas lies Laguna Nichupté. Avenida Cobá from Cancún City becomes Bulevar Kukulkán, the island's main traffic artery. Cancún's international airport is just inland from the south end of the island.

FINDING AN ADDRESS   Cancún's street-numbering system is a holdover from its early days. Addresses are still given by the number of the building lot and by the *manzana* (block) or *supermanzana* (group of blocks). The city is relatively compact, and the downtown commercial section is easy to cover on foot.

On the island, addresses are given by kilometer number on Bulevar Kukulkán or by reference to some well-known location. In Cancún, streets are named after famous Maya cities. Chichén Itzá, Tulum, and Uxmal are the names of the boulevards in Cancún, as well as nearby archaeological sites.

GETTING AROUND

BY TAXI   Taxi prices in Cancún are clearly set by zone, although keeping track of what's in which zone can take some doing. The minimum fare within the Hotel Zone is $6 per ride, making it one of the most expensive taxi areas in Mexico. In addition, taxis operating in the Hotel Zone feel perfectly justified in having a discriminatory pricing structure: Local residents pay about half of what tourists pay, and prices for guests at higher-priced hotels are about double those for budget hotel guests—these are all established by the taxi union. Rates should be posted outside your hotel; if you have a question, all drivers are required to have an official rate card in their taxis, though it's generally in Spanish.

Within the downtown area, the cost is about $1.50 (85p) per cab ride (not per person); within any other zone, it's $6 (£3.30). Traveling between two zones will also cost $6 (£3.30), and if you cross two zones, that'll cost $8 (£4.40). Settle on a price in advance, or check at your hotel. Trips to the airport from most zones cost $15 (£8.25). Taxis can also be rented for $18 (£9.90) per hour for travel around the city and Hotel Zone, but this rate can generally be negotiated down to about $15 (£8.25). If you want to hire a taxi to take you to Chichén Itzá or along the Riviera Maya, expect to pay about $30 (£17) per hour—many taxi drivers feel that they are also providing guide services.

BY BUS   Bus travel within Cancún continues to improve and is increasingly popular. In town, almost everything lies within walking distance. **Ruta 1** and **Ruta 2** (HOTELES) city buses travel frequently from the mainland to the beaches along Avenida Tulum (the main street) and all the way to Punta Nizuc at the far end of the Hotel Zone on Isla Cancún. **Ruta 8** buses go to Puerto Juárez/Punta Sam for ferries to Isla Mujeres. They stop on the east side of Avenida Tulum. All these city buses operate between 6am and 10pm daily. Beware of private buses along the same route; they charge far more than the public ones. Public buses have the fare painted on the front; at press time, the fare was 60¢.

BY MOPED   Mopeds are a convenient but dangerous way to cruise around through the very congested traffic. Rentals start at $30 (£17) for a day, and a credit card voucher is required as security. You should receive a crash helmet (it's the law) and instructions on how to lock the wheels when you park. Read the fine print on the back of the rental agreement regarding liability for repairs or replacement in case of accident, theft, or vandalism.

FAST FACTS: Cancún

American Express   The local office is at Av. Tulum 208 and Agua (🕿 998/881-4000 or -4055; www.americanexpress.com/mexico), 1 block past the Plaza México. It's open Monday through Friday from 9am to 6pm, Saturday from 9am to 1pm.

Area Code   The telephone area code is **998**.

Climate   It's hot but not overwhelmingly humid. The rainy season is May through October. August through October is hurricane season, which brings erratic weather. November through February is generally sunny but can also be cloudy, windy, somewhat rainy, and even cool.

Consulates   The **U.S. Consular Agent** is in the Plaza Caracol 2, Bulevar Kukulkán Km 8.5, 3rd level, 320–323 (🕿 998/883-0272). The office is open Monday through Friday from 9am to 2pm. The **Canadian Consulate** is in the Plaza Caracol, 3rd level, Loc. 330 (🕿 998/883-3360). The office is open Monday through Friday from 9am to 5pm. The **United Kingdom** has a consular office at the Royal Sands Hotel in Cancún (🕿 998/881-0100, ext. 65898; fax 998/848-8662; information@british consulateCancun.com). The office is open Monday through Friday from 9am to 3pm. Irish, Australian, and New Zealand citizens should contact their embassies in Mexico City.

Crime   Car break-ins are just about the only crime here. They happen frequently, especially around the shopping centers in the Hotel Zone. VW Beetles and Golfs are frequent targets.

Currency Exchange   Most banks sit downtown along Avenida Tulum and are usually open Monday through Friday from 9:30am to 4pm. Many have automated teller machines for after-hours cash withdrawals. In the Hotel Zone, you'll find banks in the Kukulcán Plaza and next to the convention center. There are also many *casas de cambio* (exchange houses). Downtown merchants are eager to change cash dollars, but island stores don't offer very good exchange rates. Avoid changing money at the airport as you arrive, especially at the first exchange booth you see—its rates are less favorable than those of any in town or others farther inside the airport concourse.

Drugstores Across the street from Señor Frog's in the Hotel Zone, at Bulevar Kukulkán Km 9.5, **Farmacías del Ahorro** (© 998/892-7291) offers 24 hour service and free delivery. Plenty of drugstores are in the major shopping malls in the Hotel Zone, and are open until 10pm. In downtown Cancún, **Farmacia Cancún** is located at Av. Tulum 17 (© 998/884-1283). You can stock up on over-the-counter and many prescription drugs without a prescription.

Emergencies To report an emergency, dial © **060,** which is supposed to be similar to 911 emergency service in the United States. For first aid, the **Cruz Roja,** or Red Cross (© **065** or 998/884-1616; fax 998/883-9218), is open 24 hours on Avenida Yaxchilán between avenidas Xcaret and Labná, next to the Telmex building. **Total Assist,** Claveles 5, SM 22, at Avenida Tulum (© **998/884-8022;** total assist@prodigy.net.mx), is a small (nine-room) emergency hospital with English-speaking doctors. It's open 24 hours and accepts American Express, MasterCard, and Visa. Desk staff may have limited command of English. **Air Ambulance** (Global Ambulance) service is available by calling © **01-800/305-9400** in Mexico.

Internet Access **Alienet** in a kiosk on the second floor of Kukulcán Plaza, Bulevar Kukulkán Km 13 (© **998/840-6099**), offers Internet access for $7 per hour. It's open daily from 10am to 10pm.

Luggage Storage & Lockers Hotels will generally tag and store luggage while you travel elsewhere.

Newspapers & Magazines Most hotel gift shops and newsstands carry English-language magazines and English-language Mexican newspapers, such as the *Miami Herald.*

Police Cancún has a fleet of English-speaking tourist police to help travelers. Dial © 998/885-2277. The **Procuraduría Federal del Consumidor (consumer protection agency),** Av. Cobá 9–11 (© 998/884-2634 or -2701), is opposite the Social Security Hospital and upstairs from the Fenix drugstore. It's open Monday through Friday from 9am to 3pm.

Post Office The main *correo* lies at the intersection of avenidas Sunyaxchen and Xel-Ha (© 998/884-1418). It's open Monday through Friday from 9am to 4pm, and Saturday from 9am to noon for the purchase of stamps only.

Safety Aside from car break-ins, there is very little crime in Cancún. People are generally safe late at night in tourist areas; just use ordinary common sense. As at any other beach resort, don't take money or valuables to the beach. See "Crime," above.

Swimming on the Caribbean side presents a danger because of the undertow. See the information on beaches in "Beaches, Watersports & Boat Tours," later in this chapter, for information about flag warnings

Seasons Technically, high season runs from December 15 to April; low season extends from May to December 15, when prices drop 10% to 30%. Some hotels are starting to charge high-season rates during June and July, when Mexican, European, and school-holiday visitors often travel, although rates may still be lower than in winter months.

Special Events The annual **Mexico-Caribbean Food Festival,** featuring special menus of culinary creations throughout town, is held each year between September and November. Additional information is available through the State Tourism Office.

2 Where to Stay

Island hotels—almost all of them offering modern facilities and English-speaking staffs—line the beach like concrete dominoes. Extravagance is the byword in the newer hotels. Some hotels, while exclusive, affect a more relaxed attitude. The water on the upper end of the island facing Bahía de Mujeres is placid, while beaches lining the long side of the island facing the Caribbean are subject to choppier water and crashing waves on windy days. (For more information on swimming safety, see "Beaches, Watersports & Boat Tours," later in this chapter.) Be aware that the farther south you go on the island, the longer it takes (20–30 min. in traffic) to get back to the "action spots," which are primarily between the Plaza Flamingo and Punta Cancún on the island and along Avenida Tulum on the mainland.

Following Hurricane Wilma's devastation, the news item that received the most coverage was the destruction of Cancún's famed white-sand beaches, certainly key to selecting a hotel location for many. Immediately following the storm, literally all of the sand was washed away from the northern border of Isla Cancún, and Punta Cancún. However, thanks in part to Mother Nature, and in part to a more than $20-million effort by Mexico's government to pump the dislocated sand back to the beach, by spring of 2006, this was no longer an issue. The southern beaches of Isla Cancún actually benefited from the storm, and those areas enjoyed especially wide beachfronts.

Almost all major hotel chains are represented on Cancún Island, so this list can be viewed as a representative summary, with a select number of notable places. The reality is that Cancún is so popular as a package destination from the U.S. that prices and special deals are often the deciding factor for those traveling here (see "Packages for the Independent Traveler," in chapter 2). Ciudad Cancún offers independently owned, smaller, less-expensive lodging; prices are lower here off season (May–early Dec). For condo, home, and villa rentals, check with **Cancún Hideaways** (© 817/ 522-4466; fax 817/557-3483; www.cancun-hideaways.com), a company specializing in luxury properties, downtown apartments, and condos—many at prices much lower than comparable hotel stays. Owner Maggie Rodriguez, a former resident of Cancún, has made this niche market her specialty.

The hotel listings in this chapter begin on Cancún Island and finish in Cancún City (the real downtown), where bargain lodgings are available. Parking is free at all island hotels.

CANCUN ISLAND
VERY EXPENSIVE
Fiesta Americana Grand Coral Beach ★★★   This spectacular hotel, which opened in 1991, has one of the best locations in Cancún, with 300m (984 ft.) of prime beachfront and proximity to the main shopping and entertainment centers. The all-suites hotel includes junior suites with sunken sitting areas, white-washed furniture, marble bathrooms, and soothing California colors. Service throughout this five-diamond

> ### ⟨Tips⟩ **Important Note on Hotel Prices**
>
> Cancún's hotels, in all price categories, generally set their rates in dollars, so they are immune to swings in the peso. Travel agents and wholesalers always have air/hotel packages available, and Sunday papers often advertise inventory-clearing packages at prices much lower than the rates listed here. Cancún also has numerous all-inclusive properties, which allow you to take a fixed-cost vacation. Note that the price quoted when you call a hotel's reservation number from the United States may not include Cancún's 12% tax. Prices can vary considerably throughout the year, so it pays to consult a travel agent or shop around.

property is gracious and attentive, and the expansive lobby is embellished with elegant dark-green granite and an abundance of marble. The hotel's great Punta Cancún location (opposite the Cancún Center) has the advantage of facing the beach to the north, meaning that the surf is calm and perfect for swimming.

Bulevar Kukulkán Km 9.5, 77500 Cancún, Q. Roo. ⟨℃⟩ 800/343-7821 in the U.S., or 998/881-3200. Fax 998/881-3273. www.fiestamericana.com. 602 units. High season $519 (£285) and up double, $639 (£351) and up club-floor double; low season $339 (£186) and up double, $459 (£252) and up club-floor double. AE, MC, V. **Amenities:** 3 restaurants; poolside snack bar; 5 bars; outdoor pool w/swim-up bars; 3 indoor tennis courts; fitness center; sauna; watersports equipment/rentals; concierge; travel agency; car-rental desk; business center; salon; room service; massage; babysitting; laundry service; concierge floor. *In room:* A/C, TV, minibar, hair dryer, coffeemaker, iron, safe.

Hilton Cancún Beach & Golf Resort ⟨★★⟩ ⟨Kids⟩   Grand, expansive, and fully equipped, this is a true resort in every sense of the word. The Hilton Cancún sits on 100 hectares (247 acres) of prime beachside property, a location that gives every room a sea view (some have both sea and lagoon views), with an 18-hole par-72 golf course across the street. Like the sprawling resort, rooms are grandly spacious and immaculately decorated in minimalist style, and following Hurricane Wilma, all received an update. It's a very kid-friendly hotel, with one of the island's best children's activity programs, special children's pool, and babysitting available. The hotel's spectacular multisection swimming pool stretches out to the gorgeous beach. The Hilton is especially appealing to golfers because it's one of only two in Cancún with an on-site course (the other is the Meliá). Greens fees for guests are $99 (£54) for 9 holes, $149 (£82) for 18 holes, and include the use of a cart. The Wellness Spa includes oceanfront massage cabañas, yoga, and aromatherapy. This Hilton has a friendly and energetic vibe and boasts wonderful service for such a large resort.

Bulevar Kukulkán Km 17, Retorno Lacandones, 77500 Cancún, Q. Roo. ⟨℃⟩ 800/228-3000 in the U.S., or 998/881-8000. Fax 998/881-8080. www.hiltoncancun.com. 426 units. High season $249–$349 (£137–£192) double, $440–$585 (£242–£322) Beach Club double, $555–$779 (£305–£428) suite; low season $119–$300 (£65–£165) double, $350–$550 (£193–£303) Beach Club double, $395–$500 (£217–£275) suite. AE, DC, MC, V. **Amenities:** 5 restaurants; 2 bars; 7 interconnected outdoor pools w/swim-up bar; golf course across the street; 2 lighted tennis courts; Wellness Spa w/spa services and fully equipped gym; 2 whirlpools; watersports center; Kids' Club; concierge; tour desk; car-rental desk; salon; room service; babysitting; laundry service. *In room:* A/C, TV, minibar, coffeemaker, hair dryer, iron, safe, bathrobes.

JW Marriott ⟨★★★⟩   One of Cancún's most upscale and appealing properties, the JW Marriott offers elegance without pretense. From the expansive marble and flower-filled lobby to the luxurious oceanview guest rooms, the hotel combines classic and Caribbean styling with warm Mexican service. Guest rooms feature beautiful marble bathrooms with separate tub and shower, private balconies, flat-screen TVs, bathrobes

Isla Cancún (Zona Hotelera)

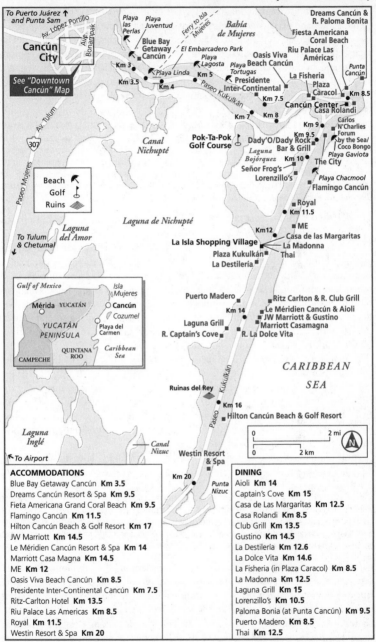

ACCOMMODATIONS

Blue Bay Getaway Cancún **Km 3.5**
Dreams Cancún Resort & Spa **Km 9.5**
Fieta Americana Grand Coral Beach **Km 9.5**
Flamingo Cancún **Km 11.5**
Hilton Cancún Beach & Golf Resort **Km 17**
JW Marriott **Km 14.5**
Le Méridien Cancún Resort & Spa **Km 14**
Marriott Casa Magna **Km 14.5**
ME **Km 12**
Oasis Viva Beach Cancún **Km 8.5**
Presidente Inter-Continental Cancún **Km 7.5**
Ritz-Carlton Hotel **Km 13.5**
Riu Palace Las Americas **Km 8.5**
Royal **Km 11.5**
Westin Resort & Spa **Km 20**

DINING

Aioli **Km 14**
Captain's Cove **Km 15**
Casa de Las Margaritas **Km 12.5**
Casa Rolandi **Km 8.5**
Club Grill **Km 13.5**
Gustino **Km 14.5**
La Destilería **Km 12.6**
La Dolce Vita **Km 14.6**
La Fisheria (in Plaza Caracol) **Km 8.5**
La Madonna **Km 12.5**
Laguna Grill **Km 15**
Lorenzillo's **Km 10.5**
Paloma Bonia (at Punta Cancún) **Km 9.5**
Puerto Madero **Km 8.5**
Thai **Km 12.5**

525

and slippers, and twice daily maid service. The inviting free-form infinity pool extends to the white-sand beach, and families feel as comfortable here as romance-seeking couples. A spectacular 3,252-sq.-m (35,000-sq.-ft.) spa includes an indoor pool and Jacuzzi, high-tech fitness center, and full range of massages, body scrubs and polishes, facials, and healing water treatments. Gustino is an outstanding Italian restaurant seated off the lobby (see "Where to Dine" later in this chapter), and afternoon tea with a musical trio is offered in the lobby lounge. Guests here also enjoy access to the adjacent Marriott Casa Magna.

Bulevar Kukulkán Km 14.5, 77500 Cancún, Q. Roo. © 800/223-6388 in the U.S., or 998/848-9600. Fax 998/848-9601. www.jwmarriottcancun.com. 448 units. High season $554–$653 (£305–£359) double; low season $300–$400 (£165–£220) double. AE, DC, MC, V. Small pets allowed with prior reservation. **Amenities:** 3 restaurants; deli; lobby bar and pool bar; expansive outdoor pool; indoor pool; full-service spa; 3 whirlpools; sauna; steam room; access to Kids' Club at Marriott Casa Magna; concierge; travel agency; car rental; business center; shopping arcade; gift shop; salon; room service; medical services; laundry service; club floor w/special amenities and complimentary cocktails. *In room:* A/C, flat-screen TV, Wi-Fi, minibar, hair dryer, iron, safe.

Le Méridien Cancún Resort & Spa ★★   Le Méridien is among the most inviting of Cancún's luxury options, with a refined yet welcoming sense of personal service. From the intimate lobby and reception area to the best concierge service in Cancún, guests feel immediately pampered. The relatively small establishment is more elegant boutique hotel than immense resort—a welcome relief. The decor throughout the rooms and common areas is classy and comforting, not overdone. Rooms are generous in size with small balconies overlooking the pool; due to the hotel's design, rooms do not have ocean views. Each has a large marble bathroom with a separate tub and glassed-in shower. The hotel attracts many Europeans as well as younger, sophisticated travelers, and it is ideal for a second honeymoon.

A highlight of—or even a reason for—staying here is the **Spa del Mar,** one of Mexico's most complete European spa facilities, with more than 4,570 sq. m (49,190 sq. ft.) of services dedicated to your body and soul. A complete fitness center with extensive cardio and weight machines is on the upper level. The spa consists of a health snack bar, a full-service salon, and 14 treatment rooms, as well as men's and women's steam rooms, saunas, whirlpools, cold plunge pool, inhalation rooms, tranquillity rooms, lockers, and changing areas.

Aioli is a splendid fine-dining value (see "Where to Dine," later in this chapter).

Retorno del Rey Km 14, Zona Hotelera, 77500, Cancún, Q. Roo. © 800/543-4300 in the U.S., or 998/881-2200. Fax 998/881-2201. www.meridiencancun.com.mx. 213 units. High season $593 (£326) double, $680 (£374) suite; low season $340 (£187) double, $470 (£259) suite. Ask about special spa packages. AE, DC, MC, V. Small pets accepted with prior reservation. **Amenities:** 2 restaurants; lobby bar; 3 cascading outdoor pools; 2 lighted championship tennis courts; whirlpool; watersports equipment/rentals; supervised children's program w/clubhouse, play equipment, wading pool; concierge; tour desk; car rental; business center; small shopping arcade; room service; massage *palapa* on the beach; babysitting; laundry service. *In room:* A/C, TV, minibar, hair dryer, iron, safe.

Ritz-Carlton Cancún ★★★ *Kids*   The Ritz-Carlton's $15-million, post-Wilma restoration shows off this luxurious hotel to spectacular effect. The hotel fronts a (mostly) recovered 366m (1,200-ft.) white-sand beach, and all rooms overlook the ocean and pools. Several new features will enhance your stay, including: a culinary center that schedules not just daily Mexican and Mayan cooking classes, but wine and tequila tastings as well; and a group of specially designed "Itzy Bitzy Ritz Kids" guest rooms that offer cribs, changing tables, and the option of ordering formula, diapers, and other essentials before your arrival. Rooms and public areas have the low-key elegance that's a hallmark of the Ritz chain—think plush carpets, chandeliers, and fresh

flowers, and rooms with marble baths, fluffy featherbeds, and 400-count bed linens. The beachfront Kayantá Spa bases many of its treatments on traditional Maya rituals and therapies. The hotel's newest restaurant, **Casitas,** is the only oceanside dining spot in Cancún, where you can dine on steakhouse fare in one of 16 candlelit cabañas. The hotel's primary restaurant, **Club Grill,** is reviewed in the "Where to Dine" section, later in this chapter.

Retorno del Rey 36, off Bulevar Kukulkán Km 13.5, 77500 Cancún, Q. Roo. (C) 800/241-3333 in the U.S. and Canada, or 998/881-0808. Fax 998/881-0815. www.ritzcarlton.com. 365 units. Apr 10–Dec 20 $279–$569 (£155–£316) double, $439–$899 (£244–£499) club floor and suites; Dec 21–Apr 9 $459–$989 (£255–£549) double, $679–$1,329 (£377–£738) club floor and suites. Ask about golf, spa, and weekend packages. AE, MC, V. **Amenities:** 5 restaurants; lounge w/ceviche bar; 2 outdoor pools (heated in winter); 3 lighted tennis courts; fully equipped fitness center; Kayantá Spa; culinary center; Kids Camp program; concierge; travel agency; business center; shopping arcade; salon; room service; babysitting; laundry service; dry cleaning; club floors. *In room:* A/C, TV, minibar, hairdryer, iron, safe.

Riu Palace Las Américas ✿   The all-inclusive Riu Palace is part of a family of Riu resorts in Cancún known for their grand, opulent style. This one is the smallest of the three, and the most over the top, steeped in pearl-white Greco style. The location is prime—near the central shopping, dining, and nightlife centers, just 5 minutes walking to the Convention Center. All rooms are spacious junior suites with ocean or lagoon views, a separate seating area, and a balcony or terrace. Eight also feature a Jacuzzi. Two beautiful central pools overlook the ocean and a wide stretch of beach, with one heated during winter months. The hotel offers guests virtually 24 hours of all-inclusive snacks, meals, and beverages. And, if that's not enough, guests have exchange privileges at the Riu Cancún, next door. The hotel's European opulence stands in contrast to the mostly informal North American guests.

Bulevar Kukulkán, Lote 4, 77500 Cancún, Q. Roo. (C) 888/666-8816 in the U.S., or 998/891-4300. www.riu.com. 372 units. High season $390–$790 (£215–£435) double; low season $337–$530 (£185–£292) double. Rates are all-inclusive. AE, MC, V. **Amenities:** 6 restaurants; 5 bars; 2 outdoor pools; access to golf and tennis; fitness center; spa (extra charges apply); solarium; room service; sports program; nonmotorized watersports. *In room:* A/C, TV, hair dryer, iron, safe.

Royal ✿✿   Opened in early 2007, this adults-only luxury hotel sits at the pinnacle of Cancún's all-inclusive establishments, offering a level of services and amenities unmatched almost anywhere. From the stunning infinity pools and gorgeous beach to the gourmet restaurants and sophisticated spa, the owners have spared no expense making this Cancún's Bellagio equivalent. The elegant marble lobby looks out one side to the Caribbean and the other to the lagoon. All of the innovative suites feature flat-screen TVs with CD/DVD players, marble bathrooms with rain showers, two-person Jacuzzis, and oceanview balconies with hammocks. Swim-up master suites have private plunge pools facing the resort's pool and beach; guests in the top-category suites have access to BMW Mini Coopers. The Mayan-inspired oceanview spa includes a massage room, Jacuzzi, sauna, traditional *temazcal* steam bath, massage waterfall, and a state-of-the-art fitness center. Actually, the range of services is almost hard to believe, except that you will be paying top dollar for it. The all-inclusive package includes gourmet meals, premium drinks, and evening entertainment.

Bulevar Kukulkán Km 11.5, 77500 Cancún, Q. Roo. (C) 800/760-0944 in the U.S., or 998/881-7340. www.realresorts. com.mx. 285 units. $446–$804 (£245–£442) double suite. AE, DC, MC, V. No children younger than 16. **Amenities:** 6 restaurants; 8 bars; expansive outdoor pool; tennis court; well-equipped fitness center; full-service-spa; sauna; steam room; concierge; travel agency; car rental; business center; salon; room service; laundry service; club floor w/special amenities and complimentary cocktails. *In room:* A/C, flat-screen TV, Wi-Fi, minibar, hair dryer, iron, safe.

EXPENSIVE

Dreams Cancún Resort & Spa ✦ *Kids*   Formerly the Camino Real Cancún, the all-inclusive Dreams Resort is among the island's most appealing places to stay, located on 1.5 hectares (3¾ acres) at the tip of Punta Cancún. The setting is casual, and the hotel welcomes children. The architecture of Dreams is contemporary and sleek, with bright colors and strategic angles. Rooms in the newer 17-story club section have extra services and amenities. The lower-priced rooms offer lagoon views. The all-inclusive concept here includes gourmet meals, 24-hour room service, and premium brand drinks, as well as the use of all resort amenities, nonmotorized watersports, theme-night entertainment, and tips. The fitness center and spa are excellent.

Bulevar Kukulkán, 77500 Punta Cancún (Apdo. Postal 14), Cancún, Q. Roo. © 866/237-3267 in the U.S., or 998/848-7000. Fax 998/848-7001. www.dreamscancun.com. 379 units. High season $500 (£275) double, $560 (£308) club double; low season $370 (£204) double, $430 (£237) club double. AE, DC, MC, V. **Amenities:** 4 restaurants; night-club; 2 outdoor pools; private saltwater lagoon w/dolphins and tropical fish; 2 lighted tennis courts; fitness center w/steam bath; watersports; kayaks; paddleboats; Kids' Club; travel agency; car rental; business center; salon; room service; massage; babysitting (w/advance notice); beach volleyball. *In room:* A/C, TV, minibar, hair dryer, iron, safe.

Marriott Casa Magna ✦✦ *Kids*   This sprawling Marriott resort is one of the most enticing family destinations in Cancún. Entering through a half-circle of Roman columns, you pass through a domed foyer to a wide, lavishly marbled lobby filled with plants and shallow pools. It looks out to the sparkling pool and Jacuzzi at the edge of the beach. Guest rooms are decorated with Mexican-Caribbean furnishings and tiled floors; most have oceanview balconies. The hotel caters to family travelers with specially priced packages (up to two children stay free with parent) and the Kids' Club Amigos supervised children's program. Among the many places to dine here, the *teppanyaki*-style (cook-at-your-table) Mikado Japanese restaurant is the best.

Bulevar Kukulkán Km 14.5, 77500 Cancún, Q. Roo © 800/228-9290 in the U.S., or 998/881-2000. Fax 998/881-2085. www.marriott.com. 452 units. $249–$309 (£137–£170) double; $454 (£250) and up suite. Ask about packages. AE, MC, V. **Amenities:** 6 restaurants; lobby bar w/live music; outdoor pool; 2 lighted tennis courts; health club w/saunas, whirlpool, aerobics, and juice bar; concierge; business center; travel agency; car rental; spa; salon w/massage and facials; room service; babysitting; laundry service. *In room:* A/C, TV, minibar, coffeemaker, hair dryer, iron, safe.

ME ✦   This latest opening of the Spanish ME hotel by Meliá brings to Cancún a new level of minimalist chic. Bathed in hues of beige and mauve, with polished marble, onyx lamps, and modern artwork, the hotel creates its own fashion statement—and the hip clientele reflects it. The modern lobby feels a bit like an upscale cocktail lounge, with trendy bars, sensual artwork, and chill-out music filling the space. Guest rooms have distinctive contemporary furnishings, plasma TVs, CD players, and marble bathrooms with rain showers and Aveda bath products; half look to the Caribbean Sea and the other half to the lagoon. The super-stylish Yhi Spa overlooks the ocean and offers body glows and exfoliations, aromatherapy massages, body masks, and wraps—this is a place to indulge yourself until you're entirely rejuvenated.

Bulevar Kukulkán Km 12, 77500 Cancún, Q. Roo. © 866/436-3542 in the U.S., or 998/881-2500. Fax 998/881-2502. www.mebymelia.com. 448 units. $357 (£196) and up double. AE, MC, V. **Amenities:** 3 restaurants; internet cafe; 2 bars; 3 outdoor pools; beach club; fitness center; full-service luxury spa; whirlpool; salon; concierge; boutique; art gallery; concierge floor. *In room:* A/C, plasma TV, wireless Internet, minibar, hair dryer, safe.

The Westin Resort & Spa Cancún   The strikingly austere architecture of The Westin Resort, impressive with its elegant use of stone and marble, is the stamp of leading Latin American architect Ricardo Legorreta. The hotel consists of two sections, the main building and the more exclusive six-story Royal Beach Club. Guest rooms offer contemporary white furnishings and, while spacious, can feel a bit cold. Those on the sixth floor have balconies, and first-floor rooms include terraces. Rooms in the tower boast ocean or lagoon views, furniture with Olinalá lacquer accents, Berber area rugs, oak tables and chairs, and terraces with lounge chairs. It's important to note that this hotel is a 15- to 20-minute ride from the liveliest section of the hotel zone, making it a preferred choice for those who want a little more seclusion than Cancún typically offers. However, it's easy to join the action—buses stop in front, and taxis are readily available. The Westin renovated after Hurricane Wilma damaged the resort.

Bulevar Kukulkán Km 20, 77500 Cancún, Q. Roo. ℂ 800/228-3000 in the U.S., 01-800/215-7000 in Mexico, or 998/848-7400. Fax 998/885-0666. www.starwoodhotels.com/westin. 379 units. High season $319–$499 (£175–£274) double; low season $139–$299 (£76–£164) double. AE, DC, MC, V. **Amenities:** 3 restaurants; 2 bars; 8 outdoor pools; 2 lighted tennis courts; gym w/Stairmaster, bicycle, weights, and aerobics; sauna; *temazcal* (sweat lodge); concierge; travel agency; car rental; pharmacy/gift shop; salon; room service; massage; babysitting; laundry service. *In room:* A/C, TV, Wi-Fi, minibar, coffeemaker, hair dryer, iron, safe.

MODERATE

Blue Bay Getaway & Spa Cancún ⟨★⟩

This adults-only getaway is a spirited, sexy all-inclusive resort favored by people looking for significant social interaction. By day, pool time is all about flirting, seducing, and getting a little wacky with adult games. Come night, theme dinners, shows, and other live entertainment keep the party going. Note that clothing is optional on the beaches of Blue Bay, which boasts calm waters for swimming. The comfortable, modern rooms are housed in two sections with lagoon, garden, or ocean views. Surrounded by acres of tropical gardens, this moderate hotel is ideally located at the northern end of the Hotel Zone, close to the major shopping plazas, restaurants, and nightlife.

Bulevar Kukulkán Km 3.5, 77500 Cancún, Q. Roo. ℂ 800/211-1000 in the U.S., or 998/848-7900. Fax 998/848-7994. www.bluebaycancun.com. 385 units. High season $286–$325 (£157–£179) double; low season $225–$260 (£124–£143) double. Rates include food, beverages, and activities. AE, MC, V. Guests must be at least 21 years old. **Amenities:** 5 restaurants; 5 bars; 3 outdoor pools; 4 whirlpools; exercise room w/daily aerobics classes; nonmotorized watersports equipment; snorkeling and scuba lessons; marina; bikes; game room w/pool and Ping-Pong tables. *In room:* A/C, TV, hair dryer.

Flamingo Cancún

The all-inclusive Flamingo seems to have been inspired by the dramatic, slope-sided architecture of the Dreams Cancún, but the Flamingo is considerably smaller and less expensive (guests have the option of opting out of the all-inclusive package, which includes three meals and domestic drinks). With two pools and a casual vibe, it's also a friendly, accommodating choice for families. The brightly colored blue and yellow guest rooms—all with balconies—border a courtyard facing the interior swimming pool and *palapa* pool-bar. The Flamingo lies in the heart of the island hotel district, opposite the Flamingo Shopping Center and close to other hotels, shopping centers, and restaurants.

Bulevar Kukulkán Km 11.5, 77500 Cancún, Q. Roo. ℂ 998/848-8870. Fax 998/883-1029. www.flamingocancun.com. 221 units. High season $190 (£105) double, low season $150 (£83) double; all-inclusive plan high season $280 (£154) double, low season $240 (£132) double. AE, MC, V. **Amenities:** 2 restaurants; 2 bars; 2 pools; fitness center; kids' club; travel agency; room service; safe. *In room:* A/C, TV, hair dryer, minibar.

Oasis Viva Beach Cancún

From the street, this all-inclusive hotel may not be much to look at, but on the ocean side you'll find a small but pretty patio garden and Cancún's best beach for safe swimming. The location is ideal, close to all the shops and restaurants near Punta Cancún and the Cancún Center. Rooms overlook the lagoon or the ocean, and all were remodeled post–Hurricane Wilma. They are large, with simple decor, marble floors, and either two double beds or a king-size bed. Several studios have kitchenettes. There is wheelchair access within the hotel's public areas.

Bulevar Kukulkán Km 8.5, 77500 Cancún, Q. Roo. © 800/221-2222 in the U.S., or 998/883-0800. Fax 998/883-2087. 216 units. High season $316 (£174); low season $185–$200 (£102–£110) double. Rates are all-inclusive. Discounted rate for children. AE, MC, V. **Amenities:** 4 restaurants; 5 bars; 2 outdoor pools (1 for adults, 1 for children); marina. *In room:* A/C, TV.

CANCUN CITY
MODERATE

Hotel Margaritas   Located in downtown Cancún, this four-story hotel (with elevator) is comfortable and unpretentious. The pleasantly decorated rooms, with white-tile floors and small balconies, are exceptionally clean and bright. Lounge chairs surround the small courtyard, which has a wading pool for children. The hotel offers complimentary safes at the front desk.

Av. Yaxchilán 41, SM22, Centro, 77500 Cancún, Q. Roo. © 01-800/640-7473 in Mexico, or 998/881-7870. Fax 998/884-1324. www.margaritascancun.com. 100 units. High season $112 (£62) double; low season $90 (£50) double. AE, MC, V. **Amenities:** Restaurant; outdoor pool; travel agency; Internet; room service; babysitting; billiards; currency exchange. *In room:* A/C, TV.

Radisson Hacienda Cancún ★ *Value*   This is the top hotel in downtown Cancún, and one of the best values in the area. The Radisson offers all the expected comforts of a chain, yet in an atmosphere of Mexican hospitality. Resembling a hacienda, the business-friendly hotel has rooms that are set off from a large rotunda-style lobby, lush gardens, and a pleasant pool area. All have brightly colored fabric accents; views of the garden, the pool, or the street; and a small sitting area and balcony. Guests have access to shuttle service to Isla Cancún's beaches. The hotel lies within walking distance of downtown Cancún dining and shopping.

Av. Nader 1, SM2, Centro, 77500 Cancún, Q. Roo. © 800/333-3333 in the U.S., or 998/881-6500. Fax 998/884-7954. www.radissoncancun.com. 248 units. $140 (£77) double; $168 (£92) junior suite. AE, MC, V. **Amenities:** 2 restaurants; lively lobby bar; outdoor pool w/adjoining bar and separate wading area for children; lighted tennis courts; small gym; sauna; travel agency; car rental; salon. *In room:* A/C, TV, coffeemaker, hair dryer, iron, safe.

Rey del Caribe Hotel ★★ *Finds*   This ecological hotel is a unique oasis where every detail has been thought out to achieve the goal of creating an environmentally friendly accommodation. You might easily forget you're in the midst of downtown Cancún in the tropical garden setting, with blooming orchids and other flowering plants. The lovely grounds include statues of Mayan deities, hammocks, and a tiled swimming pool. There's a regularly changing schedule of yoga, Tai Chi, and meditation sessions, as well as special classes on astrology, tarot, and other subjects. The on-site spa offers facial and body treatments. Rooms are large and sunny, with your choice of one king-size or two full-size beds and terrace. The detail of ecological sensitivity is truly impressive, ranging from the use of collected rainwater to waste composting. Recycling is encouraged, and solar power is used wherever possible.

Av. Uxmal SM 2A (corner of Nader), 77500 Cancún, Q. Roo. © 998/884-2028. Fax 988/884-9857. www.reycaribe.com. 31 units. High season $82 (£45) double; low season $55 (£30) double. Rates include breakfast. MC, V. **Amenities:** Outdoor pool; spa; massages; classes. *In room:* A/C, kitchenette.

INEXPENSIVE

Hotel Hacienda *Value*   This simple little hotel is a great value. The facade has been remodeled to look like a hacienda. Guest rooms are very basic; all have dark wood furnishings, white-washed walls, small tiled bathrooms, and two double beds—but no views. There's a nice small pool and cafe under a shaded *palapa* in the back. You can easily walk to anywhere in downtown from here.

Sunyaxchen 39–40, 77500 Cancún, Q. Roo. (*C*) **998/884-3672**. Fax 998/884-1208. www.berny.com.mx. 36 units. High season $50 (£28) double; low season $45 (£25) double. Street parking. From Av. Yaxchilán, turn west on Sunyaxchen; it's on the right next to the Hotel Caribe International, opposite 100% Natural. **Amenities:** Outdoor pool. *In room:* A/C, TV, safe.

Refugio del Pirata Morgan *(Finds)*   Although not actually in the town of Cancún, but on the highway leading north from Cancún to Punta Sam, this is the place for those who want a simple and secluded beach vacation. A pirate's flag greets you at the entrance, and an international kite-surfing school is located on the premises. This ecological hotel lies on a wide, virgin stretch of beach, away from the crowd of hotels and nightlife; there are no phones or television, just blissful peace and quiet. Ten simple cabañas named for the predominate color of the decor feature *palapa* roofs, beds, and hammocks. A small restaurant offers a basic selection celebrating fresh fish—otherwise, the nearest restaurant is 2km (1¼ miles) away.

Carretera Punta Sam, Isla Blanca, Km 9, 77500 Cancún, Q. Roo. (*C*) **998/860-3386** (within Mexico dial 044 first, as this is a cellphone). 10 units. $50 (£28) room; $5 (£2.75) hammock. Camping available $6 (£3.30) adult, $3 (£1.65) children. No credit cards. **Amenities:** Restaurant; kite-surfing school; kayaks and snorkeling equipment for rent. *In room:* Fan, no phone.

Xbalamqué   Creatively designed to resemble a Mayan temple, this downtown hotel features a full-service spa, lovely pool and waterfall, and an authentic Mexican cantina. Live music plays evenings in the bookstore/cafe adjacent to the lobby. Guest rooms have rustic furnishings with regional touches, colorful tile-work, and small bathrooms with showers. Ask for a room overlooking the ivy-filled courtyard. A tour desk is available to help you plan your vacation activities, and the spa offers some of the best rates of any hotel in Cancún.

Av. Yaxchilán 31, Sm. 22, Mza. 18, 77500 Cancún, Q. Roo. (*C*) **998/884-9690**. Fax 998/884-9690. www.xbalamque.com. 108 units. High season $95 (£52) double; low season $75 (£41) double. AE, MC, V. **Amenities:** Restaurant; cantina; cafe; outdoor pool; spa; travel agency. *In room:* A/C, TV.

3 Where to Dine

U.S.-based franchise chains, which really need no introduction, dominate the Cancún restaurant scene. These include Hard Rock Cafe, Rainforest Cafe, Tony Roma's, T.G.I. Friday's, Ruth's Chris Steak House, and the gamut of fast-food burger places. The establishments listed here are locally owned, one-of-a-kind restaurants or exceptional selections at area hotels. Many schedule live music. Unless otherwise indicated, parking is free.

One unique way to combine dinner with sightseeing is aboard the **Lobster Dinner Cruise** (*C* **998/849-4748**). Cruising around the tranquil, turquoise waters of the lagoon, passengers feast on lobster dinners accompanied by wine. Cost is $79 per person. There are two daily departures from the Aquatours Marina (Bulevar Kukulkán 6.5). A sunset cruise leaves at 5pm during the winter and 5:30pm during the summer; a moonlight cruise leaves at 8pm winter, 8:30pm summer. Another—albeit livelier—lobster dinner option is the **Captain Hook Lobster Dinner Cruise** (*C* **998/849-4451**), which is similar, but with the added attraction of a pirate show, making this the choice for families. It costs $83 (£46) per person, departs at 7pm from El Embarcadero, and returns at 10:30pm.

CANCUN ISLAND
VERY EXPENSIVE

Aioli ⭐⭐ FRENCH   The quality and originality of the cuisine and excellence of service make this a top choice for fine-dining in Cancún. The Provençal—but definitely not provincial—Aioli offers exquisite French and Mediterranean gourmet specialties in a warm and cozy country French setting. Though it serves perhaps the best breakfast buffet in Cancún (for $24/£13), most diners from outside the hotel come here in the evening, when low lighting and superb service promise a romantic experience. Delectable starters include *foie gras* and risotto with wild mushrooms; among the best main course are pan-seared sea scallops, roasted lamb with a tarragon crust, and breast of duck. Desserts are decadent, especially the signature "Fifth Element," rich with chocolate.

In Le Méridien Cancún Resort & Spa, Retorno del Rey Km 14. © 998/881-2200. Reservations recommended. Main courses $24–$37 (£13–£20). AE, MC, V. Daily 6:30am–11pm.

Club Grill ⭐⭐⭐ INTERNATIONAL   This is the place for that special night out. Cancún's most elegant and stylish restaurant is also among its most delicious. Even rival restaurateurs give it envious thumbs up. The gracious service starts as you enter the anteroom, with its comfortable seating and selection of fine drinks. It continues in a candlelit dining room with shimmering silver and crystal. Elegant plates of peppered scallops, truffles, and potatoes in tequila sauce; grilled lamb; or mixed grill arrive at a leisurely pace. The restaurant has smoking and nonsmoking sections. A band plays romantic music for dancing from 8pm on.

In the Ritz-Carlton Cancún, Retorno del Rey, 36 Bulevar Kukulkán Km 13.5. © 998/881-0808. Reservations required. No sandals or tennis shoes; men must wear long pants. Main courses $11–$40 (£6.05–£22). AE, DC, MC, V. Tues–Sun 7–11pm.

Lorenzillo's ⭐⭐⭐ *Kids* SEAFOOD   Live lobster is the overwhelming favorite, and part of the appeal is selecting your dinner out of the giant lobster tank set in the lagoon (Lorenzillo's sits right on the lagoon under a giant *palapa* roof). A dock leads down to the main dining area, and when that's packed (which is often), a wharf-side bar handles the overflow. In addition to lobster—which comes grilled, steamed, or stuffed—good bets are shrimp stuffed with cheese and wrapped in bacon, the *pescador* (Caribbean grouper prepared to taste), and seafood-stuffed calamari. Desserts include the tempting "Martinique": warm apples, raisins, and walnuts caramelized with rum and wrapped in a pastry with vanilla ice cream. The sunset pier offers a lighter menu of cold seafood, sandwiches, and salads. There's a festive, friendly atmosphere, and children are very welcome—after all, most of the patrons are wearing bibs!

Bulevar Kukulkán Km 10.5. © 998/883-1254. www.lorenzillos.com.mx. Reservations recommended. Main courses $19–$44 (£10–£24). AE, MC, V. Daily 1pm–12:30am.

EXPENSIVE

Casa de las Margaritas ⭐ MEXICAN   La Casa de las Margaritas is a celebration of the flavors and *¡fiesta!* spirit of Mexico. With a decor as vibrant as a *piñata,* and a soundtrack of background music that ranges from mariachi to *marimba,* the experience here is a crash course in the festive spirit of this colorful country. On the menu, best bets include the Margarita shrimp, sautéed in garlic, cream, and chipotle chile sauce; chicken breast served with three flavorful *mole* sauces; or the platter of chicken enchiladas topped with tomato-and-sun-dried-pepper sauce. Located inside La Isla shopping center, Casa de las Margaritas also serves a spectacular Sunday brunch. Live music is offered nightly.

Paseo Kukulkán Km 12.5, La Isla Shopping Mall, Loc. E-17. ✆ **998/883-3222** or -3054. www.lacasadelasmargaritas. com. Reservations recommended. Main courses $6–$38 (£3.30–£21). AE, MC, V. Mon–Sat 11am–midnight; Sun brunch noon–5pm.

Casa Rolandi ★★ SWISS/ITALIAN

Like its sister location in Isla Mujeres, Casa Rolandi blends sophisticated Swiss-Italian cuisine with fresh Caribbean fish and Mexican produce. Famous personalities, from international actors to American presidents, have dined here. The casually elegant restaurant offers white linen tables and candles at night, but welcomes informal dress. Among the creative selections are homemade ravioli stuffed with wild mushrooms over a creamy Alba truffle sauce, taglioni with sautéed shrimp and ginger sprinkled with white wine, and fresh fish (usually snapper or sea bass) baked in salt and accompanied by fresh vegetables and seasoned mashed potatoes. Finish with the sublime tiramisu served with chocolate and rum cream. Service is personalized and friendly.

Bulevar Kukulkán Km 8.5, in Plaza Caracol. ✆ **998/883-2557.** Reservations recommended. Main courses $15–$35 (£8.25–£19). AE, MC, V. Sun–Thurs 1–11:30pm; Fri–Sat 1pm–2am.

Gustino ★★ ITALIAN

JW Marriott's signature restaurant Gustino offers romantic Italian dining unsurpassed in Cancún. The refined dining room includes a gorgeous centerpiece candle display, floor-to-ceiling windows looking out to a lazy manmade lagoon and the beach beyond, and live saxophone. Among the rich selection of *antipasti,* the black shell mussels, minestrone, and *Festival dei Frutti de Mare* for two are the best. For a main course, consider homemade pasta, the veal scaloppine, or filet of beef tenderloin in a red wine sauce served with fresh vegetables. There's also a wide selection of fresh fish and seafood. Gustino boasts an open kitchen and wine cellar with an excellent variety of international grapes. Service is outstanding.

In the JW Marriott, Bulevar Kukulkán Km 14.5. ✆ **998/848-9600.** Reservations required. Main courses $14–$27 (£7.70–£15). AE, DC, MC, V. Daily 6–11pm.

Laguna Grill ★★ FUSION

Laguna Grill offers diners a contemporary culinary experience in a picturesque setting overlooking the lagoon. A tropical garden welcomes you at the entrance, while a small creek traverses the restaurant set with tables made from the trunks of tropical trees. As magical as the decor is, the real star here is the kitchen, with its selection of Pacific Rim cuisine fused with regional flavors. Starters include martini *gyoza* (steamed dumplings), filled with shrimp and vegetables, or seafood ceviche in sesame oil and curry. Fish and seafood dominate the menu, in preparations that combine Asian and Mexican flavors such as ginger, cilantro, garlic, and hoisin sauce. Grilled shrimp are marinated in rum, mint, and lime; surf and turf fusion dishes may include grilled lobster, beef, and shrimp skewers. For beef-lovers, the rib-eye served over garlic, spinach, and sweet-potato mash is sublime. Desserts are as creative as the main dishes; the pineapple-papaya strudel in Malibu rum sauce stands out. If you're an early diner, request a table on the outside deck for a spectacular sunset view. An impressive selection of wines is available.

Bulevar Kukulkán Km 16.5. ✆ **998/885-0267.** www.lagunagrill.com.mx. Reservations recommended. Main courses $11–$34 (£6.05–£19). AE, MC, V. Daily 2pm–midnight.

Paloma Bonita ★ Kids REGIONAL/MEXICAN/NOUVELLE MEXICAN

In a stylish setting overlooking the water, Paloma Bonita captures the essence of Mexico through its music and food. Since Paloma Bonita lies in a hotel (Dreams Cancún), prices are higher than at traditional Mexican restaurants in Ciudad Cancún, but this is a good choice for the Hotel Zone. There are three sections: La Cantina Jalisco, with an open kitchen and tequila bar; the Salón Michoacán, which features that state's cuisine; and the Patio Oaxaca. The menu encompasses the best of Mexico's other cuisines, with a few international dishes. Prix-fixe dinners include appetizer, main course, and dessert. Jazz trios, *marimba* and *Jarocha* music, and mariachis serenade you while you dine. A nice starter is Mitla salad, with slices of the renowned Oaxaca cheese dribbled with olive oil and coriander dressing. Wonderful stuffed chile La Doña—a mildly hot poblano pepper filled with lobster and *huitlacoche* (a type of mushroom that grows on corn) in a cream sauce—comes as an appetizer or a main course.

In the Hotel Dreams, Punta Cancún (enter from the street). (© 998/848-7000, ext. 7965. Reservations recommended. Prix-fixe dinner $30–$45 (£17–£25); main courses $25–$35(£14–£19). AE, DC, MC, V. Daily 6:30pm–11:30pm.

Puerto Madero   ARGENTINE/STEAKS/SEAFOOD   As a tribute to the famed Puerto Madero of Buenos Aires, this restaurant has quickly earned a reputation for its authentic Argentine cuisine and ambience. Overlooking the Nichupté Lagoon, the decor re-creates a 20th-century dock warehouse, with elegant touches of modern architecture. Puerto Madero offers an extensive selection of prime quality beef cuts, pastas, grilled fish, and shellfish, meticulously prepared with Buenos Aires gusto. In addition to the classic *carpaccio,* the tuna tartar and halibut steak are favorites, but the real standouts here are the tender grilled steaks (particularly the rib-eye), served in ample portions. Enjoy a cocktail or glass of wine from the extensive selection, while viewing the sunset from the lagoon-side deck. Service is excellent.

Marina Barracuda, Bulevar Kukulkán Km 14. (© 998/885-2829 or -2830. www.puertomaderocancun.com. Reservations recommended. Main courses $14–$52 (£7.70–£29). AE, MC, V. Daily 1pm–1am.

MODERATE
La Destilería MEXICAN   To experience Mexico's favorite export on an enticing terrace overlooking the lagoon, this is your place (keep an eye out for Tequila, the lagoon crocodile who often comes to visit). La Destilería is more than a tequila-inspired restaurant; it's a minimuseum honoring the "spirit" of Mexico. It serves over 150 brands of tequila, including some treasures that never find their way across the country's northern border. No surprise, the margaritas are among the best on the island. When you decide to order some food with your tequila, you'll find an authentic Mexican menu, with everything from quesadillas with squash blossom flowers, to shrimp in a delicate tequila-lime sauce. There are even *escamoles* (crisp-fried ant eggs) as an appetizer for the adventurous—or for those whose squeamishness has been diminished by the tequila!

Bulevar Kukulkán Km 12.65, across from Kukulcán Plaza. (© 998/885-1086 or -1087. www.cmr.ws. Main courses $12–$28. AE, MC, V. Daily 1pm–midnight.

La Fisheria   SEAFOOD   Seafood lovers will find heavenly bliss at this casual yet inviting restaurant overlooking Bulevar Kukulkán and the lagoon. The expansive menu includes shrimp bisque, seafood salad, and ceviche tostadas. For a main course, consider the calamari steak with shrimp, seafood paella, surf and turf, or fresh fish prepared any way you want, including the specialty grouper filet stuffed with seafood in lobster sauce. The menu changes daily, but there's always *tikin xik,* that great Yucatecan grilled fish marinated in *achiote* (a spice) sauce. For those not inclined toward seafood, a pizza from the wood-burning oven, or perhaps a grilled chicken or beef dish, might do. La Fisheria has a nonsmoking section.

Plaza Caracol shopping center, Bulevar Kukulkán Km 8.5, 2nd floor. ℂ **998/883-1395**. Main courses $9–$33 (£4.95–£18). AE, MC, V. Daily 11am–11pm.

Thai ★★★ *(Moments)* THAI   This feels a lot more like Thailand than the edge of a Mexican shopping plaza. With a backdrop that includes three dolphins cavorting in an enormous aquarium, Thai restaurant offers a unique and calming setting with individual *palapas* (each with its own table and sofa) built over the expansive lagoon. Unobtrusive service, soft red and blue lighting, and Asian chill and lounge music contribute to the romantic ambience. Such classic Thai specialties as spicy chicken soup, Thai salad, chicken satay, and chicken and shrimp curries are served in an ultrachic atmosphere. A DJ works the bar on weekends. The restaurant opens at sunset.

La Isla Shopping Center, Loc. B-4. ℂ **998/144-0364**. Reservations recommended during high season. Main courses $7.50–$28 (£4.15–£15). AE, MC, V. Daily 6pm–1am.

CANCUN CITY
EXPENSIVE
La Habichuela ★★★ *(Moments)* GOURMET SEAFOOD   In a musically accented garden setting with flowering hibiscus trees, this downtown restaurant is ideal for a romantic evening. For an all-out culinary adventure, try *habichuela* (string bean) soup; shrimp in any number of sauces, including Jamaican tamarind, tequila, or ginger and mushroom; and Mayan coffee with *xtabentun* (a strong, sweet, anise-based liqueur). Grilled seafood and steaks are excellent, and the menu includes luscious ceviches, Caribbean lobsters, an inventive seafood "parade," and shish kabob flambé. For something divine, try *cocobichuela,* lobster and shrimp in curry served in a coconut shell and topped with fruit. Top it off with one of the boozy butterscotch crepes. Service here is fabulous.

Margaritas 25. ℂ **998/884-3158**. www.lahabichuela.com. Reservations recommended in high season. Main courses $13–$43 (£7.15–£24). AE, MC, V. Daily noon–midnight.

Périco's ★★ *(Finds)* MEXICAN/SEAFOOD/STEAKS   Périco's is a joyous parade of performance, play, and brightly colored hilarity. The unique restaurant features entertaining waiters dressed in a variety of festive costumes, murals that seem to dance off the walls, a bar area with saddles for barstools, and leather tables and chairs. Its extensive menu offers well-prepared steak, seafood, and traditional Mexican dishes for reasonable rates (except for lobster). This is a place not only to eat and drink, but also to let loose and join in the fun, so don't be surprised if diners drop their forks and don sombreros to shimmy and shake in a conga line around the dining room. The entertainment kicks off at 7:30pm.

Yaxchilán 61. ℂ **998/884-3152**. www.pericos.com.mx. Reservations recommended. Main courses $14–$39 (£7.70–£21). AE, MC, V. Daily noon–1am.

MODERATE
Labná ★★ YUCATECAN   To steep yourself in Yucatecan cuisine and music, head directly to this showcase of Mayan moods and regional foods. Specialties served here include a sublime lime soup, *poc chuc* (marinated, barbecue-style pork), chicken or pork *pibil* (sweet and spicy barbecue sauce served over shredded meat), and appetizers such as *papadzules* (tortillas stuffed with boiled eggs in a pumpkin seed sauce). The Labná Special is a sampler of four typically Yucatecan main courses, including *poc chuc,* while another specialty of the house is baked suckling pig, served with guacamole. The refreshing Yucatecan beverage, *agua de chaya*—a blend of sweetened

water and the leaf of the *chaya* plant, abundant in the area, to which sweet Xtabentun liquor (a type of anise) can be added for an extra kick—is also served here. The vaulted ceiling dining room is decorated with black-and-white photographs of the region dating from the 1900s. A local trio plays weekend afternoons.

Margaritas 29, next to City Hall and the Habichuela restaurant. ℂ **998/892-3056**. Main courses $7–$20 (£3.85–£11). AE, MC, V. Daily noon–10pm.

INEXPENSIVE

100% Natural ⚘ VEGETARIAN/MEXICAN   If you want a healthy reprieve from an overindulgent night—or just like your meals as fresh and natural as possible—this is your oasis. No matter what your dining preference, you owe it to yourself to try a Mexican tradition, the fresh-fruit *licuado*. These smoothie-like drinks combine fresh fruit, ice, and water or milk. More creative combinations may mix in yogurt, granola, or other goodies. 100% Natural serves more than just meal-quality drinks—there's a bountiful selection of simple Mexican fare and terrific sandwiches served on whole-grain bread, with options for vegetarians. Breakfast is delightful and easy on the wallet. The space abounds with plants and cheery colors, and there's an attached bakery featuring all-natural baked goods. There are several 100% Natural locations in town, including branches at Playa Chac-Mool, across from Señor Frog's, and downtown.

Av. Sunyaxchen 63. ℂ **998/884-0102**. www.100natural.com.mx. Reservations not accepted. Main courses $5–$15 (£2.75–£8.25). MC, V. Daily 7am–11pm.

Pizza Rolandi ⚘ *Kids* ITALIAN   This is an institution in Cancún, and the Rolandi name is synonymous with dining in both Cancún and neighboring Isla Mujeres. Pizza Rolandi and its branch in Isla Mujeres (see chapter 14) have become standards for dependably good casual fare. At this shaded outdoor patio restaurant, you can choose from almost two dozen delicious, if greasy, wood-oven pizzas and a full selection of spaghetti, calzones, Italian-style chicken and beef, and desserts.

Cobá 12. ℂ **998/884-4047**. Fax 998/884-4047. www.rolandi.com. Pasta $8–$11 (£4.40–£6.05); pizza and main courses $7–$13 (£3.85–£7.15). AE, MC, V. Daily noon–11pm.

Roots INTERNATIONAL   This popular hangout for local residents is also a fun spot for visitors to Cancún. Located in the heart of downtown, this restaurant and jazz club offers a unique cosmopolitan ambience. The Caribbean-themed menu offers a range of casual dining choices, including salads, pastas, and even fresh squid. It's accompanied by live music, including reggae, flamenco, jazz, and fusion. Decking the walls are original works of art by local painters.

Tulipanes 26, SM 22. ℂ **998/884-2437**. roots@Cancun.com. Main courses $6–$17 (£3.30–£9.35). MC, V. Tues–Sat 6pm–1am.

4 Beaches, Watersports & Boat Tours

THE BEACHES   Big hotels dominate the best stretches of beach. All of Mexico's beaches are public property, so you can use the beach of any hotel by walking through the lobby or directly onto the sand. Be especially careful on beaches fronting the open Caribbean, where the undertow can be quite strong. By contrast, the waters of Bahía de Mujeres (Mujeres Bay), at the north end of the island, are usually calm and ideal for swimming. Get to know Cancún's water-safety pennant system, and make sure to check the flag at any beach or hotel before entering the water. Here's how it goes:

White	Excellent
Green	Normal conditions (safe)
Yellow	Changeable, uncertain (use caution)
Black or red	Unsafe—use the swimming pool instead!

In the Caribbean, storms can arrive and conditions can change from safe to unsafe in a matter of minutes, so be alert: If you see dark clouds heading your way, make for the shore and wait until the storm passes.

Playa Tortuga (Turtle Beach), Playa Langosta (Lobster Beach), Playa Linda (Pretty Beach), and Playa Las Perlas (Beach of the Pearls) are some of the public beaches. At most beaches, you can rent a sailboard and take lessons, ride a parasail, or partake in a variety of watersports. There's a small but beautiful portion of public beach on **Playa Caracol,** by the Xcaret Terminal. It faces the calm waters of Bahía de Mujeres and, for that reason, is preferable to those facing the Caribbean.

WATERSPORTS   Many beachside hotels offer watersports concessions that rent rubber rafts, kayaks, and snorkeling equipment. On the calm Nichupté lagoon are outlets for renting **sailboats, jet skis, sailboards,** and **water skis.** Prices vary and are often negotiable, so check around.

DEEP-SEA FISHING   You can arrange a day of deep-sea fishing at one of the numerous piers or travel agencies for $220 to $360 (£121–£198) for 4 hours, $420 (£231) for 6 hours, and $520 (£286) for 8 hours for up to four people; for up to eight people, the prices are $420 (£231) for 4 hours, $550 (£303) for 6 hours, or $680 (£374) for 8 hours. Marinas will sometimes assist in putting together a group. Charters include a captain, a first mate, bait, gear, and beverages. Rates are lower if you depart from Isla Mujeres or from Cozumel—and frankly, the fishing is better closer to those departure points.

SCUBA & SNORKELING   Known for its shallow reefs, dazzling color, and diversity of life, Cancún is one of the best places in the world for beginning scuba diving. Punta Nizuc is the northern tip of the **Gran Arrecife Maya (Great Mesoamerican Reef),** the largest reef in the Western Hemisphere and one of the largest in the world. In addition to the sea life along this reef system, several sunken boats add a variety of dive options. Inland, a series of caverns and *cenotes* (wellsprings) are fascinating venues for the more experienced diver. Drift diving is the norm here, with popular dives going to the reefs at **El Garrafón** and the **Cave of the Sleeping Sharks**—although be aware that the famed "sleeping sharks" have departed, driven off by too many people watching them snooze.

A variety of hotels offer resort courses that teach the basics of diving—enough to make shallow dives and slowly ease your way into this underwater world of unimaginable beauty. One preferred dive operator is **Scuba Cancún,** Bulevar Kukulkán Km 5 (© **998/ 849-4736;** www.scubacancun.com.mx), on the lagoon side. Full certification takes 3 days and costs $410 (£226). Scuba Cancún is open daily from 7am to 8pm, and accepts MasterCard and Visa. For certified divers, Scuba Cancún also offers diving trips in good weather to 18 nearby reefs, as well as to Cenotes Caverns (9m/30 ft.) and Cozumel. The average dive is around 11m (36 ft.), while advanced divers descend further (up to 18m/60 ft). Two-tank dives to reefs around Cancún cost $68 (£37); those to farther destinations cost $140 (£77). Discounts apply if you bring your own equipment. Dives usually start around 9:30am and return by 1:30pm. Snorkeling trips cost $27 (£15) and leave every afternoon at 1:30pm and 4pm for shallow reefs about a 20-minute boat ride away.

The largest dive operator is **Aquaworld,** across from the Meliá Cancún at Bulevar Kukulkán Km 15.2 (© **998/848-8327;** www.aquaworld.com.mx). It offers resort courses and diving from a man-made anchored dive platform, Paradise Island. Aquaworld has the **Sub See Explorer,** a boat with picture windows that hang beneath the surface. The boat doesn't submerge—it's an updated version of a glass-bottom boat—but it does provide nondivers with a look at life beneath the sea. This outfit is open 24 hours a day and accepts all major credit cards.

Besides snorkeling at **El Garrafón Natural Park** (see "Boating Excursions," below), travel agencies offer an all-day excursion to the natural wildlife habitat of **Isla Contoy,** which usually includes time for snorkeling. The island, 90 minutes past Isla Mujeres, is a major nesting area for birds and a treat for nature lovers. You can call any travel agent or see any hotel tour desk to get a selection of boat tours to Isla Contoy. Prices range from $45 to $70 (£25–£39), depending on the length of the trip, and generally include drinks and snorkeling equipment.

The Great Mesoamerican Reef also offers exceptional snorkeling opportunities. In Puerto Morelos, 37km (23 miles) south of Cancún, the reef hugs the coastline for 15km (9⅓ miles). The reef is so close to the shore (about 460m/1,509 ft.) that it forms a natural barrier for the village and keeps the waters calm on the inside of the reef. The water here is shallow, from 1.5 to 9m (5–30 ft.), resulting in ideal conditions for snorkeling. Stringent environmental regulations implemented by the local community have kept the reef here unspoiled. Only a select few companies are allowed to offer snorkel trips, and they must adhere to guidelines that will ensure the reef's preservation. **Cancún Mermaid** (© **998/843-6517;** www.cancunmermaid.com) is considered the best—it's a family-run ecotour company that has operated in the area since the 1970s. It's known for highly personalized service. The tour typically takes snorkelers to two sections of the reef, spending about an hour in each area. When conditions allow, the boat drops off snorkelers and then follows them along with the current—an activity known as "drift snorkeling," which enables snorkelers to see as much of the reef as possible. The trip costs $50 (£28) for adults, $35 (£19) for children, and includes boat, snorkeling gear, life jackets, a light lunch, bottled water, sodas, and beer, plus round-trip transportation to and from Puerto Morelos from Cancún hotels. Departures are Monday through Saturday at 9am. For snorkelers who just can't get enough, a combo tour for $30 (£17) more adds a bicycle tour to additional snorkeling destinations. Reservations are required at least 1 day in advance; MasterCard and Visa are accepted.

JET-SKI TOURS   Several companies offer the popular **Jungle Cruise,** which takes you by small boat or WaveRunner (you drive your own watercraft) through Cancún's lagoon and mangrove estuaries out into the Caribbean Sea and a shallow reef. The excursion runs about 2½ hours and costs $55 (£30), including snorkeling equipment and bottled water. Many people prefer the companies offering two-person boats rather than WaveRunners, since they can sit side by side rather than one behind the other.

Jet-ski operators and names offering excursions change often. To find out what's available, check with a local travel agent or hotel tour desk. The popular **Aquaworld,** Bulevar Kukulkán Km 15.2 (© **998/848-8327**), calls its trip the Jungle Tour and charges $55 (£30) for the 2½-hour excursion, which includes 45 minutes of snorkeling time. It even gives you a free snorkel, but has the less desirable one-behind-the-other seating configuration. Departures are daily every hour between 8am and 3pm.

BOATING EXCURSIONS

ISLA MUJERES   The island of **Isla Mujeres,** just 13km (8 miles) offshore, is one of the most pleasant day trips from Cancún. At one end is **El Garrafón Natural Park,** which is good for snorkeling. At the other end is a captivating village with small shops, restaurants, and hotels, and **Playa Norte,** the island's best beach. If you're looking for relaxation and can spare the time, it's worth several days. For complete information about the island, see chapter 14.

There are four ways to get there: **public ferry** from Puerto Juárez, which takes between 15 and 20 minutes; **shuttle boat** from Playa Linda or Playa Tortuga—an hour-long ride, with irregular service; **watertaxi** (more expensive, but faster), next to the Xcaret Terminal; and daylong **pleasure-boat trips,** most of which leave from the Playa Linda pier.

The inexpensive but fast Puerto Juárez **public ferries** lie just a few kilometers from downtown Cancún. From Cancún City, take the Ruta 8 bus on Avenida Tulum to Puerto Juárez. The air-conditioned *Caribbean Express* and *Ultramar* boats (15–20 min.) cost $4 (£2.20) per person. Departures are every half-hour from 6 to 8:30am and then every 15 minutes until 8:30pm. The slower *Caribbean Savage* (45–60 min.) costs about $3.50 (£1.95). It departs every 2 hours, or less frequently depending on demand. Upon arrival, the ferry docks in downtown Isla Mujeres near all the shops, restaurants, hotels, and Norte beach. You'll need a taxi to get to El Garrafón park at the other end of the island. You can stay as long as you like on the island and return by ferry, but be sure to confirm the time of the last returning ferry.

Pleasure-boat cruises to Isla Mujeres are a favorite pastime. Modern motor yachts, catamarans, trimarans, and even old-time sloops—more than 25 boats a day—take swimmers, sun lovers, snorkelers, and shoppers out on the translucent waters. Some tours include a snorkeling stop at El Garrafón, lunch on the beach, and a short time for shopping in downtown Isla Mujeres. Most leave at 9:30 or 10am, last about 5 or 6 hours, and include continental breakfast, lunch, and rental of snorkel gear. Others, particularly sunset and night cruises, go to beaches away from town for pseudo-pirate shows and include a lobster dinner or Mexican buffet. If you want to actually see Isla Mujeres, go on a morning cruise, or travel on your own using the public ferry from Puerto Juárez. Prices for the day cruises run around $45 (£25) per person.

An all-inclusive entrance fee of $65 (£36) to **Garrafón Natural Reef Park** (© 998/849-4748; www.garrafon.com) includes transportation from Cancún, meals, drinks, access to the reef and a museum, as well as use of snorkel gear, kayaks, inner tubes, life vests, the pool, hammocks, and public facilities and showers (but not towels, so bring your own). There are also nature trails and several on-site restaurants.

Tips   An All-Terrain Tour

Cancún Mermaid (© 998/843-6517; www.cancunmermaid.com) offers all-terrain-vehicle (ATV) jungle tours for $72 (£30) per person or $55 (£30) per person if riding double. The ATV tours travel through the jungles of Cancún and emerge on the beaches of the Riviera Maya. The 5-hour tour (including transportation time to the destination) includes equipment, instruction, the services of a tour guide, lunch, and bottled water; it departs daily at 8am, 10:30am, and 1:30pm. The company picks you up at the Plaza Kukulcán.

Other excursions go to the **reefs** in glass-bottom boats, so you can have a near-scuba-diving experience and see many colorful fish. However, the reefs are some distance from the shore and are impossible to reach on windy days with choppy seas. They've also suffered from overvisitation, and their condition is far from pristine. Nautibus's **Atlantis Submarine** (© **987/872-5671;** www.atlantisadventures.com) takes you close to the aquatic action. Departures vary, depending on weather conditions. Prices are $79 (£43) for adults, $45 (£25) for children ages 4 to 12. The submarine descends to a depth of 30m (98 ft.). Atlantis Submarine departs Monday to Saturday every hour from 8am until 2pm; the tour lasts about an hour. The submarine departs from Cozumel, so you either need to take a ferry to get there or purchase the package that includes round-trip transportation from your hotel in Cancún ($103/£57 adults, $76/£42 children 4–12). Reservations are recommended.

5 Outdoor Activities & Attractions

OUTDOOR ACTIVITIES

DOLPHIN SWIMS   On Isla Mujeres, you have the opportunity to swim with dolphins at **Dolphin Discovery** ✦✦ (© 998/877-0207 or 849-4757; www.dolphin discovery.com). Groups of eight people swim with two dolphins and one trainer. Swimmers view an educational video and spend time in the water with the trainer and the dolphins before enjoying 15 minutes of free swimming time with them. Reservations are recommended, and you must arrive an hour before your assigned swimming time, at 10:30am, noon, 2pm, or 3:30pm. The cost is $139 (£76) per person for the Dolphin Royal Swim. There are less expensive programs that allow you to learn about, touch, and hold the dolphins (but not swim with them) starting at $79 (£43). Ferry transfers from Playa Langosta in Cancún are available.

La Isla Shopping Center, Bulevar Kukulkán Km 12.5, has an impressive **Interactive Aquarium** (© **998/883-0411;** -0436, or -0413; www.aquariumcancun.com.mx), with dolphin swims and shows and the chance to feed a shark while immersed in the water in an acrylic cage. Guides inside the main tank use underwater microphones to point out the sea life, and even answer your questions. Open exhibition tanks enable visitors to touch a variety of marine life, including sea stars and manta rays. The educational dolphin program costs $65 (£36), while the dolphin swim is $135 (£74) and the shark-feeding experience runs $65 (£36). The entrance fee to the aquarium is $13 (£7.15) for adults, $9 (£4.95) for children, and it's open daily from 9am to 6pm.

GOLF & TENNIS   The 18-hole **Pok-Ta-Pok Club,** or Club de Golf Cancún (© **998/883-0871**), is a Robert Trent Jones, Sr., design on the northern leg of the island. Greens fees run $105 (£58) for 18 holes including golf cart (discounted twilight fees), with clubs renting for $40 (£22). A caddy costs $20 (£11). The club is open daily from 6:30am to 6:30pm, accepts American Express, MasterCard, and Visa, and has tennis courts.

The **Hilton Cancún Golf & Spa Resort** (© 998-881-8016) has a championship 18-hole, par-72 course around the Ruinas Del Rey. Greens fees for the public are typically $199 (£109) for 18 holes and $149 (£82) for 9 holes; Hilton Cancún guests pay discounted rates of $149 (£82) for 18 holes, or $99 (£54) for 9 holes, which includes a golf cart. Low season and twilight discounts are available. Golf clubs and shoes are available for rent. The club is open daily from 6am to 6pm and accepts American Express, MasterCard, and Visa. The **Gran Meliá Cancún** (© 998/881-1100) has a 9-hole executive course; the fee is $53 (£29). The club is open daily from 7am to 3pm and accepts American Express, MasterCard, and Visa.

The first Jack Nicklaus Signature Golf Course in the Cancún area has opened at the **Moon Palace Spa & Golf Club** (© **998-881-6000;** www.palaceresorts.com), along the Riviera Maya. The $260 (£143) green fee includes cart, snacks, and drinks.

HORSEBACK RIDING   **Cancún Mermaid** (© **998/843-6517;** www.cancun mermaid.com), about 30 minutes south of town at the Rancho Loma Bonita, is a popular option for horseback riding. Five-hour packages include 2 hours of riding through the mangrove swamp to the beach, where you have time to swim and relax. The tour costs $72 (£40) for adults and children. The ranch also offers a four-wheel ATV ride on the same route as the horseback tour. It costs $72 (£40) per person if you want to ride on your own, $55 (£30) if you double up. Prices for both tours include transportation to the ranch, riding, soft drinks, and lunch, plus a guide and insurance. Only cash or travelers checks are accepted.

ATTRACTIONS

A MUSEUM   Cancún is not that big on culture, but one option is the **Museo de Arte Popular Mexicano** (© **998/849-7777**), on the second floor of the El Embarcadero Marina, Bulevar Kukulkán Km 4. It displays a representative collection of masks, regional folkloric costumes, nativity scenes, religious artifacts, musical instruments, Mexican toys, and gourd art, spread over 1,370 sq. m (14,747 sq. ft.) of exhibition space. Admission is $10 (£5.50), with kids younger than 12 paying half price. The museum is open daily from 11am to 11pm.

BULLFIGHTS   Cancún has a small bullring, **Plaza de Toros** (© **998/884-8372;** bull@prodigy.net.mx), near the northern (town) end of Bulevar Kukulkán. Bullfights take place every Wednesday at 3:30pm during the winter tourist season. A sport introduced to Mexico by the Spanish viceroys, bullfighting is now as much a part of Mexican culture as tequila. The bullfights usually include four bulls, and the spectacle begins with a folkloric dance exhibition, followed by a performance by the *charros* (Mexico's sombrero-wearing cowboys). You're not likely to see Mexico's best bullfights in Cancún—the real stars are in Mexico City. Keep in mind that if you go to a bullfight, *you're going to see a bullfight,* so stay away if you're an animal lover or you can't bear the sight of blood. Travel agencies in Cancún sell tickets, which cost $40 for adults and are free for children younger than 6; seating is by general admission. American Express, MasterCard, and Visa are accepted

6 Shopping

Despite the surrounding natural splendor, shopping has become a favorite activity. Cancún is known throughout Mexico for its diverse shops and festive malls catering to international tourists. Visitors from the United States may find apparel more expensive in Cancún, but the selection is much broader than at other Mexican resorts. Numerous duty-free shops offer excellent value on European goods. The largest is **Ultrafemme,** Avenida Tulum, Supermanzana 25 (© **998/884-1402**), specializing in imported cosmetics, perfumes, and fine jewelry and watches. The downtown Cancún location offers slightly lower prices than branches in Plaza Caracol and Kukulcán Plaza.

Handicrafts are more limited and more expensive in Cancún than in other regions of Mexico because they are not produced here. They are available, though; several **open-air crafts markets** are on Avenida Tulum in Cancún City and near the convention center in the Hotel Zone. One of the biggest is **Coral Negro,** Bulevar Kukulkán Km 9.5, open daily from 7am to 11pm. A small restaurant inside, Xtabentun, serves Yucatecan food and pizza, and morphs into a dance club around 9 to 11pm.

Cancún's main venues are the **malls**—not quite as grand as their U.S. counterparts, but close. All are air-conditioned, sleek, and sophisticated. Most are on Bulevar Kukulkán between Km 7 and Km 12. They offer everything from fine crystal and silver to designer clothing and decorative objects, along with numerous restaurants and clubs. Stores are generally open daily from 10am to 10pm.

The **Kukulcán Plaza** (© 998/885-2200; www.kukulcanplaza.com) offers a large selection—more than 300—of shops, restaurants, and entertainment. There's a bank; a theater with U.S. movies; an Internet-access kiosk; several crafts stores; a liquor and tobacco store; several bathing-suit specialty stores; record and tape outlets; a leather goods store (including shoes and sandals); and a store specializing in silver from Taxco. The Fashion Gallery features designer labels, such as Louis Vuitton, Salvatore Ferragamo, and Ultrafemme. In the food court are a number of U.S. franchise restaurants, including Ruth's Chris Steak House, plus one featuring specialty coffee. There's also a large indoor parking garage. The mall is open daily from 10am to 10pm, until 11pm during high season. Assistance for those with disabilities is available upon request, and wheelchairs, strollers, and lockers are available at the information desk.

The long-standing **Plaza Caracol** (© 998/883-1038; www.caracolplaza.com) holds, among other things, Cartier jewelry, Señor Frog's clothing, Samsonite luggage, and La Fisheria and Casa Rolandi restaurants. It's just before you reach the convention center as you come from downtown Cancún.

Because the entertainment-oriented **Forum by the Sea,** Bulevar Kukulkán Km 9 (© 998/883-4425), suffered extensive hurricane damage, it received a complete facelift. Most people come here for the food and fun, choosing from Hard Rock Cafe, CoCo Bongo, and Rainforest Cafe, plus an extensive food court. Shops include Tommy Hilfiger, Diesel, Harley Davidson, Sunglass Island, and Children's World. The mall is open daily from 10am to midnight (bars remain open later).

The most intriguing mall is the **La Isla Shopping Village,** Bulevar Kukulkán Km 12.5 (© 998/883-5025; www.laislacancun.com.mx), an open-air festival mall that looks like a small village. Walkways lined with shops and restaurants cross little canals. It also has a "riverwalk," alongside the Nichupté lagoon, and an interactive aquarium and dolphin swim facility, as well as the Spacerocker and River Ride Tour—great for kid-friendly fun. Shops include Bulgari, Diesel, DKNY, Guess, Nautica, Tommy Hilfiger, Ultrafemme, and Zara. Dining choices include Johnny Rockets, Häagen-Dazs, the fun-filled Mexican restaurant La Casa de las Margaritas, and the romantic Thai restaurant. You will also find a movie theater, video arcade, and several bars, including La Madonna.

7 Cancún after Dark

One of Cancún's main draws is its active nightlife. The hottest centers of action include **Plaza Dady'O, Forum by the Sea,** and **La Isla Shopping Village.** These places transform into spring break madness for most of March and April. Hotels also play in the nightlife scene, with happy-hour entertainment and special drink prices to entice visitors and guests from other resorts. Lobby bar-hopping at sunset is one way to investigate where you might want to spend next year's Cancún vacation.

THE CLUB & MUSIC SCENE

Clubbing in Cancún is a favorite part of the vacation experience and can go on each night until the sun rises over that incredibly blue sea. Several big hotels have nightclubs or schedule live music in their lobby bars. At the clubs, expect to stand in long lines on weekends, pay a cover charge of about $40 (£22) with open bar, or $15 to $25 (£8.25–£14) without open bar and then pay $8 to $10 (£4.40–£5.50) for a drink. Some of the higher-priced clubs include live entertainment. The places listed in this section are air-conditioned and accept American Express, MasterCard, and Visa.

A great idea to get you started is the **Bar Hopper Tour** ★★ with tickets available at Señor Frog's or various travel agencies around town. For $65 (£36), it takes you by bus to the Congo Bar, Dady Rock, Señor Frog's, and CoCo Bongo, where you bypass any lines and spend about an hour at each establishment. The price includes entry to the bars, one welcome drink at each, and transportation by air-conditioned bus, allowing you to get a great sampling of the best of Cancún's nightlife. The tour runs from 8pm into the wee hours, with the meeting point at the Congo Bar.

Numerous restaurants, such as **Carlos 'n' Charlie's, Hard Rock Cafe, Señor Frog's,** and **T.G.I. Friday's,** double as nighttime party spots, offering wildish fun at a fraction of the price of more costly clubs.

Bling ★★   This is one of the coolest nightspots to have opened in Cancún, featuring a chic outdoor terrace overlooking the lagoon. A fashionable 30-something crowd congregates amidst sofas under the stars, a killer sound system, and flowing cocktails; a sushi and sashimi bar is also offered. This upscale lounge is considerably more sophisticated than Cancún's typical frat-style bars, and it's open daily from 9pm to 4am. Bulevar Kukulkán, Km 13.5. ✆ 998/840-6014.

The City ★★★   Cancún's hottest and largest nightclub, The City features progressive electronic music spun by some of the world's top DJs (the DJ station looks like an airport control tower). This is where Paris Hilton parties when she comes to town. With visiting DJs from New York, L.A., and Mexico City, the music is sizzling. You actually need never leave, as The City is a day-and-night club. The City Beach Club opens at 10am and features a pool with a wave machine for surfing and boogie-boarding, a tower-high waterslide, food and bar service, plus beach cabañas. The Terrace Bar, overlooking the action on Bulevar Kukulkán, serves food and drinks all day long. For a relaxing evening vibe, the Lounge features comfy couches, chill music, and an extensive menu of martinis, snacks, and desserts. Open at 10:30pm, the 2,500-sq.-m (26,910-sq.-ft.) nightclub features nine bars, stunning light shows, and several VIP areas. Bulevar Kukulkán, Km 9.5. ✆ 998/848-8380. www.thecitycancun.com. Cover $30–$40 (£17–£22) with open bar.

CoCo Bongo ★★   Continuing its reputation as one of the hottest spots in town, CoCo Bongo's appeal is that it combines an enormous dance club with extravagant theme shows. It has no formal dance floor, so you can dance anywhere—and that includes on the tables, on the bar, or even on the stage with the occasional live band. This place can—and regularly does—pack in as many as 3,000 people. You have to experience it to believe it. Despite its capacity, lines are long on weekends and in high season. The music alternates between Caribbean, salsa, house, hip-hop, techno, and classics from the 1970s, '80s, and '90s. Open from 10:30pm to 3:30am, CoCo Bongo draws a hip young crowd. Forum by the Sea, Bulevar Kukulkán Km 9.5. ✆ **998/883-5061.** www.cocobongo.com.mx. Cover $40–45 (£22–£25) with open bar.

Dady'O   This is a popular rave among the young and brave with frequent long lines. It opens nightly at 10pm and has a giant dance floor and awesome light system. Bulevar Kukulkán Km 9.5. *©* **998/883-3333**. www.dadyo.net. Cover $20 (£11); $40 (£22) with open bar.

Dady Rock Bar and Grill   The offspring of Dady'O, it opens at 7pm and goes as long as any other nightspot, offering a combination of live bands and DJs spinning music, along with an open bar, full meals, a buffet, and dancing. Bulevar Kukulkán Km 9.5. *©* **998/883-1626**. Cover $16; $35 (£19) with open bar

La Madonna   This martini bar and restaurant emerges unexpectedly from La Isla shopping center like a chic gem along the canal. With over 180 creative martini selections accompanied by relaxing lounge music, La Madonna also offers authentic Italian and Swiss cuisine. Enjoy your red mandarin, lychee, or vanilla peach martini elbow to elbow with Cancún's beautiful people on one of the red leather chairs on the expansive patio. It's open daily from noon to 1am. La Isla Shopping Village, Bulevar Kukulkán Km 12.5. *©* **998/883-2222**.

The Lobby Lounge *☆*   The most refined and upscale of Cancún's nightly gathering spots, with a terrace overlooking the lagoon, a special martini collection, and a list of more than 80 premium tequilas for tasting or sipping. There's also a sushi and seafood bar, as well as a humidor collection of Cuban cigars. It's open daily from 5pm to 1am, with live music Thursday through Sunday. Ritz-Carlton Cancún, Retorno del Rey 36, off Bulevar Kukulkán Km 13.5. *©* **998/881-0808**.

THE PERFORMING ARTS

Several hotels host **Mexican fiesta nights,** including a buffet dinner and a folkloric dance show; admission, including dinner, ranges from $35 to $50 (£19–£28), unless you're at an all-inclusive resort that includes this as part of the package.

Tourists mingle with locals at the downtown **Parque de las Palapas** (the main park) for Noches Caribeñas, which involves children-oriented performances (such as clown shows) and free live tropical music. Performances begin at 7:30pm on Sunday, and sometimes there are events on Friday and Saturday.

14

Isla Mujeres & Cozumel

by Juan Cristiano & David Baird

Mexico's two main Caribbean islands are idyllic places to get away from the hustle and bustle of Cancún and the Riviera Maya. Neither Isla Mujeres nor Cozumel is particularly large, and they have that island feel—small roads that don't go very far, lots of mopeds, few (or no) buses and trucks, and a sense of being set apart from the rest of the world. Yet they're just a short ferry ride from the mainland. Both offer a variety of lodging choices, ample outdoor activities, and a laid-back atmosphere that makes a delightful contrast with the mainland experience.

EXPLORING MEXICO'S CARIBBEAN ISLANDS

ISLA MUJERES   A day trip to Isla Mujeres on a party boat is one of the most popular excursions from Cancún. This fish-shaped island is just 13km (8 miles) northeast of Cancún, a quick boat ride away, allowing ample time to get a taste of the peaceful pace of life. To fully explore the village and its shops and cafes, relax at the broad, tranquil Playa Norte, or snorkel or dive Garrafón Natural Reef Park (an underwater park), you'll need more time. Overnight accommodations range from rustic to offbeat chic.

Passenger ferries go to Isla Mujeres from Puerto Juárez, and car ferries leave from Punta Sam, both near Cancún. More expensive passenger ferries, with less frequent departures, leave from the Playa Linda pier on Cancún Island.

COZUMEL   Cozumel is larger than Isla Mujeres and farther from the mainland (19km/12 miles off the coast from Playa del Carmen). It has its own international airport. Life here turns around two major activities: scuba diving and being a port of call for cruise ships. It is far and away the most popular destination along this coast for both. Despite the cruise-ship traffic and all the stores that it has spawned, life on the island moves at a relaxed and comfortable pace. There is just one town, San Miguel de Cozumel. North and south of town are resorts; the rest of the shore is deserted and predominantly rocky, with a scattering of small sandy coves that you can have practically all to yourself.

1 Isla Mujeres ★★★

13km (8 miles) N of Cancún

Isla Mujeres (Island of Women) is a casual, laid-back refuge from the conspicuously commercialized action of Cancún, visible across a narrow channel. It's known as the best value in the Caribbean, assuming that you favor an easygoing vacation pace and prefer simplicity to pretense. This is an island of white-sand beaches and turquoise waters, complemented by a town filled with Caribbean-colored clapboard houses and rustic, open-air restaurants. Most hotels here are clean, comfortable and beachy, with

> ## (Tips) The Best Websites for Isla Mujeres & Cozumel
>
> - **Isla Mujeres Tourist Information: www.isla-mujeres.net** The official site of the Isla Mujeres Tourism Board provides complete information on Isla, from getting there to where to stay.
> - **My Isla Mujeres: www.myislamujeres.com** Get a local's view of the island; especially notable are the active chat room and message boards on this site.
> - **Cozumel.net: www.cozumel.net** This site is a cut above the typical dining/lodging/activities sites. Click on "About Cozumel" to find schedules for ferries and island-hop flights, and to check the latest news. There's also a comprehensive listing of B&Bs and vacation-home rentals.
> - **Cozumel Travel Planner: www.go2cozumel.com** This is a well-done guide to area businesses and attractions, by an online Mexico specialist.
> - **Cozumel Hotel Association: www.islacozumel.com.mx** Operated by the tourism-promotion arm of the hotel association, this site gives more than just listings of the member hotels. There's info on packages and specials, plus brief descriptions of most of the island's attractions, restaurants, and recreational activities.

a few luxury boutique hotels dotting the island. But, in general, if you're looking for lots of action or opulence, you're likely to prefer Cancún.

Francisco Hernández de Córdoba, seeing figurines of partially clad females along the shore, gave the island its name when he landed in 1517. These are now believed to have been offerings to the Mayan goddess of fertility and the moon, Ixchel. Their presence indicates that the island was probably sacred to the Maya.

At midday, suntanned visitors hang out in open-air cafes and stroll pedestrian streets lined with zealous souvenir vendors. Calling attention to their bargain-priced wares, they give a carnival atmosphere to the hours when tour-boat traffic is at its peak. Befitting the size of the island, most of the traffic consists of golf carts, *motos* (mopeds), and bicycles. Once the tour boats leave, however, Isla Mujeres reverts to its more typical, tranquil way of life.

Days in "Isla"—as the locals call it—can alternate between adventurous activity and absolute repose. Trips to the Isla Contoy bird sanctuary are popular, as are the excellent diving, fishing, and snorkeling—in 1998, the island's coral coast became part of Mexico's Marine National Park system. Although the reef suffered substantial hurricane damage in 2005, it is now largely back to normal. The incredible water clarity illuminates the wonderful array of coral and tropical fish living here. Among the underwater life you are likely to see are French angelfish, longspine squirrelfish, trumpet fish, four-eye butterfly fish, green angelfish, stoplight parrotfish, southern stingrays, sharp-nose puffer fish, blue tang, and great barracuda.

An upside of Hurricane Wilma's impact is that Playa Norte received an infusion of white sand, and is now broader and more beautiful than ever, despite the "haircuts" suffered by many of the palm trees. The island and several of its traditional hotels attract regular gatherings of yoga practitioners. In the evening, most people find the

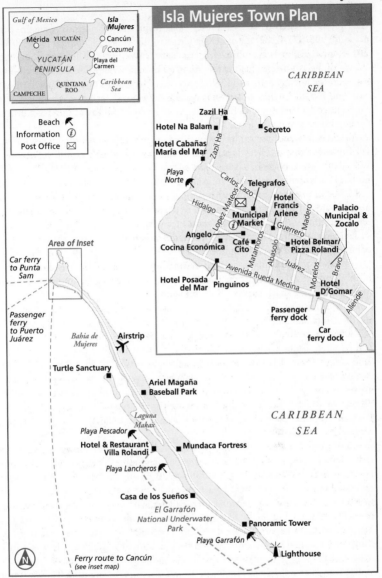

Isla Mujeres Town Plan

slow, casual pace one of the island's biggest draws. The cool night breeze is a perfect accompaniment to casual open-air dining and drinking in small street-side restaurants. Many people pack it in as early as 9 or 10pm, when most of the businesses close. Those in search of a party, however, will find kindred souls at the bars on Playa Norte that stay open late.

ESSENTIALS

GETTING THERE & DEPARTING   Puerto Juárez, just north of Cancún, is the **dock** (© 998/877-0382) for passenger ferries to Isla Mujeres. *Ultramar* (© 998/843-2011; www.granpuerto.com.mx) has fast boats leaving every half-hour from "Gran Puerto" in Puerto Juárez, making the trip in 15 minutes. There is storage space for luggage and the fare is about $4 (£2.20) each way. These boats operate daily, starting at 6am and usually ending at 10:30pm (check beforehand for latest schedules). They might leave early if they're full, so arrive ahead of schedule. Pay at the ticket office—or, if the ferry is about to leave, aboard.

Note: Upon arrival by taxi or bus in Puerto Juárez, be wary of pirate "guides" who tell you either that the ferry is canceled or that it's several hours until the next ferry. They'll offer the services of a private *lancha* (small boat) for about $40 (£22)—and it's nothing but a scam. Small boats are available and, on a co-op basis, charge $15 to $25 (£8.25–£14) one-way, based on the number of passengers. They take about 50 minutes and are not recommended on days with rough seas. Check with the clearly visible ticket office—the only accurate source for information.

Taxi fares are posted by the street where the taxis park, so be sure to check the rate before agreeing to a taxi for the ride back to Cancún. Rates generally run $12 to $15 (£6.60–£8.25), depending upon your destination. Moped and bicycle rentals are also readily available as you depart the ferry. This small complex also has public bathrooms, luggage storage, a snack bar, and souvenir shops.

Isla Mujeres is so small that a vehicle isn't necessary, but if you're taking one, you'll use the **Punta Sam** port a little beyond Puerto Juárez. The 40-minute car ferry (© 998/877-0065) runs five or six times daily between 8am and 8pm, year-round except in bad weather. Times are generally as follows: Cancún to Isla 8 and 11am and 2:45, 5:30, and 8:15pm; Isla to Cancún 6:30 and 9:30am and 12:45, 4:15, and 7:15pm. Always check with the tourist office in Cancún to verify this schedule. Cars should arrive an hour before the ferry departure to register for a place in line and pay the posted fee, which varies depending on the weight and type of vehicle. A gas pump in Isla is at the intersection of Avenida Rueda Medina and Calle Abasolo, just northwest of the ferry docks.

There are also ferries to Isla Mujeres from the **Playa Linda,** known as the Embarcadero pier in Cancún, but they're less frequent and more expensive than those from Puerto Juárez. A **Water Taxi** (© 998/886-4270 or -4847; asterix@cablered.net.mx) to Isla Mujeres operates from **Playa Caracol,** between the Fiesta Americana Coral Beach Hotel and the Xcaret terminal on the island, with prices about the same as those from Playa Linda and about four times the cost of the public ferries from Puerto Juárez. Scheduled departures are at 9 and 11am and 1pm, with returns from Isla Mujeres at noon and 5pm. Adult round-trip fares are $15 (£8.25); kids ages 3 to 12 pay $7.50 (£4.15); free for children younger than 3.

To get to Puerto Juárez or Punta Sam from **Cancún,** take any Ruta 8 city bus from Avenida Tulum. If you're coming from **Mérida,** you can fly to Cancún and proceed to Puerto Juárez, or take a bus directly to Puerto Juárez. From **Cozumel,** you can fly to Cancún (there are daily flights), or take a ferry to Playa del Carmen (see "Cozumel," later in this chapter), and then travel to Puerto Juárez.

Arriving   Passenger ferries arrive at the docks in the center of town (car ferries arrive just north of town). The main road that passes in front is Avenida Rueda Medina. Most hotels are close by. Tricycle taxis are the least expensive and most fun way to get to your hotel; you and your luggage pile in the open carriage compartment, and the driver pedals through the streets. Regular taxis are always lined up in a parking lot to the right of the pier, with their rates posted. If someone on the ferry offers to arrange a taxi for you, politely decline, unless you'd like some help with your luggage down the short pier—it just means an extra, unnecessary tip for your helper.

VISITOR INFORMATION   The **City Tourist Office** (©/fax **998/877-0767** or -0307) is at Av. Rueda Medina 130, just across the street from the pier. It's open Monday through Friday from 9am to 4pm, closed on Saturdays and Sundays. Also look for *Islander,* a free publication with local information, advertisements, and event listings.

ISLAND LAYOUT   Isla Mujeres is about 8km (5 miles) long and 4km (2½ miles) wide, with the town at the northern tip. "Downtown" is a compact 4 blocks by 6 blocks, so it's very easy to get around. The **passenger ferry docks** are at the center of town, within walking distance of most hotels, restaurants, and shops. The street running along the waterfront is **Avenida Rueda Medina,** commonly called the *malecón* **(boardwalk).** The **Mercado Municipal (town market)** is by the post office on **Calle Guerrero,** an inland street at the north edge of town, which, like most streets in the town, is unmarked.

GETTING AROUND   A popular form of transportation on Isla Mujeres is the electric **golf cart,** available for rent at many hotels or rental shops for $15 (£8.25) per hour or $45 (£25) per day. Prices are set the same at all rental locations. **El Sol Golf Cart Rental,** Av. Benito Juárez Mza 3 #20 (corner of Matamoros; © **998/877-0791**) is one good option in the town center. The golf carts don't go more than 30kmph (20 mph), but they're fun. Anyway, you aren't on Isla Mujeres to hurry. Many people enjoy touring the island by *moto* **(motorized bike or scooter).** Fully automatic versions are available for around $30 (£17) per day or $8 (£4.40) per hour. They come with helmets and seats for two people. There's only one main road with a couple of offshoots, so you won't get lost. Be aware that the rental price does not include insurance, and any injury to yourself or the vehicle will come out of your pocket. **Bicycles** are also available for rent at some hotels for $4 (£2.20) per hour or $10 (£5.50) per day, usually including a basket and a lock.

   If you prefer to use a taxi, rates are about $2.50 (£1.40) for trips within the downtown area, or $4.50 (£2.50) for a trip to the southern end of Isla. You can also hire them for about $10 (£5.50) per hour. The number to call for taxis is © **998/877-0066.**

FAST FACTS: Isla Mujeres

Area Code   The telephone area code is **998.**

Consumer Protection   You can reach the local branch of **Profeco** consumer protection agency at © **998/887-3960.**

Currency Exchange   Isla Mujeres has numerous *casas de cambio,* or currency exchanges, that you can easily spot along the main streets. Most of the hotels listed here change money for their guests, although often at less favorable rates than the commercial enterprises. There is only one bank in Isla, **HSBC Bank** (© **998/877-0005**), across from the ferry docks. It's open Monday through Friday from 8:30am to 6pm, and Saturdays from 9am to 2pm.

Drugstore **Isla Mujeres Farmacía** (© **998/877-0178**) has the best selection of prescription and over-the-counter medicines.

Emergencies To report an emergency, dial © **065** from any phone within Mexico.

Hospital The **Hospital de la Armada** is on Avenida Rueda Medina at Ojón P. Blanco (© **998/877-0001**). It's less than a kilometer (a half mile) south of the town center. It will only treat you in an emergency. Otherwise, you're referred to the **Centro de Salud** on Avenida Guerrero, a block before the beginning of the *malecón* (© **998/877-0117**).

Internet Access Owned by a lifelong resident of Isla, **Cyber Isla Mujeres.com,** Av. Francisco y Madero 17, between Hidalgo and Juárez streets (© **998/877-0272**), offers Internet access for $1.50 (85p) per hour, daily 7am to 10pm, and serves complimentary Veracruzano coffee all day.

Post Office The *correo* is at Calle Guerrero 12 (© **998/877-0085**), at the corner of López Mateos, near the market. It's open Monday through Friday from 9am to 4pm.

Taxis To call for a taxi, dial © **998/877-0066**.

Telephone Ladatel phones accepting coins and prepaid phone cards are at the plaza and throughout town.

Tourist Seasons Isla Mujeres's tourist season (when hotel rates are higher) is a bit different from that of other places in Mexico. High season runs December through May, a month longer than in Cancún. Some hotels raise their rates in August, and some raise their rates beginning in mid-November. Low season is from June to mid-November.

BEACHES & OUTDOOR ACTIVITIES

THE BEACHES   The most popular beach in town is **Playa Norte** ⟨*⟩. The long stretch of beach extends around the northern tip of the island, to your left as you get off the boat. This is perhaps the world's best municipal beach—a wide swath of fine white sand and calm, translucent, turquoise-blue water. The beach is easily reached on foot from the ferry and from all downtown hotels. Watersports equipment, beach umbrellas, and lounge chairs are available for rent. Areas in front of restaurants usually cost nothing if you use the restaurant as your headquarters for drinks and food, and the best of them have hammocks and swings from which to sip your piña coladas.

   Garrafón Natural Reef Park ⟨**⟩ (see "Snorkeling," below) is best known as a snorkeling area, but there is a nice stretch of beach on either side of the park. **Playa Lancheros** is on the Caribbean side of Laguna Makax. Local buses go to Lancheros, and then turn inland and return downtown. The beach at Playa Lancheros is nice, with a variety of casual restaurants.

SWIMMING   Wide Playa Norte is the best swimming beach, with Playa Lancheros second. There are no lifeguards on duty on Isla Mujeres, which does not use the system of water-safety flags employed in Cancún and Cozumel. The bay between Cancun and Isla Mujeres is calm, with warm, transparent waters ideal for swimming, snorkeling, and diving. The east side of the island facing the open Caribbean Sea is typically rougher with much stronger currents.

SNORKELING   By far the most popular place to snorkel is **Garrafón Natural Reef Park** ★★ (© 998/849-4748; www.garrafon.com). It lies at the southern end of the island, where you'll see numerous schools of colorful fish. The pricy but well-equipped park has two restaurant/bars, beach chairs, a swimming pool, kayaks, changing rooms, rental lockers, showers, a gift shop, and snack bars. Once a public national underwater park, Garrafón is now operated by a private company. Public facilities have been vastly improved, with new attractions and facilities added each year. Activities at the park include snorkeling and Snuba (a tankless version of scuba diving, when you descend while breathing through a long air tube), "Sea Trek," which allows you to explore the Caribbean seabed wearing a helmet with compressed air, crystal-clear canoes for viewing underwater life, and a zip-line that takes you over the water. On land, there are tanning decks, shaded hammocks, a 12m (40-ft.) climbing tower, and—of course!—a souvenir superstore. Several restaurants and snack bars are available. Admission for the Garrafón Discovery package (required for entry) includes sea transfer from Cancún, continental breakfast, open bar, lunch buffet, and snorkeling equipment for $65 (£36) for adults, $49 (£27) for children (American Express, MasterCard, and Visa are accepted). More expensive packages that include swims with dolphins at Dolphin Discovery are available. The park is open daily from 9am to 5pm.

Also good for snorkeling is **Manchones Reef,** off the southeastern coast. The reef is just offshore and accessible by boat.

Another excellent location is around *el faro* (the lighthouse) in the **Bahía de Mujeres** at the southern tip of the island, where the water is about 2m (6½ ft.) deep. Boatmen will take you for around $25 (£14) per person if you have your own snorkeling equipment or $30 (£17) if you use theirs.

DIVING   Most of the dive shops on the island offer the same trips for the same prices: one-tank dives cost about $50 (£28), two-tank dives about $70. **Bahía Dive Shop,** Rueda Medina 166, across from the car-ferry dock (© 998/877-0340), is a full-service shop that offers dive equipment for sale or rent. The shop is open daily from 10am to 7pm, and accepts MasterCard and Visa. Another respected dive shop is **Coral Scuba Center,** at Matamoros 13A and Rueda Medina (© 998/877-0061 or -0763). It's open daily from 8am to 12:30pm and 4 to 10pm. Both offer 2-hour snorkeling trips for about $20 (£11).

Cuevas de los Tiburones (Caves of the Sleeping Sharks) is Isla's most renowned dive site—but the name is slightly misleading, as shark sightings are rare these days. Two sites where you could traditionally see the sleeping shark are the Cuevas de Tiburones and **La Punta,** but the sharks have mostly been driven off, and a storm collapsed the arch featured in a Jacques Cousteau film showing them, but the caves survive. Other dive sites include a **wreck** 15km (9½ miles) offshore; **Banderas** reef, between Isla Mujeres and Cancún, where there's always a strong current; **Tabos** reef on the eastern shore; and **Manchones** reef, 1km (a half mile) off the southeastern tip of the island, where the water is 4.5 to 11m (15–36 ft.) deep. **The Cross of the Bay** is close to Manchones reef. A bronze cross, weighing 1 ton and standing 12m (40 ft.) high, was placed in the water between Manchones and Isla in 1994, as a memorial to those who have lost their lives at sea.

FISHING   To arrange a day of fishing, ask at the **Sociedad Cooperativa Turística** (the boatmen's cooperative), on Avenida Rueda Medina (© 998/877-1363), next to Mexico Divers and Las Brisas restaurant, or the travel agency mentioned in "A Visit to Isla Contoy," below. Four to six others can share the cost, which includes lunch and drinks. Captain Tony Martínez (© 998/877-0274) also arranges fishing trips aboard the *Marinonis,* with advanced reservations recommended. Year-round you'll find bonito, mackerel, kingfish, and amberjack. Sailfish and sharks (hammerhead, bull, nurse, lemon, and tiger) are in good supply in April and May. In winter, larger grouper and jewfish are prevalent. Four hours of fishing close to shore costs around $110 (£61); 8 hours farther out goes for $250 (£138). The cooperative is open Monday through Saturday from 8am to 1pm and 5 to 8pm, and Sunday from 7:30 to 10am and 6 to 8pm.

YOGA   Increasingly, Isla is becoming known as a great place to combine a relaxing beach vacation with yoga practice and instruction. The trend began at **Hotel Na Balam** ✸✸ (© **998/877-0279** or -0058; www.nabalam.com), which offers yoga classes under its large poolside *palapa,* complete with yoga mats and props. The classes, which begin at 9am Monday through Friday, are free to guests, $15 (£8.25) per class to visitors. Na Balam is also the site of frequent yoga instruction vacations featuring respected teachers and a more extensive practice schedule; the current schedule of yoga retreats is posted on their website. Local yoga culture extends down the island to **Casa de los Sueños Resort and Zenter** (© **998/877-0651;** www.casadelos suenosresort.com), where yoga classes, as well as chi gong and Pilates, are regularly held.

MORE ATTRACTIONS

DOLPHIN DISCOVERY ✸✸   You can swim with live dolphins (© **998/877-0207** or 849-4757; fax 998/849-4751; www.dolphindiscovery.com) in an enclosure at Treasure Island, on the side of Isla Mujeres that faces Cancún. Groups of eight people swim with two dolphins and one trainer. Swimmers view an educational video and spend time in the water with the trainer and the dolphins before enjoying 15 minutes of free swimming time with them. Reservations are recommended, and you must arrive an hour before your assigned swimming time, at 10:30am, noon, 2 or 3:30pm. The cost is $139 (£76) per person for the Dolphin Royal Swim. There are less-expensive programs that allow you to learn about, touch, and hold the dolphins (but not swim with them) starting at $79 (£43).

A TURTLE SANCTUARY ✸✸   As recently as 20 years ago, fishermen converged on the island nightly from May to September, waiting for the monster-size turtles to lumber ashore to deposit their Ping-Pong-ball-shaped eggs. Totally vulnerable once they begin laying their eggs, and exhausted when they have finished, the turtles were easily captured and slaughtered for their highly prized meat, shell, and eggs. Then a concerned fisherman, Gonzalez Cahle Maldonado, began convincing others to spare at least the eggs, which he protected. It was a start. Following his lead, the fishing secretariat founded the **Centro de Investigaciones;** although the local government provided assistance in the past, now the center relies solely on private donations. Since opening, tens of thousands of turtles have been released, and every year local schoolchildren participate in the event, thus planting the notion of protecting the turtles for a new generation of islanders.

Six species of sea turtles nest on Isla Mujeres. An adult green turtle, the most abundant species, measures 1 to 1.5m (3¼–5 ft.) in length and can weigh as much as 450 pounds. At the center, visitors walk through the indoor and outdoor turtle pool areas, where the creatures paddle around. The turtles are separated by age, from newly hatched up to 1 year. People who come here usually end up staying at least an hour, especially if they opt for the guided tour, which I recommend. They also have a small gift shop and snack bar. The sanctuary is on a piece of land separated from the island by Bahía de Mujeres and Laguna Makax, at Carr. Sac Bajo #5; you'll need a taxi to get there. Admission is $3 (£1.65); the shelter is open daily from 9am to 5pm. For more information, call ② **998/877-0595.**

SIGHTS OF PUNTA SUR 🎭🎭   At Punta Sur (the southern point of the island, just inland from **Garrafón National Reef Park;** call ② **998/877-1100** or go to www.garrafon.com) and part of the park, is Isla's newest attraction, the **Panoramic Tower.** At 50m (164-ft.) high, the tower offers visitors a bird's-eye view of the entire island. The tower holds 20 visitors at a time, and rotates for 10 minutes while you snap photos or simply enjoy the scenery. However, it was closed for renovations at press time.

Next to the tower you'll find **Sculptured Spaces,** an impressive and extensive garden of large sculptures donated to Isla Mujeres by internationally renowned sculptors as part of the 2001 First International Sculpture Exhibition. Among Mexican sculptors represented by works are José Luis Cuevas and Vladimir Cora.

Nearby is the **Caribbean Village,** with narrow lanes of colorful clapboard buildings that house cafes and shops displaying folkloric art. Plan to have lunch or a snack here at the kiosk and stroll around, before heading on to the lighthouse and Maya ruins.

Also at this southern point of the island, and part of the ruins, is **Cliff of the Dawn,** the southeasternmost point of Mexico. Services are available from 9am to 5pm, but you can enter at any time; if you make it there early enough to see the sunrise, you can claim you were the first person in Mexico that day to be touched by the sun!

A MAYA RUIN 🎭🎭   Just beyond the lighthouse, at the southern end of the island, are the strikingly beautiful remains of a small Maya temple, believed to have been built to pay homage to the moon and fertility goddess Ixchel. The location, on a lofty bluff overlooking the sea, is worth seeing and makes a great place for photos. It is believed that Maya women traveled here on annual pilgrimages to seek Ixchel's blessings of fertility. If you're at Garrafón park and want to walk, it's not too far. Turn right from Garrafón. When you see the lighthouse, turn toward it down the rocky path.

A PIRATE'S FORTRESS   The Fortress of Mundaca is about 4km (2½ miles) in the same direction as Garrafón, less than a kilometer (about half a mile) to the left. A slave trader who claimed to have been the pirate Mundaca Marecheaga built the fortress. In the early 19th century, he arrived at Isla Mujeres and set up a blissful paradise, while making money selling slaves to Cuba and Belize. According to island lore, he decided to settle down and build this hacienda after being captivated by the charms of an island girl. However, she reputedly spurned his affections and married another islander, leaving him heartbroken and alone on Isla Mujeres. Admission is $2 (£1.10); the fortress is open daily from 10am to 6pm.

A VISIT TO ISLA CONTOY 🎭   If possible, plan to visit this pristine uninhabited island—30km (20 miles) by boat from Isla Mujeres—that became a national wildlife reserve in 1981. Lush vegetation covers the oddly shaped island, which is 6km (3¾ miles) long and harbors 70 species of birds as well as a host of marine and animal life. Bird species that nest on the island include pelicans, brown boobies, frigates, egrets, terns, and cormorants. Flocks of flamingos arrive in April. June, July, and August are good months to spot turtles burying their eggs in the sand at night. Most excursions troll for fish (which will be your lunch), anchor en route for a snorkeling expedition, skirt the island at a leisurely pace for close viewing of the birds without disturbing the habitat, and then pull ashore. While the captain prepares lunch, visitors can swim, sun, follow the nature trails, and visit the fine nature museum, which has bathroom facilities. The trip from Isla Mujeres takes about 45 minutes each way and can be longer if the waves are choppy. Because of the tight-knit boatmen's cooperative, prices for this excursion are the same everywhere: $40 (£22). You can buy a ticket at the **Sociedad Cooperativa Turística** on Avenida Rueda Medina, next to Mexico Divers and Las Brisas restaurant (© **998/877-1363**). Isla Contoy trips leave at 9am and return around 4:30pm. The price (cash only) is $55 (£30) for adults, $28 (£15) for children. Boat captains should respect the cooperative's regulations regarding ecological sensitivity and boat safety, including the availability of life jackets for everyone on board. If you're not given a life jacket, ask for one. Snorkeling equipment is usually included in the price, but double-check before heading out.

SHOPPING

Shopping is a casual activity here. There are only a few shops of any sophistication. Shop owners will bombard you, especially on Avenida Hidalgo, selling Saltillo rugs, onyx, silver, Guatemalan clothing, blown glassware, masks, folk art, beach paraphernalia, and T-shirts in abundance. Prices are lower than in Cancún or Cozumel, but with such overeager sellers, bargaining is necessary.

The one treasure you're likely to take back is a piece of fine jewelry—Isla is known for its excellent, duty-free prices on gemstones and handcrafted work made to order. Diamonds, emeralds, sapphires, and rubies can be purchased as loose stones and then mounted while you're off exploring. The superbly crafted gold, silver, and gems are available at very competitive prices in the workshops near the central plaza. The stones are also available in the rough. **Von Hauste** (© **998/877-0331**) located at the corner of Morelos and Juárez streets, is the grandest store, with a broad selection of jewelry including diamonds, emeralds, sapphires, and tanzanites at competitive prices. It's open daily from 9am to 5:30pm and accepts all major credit cards.

WHERE TO STAY

You'll find plenty of hotels in all price ranges on Isla Mujeres. Rates peak during high season, which is the most expensive and most crowded time to go. Elizabeth Wenger of **Yucatan Peninsula Travel** in Montello, Wisconsin (© **800/552-4550** in the U.S.), specializes in Mexico travel and books a lot of hotels in Isla Mujeres. Her service is invaluable in the high season. Those interested in private home rentals or longer-term stays can contact **Mundaca Travel and Real Estate** in Isla Mujeres (© **998/877-0025;** fax 998/877-0076; www.mundaca.com.mx), or book online with **Isla Beckons** property rental service (www.islabeckons.com).

VERY EXPENSIVE

Casa de los Sueños Resort & Spa Zenter ★★★ This "house of dreams" is easily Isla Mujeres's most intimate, sophisticated, and relaxing property. Though it was originally built as a private residence, luckily it became an upscale, adults-only boutique hotel in early 1998 (it has since changed ownership), and now caters to guests looking for a rejuvenating experience, with the adjoining Zenter offering spa services and yoga classes. Its location on the southern end of the island, adjacent to Garrafón Natural Reef Park, also makes it ideal for snorkeling and diving enthusiasts. The captivating design features vivid sherbet-colored walls—think watermelon, mango, and blueberry—and a sculpted architecture. There's a large, open interior courtyard; tropical gardens; a sunken living area (with Wi-Fi access); and an infinity pool that melts into the cool Caribbean waters. All rooms have balconies or terraces and face west, offering stunning views of the sunset over the sea, as well as the night lights of Cancún. In addition, the rooms—which have names such as Serenity, Peace, and Love—also have large marble bathrooms, Egyptian cotton bedding, and luxury bath amenities, and they are decorated in a serene style that blends Asian simplicity with Mexican details. One master suite ideal for honeymooners has an exceptionally spacious bathroom area, complete with whirlpool and steam room/shower, plus other deluxe amenities. Complimentary continental breakfast is served in your room, and a restaurant adjacent to their private pier serves healthful fusion cuisine—it's open to nonguests as well. The Zenter offers a very complete menu of massages and holistic spa treatments, as well as yoga classes, held either outdoors or in a serene indoor space.

Carretera Garrafón s/n, 77400 Isla Mujeres, Q. Roo. © 998/877-0651 or -0369. Fax 998/877-0708. www.casadelos suenosresort.com. 9 units. High season $350–$450 (£193–£248) double; low season $300–$400 (£165–£220) double. Rates include continental breakfast and taxes. MC, V. No children younger than 15. **Amenities:** Restaurant; infinity pool; spa; open-air massage area; room service; yoga center. In room: TV/VCR, hair dryer, iron, safe.

Hotel Villa Rolandi Gourmet & Beach Club ★★★ (Moments)
Set on the Caribbean like a hidden jewel, Villa Rolandi is a romantic escape on one of Mexico's most idyllic islands. A private yacht brings the privileged guests from Cancun directly to the hotel, which lies on a sheltered cove with a pristine white-sand beach, interrupted only by a sailboat and set of kayaks waiting to be taken to the sea. Each of the luxurious suites holds a separate sitting area and large terrace or balcony with private whirlpool overlooking the sea. Flat-screen TVs offer satellite music and movies, and all rooms feature sophisticated in-room sound systems, subtle lighting, and deep-hued Tikal marble. The beautiful bathrooms have Bulgari products and enticing showers with multiple showerheads that convert into steam baths. In-room breakfast is delivered through a small closet-like door. The luxurious hotel spa also offers an outdoor Thalasso therapy whirlpool and beachside massages.

Dining is an integral part of a stay at Villa Rolandi. The owner is a Swiss-born restaurateur who made a name for himself with his restaurants on Isla Mujeres and in Cancún (see **Casa Rolandi** and **Pizza Rolandi** under "Where to Dine," below). This intimate hideaway is ideal for honeymooners, who receive a complimentary bottle of domestic champagne upon arrival (when the hotel is notified in advance). Service throughout this beautiful property is gracious and refined.

Fracc. Lagunamar, SM 7, Mza. 75, Locs. 15 and 16, 77400 Isla Mujeres, Q. Roo. © 998/877-0700. Fax 998/877-0100. www.villarolandi.com. 28 units. High season $380–$450 (£209–£248) double; low season $290–$350 (£160–£193) double. Rates include round-trip transportation from Playa Linda in Cancún aboard private catamaran yacht, continental breakfast, and a la carte lunch or dinner in the on-site restaurant. AE, MC, V. Children younger than 13 not accepted. **Amenities:** Restaurant (see "Where to Dine," below); infinity pool w/waterfall; small fitness room and open-air massage area; concierge; tour desk; room service. In room: TV, Wi-Fi, minibar, hair dryer, iron, safe.

EXPENSIVE
Hotel Na Balam ★★ (Finds)
Na Balam is known as a haven for yoga students and those interested in an introspective vacation. This popular, two-story hotel near the end of Playa Norte has comfortable rooms on a quiet, ideally located portion of the beach. Rooms are in three sections; some face the beach, and others are across the street in a garden setting with a swimming pool. All rooms have a terrace or balcony with hammocks. Each spacious suite contains a king-size or two double beds, a seating area, and folk-art decorations. Master suites have additional amenities, including small pools with hydromassage situated under coconut trees—ask if these are available for the best of Na Balam. Though other rooms are newer, the older section is well

kept, with a bottom-floor patio facing the peaceful, palm-filled, sandy inner yard and Playa Norte. Yoga classes (free for guests; $15/£8.25 per class for nonguests) start at 9am Monday through Friday. The restaurant, **Zazil Ha,** is one of the island's most popular (see "Where to Dine," below). A beachside bar serves a selection of natural juices and is one of the most popular spots for sunset watching.

Zazil Ha 118, 77400 Isla Mujeres, Q. Roo. © 998/877-0279. Fax 998/877-0446. www.nabalam.com. 33 units. High season $240–$450 (£132–£248) suite; low season $180–$388 (£99–£213) suite. Ask about weekly and monthly rates. AE, MC, V. **Amenities:** 2 restaurants; 2 bars; outdoor swimming pool; yoga classes; spa; mopeds, golf carts, and bikes for rent; game room w/TV; diving and snorkeling trips available; salon; in-room massage; babysitting; laundry service; Wi-Fi. *In room:* A/C, fan.

Secreto ★★ *(Finds)* This boutique hotel resembles a chic Mediterranean villa and is one of the best B&B values in the Caribbean. It offers nine suites that overlook an infinity-edge pool and the open sea beyond. Located on the northern end of the island, Secreto lies within walking distance of town, yet feels removed enough to make for an idyllic retreat. Tropical gardens surround the pool area, and an outdoor living area offers comfy couches and places to dine. Guest rooms are characterized by contemporary designs featuring clean, white spaces and original artwork. Each features a veranda with private cabaña ideal for ocean-gazing beyond Halfmoon Beach. Three suites include king-size beds draped in mosquito netting, while the remaining six have two double beds; all rooms are nonsmoking. Transportation from Cancún airport can be arranged on request, for an additional $50 (£28) per van (not per person). Secreto is distinguished by its stunning and secluded location and gracious service.

Sección Rocas, Lote 1, 77400 Isla Mujeres, Q. Roo. © 998/877-1039. Fax 998/877-1048. www.hotelsecreto.com. 9 units. $225–$250 (£124–£138) double. Extra person $25 (£14). 1 child younger than 5 stays free in parent's room. Rates include continental breakfast. AE, MC, V. **Amenities:** Outdoor pool; private cove beach; tours, diving, and snorkeling available; dinner delivery from Rolandi's restaurant available. *In room:* A/C, TV, fridge, safe, CD player, bathrobes.

MODERATE

Hotel Cabañas María del Mar ★ A good choice for simple beach accommodations, the Cabañas María del Mar is on the popular Playa Norte. The older two-story section behind the reception area and beyond the garden offers nicely outfitted rooms facing the beach. All have two single or double beds, refrigerators, and oceanview balconies strung with hammocks. Eleven single-story cabañas closer to the reception area are decorated in a rustic Mexican style. The third section, **El Castillo,** is located across the street, over and beside Buho's restaurant. It contains all "deluxe" rooms, but some are larger than others; the five rooms on the ground floor have large patios. Upstairs rooms have small balconies. Most have ocean views and predominantly white decor. The lush central courtyard contains a small pool and enchanting lighting at night.

Av. Arq. Carlos Lazo 1 (on Playa Norte, one-half block from the Hotel Na Balam), 77400 Isla Mujeres, Q. Roo. © 800/ 223-5695 in the U.S., or 998/877-0179. Fax 998/877-0213. www.cabanasdelmar.com. 73 units. High season $121–$133 (£67–£73) double; low season $75–$99 (£41–£54) double. MC, V. **Amenities:** Outdoor pool; bus for tours and boat for rent; golf cart and *moto* rentals. *In room:* A/C, fridge.

INEXPENSIVE

Hotel Belmar ★★ Situated in the center of Isla's small-town activity, this charming hotel sits above Pizza Rolandi (be sure to consider the restaurant noise) and is run by the same people. Each of the simple but stylish tile-accented rooms comes with two twin or double beds. Prices are a bit high considering the lack of views, but the rooms are appealing. This is one of the few island hotels that offer televisions (with U.S.

channels) in rooms. It has one large colonial-decorated suite with a sitting area, large patio, and whirlpool. Note that most rooms are accessed by a series of stairs.

Av. Hidalgo 110 (between Madero and Abasolo, 3½ blocks from the passenger-ferry pier), 77400 Isla Mujeres, Q. Roo. ✆ 998/877-0430. Fax 998/877-0429. www.rolandi.com. 11 units. High season $56–$95 (£31–£52) double; low season $35–$95 (£19–£52) double. AE, MC, V. **Amenities:** Restaurant/bar (see "Where to Dine," below); room service; laundry service. *In room:* A/C, TV, fan.

Hotel D'Gomar (Value)   This hotel is known for comfort at reasonable prices. You can hardly beat the value for basic accommodations, which are regularly updated. Rooms have two double beds and a wall of windows offering great breezes and views. The higher prices are for air-conditioning, which is hardly needed with the breezes and ceiling fans. The only drawback is that there are four stories and no elevator. But it's conveniently located cater-cornered (look right) from the ferry pier, with exceptional rooftop views. The name of the hotel is the most visible sign on the "skyline."

Rueda Medina 150, 77400 Isla Mujeres, Q. Roo. ✆/fax **998/877-0541.** www.hoteldgomar.com. 16 units. High season $55–$65 (£30–£36) double; low season $50–$60 (£28–£33) double. MC, V. *In room:* A/C (in some), fan.

Hotel Francis Arlene ⚘   The Magaña family operates this neat little two-story inn built around a small, shady courtyard. This hotel is very popular with families and seniors, and it welcomes many repeat guests. You'll notice the tidy cream-and-white facade from the street. Some rooms have ocean views, and all are remodeled or updated each year. They are comfortable, with tile floors, tiled bathrooms, and a very homey feel. Each downstairs room has a coffeemaker, refrigerator, and stove; each upstairs room comes with a refrigerator and toaster. Some have either a balcony or a patio. Higher prices are for the 14 rooms with air-conditioning; other units have fans. Rates are substantially better if quoted in pesos; in dollars they are 15% to 20% higher.

Guerrero 7 (5½ blocks inland from the ferry pier, between Abasolo and Matamoros), 77400 Isla Mujeres, Q. Roo. ✆/fax **998/877-0310** or -0861. www.francisarlene.com. 26 units. High season $55–$85 (£30–£47) double; low season $45–$65 (£25–£36) double. MC, V. **Amenities:** Safe; currency exchange. *In room:* A/C (in some), kitchenettes (in some), fridge, no phone.

Hotel Posada del Mar (Kids)   Simply furnished, quiet, and comfortable, this long-established hotel faces the water and a wide beach 3 blocks north of the ferry pier. This is probably the best choice in Isla for families. For the spaciousness of the rooms (half of which have ocean views) and the location, it's also among the island's best values. A wide, appealing but seldom-used stretch of Playa Norte lies across the street, where watersports equipment is available for rent. A great, casual *palapa*-style bar and a lovely pool are on the back lawn along with hammocks, and the restaurant **Pinguinos** (see "Where to Dine," below) is by the sidewalk at the front of the property, and also provides room service to hotel guests.

Av. Rueda Medina 15 A, 77400 Isla Mujeres, Q. Roo. ✆ **800/544-3005** in the U.S., or 998/877-0044. Fax 998/877-0266. www.posadadelmar.com. 52 units. High season $100 (£55) double; low season $60 (£33) double. Children younger than 12 stay free in parent's room. AE, MC, V. **Amenities:** Restaurant/bar; outdoor pool. *In room:* A/C, TV, fan.

WHERE TO DINE

At the **Municipal Market,** next to the telegraph office and post office on Avenida Guerrero, obliging, hardworking women operate several little food stands. At the **Panadería La Reyna** (no phone), at Madero and Juárez, you can pick up inexpensive sweet bread, muffins, cookies, and yogurt. It's open Monday through Saturday from 7am to 9:30pm.

Cocina económica (literally, "economical cuisine") restaurants usually aim at the local population. These are great places to find good food at rock-bottom prices, and especially so on Isla Mujeres, where you'll find several, most of which feature delicious regional specialties. But be aware that the hygiene is not what you'll find at more established restaurants, so you're dining at your own risk.

EXPENSIVE

Casa Rolandi ⭐ SWISS/ITALIAN   The gourmet Casa Rolandi restaurant and bar has become Isla's favored fine-dining experience. It boasts a wonderful view of the Caribbean and the most sophisticated menu in the area. There's a colorful main dining area as well as a more casual, open-air terrace. The food is the most notable on the island. Along with fresh fish, seafood, and northern Italian specialties, the famed wood-burning-oven pizzas are delicious. Careful—the wood-oven-baked bread, which arrives looking like a puffer fish—is so divine that you're likely to fill up on it. This is a great place to enjoy the sunset, and it offers a selection of fine international wines and more than 80 premium tequilas. Service is personalized and attentive.

On the pier of Villa Rolandi, Lagunamar SM 7. ⓒ **998/877-0700.** Main courses $8–$35 (£4.40–£19). AE, MC, V. Daily noon–11pm.

MODERATE

Angelo ⭐ ITALIAN   An authentic Italian restaurant in the pedestrian-friendly town center, Angelo offers an enticing selection of antipasti, pastas, grilled seafood, and wood oven-baked pizzas. The Sardinian-born owner instills his menu with the flavors of his homeland, including a rich tomato sauce. Consider starting with a bowl of seafood soup or black mussels *au gratin* and continuing with the grilled shrimp kabobs or seafood pasta in an olive oil and white-wine sauce. The open-air restaurant includes an inviting sidewalk terrace and lies across the street from a casual Cuban restaurant also owned by Angelo.

Av. Hidalgo 14 (between Lopez Mateos and Matamoros). ⓒ **998/877-1273.** Main courses $6.50–$12 (£3.60–£6.60). MC, V. Daily 4pm–midnight.

Pinguinos MEXICAN/SEAFOOD   The best seats on the waterfront stretch across the deck of this open-air restaurant and bar. Come late evening, islanders and tourists arrive to dance and party. This is the place to feast on sublimely fresh lobster—you'll get a large, beautifully presented lobster tail with a choice of butter, garlic, and secret sauces. The grilled seafood platter, seafood casserole, and fajitas are all spectacular. Breakfasts include fresh fruit, yogurt, and granola, or sizable platters of eggs, served with homemade wheat bread.

In front of the Hotel Posada del Mar (3 blocks west of the ferry pier), Av. Rueda Medina 15. ⓒ **998/877-0044,** ext. 157. Breakfast $1.50–$7.50 (85p–£4.15); main courses $4.50–$17 (£2.50–£9.35). AE, MC, V. Daily 7am–11pm; bar closes at midnight.

Pizza Rolandi ⭐⭐ ITALIAN/SEAFOOD   You're bound to dine at least once at Rolandi's, which is practically an Isla institution. The plate-size pizzas and calzones feature exotic ingredients—including lobster, black mushrooms, pineapple, and Roquefort cheese—as well as more traditional tomatoes, olives, basil, and salami. A wood-burning oven provides the signature flavor of the pizzas, as well as baked chicken, roast beef, and mixed seafood casserole with lobster. The extensive menu also offers a selection of salads and light appetizers, as well as an ample array of flavorful homemade pasta dishes, steaks, fish, and scrumptious desserts. The setting is the open courtyard of the Hotel Belmar, with a porch overlooking the action on Avenida Hidalgo.

Av. Hidalgo 10 (3½ blocks inland from the pier, between Madero and Abasolo). ✆ **998/877-0430**, ext. 18. Main courses $7–$16 (£3.85–£8.80). AE, MC, V. Daily 11am–11:15pm.

Zazil Ha ★★ CARIBBEAN/INTERNATIONAL Here you can enjoy some of the island's best food while sitting at tables on the sand among palms and gardens. Come night, candlelit tables sparkle underneath the open-air palapa. Specialties include Mayan chicken stuffed with corn mushroom and goat cheese, black pasta with squid rings and pesto sauce, and fish of the day with *achiote* sauce draped in a banana leaf. A selection of fresh juices complements the vegetarian options, and there's even a special menu for those participating in yoga retreats. The delicious breads are baked in house. Between the set meal times, you can order all sorts of enticing food, such as tacos and sandwiches, ceviche, terrific nachos, and vegetable and fruit drinks.

At the Hotel Na Balam (at the end of Playa Norte, almost at the end of Calle Zazil Ha). ✆ **998/877-0279.** Fax 998/877-0446. Breakfast $3.50–$9.50 (£1.95–£5.25); main courses $8.50–$22 (£4.70–£12). AE, MC, V. Daily 7:30am–10:30pm.

INEXPENSIVE

Café Cito ★ CREPES/ICE CREAM/COFFEE/FRUIT DRINKS Brisa and Luis Rivera own this adorable, Caribbean-blue corner restaurant where you can begin the day with flavorful coffee and a croissant and cream cheese (this is the only place in town where you can have breakfast until 2pm), or end it with a hot-fudge sundae. Terrific crepes come with yogurt, ice cream, fresh fruit, or *dulce de leche* (similar to caramel, but made with goat's milk) sauce, as well as ham and cheese. The two-page ice cream menu satisfies almost any craving, even one for waffles with ice cream and fruit. The three-course fixed-price dinner includes soup, a main course (such as fish or curried shrimp with rice and salad), and dessert.

Calle Matamoros 42, at Juárez (4 blocks from the pier). ✆ **998/877-1470.** Crepes $3–$6 (£1.65–£3.30); breakfast $3.50–$5.50 (£1.95–£3); sandwiches $3.50–$4.50 (£1.95–£2.50). No credit cards. Daily 8am–2pm; high season Fri–Wed 5:30pm–10:30 or 11:30pm.

ISLA MUJERES AFTER DARK

Those in a party mood by day's end may want to start out at the beach bar of the **Na Balam** hotel on Playa Norte, which usually hosts a crowd until around midnight. On Saturday and Sunday, live music plays between 4 and 7pm. **Jax Bar & Grill** on Avenida Ruedo Medina, close to Hotel Posada del Mar, is a Texas-style sports bar offering live music nightly. **Las Palapas Chimbo's** restaurant on the beach becomes a jammin' dance joint with a live band from 9pm until whenever. Farther along the same stretch of beach, **Buho's,** the restaurant/beach bar of the Cabañas María del Mar, has its moments as a popular, low-key hangout, complete with swinging seats over the sand! **Pinguinos** in the Hotel Posada del Mar offers a convivial late-night hangout, where a band plays nightly during high season from 9pm to midnight. If you want to sample one of nearly 100 tequila brands on a relaxing sidewalk terrace, stop by **La Adelita,** located at Av. Hidalgo 12 and open nightly from 5:30pm to 2:30am. Near Matamoros and Hidalgo, **KoKo Nuts** caters to a younger crowd, with international music for late-night dancing. **Om Bar and Chill Lounge,** on Calle Matamoros, serves cocktails in an atmosphere that includes jazzy Latino music, open from 6pm to 2am. For a late night dance club, **Club Nitrox,** on Avenida Guererro, is open Wednesday to Sunday from 9pm to 3am. In general, the crowds hitting these bars are in their 20s.

2 Cozumel ★ ★ ★

70km (43 miles) S of Cancún; 19km (12 miles) SE of Playa del Carmen

Cozumel has ranked for years among the top five dive destinations in the world. Tall reefs line the southwest coast, creating towering walls that offer divers a fairy-tale landscape to explore. For nondivers, it has the beautiful water of the Caribbean with all the accompanying watersports and seaside activities. The island gets a lot more visitors from North America than Europe for reasons that probably have to do with the limited flights. It is in many ways more cozy and mellow than the mainland—no big highways, no big construction projects. It's dependable. And one of my favorite things about this island is that the water on the protected side (western shore) is as calm as an aquarium, unless a front is blowing through. The island is 45km (28 miles) long and 18km (11 miles) wide, and lies 19km (12 miles) from the mainland. Most of the terrain is flat and clothed in a low tropical forest.

The only town on the island is San Miguel, which, despite the growth of the last 20 years, can't be called anything more than a small town. It's not a stunningly beautiful town, but it and its inhabitants are agreeable—life moves along at a slow pace, and every Sunday evening, residents congregate around the plaza to enjoy live music and see their friends. Staying in town can be fun and convenient. You get a choice of a number of restaurants and nightspots.

Because Cozumel enjoys such popularity with the cruise ships, the waterfront section of town holds wall-to-wall jewelry stores, duty-free, and souvenir shops. When Hurricane Wilma hit the island in October of 2005, this section, including the attractive shoreline boulevard Avenida Rafael Melgar, was severely damaged. But so extreme was the effort of the town's merchants and the local and federal government that by early 2006 all signs of the destruction were gone, and a casual visitor would never have guessed how serious the devastation from the hurricane was. This and the area around the town's main square are about as far as most cruise-ship passengers venture into town.

Should you come down with a case of island fever, **Playa del Carmen** and the mainland are a 40-minute ferry ride away. Some travel agencies on the island can set you up with a tour of the major ruins on the mainland, such as **Tulum** or **Chichén Itzá**, or a visit to a nature park such as **Xel-Ha** or **Xcaret** (see "Trips to the Mainland," later in this chapter).

The island has its own ruins, but they cannot compare with the major sites of the mainland. During pre-Hispanic times, Maya women would cross over to the island to make offerings to the goddess of fertility, Ixchel. More than 40 sites containing shrines remain around the island, and archaeologists still uncover the small dolls that were customarily part of those offerings.

ESSENTIALS
GETTING THERE & DEPARTING

BY PLANE   There are fewer international commercial flights in and out of Cozumel than charter flights. You might inquire about buying a ticket on one of these charters. Some packagers, such as **Funjet** (www.funjet.com), will sell you just a ticket. But look into packages, too. Several of the island's independent hotels work with packagers. Flight availability changes between high season and low season. **Continental** (© 800/231-0856 in the U.S., or 987/872-0596) flies to and from Houston and Newark. **US Airways** (© 800/428-4322 in the U.S., or 01-800/007-8800 in Mexico) flies to and from Charlotte. **American Airlines** (© 800/433-7300 in the U.S., or 01-800/904-

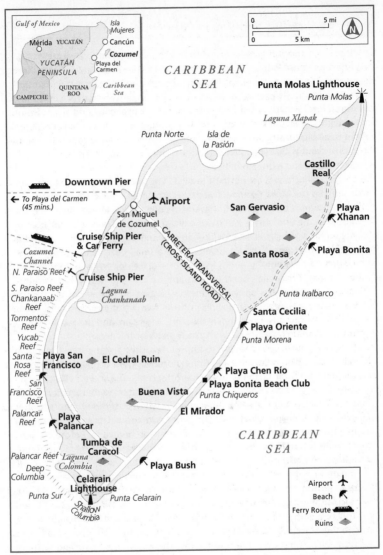

Cozumel

- Gulf of Mexico
- Isla Mujeres
- Mérida — YUCATÁN
- Cancún
- *Cozumel*
- Playa del Carmen
- YUCATÁN PENINSULA
- CAMPECHE
- QUINTANA ROO
- *Caribbean Sea*

CARIBBEAN SEA

Punta Molas Lighthouse
Punta Molas

Laguna Xlapak

Punta Norte
Isla de la Pasión

Castillo Real

Downtown Pier

← To Playa del Carmen (45 mins.)

✈ Airport

San Miguel de Cozumel

San Gervasio

Playa Xhanan

Cruise Ship Pier & Car Ferry

Cozumel Channel

N. Paraíso Reef

Cruise Ship Pier

CARRETERA TRANSVERSAL (CROSS ISLAND ROAD)

Santa Rosa

Playa Bonita

S. Paraíso Reef
Chankanaab Reef

Laguna Chankanaab

Punta Ixalbarco

Tormentos Reef
Yucab Reef

Santa Cecilia

Playa Oriente

Punta Morena

Santa Rosa Reef
Playa San Francisco

El Cedral Ruin

Playa Chen Río

San Francisco Reef

Buena Vista

Playa Bonita Beach Club
Punta Chiqueros

Palancar Reef
Playa Palancar

El Mirador

CARIBBEAN SEA

Tumba de Caracol

Palancar Reef
Laguna Colombia
Deep Columbia

Playa Bush

Celarain Lighthouse

Punta Sur
Shallow Columbia
Punta Celarain

Airport ✈
Beach ✗
Ferry Route ⛴
Ruins ≋

6000 in Mexico) offers nonstop service to/from Dallas. **Mexicana** (© **800/531-7921** in the U.S. or 987/872-0157) and **AeroMéxico** (© **800/237-6639** in the U.S., or 01-800/021-4000 in Mexico) fly from Mexico City.

BY FERRY   Passenger ferries run to and from Playa del Carmen. **Barcos México** (© **987/872-1508** or -1588) and **Ultramar** (© **987/869-2775**) offer departures almost every hour in the morning and about every 2 hours in the afternoon. The schedules change according to seasons. The trip takes 30 to 45 minutes, depending on conditions, and costs $11 (£6.05) one-way. The boats are air-conditioned. In Playa del

An All-Inclusive Vacation in Cozumel

Booking a room at an all-inclusive should be done through a vacation packager. Booking lodging directly through the hotel usually doesn't make sense, even with frequent-flier mileage to burn, because the discounts offered by most packagers are so deep. I include websites for you to find out more info about the properties, but don't expect to find clear info on rates. The game of setting rates with these hotels is complicated and always in flux. All these beach properties made significant upgrades to the rooms when they made repairs after the hurricane, so expect such things as new mattresses and extra amenities.

Two all-inclusives are north of town: **El Cozumeleño** (www.elcozumeleno.com) and the **Meliá Cozumel** (www.meliacozumel.com). Both occupy multistory modern buildings. Both have attractive rooms. El Cozumeleño is the larger of the two resorts and has the nicest hotel pool on the island. It's best suited for active types. The Meliá is quieter and offers golf discounts for the nearby golf course. The Cozumeleño has a small beach that was lost with Wilma, but the hotel brought in sand to replace what was lost and is back to normal. The Meliá's beach is long and narrow and pretty, but occasionally seaweed washes up, which doesn't happen on the rest of the island's coast. The advantages of staying in these two are the proximity to town, with its restaurants, clubs, movie theaters, and so on, and the fact that most rooms at these hotels come with lovely views of the ocean.

Of the all-inclusives to the south, my favorites are the two **Occidental** properties (**Allegro Cozumel** and **Grand Cozumel**; www.occidentalhotels.com) and the **Iberostar Cozumel** (www.iberostar.com). These are "village" style resorts with two- and three-story buildings, often with thatched roofs, spread over a large area at the center of which is the pool and activities area. The Allegro is older than the other two and has the plainest rooms, but these were completely remodeled after the hurricane. Before the hurricane this hotel had the broadest beach, and all three of these properties gained beach from Wilma. The Grand Cozumel, next door to the Allegro, is the newest property. Its rooms are larger and more attractive than the Allegro, and staying here gives you access to both Occidental resorts. Like the Occidental chain, Iberostar has several properties in the Mexican Caribbean. This one is the smallest. I like its food and service and the beauty of the grounds. The rooms are attractive and well maintained. The added sand from Wilma improved the resort a lot. The advantage to staying in these places is that you're close to a lot of dive sites; the disadvantage is that you're somewhat isolated from town, and you don't have the lovely views that the taller buildings in the north give you.

Of the other all-inclusives, I've heard several complaints about the service at the **Reef Club** (unless you stay in the VIP section), and I think the rooms are too closely set together. The **Costa Club** is on the inland side of the road in a crowded section of the island.

Carmen, the ferry dock is 1½ blocks from the main square. In Cozumel, the ferries use Muelle Fiscal, the town pier, a block from the main square. Luggage storage at the Cozumel dock costs $2 (£1.10) per day.

The car ferry that used to operate from Puerto Morelos now uses the Calica pier just south of Playa del Carmen. The fare for a standard car is $80 (£44). **Marítima Chancanaab** (© 987/872-7671 or -7504) has four departures daily from Calica at 4am, 8am, 1:30pm, and 6pm. Arrive 1 hour before departure. The schedule is subject to change, so double-check it. The ferry docks in Cozumel at the **Muelle Internacional** (the **International Pier,** which is south of town near La Ceiba Hotel).

BY BUS   If you plan to travel on the mainland by bus, there is a ticket office for **ADO buses** called **Ticket Bus** where you can purchase tickets in advance. One is located on the municipal pier and is open while the ferries are running. Another is on Calle 2 Norte and Avenida 10 (© **987/872-1706**). Hours are from 8am to 9pm daily.

ORIENTATION

ARRIVING   Cozumel's **airport** is inland from downtown. **Transportes Terrestres** provides hotel transportation in air-conditioned Suburbans. Buy your ticket as you exit the terminal. To hotels downtown, the fare is $5 (£2.75) per person; to hotels along the north shore, $7 (£3.85), and to hotels along the south shore, $8 to $15 (£4.40–£8.25). Passenger ferries arrive at the Muelle Fiscal, the municipal pier, by the town's main square. Cruise ships dock at the **Punta Langosta** pier, several blocks south of the Muelle Fiscal, and at the **International Pier,** which is at Km 4 of the southern coastal road. A third cruise ship pier, the **Puerta Maya,** suffered the most damage from Hurricane Wilma and will be nonoperational for at least another year. The International Pier was also damaged, but one side was working when I was last on the island. On days when several cruise ships arrive, some of the boats will anchor offshore, and tender boats will ferry passengers and crew to land. It seems to be working smoothly—I heard no complaints from passengers.

VISITOR INFORMATION   The **Municipal Tourism Office** (©/fax **987/869-0212**) has an information booth at the municipal ferry pier, on the main square. It's open 8am to 8pm Monday to Saturday. There are other information booths at each of the ferry piers and at the airport.

CITY LAYOUT   San Miguel's main waterfront street is **Avenida Rafael Melgar.** Running parallel to Rafael Melgar are other *avenidas* numbered in multiples of five—5, 10, 15. **Avenida Juárez** runs perpendicular to these, heading inland from the ferry dock. Avenida Juárez divides the town into northern and southern halves. The *calles* (streets) that parallel Juárez to the north have even numbers. The ones to the south have odd numbers, with the exception of Calle Rosado Salas, which runs between calles 1 and 3.

ISLAND LAYOUT   One road runs along the western coast of the island, which faces the Yucatán mainland. It has different names. North of town it's **Santa Pilar** or **San Juan;** in the city it is **Avenida Rafael Melgar;** south of town it's **Costera Sur.**

Be Streetwise

North-south streets—the *avenidas*—have the right of way, and traffic doesn't slow down or stop.

Hotels stretch along this road north and south of town. The road runs to the southern tip of the island (Punta Sur), passing **Chankanaab National Park. Avenida Juárez** (and its extension, the **Carretera Transversal**) runs east from the town across the island. It passes the airport and the turnoff to the ruins of San Gervasio before reaching the undeveloped ocean side of the island. It then turns south and follows the coast to the southern tip of the island, where it meets the Costera Sur.

GETTING AROUND   You can walk to most destinations in town. Getting to outlying hotels and beaches requires a taxi, rental car, or moped.

Car rentals are roughly the same price as on the mainland, depending on demand. **Avis** (© **987/872-0099**) and **Executive** (© **987/872-1308**) have counters in the airport. Other major rental companies have offices in town. Rentals are easy to arrange through your hotel or at any of the many local rental offices.

Moped rentals are readily available and cost $20 to $40 (£11–£22) for 24 hours, depending upon the season. If you rent a moped, be careful. Riding a moped made a lot more sense when Cozumel had less traffic; now it involves a certain amount of risk as taxi drivers and other motorists have become more numerous and pushier. Moped accidents easily rank as the greatest cause of injury in Cozumel. Before renting one, inspect it carefully to see that all the gizmos—horn, light, starter, seat, mirror—are in good shape. I've been offered mopeds with unbalanced wheels, which made them unsteady at higher speeds, but the renter quickly exchanged them upon my request. You are required to stay on paved roads. It's illegal to ride a moped without a helmet outside of town (subject to a $25/£14 fine).

Cozumel has lots of **taxis** and a strong drivers' union. Fares have been standardized—there's no bargaining. Here are a few sample fares for two people (there is an additional charge for extra passengers to most destinations): island tour, $60 (£33); town to southern hotel zone, $6 to $18 (£3.30–£9.90); town to northern hotels, $5 to $7 (£2.75–£3.85); town to Chankanaab, $9 (£4.95) for up to four people; in and around town, $3 to $4 (£1.65–£2.20).

FAST FACTS: Cozumel

Area Code   The telephone area code is **987**.

Climate   From October to December there can be strong winds all over the Yucatán, as well as some rain. June through October is the rainy season.

Clinics   **Médica San Miguel** (© **987/872-0103**) works for most things and includes intensive-care facilities. It's on Calle 6 Norte between Av. 5 and 10. **Centro Médico Cozumel** (© **987/872-3545**) is an alternative. It's at the intersection of Calle 1 Sur and Av. 50.

Currency Exchange   The island has several banks and *casas de cambio,* as well as ATMs. Most places accept dollars, but you usually get a better deal paying in pesos.

Diving   Bring proof of your diver's certification and your log. Underwater currents can be strong, and many of the reef drops are quite steep, so dive operators want to make sure divers are experienced.

Emergencies   To report an emergency, dial © **065**, which is similar to 911 emergency service in the United States.

Internet Access Several cybercafes are in and about the main square. If you go just a bit off Avenida Rafael Melgar and the main square, prices drop. **Modu-tel,** Av. Juárez 15 (at Av. 10), offers good rates. Hours are Monday through Saturday from 10am to 8pm.

Post Office The *correo* is on Avenida Rafael Melgar at Calle 7 Sur (✆ **987/872-0106**), at the southern edge of town. It's open Monday through Friday from 9am to 3pm, Saturday from 9am to noon.

Recompression Chamber There are four *cámaras de recompresión.* The best are **Buceo Médico Mexicano,** staffed 24 hours, at Calle 5 Sur 21-B, between Avenida Rafael Melgar and Avenida 5 Sur (✆ **987/872-2387** or -1430); and the **Hyperbaric Center of Cozumel** (✆ **987/872-3070**) at Calle 6 Norte, between avenidas 5 and 10.

Seasons High season is August and from Christmas to Easter.

EXPLORING THE ISLAND

For **diving** and **snorkeling,** there are plenty of dive shops to choose from, including those recommended below. For **island tours, ruins tours** on and off the island, **evening cruises,** and other activities, go to a travel agency. I recommend **InterMar Cozumel Viajes,** Calle 2 Norte 101-B, between avenidas 5 and 10 (✆ **987/872-1535** or -2022; fax 987/872-0895; cozumel@travel2mexico.com). Office hours are Monday through Saturday from 8am to 8pm, Sunday from 9am to 5pm.

WATERSPORTS

SCUBA DIVING   Cozumel is the number-one dive destination in the Western Hemisphere. Don't forget your dive card and dive log. Dive shops will rent you scuba gear, but won't take you out on a boat until you show some documentation. If you have a medical condition, bring a letter signed by a doctor stating that you've been cleared to dive. A two-tank morning dive costs around $60 (£33); some shops offer an additional afternoon one-tank dive for $15 (£8.25) for those who took the morning dives. A lot of divers save some money by buying a dive package with a hotel. These usually include two dives a day.

Diving in Cozumel is drift diving, which can be a little disconcerting for novices. The current that sweeps along Cozumel's reefs, pulling nutrients into them and making them as large as they are, also dictates how you dive here. The problem is that it pulls at different speeds at different depths and in different places. When it's pulling strong, it can quickly scatter a dive group. The role of the dive master becomes more important, especially with choosing the dive location. Cozumel has a lot of dive locations. To mention but a few: the famous **Palancar Reef,** with its caves and canyons, plentiful fish, and a wide variety of sea coral; the monstrous **Santa Rosa Wall,** famous for its depth, sea life, coral, and sponges; the **San Francisco Reef,** which has a shallower drop-off wall and fascinating sea life; and the **Yucab Reef,** with its beautiful coral.

Moments Carnaval

Carnaval (similar to Mardi Gras) is Cozumel's most colorful fiesta. It begins the Thursday before Ash Wednesday, with daytime street dancing and nighttime parades on Thursday, Saturday, and Monday (the best).

I've seen a number of news reports about reef damage caused by hurricane Wilma. Almost all of it occurred in the shallower parts, above 15m (50 ft.). In deeper areas, the currents produced by Wilma actually improved matters by clearing sand away from parts of the reef, and in some cases exposing new caverns. Wildlife is plentiful. In the shallow parts it will take a year or two for things such as fan coral to grow back. The greatest impact here is to the snorkeling.

Finding a dive shop in town is even easier than finding a jewelry store. Cozumel has more than 50 dive operators. I know and can recommend Bill Horn's **Aqua Safari,** which has a location on Avenida Rafael Melgar at Calle 5 (℗ 987/872-0101; fax 987/872-0661; www.aquasafari.com). I also know Roberto Castillo at **Liquid Blue Divers** (℗ **987/869-2812;** www.liquidbluedivers.com), on Avenida 5 between Rosado Salas and Calle 3 Sur. He does a good tour, has a fast boat, and keeps the number of divers to 12 or fewer. His wife, Michelle, handles the Internet inquiries and reservations and is quick to respond to questions.

A popular activity in the Yucatán is *cenote* diving. The peninsula's underground *cenotes* (seh-*noh*-tehs)—sinkholes or wellsprings—lead to a vast system of underground caverns. The gently flowing water is so clear that divers seem to float on air through caves complete with stalactites and stalagmites. If you want to try this but didn't plan a trip to the mainland, contact **Yucatech Expeditions,** Avenida 5, on the corner of Calle 3 Sur (℗/fax **987/872-5659;** www.yucatech.net), which offers a trip five times a week. *Cenotes* are 30 to 45 minutes from Playa del Carmen, and a dive in each *cenote* lasts around 45 minutes. Dives are within the daylight zone, about 40m (131 ft.) into the caverns, and no more than 18m (59 ft.) deep. Company owner Germán Yañez Mendoza inspects diving credentials carefully, and divers must meet his list of requirements before cave diving is permitted. For information and prices, call or drop by the office.

SNORKELING   Anyone who can swim can snorkel. When contracting for a snorkel tour, stay away from the companies that cater to the cruise ships. Those tours are crowded and not very fun. For a good snorkeling tour, contact **Victor Casanova** (℗ **987/872-1028;** wildcatcozumel@hotmail.com). He speaks English, owns a couple of boats, and does a good 5-hour tour. He takes his time and doesn't rush through the trip. You can also try the **Kuzamil Snorkeling Center,** 50 Av. bis 565 Int. 1, between 5 Sur and Hidalgo, Colonia Adolfo López Mateos (℗ **987/872-4637** or -0539). Even though you won't see a lot of the more delicate structures, such as fan coral, you will still see plenty of sea creatures and enjoy the clear, calm water of Cozumel's protected west side.

BOAT TRIPS   Travel agencies and hotels can arrange boat trips, a popular pastime on Cozumel. There are evening cruises, cocktail cruises, glass-bottom boat cruises, and other options. One novel boat ride is offered by **Atlantis Submarines** (℗ **987/872-5671**). The sub can hold 48 people. It operates almost 3km (2 miles) south of town in front of the Casa del Mar hotel and costs $81 (£45) per adult, $47 (£26) for kids ages 4 to 12. This is a superior experience to the **Sub See Explorer** offered by **Aqua World,** which is really just a glorified glass-bottom boat.

FISHING   The best months for fishing are March through June, when the catch includes blue and white marlin, sailfish, tarpon, and swordfish. The least expensive option would be to contact a boat owner directly. Try Victor Casanova, listed above under "Snorkeling." Or try an agency such as **Aquarius Travel Fishing,** Calle 3 Sur 2 between Avenida Rafael Melgar and Avenida 5 (℗ **987/872-1092;** gabdiaz@yahoo.com).

San Miguel de Cozumel

DINING ◆
Capicúa **2**
Cocos Cozumel **8**
Comida Casera Toñita **11**
El Amigo Mario **16**
French Quarter **12**
Guido's **4**
La Choza **13**
La Cocay **3**
Le Chef **14**
Prima **10**
Restaurant del Museo **5**
Zermatt **7**

ACCOMMODATIONS ■
Hacienda de San Miguel **1**
La Casona Real **17**
Suites Colonial **9**
Suites Vima **6**
Vista del Mar **15**

Information ⓘ
Pedestrian Only ////
Post Office ✉

To Airport ➔

Bulevard Aeropuerto Internacional

Calle 14 Norte   Calle 14 Norte
Calle 12 Norte
Calle 10 Norte
Calle 8 Norte
Calle 6 Norte
Calle 4 Norte
Calle 2 Norte

↑ To Hotels North

5 Avenida Norte
10 Avenida Norte
15 Avenida Norte
20 Avenida Norte
25 Avenida Norte
30 Avenida Norte
35 Avenida Norte
40 Avenida Norte

Avenida Rafael Melgar

CARIBBEAN SEA

■ **Museo de Cozumel**

← To Playa del Carmen

Plaza ⓘ

Avenida Benito Juárez   Carretera Transversal

Calle 1 Sur

30 Avenida Sur
Calle S/N
35 Avenida Sur
40 Avenida Sur

Market
Calle Dr. Adolfo Rosado Salas

San Miguel de Cozumel

COZUMEL ISLAND

15 Avenida Sur
20 Avenida Sur
25 Avenida Sur

5 Av. Sur
10 Av. Sur

Calle 3 Sur
Calle 5 Sur
Calles Morelos

Recompression Chamber

✉ Calle 7 Sur

To Hotels South & Cruise/Car Pier ↓

Calle Hidalgo

0   1/8 mi
0   125 meters
N

CHANKANAAB NATIONAL PARK & PUNTA SUR ECOLOGICAL RESERVE

Chankanaab National Park ⚘ is the pride of many islanders. In Mayan, Chankanaab means "little sea," which refers to a beautiful land-locked pool connected to the sea through an underground tunnel—a sort of miniature ocean. There was some hurricane damage to this natural pool, but it was mostly surface wear. Snorkeling in this natural aquarium is not permitted, but the park has a lovely ocean beach for sunbathing and snorkeling. Arrive early to stake out a chair and *palapa* before the cruise-ship crowd arrives (9 to 10am). Likewise, the snorkeling is best before noon. There are bathrooms, lockers, a gift shop, several snack huts, a restaurant, and a *palapa* for renting snorkeling gear.

You can also swim with dolphins. **Dolphin Discovery** (*©* 800/293-9698; www. dolphindiscovery.com) has several programs for experiencing these sea creatures. These are popular, so plan ahead—you should make reservations well in advance. The surest way is through the website—make sure to pick the Cozumel location, as there are a couple of others on this coast. There are three different programs for swimming with dolphins. The one of longest duration costs $125 (£69) and features close interaction with the beautiful swimmers. There are also swim and snorkel programs for $75 and $99 (£41–£54) that get you in the water with these creatures.

Surrounding the land-locked pool is a botanical garden that did suffer greatly from the hurricane and will take some time to come back. Admission to the park is expensive, costing $16 (£8.80) for adults, $8 (£4.40) for children 9 to 12. I think the authorities are trying to recoup some of the money spent restoring the park, and it is being marketed to the cruise ship crowd. The park is open daily from 8am to 5pm. It's south of town, just past the Fiesta Americana Hotel. Taxis run constantly between the park, the hotels, and town ($10/£5.50 from town for up to four people).

Punta Sur Ecological Reserve (admission $10/£5.50) is a large area that encompasses the southern tip of the island, including the Columbia Lagoon. The only practical way of going there is to rent a car or scooter; there is no taxi stand, and, usually, few people. This is an ecological reserve, not a park, so don't expect much infrastructure. The reserve has an information center, several observation towers, and a snack bar. The observation towers were destroyed in the hurricane and were still not reconstructed on my last visit. The information center was struck hard, too. And many of the trees on this side of the island came down, while others completely lost their leaves. These, I am told, will make a comeback, but before you go all the way out to the park and pay admission, ask around about the condition of the vegetation—it adds a good bit to a visit here. Punta Sur has some interesting snorkeling (bring your own gear), and lovely beaches that are kept as natural as possible. Regular hours are daily 9am to 5pm.

THE BEACHES

Along both the west and east sides of the island you'll see signs advertising beach clubs. A "beach club" in Cozumel can mean just a *palapa* hut that's open to the public and serves soft drinks, beer, and fried fish. It can also mean a recreational beach with the full gamut of offerings from banana boats to parasailing. They also usually have locker rooms, a pool, and food. The two biggest of these are **Mr. Sancho's** (*©* 987/879-0021; www.mrsanchos.com) and **Playa Mía** (*©* 987/872-9030; www.playamia. com). They get a lot of business from the cruise ships. Mr. Sancho's is free, while Playa Mía charges between $12 (£6.60) for simple admission to $42 (£23) for the full all-inclusive package. Quieter versions of beach clubs are **Playa San Francisco** (no phone), **Paradise Beach** (no phone, next to Playa San Francisco), and **Playa Palancar** (no phone). All of these beaches are south of Chankanaab Park and easily visible from the road. Several have swimming pools with beach furniture, a restaurant, and snorkel rental. Most of these beaches cost around $5 (£2.75).

Once you get to the end of the island, the beach clubs become simple places where you can eat and drink and lay out on the beach for free. **Paradise Cafe** is on the southern tip of the island across from Punta Sur nature park, and as you go up the eastern side of the island you pass **Playa Bonita, Chen Río,** and **Punta Morena** (not yet back in business on my last visit). Except on Sunday, when the locals head for the beaches, these places are practically deserted. Most of the east coast is unsafe for swimming because of the surf. The beaches tend to be small and occupy gaps in the rocky coast.

TOURS OF THE ISLAND

Travel agencies can arrange a variety of tours, including horseback, Jeep, and ATV tours. Taxi drivers charge $60 (£33) for a 4-hour tour of the island, which most people would consider only mildly amusing, depending on the driver's personality. The best horseback tours are offered at **Rancho Palmitas** (no phone) on the Costera Sur highway, across from the Occidental Cozumel resort. Unless you're staying in one of the resorts on the south end, the easiest way to arrange a tour is probably to talk to the owners of Cocos Cozumel restaurant (see the listing later in this chapter, making sure to note the limited hours). Rides can be from 1 to 2½ hours long and cost $20 to $30 (£11–£17).

OTHER ATTRACTIONS

MAYA RUINS   One of the most popular island excursions is to **San Gervasio** (100 B.C.–A.D. 1600). Follow the paved transversal road. You'll see the well-marked turnoff about halfway between town and the eastern coast. About 3km (2 miles) farther, pay the $5.50 (£3.05) fee to enter; still and video camera permits cost $5 (£2.75) each. A small tourist center at the entrance sells cold drinks and snacks. The ruins are open from 7am to 4pm.

When it comes to Cozumel's Maya ruins, getting there is most of the fun—do it for the mystique and for the trip, not for the size or scale of the ruins. The buildings, though preserved, are crudely made and would not be much of a tourist attraction if they were not the island's principal ruins. More significant than beautiful, this site was once an important ceremonial center where the Maya gathered, coming even from the mainland. The important deity was Ixchel, the goddess of weaving, women, childbirth, pilgrims, the moon, and medicine. Although you won't see any representations of Ixchel at San Gervasio today, Bruce Hunter, in his *Guide to Ancient Maya Ruins,* writes that priests hid behind a large pottery statue of her and became the voice of the goddess, speaking to pilgrims and answering their petitions. Ixchel was the wife of Itzamná, the sun god.

Guides charge $20 (£11) for a tour for one to six people. A better option is to find a copy of the green booklet *San Gervasio,* sold at local checkout counters and bookstores, and tour the site on your own. Seeing it takes 30 minutes. Taxi drivers offer a tour to the ruins for about $30 (£17); the driver will wait for you outside the ruins.

A HISTORY MUSEUM   The **Museo de la Isla de Cozumel** *&*, Avenida Rafael Melgar between calles 4 and 6 Norte (© **987/872-1475**), is more than just a nice place to spend a rainy hour. On the first floor an exhibit illustrates endangered species, the origin of the island, and its present-day topography and plant and animal life, including an explanation of coral formation. The second-floor galleries feature the history of the town, artifacts from the island's pre-Hispanic sites, and colonial-era cannons, swords, and ship paraphernalia. It's open daily from 9am to 5pm. Admission is $3 (£1.65). A rooftop restaurant serves breakfast and lunch (and you don't need to pay admission to eat there).

GOLF   Cozumel has a new 18-hole course designed by Jack Nicklaus. It's at the **Cozumel Country Club** (© **987/872-9570**), just north of San Miguel. Greens fees are $165 (£91) for a morning tee time, including cart rental and tax. Afternoon tee times cost $99 (£54). Tee times can be reserved 3 days in advance. A few hotels have special memberships with discounts for guests and advance tee times; guests at Playa Azul Golf and Beach Club pay no greens fees, but the cart costs $25 (£14).

TRIPS TO THE MAINLAND

PLAYA DEL CARMEN & XCARET   Going on your own to the nearby seaside village of **Playa del Carmen** and the **Xcaret** nature park is as easy as a quick ferry ride from Cozumel (for ferry information, see "Getting There & Departing," earlier in this chapter). For information on Playa and Xcaret, see chapter 15. Cozumel travel agencies offer an Xcaret tour that includes the ferry ride, transportation to the park, and the admission fee. The price is $100 (£55) for adults, $55 (£30) for kids. The tour is available Monday through Saturday.

CHICHEN ITZA, TULUM & COBA   Travel agencies can arrange day trips to the ruins of **Chichén Itzá** ඝඝඝ by air or bus. The ruins of **Tulum** ඝ, overlooking the Caribbean, and **Cobá** ඝ, in a dense jungle setting, are closer and cost less to visit. These latter two cities are quite a contrast to Chichén Itzá. Cobá is a large, mostly unrestored city beside a lake in a remote jungle setting, while Tulum is smaller, more compact, and right on the beach. It's more intact than Cobá. A trip to both Cobá and Tulum begins at 8am and returns around 6pm. A shorter, more relaxing excursion goes to Tulum and the nearby nature park of Xel-Ha.

SHOPPING

If you're looking for silver jewelry or some of the usual souvenirs, go no further than the town's coastal avenue, Rafael Melgar. Along this road you find one store after another—jewelry, souvenirs, and duty-free merchandise. But, if you're looking for something original, seek out a gallery and store called **Inspiración** (© **987/869-8293**) on Avenida 5 between Rosado Salas and Calle 3. Owner Dianne Hartwig displays the creations of some of the best-known folk artists in the Yucatan—objects that are very hard to come by if you don't actually go the villages where many of these artists live. She also represents some talented contemporary local artists. Stores carrying Mexican handicrafts include **Los Cinco Soles** (© **987/872-2040**), **Indigo** (© **987/872-1076**), and **Viva México** (© **987/872-5466**). All of these are on Avenida Rafael Melgar. There are also some import/export stores in the Punta Langosta Shopping Center in the southern part of town in front of the cruise ship pier. Prices for serapes, T-shirts, and the like are lower on the side streets off Avenida Melgar.

WHERE TO STAY

I've grouped Cozumel's hotels by location—**north** of town, **in town,** and **south** of town—and I describe them in that order. The prices I've quoted are rack rates and include the 12% tax. High season is from December to Easter. Expect rates from Christmas to New Year's to be still higher than the regular high-season rates quoted here. Low season is the rest of the year, though a few hotels raise their rates in August when Mexican families go on vacations.

All of the beach hotels in Cozumel, even the small ones, have deals with vacation packagers. Keep in mind that some packagers will offer last-minute deals to Cozumel with hefty discounts; if you're the flexible sort, keep an eye open for these.

Most hotels have an arrangement with a dive shop and offer dive packages. These can be good deals, but if you don't buy a dive package, it's quite okay to stay at one hotel and dive with a third-party operator—any dive boat can pull up to any hotel pier to pick up customers. Most dive shops won't pick up from the hotels north of town.

All the beach hotels suffered damage from the two hurricanes that passed through here. All were closed. Most took advantage of the closure to make upgrades to amenities and rooms. This is good news for those who come now. Some of the hotels in town are also remodeling, but nothing major.

As an alternative to a hotel, you can try **Cozumel Vacation Villas and Condos,** Av. Rafael Melgar 685 (between calles 3 and 5 Sur; ℂ **800/224-5551** in the U.S., or 987/ 872-0729; www.cvvmexico.com), which offers accommodations by the week.

NORTH OF TOWN

Carretera Santa Pilar, or San Juan, is the name of Avenida Rafael Melgar's northern extension. All the hotels lie close to each other on the beach side of the road a short distance from town and the airport.

Very Expensive

Playa Azul Golf-Scuba-Spa 𝕬𝕬𝕬   This quiet hotel is perhaps the most relaxing of the island's beachside properties. It's smaller than the others, and service is personal. It's an excellent choice for golfers; guests pay no greens fees, only cart rental. The hotel's small, sandy beach has been restored to its prehurricane condition, with new shade *palapas* and the return of the beach bar. Almost all the rooms have balconies and ocean views. The units in the original section are all suites—very large, with oversize bathrooms with showers. The new wing has mostly standard rooms that are comfortable and large. The corner rooms are master suites and have large balconies with Jacuzzis overlooking the sea. If you prefer lots of space over having a Jacuzzi, opt for a suite in the original building. Rooms contain a king-size bed or two double beds; suites offer two convertible single sofas in the separate living room. The hotel also offers deep-sea- and fly-fishing trips. For a family or group, the hotel rents a garden house with lovely rooms.

Carretera San Juan Km 4, 77600 Cozumel, Q. Roo. ℂ 987/869-5160 or -5165. Fax 987/869-5173. www.playa-azul. com. 50 units. High season $241 (£133) double, $285–$330 (£157–£182) suite; low season $168 (£92) double, $213–$291 (£117–£160) suite. Rates include unlimited golf and full breakfast. Internet specials sometimes available. AE, MC, V. Free guarded parking. **Amenities:** Restaurant; 2 bars; medium-size outdoor pool; unlimited golf privileges at Cozumel Country Club; spa; dive shop; watersports equipment rental; game room; tour info; room service; in-room massage; babysitting; laundry service, nonsmoking rooms. *In room:* A/C, TV, fridge, coffeemaker, hair dryer, safe.

Expensive

Condumel Condobeach Apartments   If you want some distance from the crowds, consider lodging here. It's not a full-service hotel, but in some ways it's more convenient. The one-bedroom apartments are designed and furnished in practical fashion—airy, with sliding glass doors that face the sea and allow for good cross-ventilation (especially in the upper units). They also have ceiling fans, air-conditioning, and two twin beds or one king-size. Each apartment has a separate living room and a full kitchen with a partially stocked fridge, so you don't have to run to the store on the first day. There's a small, well-tended beach area (with shade *palapas* and a grill for guests' use) that leads to a low, rocky fall-off into the sea.

Carretera Hotelera Norte s/n, 77600 Cozumel, Q. Roo. ℂ **987/872-0892.** Fax 987/872-0661. www.condumel.com. 10 units. High season $158 (£87) double; low season $135 (£74) double. No credit cards. *In room:* A/C, kitchen, no phone.

IN TOWN

Staying in town is not like staying in Playa del Carmen, where you can walk to the beach. The oceanfront in town is too busy for swimming, and there's no beach, only the *malecón*. Prices are considerably lower, but you'll have to drive or take a cab to the beach; it's pretty easy. English is spoken in almost all of the hotels.

Moderate

Hacienda San Miguel ⚜️ *(Value)*   This is a peaceful hotel built in Mexican colonial style around a large garden courtyard. The property is well maintained and the service is good. It's located a half block from the shoreline on the town's north side. Rooms are large and attractive and come with equipped kitchens, including full-size refrigerators. Most of the studios have a queen-size bed or two doubles. The junior suites have more living area and come with a queen-size and a twin bed. The two-bedroom suite comes with four double beds.

Calle 10 Norte 500 (between Rafael Melgar and Av. 5), 77600 Cozumel, Q. Roo. ✆ **866/712-6387** in the U.S., or 987/872-1986. Fax 987/872-7036. www.haciendasanmiguel.com. 11 units. High season $101 (£56) studio, $114 (£63) junior suite, $165 (£91) 2-bedroom suite; low season $84 (£46) studio, $102 (£56) junior suite, $131 (£72) 2-bedroom suite. Rates include continental breakfast and free entrance to Mr. Sancho's beach club. MC, V. Guarded parking on street. **Amenities:** Tour info; car rental. *In room:* A/C, TV, kitchen, hair dryer, safe, no phone.

Suites Colonial   Around the corner from the main square, on a pedestrian-only street, you'll find this pleasant four-story hotel. Standard rooms, called "studios," have large bathrooms and attractive red-tile floors, but they could be better lit. These units have one double and one twin bed and are trimmed in yellow pine, which seems oddly out of place here. The suites hold two double beds, a kitchenette, and a sitting and dining area. There's free coffee and sweet bread in the morning. When making a reservation, specify the Suites Colonial.

Av. 5 Sur 9 (Apdo. Postal 286), 77600 Cozumel, Q. Roo. ✆ **987/872-9080.** Fax 987/872-9073. www.suitescolonial. com. 28 units. $60–$70 (£33–£39) studio, $80 (£44) suite. Rates include continental breakfast. Extra person $20 (£11). Limited street parking. AE, MC, V. From the plaza, walk half a block south on Av. 5 Sur; the hotel is on the left. *In room:* A/C, TV, fridge.

Vista del Mar ⚜️   This hotel is located on the town's shoreline boulevard. All the rooms in front have ocean views. The balconies are large enough to be enjoyable and are furnished with a couple of chairs. Rooms are a little larger than your standard room, with better lighting than you find in most of the hotels in town. They are simply furnished and decorated, but come with several amenities. Bathrooms are medium-size or a little smaller and have showers. The rooms in back go for $10 (£5.50) less than the oceanview rooms and look out over a small pool and large Jacuzzi.

Av. Rafael Melgar 45 (between Calles 5 and 7 Sur), 77600 Cozumel, Q. Roo. ✆ **888/309-9988** in the U.S., or 987/ 872-0545. Fax 987/872-7036. www.hotelvistadelmar.com. 20 units. High season $84–$95 (£46–£52) double; low season $75–$86 (£41–£47). Discounts sometimes available. AE, MC, V. Limited street parking. **Amenities:** Bar; outdoor pool; Jacuzzi; tour info; car rental; in-room massage; laundry service. *In room:* A/C, TV, fridge, hair dryer, safe.

Inexpensive

La Casona Real   Five blocks from the waterfront, this two-story hotel is a bargain for those wanting a hotel with a pool. The rooms are small to medium in size but modern and attractive and come with good air conditioning. The hotel underwent a complete remodeling after the hurricanes. Management changed, too. Rooms are attractive and come with two double beds or one king-size (costing $10/£5.50 less). Bathrooms are medium in size. A courtyard with an oval pool is on the west side of the building. This is not the quietest of properties. Next door is a club that opens on weekends with drag queen shows from Acapulco (see nightlife, below). On the other side of the hotel is a fairly busy street.

Av. Juárez 501, 77600 Cozumel, Q. Roo. © **987/872-5471**. 14 units. $40–$50 (£22–£28) double. Discounts sometimes available in low season. No credit cards. Limited street parking. **Amenities:** Medium-size outdoor pool. *In room:* A/C, TV, no phone.

Suites Vima *(Value)*   This three-story hotel is 4 blocks from the main square. It offers large, plainly furnished rooms for a good price. The lighting is okay, the showers are good, and every room comes with it's own fridge, which for island visitors can be a handy feature. The rooms are fairly quiet. Choose between two doubles or one king bed. There is no restaurant, but there is a pool and lounge area. As is the case with other small hotels on the island, the staff at the front desk doesn't speak English. Reservations through e-mail can be made in English. This is one of the few hotels in town that doesn't use high season/low season rates.

Av. 10 Norte between Calles 4 and 6, 77600 Cozumel, Q. Roo. © **987/872-5118**. suitesvima@hotmail.com. 12 units. $67 (£37) double. No credit cards. Limited street parking. **Amenities:** Pool. *In room:* A/C, fridge.

SOUTH OF TOWN

The hotels in this area tend to be more spread out and farther from town than hotels to the north. Some are on the inland side of the road; some are on the beach side, which means a difference in price. Those farthest from town are all-inclusive properties. The beaches tend to be slightly better than those to the north, but all the hotels have swimming pools and piers from which you can snorkel, and all of them accommodate divers. Head south on Avenida Rafael Melgar, which becomes the coastal road **Costera Sur** (also called Carretera a Chankanaab).

Very Expensive

Presidente InterContinental Cozumel ☆☆☆   An extensive makeover after Hurricane Wilma has made this almost an entirely new property. It was already the best property on the island; now, after $25 million and more than a year of being closed, it has reopened as one of the best properties in the Yucatán. Palatial in scale and modern in style, the Presidente spreads out across a long stretch of coast with only distant hotels for neighbors. The rooms have all been redesigned top to bottom, and the smallest rooms were eliminated. Another pool has been added with a larger pool area. Rooms come in three categories depending mostly on location—pool view, ocean view, and beach front. A few differences exist in amenities and the design of the rooms, but these are minor. All come with such offerings as a pillow menu. All units are decorated in a sleek modern style that incorporates tropical, even rustic, materials. A terrace or a balcony offers the indoor/outdoor mix that's so enjoyable in a beach hotel. Downstairs rooms are beachfront, ocean suites, and reef rooms (larger and practically right up to the water), upstairs are ocean view. Pool view rooms can be either. Rooms are oversize and have large, beautifully finished bathrooms. A long stretch of sandy beach area dotted with *palapas* and palm trees fronts the entire hotel. This property is now a member of Leading Hotels of the World.

Costera Sur Km 6.5, 77600 Cozumel, Q. Roo. © **800/327-0200** in the U.S., or 987/872-9500. Fax 987/872-9528. www.intercontinentalcozumel.com. 220 units. High season $559 (£307) pool view, $648–$760 (£356–£418) ocean view/beachfront, $783 (£431–£474) ocean suites, from $861 (£747) reef rooms and other suites; low season $357 (£196) pool view, $424–$503 (£233–£277) ocean view/beachfront, $514 (£283) ocean suite, from $542 (£298) reef rooms and other suites. Internet specials sometimes available. AE, MC, V. Free valet parking. **Amenities:** 3 restaurants;

4 bars; 2 outdoor pools; wading pool; access to golf club; 2 lighted tennis courts; fully equipped fitness center; spa; dive ship; watersports equipment rental; children's club; concierge; tour desk; car rental; business center; shopping arcade; room service; 24-hour butler service in reef section; in-room massage; babysitting; laundry service; dry cleaning; nonsmoking rooms. *In room:* A/C, TV w/pay movies, Wi-Fi, minibar, coffeemaker, hair dryer, safe.

Expensive

El Cantil Condominiums *(Finds)*   A new condo property on the south side of town that rents out 30 (of the 45 total) units by the night or the week. The rates listed below are probably going to go up because they're tied to management and insurance costs, but this place is worth checking out because it's an attractive property with large rooms and convenient location. The shore here is rocky, but there's a sandy area for guests and a beautiful seaside pool and Jacuzzi, as well as a boat dock and easy entry into the sea. Extras include free long-distance calls to the U.S.

Av. Rafael Melgar, between calles 13 and 15. 77600 Cozumel, Q. Roo. © 954/323-8491 in the U.S., or 987/869-1517. Fax 987/869-2053. www.elcantilcondos.com. 30 units. $125 (£69) studio, $210 (£116) 1-bedroom, $260 (£143) 2-bedroom. AE, DISC, MC, V. Free sheltered parking. **Amenities:** Restaurant; bar; heated outdoor pool; saltwater Jacuzzi; watersports equipment rental; concierge; tour desk; car rental; business center; room service; laundry service and coin-op laundry; nonsmoking rooms. *In room:* A/C, TV, Wi-Fi or high-speed Internet, kitchens in all but studio units, hair dryer, safe.

WHERE TO DINE

The island offers a number of good restaurants. Taxi drivers will often steer you toward restaurants that pay them commissions; don't heed their advice.

Zermatt (© **987/872-1384**), a nice little bakery, is on Avenida 5 at Calle 4 Norte. **Le Chef** (© **987/876-3437**), at Avenida 5 and Calle 5 Sur, is a deli/gourmet food store. It has a daily menu of salads, pizzas, and prepared foods, as well as cold meats, cheeses, baguettes, and other makings for a picnic. For inexpensive local fare during the day, I like **Comida Casera Toñita** (© **987/872-0401**), at Calle Rosado Salas 265 between avenidas 10 and 15. It closes at 6pm. For morning tacos de *cochinita pibil* (traditionally a breakfast item), go to **El Amigo Mario** (© **987/872-0742**) on Calle 5 Sur, between Francisco Mújica and Avenida 35. The owners close at half-past noon.

Finally, there's a new restaurant in town called **The Wynston** (© **987/869-1517**). Albert Domínguez, the owner of Prima, brought a chef down from New York to run his new place at El Cantil condos. It was close to opening when I was last in Cozumel. I've heard the food described as Mediterranean fusion.

VERY EXPENSIVE

Cabaña del Pescador (Lobster House) 🌴🌴 LOBSTER   Lobster is the main attraction here. You select a lobster tail, and brothers Fernando or Enrique will weigh it, boil it with a hint of spices, and serve it with melted butter, accompanied by sides of rice, vegetables, and bread. Does lobster require anything more? This is the only thing on the menu on Fernando's side of the restaurant, but Enrique will cook up steaks, shrimp, or fish if you don't feel like lobster. The setting is quite tropical—a pair of thatched bungalows bordering a pond with lily pads and reeds, traversed by a small footbridge. The rooms are softly lit with the glow of candles and furnished with rustic tables and chairs. A year later, you could still see some of the marks left by Hurricane Wilma, but the Cabaña del Pescador has lost none of its charm. The restaurant rambles around quite a bit, so explore until you find the spot most to your taste.

Carretera Santa Pilar Km 4 (across from Playa Azul Hotel). No phone. Reservations not accepted. Lobster (by weight) $25–$35 (£14–£19). No credit cards. Daily 6–10:30pm.

EXPENSIVE

French Quarter 🎔🎔 SOUTHERN   You can dine very well here in a comfortable upstairs open-air setting. The owners are from Louisiana and care a great deal about food. You can order Southern and Creole classics, such as jambalaya and étouffée, or you can order the daily catch stuffed or blackened, or choose a steak of imported Black Angus beef. I tried a filet mignon with red-onion marmalade, which was delicious. The downstairs bar is a popular hangout for many of the locals.

Av. 5 Sur 18. ⓒ 987/872-6321. Reservations recommended during Carnaval. Main courses $10–$27 (£5.50–£15). AE, MC, V. Wed–Mon 5–11pm.

Guido's 🎔🎔 MEDITERRANEAN   The inviting interior, with director's chairs and rustic wood tables, makes this a restful place in daytime and a romantic spot at night. The specialty is oven-baked pizzas. Also keep an eye out for the daily specials, which may include an appetizer of sea bass carpaccio, a couple of meat dishes, and usually a fish dish. The other thing that people love here is the *pan de ajo*—a house creation of bread made with olive oil, garlic, and rosemary. There's a good wine list.

Av. Rafael Melgar, between calles 6 and 8 Norte. ⓒ 987/872-0946. Reservations accepted. Main courses $13–$21 (£7.15–£12); pizzas $12–$13 (£6.60–£7.15). AE, MC, V. Mon–Sat 11am–11pm.

La Cocay 🎔🎔🎔 SEAFOOD/MEDITERRANEAN   In its new, more convenient location, this restaurant offers sophisticated cooking in comfortable surroundings, either inside or out. The dining room is furnished in modern style with soft light and music. The garden in back is lovely. I tried a few tapas for appetizers, and they were beautifully seasoned concoctions of garbanzos, chorizo, bell peppers, panela cheese, and sun-dried tomatoes on small slices of bread. A couple of the main courses also showed a sure touch: pork in a Moroccan sauce and scallops with a cognac glaze. The chocolate torte that the restaurant is known for takes a little extra time to prepare— order it early.

Calle 8 Norte 208 (between avs. 10 and 15). ⓒ 987/872-5533. Reservations recommended. Main courses $9–$30 (£4.95–£17). AE, MC, V. Mon–Sat 1:30–11pm.

Prima 🎔🎔🎔 ITALIAN/INTERNATIONAL   Everything at this ever-popular hangout is fresh—pastas, vegetables, and seafood. The menu changes daily and concentrates on seafood. It might include shrimp scampi, fettuccine with pesto, and lobster and crab ravioli with cream sauce. The fettuccine Alfredo is wonderful, the salads crisp, and the steaks are Black Angus beef. Pizzas are cooked in a wood-burning oven. Desserts include Key lime pie and tiramisu. The food and the service are consistently good here. Dining is upstairs on an open-air terrace.

Calle Rosado Salas 109A (corner of Av. 5) ⓒ 987/872-4242. Reservations recommended during high season. Pizzas and pastas $6–$14 (£3.30–£7.70); seafood $12–$20 (£6.60–£11); steaks $15–$20 (£8.25–£11). AE, MC, V. Daily 4:30–10pm.

MODERATE

Capicúa TAPAS/SEAFOOD   A new restaurant for the island, Capicúa looks to attract customers bored with the usual run of the island's restaurants with some original cooking. The selection of *tapas* varies, but usually includes such things as smoked duck or abalone. And for those wanting something closer to comfort food there are barbecued chicken wings or shrimp *al ajillo* (with garlic and strips of toasted *guajillo* chile). I enjoyed the mahimahi encrusted with white and black sesame seeds, which was cooked just right. Salads can be had, too. There is an okay selection of wines and a full bar. The house in which the restaurant is located is decorated with a sense of humor; choose between a dining room with one of those beautiful, old tile floors and an old patio sheltered by a large tamarind tree.

Calle 10 Norte 299 (corner of Av. 15). ☎ **987/869-8265**. Reservations accepted. Tapas $3.50–$10 (£1.95–£5.50); main courses $9–$15 (£4.95–£8.25). MC. V. Tues–Sun 5pm–midnight.

El Moro ☞ *(Value)* REGIONAL   El Moro is an out-of-the-way place that has been around for a long time and has always been popular with the locals, who come for the food, the service, and the prices—but not the decor, which is orange, orange, orange, and Formica. Get there by taxi, which will cost a couple of bucks. Portions are generous. Any of the shrimp dishes use the real jumbo variety when available. For something different, try the *pollo Ticuleño,* a specialty from the town of Ticul, a layered dish of tomato sauce, mashed potatoes, crispy baked corn tortillas, and fried chicken breast, topped with shredded cheese and green peas. Other specialties include enchiladas and seafood prepared many ways, plus grilled steaks and sandwiches.

75 bis Norte 124 (between calles 2 and 4 Norte). ☎ **987/872-3029**. Reservations not accepted. Main courses $5–$15 (£2.75–£8.25). MC, V. Fri–Wed 1–11pm.

La Choza ☞ YUCATECAN/MEXICAN   For Mexican food, I like this place, and so do a lot of locals. Platters of poblano chiles stuffed with shrimp, grilled *brochetas* (kebobs), and *pollo en relleno negro* (chicken in a sauce of blackened chiles) are among the specialties. The table sauces and guacamole are great, and the daily specials can be good, too. This is an open-air restaurant with well-spaced tables under a tall thatched roof. Breakfasts are good as well.

Rosado Salas 198 (at Av. 10 Sur). ☎ **987/872-0958**. Reservations accepted for groups of 6 or more. Breakfast $4 (£2.20); main courses $9–$15 (£4.95–£8.25). AE, MC, V. Daily 7am–10pm.

INEXPENSIVE

Cocos Cozumel MEXICAN/AMERICAN   Cocos offers the largest breakfast menu on the island, including all the American and Mexican classics, from *huevos divorciados* (fried eggs on corn tortillas) to ham and eggs. Indulge in such stateside favorites as hash browns, corn flakes and bananas, gigantic blueberry muffins, cinnamon rolls, and bagels, or go for something with tropical ingredients, such as a blended fruit drink. The service and the food are excellent. The American and Mexican owners, Terri and Daniel Ocejo, are good folk and can set you up with a horseback ride or a fishing or snorkeling trip.

Av. 5 Sur 180 (1 block south of the main plaza). ☎ **987/872-0241**. Breakfast $4–$6 (£2.20–£3.30). No credit cards. Tues–Sun 6am–noon. Closed Sept–Oct.

Restaurant del Museo BREAKFAST/MEXICAN   The most pleasant place in San Miguel to have breakfast or lunch (weather permitting) is at this rooftop cafe above the island's museum. It offers a serene view of the water, removed from the traffic noise below and sheltered from the sun above. The tables and chairs are comfortable. Choices are limited to the mainstays of American and Mexican breakfasts, and lunch dishes such as sandwiches and enchiladas.

Av. Rafael Melgar (corner of Calle 6 Norte). ☎ **987/872-0838**. Reservations not accepted. Breakfast $4–$5 (£2.20–£2.75); lunch main courses $5–$10 (£2.75–£5.50). No credit cards. Daily 7am–2pm.

COZUMEL AFTER DARK

Most of the music and dance venues are along Avenida Rafael Melgar. **Carlos 'n' Charlie's** (© **987/869-1648** or -1646), which is in the Punta Langosta shopping center, practically next to **Señor Frog's** (© **987/869-1650**). Punta Langosta is just south of Calle 7 Sur. The **Hard Rock Cafe** (© **987/872-5271**) is also on Avenida Rafael Melgar, at #2, just north of the municipal pier.

In town, there are a few Latin music clubs. These open and close with every high season. They do well when people have cash in their pockets, but then they have to close down when the flow of tourism stops bringing in money. There's a sports bar at the corner of Avenida 5 and Calle 2 Norte called **All Sports Bar** (© **987/869-2246**), which operates as a salsa club Thursday to Saturday from 10pm to 3am. So go for sports, stay for salsa. Also, there's a working-class night club on Avenida Juárez, between avenidas 25 and 30, called **Los Delfines** (no phone), which puts on drag shows from Thursday to Sunday. These start around 11pm.

On Sunday evenings, the place to be is the main square, which usually has a free concert and lots of people strolling about and visiting with friends.

The town of San Miguel has three **movie theaters.** Your best option is **Cinépolis,** the modern multicinema in the Chedraui Plaza Shopping Center at the south end of town. It mainly shows Hollywood movies. Most of these are in English with Spanish subtitles *(película subtitulada);* before buying your tickets, make sure the movie hasn't been dubbed *(doblada).*

15

The Caribbean Coast: The Riviera Maya, Including Playa del Carmen & the Costa Maya

by David Baird

Perhaps I should go on about how the Riviera Maya has "endless stretches of pristine beaches of soft white sand gently caressed by the turquoise-blue waters of the Caribbean," yadda, yadda, yadda . . . but my bet is that you've already heard it. You've seen the ads, the brochures, and the articles in the Sunday travel section. So I'll spare you the purple prose and get right to the things you'll need to know.

The Yucatán's Caribbean coast is 380km (236 miles) long, stretching from Cancún all the way to Chetumal, at the border with Belize. The northern half of the coast has been dubbed the "Riviera Maya"; the southern half, the "Costa Maya." In between is the large Sian Ka'an Biosphere Reserve.

A long reef system, the second longest in the world, protects most of the shore. Where there are gaps in the reef—Playa del Carmen, Xpu-Ha, and Tulum—you find good beaches. The action of the surf

washes away silt and sea grass and erodes rocks, leaving a sandy bottom. Where the reef is prominent, you get good snorkeling and diving with lots of fish and other sea creatures. Here mangrove often occupies the shoreline; the beaches are usually sandy up to the water's edge, but shallow, with a silty or rocky floor.

Inland you'll find jungle, caverns, the famous *cenotes* (natural wells leading to underwater rivers), and the even more famous ruins of the Maya. Activities abound.

So do lodging options. On this coast you can stay in a variety of communities or distance yourself from all of them. There's just about every choice you can think of: rustic cabins, secluded spa resorts, boutique hotels, B&Bs, all-inclusive megaresorts, whatever you want. With so many options, you need to make some decisions. I hope that what follows will help.

EXPLORING MEXICO'S CARIBBEAN COAST

A single road, Highway 307, runs down the coast from Cancún to Chetumal. The section between Cancún's airport and Playa del Carmen (51km/32 miles) is a four-lane divided highway with speed limits up to 110kmph (68 mph). There are a couple of traffic lights and several reduced-speed zones around the major turnoffs. From Playa to Tulum (80km/50 miles) expect road construction, as the government is widening the highway to 4 lanes. The project is complete as far south as Paamul, and as of the time of this writing, construction is ongoing around Akumal. It still takes about 1½ hours to drive from the Cancún airport to Tulum.

From Tulum, the highway turns inland to skirt the edges of Sian Ka'an. The roadway is narrower, without shoulders, and in some areas the forest crowds in on both sides. The speed limit is mostly 80kmph (50 mph), but you'll need to slow down where the road passes through villages, and keep an eye out for *topes* (speed bumps). After the town of Limones, new road construction has widened and smoothed the highway. To drive from Tulum to Chetumal takes 3 hours.

PLAYA DEL CARMEN   Playa, as it is called, is the most happening place on the coast—a delightful beach (especially when the wind and currents are flowing in the right direction), hotels for every budget, a good choice of restaurants, and an active nightlife, most of which is on or around Quinta Avenida (Fifth Avenue), Playa's well-known promenade. In the last few years, the town has grown quickly, and local residents and the tourism board are working to keep it from becoming a smaller version of Cancún.

PUERTO MORELOS   This town between Playa and Cancún remains a little village affectionately known by the locals as "Muerto Morelos" (*muerto* means "dead"), for its phenomenally quiet low season. It has a few small hotels and rental houses, and nearby are a few secluded spa resorts. The coast is sandy and well protected by an offshore reef, which means good snorkeling and diving nearby, but the lack of surf means sea grass and shallow water. If you're looking for good swimming, head farther down the coast. If you're looking for a relaxing seaside retreat with a clean beach in an easygoing community, this will work for you.

PUERTO AVENTURAS   The first major town south of Playa is a modern condo-marina development with a 9-hole golf course, several restaurants, and a few hotels. I don't think it's a fun place to stay, but you might come here to go deep-sea fishing or swim with dolphins.

AKUMAL   A bit farther south is Akumal and Half Moon Bay. The community is relatively old for this shore, which means that it's already built up and doesn't have the boomtown feel of Playa and Tulum. Akumal has a strong ecological orientation and is a prominent scuba and snorkeling center. The locals are a mix of Americans and Mexicans who enjoy the unhurried lifestyle of the tropics, making this a good place to relax and work on your hammock technique. There are a few hotels; most of the lodging is rental houses and condos. Consequently, the town is a favorite with families who enjoy the calmness of the place and can save money by buying groceries and cooking for themselves.

TULUM   The town of Tulum (near the ruins of the same name) has a hotel district of about 30 *palapa* (palm-leaf roofed) hotels, which stretch down the coast of the Punta Allen peninsula. A few years ago, it was mainly a destination for backpacker types, but with some of the most beautiful beaches on this coast and many improvements in hotel amenities, it now attracts people with big budgets. Here you can enjoy the beach in relative solitude and quiet (unless your hotel is busy building additional rooms). The downside of this is that Tulum doesn't have the variety of restaurants that Playa and Cancún do, but you can still eat well.

COSTA MAYA   South of Tulum lies the large Sian Ka'an Biosphere Reserve and, beyond that, what is known as the Costa Maya, which designates the rest of the coast all the way down to Belize. The Costa Maya is a relaxing getaway. Most of the coast is along the Majahual Peninsula, which has a lot of sandy beaches with silt bottoms.

It's attractive to scuba divers, snorkelers, fly fishermen, and people who want to get away from the crowds. Farther south is Lake Bacalar, a large, clear freshwater lake. Inland from here are the impressive Maya ruins of the Río Bec area.

1 Playa del Carmen (★(★(★

32km (20 miles) S of Puerto Morelos; 70km (43 miles) S of Cancún; 10km (6½ miles) N of Xcaret; 13km (8 miles) N of Puerto Calica

Though it no longer has the feel of a village, Playa still provides that rare combination of simplicity (at its core, still primarily a beach town) and variety (many unique hotels, restaurants, and stores). There is a comfortable feel to the town. The local architecture has adopted elements of native building—rustic clapboard walls; stucco; thatched roofs; rough-hewn wood; and a ramshackle, unplanned look to many structures—that reflect the town's taste for third-world chic. Slicker architecture has appeared, with chain restaurants and stores, detracting from Playa's individuality, but Playa still retains the feel of a cosmopolitan getaway with a counterculture ethos.

Playa is perfect for enjoying the simple (and perhaps the best) pleasures of a seaside vacation—taking in the sun and the sea air while working your toes into the sand; cooling down with a swim in clear water; and strolling aimlessly down the beach, listening to the wash of waves, and feeling the light touch of tropical breezes. A strong European influence has made topless sunbathing (nominally against the law in Mexico) a nonchalantly accepted practice anywhere there's a beach. The beach grows and shrinks, from broad and sandy to narrower with rocks, depending on the currents and wind. When this happens, head to the beaches in north Playa.

From Playa, it's easy to shoot out to Cozumel on the ferry, drive south to the nature parks and the ruins at Tulum and Cobá, or drive north to Cancún. Directly south of

---

Tips Driving the Riviera Maya

Driving along this coast isn't difficult. There's only one highway, so you can't get lost. Speed limits are clearly posted, but lots of cars ignore them, *except around Playa,* where police are known to ticket drivers. Watch your speed when you're passing through town. Maximum speed for the center lanes is 60kmph (40 mph) and, for the outside lanes, it's 40kmph (25 mph).

South of Playa, the highway is a two-lane undivided highway with wide shoulders, but that might be changing with new road construction. If you find that it's still undivided, you should know that you're not allowed to stop on the highway to make a left turn. You're supposed to pull over to the right and wait for traffic in both directions to clear before crossing the road. Another tip: It's customary for drivers here to pretend that there's a center passing lane. Oncoming traffic moves to the right to make room for the passing vehicle. You do the same, but when you do so look out for cyclists and cars on the shoulder. This is why I recommend that you not drive at night. As far as gas availability goes, there are several more gas stations in the Riviera Maya now, so you shouldn't have a problem getting gas. But pay attention and make sure that the gasoline-station attendant gives you back the right amount of money—I've had people try to short-change me.

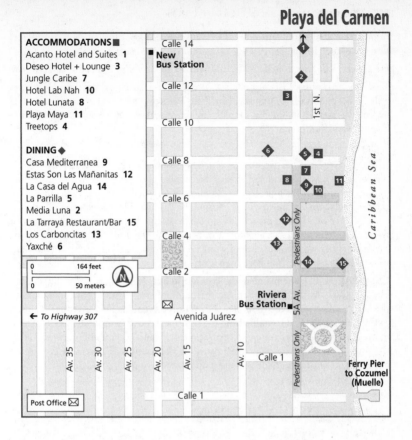

ACCOMMODATIONS ■
Acanto Hotel and Suites **1**
Deseo Hotel + Lounge **3**
Jungle Caribe **7**
Hotel Lab Nah **10**
Hotel Lunata **8**
Playa Maya **11**
Treetops **4**

DINING ◆
Casa Mediterranea **9**
Estas Son Las Mañanitas **12**
La Casa del Agua **14**
La Parrilla **5**
Media Luna **2**
La Tarraya Restaurant/Bar **15**
Los Carboncitas **13**
Yaxché **6**

town is the Playacar development, which has a golf course, several large all-inclusive resorts, and a residential development.

ESSENTIALS
GETTING THERE & DEPARTING

BY AIR   You can fly into Cancún and take a bus directly from the airport (see "By Bus," below), or fly into Cozumel and take the passenger ferry.

BY CAR   Highway 307 is the only highway that passes through Playa. As you approach Playa from Cancún, the highway divides. Keep to the inside lanes to permit turning left at any of the traffic lights. The two main arteries into Playa are Avenida Constituyentes, which works well for destinations in northern Playa, and Avenida Juárez, which leads to the town's main square. If you stay in the outside lanes, you will need to continue past Playa until you get to the turnaround, then double back, staying to your right.

BY FERRY   Air-conditioned passenger ferries to Cozumel leave from the town's pier 1 block from the main square. There is also a car ferry to Cozumel from the Calica pier just south of the Playacar development. The schedule for the passenger ferries has been in flux since the hurricanes. As of the latest information, ferries have been departing every hour in the mornings, and every 2 hours in the afternoons. For more information about both ferries, see "Getting There & Departing" in the Cozumel section of chapter 14.

BY TAXI   Taxi fares from the Cancún airport are about $50 to $60 (£28–£33) one-way.

BY BUS   Autobuses Riviera offers service from the Cancún airport about 12 times a day. Cost is $8 (£4.40) one-way. You'll see a ticket counter in the corridor leading out of the airport. From the Cancún bus station there are frequent departures—almost every 30 minutes.

ORIENTATION

ARRIVING   Playa has two **bus** stations. Buses coming from Cancún and places along the coast, such as Tulum, arrive at the Riviera bus station, at the corner of Juárez and Quinta Avenida, by the town square. Buses coming from destinations in the interior of the peninsula arrive at the new ADO station, on Avenida 20 between calles 12 and 14.

A word of caution: Approach any timeshare salesperson as you would a wounded rhino. And remember that whatever free trinket is offered for simply viewing apartments, it either won't materialize or won't be worth the time you invest in your dealings with these people. You have been warned.

CITY LAYOUT   The main street, **Avenida Juárez,** leads to the town square from Highway 307. As it does so, it crosses several numbered avenues that run parallel to the beach, all of which are multiples of 5. **Quinta Avenida (Fifth Avenue)** is closest to the beach; it's closed to traffic from the *zócalo* to Calle 6 (and some blocks beyond, in the evening). On this avenue are many hotels, restaurants, and shops. Almost all of the town is north and west of the square. To the south is "Playacar" a golf-course development of private residences and a dozen resort hotels.

FAST FACTS: **Playa del Carmen**

Area Code The telephone area code is **984**.

Currency Exchange Playa has several banks and ATMs. Many currency-exchange houses are close to the pier or along Quinta Avenida at Calle 8.

Doctor For serious medical attention, go to **Hospitén** in Cancún (© **998/881-3700**). In Playa, **Dr. G. Ambriz** speaks English and was trained in the U.S. and Europe. His office is at the corner of Avenida 30 and Calle 14 (© **984/109-1245**).

Drugstore The **Farmacía del Carmen,** Avenida Juárez between avenidas 5 and 10 (© **984/873-2330**), is open 24 hours.

Internet Access Internet cafes are all over town; most have fast connection speeds.

Parking Most parking in Playa is on the street. Spots can be hard to come by. The most accessible parking lot is the Estacionamiento México, at avenidas Juárez and 10 (where the entrance is located). It's open daily 24 hours and charges $1.25 (70p) per hour, $10 (£5.50) per day. There's also a 24-hour lot a block from the pier, where you can leave your car while you visit Cozumel.

Post Office The *correo,* on Avenida Juárez, 3 blocks from the plaza, is on the right past the Hotel Playa del Carmen and the launderette.

Seasons The main high season is from mid-December to Easter. There is a mini high season in August. Low season is all other months.

EXPLORING PLAYA & THE RIVIERA MAYA

The main activity in Playa is hanging out on the beach and enjoying Quinta Avenida. But there are actually plenty of activities to do up and down this coast. The following is a brief list to help you consider your options.

GOLF & TENNIS   If golf is your bag, the Playacar Golf Club (© **984/873-4990;** www.palace-resorts.com/playacar-golf-club) has an 18-hole **golf course** designed by Robert von Hagge. It's operated by the Palace Resorts hotel chain, which offers golf packages. Greens fees are $180 (£99) in the morning (including tax and cart) and $120 (£66) after 2pm; club rental costs $30 (£17). The club also has two **tennis** courts, which cost $10 (£5.50) per hour.

HORSEBACK RIDING   There are a few places along the highway that offer horseback rides. The best of these, **Rancho Punta Venado,** is just south of Playa past the Calica Pier. This ranch is less touristy than the others, and the owner takes good care of his horses. It has a nice stretch of coast with a sheltered bay and offers kayaking and snorkeling outings. It's best to make arrangements ahead of time and tell them you're a Frommer's reader, so that they can schedule you on a day when they have fewer customers. You can contact them through e-mail (ptavenado@yahoo.com) or by calling their office at © **984/803-5224** or by calling directly to the ranch's cell phone when in Mexico (© **044-984/116-3213**); there is a charge for the call. Talk to Gabriela or Francisco; both speak English. You might also try dropping by. The turn-off for the ranch is 2km (1¼ miles) south of the Calica overpass near Km 279.

DAY SPA   To relax after all that exertion, try **Spa Itzá** (used to be called Itzá Spa, but they must have gotten tired of all the jokes). It's in downtown Playa between calles 12 and 14 in a retail area called Calle Corazón. The phone number is © **984/803-2588.**

VISITING THE RUINED CITIES OF THE MAYA   There are four cities within easy reach of Playa and most of the coast. The easiest to reach is **Tulum** (see the section on Tulum later in this chapter). A half-hour inland from Tulum on a pockmarked road is **Cobá,** rising up from a jungle setting. This city has not been reconstructed to the same degree as the other three and doesn't have the rich imagery or clearly delineated architecture. Its description is also in the Tulum section. The other two cites, **Chichén Itzá** and **Ek Balam,** are 2½ hours distant in the interior of the peninsula. My favorite way of seeing them is to rent a car and drive to Chichén in the afternoon, check into a hotel (perhaps one with a pool), see the sound-and-light show that evening, and then tour the ruins in the cool of the morning before the big bus tours arrive. Then drive back via Valladolid and Ek Balam. See chapter 16 for a description of these places.

TOURS   From Playa and the rest of the coast there are tours to all of the above-mentioned ruins. The tour buses usually stop at a few places along the way for refreshments and souvenirs, which is why I prefer the small tours. Some combine the ruins of Tulum with a visit to a nature park. There is a tour agency in Playa called **Alltournative** (© **984/873-2036;** www.alltournative.com), which offers small tours that combine a little of everything: culture (visit a contemporary Maya village), adventure (kayaking, rappelling, snorkeling, *cenote* diving), natural history, and ruins. It offers these tours daily using vans for transportation. The tours are fun. You can call the agency directly or arrange a tour through your hotel; they pick up at most of the large resorts along the coast. **Selvática** (© **998/849-5510;** www.selvatica.com.mx), operating out of offices in Cancún, offers guests a little adventure tourism in the jungle, with

2.5km (1½ miles) of zip lines strung up in the forest canopy. There are also tours involving mountain biking and swimming in *cenotes.* They pick up from hotels in the lower Riviera Maya on Tuesdays and Thursdays and from Playa and surrounding area almost every day of the week for the morning tours. The $75 (£41) cost includes transportation, activities, a light lunch, locker, and all equipment. Buy tickets and get more information at any travel agency in Playa. Another interesting option is an ecological tour of the **Sian Ka'an Biosphere Reserve.** To do this, however, you have to get to Tulum. See the Tulum section, later in this chapter.

DEEP-SEA FISHING   The largest marina on the coast is at **Puerto Aventuras,** not far south of Playa. Here's where you'll find most of your options for boating and fishing. See p. 599.

SCUBA & SNORKELING   In Playa, **Cyan-Ha Dive Center** (© 984/803-2517; www.cyanha.com) arranges reef and cavern diving. The owner, Carlos Quintanar, has been in Playa for over 20 years. His shop is in the Shangri-la Caribe Resort, and he and his staff speak English. Snorkeling trips cost around $20 (£11) and include soft drinks and equipment. Two-tank dive trips are $60 (£33); resort courses with SSI and PADI instructors cost $80 (£44). The area around Akumal has a number of underwater caverns and *cenotes* that have become popular scuba and snorkeling destinations. The **Akumal Dive Shop** specializes in cavern diving and offers a variety of dives. But the easiest way to try cavern diving or snorkeling is through **Hidden Worlds Cenotes,** which is right on the highway 15km (9 miles) south of Akumal. They provide everything, including wet suit. See "South of Playa del Carmen," later in this chapter.

SWIMMING WITH DOLPHINS   In the two nature parks south of Playa, Xcaret and Xel-Ha, you can have the opportunity of interacting with these intelligent creatures. Also, there's an outfit in Puerto Aventuras called **Dolphin Discovery** that is quite good. See "South of Playa del Carmen," later in this chapter.

THE NATURE PARKS: XCARET & XEL-HA   These parks make full-day excursions, offering opportunities for swimming, snorkeling, and other seaside activities, and educational tours about the region's natural history and local Maya culture and entertainment. They are completely self-contained and offer food, drink, watersports equipment, and various kinds of merchandise. Xcaret is just south of Playa, while Xel-Ha is farther south, almost to Tulum. (See section 3, later in this chapter.)

Cozumel is a half-hour away by ferry; in my opinion, it makes for a poor day trip unless you simply want to shop. You'll see exactly what the cruise-ship passengers see—lots of duty-free, souvenir, and jewelry stores. To enjoy Cozumel best, you have to spend at least a couple of nights there to explore the island. See chapter 14.

WHERE TO STAY

Playa has a lot of small hotels with affordable prices that give you a better feel for the town than staying in one of the resorts in Playacar. Don't hesitate to book a place that's not on the beach. Town life here is much of the fun, and staying on the beach in Playa has its disadvantages—in particular, the noise from a couple of beach bars. Beaches are public property in Mexico, and you can lay out your towel anywhere you like. There are some beach clubs in north Playa where, for a small sum, you can have the use of lounge chairs, towels, and food and drink.

High season is from mid-December to Easter. August is also high season for some hotels but not others. During other times of the year, you can come to Playa and look for walk-in offers. The rates listed below include the 12% hotel tax. I don't include the rates for Christmas to New Year's, which are still higher than the standard high-season rates.

VERY EXPENSIVE

Acanto Hotel & Suites &&& *(Finds)*   In my view, this property is (dare I say it) the most romantic in Playa. There is intimacy and drama and an even a sense of isolation. Seven stylish suites endowed with color and texture encircle a pool and softly lit courtyard. Figures of Buddhas and Asian decoration add an exotic feel and draw a division between this small enclave and the larger world outside the hotel's door. The suites come with kitchens so you can, should you choose, limit your comings and goings. The rooms are large and comfortable and come with a queen bed and small sitting area. The location is great, just around the corner from Quinta Avenida, on a secluded street.

Calle 16 Bis (between Avs. 5th and 1st) 77710 Playa del Carmen, Q. Roo. © **631/882-1986** in the U.S. or 984/873-1252. www.acantohotels.com. 7 units. $170–$300 (£94–£165) suite. 3-night minimum stay for holiday season. AE, MC, V. Street parking. **Amenities:** Small outdoor pool; tour info; in-room massage; laundry service; nonsmoking rooms. *In room:* A/C, TV, coffeemaker, hair dryer, safe, CD player, no phone.

Deseo Hotel + Lounge &&&   In a town where being hip is a raison d'être, there is no hotel hipper than this one. Its creators, the owners of **Habita** in Mexico City, seek to redefine our notions of a hotel by designing an environment that fosters social interaction. The lounge plays the central role, appropriating all the functions of lobby, restaurant, bar, and pool area. It's a raised open-air platform with bar, pool, and self-serve kitchen furnished with large daybeds for sunning or for enjoying an evening drink when the bar is in full swing. The rooms face two sides of the lounge. The clientele is predominantly 25- to 45-year-olds, and the music seems by design to provide an artsy background that's sufficiently monotonous not to compete with the setting.

The guest rooms play their part. They are comfortable, original, and visually striking, but, unlike the usual plush hotel room, they don't tempt one to isolation amidst an array of amenities—no TV, no cushy armchair. There is a simplicity that gives them an almost Asian feel, heightened by nice touches such as sliding doors of wood and frosted glass. The mattresses, however, are thick and luxurious. All rooms have king-size beds. From the bottom of each bed, a little drawer slides out with a night kit containing three things: incense, earplugs, and condoms.

And if Deseo doesn't work for you, the owners have opened another archly styled hotel 2 blocks down called **Hotel Básico** (© **984/879-4448;** www.hotelbasico.com). It's a fun mix of industrial and '50s styles, built with materials that have found a lot of favor with architects these days: concrete, plywood, and plastics. Along with all this you get a cushy bed and a forceful shower. As with Deseo, the common areas are not wasted space.

Av. 5 (at Calle 12), 77710 Playa del Carmen, Q. Roo. © **984/879-3620.** Fax 984/879-3621. www.hoteldeseo.com. 15 units. $180 (£99) lounge view; $199 (£109) balcony; $244 (£134) suite. Rates include continental breakfast. AE, MC, V. No parking. Children younger than 18 not accepted. **Amenities:** Bar; small rooftop pool; Jacuzzi; tour info; room service; in-room massage; laundry service. *In room:* A/C, minibar, hair dryer (on request), safe.

Shangri-La Caribe &&&   This hotel—a grouping of cabañas on one of the best beaches in Playa—is hard to beat for sheer fun and leisure. And it's far enough from the center of town to be quiet. The older, south side of the hotel (the "Caribe" section) consists of one- and two-story cabañas. The north side ("Playa" section) has a few larger buildings, holding four to six rooms. A preference for one or the other section is a matter of taste; the units in both are similar in amenities, privacy, and price.

All rooms have a patio or porch complete with hammock. Rooms come with two double beds or a king-size bed. Windows are screened, and ceiling fans circulate the breeze. The real difference in price depends on the proximity to the water—oceanfront, ocean view, or garden view. Garden view is the best bargain, being only a few steps farther from the water. Book well in advance during high season.

Calle 38 (Apdo. Postal 253), 77710 Playa del Carmen, Q. Roo. (✆ 800/538-6802 in the U.S. and Canada, or 984/873-0611. Fax 984/873-0500. www.shangrilacaribe.net. 107 units. High season $200–$245 (£135) garden view, $255 (£140) ocean view, $310 (£171) oceanfront; low season $150–$190 (£83–£105) garden view, $200–$220 (£110–£121) ocean view, $250–$270 (£138–£149) oceanfront. Rates include breakfast and dinner. AE, MC, V. Free guarded parking. From Hwy. 307 from Cancún, U-turn at the light for Av. Constituyentes, making sure to get into the far right lane; backtrack to the Volkswagen dealership, turn right, and head for the beach—this will be Calle 38. **Amenities:** 2 restaurants; poolside grill; 3 bars; 2 outdoor pools; whirlpool; watersports equipment; dive shop; game room; tour desk; car rental; in-room massage; babysitting; laundry service. *In room:* A/C, hair dryer, no phone.

EXPENSIVE

Hotel Lunata ✦✦ In the middle of Playa there isn't a more comfortable or more attractive place to stay than this small hotel on Quinta Avenida. The rooms offer character, good looks, and polish. There are a few standard rooms, which are midsize and come with a queen-size or a double bed. Deluxe rooms are large and come with a king-size bed and small fridge. Junior suites come with two doubles. Bathrooms are well designed and have good showers. Light sleepers should opt for a room facing the garden. On my last stay, I took a room facing the street with double-glazed glass doors that opened to a balcony. I enjoyed looking out over Quinta Avenida, and, with the doors shut, the noise was not bothersome.

Av. 5 (between calles 6 and 8), 77710 Playa del Carmen, Q. Roo. (✆ 984/873-0884. Fax 984/873-1240. www.lunata. com. 10 units. High season $110 (£61) standard, $140–$155 (£77–£85) deluxe and junior suite; low season $95 (£52) standard, $115–$135 (£63–£74) deluxe and junior suite. Rates include continental breakfast. Promotional rates available. AE, MC, V. Secure parking $5 (£2.75). No children younger than 13 allowed. **Amenities:** Free use of bike and watersports equipment; tour desk; in-room massage; laundry service; nonsmoking rooms. *In room:* A/C, TV, fridge (in some), hair dryer (on request), safe, no phone.

Playa Maya ✦ (Value Of the beach hotels in downtown Playa, this one would be my first choice. There are a lot of reasons to like it (good location, good price, comfortable rooms, and friendly and helpful management), but one thing that really strikes my fancy is that you enter this hotel from the beach. This little, seemingly inconsequential detail shouldn't be any reason for picking a hotel, but it just sets the mood of the place and creates a little separation from the busy street scene. To get back to more practical matters, the design and location make it a quiet hotel, too, as it is a couple of blocks away from the nearest beach bar and it's sheltered by the neighboring hotels. The pool and sunning terrace are attractive and nicely set apart. Rooms are large with midsize bathrooms. A couple come with private garden terraces with Jacuzzis; others have balconies facing the beach.

Zona FMT (between calles 6 and 8 Norte), 77710 Playa del Carmen, Q. Roo. (✆ 984/803-2022. www.playa-maya. com. 20 units. High season $140–$175 (£77–£96) double; low season $100–$140 (£55–£77) double. Rates include continental breakfast. MC, V. Limited street parking. **Amenities:** Restaurant; bar; outdoor pool; Jacuzzi; tour info; room service; massage; laundry service. *In room:* A/C, TV, Wi-Fi, fridge, hair dryer, safe.

MODERATE

Hotel Jungla Caribe Located right in the heart of the action, "La Jungla" is an imaginative piece of work—a colorful execution of neoclassical *a la tropical*. It's the right place for those who enjoy original lodging and seek out the commotion that comes with the location, which quiets down around 11pm. All but the eight *sencilla* (standard) rooms are large, with gray-and-black marble floors, air-conditioning, large bathrooms, and the occasional Roman column. Doubles and junior suites face Quinta Avenida and come with two double beds. Catwalks lead from the main building to the "tower" section of suites in back (the quietest). The *sencilla* rooms face Calle 8, are small with ample bathrooms, and have no air-conditioning. They come with one double bed and a balcony. It is best for people who go to bed late because of the mariachis who play across the street. There's an attractive pool in the courtyard surrounded by vegetation and shaded by a giant *ramón* tree.

Av. 5 Norte (at Calle 8), 77710 Playa del Carmen, Q. Roo. ⓒ/fax **984/873-0650.** www.jungla-caribe.com. 25 units. High season $70 (£39) *sencilla*, $90 (£50) double, $120–$130 (£66–£72) suite; low season $50 (£28) *sencilla*, $65 (£36) double, $90–$100 (£50–£55) suite. AE, MC, V. Limited street parking. **Amenities:** Restaurant; 2 bars; outdoor pool; tour info; room service. *In room:* A/C, TV, no phone.

Treetops Hotel ⓕ *Value*   The rooms at Treetops encircle a patch of preserved jungle (and a small *cenote*) that shades the hotel and lends it the proper tropical feel. Rooms are large and have balconies or patios that overlook the "jungle." Some of the upper rooms have the feel of a treehouse, especially the "treehouse" suite. The two other suites are large, with fully loaded kitchenettes—good for groups of four. The location is excellent: a half-block from the beach, a half-block from Quinta Avenida. The American owners are helpful, attentive hosts.

Calle 8 s/n, 77710 Playa del Carmen, Q. Roo. ⓒ/fax **984/873-0351.** www.treetopshotel.com. 22 units. High season $94 (£52) double, $105 (£58) kitchen studio, $147–$176 (£81–£97) suite; low season $85 (£47) double, $94 (£52) kitchen studio, $116–$145 (£64–£80) suite. MC, V. Limited street parking. **Amenities:** Restaurant; bar; small outdoor pool. *In room:* A/C, kitchenette (in some), fridge, no phone.

INEXPENSIVE
Hotel Lab Nah *Value*   Good rooms in a central location for a good price are the main attraction at this economy hotel in the heart of Playa. The cheapest rooms have windows facing Quinta Avenida. There was some noise—mostly late-night bar hoppers. It didn't bother me too much. Nevertheless, I think it's worth the money to get one of the partial oceanview standards with balcony on the third floor. Not so much for the view of the water (which could cease if the hotel next door decides to build higher), but because they are quieter and larger. The gardenview rooms are directly below the oceanview, are just as large and quiet, but not quite as fixed up. And the difference in price is very little.

Calle 6 (and Av. 5), 77710 Playa del Carmen, Q. Roo. ⓒ 984/873-2099 www.labnah.com. 33 units. High season $50–$100 (£28–£55) double; low season $40–$72 (£22–£40) double. Rates include continental breakfast. MC, V. Limited street parking. **Amenities:** Small outdoor pool; tour info; dry cleaning; laundry service; nonsmoking rooms. *In room:* A/C.

WHERE TO DINE
Aside from the restaurants listed below, I would point you in the direction of a few that don't need a full review. For fish tacos and inexpensive seafood, try **El Oasis,** on Calle 12, between avenidas 5 and 10 (no phone). For delicious quick food in an informal surrounding, try **Los Burritos del Gordo** (no phone) on Avenida 15 between Calle 10 and Calle 10 Bis. The owners (from Guadalajara) make these outrageous burritos with carne asada—cheap and delicious. For *arrachera* (fajita) tacos, the place to go is **Super Carnes H C de Monterrey** (ⓒ **984/803-0488**) on Calle 1 Sur between avenidas 20 and 25.

EXPENSIVE

La Casa del Agua ☆☆ EUROPEAN/MEXICAN   This restaurant has excellent food in inviting surroundings. Instead of obtrusive background music, you hear the sound of falling water. The German owners work at presenting what they like best about the Old and New worlds. They do a good job with seafood—try the grilled seafood for two. There's a tantalizing dish of duck breast in an orange and tamarind sauce. For a mild dish, try chicken in a wonderfully scented sauce of fine herbs accompanied by fettuccine; for something heartier, there's the tortilla soup listed as "Mexican soup." The restaurant offers a number of cool and light dishes that would be appetizing for lunch or an afternoon meal, for example, an avocado stuffed with shrimp and flavored with a subtle horseradish sauce on a bed of alfalfa sprouts and julienne carrots—a good mix of tastes and textures. For dessert, try the chocolate mousse. This is an upstairs restaurant under a large and airy *palapa* roof.

Av. 5 (at Calle 2). ☎ 984/803-0232. Reservations recommended in high season. Main courses $15–$25 (£8.25–£14). MC, V. Daily 10am–midnight.

La Parrilla MEXICAN/GRILL   Still a fun place, but it's having problems handling its success. Prices have gone up, and service is slower. But the fajitas remain good as well as many of the Mexican standards such as tortilla soup, enchiladas, and quesadillas. Mariachis show up around 8pm; plan accordingly.

Av. 5 (at Calle 8). ☎ 984/873-0687. Reservations recommended in high season. Main courses $10–$25 (£5.50–£14). AE, MC, V. Daily noon–1am.

Yaxché ☆☆☆ YUCATECAN   The menu here makes use of many native foods and spices to present a more elaborate regional cooking than the usual offerings at Yucatecan restaurants—and it was about time for someone to show a little creativity with such an interesting palette of tastes. Excellent examples are a cream of *chaya* (a native leafy vegetable), and an *xcatic* chile stuffed with *cochinita pibil*. I also like the classic Mexican-style fruit salad with lime juice and dried powdered chile. There are several seafood dishes; the ones I had were fresh and well prepared.

Calle 8 (between avs. 5 and 10). ☎ 984/873-2502. Reservations recommended in high season. Main courses $10–$25 (£5.50–£14). AE, MC, V. Daily noon–midnight.

MODERATE

Casa Mediterránea ☆☆☆ ITALIAN   Tucked away on a quiet little patio off Quinta Avenida, this small, homey restaurant serves excellent food. Maurizio Gabrielli and Mary Michelon are usually there to greet customers and make recommendations. Maurizio came to Mexico to enjoy the simple life, and this inclination shows in the restaurant's welcoming, unhurried atmosphere. The menu is mostly northern Italian, with several dishes from other parts of Italy. There are daily specials, too. Pastas (except penne and spaghetti) are made in-house, and none is precooked. Try fish and shrimp ravioli or penne alla Veneta. There are several wines, mostly Italian, to choose from. The salads are good and carefully prepared—dig in without hesitation.

Av. 5 (between calles 6 and 8; look for a sign for Hotel Marieta). ☎ 984/876-3926. Reservations recommended in high season. Main courses $8–$15 (£4.40–£8.25). No credit cards. Daily 1–11pm.

El Asador de Manolo ☆☆ STEAKS/ARGENTINE   If I want a steak in Playa, this is where I go. (Well, actually, I would try the address listed below in hopes that the restaurant pulled off the move as planned, but this being Mexico, I would be prepared to find it back at it's old location on Avenida 10 between 24 and 26.) The owner is an

Argentine who has been living in Mexico so long, he's gone Mexican. But the food is faithful to his native land: steaks, good *empanadas,* and southern-style pastas, and you can't go wrong with any of the soups. When ordering a steak, remember that "termino medio" means medium-rare, while "tres cuartos" means medium. For dessert there are crepes, mousse, and flan, usually.

Calle 28 (at Av. 10). © **984/803-0632**. Reservations recommended in high season. Main courses $7–$20 (£3.85–£11); steaks $14–$30 (£7.70–£17). MC, V. Mon–Fri 1–11pm; Sat–Sun 4pm–midnight.

Estas Son Las Mañanitas MEXICAN/ITALIAN   For dependable food in an advantageous spot for people-watching, try this restaurant. It's simple outdoor dining on "la Quinta"—comfortable chairs and tables under *palapa* umbrellas. The Italian owner is vigilant about maintaining quality and consistency. He offers an excellent *sopa de lima* (tortilla soup garnished with slices of a regional citrus fruit called lima), a large seafood pasta, and Tex-Mex specialties such as fajitas. The hot sauces are good.

Av. 5 (between calles 4 and 6). © **984/873-0114**. Main courses $8–$15 (£4.40–£8.25). AE, MC, V. Daily 7am–11:30pm.

La Cueva del Chango ☆ HIPPIE MEXICAN   Good food in original surroundings with a relaxed "mañana" attitude. True to its name ("The Monkey's Cave"), the place suggests a cave and has little waterways meandering through it, and there are two spider monkeys that hang about in the back of the place. But take away the water and the monkeys, and, oddly enough, it brings to mind the Flintstones. You'll enjoy great juices, blended fruit drinks, salads, soups, Mexican specialties with a natural twist, and handmade tortillas. The fish is fresh and delicious. Mosquitoes can sometimes be a problem at night, but the management has bug spray for the guests.

Calle 38 (between Av. 5 and the beach, near the Shangri-la Caribe). © **984/116-3179**. Main courses $6–$12 (£3.30–£6.60). No credit cards. Mon–Sat 8am–11pm; Sun 9am–4pm.

La Vagabunda ITALIAN/MEXICAN   This place is old-style Playa in its simplicity and charm. A large *palapa* shelters several simple wood tables sitting on a gravel floor. It's low-key and quiet—a good place for breakfast, with many options, including delicious blended fruit drinks, waffles, and omelets. The specials are a good value. In the afternoon and evening you can order light fare such as panini, pastas, and ceviche.

Av. 5 (between calles 24 and 26). © **984/873-3753**. Breakfast $4–$6 (£2.20–£3.30); main courses $7–$12 (£3.85–£6.60). MC, V. High season daily 7am–11:30pm; low season daily 7am–3:30pm.

Media Luna ☆☆☆ FUSION   This restaurant has an inventive menu that favors grilled seafood, sautés, and pasta dishes. Everything is fresh and prepared beautifully. Try the very tasty pan-fried fish cakes with mango and honeyed hoisin sauce. Another choice is the black pepper–crusted fish. Be sure to eye the daily specials. For lunch you can get sandwiches and salads, as well as black-bean quesadillas and crepes. The decor is primitive-tropical chic.

Av. 5 (between calles 12 and 14). © **984/873-0526**. Breakfast $4–$6 (£2.20–£3.30); sandwich with salad $5–$7 (£2.75–£3.85); main courses $8–$15 (£4.40–£8.25). No credit cards. Daily 8am–11:30pm.

INEXPENSIVE

La Tarraya Restaurant/Bar *(Value* SEAFOOD/YUCATECAN   THE RESTAURANT THAT WAS BORN WITH THE TOWN, proclaims the sign. It's right on the beach, with the water practically lapping at the foundations. Because the owners are fishermen, the fish is so fresh, it's still practically wiggling. The wood hut doesn't look like much, but

Choosing an All-Inclusive in the Riviera Maya

There are more than 40 all-inclusive resorts on this coast. Most people are familiar with the concept—large hotels that work with economies of scale to offer lodging, food, and drink all for a single, low rate. All-inclusives offer convenience and economy, especially for families with many mouths to feed. And, because they are enclosed areas, they make it easy for parents to keep an eye on their children.

There is a certain sameness about these hotels so that a lot can be said that applies to all. They're usually built around a large pool with activities and an activities organizer. There is often a quiet pool, too. One large buffet restaurant and a snack bar serve the needs of most guests, but there will be a couple of specialty restaurants at no extra charge but for which the guest has to make reservations. Colored bracelets serve to identify guests. In the evenings a show is presented at the hotel's theater.

These resorts work best for those who are looking for a relaxing beach vacation and to get away from the cold weather. They don't work for those who aim to get away from crowds—these hotels are large and operate with a high occupancy rate. Yes, staying at these all-inclusives is convenient and hassle-free. They make everything easy, including taking tours and day trips—all the organizing is done for you. On the downside, you don't often get the spontaneity or the sense of adventure that comes with other styles of travel. The question you have to ask yourself is "what kind of vacation am I looking for?"

The best way to get a room at an all-inclusive is through a vacation packager or one of its travel agents. You get a better deal than by contacting the hotel directly. Even if you have frequent-flier miles to burn, you will still find

they also have tables right on the beach. You can have your fish prepared in several ways. If you haven't tried the Yucatecan specialty *tik-n-xic*—fish with *achiote* and bitter-orange sauce, cooked in a banana leaf—this is a good place to do so. I can also recommend the ceviches and the beer.

Calle 2 Norte. © **984/873-2040.** Main courses $5–$10 (£2.75–£5.50); whole fish $9 (£4.95) per kilo (2.2 lbs.). No credit cards. Daily noon–9pm.

Los Carboncitos ⚐ MEXICAN   The restaurant's owner is from Mexico City, and he brings with him the tastes of central highland Mexico. The menu is simple, but there's hardly anything to steer clear of. One of the main things to order are the tacos, which are primarily grilled meat, such as the fajitas (also called *arrachera*) or *al pastor* (soft tacos with marinated, grilled pork, served with onions, cilantro and pineapple.) These are served with a great collection of salsas. I can also recommend the soups, which are well made, especially the *caldo xochitl* (Mexican-style chicken soup) and the traditional *pozole.* For the seafood, you can try the shrimp al chipotle or the shrimp kebobs. Also, try the good sides, commonly served in Mexico City taco places, such as *chicharrón de queso* (fried crispy cheese) and the guacamole.

it difficult to match the rates of a full package offered by one of the biggies like Funjet.

Of the many all-inclusives in the Riviera Maya, there are a few that are my favorites and might bear looking into.

Of the several all-inclusives that are in Playa del Carmen/Playacar, I like **Iberostar Quetzal** or **Tucán** (two names for different halves of the same hotel; www.iberostar.com). The food is better than at most, and the central part of the hotel is made of raised walkways and terraces over the natural mangrove habitat.

The **Hotel Copacabana** in Xpu-Ha (www.hotelcopacabana.com) has raised walkways, preserving much of the flora and making it visually interesting. And Xpu-Ha is blessed with a stunning beach.

Also in Xpu-Ha is the **Xpu-Ha Palace** (www.palaceresorts.com), built on the grounds of a failed nature park. It has some keen features, including lagoons and jungle and offers several facilities for kids, including a small crocodile hatchery. The hotel is spread out over a large area and necessarily involves a good bit of walking, but this also makes it feel like more of a getaway.

Aventura Spa Palace (www.palaceresorts.com) is another hotel in the Palace chain—this one is just for grownups. It has a large spa and gym and attractive common areas and guest rooms. There is a large pool but no beach; guests can take a shuttle to the Xpu-Ha property if they want.

Freedom Paradise (www.freedomparadise.com) is billed as the first size-friendly vacation resort. The management has worked hard to create an environment that large people will find comfortable. I like it because it doesn't have all the froufrou of so many other resorts—it's friendly and unpretentious.

Calle 4 (between Avs. 5 and 10). 984/873-1382. Main courses $6–$11 (£3.30–£6.05); order of tacos $4–$6 (£2.20–£3.30). No credit cards. Daily 9am–1am.

PLAYA DEL CARMEN AFTER DARK

It seems as if everyone in town is out strolling along "la Quinta" until midnight; there's pleasant browsing, dining, and drinking available at the many establishments on the street. Here's a quick rundown of the bars that you won't find on Quinta Avenida. The beach bar that is an institution in Playa is the **Blue Parrot** (© **984/873-0083**). It gets live acts, mostly rock, and attracts a mixed crowd. It's between calles 12 and 14. Just to the south is **Om** (no phone), which gets a younger crowd with louder musical acts. For salsa, go to **Mambo Café** (© **984/803/2656**) on Calle 6 between avenidas 5 and 10.

Alux (© **984/110-5050**) is a one-of-a-kind club occupying a large cave with two dramatically lit chambers and several nooks and sitting areas. It's worth going to, if only for the novelty. The local conservancy group approved all the work, and great care was taken not to contaminate the water, which is part of a larger underground river system. The club books a variety of music acts, usually with no cover. Often there's belly dancing, which is quite in keeping with the surroundings, and I couldn't help but think that I had stepped into a scene from a James Bond film. The bar is cash only and is open Tuesday to Sunday from 7pm to 2am. Take Avenida Juárez across to the other side of the highway—2 blocks down on your left.

For movie going, **Cine Hollywood,** Avenida 10 and Calle 8, in the Plaza Pelícanos shopping center, shows a lot of films in English with Spanish subtitles. Before you buy your ticket, make sure the film is subtitled *(subtitulada)* and not dubbed *(doblada).*

2 North of Playa del Carmen
BETWEEN PLAYA AND PUERTO MORELOS
The coast north of Playa del Carmen holds several roadside attractions, all-inclusive hotels, small cabaña hotels, spa resorts, and a new golf development that looks super expensive. The distance between Puerto Morelos and Playa is only about 30km (20 miles).

ROADSIDE ATTRACTIONS   Near the Puerto Morelos turnoff is **Rancho Loma Bonita,** which has all the markings of a tourist trap and offers horseback riding and ATV tours. For this sort of activity, I prefer Rancho Punto Venado, just south of Playa (see "Exploring Playa and the Riviera Maya" earlier in this chapter). You'll also come across **Jardín Botánico Dr. Alfredo Barrera** (no phone). Opened in 1990 and named after a biologist who studied tropical forests, the botanical garden is open Monday to Saturday from 9am to 5pm. Admission is $7 (£3.85). This place is disappointing because it's not being maintained well. It will be of most interest to gardeners and plant enthusiasts, but I'm afraid it will bore children. They are much more likely to enjoy the interactive zoo, **CrocoCun** (© **998/850-3719**). It's a zoological park a mile north of Puerto Morelos. It raises crocodiles from eggs and keeps several species of animals native to the Yucatán Peninsula. A visit to the reptile house is fascinating, though it may make you think twice about venturing into the jungle. The rattlesnakes and boa constrictors are particularly intimidating, and the tarantulas are downright enormous. The guided tour lasts 1½ hours. Children enjoy the guides' enthusiasm and are entranced by the spider monkeys and wild pigs. Wear plenty of bug repellent. There's a restaurant on site. CrocoCun is open daily from 8:30am to 5:30pm. As with other attractions along this coast, entrance fees are high: $18 (£9.90) adults, $12 (£6.60) children 6 to 12, free for children younger than 6.

BEACH CABAÑAS   Five kilometers (3 miles) north of Playa are some economical lodgings on a mostly rocky beach. A sign that says PUNTA BETE marks the access road to Xcalacoco; in a short time you arrive at the water. Before you do, the road forks off in a few places, and you'll see signs for different cabañas. The word conjures up visions of idyllic native-style dwellings with thatched roofs, but as often as not on the Yucatecan coast, it means simple lodging. This is mostly the case here, with rates running $45 to $60 (£25–£33) a night for two people. Of the four groupings of cabañas in Xcalacoco, the one I like best is **Coco's Cabañas** (for reservations © **998/874-7056;** for info see www.travel-center.com). It's a grouping of a handful of rooms with electricity and ceiling fans; a good, inexpensive little restaurant; and a small pool. Two of the rooms have air-conditioning. Next door is the Tides Riviera Maya, a spa resort (see "Spa Resorts," below).

La Posada del Capitan Lafitte ★★   Two kilometers (1¼ miles) from the highway, down an unpaved road, this lovely seaside retreat sits on a solitary stretch of sandy beach. I like this hotel for its simplicity and seclusion. You can enjoy relative isolation

The Yucatán's Upper Caribbean Coast

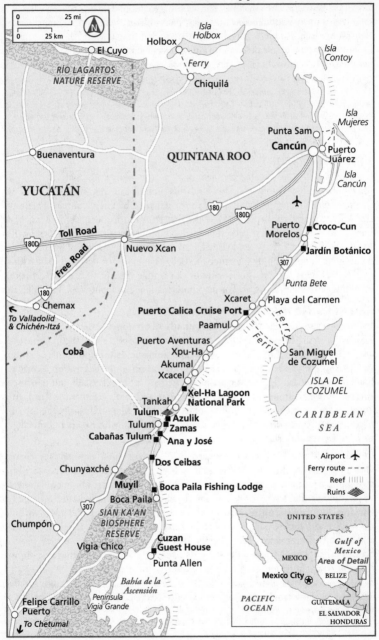

while still having all the amenities of a relaxing vacation. The beach is powdery white sand with a rocky bottom below the water. The two-story white-stucco bungalows hold four rooms each. Rooms are medium size and comfortable, with tile floors and bathrooms, either two double beds or one king-size bed, and an oceanfront porch. Service is personal and attentive. Twenty-nine bungalows have air-conditioning; the rest have fans.

Carretera Cancún–Tulum Km 62, 77710 Playa del Carmen, Q. Roo. © 800/538-6802 in the U.S. and Canada, or 984/873-0214. Fax 984/873-0212. www.mexicoholiday.com. 57 units. High season $235–$250 (£129–£138) double; low season $185–$200 (£102–£110) double. Christmas and New Year's rates are higher. Minimum 2–4 nights. Rates include breakfast and dinner. MC, V. Free guarded parking. **Amenities:** Restaurant; poolside grill; bar; midsize outdoor pool; watersports equipment; dive shop; activities desk; car rental; room service; laundry service. *In room:* A/C (in some), minibar.

NEW GOLF RESORT

Competition for the luxury tourism market just heated up with the arrival of **Mayakoba.** I don't know who is behind this project, but they definitely know what they're doing. They started with a golf course designed by Greg Norman. Then organized a PGA tour event here in 2007—the first PGA tournament ever in Mexico. And they've lined up a dazzling collection of resort properties: Fairmount, Viceroy, Rosewood, and Banyan Tree. When I visited, only the Fairmount was open, but the rest were going to be in operation by sometime in 2008. The resorts are designed to be a kind of connected endeavor—guests of one resort can sample the amenities of the other three, including restaurants and spas. For more information, check out www.mayakoba.com.

SPA RESORTS 🏯🏯🏯

In the area around Puerto Morelos, four spa resorts offer different versions of the hedonistic resort experience. Only 20 to 30 minutes from the Cancún airport, they are well situated for a quick weekend escape from the daily grind. You can jet down to Cancún, get whisked away by the hotel car, and be on the beach with a cocktail in hand before you can figure out whether you crossed a time zone. All four resorts pride themselves on their service, amenities, and spa and salon treatments. Being in the Yucatán, they like to add the healing practices of the Maya, especially the use of the native steam bath, called *temazcal.* Rates quoted below include taxes but not the 5% to 10% service charge.

Ceiba del Mar   This resort reopened in August of 2006, substantially changed, with a tad fewer rooms and more amenities. It now consists of seven three-story buildings set on a landscape of ponds and pools. The rooftop sections have been converted to penthouses, and the other rooms have been remodeled and look much finer. They are large and have a terrace or balcony. The bathrooms are large and come with both a shower and a tub, and stone counter surfaces. Service remains the same—attentive and unobtrusive, as exemplified by the delivery of coffee and juice each morning, accomplished without disturbing the guests through the use of a blind pass-through. The spa area is quite attractive and has quite a bit of space.

Av. Niños Héroes s/n, 77580 Puerto Morelos, Q. Roo. © 877/545-6221 in the U.S., or 998/872-8060. Fax 998/872-8061. www.ceibadelmar.com. 88 units. High season $450–$500 (£250–£275) deluxe and junior suite, from $850 (£468) suite; low season $415–$470 (£228–£259) deluxe and junior suite, from $800 (£440) suite. Rates include continental breakfast. Spa packages available. AE, MC, V. Free parking. **Amenities:** 2 restaurants; 2 bars; 2 outdoor pools (1 heated); lighted tennis court; complete state-of-the-art gym w/sauna, steam room, whirlpool, and Swiss showers; spa offering a wide variety of treatments; dive shop w/watersports equipment; bikes; concierge; tour info; car rental; salon; room service; babysitting, laundry service; nonsmoking rooms. *In room:* A/C, TV/VCR, Wi-Fi, minibar, hair dryer, safe, CD player.

Maroma This resort has been around the longest, owns a large parcel of land inland that it protects from development, and has a gorgeous beach and beautifully manicured grounds. Two- and three-story buildings contain the large guest rooms; most have king-size beds. The grounds are lovely, and the beach is fine white sand. The hotel has also spent a lot of effort and money on upgrades to the rooms. Nine new suites are outrageous examples of extravagance. There is a new beach bar that makes for an enjoyable place to pass the evening hours; it's a little more glitzy than the old one but still comfy. As at Tides Riviera Maya (see below), but to a lesser degree, the smaller size makes for more personal service and a deeper sense of escape.

Carretera 307 Km 51, 77710 Q. Roo. ℂ 866/454-9351 in the U.S., or 998/872-8200. Fax 998/872-8220. www.maroma hotel.com. 65 units. $480 (£264) garden-view double; $540–$740 (£297–£407) premium or deluxe double; $770–$850 (£407–£424) oceanfront double; from $940 (£517) suite. Rates include ground transfer, full breakfast, snorkeling tour. AE, MC, V. Free valet parking. No children younger than 16 allowed. **Amenities:** Restaurant; 3 bars; 3 outdoor spring-fed pools; fitness center; spa; Jacuzzi; steam bath; watersports equipment rental; game room; concierge; tours; car rental; salon; room service; in-room massage; laundry service; dry cleaning. In room: A/C, hair dryer.

Paraíso de la Bonita This resort has the most elaborate spa of all. I'm not a spa-goer and cannot discuss the relative merits of different treatments, but my work takes me to plenty of spas, and this one, which operates under the French system of thalassotherapy, is beyond anything I've seen. It uses seawater, sea salts, and sea algae in its treatments. I was impressed just in viewing the different apparatus. The beach is lovely and open. The pool area and the common areas of the spa are uncommonly attractive. The rooms occupy some unremarkable three-story buildings. They are, in decor and furnishings, more impressive than the rooms of the three other resorts reviewed in this section. The ground-floor rooms have a plunge pool; upstairs rooms come with a balcony. This resort was still closed for remodeling when I was last on the coast.

Carretera Cancún–Chetumal Km 328, Bahía Petenpich, 77710 Q. Roo. ℂ 866/751-9175 in the U.S., or 998/872-8300. Fax 998/872-8301. www.paraisodelabonita.com. 90 units. High season from $896 (£493) suite; low season from $778 (£428) suite. Rates include ground transfer. AE, MC, V. Free valet parking. No children younger than 12 allowed. **Amenities:** 2 restaurants; 2 bars; 4 outdoor pools; 1 lighted tennis court; spa; 2 Jacuzzis; watersports equipment rental; concierge; tour info; rental cars; salon; room service; in-room massage; laundry service; dry cleaning; nonsmoking rooms. In room: A/C, TV/DVD, minibar, hair dryer, safe.

The Tides Riviera Maya (formerly Ikal del Mar) The smallest of the four resorts in this section, this property is all about privacy and tranquillity. Thirty well-separated bungalows, each with its own piece of jungle, a little pool, and an outdoor shower are connected by lit pathways through the vegetation. The bungalows are large, filled with amenities, and decorated in a modern, sophisticated, spare style. The bathrooms have only a shower. Service here is the most personal of the four—everything can be brought to your bungalow. But if you do feel like socializing, the bar and restaurant (with excellent food), overlooking an inviting pool, make for an attractive common area. And of course, there's the spa. The beach was narrow and rocky, but the hurricane brought a lot of sand and widened it considerably. The new owners have made numerous improvements in the rooms and the spa.

Playa Xcalacoco, Carretera Cancún–Tulum, 77710 Q. Roo. ℂ 800/578-0281 in the U.S. and Canada, or 984/877-3000. Fax 713/528-3697. www.ikaldelmar.com. 30 units. High season from $770 (£424) villa; low season from $655 (£360) double. Rates include full breakfast. AE, MC, V. Free secure parking. Children younger than 18 not accepted. **Amenities:** Restaurant; 2 bars; large outdoor pool; spa; 2 Jacuzzis; steam bath; watersports equipment; concierge; tour info; car rental; courtesy shuttle to Playa; salon; room service; in-room massage; laundry service. In room: A/C, TV/DVD, fridge, hair dryer, safe.

PUERTO MORELOS

Puerto Morelos remains a quiet place—perfect for a relaxed vacation of lying on the white-sand beach and reading, with perhaps the occasional foray into watersports, especially snorkeling, diving, kitesurfing, windsurfing, and kayaking. Offshore lies a prominent reef, which has been declared a national park for its protection. It's shallow and makes for easy snorkeling, and it protects the coast from storm surges. The beaches are great and are maintained by the local government. The water is shallow, calm, and clear, with sea grass growing on the bottom. The town has a good bit of community spirit and a relaxed feel. There is a large English-language new and used bookstore that stocks 20,000 titles that you might want to check out if you forgot to bring beach reading. The ferry that used to depart from here for Cozumel has moved down the coast to the Calica pier just south of Playa del Carmen.

ESSENTIALS

GETTING THERE **By Car** At Km 31 there's a traffic light at the intersection, and a large sign pointing to Puerto Morelos.

By Bus Buses from Cancún to Tulum and Playa del Carmen usually stop here, but be sure to ask in Cancún if your bus makes the Puerto Morelos stop.

EXPLORING IN & AROUND PUERTO MORELOS

Puerto Morelos attracts visitors who seek seaside relaxation without crowds and high prices. The town has several hotels and a few restaurants. For outdoor recreation, there are two dive shops and plenty of recreational boats for fishing or snorkeling. On the main square, you'll find the bookstore, **Alma Libre** (✆ **998/871-0713;** www.alma librebooks.com). It has more English-language books than any other in the Yucatán, and not just whodunits, sci-fi, and spy novels. The owners, a couple of Canadians named Joanne and Rob Birce, stock everything from volumes on Maya culture to English classics to maps of the region. The store is open October through the first week in June, Tuesday to Sunday from 10am to 3pm and 6 to 9pm.

The reef directly offshore is very shallow and is protected by law. Snorkelers are required to wear a life vest to prevent them from diving down to the reef. I'm unaccustomed to snorkeling in a vest and found it a bit bothersome, but it didn't prevent me from getting a close look at the reef, which is quite shallow—3m (10 ft.) at its deepest, rising to within a foot of the surface. In a short time, I spotted four different eels and sea snakes, lots of fish, and a ray.

WHERE TO STAY

Hurricane Wilma did a good bit of damage to Puerto Morelos and the surrounding area. You can still see a few signs of it, but for the most part properties are up and running. For vacation rentals check out the website of Alma Libre books (see above).

Amar Inn Simple, rustic rooms on the beach, in a home-style setting, make this small inn a good place for those wanting a quiet seaside retreat. The cordial hostess, Ana Luisa Aguilar, is the daughter of Luis Aguilar, a Mexican singer and movie star of the 1940s and 1950s. She keeps busy promoting environmental and equitable-development causes. She can line up snorkeling and fishing trips and jungle tours for guests with local operators. There are three cabañas in back, opposite the main house, and six upstairs rooms with views of the beach. The most expensive rooms are the third-story "penthouse" rooms with a great view of the ocean. The cabañas get less of a cross-breeze than the rooms in the main house but still have plenty of ventilation. They are large and come with kitchenettes and are the most economical. Rooms in the main building are medium to large. Bedding choices include one or two doubles, one king-size, or five twin beds. Most of the mattresses were replaced after the hurricane with newer, cushier ones. A full Mexican breakfast is served in the garden.

Av. Javier Rojo Gómez (at Lázaro Cárdenas), 77580 Puerto Morelos, Q. Roo. © 998/871-0026. amar_inn@hotmail. com. 9 units. High season $60–85 (£33–£47) double; low season $50–$75 (£28–£41) double. Rates include full breakfast. No credit cards. From the plaza, turn left; it's 1km (half a mile) down, past the Hotel Ojo de Agua. Limited free parking. **Amenities:** Tour and rental info. *In room:* Fan, fridge, no phone.

Hotel Ojo de Agua ★ (Value

What I like best about this hotel is that it offers the convenience and service of a higher-priced hotel, including a good dive shop and watersports instruction and equipment rental. Two three-story buildings stand on the beach at a right angle to each other. The simply furnished rooms have balconies or terraces; most have a view of the ocean. Standard rooms have one queen bed with new mattresses. Deluxe rooms are large and have two doubles. Studios have a double and two twins and a small kitchenette but no air-conditioning (the rest of the rooms do have air-conditioning). Some rooms come with TV and phone. If you've wanted to try windsurfing or kitesurfing, this is a good place: The American who rents the boards takes his time with customers and is quite helpful.

Av. Javier Rojo Gómez, Supermanzana 2, Lote 16, 77580 Puerto Morelos, Q. Roo. © 998/871-0027 or -0507. Fax 998/871-0202. www.ojo-de-agua.com. 36 units. High season $65 (£36) double, $65–$80 (£36–£44) studio or deluxe; low season $50 (£28) double, $55–$70 (£30–£39) studio or deluxe. Weekly and monthly rates available. AE, MC, V. Limited free parking. **Amenities:** Restaurant; bar; outdoor pool; watersports equipment; dive shop; tour info; room service. *In room:* A/C (in some), TV (in some), kitchenette (in some), no phone (in some).

WHERE TO DINE

Puerto Morelos has a few restaurants. Most are on or around the main square and include **Los Pelícanos** for seafood; **Bodo's** (in the hotel Hacienda Morelos) for good lunch specials and a few German dishes, **Hola Asia** for Asian food; and **Le Café d'Amancia** for coffee and pastries. The most expensive restaurant in town is **John Grey's**, which is a couple of blocks north of the plaza and about 3 blocks inland. It's open for dinner except on Sundays. The owner is a former chef for the Ritz-Carlton.

3 South of Playa del Carmen

South of Playa del Carmen you'll find a succession of small communities and resorts and two nature parks. From north to south, this section covers them in the following order: Xcaret, Paamul, Puerto Aventuras, Xpu-Ha, Akumal, Xel-Ha, Punta Solimán, and Tankah. This section spans about 56km (35 miles).

HEADING SOUTH FROM PLAYA DEL CARMEN   Renting a car is the best way to move around down here. Southbound buses depart regularly from Playa, but the best they might do is get you close to your destination. And from the highway it can be a hot walk to the coast. Another option is to hire a car and driver.

Beyond Paamul, you'll see signs for this or that *cenote* or cave. There are thousands of *cenotes* in the Yucatán, and each is slightly different. These turnoffs are less visited than the major attractions and can make for a pleasant visit. Two major attractions bear specific mention: **Hidden Worlds,** offering remarkable snorkeling and diving tours of a couple of *cenotes,* and **Aktun Chen** cavern with a small nature park. Both are south of Akumal and described later in this chapter.

XCARET: A PARK CELEBRATING THE YUCATAN

A billboard in the airport of faraway Guadalajara reads in Spanish "And when visiting Xcaret, don't forget to enjoy the pleasures of the Riviera Maya, too." An exaggeration, but its point is well taken: Xcaret (pronounced "eesh-ca-*ret*") is the biggest attraction in these parts and is practically a destination unto itself. It even has its own resort (not recommended). If you're coming to these shores to avoid crowds, avoid this place. If you're here for entertainment and activities, you should consider visiting Xcaret. What Xcaret does, it does very well, and that is to present in one package a little bit of everything that the Yucatán (and the rest of Mexico for that matter) has to offer.

Think of the activities that people come to the Yucatán for: hanging out on the beach, scuba and snorkeling, cavern diving, visiting ruins, taking a siesta in a hammock under a grove of palm trees, hiking through tropical forest, meeting native Maya peoples—Xcaret has all that plus handicraft exhibitions; a bat cave; a butterfly pavilion; mushroom and orchid nurseries; and lots of wildlife on display, including native jaguars, manatees, sea turtles, monkeys, macaws, flamingos, and a petting aquarium. Children love it. What probably receives most of the comments is the underground river (a natural feature of the park and common in much of the Yucatán) that's been opened in places to allow snorkelers to paddle along with the current. What else? A number of tours and shows, including *charros* (Mexican cowboys) from the state of Jalisco, and the Totonac Indian *voladores* ("flyers" who do a daring pole dance high above the ground) from the state of Veracruz.

The park is famous for its evening spectacle that is a celebration of the Mexican nation. I've seen it and have to say that it is some show, with a large cast and lots of props. It starts with the Maya and an interpretation of how they may have played the pre-Hispanic game/ritual known as *pok-ta-pok,* and then to another version of a ball game still practiced in the western state of Michoacán. From there it moves on to the arrival of the Spanish and eventually to the forging of the new nation, its customs, its dress, and its music and dance.

Xcaret is 10km (6½ miles) south of Playa del Carmen (you'll know when you get to the turnoff). It's open daily from 8:30am to 9pm. Admission prices are $59 (£32) for adults, $41 (£23) for children 5 to 12. Certain activities cost extra: horseback ride $30 (£17), snuba/sea trek/snorkel tour $45 (£25), scuba $50 to $75 (£28–£41), swimming with dolphins $115 (£63). Other costs: lockers $2 (£1.10) per day, snorkel equipment $10 (£5.50) per day, food and drink variable. The park is an all-day affair; it's best to arrive early and register for tours and activities as soon as you can. For more info call © **998/883-3143** or visit www.xcaret.net.

Four kilometers (2½ miles) south of the entrance to Xcaret is the turnoff for **Puerto Calica,** the cruise-ship pier. Passengers disembark here for tours of Playa, Xcaret, the ruins, and other attractions on the coast.

Here's a tip: Fewer ships arrive on weekends than on weekdays, which makes the weekend a good time for visiting the major attractions on this coast.

PAAMUL: SEASIDE GETAWAY

About 15km (10 miles) beyond Xcaret and 25km (15 miles) from Playa del Carmen is Paamul, which in Mayan means "a destroyed ruin." The exit is clearly marked. At Paamul (also written Pamul), you can enjoy the Caribbean with relative quiet; the water at the out-of-the-way beach is wonderful, but the shoreline is rocky. There are four rooms for rent, a restaurant, and many trailer and RV lots with hookups.

There's also a dive shop. **Scuba-Mex** (℃ **984/873-0667;** fax 984/874-1729; www. scubamex.com) is a fully equipped PADI-, NAUI-, and SSI-certified dive shop next to the cabañas. Using two boats, the staff takes guests on dives 8km (5 miles) in either direction. If it's too choppy, the reefs in front of the hotel are also good. The cost for a two-tank dive is $50 (£28), plus $25 (£14) to rent gear. Snorkeling is also excellent in this protected bay and the one next to it. The shop offers a great 3-hour snorkeling trip ($25/£14).

WHERE TO STAY & DINE

Cabañas Paamul ✿   Hurricane Emily destroyed the cabañas that used to be here, and the owner, instead of replacing them, decided to go upscale, building six units in a two-story building right on the water's edge (two units are permanently occupied). They are large and come with a well-equipped kitchenette and two queen beds. Balconies offer a great view of the small bay. The trailer park has largely come back from the hurricane. Trailer guests have access to 12 showers and separate bathrooms for men and women. Laundry service is available nearby. The large, breezy *palapa* restaurant is a Brazilian-style grill under the management of Kalú da Silva, a retired Brazilian soccer player, who closed his restaurant in León, Guanajuato, to live on the coast. Restaurant customers are welcome to use the beach.

Carretera Cancún–Tulum Km 85. ℃ **984/875-1053.** paamulmx@yahoo.com. 4 units; 190 trailer spaces (all with full hookups). $100–$150 (£55–£83) double. RV space with hookups $25 (£14) per day, $500 (£275) per month. No credit cards. Ask about discount for stays longer than 1 week. Free parking. **Amenities:** Restaurant; bar. *In room:* A/C, TV, kitchenette.

PUERTO AVENTURAS: A RESORT COMMUNITY

Five kilometers (3 miles) south of Paamul and 104km (65 miles) from Cancún is the glitzy development of Puerto Aventuras, on Chakalal Bay. It's a condo/marina community with a 9-hole golf course. At the center of the development is a collection of restaurants bordering a dolphin pool. They offer a variety of food—Mexican, Italian, steaks, even a popular pub. The major attraction is the dolphins. To swim with them in a highly interactive program, you must make reservations by contacting **Dolphin Discovery** (℃ **998/849-4757;** www.dolphindiscovery.com). Make reservations well in advance—the surest way is by e-mail to salesinternet@dolphindiscovery.com.mx or through the link on the website. A 1-hour session costs $125 (£69). There are shorter programs that cost less.

This is also the place to come for boating and deep-sea fishing. I recommend **Capt. Rick's Sportfishing Center** (℃ **984/873-5195** or -5387; www.fishyucatan.com). The best fishing on this coast is from March to August. The captain will be happy to combine a fishing trip with some snorkeling, which makes for a leisurely day.

Tips In Case of Emergency

The Riviera Maya, south of Puerto Aventuras, is susceptible to power failures that can last for hours. Gas pumps and cash machines shut down when this happens, and once the power returns, they attract long lines. It's a good idea to keep a reserve of gas and cash.

I don't find Puerto Aventuras to be an interesting place for lodging and prefer to stay elsewhere on the coast. It's like a mini Cancún, but lacking Cancún's vibrancy. There are a couple of fancy hotels. The main one is the **Omni Puerto Aventuras** (© 800/843-6664 in the U.S., or 984/873-5101). It looks larger than its 30 rooms would indicate and was probably intended to be bigger but didn't get the expected traffic.

XPU-HA: BEAUTIFUL BEACH

Three kilometers (2 miles) beyond Puerto Aventuras is **Xpu-Ha** (eesh-poo-*hah*) ✶✶✶, a wide bay lined by a broad, beautiful sandy beach. Much of the bay is taken up by private houses and condos. There are a few all-inclusive resorts. One is **Xpu-Ha Palace** and another is the **Copacabana.** These suffered a lot of damage with Hurricane Emily but are open and back in business. The beach is big enough to accommodate the hotel guests, residents, and day-trippers without feeling crowded.

Also on the beach are a few small hotels. Two of these are expensive: **Al Cielo Hotel** (© 984/840-9012; www.alcielohotel.com) and **Esencia** (© 984/873-4830; www.hotelesencia.com). They are lovely places that offer personal service and attractive rooms away from the crowds. Both are close to Xpu-Ha Palace. And there are a few simple hotels offering basic lodging—a couple of beds, a cement floor, small private bathroom, and minimum decoration. These are rented on a first-come, first-served basis. Rates vary from $40 to $70 (£22–£39) a night, depending upon how busy they are. Lodging options are better in nearby Akumal, and, if you're renting a car, you can come for the day to enjoy the beach.

AKUMAL: BEAUTIFUL BAYS & CAVERN DIVING

Continuing south on Highway 307 for 2km (1¼ miles), you'll come to the turnoff for Akumal, marked by a traffic light. This is a small, ecologically oriented community built on the shores of two beautiful bays. Akumal has been around long enough that it feels more relaxed than booming places such as Playa and Tulum, and lodging tends to go for less here. Akumal draws a lot of families, who can save money by renting a unit with a kitchen to fix meals. Less than 1km (a half mile) down the road is a white arch. Just before it are a couple of grocery stores (the one named Super Chomak has an ATM) and a laundry service. Just after it (to the right) is the Hotel Akumal Caribe. If you follow the road to the left and keep to the left, you'll come to Half Moon Bay, lined with two- and three-story condos, and eventually to Yal-ku Lagoon, which is a snorkeling park. For renting a condo, contact **Info-Akumal** (© 800/381-7048 in the U.S.; www.info-akumal.com), **Akumal Vacations** (© 800/448-7137 in the U.S.; www.akumalvacations.com), or **Loco Gringo** (www.locogringo.com).

Both bays have sandy beaches with rocky or silt bottoms. This is a popular diving spot. There are three dive shops in town and at least 30 dive sites offshore. The **Akumal Dive Shop** (© 984/875-9032; www.akumal.com), one of the oldest and best dive shops on the coast, offers courses in technical diving and cavern diving trips. It and **Akumal Dive Adventures** (© 984/875-9157), at the Vista del Mar hotel on Half Moon Bay, offer resort courses as well as complete certification.

Yal-ku Lagoon snorkeling park is like a miniature and more primitive Xel-Ha. It's open daily from 8am to 5:30pm. Admission is $7 (£3.85) for adults, $4 (£2.20) for children 3 to 14. The lagoon is about 700m (2,296 ft.) long and about 200m (656 ft.) at its widest. You can paddle around comfortably in sheltered water with little current and see fish and a few other creatures. It makes for a relaxing outing, but for sheer variety, I prefer snorkeling along the reefs.

WHERE TO STAY

Rates below are for two people and include taxes. Most hotels and condo rentals charge higher rates than those listed here for the holidays.

Hotel Akumal Caribe ☆☆ *Kids*   The hotel rooms and garden bungalows of this hotel sit along Akumal Bay. Both are large and comfortable, with tile floors and good-size bathrooms. The 40 **bungalows** are simply and comfortably furnished and have kitchenettes. The 21 rooms in the three-story beachside **hotel** are more elaborately furnished and come with refrigerators. They have a king-size bed or two queen-size beds, tile floors, and Mexican accents. There is a large pool on the grounds. Other rooms belonging to the hotel are condos and the lovely **Villas Flamingo** on Half Moon Bay. The villas have two or three bedrooms and large living, dining, and kitchen areas, as well as lovely furnished patios just steps from the beach. The four villas share a pool.

Carretera Cancún–Tulum (Hwy. 307) Km 104. ☎ **984/875-9010.** www.hotelakumalcaribe.com. (Reservations: P.O. Box 13326, El Paso, TX 79913; ☎ **800/351-1622** in the U.S., 800/343-1440 in Canada, or 915/584-3552.) 70 units. High season $120 (£66) bungalow, $130–$150 (£72–£83) hotel room, $250–$500 (£138–£275) villa or condo; low season $75 (£41) bungalow, $93 (£51) hotel room, $180–$350 (£99–£193) villa or condo. Reservations with prepayment by check only. AE, MC, V. Free parking. Low-season packages available. **Amenities:** 2 restaurants; bar; large outdoor pool; dive shop; tour desk; children's activities (seasonal); in-room massage; babysitting. *In room:* A/C, kitchenette (in some), fridge, coffeemaker, no phone.

Vista del Mar Hotel and Condos ☆ *Value*   This beachside property is a great place to stay for several reasons. It offers hotel rooms at good prices, and large, fully equipped condos that you don't have to rent by the week. The lovely, well-tended beach in front of the hotel has chairs and umbrellas. There's an on-site dive shop, which eliminates the hassle of organizing dive trips. Hotel rooms are small and contain either a queen-size bed or a double and a twin bed. They consist of a well-equipped kitchen, a living area, two or three bedrooms, and one to three bathrooms. All have balconies or terraces facing the sea and are furnished with hammocks. Several rooms come with whirlpool tubs.

Half Moon Bay, 77760 Akumal, Q Roo. ☎ **877/425-8625** in the U.S. Fax 505/988-3882. www.akumalinfo.com. 27 units. High season $90 (£50) double, $220–$290 (£121–£160) condo; low season $75 (£41) double, $110–$175 (£61–£96) condo. MC, V. Limited free parking. **Amenities:** Restaurant; bar; small outdoor pool; watersports equipment rental; dive shop. *In room:* A/C, TV, CD player, kitchenette, fridge, coffeemaker, no phone.

WHERE TO DINE

There are about 10 places to eat in Akumal, and there's a convenient grocery store, **Super Chomak,** by the archway. The **Turtle Bay Café and Bakery** is good (not open for supper in low season), as is **La Buena Vida,** on Half Moon Bay.

XEL-HA: SNORKELING & SWIMMING ☆☆

Before you get to Xel-Ha (shell-*hah*) nature park, you'll pass the turnoff for **Aktun Chen** ☆ cavern (a bit beyond Akumal). Of the several caverns that I've toured in the Yucatán, this is one of the best—it has lots of geological features, good lighting, several underground pools, and large chambers, all carefully preserved. The tour takes about an hour and requires a good amount of walking, but the footing is good. You exit not far from where you enter. There is also a zoo with specimens of the local fauna. Some of the critters are allowed to run about freely. In my opinion, the cost of admission is high—$17 (£9.35) for adults, $9 (£4.95) for children—but this is true of several attractions on this coast. The cavern is open 9am to 5pm daily. The turnoff is to the right, and the cave is about 4km (2½ miles) from the road.

Thirteen kilometers (8 miles) south of Akumal is **Xel-Ha** (© **998/884-9422** in Cancún, 984/873-3588 in Playa, or 984/875-6000 at the park; www.xelha.com.mx). The centerpiece of Xel-Ha is a large, beautiful lagoon where freshwater and saltwater meet. You can swim, float, and snorkel in beautifully clear water surrounded by jungle. A small train takes guests upriver to a drop-off point. There, you can store all your clothes and gear in a locked sack that is taken down to the locker rooms in the main part of the building. The water moves calmly toward the sea, and you can float along with it. Snorkeling here offers a higher comfort level than the open sea—there are no waves and currents to pull you about, but there are a lot of fish of several species, including rays.

Inside the park, you can rent snorkeling equipment and an underwater camera. Platforms allow nonsnorkelers to view the fish. Another way to view fish is to use the park's snuba gear—a contraption that allows you to breathe air through 6m (20-ft.) tubes connected to scuba tanks floating on the surface. It frees you of the cumbersome tank while allowing you to stay down without having to hold your breath. Rental costs $45 (£25) for approximately an hour. Like snuba but more involved is sea-trek, a device consisting of an elaborate plastic helmet with air hoses. It allows you to walk around on the bottom breathing normally and perhaps participate in feeding the park's stingrays.

The park has completely remodeled and enlarged the dolphin area. This has improved the experience of swimming with these intelligent, powerful creatures. A 1-hour swim costs $115 (£63) plus park admission. You can also participate in a program that includes transportation from most hotels in the Riviera Maya and takes you to the dolphin area. It includes locker and equipment, too, all for $139 (£76). Make reservations (© **998/887-6840**) at least 24 hours in advance.

Other attractions include a plant nursery; an apiary for the local, stingerless Maya bees; and a lovely path through the tropical forest bordering the lagoon. Xel-Ha is open daily from 8:30am to 5pm. Parking is free. Admission is $33 (£18) adults, and $23 (£13) children ages 5 to 11; children younger than 5 enter free. Admission includes use of inner tubes, life vest, and shuttle train to the river, and the use of changing rooms and showers. (Though not listed on the website, the park often has discount admission during the weekend.) An all-inclusive option includes snorkeling equipment rental, locker rental, towels, food, and beverages. Adults can visit all week long for $59 (£32), and children visit for $41 (£23). These prices are not discounted on the weekend. The park has five restaurants, two ice-cream shops, and a store. It accepts American Express, MasterCard, and Visa, and it has an ATM.

Signs clearly mark the turnoff to Xel-Ha. Xel-Ha is close to the ruins of Tulum. A popular day tour from Cancún or Playa combines the two. If you're traveling on your own, the best time to enjoy Xel-Ha without the crowds is during the weekend from 9am to 2pm.

About 2km (1 mile) south of Xel-Ha are the **Hidden Worlds Cenotes** (©️©️©️ (© **984/877-8535;** www.hiddenworlds.com.mx), which offers an excellent opportunity to snorkel or dive in a couple of nearby caverns. The caverns are part of a vast network that makes up a single underground river system. The water is crystalline (and cold) and the rock formations impressive. These caverns were filmed for the IMAX production *Journey into Amazing Caves*. The people running the show are resourceful. The snorkel tour costs $40 (£22) and takes you to two different caverns (a half tour costs $25/£14). The main form of transportation is "jungle mobile," with a guide who throws in tidbits of information and lore about the jungle plant life that you see. There is some walking involved, so take shoes or sandals. I've toured several caverns, but floating through one gave me an entirely different perspective. For divers, a one-tank dive is $50 (£28), a two-tank experience is $90 (£50). The owners have also installed a 180m (590-ft.) zip line on the property. I haven't tried it, but it looks fast.

PUNTA SOLIMAN & TANKAH BAYS

The next couple of turnoffs lead to Punta Solimán and Tankah bays. On Punta Solimán Bay is a beach restaurant called **Oscar y Lalo's.** Here you can rent kayaks and snorkel equipment and paddle out to the reefs for some snorkeling. Three kilometers (2 miles) farther is the turnoff for Tankah Bay, where there are a handful of lodgings. The most interesting is **Casa Cenote** (© **998/874-5170;** www.casacenote.com). It has an underground river that surfaces at a *cenote* in the back of the property then goes underground and bubbles up into the sea just a few feet offshore. Casa Cenote has seven rooms, all on the beach. The double rate is around $150 (£83). The American owner provides kayaks and snorkeling gear and can arrange dives, fishing trips, and sailing charters.

A beach road connects the two bays. I found the snorkeling in Tankah better than in Punta Solimán. Snorkeling in the latter was both interesting and frustrating. I've never before experienced so many thermoclines, which are produced by freshwater seeping from the floors of the bay and coming in contact with the warmer saltwater. Light passing through the water is refracted in funny ways. At first I found the effect interesting—it lent an ethereal shininess to everything I was seeing—but then it just got annoying as it cut down sharply on visibility. At one point I was floating through some of the worst of it, trying not to stir up the water, when a giant silvery barracuda came ghostlike through the shimmering water and crossed my field of vision about 2m (6 ft.) away. As he passed slowly by me, I was astonished at how beautiful and luminescent he looked. Still, I will take clear water over shimmering water every time.

4 Tulum ⟨★⟨★⟨★, Punta Allen & Sian Ka'an

Tulum *pueblo* (130km/80 miles from Cancún) is a small town on Highway 307 where it intersects the road to Cobá. Nearby is an incredible beach, which has become the Tulum hotel zone—a collection of about 30 *palapa* hotels stretching from the Tulum ruins southward, along the Punta Allen Peninsula, all the way to the entrance to the Sian Ka'an Biosphere Reserve. The Tulum ruins are a walled Maya city of the post-Classic age perched on a rocky cliff overlooking the Caribbean. Tulum beach used to be a destination for backpackers, but the *palapa* hotels have gone upscale, and the beach now attracts a well-heeled crowd that seeks to get away from the bustle of the big hotels and resorts. The town of Tulum has several modest hotels, more than a dozen restaurants, several stores and pharmacies, three cybercafes, a few dive shops, a bank, two ATMs, and a new bus station.

For those who really want to leave the modern world behind, there's the Punta Allen Peninsula. Getting to the end of the peninsula from Tulum can take 1½ to 3 hours, depending on the condition of the road, which can be downright ugly. It's a quiet, out-of-the-way place; the generator (if there is one) shuts down at 10pm. For most people, Tulum will be far enough away from the crowds. But in Punta Allen, you'll find great fishing and snorkeling, the natural riches of the Sian Ka'an Biosphere Reserve, and a chance to rest up at what truly feels like the end of the road. A few beach cabañas offer reliable power, telephones, and hot showers.

> ### ⌒ *Tips* Getting to the Beach
>
> If you're staying elsewhere but want some beach time in Tulum, the easiest thing to do is drive to El Paraíso Beach Club. It's about 1km (a half mile) south of the ruins (take a left at the "T" junction). This is a great place—there's a long, broad beach that is pure sand, and access is free. The owners make money by selling food and drink (there's a nice little beach bar) so they ask you not to bring your own. The property was sold last year. The new owners are planning to build some kind of hotel or condos. No one is sure when this will happen. There might be a problem with permits. Until construction begins, the beach club will remain open. If you want a beach all to yourself, you can drive down the dirt road towards Punta Allen. After you pass the last of the beach hotels there are a couple of places where the beach comes into view. You can pull over and spread out your beach towel.

ORIENTATION   To visit the Tulum area, get a rental car; it will make everything much easier. Coming from the north you'll pass the entrance to the ruins before arriving at the town. You'll come to a highway intersection with a traffic light. To the right is the highway leading to the ruins of Cobá (see "Cobá Ruins," later in this chapter); to the left is the Tulum hotel zone, which begins about 2km (1½ miles) away. The road sign reads BOCA PAILA, which is a place halfway down the **Punta Allen Peninsula.** This road eventually goes all the way to the tip of the peninsula and the town of Punta Allen, a lobstering and fishing village. It is a rough road that is slow going for most of the way. A few kilometers down the road, you will enter the **Biosphere Reserve.**

The town of Tulum is growing quickly. It now extends for 3 or more blocks in either direction from the highway. The highway widens here and is called Avenida Tulum. It is lined with stores, restaurants, and the offices of service providers. One place that I find handy to visit is a travel agency/communications/package center called **Savana** (⌀ **984/871-2081**) on the east side of Avenida Tulum between calles Orion and Beta. The staff, for the most part, speaks English and can answer questions about tours and calling home.

EXPLORING THE TULUM ARCHEOLOGICAL SITE

Thirteen kilometers (8 miles) south of Xel-Ha are the ruins of Tulum, a Maya fortress-city on a cliff above the sea. The ruins are open to visitors daily from 7am to 5pm in the winter, 8am to 6pm in the summer. It's always best to go early, before the crowds start showing up (around 9:30am). The entrance to the ruins is about a 5-minute walk from the archaeological site. There are artisans' stands, a bookstore, a museum, a restaurant, several large bathrooms, and a ticket booth. Admission fee to the ruins is $4 (£2.20). If you want to ride the shuttle from the visitor center to the ruins, it's another $1.50 (85p). Parking is $3 (£1.65). A video camera permit costs $4 (£2.20). Licensed guides have a stand next to the path to the ruins and charge $20 (£11) for a 45-minute tour in English, French, or Spanish for up to four persons. In some ways, they are like performers and will tailor their presentation to the responses they receive from you. Some will try to draw connections between the Maya and Western theology, and they will point out architectural details that you might otherwise miss.

By A.D. 900, the end of the Classic period, Maya civilization had begun its decline, and the large cities to the south were abandoned. Tulum is one of the small city-states that rose to fill the void. It came to prominence in the 13th century as a seaport, controlling maritime commerce along this section of the coast, and remained inhabited well after the arrival of the Spanish. The primary god here was the diving god, depicted on several buildings as an upside-down figure above doorways. Seen at the Palace at Sayil and Cobá, this curious, almost comical figure is also known as the bee god.

The most imposing building in Tulum is a large stone structure above the cliff called the **Castillo** (castle). Actually a temple as well as a fortress, it was once covered with stucco and painted. In front of the Castillo are several unrestored palacelike buildings partially covered with stucco. On the **beach** below, where the Maya once came ashore, tourists swim and sunbathe, combining a visit to the ruins with a dip in the Caribbean.

The **Temple of the Frescoes,** directly in front of the Castillo, contains interesting 13th-century wall paintings, though entrance is no longer permitted. Distinctly Maya, they represent the rain god Chaac and Ixchel, the goddess of weaving, women, the moon, and medicine. On the cornice of this temple is a relief of the head of the rain god. If you pause a slight distance from the building, you'll see the eyes, nose, mouth, and chin. Notice the remains of the red-painted stucco—at one time all the buildings at Tulum were painted bright red.

Much of what we know of Tulum at the time of the Spanish Conquest comes from the writings of Diego de Landa, third bishop of the Yucatán. He wrote that Tulum was a small city inhabited by about 600 people who lived in platform dwellings along a street and who supervised the trade traffic from Honduras to the Yucatán. Though it was a walled city, most of the inhabitants probably lived outside the walls, leaving the interior for the residences of governors and priests and ceremonial structures. Tulum survived about 70 years after the conquest, when it was finally abandoned. Because of the great number of visitors this site receives, it is no longer possible to climb all of the ruins. In many cases, visitors are asked to remain behind roped-off areas to view them.

WHERE TO STAY

If you can afford staying at one of the small beach hotels in Tulum, do so. The experience is enjoyable and relaxing. But most are on the expensive side. Demand is high, supply is limited, and the hotels have to generate their own electricity (bring a flashlight). Most of the inexpensive hotels are not that comfortable. If you're on a budget, you will be more comfortable staying in Akumal or in one of the modest hotels in town and be a day-tripper to the beach.

Take the Boca Paila road from Highway 307. Three kilometers (2 miles) ahead, you come to a T-junction. To the south are most of the *palapa* hotels; to the north are several, too. The rates listed below don't include the week of Christmas and New Year, when prices go above regular high-season rates.

Very Expensive

Ana y José ★★   This *palapa* hotel has gone "boutique" with a spa, suites, and serious remodeling of rooms. It's a far cry now from what it used to be—a simple collection of cabins and a restaurant on the beach. Now there are marble countertops and marble tile floors. Rooms are large and comfortable. There's A/C in all the lower rooms that don't catch the sea breeze. The two beachfront rock cabins in front of the property have remained unchanged and are a little lower in price than the other beachfront and oceanview rooms. The beach here is excellent. Ana y José is 6.5km (4 miles) south of the Tulum ruins.

Carretera Punta Allen Km 7 (Apdo. Postal 15), 77780 Tulum, Q. Roo. (*) **998/887-5470.** Fax 998/887-5469. www. anayjose.com. 22 units. $233–$255 (£128–£140) garden and pool view; $306–$373 (£168–£205) beachfront and ocean view. AE, MC, V. Free parking. **Amenities:** Restaurant; outdoor pool; spa; tour info; car rental. *In room:* A/C in some rooms, safe, no phone.

Azulik 🐟🐟

Azulik is all about slowing down, leaving civilization behind (except for such niceties as indoor plumbing and room service), and enjoying the simple life (with or without clothes). I enjoyed the simple life during an all-too-brief stay here, and what I liked most about Azulik was the design and positioning of the individual cabañas. All but three of them sit on a stone ledge next to, and a little above, the sea. The ledge is just high enough to provide privacy while you sit out on the semi-shaded wood deck in front of your cabaña enjoying either the sun or the stars. For that purpose, they come with chairs, hammocks, and a wooden tub for soaking. (There is a larger wooden tub indoors for bathing.) Each cabaña is constructed entirely of wood and glass and thatch. There is no electricity, only candles. Each has a king-size bed with mosquito netting and a queen-size bed, suspended on ropes, for lounging during the day. This property shares a good restaurant and a good spa with a sister hotel.

Carretera Boca Paila Km 5.5, 77780 Tulum, Q. Roo. (*) **877/532-6737** in the U.S. and Canada. www.azulik.com. 15 units. High season $240–$260 (£132–£143) double; low season $190–$210 (£105–£116) double. MC, V. Limited free parking. Children younger than 18 not accepted. **Amenities:** Restaurant; bar; spa; room service. *In room:* Safe, no phone.

Moderate

Posada Dos Ceibas 🐟

Of all the places along this coast, this one reminds me the most of the way hotels in Tulum used to be. Simple, quiet, and ecological without being pretentious. This is a good choice for a no-fuss beach vacation. The one- and two-story cottages are spread out through the vegetation. Rooms are simply furnished and come with ceiling fans, and almost all have private patios or porches. Price varies according to the size of the rooms. The grounds are well tended. The electricity is solar generated and comes on at 6pm. There is a pure sand beach.

Carretera Tulum-Boca Paila Km 10, 77780 Tulum, Q. Roo. (*) **984/877-6024.** www.dosceibas.com. 8 units. High season $100–$220 (£55–£121) double; low season $75–$145 (£41–£80). MC, V. **Amenities:** Restaurant; massage; yoga classes. *In room:* No phone.

Zamas 🐟🐟

The owners of these cabañas, a couple from San Francisco, have made their rustic getaway most enjoyable by concentrating on the essentials: comfort, privacy, and good food. The cabañas are simple, attractive, well situated for catching the breeze, and not too close together. Most rooms are in individual structures; the suites and oversize rooms are in modest two-story buildings. For the money, I like the individual garden *palapas,* which are attractive, spacious, and comfortable, and come with a queen-size bed and a twin or a king- and queen-size bed. Two small beachfront cabañas with one queen-size bed go for a little less. The most expensive rooms are the upstairs oceanview units, which enjoy a large terrace and lots of sea breezes. They come with a king-size and a queen-size bed or two queen-size beds. The restaurant serves the freshest seafood—I've actually seen the owner flag down passing fishermen to buy their catch. A white-sand beach stretches between large rocky areas.

Carretera Punta Allen Km 5, 77780 Tulum, Q. Roo. (*) **415/387-9806** in the U.S. www.zamas.com. 20 units. High season $105–$150 (£58–£83) beachfront double, $110–$135 (£61–£74) garden double, $180 (£99) oceanview double; low season $85–$95 (£47–£52) beachfront double, $80–$115 (£44–£63) garden double, $135 (£74) oceanview double. No credit cards. Limited free parking. **Amenities:** Restaurant. *In room:* No phone.

Inexpensive

Cabañas Tulum   Next to Ana y José is a row of cinderblock bungalows facing the same beautiful ocean and beach. Rooms are simple and poorly lit, with basic bathrooms. All rooms have two double beds (most with new mattresses), screens on the windows, a table, one electric light, and a porch facing the beach. Electricity is available from 7 to 11am and 5 to 11pm.

Carretera Punta Allen Km 7 (Apdo. Postal 63), 77780 Tulum, Q. Roo. © **984/879-7395.** Fax 984/871-2092. www.hotels tulum.com. 32 units. $60–$80 (£33–£44) double. No credit cards. Limited free parking. **Amenities:** Restaurant; game room. *In room:* No phone.

WHERE TO DINE

There are several restaurants in the town of Tulum. They are reasonably priced and do an okay job. On the main street are **Charlie's** (© **984/871-2136**), my favorite for Mexican food, and **Don Cafeto's** (© **984/871-2207**). A good Italian-owned Italian

The Sian Ka'an Biosphere Reserve

Down the peninsula a few miles south of the Tulum ruins, you'll pass the guardhouse of the Sian Ka'an Biosphere Reserve. The reserve is a tract of 500,000 hectares (1.3 million acres) set aside in 1986 to preserve tropical forests, savannas, mangroves, coastal and marine habitats, and 110km (70 miles) of coastal reefs. The area is home to jaguars; pumas; ocelots; margays; jaguarundis; spider and howler monkeys; tapirs; white-lipped and collared peccaries; manatees; brocket and white-tailed deer; crocodiles; and green, loggerhead, hawksbill, and leatherback sea turtles. It also protects 366 species of birds—you might catch a glimpse of an ocellated turkey, a great curassow, a brilliantly colored parrot, a toucan or trogon, a white ibis, a roseate spoonbill, a jabiru (or wood stork), a flamingo, or one of 15 species of herons, egrets, and bitterns.

The park has three parts: a "core zone" restricted to research; a "buffer zone," to which visitors and families already living there have restricted use; and a "cooperation zone," which is outside the reserve but vital to its preservation. There are two principal entrances to the biosphere reserve: one is from the community of Muyil, which is off Highway 307, south of Tulum (you take a boat down canals built by the Maya that connect to the Boca Paila lagoon); the other is from the community of Punta Allen (by Jeep down the peninsula, which separates the Boca Paila Lagoon from the sea).

Visitors can arrange day trips in Tulum from a few different outfits, whose offices are just a couple of blocks apart and even have similar names. **Sian Ka'an Tours** (© **984/871-2363**; siankaan_tours@hotmail.com) is on the west side of Avenida Tulum, next to El Basilico Restaurant, at the corner of Calle Beta. **Community Tours Sian Ka'an** is on the same side of the road, 2 blocks north between Orion and Centauro streets (© **984/114-0750**; www. siankaantours.org). The latter is a community organization of Muyil and Punta Allen. Both will pick up customers from any of the area hotels.

restaurant, **Il Giardino** (© **984/804-1316;** closed Wed), is a block off the highway on the town's northern-most cross street, Satelite. At **Azafrán** (© **984/129-6130**) you can get amazingly sophisticated cooking served in a small, rustic dining room. Also in town are a couple of roadside places that grill chicken and serve it with rice and beans. And there's a local people's restaurant at the southern end of town called **Doña Tina.** Meals on the coast are going to be more expensive but more varied. Many of the hotels have restaurants—I've eaten well at **Copal** and **Mezzanine,** which are both north of the T-junction, and **Zamas,** which is south.

EXPLORING THE PUNTA ALLEN PENINSULA

If you've been captured by an adventurous spirit and have an excessively sanguine opinion of your rental car's off-road capabilities, you might want to take a trip down the Punta Allen Peninsula, especially if your interests lie in fly-fishing, birding, or simply exploring new country. The far end of the peninsula is only 50km (30 miles) away, but it can be a very slow and bouncy trip (up to 3 hr., depending on the condition of the road). Not far from the last cabaña hotel is the entrance to the 500,000-hectare (1.3-million-acre) **Sian Ka'an Biosphere Reserve** (see below).

Halfway down the peninsula, at a small bridge, is the **Boca Paila Fishing Lodge** (www.bocapaila.com). Not for the general traveler, it specializes in hosting fly-fishers, with weeklong all-inclusive fishing packages. At this point, the peninsula is quite narrow. You can see the Boca Paila lagoon on one side and the sea on the other. Another 25km (15 miles) gets you to the village of Punta Allen. Before the town is a little hotel called **Rancho Sol Caribe.** It has only four rooms and a lovely beach all to itself. Punta Allen is a lobstering and fishing village on a palm-studded beach. Isolated and rustic, it's very much the laid-back end of the line. It has a lobster cooperative, a few streets with modest homes, and a lighthouse. The **Cuzan Guesthouse** (www.fly fishmx.com) is a collection of 12 cabins and one restaurant on a nice sandy beach. Its main clientele is fly-fishers, and it offers all-inclusive fishing packages. But co-owner Sonia Litvak, a Californian, will rent to anyone curious enough to want to go down there. She also offers snorkeling trips and boat tours.

5 Cobá Ruins

168km (104 miles) SW of Cancún

Older than most of Chichén Itzá and much larger than Tulum, Cobá was the dominant city of the eastern Yucatán before A.D. 1000. The site is large and spread out, with thick forest growing between the temple groups. Rising high above the forest canopy are tall and steep pyramids of the Classic Maya style. Of the major sites, this one is the least reconstructed and so disappoints those who expect another Chichén Itzá. The stone sculpture here has worn off and has become impossible to make out. But the structures themselves and the surrounding jungle and twin lakes make the experience enjoyable. This is not a *cenote* area, and the water has nowhere to go but stay on the surface. The forest canopy is also higher than in the northern part of the peninsula.

ESSENTIALS

GETTING THERE & DEPARTING   By Car   The road to Cobá begins in Tulum and continues for 65km (40 miles). Watch out for both *topes* (speed bumps) and potholes. The road is going to be repaved and widened this year. Close to the village of Cobá you will come to a triangle offering you three choices: Nuevo Xcan, Valladolid, and Cobá. Make sure not to get on the other two roads. The entrance to the ruins is a short distance down the road past some small restaurants and the large lake.

By Bus   Several buses a day leave Tulum and Playa del Carmen for Cobá. Several companies offer bus tours.

EXPLORING THE COBA RUINS

The Maya built many intriguing cities in the Yucatán, but few grander than Cobá ("water stirred by wind"). Much of the 67-sq.-km (26-sq.-mile) site remains unexcavated. A 100km (62-mile) *sacbé* (a pre-Hispanic raised road or causeway) through the jungle linked Cobá to Yaxuná, once an important Maya center 50km (30 miles) south of Chichén Itzá. It's the Maya's longest known *sacbé*, and at least 50 shorter ones lead from here. An important city-state, Cobá flourished from A.D. 632 (the oldest carved date found here) until after the rise of Chichén Itzá, around 800. Then Cobá slowly faded in importance and population until it was finally abandoned. Scholars believe Cobá was an important trade link between the Yucatán Caribbean coast and inland cities.

Once at the site, keep your bearings—you can get turned around in the maze of dirt roads in the jungle. And bring bug spray. As spread out as this city is, renting a bike (which you can do at the entrance for $2.50/£1.40) is a good option. Branching off from every labeled path, you'll notice unofficial narrow paths into the jungle, used by locals as shortcuts through the ruins. These are good for birding, but be careful to remember the way back.

The **Grupo Cobá** holds an impressive pyramid, **La Iglesia (the Temple of the Church),** which you'll find if you take the path bearing right after the entrance. Though the urge to climb the temple is great, the view is better from El Castillo in the Nohoch Mul group farther back.

From here, return to the main path and turn right. You'll pass a sign pointing right to the ruined *juego de pelota* **(ball court),** but the path is obscure.

Continuing straight ahead on this path for 5 to 10 minutes, you'll come to a fork in the road. To the left and right you'll notice jungle-covered, unexcavated pyramids, and at one point, you'll see a raised portion crossing the pathway—this is the visible remains of the *sacbé* to Yaxuná. Throughout the area, carved stelae stand by pathways or lie forlornly in the jungle underbrush. Although protected by crude thatched roofs, most are weatherworn enough that they're indiscernible.

The left fork leads to the **Nohoch Mul Group,** which contains **El Castillo.** With the exception of Structure 2 in Calakmul, this is the tallest pyramid in the Yucatán (rising even higher than the great El Castillo at Chichén Itzá and the Pyramid of the Magician at Uxmal). Visitors are permitted to climb to the top. From this lofty perch, you can see unexcavated jungle-covered pyramidal structures poking up through the forest canopy all around.

The right fork (more or less straight on) goes to the **Conjunto Las Pinturas.** Here, the main attraction is the **Pyramid of the Painted Lintel,** a small structure with traces of its original bright colors above the door. You can climb up to get a close look. Though maps of Cobá show ruins around two lakes, there are really only two excavated groups.

Admission is $4 (£2.20), free for children younger than age 12. Parking is $1 (55p). A video camera permit costs $4 (£2.20). The site is open daily from 8am to 5pm, sometimes longer.

WHERE TO STAY & DINE

If nightfall catches you in Cobá, you have limited lodging choices. There is one tourist hotel called **Villas Arqueológicas Cobá,** which fronts the lake and is operated by Club Med. Though smaller than its sister hotels in Uxmal and Chichén Itzá, it's the same in style—modern rooms that are attractive and functional, so long as you're not too tall. It has a restaurant that serves all three meals. It could be empty or full since most of its business comes from bus tours. To make reservations, call ℰ **800/258-2633** in the U.S. or 55/5203-3086 in Mexico. It has a swimming pool. There's also a cheap hotel in town called **El Bocadito** (no phone) with simple rooms for $25 (£14) per night. It has a small restaurant, and there are a couple more in the town as well.

EN ROUTE TO THE LOWER CARIBBEAN COAST: FELIPE CARRILLO PUERTO

Mexico's lower Caribbean coast is officially called the Costa Maya. This area attracts fishermen, divers, archeology enthusiasts, birders, and travelers looking to get away from the crowds. For divers there is some great diving along the coastal reefs and at the Chinchorro Reef, which lies about 30km (20 miles) offshore (see below). You'll find sandy beaches good for sunbathing, but not for swimming because of the prominent coastal reef. But if you want to snorkel or dive among less-visited reefs, kayak in calm turquoise water, or perhaps do some fly-fishing away from the crowds, this area is a great option. And there's fine swimming in Lake Bacalar.

You also might enjoy the astounding Maya ruins in the Río Bec area, west of Bacalar. Here, too, you'll find a richer ecosystem than the northern part of the peninsula. The forest canopy is higher, and the wildlife is more abundant. If you're interested in exploring this territory, see "Side Trips to Maya Ruins from Chetumal," later in this chapter.

Continue south on Highway 307 from Tulum. The road narrows, the speed limit drops, and you begin to see *topes.* Down the road some 25km (15 miles), a sign points to the small but interesting ruins of **Muyil.** Take bug spray. The principal ruins are a small group of buildings and a plaza dominated by the Castillo, a pyramid of medium height but unusual construction. From here, a canal dug by the Maya enters what is now the Sian Ka'an Biosphere Reserve and empties into a lake, with other canals going from there to the saltwater estuary of Boca Paila. The local community offers a boat ride through these canals and lakes. The 3½-hour tour includes snorkeling the canal and letting the current carry you along. Soft drinks are also included. This is much the same Sian Ka'an tour offered by travel agencies in Tulum, but without some of the infrastructure. The agencies charge more but provide transportation, better interpretation, and lunches.

Felipe Carrillo Puerto (pop. 60,000) is the first large town you pass on the road to Ciudad Chetumal. It has two gas stations, a market, a bus terminal, and a few modest hotels and restaurants. Next to the gas station in the center of town is a bank with an ATM. Highway 184 goes from here into the interior of the peninsula, leading

---

For Your Comfort at Cobá

Visit Cobá in the morning or after the heat of the day has passed. Mosquito repellent, drinking water, and comfortable shoes are imperative.

Last Gas

It's a good idea to fill up in Felipe Carrillo Puerto, the last gas station before Bacalar.

eventually to Mérida, which makes Carrillo Puerto a turning point for those making the "short circuit" of the Yucatán Peninsula.

The town is of interest for having been a rebel stronghold during the War of the Castes and the center of the intriguing millenarian cult of the "Talking Cross." The town is still home to a strong community of believers in the cult who practice their own brand of religion and are respected by the whole town. Every month, a synod of sorts is held here for the church leaders of 12 neighboring towns.

6 Majahual, Xcalak & the Chinchorro Reef

South of Felipe Carrillo Puerto, the speed bumps begin in earnest. In 45 minutes you reach the turnoff for Majahual and Xcalak, which is after the town of Limones. From here, the highway has been widened and repaved. The roadwork was done to facilitate bus tours from the cruise-ship pier in **Majahual** (mah-hah-*wahl*) to some of the Maya ruins close by. Many passengers elect to enjoy some beach time in Majahual instead. The best option is to keep your distance from the pier and stay either in the lower Majahual area or at the bottom of the peninsula near Xcalak. You'll come to the turnoff for Xcalak before you get to Majahual. Xcalak has a decent dive shop. From Majahual to Xcalak takes a little less than an hour.

Xcalak (eesh-kah-*lahk*) is a depopulated, weather-beaten fishing village with a few comfortable places to stay and a couple of restaurants. It once had a population as large as 1,200 before the 1958 hurricane washed most of the town away; now it has only 300 permanent residents. It's charming in a run-down way, and you'll certainly feel miles away from the crush of the crowds. From here you work your way back up the coast to get to one of the several small inns just beyond the town.

ORIENTATION

ARRIVING   By Car   Driving south from Felipe Carrillo Puerto, you'll come to the clearly marked turnoff onto Highway 10, 2.5km (1½ miles) after Limones, at a place called Cafetal. From there it's a 50km (30-mile) drive to the coast, and Majahual. The pier is north of the road; Hotel Balamkú, which I like, is to the south. If you're going to Xcalak, the turn-off will be 2km (1¼ miles) before Majahual, at a military checkpoint. The road is paved, but usually with some potholes. It's 55km (34 miles) long.

DIVING THE CHINCHORRO REEF

The **Chinchorro Reef Underwater National Park** is 38km (24 miles) long and 13km (8 miles) wide. The oval reef is as shallow as 1m (3¼ ft.) on its interior and as deep as 900m (2,952 ft.) on its exterior. It lies some 30km (19 miles) offshore. Locals claim it's the last virgin reef system in the Caribbean. It's invisible from the ocean side; hence, one of its diving attractions is the **shipwrecks**—at least 30—that decorate the underwater landscape. One is on top of the reef. Divers have counted 40 cannons at one wreck site. On the west side are walls and coral gardens.

The Yucatán's Lower Caribbean Coast

To Valladolid

0   25 mi
0   25 km

N

To Cancún

■ Zamas
Ana y José ■

Cabañas Tulum ■

Chumpón

Dos Ceibas ■   Laguna
San Felipe

Boca Paila
Fishing Lodge ■

Punta Allen ○   ■ Cuzan Guest
House

Bahía de la
Ascensión

Peninsula Vigia
Grande

SIAN KA'AN

BIOSPHERE

RESERVE

● Pta. Sta. Rosa
Bahía
del Espíritu
Santo
● Pta. Herrero

○ Mosquitero

QUINTANA

ROO

To Ticul & Uxmal

Polyuc ○

Felipe Carrillo
Puerto
(Chan Santa Cruz)

Caribbean
Sea

○ Los Limones

○ Cafetal

○ Placer

Cayo Norte

○ Majahual

Banco Chinchorro
(Chinchorro Reef)

Balamkú Inn
on the Beach ■

Cayo
Lobos

Rancho
Encantado ○
Bacalar ○
Lago
Bacalar

Bahía
de
San José

Cenote Azul ○

○ Calderitas
✈ Chetumal

To Escárcega
& Rio Bec Ruins

Bahía Chetumal

■ Tierra Maya

■ Costa de Cocos
Dive Resort

Xcalak ○

BELIZE

UNITED STATES

Gulf of
Mexico

MEXICO

Area of detail
BELIZE

Mexico City ✪

PACIFIC
OCEAN

GUATEMALA
EL SALVADOR
HONDURAS

Airport ✈
Ruins

Aventuras XTC (© **983/831-0461;** www.xtcdivecenter.com) is a fully equipped dive shop in Xcalak (technical diving, Nitrox, snorkel and fishing trips). You can arrange dives to the local reefs, San Pedro in Belize, and to the Chinchorro Reef, weather permitting.

WHERE TO STAY & DINE

Balamkú Inn on the Beach ⭑⭑   This is a comfortable and friendly place to stay
in south Majahual. Rooms are in one- and two-story thatched bungalows distributed across 110m (360 ft.) of beautiful white beach. They are large and breezy with large attractive bathrooms and comfortable mattresses. All have terraces facing the beach. This hotel is very ecological. All the energy is produced by wind and sun. To run this kind of operation takes a rare combination of skill and talent, which these owners have in ample supply.

Carretera Costera Km 5.7, Majahual, Q. Roo. © 983/839-5332. www.balamku.com. 10 units. $75–$85 (£41–£47) double. Rates include full breakfast. AE, MC, V for deposits only; no credit cards at hotel. Free guarded parking. **Amenities:** Watersports equipment; activities arranged; airport transportation arranged; in-room massage; non-smoking rooms. *In room:* No phone.

Costa de Cocos Dive & Fly-Fishing Resort ⭑⭑   Several freestanding cabañas sit
around a large, attractive sandy beach graced with coconut palms. The cabañas are comfortable and have a lot of cross-ventilation, ceiling fans, hot water, and comfortable beds. They also come with 24-hour electricity using wind and solar power and purified tap water. One is a two-bedroom unit with two bathrooms.

Activities for guests include kayaking, snorkeling, scuba diving, and fly-fishing. The resort has experienced English-speaking fishing guides and a dive instructor. It has a large dive boat capable of taking divers to the Chinchorro Reef. The casual restaurant/bar offers good home-style cooking.

Carretera Majahual–Xcalak Km 52, Q. Roo. No phone. www.costadecocos.com. 16 cabañas. High season $75 (£41) double; low season $70 (£39) double. Dive and fly-fishing packages available by e-mail request. Rates include breakfast buffet. AE, MC, V. Free parking. **Amenities:** Restaurant; bar; watersports equipment; dive shop. *In room:* No phone.

Hotel Tierra Maya ⭑   This is a comfortable, modern-style hotel on the beach.
Rooms in the two-story building are spacious and designed to have good cross ventilation. They come with ceiling fans, and some rooms have the option of air-conditioning for an extra charge. All have private balconies or terraces looking out to the sea, hammocks, and bottled purified water. Solar generators provide electricity. Bathrooms are large, and beds are either twins or queen-size beds. The owners arrange diving, fishing, and snorkeling trips for guests. Guests have Internet access and the use of kayaks and bikes.

Carretera Majahual–Xcalak Km 54, Q. Roo. No phone. www.tierramaya.net. 7 units. High season $90–$110 (£50–£61) double; low season $70–$90 (£39–£50) double. Rates include continental breakfast. MC, V for advance payments. Limited free parking. **Amenities:** Restaurant; bar; watersports equipment; bikes; Internet access. *In room:* A/C (in some), no phone.

7 Lago Bacalar ⭑⭑⭑

104km (65 miles) SW of Felipe Carrillo Puerto; 37km (23 miles) NW of Chetumal

Bacalar Lake is an elaborate trick played upon the senses. I remember once standing on a pier on the lake and gazing down into perfectly clear water. As I lifted my eyes I could see the blue tint of the Caribbean. Beyond lay a dense tropical forest. A breeze blowing in from the sea smelled of the salt air, and though I knew it to be untrue, I couldn't help but believe that the water I was gazing on was, in fact, an inlet of the sea and not a lake at all—perhaps a well-sheltered lagoon like Xel-Ha. Lakes in tropical lowlands, especially those surrounded by tropical jungle, are turbid and muddy. How could this one be so clear? The answer is that Bacalar is not fed by surface runoff, but by several *cenotes* that lie beneath its surface. Only in the Yucatán is such a thing possible.

This is the perfect spot for being bone idle. But there's plenty to do, too. You can explore the jungle, visit some particularly elegant Maya ruins in the nearby Río Bec area, or take in a wonderful museum about the Maya in Chetumal. The town of Bacalar is quiet and quaint. There are a few stores and a couple of restaurants. An 18th-century fort with a moat and stout bastions is by the lake. Inside the fort is a small museum (admission is 50¢) that has several artifacts on display. All text is in Spanish.

ORIENTATION   Driving south on Highway 307, the town of Bacalar is 1½ hours beyond Felipe Carrillo Puerto, clearly marked by signs. If you're driving north from Chetumal, it takes about a half-hour. Buses going south from Cancún and Playa del Carmen stop here, and there are frequent buses from Chetumal.

WHERE TO STAY

Hotel Laguna   The Laguna overlooks the lake from a lovely vantage point. All the rooms share the view and have little terraces that make enjoyable sitting areas. The midsize rooms have ceiling fans, and most come with two double beds. The mattresses in the bungalows aren't good. The bathrooms are simple but have no problem delivering hot water. A restaurant that shares the same view is open from 7am to 9pm. The bar makes a credible margarita. The highest occupancy rates are from July to August and December to January, when you should make a reservation. The hotel is hard to spot from the road; look for the sign about 1km (half a mile) after you pass through the town of Bacalar.

Bulevar Costera de Bacalar 479, 77010 Lago Bacalar, Q. Roo. © **983/834-2206.** Fax 983/834-2205. 34 units. $50 (£28) double; $80–$95 (£44–£52) bungalow for 5–8 persons. No credit cards. Free parking. **Amenities:** Restaurant; bar; small outdoor pool. *In room:* No phone.

Rancho Encantado Cottage Resort 🐾🐾   This beautiful, serene lakeside retreat consists of 13 white-stucco cottages scattered over a shady lawn beside the smooth Lago Bacalar. Each is large and has mahogany louvered windows, a red-tile floor, a dining table and chairs, a living room or sitting area, a porch with chairs, and hammocks strung between trees. Some rooms have cedar ceilings and red-tiled roofs, and others have thatched roofs. All are decorated with folk art and murals inspired by Maya ruins. There are four waterfront cottages (nos. 9–12). Beds come in different combinations of doubles and twins. There is also a new "laguna suite," a one-bedroom townhouse with study, air-conditioning, and private dock; it rents by the week. Orange, lime, mango, sapote, Ceiba, banana, palm, and oak trees; wild orchids; and bromeliads on the grounds make great bird shelters, attracting flocks of chattering parrots, turquoise-browed motmots, toucans, and many more species.

The hotel offers almost a dozen excursions. Among them are day trips to the **Río Bec** ruin route, an extended visit to **Calakmul,** outings to the **Majahual Peninsula,** and a riverboat trip to the Maya ruins of **Lamanai,** deep in a Belizean forest. Excursions cost $55 to $115 (£30–£63) per person, depending on the length and difficulty of the trip, and several have a three-person minimum. To find the Rancho, look for the hotel's sign on the left about 3km (2 miles) before Bacalar.

Carretera Bacalar–Felipe Carrillo Puerto Km 3, 77930 Chetumal, Q. Roo. ℂ/fax 983/101-3358. www.encantado.com. (Reservations: P.O. Box 1256, Taos, NM 87571. ℂ 800/505-6292 in the U.S., or ℂ/fax 505/894-7074.) 13 units. High season $150–$200 (£83–£110) double; low season $100–$135 (£55–£74) double. Rates include continental breakfast and dinner. MC, V. Free parking. **Amenities:** Restaurant; bar; large outdoor whirlpool; spa; watersports equipment; tour desk; massage. *In room:* Fridge, coffeemaker.

WHERE TO DINE

Besides the restaurants at the hotels discussed above, you may enjoy the **Restaurante Cenote Azul,** a comfortable open-air thatched-roof restaurant on the edge of the beautiful Cenote Azul. Main courses cost $5 to $12 (£2.75–£6.60). To get to Restaurant Cenote Azul, follow the highway to the south edge of town and turn left at the restaurant's sign; follow the road around to the restaurant. At the restaurant, you can take a dip in placid Cenote Azul as long as you don't have creams or lotions on your skin.

8 Chetumal

251km (156 miles) S of Tulum; 37km (23 miles) S of Lago Bacalar

Capital of the state, and the second-largest city (after Cancún), Chetumal (pop. 210,000) is not a tourist destination. The old part of town, down by the river (Río Hondo), has a Caribbean feel, but the rest is unremarkable. Chetumal is the gateway to Belize, Tikal, and the Río Bec ruins. If you're going to spend the night here, visit the **Museo de la Cultura Maya** (ℂ 983/832-6838), especially if you plan to follow the Río Bec ruin route (see "Side Trips to Maya Ruins from Chetumal," below).

ESSENTIALS
GETTING THERE & DEPARTING
BY PLANE   Aviacsa (ℂ 983/872-7698) has a direct flight to and from Mexico City. The airport is west of town, just north of the entrance from the highway.

BY CAR   It's a little more than 3 hours from Tulum. If you're heading to Belize, you won't be able to take your rental car because the rental companies won't allow it. To get to the ruins of Tikal in Guatemala, you must go through Belize to the border crossing at Ciudad Melchor de Mencos.

BY BUS   The main bus station (ℂ 983/832-5110) is 20 blocks from the town center on Insurgentes at Niños Héroes. Buses go to Cancún, Tulum, Playa del Carmen, Puerto Morelos, Mérida, Campeche, Villahermosa, and Tikal, Guatemala.

   To Belize: Buses depart from the Lázaro Cárdenas market (most often called *el mercado nuevo*). Ask for **Autobuses Novelo.** The company has local service every 45 minutes ($12/£6.60) and four express buses per day ($16/£8.80).

VISITOR INFORMATION
The **State Tourism Office** (ℂ 983/835-0860, ext. 1811) is at Calzada del Centenario 622, between Comonfort and Ciricote. Office hours are Monday to Friday from 9am to 6pm.

ORIENTATION
The telephone **area code** is **983.**

   All traffic enters the city from the west and feeds onto Avenida Obregón into town. Avenida Héroes is the main north-south street.

A MUSEUM NOT TO MISS

Museo de la Cultura Maya ✹✹✹   This modern museum unlocks the complex world of the Maya through interactive exhibits and genuine artifacts. Push a button, and an illustrated description appears, explaining the medicinal and domestic uses of plants with their Mayan and scientific names; another exhibit describes the social classes of the Maya by their manners of dress. One of the most fascinating exhibits describes the Maya's ideal of personal beauty and the subsequent need to deform craniums, scar the face and body, and induce cross-eyed vision. An enormous screen flashes images taken from an airplane flying over more than a dozen Maya sites from Mexico to Honduras. Another large television shows the architectural variety of Maya pyramids and how they were probably built. Then a walk on a glass floor takes you over representative ruins in the Maya world. In the center of the museum is the three-story, stylized, sacred Ceiba tree, which the Maya believed connected Xibalba (the underworld), Earth, and the heavens. If you can arrange it, see the museum before you tour the Río Bec ruins.

Av. Héroes s/n. ② **983/832-6838.** Admission $6 (£3.30). Tues–Thurs 9am–7pm; Fri–Sat 9am–8pm. Between Colón and Gandhi, 8 blocks from Av. Obregón, just past the Holiday Inn.

WHERE TO STAY

Hotel Holiday Inn Puerta Maya   This modern hotel (formerly the Hotel Continental) has the best air-conditioning in town and is only a block from the Museo de la Cultura Maya. Most rooms are midsize and come with two double beds or one king-size bed. Bathrooms are roomy and well lit.

Av. Héroes 171, 77000 Chetumal, Q. Roo. ② **800/465-4329** in the U.S., or 983/835-0400. Fax 983/832-1676. 85 units. $125 (£69) double. AE, MC, V. Free secure parking. From Av. Obregón, turn left on Av. Héroes, go 6 blocks, and look for the hotel on the right. **Amenities:** Restaurant; bar; midsize outdoor pool; room service; laundry service. *In room:* A/C, TV.

Hotel Nachancán   One block from *el mercado nuevo* (the new market), this hotel offers plain rooms, with one or two double beds. Bathrooms are small, with no counter space, but they offer plenty of hot water. A cab to the Museo de la Cultura Maya costs $1 (55p).

Calzada Veracruz 379, 77000 Chetumal, Q. Roo. ② **983/832-3232.** 20 units. $33 (£18) double; $45 (£25) suite. No credit cards. Drive the length of Av. Obregón to where it stops at Calzada Veracruz, turn left, and drive 2km (1¼ miles); the hotel will be on the right. Limited street parking. **Amenities:** Restaurant; bar. *In room:* A/C, TV, no phone.

WHERE TO DINE

If you want to eat in air-conditioned surroundings in a modern, comfortable setting, try **Espress Café & Restaurant,** Calle 22 de Enero 141, corner of Bulevar Bahía (② **983/833-3013**). It serves well-prepared Mexican food, light fare such as sandwiches, and good breakfasts. It's open daily from 8am to midnight. For an economical meal with some local atmosphere, try **Restaurante Pantoja,** on the corner of calles Ghandi and 16 de Septiembre (no phone), 2 blocks east of the Museum of Maya Culture. It offers a cheap daily special, good green enchiladas, and such local specialties as *poc chuc* (grilled marinated pork). It's open Monday to Saturday from 7am to 9pm. To sample excellent *antojitos,* the local supper food, go to **El Buen Gusto,** on Calzada Veracruz across from the market (no phone). A Chetumal institution, it serves excellent *salbutes* and *panuchos* (both dishes are similar to *gorditas*), tacos, and sandwiches. Doors open around 7pm and close around midnight every night. If for some reason it's closed, go next door **La Ideal,** which many locals hold to be the better of the two supper joints. It has delicious *tacos de pierna* (soft tacos with thinly sliced pork shoulder) and *agua de horchata* (water flavored with rice, vanilla, and toasted pumpkin seed).

ONWARD FROM CHETUMAL

From Chetumal you have several choices. The Maya ruins of Lamanai, in Belize, are an easy day trip if you have transportation (not a rental car). You can explore the Río Bec ruin route directly west of the city (see below) by taking Highway 186.

9 Side Trips to Maya Ruins from Chetumal

West of Bacalar and Chetumal is the **Río Bec** area, where you can visit several Maya cities. These are picturesque and display a style of architecture that's very different from the northern Yucatán sites. From Highway 307, take Highway 186 west. The road, a clearly marked federal highway, heads into the state of Campeche. Along the way are several ruins, some very close to the road, others a bit of a drive. You could fit visits to several of the ruins into a day trip, or you could spend the night in the area. There are a few jungle hotels in the area. Here they are in order of most expensive to least expensive: The **Explorean** (✆ **888/679-3748** in the U.S.; www.theexplorean. com) is an ecolodge for adventure travelers who like their comfort. It sits all alone on the crest of a small hill not far from the ruins of Kohunlich. The **Chicanná Eco Village** (✆ **983/816-2233** in Campeche for reservations), is just beyond the town of Xpujil. **Puerta Calakmul Hotel** (www.puertacalakmul.com.mx), at the turnoff for the ruins of Calakmul, was recently purchased by the owners of Chicanná Eco Village. **Río Bec Dreams** (✆ **983/871-6057;** www.riobecdreams.com) is a good choice because the owners live on the premises and keep maintenance and service sharp. It's 11km (7 miles) west of Xpujil. **Restaurant y Hotel Calakmul** (✆ **983/871-6029**) is in the town of Xpujil.

The following section lists sites in the order in which you would see them driving from Bacalar or Chetumal. For a map of this area, consult the Yucatán Peninsula map (in the color insert in the front of this book). Entry to each site costs $2 to $4 (£1.10–£2.20). Informational signs at each building within the sites are in Mayan, Spanish, and English. Keep the mosquito repellent handy.

Dzibanché (tzee-bahn-*cheh*) means "place where they write on wood." Two large adjoining plazas have been cleared. Despite centuries of an unforgiving wet climate, a wood lintel in good condition with a date carving (indicating A.D. 733) still supports a partially preserved corbelled arch on top of this building. Inside the Temple of the Owl, the tomb of a queen was discovered.

Kohunlich ✺✺ (koh-*hoon*-leek), 42km (26 miles) from the turnoff for Highway 186, dates from around A.D. 400. The turnoff is well marked on the left. The ruins are only 8km (5 miles) from the highway. You'll find a large, shady ceremonial area flanked by four large pyramids. Continue walking, and just beyond this grouping you'll come to Kohunlich's famous Pyramid of the Masks under a thatched covering.

Xpujil (eesh-poo-*heel*), **Becán** ✺✺✺ (beh-*kahn*), and **Chicanná** (chee-kah-*nah*) are close to the highway just past the border that separates Quintana Roo from Campeche. Here you'll find the elegant high-pitched roofs and decorative staircases that are a principal feature of the sites in this region. Becán has an impressive arrangement of plazas with several tall pyramids. A temple on top of Structure 1 had a ritual doorway, in the form of the Earth Monster's mouth, which could be reached by a secret stairway. Some large chambers beneath another structure were closed on my last visit due to hurricane damage. Beside the ball court is a richly decorated figure of a Maya nobleman with an elaborate headdress. Chicanná was a large walled city; several of its buildings have been restored. This area is a little over 150km (100 miles) from Chetumal.

Calakmul 🐾🐾🐾 is another walled city. The site is quite large and beautiful, but it's also 90 minutes from the highway on a one-lane paved road. Its grand pyramid is the tallest pyramid in the Yucatán, at 54m (177 ft.). It has several elegant structures and many stelae, most of which are thoroughly weathered and unreadable.

Balamkú 🐾🐾, close to the highway not far beyond the turnoff for Calakmul, has some buildings in beautiful condition. In one you'll find a chamber with three large sculpted figures descending into the underworld in the gaping mouths of animals.

16

Mérida, Chichén Itzá &
the Maya Interior

by David Baird

Ask most people about the Yucatán, and they think of Cancún, the Caribbean coast, and Chichén Itzá. But there's much more to visit than just those places. With a little exploring, you'll find a variety of things to do. You might spend a morning scrambling over Maya ruins and in the afternoon take a dip in the cool, clear water of a *cenote* (natural well). The next day may find you strolling along a lonely beach or riding in a skiff through mangroves to visit a colony of pink flamingos, and by the evening you might be dancing in the streets of **Mérida.** This chapter covers the interior of the Yucatán peninsula, including the famous Maya ruins at **Chichén Itzá** and **Uxmal,** the flamingo sanctuaries at **Celestún** and **Río Lagartos,** as well as many other spots that might find special favor with you.

EXPLORING THE YUCATAN'S MAYA HEARTLAND

The best way to see the Yucatán is by car. The terrain is flat, there is little traffic once you get away from the cities, and the main highways are in good shape. If you drive at all around this area, you will add at least one new word to your Spanish vocabulary—*topes* (toh-pehs), meaning speed bumps. And along with *topes* you might learn a few new curse words. *Topes* come in varying shapes and sizes and with varying degrees of warning. Don't let them surprise you.

Off the main highways, the roads are narrow and rough, but hey—you'll be driving a rental car. Rentals are, in fact, a little pricey compared with those in the U.S. (due perhaps to wear and tear?), but some promotional deals are available, especially in low season. For more on renting a car, see "By Car," in "Mérida: Gateway to the Maya Heartland," below.

Plenty of buses ply the roads between the major towns and ruins. And plenty of tour buses circulate, too. But buses to the smaller towns and ruins and the haciendas are infrequent. One bus company, Autobuses del Oriente (ADO), controls most of the first-class bus service and does a good job with the major destinations. Second-class buses go to some out-of-the-way places, but they can be slow, stop a lot, and usually aren't air-conditioned. I will take them when going short distances. If you don't want to rent a car, a few tour operators take small groups to more remote attractions such as ruins, *cenotes,* and villages.

The Yucatán is *tierra caliente* (the hot lands). Don't travel in this region without a hat, sun block, mosquito repellent, and water. The coolest weather is from November to February; the hottest is from April to June. From July to October, thundershowers moderate temperatures. More tourists come to the interior during the winter months, but not to the same extent as on the Caribbean coast. The high-season/low-season distinction is less pronounced here.

Should you decide to travel into this part of the world, don't miss **Mérida.** It is, and has been for centuries, the cultural and commercial center of the Yucatán. You won't find a more vibrant tropical city anywhere. Every time I visit, there is some festival or celebration to attend, on top of the nightly performances that the city offers its citizens and visitors. It's also the Yucatán's shopping center, where you can buy the area's specialty items, such as hammocks, Panama hats, and the embroidered native blouses known as *huipiles.* Aside from Mérida, here are some other places to consider.

CHICHEN ITZA & VALLADOLID These destinations are almost midway between Mérida and Cancún. From Mérida it's 2½ hours by car to Chichén on the new *autopista* (toll road). You can spend a day at the ruins and then stay at one of the nearby hotels—or drive 40km (25 miles) to Valladolid, a quiet, charming colonial town with a pleasant central square. Valladolid features two eerie *cenotes.* The spectacular ruins at Ek Balam are only 40km (25 miles) to the north. Also in the area is the Río Lagartos Nature Reserve, teeming with flamingos and other native birds.

CELESTUN NATIONAL WILDLIFE REFUGE These flamingo-sanctuary wetlands along the Gulf coast contain a unique shallow-water estuary where freshwater from *cenotes* mixes with saltwater, creating the perfect feeding ground for flamingos. Touring this area by launch is relaxing and rewarding. Only 1½ hours from Mérida, Celestún makes for an easy day trip.

DZIBILCHALTUN This Maya site, now a national park, is 14km (8⅔ miles) north of Mérida along the road to Progreso. Here you'll find pre-Hispanic ruins, nature trails, a *cenote,* and the Museum of the Maya. You can make this the first stop in a day trip to Progreso and other attractions north of Mérida.

PROGRESO A modern city and Gulf Coast beach escape 34km (21 miles) north of Mérida, Progreso has a wide beach and oceanfront drive that's popular on the weekends and during the summer. The recent arrival of cruise ships might make Progreso even more popular, but with so much beach, you'll easily have a place to yourself. From Progreso, you can drive down the coast to **Uaymitún** to see some flamingos and visit the recently excavated ruins of **Xcambó.**

UXMAL Smaller than Chichén, but architecturally more striking and mysterious, Uxmal is about 80km (50 miles) south of Mérida. You can see it in a day, though it's a good idea to extend that somewhat to see the sound-and-light show and spend the night at one of the hotels by the ruins. Several other nearby sites make up the Puuc route and can be explored the following day. It's also possible, though a bit rushed, to see Uxmal and the other ruins on a 1-day trip by special excursion bus from Mérida.

CAMPECHE This beautiful, walled colonial city has been so meticulously restored that it's a delight just to stroll down the streets. Campeche is about 3 hours southwest of Mérida in the direction of Palenque. A full day should give you enough time to see

---

Tips **Mapping the Region**

To check out the region surrounding Mérida, see "The Yucatán Peninsula" map in the color insert in the front of this book.

> ⌒Tips **The Best Websites for Mérida, Chichén Itzá &
> the Maya Interior**
>
> • **Maya: Portraits of a People: www.nationalgeographic.com/explorer/maya/
>   more.html** A fascinating collection of articles from *National Geographic*
>   and other sources.
> • **Yucatán Travel Guide: www.mayayucatan.com** Yucatán's Ministry of
>   Tourism maintains this site. It has an update section and good general
>   info on different destinations in the state.
> • **Mexico's Yucatán Directory: www.mexonline.com/yucatan.htm** A nice
>   roundup of vacation rentals, tour operators, and information on the
>   Maya sites. For more information on Mexico's indigenous history, see the
>   links on the pre-Columbian page (www.mexonline.com/precolum.htm).

its highlights and museums, but there is something about Campeche that makes you
want to linger.

1 Mérida: Gateway to the Maya Heartland ⊛⊛

1,440km (893 miles) E of Mexico City; 320km (198 miles) W of Cancún

Mérida is the capital of the state of Yucatán and has been the dominant city in the
region since the Spanish Conquest. It is a busy city and suffers from the same problems that plague other colonial cities in Mexico—traffic and noise. Still, it is a fun city
and has many admirers. I get comments from people all the time about how much
they enjoyed Mérida. People there know how to have a good time, and they seem
driven to organize concerts, theater productions, art exhibits, and such. In recent years
the city has been in the midst of a cultural explosion.

ESSENTIALS
GETTING THERE & DEPARTING
BY PLANE AeroMéxico (⌀ 01-800/021-4000 in Mexico, or 999/927-9277; www.
aeromexico.com) flies nonstop to/from Miami and Mexico City. **Mexicana** (⌀ 01-
800/502-2000 in Mexico, or 999/924-6633; www.mexicana.com.mx) has nonstop
service to and from Mexico City. **Continental** (⌀ 999/946-1888 or -1900; www.
continental.com) has nonstop service to and from Houston. **Click** (⌀ 01-800/122-
5425 in Mexico), a Mexican budget airline, provides nonstop service to and from
Mexico City and Veracruz. **Aviacsa** (⌀ 01-800/006-2000 in Mexico) provides nonstop service to and from Villahermosa and Mexico City.

BY CAR **Highway 180** is the old *carretera federal* (federal highway) between Mérida
and Cancún. The trip takes 6 hours, and the road is in good shape; you will pass
through many Maya villages. A four-lane divided *cuota,* or *autopista* (toll road) parallels Highway 180 and begins at the town of Kantunil, 56km (35 miles) east of Mérida.
By avoiding the tiny villages and their not-so-tiny speed bumps, the *autopista* cuts 2
hours from the journey between Mérida and Cancún; one-way tolls cost $30 (£17).
Coming from the direction of Cancún, Highway 180 enters Mérida by feeding into
Calle 65, which passes 1 block south of the main square.

Coming from the south (Campeche or Uxmal), you will enter the city on Avenida Itzáes. To get to the town center, turn right on Calle 59 (the first street after the zoo).

A *periférico* (loop road) encircles Mérida, making it possible to skirt the city. Directional signs into the city are generally good, but going around the city on the loop requires vigilance.

BY BUS   There are five bus stations in Mérida, two of which offer first-class buses; the other three provide local service to nearby destinations. The larger of the first-class stations, **CAME,** is on Calle 70, between calles 69 and 71 (see "City Layout," below). The ADO bus line and its affiliates operate the station. When you get there, you'll see a row of ticket windows; all but the last couple to the right sell first-class tickets. The last two windows sell tickets for ADO's deluxe services, ADO-GL and UNO. The former is only slightly better than first class; the latter has super-wide roomy seats. Unless it's a long trip, I generally choose the bus that has the most convenient departure time. Tickets can be purchased in advance; just ask the ticket agent for the different options and departure times for the route you need.

The other first-class station is the small **Maya K'iin** used by the bus company **Elite.** It's at Calle 65 no. 548, between calles 68 and 70.

To and from Cancún: You can pick up a bus at the CAME (almost every hour) or through Elite (five per day). Both bus lines also pick up passengers at the Fiesta Americana Hotel, across from the Hyatt (12 per day). You can buy a ticket in the hotel's shopping arcade at the **Ticket Bus** agency or at the Elite ticket agency. Cancún is 4 hours away; a few buses stop in **Valladolid.** If you're downtown, you can purchase tickets from the agency in Pasaje Picheta, on the main square a couple of doors down from the Palacio de Gobierno.

To and from Chichén Itzá: Three buses per day (2½-hr. trip) depart from the CAME. Also, check out tours operating from the hotels in Mérida if you want to visit for the day.

To and from Playa del Carmen, Tulum, and Chetumal: From the CAME, there are 10 departures per day for Playa del Carmen (5-hr. trip), six for Tulum (6-hr. trip), and eight for Chetumal (7-hr. trip). From Maya K'iin there are three per day to Playa, which stop at the Fiesta Americana.

To and from Campeche: From the CAME station, there are 36 departures per day. Elite has four departures per day. It's a 2½-hour trip.

To and from Palenque and San Cristóbal de las Casas: There is service to San Cristóbal twice daily from the CAME, and once daily on Elite. To Palenque there are three and one, respectively. There have been reports of minor theft on buses to Palenque. You should do three things: Don't take second-class buses to this destination; check your luggage so that it's stowed in the cargo bay; and put your carry-on in the overhead rack, not on the floor.

The main **second-class bus station** is around the corner from the CAME on Calle 69, between calles 68 and 70.

To and from Uxmal: There are four buses per day. (You can also hook up with a tour to Uxmal through most hotels or any travel agent or tour operator in town.) One bus per day combines Uxmal with the other sites to the south (Kabah, Sayil, Labná, and Xlapak—known as the Puuc route) and does the whole round-trip in a day. It stops for 2 hours at Uxmal and 30 minutes at each of the other sites.

To and from Progreso and Dzibilchaltún: Transportes AutoProgreso offers service to/from its station at Calle 62 no. 524, between calles 65 and 67. The trip to Progreso takes an hour by second-class bus.

To and from Celestún: The Celestún station is at Calle 50 between calles 65 and 67. The trip takes 1½ to 2 hours, depending on how often the bus stops. There are 10 buses per day.

To and from Izamal: The bus station is at the corner of Calle 65 and Calle 48. Departures are every half-hour. The trip takes 1½ hours.

ORIENTATION

ARRIVING BY PLANE   Mérida's airport is 13km (8 miles) from the city center on the southwestern outskirts of town, near the entrance to Highway 180. The airport has desks for renting a car, reserving a hotel room, and getting tourist information. Taxi tickets to town ($16/£8.80) are sold outside the airport doors, under the covered walkway.

VISITOR INFORMATION   There are city tourism offices and state tourism offices, which have different resources; if you can't get the information you're looking for at one, go to the other. I have better luck with the city's **visitor information office** (*©* **999/942-0000,** ext. 80119), which is on the ground floor of the Ayuntamiento building facing the main square on Calle 62. Look for a glass door under the arcade. Hours are Monday to Saturday from 8am to 8pm and Sunday from 8am to 2pm. Monday through Saturday, at 9:30am, the staff offers visitors a free tour of the area around the main square. The state operates two downtown tourism offices: One is in the **Teatro Peón Contreras,** facing Parque de la Madre (*©* **999/924-9290**); and the other is on the main plaza, in the **Palacio de Gobierno,** immediately to the left as you enter. These offices are open daily from 8am to 9pm. There are also information booths at the airport and the CAME bus station.

Also keep your eye out for the free monthly magazine *Yucatán Today;* it's a good source of information for Mérida and the rest of the region.

CITY LAYOUT   Downtown Mérida has the standard layout of towns in the Yucatán: Streets running north-south are even numbers; those running east-west are odd numbers. The numbering begins on the north and the east sides of town, so if you're walking on an odd-numbered street and the even numbers of the cross streets are increasing, then you are heading west; likewise, if you are on an even-numbered street and the odd numbers of the cross streets are increasing, you are going south.

Address numbers don't tell you anything about what cross street to look for. This is why addresses almost always list cross streets, usually like this: "Calle 60 no. 549 × 71 y 73." The "×" is a multiplication sign—shorthand for the word *por* (meaning "by")—and *y* means "and." So this place would be on Calle 60 between calles 71 and 73. Outside of the downtown area, the numbering of streets gets a little crazy, so it's important to know the name of the neighborhood where you're going. This is the first thing taxi drivers will ask you.

The town's main square is the busy **Plaza Mayor,** referred to simply as **El Centro.** It's bordered by calles 60, 62, 61, and 63. Calle 60, which runs in front of the cathedral, is an important street to remember; it connects the main square with several smaller plazas, some theaters and churches, and the University of Yucatán, just to the north. Here, too, you'll find a concentration of handicraft shops, restaurants, and hotels. Around Plaza Mayor are the cathedral, the Palacio de Gobierno (state government building), the

Moments Festivals & Special Events in Mérida

Many Mexican cities offer weekend concerts in the park and such, but Mérida surpasses them all by offering performances every day of the week. Unless otherwise indicated, admission to the following is free.

Sunday Each Sunday from 9am to 9pm, there's a fair called *Mérida en Domingo* (Mérida on Sunday). The main plaza and a section of Calle 60 from El Centro to Parque Santa Lucía close to traffic. Parents come with their children to stroll around and take in the scene. There are booths selling food and drink, along with a lively little flea market and used-book fair, children's art classes, and educational booths. At 11am in front of the Palacio del Gobierno, musicians play everything from jazz to classical and folk music. Also at 11am, the police orchestra performs Yucatecan tunes at the Santa Lucía park. At 11:30am, you'll find bawdy comedy acts at the Parque Hidalgo, on Calle 60 at Calle 59. There's a lull in the midafternoon, and then the plaza fills up again as people walk around and visit with friends. Around 7pm in front of the Ayuntamiento, a large band starts playing mambos, rumbas, and cha-chas with great enthusiasm; you may see 1,000 people dancing in the street. Afterward, folk ballet dancers reenact a typical Yucatecan wedding inside.

Monday Every Monday at 9pm in front of the *Palacio Municipal* performers play *Vaquería regional,* traditional music and dancing to celebrate the Vaquerías feast, which was associated originally with the branding of cattle on Yucatecan haciendas. Among the featured performers are dancers with trays of bottles or filled glasses balanced on their heads—a sight to see.

Tuesday At 9pm in Parque Santiago, Calle 59 at Calle 72, the Municipal Orchestra plays Latin and American big-band music from the 1940s.

Wednesday At 9pm in the Teatro Peón Contreras, Calle 60 at Calle 57, the University of Yucatán Ballet Folklórico presents "Yucatán and Its Roots." Admission is $5 (£2.75).

Thursday Yucatecan *trova* music (boleros, baladas) and dance are presented at the Serenata in Parque Santa Lucía at 9pm.

Friday At 9pm in the courtyard of the University of Yucatán, Calle 60 at Calle 57, the University of Yucatán Ballet Folklórico performs typical regional dances from the Yucatán.

Saturday Noche Mexicana at the park at the beginning of Paseo de Montejo begins at 9pm. It features several performances of traditional Mexican music and dance. Some of the performers are amateurs who acquit themselves reasonably well; others are professional musicians and dancers who thoroughly know their craft. Food stands sell very good *antojitos* (finger foods), as well as drinks and ice cream.

Ayuntamiento (town hall), and the Palacio Montejo. The plaza always has a crowd, and it's full on Sunday, when it holds a large street fair. (See "Festivals & Special Events in Mérida," above.) Within a few blocks are several smaller plazas and the bustling market district.

Mérida's most fashionable district is the broad, tree-lined boulevard **Paseo de Montejo** and its surrounding neighborhood. The Paseo de Montejo parallels Calle 60 and begins 7 blocks north and a little east of the main square. There are a number of trendy restaurants, modern hotels, offices of various banks and airlines, and a few clubs here, but the boulevard is mostly known for its stately mansions built during the boom times of the henequén industry. Near where the Paseo intersects Avenida Colón, you'll find the two fanciest hotels in town: the Hyatt and the Fiesta Americana.

GETTING AROUND   By Car   In general, reserve your car in advance from the U.S. to get the best weekly rates during high season (Nov–Feb); in low season, I usually do better renting a car once I get to Mérida. The local rental companies are competitive and have promotional deals that you can get only if you are there. When comparing, make sure that it's apples to apples; ask if the price quote includes the IVA tax and insurance coverage. Practically everybody offers free mileage. For tips on saving money on car rentals, see "Getting Around," in chapter 2. Rental cars are generally a little more expensive (unless you find a promotional rate) than in the U.S. By renting for only a day or two, you can avoid the high cost of parking lots in Mérida. These *estacionamentos* charge one price for the night and double that if you leave your car for the following day. Many hotels offer free parking, but make sure they include daytime parking in the price.

By Taxi   Taxis are easy to come by and much cheaper than in Cancún.

By Bus   City buses are a little tricky to figure out but aren't needed very often because almost everything of interest is within walking distance of the main plaza. Still, it's a bit of a walk from the plaza to the Paseo de Montejo, and you can save yourself some work by taking a bus, minibus, or *colectivo* (Volkswagen minivan) that is heading north on Calle 60. Most of these will take you within a couple of blocks of the Paseo de Montejo. The *colectivos* or *combis* (usually painted white) run out in several directions from the main plaza along simple routes. They usually line up along the side streets next to the plaza.

FAST FACTS: Mérida

American Express   The office is at Paseo de Montejo 492 (© 999/942-8200). It's open for travelers' services weekdays from 9am to 2pm and 4 to 6pm.

Area Code   The telephone area code is **999**.

Bookstore   A new English-language bookstore, called **Amate Books** (© 999/924-2222), is open for business at Calle 60 453-A, by Calle 51. **The Librería Dante,** Calle 59 between calles 60 and 62 (© 999/928-3674), has a small selection of English-language cultural-history books on Mexico. Both keep general business hours.

Business Hours   Generally, businesses are open Monday to Saturday from 10am to 2pm and 4 to 8pm.

Climate   From November to February, the weather can be pleasantly cool and windy. In other months, it's just hot, especially during the day. Rain can occur any time of year, especially during the rainy season (July–Oct), and usually comes in the form of afternoon tropical showers.

Consulates The **American Consulate** has moved. It's now at Calle 60 no. 338-K, 1 block north of the Hyatt hotel (Col. Alcalá Martín). The phone number is © **999/942-5700.** Office hours are Monday to Friday from 9am to 1pm.

Currency Exchange I prefer *casas de cambio* (currency exchange offices) over banks. There are many of these; one called **Cambios Portales,** Calle 61 no. 500 (© **999/923-8709**), is on the north side of the main plaza in the middle of the block. It's open daily from 8:30am to 8:30pm. There are also many ATMs; one is on the south side of the same plaza.

Drugstore **Farmacía Yza,** Calle 63 no. 502, between calles 60 and 62 (© **999/ 924-9510**), on the south side of the plaza, is open 24 hours.

Hospitals The best hospital is **Centro Médico de las Américas,** Calle 54 no. 365 between 33-A and Avenida Pérez Ponce. The main phone number is © **999/ 926-2619;** for emergencies, call © **999/927-3199.** You can also call the **Cruz Roja (Red Cross)** at © **999/924-9813.**

Internet Access There are so many Internet access providers in town that you hardly have to walk more than a couple of blocks to find one.

Police Mérida has a special body of police to assist tourists. They patrol the downtown area and the Paseo de Montejo. They wear white shirts bearing the words POLICIA TURISTICA. Their phone number is © **999/925-2555.**

Post Office The *correo* is near the market at the corner of calles 65 and 56. A branch office is at the airport. Both are open Monday to Friday from 8am to 7pm, Saturday from 9am to noon.

Seasons There are two high seasons for tourism, but they aren't as pronounced as on the coast. One is in July and August, when Mexicans take their vacations, and the other is between November 15 and Easter Sunday, when Canadians and Americans flock to the Yucatán to escape winter weather.

Spanish Classes Maya scholars, Spanish teachers, and archaeologists from the United States are among the students at the **Centro de Idiomas del Sureste,** Calle 14 no. 106 at Calle 25, Col. México, 97000 Mérida, Yuc. (© **999/926-1155;** fax 999/926-9020). The school has two locations: in the Colonia México, a northern residential district, and on Calle 66 at Calle 57, downtown. Students live with local families or in hotels; sessions running 2 weeks or longer are available for all levels of proficiency and areas of interest. For brochures and applications, contact the director, Chloe Conaway de Pacheco.

Telephones There are long-distance phone service centers at the airport and the bus station. In the downtown area is **TelWorld,** Calle 59 no. 495-4 between calles 56 and 58. To use the public phones, buy a **Ladatel** card from just about any newsstand or store. The cards come in a variety of denominations and work for long distance within Mexico and even abroad.

EXPLORING MERIDA

Most of Mérida's attractions are within walking distance from the downtown area. To see a larger area of the city, take a popular **bus tour** by **Transportadora Carnaval.** The owner bought a few buses, painted them bright colors, pulled out the windows, raised the roof several inches, and installed wooden benches so that the buses remind you of the folksy buses of coastal Latin America, known as *chivas* in Colombia and Venezuela or as *guaguas* in other places. You can find these buses on the corner of calles 60 and 55 (next to the church of Santa Lucía) at 10am and 1, 4, and 7pm. The tour costs $7 (£3.85) per person and lasts 2 hours. A national company, called Turibus, operates another city tour in large, modern, bright-red, double-decker buses. You can pick them up in front of the cathedral every half hour. The tour costs $8 (£4.40). Another option for seeing the city is a **horse-drawn carriage.** A 45-minute ride around central Mérida costs $25 (£14). You can usually find the carriages beside the cathedral on Calle 61.

EXPLORING PLAZA MAYOR   Downtown Mérida is a great example of a lowland colonial city. The town has a casual, relaxed feel. Buildings lack the severe baroque and neoclassical features that characterize central Mexico; most are finished in stucco and painted light colors. Mérida's gardens add to this relaxed, tropical atmosphere. Gardeners don't strive for control over nature. Here, natural exuberance is the ideal, with plants growing in a wild profusion that disguises human intervention. Mérida's plazas are a slightly different version of this aesthetic: Unlike the highland plazas, with their carefully sculpted trees, Mérida's squares are typically built around large trees that are left to grow as tall as possible. Hurricane Isidore blew down several of these in 2002, and has changed the appearance of these plazas as well as the Paseo de Montejo.

Plaza Mayor has been relandscaped after the hurricane and is now the exception to the rule. It still remains a comfortable and informal place to meet up with friends. Even when there's no orchestrated event in progress, the park is full of people sitting on the benches, talking, or taking a casual stroll. A plaza like this is a great advantage for a big city such as Mérida, giving it a personal feel and a sense of community. Notice the beautiful scale and composition of the major buildings surrounding it. The most prominent of these is the cathedral.

The oldest **cathedral** on the continent, it was built between 1561 and 1598. Much of the stone in the cathedral's walls came from the ruined buildings of Tihó, the former Maya city. The original finish was stucco, and you can see some remnants still clinging to the bare rock. However, people like the way the unfinished walls show the cathedral's age. Notice how the two top levels of the bell towers are built off-center from their bases—an uncommon feature. Inside, decoration is sparse, with altars draped in fabric colorfully embroidered like a Maya woman's shift. The most notable item is a picture of Ah Kukum Tutul Xiú, chief of the Xiú people, visiting the Montejo camp to make peace; it's hanging over the side door on the right.

To the left of the main altar is a small shrine with a curious figure of Christ that is a replica of one recovered from a burned-out church in the town of Ichmul. In the 1500s a local artist carved the original figure from a miraculous tree that was hit by lightning and burst into flames—but did not char. The statue later became blistered in the church fire at Ichmul, but it survived. In 1645 it was moved to the cathedral in Mérida, where the locals attached great powers to the figure, naming it *Cristo de las Ampollas* (Christ of the Blisters). It did not, however, survive the sacking of the cathedral in 1915 by revolutionary forces, so another figure, modeled after the original, was made. Take a look in the side chapel (daily 8–11am and 4:30–7pm), which contains a life-size diorama of the Last Supper. The Mexican Jesus is covered with prayer crosses brought by supplicants asking for intercession.

Next door to the cathedral is the old bishop's palace, now converted into the city's contemporary art museum, **Museo de Arte Contemporáneo Ateneo de Yucatán** (© **999/928-3236**). The palace was confiscated and rebuilt during the Mexican Revolution in 1915. The museum's entrance faces the cathedral from the recently constructed walkway between the two buildings called the Pasaje de la Revolución. The 17 exhibition rooms display work by contemporary artists, mostly from the Yucatán. (The best known are Fernando García Ponce and Fernando Castro Pacheco, whose works also hang in the government palace described below.) Nine of the rooms hold the museum's permanent collection; the rest are for temporary exhibits. It's open Wednesday to Monday from 10am to 6pm. Admission is free.

Moving clockwise around the plaza, on the south side is the **Palacio Montejo.** Its facade, with heavy decoration around the doorway and windows, is a good example of the Spanish architectural style known as plateresque. But the content of the decoration is very much a New World creation. Conquering the Yucatán was the Montejo family business, begun by the original Francisco Montejo and continued by his son and nephew, both named Francisco Montejo. Construction of the house started in 1542 under the son, Francisco Montejo El Mozo ("The Younger"). Bordering the entrance are politically incorrect figures of conquistadors standing on the heads of vanquished Indians—borrowed, perhaps, from the pre-Hispanic custom of portraying victorious Maya kings treading on their defeated foes. The posture of the conquistadors and their facial expression of wide-eyed dismay make them less imposing than the Montejos might have wished. A bank now occupies the building, but you can enter the courtyard, view the garden, and see for yourself what a charming residence it must have been for the descendants of the Montejos, who lived here as recently as the 1970s. (Curiously enough, not only does Mérida society keep track of who is descended from the Montejos, but it also keeps track of who is descended from the last Maya king, Tutul Xiú.)

In stark contrast to the severity of the cathedral and Casa Montejo is the light, unimposing **Ayuntamiento** or **Palacio Municipal (town hall).** The exterior dates from the mid–19th century, an era when a tropical aesthetic tinged with romanticism began asserting itself across coastal Latin America. On the second floor, you can see the meeting hall of the city council and enjoy a view of the plaza from the balcony. Next door to the Ayuntamiento is a recently completed building called **El Nuevo Olimpo (The New Olympus).** It took the place of the old Olimpo, which a misguided town council demolished in the 1970s, to the regret of many older Meridanos. The new building tries to incorporate elements of the original while presenting something new. It holds concert and gallery space, a bookstore, and a lovely courtyard. There is a comfortable cafe under the arches, and a bulletin board at the entrance to the courtyard with postings of upcoming performances.

Cater-cornered from the Nuevo Olimpo is the old **Casa del Alguacil (Magistrate's House).** Under its arcades is something of an institution in Mérida: the **Dulcería y Sorbetería Colón,** an ice-cream and sweet shop that will appeal to those who prefer less-rich ice creams. A spectacular side doorway on Calle 62 bears viewing, and across the street is the **Cine Mérida,** with two movie screens showing art films and one stage for live performances. Returning to the main plaza, down a bit from the ice-cream store, is a **shopping center** of boutiques and convenience food vendors called **Pasaje Picheta.** At the end of the arcade is the **Palacio de Gobierno (state government building),** dating from 1892. Large murals by the Yucatecan artist Fernando Castro

Pacheco, executed between 1971 and 1973, decorate the walls of the courtyard. Scenes from Maya and Mexican history abound, and the painting over the stairway depicts the Maya spirit with ears of sacred corn, the "sunbeams of the gods." Nearby is a painting of mustachioed Lázaro Cárdenas, who as president, in 1938, expropriated 17 foreign oil companies and was hailed as a Mexican liberator. Upstairs is a long, wide gallery with more of Pacheco's paintings, which achieve their effect by localizing color and imitating the photographic technique of double exposure. The palace is open Monday to Saturday from 8am to 8pm, Sunday from 9am to 5pm. There is a small tourism office to the left as you enter.

Farther down Calle 61 is the **Museo de la Ciudad (City Museum).** It faces the side of the cathedral and occupies the former church of San Juan de Dios. An exhibit outlining the history of Mérida will be of interest to those curious about the city; there is explanatory text in English. Hours are Monday to Friday from 10am to 2pm and 4 to 8pm, Saturday and Sunday from 10am to 2pm. Admission is free.

EXPLORING CALLE 60   Heading north from Plaza Mayor up Calle 60, you'll see many of Mérida's old churches and squares. Several stores along Calle 60 sell gold-filigree jewelry, pottery, clothing, and folk art. A stroll along this street leads to the Parque Santa Ana and continues to the fashionable boulevard Paseo de Montejo and its **Museo Regional de Antropología (Anthropology Museum).**

The first place of interest is the **Teatro Daniel de Ayala,** only because it sometimes schedules interesting performances. On the right side of Calle 60 will be a small park called **Parque Cepeda Peraza** (or Parque Hidalgo). Named for 19th-century General Manuel Cepeda Peraza, the *parque* was part of Montejo's original city plan. Small outdoor restaurants front hotels on the park, making it a popular stopping place at any time of day. Across Calle 59 is the **Iglesia de Jesús,** or El Tercer Orden (the Third Order). Built by the Jesuit order in 1618, it has the richest interior of any church in Mérida, making it a favorite spot for weddings. The entire block on which the church stands belonged to the Jesuits, who are known as great educators. The school they left behind after their expulsion became the Universidad de Yucatán.

On the other side of the church is the **Parque de la Madre.** The park contains a modern statue of the Madonna and Child, a copy of the work by Renoir. Beyond the Parque de la Madre and across the pedestrian-only street is the **Teatro Peón Contreras,** an opulent theater designed by Italian architect Enrico Deserti a century ago. The theater is noted for its Carrara marble staircase and frescoed dome. Try to get a peek at it, and look at the performance schedule to see if anything of interest will take place during your stay. National and international performers appear here frequently. In the southwest corner of the theater, facing the Parque de la Madre, is a **tourist information office.** Across Calle 60 is the main building of the **Universidad de Yucatán.** Inside is a flagstone courtyard where the *ballet folklórico* performs on Friday nights.

A block farther north is **Parque Santa Lucía.** Bordered by an arcade on the north and west sides, this park was where visitors first alighted from the stagecoach. On Sunday, Parque Santa Lucía holds a used-book market, and several evenings a week it hosts popular entertainment. On Thursday nights, performers present Yucatecan songs and poems. Facing the park is the **Iglesia de Santa Lucía** (1575).

Four blocks farther up Calle 60 is **Parque Santa Ana;** if you turn right, you'll come to the beginning of the Paseo de Montejo in 2 blocks.

EXPLORING THE PASEO DE MONTEJO   The Paseo de Montejo is a broad, tree-lined boulevard that runs north-south starting at Calle 47, 7 blocks north and

2 blocks east of the main square. In the late 19th century, stalwarts of Mérida's upper crust (mostly plantation owners) decided that the city needed something grander than its traditional narrow streets lined by wall-to-wall town houses. They built this monumentally proportioned boulevard and lined it with mansions. Things went sour with the henequén industry went bust, but several of these mansions survive—some in private hands, others as offices, restaurants, or consulates. Today, this is the fashionable part of town, with many restaurants, trendy dance clubs, and expensive hotels.

Of the mansions that survived, the most notable is the Palacio Cantón, which houses the **Museo Regional de Antropología (Anthropology Museum)** 𝖆𝖆 (𝓒 **999/ 923-0557**). Designed and built by Enrico Deserti, the architect of the Teatro Peón Contreras, it was constructed between 1909 and 1911, during the last years of the Porfiriato. It was the residence of General Francisco Cantón Rosado, who enjoyed his palace for only 6 years before dying in 1917. For a time the mansion served as the official residence of the state's governor. Viewing the museum affords you an opportunity to see some of the surviving interior architecture.

The museum's main focus is the pre-Columbian cultures of the peninsula, especially the Maya. Topics include cosmology, history, and culture. Starting with fossil mastodon teeth, the exhibits take you through the Yucatán's history, paying special attention to the daily life of its inhabitants.

Exhibits illustrate such strange Maya customs as tying boards to babies' heads to create the oblong shape that they considered beautiful, and filing teeth or perforating them to inset jewels. There are enlarged photos of several archaeological sites and drawings that illustrate the various styles of Maya dwellings. Captions for the permanent displays are mostly in Spanish, but even if you know only a little Spanish, this is a worthwhile stop, and it provides good background for explorations of Maya sites. The museum is open Tuesday to Saturday from 8am to 8pm, Sunday from 8am to 2pm. Admission is $3.50 (£1.95).

SHOPPING

Mérida is known for hammocks, *guayaberas* (lightweight men's shirts worn untucked), and Panama hats. Baskets and pottery made in the Yucatán are for sale in the **central market.** Mérida is also the place to pick up prepared *adobo,* a pastelike mixture of ground *achiote* seeds (annatto), oregano, garlic, and other spices used as a marinade for making dishes such as *cochinita pibil* (pit-baked pork). Simply mix the paste with sour orange to a soupy consistency before applying to the meat. Try it on chicken for *pollo pibil.* It can be purchased in a bottle, too.

EXPLORING THE MARKET Mérida's bustling **market district** is a few blocks southeast of the Plaza Mayor. The market and surrounding few blocks make up the commercial center of the city. Hordes of people come here to shop and work. It is by far the most crowded part of town, and the city government is refurbishing the whole area to relieve the traffic congestion. Behind the post office (at calles 65 and 56) is the oldest part of the market, the **Portal de Granos (Grains Arcade),** a row of maroon arches where the grain merchants used to sell their goods. Just east, between calles 56 and 54, is the market building, Mercado Lucas de Gálvez. The city has built a new municipal market building on the south side of this building, but it was having difficulty persuading the market venders to move. When this happens the city's plan is to tear down the Lucas de Gálvez and replace it with a plaza. Inside, chaos seems to reign, but after a short while a certain order emerges. Here you can find anything from fresh fish to flowers to leather goods. In and around the market, you can find more locally manufactured goods; a secondary market is on Calle 56, labeled **Bazaar de Artesanías (crafts market)** in big letters. Another crafts market, **Bazaar García Rejón,** lies a block west of the market on Calle 65 between calles 58 and 60.

CRAFTS

Casa de las Artesanías ⟨ This store occupies the front rooms of a restored monastery. Here you can find a wide selection of crafts, 90% of which come from the Yucatán. For the most part, the quality of work is higher than elsewhere, but so are the prices. The monastery's back courtyard is used as a gallery, with rotating exhibits on folk and fine arts. It's open Monday to Saturday from 9am to 8pm, Sunday from 9am to 1pm. Calle 63 no. 513 (between calles 64 and 66). ✆ 999/928-6676.

Miniaturas This fun little store is packed to the rafters with miniatures, a traditional Mexican folk art form that has been evolving in a number of directions, including social and political satire, pop art, and bawdy humor. Alicia Rivero, the owner, collects them from several parts of Mexico and offers plenty of variety, from traditional miniatures, such as dollhouse furniture, to popular cartoon characters and celebrities. The store also sells other forms of folk art such as masks, games, and traditional crafts. Hours are Monday to Saturday from 10am to 8pm. Calle 59 no. 507A-4 (between calles 60 and 62). ✆ 999/928-6503.

GUAYABERAS

Business suits are hot and uncomfortable in Mérida's tropical climate, so businessmen, bankers, and bus drivers alike wear the *guayabera,* a loose-fitting shirt decorated with narrow tucks, pockets, and sometimes embroidery, worn over the pants rather than tucked in. Mérida is famous as the best place to buy *guayaberas,* which can go for less than $15 (£8.25) at the market or for more than $50 (£28) custom-made. A *guayabera* made of linen can cost about $80 (£44). Most are made of cotton, although other materials are available. The traditional color is white.

Most shops display ready-to-wear shirts in several price ranges. *Guayabera* makers pride themselves on being innovators. I have yet to enter a shirt-maker's shop in Mérida that did not present its own version of the *guayabera.* When looking at *guayaberas,* here are a few things to keep in mind: When Yucatecans say *seda,* they mean polyester; *lino* is linen or a linen/polyester combination. Take a close look at the stitching and such details as the way the tucks line up over the pockets; with *guayaberas,* the details are everything.

Guayaberas Jack The craftsmanship here is good, the place has a reputation to maintain, and some of the salespeople speak English. Prices are as marked. This will give you a good basis of comparison if you want to hunt for a bargain elsewhere. If the staff does not have the style and color of shirt you want, they will make it for you in about 3 hours. This shop also sells regular shirts and women's blouses. Hours are Monday to Saturday from 10am to 8pm, Sunday from 10am to 2pm. Calle 59 no. 507A (between calles 60 and 62). ✆ 999/928-6002.

HAMMOCKS

Natives across tropical America used hammocks long before the Europeans arrived in the New World. The word comes from the Spanish *hamaca,* which is a borrowing from Taino, a Caribbean Indian language. Hammocks are still in use throughout Latin America and come in a wide variety of forms, but none is so comfortable as the

Yucatecan hammock, which is woven with cotton string in a fine mesh. For most of us, of course, the hammock is lawn furniture, something to relax in for an hour or so on a lazy afternoon. But for the vast majority of Yucatecans, hammocks are the equivalent of beds, and they greatly prefer hammocks to mattresses. I know a hotel owner who has 150 beds in his establishment but won't sleep on any of them. When he does, he complains of waking up unrested and sore. Many well-to-do Meridanos keep a bed just for show. In hotels that cater to Yucatecans, you will always find hammock hooks in the walls because many Yucatecans travel with their own hammock.

My advice to the hammock buyer: The woven part should be cotton, it should be made with fine string, and the strings should be so numerous that when you get in it and stretch out diagonally (the way you're supposed to sleep in these hammocks), the gaps between the strings remain small. Don't pay attention to the words used to describe the size of a hammock; they have become practically meaningless. Good hammocks don't cost a lot of money ($20–$35/£11–£19). If you want a superior hammock, ask for one made with fine crochet thread *hilo de crochet* (the word *crochet* is also sometimes bandied about, but you can readily see the difference). This should run about $100 (£55).

Nothing beats a tryout; the shops mentioned here will gladly hang a hammock for you to test-drive. When it's up, look to see that there are no untied strings. You can also see what street vendors are offering, but you have to know what to look for, or they are likely to take advantage of you.

Hamacas El Aguacate El Aguacate sells hammocks wholesale and retail. It has the greatest variety and is the place to go for a really fancy or extra-large hammock. A good hammock is the no. 6 in cotton; it runs around $35 (£19). The store is open Monday to Friday from 8:30am to 7:30pm, Saturday from 8am to 5pm. It's 6 blocks south of the main square. Calle 58 no. 604 (at Calle 73). ✆ **999/928-6429.**

Tejidos y Cordeles Nacionales This place near the municipal market sells only cotton hammocks, priced by weight—a pretty good practice because hammock lengths are fairly standardized. The prices are better than at El Aguacate, but quality control isn't as good. My idea of a good hammock is one that weighs about 1½ kilograms (3½ lb.) and runs about $30 (£17). Calle 56 no. 516-B (between calles 63 and 65). ✆ **999/928-5561.**

PANAMA HATS

Another useful and popular item is this soft, pliable hat made from the fibers of the jipijapa palm in several towns south of Mérida along Highway 180, especially Becal, in the neighboring state of Campeche. The hat makers in these towns work inside caves so that the moist air keeps the palm fibers pliant.

Jipi hats come in various grades determined by the quality (pliability, softness, and fineness) of the fibers and closeness of the weave. The difference in weave is easy to see, as a fine weave improves the shape of a hat. It has more body and retains its shape better. You'll find Panama hats for sale in several places, but often without much selection. There is a hat store in one of the market buildings: Walk south down Calle 56 past the post office; right before the street ends in the market place, turn left into a passage with hardware stores at the entrance. The fourth or fifth shop is the **Casa de los Jipis.**

WHERE TO STAY

Mérida is easier on the budget than the resort cities. The stream of visitors is steadier than on the coast, so most hotels no longer use a high-season/low-season rate structure. Still, you are more likely to find promotional rates during low season. Mérida has

Where to Stay & Dine in Mérida

ACCOMMODATIONS ■

Casa Mexilio Guest House **6**
Casa San Juan **18**
Fiesta American Mérida **1**
Hotel Caribe **13**
Hotel Dolores Alba **17**
Hotel Maison Lafitte **8**
Hotel Medio Mundo **4**
Hotel Mucuy **10**
Hyatt Regency Mérida **2**

DINING ◆

Alberto's Continental **7**
Café Alameda **9**
Eladio's **15**
El Templo **16**
La Flor de Santiago **5**
Restaurante Amaro **11**
Restaurante Kantún **3**
Restaurant Los Almendros **14**
Vito Corleone **12**

a convention center, which attracts large trade shows that can fill the city's hotels, so it's a good idea to make reservations. The rates quoted here include the 17% tax. When inquiring about prices, always ask if the price quoted includes tax. Most hotels in Mérida offer at least a few air-conditioned rooms, and some also have pools. But many inexpensive hotels haven't figured out how to provide a comfortable bed. Either the mattresses are poor quality, or the bottom sheet is too small to tuck in properly. Some hotels here would offer a really good deal if only they would improve their beds. One last thing to note: Without exception, every hotel in Mérida that doesn't have its own parking has an arrangement with a nearby parking garage, where for a fee you can park your car. Or you can park on the street, where for the most part cars are safe from vandalism. In Mérida, free parking is a relative concept—for many hotels, free parking means only at night; during the day there may be a charge.

VERY EXPENSIVE

Fiesta Americana Mérida 🌟🌟   This six-story hotel on the Paseo de Montejo is built in the grand *fin-de-siècle* style of the old mansions along the Paseo. Guest rooms are off the cavernous lobby, so all face outward and have views of one or another of the avenues. The rooms are comfortable and large, with furnishings and decorations striving for, and achieving, innocuousness in light, tropical colors. The floors are tile and the bathrooms large and well equipped. Service is very attentive, better than at the Hyatt. There is a shopping center on the ground floor, below the lobby.

Av. Colón 451, corner of Paseo Montejo, 92127 Mérida, Yuc. ℂ 800/343-7821 in the U.S. and Canada, or 999/942-1111. Fax 999/942-1112. www.fiestaamericana.com.mx. 350 units. $210 (£116) double; $240 (£132) executive level; $260 (£143) junior suite. AE, DC, MC, V. Free secure parking. **Amenities:** 2 restaurants; bar; midsize outdoor pool; tennis court; health club w/saunas, men's steam room, unisex whirlpool; children's programs; concierge; tour desk; small business center; shopping arcade; room service; massage; babysitting; laundry service; dry cleaning; executive-level rooms. *In room:* A/C, TV w/pay movies, high-speed Internet, minibar, coffeemaker, hair dryer, safe.

Hyatt Regency Mérida 🌟🌟   This Hyatt is much like Hyatts elsewhere, wherein lies this hotel's chief asset. The rooms are dependably comfortable and quiet, the quietest in a noisy city. They're carpeted and well furnished, with great bathrooms. In decoration and comfort, I find them superior to those of the Fiesta Americana, but they certainly don't have any local flavor. The Hyatt's facilities, especially its tennis courts and health club, also rank above the Fiesta Americana's. The pool is more attractive and larger, but its location keeps it in the shade for most of the day, and the water never gets a chance to heat up. Rising 17 stories, the Hyatt is not hard to find in Mérida's skyline; it's near the Paseo de Montejo and across Avenida Colón from the Fiesta Americana.

Calle 60 no. 344 (at Av. Colón), 97000 Mérida, Yuc. ℂ 800/223-1234 in the U.S. and Canada, or 999/942-1234. Fax 999/925-7002. www.merida.regency.hyatt.com. 299 units. $175 (£96) standard double; $200 (£110) Regency Club double. Ask about promotional rates. AE, DC, MC, V. Free guarded parking. **Amenities:** 2 restaurants; 2 bars (1 swim-up, open seasonally); large outdoor pool; 2 lighted tennis courts; state-of-the-art health club w/men's and women's whirlpool, sauna, and steam room; children's activities (seasonal); concierge; tour desk; car rental; business center; shopping arcade; room service; massage; babysitting; laundry service; dry cleaning; nonsmoking rooms; executive-level rooms. *In room:* A/C, TV, minibar, hair dryer.

MODERATE

Casa Mexilio Guest House 🌟 *Moments*   This bed-and-breakfast is unlike any other I know. The owners are geniuses at playing with space in an unexpected and delightful manner. Rooms are at different levels, creating private spaces joined to each other and to rooftop terraces by stairs and catwalks. Most are spacious and airy, furnished and decorated in an engaging mix of new and old, polished and primitive. Five come with air-conditioning. A small pool with a whirlpool and profuse tropical vegetation take up most of the central patio. Breakfasts are great. It's 4 blocks west of the plaza. A small bar serves drinks during happy hour, and, weather permitting, you can have your cocktail on one of the rooftop terraces.

Calle 68 no. 495 (between calles 57 and 59), 97000 Mérida, Yuc. © 877/639-4546 in the U.S. and Canada, or 999/928-2505. www.casamexilio.com. 9 units. $50–$85 (£28–£47) double; $120 (£66) penthouse. Rates include full breakfast. MC, V. Limited street parking. **Amenities:** Bar; small outdoor pool; whirlpool; nonsmoking rooms. *In room:* A/C (in some), no phone.

Hotel Caribe   This three-story colonial-style hotel (no elevator) is great for a couple of reasons: Its location at the back of Plaza Hidalgo is both central and quiet, and it has a nice little pool and sun deck on the rooftop with a view of the cathedral. The rooms are moderately comfortable, though they aren't well lit, and have only small windows facing the central courtyard. Thirteen *clase económica* rooms don't have air-conditioning, but standard rooms do; and superior rooms (on the top floor) have been remodeled and have safes, hair dryers, larger windows, and quieter air-conditioning. Avoid the rooms on the ground floor. The hotel offers a lot of variety in bedding arrangements, mostly combinations of twins and doubles. Mattresses are often softer than standard. The TVs add little value to the rooms. Nearby parking is free at night but costs extra during the day beginning at 7am. The restaurant serves good Mexican food.

Calle 59 no. 500 (at Calle 60), 97000 Mérida, Yuc. © 888/822-6431 in the U.S. and Canada, or 999/924-9022. Fax 999/924-8733. www.hotelcaribe.com.mx. 53 units. $48 (£26) *clase económica* double; $60–$70 (£33–£39) standard or superior double. AE, MC, V. Free nearby night parking. **Amenities:** Restaurant; bar; small outdoor pool; tour desk; room service; laundry service. *In room:* A/C (in some), TV, hair dryer (in some), safe (in some).

Hotel Maison Lafitte ☆   This new three-story hotel offers modern, attractive rooms with good air-conditioning as well as tropical touches such as wooden louvers over the windows, and light furniture with caned backs and seats. Rooms are medium to large, with midsize bathrooms that have great showers and good lighting. Most rooms come with either two doubles or a king-size bed. Rooms are quiet and look out over a pretty little garden with a fountain. A couple of rooms don't have windows. The location is excellent.

Calle 60 no. 472 (between calles 53 and 55), 97000 Mérida, Yuc. © 800/538-6802 in the U.S. and Canada, or 999/928-1243. Fax 999/923-9159. www.maisonlafitte.com.mx. 30 units. $90 (£50) double. Rates include full breakfast. AE, MC, V. Free limited secure parking for compact cars. **Amenities:** Restaurant; bar; small outdoor pool; tour desk; car rental; room service; in-room massage; laundry service; dry cleaning. *In room:* A/C, TV, Wi-Fi, minibar, hair dryer, safe.

Hotel MedioMundo ☆ *(Finds)*   This is a quiet courtyard hotel with beautiful rooms and a good location 3 blocks north of the main plaza. The English-speaking owners have invested their money in the right places, going for high-quality mattresses, good lighting, quiet air-conditioning units, lots of space, and good bathrooms with strong showers. What they didn't invest in were TVs, which adds to the serenity. Higher prices are for the eight rooms with air-conditioning, but all units have windows with good screens and get ample ventilation. Breakfast is served in one of the two attractive courtyards.

Calle 55 no. 533 (between calles 64 and 66), 97000 Mérida, Yuc. ©/fax 999/924-5472. www.hotelmediomundo.com. 12 units. $60–$80 (£33–£44) double. MC, V. Limited street parking. **Amenities:** Small outdoor pool; tour info; in-room massage; laundry service; nonsmoking rooms. *In room:* A/C (in some), no phone.

Of Haciendas & Hotels

Haciendas in the Yucatán have had a bumpy history. During the colonial period they were isolated, self-sufficient fiefdoms—not terribly efficient, but they didn't have to be. Mostly they produced foodstuffs—enough for the needs of the owners and peasants plus a little extra that the owners could sell for a small sum in the city. The owners, though politically powerful, especially within the confines of their large estates, were never rich.

This changed in the 19th century, when the expanding world market created high demand for henequén, the natural fiber of the sisal plant, which was used to bale hay. In a few years, all of the haciendas shifted to mass production of this commodity. Prices and profits kept climbing through the end of the century and into the 20th. Hacienda owners now had lots of cash to spend on their estates and on heavy machinery to process the henequén fiber more efficiently. Then came the bust. Throughout the 1920s, prices and demand fell, and there was no other commodity that could replace sisal. The haciendas entered a long decline, but by then, the cultivation and processing of the sisal plant had become part of local culture.

To see and understand what things were like during the golden age, you can visit a couple of haciendas. One, by the name of **Sotuta de Peón,** has recently been thoroughly refurbished and operates much like in the old days—a living museum involving an entire community (see "Side Trips from Mérida," later in this chapter). At the other one, **Yaxcopoil** (see "En Route to Uxmal," later in this chapter), you can stroll through the shell of a once bustling estate and look for remnants of faded splendor.

Now another boom of sorts has brought haciendas back; this time as retreats, country residences, and hotels. The hotels convey an air of the past—elegant gateways, thick walls, open arches, and high ceilings—you get the feel of an era gone by. Indeed, there are a few features that make a guest feel like lord and master, especially the extravagant suites and personal service. But what strikes me the most when I visit these haciendas is the contrast between them and the world outside. They are like little islands of order and tranquillity in the sea of chaos that is the Yucatán.

There are five luxury hacienda hotels. The most opulent of these is **La Hacienda Xcanatún** (© 888/883-3633 in the U.S.; www.xcanatun.com). It's

INEXPENSIVE

Casa San Juan ⚘ *Value* This B&B, in a colonial house, is loaded with character and provides a good glimpse of the old Mérida that lies behind the colonial facades in the historic district. Guest rooms are beautifully decorated, large, and comfortable. Those in the original house have been modernized but maintain a colonial feel, with 7m (23-ft.) ceilings and 45cm-thick (18-inch) walls. The modern rooms in back look out over the rear patio. The lower rate is for the three rooms without air-conditioning (they have ceiling and floor fans). Choice of beds includes one queen-size, one double, or two on the outskirts of Mérida, off the highway to Progreso. The suites are large and have extravagant bathrooms. The decor is in muted colors with rich materials and modern pieces that evoke the simplicity of an earlier age. It has the best restaurant in the Mérida area and a complete spa. The owners personally manage their hotel and keep the service sharp.

The other four luxury hotels are all owned by Roberto Hernández, one of the richest men in Mexico. The hospitality and reservation system are handled by **Starwood Hotels** (© 800/325-3589 in the U.S. and Canada; www.luxurycollection.com). The owner has taken great pains to restore all four haciendas to original condition, and all are beautiful. **Temozón,** off the highway to Uxmal, is the most magnificent. **Uayamón,** located between the ruins of Edzná and the colonial city of Campeche, is perhaps the most romantic. **Hacienda San José Cholul,** located east of Mérida towards Izamal, is my personal favorite, and picturesque **Santa Rosa** lies southwest of Mérida, near the town of Maxcanú. Packages are available for staying at two or more of these haciendas. All offer personal service, activities, and spas.

Two haciendas offer economical lodging. On the western outskirts of Mérida by the highway to Chichén Itzá and Cancún is **Hacienda San Pedro Nohpat** (© 999/988-0542; www.haciendaholidays.com). It retains only the land that immediately surrounds the residence, but it offers a great bargain in lodging—large, comfortable rooms and an attractive garden area and pool. The other is **Hacienda Blanca Flor** (© 999/925-8042; www.mexonline. com/blancaflor.htm), which lies between Mérida and Campeche just off the highway. It's the only hacienda hotel that actually operates like one, producing most of the food served there. The owners work with bus tours but also welcome couples and individuals. Rooms are in a modern building and are large and simply furnished.

Two other haciendas can be leased by small groups for retreats and group vacations: **Hacienda Petac** (© 800/225-4255 in the U.S.; www.hacienda petac.com) and **San Antonio Hacienda** (© 999/910-6144; www.hacienda sanantonio.com.mx). Both have beautiful rooms, common areas, and grounds.

twins, all with good mattresses and sheets. Breakfast includes fruit or juice, coffee, bread, and homemade preserves. Casa San Juan is 4 blocks south of the main square.

Calle 62 no. 545a (between calles 69 and 71), 97000 Mérida, Yuc. ©/fax 999/986-2937. www.casasanjuan.com. 8 units (7 with private bathroom). $30–$60 (£17–£33) double. Rates include continental breakfast. No credit cards. Parking nearby $2 (£1.10). *In room:* A/C (in some), no phone.

Hotel Dolores Alba (Value)
The Dolores Alba offers attractive, comfortable rooms, an inviting swimming pool, good A/C, and free parking, all for a great price. The three-story section (with elevator) surrounding the back courtyard offers large rooms with good-size bathrooms. Beds (either two doubles or one double and one twin) have

supportive foam-core mattresses, usually in a combination of one medium-firm and one medium-soft. All rooms have windows or balconies looking out over the pool. An old mango tree shades the front courtyard. The older rooms in this section are decorated with local crafts and have small bathrooms. The family that owns the Hotel Dolores Alba outside Chichén Itzá manages this hotel; you can make reservations at one hotel for the other. This hotel is 3½ blocks from the main square.

Calle 63 no. 464 (between calles 52 and 54), 97000 Mérida, Yuc. ✆ **999/928-5650.** Fax 999/928-3163. www.dolores alba.com. 100 units. $40–$45 (£22–£25) double. MC, V (with 8% surcharge). Internet specials available. Free guarded sheltered parking. **Amenities:** Restaurant; outdoor pool; tour desk; room service; laundry service; Laundromat. *In room:* A/C, TV, safe.

Hotel Mucuy *Value* The Mucuy is a simple, quiet, pleasant hotel in a great location. The gracious owners strive to make guests feel welcome, with conveniences such as a communal refrigerator in the lobby and, for a small extra charge, the use of a washer and dryer. Guest rooms are basic; most contain two twin beds or a queen (with comfortable mattresses) and some simple furniture. A neat garden patio with comfortable chairs is the perfect place for sitting and reading. The Mucuy is named for a small dove said to bring good luck to places where it alights. The hotel has a few rooms with A/C, which cost $5 (£2.75) more. English is spoken.

Calle 57 no. 481 (between calles 56 and 58), 97000 Mérida, Yuc. ✆ **999/928-5193.** Fax 999/923-7801. www.mucuy. com or cofelia@yahoo.com.mx. 21 units. $22 (£12) double. No credit cards. Limited street parking. **Amenities:** Small outdoor pool; tour info; self-serve laundry. *In room:* A/C (in some), no phone.

WHERE TO DINE

The people of Mérida have strong ideas and traditions about food. Certain dishes are always associated with a particular day of the week. In households across the city, Sunday would feel incomplete without *puchero* (a kind of stew). On Monday, at any restaurant that caters to locals, you are sure to find *frijol con puerco* (pork and beans). Likewise, you'll find *potaje* (potage) on Thursday; fish, of course, on Friday; and *chocolomo* (a beef dish) on Saturday. These dishes are heavy and slow to digest; they are for the midday meal, and not suitable for supper. What's more, Meridanos don't believe that seafood is a healthy supper food. All seafood restaurants in Mérida close by 6pm unless they cater to tourists. The preferred supper food is turkey (which, by the way, is said to be high in tryptophan, a soporific), and it's best served in the traditional *antojitos*—*salbutes* (small thin rounds of *masa* fried and topped with turkey, pork, or chicken, and onions, tomatoes, and lettuce) and *panuchos* (sliced open and lightly stuffed with bean paste, before having toppings added)—and turkey soup.

Another thing you may notice about Mérida is the surprising number of Middle Eastern restaurants. The city received a large influx of Lebanese immigrants around 1900. This population has had a strong influence on local society, to the point where Meridanos think of kibbe the way Americans think of pizza. Speaking of pizza, if you want to get some to take back to your hotel room, try **Vito Corleone,** on Calle 59 between calles 60 and 62. Its pizzas have a thin crust with a slightly smoky taste from the wood-burning oven.

It's becoming more difficult to recommend good restaurants for fine dining in the downtown area. Most of the best places are in the outlying districts, near the upper-class neighborhoods and shopping plazas. They are a little difficult to get to. If you want something special, I would recommend dining at the Hacienda Xcanatún on the outskirts of town, off the Progreso road. (See "Of Haciendas & Hotels," above.)

EXPENSIVE

Alberto's Continental ✿ LEBANESE/YUCATECAN/ITALIAN   There's nothing quite like dining here at night in a softly lit room or on the wonderful old patio framed in Moorish arches. Nothing glitzy—just elegant *mudejar*-patterned tile floors, simple furniture, decoration that's just so, and the gurgling of a fountain creating a romantic mood. I find the prices on the expensive side. For supper, you can choose a sampler plate of four Lebanese favorites, or traditional Yucatecan specialties, such as *pollo pibil* or fish Celestún (bass stuffed with shrimp). You can finish with Turkish coffee.

Calle 64 no. 482 (at Calle 57). ✆ **999/928-5367.** Reservations recommended. Main courses $8–$20 (£4.40–£11). AE, MC, V. Daily 1–11pm.

MODERATE

El Príncipe Tutul Xiú ✿ *(Finds)* REGIONAL   This restaurant serves Yucatecan specialties from a limited menu. The original is in the town of Maní—the owner opened this restaurant because he got tired of hearing Meridanos asking him why he didn't open one in the capital. It's a short taxi ride from downtown, and to return you can pick up a local bus that passes by the restaurant. This is a great place to try the famous *sopa de lima,* and one of the six typical main courses. These are served with great handmade tortillas. And you can order, with confidence, one of the flavored waters such as an *horchata* or *tamarindo.*

Calle 123 no. 216 (between calles 46 and 46b), Colonia Serapio Rendón. ✆ **999/929-7721.** Reservations not accepted. Main courses $6 (£3.30). MC, V. Daily 11am–6pm.

El Templo ✿ MEXICAN NUEVA COCINA   I'm hoping that this recently opened restaurant survives. The chef-owner offers out-of-the-ordinary dining, which is something that Mérida really needs. The odd layout of the place and the decor, which plays loosely with Mexican popular culture and iconography, are amusing. And the triptych menu, divided into Yucatecan, Mexican, and original, holds a lot of uncommon choices, plus a couple of daily specials. Sample dishes include the Cornish game hen in a guava-lime glaze and a salmon in a tamarind and black sesame sauce. I get the feeling that chef hasn't settled down into a groove yet, but there is no denying his enthusiasm. I just hope the locals enjoy this place as much as I do.

Calle 59 no. 438 (between calles 50 and 52). ✆ **999/930-9303.** Reservations accepted. Main courses $7–$10 (£3.85–£5.50). MC, V. Mon–Sat 11am–midnight.

Restaurant Amaro REGIONAL/VEGETARIAN   The menu in this courtyard restaurant offers some interesting vegetarian dishes, such as *crema de calabacitas* (cream of squash soup), apple salad, and avocado pizza. There is also a limited menu of fish and chicken dishes; you might want to try the Yucatecan chicken. The *agua de chaya* (chaya is a leafy vegetable prominent in the Maya diet) is refreshing on a hot afternoon. All desserts are made in-house. The restaurant is a little north of Plaza Mayor.

Calle 59 no. 507 Interior 6 (between calles 60 and 62). ✆ **999/928-2451.** Main courses $5–$9 (£2.75–£4.95). MC, V. Mon–Sat 11am–2am.

Restaurante Kantún ✿ *(Value)* SEAFOOD   This modest little restaurant serves up the freshest seafood for incredibly low prices. The owner-chef is always on the premises taking care of details. The menu includes excellent ceviches and seafood cocktails and fish cooked in a number of ways. I had the *especial Kantún,* which was lightly battered and stuffed with lobster, crab, and shrimp. The dining room is air-conditioned, the furniture comfortable, and the service attentive.

Calle 45 no. 525-G (between calles 64 and 66). ℂ **999/923-4493.** Reservations recommended. Main courses $6–$12 (£3.30–£6.60). MC, V. Daily noon–8pm (occasionally closes Mon).

Restaurant Los Almendros *(Overrated)* YUCATECAN   Ask where to eat Yucatecan food, and locals will inevitably suggest this place because of its reputation. After all, this was the first place to offer tourists such Yucatecan specialties as *salbutes, panuchos* and *papadzules* (both similar to *gorditas*), *cochinita pibil,* and *poc chuc.* The menu even comes with color photographs to facilitate acquaintance with these strange-sounding dishes. The food is okay and not much of a risk, but you can find better elsewhere. Still, it's a safe place to try Yucatecan food for the first time, and it's such a fixture that the idea of a guidebook that doesn't mention this restaurant is unthinkable. It's 5 blocks east of Calle 60, facing the Parque de la Mejorada.

Calle 50A no. 493. ℂ **999/928-5459.** Main courses $5–$9 (£2.20–£4.95); daily special $5–$9 (£2.75–£4.95). AE, MC, V. Daily 10am–11pm.

INEXPENSIVE

Café Alameda MIDDLE EASTERN/VEGETARIAN   The trappings here are simple and informal (metal tables, plastic chairs), and it's a good place for catching a light meal. The trick is figuring out the Spanish names for popular Middle Eastern dishes. Kibbe is *quebbe bola* (not *quebbe cruda*), hummus is *garbanza,* and shish kabob is *alambre.* I leave it to you to figure out what a spinach pie is called (and it's excellent). Café Alameda is a treat for vegetarians, and the umbrella-shaded tables on the patio are perfect for morning coffee and *mamules* (walnut-filled pastries).

Calle 58 no. 474 (between calles 55 and 57). ℂ **999/928-3635.** Main courses $2–$5 (£1.10–£2.75). No credit cards. Daily 8am–5pm.

Eladio's *✿* YUCATECAN   This is where locals come to relax in their off hours, drink very cold beer, and snack or dine on Yucatecan specialties. There are 4 or 5 of these restaurant scattered about the city; this is the closest to the center of downtown. You have two choices: order a beer and enjoy *una botana* (a small portion that accompanies a drink, in this case usually a Yucatecan dish), or order from the menu. *Cochinita, poc chuc,* and *relleno negro* (turkey flavored with burnt chiles) are all good. Or try the *panuchos* or *salbutes.* Often there is live music in this open-air restaurant, which is 3 blocks east of Parque de la Mejorada.

Calle 59 (at Calle 44). ℂ **999/923-1087.** Main courses $4–$8 (£2.20–£4.40). AE, MC, V. Daily noon–9pm.

La Flor de Santiago REGIONAL   I enjoy the food here as much as anywhere else in the downtown area, but often it can be annoying because the cooks run out of food. The restaurant has its own bakery with a wood-fired stove for baking sweet breads for breakfast and supper. On the menu are several of the regional dishes that you see elsewhere, such as *panuchos* and *salbutes,* and some things that aren't so commonly on the menu, such as *pibito,* also called *mucbil pollo;* a traditional food for Day of the Dead, it's much like a tamal on the outside, with chicken and a soft center on the inside. There are also several sandwiches, *comida corrida,* and a large choice of beverages. The dining area is classic, with its high ceiling, plain furniture, and local clientele.

Calle 70 no. 478 (between calles 57 and 59). ℂ **999/928-5591.** *Comida corrida* $3.50 (£1.95); main courses $3–$6 (£1.65–£3.30). No credit cards. Daily 7am–11pm.

MERIDA AFTER DARK

For nighttime entertainment, see the box, "Festivals & Special Events in Mérida," earlier in this chapter, or check out the theaters noted here.

Teatro Peón Contreras, Calle 60 at Calle 57, and **Teatro Ayala,** Calle 60 at Calle 61, feature a wide range of performing artists from Mexico and around the world. **El Nuevo Olimpo,** on the main square, schedules frequent concerts; and **Cine Mérida,** a half-block north of the Nuevo Olimpo, has two screens for showing classic and art films, and one live stage.

Mérida's club scene offers everything from ubiquitous rock/dance to some one-of-a-kind spots that are nothing like what you find back home. Most of the dance clubs are in the big hotels or on Paseo de Montejo. For dancing, a small cluster of clubs on Calle 60, around the corner from Santa Lucía, offer live rock and Latin music. For salsa, go to **Mambo Café** in the Plaza las Américas shopping center.

La Trova *(Moments* It's hard to overstate the importance of *música de trío* or *trova* in Mexican popular culture. This music, mainly in the form of songs called boleros, may have been at its most popular in the 1940s and 1950s, but every new Mexican pop-music heartthrob feels compelled to release a new version of the classics. I like the originals best, and so do most Mexicans. And, if you understand colloquial Spanish, all the better; the language of boleros is vivid, passionate, and quite Mexican. The Yucatán is especially well known for its *trova*—so much so, that Mérida has built a museum to popular song (Museo de la Canción Yucateca). But I prefer listening to it live. The best place by far to do this is La Trova, a cozy and comfortable bar in the old Mérida Misión Hotel at the corner of calles 60 and 57. The musical director for the bar is a local legend, and he lines up some of the best trios I've ever heard. It's open Monday to Saturday from 9pm to 2am. Calle 60 no. 491. ℂ **999/923-9500.** Cover $9 (£4.95).

ECOTOURS & ADVENTURE TRIPS

The Yucatán Peninsula has seen a recent explosion of companies that organize nature and adventure tours. One well-established outfit with a great track record is **Ecoturismo Yucatán,** Calle 3 no. 235, Col. Pensiones, 97219 Mérida (ℂ **999/920-2772;** fax 999/925-9047; www.ecoyuc.com). Alfonso and Roberta Escobedo create itineraries to meet just about any special or general interest you may have for going to the Yucatán or southern Mexico. Alfonso has been creating adventure and nature tours for more than a dozen years. Specialties include archaeology, birding, natural history, and kayaking. The company also offers day trips that explore contemporary Maya culture and life in villages in the Yucatán. Package and customized tours are available.

SIDE TRIPS FROM MERIDA
SOTUTA DE PEON

What started out as one man's hobby—to restore an old hacienda for a weekend getaway and perhaps see what it takes to plant a couple of acres of henequén—spiraled out of control until it grew into one of the best living-museums you'll see anywhere; it has engrossed the imagination of an entire rural community. Presto! You have a completely functional *hacienda henequenera.*

You can arrange transportation from any of Mérida's hotels by calling **Hacienda Sotuta de Peón** at ℂ **999/941-8639.** Call to make a reservation even if you have your own car, and be sure to bring your bathing suit; there's a cool *cenote* on the property. The best days to visit are when the giant fiber-extracting machine is in operation—Tuesday, Thursday, or Saturday. The tour starts with a visit to the henequén fields via mule-drawn carts, the same as are used to transport the leaves of the plant to the hacienda's headquarters. You get to see it being harvested, and later, processed at the *casa de máquinas,* and even used in the manufacturing of twine and such. Along the way you get a glimpse into the local culture surrounding henequén production. You visit a house of one of the workers, as well as the house of the *hacendado* (the owner). You can also try some of the regional cooking—there's a restaurant on the premises. Transportation and tour (in English or Spanish) costs $45 (£25) per person, but check this because the hacienda is a newly operating business, and there might be some price adjustments. For more information see **www.haciendatour.com**.

IZAMAL

Izamal is a sleepy town some 80km (50 miles) east of Mérida, an easy day trip by car. You can visit the famous Franciscan convent of San Antonio de Padua and the ruins of four large pyramids that overlook the center of town. One pyramid is partially reconstructed. Life in Izamal is easygoing in the extreme, as evidenced by the *victorias,* the horse-drawn buggies that serve as taxis here. Even if you come by car, you should make a point of touring the town in one of these. There is also a sound and light show in the old convent. The half-hour show costs $4.50 (£1.95) and is held on Tuesday, Thursday, Friday, and Saturday at 8:30pm. It's in Spanish, but you can rent headphones in other languages for $2.50 (£1.40).

CELESTUN NATIONAL WILDLIFE REFUGE: FLAMINGOS & OTHER WATERFOWL

On the coast, west of Mérida, is a large wetlands area that has been declared a biopreserve. It is a long, shallow estuary where freshwater mixes with Gulf saltwater, creating a habitat perfect for flamingos and many other species of waterfowl. This *ría* (estuary), unlike others that are fed by rivers or streams, receives fresh water through about 80 *cenotes,* most of which are underwater. It is very shallow (.3–1m/1–4 ft. deep) and thickly grown with mangrove, with an open channel .5km (a quarter mile) wide and 50km (31 miles) long, sheltered from the open sea by a narrow strip of land. Along this corridor, you can take a launch to see flamingos as they dredge the bottom of the shallows for a species of small crustacean and a particular insect that make up the bulk of their diet.

You can get here by car or bus; it's an easy 90-minute drive. (For information on buses, see "Getting There & Departing: By Bus," earlier in this chapter.) To drive, leave downtown Mérida on Calle 57. Shortly after Santiago Church, Calle 57 ends and there's a dogleg onto Calle 59-A. This crosses Avenida Itzáes, and its name changes to Jacinto Canek; continue until you see signs for Celestún Highway 178. This will take you through Hunucmá, where the road joins Highway 281, which takes you to Celestún. You'll know you have arrived when you get to the bridge.

In the last few years, the state agency CULTUR has come into Celestún and established order where once there was chaos. Immediately to your left after the bridge, you'll find modern facilities with a snack bar, clean bathrooms, and a ticket window. Prices for tours are fixed. A 75-minute tour costs about $50 (£28) and can accommodate up to six people. You can join others or hire a boat by yourself. On the tour you'll definitely see some flamingos; you'll also get to see some mangrove close up, and one of the many underwater springs. Please do not urge the boatmen to get any closer to the flamingos than they are allowed to; if pestered too much, the birds will abandon the area for another, less fitting habitat. The ride is quite pleasant—the water is calm, and CULTUR has supplied the boatmen with wide, flat-bottom skiffs that have canopies for shade.

In addition to flamingos, you will see frigate birds, pelicans, spoonbills, egrets, sandpipers, and other waterfowl feeding on shallow sandbars at any time of year. At least 15 duck species have been counted, and there are several species of birds of prey. Of the 175 bird species that are here, some 99 are permanent residents. Nonbreeding flamingos remain here year-round; the larger group of breeding flamingos takes off around April to nest on the upper Yucatán Peninsula east of Río Lagartos, returning to Celestún in October.

Hotel Eco Paraíso Xixim 🐸🐸 Eco Paraíso is meant to be a refuge from the modern world. It sits on a deserted 4km (2½-mile) stretch of beach that was once part of a coconut plantation. It attracts much the same clientele as the former-haciendas-turned-luxury-hotels, but in some ways it has more going for it (like the beach). Some guests come here for a week of idleness; others use this as a base of operations for visiting the biopreserve and making trips to the Maya ruins in the interior. The hotel offers its own tours to various places. Rooms are quite private; each is a separate bungalow with *palapa* roof. Each comes with two comfortable queen-size beds, a sitting area, ceiling fans, and a private porch with hammocks. On my last visit, the food was very good, and the service was great. The hotel composts waste, and treats and uses wastewater.

Antigua Carretera a Sisal Km 10, 97367 Celestún, Yuc. ✆ **988/916-2100.** Fax 988/916-2111. www.ecoparaiso.com. 15 units. High season $198 (£109) double; low season $172 (£95) double. Rates include 2 meals per person. AE, MC, V. Free parking. **Amenities:** Restaurant; bar; midsize outdoor pool; tour desk. *In room:* Coffeemaker, hair dryer, safe.

DZIBILCHALTUN: MAYA RUINS & MUSEUM

This destination makes for a quick morning trip that will get you back to Mérida in time for a siesta, or it could be part of a longer trip to Progreso, Uaymitún, and Xcambó. It's located 14km (8⅔ miles) north of Mérida along the Progreso road and 4km (2½ miles) east of the highway. To get there, take Calle 60 all the way out of town and follow signs for Progreso and Highway 261. Look for the sign for Dzibilchaltún, which also reads UNIVERSIDAD DEL MAYAB; it will point you right. After a few miles, you'll see a sign for the entrance to the ruins and the museum. If you don't want to drive, take one of the *colectivos* that line up along Parque San Juan.

Dzibilchaltún was founded about 500 B.C., flourished around A.D. 750, and was in decline long before the coming of the conquistadors. Since the ruins were discovered in 1941, more than 8,000 buildings have been mapped. The site covers an area of almost 15 sq. km (6 sq. miles) with a central core of almost 25 hectares (62 acres), but the area of prime interest is limited to the buildings surrounding two plazas next to the *cenote,* and another building, the Temple of the Seven Dolls, connected to these by a *sacbé* (causeway). Dzibilchaltún means "place of the stone writing," and at least 25 stelae have been found.

Start at the **Museo del Pueblo Maya,** which is worth seeing. It's open Tuesday to Sunday from 8am to 4pm. Admission is $6 (£3.30). The museum's collection includes artifacts from various sites in the Yucatán. Explanations are printed in bilingual format and are fairly thorough. Objects include a beautiful example of a plumed serpent from Chichén Itzá and a finely designed incense vessel from Palenque. From this general view of the Maya civilization, the museum moves on to exhibit specific artifacts found at the site of Dzibilchaltún, including the rather curious dolls that have given one structure its name. Then there's an exhibit on Maya culture in historical and present times, including a collection of *huipiles,* the woven blouses that Indian women wear. From here a door leads out to the site.

The first thing you come to is the *sacbé* that connects the two areas of interest. To the left is the **Temple of the Seven Dolls.** The temple's doorways and the *sacbé* line up with the rising sun at the spring and autumnal equinoxes. To the right are the buildings grouped around the Cenote Xlacah, the sacred well, and a complex of buildings around **Structure 38,** the **Central Group** of temples. The Yucatán State Department of Ecology has added nature trails and published a booklet (in Spanish) of birds and plants seen along the mapped trail.

PROGRESO, UAYMITUN & XCAMBO: GULF COAST CITY, FLAMINGO LOOKOUT & MORE MAYA RUINS

For a beach escape, go to the port of Progreso, Mérida's weekend beach resort. This is where Meridanos have their vacation houses and where they come in large numbers in July and August. It is also the part-time home of some Americans and Canadians escaping northern winters. Except for July and August, it is a quiet place where you can enjoy the Gulf waters in peace. Along the *malecón,* the wide oceanfront drive that extends the length of a sandy beach, you can pull over and enjoy a swim anywhere you like. The water here isn't the blue of the Caribbean, but it's clean. A long pier extends several kilometers into the gulf to load and unload large ships. Cruise ships dock here twice a week. Along or near the *malecón* are several hotels and a number of restaurants where you can get good fresh seafood.

From Mérida, buses to **Progreso** leave from the bus station at Calle 62 no. 524, between calles 65 and 67, every 15 minutes, starting at 5am. The trip takes almost an hour and costs $3 (£1.65).

If you have a car, you might want to drive down the coastal road east toward Telchac Puerto. After about 20 minutes, at the right side of the road you'll see a large, solid-looking wooden observation tower for viewing flamingos. A sign reads UAYMITUN. The state agency CULTUR constructed the tower, operates it, and provides binoculars free of charge. A few years ago, flamingos from Celestún migrated here and established a colony. Your chances of spotting them are good, and you don't have to pay for a boat.

Twenty minutes farther down this road, there's a turnoff for the road to Dzemul. On my last trip I didn't see any flamingos at Uaymitún, but just after turning here, I found a flock of 500, only 30m (98 ft.) from the highway. After a few minutes, you'll see a sign for **Xcambó** that points to the right. This Maya city is thought to have prospered as a production center for salt, a valuable commodity. Archaeologists have reconstructed the small ceremonial center, which has several platforms and temples. Admission is free. After viewing these ruins, you can continue on the same road through the small towns of Dzemul and Baca. At Baca, take Highway 176 back to Mérida.

EN ROUTE TO UXMAL

Two routes go to Uxmal, about 80km (50 miles) south of Mérida. The most direct is Highway 261 via Umán and Muna. On the way, you can stop to see Hacienda Yaxcopoil, which is 30km (20 miles) from Mérida. If you have the time and want a more scenic route, try the meandering State Highway 18. This is sometimes referred to as the Convent Route, but all tourism hype aside, it makes for a pleasant drive with several interesting stops. One thing you might do is make your trip to Uxmal into a loop by going one way and coming back the other with an overnight stay at Uxmal. You could plan on arriving in Uxmal in the late afternoon, attend the sound-and-light show in the evening, and see the ruins the next morning while it is cool and uncrowded.

While traveling in this area you'll pass through a number of small villages without directional signs, so get used to poking your head out the window and saying *"Buenos días, ¿dónde está el camino para . . . ?"* which translates as "Good day, where is the road to . . . ?" This is what I do, and I ask more than one person. The streets in these villages are full of children, bicycles, and livestock, so drive carefully and, as always, keep an eye out for unmarked *topes.* The attractions on these routes all have the same hours: Churches are open daily from 10am to 1pm and 4 to 6pm; ruins are open daily from 8am to 5pm.

HIGHWAY 261: YAXCOPOIL & MUNA   From downtown, take Calle 65 or 69 to Avenida Itzáes and turn left; this feeds onto the highway. You can save some time by looping around the busy market town of Umán. To do so, take the exit for Highway 180 Cancún and Campeche, and then follow signs towards Campeche. You'll be on 180 headed south; take it for a few miles to where it intersects with Highway 261; take the exit labeled UXMAL. Very shortly you'll come to the town and **Hacienda Yaxcopoil** (yash-koh-*poyl;* ℭ **999/900-1193;** www.yaxcopoil.com), a ruined hacienda in plain sight on the right side of the road. In the front courtyard—now a parking lot— is a giant Indian laurel tree. You can take a half-hour tour of the place, including the manor, and the henequén factory. It's open from Monday to Saturday from 8am to 5pm and Sunday 9am to 1pm. Admission is $5 (£2.75). It's a little overpriced because the owners have not put much effort into making this a special attraction, but the grounds are attractive, and there are some things of interest to examine.

After Yaxcopoil comes the little market town of **Muna** (65km/40 miles from Mérida). Here you can find excellent **reproductions of Maya ceramics.** An artisan named Rodrigo Martín Morales has worked 25 years perfecting the style and methods of the ancient Maya. He and his family have two workshops in town. They do painstaking work and sell a lot of their production to archeologists and museum stores. The first store is on the right at the junction of a bypass for Muna. Look for a typical Maya dwelling and a small store. The main store is 3km (2 miles) farther on, just as you enter Muna. Keep an eye out for two large Ceiba trees growing on the right-hand side of the road. Under the trees is a small plaza with stalls selling handcrafts or food. Make a right turn and go down 46m (151 ft.). On your left will be a store. It's not well marked, but it will be obvious when you get there. The name of the place is **Taller de Artesanía Los Ceibos** (ℭ **997/971-0036**). The family will be working in the back. Only Spanish is spoken. The store is open from 9am to 6pm daily. In addition to ceramics, Rodrigo works in stone, wood, and jade. Uxmal is 15km (9⅓ miles) beyond Muna.

HIGHWAY 18 (THE CONVENT ROUTE): KANASIN, ACANCEH, MAYAPAN & TICUL   From downtown take Calle 63 east to Circuito Colonias and turn right; look for a traffic circle with a small fountain and turn left. This feeds onto Highway 18 to Kanasín (kah-nah-*seen*) and then Acanceh (ah-kahn-*keh*). In **Kanasín,** the highway divides into two roads, and a sign will tell you that you can't go straight; instead, you go to the right, which will curve around and flow into the next parallel street. Go past the market, church, and the main square on your left, and then stay to the right when you get to a fork.

Shortly after Kanasín, the highway has been upgraded and now bypasses a lot of villages. After a few of these turnoffs you'll see a sign pointing left to Acanceh. Across the street from and overlooking Acanceh's church is a restored pyramid. On top of this pyramid, under a makeshift roof, are some large stucco figures of Maya deities. The caretaker, Mario Uicab, will guide you up to see the figures and give you a little explanation (in Spanish). Admission is $2.50 (£1.40). There are some other ruins a couple of blocks away called **El Palacio de los Estucos.** In 1908, a stucco mural was found here in mint condition. It was left exposed and has deteriorated somewhat. Now it is sheltered, and you can still easily distinguish the painted figures in their original colors.

To leave Acanceh, head back to the highway on the street that passes between the church and the plaza.

The next turnoff will be for **Tecoh** on the right side. Tecoh's parish church sits on a massive pre-Columbian raised platform—the remains of a ceremonial complex that was sacrificed to build the church. With its rough stone and simple twin towers that are crumbling around the edges, the church looks ancient. Inside are three carved *retablos* (altarpieces) covered in gold leaf and unmistakably Indian in style. In 1998, they were refurbished and are well worth seeing.

Also in Tecoh are some caverns, shown by a local. The bad news is that the owner doesn't have a very good flashlight, and I found myself groping around in the dark. You'll find them as you leave town heading back to the highway. Then it's on to the ruins of Mayapán.

MAYAPAN 𝕮

Founded, according to Maya lore, by the man-god Kukulkán (Quetzalcoatl in central Mexico) in about A.D. 1007, Mayapán quickly established itself as the most important city in northern Yucatán. For almost 2 centuries, it was the capital of a Maya confederation of city-states that included Chichén Itzá and Uxmal. But before 1200, the rulers of Mayapán ended the confederation by attacking and subjugating the other two cities. Eventually, a successful revolt by the other cities brought down Mayapán, which was abandoned during the mid-1400s.

The city extended out at least 4 sq. km (1½ sq. miles), but the ceremonial center is quite compact. In the last few years, archaeologists have been busy excavating and rebuilding it, and work continues. Several buildings bordering the principal plaza have been reconstructed, including one that is similar to El Castillo in Chichén Itzá. The excavations have uncovered murals and stucco figures that provide more grist for the mill of conjecture: atlantes (columns in the form of a human figure supporting something heavy, in the way Atlas supported the sky in Greek myth), skeletal soldiers, macaws, entwined snakes, and a stucco jaguar. This place is definitely worth stopping to see.

The site is open daily from 8am to 5pm. Admission is $3.50 (£1.95). Use of a personal video camera is $4 (£2.20).

FROM MAYAPAN TO TICUL   About 20km (12 miles) after Mayapán, you'll see the highway for **Mama** on your right. This will put you on a narrow road that quickly enters the town. For some reason I really like this village; some parts of it are quite pretty. It's often called Mamita by the locals, using the affectionate diminutive suffix. The main attraction is the church and former convent. Inside are several fascinating *retablos* sculpted in a native form of baroque. During the restoration of these buildings, colonial-age murals and designs were uncovered and restored. Be sure to get a peek at them in the sacristy. From Mama, continue on for about 20km (12 miles) to Ticul, a large (for this area) market town with a couple of simple hotels.

TICUL

Best known for the cottage industry of *huipil* (native blouse) embroidery and for the manufacture of women's dress shoes, Ticul isn't the most exciting stop on the Puuc route, but it's a convenient place to wash up and spend the night. It's also a center for large commercially produced pottery; most of the widely sold sienna-colored pottery painted with Maya designs comes from here. If it's a cloudy, humid day, the potters may not be working (part of the process requires sun drying), but they still welcome visitors to purchase finished pieces.

Ticul is only 20km (12 miles) northeast of Uxmal, so thrifty tourists stay either here or in Santa Elena instead of the more expensive hotels at the ruins. On the main square is the **Hotel Plaza,** Calle 23 no. 202, near the intersection with Calle 26 (© **997/ 972-0484**). It's a modest but comfortable hotel. A double room with air-condition-ing costs $30 (£17); without air-conditioning, $25 (£14). In both cases, there's a 5% charge if you want to pay with a credit card (MasterCard and Visa accepted). Get an interior room if you're looking for quiet, because Ticul has quite a lively plaza. From Ticul, you can do one of two things: head straight for Uxmal via Santa Elena, or loop around the Puuc Route, the long way to Santa Elena. For information on the Puuc route, see "The Puuc Maya Route & Village of Oxkutzcab," below.

FROM TICUL TO UXMAL   Follow the main street (Calle 23) west through town. Turn left on Calle 34. It's 15km (9⅓ miles) to Santa Elena; and from there another 15km (9⅓ miles) to Uxmal. In Santa Elena, by the side of Highway 261, is a clean restaurant with good food, **El Chaac Mool,** and on the opposite side of the road is the **Flycatcher Inn B&B** (see listing, below).

2 The Ruins of Uxmal ★ ★ ★

80km (50 miles) SW of Mérida; 19km (12 miles) W of Ticul; 19km (12 miles) S of Muna

The ceremonial complex of Uxmal (pronounced "oosh-*mahl*") is one of the master-works of Maya civilization. It is strikingly different from all other cities of the Maya for its expansive and intricate facades of carved stone. Unlike other sites in northern Yucatán, such as Chichén Itzá and Mayapán, Uxmal isn't built on a flat plane. The builders worked into the composition of the ceremonial center an interplay of eleva-tions that adds complexity. And then, there is the strange and beautiful oval-shaped Pyramid of the Magician, which is unique among the Maya. The great building period took place between A.D. 700 and 1000, when the population probably reached 25,000. After 1000, Uxmal fell under the sway of the Xiú princes (who may have come from central Mexico). In the 1440s, the Xiú conquered Mayapán, and not long afterward the age of the Maya ended with the arrival of the Spanish conquistadors.

Close to Uxmal, four smaller sites—**Sayil, Kabah, Xlapak,** and **Labná**—can be visited in quick succession. With Uxmal, these ruins are collectively known as the **Puuc route.** See "Seeing Puuc Maya Sites," below, if you want to explore these sites.

ESSENTIALS

GETTING THERE & DEPARTING   By Car   Two routes to Uxmal from Mérida, Highway 261 and State Highway 18, are described in "En Route to Uxmal," above. *Note:* There's no gasoline at Uxmal.

By Bus   See "Getting There & Departing" in "Mérida: Gateway to the Maya Heart-land," earlier in this chapter, for information about bus service between Mérida and Uxmal. To return, wait for the bus on the highway at the entrance to the ruins. To see the sound-and-light show, don't bother with regular buses; sign up with a tour opera-tor in Mérida.

ORIENTATION   Entrance to the ruins is through the visitor center where you buy your tickets (two per person, hold on to both). It has a restaurant; toilets; a first-aid station; shops selling soft drinks, ice cream, film, batteries, and books; a state-run Casa de Artesanía (crafts house); and a small museum, which isn't very informative. The site is open daily from 8am to 5pm. Admission to the archaeological site is around $11

(£6.05), which includes admission to the nightly sound-and-light show. Bringing in a video camera costs $3 (£1.65). Parking costs $1 (55p). If you're staying the night in Uxmal, it is possible (and I think preferable) to get to the site late in the day and buy a ticket that allows you to see the sound-and-light show that evening and lets you enter the ruins the next morning to explore them before it gets hot. Just make sure that the ticket vendor knows what you intend to do and keep the ticket.

Guides at the entrance of Uxmal give tours in a variety of languages and charge $40 (£22) for a single person or a group. The guides frown on unrelated individuals joining a group. They'd rather charge you as a solo visitor, but you can ask other English speakers if they'd like to join you in a tour and split the cost. As at other sites, the guides vary in quality but will point out areas and architectural details that you might otherwise miss. You should think of these guided tours as performances—the guides try to be as entertaining as possible and adjust their presentations according to the interests of the visitors.

Included in the price of admission is a 45-minute **sound-and-light show,** staged each evening at 7pm. It's in Spanish, but headsets are available for rent ($2.50/£1.40) for listening to the program in several languages. The narrative is part Hollywood, part high school, but the lighting of the buildings is worth making the effort to see it. After the show, the chant *"Chaaac, Chaaac"* will echo in your mind for weeks.

A TOUR OF THE RUINS

THE PYRAMID OF THE MAGICIAN   As you enter the ruins, note a *chultún,* or cistern, where Uxmal stored its water. Unlike most of the major Maya sites, Uxmal has no *cenote* to supply fresh water. The city's inhabitants were much more dependent on rainwater, and consequently venerated the rain god Chaac much more than in other places.

Rising in front of you is the Pirámide del Adivino. The name comes from a myth told to John Lloyd Stephens on his visit in the 19th century. It tells the story of a magician-dwarf who reached adulthood in a single day after being hatched from an egg and built this pyramid in one night. Beneath it are five earlier structures. The pyramid has an oval base and rounded sides. You are looking at the east side. The main face is on the west side. Walk around the left or south side to see the front. The pyramid was designed in such a manner that the east side rises less steeply than the west side so that the crowning temples are shifted to the west of the central axis of the building, causing them to loom above the plaza below. The temple doorway's heavy ornamentation, a characteristic of the Chenes style, features 12 stylized masks of what many think are a representation of Chaac.

THE NUNNERY QUADRANGLE   From the plaza you're standing in, you want to go to the large Nunnery Quadrangle. Walk out the way you walked into the plaza, turn right, and follow the wall of this long stone building until you get to the building's main door—a corbelled arch that leads into the quadrangle. You'll find yourself in a plaza bordered on each side by stone buildings with elaborate facades. The 16th-century Spanish historian Fray Diego López de Cogullado gave the quadrangle its name when he decided that its layout resembled a Spanish convent.

The quadrangle does have a lot of small rooms, about the size of a nun's cell. You might poke you're head into one just to see the shape and size of it, but don't bother trying to explore them all. These rooms were long ago abandoned to the swallows, which are almost always flying above the city. No interior murals or stucco work have been found here—at least, not yet. No, the richness of Uxmal lies in the stonework on its exterior walls.

The Nunnery is a great example of this. The first building your eye latches onto when you enter the plaza is the north building in front of you. It is the tallest, and the view from the top includes all the major buildings of the city, making it useful for the sound-and-light show. The central stairway is bordered by a common element in Puuc architecture, doorways supported by rounded columns. The remnants of the facade on the second level show elements used in the other three buildings and elsewhere throughout the city. There's a crosshatch pattern and a pattern of square curlicues, called a step-and-fret design, and the long-nosed god mask repeated vertically, used often to decorate the corners of buildings—what I call a Chaac stack. Though the facades of these buildings share these common elements and others, their composition varies. On the west building you'll see long feathered serpents intertwined at head and tail. A human head stares out from a serpent's open mouth. I've heard and read a number of interpretations of this motif, repeated elsewhere in Maya art, but they all leave me somewhat in doubt. And that's the trouble with symbols: They are usually the condensed expression of multiple meanings, so any one interpretation could be true, but only partially true.

THE BALL COURT   Leaving the Nunnery by the same way you entered, you will see straight ahead a ball court. What would a Maya city be without a ball court? And this one is a particularly good representative of the hundreds found elsewhere in the Maya world. Someone has even installed a replica of one of the stone rings that were the targets for the players, who would make use of their knees, hips, and maybe their arms to strike a solid rubber ball (yes, the Maya knew about natural rubber and extracted latex from a couple of species of rubber trees). The inclined planes on both sides of the court were in play and obviously not an area for spectators, who are thought to have observed the game from atop the two structures.

THE GOVERNOR'S PALACE   Continuing in the same direction (south), you come to the large raised plaza on top of which sits the Governor's Palace, running in a north-south direction. The surface area of the raised plaza measures 140m×170m (459 ft.×558 ft.), and it is raised about 10m (33 ft.) above the ground—quite a bit of earth-moving. Most of this surface is used as a ceremonial space facing the front (east side) of the palace. In the center is a double-headed jaguar throne, which is seen elsewhere in the Maya world. From here, you get the best view of the building's remarkable facade. Like the rest of the palaces here, the first level is smooth, and the second is ornate. Moving diagonally across a crosshatch pattern is a series of Chaac masks. Crowning the building is an elegant cornice projecting slightly outward from above a double border, which could be an architectural reference to the original crested thatched roofs of the Maya. Human figures adorned the main doors, though only the headdress survives of the central figure.

THE GREAT PYRAMID   Behind the palace, the platform descends in terraces to another plaza with a large pyramid on its south side. This is known as the Great Pyramid. On top is the Temple of the Macaws, for the repeated representation of macaws on the face of the temple, and the ruins of three other temples. The view from the top is wonderful.

THE DOVECOTE   This building is remarkable in that roof combs weren't a common feature of temples in the Puuc hills, although you'll see one (of a very different style) on El Mirador at Sayil.

WHERE TO STAY

Flycatcher Inn B&B *Value*   This pleasant little bed-and-breakfast is in the neighboring village of Santa Elena, just off Highway 261. The rooms are quiet, attractive, and spacious and come with queen-size beds and lots of decorative ironwork made by one of the owners, Santiago Domínguez. The other owner is Christine Ellingson, an American from the Northwest who has lived in Santa Elena for years and is happy to help her guests with their travels.

Carretera Uxmal–Kabah, 97840 Santa Elena, Yuc. No phone. www.flycatcherinn.com. 5 units. $40–$60 (£22–£33) double; $70 (£39) suite. Rates include breakfast. No credit cards. Free secure parking.

Hacienda Uxmal and The Lodge at Uxmal *GGG*   The Hacienda is the oldest hotel in Uxmal. Located just up the road from the ruins, it was built for the archaeology staff. Rooms are large and airy, exuding a feel of days gone by, with patterned tile floors, heavy furniture, and louvered windows. Room nos. 202 through 214 and 302 through 305 are the nicest of the superiors. Corner rooms are labeled A through F and are even larger and come with Jacuzzi tubs. A handsome garden courtyard with towering royal palms, a bar, and a pool adds to the air of tranquillity. A guitar trio usually plays on the open patio in the evenings.

The Lodge is at the entrance to the ruins. It comprises several two-story thatched buildings situated around two pools and surrounded by landscaped grounds. Each building has a large, open breezeway with ceiling fans and rocking chairs. Rooms are extra large and attractively finished with details such as carved headboards. Bathrooms are large and come with stone countertops and either a bathtub or a Jacuzzi tub. Upstairs rooms have thatched roofs.

High season is from January through April except for a few days surrounding the spring equinox. For those days, the month of November, and Christmas vacation there is a higher rate than what is listed below. Low season is the first 3 weeks of December and May through October.

Carretera Mérida–Uxmal Km 80, 97844 Uxmal, Yuc. *C* **997/976-2011.** www.mayaland.com. (Reservations: Mayaland Resorts, Robalo 30 SM3, 77500 Cancún, Q. Roo; *C* 800/235-4079 in the U.S., or 998/887-2450; fax 998/887-4510.) 113 units. High season $173 (£95) superior, $255 (£140) superior with Jacuzzi, $438–$556 (£241–£306) Lodge bungalow; low season $91 (£50) superior, $145 (£80) superior with Jacuzzi, $192–$285 (£106–£157) Lodge bungalow. AE, MC, V. Free guarded parking. **Amenities:** 2 restaurants; bar; 4 outdoor pools; tour info; laundry service; nonsmoking rooms. *In room:* A/C, TV, minibar, coffeemaker, hair dryer (upon request).

Villas Arqueológicas Uxmal *G*   This hotel is associated with Club Med, but it is just a hotel, not a self-contained vacation village. A two-story layout surrounds a garden patio and a pool. At guests' disposal are a tennis court, a library, and an audiovisual show on the ruins in English, French, and Spanish. Each of the modern, medium-size rooms has a double and a twin bed that fit into spaces that are walled on three sides. Very tall people should stay elsewhere. You can also ask for rates that include half- or full board.

Ruinas Uxmal, 97844 Uxmal, Yuc. *C* **800/258-2633** in the U.S., or 997/976-2018. 48 units. $110 (£61) double. Rates include continental breakfast. Half-board (breakfast plus lunch or dinner) $18 (£9.90) per person; full board (3 meals) $35 (£19) per person. AE, MC, V. Free guarded parking. **Amenities:** Restaurant; bar; outdoor pool; tennis court, laundry service. *In room:* A/C, hair dryer.

WHERE TO DINE

I've eaten well at the hotel restaurant of the Lodge at Uxmal, ordering the Yucatecan specialties, which were fresh and well prepared. I've also eaten well at the hotel restaurant at the Villas Arqueológicas, but again, keeping it simple. There are some *palapa* restaurants by the highway as you approach the ruins from Mérida. I've had good and bad experiences at these. They do a lot of business with bus tours, so the best time to try them is early afternoon.

THE PUUC MAYA ROUTE & VILLAGE OF OXKUTZCAB

South and east of Uxmal are several other Maya cities worth visiting. Though smaller in scale than Uxmal or Chichén Itzá, each contains gems of Maya architecture. The Palace of Masks at **Kabah,** the palace at **Sayil,** and the fantastic caverns of **Loltún** are well worth viewing.

Kabah is 28km (17 miles) southeast of Uxmal via Highway 261 through Santa Elena. From there it's only a couple kilometers to Sayil. Xlapak is almost walking distance (through the jungle) from Sayil, and Labná is just a bit farther east. A short drive beyond Labná brings you to the caves of Loltún. Oxkutzcab is at the road's intersection with Highway 184, which you can follow west to Ticul or east all the way to Felipe Carrillo Puerto. If you aren't driving, a daily bus from Mérida goes to all these sites, with the exception of Loltún. (See "By Bus" in "Getting There & Departing," earlier in this chapter.)

PUUC MAYA SITES

KABAH ⟨ To reach Kabah from Uxmal, head southwest on Highway 261 to Santa Elena (1km/½ mile), then south to Kabah (13km/8 miles). The ancient city of Kabah lies along both sides of the highway. Turn right into the parking lot.

The most outstanding building at Kabah is the **Palace of Masks,** or Codz Poop ("rolled-up mat"), named for its decorative motif. You'll notice it to the right as you enter. Its outstanding feature is the Chenes-style facade, completely covered in a repeated pattern of 250 masks of Chaac, each one with curling remnants of Chaac's elephant-trunk-like nose. There's nothing else like this facade in all of Maya architecture. For years, parts of this building lay lined up in the weeds like pieces of a puzzle awaiting the master puzzle-solver to put them into place. Sculptures from this building are in the anthropology museums in Mérida and Mexico City.

Just behind and to the left of the Codz Poop is the **Palace Group** (also called the East Group), with a fine Puuc-style colonnaded facade. Originally it had 32 rooms. On the front are seven doors, two divided by columns, a common feature of Puuc architecture. Across the highway is what was once the **Great Temple.** Past it is a **great**

⟨Tips Seeing Puuc Maya Sites

All of these sites are currently undergoing excavation and reconstruction, and some buildings may be roped off when you visit. The sites are open daily from 8am to 5pm. Admission is $2 to $3 (£1.10–£1.65) for each site, and $5 (£2.75) for Loltún. Loltún has specific hours for tours—9:30 and 11am, and 12:30, 2, 3, and 4pm. Even if you're the only person at the cave at one of these times, the guide must give you a tour, and he can't try to charge you more money as if you were contracting his services for an individual tour. Sometimes the guides try to do this. Use of a video camera at any time costs $4 (£2.20); if you're visiting Uxmal in the same day, you pay only once for video permission and present your receipt as proof at each ruin.

arch, which was much wider at one time and may have been a monumental gate into the city. A *sacbé* linked this arch to a point at Uxmal. Compare this corbelled arch to the one at Labná (see below), which is in much better shape.

SAYIL   About 4km (2½ miles) south of Kabah is the turnoff (left, or east) to Sayil, Xlapak, Labná, Loltún, and Oxkutzcab. The ruins of **Sayil** ("place of the ants") are 4km (2½ miles) along this road.

Sayil is famous for **El Palacio** 𝕬𝕬. This palace of more than 90 rooms is impressive for its size alone. At present it is roped off because of some damage suffered in the last hurricane. Climbing is not permitted. But this is unimportant because what makes it a masterpiece of Maya architecture is the facade, which is best appreciated from the ground. It stretches across three terraced levels, and its rows of columns give it a Minoan appearance. On the second level, notice the upside-down stone figure known to archaeologists as the Diving God, or Descending God, over the doorway; the same motif was used at Tulum a couple of centuries later. The large circular basin on the ground below the palace is an artificial catch basin for a *chultún* (cistern); this region has no natural *cenotes* (wells) to use to irrigate crops.

In the jungle past El Palacio is **El Mirador,** a small temple with an oddly slotted roof comb. Beyond El Mirador, a crude stele (tall, carved stone) has a phallic idol carved on it in greatly exaggerated proportions. Another cluster of buildings, the Southern Group, is a short distance down a trail that branches off from the one heading to El Mirador.

XLAPAK   Xlapak (*shla*-pahk) is a small site with one building; it's 5.5km (3½ miles) down the road from Sayil. The Palace at Xlapak bears the masks of the rain god Chaac. You won't miss much if you skip this place.

LABNA   Labná, which dates from between A.D. 600 and 900, is 30km (19 miles) from Uxmal and only 3km (2 miles) past Xlapak. Descriptive placards fronting the main buildings are in Spanish, English, and German. The first thing you see on the left as you enter is **El Palacio,** a magnificent Puuc-style building much like the one at Sayil, but in poorer condition. Over a doorway is a large, well-conserved mask of Chaac with eyes, a huge snout nose, and jagged teeth around a small mouth that seems on the verge of speaking. Jutting out on one corner is a highly stylized serpent's mouth from which pops a human head with an unexpectedly serene expression. From the front, you can gaze out to the enormous grassy interior grounds flanked by vestiges of unrestored buildings and jungle.

From El Palacio, you can walk across the interior grounds on a reconstructed *sacbé* leading to Labná's **corbelled arch.** At one time, there were probably several such arches spread through the region. This one has been extensively restored, although only remnants of the roof comb can be seen. It was once part of a more elaborate structure that is completely gone. Chaac's face is on the corners of one facade, and stylized Maya huts are fashioned in stone above the two small doorways.

You pass through the arch to **El Mirador,** or El Castillo. Towering above a large pile of rubble is a singular room crowned with a roof comb etched against the sky.

There's a snack stand with toilets at the entrance.

LOLTUN   The caverns of Loltún are 31km (19 miles) past Labná on the way to Oxkutzcab, on the left side of the road. These fascinating caves, home of ancient Maya, were also used as a refuge during the War of the Castes (1847–1901). Inside are statuary, wall carvings and paintings, *chultunes* (cisterns), and other signs of Maya habitation. Guides will explain much of what you see. When I was there, the guide spoke English but was a little difficult to understand.

The admission price includes a 90-minute **tour;** tours begin daily at 9:30 and 11am, and 12:30, 2, 3, and 4pm. The floor of the cavern can be slippery in places; if you have a flashlight, take it with you. Admission is $5 (£2.75). What you see is quite interesting. I've heard reports of guides canceling the regularly scheduled tour so that they can charge for a private tour. Don't agree to such a thing.

To return to Mérida from Loltún, drive the 7km (4½ miles) to Oxkutzcab. From there, you have a couple of options for getting back to Mérida: The slow route is through Maní and Teabo, which will allow you to see some convents and return by Highway 18, known as the "Convent Route" (see "En Route to Uxmal," earlier in this chapter). Alternately, you can head towards Muna to hook up with Highway 261 (also described earlier).

OXKUTZCAB

Oxkutzcab (ohsh-kootz-*kahb*), 11km (7 miles) from Loltún, is the center of the Yucatán's fruit-growing region. Oranges abound. The tidy village of 21,000 centers on a beautiful 16th-century church and the market. **Su Cabaña Suiza** (no phone) is a good restaurant in town. The last week of October and first week of November is the **Orange Festival,** when the village turns exuberant, with a carnival and orange displays in and around the central plaza.

EN ROUTE TO CAMPECHE

From Oxkutzcab, head back 43km (27 miles) to Sayil, and then drive south on Highway 261 to Campeche (126km/78 miles). After crossing the state line, you'll pass through the towns of Bolonchén and Hopelchén. The drive is pleasant, and there's little traffic. Both towns have gas stations. When going through the towns, watch carefully for directional traffic signs so that you stay on the highway. From Hopelchén, Highway 261 heads west. After 42km (26 miles), you'll find yourself at Cayal and the well-marked turnoff for the ruins of the city of Edzná, 18km (11 miles) farther south.

EDZNA ⟨ This city is interesting for several reasons. The area was populated as early as 600 B.C., with urban formation by 300 B.C. From that point forward, Edzná grew impressively in a manner that suggests considerable urban-planning skills. An ambitious and elaborate canal system was dug, which must have taken decades to complete, but would have allowed for a great expansion in agricultural production and, hence, concentration of population. This made Edzná the preeminent city for a wide territory.

Another boom in construction began around A.D. 500, during the middle of the Classic period. This would have been when the city's most prominent feature, the **Great Acropolis,** was started.

Sitting on top of this raised platform are five main pyramids, the largest being the much-photographed **Pyramid of Five Stories.** It combines the features of temple platform and palace. In Maya architecture, you have palace buildings with many vaulted chambers and you have solid pyramidal platforms with a couple of interior temples or burial passages. These are two mutually exclusive categories—but not here. Such a mix is found only in the Puuc and Río Bec areas and only in a few examples, and none similar to this, which makes this pyramid a bold architectural statement. The four lesser pyramids on the Acropolis are each constructed in a different style, and each is a pure example of that style. It's as if the rulers of this city were flaunting their cosmopolitanism, showing that they could build in any style they chose but preferred creating their own, superior architecture.

West of the Acropolis, across a large open plaza, is a long, raised building whose purpose isn't quite clear. But its size, as well as that of the plaza, makes you wonder just how many people this city actually held to necessitate such a large public space.

The site takes an hour to see, and is open daily from 8am to 5pm. Admission is $4 (£2.20), plus it's around $4 (£2.20) to use your video camera.

3 Campeche ⟨★⟨★

251km (156 miles) SW of Mérida; 376km (233 miles) NE of Villahermosa

Campeche, the capital of the state of the same name, is a beautifully restored colonial city. The facades of all the houses in the historic center of town have been repaired and painted, all electrical and telephone cables have been routed underground, and the streets have been paved to look cobbled. Several Mexican movie companies have taken advantage of the restoration to shoot period films here.

Despite its beauty, not many tourists come to Campeche. Those who do, tend to be either on their way to the ruins at Palenque (see chapter 11) or the Río Bec region (see chapter 15) or the kind of travelers who are accidental wanderers. A couple of things do need to be said: Campeche is not geared to foreign tourism the way Mérida is, so expect less in the way of English translations and such at museums and other sights. Also, expect less in the way of nightlife, except on weekend nights when they block off the main square for a street party.

If you're interested in seeing the ruins along the Río Bec route, see the section "Side Trips to Maya Ruins from Chetumal," in chapter 15. **Calakmul** ★★★ is a large and important site, with the tallest pyramid in the Yucatán peninsula, and if you're going that far, you should stop at Balamkú and perhaps a few other ruins in the area. From the Campeche side you can get information and contract a tour with one of several tour operators. You can also rent a car. Calakmul is too far away for a day trip. There are a few small hotels in the area. Hotel Del Mar in Campeche has two: **Chicanná Eco-village** and **Puerta Calakmul.**

From the Calakmul area, it's easy to cross over the peninsula to Yucatán's southern Caribbean coast. Then you can head up the coast and complete a loop of the peninsula.

Campeche has an interesting history. The conquistadors arrived in 1517, when Francisco de Córdoba landed here while exploring the coast and stayed just long enough to celebrate Mass. Attempts to settle here were unsuccessful because of native resistance until Montejo The Younger was able to secure a settlement in 1540.

In the 17th and 18th centuries, pirates repeatedly harassed the city. The list of Campeche's attackers reads like a who's who of pirating. On one occasion, several outfits banded together under the famous Dutch pirate Peg Leg (who most likely was the inspiration for the many fictional one-legged sailors) and managed to capture the city. The Campechanos grew tired of hosting pirate parties and erected walls around the city, showing as much industry then as they now show in renovating their historic district. The walls had a number of *baluartes* (bastions) at critical locations. For added security, they constructed two forts, complete with moats and drawbridges, on the hills flanking the city. There were four gates to the city, and the two main ones are still intact: the Puerta de Mar (Sea Gate) and the Puerta de Tierra (Land Gate). The pirates never cared to return, but, in Mexico's stormy political history, the city did withstand a couple of sieges by different armies. Eventually, in the early 1900s, the wall around the city was razed, but the bastions and main gates were left intact, as were the two hilltop fortresses. Most of the bastions and both forts now house museums.

ESSENTIALS

GETTING THERE & DEPARTING   By Plane   AeroMéxico (𝄞 **981/816-6656;** www.aeromexico.com.mx) flies once daily to and from Mexico City. The **airport** is several kilometers northeast of the town center, and you'll have to take a taxi into town (about $5/£2.75).

By Car   Highway 180 goes south from Mérida, passing near the basket-making village of Halacho and near Becal, known for its Panama-hat weavers. The trip takes 2½ hours. At Tenabo, take the shortcut (right, Highway 24) to Campeche rather than going farther to the crossroads near Chencoyí. The longer way from Mérida is along Highway 261 past Uxmal.

When returning to Mérida via Highway 180, go north on Avenida Ruiz Cortines, bearing left to follow the water (this becomes Avenida Pedro Sainz de Baranda, but there's no sign). Follow the road as it turns inland to Highway 180, where you turn left (there's a gas station at the intersection).

If you're leaving Campeche for Edzná and Uxmal, go north on either Ruiz Cortines or Gobernadores and turn right on Madero, which feeds onto **Highway 281.** To go south to Villahermosa, take Ruiz Cortines south.

By Bus   ADO (𝄞 **981/816-2802**) offers a first-class *de paso* (passing through) bus to Palenque (6 hr.; $15/£8.25) four times a day and buses to Mérida (2½ hr.; $8/£4.40) every hour from 5:30am to midnight. The ADO **bus station** is on Avenida Patricio Trueba, a kilometer (a half-mile) from the Puerta de Tierra.

INFORMATION   The **State of Campeche Office of Tourism** (𝄞/fax **981/816-6767;** www.campechetravel.com) is in Plaza Moch-Couoh, Avenida Ruiz Cortines s/n, 24000 Campeche. This is in one of the state buildings between the historic center and the shore. There are also information offices in the bastions of Santa Rosa, San Carlos, and Santiago. It's open Monday to Friday from 9am to 2pm and 4 to 7pm.

CITY LAYOUT   The most interesting part of the city is the restored old part, most of which once lay within the walls. Originally, the seaward wall was at the water's edge, but now land has been gained from the sea between the old walls and the coastline. This is where you'll find most of the state government buildings, which were built in a glaringly modernist style around **Plaza Moch-Couoh:** buildings such as the office tower **Edificio de los Poderes (Judicial Building)** or **Palacio de Gobierno (headquarters for the state of Campeche),** and the futuristic **Cámara de Diputados (Chamber of Deputies),** which looks like a cubist clam.

Campeche's system of street numbering is much like that of other cities in the Yucatán, except that the numbers of the north-south streets increase as you go east instead of the reverse. (See "City Layout" in "Mérida: Gateway to the Maya Heartland," earlier in this chapter.)

GETTING AROUND   Most of the recommended sights, restaurants, and hotels are within walking distance of the old city, except for the two fort-museums. Campeche isn't easy to negotiate by bus, so take taxis for anything beyond walking distance—they are inexpensive.

FAST FACTS: Campeche

American Express Local offices are at Calle 59 no. 4 and 5 (© **981/811-1010**), in the Edificio Del Mar, a half-block toward town from the Hotel Del Mar. Open Monday to Friday from 9am to 2pm and 5 to 7pm, and Saturday from 9am to 1pm. This office does not cash traveler's checks.

Area Code The telephone area code is **981**.

ATMs There are more than 10 cash machines in and around the downtown area.

Emergencies To report an emergency, dial © **060**, which is supposed to be similar to 911 emergency service in the United States.

Internet Access There are plenty of places to check e-mail, too—just look for signs with the words INTERNET or CYBERCAFE.

Post Office The *correo* is in the Edificio Federal at the corner of Avenida 16 de Septiembre and Calle 53 (© **981/816-2134**), near the Baluarte de Santiago; it's open Monday to Saturday from 7:30am to 8pm. The telegraph office is here as well.

EXPLORING CAMPECHE

With beautiful surroundings, friendly people, and an easy pace of life, Campeche is worthy of at least a day on your itinerary. It has some interesting museums, one outstanding restaurant, and plenty to do.

INSIDE THE CITY WALLS

A good place to begin is the pretty *zócalo,* or **Parque Principal,** bounded by calles 55 and 57 running east and west and calles 8 and 10 running north and south. On Saturday nights and Sundays, the city closes the main square to traffic and contracts bands to play. People set up tables in the streets and the entire scene becomes a fun kind of block party. Construction of the church on the north side of the square began in 1650 and was finally completed 150 years later. A pleasant way to see the city is to take the *tranvía* (trolley) tour that leaves three or four times a day from the main plaza; check with one of the tourist information offices for the schedule. The cost is $7 (£3.85) for a 45-minute tour.

Baluarte de la Soledad   This bastion next to the sea gate houses Maya stelae recovered from around the state. Many are badly worn, but the line drawings beside the stones allow you to appreciate their former design.

Calle 57 and Calle 8, opposite Plaza Principal. No phone. Admission $2.50 (£1.40). Tues–Sat 9am–8pm; Sun 9am–1pm.

Baluarte de San Carlos/Museo de la Ciudad   The city museum deals primarily with the design and construction of the fortifications. A model of the city shows how it looked in its glory days and provides a good overview for touring within the city walls. There are several excellent ship models as well. All text is in Spanish.

Circuito Baluartes and Av. Justo Sierra. No phone. Admission $2.50 (£1.40). Tues–Sat 9am–8pm; Sun 9am–1pm.

Baluarte de Santiago   The Jardín Botánico Xmuch'haltun is a jumble of exotic and common plants within the stone walls of this bastion. More than 250 species of plants and trees share a small courtyard.

Av. 16 de Septiembre and Calle 49. No phone. Free admission. Mon–Fri 9am–8pm; Sat–Sun 9am–1pm.

Casa no. 6 Centro Cultural   In this remodeled colonial house, you'll see some rooms decorated with period furniture and accessories. The patio of mixtilinear arches supported by simple Doric columns is striking. Exhibited in the patio are photos of the city's fine colonial architecture. Several of the photographed buildings have recently been renovated. There is also a small bookstore in back, as well as temporary exhibition space.

Calle 57 no. 6. No phone. Free admission. Daily 9am–9pm.

Puerta de Tierra   At the Land Gate is a small museum displaying portraits of pirates and the city founders. The 1732 French 5-ton cannon in the entryway was found in 1990. On Tuesday, Friday, and Saturday at 8pm, there's a light-and-sound show, as long as 15 or more people have bought tickets. Some shows are in English and some are in Spanish; it depends on the audience. The show is amusing.

Calle 59 at Circuito Baluartes/Av. Gobernadores. No phone. Free admission to museum; show $3 (£1.65) adults, $1 (55p) children younger than 11. Daily 9am–9pm.

OUTSIDE THE WALLS: SCENIC VISTAS

Fuerte–Museo San José el Alto   This fort is higher and has a more sweeping view of Campeche and the coast than Fuerte San Miguel, but it holds only a small exhibit of 16th- and 17th-century weapons and scale miniatures of sailing vessels. This is a nice place for a picnic. Take a cab. On the way, you will pass by an impressive statue of Juárez.

Av. Morazán s/n. No phone. Admission $2.50 (£1.40). Tues–Sun 8am–8pm.

Fuerte–Museo San Miguel ★★   For a good view of the city and a great little museum, take a cab ($2–$3/£1.10–£1.65) up to Fuerte–Museo San Miguel. San Miguel is a small fort with a moat and a drawbridge. Built in 1771, it was the most important of the city's defenses. General Santa Anna captured it when he attacked the city in 1842. The museum of the Maya world was renovated in 2000 and is well worth seeing. It groups the artifacts around central issues in Maya culture. In a room devoted to Maya concepts of the afterlife, there's a great burial scene with jade masks and jewelry from Maya tombs at Calakmul. Another room explains Maya cosmology, another depicts war, and another explains the gods. There are also exhibits on the history of the fort.

Ruta Escénica s/n. No phone. Admission $2.50 (£1.40). Tues–Sat 9am–8pm; Sun 8am–noon.

SHOPPING

Casa de Artesanías Tukulná   This store, run by DIF (a government family-assistance agency), occupies a restored mansion. There is an elaborate display of regional arts and crafts in the back. The wares in the showrooms represent everything that is produced in the state. There are quality textiles, clothing, and locally made furniture. Open Monday to Saturday from 9am to 8pm. Calle 10 no. 333 (between calles 59 and 61). ⓒ 981/816-9088.

WHERE TO STAY

Rates quoted include the 17% tax.

VERY EXPENSIVE

Hacienda Puerta Campeche ★★★   This hotel was created from several adjoining colonial houses. It's a beautiful and original property just inside the Puerta de Tierra in Campeche's colonial center. There is a tropical garden in the center and a pool that runs through the ruined walls of one of the houses. It's quite picturesque. Rooms are colonial with flare—large with old tile floors, distinctive colors, and beamed ceilings. "Hacienda" is in the name to make it apparent that this is one of the properties connected to the four haciendas managed by Starwood hotels. (See "Of Haciendas & Hotels" in the Mérida section, earlier in this chapter.)

Calle 59 71, 24000 Campeche, Camp. (C) **800/325-3589** in the U.S. or Canada, or 981/816-7508. www.luxurycollection. com. 15 units. $305 (£168) superior; $360 (£198) junior suite; $450 (£248) master suite. AE, MC, V. Free guarded parking. **Amenities:** Restaurants; 2 bars; outdoor pool; spa services; concierge; tours; car-rental desk; airport transportation; room service; babysitting; laundry service. *In room:* A/C, TV, high-speed Internet, minibar, fridge, coffeemaker, hair dryer, iron.

EXPENSIVE

Hotel Del Mar 🍄 Rooms in this four-story hotel are large, bright, and comfortably furnished. All have balconies that face the Gulf of Mexico. The beds (two doubles or one king-size) are comfortable. The Del Mar is on the main oceanfront boulevard, between the coast and the city walls. It offers more services than the Baluartes and is a little more expensive. You can make a reservation here to stay in the Río Bec area, or you can buy a package that includes guide and transportation. The hotel also offers a tour to Edzná.

Av. Ruiz Cortines 51, 24000 Campeche, Camp. (C) **981/811-9192** or -9193. Fax 981/811-1618. www.delmarhotel. com.mx. 146 units. $135 (£74) double; $150 (£83) executive-level double. AE, MC, V. Free parking. **Amenities:** 2 restaurants; bar; large outdoor pool; gym w/sauna; travel agency; car-rental desk; business center; room service; babysitting; laundry service; nonsmoking rooms; executive level. *In room:* A/C, TV, safe.

MODERATE

Hotel Baluartes 🍄 Between the Sea Gate and the Gulf of Mexico, this was the city's original luxury hotel. All the rooms have been completely refurbished with new tile floors, new furniture, and new mattresses—one king-size bed or two doubles. They are cheerful and have good lighting, but the bathrooms are small.

Av. 16 de Septiembre no. 128, 24000 Campeche, Camp. (C) **981/816-3911.** Fax 981/816-2410. www.baluartes. com.mx. 156 units. $95 (£52) double; $125 (£69) suite. Rates include breakfast buffet. AE, MC, V. Free guarded parking. **Amenities:** 2 restaurants; bar; large outdoor pool; travel agency; car rental; room service; laundry service; nonsmoking rooms. *In room:* A/C, TV, hair dryer, safe.

Hotel Francis Drake 🍄 (Value A three-story hotel in the *centro histórico* (historical district) with comfortable, attractive rooms at good prices. Rooms are midsize and come with tile floors and one king-size bed, two doubles, or two twins. The bathrooms are modern with large showers. Suites are larger and better furnished. The location is excellent.

Calle 12 no. 207 (between calles 63 and 65), 24000 Campeche, Camp. (C) **981/811-5626** or -5627. www.hotelfrancis drake.com. 24 units. $75 (£41) double; $90 (£50) junior suite; $93 (£51) suite. AE, MC, V. Limited free parking. **Amenities:** Restaurant; tour info; car-rental desk; room service; laundry service. *In room:* A/C, TV, minibar, hair dryer.

INEXPENSIVE

Hotel Colonial (Moments What, you may ask, in a cheap hotel could possibly qualify for a Frommer's Mexican Moment? Well, first of all is the fact that the hotel hasn't changed in 50 years; it exudes an air of the past long since disappeared with the coming of globalization. The rooms have the original tiles—once made in Mérida, but alas, no longer—beautiful things with lovely colors in swirls and geometrics; each room has a different pattern. And then there's the plumbing, which, in my room was so bodacious in design and execution that to hide it within the walls would have been pure Philistinism. Remarkable, too, are the bathroom fixtures, the four-color paint job, and the '40s-style furniture. Sure, you have to make sacrifices for such character—the rooms and bathrooms are small, and the mattresses aren't the best—but even character aside, this hotel is cleaner and more cheerful than any in its class.

Calle 14 no. 122, 24000 Campeche, Camp. (℃ 981/816-2222. 30 units. $25 (£14) double; $35 (£19) double with A/C. No credit cards. *In room:* A/C (some units), no phone.

WHERE TO DINE

Campeche is a fishing town, so seafood predominates. The outstanding restaurant is **La Pigua.** For breakfast, you have your hotel restaurant or one of the traditional eateries such as **La Parroquia.** For a light supper, either get some *antojitos* (small dishes) in the old *barrio* of San Francisco, or have supper above the main plaza at **La Casa Vieja.** If you want a steak, your best bet is **Cactus.**

MODERATE

Cactus STEAKS/MEXICAN   If seafood isn't to your taste, try this steakhouse; it's a favorite with the locals. The rib-eyes are good, as is everything but the *arrachera*, which is the same cut of meat used for fajitas and is very tough.

Av. Malecón Justo Sierra. (℃ 981/811-1453. Main courses $9–$18 (£4.95–£9.90). No credit cards. Daily 7am–2am.

Casa Vieja MEXICAN/INTERNATIONAL   I'm afraid that Casa Vieja has gotten a little old. There's been a drop in effort here, but it still has the prettiest dining space in the city—an upstairs arcade overlooking the main square. Your best option is to order something simple, and it just might be your luck that changes have been made in the kitchen.

Calle 10 no. 319. (℃ 981/811-1311. Reservations not accepted. Main courses $6–$16 (£3.30–£8.80). No credit cards. Tues–Sun 9am–2am; Mon 5:30pm–2am.

La Pigua ✸✸✸ SEAFOOD   The dining area is an air-conditioned version of a traditional Yucatecan cabin, but with walls of glass looking out on green vegetation. The owner has recently remodeled and enlarged his restaurant so that there's less trouble getting a table these days. He also is now opening in the evenings to accommodate tourists. Spanish nautical terms pepper the large menu as the headings for different courses. Sure to be on the menu is fish stuffed with shellfish, which I wholeheartedly recommend. If you're lucky, you might find pompano in a green-herb sauce seasoned with a peppery herb known as *hierba santa*. Other dishes that are sure to please are coconut-battered shrimp with applesauce and *chiles rellenos* with shark. Service is excellent, and the accommodating owner can have your favorite seafood prepared in any style you want.

Av. Miguel Alemán no. 179A. (℃ 981/811-3365. Reservations recommended. Main courses $10–$20 (£5.50–£11). AE, MC, V. Daily noon–8pm. From Plaza Principal, walk north on Calle 8 for 3 blocks; cross Av. Circuito by the botanical garden where Calle 8 becomes Miguel Alemán; the restaurant is 1½ blocks farther up, on the right side of the street.

INEXPENSIVE

Cenaduría Portales ✸ ANTOJITOS   This is the most traditional of supper places for Campechanos. It's a small restaurant under the stone arches that face the Plaza San Francisco in the *barrio* (neighborhood) of San Francisco. This is the oldest part of town, but it lies outside the walls just to the north. Don't leave without ordering the *horchata* (a sweet milky-white drink made of a variety of things, in this case coconut). For food, try the turkey soup, which is wonderful, and the *sincronizadas* (tostadas) and *panuchos*.

Calle 10 no. 86, Portales San Francisco. (℃ 981/811-1491. *Antojitos* 40¢–$1.50 (22p–85p). No credit cards. Daily 6pm–midnight.

La Parroquia MEXICAN   This local hangout offers good, inexpensive fare. It's best for breakfasts and the afternoon *comida corrida*. Selections on the *comida corrida* might include pot roast, meatballs, pork, or fish, with rice or squash, beans, tortillas, and fresh-fruit-flavored water.

Calle 55 no. 9. ✆ 981/816-8086. Breakfast $4 (£2.20); main courses $4–$12 (£2.20–£6.60); *comida corrida* (served noon–3pm) $4–$5 (£2.20–£2.75). MC, V. Daily 24 hr.

4 The Ruins of Chichén Itzá ★★★

179km (111 miles) W of Cancún; 120km (74 miles) E of Mérida

The fabled ruins of Chichén Itzá (no, it doesn't rhyme with "chicken pizza"; the accents are on the last syllables: chee-*chen* eet-*zah*) are the Yucatán's best-known ancient monuments. They are plenty hyped, but Chichén merits a visit. Walking among these stone platforms, pyramids, and ball courts gives you an appreciation for this ancient civilization that books cannot convey. The city is built on a scale that evokes a sense of wonder: To fill the plazas during one of the mass rituals that occurred here a millennium ago would have required an enormous number of celebrants. Even today, with the mass flow of tourists through these plazas, the ruins feel empty.

When visiting the ruins, keep in mind that much of what is said about the Maya (especially by tour guides, who speak in tones of utter certainty) is merely educated guessing. This much we do know: The area was settled by farmers as far back as the 4th century A.D. The first signs of an urban society appear in the 7th century in the construction of stone temples and palaces in the traditional Puuc Maya style. These buildings can be found in the "Old Chichén" section of the city. Construction continued for a couple hundred years. In the 10th century (the post-Classic era), the city came under the rule of the Itzáes, who arrived from central Mexico by way of the Gulf Coast. They may have been a mix of highland Toltec Indians (the people who built the city of Tula in central Mexico) and lowland Putún Maya, who were a commercial people thriving on trade between the different regions of the area. In the following centuries, the city saw its greatest growth. Most of the grand architecture was built during this age in a style that is clearly Toltec influenced. The new rulers may have been refugees from Tula. There is a mythological story told in pre-Columbian central Mexico about a fight that occurred between the gods Quetzalcoatl and Tezcatlipoca, which resulted in Quetzalcoatl being forced to leave his homeland and venture east. This may be a shorthand account of a civil war in Tula, different religious factions, with the losers fleeing to the Yucatán, where they were welcomed by the local Maya. Over time, the Itzáes adopted more and more the ways of the Maya. Sometime at the end of the 12th century, the city was captured by its rival, the city of Mayapán.

Though it's possible to make a day trip from Cancún or Mérida, it's preferable to overnight here or in nearby Valladolid. It makes for a more relaxing trip. You can see the light show in the evening and return to see the ruins early the next morning when it is cool and before the tour buses arrive.

ESSENTIALS

GETTING THERE & DEPARTING   **By Plane**   Travel agents in the United States, Cancún, and Cozumel can arrange day trips from Cancún and Cozumel.

By Car   Chichén Itzá is on old Highway 180 between Mérida and Cancún. The fastest way to get there from either city is to take the *autopista* (or *cuota*). The toll is $7 (£3.85) from Mérida, $22 (£12) from Cancún. Once you have exited the *autopista*, you will turn onto the road leading to the village of Pisté. Once in the village, you'll reach a T junction at Highway 180 and turn left to get to the ruins. The entrance to the ruins is well marked. If you stay on the highway for a few kilometers more you'll come to the exit for the hotel zone at Km 121 (before you reach the turn-off, you'll pass the eastern entrance to Mayapán, which is usually closed). Chichén is 1½ hours from Mérida and 2½ hours from Cancún.

By Bus   From Mérida, there are three first-class ADO buses per day. There are also a couple of first-class buses to Cancún and Playa. Otherwise, you can buy a second-class bus ticket to Valladolid and a first-class from there. If you want to take a day trip from Mérida or Cancún, go with a tour company.

AREA LAYOUT   The village of **Pisté,** where most of the economical hotels and restaurants are located, is about 2.5km (1½ miles) to the west of the ruins. Public buses can drop you off here. And located on the old highway 2.5km (1½ miles) east from the ruins is another economical hotel, the Hotel Dolores Alba (see "Where to Stay," below). Situated at the ruins of Chichén Itzá are three luxury hotels.

EXPLORING THE RUINS

The site occupies 6.5 sq. km (2½ sq. miles), and it takes most of a day to see all the ruins, which are open daily from 8am to 5pm. Service areas are open from 8am to 10pm. Admission is $10 (£5.50), free for children younger than age 12. A video camera permit costs $4 (£2.20). Parking is extra. *You can use your ticket to re-enter on the same day.* The cost of admission includes the **sound-and-light show,** which is worth seeing since you're being charged for it anyway. The show, held at 7 or 8pm depending on the season, is in Spanish, but headsets are available for rent in several languages. The narrative is okay, but the real reason for seeing the show is the lights, which show off the beautiful geometry of the city.

The large, modern visitor center, at the main entrance where you pay the admission charge, is beside the parking lot and consists of a museum, an auditorium, a restaurant, a bookstore, and bathrooms. You can see the site on your own or with a licensed guide who speaks English or Spanish. Guides usually wait at the entrance and charge around $45 (£25) for one to six people. Although the guides frown on it, there's nothing wrong with approaching a group of people who speak the same language and asking if they want to share a guide. These guides can point out architectural details often missed when visiting on your own. Chichén Itzá has two parts: the central (new) zone, which shows distinct Toltec influence, and the southern (old) zone, with mostly Puuc architecture.

EL CASTILLO   As you enter from the tourist center, the magnificent 25m (82-ft.) El Castillo pyramid (also called the Pyramid of Kukulkán) will be straight ahead across a large open area. It was built with the Maya calendar in mind. The four stairways leading up to the central platform each have 91 steps, making a total of 364, which when you add the central platform equals the 365 days of the solar year. On either side of each stairway are nine terraces, which makes 18 on each face of the pyramid, equaling the number of months in the Maya solar calendar. On the facing of these terraces are 52 panels (we don't know how they were decorated), which represent the 52-year cycle when both the solar and religious calendars would become realigned. The pyramid's alignment is such that on the **spring** or **fall equinox** (Mar 21 or Sept 21) a curious event occurs. The setting sun casts the shadow of the terraces onto the ramp of the northern stairway. A diamond pattern is formed, suggestive of the geometric designs on some snakes. Slowly it descends into the earth. The effect is more conceptual than visual, and to view it requires being with a large crowd. It's much better to see the ruins on other days when it's less crowded.

El Castillo was built over an earlier structure. A narrow stairway at the western edge of the north staircase leads inside that structure, where there is a sacrificial altar-throne—a red jaguar encrusted with jade. The stairway is open from 11am to 3pm and is cramped, usually crowded, humid, and uncomfortable. A visit early in the day is best. Photos of the jaguar figure are not allowed.

JUEGO DE PELOTA (MAIN BALL COURT)   Northwest of El Castillo is Chichén's main ball court, the largest and best preserved anywhere, and only one of nine ball courts built in this city. Carved on both walls of the ball court are scenes showing Maya figures dressed as ball players and decked out in heavy protective padding. The carved scene also shows a headless player kneeling with blood shooting from his neck; another player holding the head looks on.

Players on two teams tried to knock a hard rubber ball through one of the two stone rings placed high on either wall, using only their elbows, knees, and hips. According to legend, the losing players paid for defeat with their lives. However, some experts say the victors were the only appropriate sacrifices for the gods. One can only guess what the incentive for winning might be in that case. Either way, the game must have been riveting, heightened by the wonderful acoustics of the ball court.

THE NORTH TEMPLE   Temples are at both ends of the ball court. The North Temple has sculptured pillars and more sculptures inside, as well as badly ruined murals. The acoustics of the ball court are so good that from the North Temple, a person speaking can be heard clearly at the opposite end, about 135m (443 ft.) away.

TEMPLE OF JAGUARS   Near the southeastern corner of the main ball court is a small temple with serpent columns and carved panels showing warriors and jaguars. Up the steps and inside the temple, a mural was found that chronicles a battle in a Maya village.

TZOMPANTLI (TEMPLE OF THE SKULLS)   To the right of the ball court is the Temple of the Skulls, an obvious borrowing from the post-Classic cities of central Mexico. Notice the rows of skulls carved into the stone platform. When a sacrificial victim's head was cut off, it was impaled on a pole and displayed in a tidy row with others. Also carved into the stone are pictures of eagles tearing hearts from human victims. The word *Tzompantli* is not Mayan but comes from central Mexico. Reconstruction using scattered fragments may add a level to this platform and change the look of this structure by the time you visit.

PLATFORM OF THE EAGLES   Next to the Tzompantli, this small platform has reliefs showing eagles and jaguars clutching human hearts in their talons and claws, as well as a human head emerging from the mouth of a serpent.

PLATFORM OF VENUS   East of the Tzompantli and north of El Castillo, near the road to the Sacred Cenote, is the Platform of Venus. In Maya and Toltec lore, a feathered monster or a feathered serpent with a human head in its mouth represented Venus. This is also called the tomb of Chaac-Mool because a Chaac-Mool figure was discovered "buried" within the structure.

SACRED CENOTE   Follow the dirt road (actually an ancient *sacbé,* or causeway) that heads north from the Platform of Venus; after 5 minutes you'll come to the great natural well that may have given Chichén Itzá (the Well of the Itzáes) its name. This well was used for ceremonial purposes. Sacrificial victims were thrown in. Anatomical research done early in the 20th century by Ernest A. Hooten showed that bones of both children and adults were found in the well.

Edward Thompson, who was the American consul in Mérida and a Harvard professor, purchased the ruins of Chichén early in the 20th century and explored the *cenote* with dredges and divers. His explorations exposed a fortune in gold and jade. Most of the riches wound up in Harvard's Peabody Museum of Archaeology and Ethnology—a matter that continues to disconcert Mexican classicists today. Excavations in the 1960s unearthed more treasure, and studies of the recovered objects detail offerings from throughout the Yucatán and even farther away.

TEMPLO DE LOS GUERREROS (TEMPLE OF THE WARRIORS)   Due east of El Castillo is one of the most impressive structures at Chichén: the Temple of the Warriors, named for the carvings of warriors marching along its walls. It's also called the Group of the Thousand Columns for the rows of broken pillars that flank it. During the recent restoration, hundreds more of the columns were rescued from the rubble and put in place, setting off the temple more magnificently than ever. A figure of Chaac-Mool sits at the top of the temple, surrounded by impressive columns carved in relief to look like enormous feathered serpents. South of the temple was a square building that archaeologists call **El Mercado (The Market);** a colonnade surrounds its central court. Beyond the temple and the market in the jungle are mounds of rubble, parts of which are being reconstructed.

The main Mérida-Cancún highway once ran straight through the ruins of Chichén, and though it has been diverted, you can still see the great swath it cut. South and west of the old highway's path are more impressive ruined buildings.

TUMBA DEL GRAN SACERDOTE (TOMB OF THE HIGH PRIEST)   Past the refreshment stand to the right of the path is the Tomb of the High Priest, which stood atop a natural limestone cave in which skeletons and offerings were found, giving the temple its name.

CASA DE LOS METATES (TEMPLE OF THE GRINDING STONES)   This building, the next one on your right, is named after the concave corn-grinding stones the Maya used.

TEMPLO DEL VENADO (TEMPLE OF THE DEER)   Past Casa de los Metates is this fairly tall though ruined building. The relief of a stag that gave the temple its name is long gone.

CHICHANCHOB (LITTLE HOLES)   This next temple has a roof comb with little holes, three masks of the rain god Chaac, three rooms, and a good view of the surrounding structures. It's one of the oldest buildings at Chichén, built in the Puuc style during the late Classic period.

EL CARACOL (OBSERVATORY)   Construction of the Observatory, a complex building with a circular tower, was carried out over centuries; the additions and modifications reflected the Maya's careful observation of celestial movements and their need for increasingly exact measurements. Through slits in the tower's walls, astronomers could observe the cardinal directions and the approach of the all-important spring and autumn equinoxes, as well as the summer solstice. The temple's name, which means "snail," comes from a spiral staircase within the structure.

On the east side of El Caracol, a path leads north into the bush to the **Cenote Xtoloc,** a natural limestone well that provided the city's daily water supply. If you see any lizards sunning there, they may well be *xtoloc,* the species for which this *cenote* is named.

TEMPLO DE LOS TABLEROS (TEMPLE OF PANELS)   Just south of El Cara-col are the ruins of a *temazcalli* (a steam bath) and the Temple of Panels, named for the carved panels on top. This temple was once covered by a much larger structure, only traces of which remain.

EDIFICIO DE LAS MONJAS (EDIFICE OF THE NUNS)   If you've visited the Puuc sites of Kabah, Sayil, Labná, or Xlapak, the enormous nunnery here will remind you of the palaces at those sites. Built in the late Classic period, the new edifice was constructed over an older one. Suspecting that this was so, Le Plongeon, an archaeol-ogist working early in the 20th century, put dynamite between the two and blew away part of the exterior, revealing the older structures within. You can still see the results of Le Plongeon's indelicate exploratory methods.

On the east side of the Edifice of the Nuns is **Anexo Este (annex)** constructed in highly ornate Chenes style with Chaac masks and serpents.

LA IGLESIA (THE CHURCH)   Next to the annex is one of the oldest buildings at Chichén, the Church. Masks of Chaac decorate two upper stories. Look closely, and you'll see other pagan symbols among the crowd of Chaacs: an armadillo, a crab, a snail, and a tortoise. These represent the Maya gods, called *bacah,* whose job it was to hold up the sky.

AKAB DZIB (TEMPLE OF OBSCURE WRITING)   Beloved of travel writers, this temple lies east of the Edifice of the Nuns. Above a door in one of the rooms are some Mayan glyphs, which gave the temple its name because the writings have yet to be deciphered. In other rooms, traces of red handprints are still visible. Reconstructed and expanded over the centuries, Akab Dzib may be the oldest building at Chichén.

CHICHEN VIEJO (OLD CHICHEN)   For a look at more of Chichén's oldest buildings, constructed well before the time of Toltec influence, follow signs from the Edifice of the Nuns southwest into the bush to Old Chichén, about 1km (a half-mile) away. Be prepared for this trek with long trousers, insect repellent, and a local guide. The attractions here are the **Templo de los Inscripciones Iniciales (Temple of the First Inscriptions),** with the oldest inscriptions discovered at Chichén, and the restored **Templo de los Dinteles (Temple of the Lintels),** a fine Puuc building. Some of these buildings have recently undergone restoration.

WHERE TO STAY

The expensive hotels in Chichén all occupy beautiful grounds, are close to the ruins, and serve decent food. All have toll-free reservations numbers. These hotels do a lot of business with tour operators—they can be empty one day and full the next. From these hotels you can easily walk to the back entrance of the ruins, next to the Hotel Mayaland. There are several inexpensive hotels in the village of Pisté, just to the west of the ruins. There is no advantage to staying in Pisté other than the proximity to Chichén Itzá. It is an unattractive village with little to recommend it. Another option is to stay in the colonial town of Valladolid, 40 minutes away.

EXPENSIVE

Hacienda Chichén Resort ★★   This is the smallest and most private of the hotels at the ruins. It is also the quietest. This former hacienda served as the headquarters for the Carnegie Institute's excavations in 1923. Several bungalows scattered about the property were built to house the institute's staff. Each one houses one or two units. Rooms come with a dehumidifier, a ceiling fan, and good air-conditioning. The floors are ceramic tile, the ceilings are stucco with wood beams, and the walls are decorated with carved stone trim. Trees and tropical plants fill the manicured gardens. You can enjoy these from your room's porch or from the terrace restaurant, which occupies part of the original hacienda owner's house. Standard rooms come with a queen-size, two twin, or two double beds. Suites are bigger and have sitting areas with sleeper-sofas. These come with king-size beds. The main building belonged to the hacienda; it houses the terrace restaurant.

Zona Arqueológica, 97751 Chichén Itzá, Yuc. ℂ/fax 985/851-0045. www.haciendachichen.com. (Reservations: Casa del Balam, Calle 60 no. 488, 97000 Mérida, Yuc.; ℂ 800/624-8451 in the U.S., or 999/924-2150; fax 999/924-5011.) 28 units. $175 (£96) double; $200 (£110) junior suite. AE, MC, V. Free guarded parking. **Amenities:** Restaurant; 2 bars; large outdoor pool. *In room:* A/C, minibar, hair dryer, no phone.

Hotel & Bungalows Mayaland ★★★
The main doorway frames El Caracol (the Observatory) in a stunning view—that's how close this hotel is to the ruins. The long main building is three stories high. The rooms are large, with comfortable beds and large tiled bathrooms. Bungalows, scattered about the rest of the grounds, are built native style, with thatched roofs and stucco walls; they're a good deal larger than the rooms. The grounds are gorgeous, with huge trees and lush foliage—the hotel has had 75 years to get them in shape. The suites are on the top floor of the main building and come with terraces and two-person Jacuzzis. The "lodge section" consists of two groupings of larger bungalows in the back of the property surrounded by a lovely garden and pool area. Rates for November, Christmas, and the spring equinox are a little higher than posted here.

Zona Arqueológica, 97751 Chichén Itzá, Yuc. ℂ 985/851-0100. www.mayaland.com. (Reservations: Mayaland Resorts, Robalo 30 SM3, 77500 Cancún, Q. Roo; ℂ 800/235-4079 in the U.S., or 998/887-2495; fax 998/887-4510.) 97 units. High season $192 (£106) double, $278 (£153) bungalow, $316 (£174) suite, $438–$520 (£241–£286) lodge bungalows; low season $103 (£57) double, $168 (£92) bungalow, $230 (£127) suite, $192–$248 (£106–£136) lodge bungalows. Higher rates are for units with Jacuzzis. AE, MC, V. Free guarded parking. **Amenities:** 2 restaurants; bar; 3 outdoor pools; tour desk; room service; babysitting; laundry service. *In room:* A/C, TV, minibar, coffeemaker.

MODERATE
Villas Arqueológicas Chichén Itzá ★
This hotel is built around a courtyard and a pool. Two massive royal Poinciana trees tower above the grounds, and bougainvillea drapes the walls. This chain has similar hotels at Cobá and Uxmal, and is connected with Club Med. The rooms are modern and comfortable, unless you're 1.9m (6 ft., 2 in.) or taller—each bed is in a niche, with walls at the head and foot. Most rooms have one double bed and a twin bed. You can book a half- or full-board plan or just the room.

Zona Arqueológica, 97751 Chichén Itzá, Yuc. ℂ 800/258-2633 in the U.S., or 985/851-0034 or 985/856-2830. 40 units. $100 (£55) double. Rates include continental breakfast. Half-board (breakfast plus lunch or dinner) $18 (£9.90) per person; full board (3 meals) $35 (£19) per person. AE, MC, V. Free parking. **Amenities:** Restaurant; bar; large outdoor pool; tennis court; tour desk. *In room:* A/C, hair dryer.

INEXPENSIVE
Hotel Dolores Alba *Value*
This place is of the motel variety, perfect if you come by car. It is a bargain for what you get: two pools (one really special), *palapas* and hammocks around the place, and large, comfortable rooms. The restaurant serves good meals at moderate prices. There is free transportation to the ruins and the Caves of

Balankanché during visiting hours, though you will have to take a taxi back. The hotel is on the highway 2.5km (1½ miles) east of the ruins (toward Valladolid). Rooms come with two double beds.

Carretera Mérida–Valladolid Km 122, Yuc. © **985/858-1555**. www.doloresalba.com. (Reservations: Hotel Dolores Alba, Calle 63 no. 464, 97000 Mérida, Yuc.; © 999/928-5650; fax 999/928-3163.) 40 units. $45 (£25) double. MC, V (8% service charge). Free parking. **Amenities:** Restaurant; bar; 2 outdoor pools; room service. *In room:* A/C, TV, no phone.

WHERE TO DINE

Although there's no great food in this area, there is plenty of decent food. The best idea is to stick to simple choices. The restaurant at the visitor center at the ruins serves decent snack food. The hotel restaurants mostly do a fair job, and, if you're in the village of Pisté, you can try one of the restaurants along the highway there that cater to the bus tours, such as **Fiesta** (© **985/851-0111**). The best time to go is early lunch or regular supper hours, when the buses are gone.

OTHER ATTRACTIONS IN THE AREA

Ik-Kil is a large *cenote* on the highway just across from the Hotel Dolores Alba, 2.5km (1½ miles) east of the main entrance to the ruins. And it's deep, with lots of steps leading down to the water's edge. Unlike Dzitnup, these steps are easy to manage. The view from both the top and the bottom is dramatic, with lots of tropical vegetation and curtains of hanging tree roots stretching all the way to the water's surface. Take your swimsuit and enjoy the cold water. The best swimming is before 11:30am, at which time bus tours start arriving from the coast. These bus tours are the main business of Ik-Kil, which also has a restaurant and souvenir shops. Ik-Kil is open from 8am to 5pm daily. Admission is $6 (£3.30) per adult, $3 (£1.65) per child 7 to 12 years old.

The **Cave of Balankanché** is 5.5km (3½ miles) from Chichén Itzá on the road to Valladolid and Cancún. Taxis will make the trip and wait. The entire excursion takes about a half-hour, but the walk inside is hot and humid. Of the cave tours in the Yucatán, this is the tamest, having good footing and requiring the least amount of walking and climbing. It includes a cheesy and uninformative recorded tour. The highlight is a round chamber with a central column that gives the impression of being a large tree. You come up the same way you go down. The cave became a hideaway during the War of the Castes. You can still see traces of carving and incense burning, as well as an underground stream that served as the sanctuary's water supply. Outside, take time to meander through the botanical gardens, where most of the plants and trees are labeled with their common and botanical names.

Admission is $5 (£2.75), free for children 6 to 12. Children younger than age 6 are not admitted. Use of a video camera costs $4 (£2.20) or it's free if you've already bought a video permit in Chichén the same day. Tours in English are at 11am and 1 and 3pm, and, in Spanish, at 9am, noon, and 2 and 4pm. Double-check these hours at the main entrance to the Chichén ruins.

5 Valladolid

40km (25 miles) E of Chichén Itzá; 160km (100 miles) SW of Cancún

Valladolid (pronounced "bah-yah-doh-*leed*") is a small, pleasant colonial city halfway between Mérida and Cancún. The people are friendly and informal, and, except for the heat, life is easy. The city's economy is based on commerce and small-scale manufacturing. There is a large *cenote* in the center of town and a couple more 4km (2½ miles) down the road to Chichén. Not far away are the intriguing ruins of Ek Balam, the flamingo-infested waters of Rio Lagarto, and the sandy beaches of Holbox (see "Side Trips from Valladolid," below).

ESSENTIALS

GETTING THERE & DEPARTING   By Car   From Mérida or Cancún, you have two choices: the *cuota* (toll road) or Highway 180. The toll from Cancún is $18 (£9.90), from Mérida $10 (£5.50). The *cuota* passes 2km (1¼ miles) north of the city; the exit is at the crossing of Highway 295 to Tizimín. **Highway 180** takes significantly longer because it passes through a number of villages (with their requisite speed bumps). Both 180 and 295 lead directly to downtown. Leaving is just as easy: from the main square, Calle 41 turns into 180 East to Cancún; Calle 39 heads to 180 West to Chichén Itzá and Mérida. To take the *cuota* to Mérida or Cancún, take Calle 40 (see "City Layout," below).

By Bus   There are several direct buses to Mérida (13 per day) or Cancún (five per day). Each runs $11 (£6.05). You can also get direct buses for Playa (five per day) and Tulum (four per day). Buses to Playa take the toll road and cost $14 (£7.70); buses to Tulum take the shortcut via Chemax and cost $6 (£3.30). To get to Chichén Itzá, take a second-class bus, which leaves every hour and sometimes on the half-hour. The recently remodeled bus station is at the corner of calles 39 and 46.

There is now a daily bus to Ek Balam that departs from in front of the Palacio Municipal (see "Ek Balam: Dark Jaguar," below).

VISITOR INFORMATION   The small **tourism office** is in the Palacio Municipal. It's open daily from 9am to 8pm, Sunday 9am to 1pm.

CITY LAYOUT · Valladolid has the standard layout for towns in the Yucatán: Streets running north-south are even numbers; those running east-west are odd numbers. The main plaza is bordered by Calle 39 on the north, 41 on the south, 40 on the east, and 42 on the west. The plaza is named Parque Francisco Cantón Rosado, but everyone calls it **El Centro.** Taxis are easy to come by.

EXPLORING VALLADOLID

Before it became Valladolid, the city was a Maya settlement called Zací (zah-*kee*), which means "white hawk." There is one *cenote* in town: **Cenote Zací,** at the intersection of calles 39 and 36, in a small park. A trail leads down close to the water. Caves, stalactites, and hanging vines contribute to a wild, prehistoric feel. The park has a large *palapa* restaurant. Admission is $2 (£1.10).

Ten blocks to the southwest of the main square is the Franciscan monastery of **San Bernardino de Siena** (1552). Most of the compound was built in the early 1600s; a large underground river is believed to pass under the convent and surrounding neighborhood, which is called Barrio Sisal. "Sisal" is, in this case, a corruption of the Mayan phrase *sis-ha,* meaning "cold water." The *barrio* has undergone extensive restoration and is a delight to behold.

Valladolid's main square is the social center of town and a thriving market for Yucatecan dresses. On its south side is the principal church, **La Parroquia de San Servacio.** Vallesoletanos, as the locals call themselves, believe that almost all cathedrals in Mexico point east, and they cherish a local legend to explain why theirs points north—but don't believe a word of it. On the east side of the plaza is the municipal building, **El Ayuntamiento.** Get a look at the highly dramatic paintings outlining the

Sweet as Honey

Valladolid also produces a highly prized honey made from the *tzi-tzi-ché* flower. You can find it and other goods at the **town market,** Calle 32 between calles 35 and 37. The best time to see the market is Sunday morning

history of the peninsula. My personal favorite depicts a horrified Maya priest foreseeing the arrival of Spanish galleons. On Sunday nights, beneath the stone arches of the Ayuntamiento, the municipal band plays *jaranas* and other traditional music of the region.

SHOPPING

The **Mercado de Artesanías de Valladolid (crafts market),** at the corner of calles 39 and 44, gives you a good idea of the local merchandise. Perhaps the main handicraft of the town is embroidered Maya dresses, which can be purchased here or from women around the main square. The area around Valladolid is cattle country; locally made leather goods such as *huaraches* (sandals) and bags are inexpensive and plentiful. On the main plaza is a small shop above the municipal bazaar. A good sandal maker has a shop called **Elios,** Calle 37 no. 202, between calles 42 and 44 (no phone). An Indian named **Juan Mac** makes *alpargatas,* the traditional sandals of the Maya, in his shop on Calle 39, near the intersection with Calle 38, 1 block from the main plaza. It's almost on the corner, across from the Bar La Joya. There's no sign, but the door jamb is painted yellow. Juan Mac can be found there most mornings. Most of his output is for locals, but he's happy to knock out a pair for visitors. He also makes a dress *alpargata,* but I like the standard ones better.

WHERE TO STAY

Aside from the hotels listed below, you can stay in town at **Hotel Zací,** Calle 44 between calles 37 and 39 (© 985/856-2167). Another option is the **Ecotel Quinta Regia** (© 985/856-3472; www.ecotelquintaregia.com.mx) a few blocks farther from the main square on Calle 48 between calles 27 and 29.

For something a bit different, you can stay in a small ecohotel in the nearby village of Ek Balam, close to the ruins: **Genesis Retreat Ek Balam** (© 985/858-9375; www.genesisretreat.com). It is owned and operated by a Canadian woman, Lee Christie. She takes guests on tours of the village showing what daily life is like among the contemporary Maya. There are other activities, too. She rents out some simple cabañas (with shared or private bathrooms) that surround a lovely pool and a restaurant.

El Mesón del Marqués ★ This was originally a small colonial hotel that has grown large and modern. The first courtyard surrounds a fountain and abounds with hanging plants and bougainvillea. This was the original house, now occupied mostly by the restaurant (see "Where to Dine," below). In back are the new construction and the pool. Rooms are medium to large and are attractive. Most come with two double beds. The hotel is on the north side of El Centro, opposite the church.

Calle 39 no. 203, 97780 Valladolid, Yuc. © 985/856-3042 or -2073. Fax 985/856-2280. www.mesondelmarques.com. 90 units. $55 (£30) double; $70 (£39) superior; $105 (£58) junior suite. AE. Free secure parking. **Amenities:** Restaurant; bar; outdoor pool; room service; laundry service. *In room:* A/C, TV.

Hotel María de la Luz The three-story María de la Luz is on the west side of the main square. The guest rooms have tile floors and bathrooms; three have balconies overlooking the main square. The wide interior space holds a restaurant that is comfortable and airy for most of the day.

Calle 42 no. 193, 97780 Valladolid, Yuc. ⓒ/fax **985/856-2071** or -1181. www.mariadelaluzhotel.com. 70 units. $45 (£25) double. MC, V. Free secure parking. **Amenities:** Restaurant; bar; midsize outdoor pool; tour desk. *In room:* A/C, TV.

WHERE TO DINE

Valladolid is not a center for haute cuisine, but you can try some of the regional specialties. Some of the best food I had was at **El Mesón del Marqués** right on the main square. There is another restaurant on the main square called **Las Campanas,** which is okay. Locals like to eat at one of the stalls in the **Bazar Municipal,** next door to the Mesón del Marqués. They also frequent the **taco stands** that set up around the square. I did a quick sampling of *cochinita pibil, carnitas,* and *lechón asado* (all pork dishes) at the three most popular taco stands. I enjoyed it all and wasn't the worse for the wear. These stands serve customers only until around noon.

SIDE TRIPS FROM VALLADOLID
CENOTES DZITNUP & SAMMULA

The **Cenote Dzitnup** 🐦 (also known as Cenote Xkekén) is 4km (2½ miles) west of Valladolid off Highway 180 in the direction of Chichén Itzá. It is worth a side trip, especially if you have time for a dip. You can take the bike trail there. Antonio Aguilar, who owns a sporting goods store at Calle 41 no. 225, between calles 48 and 50, rents bikes. Once you get there, you descend a short flight of rather perilous stone steps, and at the bottom, inside a beautiful cavern, is a natural pool of water so clear and blue that it seems plucked from a dream. If you decide to swim, be sure that you don't have creams or other chemicals on your skin—they damage the habitat of the small fish and other organisms living there. Also, no alcohol, food, or smoking is allowed in the cavern. Admission is $2 (£1.10). The *cenote* is open daily from 7am to 7pm. If it's crowded, about 90m (295 ft.) down the road on the opposite side is another recently discovered *cenote,* **Sammulá,** which is also worth a visit and a swim. Admission is $2 (£1.10).

EK BALAM: DARK JAGUAR 🐦🐦🐦

About 18km (11 miles) north of Valladolid, off the highway to Río Lagartos, are the spectacular ruins of **Ek Balam,** which, owing to a certain ambiguity in Mayan, means either "dark jaguar" or "star jaguar." Relatively unvisited by tourists, the Ek Balam ruins are about to hit it big. A new road now runs from the highway to the ruins. There is a daily air-conditioned bus from Valladolid that departs from the main square at 9am, allows a couple of hours at the ruins, and returns at 1pm. The fare is $4 (£2.20) round-trip.

Take Calle 40 north out of Valladolid to Highway 295; go 20km (12 miles) to a large marked turnoff. Ek Balam is 13km (8 miles) from the highway; the entrance fee is $5 (£2.75), plus $4 (£2.20) for each video camera. The site is open daily from 8am to 5pm.

In the last few years, a team of archeologists have been doing extensive excavation and renovation. What they have found has the world of Mayan scholars all aquiver. Built between 100 B.C. and A.D. 1200, the smaller buildings are architecturally unique—especially the large, perfectly restored **Caracol.** Flanked by two smaller pyramids, the imposing central pyramid is about 160m (525 ft.) long and 60m (197 ft.) wide. At more than 30m (100 ft.) high, it is easily taller than the highest pyramid in Chichén Itzá. On the left side of the main stairway, archaeologists have uncovered a large ceremonial doorway of perfectly preserved stucco work. It is an astonishingly elaborate representation of the gaping mouth of the underworld god. Around it are several beautifully detailed human figures. Excavation inside revealed a long chamber filled with Mayan hieroglyphic writing. From the style, it appears that the scribes probably came from Guatemala. So far this chamber is closed to the public. From this script, an epigrapher, Alfonso Lacadena, has found the name of one of the principal kings of the city—Ukit Kan Le'k. If you climb to the top of the pyramid, in the middle distance you can see untouched ruins looming to the north. To the southeast, you can spot the tallest structures at **Cobá,** 50km (31 miles) away.

Also visible are the **raised causeways** of the Maya—the *sacbé* appear as raised lines in the forest vegetation. More than any of the better-known sites, Ek Balam inspires a sense of mystery and awe at the scale of Maya civilization and the utter ruin to which it came.

RIO LAGARTOS NATURE RESERVE 𝒢

Some 80km (50 miles) north of Valladolid (40km/25 miles north of Tizimín) on Highway 295 is Río Lagartos, a 50,000-hectare (123,500-acre) refuge established in 1979 to protect the largest nesting population of flamingos in North America. The nesting area is off limits, but you can see plenty of flamingos as well as many other species of fowl and take an enjoyable boat ride around the estuary here.

To get to Río Lagartos, you pass through Tizimín, which is about 30 minutes away. If you need to spend the night there, try **Hotel 49,** Calle 49 373-A (© **986/863-2136**), by the main square. There is not much to do in Tizimín unless you are there during the first 2 weeks of January, when it holds the largest fair in the Yucatán. The prime fiesta day is January 6.

SEEING THE RIO LAGARTOS REFUGE   Río Lagartos is a small fishing village of around 3,000 people who make their living from the sea and from the occasional tourist who shows up to see the flamingos. Colorfully painted houses face the *malecón* (the oceanfront street), and brightly painted boats dock here and there.

When you drive into town, keep going straight until you get to the shore. Look for where Calle 10 intersects with the *malecón;* it's near a modern church. There, in a little kiosk, is where the guides can be found (no phone). The sign reads PARADOR TURISTICO NAHOCHIN. There you can make arrangements for a 2-hour tour, which will cost $50 to $60 (£28–£33) for two to three people. The best time to go is in the early morning, so it's best to overnight here at one of the cheap hotels along the *malecón.* I looked at a few and liked **Posada Lucy** (no phone; $25/£14 for two).

I had a very pleasant ride the next morning, and saw several species of ducks, hawks, cranes, cormorants, an osprey, and, of course, lots of flamingos. The guide also wanted to show me how easy it was to float in some evaporation pools used by the local salt producer at Las Coloradas (a good source of employment for the locals until it was mechanized) and a place where fresh water bubbles out from below the saltwater estuary.

ISLA HOLBOX 𝒢

A sandy strip of an island off the northeastern corner of the Yucatán Peninsula, Holbox (pronounced "hohl-*bosh*") was a remote corner of the world with only a half-deserted fishing village, until tourists started showing up for the beach. Now it's a semiprosperous little community that gets its livelihood from tourist services, employment at the beach hotels, and tours. It's most popular with visitors from May to September, when over a hundred **whale sharks** congregate in nearby waters (why precisely they come here is not known). These gentle giants swim slowly along the surface of the water and don't seem to mind the boat tours and snorkelers that come to experience what it's like to be in the wild with these creatures. Whale sharks don't fit the common picture of a shark; they are much larger, attaining a length of up to 18m (59 ft.), and they are filter feeders for the most part, dining on plankton and other small organisms. That said, they can do some mischief if you annoy them.

The beach here is broad and sandy (with fine-textured sand). It is also shallow. Instead of the amazing blue color of the Caribbean, it's more of a dull green. There are several beach hotels just beyond town. These experienced lots of damage from Hurricane Emily in the summer of 2005, but they've since come back: **Villas Flamingos** (© 800/538-6802 in the U.S. and Canada) and **Villas Delfines,** which has an office in Cancún (© 998/884-8606 or 984/875-2197; www.holbox.com). The latter is a personal favorite. Rates run between $100 and $150 (£55–£83) for a large free-standing beach bungalow with a large porch, a thatched roof, mosquito netting, and plenty of cross-ventilation. This is very much an ecohotel, with composting toilets and solar water heaters. There is a pool, a good restaurant, and lovely grounds. If you want A/C, try **Casa Sandra** (© 984/875-2171).

From Valladolid, take Highway 180 east for about 90km (56 miles) toward Cancún; turn north after Nuevo Xcan at the tiny crossroads of El Ideal. Drive nearly 100km (62 miles) north on a state highway to the tiny port of Chiquilá, where you can park your car in a secure parking lot; walk 180m (590 ft.) to the pier, and catch the ferry to the island. It runs 10 times per day. When you get off in the village, you can contract with one of the golf cart taxis for a ride to your hotel.

17

The Copper Canyon

by David Baird

The first time I went to the Copper Canyon, I had a vision of the Grand Canyon because I had read many remarks comparing the two. This turned out to be misleading. Comparing the two does neither place justice. The canyons are not alike; they have different topography, geology, climate, flora, and fauna, and different local cultures, too.

If you are interested in viewing a rugged and beautiful land, if you're interested in taking one of the most remarkable train trips in the world, if you're interested in hiking or riding horseback through remote areas to see an astonishing variety of plants and animals, or if you're curious about a land still populated by indigenous people living pretty much the way they have for centuries, the Copper Canyon is the place to go.

When people say **Copper Canyon,** they are referring to a section of the Sierra Madre of northwestern Mexico known as the **Sierra Tarahumara** (after the Indians who live there). The area was formed through violent volcanic uplifting followed by the gradual process of erosion that carved a vast network of canyons into the soft volcanic stone. In geological terms, it's much newer than the Grand Canyon.

Crossing the Sierra Tarahumara is the famed **Chihuahua al Pacífico (Chihuahua to the Pacific)** railway. Acclaimed as an engineering marvel, the 624km (387-mile) railroad has 39 bridges—the highest is more than 300m (984 ft.) above the Chinipas River and the longest is about .5km (one-third mile) long—and 86 tunnels, including one more than 1.5km (1 mile) long. It climbs from **Los Mochis,** at sea level, up nearly 2,425m (7,954 ft.) through some of Mexico's most magnificent scenery—thick pine forests, jagged peaks, and shadowy canyons—before descending to the city of **Chihuahua.**

EXPLORING THE COPPER CANYON

The principal airports for the region are Los Mochis and Chihuahua, the two terminal points of the railroad. This chapter covers these cities and how to get to them.

It's easier now than ever before to get to the region, thanks to improved connecting flights out of Chihuahua and Los Mochis. But moving through the canyon still requires planning. Train tickets and hotel rooms are limited, and in high season (Mar–Apr and Oct–Nov) tour companies buy up large blocks of both. If going in high season, you should work your trip around an itinerary, and have train tickets and hotel reservations *in hand* when you arrive in the region. You can make arrangements on your own or go through a travel agent or tour operator. (For tips, see "Choosing a Package or Tour Operator," below.) During the rest of the year it's possible to buy train tickets as you need them and make last-minute reservations or no reservations at all.

The Copper Canyon

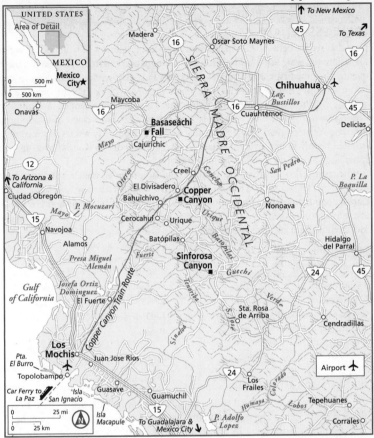

There is a small risk that you might run into a large group that has taken all the hotel rooms, but in most locations now, somebody usually has an inexpensive cabin for rent. The most plentiful lodging is to be found in Creel, and it would make a good base of operations for a minimally planned trip.

WHEN TO GO   There are two high seasons for the Sierra: from mid-October to mid-November and March through April. These months are the most popular because of the likelihood of moderate temperatures—but even in these months, temperatures in the bottom of the canyon will be warm. Most canyon visitors stay up in the rim country. To avoid the crowds and get cheaper prices, I suggest **going in August or September** (the rainy season). During that time, barring drought, you'll find occasional afternoon thundershowers (very pretty in the canyon land), green vegetation, flowing water, and comfortable temperatures up along the rim. If you plan to do some serious hikes into the canyon, consider going in the winter, when temperatures at the bottom will be the least tropical. **Avoid the Sierra from late April through June.** This is the driest part of the year, with chronic water shortages in many of the towns and hotels; the vegetation is brown, and the canyons can be hazy.

1 The Copper Canyon Train & Stops along the Way

TRAIN ESSENTIALS

First-class service between Chihuahua and Los Mochis operates daily in both directions. Departure times are listed below. Second-class trains also run daily. They stop more frequently than the first-class trains and are slower. First-class service has undergone major improvements. The passenger cars have been revamped, with clean bathrooms that work and improved seating and windows. (They already were air-conditioned in summer and heated in winter.) The train now hauls both a dining car and a club car. In addition, it makes fewer stops than before. The new owner, **Ferromex** (www.ferromex.com.mx), invested heavily in improving the tracks, making delays due to landslides less frequent. It has also spruced up some of the local stations.

The train makes 12 stops; the five of principal interest to travelers are described in detail below. The schedule is a word problem that would gratify any high school algebra teacher: two trains depart from opposite ends of the line (Chihuahua and Los Mochis) at the same time (6am) to meet at point x. So that you don't have to solve for y, I've included the "official" schedule below.

Train Departure Times

From Los Mochis		From Chihuahua	
Los Mochis	6am	Chihuahua	6am
El Fuerte	9am	Creel	11:35am
Bahuichivo/Cerocahui	1:10pm	El Divisadero	1:30pm
Barrancas	2:25pm	Barrancas	2pm
El Divisadero	2:35pm	Bahuichivo/Cerocahui	3:15pm
Creel	4:50pm	El Fuerte	7:20pm
Chihuahua (arrives)	10:25pm	Los Mochis (arrives)	10:25pm

Actual times vary. The local people at each stop are well attuned to train times, so it's good to ask them. The stops are short except at **El Divisadero,** where you have 20 minutes to get out and walk down the steps to the overlook for a spectacular panorama of the canyon, and perhaps time to buy a trinket or a taco from one of the many vendors.

DELAYS   Travelers may have to contend with delays because of landslides, minor derailments, or maintenance projects. Traveling in this region requires some flexibility and patience. In case of a major service interruption, you can travel on a highway that parallels the railway from Chihuahua as far as Cerocahui, but the final stretch from Cerocahui to El Fuerte is not much of an option because it requires four-wheel-drive.

⌜Tips⌝ Which Direction Should I Travel?

For sightseeing, **Los Mochis,** the western terminus, is the better starting place: The most scenic part of the 15- to 16-hour journey comes between **El Fuerte** and **Bahuichivo/Cerocahui,** which you are guaranteed to see in daylight if you come from Los Mochis. The train that starts in Chihuahua often gets to this area in darkness. This chapter lists the stops in order from Los Mochis to Chihuahua.

Tips Choosing a Package or Tour Operator

A number of tour operators and packagers offer trips to the Copper Canyon. You can purchase your package through a travel agency; those that do frequent business with Copper Canyon trips have better knowledge of what's out there. Keep in mind that the travel agent may try to steer you toward one package over another because it pays a higher commission.

The industry breaks down into the following categories:

BUS TOURS Some outfits run buses from El Paso to Chihuahua or Tucson to Los Mochis, then put their customers on the train. The usual length of stay in the Sierra is 2 nights before returning by bus to the U.S. These tours involve a lot of sitting on a bus or train, but they are the least expensive.

TRAIN TOURS Sierra Madre Express, P.O. Box 26381, Tucson, AZ 85726 (© 800/666-0346 in the U.S.), runs its own deluxe trains, complete with dining and Pullman cars, through the canyon. The trip takes a week, with 2 nights in the canyon. **Tauck Tours** (© 800/468-2825 in the U.S.) uses this train.

STANDARD PACKAGES This option merely bundles airfare, train tickets, and lodging. Hotels in the canyon send drivers to meet the train, so getting to your hotel is not hard once you're in the canyon. With these tours, you can have more time in the canyon, but once you're there, it's up to you to line up activities.

CUSTOM TOUR OPERATORS These outfits sell fixed package tours through travel agents only because it simplifies the agent's job. If you eliminate the middle person and call any of the outfits directly, you might be able to arrange a custom trip. Travel through these companies generally allows you more time in the canyon and a better experience. Some assemble small groups with a guide; some allow you to travel by yourself and supply you with contacts in different locations. As the number of people visiting the Sierra increases, these companies are taking people deeper into the mountains to get away from the effects of mass tourism. The best of the bunch is **Canyon Travel** (formerly Columbus), 900 Ridge Creek Lane, Bulverde, TX 78163-2872 (© 800/843-1060 in the U.S. and Canada, or 830/885-2000; www.canyontravel.com). Canyon Travel is pretty much in a class by itself. It has lined up some beautiful small lodges in the canyons and in El Fuerte and staffed them with talented local guides. It also offers a lot of flexibility, and it responds quickly to problems.

Other operators that provide good service are **The California Native,** 6701 W. 87th Place, Los Angeles, CA 90045 (© 800/926-1140 in the U.S.; www. calnative.com), and **Native Trails,** 613 Querétaro, El Paso, TX 79912-2210 (© 800/884-3107 in the U.S.; www.nativetrails.com).

BUYING A TICKET   The train offers no rail pass; you must buy a ticket for a particular day, point of departure, and destination. This is not usually a problem during the off season. You can buy a ticket for the first leg of your trip when you get to Los Mochis or Chihuahua, and then buy the rest each time you board the train. You're not

---

Tips **Going Solo: Not a Good Idea**

If you're planning to do any hiking in the Copper Canyon, it's a good idea to have company, especially someone who knows the area. Guides tell me that they come across lost hikers all the time. Also, ankles can get sprained, knees can give out—it helps to have someone who knows where to get the nearest horse and such.

---

going to have a guaranteed seat, but there's usually abundant seating during this part of the year. If you have an itinerary, you'll have guaranteed seating throughout the trip. You may not get to choose which seat, but that's a minor issue. Should you deviate from your itinerary, you can buy a new ticket at the local station or aboard the train. The cost of a ticket for the entire trip one-way is $130 (£72).

To reserve tickets ahead of time, call the railway directly (© **888/484-1623** in the U.S. or Canada, or 614/439-7212). A few days before your trip, you will need to call again to reconfirm your reservations. Then you can buy the tickets at the station the morning of your departure with cash or credit card (MasterCard or Visa). For more information, see www.chepe.com.mx. If you actually want to purchase tickets ahead of time, you can do so from a local travel agency in Chihuahua or Los Mochis. To start out in Chihuahua, contact **Turismo al Mar** (© 614/410-9232 or 416-5950; www.copper-canyon.net); from Los Mochis, contact **Viajes Araceli** (© **668/815-5780;** fax 668/815-8787; ventasaracely@viajearacely.com) or **Viajes Flamingo** (© **668/812-1613;** fax 668/812-0046; www.mexicoscoppercanyon.com). Travel agencies outside of Mexico sell tickets only as part of a package that includes transportation to the region and hotel accommodations. A wide variety of packages and custom trips are available. Look into these carefully before you book (see "Choosing a Package or Tour Operator," below).

LODGING   If you spend a night at any spot en route, you'll have roughly 24 hours to explore, unless you're heading back in the direction you came. Drivers from all canyon hotels pick up guests from the train station; if you don't have a reservation, ask a driver about room availability. Standard accommodations in the canyon are getting more expensive, especially in El Divisadero and Cerocahui. In high season, I wouldn't arrive at either place without reservations. Rates for hotels in both of these towns usually include meals. The number of rooms is limited, and with groups of 40 or 50 people going through the Sierra, a hotel can be empty one day and full the next. When hotels are full, you'll notice a decline in service in the dining room, or you'll have to wait in line at the buffet even if you're not part of the group. Overbooking rooms also seems to be a problem with some of the large hotels, though it's not common enough that you should worry about it. In Creel, you find the greatest variety of accommodations and restaurants. This is where most of the economical hotels are.

CLIMATE   Los Mochis and El Fuerte are warm year-round. Chihuahua can be warm in summer, windy at almost any time, and freezing in winter. The canyon rim may experience freezes from November through March; the bottom of the canyon may get cool enough for a sweater. In the other half of the year, it's hot below and cool above.

STOP 1: EL FUERTE ✪

El Fuerte is on the coastal plain before the foothills of the Sierra Madre. It has charming cobblestone streets and handsome colonial mansions and is the prettiest town along the train route. At only 80m (262 ft.) above sea level, it is most comfortable in winter. The town owes its origin to silver mining, and its existence in recent times to booming agriculture. From the late 18th century onward, the town has been under the control of a few families, and to this day, much of the real estate in and about the center of town remains in their hands. The town's plaza is quaint and handsome, with a 19th-century bandstand surrounded by graceful palms. One way to see the town is to take a taxi from Los Mochis and pick up the train the next day. An added advantage to this plan is that it allows you an extra hour in bed. The train station is a few kilometers from town.

EXPLORING THE TOWN   Possible activities include visiting nearby villages, birding, fishing for black bass and trout, and hunting for duck and dove. Hotels can arrange guides and all equipment if notified in advance.

WHERE TO STAY & DINE

Besides the restaurants at the hotels mentioned here, there are inexpensive restaurants on and near the central plaza.

Hotel El Fuerte ⭐   This is a charming inn loaded with character. Rooms have double or king-size beds, tiled bathrooms, and colonial furnishings. The courtyard and common areas are shady and cool. This hotel usually books up with tour groups for much of the high season, but for the rest of the year it is a good option.

Montesclaro 37, 81820 El Fuerte, Sin. ℂ 698/893-0226. Fax 698/893-1246. www.hotelelfuerte.com.mx. 32 units. $120 (£66) double. MC, V. Free parking. **Amenities:** Restaurant; bar; Jacuzzi; tour info; laundry service. *In room:* A/C, no phone.

Hotel La Choza   Two stories of rooms are arranged around a modern courtyard/parking lot. The upstairs rooms are nicer, as they come with a bóveda ceiling, but all are comfortable and colorfully decorated and have nice, midsize bathrooms. Most have two double beds.

Cinco de Mayo 101, 81820 El Fuerte, Sin. ℂ 698/893-1274. www.hotellachoza.com. 32 units. $80 (£44) double. MC, V. Free secure parking. **Amenities:** Restaurant; bar/dance club; outdoor pool; room service. *In room:* A/C, TV, no phone.

Hotel Posada del Hidalgo ⭐⭐   This handsome hotel is one of the Balderrama properties and can be booked through the central reservations office in Los Mochis. It, too, gets several tour groups. The mansion section, with open arcades around a central patio, belonged to silver barons in the 18th century; there's even a steep carriage ramp from its days as a stagecoach stop. There are three courtyards, each in a different style, with bougainvillea and tall palm trees. The guest rooms are nicely finished with lovely tile or hardwood floors, attractive furniture, and good bathrooms. All have two double beds.

Hidalgo 101, 81820 El Fuerte, Sin. ℂ 800/896-8196 in the U.S. (to the Hotel Santa Anita in Los Mochis) or 698/893-1194 in El Fuerte. Fax 698/893-1194. www.hotelposadadelhidalgo.com. 58 units. $140 (£77) double. AE, MC, V. Free parking. **Amenities:** Restaurant; bar; outdoor pool; Jacuzzi. *In room:* A/C, no phone.

⟮Tips⟯ Money Changing: Be Prepared

Be sure to start the journey with adequate funds, because exchanging money outside of Creel is almost impossible; even credit cards are only good at the expensive hotels. (I won't use a credit card at some of the hotels listed in this chapter because they use radio communication to the main office to confirm a card—hardly a secure system.)

Río Vista Lodge *(Finds)* Free-spirited owner Chal Gámez has done it his way in this small hotel on a hill atop the town. The common areas and rooms hold fanciful murals, artifacts of Yaqui and Maya Indians, decorations from northern Mexico, and a few things reminiscent of the Old West. The outdoor dining area is a lovely place to gaze out over the river or watch the swarms of hummingbirds that feast at Chal's feeders. These birds seem little bothered by the proximity of humans—you can even put your hand under the feeder and be fanned by their wings. Meals are simple but good.

Cerro de la Pilas s/n, 81820 El Fuerte, Sin. ℂ/fax **698/893-0413**. hotelriovista@hotmail.com. 18 units. $55 (£30) double. MC, V. Free parking. **Amenities:** Restaurant. *In room:* A/C, hair dryer, no phone.

STOP 2: BAHUICHIVO & CEROCAHUI ✦✦✦

This is the first train stop in canyon country. **Bahuichivo** is merely the train depot and didn't exist before the railroad's construction. The village of **Cerocahui** (elevation 1,670m/5,478 ft.) dates from before the colonial era. It's home to 600 people and is in a valley about 10km (6¼ miles) from the train stop. The road is unpaved, so the trip takes about 30 minutes. The most dramatic part of the train ride is the section between El Fuerte and Bahuichivo.

EXPLORING CEROCAHUI Built around a sweet-looking mission church, Cerocahui consists of little more than rambling unpaved streets and 100 or so houses. It enjoys a wonderful view of the mountains, but you have to take an excursion to get real canyon vistas. All hotels can arrange horseback rides to nearby waterfalls and other scenic spots, as well as trips to **Cerro Gallego,** a famous lookout point with a beautiful vista of Urique canyon. It's possible to see the waterfall on arrival, schedule the Gallego trip for the next morning, have lunch, and still make the train, but I like the quiet of Cerocahui and recommend staying here as long as you can, provided you like hiking or horseback riding. There are a number of secluded places, both near and far, to visit. One possible trip is a hike down to the mining town of **Urique** at the bottom of the Urique Canyon (one of several canyons that make up the Copper Canyon), then a car ride back up. There are a few simple but comfortable hotels where you can stay for between $30 and $40 (£17–£22) a night. The nicest is **Hotel Barrancas Urique** (ℂ **635/456-6076**). It can provide you with a guide if you feel like doing some more hiking. The rooms come with fans, but the hotel might install air-conditioning units in a couple of the rooms.

WHERE TO STAY & DINE

Rates for doubles in the two hotels listed below include all meals for two people and transportation to and from the train station. The Paraíso del Oso is less than a kilometer (about a mile) short of the village. The mission is in Cerocahui proper. In the town, you can find simple lodging for a fraction of the cost of the other places. There are also some cabins for rent up above town. They go for $60 (£33) for two people and include transportation from the train station. You can reserve a cabin through Río Vista Lodge (see above) or by calling ℂ **635/456-5257** and saying you want a cabin in Cerocahui (the staff speaks English).

Hotel Misión Cerocahui ✦ Established years ago, the Hotel Misión is right on the town's little plaza. Guest rooms have hot water and electricity. The lobby and restaurant area surrounds a large rock fireplace where a local guitarist and singer sometimes entertain in the evenings. The food is usually good, and the ranch-style rooms (with tile floors, wood-burning stoves, and kerosene lanterns) are comfortable. The hotel offers several tours, including rides to Cerro Gallego, Urique, and the local waterfalls. There are also hiking, mountain biking, and horseback riding trips.

Domicilio Conocido, Cerocahui. www.hotelmision.com. (Reservations: Hotel Santa Anita, Apdo. Postal 159, 81200 Los Mochis, Sin. (*) **800/896-8196** in the U.S.) 38 units. $230 (£127) double. Rates include meals. AE, MC, V. Free parking. **Amenities:** Restaurant.

Paraíso del Oso ⛰ *(Moments* Opened in 1990, Paraíso del Oso sits in a sheltered hollow with a backdrop of impressive stone palisades less than a kilometer (about a half-mile) from the town. Owner Doug Rhodes is an avid horseman and takes guests for rides that can last anywhere from 3 hours to more than a week. Rooms come with two double beds and ranch furniture. They are comfortable, with wood-burning stoves and plenty of hot water. Solar-generated electricity fuels such vital services as refrigeration, while lanterns provide light. This and the utter solitude of the area are charming traits that make you feel more in touch with the Sierra than the big canyon hotels along the railroad tracks do. There is a cash bar, a small but good library (with both novels and books on Mexican history), and topographical maps of the area.

Cerocahui. (*) **800/884-3107** or 915/833-3107 in the U.S., or 614/421-3372. Fax 614/421-3372. www.mexicohorse. com. (Reservations: Paraíso del Oso, P.O. Box 31089, El Paso, TX 79931.) 21 units. $165 (£91) double. Rates include meals. No credit cards. Free parking. **Amenities:** Bar. *In room:* No phone.

STOPS 3 & 4: BARRANCAS/EL DIVISADERO ⛰⛰

Between Bahuichivo and here, the train stops at San Rafael to change crews. By the time it arrives in this area, it is at the highest part of its journey. Many packages include at least a night here for soaking up the great views of the canyons. Two nights would be better if you want to do some hiking or horseback riding.

Barrancas and El Divisadero are less than 3km (2 miles) apart. Coming from Los Mochis, you'll arrive at Barrancas first. At this stop, drivers from the **Hotel Mirador,** the **Hotel Rancho,** and the **Mansion Tarahumara** meet passengers. Then the train takes you to El Divisadero (elevation 2,240m/7,347 ft.), where you'll find the **Hotel Divisadero-Barrancas,** taco stands (at train time), and the most **spectacular view of the canyon** that you'll get if you are making no overnight stops. The train stops for 20 minutes—time enough to walk down the steps to the lookout to enjoy the view and purchase one or two mementos from the Tarahumara Indians who sell sweet-smelling pine-needle baskets, homemade violins, and wood and cloth dolls. Hotels arrange various excursions, including a visit to a cave-dwelling Tarahumara family, hiking, and horseback riding. All hotels listed below offer free secure parking.

WHERE TO STAY & DINE

Hotel Divisadero-Barrancas ⛰⛰ This location, on the edge of the canyon overlook, provides the most spectacular view of any hotel in the canyon. The restaurant has a large picture window, perfect for hours of sitting and gazing at the canyon. The rooms are in four sections. The newest section (nos. 35–48) is a two-story building perched on the edge of the canyon. These rooms have sliding glass doors that open on to balconies with a view. The bathrooms are midsize and modern. These are also probably the quietest rooms. I also like the original section with rooms 1 through 10. These are made of logs and stones and are more rustic, which for me is a good part of their appeal.

El Divisadero. (*) **800/232-4219** in the U.S. and Canada, or 635/578-3060. www.hoteldivisadero.com. (Reservations: Av. Mirador 4516, Apdo. Postal 661, Col. Residencial Campestre, 31238 Chihuahua, Chih.; (*) 614/415-1199; fax 614/415-6575.) 52 units. High season $215 (£118) double; low season $160 (£88) double. Rates include meals and 2 tours. AE, MC, V. **Amenities:** Restaurant; bar; tours. *In room:* Coffeemaker.

Hotel Mirador ⛰⛰ *(Moments* The Mirador sits on the edge of the canyon 5 minutes up the mountain from its sister hotel, the Hotel Rancho (see below). Every room has a dramatic balcony that seems to hang right over the cliff's edge. The views are beautiful. Rooms have attractive decorations and furniture, with bold Mexican color combinations; most hold two double beds. Each room has its own heater. The common areas are also comfortable and attractive.

El Divisadero. ☎ 635/578-3020. www.mexicoscoppercanyon.com/mirador. (Reservations: Hotel Santa Anita, Apdo. Postal 159, 81200 Los Mochis, Sin.; ☎ 800/896-8196 in the U.S.); fax 668/812-0046. 61 units. $265 (£146) double. Rates include meals. AE, MC, V. **Amenities:** Restaurant; bar; tour info; transportation to and from train station. *In room:* No phone.

Hotel Rancho   The train stops right in front of this inn. Rooms are comfortable, with two double beds and a wood-burning iron stove. Like those in other lodges, meals are a communal affair in the cozy living and restaurant area, and the food is good. You can rent horses or hike to the Tarahumara caves and to the rim of the canyon, where a more expensive sister hotel, the Hotel Mirador (see above), has a beautiful restaurant and bar with a magnificent view. This hotel sometimes accommodates overbooking at its sister hotel.

El Divisadero. ☎ 635/578-3020. (Reservations: Hotel Santa Anita, Apdo. Postal 159, 81200 Los Mochis, Sin.; ☎ 800/896-8196 in the U.S.); fax 668/812-0046. www.mexicoscoppercanyon.com/rancho. 25 units. $220 (£121) double. Rates include meals. AE, MC, V. **Amenities:** Restaurant; bar; transportation to and from train station. *In room:* No phone.

Mansion Tarahumara ⭐   The Mansion Tarahumara spreads across a mountainside above the train stop at Posada Barrancas. The setting is lovely. The cabin rooms offer more privacy and space than the hotel rooms, but not direct views of the canyon. Made of stone and wood, each room has a big fireplace, a wall heater, and two double beds. The castle-like structure, which is the first thing that catches the guest's eye, houses the restaurant and bar. It offers lovely views from its big windows and good food from its kitchen.

El Divisadero. ☎ 635/578-3030. (Reservations: Mansion Tarahumara, Calle Juárez 1602-A, Col. Centro, 31000 Chihuahua, Chih.; ☎ 614/415-4721; fax 614/416-5444.) www.mansiontarahumara.com.mx. 60 units. $172 (£95) double. Rates include meals. MC, V. **Amenities:** Restaurant; bar; heated outdoor pool; Jacuzzi; tours; transportation to and from train station. *In room:* No phone.

STOP 5: CREEL ⭐

This rustic logging town with a handful of paved streets offers the most economical lodgings in the canyon. Creel (rhymes with "feel") is also the starting point for some of the best side trips, especially hiking and overnight camping.

ESSENTIALS
GETTING THERE & DEPARTING   By Train   See the chart on p. 674 for "official" arrival and departure times.

By Car   From Chihuahua, follow the signs to La Junta until you see signs for Hermosillo. Follow those signs until you see signs to Creel (left). The trip takes about 4 hours on a paved road.

By Bus   Estrella Blanca (☎ 635/456-0073), next to the Hotel Korachi, has six trips to Chihuahua per day. The trip takes 4 hours and costs $17 (£9.35). This is a lot cheaper and faster than the train.

ORIENTATION   The train station, around the corner from the Mission Store and the main plaza, is in the heart of the village and within walking distance of all lodgings except the Copper Canyon Sierra Lodge. Look for your hotel's van waiting at the station (unless you're staying at the Casa de Huéspedes Margarita, which is only 2 blocks away). There's one main street, **López Mateos,** and almost everything is within a couple of blocks.

FAST FACTS   The telephone **area code** is **635.** Electricity is available 24 hours daily in all Creel hotels. (In other parts of the canyon, electricity is sporadic or not available.) Creel has one ATM, one bank, and one *casa de cambio.* The best sources of **information** are the Mission Store and the hotels. Several businesses and many of the hotels offer long-distance **telephone** service; look for LARGA DISTANCIA signs or ask at your hotel. Creel sits at an **elevation** of 2,210m (7,248 ft.) and has a **population** of around 6,000. It's the largest town in the canyon area.

EXPLORING CREEL

You'll occasionally see the Tarahumara as you walk around town, but mostly, you'll see rugged logging types and tourists from around the world.

Several stores around Creel sell Tarahumara arts and crafts. The best is **Artesanías Misión (Mission Crafts),** which sells quality merchandise at reasonable prices; all profits go to the Mission Hospital run by Father Verplancken, a Jesuit, and benefit the Tarahumara. Here you'll find dolls, pottery, woven purses and belts, drums, violins (an instrument borrowed from the Spanish), bamboo flutes, bead necklaces, bows and arrows, cassettes of Tarahumara music, woodcarvings, baskets, and heavy wool rugs, as well as an excellent supply of books and maps relating to the Tarahumara and the region. It's open daily from 9:30am to 1pm, and Monday through Saturday from 3 to 6pm. It's beside the railroad tracks on the main plaza.

WHERE TO STAY

Though a small town, Creel has several places to stay, all with free parking. A lot of these hotels cater to backpackers. It's advisable to make reservations during high season.

Expensive

The Lodge at Creel   Each of this Best Western hotel's cheerfully decorated cabins holds four units, built completely of pine, including the furniture. Most have two double beds, and some have their own porches. Their construction, decor, and layout remind me of old-style motels that you find next to U.S. national parks. The lobby, next to the dining area, has a phone for guests' use and a small gift shop. The hotel offers 3-night backpacking trips to the bottom of the canyon, among other tours, for 4 to 10 people. The on-site restaurant serves all three meals. The van meets all trains.

Av. López Mateos 61, 33200 Creel, Chih. ⓒ 888/879-4071 in the U.S., or 635/456-0071. Fax 635/456-0082. www.thelodgeatcreel.com. 38 units. $120 (£66) double. AE, MC, V. **Amenities:** Restaurant; bar; fitness room; Jacuzzi; sauna; tours; room service; nonsmoking rooms. *In room:* TV, high-speed Internet, coffeemaker, hair dryer, safe, no phone.

Copper Canyon Sierra Lodge ★★ *Finds*   About 20 minutes (22km/14 miles) southwest of Creel, the Sierra Lodge has everything you hope for in a mountain lodge—rock walls, beamed ceilings, lantern lights, and wood-burning stoves; in other words, rustic charm and no electricity. Its out-of-town location is a great starting point for self-guided hikes and walks in the mountains to the Cusárare Waterfalls. This hotel has a sister lodge in Batopilas, which is beautiful and runs about the same per room.

Apdo. Postal 3, 33200 Creel, Chih. ⓒ 800/776-3942 in the U.S. Fax 635/456-0036 (in Creel). www.sierratrail.com. 22 units. $140 (£77) double. Rates include meals. No credit cards. *In room:* No phone.

Moderate

Hotel Parador de la Montaña   This is the largest hotel in town, located 4 blocks west of the plaza. The comfortable rooms have two double beds, high wood-beamed ceilings, central heating, tiled bathrooms, and thin walls. Guests congregate in the restaurant, bar, and lobby, which has a roaring fireplace. The hotel caters to groups and offers some 10 overland tours, priced from $20 to $70 (£11–£39).

Av. López Mateos s/n, 33200 Creel, Chih. ⓒ 635/456-0023. Fax 635/456-0085. (Reservations: Calle Allende 1414, 31300 Chihuahua, Chih.; ⓒ 614/410-4580; fax 635/415-3468.) www.hotelparadorcreel.com. 50 units. $93 (£51) double. AE, MC, V. **Amenities:** Restaurant; bar; tours. *In room:* TV, no phone.

Inexpensive
Hotel Nuevo   The Nuevo has two sections: the older one, across the tracks from the train station and next to the restaurant and variety store, and newer log cabañas in back. Rooms are small to midsize and not as attractive as the higher-priced (and carpeted) cabañas. Half the rooms have TVs. The nice hotel restaurant is open from 8:30am to 8pm, and the small general store carries local crafts as well as basic supplies. Ask at the store about rooms.

Francisco Villa 121, 33200 Creel, Chih. ⓒ 635/456-0022. Fax 635/456-0043. 27 units. $30–$80 (£17–£44) double. MC, V. **Amenities:** Restaurant; general store. *In room:* TV (in some), no phone.

WHERE TO DINE
There are several places to eat in Creel, but no standouts. Aside from the restaurants at the hotels, you might want to try one of the establishments on López Mateos, such as the **Caballo Bayo, Tío Molcas,** or **Verónica's.**

NEARBY EXCURSIONS
Close by are several canyons, waterfalls, a lake, hot springs, Tarahumara villages and cave dwellings, and an old Jesuit mission. Ten kilometers (6 miles) north of town is an ecotourism complex, **San Ignacio de Arareko** (ⓒ 635/456-0126). It has a lake, hiking and biking trails, horses, cabins, and a crafts shop, all run by indigenous peoples of the *ejido* (cooperative)—a change from the *mestizo* population's almost total control of tourism in Mexico. **Batopilas,** an 18th-century silver-mining town at the bottom of the canyon, requires an overnight excursion. You can ask for information about these and other things to do at your hotel, or go by the office of **The 3 Amigos** (ⓒ 635/456-0036; www.the3amigoscanyonexpeditions.com) at Av. López Mateos 46 in downtown Creel. These guys rent pickups with crew cabs or mountain bikes and can give you maps and advice on where to go, depending on your interests.

From Creel, you can drive to **El Divisadero** (see "Stops 3 & 4: Barrancas/El Divisadero," above, for details) on a recently paved road. The trip takes about an hour.

ORGANIZED TOURS   Hotels offer 2- to 10-hour organized tours that cost $15 to $90 (£8.25–£50) per person (four people minimum). All tour availability depends on whether a group can be assembled; your best chance is at the **Hotel Parador de la Montaña.**

BASASEACHIC FALLS   This is an exhausting day tour to what is billed as the tallest single cascade in North America. The best time to go is during the rainy season, from July to September. The tour costs around $50 (£28) per person and takes about 11 hours. Driving time is 4 hours one-way, and the strenuous hike to the bottom and back up takes 3 hours—not a lot of time to be by the falls. Another option is to stay in one of the simple accommodations that have opened near the falls, if you can get transportation back the next day. Ask around Creel.

BATOPILAS   You can make an overnight side trip from Creel to the old silver-mining town of Batopilas, founded in 1708. It's 7 to 9 hours from Creel by town bus, 5 hours by

---

Tips **Caution: Don't Be a Dope**

It's no secret that marijuana farmers use clandestine farmlands in the Copper Canyon, and that rumors link prominent names in the state to their activities. This has never affected any of my trips to the region. If you are hiking the backwoods and happen upon a field of marijuana, simply leave the area.

---

sport utility vehicle, along a narrow, winding dirt road through some of the most spectacular scenery in the Copper Canyon. In Batopilas, which lies beside a river at the bottom of a deep canyon, the weather is tropical, though it can get cool in the evenings. You can visit a beautiful little church and do several walks, including one to **Misión Satevó,** a ruined mission church that dates from the early 18th century. The place has many colorful little details: The dry-goods store has the original shelving and cash register, cobblestone streets twist past whitewashed homes, miners and ranchers come and go on horseback, and the Tarahumara frequently visit. A considerable number of pigs, dogs, and flocks of goats roam at will—this is, after all, Chihuahua's goat-raising capital.

Getting There   From Creel, take the **bus** from the Restaurant Herradero, López Mateos s/n, three doors past the turnoff to Hotel Plaza Mexicana. It goes to Batopilas on Tuesday, Thursday, and Saturday, leaving Creel at 7am and arriving midafternoon. Tickets are sold at the restaurant. Several Suburban-type **vans** offer transportation. One leaves on Monday, Wednesday, and Friday at 10:30am and arrives midafternoon. Both bus and van return the following day. There are no bathrooms, restaurants, or other conveniences of civilization along the way, but the bus may stop to allow passengers to stretch and find a bush.

Where to Stay & Dine   Batopilas has a few little restaurants and inns. There are no telephones, though, so don't expect to make reservations. One night probably isn't enough for a stay here, since you arrive midafternoon and must leave at 7am or 10:30am the next day.

The staff at the Hotel Parador de la Montaña in Creel provides information about vacancies at the basic, comfortable, 10-room **Hotel Mary** (formerly Parador Batopilas). All rooms have private bathrooms and cost around $20 (£11) double per night. There are also the rustic **Hotel Batopilas** and **Hotel Las Palmeras,** with five or six rooms each; if all else fails, you can probably find a family willing to let you stay in an extra room.

Restaurants in Batopilas are informal, so bring along some snacks and bottled water to tide you over; snacks are available at the general store. The place to eat in Batopilas is **Doña Mica's,** facing a little plaza tucked behind the main square. Ask anyone for directions (everyone knows her). She serves meals on her front porch surrounded by plants, but it's best to let her know in advance when to expect you. On short notice, she can probably rustle up some scrambled eggs.

2 Los Mochis: The Western Terminus

202km (121 miles) SW of Alamos; 80km (50 miles) SW of El Fuerte; 309km (192 miles) SE of Guaymas; 416km (258 miles) NW of Mazatlán

Los Mochis, in Sinaloa State, is a coastal city of 350,000 founded in 1893 by Benjamin Johnson of Pennsylvania. It is a wealthy city in a fertile agricultural area, but holds little of interest for the visitor. The most important aspects of the city are that it is a boarding point for the train, it has an airport, and it is connected to La Paz, Baja California, by ferry, and to the U.S. border by highway.

ESSENTIALS

GETTING THERE & DEPARTING   By Plane   AeroMéxico/Aerolitoral (© 800/ 237-6639 in the U.S., or 668/815-2570 for reservations; www.aeromexico.com.mx) has direct service from Phoenix, Chihuahua, Hermosillo, Mazatlán, and La Paz. The airport is 21km (13 miles) north of town; transportation is by *combi* (collective minivan) or airport taxi ($10/£5.50).

By Train   The first-class **Chihuahua al Pacífico (Copper Canyon train)** runs between Los Mochis and Chihuahua once daily, departing at 6am. First-class fare is $130 (£72).

By Car   **Coastal Highway 15** is well maintained in both directions leading into Los Mochis.

By Ferry   A ferry plies the waters between La Paz and Topolobampo, the port for Los Mochis carrying passengers, vehicles, and cargo. The company, **Baja Ferries** (© 668/ **817-3752** or -3864; www.bajaferries.com), uses a larger and more dependable ship than the company that used to operate this ferry route. There's one departure per day leaving at 11pm.

By Bus   Buses serve Los Mochis, however marginally. Most are *de paso*—passing through. All bus stations are downtown, within walking distance of the hotels. The **first-class station** is near Juárez at Degollado 200. From here, Elite buses go to and from Tijuana, Monterrey, Nogales, and Ciudad Juárez. Auto-transportes Transpacíficos, in the same station, serves Nogales, Tijuana, Mazatlán, Guadalajara, Querétaro, and Mexico City. A lot of travelers who arrive in Los Mochis prefer to go directly to El Fuerte, spend the night there, and then catch the train. There are two places to catch the bus to El Fuerte (1½–2 hr.). The first is at the **Mercado Independencia;** the bus stops at the corner of Independencia and Degollado. The other is at the **corner of Cuauhtémoc and Prieto,** near the Hotel América. Ask hotel desk clerks or the tourism office for a schedule. These are second-class buses, which stop frequently, prolonging the trip well beyond the normal 1-hour travel time.

CITY LAYOUT   Los Mochis contains no central plaza, and streets run northwest to southeast and southwest to northeast.

FAST FACTS   The local **American Express** representative is **Viajes Araceli,** Av. Alvaro Obregón 471-A Poniente (© 668/815-5780; fax 668/815-8787). *Note:* Changing money outside of Los Mochis is difficult, so stock up on pesos before boarding the train. Most places in the canyons do not accept credit cards. The telephone **area code** for Los Mochis is **668.**

EXPLORING LOS MOCHIS

For most travelers, Los Mochis is a stopover en route to somewhere else. There isn't much here, but the town is pleasant, and you can enjoy some excellent seafood. The **Viajes Flamingo** travel agency, on the ground floor of the Hotel Santa Anita (© 668/812-1613 or -1929), arranges a city tour, hunting and fishing trips, and a harbor tour around **Topolobampo Bay.** The harbor tour is fun. The agency is open Monday through Saturday from 8:30am to 1pm and 3 to 6:30pm. The boat ride is really just a spin in the bay and not especially noteworthy, although the bay is pretty and dolphins often show up.

WHERE TO STAY

Hotel Corintios   Behind a campy entrance with Greek columns and mirrored glass are two stories of rooms with ample light, carpeted floors, and adequate space for two comfortable double beds and luggage. The bathrooms are midsize and have marble tub/showers but poor lighting. The junior suites come with a king-size bed.

Obregón 580 Poniente, 81200 Los Mochis, Sin. ✆ 668/818-2300 or 01-800/690-3000 in Mexico. Fax 668/818-2277. 59 units. $80 (£44) double, $88 (£48) junior suite. AE, MC, V. Rates include continental breakfast. Free parking. **Amenities:** Restaurant; Jacuzzi; room service; laundry service. *In room:* A/C, TV.

Hotel Las Fuentes   Of the inexpensive hotels in town, I like this one the best. The rooms are cheerful and clean and the staff is helpful. Rooms come with one or two double beds, and the cost varies accordingly. Bathrooms are midsize with a shower. The hotel is 5 minutes from downtown on one of the main arteries.

Bulevar Adolfo López Mateos 1251-A Norte, 81220 Los Mochis, Sin. ✆ 668/818-8871 or -8172. Fax 668/812-5983. las fuenteshotel@lmm.megared.net.mx. 38 units. $42–$50 (£23–£28) double. AE, MC, V. Free secure parking. **Amenities:** Restaurant; bar; room service; laundry service. *In room:* A/C, TV.

Hotel Santa Anita   The Santa Anita is the choice of most going to the canyon; not only is it a comfortable, quiet hotel, but it offers reliable transportation to and from the train station. The rooms are modern and well furnished but vary a good deal in size. All are carpeted and have comfortable beds, color TVs with U.S. channels, and tap water purified for drinking. The hotel's popular restaurant is just off the lobby. There are two bars, one with live music at least 1 day a week.

Leyva, at the corner of Hidalgo (Apdo. Postal 159), 81200 Los Mochis, Sin. ✆ 800/896-8196 in the U.S., or 668/818-7046. Fax 668/812-0046. 116 units. $140 (£77) double. AE, MC, V. Free parking. **Amenities:** Restaurant; bar; transportation to and from the train station; business center; room service; laundry service; nonsmoking rooms. *In room:* A/C, TV, hair dryer.

WHERE TO DINE

El Farallón ★★ SEAFOOD   If you like seafood, there's no reason to eat anywhere else in Los Mochis. Don't be put off by the menu, which is confusing—to put it simply, you can order seafood cooked any way you want. Try a Mexican style such as *al ajillo*, with toasted *guajillo* chiles. If you're hungry, I recommend the *mariscada* for two or more, which comes with a cold and a hot platter of a variety of fish and shellfish. Try *calamares* (squid), the cheapest thing on the platter. Forget about those rubbery rings fried up in other restaurants; because the squid get to be giant-size in this region's waters, the meat comes in big, tender chunks. One of my favorites is *machaca*, made with either shrimp or smoked marlin (cooked in a reduced fish stock, which is mild and satisfying). The atmosphere is casual, the air-conditioning functions with gusto, and the white-tiled dining area is simply furnished.

Obregón, at Angel Flores. ✆ 668/812-1428. Main courses $8–$17 (£4.40–£9.35). AE, MC, V. Daily 8am–11pm. From the Hotel Santa Anita, turn right on Leyva and right again for 1 block on Obregón; it's on your left.

El Taquito *Value* MEXICAN   Any time of the day or night, El Taquito serves standard Mexican fare at a good price. With orange booths and Formica tables, the cafe looks like an American fast-food place. Tortilla soup comes in a large bowl, and both breakfast and main-course portions are quite generous.

Leyva at Barrera. ✆ 668/812-8119. Breakfast $3–$5 (£1.65–£2.75); main courses $4–$8 (£2.20–£4.40). AE, DC, MC, V. Daily 24 hr. From the Hotel Santa Anita, turn left on Leyva, cross Hidalgo and go 1 block; it's on your right.

Restaurante España STEAK/SEAFOOD This Spanish-style restaurant is a favorite among downtown professionals, who feast on large plates of paella (available Thurs and Sun after 1pm; at other times it's made to order, taking 45 min.). The decor is upscale for Los Mochis, with a splashing fountain in the dining room and heavy, carved-wood tables and chairs.

Obregón 525 Pte. ℂ 668/812-2221. Breakfast $4–$6 (£2.20–£3.30); main courses $9–$13 (£4.95–£7.15). AE, MC, V. Daily 7am–11pm. From the Hotel Santa Anita, turn right out the front door to Obregón, then right on Obregón for 1½ blocks; it's on your right.

3 Chihuahua: The Eastern Terminus ✦

341km (211 miles) S of El Paso; 440km (273 miles) NW of Torreón

Chihuahua, a city of wide boulevards and handsome buildings, is the capital of the state of Chihuahua, the largest and richest in Mexico. The wealth comes from mining, timber, cattle raising, *maquiladoras* (assembly plants for export goods), and tourism. The city has grown a lot in the last 30 years, thanks mainly to an increase in manufacturing plants, and has lost its frontier feeling. But the historic center of Chihuahua retains much of its character and holds a few museums and buildings worth visiting, including the house where Pancho Villa once lived.

ESSENTIALS

GETTING THERE & DEPARTING **By Plane** **Continental** (ℂ 800/525-0280 in the U.S., or 01-800/900-5000 in Mexico; www.continental.com) has nonstop service to and from Houston on a 50-seat jet. **AeroMéxico/Aerolitoral** (ℂ 800/237-6639 in the U.S., or 614/415-6303; www.aeromexico.com.mx) flies direct from El Paso, Phoenix, Guadalajara, Hermosillo, Mexico City, Monterrey, Torreón, Tijuana, Culiacán, La Paz, and Los Mochis, with connecting flights from Los Angeles and San Antonio. **Transportes Terrestre** (ℂ 614/420-3366) controls minivan service from the airport ($7/£3.85 per person, $10/£5.50 if it's an early flight). Taxis from town charge $15 (£8.25) for up to four people.

By Train The **Chihuahua al Pacífico** (ℂ 614/439-7212; fax 614/439-7208) leaves Chihuahua daily for Los Mochis by way of the Copper Canyon country. The complete train schedule and the train route appear in "The Copper Canyon Train & Stops along the Way," earlier in this chapter. In that section you'll find information on purchasing tickets. It is easier to go through a travel agency than to deal directly with the company. The train is scheduled to leave at 6am daily. To get to the station in time, it's best to arrange transportation through one of the travel agencies recommended under "Canyon Arrangements" in "Fast Facts: Chihuahua," below. They pick up clients taking the train each morning.

By Car **Highway 45** leads south from Ciudad Juárez; **Highway 16** south from Ojinaga; and **Highway 49** north from Torreón. For the drive to Creel, see "Getting There & Departing" under "Stop 5: Creel," earlier in this chapter.

By Bus The Central Camionera **Terminal de Autobuses (bus station)** is on Avenida Juan Pablo II, 8km (5 miles) northeast of town en route to the airport. Buses leave hourly for major points inland and north and south on the coast. Transportes Chihuahuenses, the big local line, offers first-class service to Ciudad Juárez every half-hour; the trip takes 4 hours. Transportes del Norte and Autobuses Estrella Blanca also run buses hourly from the border through Chihuahua to points south. Omnibus de

Chihuahua

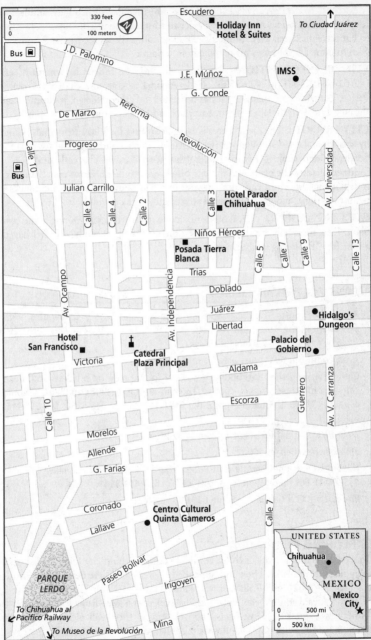

Escudero

Holiday Inn
Hotel & Suites

To Ciudad Juárez

0 ——— 330 feet
0 ——— 100 meters

Bus 🚌

J.D. Palomino

J.E. Múñoz

G. Conde

IMSS

Reforma

De Marzo

Revolución

Progreso

Calle 10
Bus

Julian Carrillo

Av. Universidad

Calle 6
Calle 4
Calle 2
Calle 3

Hotel Parador
Chihuahua

Niños Héroes

Posada Tierra
Blanca

Calle 5
Calle 7
Calle 9
Calle 13

Trias

Doblado

Av. Ocampo

Av. Independencia

Juárez

Libertad

Hidalgo's
Dungeon

Hotel
San Francisco

Catedral
Plaza Principal

Palacio del
Gobierno

Victoria

Aldama

Escorza

Guerrero

Av. V. Carranza

Calle 10

Morelos

Allende

G. Farias

Coronado

Centro Cultural
Quinta Gameros

Calle 7

Lallave

PARQUE
LERDO

Paseo Bolívar

Irigoyen

To Chihuahua al
Pacifico Railway

To Museo de la Revolución

Mina

UNITED STATES

Chihuahua

MEXICO

Mexico
City

0 ——— 500 mi
0 ——— 500 km

México has *servicio ejecutivo* (deluxe service) from Juárez, Mexico City, and Monterrey. Futura/Turistar also has deluxe service to Monterrey and Durango.

For travel to Creel, look for the Estrella Blanca line. Buses leave every 2 hours from 6am to 6pm. Direct buses make the trip in 4 hours.

VISITOR INFORMATION   For basic info, visit the **tourist information center** (© 614/410-1077 or 429-3596), Calle Aldama at Carranza in the Government Palace, just left of the altar and murals dedicated to Father Hidalgo. It's open Monday through Friday from 9am to 6pm, Saturday and Sunday from 10am to 5pm.

CITY LAYOUT   The town center is laid out around the **Plaza Principal,** bounded by avenidas Libertad and Victoria (which run northeast-southwest) and Avenida Independencia and Calle 4 (which run northwest-southeast). The **cathedral** is at the southwest end of the plaza, and the city offices are on the northeast end. Standing on Independencia with the cathedral on your left, odd-numbered streets and blocks will be to your right, and even-numbered streets and blocks to your left.

GETTING AROUND   Local buses run along main arteries beginning at the central plaza. Taxis are readily available. If you want to see the sights and have only 1 day, take a tour (see "Exploring Chihuahua," below).

FAST FACTS: Chihuahua

American Express   The local representative is **Viajes Rojo y Casavantes,** with one agent in the Hotel San Francisco and a full office at Vicente Guerrero 1207 (© 614/415-4636; fax 614/415-5384).

Area Code   The telephone area code is **614.**

Canyon Arrangements   If you have waited to purchase train tickets and make canyon hotel reservations, contact **Turismo al Mar,** Calle Berna 2202, Colonia Mirador, 31270 Chihuahua, Chih. (© 614/410-9232 or 416-5950; fax 614/416-6589).

Elevation   Chihuahua sits at 1,425m (4,374 ft.).

Emergencies   Call © 060.

Hospital   **Clínica del Parque** is at Pedro Leal del Rosal and de la Llave (© 614/415-7411). For medical emergencies, call © 614/411-8141.

Population   Chihuahua has some 670,000 residents.

EXPLORING CHIHUAHUA

To see Chihuahua's sights in 1 day, consider taking a 3-hour city tour; English-speaking guides are available. Three recommended agencies are **Torre del Sol,** Independencia 116-2 (© 614/415-7380), in the Hotel Palacio del Sol; **Turismo al Mar** (see "Canyon Arrangements" in "Fast Facts," above); and **Viajes Rojo y Casavantes** (see "American Express" in "Fast Facts," above). Any of these will pick you up at your hotel. A half-day city tour includes visits to the museums, the churches, the colonial aqueduct, the state capital building, the state penitentiary, and more. A 7-hour trip to the Mennonite village near Cuauhtémoc costs about $35 (£19) per person, with a minimum of four people. Unless you have a particular interest in cheese making or the Mennonites, it's not worth your time.

SIGHTS IN TOWN

Hidalgo's Dungeon   Father Miguel Hidalgo y Costilla was a priest in Dolores, Guanajuato, when he started the War of Independence on September 15, 1810. Six months later, he was captured by the Spanish, brought to Chihuahua, and thrown in a dungeon for 98 days. He was then shot along with his lieutenants, Allende, Aldama, and Jiménez. The four were beheaded, and their heads hung in iron cages for 9½ years on the four corners of the Alhóndiga granary in Guanajuato (see chapter 6) as examples of the fate revolutionaries would meet. In this cell, Hidalgo lived on bread and water before his execution. The night before his death, he wrote a few words on the wall with a piece of charcoal to thank his guard and the warden for the good treatment they gave him. A bronze plaque commemorates his final message.

In the Palacio Federal, Av. Juárez at Guerrero. No phone. Admission 50¢ (30p). Tues–Sun 10am–6pm. From Plaza Principal, walk on pedestrian-only Calle Libertad for 3 long blocks to Guerrero, turn left, and walk to corner of Juárez; turn right and go a half-block; museum entrance is on the right, below the post office.

Museo de la Revolución 🔎 _Finds_   The Revolution Museum is Pancho Villa's house, where Luz Corral de Villa, Pancho Villa's widow, lived until her death in 1981. Exhibits include Villa's weapons, some personal effects, lots of period photos, and the 1922 Dodge in which he was shot in 1923 (you'll see the bullet holes). I found it interesting and recommend seeing the place with a guide, who can add lots of biographical details about this larger-than-life character. Be sure to ask about Villa's opinions on marriage and about the total number of his offspring and grandchildren.

Calle 10 no. 3014 (at Méndez). ✆ 614/416-2958. Admission $1 (55p). Tues–Sat 9am–1pm and 3–7pm. Bus: Colonia Dale (runs west on Juárez, then south on Ocampo); exit at corner of Ocampo and Méndez.

Palacio del Gobierno   The Palacio del Gobierno is a magnificent, ornate structure dating in part from 1890; the original building, the Jesuit College, was built in 1718. A colorful, expressive mural encompasses the first floor of the large central courtyard and tells the history of the area around Chihuahua from the time of the first European visitation through the Revolution. In the far right corner, note the scene depicting Benito Juárez flanked by Abraham Lincoln and Simón Bolívar, liberator of South America. In the far left rear courtyard are a plaque and altar commemorating the execution in 1811 of Miguel Hidalgo, the father of Mexican independence; the plaque marks the spot where the hero was executed in the old building, and the mural portrays the scene.

Av. Aldama (between Guerrero and Carranza). ✆ 614/410-6324. Free admission. Daily 8am–10pm. With the cathedral on your right, walk along Independencia 1 block, turn left on Aldama, continue 2 long blocks, and cross Guerrero; entrance is on the left.

Quinta Gameros 🔎   Quinta Gameros is a neoclassical, French Second Empire–style mansion with a beautiful Art Nouveau interior. Built in 1910 for Manuel Gameros, the mansion became a museum in 1961. Pancho Villa used it briefly as a headquarters. The interior walls, floors, and ceilings are lavishly decorated, which inspired the transfer of a beautiful collection of fine Mexican Art Nouveau furnishings from Mexico City to this museum. If you like design and beautiful antiques, especially Art Nouveau, don't miss this place.

Quinta Gameros, Paseo Bolívar 401. ✆ 614/416-6684. Admission $2 (£1.10). Tues–Sun 11am–2pm and 4–7pm. Heading away from the Plaza Principal with the cathedral on your right, walk 7 blocks on Independencia to Bolívar, turn right, and walk 1 block; museum is on the right.

WHERE TO STAY
EXPENSIVE
Holiday Inn Hotel and Suites ♠ This Holiday Inn offers the most comfortable rooms in the downtown area. All units are suites, with kitchenettes that include stove, refrigerator, and coffeemaker. There's a sitting area, large writing table, and a choice of one king-size bed or two doubles. Guests have the use of a video library. The hotel staff is helpful and efficient. They can provide a continental breakfast for people heading off on the train, as well as a box lunch. The hotel is a 5-minute walk from downtown.

Calle Escudero 702 (between Av. Universidad and Av. de Montes), 31240 Chihuahua, Chih. ℂ **800/465-4329** in the U.S., or 614/439-0000. Fax 614/414-3313. 74 units. $150 (£83) double. Rates include breakfast buffet. AE, MC, V. Free secure parking. **Amenities:** Restaurant; bar; 2 pools (1 indoor); fitness room; Jacuzzi; steam room; game room; business center; room service; babysitting; laundry service; coin-op laundry; nonsmoking rooms. *In room:* A/C, TV, high-speed Internet, kitchenette, fridge, coffeemaker, hair dryer, iron, safe.

Quality Inn Chihuahua San Francisco   The good location and comfortable mid-size rooms are the main attractions here. Rooms are well furnished. The bathrooms are well equipped and have ample counter space. Bed choices include two doubles, a queen, or a king. Mattresses are firm. Don't worry about getting a view; ask for something quiet. This used to be called the Hotel San Francisco.

Victoria 409, 31000 Chihuahua, Chih. ℂ **800/847-2546** in the U.S., or 614/439-9000. Fax 614/415-3538. www.quality innchihuahua.com. 131 units. $110 (£61) double. AE, MC, V. Free covered parking and continental breakfast. From the cathedral, walk to Victoria and turn right; the hotel is 1½ blocks down on your right, before Av. Ocampo. **Amenities:** Restaurant (see review for Degá, below); bar; fitness room; travel agency; car rental; business center; room service; laundry service. *In room:* A/C, TV, coffeemaker, hair dryer, iron, safe.

MODERATE
Hotel Posada Tierra Blanca   A downtown hotel with an attractive large pool area shaded by trees. Rooms are in two- and three-story buildings. They are large and quiet (none have windows facing the street). Bathrooms are midsize with good counter space and better lighting than most of the hotels in Chihuahua.

Niños Héroes 102, 31000 Chihuahua, Chih. ℂ **614/415-0000.** www.posadatierrablanca.com.mx. 90 units. $70 (£39) double. AE, MC, V. Free secure parking. **Amenities:** Restaurant; bar; large outdoor pool; fitness room; room service; laundry service. *In room:* A/C, TV.

INEXPENSIVE
Hotel Parador Chihuahua   I like this motel for the price, the downtown location, and the well-maintained rooms. It occupies the interior of a small city block, with the rooms built around the pool and the garden area. The midsize rooms are carpeted and furnished rather plainly. Choice of one king-size bed or two doubles. Bathrooms are midsize.

Calle 3, no. 304 (between Julian Carrillo and Niños Héroes), 31000 Chihuahua, Chih. ℂ **614/415-0827.** www. paradorchihuahua.com. 34 units. $52 (£29) double. AE, MC, V. Free secure parking. **Amenities:** Restaurant; bar; small outdoor pool; room service; laundry service. *In room:* A/C, TV.

WHERE TO DINE
Dining in Chihuahua is fine so long as you don't rely too heavily on the city's sophistication. Stick with steaks and Mexican food.

Degá MEXICAN/INTERNATIONAL   This restaurant bar at the Quality Inn Chihuahua San Francisco hotel draws both downtown workers and travelers. The breakfast buffet features made-to-order omelets. The steaks and Mexican dishes are well priced; try the *plato mexicano,* a popular dish that comes with a tamal, chile relleno, beans, chips, and guacamole.

In the Quality Inn Chihuahua San Francisco, Calle Victoria 409. *C* **614/416-7550**. Breakfast $4–$7 (£2.20–£3.85); breakfast buffet $8 (£4.40); main courses $5–$17 (£2.75–£9.35); Sun buffet $10 (£5.50). AE, MC, V. Daily 7am–11pm.

La Calesa STEAKS/MEXICAN   The dining room, with its heavy furniture, wood paneling, and bound menus, gets the message across that this is Chihuahua's establishment restaurant. Some of the steaks go by different names here, but the waiters are familiar with all the cuts. A piano serenades diners from 2:30 to 5pm and 9pm to midnight.

Av. Colón 3300, corner of Av. Juárez. *C* **614/410-1038**. Steaks $11–$21 (£6.05–£12); Mexican dishes $7–$10 (£3.85–£5.50). AE, MC, V. Daily 12:30pm–midnight.

Restaurante Todo de Maíz *Finds* MEXICAN   To eat cheaply and eat well in Chihuahua is a bit of a trick—unless you go here. Señora María Matilde Salazar is a great cook and an unabashed leftist. She keeps quality and freshness up by keeping the menu simple. Between 1 and 2:30pm she offers a *comida corrida* that's a bargain. And the rest of the time she makes tacos, quesadillas, tostadas, and *peneques* (a local form of *antojito* that's like a *gordita*) all made with corn *masa*, as the restaurant's name suggests. This place is down the street from the Holiday Inn.

Calle Escudero 2103 (between calles 21 and 23). *C* **614/414-5778**. *Comida corrida* $3 (£1.65); *antojitos* $1–$2 (55p–£1.10). No credit cards. Mon–Fri 9am–5pm; Sat 11am–5pm.

Rincón Mexicano *✦* MEXICAN   The Rincón serves great Mexican food and offers a substantial number of choices. Good appetizers include *quesadillas de huitlacoche* (corn empanadas with cheese and corn fungus) for the adventurous, and *chile con asadero* (melted spicy cheese). For a main dish that gives you a little of everything, try *enchiladas tres moles*. As you would expect of a restaurant in Chihuahua, the emphasis is on beef, prepared in very Mexican ways such as *puntas en chile pasado* (beef tips cooked in a dried chile sauce) or *molcajete de res* (fajitas cooked and served in a steaming stone vessel accompanied by tortillas). The interior is easy on the eyes, with muted tones of yellow and orange, good lighting, and tablecloths. A guitar trio occasionally performs soft music in the evenings. The restaurant is a short taxi ride from downtown.

Av. Cuauhtémoc 2224. *C* **614/411-1510** or -1427. Main courses $8–$15 (£4.40–£8.25). AE, MC, V. Daily noon–midnight.

CHIHUAHUA AFTER DARK

Most nighttime action takes place in hotel lobby bars (see "Where to Stay," above). At the **Quality Inn Chihuahua San Francisco,** there's live music Monday through Saturday, with happy hour from 5 to 8pm. The lobby bar at the **Hotel Palacio del Sol** schedules live entertainment nightly.

18

Los Cabos & Baja California

by Lynne Bairstow & Emily Hughey Quinn

B aja California is a place of complementary contrasts: hot desert and cool ocean, manicured golf greens and craggy mountains, glistening resorts and frontier land. Baja lays claim to a striking and peculiar blend of Mexican and American cultures, and it can't be found anywhere else in Mexico.

The Baja Peninsula is and is not part of Mexico. Attached mostly to the United States and separated from all but a sliver of Mexico by the Sea of Cortez (Gulf of California), the peninsula consists of one long granite ridge extending about 1,500km (930 miles)—longer than Italy—from Mexico's northernmost city of **Tijuana** to **Cabo San Lucas** at its southern tip. Desert terrain rises from both coasts; forests of cardón cactus, spiky elephant trees, and spindly ocotillo bushes populate the raw landscape. Long stretches of open highway criss-crossed by roadrunners and tumbleweed are interrupted by the occasional dusty pueblo and jaw-dropping coastline. Baja is part Wild West, part country club, part seafaring paradise, part adventure wonderland, and there's room for all of its visitors to blaze their own trails. For more in-depth coverage of this region, consult *Frommer's Los Cabos & Baja.*

EXPLORING THE REGION

The weather in this land of extremes can be sizzling hot in summer and cold and windy in winter. Winter is often warm enough for watersports, but bring a wetsuit if you're a serious diver or snorkeler, as well as warmer clothes for chilly weather. Although Baja's weather varies greatly by season, it is predictable—an important quality for the increasing number of golfers looking for sunny skies. Rainy days are few and far between, with most showers concentrated in September.

THE TWO CABOS Nearly 2 million visitors and growing are lured to Los Cabos (the capes), the twin towns at the peninsula's southernmost tip, each year. **Cabo San Lucas** holds court on the Western cape and **San José del Cabo** rounds out the Eastern cape. Connected only by the **Tourist Corridor,** 33km (21 miles) of coastline studded with golf courses, luxury resorts and master-planned communities, the two capes could not be more different.

Cabo San Lucas, also known as Land's End, is twofold. Most obviously, she's the rowdy younger sister who takes tequila shots from a holster while dancing on the table chanting, "What happens in Cabo stays in Cabo," and wraps up the night at a local American fast-food joint. The other side of San Lucas is a bling-flashing older brother who frequents swanky clubs, sips champagne in his oceanfront Jacuzzi, or cruises the

The Baja Peninsula

Tijuana
Rosarito
Punta Salsipuedes
Valle de Guadalupe
Ensenada
San Vicente
San Quintín
SIERRA DE JUÁREZ
BAJA CALIFORNIA
SIERRA DE COLOMBIA
Mexicali
Yuma
Colorado
La Ventana
San Felipe
DESIERTO DE ALTAR
8
2
3
5
3
1
1
8
2

THE BAJA PENINSULA
UNITED STATES
PACIFIC OCEAN
MEXICO
Mexico City ★
Gulf of Mexico
0   500 mi
0   500 km

Nogales
Caborca
Santa Ana
2

Isla Ángel de la Guarda
Punta Prieta
Isla Cedros
Bahía de Sebastián Vizcaíno
Isla Tiburón
SONORA
Hermosillo
15
16

Guerrero Negro
Scammon's Lagoon
Península de Vizcaíno
DESIERTO DE VIZCAÍNO
San Ignacio Lagoon
Santa Rosalía
Mulegé
BAJA CALIFORNIA SUR
Bahía Concepción
Guaymas
Ciudad Obregon
15
1
1

PACIFIC OCEAN
Las Barrancas
Loreto
Isla Del Carmen
Los Mochis
Gulf
of
California
Puerto Adolfo López Mateos
Ciudad Insurgentes
Ciudad Constitución
Puerto San Carlos
Bahía Magdalena
Isla Santa Margarita
Isla San José
1
Isla Espíritu Santo
Sea of Cortez
La Paz
Las Cruces

Airport ✈
Ferry ⛴

0   50 mi
0   50 km

Todos Santos
19
1
La Rivera
Cabo San Lucas
San José del Cabo

Car Ferry to Mazatlán →

(Tips **The Best Websites for Los Cabos & Baja**

- All About Cabo: www.allaboutcabo.com
- Baja Quest: www.bajaquest.com
- Baja Insider: www.bajainsider.com
- Visit Los Cabos: www.visitloscabos.org

bay in his luxury yacht. Somewhere in between are the fun-loving aunts and uncles who've come to fish for marlin and/or for a peep at Sammy Hagar.

On the other hand, San José del Cabo, on the eastern side of Baja's tip, is a decidedly more "Mexican" experience. Colorful 18th century homes-turned-artisan shops, vibrant flowering trees, world-class waves, and exquisite restaurants draw well-tanned West Coast surfers; jolly snowbirds in search of sun and margaritas; celebrities and executives looking for respite from the rat race; and couples and families who wake up early to walk on the beach, go for a swim, take a tour, and spend the afternoon relaxing before enjoying a nice dinner on the town. The tree-lined streets of the downtown area are particularly enchanting, and the melodies of Ranchero or Banda music float from century-old homes still inhabited after generations.

Baja can seem like one of the least crowded corners of Mexico. **Todos Santos,** an artistic community on the Pacific side of the coastal curve (one hour north of the tip), and Baja's **East Cape,** draw travelers who find that Los Cabos has outgrown them. **La Paz,** capital of Baja Sur, remains an easygoing maritime port skirted by white-sand beaches and a smattering of islands worth exploring.

MID BAJA   Among the highlights of the mid-Baja region are the east-coast towns of **Loreto, Bahía Magdalena, Mulegé,** and **Santa Rosalía.** These towns have a much richer cultural heritage than those in Baja Sur. Although Loreto is experiencing growth—driven by a real estate project just outside of town—the remaining east coast towns have all but escaped the tourism boom experienced by the two Cabos.

These mid-Baja towns were the center of the 18th-century Jesuit mission movement. Today, they attract travelers who are drawn to Baja's wild natural beauty but find the popularity of Los Cabos a bit overwhelming. This area's natural attractions have made it a center for sea kayaking, sportfishing, diving, and hiking—including excursions to view indigenous cave paintings.

This also is the area to visit if you're interested in whale-watching; many tour companies operate out of Loreto and the smaller neighboring towns (see "Whale-watching in Baja," later in this chapter).

BAJA NORTE   **Tijuana** has the dubious distinction of being the most visited and perhaps most misunderstood town in all of Mexico. New cultural and sporting attractions, extensive shopping, and strong business growth—of the reputable kind—are brightening Tijuana's image.

Tranquil **Rosarito Beach** also has reemerged as a resort town; it got a boost after the movies *Titanic* and *Master and Commander* were filmed there, and Fox Studios converted the former set into a film-themed amusement park. Farther south on the Pacific Coast is the lovely port town of **Ensenada,** also known for its surfing and sportfishing. Tours of nearby inland vineyards (Mexico's wine country) are growing in popularity.

1 Los Cabos: Resorts, Watersports & Golf ⋆⋆⋆

The two towns at the southern tip of the rugged Baja Peninsula are grouped together as Los Cabos, although they couldn't be more different. San José del Cabo and Cabo San Lucas are separated not just by 33km (21 miles), but also by distinct attitudes and ways of life. Where Cabo San Lucas mirrors a spirited version of the Los Angeles lifestyle, San José del Cabo remains a traditional, tranquil Mexican small town, although recent gentrification is turning it into the more sophisticated of the two resorts.

The golden days of Los Cabos began when silver-screen greats such as Bing Crosby, John Wayne, and Ava Gardner ventured south in the 1950s. Sportfishing was the first draw, but the transfixing landscape, rich waters, and nearly flawless climate quickly gained the favor of other explorers. The only way to get to the soon-to-be "marlin capital of the world" was by boat or private airplane. As such, Los Cabos was born of exclusivity and extravagance. Fishing remains a lure today, although golf may have overtaken it as the principal attraction. By the early 1980s, the Mexican government realized the growth potential of Los Cabos and invested in new highways, airport facilities, golf courses, and marine facilities. The increase in air access and the opening of Transpeninsular Highway 1 (in 1973) paved the way for spectacular growth.

Today, Los Cabos is not just about marlin and the links. The destination has become a hub for surfing, hiking, diving, whale-watching, sea kayaking, and even spa going. And there's always an isolated, wild beach on which to picnic, camp, or simply watch the tide come in.

The road that connects Cabo San Lucas and San José del Cabo is the centerpiece of resort growth. Known as the "Tourist Corridor," or simply "the Corridor," this four-lane stretch offers cliff-top vistas and an easy ride between the towns, but still has no nighttime lighting and bears too many roadside memorials to count—fair warning that cautious driving is imperative, especially at night. The area's deluxe resorts and renowned golf courses are here, along with a collection of dramatic beaches and coves. The view is especially outstanding in January and February, when gray whales often spout close to shore.

The Los Cabos area is more expensive than other Mexican resorts because luxury is the norm among local hotels, and real estate prices make the San Diego market seem tame. However, a new boon in all-inclusive resorts and off-season travel deals is making Los Cabos vacations more affordable.

You should consider renting a car, even if only for a day or two, because there's too much to see to spend an hour waiting at the bus stop or hundreds of dollars on expensive taxis. For those who like the freedom to explore on their own terms, a rental car is essential, not to mention economical. And to best understand Los Cabos, both capes need your attention.

Because of the distinctive character and attractions of each of the Cabos, they are treated separately here. It is common to stay in one—or in the Corridor between—and make day trips to the other.

SAN JOSE DEL CABO

180km (112 miles) SE of La Paz; 33km (21 miles) NE of Cabo San Lucas; 1,760km (1,091 miles) SE of Tijuana

San José del Cabo, with its pastel cottages and narrow streets lined with flowering trees, retains the air of a provincial Mexican town. The main square, adorned with a wrought-iron bandstand and shaded benches, faces the cathedral, which was built on the site of an early mission. San José is becoming increasingly sophisticated, with a collection of noteworthy cafes, art galleries, interesting shops, and intriguing inns adding a newly refined flavor to the downtown area. This is the best choice for those who want to enjoy the paradoxical landscape but still be aware that they're in Mexico.

ESSENTIALS
Getting There & Departing

By Plane   **AeroMéxico** (© 800/237-6639 in the U.S., 01-800/021-4000 in Mexico, or 624/146-5098 or -5097; www.aeromexico.com), flies nonstop from San Diego and Ontario and has connecting flights from other cities; **American Airlines** (© 800/223-5436 in the U.S., or 624/146-5300 or -5309; www.aa.com) flies from Dallas/Ft. Worth, Los Angeles, Chicago, and New York; **US Airways/America West** (© 800/235-9292 in the U.S., or 624/146-5380; www.usairways.com) operates nonstop flights from Phoenix, Las Vegas, Oakland, and San Diego; **Alaska Airlines** (© 800/252-7522 in the U.S., or 624/146-5100 or -5101; www.alaskaair.com) flies from Los Angeles, Portland, San Diego, Seattle, and San Francisco; **Continental** (© 800/537-9222 in the U.S., or 624/146-5040 or -5080; www.continental.com) flies nonstop from Houston and Newark; **Delta** (© 800/241-4141 in the U.S. or 624/146-5003; www.delta.com) has flights from Atlanta, Cincinnati, New York, and Salt Lake City; **Frontier** (© 800/432-1359 in the U.S. or 624/146-5421; www.frontierairlines.com) has nonstop service from Denver, Kansas City, Los Angeles, Sacramento, and San José; **Mexicana** (© 800/531-7921 in the U.S., or 624/146-5001 or 143-5352; www.mexicana.com) has direct or connecting flights from Guadalajara, Las Vegas, Los Angeles, Sacramento, and Mexico City; **United Airlines** (© 800/538-2929 in the U.S., or 624/146-5433; www.united.com) flies nonstop from Chicago, San Francisco, and Denver; **Aereo Calafia** (© 624/143-4302; www.Aereocalafia.com) offers regular flights within Baja as well as from Mazatlán and Puerto Vallarta.

By Car   From San Diego, drive south on Highway 1—as night driving is not recommended, the drive takes about two and a half days. From La Paz, take Highway 1 south; the drive takes 3 to 4 hours. Or take Highway 1 south just past the village of San Pedro, then take Highway 19 south (a less winding road) through Todos Santos to Cabo San Lucas, where you pick up Highway 1 east to San José del Cabo. From Cabo San Lucas, it's a half-hour drive to San José.

By Bus   The **Terminal de Autobuses (bus station),** on Valerio Gonzalez, a block east of Highway 1 (© 624/142-1100), is open daily from 5:30am to 8pm.

Orientation

ARRIVING   Los Cabos International **Airport** (© 624/146-5111) serves both Cabos and the Corridor in between. San José is 13km (8 miles) from the airport and Cabo San Lucas is a 48km (30 miles) drive. As Los Cabos grows in popularity, the number of flights coming into the destination has increased steadily each year—from 18,963 flights in 2005 to 20,898 in 2006—justifying continuous construction and two separate terminals. Be sure to request the correct terminal when you head home. Upon arriving, pass customs and baggage claim, and turn right once you exit the sliding doors. Ask for the shuttle desk while breezing past the timeshare booths that hawk free amenities in exchange for attending their sales pitch presentation. You'll have plenty of encounters with timeshare salespeople—especially in Cabo San Lucas—so feel free to head straight for a taxi or shuttle if you want to get to the beach in a hurry. At about $10 to $17 (£5.50–£9.35) per person, depending on the location of your hotel, shuttles are the most economic transportation option, and **Josefinos** (© 624/146-5354) is located in the airport. A private van for up to five passengers is $70

San José del Cabo

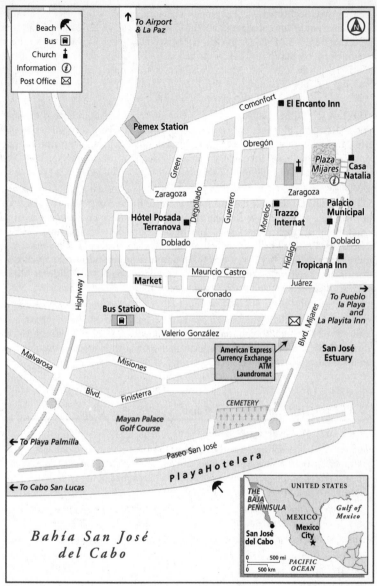

Key:
- Beach
- Bus
- Church
- Information
- Post Office

Comonfort · El Encanto Inn

Pemex Station

Obregón

Green

Plaza Mijares · Casa Natalia

Degollado

Zaragoza

Zaragoza

Guerrero

Morelos

Palacio Municipal

Hótel Posada Terranova

Trazzo Internat

Doblado

Doblado

Mauricio Castro

Hidalgo

Tropicana Inn

Highway 1

Market

Coronado

Juárez

Bus Station

To Pueblo la Playa and La Playita Inn

Valerio González

American Express Currency Exchange ATM Laundromat

Blvd. Mijares

San José Estuary

Malvarosa

Misiones

Blvd.

Finisterra

CEMETERY

Mayan Palace Golf Course

Paseo San José

← To Playa Palmilla

p l a y a H o t e l e r a

← To Cabo San Lucas

Bahía San José del Cabo

UNITED STATES

THE BAJA PENINSULA

MEXICO · Gulf of Mexico

San José del Cabo

Mexico City ★

0 500 mi
0 500 km

PACIFIC OCEAN

(£39) and may be able to whisk away your large group more quickly than a regular shuttle. Taxis charge about $20 to San José and upwards of $35 (£19) to San Lucas.

For those who like their freedom, it's helpful to have a car in Los Cabos, and rental is very affordable when booked online in advance. However, the major car-rental agencies all have counters at the airport, open during flight arrivals for last-minute booking. **Avis** (© **800/331-1212** in the U.S., or 624/146-0201; www.avis.com) is open daily 7am to 9pm; **Budget** (© **800/527-0700** in the U.S., 624/146-5333 at the airport, or 624/143-4190 in Cabo San Lucas; www.budget.com) is open daily 8am to 10pm; **Hertz** (© **800/654-3131** in the U.S., 624/146-1803 in San José del Cabo, or 624/105-1428 in Cabo San Lucas; www.hertz.com) is open daily 8am to 8pm; and **National** (© **800/328-4567** in the U.S., 624/146-5022 at the airport, or 624/142-2424 in San José del Cabo; www.nationalcar.com) is open daily 8am to 8pm.

VISITOR INFORMATION San José's city tourist information office (©/fax **624/142-3310** or -9628) is in the old post office building on Zaragoza at Mijares. It offers maps, free local publications, and other basic information about the area. It's open Monday through Friday from 8:30am to 3pm. Prior to arrival, contact the **Los Cabos Tourism Board** (© **866/567-2226** in the U.S., or 624/143-4777; www.visitlos cabos.org).

CITY LAYOUT San José del Cabo sprawls from the airport halfway to San Lucas, but two main areas are most enticing to visitors: **downtown,** or *el centro,* has restaurants, shopping, sophisticated inns, and traditional budget hotels, while the **hotel zone** is lined with all-inclusive resorts along the beach. **Zaragoza** is the main street leading from the highway into town; **Paseo San José** runs parallel to the beach and is the principal boulevard of the hotel zone. The 1.6km-long (1 mile) **Bulevar Mijares** connects the two areas, and is the center of most tourist activity in San José.

GETTING AROUND There is no local bus service between downtown and the beach, but it's about a 30-minute walk from the center of downtown to the sand, and **taxis** (© **624/142-0580**) connect the two for about $5 (£2.75) each way. For day trips to **Cabo San Lucas,** ask your concierge if your hotel has a daily shuttle or just catch a **bus** (see "Getting There & Departing," above) or a cab.

FAST FACTS: San José del Cabo

Area Code The local telephone area code is **624**.

Banks Banks exchange currency during business hours, which are generally Monday through Friday from 8:30am to 6pm, and Saturday from 10am to 2pm. There are several major banks with ATMs on Zaragoza between Morelos and Degollado and in the downtown.

Drugstores **Farmacía ISSSTE,** Carretera Transpeninsular Km 34, Plaza California, Loc. 7 (© **624/142-2645**), is open daily from 8am to 8pm.

Emergencies Dial © **066,** or the local police number at City Hall: © **624/142-0361.**

Hospital **Hospital General** is at Retorno Atunero s/n, Col. Chamizal (© **624/142-0013**).

Internet Access **Trazzo Internet,** on the corner of Zaragoza and Morelos, across from the cathedral downtown (© **624/142-0303;** fax 624/142-1220; www.trazzo digital.com) is open Monday through Friday 8am to 9pm, and Saturday from 9am to 7pm. They charge $2.50 (£1.40) for 30 minutes or less of high-speed access. They also have printing, copy, and fax services available.

Post Office The *correo,* Bulevar Mijares 1924, at Valerio Gonzalez (✆ **624/142-0911**), is open Monday through Friday from 8am to 6pm, Saturday from 9am to noon. For more substantial mailings, Mail Boxes Etc., Plaza Las Palmas Km 31 (✆ **624/142-4355**), is open Monday through Friday from 8:30am to 5:30pm and Saturday from 9am to noon.

OUTDOOR ACTIVITIES: BEACHES, SPORTS & MORE

Although the water activities hub is on Cabo San Lucas's Medano Beach, San José is tops for outdoor adventure, and its relaxed pace also makes it an ideal place to unwind in the sand. From quiet coves to advanced surf breaks and untouched beaches to a living estuary, San José has relaxation and adventure by land and by sea.

ADVENTURE TOURS **Tío Sports** (✆ **624/143-3399;** www.tiosports.com) arranges a variety of land- and water-based adventure and nature tours, including popular ATV tours to La Candelaria; parasailing; and kayak, catamaran, snorkeling, and diving trips. The website gives current prices. **Baja Wild** (✆ **624/172-6300;** www.bajawild.com) is ideal for a wide range of adventure, as they offer every excursion imaginable in Los Cabos from rock climbing to kayaking, hiking to rappelling, and more. **Baja Outback** (✆ **624/142-9215;** www.bajaoutback.com) provides single- and multiday adventure tours throughout Southern Baja. Armed with a naturalist guide and an expedition guide, who provide information and offer driving instruction over the two-way radios that connect each Hummer in the caravan, you take the wheel of your own H2 Hummer and discover mountain, desert, and sea.

BEACHES The best beach safe for swimming is **Palmilla Beach** ★★★, which fronts the glitzy One&Only Palmilla resort 8km (5 miles) west of San José. With its rocky coves, soft sand, and visible sea life, this beach has been home to fishermen for centuries and is the preeminent picnic destination for Mexican families on Sunday afternoons. Past the rock formations, the beach curves east and the culminating swim is well worth the pebble-strewn stroll. Locals agree there's just something about the water on the other side of the rocks. Perfect for swimming, the water in Palmilla Bay has a sort of magic unlike anywhere else and, when you emerge, you'll feel it for yourself. To reach Playa Palmilla, enter the lush Palmilla community at Km 27.5 on the highway, take the road toward the beach, and then take the fork to the left (without entering the hotel grounds) and park in the lot.

Estero San José, a natural freshwater estuary on which the ancient Pericúe Indians built their civilization centuries ago, has at least 270 species of birds and is on the east

Tips Swimming Safety

Although this area is ideal for watersports, occasional strong currents and undertows can make swimming dangerous at most **beaches in San José, the Tourist Corridor,** and **Cabo San Lucas.** Check conditions before entering the surf. Swimming is generally safe at **Palmilla Beach** (see "Beaches," above), though it, too, can be rough. The safest area beach for swimming is **Medano Beach** in Cabo San Lucas.

end of the hotel zone. The estuary is a protected ecological reserve and merits a sunset beach walk from the Hotel Presidente InterContinental to the river mouth where the spring-fed estuary meets the Sea of Cortez.

For a list of other nearby beaches worth exploring if you have a rental car, see "Outdoor Activities: Fishing, Golf & More," under "Cabo San Lucas," later in this chapter.

FISHING   The least expensive way to enjoy deep-sea fishing is to pair up with another angler and charter a *panga,* a 7m (23-ft.) skiff used by local fishermen, from Pueblo la Playa, the beach near the new Puerto Los Cabos Marina. Several *panga* fleets offer 6-hour sportfishing trips, usually from 6am to noon, for $200 to $500 (£110—£275). Two or three people can split the cost. For information, visit the fishermen's cooperative in Pueblo la Playa (no phone) or contact **Gordo Banks Pangas** (© **624/142-1147;** www.gordobanks.com). For larger charter boats, you'll depart from the marina in Cabo San Lucas (see "Outdoor Activities: Fishing, Golf & More," under "Cabo San Lucas," later in this chapter).

GOLF   Los Cabos has become Latin America's leading golf destination, with a collection of top signature courses and others under construction. The lowest greens fees in the area are at the 9-hole **Mayan Palace Golf Los Cabos,** Paseo Finisterra 1 (© **624/142-0900** or -0901), which is the first right turn east of the yellow Fonatur statue in the highway roundabout. See p. 716 for fees.

HORSEBACK RIDING   Horses can be rented near the Presidente InterContinental, Fiesta Inn, and in the Costa Azul Canyon for $15 to $20 (£8.25–£11) per hour. Most people choose to ride on the beach, but a trip up the arroyo also could prove scenic. For a more organized riding experience—English or Western—there's **Cuadra San Francisco Equestrian Center,** Km 19.5, along the Corridor, in front of the Casa del Mar resort (© **624/144-0160;** www.loscaboshorses.com). Owned by master horseman Francisco Barrena, his more than 30 years of experience in training horses and operating equestrian schools will comfort any level rider, as will his expertise in selecting and fitting a horse to riders' skill levels. A 2-hour canyon ride in and around Arroyo San Carlos or Venado Blanco costs $85 (£47); a 1-hour ride to the beach or desert is $40 (£22). Private tours go for $55 (£30) per hour and equestrian aficionados may schedule a dressage class for $80 (£44).

SEA KAYAKING   Fully guided, ecologically oriented **ocean kayak tours** are available through **Ramon's Ecotours** (© **624/122-3696;** www.ramonsecotours.com), **Cabo Expeditions** (© **624/143-2700**), and **Cabo Acuadeportes** (© **624/143-0117;** www.allaboutcabo.com/cabosanlucaswatersports.htm). Most ocean kayaking tours depart from Cabo San Lucas, curve around the bay toward the Arch, and break for snorkeling at Lover's Beach.

SNORKELING & DIVING   **Manta** (© **624/144-3871;** www.caboscuba.com) and **Amigos del Mar** in Cabo San Lucas (© **800/344-3349** in the U.S., or 624/143-0505; www.amigosdelmar.com) are two of the most reputable dive operations in Los Cabos. Manta offers everything from advanced dive trips to PADI open water diver certification. Prices start at $50 (£28) for a one-tank dive and at $150 (£83) for 2 days of diving. Night dives are $65 per person. The 4-day PADI certification course, which certifies you to scuba dive anywhere in the world, costs $430 (£237). Among the area's best dive sites are **Gordo Banks** and **Cabo Pulmo.** Gordo Banks is an advanced dive site where you can see whale sharks and hammerhead sharks. It's a deep dive—27 to 30m (90–98 ft.)—with limited visibility (9–12m/30–40 ft.). Most dives are drift dives, and wetsuits are highly recommended. Cabo Pulmo, a protected marine park 72km (45 miles) northeast of San José, has seven sites geared for divers of all experience levels, plus some of the most beautiful stretches of Baja beach, so it never feels crowded. **Cabo Pulmo Beach Resort** (© **888/997-8566** in the U.S., or 624/141-0244; www.cabopulmo.com) offers charming rental bungalows to call home in between dives or long walks on the beach.

SURFING 🥾🥾   Surfing is becoming one of the hottest trends in the entire destination, drawing land-locked Midwesterners and SoCal surf aficionados alike to the wide range of waves at Baja's tip. **Playa Costa Azul,** at Km 29, on Highway 1 just south of San José, has the most popular surfing beaches in the area. The **Costa Azul Surf Shop,** Km 28, Playa Costa Azul (© **624/142-2771;** www.costa-azul.com.mx), offers surfing lessons, surfboard and snorkeling equipment rentals, and specialized surf excursions to any of the 15 local breaks. Excursions include transportation and a DVD video of the day, and owner Alejandro Olea handcrafts all rental boards. Just $20 (£11) per day will get you a board, leash, shade umbrella, beach chair, and rack for your rental car. One-hour lessons are $55 (£30), and other special packages are available. **Cabo Surf Hotel** (© **624/172-6188;** www.cabosurfhotel.com) also offers surf lessons and daily board rentals for $35 (£19).

The surf switches sides with the seasons, so the waves break on the eastern side of the peninsula in the spring and summer (Mar–Oct) and the Pacific plays host to surfers in the fall and winter (Nov–Mar). The most popular summer breaks start at Acapulquito and extend up the East Cape, while the hot spot for winter waves is Los Cerritos Beach, south of Todos Santos. As every break has its secret—from rocks covered in sea urchins to territorial locals—your best bet is to hook up with a reputable surf shop or guide to take you to the break that's right for you.

TENNIS   Tennis is available at many resorts throughout Los Cabos, but if you're staying somewhere tennis isn't available, the two courts at the **Mayan Palace Resort Golf Los Cabos,** Paseo Finisterra 1 (© **624/142-0905**), rent for $14 (£7.70) an hour during the day, $28 (£15) an hour at night. Call the club to reserve. Club guests also can use the swimming pool.

WHALE-WATCHING   From January through March, migrating gray and humpback whales visit Los Cabos to breed and bear their calves, creating one of Baja's most impressive spectacles. Practically every local tour company advertises whale-watching tours that range from an hour to a half-day. Options include Zodiac-style rafts, sportfishing boats, glass-bottom boats, and cruise catamarans, all of which depart from the Cabo San Lucas Marina and cost $35 to $50 (£19–£28), depending on the type of boat and whether the trip includes snacks and beverages. The ultimate whale excursion is a trip to **Magdalena Bay. BookCabo.com** (© **624/142-9200;** www.bookcabo.com) offers luxury bus tours from San José to San Carlos, where lobster dinners await in your 2-night stay at the quaint Alcatraz Hotel. The next morning entails cruising around the bay observing the whales and, hours later, lunching on Margarita Island. The cost is $227 per person (£125) based on double occupancy and $126 (£69) for kids 3 to 10 years old. Flying tours on Baja-based airline, **Aereo Calafia** (© **624/143-4302;** www.Aereocalafia.com), fly from San Lucas—a 75-minute flight—to Magdalena, where you board a *panga* and spend 3 hours watching gray whales and humpbacks loll around the coastal lagoons before returning the same day. This tour is $420 (£231), including air transportation, the tour, and lunch. You also can spot whales from the shore in Los Cabos; good spots include the beach by the Westin Resort & Spa; at Esperanza Resort in the Punta Ballena community, and along the beaches and cliffs of the Corridor.

SHOPPING

San José is the two capes' seat of artisan finery, design boutiques, and hip art galleries. They cluster around **Bulevar Mijares** and **Zaragoza.** Start in the main plaza and head northwest toward the historic gallery district for a peek at the paintings and sculptures of Pez Gordo Gallery, the Fine Art Annex, Old Towne Gallery, and Galería de Ida Victoria. Head any other direction from the main plaza for boutiques specializing in crafts. The following businesses accept credit cards (American Express, MasterCard, and Visa).

Las Tiendas de Palmilla   The ultimate in luxury, style, and home design can be found in San José's opulent shopping center, located on the grounds of the One&Only Palmilla Resort. Among other shops, **Casa Vieja** sells fine linen dresses and Pineda Covalín silk scarves, **Cabana** sells chic women's clothing and resort wear, **Tiki Lounge** is the local Tommy Bahama outpost, **Q Boutique** houses Diamonds International's connoisseur collection, and the Guadalajara-headquartered **Antigua de México** sells furniture from the state of Jalisco. Store hours vary. Km. 27.5 Carretera Transpeninsular. www.lastiendasdepalmilla.com.

Los Amigos Smokeshop and Cigar Bar   For fine Cuban cigars and cigarettes, a visit here is a must. They sell not only high quality cigars, but also a whole range of smoking accessories. Also available is a bar with an excellent selection of single malts and California wines. Open Monday through Wednesday 9am to 8pm; Thursday through Saturday from 9am to 1pm. At the intersection of Doblado and Morelos, across from the French Riviera bakery. ℂ 624/142-1138.

Mejicanissmo   This shop sells everything from locally made soaps and Damiana tea to embroidered linens and exquisite Emilia Castillo sterling-silver-embedded porcelain. The luminous owner, Magdalena del Río, supplies most of the area's luxury resorts with their fine Oaxacan embroidery, often used for tablecloths and throw pillows. Right across from the plaza, it can't be missed. Open Monday through Saturday from 10am to 9pm. Zaragoza, across from the cathedral. ℂ 624/142-3090.

Necri 🖈   This shop sells the finest in Talavera ceramics and pewter accessories. Shipping is available. Open Monday through Saturday from 9am to 9pm. Zaragoza at Hidalgo, fronting the giant fig tree in the plaza. ℂ 624/142-2777.

SAX   For unusual and well-priced jewelry, visit this small shop where two local designers (who also happen to be sisters) create one-of-a-kind pieces using silver, coral, and semiprecious stones. They'll even create a special request design for you, and have it ready in 24 hours. Open Monday through Saturday from 10am to 9pm, closed Sunday. On Mijares next to Casa Natalia. ℂ 624/142-0704.

WHERE TO STAY

There's more demand than supply in Baja Sur—especially during the idyllic winter months—so prices tend to be higher than those for equivalent accommodations in other parts of Mexico. It's best to call ahead for reservations. Properties in the beachside hotel zone often offer package deals that bring room rates down to the moderate range, especially during summer months. Check with your travel agent. High season generally denotes December through April and low season is from May through

November. Rates listed below do not include tax, which is 15%, and most resorts in Los Cabos offer free parking, although that, too, is changing.

Expensive

Casa Natalia ⭐⭐⭐ *(Finds)*   This acclaimed boutique hotel is exquisite. Owners Nathalie and Loic have transformed a former residence into a beautiful amalgam of palms, waterfalls, and flowers. The inn is a completely renovated historic home that combines modern architecture with traditional Mexican touches. All rooms have sliding glass doors that open onto small private terraces or balconies with hammocks and chairs, shaded by bougainvillea and bamboo. Rooms are equipped with CD and DVD players, along with a small collection of DVDs. The two spa suites each have a private terrace with a whirlpool and hammock. Tall California palms surround a small courtyard pool, and the terraces face onto it. Casa Natalia offers its guests privacy, style, and romance. It's in the heart of downtown San José, just off the central plaza, and the restaurant, **Mi Cocina** (reviewed in "Where to Dine," below), is often visitors' favorite dining experience of an entire trip.

Bulevar Mijares 4, 23400 San José del Cabo, B.C.S. (C) **888/277-3814** in the U.S., 866/826-1170 in Canada, or 624/142-5100. Fax 624/142-5110. www.casanatalia.com. 20 units. High season $295 (£162) double, $475 (£261) spa suite; low season $220 (£121) double, $350 (£193) spa suite. AE, MC, V. Children younger than 14 not accepted. Free parking. **Amenities:** Gourmet restaurant; bar; heated outdoor pool w/waterfall and swim-up bar; access and transportation to private beach club; concierge; room service; in-room spa services; laundry service. *In room:* A/C, TV/DVD, high-speed Internet, hair dryer, safe, fan.

Moderate

El Encanto Inn ⭐ *(Value)*   On a quiet street in the historic downtown district, this charming inn borders a grassy courtyard with a fountain and small pool. It offers a relaxing alternative to busy hotels, as well as excellent value. Rooms are decorated with rustic wood and contemporary iron furniture. Nice-size bathrooms have colorful tile accents. Rooms have two double beds, while suites have king-size beds and a sitting room. A pool area with a *palapa* bar and 14 impeccable poolside suites were recently added. These newer suites have minibars and other extras, while all rooms offer DirecTV satellite. The owners, Cliff and Blanca (a lifelong resident of San José), can help arrange fishing packages and golf and diving outings. The inn is a half-block from the church.

Morelos 133 (between Obregón and Comonfort), 23400 San José del Cabo, B.C.S. (C) **210/858-6649** or 624/142-0388. www.elencantoinn.com. 26 units. $75 (£41) double; $105–$175 (£58–£96) suite. MC, V. Limited street parking available. **Amenities:** Restaurant, small outdoor pool; *palapa* bar; spa. *In room:* A/C, TV, coffeemaker, fan.

La Playita Hotel   Removed from even the slow pace of San José, this courtyard hotel is older yet impeccably clean and friendly, and it's ideal for fishermen and those looking for something different from a traditional resort vacation. As it's smack in the middle of the Puerto Los Cabos master-planned community, it's not the quiet getaway it once was. However, it's the only hotel on the only beach in San José that's considered safe for swimming. Just steps from the water and the lineup of fishing *pangas*, the two stories of sunlit rooms frame a patio with a pool just large enough to allow you to swim laps. Each room is spacious, with high-quality basic furnishings, screened windows, a nicely tiled bathroom, and cable TV. Two large suites on the second floor have full kitchens. Next door, the hotel's La Playita Grill will serve breakfast and Bloody Marys from 7am until noon, and Tommy's Barefoot Bar, open daily from noon to 9pm, offers a great mix of seafood and standard favorites, plus occasional live jazz or tropical music.

Pueblo la Playa, Apdo. Postal 437, 23400 San José del Cabo, B.C.S. ⓒ/fax **624/142-4166.** www.laplayitahotel.com. 26 units. $69 (£38) for a double and $99–$159 (£54–£87) suite. MC, V. Free parking. From Bulevar Mijares, follow sign pointing to Pueblo la Playa (dirt road) for about 3km (2 miles); hotel is on the left. **Amenities:** Restaurant; outdoor pool; kayak rental. *In room:* A/C, TV.

Tropicana Inn ✦ This hacienda-style hotel, a longstanding favorite in San José, welcomes many repeat visitors. Just behind the Tropicana Bar and Grill, it frames a plant-filled courtyard with a graceful arcade bordering the rooms and inviting swimming pool. Each nicely furnished, medium-size room in the L-shaped building (which has a two- and a three-story wing) has tile floors, two double beds, a window looking out on the courtyard, and a brightly tiled bathroom with shower. Each morning, freshly brewed coffee, delicious sweet rolls, and fresh fruit are set out for hotel guests. There's room service until 10pm from the adjacent Tropicana Bar and Grill (owned by the hotel).

Bulevar Mijares 30 (1 block south of the town square), 23400 San José del Cabo, B.C.S. ⓒ **624/142-0907** or -1580. Fax 624/142-1590. 38 units. High season $79 (£43) double; low season 10% less. Rates include continental breakfast. AE, MC, V. Free limited parking. **Amenities:** Restaurant/bar; small outdoor pool; tour desk; room service; laundry service. *In room:* A/C, TV, minibar, coffeemaker.

Inexpensive
Hotel Posada Terranova This small family-owned hotel is so famous for its traditional Mexican breakfasts and charming outdoor dining terrace that locals often forget it's even a hotel. However, while local Mexicans and expats love it for weekend brunch, the budget traveler will love it for its spare decor, clean rooms, soft sheets, ideal location in the center of downtown San José and, yes, for its huevos rancheros and fresh-squeezed OJ in the morning.

Degollado, between Doblado and Zaragoza, 23400 San José del Cabo, B.C.S. ⓒ **624/142-0534.** Fax 624/142-0902. www.hterranova.com.mx. 25 units. $60 (£33) single and double. Seasonal rates available. Rates include continental breakfast. MC, V. Free parking. **Amenities:** Restaurant, bar, room service. *In room:* Satellite TV, A/C, fan, no phone.

WHERE TO DINE
Expensive
Baan Thai ✦✦ *Finds* PAN-ASIAN Asian food is hard to come by in Los Cabos, and Baan Thai—set in one of San José's lovely historic buildings—does an impressive job of innovating these flavors to blend in a hint of Mexico. Move beyond such traditional starters as spring rolls or satay to one of Baan Thai's more unique offerings, such as blue crab stir fried with chile, garlic, and tomatoes, or mild chiles stuffed with smoked marlin and served with a soy-ginger dipping sauce. From there, move on to entrees such as wok-tossed salmon; steamed Baja mussels in a coconut herb broth, or seared steak tossed with mangos, green apples, and chiles. An impressive wine list and full bar service are available to complement your meal. Dine outdoors on the exotic garden patio or take a seat in the air-conditioned indoor dining room.

Morelos s/n, 1 block behind the church and plaza. ⓒ **624/142-3344.** Reservations recommended. Main courses $8–$21 (£4.40–£12). MC, V. Mon–Sat noon–10:30pm.

Don Emiliano ✦✦✦ *Finds* MEXICAN If years of queso dip and fried chimichangas have framed your vision of Mexican food, be prepared for your world to come crashing delightfully down. Sparkling seasonal menus rooted in such Mexican traditions as Day of the Dead and Independence Day bring rare *mole* sauces and stuffed chiles drenched in walnut cream sauce and pomegranate seeds *(chile en nogada)*, while traditional staples such as flavored tamales and grilled farm cheese atop roasted tomatillo salsa grace the menu on a regular basis. An extensive Mexican and imported wine list and ample supply of fresh-mint mojitos paired with the warmth of the staff and perfect portions ensure a festive evening that will change the way you view Mexican food. For nearly a decade, Chef Margarita C. de Salinas has been the official gala chef for the Mexican government, which means she travels the world preparing gourmet Mexican fare for heads of state while her son, Angel, holds down the fort with such graciousness and culinary precision it must be a secret family recipe. Try the tasting menu or create your own, but whatever you do, don't miss the locally made *queso corazón* (a local cow's milk cheese) to start.

Bulevar Mijares 27, downtown San José. ℂ **624/142-0266.** www.donemiliano.com.mx. Reservations recommended. Main courses $18–$25 (£9.90–£14). AE, MC, V. Daily 6–10pm.

Mi Cocina ✿✿✿ NOUVELLE MEXICAN/EURO   Widely appreciated as one of Los Cabos' finest restaurants, Mi Cocina doesn't rely solely on the romance of its setting—the food is superb, creative, and consistently flavorful. Notable starters include steamed baby clams topped with a creamy cilantro sauce and served with garlic croutons, or a healthy slice of Camembert cheese, fried and served with homemade toast and grapes. Among the favorite main courses are the baked baby rack of lamb served with grilled vegetables, and the Provençal-style shrimp served with risotto, roasted tomato, basil, and cilantro-fish consommé. Save room for dessert; choices include their famous chocolate-chocolate cake and a perfect crème brûlée. The full-service *palapa* bar offers an excellent selection of wines, premium tequilas, and single-malt scotches. Be adventurous and try one of their special martinis—like the Flor de México, an adaptation of the Cosmo, using Jamaica (hibiscus flower infusion) rather than cranberry juice.

In the Casa Natalia hotel, Bulevar Mijares. ℂ **624/142-5100.** www.casanatalia.com/dining.cfm. Reservations recommended. Main courses $15–$32 (£8.25–£18). AE, MC, V. Daily 6:30am–10pm (hotel guests only 6:30am–6pm).

Tequila Restaurant ✿ MEDITERRANEAN/ASIAN   Contemporary fusion cuisine with a light and flavorful touch is the star attraction here, although the garden setting is lovely, with rustic *equipal* furniture and lanterns scattered among palms and mango trees. Organic produce and good greens are hard to find in these parts, so Tequila's homegrown produce, harvested from owner Enrique Silva's ranch, is a welcome dose of light-and-fresh fare that accompanies almost every entree. Try the shrimp risotto or beef tenderloin in rosemary-cabernet sauce. Other enjoyable options include perfectly seared tuna with cilantro and ginger and rack of lamb topped with tamarind sauce. The accompanying whole-grain bread arrives fresh and hot with a pesto-infused olive oil, and attentive service complements the fine meal. Cuban cigars and an excellent selection of tequilas are available, as is an extensive wine list emphasizing California vintages.

Manuel Doblado s/n, near Hidalgo. ℂ **624/142-1155** or -3753. www.tequilarestaurant.com. Reservations recommended. Lunch $9–$22 (£4.95–£12); dinner main courses $10–$45 (£5.50–£25). AE. Daily 5:30–10:30pm.

Moderate

French Riviera Restaurant & Bakery FRENCH/PASTRIES/COFFEE   This casual restaurant, in a classic historic building in San José, not only serves tempting French fare, but irresistible sweets. Its on-site bakery, with an exhibition window for watching the pastry chefs at work, results in smells so delectable, I dare you to leave without a sweet something. Start the day with a croissant and cappuccino, perk up your afternoon with a dark-chocolate-dipped macaroon, and ease into evening with a tastefully spiked coffee beverage. A second location in Cabo San Lucas offers a more traditional—yet stunning—restaurant setting on a bluff overlooking the Arch, with a great selection of wines and an excellent menu of French entrees. It's found in Plaza del Rey, next to the Misiones del Cabo entrance on the highway, Km 6, and it's open from noon until 11pm (© **624/104-3125**).

Corner of Hidalgo and Manuel Doblado s/n. © **624/142-3350**. www.frenchrivieraloscabos.com. Breakfast $4–$12 (£2.20–£6.60); dinner $7–$23 (£3.85–£13). MC, V. Daily 7:30am–11pm.

Tropicana Bar and Grill SEAFOOD/MEAT The Tropicana is a popular mainstay, especially for tourists. The lively restaurant and bar maintain a steady buzz day and night, rewarding guests with live nightly mariachi music and special sporting events on satellite TV. The dining area is in a courtyard pavilion with a tiled mural at one end. Cafe-style sidewalk dining is also available. The menu is too extensive to lay claim to any specialty; it aims to please everyone, but the appetizer sampler for two offers a well-done selection of traditional Mexican *botanas,* or appetizers, that are sure to please the table.

Bulevar Mijares 30, 1 block south of the Plaza Mijares. © **624/142-1580** or -0907. Breakfast $4–$6 (£2.20–£3.30); main courses $10–$25 (£5.50–£14). AE, MC, V. Daily 8am–midnight.

Zipper's 🎯🎯 MEXICAN/BEACHFRONT GRILL If cheeseburgers in paradise is your mission, Zipper's is the real deal. Located along the Corridor near San José del Cabo, surfers downing icy Pacíficos and fresh shrimp ceviche merge with fishermen bolting Sauza and fried-fish tacos. However, the not-so-humble cheeseburger is the star of Zipper's gringo-fabulous menu. Service is slow, so pass the time watching pelicans swoop the swells, catching rays in board shorts and bikinis, and blissing out to the Jimmy Buffet–laced Radio Margaritaville, which is Zipper's 24/7 soundtrack. You won't find dance contests and Jet Ski vendors here; located beneath a beachfront palapa that faces a surf break of the same name, Zipper's is a stripped-down sensory experience that rivals even the swankiest Los Cabos restaurant—at a slightly lesser price tag.

Km 28.5 on Transpeninsular Highway, in Playa Costa Azul, just south of San José. © **624/172-6162**. Cheeseburgers and sandwiches $8–$10 (£4.40–£5.50); main courses $13–$18 (£7.15–£9.90). No credit cards. Daily 11am–10:30pm.

Inexpensive

Las Guacamayas 🎯🎯🎯 *Finds* TACOS This off-the-beaten-path dive is home to the most delectable tacos in all of Los Cabos. If you can get over the plastic chairs, occasional wandering roosters, and low-hanging fruit trees in this packed-nightly courtyard, you'll be mesmerized by this meticulously operated gringo and Mexican hotspot. Traditionalists wisely go for the *tacos al pastor*—shaved pork tacos with onion, cilantro, and pineapple in a corn or flour tortilla, but the *quesadillas chilangas*—crispy fried tortillas stuffed with an assortment of fillings—are a blissful indulgence. Pace yourself. The addicting flavors and rock-bottom prices may inspire you to stay all night.

Driving east on Transpeninsular Hwy., turn left at the Pescador street sign. The street winds into the Chamizal neighborhood. Take your second left and look for the neon sign. Guacamayas is on the right-hand side. © **624/172-6162**. Tacos, stuffed potatoes, and more $1.50–$7 (85p–£3.85). No credit cards. Weekdays 6pm–midnight; 'til 4am Fri–Sat. Closed on Tues.

SAN JOSE AFTER DARK

The nightlife in San José may seem a bit more understated than its wild-nights counterpart in San Lucas, yet a new crop of swanky clubs, wine bars, and neighborhood hangouts, all pumped with electronic DJ music till 2 or 3am on the weekends, is offering a nighttime release for locals and San José visitors alike. Those intent on American music and bump-and-grind dance clubs will have better luck in San Lucas.

El Moro   Located in San José's gallery district in the old brick building formerly known as Rawhide, Pez Gordo Gallery owner, Dana Lieb, has opened this rustic bar for locals looking for a place to kick back and, well, drink. Obregón and Zaragoza,. No phone.

La Santa Wine Bar ⭐   This posh cavern of fine wine and comfortable lounge décor serves light food, desserts, and electronic music in San José's gallery district. Hidalgo and Obregón. ✆ **624/172-6767.**

O2 Restaurant, Dance Club and Oxygen Bar   The one place to dance to American hip-hop in San José is also the area's only public beach club. It's located right on the beach on the north side of the hotel zone. Take in a hit of pure oxygen before heading home. On the beach in Plaza Los Soles, behind Mega supermarket. No phone.

Red ⭐⭐   A sleek martini bar facing the hotel zone, this San Lucas spin-off also offers light meals, awesome wood-fired pizza, and DJ music. Paseo San José, adjacent to the roundabout behind Mega supermarket. No phone.

Tropicana   This bar features American sports events and live mariachi music nightly from 6 to 9pm, with live Mexican and Cuban dance music playing from 9:30pm until about 1am on weekends. Bulevar Mijares, ✆ **624/142-1580.**

THE CORRIDOR: BETWEEN THE TWO CABOS

The Corridor between the towns of San José del Cabo and Cabo San Lucas contains some of Mexico's most lavish resorts. Most growth at the tip of the peninsula is occurring along the Corridor, which already has become center stage for championship golf. The five major resort areas are **Palmilla, Querencia, Cabo Real, Cabo del Sol,** and **Punta Ballena** and each is an enclosed master-planned community sprinkled with multimillion-dollar homes (or the promise of them). All but Punta Ballena have championship golf and all but Querencia, which is a private residential community, have ultraluxury resorts within their gates. If you plan to explore the region while staying at a Corridor hotel, you'll need a rental car (available at the hotels) for at least 1 or 2 days. Even if you're not staying here, the beaches and dining options are worth investigating. All hotels listed here offer free parking and qualify as very expensive; quoted rates do not include tax, which is 12% in Baja, and some of the more luxurious resorts also add a 15% service charge to the tab to save guests from having to tip hotel staff. Most resorts offer golf and fishing packages.

WHERE TO STAY

Casa del Mar Beach Golf & Spa Resort ⭐ *Finds*   A little-known treasure, this intimate resort is one of the best values along the Corridor and its 2006 renovation makes it even better. The hacienda-style building offers luxury accommodations in an intimate setting, as well as an on-site spa and nearby golf facilities. It's convenient to the 18-hole championship Cabo Real, a Robert Trent Jones, Jr., golf course. Guest rooms have a bright feel, with white marble floors, light wicker furnishings, a separate sitting area, and a large whirlpool tub plus separate shower. Balconies have oversize chairs with a view of the ocean beyond the pool. It's a romantic hotel for couples and honeymooners; it's known for welcoming, personalized service.

Km 19.5 on Hwy. 1, Cabo San Lucas, B.C.S. ✆ **888/227-9621** in the U.S., or 624/144-0030 or 145-7700. Fax 624/144-0034. www.casadelmarmexico.com. 56 units. High season $470 (£259) double, $500 (£275) suite; low season $290 (£160) double, $340 (£187) suite. AE, MC, V. **Amenities:** Restaurant; lobby and pool bars; beach club (adults only) w/outdoor pool and hot tub; 6 other outdoor pools; privileges at Cabo Real golf club; 2 lighted tennis courts; small workout room; full-service spa; tour desk; room service; babysitting; laundry service; dry cleaning. *In room:* A/C, TV, minibar, hair dryer, safe, Jacuzzi.

The Two Cabos & the Corridor

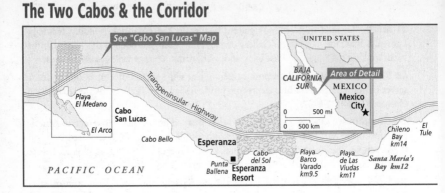

Esperanza ✦✦✦   Although this new luxury resort along Cabo's over-the-top Corridor sits on a bluff overlooking two small, rocky coves, the absence of a sandy beach doesn't seem to matter much to its guests—the hotel more than makes up for it in terms of pampering services and stylish details. Created by the famed Auberge Resorts group, the architecture of this hotel is dramatic, elegant, and comfortable. The casitas and villas are spread across 7 hectares (17 acres), designed to resemble a Mexican village, and are connected to the resort facilities by stone footpaths. The top-floor suites have handmade *palapa* ceilings and a private outdoor whirlpool spa. All rooms are exceptionally spacious, with woven wicker and tropical wood furnishings, original art, rugs and fabrics in muted colors with jewel-tone color accents, and Frette linens gracing the extra-comfortable feather beds. Terraces are large, extending the living area to the outdoors, and all have hammocks and views of the Sea of Cortez. The oversize bathrooms have separate tubs and showers with dual showerheads.

Carretera Transpeninsular Km 7 on Hwy. 1, at Punta Ballena, Cabo San Lucas, B.C.S. **②** **866/311-2226** in the U.S., or **624/145-6400.** Fax 624/145-6403. www.esperanzaresort.com. 50 suites, 6 villas. High season $875–$1,225 (£481–£674) oceanview casita, $1,075–$1,325 (£591–£789) beachfront casita, $4,000–$5,500 (£2,200–£3,025) oceanfront suite; low season $675–$1,025 (£371–£564) oceanview casita, $675–$1,025 (£371–£564) beachfront casita, $2,500–$3,500 (£1,375–£1,925) oceanfront suite. AE, MC, V. **Amenities:** Oceanfront restaurant; sushi & ceviche bar; swimming pool; golf privileges; fitness center; full-service luxury spa; yoga studio with complimentary daily classes; art gallery; concierge; gourmet market; room service; babysitting; laundry service; dry cleaning; private beach w/club. *In room:* A/C, plasma TV w/DVD, stereo, Wi-Fi, in-suite bar, hair dryer, safe.

Las Ventanas al Paraíso ✦✦✦   Las Ventanas is known for its luxury accommodations and attention to detail. The architecture, with adobe structures and rough-hewn wood accents, provides a soothing complement to the desert landscape. The only color comes from the dazzling *ventanas* (windows) of pebbled rainbow glass handmade by regional artisans. Richly furnished, Mediterranean-style rooms are large (starting at 300 sq. m/3,229 sq. ft.) and appointed with every conceivable amenity, from wood-burning fireplaces, iPods, and aromatherapy turn-down service to computerized telescopes for star or whale gazing. Sizable whirlpool tubs overlook the room and may be closed off for privacy. Larger suites offer extras such as rooftop terraces, sunken whirlpools on a private patio, or a personal pool. Note that Las Ventanas is also booking the surrounding Las Ventanas condominiums as part of its room inventory, so be certain to verify where you'll be placed if this is not your preference. Although spacious and boasting a full kitchen, the condominiums do lack the views of the resort rooms and suites. The spa is considered among the best in Mexico, and the resort's three new Spa Suites offer a suite-contained resort spa experience tailored

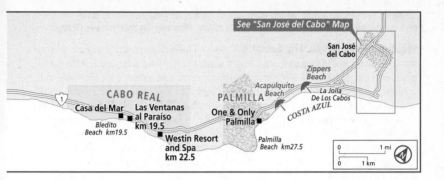

See "San José del Cabo" Map

San José del Cabo

Zippers Beach

Acapulquito Beach

La Jolla De Los Cabos

CABO REAL
Casa del Mar   Las Ventanas al Paraíso km 19.5
Bledito Beach km19.5

PALMILLA
One & Only Palmilla

COSTA AZUL

Westin Resort and Spa km 22.5

Palmilla Beach km27.5

0   1 mi
0   1 km

to the guest's goals and needs ranging from health and beauty to fitness and weight loss. With a staff that outnumbers guests by four to one and a focus on holistic healing, this is the place for those who want (and can afford) to be seriously spoiled. They even have Porsche Boxsters for guest rental and special packages for pampered pets. The 15% service charge is not included in the prices below, which do include taxes.

Km 19.5 on Hwy. 1, 23410 San José del Cabo, B.C.S. © **888/525-0483** or 888/767-3966 in the U.S., or 624/144-2800. Fax 624/144-2801. www.lasventanas.com. 61 suites. High season $700 (£385) garden-view double, $950 (£523) oceanview double, $1,150 (£633) split-level oceanview suite with rooftop terrace, $1,325 (£729) split-level oceanfront suite with rooftop terrace, $2,800–$5,500 (£1,540–£3,025) luxury suites (1–3 bedrooms); low season $500 (£275) garden-view double, $700 (£385) oceanview double, $850 (£468) split-level oceanview suite with rooftop terrace, $975 (£536) split-level oceanfront suite with rooftop terrace, $2,000–$4,300 (£1,100–£2,365) luxury suites. Spa Suites packages start at $13,425 (£7,384) for a 4-night program for 2. Spa and golf packages and inclusive meal plans available. AE, DC, MC, V. Free valet parking. **Amenities:** Infinity swimming pool; oceanview restaurant; terrace bar w/live music; seaside grill; fresh-juice bar; access to adjoining championship Cabo Real golf course; deluxe European spa w/complete treatment and exercise facilities; watersports; tour services; Porsche Boxster rental; shuttle services; room service; laundry service; sportfishing and luxury yachts; pet packages, including treats and massages. In room: A/C, TV/DVD, Wi-Fi, minibar, hair dryer, iron, safe, CD player.

One&Only Palmilla *(Overrated* One of the most luxurious hotels in Mexico, the One&Only Palmilla completed a thorough renovation in late 2003, making it among the most spectacular resort hotels anywhere. The new decor features muted desert colors and luxury fabrics, with special extras such as flat-screen TVs with DVD/CD players, and Bose surround-sound systems. Guests receive twice-daily maid service, a personal butler, and an aromatherapy menu. However, unless you're a Fortune 500 CEO or a Hollywood A-lister, the royal treatment is hard to come by and, although there are exceptions, staff runs the gamut from indifferent to defiant. Nonetheless, Charlie Trotter's C restaurant, offers impeccable 24-hour in-room dining and the *palapa*-topped Agua restaurant, with "Mexiterranean" cuisine, is a high point of the destination. The guest-only spa and its 13 private treatment villas offer a spectacular bit of pampering and are reason enough to put up with the resort's too-cool attitude. Across the highway, the resort's own championship golf course, designed by Jack Nicklaus, is available for guests. The lush tropical resort also has two lighted tennis courts, a 600 sq. m (6,458-sq. ft.) fitness center, and a yoga garden.

Carretera Transpeninsular Km 7.5, 23400 San José del Cabo, B.C.S. © **800/637-2226** in the U.S., or 624/146-7000. Fax 624/144-5100. www.oneandonlypalmilla.com. 172 units. High season $600 (£330) double, $1,025–$2,600 (£564–£1,430) suite; low season $450 (£248) double, $825–$2,050 (£454–£1,128) suite. AE, MC, V. **Amenities:** 2 restaurants; 2 bars; pool bar; 2 infinity swimming pools; championship Palmilla golf course; deluxe European spa w/complete treatment and exercise facilities; watersports; tour services; car rental; room service; laundry service; dry cleaning; yoga garden; sportfishing. *In room:* A/C, TV/DVD, minibar, coffeemaker, hair dryer, iron, safe, CD player.

Westin Resort & Spa, Los Cabos 🦊🦊 *Kids*   The architecturally dramatic Westin sits at the end of a long paved road atop a seaside cliff. Vivid terra cotta, yellow, and pink walls rise against a landscape of sandstone, cacti, and palms, with fountains and gardens lining the long pathways from the lobby to the rooms. The rooms, all of which are ocean view, are sleek and spacious, with fluffy Heavenly Beds and walk-in showers separate from the bathtubs. The seaside 18-hole putting green, first-rate fitness facility, and freshly renovated La Cascada restaurant set this property apart from other Corridor resorts. Plus, it's one of the best among our selections for families vacationing along the corridor; it is smoke-free and offers a wealth of activities for children—not to mention Heavenly Dog Beds for beloveds of the canine persuasion.

Hwy. 1 Km 22.5, San José del Cabo, B.C.S. ✆ **800/228-3000** in the U.S., or 624/142-9000. Fax 624/142-9010. www.westin.com/loscabos. 243 units. High season $529 (£291) oceanview double; $835 (£459) suite; low season $239 (£131) oceanview double, $535 (£294) suite. AE, DC, MC, V. **Amenities:** 6 restaurants; 2 bars; 3 outdoor pools; nearby Palmilla and Cabo Real golf courses; 18-hole putting course; 2 tennis courts; full fitness center and spa; children's activities; concierge; Xplora Adventours services; car rental; business services; salon; 24-hr. room service; babysitting; laundry service. *In room:* A/C, TV, high-speed Internet, minibar, hair dryer, safe.

WHERE TO DINE

C 🦊🦊🦊 GOURMET   Under the direction of renowned Chicago chef Charlie Trotter (this is his first restaurant outside the U.S.), a table for dinner at C is the most coveted reservation in Cabo. Baja's influence on Trotter's culinary innovation is obvious in the menu selections, which change daily but emphasize seafood and indigenous ingredients, although there are also selections of meat and game. To experience the best, order the signature *degustation* menu, offering a variety of small courses, each paired with individual wine selection. The 110-seat dining room is L.A.-chic and gives no hint that you're in Mexico, despite the prevalent water theme and the series of blue cylindrical aquariums that separate the dining room from the exhibition kitchen. There are also two glass-enclosed wine rooms in the main dining area, and the overall atmosphere is bright and a bit loud. C also offers a 10-seat private dining room, and an invitation-only Chef's Kitchen Table, seating eight. Many consider a meal at C worth the trip to Cabo, and although the setting is visually stunning and the flavors superb, I found the service pretentious and the prices excessive—even for Cabo, which is saying a lot. Formal resort attire is requested, and reservations are an absolute must during high season.

One&Only Palmilla, Hwy. 1, Km 7.5. ✆ 624/146-7000. www.oneandonlyresorts.com. Reservations required during high season. Main courses $45–$200 (£25–£110). AE, MC, V. Daily 5–11pm.

Nick-San 🦊🦊🦊 JAPANESE/SUSHI   If you eat one meal out in Los Cabos, do it at Nick-San. No matter your fancy—raw, cooked, vegetarian, carnivorous, traditional, or out there—this dining experience is so superb, it may shift your world view. Owned by Masayuki Niikura, Angel Carbajal, and his sister, Carmen Carbajal, who started their sushi dynasty 12 years ago at the original Nick-San in downtown Cabo San Lucas, the newer and swankier outpost at Las Tiendas de Palmilla assures a taste of teppanyaki Nirvana on both ends of the Corridor. The fire of Mexico meets traditional Japanese ingredients in such delicacies as tuna tostada, locally caught sea bass sashimi, and lobster with curried cream sauce. The low-lit atmosphere suits an intimate occasion or a night out with friends, and the meticulous service is always warm and personal. Because the entire menu is too delectable to pick one thing, let someone else make the decision for you: ask for the chef's tasting plate and, whatever you do, do not miss the lobster tempura roll or the salmon yuzu. Just be sure to let your server know when you've had enough or the plates will keep on coming. By the time the check rolls around, you'll be so enamored it won't even faze you.

Tiendas de Palmilla, Hwy. 1, Km 27.5 (✆ **624/144-6262** or -6263. www.nicksan.com. Reservations required unless you care to sit at the bar. Sashimi, rolls, and main courses $15–$50 (£8.25–£28). AE, MC, V. Tues–Sun 12:30–10:30pm.

CABO SAN LUCAS

183km (114 miles) S of La Paz; 33km (21 miles) W of San José del Cabo; 1,792km (1,111 miles) SE of Tijuana

The hundreds of luxury hotel rooms along the Corridor north of Cabo San Lucas have transformed this formerly rustic and rowdy outpost. Although it retains boisterous nightlife, Cabo San Lucas is no longer the simple town Steinbeck wrote about. Once legendary for big-game fish, Cabo San Lucas now draws more people for its nearby world-class fairways and greens. This has become Mexico's most elite resort destination. Travelers enjoy a growing roster of adventure-oriented activities as well as sumptuous spa services, and the nightlife is as hot as the desert in July. A collection of popular restaurants and bars along Cabo's main street stay open and active until the morning's first fishing charters head out to sea. Despite the growth in diversions, Cabo remains more or less a one-stoplight town, with almost everything along the main strip.

ESSENTIALS

GETTING THERE & DEPARTING   By Plane   For information, see "Getting There & Departing," earlier, under San José del Cabo. Local airline numbers are as follows: **Alaska Airlines** (✆ **624/146-5100** or -5101) and **Mexicana** (✆ **624/143-5352** or -5353, or 146-5001).

By Car   From La Paz, the best route is **Highway 1** south past the village of San Pedro, then **Highway 19** south through Todos Santos to Cabo San Lucas, a 2-hour drive.

By Bus   The **bus terminal** (✆ **624/143-5020**) is on Héroes at Morelos; it is open daily from 7am to 10pm. Buses go to La Paz every 2 hours starting at 7:15am, with the last departure at 8:15pm. To and from San José, the more convenient and economical **Suburcabos** public bus service runs every 15 minutes and costs $2.50.

Arriving   At the airport, either buy a ticket for a *colectivo* (shuttle) from **Josefinos** (✆ **624/146-5354**), the authorized transportation booth inside the building (about $13/£7.15), or arrange for a rental car, the most economical way to explore the area. Up to four people can share a private taxi, which costs about $60 (£33).

VISITOR INFORMATION   The **Los Cabos Tourism Office** (✆ **624/146-9628**) is in San José, in the Plaza San José, Locs. 3 and 4, and is open daily from 8am to 3pm. The English-language *Los Cabos Guide, Los Cabos News, Destino Los Cabos* and the irreverent and extremely entertaining *Gringo Gazette* are distributed free at most hotels and shops and have up-to-date information on new restaurants and clubs. If you fall so deeply in love with Los Cabos as to want to own a piece of it, the *Baja Real Estate Guide* is a great place to start (www.tregintl.com).

CITY LAYOUT   The small town spreads out north and west of the harbor of **Cabo San Lucas Bay,** edged by foothills and desert mountains to the west and south. The main street leading into town from the airport and San José del Cabo is **Lázaro Cárdenas;** as it nears the harbor, **Bulevar Marina** branches off from it and becomes the main artery that curves around the waterfront.

GETTING AROUND   Taxis are easy to find but expensive, in keeping with the high cost of everything else. Expect to pay about $15 to $25 (£8.25–£14) for a taxi between Cabo and the Corridor hotels.

For day trips to San José del Cabo, take the Suburcabos (see "Getting There & Departing," above) or a cab. You'll see car-rental specials advertised in town, but before signing on, be sure you understand the total price after insurance and taxes are added. Rates can run between $50 and $75 (£28–£41) per day, with insurance an extra $10 (£5.50) per day. One of the best and most economical agencies is **Advantage Rent-A-Car** (✆ **624/143-0909;** ✆/fax 624/143-0466), on Lázaro Cárdenas between Leona Vicario and Morelos. VW sedans rent for $80 (£44) per day, and weekly renters receive 1 free day. A collision damage waiver will add $22 (£12) per day to the price. If you pick up the car downtown, you can return it to the airport at no extra charge.

FAST FACTS: Cabo San Lucas

Area Code   The telephone area code is **624.**

Beach Safety   Before swimming in the open water, *check if conditions are safe.* Undertows and large waves are common. **Medano Beach,** close to the marina and town, is the principal beach that's safe for swimming. The ME Cabo resort on Medano Beach has a roped-off swimming area to protect swimmers from personal watercraft and boats. Colored flags to signal swimming safety aren't generally found in Cabo, and neither are lifeguards, so be aware.

Currency Exchange   Banks exchange currency during normal business hours, generally Monday through Friday from 9am to 6pm, Saturday from 10am to 2pm. Currency-exchange booths, throughout Cabo's main tourist areas, aren't as competitive, but they're more convenient. ATMs are widely available and even more convenient, dispensing pesos—and, in some cases, dollars—at bank exchange rates.

Drugstore   A drugstore with a wide selection of toiletries as well as medicine is **Farmacía Aramburo,** in Plaza Aramburo, on Lázaro Cárdenas at Zaragoza (✆ **624/143-1489**). It's open daily from 8am to 10pm, and accepts MasterCard and Visa.

Emergencies & Hospital   In Cabo, **Amerimed** (✆ **624/143-9671**) is a 24-hour, American-standards clinic with bilingual physicians, emergency air evacuation services, and accepts major credit cards. Most of the larger hotels have a doctor on call.

Internet Access   **Cabo Mail** (✆ **624/143-7796**), Plaza Aramburo on Lázaro Cárdenas, charges $1 (55p) for 1 to 10 minutes, and 10¢ (5p) for each additional minute. They also offer long-distance VOIP access, fax, copies, memory-stick photo downloads, color printing, and CD/DVD recording. It's open Monday through Friday from 9am to 9pm, Saturday from 9:30am to 6pm, and Sundays from noon to 6pm.

Post Office   The *correo* is at Lázaro Cárdenas between Medano and Gomez Farías (✆ **624/143-0048**), on the highway to San José del Cabo, east of the bar El Squid Roe. It's open Monday through Friday from 9am to 5pm, Saturday from 9am to 3pm.

Cabo San Lucas

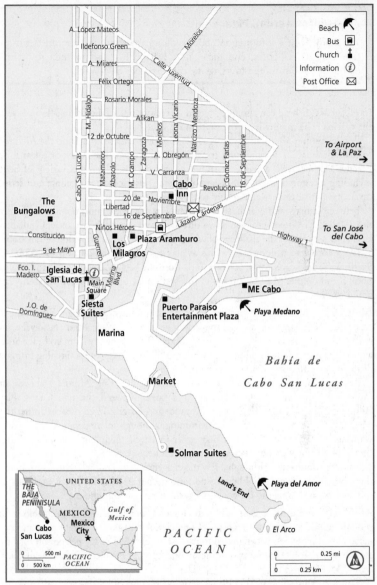

Legend:
- Beach
- Bus
- Church
- Information
- Post Office

A. López Mateos
Ildefonso Green
A. Mijares
Félix Ortega
Rosario Morales
Alikan
12 de Octubre
Morelos
Calle Juventud
M. Hidalgo
Cabo San Lucas
Matamoros
Abasolo
M. Ocampo
I. Zaragoza
A. Obregón
V. Carranza
Leona Vicario
Narcizo Mendoza
Gómez Farías
16 de Septiembre
Revolución
Lázaro Cárdenas
Cabo Inn
20 de Noviembre
Libertad
16 de Septiembre
The Bungalows
Constitución
5 de Mayo
Niños Héroes
Los Milagros
Plaza Aramburo
Fco. I. Madero
Iglesia de San Lucas
Main Square
Guerrero
Marina Blvd
J.O. de Domínguez
Siesta Suites
Marina
Puerto Paraiso Entertainment Plaza
ME Cabo
Playa Medano
Highway 1
To Airport & La Paz →
To San José del Cabo →
Market
Bahía de Cabo San Lucas
Solmar Suites
Land's End
Playa del Amor
El Arco
PACIFIC OCEAN

UNITED STATES
THE BAJA PENINSULA
MEXICO
Gulf of Mexico
Cabo San Lucas
Mexico City
PACIFIC OCEAN
0   500 mi
0   500 km

0   0.25 mi
0   0.25 km

OUTDOOR ACTIVITIES: FISHING, GOLF & MORE

Although superb sportfishing put Cabo San Lucas on the map, there's more to do than drop your line and wait for the Big One. For most cruises and excursions, try to make fishing reservations at least a day in advance; keep in mind that some trips require a minimum number of people. Most sports and outings can be arranged through a

> **Tips Information, Please**
>
> The many "visitor information" booths along the street in Cabo are actually timeshare sales booths, and their staffs will pitch a visit to their resort in exchange for discounted tours, rental cars, or other giveaways.

travel agency; fishing can also be arranged directly at one of the fishing-fleet offices at the marina. The marina is on the south side of the harbor.

Besides fishing, there are kayaking ($65/£36 for a sunset trip around the Arch rock formation; $40/£22 for morning trips) and boat trips to Los Arcos or uninhabited beaches. All-inclusive daytime or sunset cruises are available on a variety of boats, including a restored pirate ship. Many of these trips include snorkeling; and serious divers have great underwater venues to explore.

Between January and March, whale-watching is one of the most popular local activities. Guided ATV tours take you down dirt roads and canyons to an ancient Indian village. And then there's the challenge of world-class golf, a major attraction of Los Cabos.

For a complete rundown of what's available, look to **Book Cabo** (© **624/142-9200;** www.bookcabo.com). It offers tours from the best local companies and you can book ahead online. Most businesses in this section are open daily from 10am to 2pm and 4 to 7pm.

BEACHES   All along the curving sweep of sand known as Medano Beach, on the east side of the bay, you can rent snorkeling gear, boats, Wave Runners, kayaks, and sailboards. You can also take windsurfing lessons. This is the town's main beach and is a great place for safe swimming, happy hour imbibing, and people-watching from one of the many outdoor restaurants along its shore.

Beach aficionados may want to rent a car (see "Getting Around," above) and explore the five more remote beaches and coves between the two Cabos: Playa Palmilla, Chileno, Santa María, Barco Varado, and Lover's Beach. Beaches other than Medano are not considered safe for swimming, although many people don't heed the warning. Experienced snorkelers may wish to check them out, but other visitors should go for the view only. Always check at a hotel or travel agency for directions and swimming conditions. Although a few travel agencies run snorkeling tours to some of these beaches, there's no public transportation: Your options for beach exploring are to rent a car or have a cab drop you off at the beach of your choice.

ATV TRIPS   Expeditions on ATVs to visit La Candelaria, an Indian pueblo in the mountains, are available through travel agencies. A 440-pound weight limit per two-person vehicle applies. Most guided tours cost around $45 (£25) per person on a single vehicle, or $60 (£33) for two riding on one ATV. The vehicles are also available for rent ($35/£19 for 3 hr.).

Tío Sports (© **624/143-3399;** www.tiosports.com) offers day trips to La Candelaria, an isolated Indian village in the mountains 40km (25 miles) north of Cabo San Lucas. Described in *National Geographic,* the old pueblo is known for the practice of white and black witchcraft, but the locals chuckle at the mention of *brujería.* Lush with palms, mango trees, and bamboo, the settlement gets its water from an underground river that emerges at the pueblo. The return trip of the tour travels down a steep canyon, along a beach (giving you time to swim), and through town. Departing at 9am, the 5-hour La Candelaria tour costs around $80 (£44) per person or $100 (£55) for two on the same ATV.

CRUISES   **Glass-bottom boats** leave from the town marina daily every 45 minutes between 9am and 4pm. They cost about $14 (£7.70) for a 1-hour tour, which passes sea lions and pelicans on its way to the famous **El Arco (the Arch)** at Land's End, where the Pacific and the Sea of Cortez meet. Boats drop you off at Playa de Amor; make sure you confirm with your driver which boat will pick you up—it's usually a smaller one run by the same company that ferries people back at regular intervals— and when. Check the timing to make sure you have the correct boat, or expect an additional $10 (£5.50) charge for boarding the boat of an eager competitor.

A number of **daylong** and **sunset cruises** come in a variety of boats and catamarans. They cost $30 to $50 (£17–£28) per person, depending on the boat, duration of cruise, and amenities. A sunset cruise on the 13m (43-ft.) catamaran *Pez Gato* (🕾 624/143-3797; www.pezgatocabo.com) departs from the Tesoro Resort dock (Dock #4, 50m/164 ft. from the main dock) between 4:30 and 5:30pm, depending on the season. A 2-hour cruise costs $35 (£19) and includes an open bar and appetizers. The seasonal (winter) whale-watching tour leaves at 10:30am and returns at 1:30pm. It costs $35 (£19) and includes open bar and snacks. Similar boats leave from the marina and the Tesoro Resort. Check with travel agencies or hotel tour desks.

DRIVING TOURS   A uniquely "Cabo" experience is offered by **Baja Outback** (🕾 624/142-9215; fax 624/142-3166; www.bajaoutback.com) via their caravan-style Hummer Adventures. You drive these luxury Hummer H2s, going off-road to cruise desert and beachfront terrain in style, while learning about the surrounding area through expert guides. Communication links as many as 10 vehicles in the caravan, allowing you to listen to the narrations of the guide. There's a choice of four routes, which include treks to Todos Santos, the East Cape, Santiago and Cañón de la Zorra, and Rancho la Verdad. Tours depart at 9am and return at 3pm, with prices ranging from $165 to $220 (£91–£121), depending upon the route, and include lunch. Visa, MasterCard, and American Express are accepted, and you must have your valid driver's license. Special group rates are also available.

If this sounds too tame, **Wide Open Baja Racing Experience** (🕾 888/788-2252 or 949/340-1155 in the U.S., or 624/143-4170; office in Plaza Nautica; www.wideopencabo.com) gives you the chance to drive actual Chenowth Magnum racecars at Wide Open's 600-hectare (1,482-acre) racing ranch on the Pacific Coast. There's varied terrain to drive, with twists, turns, sand washes, and plenty of bumps for thrill seekers. Session times for the **Test Drive** are at 10am and 1:30pm. The price of $250 (£138) includes shuttle transportation from downtown Cabo to the ranch, driver orientation, and safety equipment. Private group rates are also available. Wide Open Baja also offers multiday tours driving race vehicles through Cabo, Ensenada, and the entire Baja peninsula.

GOLF   Los Cabos has become the golf capital of Mexico, and although most courses are along the Corridor, people look to Cabo San Lucas for information about this sport in Baja Sur. The master plan for Los Cabos golf calls for a future total of 207 holes. Fees listed below are for 18 holes, including golf cart, water, club service, and tax. Summer rates are about 25% lower, and many hotels offer golf packages.

Several specialty tour operators offer golf packages to Los Cabos, which include accommodations, greens fees, and other amenities. These include **Golf Adventures**

(© 800/841-6570 in the U.S.; www.golfadventures.com) and **Sportours** (© 888/465-3639 in the U.S.; www.sportours.com).

The 27-hole course at the **Palmilla Golf Club** (© 800/386-2465 in the U.S., or 624/144-5250; www.oneandonlyresorts.com; daily 7am–7pm) was the first Jack Nicklaus Signature layout in Mexico, on 360 hectares (900 acres) of dramatic ocean-front desert. The course offers your choice of two back-9 options, with high-season greens fees of $255 (£140), lower after 1pm, and low-season greens fees running between $190 and $210 (£105–£116). Guests at some hotels pay discounted rates.

Just a few kilometers away is another Jack Nicklaus Signature course, the 18-hole Ocean Course at **Cabo del Sol,** the posh resort development in the Corridor (© 866/231-4677 in the U.S:, or 624/145-8200; www.cabodelsol.com). The 7,100-yard Ocean Course is known for its challenging 3 finishing holes, and greens fees start at $250 (£138) in the low season and range to $350 (£193) for the high season. Tom Weiskopf designed the new 18-hole Desert Course, for which greens fees are $220 (£121) in the high season, $185 (£102) in the low season. Desert Course twilight play ranges from $140 to $165 (£77–£91) in low and high seasons, respectively.

The 18-hole, 6,945-yard course at **Cabo Real,** by the Meliá Cabo Real Hotel in the Corridor (© 877/795-8727 in the U.S., or 624/173-9400; www.caboreal.com; daily 6:30am–6pm), was designed by Robert Trent Jones, Jr., and features holes that sit high on mesas overlooking the Sea of Cortez. Fees run $280 (£154) for 18 holes. After 3pm, rates drop to $132 (£73) in the low season and $180 (£99) in the high season. Kids 16 and younger than play for $92 (£51) year round.

An 18-hole course designed by Roy Dye is at the **Raven Club,** formerly the Cabo San Lucas Country Club (© 888/328-8501 in the U.S., or 624/143-4653; fax 624/143-5809). The entire Dye-design course overlooks the juncture of the Pacific Ocean and Sea of Cortez, including the famous rocks of Land's End. It includes a 607-yard, par-5 7th hole. High season greens fees are $186 (£102) for 18 holes, $149 (£82) for the noon rate, and $105 (£58) after 2:30pm. In the summer months, greens fees drop to $109 (£60) for 18 holes and to $79 (£43) after 10:30am.

The lowest greens fees in the area are at the public 9-hole **Mayan Palace Golf Los Cabos** (© 624/142-0900 or -0901) in San José del Cabo (see earlier in this chapter). Early morning greens fees are just $69 (£38) for 9 holes and $99 (£54) for 18 holes with equipment, from 6am to 2pm; rates drop to $80 (£44) for 18 holes after 3pm. All greens fees include the use of a cart.

HORSEBACK RIDING   You can rent **horses** through **Rancho Colín** (© 624/143-3652) for $25 (£14) per hour. Tours for sunset riding on Sea of Cortez beaches cost $35 (£19) per hour; the 2-hour desert-and-beach trail ride is $60 (£33); and the 3½-hour tour through the mountains is $80 (£44). The ranch is open daily from 8am to noon and 2 to 5pm and is across from the Hotel Club Las Cascadas. For information on the highly recommended **Cuadra San Francisco Equestrian Center,** see p. 700.

SNORKELING & DIVING   Several companies offer snorkeling; a 2-hour cruise to sites around El Arco costs $30 (£17), and a 4-hour trip to Santa María costs $55 (£30), including gear rental. Among the beaches visited on different trips are Playa de Amor, Santa María, Chileno, and Barco Varado. Snorkeling gear rents for $10 to $15 (£5.50–£8.25). Contact **Book Cabo** (© 624/142-9200; www.bookcabo.com). For scuba diving, contact **Manta Diving** (© 624/144-3871; www.caboscuba.com) and **Amigos del Mar** in Cabo San Lucas (© 800/344-3349 in the U.S., or 624/143-0505; www.amigosdelmar.com). Dives are along the wall of a canyon in San Lucas

Bay, where you can see the cascading sand falls by Anegada Rock. There are also scuba trips to Santa María Beach and more distant places, including Gordo Banks and Cabo Pulmo. Prices start at $50 (£28) for a one-tank dive and from $150 (£83) for 2 days of diving. Night dives are $65 (£36) per person. Trips to the coral outcropping at Cabo Pulmo start at $130 (£72). You'll need a wet suit for winter dives. A 5-hour resort course is available for $100, and open-water certification costs $4,300 (£2,365).

SPORTFISHING   To make your own arrangements, go to the marina on the south side of the harbor, where you'll find several fleet operators with offices near the docks. *Panga* fleets offer the best deals; 5 hours of fishing for two or three people costs $200 to $450 (£110–£248), plus a 20% tip. But stroll around the marina and talk with the captains—you might be able to negotiate a better deal. Try **Pisces Fleet,** located in the Cabo Maritime Center, behind Tesoro Resort and next to Captain Tony's on the marina (© **624/143-1288;** www.piscessportfishing.com; daily 10am–4pm; Visa and MasterCard accepted), or **Minerva's** (© **624/143-1282;** www.minervas.com; daily 6am–8pm; American Express, MasterCard, and Visa accepted), on the corner of Bulevar Marina and Madero. A day on a fully equipped cruiser with captain and guide starts at around $800 (£440) for up to six people. For deluxe trips with everything included aboard a 12m (40-ft.) boat, you'll have to budget around $1,500 (£825) and up. If you're traveling in your own vessel, you'll need a fishing permit, which you can get at Minerva's Baja Tackle. Depending on the size of the boat, it will cost $15 to $45 (£8.25–£25) per month. Daily permits ($4–$10/£2.20–£5.50) and annual permits are also available.

The fishing here lives up to its reputation: Bringing in a 100-pound marlin is routine, although decades of pressure on Sea of Cortez fisheries should inspire you to release your prized catch. Angling is good all year, though the catch varies with the season. Sailfish and wahoo are best from June through November; yellowfin tuna, May through December; yellowtail, January through April; black and blue marlin, July through December. Striped marlin and dorado, or mahimahi, are prevalent year-round.

SURFING   Stellar surfing can be found from November through April all along the Pacific beaches north and west of town, and the East Cape is the ultimate North American surfing destination from May through October. (Also see "Surfing" in "San José del Cabo," earlier in this chapter, for details on Costa Azul and East Cape breaks).

The areas to the east and west of Los Cabos, known as the East Cape and the Pacific side, respectively, have yet to face the onslaught of development that's so rapidly changed the tip. An hour-long drive up the western coast to the little towns of Pescadero and Todos Santos can be a great surf journey, as can a summer trek up the Sea of Cortez coastline toward Cabo Pulmo. Your best bet is to visit www.costa-azul. com.mx/area-maps.htm for a detailed look at the different breaks, excursions, rental equipment, and lessons available.

Many beach breaks are ride-worthy at different times, depending on the wave conditions, but a vicious shore break and strong undertow characterize much of the beach around Todos Santos. While the unruliness of the ocean has helped keep industrial tourism at bay, it also means you have to hunt a little harder to find playful waves.

WHALE-WATCHING   Whale-watching cruises are the best way to get up close and personal with nature's most majestic seafaring mammals. See "Whale-Watching in Baja," p. 743, for information on the excursions, which operate between January and March.

Surf & Sleep

If you can't get enough of the surf, stay where this is the specialty and not just an activity. The Los Cabos area has two outposts that cater to surfers, one along Los Cabos Corridor and the other on the Pacific coast, near Todos Santos.

The **Cabo Surf Hotel** (© 858/964-5146 from the U.S., or 624/142-2666; www.cabosurfhotel.com) has 16 beachfront rooms in a secluded, gated boutique resort. It's 13km (8 miles) west of San José del Cabo, across from the Querencia golf course, on Playa Acapulquito, which is the most popular surfing beach in Los Cabos. Along with a choice of rooms and suites, it's equipped with an oceanfront terrace restaurant, surf shop, and the Mike Doyle Surf School, which offers day lessons and more intensive instruction. Rates range from $260 to $325 (£143–£179) for a double and $275 to $780 (£151–£429) for suites and villas. Promotional rates are available during summer months, which is optimum for surfers who seek the Sea of Cortez's summertime swells.

The **Pescadero Surf Camp** (© 612/130-3022 or 134-0480; www.pescadero surf.com) is a sparse Pacific getaway at Km 64 on Highway 1 toward Todos Santos. Eight poolfront casitas, each equipped with a minifridge, start at $25 (£14), and the two-story suite rents for $60 (£33) a night. Although it's a kilometer (half-mile) from the beach, this surf camp is a comfortable step up from the beach camping that's a way of life for most surf mongers and, in the winter, when the waves—and sometimes winds—are at their strongest, it's nice to have a roof overhead. The property's brand new pool has a b.y.o.b. swim-up bar that's ideal for cooling off between surf excursions, and a large outdoor kitchen provides a space to prepare your own meals. Owner Jaime Dobies also offers 1½-hour lessons for $50 (£28), board rental for $15 (£8.25) a day, boogie and skim board rental for $10 (£5.50) a day, and day-long guided surf safaris starting at $100 (£55)/person. He also repairs boards, should your baby get dinged in action.

Of course, if you're coming to Baja strictly for the surf, you may join the other hard-core wave-riders and camp along the sugary beaches of the East Cape in the summer and the Pacific in the winter. Most beaches—especially the ones fronting secluded surf breaks—are safe and accommodating for overnight stays.

A BREAK FROM SPORTS: EXPLORING CABO SAN LUCAS

FESTIVALS & EVENTS   October 12 is the festival of the patron saint of Todos Santos, a town about 105km (65 miles) north. **October 18** is the feast of the patron saint of Cabo San Lucas, celebrated with a fair, feasting, music, dancing, and other special events.

HISTORIC CABO SAN LUCAS   Watersports and outright partying are Cabo's main attractions, but there are also a few cultural and historical points of interest. The Spanish missionary Nicolás Tamaral established the **Iglesia de San Lucas (Church of**

San Lucas) on Calle Cabo San Lucas, close to the main plaza, in 1730. A large bell in a stone archway commemorates the completion of the church in 1746. The Pericúe Indians, who resisted Tamaral's demands that, among other things, they practice monogamy, eventually killed him in a violent uprising. Buildings on the streets facing the main plaza are gradually being renovated to house restaurants and shops, and the picturesque block has the most Mexican ambience in town.

DAY TRIPS   Most local and hotel travel agencies book day trips to the city of **La Paz;** they cost around $60 (£33), including beverages and a tour of the countryside along the way. Usually there's a stop at the weaving shop of Fortunato Silva, who spins his own cotton and weaves it into wonderfully textured rugs and textiles. Day trips are also available to **Todos Santos** ($60/£33), with a guided walking tour of the mission, museum, Hotel California, and various artists' homes. (For more information, see "La Paz" and "Todos Santos," later in this chapter.)

SHOPPING

San José has the better shopping of the two towns, when it comes to quality and uniqueness, but if you're after a beer-themed T-shirt, Cabo San Lucas can't be topped. Nevertheless, the **Puerto Paraíso Entertainment Plaza** (✆ 624/144-3000; www. puertoparaiso.com) does have a selection of designer clothing stores, knickknack shops, and swimwear boutiques. Opened in 2002, this is now the focal point for locals' entertainment and tourists' exploration. It's a truly world-class mall, complete with free parking, movie theaters, a video arcade, a food court, and various restaurants, not the least of which is **Ruth's Chris Steak House,** adjacent to the marina (✆ 624/ 144-3232; www.ruthschris.com.mx; daily 1–11:30pm). With more than 50,000 sq. m (538,195 sq. ft.) of air-conditioned space on three levels, it's a shame so much of the mall is still empty. Rumor has it that developers are taking their time to rent the spaces, so don't expect the equivalent of a U.S. shopping mall experience for a few years. The plaza is located marina-side, between the Plaza Bonita Mall and Marina Fiesta Resort—you can't miss it if you try. Most other shops in Cabo are on or within a block or two of Boulevard Marina and the plaza.

In addition to the mall, I recommend the following specialty stores.

Baja Body Deli   This is a true gem of a spa boutique. Fragrant candles, Baja-grown loose teas and dried herbs, handmade cut-to-order soaps, luxury bathrobes, and other pampering products make this a stylish oasis in a sea of commercial shops. They specialize in custom-scented body lotion, hair care, massage oil, sprays, and scrubs. Open Monday through Saturday 10am to 7:30pm. Matamoros, near corner of Lázaro Cardenas. ✆ 624/143-3272.

El Callejón   This has San Lucas's best selection of fine Mexican furniture and decor items, plus gifts, accessories, tableware, fabrics, and lamps. Open Monday through Saturday 9:30am to 7pm. Guerrero between Madero and Bulevar Marina (across from the main plaza). ✆ 624/143-3188.

J & J Habanos   J & J is Cabo's largest cigar shop, selling premium Cuban and fine Mexican cigars—it even has a walk-in humidor. They also sell fine tequila and espresso. Open Monday through Saturday 9am to 10pm, Sunday 9am to 9pm. Madero between Bulevar Marina and Guerrero. ✆ 624/143-6160 or -3839.

Ultrafemme   Mexico's largest duty-free shop has an excellent selection of fine jewelry and watches, including Rolex, Cartier, Omega, TAG Heuer, Tiffany, and Tissot; perfumes, including Lancôme, Chanel, Armani, Carolina Herrera; and other gift items, all at duty-free prices. Open daily 10am to 9:30pm. Plaza UltraFemme, Bulevar Marina. (C) 624/145-6090. www.ultrafemme.com.mx.

WHERE TO STAY

High-season prices are in effect from December to Easter. Several hotels offer package deals that significantly lower the nightly rate; ask your travel agent for information. Budget accommodations are scarce, but the number of small inns and B&Bs is growing; several notable ones have opened in recent years. Because most of the larger hotels are well maintained and offer packages through travel agents, I will focus on smaller, unique accommodations.

Expensive

ME Cabo ⨕⨕ If you've come to Cabo to party, this is your place. Formerly the Meliá San Lucas, the newly renovated ME Cabo is Sol Meliá's foray into hip, making it Cabo's hottest hotspot. Upgraded rooms, a new adult-focused floor called "The Level," and the addition of the swank Nikki Beach stake a glam claim on this beachfront property, which is geared toward those who'd rather party than relax. Its location on Medano Beach is central to any other action you may want to seek but, with Nikki Beach and Passion, you'll find plenty right here. Rooms are awash in fiery red and white, with a sleek, contemporary decor. All suites have ocean views and private terraces looking across to the famed El Arco. Master suites have a separate living room area. Guests gather by the beachfront pool, where oversized daybeds perfectly accommodate this lounge atmosphere. There are also VIP tepees, and the live DJ music keeps the party here going day and night.

Playa El Medano s/n; 23410 Cabo San Lucas, B.C.S. (C) 624/145-7800. Fax 624/143-0420. www.mebymelia.com. 150 units. High season $356–$540 (£196–£297) double, $1,100 (£605) chic suite, $2,100 (£1,155) loft suite; low season $311–$441 (£171–£243) double, $756 (£416) chic suite, $1,100 (£605) loft suite. AE, MC, V. Free parking. **Amenities:** Restaurant; bar/dance club; 3 outdoor pools; beach club; Jacuzzi; concierge; boutique; tour desk; car rental; room service; laundry service; dry cleaning. *In room:* A/C, TV, Wi-Fi, minibar, coffeemaker, hair dryer, safe.

Moderate

The Bungalows Hotel ⨕ *Finds* This is one of the most special places to stay in Los Cabos. Each "bungalow" is a charming retreat decorated with authentic Mexican furnishings. Terra-cotta tiles, hand-painted sinks, wooden chests, blown glass, and other creative touches make you feel as if you're a guest at a friend's home rather than a hotel. Each room has a kitchenette, purified water, VCR, and designer bedding. Rooms surround a lovely heated pool with cushioned lounges and tropical gardens. A brick-paved breakfast nook serves a gourmet breakfast with fresh-ground coffee and fresh juices. Under the owner's warm and welcoming management, this is Cabo's most spacious, comfortable, full-service inn. A 100% smoke-free environment, it is 5 blocks from downtown Cabo.

Miguel A. Herrera s/n, in front of Lienzo Charro, Cabo San Lucas, B.C.S. (C)/fax 624/143-5035 or -0585. www.cabobungalows.com. 16 units. High season $115–$165 (£63–£91) suite; low season $105–$115 (£58–£63) suite. Extra person $20 (£11). Rates include full breakfast. AE, V. Street parking available. **Amenities:** Breakfast room; outdoor pool; concierge; tour desk. *In room:* A/C, TV/VCR, kitchenette, fridge, coffeemaker.

Los Milagros Hotel The elegant whitewashed two-level buildings containing the 12 suites and rooms of Los Milagros (the Miracles) border either a grassy garden area or the small tile pool. Rooms contain contemporary iron beds with straw headboards, buff-colored tile floors, and artistic details. Some units have kitchenettes, the master suite has a sunken tub, and there's coffee service in the mornings on the patio.

Evenings are romantic: Candles light the garden and classical music plays. Request a room in one of the back buildings, where pomegranate trees buffer others' conversations. It's just 1½ blocks from the Giggling Marlin and Cabo Wabo.

Matamoros 116, 23410 Cabo San Lucas, B.C.S. ©/fax **718/928-6647** in the U.S., or 624/143-4566. www.losmilagros. com.mx. 11 units. $75 (£41) double, $90 (£50) kitchenette suite, $115 (£63) master suite. Ask about summer discounts, group rates, long-term discounts. No credit cards, but payable through PayPal. Limited street parking. **Amenities:** Small outdoor pool; rooftop terrace; business services. *In room:* A/C, cable TV, Wi-Fi.

Inexpensive

Cabo Inn 🐾🐾 *(Finds* This three-story hotel on a quiet street is a real find, and it keeps getting better. It offers a rare combination of low rates, extra-friendly management, and great, funky style. Rooms are basic and very small, with either two twin beds or one queen; although this was a bordello in a prior incarnation, everything is kept new and updated, from the mattresses to the minifridges. Muted desert colors add a spark of personality. The rooms surround a courtyard where you can enjoy satellite TV, a barbecue grill, and free coffee. The third floor has a rooftop terrace with *palapa* and a small swimming pool. Also on this floor is a suite equipped with a king-size bed and Jacuzzi. It's a colorful, *palapa*-topped, open-air room with hanging *tapetes* (woven palm mats) for additional privacy. A large fish freezer is available, and most rooms have kitchenettes. The hotel is just 2 blocks from downtown and the marina. A lively restaurant next door will even deliver pitchers of margaritas and dinner to your room.

20 de Noviembre and Leona Vicario, 23410 Cabo San Lucas, B.C.S. ©/fax **619/819-2727** in the U.S., or 624/143-0819. www.caboinnhotel.com. 23 units. Year round $39 (£21) single, $58 (£32) double, $79 (£43) triple, $120 (£66) up to 6 people; $120 (£66) suite with Jacuzzi. No credit cards. Street parking. **Amenities:** Small rooftop pool and sunning area; communal TV and barbecue. *In room:* A/C, fridge.

Siesta Suites   Reservations are a must at this immaculate, small inn that's popular with return visitors. (It's especially popular with fishermen.) The very basic rooms have white-tile floors and white walls, kitchenettes with seating areas, refrigerators, and sinks. The mattresses are firm, and the bathrooms are large and sparkling clean. Rooms on the fourth floor have two queen-size beds each. The accommodating proprietors offer free movies and VCRs, a barbecue pit and outdoor patio table on the second floor, and a comfortable lobby with a TV. They also arrange fishing trips. Weekly and monthly rates are available. The hotel is 1½ blocks from the marina, where parking is available.

Calle Emiliano Zapata between Guerrero and Hidalgo, 23410 Cabo San Lucas, B.C.S. © **866/271-0952** in the U.S., or 624/143-2773. www.cabosiestasuites.com. 20 suites (15 w/kitchenette). $55–$69 (£30–£38) double. $340–$460 (£187–£253) weekly rates. AE, MC, V. Parking available at marina. **Amenities:** Outdoor pool; barbecue pit. *In room:* A/C, VCR, kitchenette (in some), fridge, fan.

WHERE TO DINE

It's not uncommon to pay a lot for mediocre food in Cabo, so try to get a couple of unbiased recommendations. If people are only drinking and not dining, take that as a clue—many seemingly popular places are long on party atmosphere but short on food. Prices may decrease the farther you walk inland. The absolute local favorite is **Gardenia's Tacos,** a bare-bones eatery on Paseo Pescadores (same street as McDonald's) that serves Cabo San Lucas's best tacos. Streets to explore for other good restaurants include Hidalgo and Lázaro Cárdenas, plus the marina at the Plaza Bonita. Note that many restaurants automatically add the tip (15%) to the bill; make sure you ask.

Very Expensive

Edith's Restaurante ☆☆☆ SEAFOOD/STEAKS/MEXICAN   Prices may seem over the top and reservations hard to come by, but once you sit down at one of Edith Jiménez's cheerful tables, you will see you're not only paying for an exquisite meal, but also for the time of your life. Lanterns light the open-air way for highly trained waiters, and bouquets of fresh lilies always perfume the entrance and washrooms. No detail is overlooked and, without exception, everyone in the house is in full celebration mode. You will be, too, after a celestial pitcher of margaritas or a bottle from Edith's carefully stocked cellar. While the lobster, shrimp, seafood, and steak combinations are worth every last peso, the grilled tuna is beyond compare when it comes to quality and value. And if Mexican food is what you crave, both the Tampiqueña and the Pancho Villa offer a magnanimous sampling of some of Mexico's most prized traditional dishes, which are abundant enough for two, especially when kicked off with the squash blossom quesadillas or a Caesar salad.

Camino a Playa Medano. ✆ **624/143-0801**. www.edithscabo.com. Reservations strongly recommended. Main courses $20–$84 (£11–£46). MC, V. Daily 5–11pm.

Expensive

Nick-San ☆☆ JAPANESE/SUSHI   This is the original branch of exceptional Japanese cuisine and sushi in Los Cabos. Now joined by a second location in the Corridor near San José, Nick-San's innovative flavors have two splendid homes. See p. 710 for menu details.

Bulevar Marina, Plaza de la Danza, Loc. 2. ✆ **624/143-7342**. Reservations recommended. Main courses $15–$50 (£8.25–£28). MC, V. Tues–Sun 11:30am–10:30pm.

Moderate

La Dolce ITALIAN   This restaurant is the offspring of Puerto Vallarta's La Dolce Vita, with authentic Italian thin-crust, brick-oven pizzas, fresh pasta dishes, and other specialties. Most of its business is from local customers, underscoring the attention to detail and reasonable prices. The simple menu also features sumptuous calzones and delightful starters, plus great salads. This is the best late-night dining option, and there's also an equally loved branch on the main square in San José del Cabo that's open from 2 to 11pm.

M. Hidalgo and Zapata s/n. ✆ **624/143-4122** or -9553. Main courses $7.50–$19 (£4.15–£10). MC, V. Tues–Sun 6–11pm. Closed Mon.

Mi Casa Restaurant ☆ MEXICAN   The building's vivid cobalt-blue facade is your first clue that this place celebrates Mexico, and the menu confirms that impression. This is one of Cabo's most renowned Mexican restaurants. Traditional specialties such as *manchamanteles* (literally, "tablecloth stainers"), *cochinita pibil,* and *chiles en nogada* are menu staples. Fresh fish is prepared with delicious seasonings from throughout Mexico. Especially pleasant at night, the restaurant's tables, scattered around a large patio, are set with colorful cloths, traditional pottery, and glassware. It's across from the main plaza.

Calle Cabo San Lucas (at Madero). ✆ **624/143-1933**. www.micasarestaurant.com. Reservations recommended. Main courses $13–$40 (£7.15–£22). MC, V. Daily 1–10pm.

Inexpensive

Cafe Canela ☆ COFFEE/PASTRY/LIGHT MEALS   This cozy, tasty cafe and bistro is a welcome addition to the Cabo Marina boardwalk. Espresso drinks or fruit smoothies and muffins are good eye-openers for early risers. Enjoy a light meal or a tropical drink either inside or on the bustling waterfront terrace. The appealing menu also offers breakfast egg wraps, salads (for example, curried chicken salad with fresh fruit), sandwiches (such as blue-cheese quesadillas with smoked tuna and mango), and pastas—all reasonably priced. Full bar service is also available.

Marina boardwalk, below Tesoro Resort. ℂ **624/143-3435**. Main courses $5–$35 (£2.75–£19); coffee $1.75–$4.20 (95p–£2.30). AE, MC, V. Daily 6am–8pm.

Mocambo's ⚝ SEAFOOD   The location of this longstanding Cabo favorite is not inspiring—it's basically a large cement building—but the food obviously is. The place is always packed, generally with locals tired of high prices and small portions. Ocean-fresh seafood is the order of the day, and the specialty platter can easily serve four people. The restaurant is 1½ blocks inland from Lázaro Cárdenas.

Av. Leona Vicario and 20 de Noviembre. ℂ **624/143-6070**. Main courses $5–$30 (£2.75–£17). MC, V. Daily noon–10pm.

CABO SAN LUCAS AFTER DARK

Cabo San Lucas is the nightlife capital of Baja. After-dark fun starts with the casual bars and restaurants on Bulevar Marina or facing the marina, and transforms into a tequila-fueled dance club scene after midnight. You can easily find a happy hour with live music and a place to dance or a Mexican fiesta with mariachis.

MEXICAN FIESTAS & THEME NIGHTS   Some larger hotels have weekly fiesta nights and other buffet-plus-entertainment theme nights that can be fun as well as a good buy. Check travel agencies and the following hotels: the **Solmar** (ℂ **624/143-3535**) and the **Finisterra** (ℂ **624/143-3333**). Prices range from $25 (£14), not including drinks, tax, and tips, to $50 (£28), which covers everything, including an open bar with national drinks. Otherwise, Mi Casa (ℂ **624/143-1933** see "Where to Dine" section) is a veritable Mexican theme night every night.

SUNSET WATCHING   Come twilight, check out Land's End, where the two seas meet. At **Whale Watcher's Bar,** in the Hotel Finisterra (ℂ **624/143-3333**), not only will you get a world-class view of the sun sinking into the Pacific, but you'll get a taste of "old Cabo." Mariachis play on Friday from 6:30 to 9pm, and the bar is open daily from 10am to 11pm. Another good place to watch the sunset is at the Pueblo Bonito Sunset Beach hotel—where nothing obstructs the setting sun—on the Pacific side of San Lucas (ℂ **624/142-9999**).

HAPPY HOURS, CLUBS & HANGOUTS   If you shop around, you can usually find an *hora feliz* (happy hour) somewhere in town between noon and 7pm. The most popular places to drink and carouse until all hours are longstanding favorites such as the Nowhere Bar, the Giggling Marlin, El Squid Roe, and the Cabo Wabo Cantina.

Two places to enjoy a more refined setting are the **Sancho Panza Wine Bistro and Jazz Club** (see below) and **Red** (ℂ **624/143-5645**), a food, wine and martini bar, on Zaragoza around the corner from Squid Roe. While Sancho Panza offers live classic jazz, Red brings smooth electronica, both of which set the stage for rich conversation.

Cabo Wabo Cantina   Owned by Sammy Hagar (formerly of Van Halen) and his Mexican and American partners, this "cantina" packs in youthful crowds, especially when rumors (frequent, and frequently false, just to draw a crowd) fly that a surprise appearance by a vacationing musician is imminent. One of Cabo's few air-conditioned dance venues, it's especially popular in the summer months. When there isn't a live band, a dance club–type sound system plays mostly rock and some alternative and techno. Overstuffed furniture frames the dance floor. Beer goes for $3 (£1.65), margaritas for $5 (£2.75). For snacks, the Taco Wabo, just outside the club's entrance, stays up late, too. The cantina is open from 11am to 4am. Vicente Guerrero at Lázaro Cárdenas. © 624/143-1188. www.cabowabo.com.

El Squid Roe *(Moments*   El Squid Roe is one of the late Carlos Anderson's inspirations, and it still attracts wild, fun-loving crowds of all ages with its two stories of nostalgic decor. The eclectic food is far better than you'd expect from such a party place and, as fashionable as blue jeans, you can't come to Cabo without a visit here. Skin-to-win is the theme as the dancing on tables moves into high gear around 9pm. The scene is mostly tourists jerking to American hip-hop from early evening to around midnight, and at 1am, the local Mexican crowd—just getting their night started—flow in, and the hips don't stop shaking until first light. Open daily from noon to 4am. Bulevar Marina, opposite Plaza Bonita. © 624/143-0655. www.elsquidroe.com.

Mambo Café   Make no mistake: you go to Mambo Café to dance. Part of a chain of bars around Mexico, it features a Caribbean concept with a marine tropical ambience, playing contemporary Latin music. Tiered levels of seating lead to the expansive dance floor. High-energy live music is also featured. It's open Wednesday through Sunday from 9pm. Thursday is ladies night, which means women drink free from 9 to 11pm. Bulevar Marina Loc. 9–10, next to the Tesoro Resort. © 624/143-1484. www.mambocafe.com.mx. Cover varies with the night.

Nikki Beach   This haven of the hip hails from South Beach, Miami, and brought its ultracool vibe to the beach of the ME Cabo resort in March 2005. White-draped lounge beds scatter the outdoor area, under a canopy of umbrellas, surrounding a pool, and overlooking Cabo's best swimming beach. A teak deck offers covered dining. The music is the latest in electronic, house, and chill, with visiting DJs often playing on weekend nights. Sundays feature the signature beach brunch. It's a great choice for catching rays during the day while sipping tropical drinks, but its real appeal is the nocturnal action. Open Sunday to Wednesday from 11am to 1am (food service stops at 11pm), and Thursday to Saturday from 11am to 3am (food service stops at 1am). On the beach at the ME Cabo resort, on Medano Beach. © 624/145-7800. www.nikkibeach.com.

Passion   ME Cabo's most recent contribution to Cabo's growing high-end nightlife scene is Passion, arguably the most aphrodisiacal club in San Lucas. Champagne cocktails, the house music of resident and guest DJs, and a low-lit atmosphere prime Los Cabos' jet set for dancing and partying as long as they want. Open Sunday to Wednesday from 10am to 2am and Thursday to Saturday from 10am to 4am. In the ME Cabo resort, on Medano Beach. © 624/145-7800.

Sancho Panza Wine Bistro and Jazz Club   Sancho Panza combines a gourmet food market with a wine bar that features live jazz music plus an intriguing menu of Nuevo Latino cuisine (Mediterranean food with Latin flair). The place has a cozy neighborhood feeling, with tourists and locals sampling the selection of more than 150 wines, plus espresso drinks. During high season, make reservations. It's open daily from 4pm to midnight. Plaza Tesoro boardwalk, next to the Lighthouse. © 624/143-3212. www.sanchopanza.com.

2 Todos Santos: A Creative Oasis ✦✦✦

68km (42 miles) N of Cabo San Lucas

Although Todos Santos is well past its off-the-beaten-path days, it's still a favorite among Bohemian types looking either for regional up-and-coming artists or simply a piece of art that makes them feel good—and it's a prime destination among those simply weary of the L.A.-ization of Cabo San Lucas.

The art and artistry created here—from the kitchen to the canvas—is of an evolved type that seems to care less about commercial appeal than quality. In doing so, it becomes more of a draw. Not to be overlooked are the arts of agriculture, masonry, and weaving created by some of the town's original residents. From superb meals at **Café Santa Fe** to an afternoon browsing at **El Tecolote Libros,** Todos Santos is intriguing to its core. In fact, the Mexican government dubbed it a "Pueblo Mágico" in 2006, bringing official recognition, not to mention various infrastructure updates, to the town.

Not only is the town a cultural oasis in Baja, it's an oasis in the true sense of the word—in this desert landscape, Todos Santos enjoys an almost continuous water supply from the peaks of the Sierra de la Laguna mountains. It's just over an hour's drive up the Pacific coast from Cabo San Lucas; you'll know you've arrived when the arid coastal scenery suddenly gives way to verdant groves of palms, mangos, avocados, and papayas.

During the Mission Period of Baja, this oasis valley was deemed the only area south and west of La Paz worth settling—it had the only reliable water supply. In 1723, an outpost mission was established, followed by the full-fledged Misión Santa Rosa de Las Palmas in 1733. At the time, the town was known as Santa Rosa de Todos Santos; eventually shortened to its current name, it translates as "All Saints."

Over the next 200 years, the town alternated between prosperity and difficulty. Its most recent boom lasted from the mid-19th century until the 1950s, when the town flourished as a sugar-cane production center and began to develop a strong cultural core. Many of the buildings now being restored and converted into galleries, studios, shops, and restaurants were built during this era. It wasn't until the 1980s that a paved road connected Todos Santos with La Paz, and tourism began to draw new attention to this tranquil town.

The demand for the town's older colonial-style structures by artists, entrepreneurs, and foreign residents has resulted in a real-estate boom, and new shops, galleries, and cafes crop up continuously. The coastal strip south of Todos Santos, which once was the exclusive hideaway of impassioned surfers, has plans for development; so visit soon, before this perfect stretch of beach and desert changes. For the casual visitor, Todos Santos is easy to explore in a day, but a few tranquil inns welcome guests who want to stay a little longer.

WHAT TO SEE & DO

During the **Festival Fundador** (Oct 10–14), which celebrates the founding of the town in 1723, streets around the main plaza fill with food, games, and wandering troubadours. Many of the shops and the Café Santa Fe close from the end of September through the festival. A new **Arts Festival,** in February, seems to be gaining importance. It includes film festivals, dance and music performances, and more.

Todos Santos has at least half a dozen galleries, including the noted **Galería de Todos Santos,** corner of Topete and Legaspi (© 612/145-0500), which features a changing collection of works by regional artists. It's open daily from 11am to 4pm (closed Sun May–Nov) and doesn't accept credit cards. The new **La Galera,** on Obregón (© 612/145-0215), houses a striking collection of local and regional Mexican artists, plus some handicrafts and jewelry from mainland Mexico. Keep an eye out for the brooding paintings of local Sebastián Díaz Duarte, La Galera's featured artist. It's open Monday through Saturday from 10am to 5pm.

El Tecolote Libros 🌟🌟🌟 (© **612/145-0295**), though tiny, gets our vote for the best bookstore in Mexico. It carries an exceptional selection of Latin American literature, poetry, children's books, and reference books centering on Mexico. Both English and Spanish editions, new and used, are in stock, along with maps, magazines, cards, and art supplies. Information on upcoming writing workshops and local reading groups also is posted here. The shop is at the corner of Hidalgo and Juárez. It's open Monday through Saturday, from 9am to 5pm, and Sunday, from 10am to 3pm.

WHERE TO STAY & DINE

Consider the **Todos Santos Inn** 🌟🌟, Calle Legaspi 33, between Topete and Obregón (© **612/145-0040;** www.todossantosinn.com). An elegant place to stay, it is in a historic house that has served as a general store, cantina, school, and private residence. Now under new ownership, it retains its air of casual elegance, with luxurious white bed linens, netting draped romantically over the beds, Talavera tile bathrooms, antique furniture, and high, wood-beamed ceilings. Two rooms and four suites border a lush courtyard terrace, pool, and garden. Rates run $125 to $325 (£69–£179) per night depending on the room and the season. The suites are air-conditioned, but have neither television nor telephone. The hotel's wine bar, **La Copa,** is open to the public, serves libations Tuesdays through Saturdays from 5 to 9pm, and has an excellent selection of California and other imported wines. Currently, no credit cards are accepted. Seasonal discounts are available, but the inn closes for the month of September.

Hotel California, Calle Juárez, corner of Morelos (© **612/145-0525** or -0522), has been the stuff of legends—and the verdict is still out as to whether it's the source of inspiration for the Eagles' song of the same name. A few years back, it was a dilapidated guesthouse; however, after an extensive renovation, it's now the hippest place to stay in the area. Think Philippe Stark in the desert—the decor here is a fusion of jewel-tone colors with eclectic Mexican and Moroccan accents. Each room features a different decor, but all of it is high style, with rich hues and captivating details. Most rooms also offer an outdoor terrace or seating area. Rates for the 11 rooms range from $125 to $250 (£69–£138) in high season or $100 to $200 (£55–£110) in low season. It's so stylishly accommodating that although you can check out anytime you want— you may not want to! On the ground floor, you'll find the lobby and the low-lit library—with deep blue walls, a profusion of candles, and tin stars—as well as a small outdoor pool with sun chairs. Also at ground level is the **Emporio** boutique, which is well worth a visit for its rugs, jewelry, and glass lanterns; the **La Coronela Restaurant and Bar** (open daily 7am–11pm) is the nocturnal hot spot with live guitar, jazz, and blues on Saturday evenings. The recently added **Tequila Bar** is a small, decadently decorated spot, with red and black settees, and an extensive selection of tequilas, including their own Hotel California label.

For myself—and I would suspect many others—a meal at the **Café Santa Fe** 🌟, Calle Centenario 4 (© **612/145-0340**), is reason enough to visit Todos Santos. Much of the attention the town has received in recent years can be directly attributed to this outstanding cafe, and it continues to live up to its lofty reputation. Owners Ezio and Paula Colombo refurbished a large stucco house across from the plaza, creating an exhibition kitchen, several dining rooms, and a lovely courtyard adjacent to a flowering garden. The excellent northern Italian cuisine emphasizes local produce and seafood; try ravioli stuffed with spinach and ricotta in a Gorgonzola sauce, or ravioli with lobster and shrimp, accompanied by an organic salad. In high season, the wait for a table at lunch can be long. Everything is prepared to order, and reservations are recommended. Main courses run $10 to $20 (£5.50–£11). It's open Wednesday through Monday from noon to 9pm, closed September and October, and accepts MasterCard and Visa.

If you prefer a gourmet Mexican experience, the margaritas and the sopa tarasca, a decadent puree of white beans, chipotle peppers, and cream, at **Los Adobes** (© 612/ 145-0203) are alone enough to inspire a visit to the fine-dining restaurant on Hidalgo, just down from El Tecolote Libros.

A more casual option, and a magical place to start the day, is the garden setting of the **Café Todos Santos,** Centenario 33, down the street from the Todos Santos Inn (© 612/145-0300). Among the espresso drinks is the bowl-size *caffe latte,* accompanied by a freshly baked croissant or one of the signature cinnamon buns. Lunch or a light meal may include a *frittata* (an egg-based dish similar to quiche), a hearty sandwich on home-baked bread, or a fish filet wrapped in banana leaves with coconut milk. Main courses average $3 to $6 (£1.65–£3.30). The cafe is open Tuesday through Sunday from 7am to 9pm; credit cards are not accepted.

3 La Paz: Peaceful Port Town 🌟🌟

176km (109 miles) N of Cabo San Lucas; 195km (121 miles) NW of San José del Cabo; 1,544km (957 miles) SE of Tijuana

La Paz means "peace," and the feeling seems to float on the ocean breezes of this provincial town. Despite being an important port, home to almost 200,000 inhabitants, and the capital of the state of Baja California Sur, it remains slow-paced and relaxed. Beautiful deserted beaches just minutes away complement the lively beach and palm-fringed *malecón* (seaside boulevard) that front the town center. The easygoing city is the guardian of "old Baja" atmosphere, and it has an unmistakable air of outdoor adventure, thanks to the ubiquity of skilled anglers, competitive freedivers, Baja 1000 racers, recreational (as in, noncommercial) spear fishermen, a marina full of large yachts, and kayak rental agencies.

Adventurous travelers enjoy countless options, including hiking, rock climbing, diving, fishing, and sea kayaking. Islands and islets sit just offshore, once hiding places for looting pirates but now magnets for kayakers and beachcombers. You can even camp overnight, posh safari-style, at **Baja Camp** (www.bajacamp.com) on Espíritu Santo, or swim with sea lions on Los Islotes.

The University of Southern Baja California adds a unique cultural presence that includes museums and a theater and arts center. The surrounding tropical desert diversity and pandemic wildlife are also compelling reasons to visit. Despite its name, La Paz has historically been a place of conflict between explorers and indigenous populations. Beginning in 1535, Spanish conquistadors and Jesuit missionaries arrived and exerted their influence on the town's architecture and traditions. From the time conquistadors saw local Indians wearing pearl ornaments, mass pearl harvesting lasted through the late 1930s, when all the pearls eventually were wiped out. John Steinbeck immortalized a local legend in his novella *The Pearl.*

La Paz is ideal for anyone nostalgic for Los Cabos the way it used to be—and it has the breathtaking sunsets not always visible at Baja's tip. From accommodations to taxis, it's also one of Mexico's most outstanding beach vacation values and a great place for family travelers. However, as is the case throughout Mexico, development activity in the areas immediately surrounding La Paz may change this in the coming years, so plan a visit now to experience the pearl of La Paz in its natural state.

ESSENTIALS

GETTING THERE & DEPARTING   By Plane   Both **Alaska Airlines (② 800/ 252-7522) and **Delta** (② 800/241-4141) have nonstop flights from Los Angeles. **AeroMéxico** (② 800/237-6639 in the U.S., or 612/122-0091, -0093, or -1636) connects through Tucson and Los Angeles in the United States and flies from Mexico City and other points within Mexico. The airport is 18km (11 miles) northwest of town along the highway to Ciudad Constitución and Tijuana. Airport *colectivos* (around $12/£6.60 per person) run only from the airport to town, not vice versa, and a group shuttle is a flat charge of $25 (£14). **Taxi** service (around $27/£15) is available as well. Most major rental car agencies have booths inside the airport. **Budget**'s local number is ② 612/124-6433 or 122-7655; you can contact **Avis** at ② 612/122-2651, or **Alamo** at 612/122-6262.

By Car   From San José del Cabo, **Highway 1** north is the more scenic route, and it passes through a mountain town called San Bartolo, where heavenly homemade macaroons made of thick, fresh-cut coconut and pralines made from *cajeta* (goat's-milk caramel) are well worth the slightly longer drive; an arguably faster route is heading east of Cabo San Lucas, then north to **Highway 19** through Todos Santos. A little before San Pedro, Highway 19 rejoins Highway 1 and runs north into La Paz; both trips takes 2½ to 3 hours. From northern Baja, Highway 1 south is the only choice.

By Bus   The **Central Camionera** (main bus station) is at Jalisco and Héroes de la Independencia, about 25 blocks southwest of the center of town; it's open daily from 6am to 10pm. Bus service operates from the south (Los Cabos, 2½–3½ hr.) and north (as far as Tijuana). It's best to buy your ticket in person the day before, though reservations can be made over the phone at the bus station in your point of origin. Taxis are available in front of the station.

All routes north and south, as well as buses to Pichilingue, the ferry pier, and close to outlying beaches, are available through the **Transportes Aguila** station, sometimes called the beach bus terminal, on the *malecón* at Alvaro Obregón and Cinco de Mayo (② 612/122-7898). The station is open daily from 6am to 10pm. Buses to Pichilingue depart seven times a day from 8am to 5pm and cost $2 (£$1.10) one-way. Local buses arrive at the **beach station,** along the *malecón*. Taxis line up out front of both.

By Ferry   **Baja Ferries** serves La Paz from Topolobampo (the port for Los Mochis) daily at 11:30pm and the return trip to Topolobampo leaves La Paz at 3pm daily. Tickets are available at the Baja Ferries office in La Paz, on the corner of Allende and Marcelo Rubio (② 612/123-6600 or -1313), or at any Banamex banks throughout Mexico (make payable to Baja Ferries, SA de CV, account #7145468 sucursal 001.) The local office is open daily 8am to 6pm. For toll-free information, call ② 01-800/122-1414 within Mexico.

The ferry departs for Topolobampo daily at 11:30pm and arrives in La Paz 6 hours later. The ferries can carry 1,000 passengers, as well as accommodate vehicles and trucks. Passengers pay one fee for themselves ($68/£37 for a seat, $34/£19 for children ages 3 to 11, or $144/£79 for a cabin with four beds and one bathroom) and another for their vehicles ($100/£55). The ferries offer restaurant and bar service, as well as a coffee shop and live music, and a hot meal is included in the cost of the ticket. Disabled access is offered as well. Passengers are requested to arrive 3 hours prior to departure time. Information and updated schedules are available at www.bajaferries.com. Taxis meet each ferry as well, and cost about $8 (£4.40) to downtown La Paz.

VISITOR INFORMATION The most accessible visitor information office is on the corner of Alvaro Obregón and Nicolas Bravo (© **612/122-5939** or 612/124-0100; turismo@gbcs.gob.mx or turismo@lapaz.cromwell.com.mx). It's open daily from 8am to 8pm. The extremely helpful staff speaks English and can supply information on La Paz, Los Cabos, and the rest of the region. The official website of the La Paz Tourism Board is **www.vivalapaz.com**.

CITY LAYOUT Although La Paz sprawls well inland from the *malecón* (Paseo Alvaro Obregón), you'll probably spend most of your time in the older, more congenial downtown section within a few blocks of the waterfront. The main plaza, **Plaza Pública,** or Jardín Velasco, is bounded by Madero, Independencia, Revolución, and Cinco de Mayo.

GETTING AROUND Because most of what you'll need in town is on the *malecón* between the tourist information office and the Hotel Los Arcos, or a few blocks inland from the waterfront, it's easy to get around La Paz on foot. Public buses go to some of the beaches north of town (see "Beaches & Sports," below). To explore the many beaches within 80km (50 miles) of La Paz, your best bet is to rent a car or hire a taxi. There are several car-rental agencies on the *malecón*.

FESTIVALS & EVENTS February features the biggest and best **Carnaval/Mardi Gras** in Baja, as well as a 4- to 5-week **Festival of the Gray Whale** (starting in late Jan or early Feb, sometimes extending through early Mar). On May 3, **a festival** celebrates the city's founding by Cortez in 1535, and features *artesanía* exhibitions from throughout southern Baja. An annual **marlin-fishing tournament** is in August, with **other fishing tournaments** scheduled in September and November. On November 1 and 2, the **Days of the Dead,** altars are on display at the Anthropology Museum.

FAST FACTS: La Paz

Area Code The telephone area code is **612**.

Banks Banks generally exchange currency during normal business hours: Monday through Friday from 9am to 6pm, Saturday from 10am to 2pm. ATMs are readily available and offer bank exchange rates on withdrawals.

Drugstore One of the largest pharmacies is **Farmacía Baja California,** corner of Independencia and Madero (© **612/122-0240** or 123-4408). Open 7am to 9:30pm Monday to Saturday and Sundays from 8am to 9:30pm.

Emergencies Dial © **066** for general emergency assistance, or © **060** for the police.

Hospitals The two hospitals in the area are **Hospital Especialidades Médicas,** at Km 4.5 on the highway toward the airport (© **612/124-0400**), and **Hospital Juan María de Salvatierra** (© **612/122-1497**), Nicolás Bravo 1010, Col. Centro. Both are open 24 hours, and the former offers access to emergency air evacuation.

Internet Access In the fleeting world of Internet cafes, your best bet is to scan the *malecón* or ask your hotel concierge for their recommendations. However, **Omni Services,** which doubles as an Internet center and a real estate agency, offers Internet, Wi-Fi, fax, and long-distance VOIP phone service to the U.S. and Canada for 30¢ (17p) per minute on the *malecón,* Alvaro Obregón 460-C, close to Burger King (© **612/123-4888**; www.osmx.com). It also offers hookups for laptops, color printers, and copiers.

Post Office The *correo*, 3 blocks inland at Constitución and Revolución de 1910 (© **612/122-0388**), is open Monday through Friday from 8am to 5pm, Saturday from 8am to 1pm.

Tourism Office The office is at Carretera al Norte Km 5.5, Edificio Fidepaz, Col. Fidepaz, La Paz, B.C.S. (© **612/124-0100**). It's open daily from 8am to 3pm. A tourist information module is on the *malecón*, open daily from 8am to 8pm.

BEACHES & SPORTS

La Paz combines the unselfconscious bustle of a small capital port city with the charm of resort Mexico and beautiful, isolated beaches not far from town. Well on its way to becoming the undisputed adventure-tourism capital of Baja, it's the starting point for whale-watching, diving, sea kayaking, climbing, and hiking tours throughout the peninsula. For those interested in day adventures, travel agencies in major hotels or along the *malecón* usually can arrange all of the above, plus beach tours, sunset cruises, and visits to the sea lion colony. Agencies in the United States that specialize in Baja's natural history also book excursions (see "Special-Interest Trips," in chapter 2).

BEACHES   Within a 10- to 45-minute drive from La Paz lie some of the loveliest beaches in Baja. Many rival those of the Caribbean with their clear, turquoise water. The beach bordering the *malecón* is the most convenient in town. Although the sand in the Bay of La Paz is soft and white and the water appears turquoise and gentle, locals don't generally swim there. Because of the commercial port, the water is not considered as clean as that at the very accessible outlying beaches. With colorful playgrounds dotting the central beachfront and numerous open-air restaurants that front the water, it's best for a casual afternoon of post-sightseeing lunch and play.

The best beach nearby is immediately north of town at **La Concha Beach Resort;** nonguests may use the hotel restaurant and bar and rent equipment for snorkeling, diving, skiing, and sailing. It's 10km (6 miles) north of town on the Pichilingue Highway at Km 5.5. The other beaches are all farther north of town, but midweek you may have these distant beaches to yourself.

For more information about beaches and maps, check at the tourist information office on the *malecón*. For an overview of the beaches before deciding where to spend your precious vacation days, **Viajes Lybs,** Independencia 2050, between Mina and Galeana (© **612/122-4680;** fax 612/125-9600), offers a 4-hour beach tour for $25 (£14) per person, with stops at Balandra and El Tecolote beaches.

CRUISES   A popular and very worthwhile cruise is to **Isla Espíritu Santo** and **Los Islotes.** You visit the largest sea lion colony in Baja, stunning rock formations, and remote beaches, with stops for snorkeling, swimming, and lunch. If conditions permit, you may even be able to snorkel beside the sea lions. (*Note:* Remember sea lions are wild animals. Blowing bubbles in your face is their sign of warning, not of play, so steer clear of the giant bulls—who can be quite protective of their females—and let the curious babies come to you.) Both boat and bus tours are available to **Puerto Balandra,** where bold rock formations rising up like humpback whales frame pristine coves of crystal-blue water and ivory sand. **Viajes Lybs** (see above) and other travel agencies can arrange these all-day trips, weather permitting. Price is $80 (£44) per person.

ECOTOURS   A wide selection of ecotours and adventure activities are available through **Baja Quest** and **Grupo Fun Baja** (© 612/121-5884 or 125-2366; www. funbaja.com). In addition to diving excursions (the company's specialty) they also offer ATV tours and kite surfing. **DeSea Baja** (© 612/121-5100; www.deseabaja.com) offers driving tours in rental vehicles equipped for off-road adventures.

SCUBA DIVING   Scuba diving trips are best June through September. Fernando Aguilar's **Club Cantamar,** Obregón 1665-2 (© 612/122-1826; fax 612/122-3296; www.clubcantamar.com), arranges them. Rates start at $102 (£56) per person for a daylong two-tank dive or $125 (£69), including rental equipment. Another excellent dive operator is **Baja Quest** (© 612/123-5320; www.bajaquest.com.mx), at Rangel 10, between Sonora and Sinaloa. Day boat trips run approximately $110 (£61) for two tanks, $125 (£69) for three-tank dives. They also offer other outdoor adventures including kayaking and various wildlife watching, not to mention service in English, Spanish, and Japanese.

Also of note is **DeSea Baja** (© 612/121-5100; www.deseabaja.com), a complete tour company with expertise in diving and sportfishing. Prices are $145 (£80) for three-tank dives, including equipment, or $170 (£94), including a resort dive course. They also offer private boats with guides for underwater photo or video diving, and private divemasters or instructors for yachts or charters. DeSea also offers **freediving,** including instruction from internationally renowned freediving instructors, Aharon and Maria Teresa (MT) Solomon. Courses include yoga-based breathing exercises, mental control, and the physiology of breath hold. Beginning through advanced instruction is available, as are live-aboard charters and **spearfishing** excursions.

SEA KAYAKING   Kayaking in the many bays and coves near La Paz is a paddler's dream, and because some of the area's special sites for swimming and snorkeling are only accessible by kayak, daylong or multiday trips can't be beat. In the waters near La Paz, the water clarity gives the sensation of being suspended in the air. Bring your own equipment, or let the local companies take care of you. Several companies in the United States (see "Special-Interest Trips," in chapter 2) can book trips in advance. Locally, **Baja Quest** (see above; daytrips start at $90/£50, and multiday trips also are available) and **Mar y Aventuras (Sea and Adventures;** © 612/123-0559; fax 612/122-3559; www.kayakbaja.com) arrange extended kayak adventures.

SPORTFISHING   La Paz, justly famous for its sportfishing, attracts anglers from all over the world. Its waters are home to more than 850 species of fish. The most economical approach is to rent a *panga* boat with a captain and equipment. It costs $125 (£69) for 3 hours, but you don't go very far out. Super *pangas,* which have a shade cover and comfortable seats, start at around $180 (£99) for two persons. Larger cruisers with bathrooms start at $240 (£132). Local hotels and tour agencies arrange sportfishing trips.

You can arrange sportfishing trips locally through hotels and tour agencies. **La Paz Sportfishing** (© 310/691-8040; www.lapazsportfishing.com) rates start at $220 (£121) a day for two people. David Jones of **The Fishermen's Fleet** (© 612/122-1313; fax 612/125-7334; www.fishermensfleet.com) uses the locally popular *panga*-style fishing boat. David is superprofessional, speaks English, and truly understands area fishing.

The average price is $225 (£124) for the boat, but double-check what the price includes—you may need to bring your own food and drinks.

WHALE-WATCHING   Between January and March, and sometimes as early as December, 3,000 to 5,000 gray whales migrate from the Bering Strait to the Pacific coast of Baja. The main whale-watching spots are **Laguna San Ignacio** (on the Pacific near San Ignacio), **Magdalena Bay** (on the Pacific near Puerto López Mateos—about a 2-hr. drive from La Paz), and **Scammon's Lagoon** (near Guerrero Negro).

Most tours originating in La Paz go to Magdalena Bay, where the whales give birth to their calves in calm waters. Several companies arrange whale-watching tours that originate in La Paz or other Baja towns or in the United States; 12-hour tours from La Paz start at around $115 (£63) per person, including breakfast, lunch, transportation, and an English-speaking guide. Make reservations at **Viajes Lybs** (see above).

A BREAK FROM THE BEACHES: EXPLORING LA PAZ

Most tour agencies offer city tours of all the major sights. Tours last 2 to 3 hours, include time for shopping, and cost around $15 (£8.25) per person.

HISTORIC LA PAZ   When Cortez landed here on May 3, 1535, he named it Bahía Santa Cruz. It didn't stick. In April 1683, Eusebio Kino, a Spanish Jesuit, arrived and dubbed the place Nuestra Señora de la Paz (Our Lady of Peace). It wasn't until November 1, 1720, however, that Jaime Bravo, another Jesuit, set up a permanent mission. He used the same name as his predecessor, calling it the Misión de Nuestra Señora de la Paz. The mission church stands on La Paz's main square, on Revolución between Cinco de Mayo and Independencia.

The Anthropology Museum   The museum features large, though faded, color photos of Baja's prehistoric cave paintings. There are also exhibits on various topics, including the geological history of the peninsula, fossils, missions, colonial history, and daily life. All information is in Spanish.

Altamirano and Cinco de Mayo. ©/fax **612/122-0162** or 125-6424. Free admission (donations encouraged). Daily 9am–6pm.

El Teatro de la Ciudad   The city theater is the cultural center, with performances by visiting and local artists. Bookings include small ballet companies, experimental and popular theater, popular music, and an occasional classical concert or symphony.

Av. Navarro 700. © **612/125-0486**.

NATURAL MUSEUMS OF LA PAZ

Increasingly, La Paz is drawing numbers of travelers enchanted with the beauty of the area's diverse natural environment. Several new centers have emerged, combining entertainment with environmental education.

Aquarium   The newest of La Paz's natural museums opened in late 2003, and already is undergoing renovation to improve visitors' introduction to marine life in the Sea of Cortez. New attractions include a shark tank, a turtle exhibit, and an audiovisual center that will enable further education to students and groups. When the aquarium reopens (est. summer 2007), guided tours will be offered.

Pichilingue Km 5.5, next to the Hotel La Concha. © **612/121-5872**. Admission $5 (£2.75) adults. Tues–Sun 10am–6pm.

Cactus Sanctuary ✦   This 50-hectare (124-acre) natural reserve features 1,000 meters (3,300 ft.) of marked pathways and self-guided tours with information about the plants and animals of La Paz's desert region. Fifty unique areas have been identi-fied, which you can explore in consecutive order, or any other progression of your choosing. Route maps and guided tours are available, as well as descriptive signs for many of the plants. There's a surprising amount of wildlife to see here, from the myr-iad types of cacti, many of which are endemic to Baja California, to the numerous plants and animals that support this unique ecosystem. The sanctuary is in the Ejido El Rosario; go to the Ejido's main office (the *delegación*), and they will provide you with a key to enter the reserve.

Ejido El Rosario. (℅ 612/124-0245 (Dr. Hector Nolasco). hnolasco@cibnor.mx. $2 (£1.10) donation to enter. No fixed hours. 45 min. south of La Paz; take Hwy. 1 toward the town of El Triunfo; drive 10 min. inland along a dirt road.

Serpentarium ⚓ This mostly open-air natural museum offers plenty of opportu-nities to observe various species of reptiles that inhabit the region's ecosystem, includ-ing snakes, turtles, iguanas, lizards, and crocodiles. It's on the corner of Calle Brecha California and Calle La Posada. To get there, go to the southernmost point of the *malecón* at Calle Abasolo, where the last streetlights are, and just before the beach you'll see an unpaved street—that's Brecha California. If you're going with a group, e-mail cobra293@hotmail.com to make a reservation.

Calles Brecha California and La Posada. (℅ 612/123-5731. $8 (£4.40) adults, $5 (£2.75) children. Daily 10am–4pm.

SHOPPING

La Paz has little in the way of folk art or other treasures from mainland Mexico. The dense cluster of streets behind the **Hotel Perla,** between 16 de Septiembre and Degol-lado, is full of small shops, some tacky, others quite upscale. In this area, there is also a very small but authentic **Chinatown,** dating from the time when Chinese laborers were brought to settle in Baja. Serdán from Degollado south is home to dozens of sell-ers of dried spices, piñatas, and candy. Stores carrying crafts, folk art, clothing, hand-made furniture and accessories lie mostly along the *malecón* (Paseo Obregón) or within 1 or 2 blocks. The **municipal market,** at Revolución and Degollado, has little of interest to visitors. Something you're sure to notice if you explore around the cen-tral plaza is the abundance of stores selling electronic equipment, including stereos, cameras, and televisions. This is because La Paz is a principal port for electronic imports to Mexico from the Far East, and therefore offers some of the best prices in Baja and mainland Mexico.

Antigua California This shop manages to stay in business as others come and go. It carries a good selection of folk art from throughout Mexico. It's open Monday to Saturday from 9:30am to 8:30pm, Sunday from 10:30am to 2:30pm. Paseo Alvaro Obregón 220, at Arreola. (℅ 612/125-5230.

Artesanías Cuauhtémoc (The Weaver) If you like beautiful hand-woven table-cloths, place mats, rugs, and other textiles, it's worth the long walk or taxi ride to this unique shop. Fortunato Silva, an elderly gentleman, weaves wonderfully textured cot-ton textiles from yarn he spins and dyes himself. He charges far less than what you'd pay for equivalent artistry in the United States. Open Monday through Saturday from 10am to 3:30pm and 6pm to 7pm. On the corner of Abasolo and Oaxaca, between Jalisco and Nayarit. (℅ 612/122-4575.

Dorian's If you've forgotten essentials or want to stock up on duty-free perfume or cosmetics, head for Dorian's, La Paz's major department store. La Paz is a duty-free port city, so prices are excellent. Dorian's carries a wide selection of stylish clothing, shoes, lingerie, jewelry, and accessories as well. Open daily from 10am to 9pm. 16 de Septiembre, between Esquerro and 21 de Agosto. ℭ 612/122-8014.

Ibarra's Pottery   Here, you not only shop for tableware, hand-painted tiles, and decorative pottery, you can watch it being made. Each piece is individually hand-painted or glazed, then fired. Open Monday to Saturday from 9am to 3pm. You can call ahead to schedule a tour. Guillermo Prieto 625, between Torre Iglesias and República. ℭ 612/122-0404.

WHERE TO STAY

Grand Plaza La Paz ✦   Among La Paz's newest options in places to stay, this all-suite hotel offers travelers a comfortable sense of U.S. standards and modern conveniences. It's considered the best option for business travelers to the area, one of the few in town with a full business center, Internet access, secretarial assistance, and meeting space. Vacationers will also enjoy the hotels' location on the marina, as well as its range of helpful tour services and pleasant pool area. The clean, modern, and well-equipped rooms on three floors offer either views to the bay or overlooking the courtyard pool, with a choice of king or two double beds. Five different kinds of suites have a private balcony, and all have ocean views. The hotel is at the northern end of town, 5.6km (3½ miles) from downtown, at the Marina Fidepaz.

Lote A Marina Fidepaz, P.O. Box 482, 23090 La Paz, B.C.S. ℭ 800/227-6963 in the U.S., or 612/124-0830 or -0833. Fax 612/124-0837. www.grandplazalapaz.com. 54 suites. High season $186 (£102) double; 30% discount during low season. AE, DC, MC, V. Free guarded parking. **Amenities:** Restaurant; 2 bars; outdoor pool; fitness center; squash court; sauna; whirlpool; concierge; tour desk; business center; room service; babysitting; laundry service; Wi-Fi in lobby. *In room:* A/C, TV, coffeemaker, hair dryer, iron, safe, microwave (in some units).

Hotel Los Arcos   This three-story, neocolonial-style hotel at the west end of the *malecón* is the best place for downtown accommodations with a touch of tranquillity. Although the hotel is a bit dated, Los Arcos has functional furnishings and amenities and is filled with fountains, plants, rocking chairs, and even a Ping-Pong table. Most of the rooms and suites come with two double beds. Each has a balcony overlooking the pool in the inner courtyard or the waterfront, plus a whirlpool tub. I prefer the South Pacific-style bungalows with thatched roofs and fireplaces in the back part of the property. Satellite TVs carry U.S. channels.

Av. Alvaro Obregón 498, between Rosales and Allende (Apdo. Postal 112), 23000 La Paz, B.C.S. ℭ 800/347-2252 in the U.S., 714/450-9000, or 612/122-2744. Fax 612/125-4313. www.losarcos.com. 130 units. 52 bungalows. $100 (£55) double; $115 (£63) suite; $80–$100 (£44–£55) bungalow. AE, MC, V. Free guarded parking. **Amenities:** Cafeteria; restaurant; bar w/live music; 2 outdoor pools (1 heated); sauna; travel agency; fishing information desk; room service; laundry service. *In room:* A/C, TV, minibar.

Hotel Mediterrane ✦   Simple yet stylish, this unique inn mixes Mediterranean with Mexican, creating a cozy place for couples or friends to share. All rooms, two of which were remodeled this year, face an interior courtyard and are decorated with white-tile floors and *equipal* furniture, with colorful Mexican serapes draped over the beds. Some rooms have minifridges. All have VCRs. Its location is great—just a block from the *malecón*. The adjacent La Pazta restaurant (see "Where to Dine," below) is one of La Paz's best. Rates include use of kayaks and bicycles for exploring the town. This is a gay-friendly hotel.

Allende 36, 23000 La Paz, B.C.S. ℭ/fax 612/125-1195. www.hotelmed.com. 9 units. $66 (£36) double; $83 (£46) suite, plus $10 (£5.50) for additional person. AE, MC, V. Weekly discounts available. Street parking. *In room:* A/C, TV/VCR, Wi-Fi, no phone.

La Concha Beach Club Resort ☆   Ten kilometers (6 miles) north of downtown La Paz, this resort's setting is perfect: on a curved beach ideal for swimming and watersports. All rooms face the water and have double beds, balconies or patios, and small tables and chairs. Condos with full kitchens and one or three bedrooms are available on a nightly basis in the high-rise complex next door. They're worth the extra price for a perfect family vacation stay, although no children younger than 14 are allowed in the condos. The hotel offers scuba, fishing, and whale-watching packages.

Carretera Pichilingue Km 5, 23000 La Paz, B.C.S. ⓒ 612/121-6161. www.laconcha.com. 113 units. $95 (£52) double; $125 (£69) junior suite; $137–$259 (£75–£142) condo. AE, DC, MC, V. Free guarded parking. **Amenities:** Restaurant (w/theme nights); 2 bars; beachside pool; Jacuzzi; complete watersports center w/Wave Runners, kayaks, and paddleboats; tour desk; business center; free twice-daily shuttle to town; room service; laundry service; babysitting; beach club w/scuba program. *In room:* A/C, TV, Internet access, minibar.

Posada de Las Flores ☆   New owner Giuseppe Marceletti has continued the tradition of hospitality in this elegant B&B (formerly Posada Santa Fe), the best bet for travelers looking for a more refined place to stay in La Paz. Each room is individually decorated with high-quality Mexican furniture and antiques, hand-loomed fabrics, and exquisite artisan details. Bathrooms are especially welcoming, with marble tubs and thick towels. Breakfast is served from 8 to 11am daily, and complimentary wake-up coffee service is available on request. Telephone, fax, and Internet service are available through the office. It's at the northern end of the *malecón*.

Alvaro Obregón 440, 23000 La Paz, B.C.S. ⓒ 877/245-2860 in the U.S., or 612/125-5871. www.posadadelasflores.com. 8 units. High season $180 (£99) double, $290 (£160) suite; low season $150 (£83) double, $250 (£138) suite. Rates include full breakfast. No children younger than 12 accepted. MC, V. Street parking. **Amenities:** Small outdoor pool; Internet access; hospitality desk. *In room:* A/C, TV, minibar, hairdryer.

WHERE TO DINE

Although La Paz is not known for culinary grandeur, it has a growing assortment of small, pleasant restaurants that are good and reasonably priced. In addition to the usual seafood and Mexican dishes, you can find Italian, French, Spanish, Chinese, and vegetarian offerings. Restaurants along the *malecón* tend to be more expensive than those a few blocks inland.

MODERATE

Buffalo Bar-B-Q ☆☆ ARGENTINEAN/GRILLED HAMBURGERS   This is the ultimate send-off meal before a fishing, diving, or cruising trip, where dinner no doubt will be the daily catch. Indoor seating plays second fiddle to the outdoor courtyard, which fronts a fiery grill on which prime cuts are turned into delicacies. The hamburgers are big, flavorful, and come in so many delectable styles—from the special-sauced New Mexico burger to the standard cheeseburger—that a carnivore may just call this heaven. Otherwise, Buffalo Bar-B-Q's stellar steaks, ribs, and wine list are a worthy tribute to the chef's Argentinean roots.

Madero 1240 (corner of Cinco de Mayo and Constitución). ⓒ 612/128-8755. www.buffalo-bbq.com. Hamburgers and main courses $8–$15 (£4.40–£8.25). AE, MC, V. Wed–Mon 2pm–midnight.

La Pazta ☆ ITALIAN/SWISS   The trendiest restaurant in town, La Pazta gleams with black-lacquered tables and white tile; the aromas of garlic and espresso float in the air. The menu features local fresh seafood in items such as pasta with squid in wine-and-cream sauce, and crispy fried calamari. There's also homemade lasagna, baked in a wood-fired oven. La Pazta's daytime cafe is appealing for breakfast, too. The restaurant is in front of the Hotel Mediterrane, 1 block inland from the *malecón*.

Allende 36. ✆ **612/125-1195.** www.hotelmed.com. Breakfast $2–$4 (£1.10–£2.20); main courses $8–$15 (£4.40–£8.25). AE, MC, V. Cafe Thurs–Tues 7am–11pm, restaurant 3–11pm.

INEXPENSIVE

Café Expresso FRENCH/CAFE You'll feel as if you've suddenly been transported across the Atlantic in this incongruous but welcoming spot. Indulge in any number of espresso coffee drinks, plus French and Austrian pastries, while sitting at marble-topped bistro tables. Jazz music plays in the background.

Av. Obregón and 16 de Septiembre. ✆ **612/123-4373.** Coffees and pastries $1–$3 (55p–£1.65). No credit cards. Tues–Sun 6pm–4am.

El Quinto Sol VEGETARIAN Not only is this La Paz's principal health food market, it's a cheerful, excellent cafe for fresh fruit *licuados* (smoothies), *tortas,* daily vegetarian lunch specials, and ice creams made from in-season fruit. Tables sit beside oversize wood-framed windows with flowering planters in the sills. Sandwiches are served on whole-grain bread—also available for sale—and the potato tacos are an excellent way for vegetarians to indulge in a Mexican staple. Owner Marta Alonso also offers free nightly meditation classes to clients.

Av. Independencia and B. Domínguez. ✆ **612/122-1692.** Main courses $1.50–$7 (85p–£3.85). No credit cards. Mon–Sat 8am–4pm; store hours 8am–9pm.

LA PAZ AFTER DARK

A night in La Paz logically begins at a bar or cafe along the *malecón* as the sun sinks into the sea. A favorite ringside seat at dusk is a table at **La Terraza,** next to the Hotel Perla (✆ **612/122-0777**). La Terraza makes good schooner-size margaritas. **Pelícanos Bar,** on the second story of the Hotel Los Arcos (✆ **612/122-2744**), has a good view of the waterfront and a clubby, cozy feel. **Carlos 'n' Charlie's La Paz-Lapa** (✆ **612/122-9290**) has live music on weekends; and on the second-floor terrace above is **Casa de Villa,** where current pop music commingles with young *Paceños,* or La Paz locals, till late. **La Cabaña** nightclub (✆ **612/122-0777**), in the Hotel Perla, features Latin rhythms. It opens at 9pm, and there's a $4 (£2.20) cover on weekends. **Las Varitas,** Independencia and Domínguez (✆ **612/125-2025**), is where you'll hear Latin rock, ranchero, and salsa. It's open from 9pm to 3 or 4am, with cover charges around $5.50 (£3). Note that covers may rise or fall depending on the crowd.

4 Mid Baja: Loreto, Mulegé & Santa Rosalía

Halfway between the resort sophistication of Los Cabos and the frontier exuberance of Tijuana lies Baja's midsection, an area rich in history and culture. The indigenous cave paintings here are a UNESCO World Heritage Site, and the area was home to numerous Jesuit missions in the 1700s. These days, Mid Baja is known for its sea kayaking, freediving, sportfishing, off-road racing, and hiking.

Overlooked by many travelers (except avid sportfishermen), **Loreto** is a rare gem that sparkles under the desert sky. The purple hues of the Giganta Mountains meet the indigo waters of the Sea of Cortez, providing a spectacular backdrop of natural contrasts for the historic town. **Mulegé** is, literally, an oasis in the Baja desert. The only freshwater river (Río Mulegé) in the peninsula flows through town. And the port town of **Santa Rosalía,** while a century or so past its prime, makes a worthy detour, with its pastel clapboard houses and unusual steel-and-stained-glass church, designed by Gustave Eiffel (of Eiffel Tower fame).

The Lower Baja Peninsula

Bahía de
Sebastián Vizcaíno
Playa San Rafael
B. San Rafael

0   50 mi
0   50 km

Airport ✈
Beach 🏖

Bahía
Tortugas
Guerrero Negro
Pto. Nuevo

*Scammon's
Lagoon*

B. San Carlos
La Trinidad

Bahía Asuncion
B. La Asunción
Guadalupe
DESIERTO DE
B. Santa Ana

Bahía San Hipólito
San Ignacio
VIZCAINO
Santa Rosalía

*Laguna de
San Ignacio*
Mulegé

Gulf

*Bahía
Concepción*

San Juanico
La Purisima   San Isidro
B. San Basílio

of

SEa. COYOTE

*SIERRA DE LA
GIGANTA*

California

San Javier
Loreto
*Isla
Del Carmen*

Boca La Soledad
Va. Ignacio Zaragoza
Pto. Adolfo Lopez Mateos
Ciudad Insurgentes

Sea of Cortez

Puerto San Carlos
**Ciudad
Constitución**
B. Santa María
El Ciruelo
*Isla
San José*

Bahía Magdalena

San Ignacio
B. Coyote
*Isla La
Partida*

*PACIFIC
OCEAN*

*Isla
Espíritu Santo*

*Isla
Cerralvo*

Pichilingue
La Paz
Las Cruces

San Pedro
La Ventana
San
El Triunfo   Bartolo
*B. de los
Muertos*

Buena
Vista
*B. de
Palmas*

Los
Barriles
**La
Rivera**

Todos Santos
SIERRA DE LA LAGUNA
Santiago
Miraflores
Cabo
Pulmo

Gordo Banks

Cabo San Lucas
**San José
del Cabo**

UNITED STATES

MEXICO
*Gulf of
Mexico*

Area of
Detail
★ **Mexico
City**

0   500 mi
0   500 km

*PACIFIC
OCEAN*

737

Far enough away from the polished tourism gem of Los Cabos, the people's smiles are more sincere, and you rarely hear the timeshare salesman's grating "Hola, amiga" as you walk the streets. Nonetheless, plans may be in the works to change that. Ensenada Blanca Bay, Loreto Bay, and more are getting snapped up by north-of-the-border developers. Although mid-Baja is still a decade or more from being a hot spot for anyone besides adventurers, racing teams, and RV caravans, the plans are there, so if you want a glimpse of the Wild West, now is the time to visit Loreto, Mulegé, Santa Rosalía, and San Ignacio.

The region is also a popular jumping-off point for whale-watching tours. To find out when, where, and how to view the gentle giants, consult "Whale-Watching in Baja," later in this chapter.

LORETO & THE OFFSHORE ISLANDS

389km (241 miles) NW of La Paz; 533km (330 miles) N of Cabo San Lucas; 1,125km (698 miles) SE of Tijuana

The center of the Spanish mission effort during colonial times, Loreto was the first capital of the Californias and the first European settlement in the peninsula. Founded on October 25, 1697, it was selected by Father Juan María Salvatierra as the site of the first mission in the Californias. (California, at the time, extended from Cabo San Lucas to the Oregon border.) He held Mass beneath a figure of the Virgin of Loreto, brought from a town in Italy bearing the same name. For 132 years, Loreto served as the state capital, until an 1829 hurricane destroyed most of the town. The capital moved to La Paz the following year.

During the late 1970s and early 1980s, the Mexican government saw in Loreto the possibility for another megadevelopment along the lines of Cancún, Ixtapa, or Los Cabos. It invested in a golf course and championship tennis facility, modernized the infrastructure, and built an international airport and marina facilities at Puerto Loreto, several kilometers south of town. The economics, however, didn't make sense, and few hotel investors and even fewer tourists came. In the past 2 years, however, this effort has been revitalized, and the area is seeing a welcome influx of flights, as well as the addition of its first new hotel in years, a sprawling Inn at Loreto Bay (formerly the Camino Real). The Loreto Bay residential development has been a major part of renewed interest in the area, and it is bringing homes, condos, and other facilities to the area, with a rental program in place for vacation stays (© 877/865-6738 toll-free from the U.S., for rental information).

Soon, Loreto may become the next "new" place to go, but for now, downtown Loreto remains the heart rate–relaxing fishing village and gringo hideaway it's been for decades. The celebration of the town's 300th anniversary had the added benefit of updating the streets, plaza, and mission. Old Town Loreto is now a quaint showplace.

The *Loretanos,* Loreto-born Mexicans, are friendly and helpful; unlike the swarms of proprietary tourists that dominate the peninsula's northern and southern reaches, the mid-Baja region attracts a more unassuming set of visitors, and locals play the part of gracious hosts. Canadian and American expatriates who've settled in Loreto may be a bit more aloof with tourists, and who can blame them? They settled here when there was nothing, and they can't help but want it to stay that way for as long as possible.

The main reasons to come to Loreto center on the Sea of Cortez and the five islands just offshore, but the Sierra de La Giganta Mountains offer a wealth of opportunities for exploration as well. The reefs around Isla Coronado are home to schools of giant grouper, and beachgoers won't find a bay more beautiful than the one on Coronado's north side. Puerto Escondido shelters a growing yachting community; it's so lovely that most of the sailboats stay put year round. Kayakers launch here for trips to Isla del Carmen and Isla Danzante or down the remote mountain coast to La Paz; history buffs head for the mountains to visit some of the oldest Jesuit missions.

ESSENTIALS

The **Loreto International Airport** (© 613/135-0499 or -0498) is 6km (4 miles) southwest of town. **Taxis** (© 613/135-1255) are readily available and charge about $16 (£8.80) for the 10-minute ride to Loreto. It is serviced by **AeroMéxico** (© 800/ 237-6639 in the U.S., or 613/135-1837; fax 613/135-1838), **Alaska Airlines** (© 800/ 252-7522; www.alaskaair.com), and **Delta** (©800/241-4141 in the U.S.), which all have nonstop flights from Los Angeles. Loreto's Terminal de Autobuses, or **bus station** (© 613/135-0767), is on Salvatierra and Paseo Tamaral, a 10-minute walk from downtown. It's open 24 hours. The trip from La Paz takes 5 hours and costs $25 (£14).

The city **tourist information office** (© 613/135-0036 or -0411) is in the southeast corner of the Palacio de Gobierno building, across from the town square. It offers maps, local free publications, and other basic information about the area. It's open Monday through Friday from 8am to 3pm. Information, which may be outdated, is also available at **www.gotoloreto.com** and **www.loreto.com**.

Salvatierra is the main street that runs northeast, merging into Paseo Hidalgo, which runs toward the beach. Calle de la Playa, also known as the Malecón, parallels the water; along this road you'll find many hotels, seafood restaurants, fishing charters, and the marina. Most of the town's social life revolves around the central square, the old mission, and the Malecón. The local telephone **area code** is **613.**

WHAT TO SEE & DO

The Sea of Cortez is the star in Loreto and the five islands just offshore make for some of the best kayaking, sailing, diving, and fishing in North America. Freediving, too, is becoming more popular. Loreto is the nearest major airport and city to **Bahía de Magdalena (Magdalena Bay),** the southernmost of the major gray whale–calving lagoons on the Pacific coast of Baja. For more information on popular whale-watching spots and tour operators, see "Whale-Watching in Baja," later in this chapter.

Misión Nuestra Señora de Loreto was the first mission in the Californias, started in 1699. The original Virgen de Loreto, brought to shore by Padre Kino in 1697, is on display in the church's 18th-century gilded altar. The mission is on Salvatierra, across from the central square. Adjacent to the mission church and of equal or greater interest is the **Museo de las Misiones,** Salvatierra 16 (© 613/135-0441). It has a small but complete collection of historical and anthropological exhibits from the Jesuit mission period. The museum is open Tuesday through Sunday from 9am to 1pm and 1:45pm to 6pm. Admission is $3 (£1.65).

WHERE TO STAY

In general, accommodations in Loreto are the kind travelers to Mexico used to find all over: inexpensive and unique, with genuine, friendly owner-operators. And, as mid- Baja is a mecca of sorts for RV explorers, **Rivera Del Mar RV Park & Camping** (© 613/135-0718; www.riveradelmar.com) has deluxe hook-ups just 2 blocks from the beach. The rates quoted below do not include the 12% tax. Parking is free at all hotels in mid-Baja.

Inn at Loreto Bay ✦ *Kids*   Loreto's newest place to stay, the Inn at Loreto Bay (formerly the Camino Real) is on its own private cove a few kilometers outside of town, on a lovely beach, with calm waters perfect for swimming or kayaking. The hotel's brightly colored architecture complements sleek stone-floored guest rooms and warmtoned woven comforters. Master suites and presidential suites have large terraces and private Jacuzzis that overlook the bay. The ample space and recreational programs make this a great choice for families. Adjacent to Loreto's golf course, it's also ideal for anyone with a passion for the links. The upper-level Lobby Bar is a spectacular spot for a sunset cocktail, but the best place to take in the Sea of Cortez moonglow is from the terrace whirlpool tub.

Paseo de la Misión s/n, Nopoló, Loreto, B.C.S. (©) **877/865-6738** in the U.S., or 613/133-0010. reservations@loretobay.com. 156 units. High season $165–$190 (£91–£105) standard double, $230 (£127) junior suite, $290 (£160) master suite; low season $125–$150 (£69–£83) standard double; $210 (£116) junior suite; $270 master suite. Meal plans available. AE, MC, V. **Amenities:** 2 restaurants, 2 bars; outdoor pool; golf course; fitness center; concierge; tour desk; car rental; room service; child care; laundry service; Internet access. *In room:* A/C, satellite TV, minibar, hair dryer, safe, fan.

La Damiana Inn ✦✦ *Finds*   The location of the La Damiana Inn—in the heart of town on Calle Madero—is reason enough to book a reservation, but the warmth of color, style, and ownership make it the best accommodations value in Loreto. Debora Simmons lovingly operates this former family home, built in 1917. Today, its five rooms, all equipped with air conditioning and ceiling fans, offer a blend of twin, queen, and king beds that provide cozy resting places when you're not exploring the area. Wi-Fi throughout the hotel, laundry facilities, a shared living room, use of the kitchen, and free cuddles from two friendly house dogs are the extras that make La Damiana Inn seem more like a gracious friend's home than anything else. Pets welcome upon prior approval.

Madero, between Hidalgo and Jordan, Centro, 23880 Loreto, B.C.S. (©) **613/135-0356.** www.ladamianainn.com. 5 units. $50 (£28) double; $55 (£30) suite. No credit cards (American check accepted). **Amenities:** Wi-Fi; phone for local calls; library; complimentary bikes; TV; laundry service. *In room:* A/C, fan, no phone.

Posada de Las Flores ✦✦✦   The most luxurious place to stay in Loreto conveniently sits adjacent to the main square, in the heart of historic Loreto. Every room is beautifully decorated with fine Mexican arts and crafts, including heavy wood doors, Talavera pottery, painted tiles, candles, and Mexican scenic paintings. The colors and decor of the hotel are nouveau-colonial Mexico, with wood and tin accents. Large bathrooms have thick white towels and bamboo doors, with Frette bathrobes hanging in the closet. Every detail has been carefully selected, including the down comforters and numerous antiques tucked into corners. This hotel exudes class and refinement, from the general ambience to the warm polish of its employees. Italian-owned and operated, the sophisticated service has a European style to it. Only children older than 12 are welcome.

Salvatierra and Francisco I. Madera, Centro, 23880 Loreto, B.C.S. (©) **877/245-2860** in the U.S., or 613/135-1162. Fax 613/135-1099. www.posadadelasflores.com. 15 units. High season $180 (£99) double, $290 (£160) suite; low season $150 (£83) double, $250 (£138) suite. Rates include continental breakfast. Children 11 or younger not permitted. MC, V. Street parking. **Amenities:** Breakfast restaurant; rooftop glass-bottom swimming pool; hospitality desk. *In room:* A/C, TV, Wi-Fi, minibar, hair dryer.

An Ecoresort

Danzante Destination Resort ✦✦ *Finds*   This all-inclusive ecoresort offers guests everything that's wonderful about this area—sandy beaches, tranquillity, easy access to eco- and adventure activities—all in a lovely place to stay. It's 40km (25 miles) south of Loreto on serene Ensenada Blanca bay, home also to a tiny fishing village. The resort itself covers 4 hectares (10 acres), and is comprised of nine suites perched in a rocky hill facing the sea. Each king or queen room has a large Mexican-tile bathroom, beamed ceilings, handmade furnishings, large windows, and French doors that open onto a private thatched palm-covered terrace with hammocks. Lying in them and soaking in the view seems to be the favored activity of guests, yet there's much more you can do here—all activities are included in the room rate and include hiking, kayaking, snorkeling, and swimming at their secluded beach. Horseback riding is also available in the surrounding canyons, and diving, fishing, massage services, whale- and dolphin-watching, mission and cave painting tours, and "safari at sea" excursions can be arranged for an additional charge. For meals, included in the room rate, they serve a delicious selection of seafood, local fruits and vegetables, and organic produce from the on-site garden. The resort itself is entirely solar powered, and is owned by a couple who counts among their many accomplishments published books on Mexico travel and diving, underwater documentaries, explorations for sunken treasure, and guiding adventure tours worldwide. This may be their best achievement yet.

Highway 1 at Ligui, Ensenada Blanca, Loreto, B.C.S. ℂ 408/354-0042. www.danzante.com. info@danzante.com. 9 units. High season $199 per person (£109) queen suite, $225 per person (£124) king suite; low season $180 per person (£99) queen suite, $205 per person (£113) suite. All meals and activities included. MC, V. **Amenities:** Restaurant; bar; hilltop freshwater swimming pool; tour services; lending library; telescope for stargazing; cellphone at front desk; kayaks, horses, watersports, land and marine excursions. *In room:* Fan, hammock, no phone.

WHERE TO DINE

Dining in Loreto affords surprising variety, given the small size and laid-back nature of the town. However, don't expect anything fancy, even at the nicest restaurant. Big flavors come in humble packages in Loreto. In addition to the following hubs, the Wednesday two-for-one special at **Sushi Time** on the *malecón,* a vegetarian wood-fired pizza at **Pachamama** on Zapata, the grilled porterhouse at **El Nido** on Salvatierra, and the fried shrimp tacos at **Tacos el Rey** on Benito Juárez are all meals that will add flavor to your stay in Loreto.

Augie's Bar ⊕ PIZZA/BAR   Located on the *malecón,* this is the preeminent happy-hour hotspot for the gringo community. Augie, who hales from the California video arcade business and does fun for a living, offers dancing lessons to patrons after they've had six drinks—and he keeps good on his promise. With TV sports of all kinds, ocean views, fabulous margaritas, tortilla pizzas that drive the town crazy, and an upstairs terrace that showcases Loreto's big-sky sunsets, this is the place to be after 4pm any day of the week.

On the corner of the Malecón and Zaragoza. No phone. Pizza $5–$8 (£2.75–£4.40). No credit cards. Daily 7am–11pm.

Café Olé LIGHT FARE   Although an espresso machine is hard to come by in this town, the breezy Café Olé is the best option for breakfast. Try eggs with *nopal* cactus, hotcakes, or a not-so-light lunch of a burger and fries. Tacos and some Mexican standards are also on the menu, as are fresh-fruit smoothies, or *licuados.*

Madero 14. ℂ 613/135-0496. Breakfast $2–$5 (£1.10–£2.75); sandwiches $2–$3.50 (£1.10–£1.95). No credit cards. Mon–Sat 7am–10pm; Sun 7am–2pm.

Del Borracho ⊕ BURGERS/SANDWICHES   If you're a *Three Amigos* fan from way back, Mike and Andrea Patterson's tribute to the obscure bar in the classic comedy will not disappoint. The movie often plays on loop in the background of this wooden saloon outside of town while chili dogs, milkshakes, sandwiches, and burgers make the rounds among a happy-bellied crowd who are chugging draft beer. The only place in town to serve Modelo Light and Modelo Negro on draft, Del Borracho's real claim to fame is the $3.50 (£1.95) bowl of blow-your-mind clam chowder that comes with a side of Andrea's homemade bread. And ask about the smoked fish for sale— namely the candied dorado—from the **Loreto Smokehouse and Fish Factory** (© 613/ 113-8678; loretosmokehousefishfactory@yahoo.com); of note for sports fans, Del Borracho has the NFL Sunday Ticket.

.5km (quarter-mile) down the road to San Javier, 3.2km (2 miles) south of Loreto. © 613/137-0112. Main courses $3–$5 (£1.65–£2.75). No credit cards. Daily sunrise–sunset.

LORETO AFTER DARK

Although selection is limited, Loreto after dark seems to offer a place for almost every nightlife preference. Happy hour starts in the late afternoon and ends shortly after sundown at bars like **Augie's Bar** (see above). Cocktails, music, and tapas flow into the wee hours at **Antigua Casa del Negro Meza** on Salvatierra and Madero; and, if dancing is your game, the *malecón's* **Black&White** club gets going around 10pm Friday and Saturday nights. In addition, as is the tradition throughout Mexico, Loreto's central plaza offers a **free concert** in the bandstand every Sunday evening. However, Loretanos and their families are so hospitable that the best party may be the one to which you're unexpectedly invited. In Loreto, magic is bound to happen.

SANTA ROSALIA

61km (38 miles) N of Mulegé

Located in an *arroyo* (dry streambed) north of Mulegé, Santa Rosalía looks more like an old Colorado mining town than a Mexican port city. Founded by the French in 1855, the town has a European ambience combined with a distinctly Mexican culture. Pastel clapboard houses surrounded by picket fences line the streets, giving the town its nickname—*ciudad de madera* (city of wood). The large harbor and rusted ghost of a copper smelting facility dominate the central part of town bordering the waterfront. The town was a copper-mining center for years, and a French outfit operated here from 1885 until 1954, when the Mexicans regained the use of the land. Problems plagued the facility, which closed permanently in 1985.

Today, Santa Rosalía (pop. 14,000) is known for its man-made harbor—the recently constructed Marina Santa Rosalía, complete with concrete piers, floating docks, and full docking accommodations for up to a dozen ocean liners. Because this is the prime entry point of manufactured goods into Baja, the town abounds with auto parts and electronics stores, along with shops selling Nikes and sunglasses. The town has no real beach to speak of and few recreational attractions.

EXPLORING SANTA ROSALIA

The principal attraction in Santa Rosalía is the **Iglesia de Santa Bárbara,** a structure of galvanized steel designed by Gustave Eiffel (of Eiffel Tower fame) in 1884. It was created for the 1889 Paris World Expo, then transported here, section-by-section, and reassembled in 1897. Its somber gray exterior belies the beauty of the intricate stained-glass windows as viewed from inside.

The other sight to see is the former Fundación del Pacífico, or **Museo Histórico Minero de Santa Rosalía.** Located in a landmark wooden building, it houses a permanent display of artifacts from the days of Santa Rosalía's mining operations. It's open Monday through Saturday from 8:30am to 2pm and 5 to 7pm. Admission is $1.50 (85p).

⌒Moments   Whale-Watching in Baja

Few sights inspire as much reverence as close contact with a whale in its natural habitat. The various protected bays and lagoons on Baja's Pacific coast are the preferred winter waters for migrating gray whales as they journey south to mate and give birth to their calves. These whales are known to be so friendly and curious that they frequently come up to the boats and stay close by, and sometimes even allow people to pet them.

The experience is particularly rewarding in the protected areas of the **El Vizcaíno Biosphere Reserve**, where you can easily see many whales. This area encompasses the famous **Laguna Ojo de Liebre**—also known as **Scammon's Lagoon**—as well as Guerrero Negro, Laguna San Ignacio, and Bahía Magdalena.

Because these protected waters offer ideal conditions for gray whales during the winter, the neighboring towns have developed the infrastructure and services to accommodate whale watchers. Whale-watching season generally runs from January to March. But remember that the colder the water, the farther south the whales migrate, so check on water temperatures and whale sightings before you plan your expedition. The temperature on the boat can be quite cool, so bring a jacket.

Although you can fly from Los Cabos and La Paz, **Loreto** is the best place to launch a whale-watching journey, as it has a well-developed tourist infrastructure and a number of lovely resort hotels. Trips take you by road to Bahía Magdalena, where you board a skiff to get up close to the gentle giants. Locally based **Las Parras Tours** (© 613/135-0900; www.mexonline.com/lasparras.htm) offers excellent tours. Prices for package trips from Loreto run around $90 to $100 (£50–£55) per person for a daylong trip. Among the many groups that run longer-term expeditions, which cost upwards of $1,000 (£550) per person for a multiday trip, is San Diego-based **Baja Expeditions** (© 800/843-6967 in the U.S., or 612/125-3828; www.bajaex.com).

However, the city itself is the macro-attraction. Wooden saloons, wraparound verandas, and mountainous terrain make for a paradoxical contrast to the Mexicans milling in the streets. You can't get lost in this grid of one-way streets, so even if you're on your way some place else, a 15-minute drive through Santa Rosalía is a must. Here, in this thriving ghost town, you won't find hacienda-style architecture or red-tile roofs, but you will find the best bakery in Baja. **El Boleo**, at Avenida Obregón at Calle 4 (© 615/152-0310), has been baking French baguettes since the late 1800s, but I recommend the pitahaya, a dense sweetbread stuffed with a kind of almond paste. It's 3 blocks west of the church, and is open from 8am to 9pm Monday to Saturday, and Sunday 8am to 2pm.

WHERE TO STAY & DINE

Dining is limited in the small town of Santa Rosalía, but lunch at **El Muelle** restaurant, on Obregón, right across from the central plaza, is superb. The tacos, enchiladas in spicy fresh tomato sauce and breaded fish bathed in peppers and cheese are all good reasons to visit, but the main draw is the creamy chipotle smoked tuna dip that comes with chips before the meal. Follow it up with dessert bread from El Boleo.

Hotel Francés　Founded in 1886, the Hotel Francés once set the standard of hospitality in Baja Sur, welcoming European dignitaries and hosting the French administrators and businessmen of the mining operations. Today, it has a worn air of elegance but retains its position as the most welcoming accommodation in Santa Rosalía. Rooms are in the back, with wooden porches and balconies overlooking a small courtyard pool. Each room has individually controlled air-conditioning, plus windows that open for ventilation. Floors are wood-planked, and the small bathrooms are beautifully tiled. You have a choice of two double beds or one king. Telephone service is available in the lobby. The popular restaurant serves breakfast until noon.

Calle Jean Michel Cousteau s/n, 23920 Santa Rosalía B.C.S. ⓒ/fax **615/152-2052**. 16 units. High season $71 (£39) double; low season $65 (£36) single or double. Rates include breakfast. No credit cards. Free parking. **Amenities:** Restaurant (7am–noon); small courtyard pool. *In room:* A/C, TV, Wi-Fi, no phone.

5 Tijuana & Rosarito Beach

Northern Baja California is not only Mexico's most infamous border crossing, but it also claims to be the birthplace of the original Caesar salad and the margarita. Along the Pacific coastline south of the border, the towns of Tijuana and Rosarito Beach combine to make one of the country's most important entry points, not to mention an evolving destination.

Long notorious as a hard-partying 10-block border town, **Tijuana** has cleaned up its act a bit on its way to becoming a full-scale city. A growing number of sports and cultural attractions now augment the legendary shopping experience and wild nightlife. **Rosarito Beach,** of *Titanic* fame, remains a more tranquil resort town; the decidedly laid-back atmosphere makes enjoying its miles of beachfront easy.

TIJUANA: BAWDY BORDER TOWN

In northern Baja, 26km (16 miles) south of San Diego, the first point of entry from the West Coast of the U.S. is infamous Tijuana—a town that continues to delude travelers into thinking that a visit there means they've been to Mexico. An important border town, Tijuana is renowned for its hustling, carnival-like atmosphere and easily accessible decadence.

Tijuana's "sin city" image is gradually morphing into that of a shopper's paradise and a nocturnal playground. Vineyards associated with the expanding wine industry are nearby, and an increasing number of cultural offerings have joined the traditional sporting attractions of greyhound racing, jai alai, and bullfights.

You are less likely to find the Mexico you may be expecting here—no charming town squares and churches, no women in colorful embroidered skirts and blouses, no bougainvillea spilling out of every crevice. Tijuana has an urban culture, a profusion of U.S.-inspired goods and services, and relentless hawkers plying to the thousands of tourists who come for a taste of Mexico.

ESSENTIALS

A visit to Tijuana requires little in the way of formalities—people who stay less than 72 hours in the border zone do not need a tourist card. If you plan to stay longer, a tourist card is required and, beginning in January 2008, a passport will be required as

Tijuana

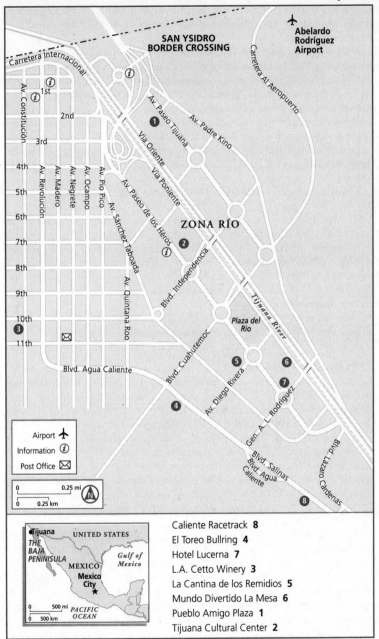

SAN YSIDRO
BORDER CROSSING

Abelardo
Rodríguez
Airport

Carretera Internacional

Carretera Al Aeropuerto

Av. Constitución

Av. 1st

2nd

3rd

4th

5th

6th

7th

8th

9th

10th

11th

Av. Revolución

Av. Madero

Av. Negrete

Av. Ocampo

Av. Pio Pico

Av. Sánchez Taboada

Av. Quintana Roo

Av. Paseo de los Heros

Av. Paseo Tijuana

Via Oriente

Via Poniente

Av. Padre Kino

ZONA RÍO

Blvd. Independencia

Blvd. Cuahutemoc

Blvd. Agua Caliente

Plaza del
Rio

Tijuana River

Av. Diego Rivera

Gen. A.L. Rodríguez

Blvd. Salinas
Blvd. Agua
Caliente

Blvd. Lázaro Cárdenas

Airport ✈
Information ⓘ
Post Office ✉

0   0.25 mi
0   0.25 km

Tijuana

UNITED STATES

THE
BAJA
PENINSULA

MEXICO

Mexico
City ★

Gulf of
Mexico

0   500 mi
0   500 km

PACIFIC
OCEAN

Caliente Racetrack **8**
El Toreo Bullring **4**
Hotel Lucerna **7**
L.A. Cetto Winery **3**
La Cantina de los Remidios **5**
Mundo Divertido La Mesa **6**
Pueblo Amigo Plaza **1**
Tijuana Cultural Center **2**

well. If you're staying 7 days or less, tourist cards are available free of charge from the border crossing station or from any immigration office, and will cost a small fee for more than 7 days.

From downtown San Diego, you also have the option of taking the **bright-red trolley** headed for San Ysidro and getting off at the last, or San Ysidro, stop (it's nicknamed the Tijuana Trolley for good reason). From here, follow the signs to walk across the border, or hop one of the buses (© **664/621-2982**), which are located next to the trolley station. It's simple, quick, and inexpensive; the one-way fare is about $2 (£1.10). The last trolley leaving for San Ysidro departs downtown San Diego around midnight; the last returning trolley from San Ysidro is at 1am. On Saturday, the trolley runs 24 hours.

Once you're in Tijuana, it's easy to get around by taxi. Cab fares from the border to downtown average $5 (£2.75). You can also hire a taxi to Rosarito for about $20 (£11) one-way.

The Tijuana airport (© **664/683-8002**) is about 8km (5 miles) east of the city. To drive to Tijuana from the U.S., take I-5 or 805 south to the Mexican border at San Ysidro. The drive from downtown San Diego takes about a half-hour, or you can leave your car in a San Ysidro parking lot and walk the 20 minutes to Avenida Revolución.

For **tourist information,** visit the Centro Cultural Tijuana, Paseo de los Héroes and Mina (© **664/687-9600**). It's in the Zona Río, the principal shopping and dining district, adjacent to the Tijuana River. For information online, visit the Tijuana Tourism board's official website, **www.seetijuana.com**. Another recommendable site is **www.tijuanaonline.org**.

There are major banks with ATMs and *casas de cambio* (money-exchange houses) all over Tijuana, but you can easily come here—or to Rosarito and Ensenada, for that matter—without changing money, because dollars are accepted everywhere.

EXPLORING TIJUANA

For many visitors, Tijuana's main event is the bustling **Avenida Revolución,** which was constructed in 1889. Beginning in the 1920s, American college students, servicemen, and hedonistic tourists discovered this street as a center for illicit fun. Some of the original attractions—gambling, back-alley cockfights (now illegal), and girlie shows—have fallen by the wayside, with drinking and shopping the main order of business these days. You'll find the action between calles 1 and 9; the landmark Jai Alai Frontón Palace anchors the southern portion. If you don't want to navigate the area on your own, the **Tijuana Convention & Visitors' Bureau** (© **664/683-1405;** www.tijuanaonline.org) offers a 1-hour guided walking tour of the city, and **Eco Baja Tours** (© **664/623-8875;** www.ecobajatours.com) offers a selection of tours, including visits to the Guadalupe Valley, La Bufadora, and Tecate.

If you're looking to see a different side of Tijuana, the best place to start is the **Centro Cultural Tijuana,** Paseo de los Héroes and Mina Zona Río (© **664/687-9600,** ext. 9650; www.cecut.gob.mx). You'll easily spot the ultramodern Tijuana Cultural Center complex, which houses an IMAX theater, the museum's permanent collection of Mexican artifacts, and a gallery of visiting exhibits. The center is open daily from 9am to 9pm. Admission to the permanent exhibits is free, there's a $2 (£1.10) charge for the special event gallery, and tickets for IMAX films are $4 (£2.20) for adults and $2.50 (£1.40) for children.

You'll find some classier shopping and a colorful local marketplace, plus go-karts and minigolf, at **Mundo Divertido La Mesa,** Vía Rápida Poniente 15035 (© **664/701-7133**). The park is open Monday through Friday from noon to 9pm and

Moments First Crush: The Annual Harvest Festival

If you enjoyed a visit to L.A. Cetto, Tijuana's winery (or Ensenada's Bodegas de Santo Tomás, discussed later in this chapter), then you might want to come back for the Harvest Festival, held each year in late August or early September. Set among the endless vineyards of the fertile Guadalupe Valley, the day's events include the traditional blessing of the grapes, wine tastings, live music and dancing, riding exhibitions, and a country-style Mexican meal. L.A. Cetto offers a group excursion from Tijuana (about an hour's drive); San Diego's **Baja California Tours** (© 800/336-5454 in the U.S., or 858/454-7166) also organizes a daylong trip from San Diego.

Sundays from 11am to 10pm. Admission is free, and several booths inside sell tickets for the various rides; most rides cost $1 to $11 (55p–£6.05).

The fertile valleys of northern Baja produce most of Mexico's finest wines and export many high-quality vintages to Europe. For an introduction to Mexican wines, stop into **Cava de Vinos L. A. Cetto (L. A. Cetto Winery),** Av. Cañón Johnson 2108, at Avenida Constitución Sur (© 664/685-3031, ext. 128, or 638-1644; www.lacetto.com). Shaped like a wine barrel, this building's striking facade is made from old oak aging barrels—call it inspired recycling. Guided tours are available Monday through Friday from 10am to 1:30pm and 4 to 6pm. On Saturdays, it's open from 10am to 4pm.

If your tastes run more toward *cerveza* than wines, plan to visit the **Tijuana Brewery,** 2951 Bulevar Fundadores, Col. Juárez (© 664/684-2406 or 638-8662; www.tjbeer.com). Here, guided tours (by prior appointment) demonstrate the beer-making process at the brewery. The family who owns the company has a long tradition of master brewers who worked in breweries in the Czech Republic, bringing their knowledge back home to Tijuana. Cerveza Tijuana was founded in January 2000, and now has select distribution in the U.S. Its lager, dark, and light beers are all available to sample in the adjoining European-style pub, which features karaoke on Monday and Tuesday nights and live music Wednesday through Saturday. A menu of appetizers and entrees is also available. Taberna TJ is open Monday to Saturday from 1pm to 2am.

Tijuana's biggest attraction is **shopping.** People come to take advantage of low prices on a variety of merchandise: terra cotta and colorfully glazed pottery, woven blankets and serapes, embroidered dresses and sequined sombreros, onyx chess sets, beaded necklaces and bracelets, silver jewelry, leather bags and *huarache* sandals, rain sticks, Cuban cigars, and Mexican liquors. You're permitted to bring $400 (£220) worth of purchases back across the border (sorry, no Cuban cigars allowed), including 1 liter (.26 gallons) of alcohol per person. Many Americans view Tijuana as a way to purchase inexpensive prescription drugs and bring them back across the border. Be aware—authorities have cracked down on this practice and are now making surprise arrests of foreigners purchasing drugs without valid prescriptions from a Mexican doctor.

If a marketplace atmosphere and spirited bargaining are what you're looking for, head to **Mercado de Artesanías (crafts market),** Calle 2 and Avenida Negrete. Here, vendors of pottery, clayware, clothing, and other crafts fill an entire city block.

Shopping malls are as common in Tijuana as in any big American city; you shouldn't expect to find typical souvenirs there, but shopping alongside residents and other intrepid visitors is often more fun than feeling like a sitting-duck tourist. One of the biggest, and most convenient, is **Plaza Río Tijuana,** Paseo de los Héroes 96 at Avenida Independencia, Zona Río (© **664/684-0402**), an outdoor plaza anchored by several department stores and featuring dozens of specialty shops and casual restaurants. **Plaza Agua Caliente** (© **664/681-7777**), at 4558 Bulevar Agua Caliente, Col. Aviación, is a more upscale shopping center, and in addition to fine shops and restaurants, is known for its emphasis on health and beauty, with day spas, gyms, and doctors offices found in abundance here. A comprehensive selection of shopping options is listed at **www.tijuanaonline.org/english/shopping/index.htm**.

OUTDOOR ACTIVITIES & SPECTATOR SPORTS

Tijuana is a spectator's (and gambler's) paradise.

BULLFIGHTING Whatever your opinion, bullfighting has a prominent place in Mexican heritage and is even considered an essential element of the culture. The skill and bravery of matadors is closely linked with cultural ideals regarding *machismo,* and some of the world's best perform at Tijuana's two stadiums. The season runs late spring to early fall (usually May–early Oct), with events held on Sunday at 4:30pm. Ticket prices range from $25 to $50 (£ 14–£28), the premium seats are on the shaded side of the arena, and can be purchased at the bullring or in advance from San Diego's **Five Star Tours** (© **619/232-5049** or 664/622-2203). **El Toreo de Tijuana** (© **664/ 686-1510** or -1219; www.bullfights.org) is 3km (2 miles) east of downtown on Bulevar Agua Caliente at Avenida Diego Rivera. **Plaza de Toros Monumental,** also called Bullring-by-the-Sea (© **664/680-1808;** www.plazamonumental.com), is 10km (6 miles) west of downtown on Highway 1-D (before the first toll station); it's perched at the edge of both the ocean and the California border.

DOG RACING There's satellite wagering on U.S. horse races at the majestic **Caliente Racetrack,** off Bulevar Agua Caliente, 5km (3 miles) east of downtown (© **619/231-1910** or 664/682-3110; www.caliente.com.mx), but only greyhounds actually kick up dust at the track. Races are held daily at 7:45pm; at 1pm on Sunday, Monday, and Tuesday; and at 2pm on Saturday. Admission is free.

A PLACE TO STAY

Hotel Lucerna Once the most chic hotel in Tijuana, Lucerna now feels slightly worn, though it still has personality. The flavor is Mexican Colonial—wrought-iron railings and chandeliers, rough-hewn heavy wood furniture, brocade wallpaper, and traditional tiles. The hotel is in the Zona Río, away from the noise and congestion of downtown, so a quiet night's sleep is easily attainable. All of the rooms in the five-story hotel have balconies or patios. Hotel rates in Tijuana are subject to a 12% tax.

Av. Paseo de los Héroes, 10902 Zona Río, Tijuana. © **664/633-3900.** 168 units. $190 (£105) double; $360 (£198) suite. AE, MC, V. Free parking. **Amenities:** Coffee shop; outdoor pool; room service. *In room:* A/C, satellite TV, coffeemaker, hair dryer, iron, fresh fruit.

WHERE TO DINE

Cien Años MEXICAN This elegant and gracious Zona Río restaurant offers artfully blended Mexican flavors (tamarind, *poblano chile,* mango) in stylish presentations. If you're interested in haute cuisine for breakfast, lunch, or dinner, the buzz around Tijuana is all about this place.

José María Velazco 1407, Zona del Río. ⓒ 888/534-6088 or 619/819-5070 in the U.S.; 664/634-3039 or -7262. Main courses $10–$20 (£5.50–£11). AE, MC, V. Mon–Thurs 8am–11pm; Fri–Sat 8am–midnight; Sun 8am–10pm.

La Cantina de los Remedios MEXICAN   This is one of Tijuana's most festive atmospheres, wildly popular with Mexicans and Americans alike for it's typical Mexican cuisine and courtyard atmosphere. Another highlight is its all-inclusive menu option, which has made it a hit in seven other cities throughout Mexico. For one price, guests can enjoy an appetizer, soup or salad, main course, dessert, and a cocktail. Here, the drink menu is extensive, inspiring the name *los remedios,* or the remedies.

Av. Diego Rivera 19 718, Zona del Río. ⓒ 664/634-3065. All-inclusive meal $18–$137 (£9.90–£75). MC, V. Mon–Thurs 1pm–1am; Fri–Sat 1pm–2am; Sun 1–10pm.

⟨Finds⟩ A Northern Baja Spa Sanctuary

One of Mexico's best-known spas is in northern Baja, just 58km (36 miles) south of San Diego. The **Rancho La Puerta** ✦✦ occupies 1,200 hectares (2,964 acres) of lush oasis surrounded by pristine countryside, which includes a 2.5-hectare (6-acre) organic garden and La Cocina Que Canta, a spa cuisine cooking school set to open in summer of 2007. Cottages can accommodate up to 150 guests per week, and the ranch has a staff of almost 400. Each cottage has its own patio garden and is decorated with Mexican folk art. Inside the rooms are spacious living-room-sized seating areas, desks, CD players, hair dryers, robes, and safes, and most rooms have fireplaces.

Three swimming pools, four tennis courts, five hot tubs, saunas, steam rooms, and eleven gyms for aerobic and restorative classes, are only a part of the facilities. Separate men and women's health centers offer the full range of spa services. Hiking trails surround the resort, and there's even a labyrinth that is a full-size replica of the ancient labyrinth found in Chartres Cathedral, for moving meditation.

There are also several lounges and shared spaces, including the library, with thousands of books to browse and read, an evening movie lounge, recreation room, and for those who can't conceive of totally disconnecting, the E-center, with 24-hour access to e-mail and Internet.

Rancho La Puerta runs weeklong programs—Saturday through Saturday—emphasizing a mind/body/spirit philosophy, and certain weeks throughout the year are geared specifically to one topic; Specialty Week themes range from couples to Pilates and dance to meditation. Prices begin at $2,690 (£1,480) for the week most of the year and $2,780 (£1,529) for the week from March through May. Included in the rates are all classes, meals, evening programs, and use of facilities. Personal spa services are an extra charge. You may be able to book shorter stays (3 nights or more); and rates may be prorated on a nightly basis.

For reservations or to request a brochure, visit www.rancholapuerta.com; call **800/443-7565** in the U.S., or fax 858/764-5500. American Express, Master Card, and Visa are accepted.

TIJUANA AFTER DARK

Avenida Revolución is the center of the city's nightlife; many compare it with Bourbon Street in New Orleans during Mardi Gras—except here it's a regular occurrence, not a once-a-year blowout.

Zona Río and Plaza Fiesta are more geared toward late-night dining and dance-clubbing than tequila swilling and barhopping. Although the nightlife scene changes regularly, perhaps the most popular dance club is **Baby Rock,** 1482 Diego Rivera (© **664/634-2404**), Zona Río, near the Guadalajara Grill restaurant, a cousin to Acapulco's lively Baby O, which features everything from Latin rock to rap. It's open from 9pm to 3am, with a cover charge of $12 (£6.60) on Saturdays.

Also popular in Tijuana are sports bars, featuring wagering on events from all over the United States as well as races from Tijuana's Caliente track. The most popular of these bars cluster in the Pueblo Amigo and Vía Oriente areas and around Plaza Rio Tijuana in the Zona Río, a center designed to resemble a colonial Mexican village. Also in Zona Río is the chic club **Karma** (Paseo de los Héroes 954713; © **664/900-6063;** Wed–Sat 9pm–3am). Just beyond Zona Río you'll find **Tangaloo** (Av. Monterrey 3215; © **664/681-8091;** www.tangaloo.com; Thurs–Sun 9pm–4am), a hip club featuring DJs spinning electronic dance music, with a changing theme each Saturday night. Two of the town's hottest clubs, which are open until 4 or 5am on the weekends, **Rodeo de Media Noche** (© **664/682-4967;** cover $8/£4.40) and **Señor Frog's** (© **664/682-4964;** no cover), are in Pueblo Amigo Plaza, which is just off of Paseo Tijuana. Pueblo Amigo Plaza is less than 3km (2 miles) from the border, a short taxi ride or—during daylight hours—a pleasant walk.

ROSARITO BEACH: BAJA'S FIRST BEACH RESORT

Just 29km (18 miles) south of Tijuana and a complete departure in ambience, Rosarito Beach is a tranquil, friendly beach town. Hollywood has played a major part in Rosarito's recent renaissance—it was the location for the sound stage and filming of the Academy Award-winning *Titanic.* The former *Titanic* Museum—now called **Foxploration**—continues to draw the fans of this film and moviegoers in general. The beaches between Tijuana and Rosarito are also known for excellent surf breaks.

GETTING THERE   Two roads run between Tijuana and Ensenada (the largest and third-largest cities in Baja)—the scenic, coast-hugging toll road (**Hwy. 1-D,** marked *cuota,* costs $2.40), and the free but slower public road (**Hwy. 1,** marked *libre*). Both roads pass through Rosarito Beach. If you're not driving, you can take a shuttle from the last trolley stop in San Ysidro. **Mexicoach** (© **619/428-9517** in the U.S., or 664/685-1470 locally; www.mexicoach.com) offers shuttle rides for about $10 (£5.50).

WHAT TO SEE & DO

A few kilometers south of Rosarito proper lies the **seaside production site** of 1997's megablockbuster *Titanic,* and more recently, *Master and Commander.* On 16 otherwise dry hectares (40 acres) along the Pacific Coast, the studio has several huge tanks that fill with water to reproduce seafaring conditions. Filled with *Titanic* memorabilia, it has now become the moviemaking theme park, **Foxploration,** devoted to the art of moviemaking. The Cinemágico area has interactive displays about filmmaking and special effects, and guided tours are available in English and Spanish. There is also a play center for kids, plus a gift shop. Admission is $12 (£6.60) for adults, $9 (£4.95) for children 3 to 11. Foxploration (© **866/369-2252** in the U.S., or 661/614-9444; www.foxploration.com) is open Wednesday through Friday from 9am to 4:30pm, and

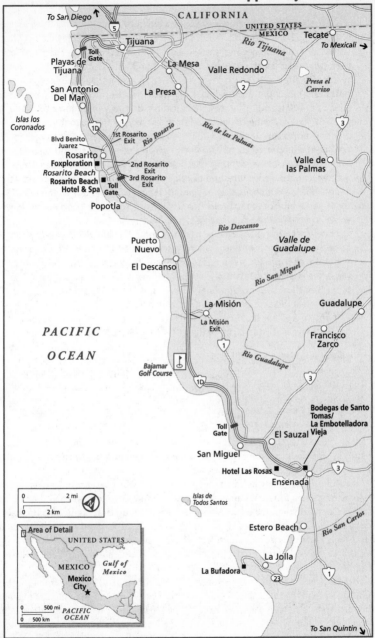

The Upper Baja Peninsula

CALIFORNIA

UNITED STATES
MEXICO

To San Diego ↑

Rio Tijuana

Tijuana

Tecate

To Mexicali →

Toll Gate

Playas de Tijuana

La Mesa

Valle Redondo

San Antonio Del Mar

La Presa

Presa el Carrizo

Islas los Coronados

Rio Rosario

Rio de las Palmas

1st Rosarito Exit

Blvd Benito Juarez

Valle de las Palmas

Rosarito

Foxploration ■

2nd Rosarito Exit

Rosarito Beach
Rosarito Beach Hotel & Spa

3rd Rosarito Exit

Toll Gate

Popotla

Rio Descanso

Valle de Guadalupe

Puerto Nuevo

El Descanso

Rio San Miguel

La Misión

Guadalupe

La Misión Exit

Francisco Zarco

PACIFIC

OCEAN

Rio Guadalupe

Bajamar Golf Course

Bodegas de Santo Tomas/ La Embotelladora Vieja

Toll Gate

El Sauzal

San Miguel

Hotel Las Rosas ■

Ensenada

Islas de Todos Santos

Estero Beach

Rio San Carlos

0   2 mi
0   2 km

La Jolla

La Bufadora ■

Area of Detail

UNITED STATES

MEXICO

Gulf of Mexico

Mexico City ★

0   500 mi
0   500 km

PACIFIC OCEAN

To San Quintin ↓

Tips Surfing, Northern Baja Style

From California and beyond, surfers come to the northern Baja coastline for perpetual right-breaking waves, cheap digs and eats, and *Endless Summer*-type camaraderie.

Undoubtedly, the most famous surf spot in all of Mexico is Killers, at Todos Santos Island. This was the location of the winning wave in the 1997–98 K2 Challenge (a worldwide contest to ride the largest wave each winter—and be photographed doing it). Killers is a very makeable wave for confident, competent surfers. To get there you need a boat. You can get a lift from the local *panga* (skiff) fleet, for about $100 (£55) for the day. That's pretty much the going rate, and the tightly knit Ensenada *pangueros* aren't eager to undercut each other. It's about 15km (10 miles) out to the island; there you'll anchor and paddle into the lineup. You must bring everything you'll need—food, drink, sunscreen, and so on.

Other less radical and easier-to-reach spots include the rocky Popotla break, just south of Rosarito, where you'll walk to the beach through the Popotla trailer park. Calafia, also just a few kilometers south of Rosarito, has a reeling right point that can get extremely heavy. San Miguel is the point break just south of the final tollbooth on the highway into Ensenada. It's an excellent wave but generally crowded.

If you're a surfer looking to get your bearings or a beginner wanting to get your feet wet, stop by **Inner Reef** (© 661/613-2065; Km 34.5 on the free road, 9.7km/6 miles south of Rosarito). This tiny shack, painted green with blue flames, offers all the essentials: wax, leashes, patch kits, custom surfboards, rentals, and ding repairs. Owner Mitch Benson is there daily from 9am to 5pm in winter and from 8am to 6pm in summer. He also has a shop in front of Rosarito Beach Hotel.

Saturday and Sunday from 10am to 5:30pm. There's a food court with Dominos pizza, Subway, and even a Starbucks coffee.

If you have only a few hours to spend in Rosarito Beach, that's still enough time to have a swim or a horseback ride at the beach, shop for souvenirs, and dine on fish tacos or tamales from one of the family-run stands along **Bulevar Benito Juárez,** the town's main (and only) drag. The dozen or so blocks of Rosarito north of the Rosarito Beach Hotel are packed with stores typical of Mexican border towns: curio shops, cigar and *licores* (liquor) stores, and *farmacías* (where such drugs as Viagra, Retin-A, Prozac, and many more are available at low cost).

Because the legal drinking age in Baja is 18, the under-21 crowd from Southern California tends to flock across the border on Friday and Saturday nights. The most popular spot in town is **Papas & Beer** (© 661/612-0444; www.papasandbeer.com). It's a relaxed come-as-you-are-type club on the beach, just a block north of the hotel. Even for those young in spirit only, it's great fun, with outdoor tables and a bar surrounding a sand volleyball court. The **Salón Mexicano** (© 661/612-0144), in the Rosarito Beach Hotel, attracts a slightly more mature evening crowd, with live music on Friday and Saturday.

WHERE TO STAY & DINE

Rosarito Beach Hotel & Spa   Although this once-glamorous family-owned resort has been holding steady since its 1920s heyday, it's currently defined by glaring night-time neon and party-mania. Despite the resort's changed personality, its unique artistic construction and lavish decoration remain. It has a wide, family-friendly stretch of beach. The stately home of the original owners has been transformed into the full-service **Casa Playa Spa**, where massages and other treatments are only slightly less costly than in the U.S. You'll pay more for a room with an ocean view, and more for the newer, air-conditioned units in the tower; the older rooms in the poolside building have only ceiling fans, but they prevail in the character department, with hand-painted trim and original tile. The mansion's dining room (Chabert's Restaurant) charges top dollar for Continental cuisine; Azteca is a casual Mexican restaurant in the main building.

Bulevar Benito Juárez, Zona Centro, 22710 Rosarito, B.C. Ⓒ 800/343-8582 in the U.S., or 661/612-0144. Fax 661/612-1125. www.rosaritobeachhotel.com. 278 units. $97–$167 (£53–£92) double; $125–$251 (£69–£138) suites. 2 children younger than 12 stay free in parent's room. Packages available. MC, V. Free parking. **Amenities:** 2 restaurants; bar; 2 outdoor pools; wading pool; spa; racquetball court; playground; room service; Wi-Fi in some areas of hotel. *In room:* A/C (in some), fan (in some), TV.

6 Ensenada: Port of Call

134km (83 miles) S of San Diego; 109km (68 miles) S of Tijuana

Ensenada is an attractive town on a lovely bay, surrounded by sheltering mountains. About 40 minutes from Rosarito, it's the kind of place that loves a celebration—be it for a bicycle race or a seafood festival.

GETTING THERE & INFORMATION   After passing through the final tollgate, **Highway 1-D** curves sharply toward downtown Ensenada.

The **Tourist and Convention Bureau booth** (Ⓒ 646/178-2411; www.enjoy ensenada.com) is at the western entrance to town, where the waterfront-hugging Bulevar Lázaro Cárdenas—also known as Bulevar Costero—curves away to the right. It's open Monday through Friday from 9am to 7pm. and Saturday and Sunday from 9am to 5pm. Taxis park along López Mateos.

EXPLORING ENSENADA

While Ensenada is technically a border town, one of its appeals is its multilayered vitality. The bustling port consumes the entire waterfront—beach access can be found only north or south of town—and the Pacific fishing trade and agriculture in the fertile valleys surrounding the city dominate the economy.

Even part-time oenophiles should pay a visit to the **Bodegas de Santo Tomás Winery** ✪✪, Av. Miramar 666, at Calle 7 (Ⓒ 646/178-3333; www.santo-tomas.com), the oldest winery in Mexico, and the largest in Baja. It uses old-fashioned methods of processing grapes, first cultivated from Spanish varietals in 1888, in the lush Santo Tomás Valley, where a Dominican mission of the same name was founded almost a century earlier. Tours in English run every hour from 9am to 5pm Monday through Saturday and from 10am to 4pm Sunday. The tour is free, and if you wish to follow it up with a tasting, $5 (£2.75) gets you a sampling of six young or low-priced wines, and the $10-option (£5.50) includes six older or high-priced wines and two reserves.

Ensenada's equivalent of Tijuana's Avenida Revolución is crowded **Avenida López Mateos,** roughly parallel to Bulevar Lázaro Cárdenas (Bulevar Costero); the highest concentration of shops and restaurants is between avenidas Ruiz and Castillo. Compared to Tijuana, there is more authentic Mexican art and craftwork in Ensenada. And Ensenada is home to a thriving adventure subculture: off-road racers, surfers, kayakers, and more flock to Ensenada in search of their adrenaline fix.

South of the city, 45 minutes by car along the rural Punta Banda peninsula, is one of Ensenada's major attractions: **La Bufadora,** a natural sea spout in the rocks. With each incoming wave, water is forced upward through the rock, creating a geyser whose loud grunt gave the phenomenon its name (it means "buffalo snort"). From downtown Ensenada, take Avenida Reforma (Hwy. 1) south to Highway 23 west. La Bufadora is at the end of the road. Once parked (about $2/£1.10 per car in crude dirt lots), you must walk downhill to the viewing platform, at the end of a 270m (986-ft.) pathway lined with souvenir stands. Also, **Picacho del Diablo,** the 10,154-foot mountain located in the Sierra de San Pedro Mártir national park, draws hikers and backpackers eager to scale its two-pronged peak about 129km (80 miles) south of Ensenada.

WHERE TO STAY

Las Rosas Hotel & Spa One of the most modern hotels in the area, Hotel Las Rosas still falls short of most definitions of luxurious, yet the pink oceanfront hotel 3km (2 miles) outside Ensenada is the favorite of many Baja aficionados. It offers most of the comforts of an upscale American hotel—which doesn't leave room for much Mexican personality, but surfers will appreciate the view of Todos Santos Island. The atrium lobby is awash in pale pink and sea foam green, a color scheme that pervades throughout—but the rooms received a welcome update in 2006. Some rooms have fireplaces, wireless Internet, and/or in-room whirlpools, and all have balconies overlooking the pool and ocean. One of the resort's main photo-ops is the swimming pool that overlooks the Pacific and features a vanishing edge that appears to merge with the ocean beyond. If you're looking to maintain the highest comfort level possible, this would be your hotel of choice.

Hwy. 1, 3km (2 miles) north of Ensenada. (C) **866/447-6727** in the U.S., or 646/174-4310. www.lasrosas.com. 48 units. $89–$142 (£49–£78) double; $125–$184 (£69–£101) suite. MC, V. Free parking. **Amenities:** Restaurant; cocktail lounge; outdoor pool; tennis court; small workout room; full-service spa; cliff-top hot tub; business center w/Internet; room service; laundry service. *In room:* TV, Wi-Fi in some, hairdryer, fan.

WHERE TO DINE

El Rey Sol ⭐ FRENCH/SEAFOOD If you've been to Ensenada without eating at El Rey Sol, you better not tell a local. *Ensenadenses* are as proud of this family-run French restaurant as they are of their festivals, and after one taste of the clams au gratin, Chateaubriand bouquetiere, farm-fresh vegetables, or mango charlotte, you will understand why. El Rey Sol, which opened in 1947, also offers a selection of traditional Mexican plates for dinner as well as coffee and French pastries at the sidewalk cafe during the day.

Av. Lopez Mateos 1000. (C) **646/178-1733.** Reservations recommended on weekends. Main courses $9–$19 (£4.95–£10). AE, MC, V. Daily 7:30am–10:30pm

ENSENADA AFTER DARK

Just like in *Casablanca,* where "everyone goes to Rick's," everyone's been going to **Hussong's Cantina,** Av. Ruiz 113, near Avenida López Mateos ((C) **646/178-3210**), since the bar opened in 1892. Nothing much has changed—the place still sports Wild

West–style swinging saloon doors, a long bar to slide beers along, and strolling mari-achis bellowing above the din. Be aware that hygiene and privacy are low priorities in the restrooms. While the crowd (a pleasant mix of tourists and locals) at Hussong's can really whoop it up, they're amateurs compared to those who frequent **Papas & Beer,** Avenida Ruiz near Avenida López Mateos (© **646/174-0145;** www.papasandbeer. com), across the street. A tiny entrance leads to the upstairs bar and dance club. The music is loud and the hip young crowd is definitely here to party. Papas & Beer has quite a reputation with the Southern California college crowd, and has opened a branch in Rosarito Beach (see above).

Appendix A:
Mexico in Depth

by David Baird

Mexico is so close to the United States, yet so different. Flying into Mexico City, you'll see what I mean when you catch a glimpse of majestic snowcapped volcanoes with the strange-sounding names Popocatépetl and Ixtaccihuatl. You're entering an exotic land of volcanoes and pyramids, mountains and jungles, where ancient civilizations have left more than just ruins and strange-sounding place names. Millions of native Mexicans still speak their languages—Náhuatl (Aztec), Maya, Zapotec, and others—and their customs and beliefs have shaped a national culture that's different from any other in the Spanish-speaking world.

1 The Land & Its People

Mexico stretches nearly 3,200km (1,984 miles) from east to west and more than 1,600km (1,000 miles) north to south. Only one-fifth the size of the United States, its territory includes trackless deserts in the north, dense jungles in the south, thousands of miles of lush seacoast and beaches along the Pacific and Caribbean, and the central highlands, crisscrossed by mountain ranges.

Mexico has more than 105 million inhabitants, with perhaps 22 million of them living in greater Mexico City. Over the last few decades, the rate of population growth has been steadily declining, from 3.2% per year in the 1970s to 1.16% at present. Mexico City has the slowest growth rate in the country, at less than 1% per year.

By most measurements, the disparity between rich and poor has increased in the last 30 years. Cycles of boom-and-bust seem to weigh heavier on the poor than on the rich. The middle class also seems to have had a rough ride. And, as a result, the ranks of the poor grow while wealth becomes increasingly concentrated in the upper rungs of society.

But in the face of all of this, Mexican society maintains its cohesiveness. It is amazingly resilient, due in some part to the way Mexicans live. They place a high value on family and friends, social gatherings, and living in the present; getting ahead and the uncertain prospects of the future take a back seat. In Mexico, there is always time to meet with friends for a drink or a cup of coffee or attend a family get-together. The many high-spirited public celebrations that Mexico is so famous for are simply another manifestation of this attitude.

SOCIAL MORES American and English travelers have often observed that Mexicans have a different conception of time and that life in Mexico obeys slower rhythms. This is true, and yet few observers go on to explain what the consequences of this are for the visitor to Mexico. This is a shame, because an imperfect appreciation of this difference causes a good deal of misunderstanding between tourists and locals.

On several occasions, Mexican acquaintances have asked me why Americans grin all the time. At first, I wasn't sure what to make of the question, and only gradually came to appreciate what was at issue. As the pace of life for Americans, Canadians, and others has quickened, they have come to skip some of the niceties of social interaction. When walking into a store, many Americans simply smile at a clerk and launch right into a question or request. The smile, in effect, replaces the greeting. In Mexico, it doesn't work that way. Mexicans misinterpret this American manner of greeting. After all, a smile when there is no context can be ambiguous; it can convey amusement, smugness, or superiority.

One of the most important pieces of advice I can offer travelers is always to give a proper greeting when addressing Mexicans. Don't try to abbreviate social intercourse. Mexican culture places a higher value on proper social form than on saving time. A Mexican must at least say *"¡Buenos días!"* or its equivalent to show proper respect. When an individual meets up with a group, he will greet each person separately, which can take quite a while. For us, the polite thing would be to keep our interruption to a minimum and give a general greeting to all.

Mexicans, like most people, will consciously or subconsciously make quick judgments about individuals they meet. Most divide the world into the *bien educado* (well raised and cultured), and the *mal educado* (poorly raised). Unfortunately, many visitors are reluctant to try out their Spanish, preferring to keep exchanges to a minimum. Don't do this. To be categorized as a foreigner isn't a big deal. What's important in Mexico is to be categorized as one of the cultured foreigners and not one of the barbarians. This makes it easier to get the attention of waiters, hotel desk clerks, and people on the street.

2 A Look at the Past

PRE-HISPANIC CIVILIZATIONS

The earliest "Mexicans" were Stone Age hunter-gatherers from the north, descendants of a race that had probably crossed the Bering Strait and reached North America around 12,000 B.C. They arrived in what is now Mexico by 10,000 B.C. Sometime between 5200 and 1500 B.C., in what is known as the **Archaic period,** they began practicing agriculture and domesticating animals.

THE PRE-CLASSIC PERIOD (1500 B.C. to A.D. 300) Eventually, agriculture improved enough to support large communities and free some of the population from agricultural work. A civilization emerged that we call the **Olmec**—an enigmatic people who settled the lower Gulf Coast in what is now Tabasco and Veracruz. Anthropologists regard them as the mother culture of Mesoamerica because they established a pattern for later civilizations in a wide area stretching from northern Mexico into Central America. The Olmec developed the basic calendar used throughout the region, established a 52-year cycle (which they used to schedule the construction of pyramids), established principles of urban layout and architecture, and originated the cult of the jaguar and the sanctity of jade.

The Maya civilization began developing in the late pre-Classic period, around 500 B.C. Our understanding of this period is sketchy, but Olmec influences are apparent everywhere. The Maya perfected the Olmec calendar and, somewhere along the way, developed an ornate system of hieroglyphic writing and early architectural concepts. Two other civilizations began the rise to prominence around this time: the people of Teotihuacán, just north of present-day Mexico

City, and the Zapotec of Monte Albán, in the valley of Oaxaca.

THE CLASSIC PERIOD (A.D. 300–900)

The flourishing of these three civilizations marks the boundaries of this period—the heyday of pre-Columbian Mesoamerican artistic and cultural achievements. These include the pyramids and palaces in Teotihuacán; the ceremonial center of Monte Albán; and the temple complexes and pyramids of Palenque and Calakmul.

The inhabitants of **Teotihuacán** (100 B.C. to A.D. 700), near present-day Mexico City, built a city that, at its zenith, is thought to have had 200,000 or more inhabitants. It was a well-organized city, covering 30 sq. km (12 sq. miles), and built on a grid with streams channeled to follow the city's plan.

Farther south, the **Zapotec,** influenced by the Olmec, raised an impressive civilization in the region of Oaxaca. Their two principal cities were **Monte Albán,** inhabited by an elite class of merchants and artisans, and **Mitla,** reserved for the high priests.

THE POST-CLASSIC PERIOD (A.D. 900–1521)

Warfare was a more conspicuous activity of the civilizations that flourished in this period. Social development was impressive but not as cosmopolitan as the Maya, Teotihuacán, and Zapotec societies. In central Mexico, a people known as the **Toltec** established their capital at Tula in the 10th century. They revered a god known as **Tezcatlipoca,** or "smoking mirror," who later became an Aztec god. The Toltec maintained a large military class divided into orders symbolized by animals. At its height, Tula may have had 40,000 people, and its influence spread across Mesoamerica. By the 13th century, however, the Toltec had exhausted themselves, probably in civil wars and in battles with the invaders from the north.

Of those northern invaders, the **Aztec** were the most warlike. At first they served as mercenaries for established cities in the valley of Mexico—one of which allotted them an unwanted, marshy piece of land in the middle of Lake Texcoco for their settlement. It eventually grew into the island city of Tenochtitlán. Through aggressive diplomacy and military action, the Aztec soon conquered central Mexico and extended their rule east to the Gulf Coast and south to the valley of Oaxaca.

During this later period, the Maya civilization flourished in northern Yucatán, especially in cities such as Chichén Itzá and Uxmal.

THE CONQUEST

In 1517, the first Spaniards arrived in what is today known as Mexico and skirmished with Maya Indians off the coast of the Yucatán Peninsula. One of the fledgling expeditions ended in shipwreck, leaving several Spaniards stranded as prisoners of the Maya. The Spanish sent out another expedition, under the command of **Hernán Cortez,** which landed on Cozumel in February 1519. Cortez inquired about the gold and riches of the interior, and the coastal Maya were happy to describe the wealth and splendor of the Aztec empire in central Mexico. Cortez promptly disobeyed all orders of his superior, the governor of Cuba, and sailed into the Gulf of Mexico, landing at what is now Veracruz.

Cortez arrived when the Aztec empire was at the height of its wealth and power. **Moctezuma II** ruled over the central and southern highlands and extracted tribute from lowland peoples. His greatest temples were literally plated with gold and encrusted with the blood of sacrificial captives. Moctezuma was a fool, a mystic, and something of a coward. Despite his wealth and military power, he dithered in his capital at Tenochtitlán, sending messengers with gifts and suggestions that Cortez leave. Meanwhile, Cortez blustered and negotiated his way into the highlands, always cloaking his real intentions. Moctezuma, terrified by the military tactics and technology of the Spaniard, convinced himself that Cortez was in fact the god Quetzalcoatl making his long-awaited return. By the time the Spaniards arrived in the Aztec capital, Cortez had gained some ascendancy over the lesser Indian states that were resentful tributaries to the Aztec. In November 1519, Cortez confronted Moctezuma and took him hostage in an effort to leverage control of the empire.

In the middle of Cortez's dangerous game of manipulation, another Spanish expedition arrived with orders to end Cortez's authority over the mission. Cortez hastened to meet the rival's force and persuade them to join his own. In the meantime, the Aztec chased the garrison out of Tenochtitlán, and either they or the Spaniards killed Moctezuma. For the next year and a half, Cortez laid siege to Tenochtitlán, with the help of rival Indians and a decimating epidemic of smallpox, to which the Indians had no resistance. In the end, the Aztec capital fell, and when it did, all of central Mexico lay at the feet of the conquistadors.

The Conquest started as a pirate expedition by Cortez and his men, unauthorized by the Spanish crown or its governor in Cuba. The Spanish king legitimized Cortez following his victory over the Aztec and ordered the forced conversion to Christianity of this new colony, to be called **New Spain.** Guatemala and Honduras were explored and conquered, and by 1540, the territory of New Spain included possessions from Vancouver to Panama. In the 2 centuries that followed, Franciscan and Augustinian friars converted millions of Indians to Christianity, and the Spanish lords built huge feudal estates on which the Indian farmers were little more than serfs. The silver and gold that Cortez looted made Spain the richest country in Europe.

THE COLONIAL PERIOD

Hernán Cortez set about building a new city upon the ruins of the old Aztec capital. To do this, he collected from the Indians the tributes once paid to the Aztec emperor, many of these rendered in labor. This arrangement, in one form or another, became the basis for the construction of the new colony. But diseases brought by the Spaniards decimated the native population over the next century and drastically reduced the pool of labor.

Cortez soon returned to Spain and was replaced by a governing council, and, later, the office of viceroy. Over the 3 centuries of the colonial period, 61 viceroys governed Mexico. Spain became rich from New World gold and silver, chiseled out by Indian labor. The colonial elite built lavish homes in Mexico City and in the countryside. They filled their homes with ornate furniture, had many servants, and adorned themselves in imported velvets, satins, and jewels.

A new class system developed. Those born in Spain (*peninsulares*) considered themselves superior to the Spanish born in Mexico (*criollos*). And, below the latter, were the other races and the *castas* (mixtures of Spanish and Indian, and African).

Discontent with the mother country simmered for years over social and political issues: taxes, royal monopolies, the bureaucracy, the superior position of *peninsulares* over *criollos,* and restrictions on commerce with Spain and other countries. In 1808, Napoleon invaded Spain and crowned his brother, Joseph, king in place of Charles IV. To many in Mexico, allegiance to France was out of the question; discontent reached the level of revolt.

INDEPENDENCE

The rebellion began in 1810, when **Father Miguel Hidalgo** gave the *grito,* a cry for independence, from his church in the town of Dolores, Guanajuato. The uprising soon became a full-fledged revolution, as Hidalgo and Ignacio Allende gathered an "army" of citizens and threatened Mexico City. Although Hidalgo ultimately failed and was executed, he is honored as "the Father of Mexican Independence." Another priest, José María Morelos, kept the revolt alive with several successful campaigns through 1815, when he, too, was captured and executed.

After the death of Morelos, prospects for independence were rather dim until the Spanish king who replaced Joseph Bonaparte decided to make social reforms in the colonies. This convinced the conservative powers in Mexico that they didn't need Spain after all. With their tacit approval, Agustín de Iturbide, then commander of royalist forces, changed sides and declared Mexico independent and himself emperor. Before long, however, internal dissension brought about the fall of the emperor, and Mexico was proclaimed a republic.

Political instability engulfed the young republic and Mexico waged a disastrous war with the U.S., losing half its territory. A central figure was **Antonio López de Santa Anna,** who assumed the leadership of his country no fewer than 11 times and was flexible enough in those volatile days to portray himself variously as a liberal, a conservative, a federalist, and a centralist. But, by 1855, he was finally left without a political comeback and ended his days in Venezuela.

Political instability persisted, and the conservative forces, with some encouragement from Napoleon III, hit upon the idea of inviting in a Habsburg to regain control (as if that strategy had ever worked for Spain). They found a willing volunteer in Archduke Maximilian of Austria, who accepted the position of Mexican emperor with the support of French troops. The ragtag Mexican forces defeated the French force—a modern, well-equipped army—in a battle near Puebla (now celebrated annually as **Cinco de Mayo**). A second attempt was more successful, and Ferdinand Maximilian Joseph of Habsburg became emperor. After 3 years of civil war, the French were finally induced to abandon the emperor's cause; Maximilian was captured and executed by a firing squad near Querétaro in 1867. His adversary and successor (as president of Mexico) was **Benito Juárez,** a Zapotec Indian lawyer and one of the great heroes of Mexican history. Juárez did his best to unify and strengthen his country before dying of a heart attack in 1872; his impact on Mexico's future was profound, and his plans and visions bore fruit for decades.

THE PORFIRIATO & THE REVOLUTION

A few years after Juárez's death, one of his generals, **Porfirio Díaz,** assumed power in a coup. He ruled Mexico from 1877 to 1911, a period now called the "Porfiriato." He stayed in power by imposing repressive measures and courting the favor of powerful nations. Generous in his dealings with foreign investors, Díaz became, in the eyes of most Mexicans, the archetypal *entreguista* (one who sells out his country for private gain). With foreign investment came the concentration of great wealth in few hands, and social conditions worsened.

In 1910, Francisco Madero called for an armed rebellion that became the **Mexican Revolution** (La Revolución in Mexico; the revolution against Spain is the Guerra de Independencia). Díaz was sent into exile; while in London, he became a celebrity at the age of 81, when he jumped into the Thames to save a drowning boy. He is buried in Paris. Madero became president but was promptly betrayed and executed by **Victoriano Huerta.** Those who had answered Madero's call responded again—to the great peasant hero **Emiliano Zapata** in the south, and to the seemingly invincible **Pancho Villa** in the central north, flanked by Alvaro Obregón and Venustiano Carranza. They eventually put Huerta to flight and began hashing out a new constitution.

For the next few years, the revolutionaries Carranza, Obregón, and Villa fought among themselves; Zapata did not seek national power, though he fought tenaciously for land for the peasants. Carranza, who was president at the time, betrayed and assassinated Zapata. Obregón finally consolidated power and probably had Carranza assassinated. He, in turn, was assassinated when he tried to break one of the tenets of the Revolution—no reelection. His successor, Plutarco Elias Calles, learned this lesson well, installing one puppet president after another, until **Lázaro Cárdenas** severed the puppeteer's strings and banished him to exile.

Until Cárdenas's election in 1934, the outcome of the revolution remained in doubt. There had been some land redistribution, but other measures took a back seat to political expediency. Cárdenas changed all that. He implemented massive redistribution of land and nationalized the oil industry. He instituted many reforms and gave shape to the ruling political party (now the **Partido Revolucionario Institucional,** or PRI) by bringing a broad representation of Mexican society under its banner and establishing mechanisms for consensus building. Most Mexicans practically canonize Cárdenas.

MODERN MEXICO

The presidents who followed were noted more for graft than for leadership. The party's base narrowed as many of the reform-minded elements were marginalized. Economic progress, a lot of it in the form of large development projects, became the PRI's main basis for legitimacy. In 1968, the government violently repressed a student protest in the Tlatelolco section of Mexico City. An

unknown number of citizens were killed. Though the PRI maintained its grip on power, it lost all semblance of being a progressive party. In 1985, a devastating **earthquake in Mexico City** brought down many of the government's new, supposedly earthquake-proof buildings, exposing shoddy construction and the widespread government corruption that fostered it. The government's handling of the relief efforts also drew heavy criticism. In 1994, a political and military **uprising in Chiapas** focused world attention on Mexico's great social problems. A new political force, the Ejército Zapatista de Liberación Nacional, or EZLN (Zapatista National Liberation Army), skillfully publicized the plight of the peasant.

In the years that followed, opposition political parties grew in power and legitimacy. Facing pressure and scrutiny from national and international organizations, and widespread public discontent, the PRI began to concede defeat in state and congressional elections throughout the '90s. Party reformers were able to make changes over the objections of many hard-liners. They instituted a partial system of primary elections to give greater voice to the rank and file. This made for successful campaigns in several states, but in other states the old-style party leaders held on to their right to appoint the official party candidate. Internal strife reached a climax with the assassination of the party's presidential candidate, Luis Donaldo Colosio. A quick compromise between different party factions resulted in the nomination of Ernesto Zedillo for president. Once in power, Zedillo proved to be a reformer. Over his 6-year term, he steadily led the country toward open and fair elections by strengthening the electoral process, gaining the public's confidence, and getting his own party to accept the possibility of losing power.

In the presidential elections of 2000, Vicente Fox, candidate for the Partido

Acción Nacional (National Action Party, or PAN), won by a landslide. It couldn't have been otherwise. For many voters this election was an experiment to see if their votes would really count. They voted for the most prominent opposition candidate to see if, in fact, he would be allowed to assume the presidency. For Mexicans, a government under the PRI was all that they had ever known.

During Fox's presidency, the three main political parties had to adjust to the new realty of power sharing. The old government party, the PRI, still had a large infrastructure for getting out the vote and still controlled the local governments of several states. Fox's center-right PAN had control of the presidency and the most seats in the legislature, while the center-left PRD (Partido de la Revolución Democrática, or Democratic Revolution Party) controlled the city government of Mexico City as well as a few southern states. Many observers anticipated gridlock. But the three parties, to their credit, handled the transition better than expected.

But by the end of Fox's term, the situation turned ugly, and Mexico's experiment with pluralistic democracy faced a difficult crisis. The Fox administration showed no finesse in dealing with the legislature and failed to pass most of its initiatives. In the off-year elections of 2004, PAN lost many seats in the legislature and several governorships.

The main beneficiary was the PRI, which looked to be in an excellent position for the presidential election of 2006, but not for long. In 2005, the party's leader, Roberto Madrazo, sought to become the party's nominee without going through primary elections. His power plays worked to make him the nominee but splintered the party badly and reminded voters of the old days when their votes didn't count for anything.

Meanwhile, the PRD's choice of nominee seemed inevitable. Mexico City mayor Andrés Manuel López Obrador (AMLO for short) was without question the most important figure in the party. He was tremendously popular for creating programs, such as a pension for the city's elderly. And his popularity soared when he became the target of political dirty tricks to make him ineligible to run for president. He was genuinely interested in helping the poor, but there was something unsettling about the way he would take political opposition personally. He dismissed a large demonstration in Mexico City against kidnapping and other crimes as the work of his political enemies and not as the expression of local citizens to highlight the need to feel safe in their city.

The PAN ended up having the only meaningful primary elections, which resulted in an underdog candidate, Felipe Calderón, becoming the party nominee. He is a social conservative and a devout Catholic who believes in privatization and market forces.

A bitter campaign between AMLO and Calderón, followed by an incredibly close election in the summer of 2006, made for a serious crisis. So close was the election that it took over a month for the elections tribunal to declare Calderón the winner. AMLO refused to recognize the verdict and launched a protest that lasted another month. Supporters in his party even tried to physically prevent Calderón from taking office by occupying the legislative chambers. All of this ended up diminishing AMLO's popularity.

The crisis shows that Mexico must continue to strengthen its political institutions. PAN now has the most seats in the legislature, but not a majority. To pass legislation it will need to compromise with the other parties. The PRD has the second highest number of seats. It must put AMLO behind it if it doesn't want to be marginalized. And the PRI must learn from its mistakes and move towards democracy and transparency. But at the moment, its legislators enjoy the role of powerbrokers between the government and a powerful opposition party. It will be the key player in deciding what gets accomplished in the next few years.

3 Recommended Books

Studying up on Mexico can be one of the most fun bits of "research" you'll ever do. If you'd like to learn more about this fascinating country before you go—which I encourage—these books are an enjoyable way to do it.

HISTORY & CULTURE For an overview of pre-Hispanic cultures, pick up a copy of Michael D. Coe's *Mexico: From the Olmecs to the Aztecs* or Nigel Davies's *Ancient Kingdoms of Mexico.* Richard Townsend's *The Aztecs* is a thorough, well-researched examination of the Aztec and the Spanish conquest. For the Maya, Michael Coe's *The Maya* is probably the best general account. For a survey of Mexican history through modern times, *A Short History of Mexico* by J. Patrick McHenry provides a complete, yet concise account.

John L. Stephens's *Incidents of Travel in the Yucatán, Vol. I and II* are considered among the great books of archaeological discovery, as well as being travel classics. The two volumes chart the course of Stephens's discoveries of the Yucatán, beginning in 1841. Before his expeditions, little was known of the region, and the Mayan culture had not been discovered.

For a more modern exploration of the archaeology of the region, Peter Tompkins's *Mysteries of the Mexican Pyramids* is a visually rich book which explores the whole of Mexico's archaeological treasures.

Lesley Byrd Simpson's *Many Mexicos* provides a comprehensive account of Mexican history within a cultural context. A classic on understanding the culture of this country is *Distant Neighbors,* by Alan Riding.

ART & ARCHITECTURE *Art and Time in Mexico: From the Conquest to the Revolution,* by Elizabeth Wilder Weismann, covers religious, public, and private architecture. *Casa Mexicana,* by Tim Street-Porter, takes readers through the interiors of some of Mexico's finest homes-turned-museums, public buildings, and private homes.

Maya Art and Architecture, by Mary Ellen Miller showcases the best of the artistic expression of this culture, with interpretations into its meanings.

For a wonderful read on the food of the Yucatán and Mexico, pick up *Mexico, One Plate at a Time,* by celebrity chef Rick Bayless.

NATURE *A Naturalist's Mexico,* by Roland H. Wauer, is a fabulous guide to birding. *A Hiker's Guide to Mexico's Natural History,* by Jim Conrad, covers flora and fauna and tells how to find the easy-to-reach as well as out-of-the-way spots he describes. *Peterson Field Guides: Mexican Birds,* by Roger Tory Peterson and Edward L. Chalif, is an excellent guide.

Appendix B:
Useful Terms & Phrases

Most Mexicans are very patient with foreigners who try to speak their language; it helps a lot to know a few basic phrases. I've included simple phrases for expressing basic needs, followed by some common menu items.

ENGLISH-SPANISH PHRASES

English	Spanish	Pronunciation
Good day	**Buen día**	Bwehn *dee*-ah
Good morning	**Buenos días**	*Bweh*-nohs *dee*-ahs
How are you?	**¿Cómo está?**	*Koh*-moh eh-*stah*
Very well	**Muy bien**	Mwee byehn
Thank you	**Gracias**	*Grah*-syahs
You're welcome	**De nada**	Deh *nah*-dah
Goodbye	**Adiós**	Ah-*dyohs*
Please	**Por favor**	Pohr fah-*bohr*
Yes	**Sí**	See
No	**No**	Noh
Excuse me	**Perdóneme**	Pehr-*doh*-neh-meh
Give me	**Déme**	*Deh*-meh
Where is . . . ?	**¿Dónde está . . . ?**	*Dohn*-deh eh-*stah*
the station	**la estación**	lah eh-stah-*syohn*
a hotel	**un hotel**	oon oh-*tehl*
a gas station	**una gasolinera**	*oo*-nah gah-soh-lee-*neh*-rah
a restaurant	**un restaurante**	oon res-tow-*rahn*-teh
the toilet	**el baño**	el *bah*-nyoh
a good doctor	**un buen médico**	oon bwehn *meh*-dee-coh
the road to . . .	**el camino a/hacia . . .**	el cah-*mee*-noh ah/*ah*-syah
To the right	**A la derecha**	Ah lah deh-*reh*-chah
To the left	**A la izquierda**	Ah lah ees-*kyehr*-dah
Straight ahead	**Derecho**	Deh-*reh*-choh
I would like	**Quisiera**	Key-*syeh*-rah
I want	**Quiero**	*Kyeh*-roh
to eat	**comer**	koh-*mehr*
a room	**una habitación**	*oo*-nah ah-bee-tah-*syohn*
Do you have . . . ?	**¿Tiene usted . . . ?**	Tyeh-neh oo-*sted*
a book	**un libro**	oon *lee*-broh
a dictionary	**un diccionario**	oon deek-syoh-*nah*-ryoh

English	Spanish	Pronunciation
How much is it?	¿Cuánto cuesta?	*Kwahn*-toh *kweh*-stah
When?	¿Cuándo?	*Kwahn*-doh
What?	¿Qué?	Keh
There is (Is there . . . ?)	(¿)Hay (. . . ?)	Eye
What is there?	¿Qué hay?	Keh eye
Yesterday	Ayer	Ah-*yer*
Today	Hoy	Oy
Tomorrow	Mañana	Mah-*nyah*-nah
Good	Bueno	*Bweh*-noh
Bad	Malo	*Mah*-loh
Better (best)	(Lo) Mejor	(Loh) Meh-*hohr*
More	Más	Mahs
Less	Menos	*Meh*-nohs
No smoking	Se prohibe fumar	Seh proh-*ee*-beh foo-*mahr*
Postcard	Tarjeta postal	Tar-*heh*-tah poh-*stahl*
Insect repellent	Repelente contra insectos	Reh-peh-*lehn*-teh *cohn*-trah een-*sehk*-tohs

MORE USEFUL PHRASES

English	Spanish	Pronunciation
Do you speak English?	¿Habla usted inglés?	*Ah*-blah oo-*sted* een-*glehs*
Is there anyone here who speaks English?	¿Hay alguien aquí que hable inglés?	Eye *ahl*-gyehn ah-*kee* keh *ah*-bleh een-*glehs*
I speak a little Spanish.	Hablo un poco de español.	*Ah*-bloh oon *poh*-koh deh eh-spah-*nyohl*
I don't understand Spanish very well.	No (lo) entiendo muy bien el español.	Noh (loh) ehn-*tyehn*-doh mwee byehn el eh-spah-*nyohl*
The meal is good.	Me gusta la comida.	Meh *goo*-stah lah koh-*mee*-dah
What time is it?	¿Qué hora es?	Keh *oh*-rah ehs
May I see your menu?	¿Puedo ver el menú (la carta)?	*Pweh*-doh vehr el meh-*noo* (lah *car*-tah)
The check, please.	La cuenta, por favor.	Lah *kwehn*-tah pohr fa-*borh*
What do I owe you?	¿Cuánto le debo?	*Kwahn*-toh leh *deh*-boh
What did you say?	¿Mande? (formal) ¿Cómo? (informal)	*Mahn*-deh *Koh*-moh

English	Spanish	Pronunciation
I want (to see) . . .	**Quiero (ver)** . . .	*kyeh*-roh (vehr)
a room	**un cuarto** or **una habitación**	oon *kwar*-toh, *oo*-nah ah-bee-tah-*syohn*
for two persons	**para dos personas**	*pah*-rah dohs pehr-*soh*-nahs
with (without) bathroom	**con (sin) baño**	kohn (seen) *bah*-nyoh
We are staying here only . . .	**Nos quedamos aquí solamente** . . .	Nohs keh-*dah*-mohs ah-*kee* soh-lah-*mehn*-teh
one night.	**una noche.**	*oo*-nah *noh*-cheh
one week.	**una semana.**	*oo*-nah seh-*mah*-nah
We are leaving . . .	**Partimos (Salimos)** . . .	Pahr-*tee*-mohs (sah-*lee*-mohs)
tomorrow.	**mañana.**	mah-*nya*-nah
Do you accept . . . ?	**¿Acepta usted** . . . ?	Ah-*sehp*-tah oo-*sted*
traveler's checks?	**cheques de viajero?**	*cheh*-kehs deh byah-*heh*-roh
Is there a	**¿Hay una**	Eye *oo*-nah lah-*bahn*-deh-*ree*-ah
laundromat . . . ?	**lavandería** . . . ?	
near here?	**cerca de aquí?**	*sehr*-kah deh ah-*kee*
Please send these clothes to the laundry.	**Hágame el favor de mandar esta ropa a la lavandería.**	Ah-gah-meh el fah-*bohr* deh mahn-*dahr* eh-stah *roh*-pah a lah lah-*bahn*-deh-*ree*-ah

NUMBERS

1	**uno** (*ooh*-noh)		17	**diecisiete** (dyeh-see-*syeh*-teh)
2	**dos** (dohs)		18	**dieciocho** (dyeh-*syoh*-choh)
3	**tres** (trehs)		19	**diecinueve** (dyeh-see-*nweh*-beh)
4	**cuatro** (*kwah*-troh)		20	**veinte** (*bayn*-teh)
5	**cinco** (*seen*-koh)		30	**treinta** (*trayn*-tah)
6	**seis** (sayes)		40	**cuarenta** (kwah-*ren*-tah)
7	**siete** (*syeh*-teh)		50	**cincuenta** (seen-*kwen*-tah)
8	**ocho** (*oh*-choh)		60	**sesenta** (seh-*sehn*-tah)
9	**nueve** (*nweh*-beh)		70	**setenta** (seh-*tehn*-tah)
10	**diez** (dyehs)		80	**ochenta** (oh-*chehn*-tah)
11	**once** (*ohn*-seh)		90	**noventa** (noh-*behn*-tah)
12	**doce** (*doh*-seh)		100	**cien** (syehn)
13	**trece** (*treh*-seh)		200	**doscientos** (do-*syehn*-tohs)
14	**catorce** (kah-*tohr*-seh)		500	**quinientos** (kee-*nyehn*-tohs)
15	**quince** (*keen*-seh)		1,000	**mil** (meel)
16	**dieciséis** (dyeh-see-*sayes*)			

Index

AARP, 50
Abbreviations, 69
Academia Falcón (Guanajuato), 200
Academia Hispano Americana (San Miguel), 187
Acanceh, 645–646
Acapulco, 3, 370–394
  accommodations, 383–388
  American Express, 376
  consular agents, 376
  getting around, 375–376
  Internet access, 376–377
  layout of, 374–375
  nightlife, 392–394
  outdoor activities, 377–381
  restaurants, 388–392
  safety, 377
  shopping, 382
  tourist police, 377
  traveling to and from, 374
  visitor information, 374
Acapulco Historical Museum, 381
Accommodations
  best, 17–20
  hotel chains, 64
  house rentals and swaps, 64–65
  landing the best room, 66
  rating system, 63–64
  saving on, 65–66
  surfing for, 65
Active vacations, 59–60. *See also* Ecotourism and adventure trips
  best, 12–13
Acuario (aquarium)
  Mazatlán, 339
  Veracruz, 490
Adventure trips. *See* Ecotourism and adventure trips
AeroMéxico Vacations, 55
Agua Azul waterfalls, 470
Aguacatenango, 479
Aguilar sisters (Ocotlán), 459

Airfares, 34–36
Airport security, 35
Airport taxes, 61
Air Tickets Direct, 35
Air travel, 1–2, 33–36
  bankrupt airlines, 43
  in Mexico, 60–61
Akab Dzib (Chichén Itzá), 664
Aktun Chen cavern, 601
Akumal, 579, 600–601
Alameda Park (Mexico City), 135
Alaska Airlines Vacations, 55–56
Alebrijes (Acapulco), 392–393
Alfarería Tlaquepaque (Puerto Vallarta), 305–306
Alma Libre (Puerto Morelos), 596
Altitude sickness, 44–45
Alux (Playa del Carmen), 591–592
Amatenango del Valle, 478–479
Amatitán, 281
Amatlán, 176
Amber, San Cristóbal, 479, 480
American Airlines Vacations, 55, 56
American Express, 41
  Acapulco, 376
  Cancún, 521
  Chihuahua, 688
  Cuernavaca, 167
  Guadalajara, 265
  Ixtapa/Zihuatanejo, 397
  Manzanillo, 362
  Mazatlán, 336
  Mérida, 625
  Mexico City, 100
  Morelia, 240
  Oaxaca City, 440
  Puebla, 504
  Puerto Vallarta, 289
  Querétaro, 213
  San Luis Potosí, 232
  San Miguel, 184
  Veracruz, 488
  Zacatecas, 222

American Express Travelers Cheque Card, 42
AMTAVE (Asociación Mexicana de Turismo de Aventura y Ecoturismo, A.C.), 59
Angahuan, 260
Annual Witches Conference, 28
Annual Yucatán Bird Festival (Mérida), 32
Año Nuevo (New Year's Day), 27
Anthropological museums
  Casa Na-Bolom (San Cristóbal), 476
  La Paz, 732
  Museo Antropología de Xalapa, 498
  Museo de la Cultura Maya (Chetumal), 616
  Museo del Pueblo Maya (Dzibilchaltún), 643
  Museo Nacional de Antropología (Mexico City), 15, 101, 120
  Museo Regional de Antropología (Mérida), 630
  Museo Regional de Antropología Carlos Pellicer Cámara (Villahermosa), 461–462
Anthropology Museum (La Paz), 732
Apple Vacations, 56
Aquarium (La Paz), 732
Aquariums. *See* Acuario
Aqueduct of Zacatecas, 225
Archaeological Conservancy, 57
Archaeological museums and exhibits
  Museo Arqueológico de Mazatlán, 340
  Museo Arqueológico de Xochimilco (Mexico City), 132
  Museo Arqueológico Guillermo Spratling (Taxco), 156

Archaeological museums and exhibits *(cont.)*
Museo de Arqueología de la Costa Grande (Ixtapa/Zihuatanejo), 398
Museo de Arqueología del Occidente de México (Guadalajara), 277
Museo del Estado (Morelia), 243–244
Museum of Archaeology and History (Manzanillo), 364
Parque-Museo La Venta (Villahermosa), 462
Puerto Vallarta, 300

Archaeological sites and ruins
Acanceh, 645
Balamkú, 618
Becán, 617
best, 11–12
Bonampak, 469–470
Cacaxtla, 514
Calakmul, 618
Chicanná, 617–618
Chichén Itzá, 661–664
Chincultic, 485
Cholula, 511–512
Cobá, 609
Cozumel, 569
Dainzú, 456
Dzibanché, 617
Dzibilchaltún, 643–644
Edzná, 653–654
Ek Balam, 669–670
El Tajín, 499–501
Isla Mujeres, 553
Izamal, 642
Kabah, 651–653
Kohunlich, 617
Labná, 652
Lambityeco, 456
Loltún, 652–653
Mayapán, 646
Mitla, 457–458
Monte Albán, 453–454
Muyil, 610
Palenque, 464–466
near Playa del Carmen, 583
Puuc Maya sites, 651–654
Río Bec area, 617
Sayil, 652
suggested itinerary, 78–80
Tecoh, 646
Teotihuacán (near Mexico City), 144–148
Tepozteco pyramid (Tepoztlán), 175–176
Tlaxcala, 512
Toniná, 470–471
Tulum, 603–605

Uxmal, 647–649
Xcambó, 644
Xlapak, 652
Xochicalco, 171
Xochitécatl, 514–515
Xpujil, 617
Yagul, 457
Yaxchilán, 470
Zaachila, 459
Zempoala (Cempoala), 495

AREA Bar and Terrace at Hotel Habita (Mexico City), 142
Arrazola, 458
Art and culture tours, 58
Artesanías Cuauhtémoc (La Paz), 733
Artesanías Misión (Creel), 681
Artesanías Vázquez (Guanajuato), 204
Artesanos de México (Mexico City), 137
Art galleries, 16
Acapulco, 382
Mexico City, 137–138
Puerto Vallarta, 304–305
Todos Santos, 725
Arts and crafts. *See* Handicrafts and folk art
Arts Festival (Todos Santos), 725
Arvil. Galería de Arte y Libros de Arte (Mexico City), 138
Ash Wednesday, 28
Assumption of the Virgin Mary, 30–31
ATC Tours and Travel, 57–58
Atlantis Submarine, Cancún, 540
ATMs (automated-teller machines), 40–41
Atotonilco el Grande, 188
Auto insurance, 38
Avándaro, 162
Avenida Revolución (Tijuana), 746, 750
Avenue of the Dead (Teotihuacán), 147
Ayuntamiento
Mérida, 628
Valladolid, 667–668
Aztec city of Tlatelolco (Mexico City), 134
Aztec ruins. *See* Archaeological sites and ruins
Azulejos Talavera Vázquez (Dolores Hidalgo), 196
Azul 96 (Puerto Vallarta), 321–322

Baby-O (Acapulco), 393
Bacalar Lake, 13, 14, 613–615
Bahía de Magdalena, 739
Bahía de Mujeres, 551
Bahías de Huatulco, 425–432
Bahuichivo, 678–679
Baja California, 6, 22, 692–694
immigration laws, 26
mid-Baja region, 694, 736–744
northern, 694, 744–755
Baja Expeditions, 60
Baja Sur, 13–14
Balamkú, 618
Balankanché, Cave of, 666
Ball court *(juego de pelota)*
Chichén Itzá, 662
Cobá, 609
El Tajín, 500
Monte Albán, 453
Palenque, 466
Uxmal, 649
Yagul, 457
Ballet Folklórico de México (Mexico City), 141
Ballet Tradiciones de México (Veracruz), 489–490
Balneario Ixtapan, 160–161
Baluarte de la Soledad (Campeche), 656
Baluarte de San Carlos/Museo de la Ciudad (Campeche), 656
Baluarte de Santiago (Campeche), 656
Baluarte Santiago (Veracruz), 490
Banderas Bay Trading Company (Puerto Vallarta), 306
Banks, 40
Barceló La Jolla de Mismaloya (near Puerto Vallarta), 291–292
Bar Constantini (Puerto Vallarta), 322
Bar Fly (Mexico City), 142–143
Bar Ocho (Guanajuato), 210
Barra de Navidad, 353–358
Barrancas, 679–680
Basílica de la Soledad (Oaxaca City), 443–444
Basílica de la Virgen de Zapopan (Guadalajara), 278
Basílica de Santa María de Guadalupe (Mexico City), 117–118
Batopilas, 682
Bay of La Paz Project, 6

Bazar del Centro (Mexico City), 138

Bazar del Sábado (Mexico City), 138–139

Bazar del Sábado (San Angel), 16

Bazar Hecht (Tlaquepaque), 281

Beaches. *See also specific beaches and entries starting with "Playa"*
Acapulco, 377–378
Bahías de Huatulco, 427–428
best beach vacations, 7, 10
Cancún, 536–537
Costa Alegre, 354
Cozumel, 568–569
Isla Mujeres, 550
Ixtapa/Zihuatanejo, 398–399
La Paz, 730
Manzanillo, 362–363
Mazatlán, 336–337
Puerto Angel, 424
Puerto Escondido, 415–417
Puerto Vallarta, 291–293
San José del Cabo, 699–700
Tulum, 604, 605
Veracruz, 491

Becán, 617

Beer Bob's Books (between Sinaloa and Guanajuato), 354

Bellas Artes/El Nigromante (Centro Cultural Ignacio Ramírez; San Miguel), 185–186

Bengala (Mexico City), 143

Benito Juárez International Airport (Mexico City), 86

Benito Juárez Market (Oaxaca City), 446

Benito Juárez's Birthday, 28

Beverages, 69

Biblioteca Palafoxiana (Puebla), 506

Biking and mountain biking
Mazatlán, 339
Oaxaca, 447
San Cristóbal, 474

Birding
Bahías de Huatulco, 429
Celestún National Wildlife Refuge, 642–643
Huitepec Cloud Forest, 479
Ixtapa/Zihuatanejo, 400
Manzanillo, 363
Mazatlán, 339
Rio Lagartos Nature Reserve, 670

Sixth Annual Yucatán Bird Festival (Mérida), 32

Teacapán, 348

Blessing of the Animals (San Miguel), 185

Bling (Cancún), 543

Boating (boat rentals)
Acapulco, 379
Ixtapa/Zihuatanejo, 400
Mazatlán, 337

Boat trips and cruises
Acapulco, 378–379
Bahías de Huatulco, 428
Cabo San Lucas, 715
Cancún, 539–540
Costa Alegre, 354
Cozumel, 566
Ixtapa/Zihuatanejo, 399–400
La Paz, 730–731
Manzanillo, 364
Mazatlán, 337
Puerto Angel, 424
Puerto Vallarta, 289, 293–294, 298–299
Veracruz, 491

Boca de Tomatlán (Puerto Vallarta), 292

Bodegas de Santo Tomás Winery (Ensenada), 753

Books, recommended, 763

Bribes and scams, 47–48

Brisas Hotels & Resorts, 64

Bucerías, 287–288, 327

Bucket shops, 34–35

Bullfights
Acapulco, 381
Cancún, 541
Mazatlán, 338
Puerto Vallarta, 299
Tijuana, 748
Zacatecas, 222

Bungee jumping, Acapulco, 392

Bus hijackings, 63

Business hours, 69–70

Bustamante, Sergio, 281

Bus travel
in Mexico, 63
into Mexico, 39

Cabo Pulmo, 14

Cabo San Lucas, 711–724
accommodations, 720–721
beaches, 714
safety, 712
day trips from, 719
emergencies and hospital, 712

getting around, 712
getting there and departing, in, 711
Internet access, 712
layout of, 711
nightlife, 723–724
outdoor activities, 713–718
restaurants, 721–723
shopping, 719–720
visitor information, 711

Cacahuamilpa Caves or Grottoes, 156

Cacaxtla-Xochitécatl (Tlaxcala), 512–513

Cacaxtla-Xochitécatl archaeological site, 514

Cactus Sanctuary (La Paz), 732–733

Cafeina (Mexico City), 143

Calakmul, 618

Calendar of events, 27–33

Caleta Beach (Acapulco), 377–379

Caletilla Beach (Acapulco), 377–379

The California Native, 60

Callejón de los Sapos (Puebla), 508

Calle 60 (Mérida), 629

Cameras and film, 70

Campeche, 6, 620, 654–660
en route to, 653–654

Cancún, 7, 516–544
accommodations, 4–5, 523–531
American Express, 521
attractions, 541
beaches, 4
beaches and outdoor activities, 536–538, 540–541
boating excursions, 539–540
climate and seasons, 521, 522
consulates, 521
currency exchange, 521–522
drugstores, 522
emergencies, 522
finding an address in, 520
getting around, 520–521
layout of, 520
nightlife, 542–544
police, 522
restaurants, 531–536
shopping, 541–542
traveling to, 517–518
visitor information, 518
websites, 518, 520

Candlemas (Día de la Candelaria), 28

Canopy Costa Azul Xtreme Tours, 6

Canopy tours, Puerto Vallarta, 296–297

Cantinas, Guanajuato, 210

Canyon Travel, 60

Capilla del Rosario (Puebla), 15, 502, 505

Caracol
Chichén Itzá, 663
Ek Balam, 669–670

Caribbean coast, 578–618. See also Riviera Maya (Costa Maya)

Caribbean Village (Isla Mujeres), 553

Carlos 'n' Charlie's
Acapulco, 393
Ixtapa, 410

Carlos O'Brian's (Puerto Vallarta), 322

Carnaval, 28
Cozumel, 565
Mazatlán, 340
Veracruz, 490

Car rentals, 62

Car travel
in Mexico, 61–63
to Mexico, 36–38

Casa Borda (Casa de la Cultura de Taxco), 155

Casa de Alfeñique (Puebla), 506

Casa de Artesanías, San Cristóbal, 479

Casa de Artesanías Tukulná (Campeche), 657

Casa de Capelo (Guanajuato), 204

Casa de Ecala (Querétaro), 214

Casa de Hidalgo (Dolores Hidalgo), 196

Casa de Juárez (Oaxaca City), 445

Casa de la Corregidora (Querétaro), 214

Casa de la Cultura de Taxco (Casa Borda), 155

Casa del Alguacil (Mérida), 628

Casa de la Marquesa (Querétaro), 216

Casa del Artesano (San Luis Potosí), 234

Casa de la Salsa (Morelia), 248–249

Casa de las Artesanías
Mérida, 631
Morelia, 244–245

Casa de las Artesanías de Michoacán/Casa de los Once Patios (Pátzcuaro), 253

Casa de las Sirenas (Mexico City), 144

Casa de la Zacatecana (Querétaro), 215–216

Casa del Feng Shui (Puerto Vallarta), 306

Casa del Habano (Puerto Vallarta), 307

Casa de los Azulejos (Mexico City), 124

Casa de los Metates (Chichén Itzá), 663

Casa de los Muñecos (Puebla), 506

Casa de los Once Patios (Pátzcuaro), 253

Casa del Tequila (Puerto Vallarta), 307

Casa Marina (Zihuatanejo), 401

Casa Museo de Morelos (Morelia), 242

Casa Na-Bolom (San Cristóbal), 476

Casa no. 6 Centro Cultural (Campeche), 657

Casa Queretana de Artesanía (Querétaro), 215

Castillo de Chapultepec/Museo Nacional de Historia (Mexico City), 128

Cathedral (Catedral)
Cuernavaca, 168–169
Guadalajara, 276
of the Immaculate Conception (Mazatlán), 341
Mérida, 627
Metropolitana (Mexico City), 15, 126, 128
Morelia, 15, 241–242
Nuestra Señora de la Soledad (Acapulco), 377
Oaxaca City, 444
Puebla, 502, 505
San Cristóbal, 476
San Luis Potosí, 233

Cava de Vinos L. A. Cetto (Tijuana), 747

Cave of Balankanché, 666

Celestún National Wildlife Refuge, 620, 642–643

Cellphones, 54

Cempoala (Zempoala), 495

Cenote Dzitnup (Cenote Xkekén), 669

Cenotes and cenote diving, 566
Chichén Itzá, 662–663
Ik-Kil, 666

Tankah Bay, 603
Valladolid area, 667, 669
Xel-Ha, 602–603

Cenote Zací (Valladolid), 667

Centers for Disease Control and Prevention, 44

Centro Artesanal (Mercado de Curiosidades; Mexico City), 139

Centro Cultural El Refugio (Guadalajara), 278

Centro Cultural Ignacio Ramírez (Bellas Artes/El Nigromante; San Miguel), 185–186

Centro Cultural Tijuana, 746

Centro Histórico
Guadalajara, 263–264
Mexico City
accommodations, 103–104
nightlife, 140
restaurants, 115–117
sights and attractions, 129, 130–132

Centro Mercado (Mazatlán), 346

Centro Mexicano la Tortuga (near Puerto Escondido), 415

Cerámica La Cruz (Guanajuato), 204

Ceramics and pottery
Amatenango del Valle, 478–479
Dolores Hidalgo, 195, 196
Guanajuato, 204
Muna, 645
Museo Pantaleón Panduro (Guadalajara), 278
National Ceramics Fair and Fiesta (Tlaquepaque), 29
Ocotlán, 459–460
Pátzcuaro, 254
San Bartolo Coyotepec, 459
San José del Cabo, 702
Talavera, 16
Dolores Hidalgo, 196
Puebla, 507–508
Ticul, 646
Tonalá, 281–282

Cerocahui, 14, 678–679

Cerro de la Bufa, 222, 224, 225

Cerro de las Campanas (Querétaro), 216

Cerro del Fortín (Oaxaca City), 445

Cerro Gallego, 678

Chacahua Lagoon National Park, 416

Chahué Bay, 428

Chamula, 478
Chankanaab National Park, 567–568
Chapultepec Park and Polanco (Mexico City)
  accommodations, 104–107
  restaurants, 111–114
  sights and attractions, 128, 129–130
  sightseeing, 136
Chávez Morado, José, 201
Chetumal, 615–617
  side trips to Maya ruins from, 617–618
Chiapas, 23, 433–434
  Zapatista movement in, 472, 474
Chicanná, 617–618
Chichanchob (Chichén Itzá), 663
Chichén Itzá, 12, 570, 583, 620, 660–666
Chichén Viejo, 664
Chihuahua, 686–691
Chiles, 67–68
Chinatown (La Paz), 733
Chinchorro Reef Underwater National Park, 611, 613
Chincua (near Morelia), 249
Chincultic, 485
Cholula, 511–512
Christine (Ixtapa), 410
Christine (Puerto Vallarta), 323
Christmas, 33
Christmas Posadas, 33
Church. See under first significant word (e.g. Santo Domingo, Church of)
Cinco de Mayo, 29, 505
Cine Bar (San Miguel), 195
The City (Cancún), 543
Classic Vacations, 56
Cliff divers, Mazatlán, 338
Cliff of the Dawn (Isla Mujeres), 553
Climate, 26–27
Club Maeva Hotel & Resort (Manzanillo), 369
Cobá, 570, 608–611
Cocinar Mexicano (Tepoztlán), 175
CoCo Bongo (Cancún), 543
Coco Cabaña Collectibles (Zihuatanejo), 402
Coffee Plantation Tour (Huatulco), 429
Collage Club (Puerto Vallarta), 323
College of San Nicolás de Hidalgo (Morelia), 243

Colonial Puebla. See Puebla
Columbus Day (Día de l a Raza), 31
Comitán, 485
Compañia, Church of the
  Guanajuato, 202
  Puebla, 505–506
Compañía de Jesús, Iglesia de la (Morelia), 243
Condesa and Roma neighborhoods (Mexico City), nightlife, 140
Condesa Beach (Acapulco), 378
Condesa/Roma (Mexico City), accommodations, 110–111
Conservatorio de las Rosas (Morelia), 243
Consolidators, 34–35
Constitution Day (Día de la Constitución), 28
Continental Airlines Vacations, 55
Continental Vacations, 56
Convento de Guadalupe, 227
Convent of San Bernardino de Siena (Mexico City), 128
Convent of Santa Clara (Querétaro), 216
Cooking classes
  Oaxaca City, 446
  Tepoztlán, 175
Cooking tours, 59
Copala, 341, 348–349
Copalitilla Cascades, 428
Copper Canyon, 13, 22, 295, 672–691
Copper Canyon Train, 674–683
Copper Museum (Santa Clara), 258
Corpus Christi, 29
Corsica (Puerto Vallarta), 304
Costa Alegre, 14, 349–359
Costa Maya (Riviera Maya), 4, 5, 14, 579–580
  all-inclusive resorts on, 590–591
  driving along, 580
  exploring, 583–584
Coyuca Lagoon, 378
Cozumel, 5, 560–577
  accommodations, 570–574
  all-inclusive resorts, 562–563
  beaches, 568–569
  clinics, 564
  exploring, 565–570
  getting around, 564
  getting there and departing, 560–561
  Internet access, 565
  layout of, 563–564

  nightlife, 577
  restaurants, 574–576
  shopping, 570
  tours, 569
  traveling to, 563
  trips to the mainland, 570
  visitor information, 563
  watersports, 565–566
Crafts. See Handicrafts and folk art
Credit cards, 41
  lost or stolen, 74–75
Creel, 680–682
Crime, 46–47
CrocoCun (near Puerto Morelos), 592
The Cross of the Bay (Isla Mujeres), 551
Cruise lines, 38–39
Cuanajo, 259
Cuernavaca, 164–174
  accommodations, 171–173
  activities and excursions, 170–171
  American Express, 167
  banks, 167
  exploring, 168–170
  Internet access, 167–168
  layout of, 167
  nightlife, 174
  restaurants, 173–174
  traveling to and from, 166
  visitor information, 167
Cuevas de los Tiburones, 551
Cuilapan, 458
Culinary Adventures, 59
Currency and currency exchange, 39–40
  scams, 48
Customs regulations, 70–71

D

Dady'O (Cancún), 544
Dady Rock Bar and Grill (Cancún), 544
Dainzú, 456
Danzantes friezes (Monte Albán), 453, 454
Day of the Dead, 31–32
Delta Vacations, 55, 56
De Santos (Puerto Vallarta), 323
Día de la Candelaria (Candlemas), 28
Día de la Constitución (Constitution Day), 28
Día de la Marina (Navy Day), 29
Día de la Raza, 31

Día de los Reyes (Three Kings' Day), 27
Día de San Pedro y San Pablo, 29
Días de los Muertos, Oaxaca City, 441–442
Disabilities, travelers with, 48–49
Diseño Artesano (Pátzcuaro), 253
Diving. *See* Scuba diving
Dog racing, Tijuana, 748
Dolores Hidalgo, 195–196
Dolphins, swimming with
  Acapulco, 382
  Cancún, 540
  Cozumel, 568
  Isla Mujeres, 552
  Playa del Carmen, 584
  Puerto Aventuras, 599
  Puerto Vallarta, 299
  Xel-Ha, 602
Dolphin shows, Acapulco, 382
Dominico de la Navidad, former convent (Tepoztlán), 176
The Dovecote (Uxmal), 649
Drinks, 69
Drug laws, 71
Drugstores, 71
Dzibanché, 617
Dzibilchaltún, 620, 643–644

Ecotourism and adventure trips, 52–53
  Cabo San Lucas, 714–715
  La Paz, 731
  Mérida, 641
  Puerto Escondido area, 416
  Puerto Vallarta, 296
  San José del Cabo, 699
Edificio de las Monjas (Chichén Itzá), 664
Edzná, 653–654
Ek Balam, 12, 583, 669–670
El Agora (Xalapa), 497
El Artesano (Querétaro), 217
El Bar de Félix (Manzanillo), 368
El Bosque (Morelia), 244
El Carmen, church and former convent of (Morelia), 244
El Castillo
  Chichén Itzá, 661–662
  Cobá, 609
El Centro (Plaza Mayor; Mérida), 623, 627
Elderhostel, 50
ElderTreks, 50
El Divisadero, 679–680, 682

Electricity, 71–72
El Encuentro (San Cristóbal), 479
El Estribo, 257
Elevation sickness, 44–45
El Faro Lighthouse Bar (Puerto Vallarta), 322–323
El Fuerte, 676–678
El Garrafón Natural Park, 538, 539, 551
El Incendio (Guanajuato), 210
El Mirador (Kabah), 652
El Nuevo Olimpo (Mérida), 628, 641
El Palacio, Kabah, 652
El Pípila (Guanajuato), 200–201
El Rosario (near Morelia), 249
El Santuario de Guadalupe (Morelia), 244
El Squid Roe (Cabo San Lucas), 724
El Tajín, 499–501
El Teatro de la Ciudad (La Paz), 732
El Tecolote Libros (Todos Santos), 726
E-mail, 54–55
Embassies and consulates, 72–73
Emergencies, 73
Enchiladas, 67
Encuentro Internacional del Mariachi (Guadalajara), 274
Enrique Estrada Park (Zacatecas), 225
Ensenada, 753–755
Entry requirements, 25–26
  car documents, 37–38
Erongarícuaro, 258
Escobilla Beach (near Puerto Escondido), 415
Escondido, 188
Escuinapa, 338
Estero San José, 699–700
Etiquette and customs, 73
Exconvento de Santa Mónica (Puebla), 506
Exconvento de Santa Rosa (Puebla), 506
Exposición Nacional de Arte Popular (FONART; Mexico City), 138

Fábrica La Aurora (San Miguel), 189
Fall Equinox (Chichén Itzá), 31
Fall of Tenochtitlán (Mexico City), 30
Families with children, information and resources, 50–51

Far Flung Adventures, 59
Feast of San Antonio Abad (Mexico City), 27–28
Feast of San Isidro, 29
Feast of the Virgin of Guadalupe, 32
Felipe Carrillo Puerto, 610–611
Female travelers, 51
Feria de Zacatecas, 222
Feria Nacional del Mole (Mexico City), 31
Festival Cervantino (Guanajuato), 31
Festival de México en el Centro Histórico (Mexico City), 29
Festival Fundador (Todos Santos), 725
Festival Internacional Cervantino (Guanajuato), 200
Festival of San Cristóbal de las Casas, 32–33
Festival of the Radishes, 33
Festival of the Virgin of Guadalupe (Puerto Vallarta), 292
Fiesta Americana and Fiesta Inn, 64
Fiesta de la Soledad (Oaxaca City), 442
Fiesta de la Virgen de Guadalupe (Oaxaca City), 442
Fiesta de los Locos (San Miguel), 185
Fiesta de los Rábanos (Festival of the Radishes), 33
Fiesta Guelaguetza (Oaxaca City), 441
Fiestas de la Vendimia (Ensenada), 30
Fiestas de Noviembre, 32
Fiestas de Octubre (Guadalajara), 31
Fireworks, 11
  Mazatlán, 347
Fishing
  Acapulco, 379
  Cabo San Lucas, 713–714, 717
  Cancún, 537
  Cozumel, 566
  Isla Mujeres, 551–552
  La Paz, 729, 731–732
  Manzanillo, 363
  Mazatlán, 337–338
  Puerto Aventuras, 584, 599
  Puerto Escondido, 416
  Puerto Vallarta, 297
  Punta Allen Peninsula, 608
  San José del Cabo, 700

Flamingos, 348, 553, 598, 620, 642–644, 670
Flights.com, 35
Floating Gardens of Xochimilco (Mexico City), 136
FlyCheap, 35
FMT (Mexican Tourist Permit), 25–26
Folk art. *See* Handicrafts and folk art
FONART (San Luis Potosí), 233–234
Fort of San Juan de Ulúa (Veracruz), 490
Fortress of Mundaca, 553
Forum by the Sea (Cancún), 542
Friday Pottery Market (Pátzcuaro), 254
Frijoles, 67
Frommers.com, 52
Fuerte de San Diego (Acapulco), 381
Fuerte-Museo San José el Alto (Campeche), 657
Fuerte-Museo San Miguel (Campeche), 657
Funjet Vacations, 56

Galería AL (Arte Latinoamericano; Puerto Vallarta), 304–305
Galería del Arcángel (Pátzcuaro), 254
Galería des Artistes (Puerto Vallarta), 305
Galería Iturbe (Pátzcuaro), 254
Galería Libertad (Querétaro), 214
Galería Omar Alonso (Puerto Vallarta), 305
Galería Pacífico (Puerto Vallarta), 305
Galería Uno (Puerto Vallarta), 305
Gallería Dante (Puerto Vallarta), 305
Garrafón Natural Reef Park, 538, 539, 551
Gasoline, 61
Gay and lesbian travelers, 49
    Mazatlán, 337
    Puerto Vallarta, 324–325
Gestures, 73
Gnats, 45
GOGO Worldwide Vacations, 57
Golf, 58
    Acapulco, 380
    Bahías de Huatulco, 429

Cabo San Lucas, 715–716
Cancún, 540–541
Costa Alegre, 354
Cozumel, 570
Cuernavaca, 170
Ixtapa/Zihuatanejo, 400–401
Manzanillo, 363–364
Mazatlán, 338–339
Playa del Carmen and environs, 583, 594
Puerto Vallarta, 297–298
San José del Cabo, 700
The Gorky González Workshop (Guanajuato), 204–205
Gourmet Festival (Puerto Vallarta), 32, 292
Governor's Palace (Uxmal), 649
Gran Arrecife Maya, 537
Gran Hotel Ciudad de México (Mexico City), 124
Gran Noche Mexicana (Acapulco), 392
Great Plaza (Monte Albán), 453
Great Pyramid
    Cholula, 512
    Uxmal, 649
Group of the Columns (Mitla), 458
Grutas de Cacahuamilpa, 156
Guadalajara, 3, 262–282
    accommodations, 266–270
    books, newspapers and magazines, 265
    bus tours, 274
    climate and dress, 265
    consulates, 265
    emergencies, 265
    exploring, 274–278
    getting around, 264
    language classes, 265–266
    layout of, 263
    neighborhoods, 263–264
    nightlife, 282
    police, 266
    restaurants, 270–274
    safety, 266
    shopping, 279–282
    traveling to and from, 262–263
    visitor information, 263
Guadalupe, 227
Guadalupe, Iglesia de (Huatulco), 427
Guanajuato, 196–210
    accommodations, 2, 205–208
    drugstores, 199
    getting around, 199
    hospitals, 199
    layout of, 199

nightlife, 210
restaurants, 2, 208–210
seasons, 200
shopping, 204–205
special events and festivals, 200
traveling to and from, 198–199
Guayaberas, Mérida, 631
Guelaguetza Dance Festival (Oaxaca), 30
Guelatao, 460
Gulf Coast, 23

Habla Hispana (San Miguel), 187
Hacienda El Lencero (Xalapa), 497–498
Haciendas, in the Yucatán, 636–637
Hacienda Style (Dolores Hidalgo), 196
Hamacas El Aguacate (Mérida), 632
Hammocks, Mérida, 631–632
Handicrafts and folk art. *See also* Markets; Pottery and ceramics; Textiles and weavings; Woodcarvings
    Campeche, 657
    Cancún, 541–542
    Creel, 681
    Guadalajara, 279
    Guanajuato, 204
    Ixtapa/Zihuatanejo, 401
    La Paz, 733
    Mazatlán, 346
    Mérida, 631
    Mexico City, 137–138
    Morelia, 244–245
    Oaxaca City, 445, 446
    Oaxaca state, 452–453
    Pátzcuaro, 16
    Pátzcuaro and nearby villages, 253, 254, 258
    Puerto Vallarta, 300, 305–307
    Querétaro, 215
    San Luis Potosí, 233–234
    San Miguel de Allende, 16
    Tepoztlán, 175
    Tijuana, 747
    Tlacolula, 457
    Tlaquepaque, 279–281
    Tonalá, 281–282
    Valladolid, 668
    Zacatecas, 225, 225
Health concerns, 43–46
Health insurance, 42–43
Hemiciclo (Mexico City), 135

Hidalgo's Dungeon (Chihuahua), 689
High-altitude hazards, 44–45
Highway 18 (the Convent Route), 645–646
Highway 175, 459–460
Highway 200, motorist advisory, 396
Highway 261, 645
Highway 307, 4
Hiking
    Bahías de Huatulco, 429
    Oaxaca, 447
Hilo (Puerto Vallarta), 323–324
History of Mexico, 757–763
Holy Week (Semana Santa), 28–29
    Oaxaca City, 441
    Taxco, 155
Hornitos Beach (Acapulco), 378
Hornos Beach (Acapulco), 378
Horseback riding
    Acapulco, 381
    Bahías de Huatulco, 429
    Cabo San Lucas, 716–717
    Cancún, 541
    Ixtapa/Zihuatanejo, 401
    Mazatlán, 339
    Paricutín volcano, 261
    Playa del Carmen, 583
    Puerto Vallarta, 298
    San Cristóbal, 477
    San José del Cabo, 700
Hostelling International México, 51
Hot Air Balloon Festival (León), 32
Hoteles Camino Real, 64
Hotels
    best, 17–20
    hotel chains, 64
    house rentals and swaps, 64–65
    landing the best room, 66
    rating system, 63–64
    saving on, 65–66
    surfing for, 65
Hot mineral springs. See Thermal spas and hot springs
House and Garden Tour (San Miguel), 187
House rentals and swaps, 64–65
Huichol Indians, 295, 303
    art, 16–17, 302–304
Huitepec Cloud Forest, 479
Humboldt House/Museo Virreinal de Taxco, 155
Hurricane season, 27

Icacos Beach (Acapulco), 378
Iglesia. See under first significant word (e.g. Compañía de Jesús, Iglesia de la)
Ihuatzio, 259
Ik-Kil, 666
Independence Day, 30
Insects, 45
Instituto Allende (San Miguel), 186
Instituto Cultural Cabañas (Guadalajara), 277
Instituto de la Artesanía Jalisciense (Guadalajara), 279
Instituto Michoacano de Cultura (Morelia), 244
Insurance, 42
    auto, 38
International Association for Medical Assistance to Travellers (IAMAT), 43–44
International Chamber Music Festival (San Miguel de Allende), 30
International Guitar Festival (Morelia), 241
International Organ Festival (Morelia), 241
Internet access, 54–55, 73. See also specific destinations
Isla Contoy, 538, 553–554
Isla de la Piedra (Mazatlán), 337
Isla de las Chivas (Mazatlán), 337
Isla Holbox, 670–671
Isla Ixtapa, 399
Isla Mujeres, 5, 10, 545–559
    accommodations, 554–557
    beaches and outdoor activities, 550–552
    emergencies, 550
    getting around, 549
    getting there and departing, 548
    layout of, 549
    nightlife, 559
    restaurants, 557–559
    seasons, 550
    shopping, 554
    visitor information, 549
    websites, 546
Itineraries, suggested, 78–84
    La Ruta Maya in 2 weeks, 82–84
    Los Cabos to Copper Canyon, 81–82

pre-Columbian treasures in a week, 78–80
western Mexico, 80–81
IVA (value-added tax), 40
Ixtapan de la Sal, 160–162
Ixtapa/Zihuatanejo, 7, 394–410
    accommodations, 402–407
    American Express, 397
    banks, 398
    beaches, 398–399
    getting around, 397
    hospitals, 398
    Internet access, 398
    layout of, 397
    nightlife, 409–410
    outdoor activities, 398–401
    restaurants, 407–409
    shopping, 401–402
    traveling to and from, 394, 396
    visitor information, 396
Izamal, 642

J & B Salsa Club (Puerto Vallarta), 324
Janitzio, 252, 257
Jardín Borda (Cuernavaca), 169
Jardín Botánico Dr. Alfredo Barrera (near Puerto Morelos), 592
Jardín Etnobotánico y Museo de Medicina Tradicional y Herbolaria (Cuernavaca), 169
Jardín Zenea (Querétaro), 214
Jesús, Iglesia de (Mérida), 629
Jet-ski tours, Cancún, 538
Jewelry
    Mazatlán, 346
    Mexico City, 138
    Puerto Vallarta, 307
    San Cristóbal, 480
    San José del Cabo, 702
Jiménez, Manuel, 458
Jornadas Alarconianas (Taxco), 155
Jorongo Bar (Mexico City), 142
Juárez, Benito, birthplace of (Guelatao), 460
Juárez Monument (Mexico City), 135
Juego de pelota (ball court)
    Chichén Itzá, 662
    Cobá, 609
    El Tajín, 500
    Monte Albán, 453
    Palenque, 466
    Uxmal, 649
    Yagul, 457

Kabah, 651–652
Kahlo, Frida, Museo (Mexico City), 118, 120
Kanasín, 645
Kayaking
    La Paz, 731
    Mazatlán, 339
    Punta Solimán, 603
    San José del Cabo, 700
Kohunlich, 617
Kukulcán Plaza (Cancún), 542

Labná, 652
La Bodeguita del Medio (Guadalajara), 282
La Bodeguita del Medio (Puerto Vallarta), 322
Labor Day, 29
La Bufadora, 754
La Calzada Fray Antonio de San Miguel (Morelia), 244
La Casa. See entries starting with "Casa"
La Cava de la Princesa (San Miguel), 194–195
L.A. Cetto Winery (Tijuana), 747
La Ciudadela (Teotihuacán), 147
La Dama de las Camelias (Guanajuato), 210
La Entrega Beach (Santa Cruz Bay), 428
La Fuente (Ixtapa), 402
La Galería (San Cristóbal), 480
Lago Bacalar, 13, 14, 613–615
Lágrimas de la Selva (San Cristóbal), 480
La Gruta, 188
Laguna de Cuyutlán, 363
Laguna de Las Garzas, 363
La Huatápera (Uruapan), 260
La Iglesia
    Chichén Itzá, 664
    Cobá, 609
La Isla Shopping Village (Cancún), 542
La Madonna (Cancún), 544
Lambityeco, 456
La Mina Club (Zacatecas), 230
La Mina "El Edén" (Zacatecas), 225–226
Language, 73. See also Spanish schools and classes
LanguagePoint (San Miguel), 186

La Noche de Rábanos (Oaxaca City), 442
La Otra Cara de México (San Miguel), 187–188
La Parroquia (San Miguel), 186
La Paz, 10, 719, 727–736
Lapidaria de Querétaro, 217
La Punta (Puerto Escondido), 415
La Quebrada (Acapulco), 377
    accommodations, 386–388
    high divers at, 380
La Ruta Maya, suggested 2-week itinerary, 82
Las Animas Beach (near Puerto Vallarta), 292
La Santa Cruz (Querétaro), 215
Las Estacas, 170–171, 176
Las Grutas de Cacahuamilpa, 176
Las Tiendas de Palmilla (San José del Cabo), 702
La Taboada, 188
La Torre Latinoamericana (Mexico City), 136
La Trova (Mérida), 641
La Valenciana, 203
Legal aid, 73
Liberty Travel, 57
Lienzo Charro de Jalisco (Guadalajara), 277–278
Liquor laws, 74
Living (Mexico City), 143
The Lobby Lounge (Cancún), 544
Loltún, 652–653
López Quiroga Gallery (Mexico City), 138
Loreto, 736, 738–742
Los Amigos Smokeshop and Cigar Bar (San José del Cabo), 702
Los Cabos, 6, 10, 692–724. See also Cabo San Lucas; San José del Cabo
    Corridor between, 707–711
Los Castillo (near Taxco), 156
Los Danzantes (Monte Albán), 453, 454
Los Mochis, 674, 683–686
Los Morros de Los Pericos islands, 399–400
Los Pinos (Mazatlán), 337
Los Pinos (Mexico City), 136
Lost and found, 74–75
Lost-luggage insurance, 43
Lucy's CuCu Cabaña (Puerto Vallarta), 306

MACG (Museo de Arte Carrillo Gil; Mexico City), 133
MACO (Museo de Arte Contemporáneo de Oaxaca), 442
Mágico Mundo Marino (Acapulco), 377–378
Mail, 75
Majahual, 611
Mama (Mamita), 646
Mama Mía (San Miguel), 195
Mambo Café (Acapulco), 393
Mambo Café (Cabo San Lucas), 724
Manchones Reef, 551
Mandara (Acapulco), 393
Mantas Típicas (Pátzcuaro), 254
Manzanillo, 359–369
    accommodations, 364–367
    getting around, 360, 362
    Internet access, 362
    layout of, 360
    nightlife, 368–369
    outdoor activities, 362–364
    restaurants, 367–368
    shopping, 364
    tours, 363
    traveling to and from, 359–360
    visitor information, 360
Mariachi Festival (Guadalajara), 30
Mariachi Loco (Puerto Vallarta), 323
Mariachis
    Encuentro Internacional del Mariachi (Guadalajara), 274
    Guadalajara, 282
    Mexico City, 142
    Puebla, 511
Marietas Islands, 293
Marina Vallarta, 287, 292, 300
    accommodations, 308–309
    nightlife, 321
    restaurants, 313
Marina Vallarta Golf Club, 297
Markets. See also Handicrafts and folk art
    Bahías de Huatulco, 429
    Guadalajara, 277
    Ixtapa/Zihuatanejo, 401, 402
    La Paz, 733
    Mérida, 630–631
    Mexico City, 138–140
    Morelia, 242
    Oaxaca City, 446
    Papantla, 501
    Pátzcuaro, 252
    Puerto Vallarta, 300, 302

Markets *(cont.)*
San Cristóbal, 476
Valladolid, 668
Zaachila, 459
MARO (Oaxaca City), 446
Mascota, 295
Masks, 15
Mayapán, 646
Maya ruins. *See* **Archaeological sites and ruins**
Mayólica Santa Rosa (Guanajuato), 205
Mazatlán, 332–349
accommodations, 341–344
American Express, 336
emergencies, 336
getting around, 335
Internet access, 336
language classes, 336
nightlife, 347
organized tours, 341
outdoor activities, 336–339
restaurants, 344–346
shopping, 346–347
side trips from, 347–349
sights and attractions, 339–341
spectator sports, 338
traveling to and from, 332, 334
visitor information, 334–335
Mazunte Beach, 415–416
Mealtimes, 68
Medical insurance, 42–43
MedjetAssist, 46
Mejicanissimo (San José del Cabo), 702
Melaque, 353
Melaque (San Patricio), 358–359
Mercado Abastos (Oaxaca City), 446
Mercado Central (Taxco), 156
Mercado de Artesanía (Oaxaca City), 446
Mercado de Artesanías
Puebla (El Parián), 508
San Miguel, 189
Tijuana, 747
Valladolid, 668
Mercado de Curiosidades (Centro Artesanal; Mexico City), 139
Mercado de Dulces (Morelia), 245
Mercado de la Ciudadela (Mexico City), 139
Mercado de la Merced (Mexico City), 139–140

Mercado González Ortega (Zacatecas), 224
Mercado Hidalgo
Guanajuato, 204
San Luis Potosí, 234
Mercado Insurgentes (Mexico City), 140
Mercado Jesús González Ortega (Zacatecas), 225
Mercado Libertad (Guadalajara), 277, 279
Mérida, 6, 620, 621–647
accommodations, 632–638
climate and seasons, 625, 626
exploring, 626–630
festivals and special events, 624
getting around, 625
getting there and departing, 621–623
hospitals, 626
layout of, 623–625
nightlife, 640–641
police, 626
restaurants, 638–640
shopping, 630–632
side trips from, 641–647
Spanish classes, 626
visitor information, 623
Mexcaltitan, 295
Mexican Art Tours, 58
Mexicana Vacations, 57
Mexican Tourist Permit (FMT), 25–26
Mexico Boutique Hotels, 57
Mexico-Caribbean Food Festival (Cancún), 523
Mexico City, 10, 85–148
accommodations, 2, 103–111
American Express, 100
architectural highlights, 124–125
arriving and departing, 86
banks, 100
bookstores, 100–101
car rentals, 100
Centro Histórico
accommodations, 103–104
nightlife, 140
restaurants, 115–117
sights and attractions, 129, 130–132
churches, 126, 128
crime, 46–47, 102–103
at night, 140, 143
currency exchange, 101
drugstores, 101
elevation, 101
emergencies, 101

finding an address in, 92–93
free Sunday concerts, 99
getting around, 95, 98–100
historic buildings and monuments, 128–129
hot lines, 101
Internet access, 102
markets, 138–140
neighborhoods, 93–95
nightlife, 140–144
organized tours, 136–137
parks and gardens, 135–136
post offices, 102
restaurants, 111–117
restrooms, 102
shopping, 137–140
side trip to the Pyramids of San Juan Teotihuacán, 144–148
sights and attractions, 117–136
taxis, 95, 98
airport taxis, 88–90
safety precautions, 89
telephones, 103
visitor information, 92
weather and clothing, 103
Mexico Travel Link Ltd., 58
Mexico Travel Net, 57
Mezcal, 69, 457
Michoacán, 3, 237–261
Million Monarch March (Michoacán), 13
Miniaturas (Mérida), 631
Misión Nuestra Señora de Loreto, 739
Misol Ha, 470
Mitla, 452, 455, 457–458
Monarch butterflies, Michoacán, 195, 248–249
Money matters, 39–42
Monte Albán, 11, 452, 453–455
Montebello National Park, 485
Monumento a la Revolución (Mexico City), 129
Monumento a los Héroes de la Independencia (Mexico City), 128
Morales, Rodolfo, 460
Morelia, 238–249
accommodations, 245–246
exploring, 241–244
getting around, 240
layout of, 240
nightlife, 248–249
restaurants, 246–248
shopping, 244–245
special events and festivals, 241

traveling to and from, 238, 240

visitor information, 240

Morelia Boys Choir, 243

Mosquitoes, 45

Mountain Travel Sobek, 60

Mulegé, 736

Mummy Museum (La Valenciana), 203

Muna, 645

Mundo Divertido La Mesa (Tijuana), 746–747

Museo Amparo (Puebla), 16, 506–507

Museo Antropología de Xalapa, 15, 498

Museo Arqueológico de Mazatlán, 340

Museo Arqueológico de Xochimilco (Mexico City), 132

Museo Arqueológico Guillermo Spratling (Taxco), 156

Museo Bello y González (Puebla), 507

Museo Casa de Allende (San Miguel), 187

Museo Casa Robert Brady (Cuernavaca), 169–170

Museo de Arqueología de la Costa Grande (Ixtapa/Zihuatanejo), 398

Museo de Arqueología del Occidente de México (Guadalajara), 277

Museo de Arte (Querétaro), 216

Museo de Arte Carrillo Gil (MACG; Mexico City), 133

Museo de Arte Colonial (Morelia), 244

Museo de Arte Contemporáneo Ateneo de Yucatán (Mérida), 628

Museo de Arte Contemporáneo de Oaxaca (MACO), 442

Museo de Arte Moderno (Mexico City), 129–130

Museo de Arte Popular (Puebla), 506

Museo de Arte Popular Mexicano (Cancún), 541

Museo de Artesanías (Tlaxcala), 512

Museo de Artes e Industrias Populares (Pátzcuaro), 253

Museo de Cuauhnáhuac (Cuernavaca), 170

Museo de Historia Natural de la Ciudad de Mexico (Mexico City), 130

Museo de la Ciudad
Campeche, 656
Ciudad de México (Mexico City), 130
Guadalajara, 278
Mérida, 629
Veracruz, 490–491

Museo de la Cultura Maya (Chetumal), 616

Museo de la Independencia (Dolores Hidalgo), 196

Museo de la Isla de Cozumel, 569

Museo del Ambar (San Cristóbal), 476–477

Museo de la Revolución (Chihuahua), 689

Museo de las Artes de la Universidad de Guadalajara, 278

Museo de las Misiones (Loreto), 739

Museo de la Toma de Zacatecas, 225

Museo del Cobre (Santa Clara), 258

Museo del Estado (Morelia), 243–244

Museo de Los Momias (La Valenciana), 203

Museo del Palacio de Bellas Artes (Mexico City), 124

Museo del Pueblo de Guanajuato (Guanajuato), 201

Museo del Pueblo Maya (Dzibilchaltún), 643

Museo del Templo Mayor (Mexico City), 122–123

Museo de Medicina Tradicional y Herbolaria (Cuernavaca), 169

Museo de Muebles (Xalapa), 497–498

Museo Diego Rivera (Guanajuato), 201

Museo Diego Rivera Anahuacalli (Mexico City), 132–133

Museo Dolores Olmedo Patiño (Mexico City), 133

Museo Estudio Diego Rivera (Mexico City), 133–134

Museo Exhacienda San Gabriel de Barrera (near La Valenciana), 204

Museo F. Goitia (Zacatecas), 226

Museo Franz Mayer (Mexico City), 130–131

Museo Frida Kahlo (Mexico City), 118, 120

Museo Histórico de Acapulco, 381

Museo Histórico Minero de Santa Rosalía, 742

Museo Histórico Naval (Veracruz), 491

Museo Iconográfico del Quijote (Guanajuato), 201

Museo José Luis Cuevas (Mexico City), 131

Museo León Trotsky (Mexico City), 134

Museo Mural Diego Rivera (Mexico City), 131

Museo Nacional de Antropología (Mexico City), 15, 101, 120

Museo Nacional de Arte (Munal; Mexico City), 132

Museo Nacional de Cerámica (Tonalá), 282

Museo Nacional de Historia (Mexico City), 128

Museo Nacional de la Estampa (Mexico City), 132

Museo Nacional de la Máscara (San Luis Potosí), 233

Museo Nacional de la Revolución (Mexico City), 129

Museo Nacional del Ferrocarril (Puebla), 507

Museo Nacional de San Carlos (Mexico City), 132

Museo Pantaleón Panduro (Guadalajara), 278

Museo Pedro Coronel (Zacatecas), 226

Museo Rafael Coronel (Zacatecas), 226–227

Museo Regional (Querétaro), 214

Museo Regional de Antropología (Mérida), 630

Museo Regional de Antropología Carlos Pellicer Cámara (Villahermosa), 461–462

Museo Regional de Guadalajara, 276

Museo Regional de la Historia (Guadalupe), 227

Museo Regional de Oaxaca (Oaxaca City), 442–443

Museo Regional La Alhóndiga de Granaditas (Guanajuato), 201–202

Museo Regional Michoacano (Morelia), 242–243

Museo Río Cuale (Puerto Vallarta), 300
Museo Rufino Tamayo (Mexico City), 130
Museo Templo y Convento Santo Domingo (San Cristóbal), 477
Museo Teotihuacán, 146
Museo Virreinal de Guadalupe, 15, 227
Museo Virreinal de Taxco, 155
Museum of Archaeology and History (Manzanillo), 364
Museum of Zapotec Art (Mitla), 457–458
Music, 11
Muyil, 610

Nacional Monte de Piedad (Mexico City), 138, 140
National Auditorium (Mexico City), 141
National Ceramics Fair and Fiesta (Tlaquepaque), 29
National Silver Fair (Taxco), 32
Natural Habitat Adventures, 59
Natural history tours, 59
NatureQuest, 59
Navy Day (Día de la Marina), 29
Necri (San José del Cabo), 702
Newspapers and magazines, 75
New Year's Day (Año Nuevo), 27
New Year's Eve, 33
NH Hoteles, 64
Nieves del Correo (Morelia), 243
Nikki Beach
   Cabo San Lucas, 724
   Puerto Vallarta, 324
Noche Mexicana (Mérida), 624
No Name Bar & Grill (Puerto Vallarta), 324
Norte season, 27
North-Central Region, 23
Northern Platform (Monte Albán), 454
The North Temple (Chichén Itzá), 662
November Festivals, 32
Nuevo Vallarta, 287, 326–327
The Nunnery Quadrangle (Uxmal), 648–649

Oaxaca (state), 3, 23, 433, 434
   social unrest in, 436

Oaxaca City, 434–460
   accommodations, 447–450
   American Express, 440
   consulates, 440
   cooking and language classes, 446–447
   exploring, 442–445
   getting around, 439
   layout of, 439
   nightlife, 452
   restaurants, 450–452
   road trips from, 452–460
   seasons, 440
   shopping, 445–446
   special events and festivals, 441
   street food, 450
   traveling to and from, 436–439
   visitor information, 439
Oaxaca Reservations/Zapotec Tours, 58
Observatory (Chichén Itzá), 663
Ocosingo, 470
Ocotlán, 459–460
Ocotlán Sanctuary (Tlaxcala), 513
October Festivals (Guada-lajara), 31
Ojo de Venado (Guanajuato), 205
Olinala (Puerto Vallarta), 306
Olmedo, Dolores, home of (Acapulco), 381
O.M.R. Gallery (Mexico City), 138
Opals, Querétaro, 217
Our Lord of the Column (San Miguel), 185
Our Lord of the Conquest (San Miguel), 185
Oxkutzcab, 653

Paamul, 598–599
Pacific coast, 22–23
   central, 283–369
   southern, 370–432
Package tours, 55–57
Palace Group (Kabah), 651
Palace of Quetzalpapalotl (Teotihuacán), 148
Palacio Clavijero (Morelia), 243
Palacio de Bellas Artes (Mexico City), 15, 141
Palacio de Gobierno
   Mérida, 628–629
   San Luis Potosí, 233
   Zacatecas, 224

Palacio de la Mala Noche (Zacatecas), 224
Palacio de las Bellas Artes (San Cristóbal), 477
Palacio del Gobierno
   Chihuahua, 689
   Guadalajara, 276
   Morelia, 242
Palacio de los Estucos (Acanceh), 645
Palacio Federal (Morelia), 244
Palacio Huitziméngari (Pátzcuaro), 254
Palacio Montejo (Mérida), 628
Palacio Municipal (City Hall)
   Mérida, 628
   San Luis Potosí, 233
Palacio Nacional (Mexico City), 15, 120, 122
Palancar Reef, 565
Palenque, 11, 463–471
Palladium (Acapulco), 393–394
Palmilla Beach (San José del Cabo), 699
Panama hats, Mérida, 632
Panoramic Tower (Isla Mujeres), 553
Panteón del Tepeyac (Mexico City), 118
Papalote, Museo del Niño (Mexico City), 130
Papantla, 499
Paradise Beach (Cozumel), 568
Paraíso Beach (Acapulco), 378
Parasailing
   Acapulco, 379–380
   Ixtapa/Zihuatanejo, 400
   Puerto Vallarta, 298
Paricutín volcano, 260–261
Parish of Nuestra Señora de Guadalupe church (Puerto Vallarta), 300
Parque Acuático el CICI (Acapulco), 382
Parque Agua Azul (Guadala-jara), 277
Parque Cepeda Peraza (Mérida), 629
Parque de la Madre (Mérida), 629
Parque-Museo La Venta (Villahermosa), 462
Parque Nacional Eduardo Ruiz (Uruapan), 259, 260
Parque Nacional Palenque, 464
Parque Principal (Campeche), 656
Parque Santa Lucía (Mérida), 629

Parroquia de San Servacio (Valladolid), 667
Paseo de Montejo (Mérida), 625, 629–630
Passion (Cabo San Lucas), 724
Passports, 25, 75
Pátzcuaro, 249–259
  accommodations, 254–256
  climate, 251–252
  exploring, 252–253
  layout of, 251
  nightlife, 257
  restaurants, 256–257
  shopping, 253
  side trips from, 257–259
  traveling to and from, 251
  visitor information, 251
Pepe's Piano Bar (Acapulco), 394
Petacalco Beach (near Ixtapa), 400
Pets, traveling with, 76
Pie de la Cuesta (near Acapulco), 378
Pirámide del Adivino (Uxmal), 648
Platform of the Eagles (Chichén Itzá), 662
Platform of Venus (Chichén Itzá), 662
Playa Anclote (near Puerto Vallarta), 292
Playa Audiencia (Manzanillo), 362
Playa Azul (Manzanillo), 363
Playa Bacocho (Puerto Escondido), 415
Playa Caracol (Cancún), 537
Playa Carrizalillo (Puerto Escondido), 415
Playa del Carmen, 10, 570, 579, 580–592
  accommodations, 584–587
  coast north of, 592–596
  coast south of, 597–603
  exploring, 583–584
  getting there and departing, 581–582
  layout of, 582
  nightlife, 591–592
  restaurants, 587–591
Playa Destiladeras (near Puerto Vallarta), 292
Playa la Angosta (Acapulco), 377
Playa Larga (Zihuatanejo), 399
Playa La Ropa (Zihuatanejo), 399

Playa Las Brisas (Manzanillo), 362
Playa las Cuatas (Ixtapa), 399
Playa Las Gatas (Zihuatanejo), 399
Playa Las Gaviotas (Mazatlán), 337
Playa Linda (near Ixtapa), 399, 401
Playa Los Muertos (Playa Olas Altas or Playa del Sol; Puerto Vallarta), 291
Playa Madera (Zihuatanejo), 398
Playa Majahua (Ixtapa), 399
Playa Manzanillo (Acapulco), 378, 400
Playa Manzanillo (Puerto Escondido), 415
Playa Marineros (Puerto Escondido), 415
Playa Miramar (Manzanillo), 362–363
Playa Mismaloya (near Puerto Vallarta), 291
Playa Municipal (Zihuatanejo), 398
Playa Norte (Isla Mujeres), 550
Playa Norte (Mazatlán), 337
Playa Olas Altas (Mazatlán), 336
Playa Palancar (Cozumel), 568
Playa Palmar (Ixtapa), 399
Playa Panteón (Puerto Angel), 424
Playa Piedras Blancas (near Puerto Vallarta), 292
Playa Principal (Puerto Escondido), 415
Playa Puerto Marqués (near Acapulco), 378
Playa Quieta (Ixtapa), 399
Playa Sábalo (Mazatlán), 337
Playa San Agustinillo, 424
Playa San Francisco (Cozumel), 568
Playa San Pedrito (Manzanillo), 362
Playa Vista Hermosa (Ixtapa), 399
Playa Zicatela (Puerto Escondido), 415
Playa Zipolite, 424
Plaza Bahía (Acapulco), 382
Plaza Caracol (Cancún), 542
Plaza Chica (Pátzcuaro), 252, 253
Plaza de Armas
  Guadalajara, 276
  San Luis Potosí, 232–233
  Zacatecas, 224

Plaza de Garibaldi (Mexico City), 142
Plaza de la Campaña (Veracruz), 489
Plaza de la República (Mexico City), 129
Plaza de la República (Veracruz), 489
Plaza de las Tres Culturas (Mexico City), 134
Plaza de los Fundadores (San Luis Potosí), 233
Plaza de los Sapos (Puebla), 511
Plaza de San Francisco (San Luis Potosí), 233
Plaza de Santa Inés (Puebla), 511
Plaza de Santo Domingo
  Mexico City, 135
  San Cristóbal, 480
Plaza de Toros (Cancún), 541
Plaza Grande (Pátzcuaro), 252, 253
Plaza Mayor (El Centro; Mérida), 623, 627
Plaza Peninsula (Puerto Vallarta), 302
Plaza Principal (Mazatlán), 341
Plazuela del Baratillo (Guanajuato), 202
Plazuela del Carmen (San Luis Potosí), 233
Plazuela Machado (Mazatlán), 340
Pleasant Holidays, 57
Polanco (Mexico City), 16
Police, 76
Pottery and ceramics
  Amatenango del Valle, 478–479
  Dolores Hidalgo, 195, 196
  Guanajuato, 204
  Muna, 645
  Museo Pantaleón Panduro (Guadalajara), 278
  National Ceramics Fair and Fiesta (Tlaquepaque), 29
  Ocotlán, 459–460
  Pátzcuaro, 254
  San Bartolo Coyotepec, 459
  San José del Cabo, 702
  Talavera, 16
    Dolores Hidalgo, 196
    Puebla, 507–508
  Ticul, 646
  Tonalá, 281–282
Prescription medications, 46
Procession of Three Falls (Taxco), 155

Progreso, 620, 644
Puebla, 4, 502–515
    accommodations, 508–510
    Battle of (1862), 505
    exploring, 504–507
    getting there and departing, 502
    layout of, 504
    nightlife, 511
    restaurants, 510–511
    shopping, 507–508
    side trips from, 511–515
    visitor information, 504
Puerco Azul (Puerto Vallarta), 306
Puerta de Tierra (Campeche), 657
Puerto Angel, 423–424
Puerto Angelito (Puerto Escondido), 415
Puerto Aventuras, 579, 599–600
Puerto Calica, 598
Puerto Escondido, 7, 410–424
    accommodations, 418–420
    beaches, 415–417
    getting around, 414
    layout of, 413–414
    nightlife, 422–423
    restaurants, 420–422
    shopping, 417–418
    side trip to Puerto Angel, 423–424
    sights and activities, 415–417
    traveling to and from, 412–413
    visitor information, 413
Puerto Marqués, 378
Puerto Morelos, 579, 594–597
Puerto Paraíso Entertainment Plaza (Cabo San Lucas), 719
Puerto Vallarta, 3, 7, 283–332
    accommodations, 307–312
    beaches, activities and excursions, 291–293
    climate, 289
    consulates, 290
    consumer assistance, 289–290
    currency exchange, 290
    getting around, 288–289
    hospitals, 290
    layout of, 287
    newspapers and magazines, 290
    nightlife, 321–325
    organized tours, 293–296
    outdoor activities, 296–299
    restaurants, 313–320
    safety, 291

    shopping, 300, 302–307
    side trips from, 325–332
    sights and attractions, 299–300
    traveling to and from, 284, 286
    visitor information, 286–287
Punta Allen Peninsula, 14, 603–608
Punta del Guitarrón (Acapulco), 378
Punta Diamante, 378
Punta Mita, 14, 288, 293, 329–330
Punta Mita Golf Club, 297
Punta Solimán, 603
Punta Sur (Isla Mujeres), 553
Punta Sur Ecological Reserve, 568
Purépecha Indians (Tarascan Indians), 237, 244, 249, 253, 258
Puuc Maya Route, 651–653
Pyramid of Five Stories (Kabah), 653–654
Pyramid of the Flowers (Xochitécatl), 514–515
Pyramid of the Magician (Uxmal), 648
Pyramid of the Moon (Teotihuacán), 148
Pyramid of the Niches (El Tajín), 500
Pyramid of the Painted Lintel (Cobá), 609
Pyramid of the Sun (Teotihuacán), 147–148

Querétaro, 2–3, 211–221
    accommodations, 216–219
    American Express, 213
    emergencies, 213
    layout of, 213
    restaurants, 219–221
    sights and attractions, 214–216
    traveling to and from, 211, 213
    visitor information, 213
Querubines (Puerto Vallarta), 307
Quetzalcoatl Fountain (Guadalajara), 277
Quimixto Beach (near Puerto Vallarta), 292
Quinta Gameros (Chihuahua), 689
Quinta Real Grand Class Hotels and Resorts, 64

Rancho Loma Bonita (near Puerto Morelos), 592
Regional Ceramics Museum (Tlaquepaque), 280
Regions of Mexico, 22–24
Residencia de Gobernadores (Zacatecas), 224
Restaurants, 66–69
    best, 20–21
Restrooms, 76
Reto al Tepozteco (Tepoztlan), 30
Revolcadero Beach (Acapulco), 378
Revolution Day, 32
Rexo (Mexico City), 143
Rhythms of the Night (Puerto Vallarta to Las Caletas), 321
Ridley turtle. See Sea turtles
Rincón Artesanal (Guanajuato), 205
Río Bec area, 617
Rio Lagartos Nature Reserve, 670
Rioma (Mexico City), 143
Rivera, Diego
    murals (Mexico City), 120, 122, 124, 131, 133
    Museo Diego Rivera (Guanajuato), 201
    Museo Diego Rivera Anahuacalli (Mexico City), 132–133
    Museo Estudio Diego Rivera (Mexico City), 133–134
    Museo Mural Diego Rivera (Mexico City), 131
River rafting, Xalapa, 498
Riviera Maya (Costa Maya), 4, 5, 14, 579–580
    all-inclusive resorts on, 590–591
    driving along, 580
    exploring, 583–584
Rodeos (charreadas), Mazatlán, 338
Roqueta Island, 378, 379
Rosario, 338
Rosarito Beach, 750–753
Rotonda de los Hombres Ilustres (Guadalajara), 276
Route 66 (Puerto Vallarta), 323
Rufino Tamayo Museo de Arte Prehispánico de México (Oaxaca City), 443
Rugs. See Textiles and weavings

Ruins and archaeological sites.
See Archaeological sites
and ruins
Ruins of Bonampak, 469–470

Sacred Cenote (Chichén Itzá),
662–663
Safari Accents (Puerto
Vallarta), 306
Safety, 46–48
St. Peter and St. Paul Day, 29
Sala German Gedovius (San
Luis Potosí), 233
Salon Q (Acapulco), 394
Sammulá, 669
San Agustín, convent of
(Querétaro), 216
San Agustín (Zacatecas),
224–225
San Bartolo Coyotepec, 459
San Bernardino de Siena,
monastery of (Valladolid),
667
San Bernardino de Siena, Con-
vent of (Mexico City), 128
Sanborn's (Acapulco), 382
Sanborn's Mexico Insurance, 38
Sanborn Tours, 50
San Cayetano, Church of
(La Valenciana), 203
Sancho Panza Wine Bistro and
Jazz Club (Cabo San Lucas),
724
San Cristóbal de las Casas,
17, 471–485
accommodations, 480–482
climate, 475
coffeehouses, 484
exploring, 476–479
getting around, 474
getting there and departing,
472
layout of, 474
nearby Maya villages and
countryside, 477–479
nightlife, 484
restaurants, 482–484
road trips from, 484–485
shopping, 479–480
Spanish classes, 475
San Diego, Church of
Guanajuato, 202
Morelia, 244
San Felipe Neri, Iglesia de
(Oaxaca City), 444
San Francisco, church and convent of (Morelia), 242
San Francisco Acatepec, 512

San Francisco Church
(Querétaro), 214
San Francisco Reef, 565
San Ignacio de Arareko, 682
San Jerónimo Tlacochahuaya,
Iglesia de (Santa María
del Tule), 456
San José del Cabo, 695–707
accommodations, 702–704
getting around, 698
getting there and departing,
696–697
Internet access, 698
layout of, 698
nightlife, 706–707
outdoor activities, 699–702
post office, 699
restaurants, 704–706
shopping, 702
visitor information, 698
San José El Mogote, 453
San Juan Chamula, 478
San Juan de Dios Church
(Oaxaca City), 444
San Juan de Ulúa (Veracruz),
489
San Juan Parangaricutiro,
Church of, 260
San Juan Teotihuacán, 144–148
San Lucas, Iglesia de (Cabo San
Lucas), 718–719
San Luis Potosí, 3, 230–236
San Marcos National Fair
(Aguascalientes), 29
San Martín Tilcajete, 459
San Miguel (Cozumel), 560
Sanmiguelada (Running of the
Bulls at San Miguel), 31
San Miguel de Allende,
2, 10–11, 179–196
accommodations, 189–192
American Express, 184
climate and seasons, 184, 185
communication and shipping
services, 184
currency exchange, 184
exploring, 185–188
getting around, 183
nightlife, 194–195
restaurants, 192–194
shopping, 188–189
side trip to Dolores Hidalgo,
195–196
Spanish schools and classes,
186–187
special events and festivals,
185
traveling to and from,
181–182
visitor information, 182–183

San Sebastián, 14, 331–332
San Sebastián Air Expedition
(Puerto Vallarta), 295
Santa Bárbara, Iglesia de
(Loreto), 742
Santa Catalina, former convent
of (Oaxaca City), 444
Santa Clara, church and former
convent of (Querétaro), 216
Santa Clara del Cobre, 258
Santa María del Tule, 455–456
Santa Mónica, Exconvento de
(Puebla), 506
Santa Prisca y San Sebastián
Church (Taxco), 15, 156
Santa Rosa, Exconvento de
(Puebla), 506
Santa Rosa de Viterbo, church
and former convent of, 216
Santa Rosalía, 736, 742–744
Santa Rosa Wall, 565
Santiago, Church of (Mexico
City), 134–135
Santiago de Querétaro,
2–3, 211–221
accommodations, 216–219
American Express, 213
emergencies, 213
layout of, 213
restaurants, 219–221
sights and attractions,
214–216
traveling to and from,
211, 213
visitor information, 213
Santo Domingo, Church of
(Zacatecas), 224
Santo Domingo, Iglesia de
Oaxaca City, 444
Puebla, 505
Santo Domingo Xocotitlán, 176
Santo Tomás Jalietza, 459
SAX (San José del Cabo), 702
Sayil, 652
Sayulita, 330–331
Scams, 47–48
Scuba diving
Acapulco, 379
Akumal, 600
Cancún, 537–538
Chinchorro Reef Underwater
National Park, 611, 613
Cozumel, 564, 565–566
Isla Mujeres, 551
Ixtapa/Zihuatanejo, 400
La Paz, 731
Manzanillo, 363
Playa del Carmen, 584
Puerto Escondido, 416
Puerto Vallarta, 296

Scuba diving *(cont.)*
  San José del Cabo, 700–701
  Xel-Ha, 602
Sculptured Spaces (Isla Mujeres), 553
Sea Kayak Adventures, 59
Sea kayaking
  La Paz, 731
  Mazatlán, 339
  Punta Solimán, 603
  San José del Cabo, 700
Seasons, 26–27
Sea Trek Ocean Kayaking Center, 59
Sea turtles, 13
  Isla Mujeres, 552–553
  Puerto Escondido, 415
SeaWatch, 6
Secretaría de Educación Pública (Mexico City), 129
Semana Santa (Holy Week), 28–29
  Oaxaca City, 441
  Taxco, 155
Senior travel, 50
Señor Frog's
  Ixtapa, 410
  Puerto Vallarta, 324
Serpentarium (La Paz), 733
Shopping, best, 16–17
Sian Ka'an Biosphere Reserve, 603, 607
Sierra Madre, 294–295
Sierra Norte, 447
Silver cities, 149, 179–236.
  See also specific cities
  exploring, 180
Silver Fair (Taxco), 155
Smoking, 76
Sna Jolobil (San Cristóbal), 480
Snorkeling
  Akumal, 600
  Cancún, 537–538
  Cozumel, 566, 568
  Isla Mujeres, 551
  Playa del Carmen, 584
  Puerto Angel, 424
  Puerto Vallarta, 296
  Punta Solimán and Tankah bays, 603
  San José del Cabo, 700–701
  Xel-Ha, 601–602
Spanish schools and classes
  Cuernavaca, 168
  Guadalajara, 265–266
  Guanajuato, 200
  Mazatlán, 336
  Mérida, 626
  Oaxaca City, 446–447

  San Cristóbal, 475
  San Miguel, 186–187
Spratling Ranch Workshop (near Taxco), 156–157
Spring Equinox (Chichén Itzá), 28
STA Travel, 35
Student travel, 51
Studio Cathy Von Rohr (Puerto Vallarta), 305
Sun exposure, 44
SunTrips, 57
Suprema Corte de Justicia (Mexico City), 129
Surfing
  Baja California, 752
  Cabo San Lucas, 717, 718
  Costa Alegre, 354
  Ixtapa/Zihuatanejo, 400
  Mazatlán, 337
  Playa Zipolite, 424
  Puerto Escondido, 415
  San José del Cabo, 701
  Sayulita, 330
Sustainable tourism/ecotourism, 52–53
Swimming, Isla Mujeres, 550

Tacos, 67
Talavera Cortés (Dolores Hidalgo), 196
Talavera Mora (Dolores Hidalgo), 196
Talavera pottery, 16
  Dolores Hidalgo, 196
  Puebla, 507–508
Talavera San Gabriel (Dolores Hidalgo), 196
Talpa de Allende, 295
Tamales, 67
Tane (Mexico City), 138
Tangolunda Bay, 428
Tankah Bay, 603
Taquerías (taco joints), 68
Tarascan Indians (the Purépecha), 23, 237, 244, 249, 253, 258
Taste of Oaxaca Festival, 31
Taxco, 149–160
  accommodations, 157–158
  exploring, 155–157
  layout of, 154
  nightlife, 159–160
  restaurants, 158–159
  traveling to and from, 152, 154
  visitor information, 154
Taxes, 76
Taxis, 63

Teacapán, 347–348
Teatro Angela Peralta (Mazatlán), 340
Teatro Calderón (Zacatecas), 225
Teatro Daniel de Ayala (Mérida), 629
Teatro Degollado (Guadalajara), 277
Teatro Juárez (Guanajuato), 202
Teatro Macedonio de Alcalá (Oaxaca City), 445
Teatro Peón Contreras (Mérida), 629, 641
Tecoh, 646
Tejidos y Cordeles Nacionales (Mérida), 632
Telephones, 53–54
Temple of Jaguars (Chichén Itzá), 662
Temple of Panels (Chichén Itzá), 664
Temple of the Columns (El Tajín), 500
Temple of the Deer (Chichén Itzá), 663
Temple of the Frescoes (Tulum), 605
Temple of the Grinding Stones (Chichén Itzá), 663
Temple of the Inscriptions (Palenque), 464–465
Temple of the Seven Dolls (Dzibilchaltún), 643–644
Temple of the Skulls (Chichén Itzá), 662
Temple of the Warriors (Chichén Itzá), 663
Templo de Cata (La Valenciana), 203–204
Templo de las Capuchinas (Morelia), 242
Templo de las Monjas (Morelia), 244
Templo de los Dinteles (Chichén Itzá), 664
Templo de los Guerreros (Chichén Itzá), 663
Templo de los Inscripciones Iniciales (Chichén Itzá), 664
Templo de los Tableros (Chichén Itzá), 664
Templo del Señor Santiago Tupátaro, 258
Templo del Venado (Chichén Itzá), 663
Templo de San Cristóbal (San Cristóbal), 477

Templo de San Francisco (Tlaxcala), 512
Templo Mayor (Mexico City), 122
Tenacatita Bay, 352–353
Tenejapa, 479
Tennis
  Acapulco, 380–381
  Bahías de Huatulco, 429
  Ixtapa/Zihuatanejo, 401
  Mazatlán, 338
  Playa del Carmen, 583
  Puerto Vallarta, 299
  San José del Cabo, 701
Teotihuacán (near Mexico City), 144–148
Teotitlán del Valle, 453, 456
Tepoznieves (Tepoztlán), 177
Tepozteco Challenge (Tepoztlán), 30
Tepozteco pyramid (Tepoztlán), 175–176
Tepoztlán, 174–178
Tequila (liquor), 69
  distilleries, 280–281
  Puerto Vallarta, 307
Tequila (town), 280
Tequila Express, 281
Terminal Central de Autobuses del Norte (Mexico City), 91
Terminal Central de Autobuses del Sur (Mexico City), 91
Terminal de Autobuses de Pasajeros de Oriente (Mexico City), 91
Terminal Poniente de Autobuses (Mexico City), 91–92
Terra Noble Art & Healing Center (Puerto Vallarta), 294
Textiles and weavings
  Ihuatzio, 259
  Oaxaca City, 446
  San Cristóbal, 479, 480
  Santo Tomás Jalietza, 459
  Tenejapa, 479
  Teotitlán del Valle, 456
  Tlacolula, 457
  Uruapan, 260
  Zihuatanejo, 401
Thermal spas and hot springs
  Ixtapan de la Sal, 160–162
  near San Miguel, 188
Three Kings' Day (Día de los Reyes), 27
Ticul, 646–647
Tierra de Vinos (Mexico City), 144
Tijuana, 744–750
Tijuana Brewery, 747

Time zones, 76
Tío Lucas (San Miguel), 195
Tipping, 76
  at restaurants, 69
Tlacolula, 457
Tlaquepaque, 264, 279–281
Tlatelolco, Aztec city of (Mexico City), 134
Tlaxcala, 512–514
Tócuaro, 258
Todos Santos, 724–727
Toll roads, 61
Tomb of the High Priest (Chichén Itzá), 663
Tonalá, 264, 281–282
Tonantzintla, 512
Topolobampo Bay, 684
Torre Latinoamericana (Mexico City), 136
Tortillas, 67
Tour Baja, 59
Tours
  package, 55–57
  special-interest, 57–60
Town and Country, 57
Transportation, 60–63
Traveler's checks, 41–42
Travelers' diarrhea (turista), 44
Travel insurance, 42–43
Trek America, 59–60
Trip-cancellation insurance, 42
Tropical illnesses, 45
Trotsky, León, Museo (Mexico City), 134
Tule Tree (Santa María del Tule), 455–456
Tulum, 5, 7, 10, 570, 579, 603–608
Tumba del Gran Sacerdote (Chichén Itzá), 663
Tupátaro, 258–259
Turista (travelers' diarrhea), 44
Turtle Museum (near Puerto Escondido), 415
Tzaráracua waterfall, 260
Tzintzuntzan, 252, 257–258
Tzompantli (Chichén Itzá), 662

Uaymitún, 644
Unión Regional de Artesanías de los Altos (San Cristóbal), 480
United Vacations, 55
Universidad Nacional Autónoma de México (UNAM; Taxco), 154
Uricho, 258
Urique, 678

Uruapan, 259–261
US Airways Vacations, 56
UXMAL, 620
Uxmal, 12, 647–654
  en route to, 644–647

Valladolid, 620, 666–671
Valle de Bravo, 162–164
VAT (value-added tax), 40
20 de Noviembre Market (Oaxaca City), 446
Ventanilla, 417
Veracruz, 4
  accommodations, 491–493
  exploring, 489–491
  getting around, 488
  getting there and departing, 487–488
  layout of, 488
  nightlife, 495
  outdoor activities, 491
  restaurants, 493–494
  visitor information, 488
Veracruz City, 486–495
Veraventuras, 60
Víctor Artes Populares Mexicanas (Mexico City), 138
Villa del Mar (near Veracruz), 491
Villahermosa, 460–463
Visas, 25–26
Visitor information, 24–25
Viva (Puerto Vallarta), 307
Viva Zapatos (Zihuatanejo), 402
Vog Disco (Manzanillo), 368–369
Voice over Internet protocol (VoIP), 54
Voladores (flyers)
  de Papantla (Puerto Vallarta), 300, 501
  El Tajín, 500

Warren Hardy Spanish (San Miguel), 187
Water, drinking, 44, 77
Watersports. See also specific watersports
  Acapulco, 379–380
  Cancún, 537
  Cozumel, 565–566
  Ixtapa/Zihuatanejo, 399–400
  Mazatlán, 338
  Puerto Angel, 424
  Xcaret, 598
Western Union, 74

Whale-watching, 13
   Baja California, 743
   Cabo San Lucas, 717
   La Paz, 729, 732
   Puerto Vallarta, 294
   San José del Cabo, 701–702
Wheelchair accessibility, 48–49
Whiskey Bar/The Terrace
   (Mexico City), 144
Wi-Fi access, 54–55
Wildlife. See also Birding;
   Whale-watching
      health concerns, 45
Wine Harvest Festival
   (Ensenada), 30
Women travelers, 51
Woodcarvings
   Arrazola, 458
   Pátzcuaro and nearby
      villages, 254, 259
   San Martín Tilcajete, 459

Xalapa, 496–499
Xcalak, 611
Xcambó, 644
Xcaret, 570, 584, 598
Xel-Ha, 584, 601–603
Xlapak, 652
Xochitécatl, 514–515
Xpu-Ha, 600
Xpujil, 617

Yagul, 457
Yal-ku Lagoon (Akumal), 600
Yaxchilán, 470
Yaxcopoil, 645
Yelapa, 292, 325
Yoga, Isla Mujeres, 552
Yucab Reef, 565
Yucatán Peninsula, 23–24
   exploring the Maya heartland,
      619–621
   websites, 621

Zaachila, 459
Zacatecas, 221–230
Zapatista movement, 472
Zempoala (Cempoala), 495
Zen (Ixtapa), 410
Zihuatanejo. See Ixtapa/
   Zihuatanejo
Zinacantán, 478
Zinco (Mexico City), 144
Zócalo (Mexico City), 135
Zona Rosa (Mexico City)
   accommodations, 107–110
   restaurants, 114–115
   sights and attractions, 128
Zoo (club in Puerto Vallarta),
   324
Z'Tai (Puerto Vallarta), 322

FROMMER'S® COMPLETE TRAVEL GUIDES

Alaska
Amalfi Coast
American Southwest
Amsterdam
Argentina & Chile
Arizona
Atlanta
Australia
Austria
Bahamas
Barcelona
Beijing
Belgium, Holland & Luxembourg
Belize
Bermuda
Boston
Brazil
British Columbia & the Canadian Rockies
Brussels & Bruges
Budapest & the Best of Hungary
Buenos Aires
Calgary
California
Canada
Cancún, Cozumel & the Yucatán
Cape Cod, Nantucket & Martha's Vineyard
Caribbean
Caribbean Ports of Call
Carolinas & Georgia
Chicago
China
Colorado
Costa Rica
Croatia
Cuba
Denmark
Denver, Boulder & Colorado Springs
Edinburgh & Glasgow
England
Europe
Europe by Rail
Florence, Tuscany & Umbria
Florida
France
Germany
Greece
Greek Islands
Hawaii
Hong Kong
Honolulu, Waikiki & Oahu
India
Ireland
Israel
Italy
Jamaica
Japan
Kauai
Las Vegas
London
Los Angeles
Los Cabos & Baja
Madrid
Maine Coast
Maryland & Delaware
Maui
Mexico
Montana & Wyoming
Montréal & Québec City
Moscow & St. Petersburg
Munich & the Bavarian Alps
Nashville & Memphis
New England
Newfoundland & Labrador
New Mexico
New Orleans
New York City
New York State
New Zealand
Northern Italy
Norway
Nova Scotia, New Brunswick & Prince Edward Island
Oregon
Paris
Peru
Philadelphia & the Amish Country
Portugal
Prague & the Best of the Czech Republic
Provence & the Riviera
Puerto Rico
Rome
San Antonio & Austin
San Diego
San Francisco
Santa Fe, Taos & Albuquerque
Scandinavia
Scotland
Seattle
Seville, Granada & the Best of Andalusia
Shanghai
Sicily
Singapore & Malaysia
South Africa
South America
South Florida
South Pacific
Southeast Asia
Spain
Sweden
Switzerland
Tahiti & French Polynesia
Texas
Thailand
Tokyo
Toronto
Turkey
USA
Utah
Vancouver & Victoria
Vermont, New Hampshire & Maine
Vienna & the Danube Valley
Vietnam
Virgin Islands
Virginia
Walt Disney World® & Orlando
Washington, D.C.
Washington State

FROMMER'S® DAY BY DAY GUIDES

Amsterdam
Chicago
Florence & Tuscany
London
New York City
Paris
Rome
San Francisco
Venice

PAULINE FROMMER'S GUIDES! SEE MORE. SPEND LESS.

Hawaii
Italy
New York City

FROMMER'S® PORTABLE GUIDES

Acapulco, Ixtapa & Zihuatanejo
Amsterdam
Aruba
Australia's Great Barrier Reef
Bahamas
Big Island of Hawaii
Boston
California Wine Country
Cancún
Cayman Islands
Charleston
Chicago
Dominican Republic
Dublin
Florence
Las Vegas
Las Vegas for Non-Gamblers
London
Maui
Nantucket & Martha's Vineyard
New Orleans
New York City
Paris
Portland
Puerto Rico
Puerto Vallarta, Manzanillo & Guadalajara
Rio de Janeiro
San Diego
San Francisco
Savannah
St. Martin, Sint Maarten, Anguila & St. Bart's
Turks & Caicos
Vancouver
Venice
Virgin Islands
Washington, D.C.
Whistler

I don't speak sign language.

A hotel can close for all kinds of reasons.

Our Guarantee ensures that if your hotel's undergoing construction, we'll let you know in advance. In fact, we cover your entire travel experience. See www.travelocity.com/guarantee for details.

travelocity®
You'll never roam alone.

There's a parking lot where my ocean view should be.

À la place de la vue sur l'océan, me voilà avec une vue sur un parking.

Anstatt Meerblick habe ich Sicht auf einen Parkplatz.

Al posto della vista sull'oceano c'è un parcheggio.

No tengo vista al mar porque hay un parque de estacionamiento.

Há um parque de estacionamento onde deveria estar a minha vista do oceano.

Ett parkeringsområde har byggts på den plats där min utsikt över oceanen borde vara.

Er ligt een parkeerterrein waar mijn zee-uitzicht zou moeten zijn.

هنالك موقف للسيارات مكان ما وجب ان يكون المنظر الخلاب المطل على المحيط .

眼前に広がる紺碧の海・・・じゃない。窓の外は駐車場！

停车场的位置应该是我的海景所在。

— I'm fluent in
pig latin.

Hotel mishaps aren't bound by geography.
Neither is our Guarantee. It covers your entire travel experience,
including the price. So if you don't get the ocean view you booked,
we'll work with our travel partners to make it right, right away. See
www.travelocity.com/guarantee for details.

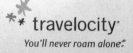